One method of reducing a part of the earth's surface is by aerial photography. The two photographs on this page are semi-controlled mosaics and are made by matching together a series of vertical aerial photographs. Although an accurate map cannot be made directly from such a mosaic, it does illustrate one way that a map can be made. Each of the mosaics is approximately the scale of its corresponding map.

On a map, cultural and physical features are represented by means of signs, symbols, and certain conventions. By comparing the mosaic with the map in each case, one can ascertain how various features on the earth have been represented on the map and how they, and other features, appear from the air. For example, the darkest areas on the Pittsburgh mosaic are wooded areas which are shown in green on the map. The heavily built-up area of Pittsburgh is depicted by a red screen on the map. The major buildings, roads, and bridges are easily recognized.

The part of the Strasburg, Virginia, Quadrangle selected lies in the folded Appalachians just east of Woodstock, Virginia, and across the "Great Valley" of the Shenandoah River. The valley, occupied by the meanders of both forks of the Shenandoah River, is divided at this point by Massanutten Mountain. The latter is a complex synclinal mass, made mostly of sandstone. The three northeast trending parallel ridges of the mountain can be readily recognized and compared. Notice that the shading on the map and the shadows on the mosaic do not agree. The photographs were taken in the morning, placing the western slopes of the ridges in shadow. The general practice of the cartographer, however, is to render the relief as if the light source was from the northwest. The comparison, nevertheless, facilitates an understanding of how contours and relief shading are used to represent surface configuration.

PITTSBURGH WEST 1:24 000
U.S. GEOLOGICAL SURVEY

GOODE'S

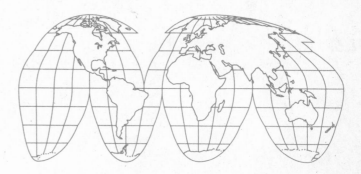

WORLD ATLAS

TWELFTH EDITION

edited by
Edward B. Espenshade, Jr.
Professor of Geography, Northwestern University

RAND McNALLY & COMPANY · CHICAGO

CONTENTS

ACKNOWLEDGMENTS

This is the twelfth edition of *Goode's World Atlas* which was first published more than thirty years ago. The name of Dr. Goode, the original editor who was a distinguished cartographer and designed the early editions, is still retained and suggests the high standards which all those who have participated in the preparation of the book have sought to attain. The practice of including systematic improvements and revisions of the maps and data with each new edition is continued.

Sources. Every effort has been made to assemble the latest and most authentic source materials for use in compiling the atlas. For the general physical-political maps, national and state surveys, recent military maps, and hydrographic charts have been utilized. For the specialized maps, the source materials are even more varied. They include both published and unpublished items in the form of maps, descriptions in articles and books, statistics, and correspondence with geographers and others. To the various agencies and organizations, official and unofficial, who have cooperated, appreciation and thanks are expressed. Noteworthy among these organizations and agencies are: Food and Agriculture Organization of The United Nations for production statistics on livestock, crop and forest products, and statistics on world trade; the Office of the Geographer, The Department of State, for the map of Surface Transport Facilities, and other items; the Office of Foreign Agricultural Relations, Department of Agriculture, for information on crop and livestock production and distribution; the Bureau of Mines, Department of the Interior, for information on mineral production; various branches of the National Military Establishment and the Weather Bureau, Department of Commerce, for information on temperature, wind, pressure, and ocean currents; the Maritime Commission and the Department of Commerce, for statistics on ocean trade; the American Geographical Society, for use of its library and permission to use the Miller cylindrical projection; The University of Chicago Press, owners of the copyright, for permission to use Goode's Homolosine equal-area projection; and McGraw-Hill Book Company, for cooperation in permitting the use of Glenn Trewartha's map of climatic regions and Petterson's diagram of zones of precipitation.

Other acknowledgments. The variety and complexity of the problems involved in the preparation of a world atlas make highly desirable the participation of specialists in some of the problems. In the preparation of the new edition of *Goode's World Atlas* the editor has been ably assisted by several such experts. He expresses his deep appreciation and thanks to all of them. He is particularly indebted to the experts listed below who have assumed primary responsibility for certain maps.

The editor's grateful thanks are due to the staff of Rand McNally & Company. It is not possible to cite individual contributions, but the varied skills of geographers, cartographers, and many others are involved. Their faithful and careful work has contributed much to the final result.

EDWARD B. ESPENSHADE, JR.
Northwestern University
May, 1964

Cooperating Experts

A. W. KÜCHLER
Department of Geography
University of Kansas

THOBURN C. LYON
Consultant
Cartography and Air Navigation

A. C. ORVEDAL
Soil Scientist
Division of Soil Survey
United States Department of Agriculture

ERWIN RAISZ
Cartographer
Cambridge, Massachusetts

GLENN T. TREWARTHA
Department of Geography
University of Wisconsin

J. PARKER VAN ZANDT
President
Aviation Research Institute

WALTER H. VOSKUIL
Mineral Economist
Illinois Geological Survey

DERWENT WHITTLESEY
Late Professor of Geography
Harvard University

BOGDAN ZABORSKI
Professor of Geography
University of Ottawa

INTRODUCTION

Utility of maps. There are many kinds of maps, and they are useful in countless ways. It would be difficult to list all the ways in which even a simple road map, for example, is or may be useful. A knowledge of location, relative size, direction, distance, or of other facts which are set down in an atlas is necessary to an understanding of much about which one reads today. The changing world and the widespread commitments of the United States place new emphasis on map study. An atlas has become a prime necessity for understanding the course of world events. Three outstanding attributes may be noted in connection with the maps of this atlas. They are characteristics common to maps of the most varied kinds and utilities.

(1) The maps show facts of areal distribution, both qualitative and quantitative. For example, the world vegetation map (pp. 16-17) is based on observations made by many hundreds of individuals. The map shows hundreds of varied vegetative units and thirty-two types of vegetation. Thousands of words would be required to state the facts portrayed by the map. These facts can be presented best on a map and can be grasped quickly from a map. The information embodied in the world vegetation map is chiefly qualitative. It was reduced from a general, undefined form to a particular, classified form, and so its utility was greatly enhanced. The world rainfall map (pp. 14-15) provides quantitative facts concerning annual precipitation, by means of isohyets (lines connecting points of equal rainfall). Here again, a single map conveys factual information far better than could be done by volumes of words and tables.

(2) The maps in *Goode's World Atlas* also serve to illustrate innumerable facts of significance that are associated with location and areal distribution. For example, the climatic-regions map (pp. 8-9) shows the areal distribution of types of climate which are determined from a synthesis of thousands of rainfall and temperature statistics.

(3) Finally, many useful comparisons may be made between different maps, between two maps in some instances, between three or more in others, with a view to establishing relationships between the various types of information entered on the maps. Useful comparisons may also be made, of course, between different places on the same map as well as between different aspects of the same place as shown on two or more maps. For example, compare the areas of dense population (pp. 20-21) with areas which have an intensive subsistence rice or non-rice agriculture (pp. 24-25). There are few agricultural areas in the world, with the exception of those in Europe, which have similar population densities. Note also on the agricultural-regions map the absence of nomadic herding in the Western Hemisphere, whereas extensive areas exist in Asia and Africa.

Reading maps. An ability to read maps is acquired through practice, in the same manner as the ability to read a written text. The effectiveness of any written text depends both on the skill of the writer and on that of the reader. Similarly, the value of a particular map depends both on the effectiveness of the cartography and on the map-reading ability of the user. Of particular importance in reading maps is a knowledge of map scales, projections, and symbolism.

Understanding scales. A function of all maps is to provide a reduced representation of the earth's surface. Since part or all of the earth's surface is depicted on a single page of this atlas, the question arises, "What is the relation of map size to earth size?" This proportional relationship is the scale of a map. The scale is given in three forms on most maps of this atlas to facilitate answering this question.

To aid further in understanding scales, a comparison of scale is given in a series of maps on the next page. A comparison of diagrams A, B, C, and D illustrates how progressively smaller-scale maps (of constant page size) increase the size of the area covered but reduce the detail which can be expressed. On the second map and on each later map, the area covered by the previous map is outlined within the map, to provide a direct comparison of the areas covered. On the first map, individual buildings are shown. On the final map, even many cities are omitted.

To aid the student in acquiring accurate concepts of the relative size of continents and of some countries and regions, uniform scales for comparable areas are used as far as possible. Continental maps are given on a uniform scale of 1:40,000,000 (one inch to 640 miles). In similar fashion, series of regions comparable in area appear in groups of maps on uniform scales of 1:16,000,000 (one inch to 250 miles), 1:12,000,000 (one inch to 190 miles), 1:4,000,000 (one inch to 64 miles), and on larger scales. The maximum size of the scale utilized for any

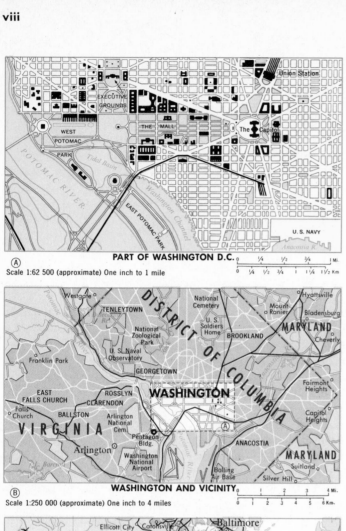

PART OF WASHINGTON D.C.

(A)

Scale 1:62 500 (approximate) One inch to 1 mile

WASHINGTON AND VICINITY

(B)

Scale 1:250 000 (approximate) One inch to 4 miles

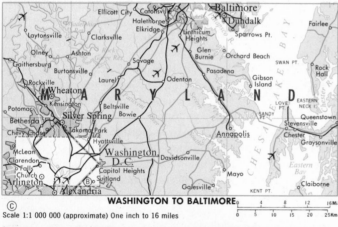

WASHINGTON TO BALTIMORE

(C)

Scale 1:1 000 000 (approximate) One inch to 16 miles

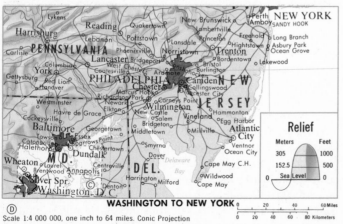

WASHINGTON TO NEW YORK

(D)

Scale 1:4 000 000, one inch to 64 miles. Conic Projection

given region is a partial measure of the importance of the region and of interest in it.

Understanding projections. There is no way of representing the curved surface of the globe on a flat surface without some distortion of the useful features desired on flat maps. On large-scale maps covering areas of only a few square miles, this distortion is negligible. In maps representing large areas, as in maps of a large country, a continent, or the whole world, the distortion inevitably is considerable, and, unless understood, it may result in serious misconceptions. The distortion may involve distances, directions, or the shapes and sizes of areas.

A map projection is an orderly system of parallels and meridians on which a map can be drawn. There are hundreds of map projections in use, but none avoids distortion of the spatial relationships that only a globe map can show truthfully. It is not possible to have truth of area, shape, angle, and scale all in the same flat map. It is possible, however, to select from the many types of projections one which is accurate for a particular property or which is a compromise (limiting the distortion of one or more elements at the expense of the others) that is relatively satisfactory for a particular need.

Truth of area is of prime importance in many maps. Most of the maps made for geographical study, particularly those used to show the areal distribution of an item, are drawn on equal-area projections. In an equal-area projection any square inch on the map represents the same number of square miles on the earth's surface as any other square inch on the map. Continents, oceans, islands, states, all are shown in their true relative size. Close to the importance of equality of area is truth of shape. This characteristic is to some extent an esthetic quality, but it is also a practical one. The student becomes familiar with the true shape of a continent or an island or a body of water as it appears on a globe map. Distortion of these shapes almost beyond recognition on a flat map is incongruous and a source of bewilderment to the student. Truth of direction is especially important in the study of the distribution of factors of significance in world relations. To show the latitudinal or zonal distribution of such factors, it is obviously desirable that lines of latitude be parallel, or better, straight lines parallel with the equator.

Most of the maps used in this atlas are drawn on projections that give equality of area, good land and ocean shapes, and parallel latitudinal directions. To provide these and other qualities desired for particular maps, some distortion of other elements is inevitable. The student should make himself aware of the nature of such distortions and make allowances for them in his use of the maps. One of the more practical procedures is to compare the projection grid of the flat map with the grid of the globe map. He should first verify the fundamental characteristics of the globe grid as listed here:

(1) On the globe map all longitude lines are equal in length and meet at the poles.

(2) All latitude lines are parallel.

(3) The length of the latitude lines, that is, the circumference of latitude circles, decreases from the equator to the points representing the poles. At latitude 60°, the circumference of the latitude circle is one-half the circumference of the equatorial circle.

(4) Distances along lines of longitude between any two latitude lines are equal.

(5) All latitude and longitude lines meet at right angles. With item (1) in mind, the student will observe that the projection used on pages 44-45 has latitude lines of equal length. This results in considerable exaggeration of areas in the higher latitudes. With item (5) in mind, he will note that the projection used on pages 6-7 has oblique angles at the junction of latitude and longitude lines in the higher latitudes, and that this partly causes distortion of land shapes in such areas as Alaska and Greenland. In this projection, however, truth of area has been maintained.

Some illustration of the construction of the more commonly used projections and indication of their properties are helpful in making clear the nature of inherent distortions. Pages 2 and 3 are designed to provide this help. They also illustrate the seven projections used in this atlas.

Few of the several hundred projections in use can be constructed graphically by methods of descriptive geometry. Most of them are derived from mathematical formulas designed to afford the properties desired. In some cases it is easier to visualize the general form and characteristics of a projection if the earth's surface is considered to be projected upon a plane, a cone, or a cylinder. The last two surfaces, when they are cut and unrolled, form a plane surface. These surfaces provide one general classification of projections: azimuthal (on a plane), conic, or cylindrical (fig. 1, 2, and 5, pp. 2 and 3). In each class the characteristics of the projections may be changed by varying the systematic arrangement or spacing of the latitude and longitude lines.

Figure 1, A (p. 2) is a true plane projection with the point of projection at the center of the globe. This geometrical projection of the earth grid on a tangent plane is called a gnomonic projection. In the illustration the plane is tangent to the equator, but it could be placed tangent to the poles, or to any other point on the earth's surface. Several other distinctive map projections can be obtained by changing the origin point of the projection. For example, the projection obtained from an origin point on the surface of the globe diametrically opposite the point of contact of the tangent plane is called a stereographic projection, and the projection from an origin point at infinity is called an orthographic projection. None of these perspective projections obtained from projection on a plane is used in this atlas, but the mathematically derived Lambert azimuthal equal-area projection (fig. 1, B, p. 2) may be considered in this general class. The polar aspect of the Lambert azimuthal equal-area projection is used for the map of the Northern Lands and Seas (p. 48); the oblique aspect is used for the series of continental maps. Besides its equal-area quality, the projection gives relatively good shapes to continental areas as a whole.

Conic projections may be thought of as derived from a tangent cone (fig. 2) or from an intersecting cone (fig. 3). In the latter case, the resulting projection is said to have "two standard parallels" along which the scale is exact (since the cone and the sphere coincide throughout the length of the parallels). In maps of areas covering a wide range of longitude, the projection used in this atlas is a modified conic of the latter type (De Lisle's). In this projection, as here used, the shapes are excellent, and the departure from the equal-area quality is almost negligible. (See Canada, pp. 86-87, and Siberia, pp. 134-135). The scale between the two standard parallels is too small along the parallels, and outside the standard parallels is too great along the parallels. The use of two standard parallels, however, provides a much better opportunity of extending the area within which the scale is reasonably accurate than the use of a single standard parallel, as in the simple conic.

Another modification of the conic principle is the Bonne projection (fig. 3, C, p. 2), used on pages 114-115 for the map of the Mediterranean lands. It has a selected standard parallel, and other parallels are arcs of concentric circles truly divided for points of intersection with the meridians. The scale along all the parallels is true everywhere, but the central meridian is the only one along which it is true. By construction, however, it is equal-area, and reasonably correct representation of shape is obtained in narrow zones along the standard parallel and central meridian, where the intersections are at right angles, or nearly so.

The polyconic projection (fig. 4, p. 2) is used for the United States and some other areas of similar position and size. In the case of the polyconic projection, the earth may be considered as made up of a series of tangent cones. As each base is developed, the result is as shown, somewhat exaggerated, in figure 4, B, page 2. The area of the projection used for the map of the United States (fig. 4, C, page 2) is the central portion of figure 4, B, beneath the word "Pole." In this projection the central meridian crosses all parallels at right angles, as on the globe; other intersections become noticeably oblique only at considerable distance from the central meridian. The scale is true on the central meridian and on each parallel. Shapes, as a result, are very good. Meridian-scale errors, however, increase rapidly with increasing distance from the central meridian. The projection is thus not well adapted to areas of wide longitudinal extent. The departure, however, from equality of area is slight where it has been used for maps in this atlas.

The cylindrical class of projections may be visualized as perspective projections on a tangent or intersecting cylinder (fig. 5, page 3). Many of the cylindrical projections in use, however, are mathematical modifications of the true perspective forms. As a general class, the cylindrical projections have the following characteristics: (1) latitude lines which are straight, parallel, and equal in length; (2) longitude lines which are straight, parallel, equal in length, and equally spaced; (3) meridians and parallels which intersect at right angles (fig. 5, page 3). Since the latitude lines are all drawn equal in length, an increasing distortion of scale occurs along the parallels with increasing distance from the standard parallel or parallels of tangency.

Mercator's projection (fig. 5, C, page 3), which belongs to this general class, is one of the better-known projections. For nearly four hundred years it has been used widely for world distributional maps, in spite of the facts (1) that it is impossible with this projection to show the entire surface of the earth, the poles being at infinity; and (2) that distances and areas grow rapidly larger with increase of latitude, until the distortion becomes enormous in higher latitudes. This is made apparent by

a comparison of the relative size of areas in figures 5, C, and 6. The distortion of area is so great that the use of the Mercator projection for world maps showing areal distributions of most kinds is pedagogically unsound and misleading. The projection was designed by Mercator primarily for use of navigators, and for that use it is incomparable. On it, the navigator can draw a straight line (called a rhumb line) between any two points, read the angle between the rhumb line and any meridian that it crosses, set his compass on that angle, and go direct to his destination without change of compass. This advantage is so great that no other projection has yet taken the place of the Mercator in marine navigation.

A variation of the Mercator is the transverse or oblique Mercator. The grid is derived from a cylinder tangent along a selected great circle (fig. 7). The resulting projection is conformal, but its grid bears no resemblance to that of the ordinary Mercator and may be mistaken for that of a conic projection. Although the transverse Mercator projection is not used in this atlas, it illustrates a special-purpose projection which is being used more and more because of its value in air navigation for maps of great-circle strips.

Miller's projection (fig. 5, D) is a recent "compromise projection." It has been used in the atlas (with permission of the American Geographical Society) for climatic maps showing barometric pressures, winds, and temperatures, and for the map of ocean communications. A continuous grid without interruptions, and straight-line parallels were desirable for the best presentation of the features listed above. Miller's projection meets these requirements and provides a compromise between the distortion of areas and shapes. Mercator's projection was not suitable because of its excessive area distortion, although shapes of areas are excellent. Use of continuous grids for the whole world which were strictly equal-area would result in considerable distortion of shapes. The student will note, however, that even on the Miller projection there is still considerable distortion of areas and shapes in the higher latitudes (cf. fig. 5, D, 5, C, and 6). Changes in scale according to latitude are indicated in the legend of the map and should be carefully noted. For example, compare on the graphic scale (page 44) a distance of one thousand miles at the equator with the same distance at latitude 60° or 80°.

Figure 6 illustrates three projections which are purely conventional in design. They cannot be readily related to the three general classes just discussed. They are not projections in the sense of being projected on a plane, a cone, or a cylinder; rather, they all are based on mathematical formulas. The sinusoidal projection (fig. 6, C, page 3) is used for the large-scale sectional maps of South America and Africa and for the map showing world surface transport facilities. It is an equal-area projection. On these continental maps it is most accurate along the equator where the two continents are widest. The placement of the central meridian through the center of the continents results in relatively little distortion of scale or shapes in the narrower southern parts of the continents. The scale is true along all parallels and the central meridian, but it increases on other meridians in conformity with their increasing obliquity. On the world map (pp. 42-43) the extent of the distortion is reduced by the technique of interrupting the projection and of using a separate central meridian for different land masses.

Mollweide's equal-area projection (fig. 6, A, page 3), designed to show the entire globe as an uninterrupted unit, gives an elliptical picture of the earth. The ellipse is drawn to enclose an area equal to that of a globe on the same scale. The central meridian is divided so that the areas of the bands between the parallels are truthfully proportional. Mollweide's projection is thus an equal-area projection, but there is little uniformity in linear scale. So that the areas of greater distortion in the outer parts of the projection will be eliminated, it, like the sinusoidal projection, may be interrupted and a new central meridian established through each continent (cf. the two forms, fig. 6, A and B, page 3).

Most of the world distribution maps in this atlas are drawn on Goode's homolosine equal-area projection (fig. 6, D, page 3). This projection is derived by combining the sinusoidal projection for latitudes up to 40° north and south with the homolographic projection (Mollweide) for areas poleward of these latitudes. In this manner an equal-area projection is obtained which has some of the better qualities of both the sinusoidal and homolographic. Further improvement of shapes is obtained by application of the principle of interruption, so that extremely oblique intersections are eliminated. The result has a number of distinct advantages: (1) It presents the entire surface of the earth, which Mercator's projection cannot do. (2) It is strictly an equal-area projection, with no distortion of the size of areas. (3) On it the parallels of latitude are represented by straight lines trending with the equator, a real advantage in the study of comparative latitudes. (4) On it the grid is interrupted in the oceans so as to give each continent in turn the advantage of being in the center of the projection, thus providing better shapes for the continents than any uninterrupted world map can give. No map projection has been devised which displays to better advantage the distribution of most world phenomena which are studied best from the equatorial aspect.

Symbolism. The signs, symbols, and conventions shown on maps are a form of "shorthand" indicating a variety of phenomena (page xii). Many of them are self-explanatory. Compare also the aerial mosaics with the adjacent topographic maps of Pittsburgh and Strasburg areas (inside cover). A complete legend (page xii) provides a key to the physical-political reference maps.

Two systems of measurement are used in connection with the maps in this atlas. The English system of measures, which is conventional in this country, is utilized, although admittedly it is somewhat irrational and cumbersome. Since much of the world uses the metric system of measurement and the centigrade thermometer, most measures are given also in these scientific terms, or conversion scales are provided. A linear scale in miles is placed alongside a linear scale in kilometers, with the zero points together. Heights and depths may be read in feet or in meters from opposite scales. Comparative scales in the margins permit ready conversion of temperature and precipitation values from one system to another.

Surface configuration on the continental and regional maps is shown in a different manner from the tenth edition of this

atlas. A combination of two techniques is utilized which gives a striking three-dimensional effect. General elevation above sea level is indicated as previously by layer-tints, altitudinal zones, each of which has a different hue and is defined by a generalized contour line. The hues for the zones, however, have been selected so that their values increases with elevation in preference to the more conventional layer-tint colors. Thus, although shades of green are still used for the lowlands below 1,000 feet, hues of light tan, buff, and yellow are used for successively higher elevations and areas of more than 10,000 feet are left white. Each of the hues increases in value with increasing elevation and thus visually appears closer to the observer.

An oblique shading in gray has been utilized to indicate local relief, particularly the direction and steepness of slopes. This has been superimposed over the layer tints and a much more realistic and readily visualized impression of the surface configuration is obtained. The three-dimensional effect is more noticeable where it is important in the higher mountainous areas whose slopes are steepest, because the shadow contrast is greatest in the very areas where the color values are highest.

This new presentation of relief is designed to overcome some of the serious weaknesses of the layer-tints system used previously. Steepness of slope, the ruggedness of the terrain, and significant relief features which have differences in elevation with a value less than the layer-tint interval are distinguished and can be visualized. No longer should the nearly level high plateau area be confused with an adjacent mountain area. The improved symbolism for representation of surface configuration should facilitate the reading of the maps and should reduce some of the misconceptions obtained when layer-tints alone were utilized.

Place Names. Place names are used to distinguish particular places and features—cities, towns, bays, peninsulas—from other similar features. Many place names consist of two parts —a specific and a generic part. For example, Lake Michigan consists of the specific term "Michigan" modifying the generic term "lake."

If the world used one alphabet and one language, no particular difficulty would arise in the use of place names. Unfortunately, people use many languages and various alphabets. Moreover, some of the people of the world, the Chinese and the Japanese, for example, use non-alphabet languages. In order to make some languages intelligible to American readers, their letters and symbols must be converted into the Roman alphabet. It has been the practice of many people to transform place names further by transcribing or translating part or all of them into English. The recent war, which brought far corners of the earth to our attention, and the increasing facilities for communication in recent years make this practice no longer desirable. In this atlas, a "local-name policy" generally has been used for the cities and towns and for all local topographic and water features. However, for a few major cities the Anglicized form is preferred and the local name is given in parentheses. In countries where more than one official language is used such as South Africa, the spelling of the name is in the form of the dominant local language. The generic parts of local names for topographic and water features are self-explanatory in many cases because of the associated map symbol or type style. A complete list of foreign generic terms is given in the glossary on page 171, and a short list of "geographical equivalents" is given on pages 6 and 7.

A distinctive feature of *Goode's World Atlas* is the pronouncing index which has been completely revised. The variable vowel sounds of English and the differences among other languages make the correct pronunciation of place names difficult. The correct pronunciation of many names differs from the pronunciation that may seem natural. Under these circumstances, the pronouncing index of more than thirty thousand names should be very helpful to the student.

Economic maps and statistics. The statistics presented in this atlas are not intended to take the place of statistical reference works. Instead of having been planned to present an absolute index to production and trade, they were planned to give a picture of the relative importance of countries and regions in the particulars involved. The maps have been reserved chiefly to present facts of distribution. However, the general magnitude of production is indicated by graded point symbols in the case of minerals, and the density of the uniform dot pattern indirectly provides a similar assessment for crop production. Marginal graphs show the relative importance of different areas by percentage values of world totals.

No single year affords, for this purpose, a satisfactory base for production and trade statistics. For this reason, the percentages and world totals used have been computed with few exceptions, from averages of a period of three or four years. The base period of years varies, but the latest year for which data are available at time of publication has been used. Few realize that there is a necessary gap of several years between the date of a publication such as this and the date of the statistics used. Organizations issuing statistical data of the sort used in the atlas require two or three years to gather, tabulate, and publish their materials. An additional year is required to incorporate and publish the data within this atlas. Publishers often are reluctant to date their statistical materials, since few users understand the reason for the gap in time. The dates of the base period used are indicated on each graph. In general the averages and percentages will provide the student with a sufficiently accurate picture of the relative importance of areas, despite the fact they are not for the current year. An exception occurs in the case of a product which is subject to major or rapid expansion or contraction of production either nationally, regionally, or on a world wide basis. This occurs more commonly in mineral products than in agricultural products. An important example is petroleum where notable shifts in proven reserves, production, and trade movements have occurred within the last five years.

EDWARD B. ESPENSHADE, JR.
Northwestern University
May, 1964

MAP SYMBOLS

CULTURAL FEATURES

Political Boundaries

-·--·--·-	International
-··--··-	Intercolonial
-·--·--·-	Secondary: State, Provincial, etc.
▅ ▅ ▅ ▅	Disputed or Indefinite
⌐⌐⌐⌐	Parks, Indian Reservations
⌐⌐⌐	City Limits

Cities, Towns and Villages
(Except for scales of 1:20,000,000 or smaller)

PARIS	1,000,000 and over
◎ Ufa	500,000 to 1,000,000
⊙ Győr	50,000 to 500,000
○ Agadir	25,000 to 50,000
° Moreno	0 to 25,000
TŌKYŌ	National Capitals
Boise	Secondary Capitals

Transportation

─────	Railroads
--------	Railroad Ferries
─────	Roads
········	Caravan Routes
✈	Airports

Other Cultural Features

∿	Dams
++++++	Pipelines
▲	Pyramids
∴	Ruins

WATER FEATURES

Lakes and Reservoirs

▭	Fresh Water
▭	Fresh Water: Intermittent
▭	Salt Water
▭	Salt Water: Intermittent

Other Water Features

▭	Salt Basins, Flats
∿	Swamps
∿	Ice Caps and Glaciers
∿	Rivers
∿	Canals
∿	Aqueducts
=====	Ship Channels
∿	Falls
∿	Rapids
♪	Springs
△	Water Depths
⊙	Fishing Banks
▨	Sand Bars
≋≋	Reefs

LAND FEATURES

△	Peaks, Spot Heights
=	Passes
∴∴	Sand
⬭	Contours

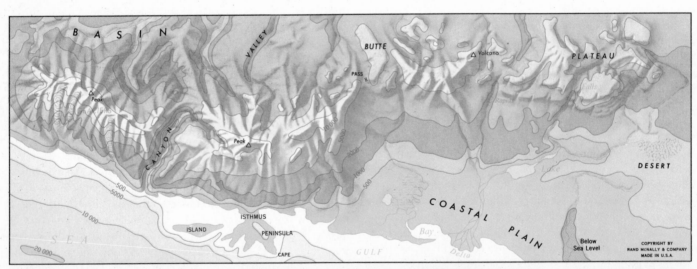

COPYRIGHT BY
RAND MCNALLY & COMPANY
MADE IN U.S.A.

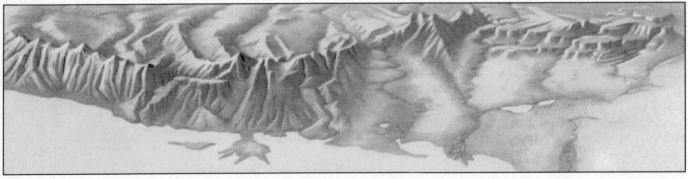

THE SEASONS

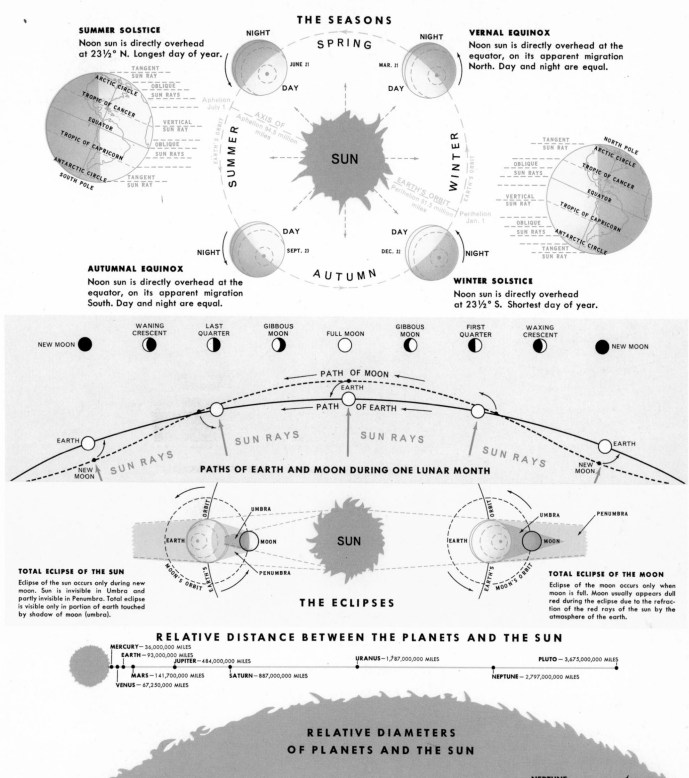

SUMMER SOLSTICE
Noon sun is directly overhead at 23½° N. Longest day of year.

SPRING

JUNE 21

NIGHT — DAY

VERNAL EQUINOX
Noon sun is directly overhead at the equator, on its apparent migration North. Day and night are equal.

MAR. 21

NIGHT — DAY

SUMMER — WINTER

Aphelion July 1

AXIS OF Aphelion 94.5 million miles

EARTH'S ORBIT

SUN

EARTH'S ORBIT Perihelion 91.5 million miles — Perihelion Jan. 1

TANGENT SUN RAY
ARCTIC CIRCLE
TROPIC OF CANCER
OBLIQUE SUN RAYS
EQUATOR
VERTICAL SUN RAY
TROPIC OF CAPRICORN
OBLIQUE SUN RAYS
ANTARCTIC CIRCLE
SOUTH POLE
TANGENT SUN RAY

TANGENT SUN RAY
NORTH POLE
ARCTIC CIRCLE
OBLIQUE SUN RAYS
TROPIC OF CANCER
VERTICAL SUN RAY
EQUATOR
TROPIC OF CAPRICORN
OBLIQUE SUN RAYS
ANTARCTIC CIRCLE
TANGENT SUN RAY

SEPT. 23

DAY — NIGHT

DEC. 22

DAY — NIGHT

AUTUMN

AUTUMNAL EQUINOX
Noon sun is directly overhead at the equator, on its apparent migration South. Day and night are equal.

WINTER SOLSTICE
Noon sun is directly overhead at 23½° S. Shortest day of year.

NEW MOON — WANING CRESCENT — LAST QUARTER — GIBBOUS MOON — FULL MOON — GIBBOUS MOON — FIRST QUARTER — WAXING CRESCENT — NEW MOON

PATH OF MOON
EARTH
PATH OF EARTH
SUN RAYS — SUN RAYS — SUN RAYS — SUN RAYS
EARTH
NEW MOON
EARTH
NEW MOON

PATHS OF EARTH AND MOON DURING ONE LUNAR MONTH

ORBIT
UMBRA
PENUMBRA
EARTH — MOON
SUN
EARTH — MOON
MOON'S ORBIT
EARTH'S
PENUMBRA
UMBRA
MOON'S ORBIT

TOTAL ECLIPSE OF THE SUN
Eclipse of the sun occurs only during new moon. Sun is invisible in Umbra and partly invisible in Penumbra. Total eclipse is visible only in portion of earth touched by shadow of moon (umbra).

THE ECLIPSES

TOTAL ECLIPSE OF THE MOON
Eclipse of the moon occurs only when moon is full. Moon usually appears dull red during the eclipse due to the refraction of the red rays of the sun by the atmosphere of the earth.

RELATIVE DISTANCE BETWEEN THE PLANETS AND THE SUN

MERCURY—36,000,000 MILES
EARTH—93,000,000 MILES
JUPITER—484,000,000 MILES
URANUS—1,787,000,000 MILES
PLUTO—3,675,000,000 MILES
MARS—141,700,000 MILES
SATURN—887,000,000 MILES
NEPTUNE—2,797,000,000 MILES
VENUS—67,250,000 MILES

RELATIVE DIAMETERS OF PLANETS AND THE SUN

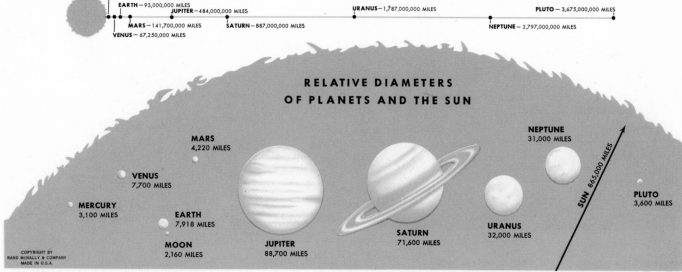

MARS 4,220 MILES

NEPTUNE 31,000 MILES

VENUS 7,700 MILES

MERCURY 3,100 MILES

EARTH 7,918 MILES

MOON 2,160 MILES

JUPITER 88,700 MILES

SATURN 71,600 MILES

URANUS 32,000 MILES

SUN 865,000 MILES

PLUTO 3,600 MILES

PROJECTIONS

A map projection is merely an orderly system of parallels and meridians on which a flat map can be drawn. There are hundreds of projections, but no one represents the earth's spherical surface without some distortion. The distortion is relatively small for most practical purposes when a small part of the sphere is projected. For larger areas, a sacrifice of some property is necessary.

Most projections are designed to preserve on the flat map some particular property of the sphere. By varying the systematic arrangement or spacing of the latitude and longitude lines, a projection may be made either equal-area or conformal. Although most projections are derived from mathematical formulas, some are easier to visualize if thought of as projected upon a plane, or upon a cone or cylinder which is then unrolled into a plane surface. Thus, many projections are classified as plane (azimuthal), conic, or cylindrical.

For a fuller discussion of map projections, see Preface. Figures with asterisks indicate projections used in this atlas.

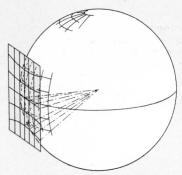

(A) GNOMONIC PROJECTION

A geometric or perspective projection on a tangent plane with the origin point at the center of the globe. Shapes and distances rapidly become increasingly distorted away from the center of the projection. Important in navigation, because all straight lines are great circles.

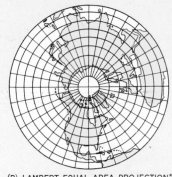

(B) LAMBERT EQUAL AREA PROJECTION*

A mathematically designed azimuthal equal-area projection. Excellent for continental areas. For larger areas away from the center, distortion of distances and shapes is appreciable.

FIGURE 1.—TYPICAL PLANE PROJECTIONS

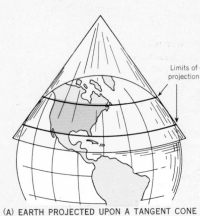

(A) EARTH PROJECTED UPON A TANGENT CONE

(B) CONE CUT FROM BASE TO APEX

A perspective projection on a tangent cone with the origin point at the center of the globe. At the parallel of tangency, all elements of the map are

(C) CONE DEVELOPED INTO A PLANE SURFACE

true- angles,distances,shapes,areas. Away from the tangent parallel, distances increase rapidly, giving bad distortion of shapes and areas.

FIGURE 2.—SIMPLE CONIC PROJECTIONS

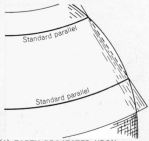

(A) EARTH PROJECTED UPON AN INTERSECTING CONE

This modification of the conic has two standard parallels, or lines of intersection. It is not an equal-area projection, the space being reduced in size between the standard parallels and

(B) CONIC PROJECTION WITH TWO STANDARD PARALLELS*

progressively enlarged beyond the standard parallels. Careful selection of the standard parallels provides, however, good representation for areas of limited latitudinal extent.

(C) BONNE PROJECTION*

An equal-area modification of the conic principle. Distances are true along all parallels and the central meridian; but away from it, increasing obliqueness of intersections and longitudinal distances, with their attendant distortion of shapes, limits the satisfactory area.

FIGURE 3.—MODIFIED CONIC PROJECTIONS

(A) EARTH CONSIDERED AS FORMED BY BASES OF CONES

(B) DEVELOPMENT OF THE CONICAL BASES

This variation is not equal-area. Parallels are non-concentric circles truly divided. Distances along the straight central meridian are also true, but

(C) POLYCONIC PROJECTION*

along the curving meridians are increasingly exaggerated. Representation is good near the central meridian, but away from it there is marked distortion.

FIGURE 4.—POLYCONIC PROJECTION

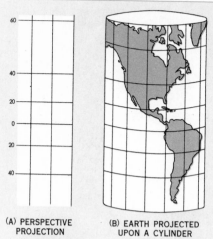

(A) PERSPECTIVE
PROJECTION

A perspective projection on a tangent cylinder. Because of rapidly increasing distortion away from the line of tangency and the lack of any special advantage, it is rarely used.

(B) EARTH PROJECTED
UPON A CYLINDER

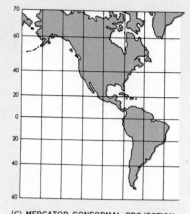

(C) MERCATOR CONFORMAL PROJECTION

Mercator's modification increases the latitudinal distances in the same proportion as longitudinal distances are increased. Thus, at any point shapes are true, but areas become increasingly exaggerated. Of value in navigation, because a line connecting any two points gives the true direction between them.

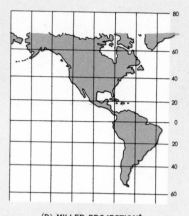

(D) MILLER PROJECTION*

This recent modification is neither conformal nor equal-area. Whereas shapes are less accurate than on the Mercator, the exaggeration of areas has been reduced somewhat.

FIGURE 5.—CYLINDRICAL PROJECTIONS

(A) MOLLWEIDE'S HOMOLOGRAPHIC PROJECTION

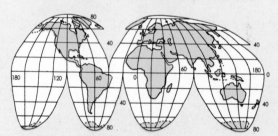

(B) GOODE'S INTERRUPTED HOMOLOGRAPHIC PROJECTION

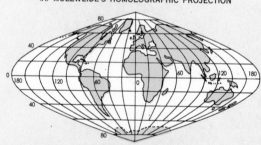

(C) SINUSOIDAL PROJECTION*

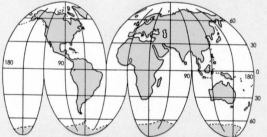

(D) GOODE'S INTERRUPTED HOMOLOSINE PROJECTION*

Although each of these projections is equal-area, differences in the spacing and arrangement of latitude and longitude lines result in differences in the distribution and relative degree of the shape and distance distortion within each grid. On the homolographic, there is no uniformity in scale. It is different on each parallel and each meridian. On the sinusoidal, only distances along all latitudes and the central meridian are true. The homolosine combines the homolographic, for areas poleward of 40°, with the sinusoidal. The principle of interruption permits each continent in turn the advantage of being in the center of the projection, resulting in better shapes.

FIGURE 6.—EQUAL AREA PROJECTIONS OF THE WORLD

A conformal projection in which a selected great circle of the globe is considered as the "equator" of the ordinary Mercator projection, with the cylinder tangent along the great circle. It is used chiefly for charts of great-circle air routes between distant cities.

FIGURE 7.—TRANSVERSE MERCATOR PROJECTION

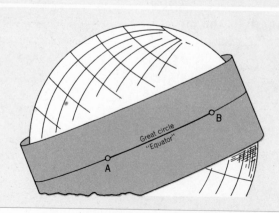

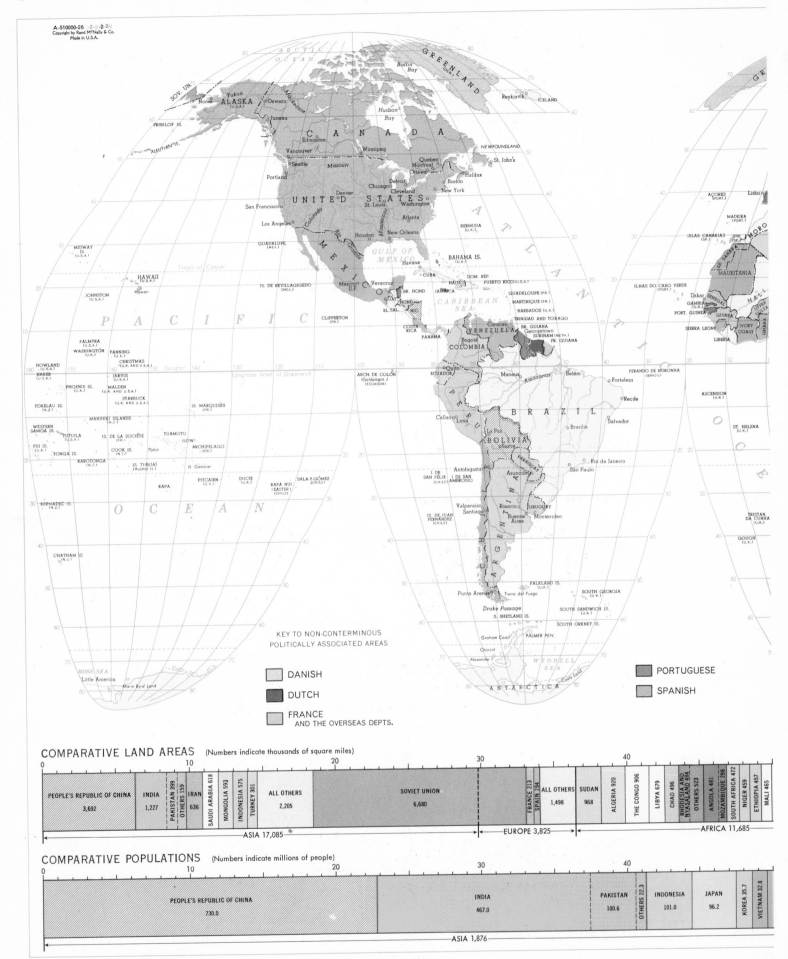

A-510000-26
Copyright by Rand McNally & Co.
Made in U.S.A.

KEY TO NON-CONTERMINOUS
POLITICALLY ASSOCIATED AREAS

DANISH

DUTCH

FRANCE
AND THE OVERSEAS DEPTS.

PORTUGUESE

SPANISH

COMPARATIVE LAND AREAS (Numbers indicate thousands of square miles)

PEOPLE'S REPUBLIC OF CHINA 3,692	INDIA 1,227	...	SOVIET UNION 6,680

PAKISTAN 399 · OTHERS 159 · IRAN 636 · SAUDI ARABIA 618 · MONGOLIA 593 · INDONESIA 575 · TURKEY 301 · ALL OTHERS 2,205

FRANCE 213 · SPAIN 194 · ALL OTHERS 1,498 · SUDAN 968 · ALGERIA 920 · THE CONGO 906 · LIBYA 679 · CHAD 496 · RHODESIA AND NYASALAND 484 · OTHERS 523 · ANGOLA 481 · MOZAMBIQUE 798 · SOUTH AFRICA 472 · NIGER 459 · ETHIOPIA 457 · MALI 465

ASIA 17,085 — EUROPE 3,825 — AFRICA 11,685

COMPARATIVE POPULATIONS (Numbers indicate millions of people)

PEOPLE'S REPUBLIC OF CHINA 730.0	INDIA 467.0	PAKISTAN 100.6	

OTHERS 22.3 · INDONESIA 101.0 · JAPAN 96.2 · KOREA 35.7 · VIETNAM 32.8

ASIA 1,876

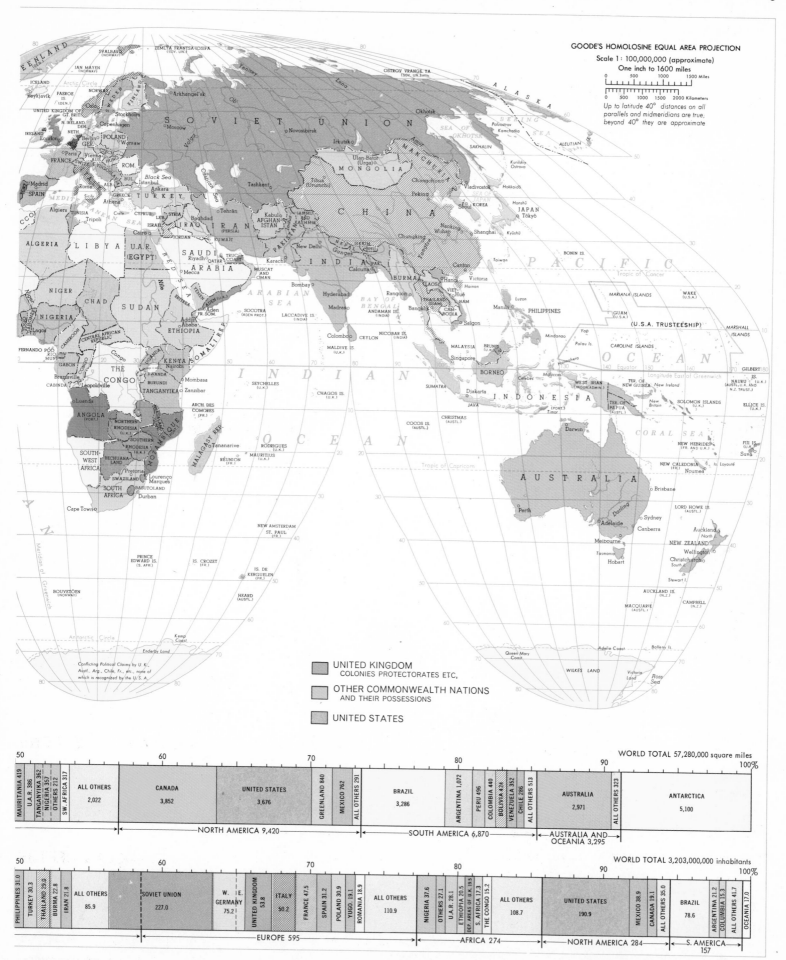

GOODE'S HOMOLOSINE EQUAL AREA PROJECTION

Scale 1 : 100,000,000 (approximate)

One inch to 1600 miles

0 500 1000 1500 Miles

0 500 1000 1500 2000 Kilometers

Up to latitude 40° distances on all parallels and midmeridians are true; beyond 40° they are approximate

UNITED KINGDOM
COLONIES PROTECTORATES ETC,

OTHER COMMONWEALTH NATIONS
AND THEIR POSSESSIONS

UNITED STATES

WORLD TOTAL 57,280,000 square miles

| MAURITANIA 419 | U.A.R. 386 | TANGANYIKA 362 | NIGERIA 357 | OTHERS 212 | SW. AFRICA 317 | ALL OTHERS 2,022 | CANADA 3,852 | UNITED STATES 3,676 | GREENLAND 840 | MEXICO 762 | ALL OTHERS 291 | BRAZIL 3,286 | ARGENTINA 1,072 | PERU 496 | COLOMBIA 440 | BOLIVIA 424 | VENEZUELA 352 | CHILE 286 | ALL OTHERS 513 | AUSTRALIA 2,971 | ALL OTHERS 323 | ANTARCTICA 5,100 |

NORTH AMERICA 9,420 — SOUTH AMERICA 6,870 — AUSTRALIA AND OCEANIA 3,295

WORLD TOTAL 3,203,000,000 inhabitants

| PHILIPPINES 31.0 | TURKEY 30.3 | THAILAND 29.0 | BURMA 22.8 | IRAN 21.8 | ALL OTHERS 85.9 | SOVIET UNION 227.0 | W. GERMANY 75.2 | UNITED KINGDOM 53.8 | ITALY 50.2 | FRANCE 47.5 | SPAIN 31.2 | POLAND 30.9 | YUGO 19.1 | ROMANIA 18.9 | ALL OTHERS 110.9 | NIGERIA 37.6 | OTHERS 27.1 | U.A.R. 28.1 | ETHIOPIA 20.5 | DEP. AREAS OF U.K. 19.5 | S. AFRICA 17.3 | THE CONGO 15.2 | ALL OTHERS 108.7 | UNITED STATES 190.9 | MEXICO 38.9 | CANADA 19.1 | ALL OTHERS 35.0 | BRAZIL 78.6 | ARGENTINA 21.2 | COLUMBIA 15.3 | ALL OTHERS 41.7 | OCEANIA 17.0 |

EUROPE 595 — AFRICA 274 — NORTH AMERICA 284 — S. AMERICA 157

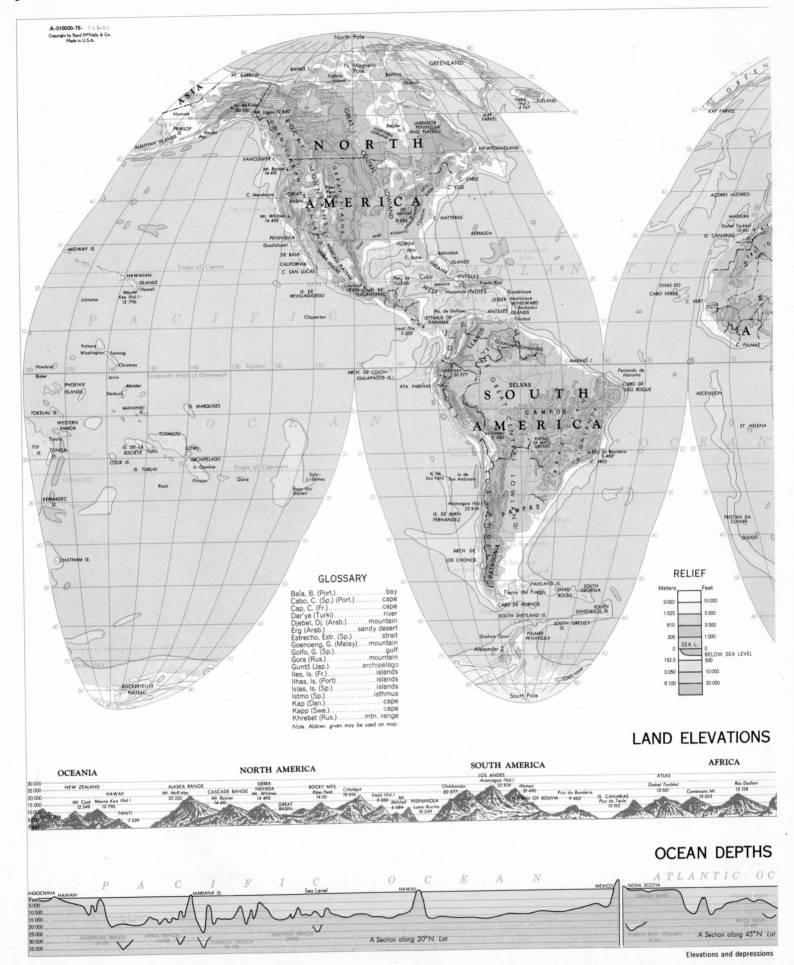

GLOSSARY

Baía, B. (Port.) .... bay
Cabo, C. (Sp.) (Port.) .... cape
Cap, C. (Fr.) .... cape
Dar'ya (Turki) .... river
Djebel, Dj. (Arab.) .... mountain
Erg (Arab.) .... sandy desert
Estrecho, Estr. (Sp.) .... strait
Goenoeng, G. (Malay) ... mountain
Golfo, G. (Sp.) .... gulf
Gora (Rus.) .... mountain
Guntō (Jap.) .... archipelago
Iles, Is. (Fr.) .... islands
Ilhas, Is. (Port) .... islands
Islas, Is. (Sp.) .... islands
Istmo (Sp.) .... isthmus
Kap (Dan.) .... cape
Kapp (Swe.) .... cape
Khrebet (Rus.) .... mtn. range

Note: Abbrev. given may be used on map.

RELIEF

LAND ELEVATIONS

OCEAN DEPTHS

Elevations and depressions

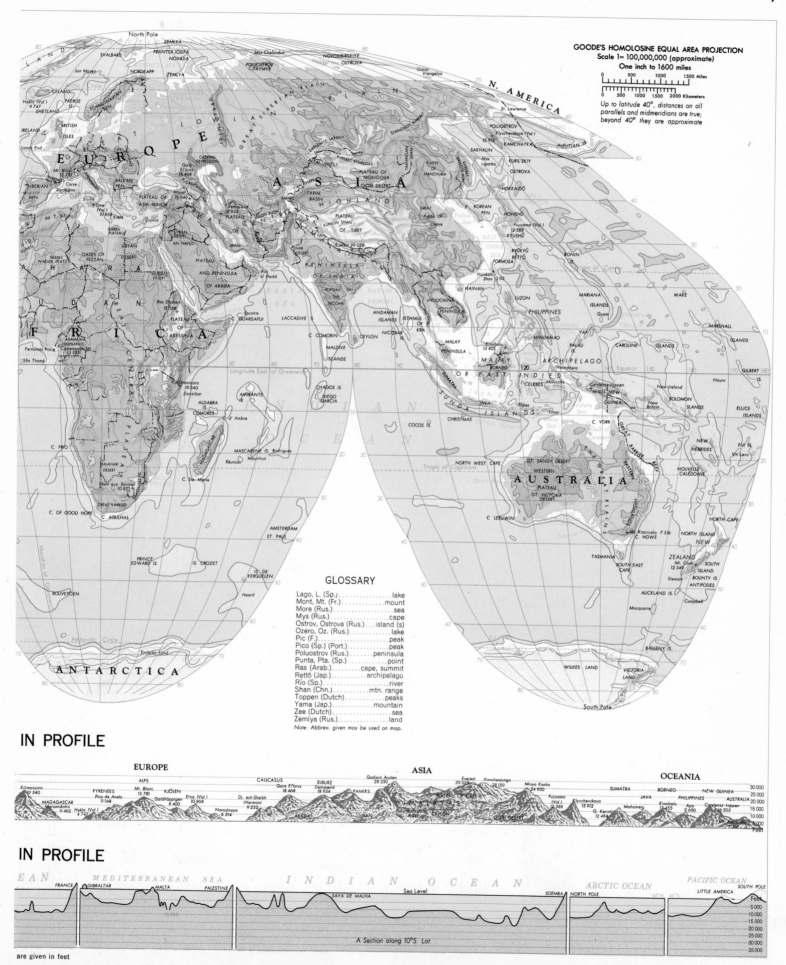

GOODE'S HOMOLOSINE EQUAL AREA PROJECTION
Scale 1= 100,000,000 (approximate)
One inch to 1600 miles

Up to latitude 40°, distances on all
parallels and midmeridians are true;
beyond 40° they are approximate

GLOSSARY

Lago, L. (Sp.)	lake
Mont, Mt. (Fr.)	mount
More (Rus.)	sea
Mys (Rus.)	cape
Ostrov, Ostrova (Rus.)	island (s)
Ozero, Oz. (Rus.)	lake
Pic (F.)	peak
Pico (Sp.) (Port.)	peak
Poluostrov (Rus.)	peninsula
Punta, Pta. (Sp.)	point
Ras (Arab.)	cape, summit
Rettō (Jap.)	archipelago
Río (Sp.)	river
Shan (Chn.)	mtn. range
Toppen (Dutch)	peaks
Yama (Jap.)	mountain
Zee (Dutch)	sea
Zemlya (Rus.)	land

Note: Abbrev. given may be used on map.

IN PROFILE

IN PROFILE

A Section along 10°S. Lat.

are given in feet

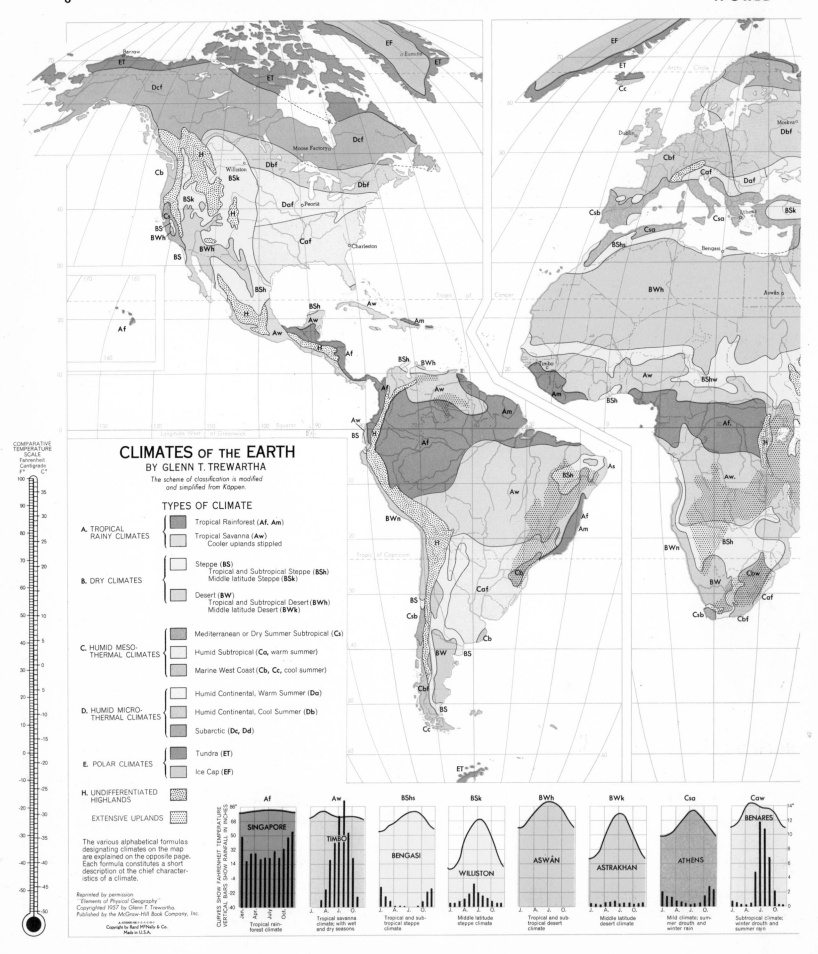

COMPARATIVE
TEMPERATURE
SCALE
Fahrenheit
Centigrade
F°   C°

CLIMATES OF THE EARTH
BY GLENN T. TREWARTHA

*The scheme of classification is modified
and simplified from Köppen.*

TYPES OF CLIMATE

**A. TROPICAL
RAINY CLIMATES**
- Tropical Rainforest (**Af, Am**)
- Tropical Savanna (**Aw**)
  Cooler uplands stippled

B. DRY CLIMATES
- Steppe (**BS**)
  Tropical and Subtropical Steppe (**BSh**)
  Middle latitude Steppe (**BSk**)
- Desert (**BW**)
  Tropical and Subtropical Desert (**BWh**)
  Middle latitude Desert (**BWk**)

**C. HUMID MESO-
THERMAL CLIMATES**
- Mediterranean or Dry Summer Subtropical (**Cs**)
- Humid Subtropical (**Ca,** warm summer)
- Marine West Coast (**Cb, Cc,** cool summer)

**D. HUMID MICRO-
THERMAL CLIMATES**
- Humid Continental, Warm Summer (**Da**)
- Humid Continental, Cool Summer (**Db**)
- Subarctic (**Dc, Dd**)

E. POLAR CLIMATES
- Tundra (**ET**)
- Ice Cap (**EF**)

**H. UNDIFFERENTIATED
HIGHLANDS**

EXTENSIVE UPLANDS

The various alphabetical formulas
designating climates on the map
are explained on the opposite page.
Each formula constitutes a short
description of the chief characteristics of a climate.

Reprinted by permission.
"Elements of Physical Geography"
Copyrighted 1957 by Glenn T. Trewartha.
Published by the McGraw-Hill Book Company, Inc.

A-510000-00-1-1-1-1-0-1
Copyright by Rand McNally & Co.
Made in U.S.A.

CURVES SHOW FAHRENHEIT TEMPERATURE
VERTICAL BARS SHOW RAINFALL IN INCHES

Af
SINGAPORE
Jan. Apr. July Oct.
Tropical rain-
forest climate

Aw
TIMBO
J. A. J. O.
Tropical savanna
climate; with wet
and dry seasons

BShs
BENGASI
J. A. J. O.
Tropical and sub-
tropical steppe
climate

BSk
WILLISTON
J. A. J. O.
Middle latitude
steppe climate

BWh
ASWÂN
J. A. J. O.
Tropical and sub-
tropical desert
climate

BWk
ASTRAKHAN
J. A. J. O.
Middle latitude
desert climate

Csa
ATHENS
J. A. J. O.
Mild climate; sum-
mer drouth and
winter rain

Caw
BENARES
J. A. J. O.
Subtropical climate;
winter drouth and
summer rain

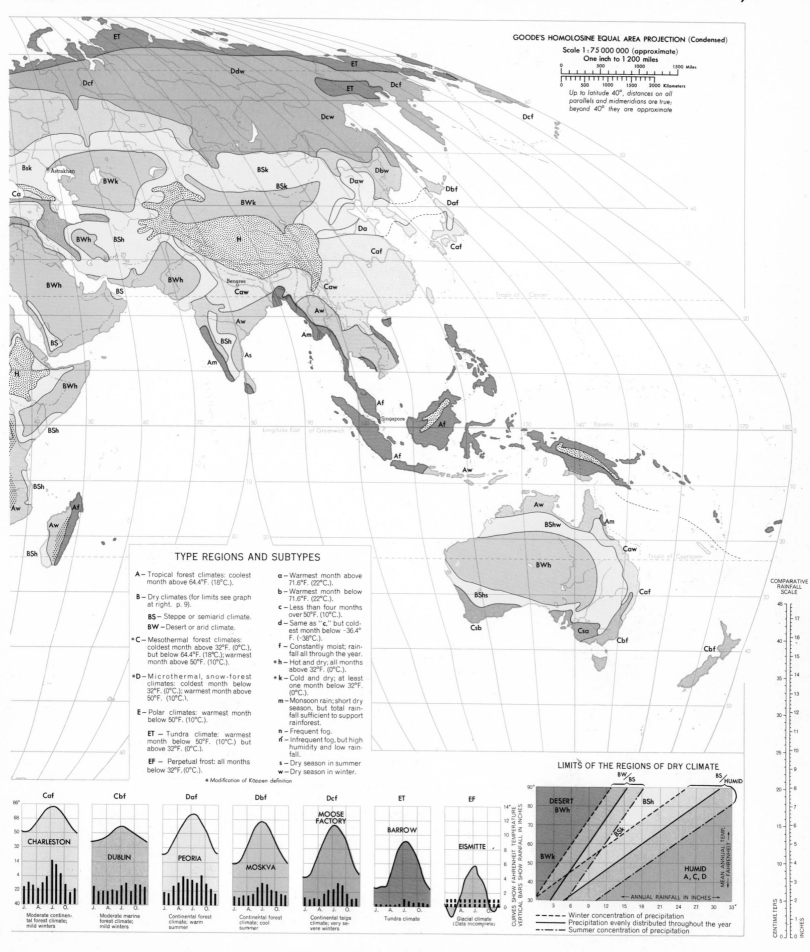

GOODE'S HOMOLOSINE EQUAL AREA PROJECTION (Condensed)

Scale 1:75 000 000 (approximate)
One inch to 1 200 miles

Up to latitude 40°, distances on all
parallels and midmeridians are true;
beyond 40° they are approximate

TYPE REGIONS AND SUBTYPES

A – Tropical forest climates: coolest month above 64.4°F. (18°C.).

B – Dry climates (for limits see graph at right. p. 9).

BS – Steppe or semiarid climate.

BW – Desert or arid climate.

*C – Mesothermal forest climates: coldest month above 32°F. (0°C.), but below 64.4°F. (18°C.); warmest month above 50°F. (10°C.).

*D – Microthermal, snow-forest climates: coldest month below 32°F. (0°C.); warmest month above 50°F. (10°C.).

E – Polar climates: warmest month below 50°F. (10°C.).

ET – Tundra climate: warmest month below 50°F. (10°C.) but above 32°F. (0°C.).

EF – Perpetual frost: all months below 32°F. (0°C.).

a – Warmest month above 71.6°F. (22°C.).

b – Warmest month below 71.6°F. (22°C.).

c – Less than four months over 50°F. (10°C.).

d – Same as "c," but coldest month below −36.4° F. (−38°C.).

f – Constantly moist; rainfall all through the year.

*h – Hot and dry; all months above 32°F. (0°C.).

*k – Cold and dry; at least one month below 32°F. (0°C.).

m – Monsoon rain; short dry season, but total rainfall sufficient to support rainforest.

n – Frequent fog.

n' – Infrequent fog, but high humidity and low rainfall.

s – Dry season in summer.

w – Dry season in winter.

* Modification of Köppen definition

LIMITS OF THE REGIONS OF DRY CLIMATE

CURVES SHOW FAHRENHEIT TEMPERATURE
VERTICAL BARS SHOW RAINFALL IN INCHES

DESERT BWh   BSh   BS HUMID

BWk   BSk   HUMID A, C, D

ANNUAL RAINFALL IN INCHES

MEAN ANNUAL TEMP. FAHRENHEIT

- - - - Winter concentration of precipitation
——— Precipitation evenly distributed throughout the year
—·—· Summer concentration of precipitation

COMPARATIVE RAINFALL SCALE

CENTIMETERS   INCHES

Caf — CHARLESTON
Moderate continental forest climate; mild winters

Cbf — DUBLIN
Moderate marine forest climate; mild winters

Daf — PEORIA
Continental forest climate; warm summer

Dbf — MOSKVA
Continental forest climate; cool summer

Dcf — MOOSE FACTORY
Continental taiga climate; very severe winters

ET — BARROW
Tundra climate

EF — EISMITTE
Glacial climate (Data incomplete)

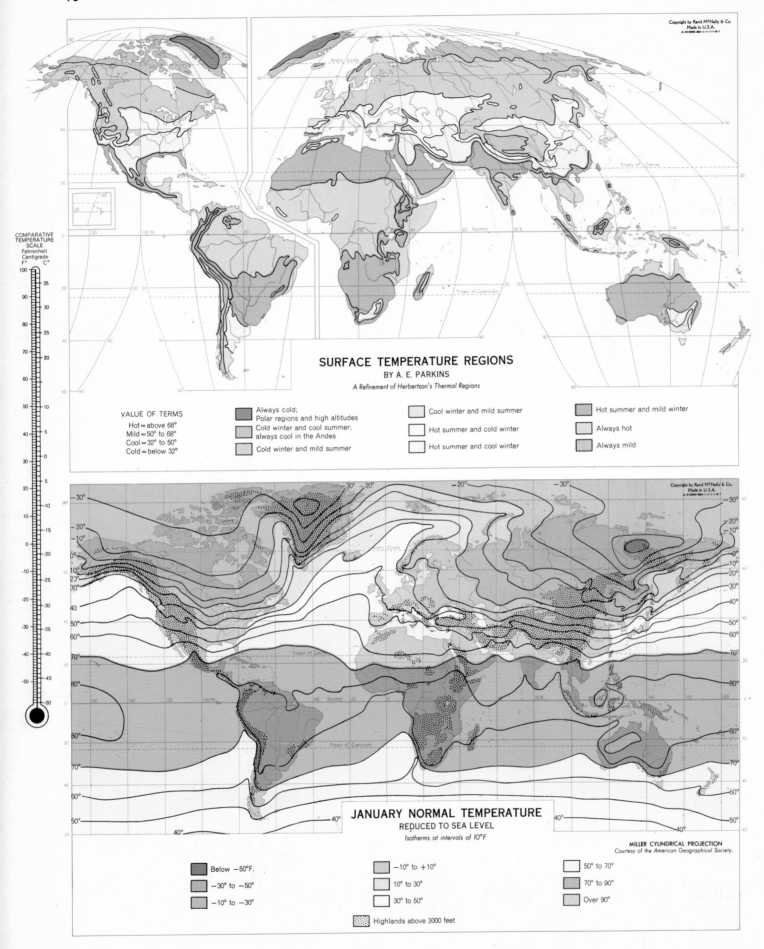

COMPARATIVE
TEMPERATURE
SCALE
Fahrenheit
Centigrade
F° C°

SURFACE TEMPERATURE REGIONS
BY A. E. PARKINS
A Refinement of Herbertson's Thermal Regions

VALUE OF TERMS

Hot = above 68°
Mild = 50° to 68°
Cool = 32° to 50°
Cold = below 32°

Always cold;
Polar regions and high altitudes

Cold winter and cool summer;
always cool in the Andes

Cold winter and mild summer

Cool winter and mild summer

Hot summer and cold winter

Hot summer and cool winter

Hot summer and mild winter

Always hot

Always mild

JANUARY NORMAL TEMPERATURE
REDUCED TO SEA LEVEL
Isotherms at intervals of 10°F

MILLER CYLINDRICAL PROJECTION
Courtesy of the American Geographical Society.

Below −50°F.

−30° to −50°

−10° to −30°

−10° to +10°

10° to 30°

30° to 50°

50° to 70°

70° to 90°

Over 90°

Highlands above 3000 feet

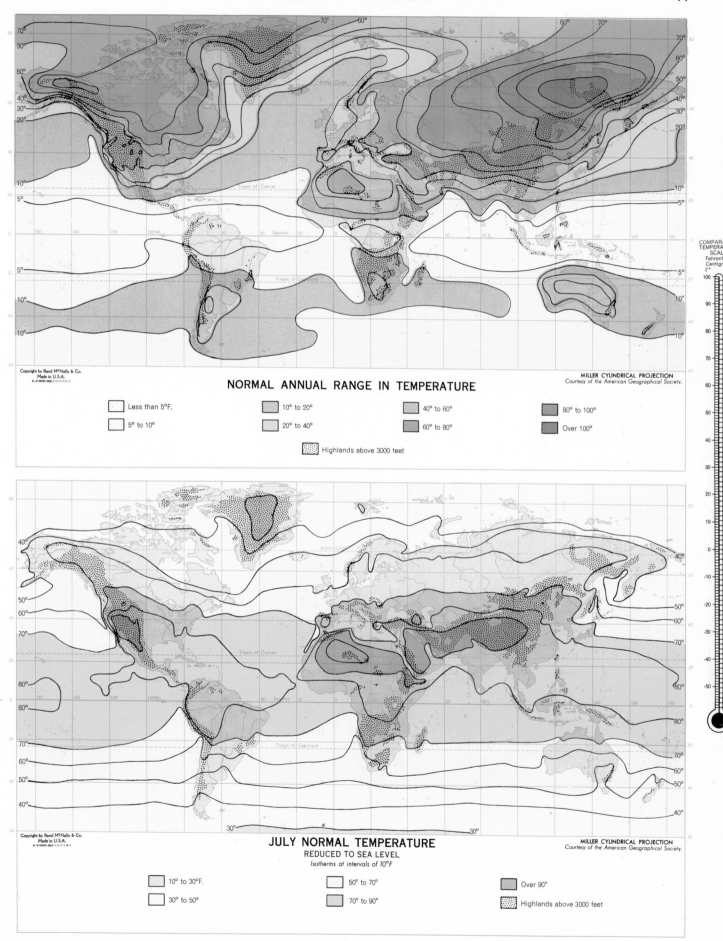

NORMAL ANNUAL RANGE IN TEMPERATURE

Copyright by Rand McNally & Co.
Made in U.S.A.
A-510000-862-1-1-1-1-1

MILLER CYLINDRICAL PROJECTION
Courtesy of the American Geographical Society.

☐ Less than 5°F.	☐ 10° to 20°	☐ 40° to 60°	☐ 80° to 100°
☐ 5° to 10°	☐ 20° to 40°	☐ 60° to 80°	☐ Over 100°

☷ Highlands above 3000 feet

JULY NORMAL TEMPERATURE
REDUCED TO SEA LEVEL
Isotherms at intervals of 10°F

Copyright by Rand McNally & Co.
Made in U.S.A.
A-510000-864-1-1-1-1-0-1

MILLER CYLINDRICAL PROJECTION
Courtesy of the American Geographical Society.

☐ 10° to 30°F.	☐ 50° to 70°	☐ Over 90°
☐ 30° to 50°	☐ 70° to 90°	☷ Highlands above 3000 feet

COMPARATIVE
TEMPERATURE
SCALE
Fahrenheit
Centigrade
F°   C°

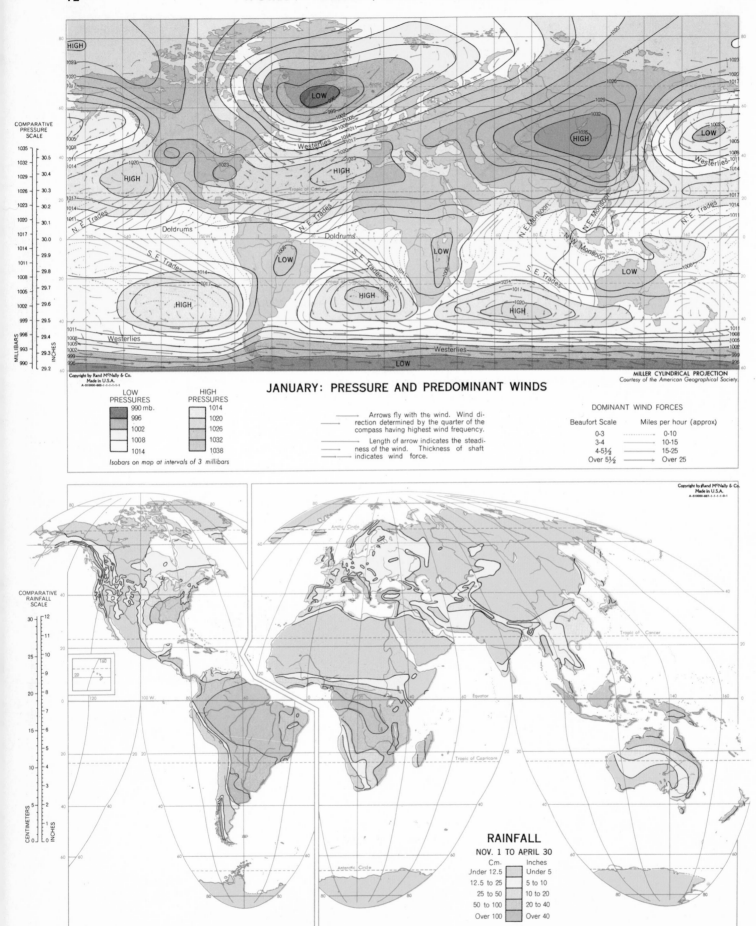

JANUARY: PRESSURE AND PREDOMINANT WINDS

MILLER CYLINDRICAL PROJECTION
Courtesy of the American Geographical Society.

Copyright by Rand McNally & Co.
Made in U.S.A.
A-510000-665-1-1-1-1-1-1

COMPARATIVE
PRESSURE
SCALE

LOW PRESSURES	HIGH PRESSURES
990 mb.	1014
996	1020
1002	1026
1008	1032
1014	1038

Isobars on map at intervals of 3 millibars

Arrows fly with the wind. Wind direction determined by the quarter of the compass having highest wind frequency.

Length of arrow indicates the steadiness of the wind. Thickness of shaft indicates wind force.

DOMINANT WIND FORCES

Beaufort Scale	Miles per hour (approx)
0-3	0-10
3-4	10-15
4-5½	15-25
Over 5½	Over 25

Copyright by Rand McNally & Co.
Made in U.S.A.
A-510000-667-1-1-1-1-0-1

COMPARATIVE
RAINFALL
SCALE

RAINFALL

NOV. 1 TO APRIL 30

Cm.	Inches
Under 12.5	Under 5
12.5 to 25	5 to 10
25 to 50	10 to 20
50 to 100	20 to 40
Over 100	Over 40

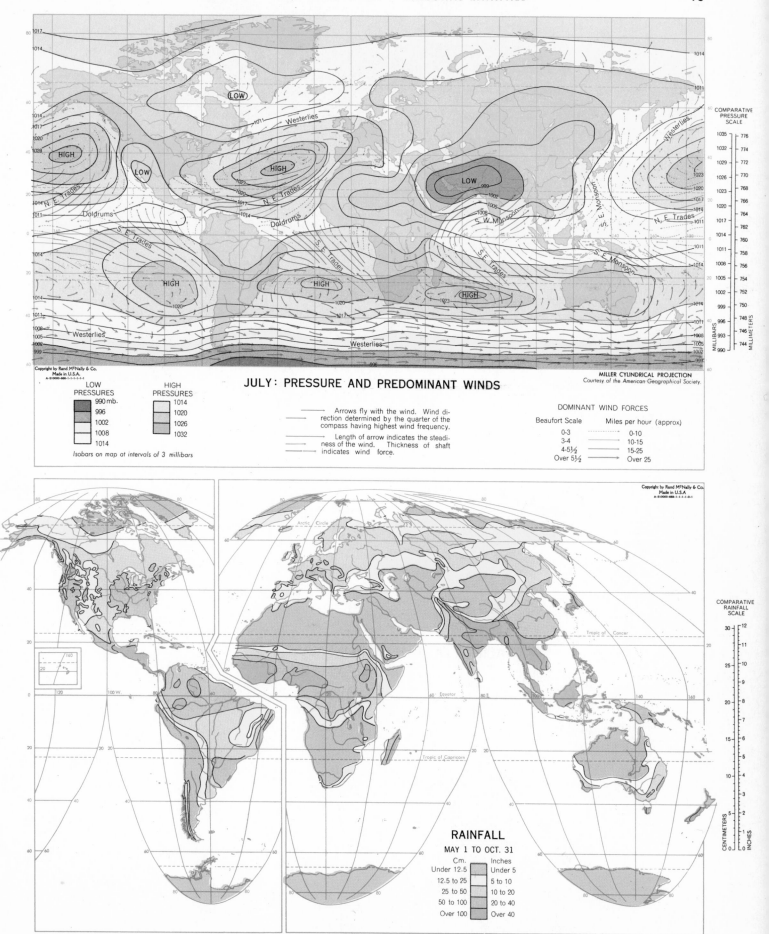

JULY: PRESSURE AND PREDOMINANT WINDS

MILLER CYLINDRICAL PROJECTION
Courtesy of the American Geographical Society.

Copyright by Rand McNally & Co.
Made in U.S.A.
A-510000-668-1-1-1-1-1

COMPARATIVE
PRESSURE
SCALE

LOW PRESSURES	HIGH PRESSURES
990 mb.	1014
996	1020
1002	1026
1008	1032
1014	

Isobars on map at intervals of 3 millibars

Arrows fly with the wind. Wind direction determined by the quarter of the compass having highest wind frequency.

Length of arrow indicates the steadiness of the wind. Thickness of shaft indicates wind force.

DOMINANT WIND FORCES

Beaufort Scale	Miles per hour (approx)
0-3	0-10
3-4	10-15
4-5½	15-25
Over 5½	Over 25

Copyright by Rand McNally & Co.
Made in U.S.A
A-510000-668-1-1-1-1-0-1

COMPARATIVE
RAINFALL
SCALE

RAINFALL

MAY 1 TO OCT. 31

Cm.	Inches
Under 12.5	Under 5
12.5 to 25	5 to 10
25 to 50	10 to 20
50 to 100	20 to 40
Over 100	Over 40

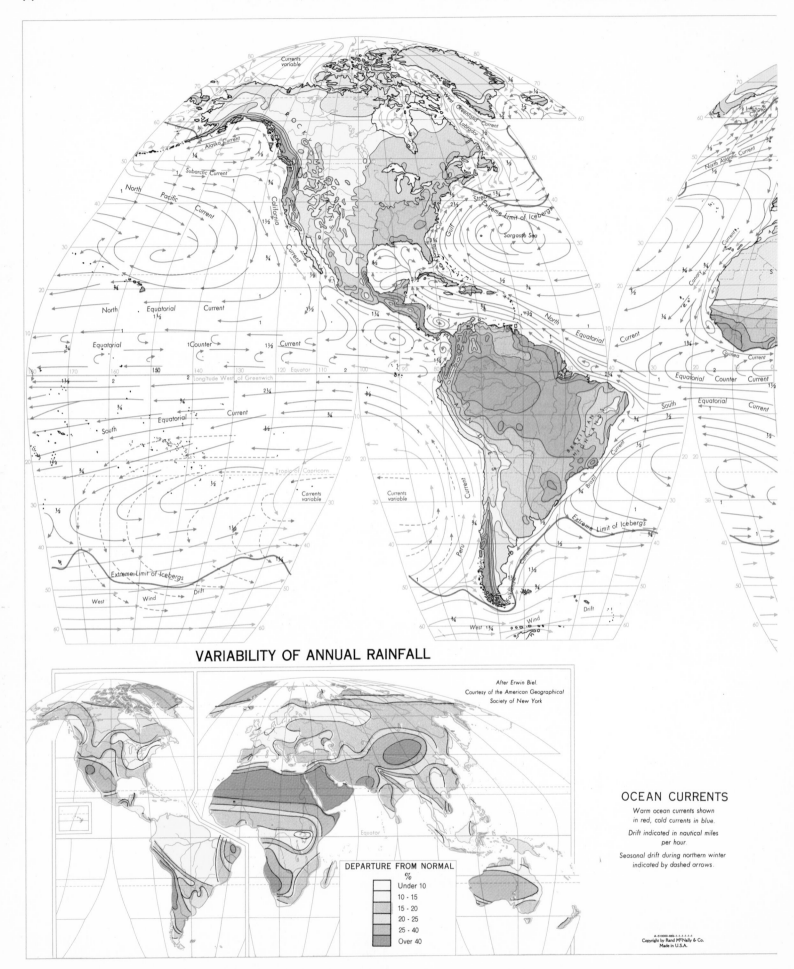

VARIABILITY OF ANNUAL RAINFALL

After Erwin Biel.
Courtesy of the American Geographical
Society of New York

OCEAN CURRENTS

Warm ocean currents shown
in red, cold currents in blue.

Drift indicated in nautical miles
per hour.

Seasonal drift during northern winter
indicated by dashed arrows.

DEPARTURE FROM NORMAL
%
Under 10
10 - 15
15 - 20
20 - 25
25 - 40
Over 40

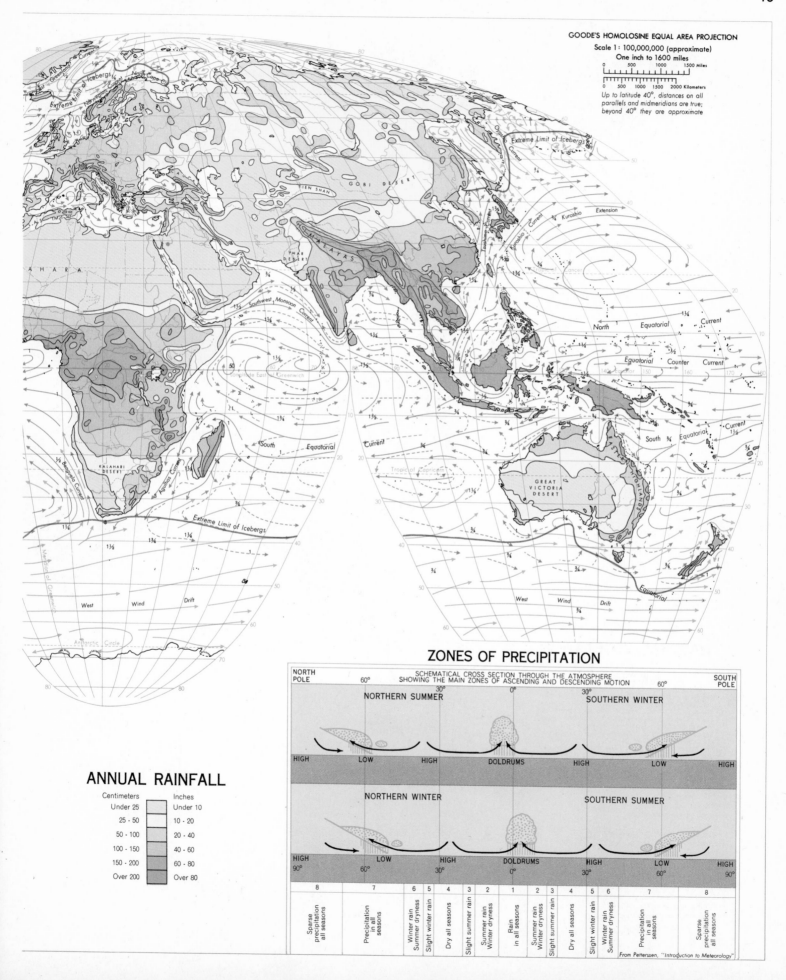

GOODE'S HOMOLOSINE EQUAL AREA PROJECTION

Scale 1 : 100,000,000 (approximate)

One inch to 1600 miles

Up to latitude 40°, distances on all
parallels and midmeridians are true;
beyond 40° they are approximate

ZONES OF PRECIPITATION

ANNUAL RAINFALL

Centimeters		Inches
Under 25		Under 10
25 - 50		10 - 20
50 - 100		20 - 40
100 - 150		40 - 60
150 - 200		60 - 80
Over 200		Over 80

NORTH POLE · SCHEMATICAL CROSS SECTION THROUGH THE ATMOSPHERE SHOWING THE MAIN ZONES OF ASCENDING AND DESCENDING MOTION · SOUTH POLE

NORTHERN SUMMER · SOUTHERN WINTER

HIGH · LOW · HIGH · DOLDRUMS · HIGH · LOW · HIGH

NORTHERN WINTER · SOUTHERN SUMMER

HIGH · LOW · HIGH · DOLDRUMS · HIGH · LOW · HIGH

From Petterssen, "Introduction to Meteorology"

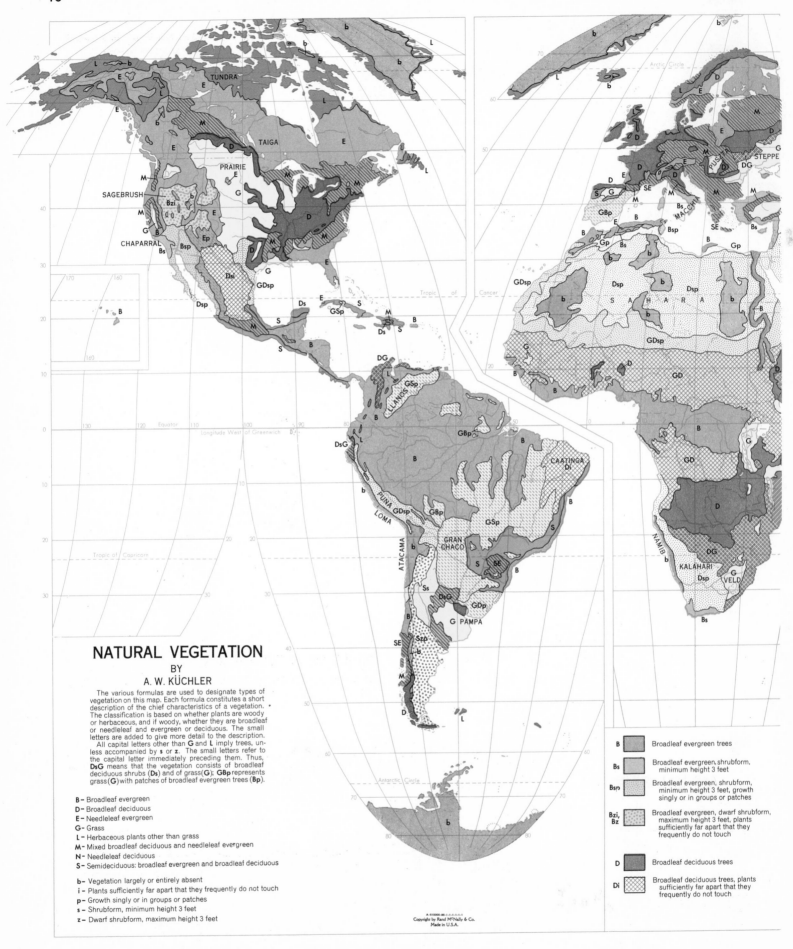

NATURAL VEGETATION

BY
A. W. KÜCHLER

The various formulas are used to designate types of
vegetation on this map. Each formula constitutes a short
description of the chief characteristics of a vegetation.
The classification is based on whether plants are woody
or herbaceous, and if woody, whether they are broadleaf
or needleleaf and evergreen or deciduous. The small
letters are added to give more detail to the description.

All capital letters other than **G** and **L** imply trees, unless accompanied by **s** or **z**. The small letters refer to
the capital letter immediately preceding them. Thus,
DsG means that the vegetation consists of broadleaf
deciduous shrubs (**Ds**) and of grass (**G**); **GBp** represents
grass (**G**) with patches of broadleaf evergreen trees (**Bp**).

B– Broadleaf evergreen
D– Broadleaf deciduous
E– Needleleaf evergreen
G– Grass
L– Herbaceous plants other than grass
M– Mixed broadleaf deciduous and needleleaf evergreen
N– Needleleaf deciduous
S– Semideciduous: broadleaf evergreen and broadleaf deciduous

b– Vegetation largely or entirely absent
i– Plants sufficiently far apart that they frequently do not touch
p– Growth singly or in groups or patches
s– Shrubform, minimum height 3 feet
z– Dwarf shrubform, maximum height 3 feet

	Broadleaf evergreen trees
B	Broadleaf evergreen trees
Bs	Broadleaf evergreen, shrubform, minimum height 3 feet
Bsn	Broadleaf evergreen, shrubform, minimum height 3 feet, growth singly or in groups or patches
Bzi, Bz	Broadleaf evergreen, dwarf shrubform, maximum height 3 feet, plants sufficiently far apart that they frequently do not touch
D	Broadleaf deciduous trees
Di	Broadleaf deciduous trees, plants sufficiently far apart that they frequently do not touch

GOODE'S HOMOLOSINE EQUAL AREA PROJECTION (Condensed)

Scale 1:75 000 000 (approximate)

One inch to 1 200 miles

Up to latitude 40°, distances on all
parallels and midmeridians are true,
beyond 40° they are approximate

	Ds	Broadleaf deciduous, shrubform, minimum height 3 feet
	Dsi	Broadleaf deciduous, shrubform, minimum height 3 feet, plants sufficiently far apart that they frequently do not touch
	Dsp	Broadleaf deciduous, shrubform, minimum height 3 feet, growth singly or in groups or patches
	Dzp	Broadleaf deciduous, dwarf shrubform, maximum height 3 feet, growth singly or in groups or patches
	DsG	Broadleaf deciduous, shrubform, minimum height 3 feet Grass and other herbaceous plants
	DG	Broadleaf deciduous trees Grass and other herbaceous plants
	DBs	Broadleaf deciduous trees Broadleaf evergreen, shrubform, minimum height 3 feet

	E	Needleleaf evergreen trees
	Ep	Needleleaf evergreen trees, growth singly or in groups or patches
	G	Grass and other herbaceous plants
	Gp	Grass and other herbaceous plants, growth singly or in groups or patches
	GBp	Grass and other herbaceous plants Broadleaf evergreen trees, growth singly or in groups or patches
	GD	Grass and other herbaceous plants Broadleaf deciduous trees
	GDp	Grass and other herbaceous plants Broadleaf deciduous trees, growth singly or in groups or patches

	GDsp	Grass and other herbaceous plants Broadleaf deciduous, shrubform, minimum height 3 feet, growth singly or in groups or patches
	GSp	Grass and other herbaceous plants Semideciduous: broadleaf evergreen and broadleaf deciduous trees, growth singly or in groups or patches
	L	Herbaceous plants other than grass
	M	Mixed: broadleaf deciduous and needleleaf evergreen trees
	N	Needleleaf deciduous trees
	ND	Needleleaf deciduous trees Broadleaf deciduous trees

	S	Semideciduous: broadleaf evergreen and broadleaf deciduous trees
	Ss	Semideciduous: broadleaf evergreen and broadleaf deciduous, shrubform, minimum height 3 feet
	SsG	Semideciduous: broadleaf evergreen and broadleaf deciduous, shrubform, minimum height 3 feet Grass and other herbaceous plants
	Szp	Semideciduous: broadleaf evergreen and broadleaf deciduous, dwarf shrubform, maximum height 3 feet, growth singly or in groups or patches
	SE	Semideciduous: broadleaf evergreen and broadleaf deciduous trees Needleleaf evergreen trees
	b	Vegetation largely or entirely absent

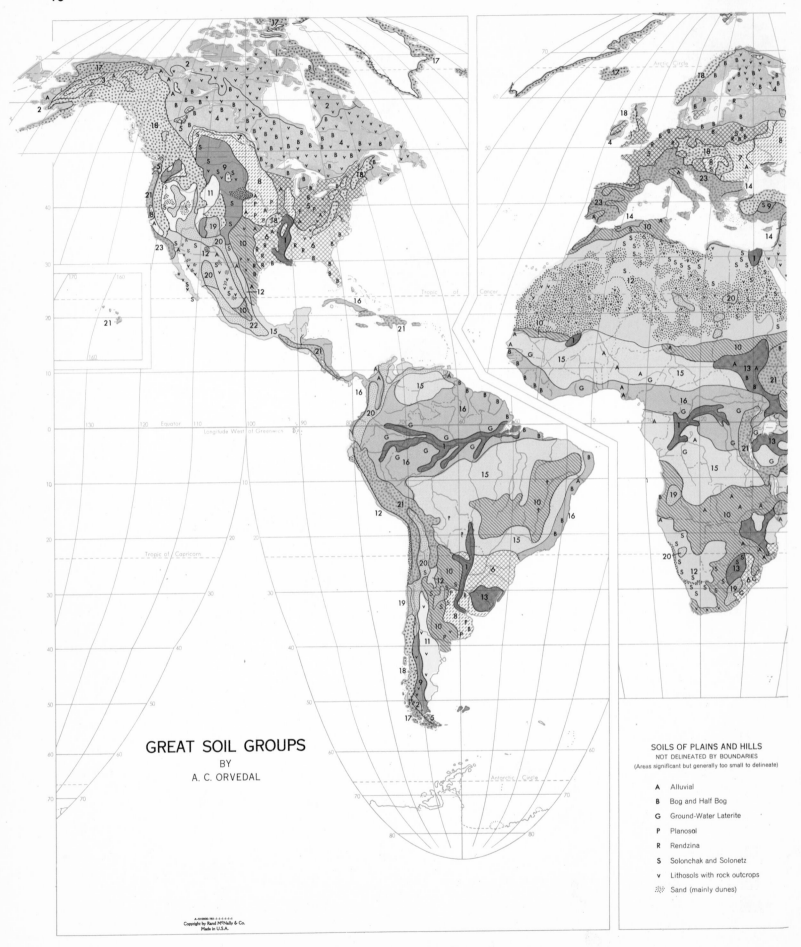

GREAT SOIL GROUPS

BY

A. C. ORVEDAL

SOILS OF PLAINS AND HILLS
NOT DELINEATED BY BOUNDARIES
(Areas significant but generally too small to delineate)

A Alluvial

B Bog and Half Bog

G Ground-Water Laterite

P Planosol

R Rendzina

S Solonchak and Solonetz

v Lithosols with rock outcrops

⋮ Sand (mainly dunes)

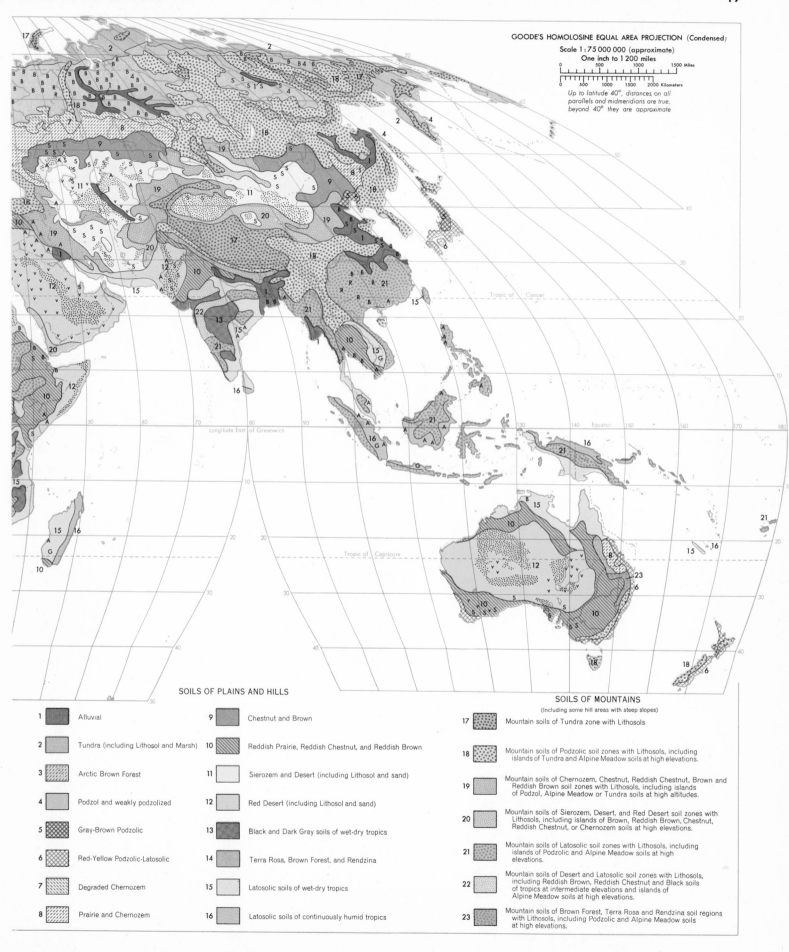

GOODE'S HOMOLOSINE EQUAL AREA PROJECTION (Condensed)
Scale 1 : 75 000 000 (approximate)
One inch to 1 200 miles

0   500   1000   1500 Miles
0 500 1000 1500 2000 Kilometers

Up to latitude 40°, distances on all
parallels and midmeridians are true,
beyond 40° they are approximate

SOILS OF PLAINS AND HILLS

1 Alluvial

2 Tundra (including Lithosol and Marsh)

3 Arctic Brown Forest

4 Podzol and weakly podzolized

5 Gray-Brown Podzolic

6 Red-Yellow Podzolic-Latosolic

7 Degraded Chernozem

8 Prairie and Chernozem

9 Chestnut and Brown

10 Reddish Prairie, Reddish Chestnut, and Reddish Brown

11 Sierozem and Desert (including Lithosol and sand)

12 Red Desert (including Lithosol and sand)

13 Black and Dark Gray soils of wet-dry tropics

14 Terra Rosa, Brown Forest, and Rendzina

15 Latosolic soils of wet-dry tropics

16 Latosolic soils of continuously humid tropics

SOILS OF MOUNTAINS
(Including some hill areas with steep slopes)

17 Mountain soils of Tundra zone with Lithosols

18 Mountain soils of Podzolic soil zones with Lithosols, including islands of Tundra and Alpine Meadow soils at high elevations.

19 Mountain soils of Chernozem, Chestnut, Reddish Chestnut, Brown and Reddish Brown soil zones with Lithosols, including islands of Podzol, Alpine Meadow or Tundra soils at high altitudes.

20 Mountain soils of Sierozem, Desert, and Red Desert soil zones with Lithosols, including islands of Brown, Reddish Brown, Chestnut, Reddish Chestnut, or Chernozem soils at high elevations.

21 Mountain soils of Latosolic soil zones with Lithosols, including islands of Podzolic and Alpine Meadow soils at high elevations.

22 Mountain soils of Desert and Latosolic soil zones with Lithosols, including Reddish Brown, Reddish Chestnut and Black soils of tropics at intermediate elevations and islands of Alpine Meadow soils at high elevations.

23 Mountain soils of Brown Forest, Terra Rosa and Rendzina soil regions with Lithosols, including Podzolic and Alpine Meadow soils at high elevations.

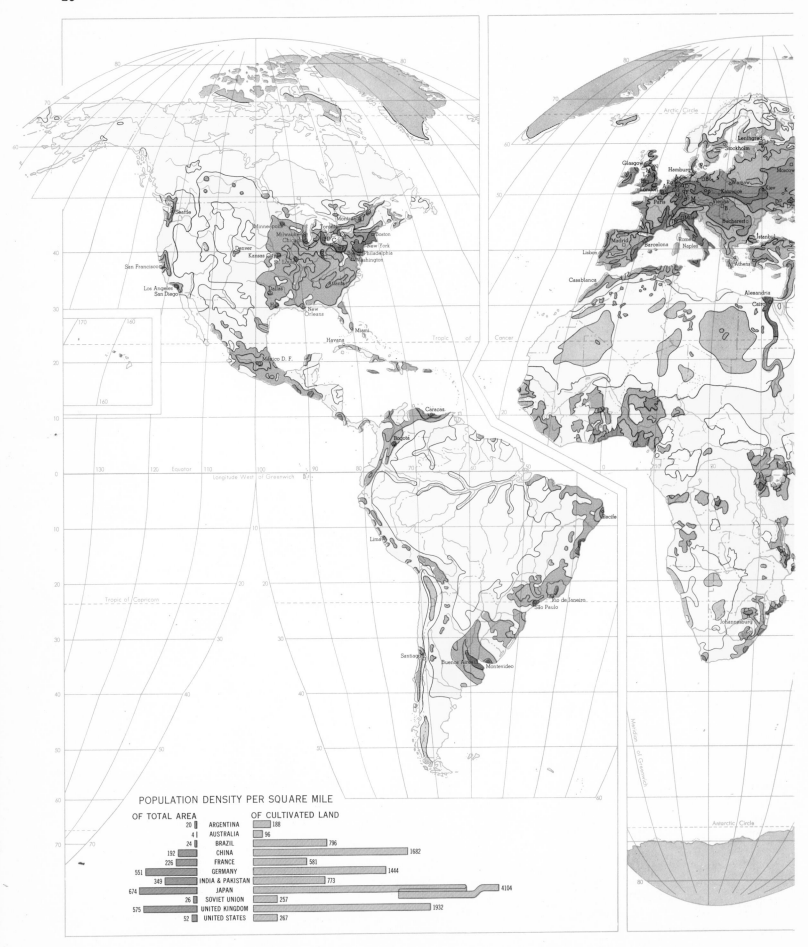

POPULATION DENSITY PER SQUARE MILE

OF TOTAL AREA | | OF CULTIVATED LAND
20	ARGENTINA	188
4	AUSTRALIA	96
24	BRAZIL	796
192	CHINA	1682
226	FRANCE	581
551	GERMANY	1444
349	INDIA & PAKISTAN	773
674	JAPAN	4104
26	SOVIET UNION	257
575	UNITED KINGDOM	1932
52	UNITED STATES	267

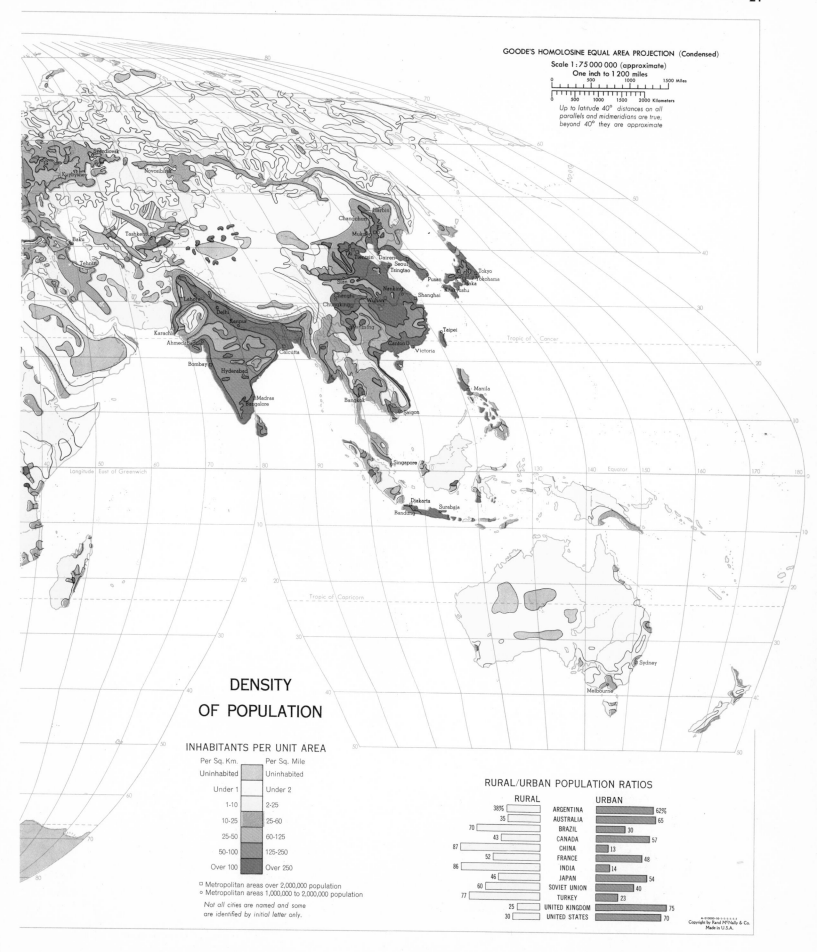

GOODE'S HOMOLOSINE EQUAL AREA PROJECTION (Condensed)

Scale 1 : 75 000 000 (approximate)

One inch to 1 200 miles

Up to latitude 40° distances on all parallels and midmeridians are true; beyond 40° they are approximate

DENSITY
OF POPULATION

INHABITANTS PER UNIT AREA

Per Sq. Km.	Per Sq. Mile
Uninhabited	Uninhabited
Under 1	Under 2
1-10	2-25
10-25	25-60
25-50	60-125
50-100	125-250
Over 100	Over 250

□ Metropolitan areas over 2,000,000 population
○ Metropolitan areas 1,000,000 to 2,000,000 population

Not all cities are named and some are identified by initial letter only.

RURAL/URBAN POPULATION RATIOS

RURAL		URBAN
38%	ARGENTINA	62%
35	AUSTRALIA	65
70	BRAZIL	30
43	CANADA	57
87	CHINA	13
52	FRANCE	48
86	INDIA	14
46	JAPAN	54
60	SOVIET UNION	40
77	TURKEY	23
25	UNITED KINGDOM	75
30	UNITED STATES	70

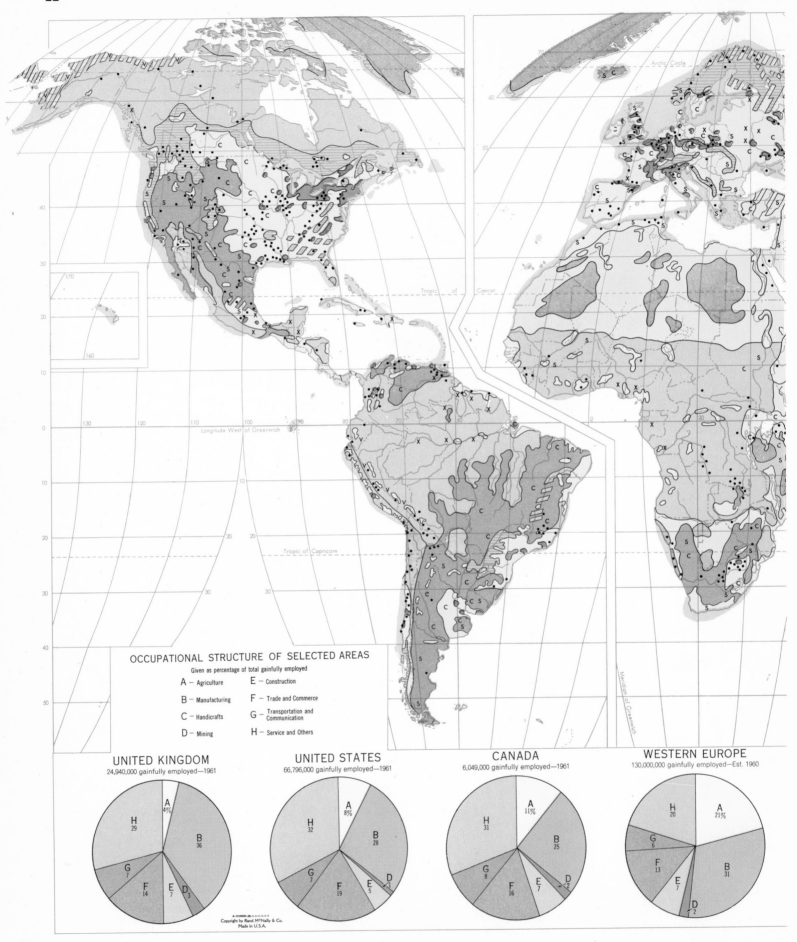

OCCUPATIONAL STRUCTURE OF SELECTED AREAS

Given as percentage of total gainfully employed

A – Agriculture   E – Construction

B – Manufacturing   F – Trade and Commerce

C – Handicrafts   G – Transportation and
                           Communication

D – Mining   H – Service and Others

UNITED KINGDOM
24,940,000 gainfully employed—1961

UNITED STATES
66,796,000 gainfully employed—1961

CANADA
6,049,000 gainfully employed—1961

WESTERN EUROPE
130,000,000 gainfully employed—Est. 1960

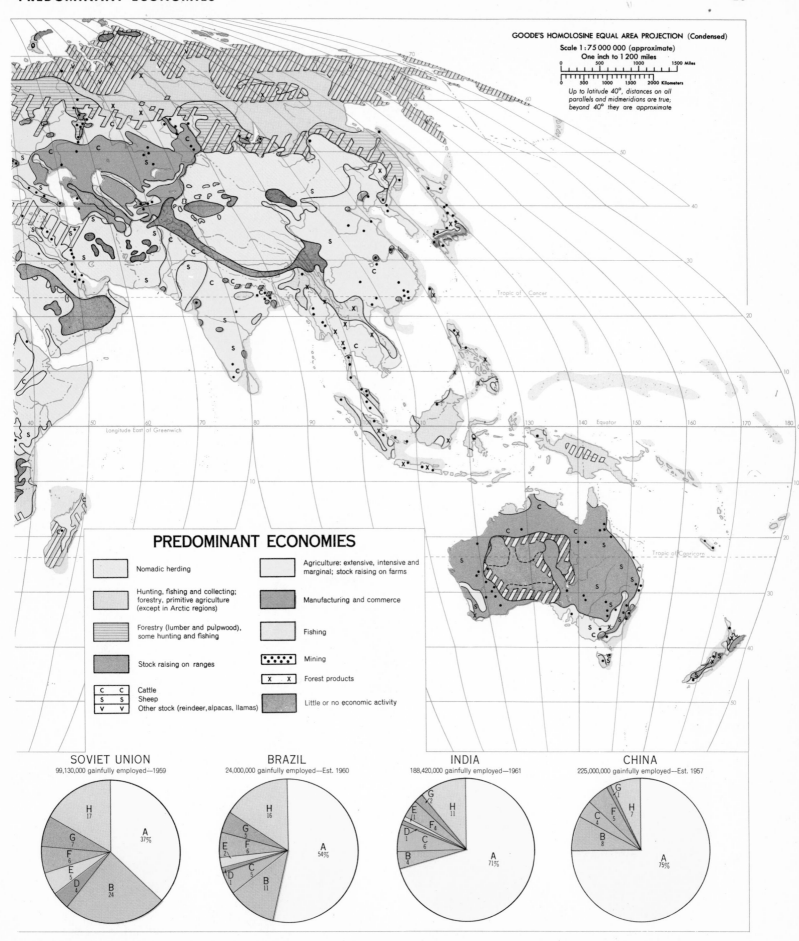

GOODE'S HOMOLOSINE EQUAL AREA PROJECTION (Condensed)

Scale 1 : 75 000 000 (approximate)
One inch to 1 200 miles

Up to latitude 40°, distances on all
parallels and midmeridians are true;
beyond 40° they are approximate

PREDOMINANT ECONOMIES

Nomadic herding

Hunting, fishing and collecting;
forestry, primitive agriculture
(except in Arctic regions)

Forestry (lumber and pulpwood),
some hunting and fishing

Stock raising on ranges

C C Cattle
S S Sheep
V V Other stock (reindeer, alpacas, llamas)

Agriculture: extensive, intensive and
marginal; stock raising on farms

Manufacturing and commerce

Fishing

Mining

Forest products

Little or no economic activity

SOVIET UNION
99,130,000 gainfully employed—1959

H 17
A 37%
G 7
F 6
E 5
D 4
B 24

BRAZIL
24,000,000 gainfully employed—Est. 1960

H 16
G 5
E 2
F 6
D 1
C 5
B 11
A 54%

INDIA
188,420,000 gainfully employed—1961

G 2
H 11
E 1
F 4
D 1
C 6
B 4
A 71%

CHINA
225,000,000 gainfully employed—Est. 1957

G 1
F 5
H 7
C 4
B 8
A 75%

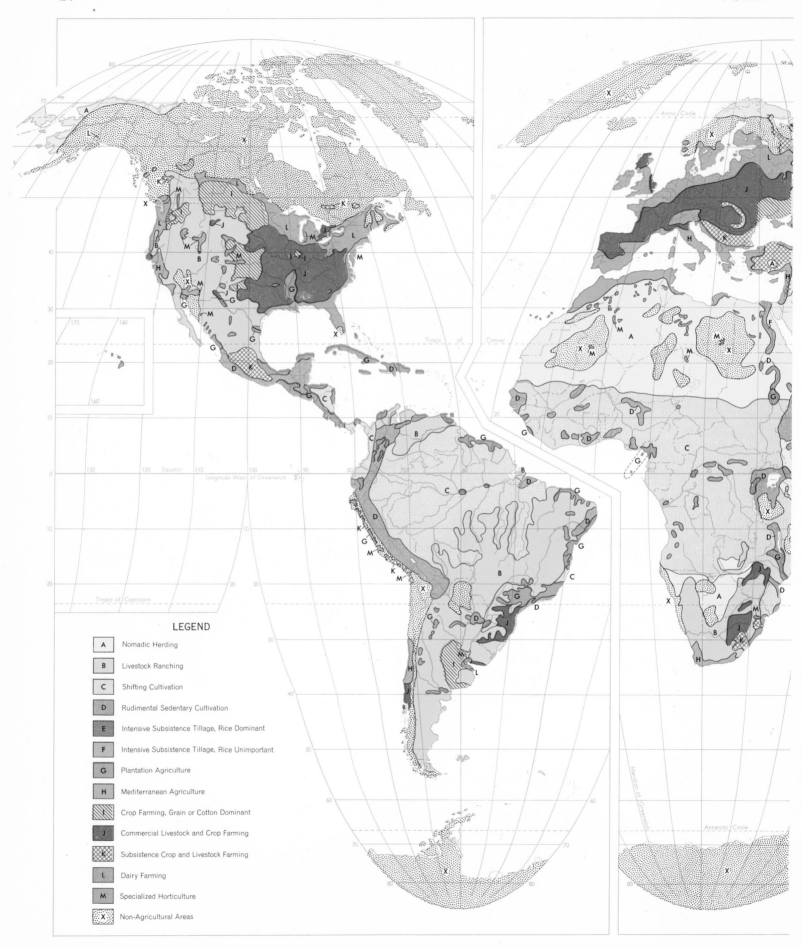

LEGEND

A	Nomadic Herding
B	Livestock Ranching
C	Shifting Cultivation
D	Rudimental Sedentary Cultivation
E	Intensive Subsistence Tillage, Rice Dominant
F	Intensive Subsistence Tillage, Rice Unimportant
G	Plantation Agriculture
H	Mediterranean Agriculture
I	Crop Farming, Grain or Cotton Dominant
J	Commercial Livestock and Crop Farming
K	Subsistence Crop and Livestock Farming
L	Dairy Farming
M	Specialized Horticulture
X	Non-Agricultural Areas

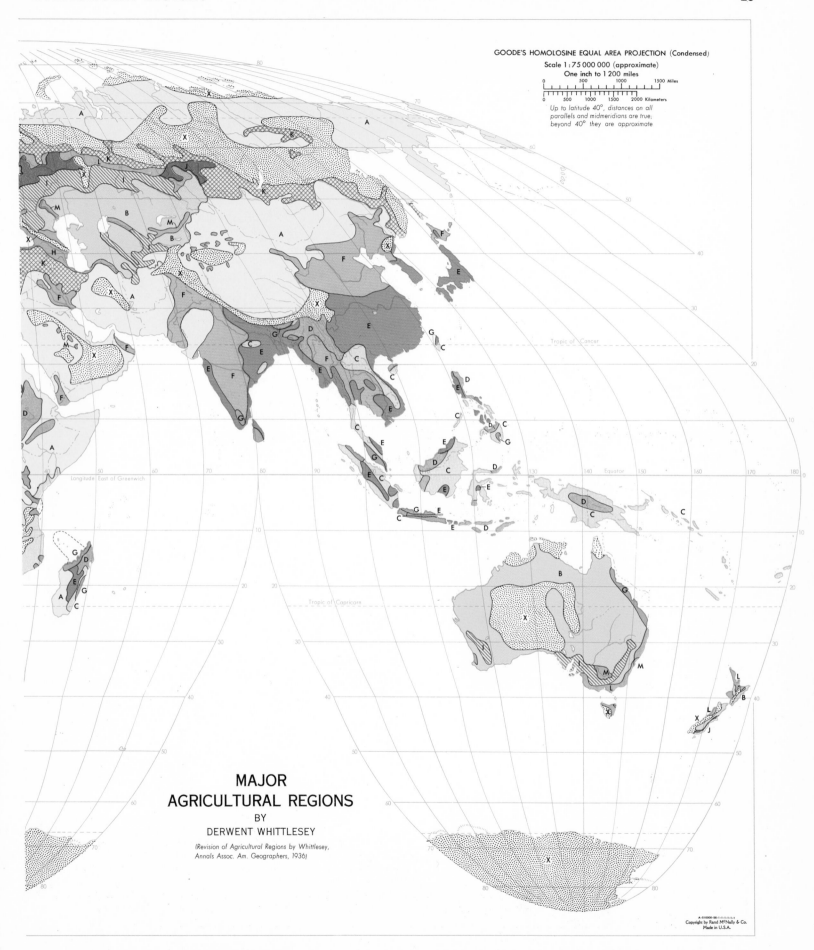

GOODE'S HOMOLOSINE EQUAL AREA PROJECTION (Condensed)
Scale 1 : 75 000 000 (approximate)
One inch to 1 200 miles

Up to latitude 40°, distances on all
parallels and midmeridians are true;
beyond 40° they are approximate

Tropic of Cancer

Longitude East of Greenwich

Equator

Tropic of Capricorn

MAJOR
AGRICULTURAL REGIONS
BY
DERWENT WHITTLESEY

(Revision of Agricultural Regions by Whittlesey,
Annals Assoc. Am. Geographers, 1936)

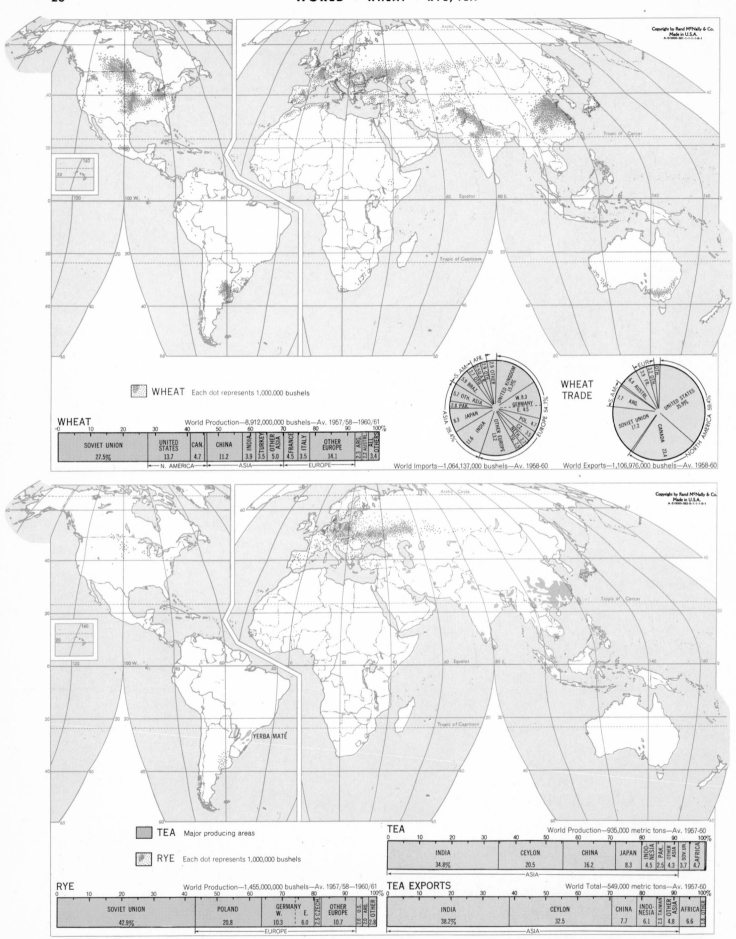

◻ **WHEAT**   Each dot represents 1,000,000 bushels

WHEAT TRADE

WHEAT
World Production—8,912,000,000 bushels—Av. 1957/58—1960/61

0	10	20	30	40	50	60	70	80	90	100%			
SOVIET UNION 27.5%				UNITED STATES 13.7	CAN. 4.7	CHINA 11.2	INDIA 3.9	TURKEY 3.5	OTHER ASIA 5.0	FRANCE 4.5	ITALY 3.5	OTHER EUROPE 14.1	ARG. 2.3 / AUSTRL. 2.2 / ALL OTHERS 3.4

← N. AMERICA → ← ASIA → ← EUROPE →

World Imports—1,064,137,000 bushels—Av. 1958-60
World Exports—1,106,976,000 bushels—Av. 1958-60

Pie chart (Imports): S. AM. — AFR. 2.9 OTHER / 2.0 AFR. / 2.4 EGYPT / 3.9 BRAZ. / 5.7 OTH. ASIA / 2.8 PAK. / 8.3 JAPAN / 11.6 INDIA — ASIA 28.4% — UNITED KINGDOM 15.3% / W. 8.3 GERMANY E. 4.5 / POL. 4.7 / NETH. 2.7 / C.) 3.5 / OTHER EUROPE 13.2 — EUROPE 54.7%

Pie chart (Exports): EUR. 13.9 OTH. / S. AM. — 1.7 / 6.4 FR. / AUSTRL. ARG. — UNITED STATES 35.9% / CANADA 23.4 — NORTH AMERICA 59.4% — SOVIET UNION 17.2

YERBA MATÉ

◻ **TEA**   Major producing areas

◻ **RYE**   Each dot represents 1,000,000 bushels

RYE
World Production—1,455,000,000 bushels—Av. 1957/58—1960/61

0	10	20	30	40	50	60	70	80	90	100%	
SOVIET UNION 42.9%					POLAND 20.8	GERMANY W. 10.3 / E. 6.0	CZECH 2.5	OTHER EUROPE 10.7	U.S. 2.0 / ARG. 2.0 / OTHER 2.8	

← EUROPE →

TEA
World Production—935,000 metric tons—Av. 1957-60

0	10	20	30	40	50	60	70	80	90	100%
INDIA 34.8%			CEYLON 20.5		CHINA 16.2		JAPAN 8.3	INDO-NESIA 4.5 / PAK. 2.5 / OTHER ASIA 4.3	SOV UN 3.7	AFRICA 4.7

← ASIA →

TEA EXPORTS
World Total—549,000 metric tons—Av. 1957-60

0	10	20	30	40	50	60	70	80	90	100%
INDIA 38.2%				CEYLON 32.5			CHINA 7.7	INDO-NESIA 6.1 / TAIWAN 2.3 / OTHER ASIA 4.8	AFRICA 6.6	OTHER 1.8

← ASIA →

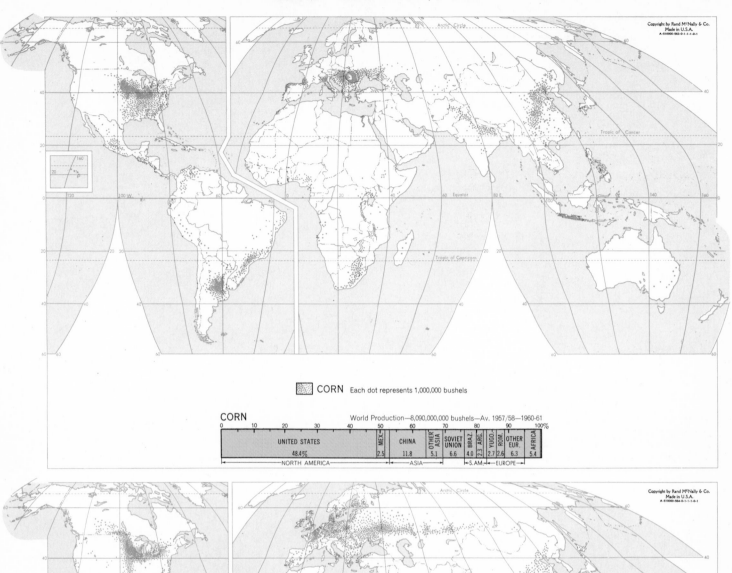

CORN Each dot represents 1,000,000 bushels

CORN

World Production—8,090,000,000 bushels—Av. 1957/58—1960-61

0	10	20	30	40	50	60	70	80	90	100%

| UNITED STATES 48.4% | MEX. 2.5 | CHINA 11.8 | OTHER ASIA 5.1 | SOVIET UNION 6.6 | BRAZ. 4.0 | ARG. 2.3 | YUGO- 2.7 | ROM. 2.6 | OTHER EUR. 6.3 | AFRICA 5.4 |

——NORTH AMERICA——   ——ASIA——   ——S. AM.——EUROPE——

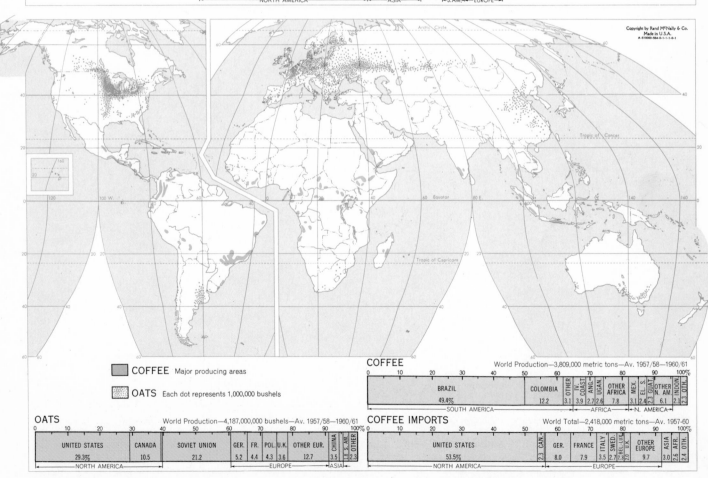

COFFEE Major producing areas

OATS Each dot represents 1,000,000 bushels

COFFEE

World Production—3,809,000 metric tons—Av. 1957/58—1960/61

0	10	20	30	40	50	60	70	80	90	100%

| BRAZIL 49.4% | COLOMBIA 12.2 | OTHER S. AM. 3.1 | IV. COAST 3.9 | ANG. 2.7 | UGAN. 2.6 | OTHER AFRICA 7.8 | MEX. 3.1 | EL S. 2.3 | GUAT. 2.4 | OTHER N. AM. 6.1 | INDON. 2.1 | OTH. 2.3 |

——SOUTH AMERICA——   ——AFRICA——   ——N. AMERICA——

OATS

World Production—4,187,000,000 bushels—Av. 1957/58—1960/61

0	10	20	30	40	50	60	70	80	90	100%

| UNITED STATES 29.3% | CANADA 10.5 | SOVIET UNION 21.2 | GER. 5.2 | FR. 4.4 | POL. 4.3 | U.K. 3.6 | OTHER EUR. 12.7 | CHINA 3.5 | S. AM. 2.3 | OTHER 2.3 |

——NORTH AMERICA——   ——EUROPE——   ——ASIA——

COFFEE IMPORTS

World Total—2,418,000 metric tons—Av. 1957-60

0	10	20	30	40	50	60	70	80	90	100%

| UNITED STATES 53.5% | CAN. 2.3 | GER. 8.0 | FRANCE 7.9 | ITALY 3.5 | SWED. 2.7 | BEL.-LUX. 2.0 | U.K. | OTHER EUROPE 9.7 | ASIA 3.0 | AFR. 2.6 | OTH. 2.4 |

——NORTH AMERICA——   ——EUROPE——

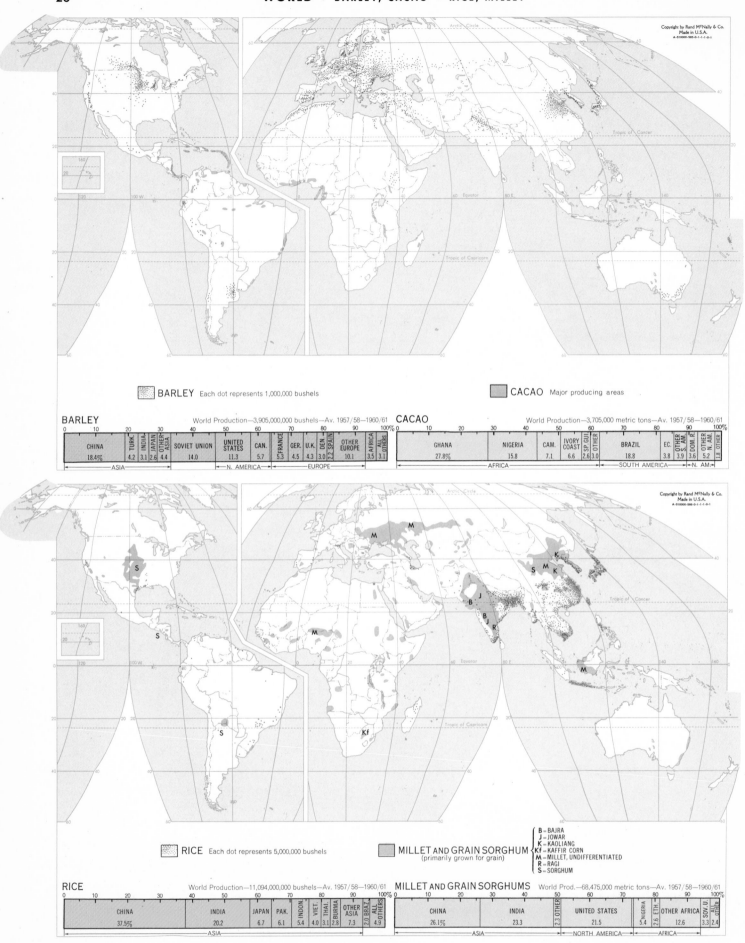

Copyright by Rand McNally & Co.
Made in U.S.A.
A-510000-565-0-1-1-1-0-1

BARLEY Each dot represents 1,000,000 bushels

CACAO Major producing areas

BARLEY
World Production—3,905,000,000 bushels—Av. 1957/58—1960/61

CHINA 18.4%	TURK. 4.2	INDIA- 3.1	JAPAN 2.6	OTHER ASIA 4.4	SOVIET UNION 14.0	UNITED STATES 11.3	CAN. 5.7	FRANCE 5.3	GER. 4.5	U.K. 4.3	DEN. 3.0	SPAIN 2.2	OTHER EUROPE 10.1	AFRICA 3.5	ALL OTHERS 3.1

ASIA — N. AMERICA — EUROPE

CACAO
World Production—3,705,000 metric tons—Av. 1957/58—1960/61

GHANA 27.8%	NIGERIA 15.8	CAM. 7.1	IVORY COAST 6.6	SP. GUI. 2.6	OTHER 3.0	BRAZIL 18.8	EC. 3.8	OTHER S. AM. 3.9	DOM. R. 3.6	OTHER N. AM. 5.2	OTHER 1.8

AFRICA — SOUTH AMERICA — N. AM.

Copyright by Rand McNally & Co.
Made in U.S.A.
A-510000-566-0-1-1-1-0-1

RICE Each dot represents 5,000,000 bushels

MILLET AND GRAIN SORGHUM
(primarily grown for grain)

B = BAJRA
J = JOWAR
K = KAOLIANG
Kf = KAFFIR CORN
M = MILLET, UNDIFFERENTIATED
R = RAGI
S = SORGHUM

RICE
World Production—11,094,000,000 bushels—Av. 1957/58—1960/61

CHINA 37.5%	INDIA 20.2	JAPAN 6.7	PAK. 6.1	INDON. 5.4	VIET. 4.0	THAI. 3.1	BURMA 2.8	OTHER ASIA 7.3	BRAZ. 2.0	ALL OTHERS 4.9

ASIA

MILLET AND GRAIN SORGHUMS
World Prod.—68,475,000 metric tons—Av. 1957/58—1960/61

CHINA 26.1%	INDIA 23.3	OTHER 2.3	UNITED STATES 21.5	NIGERIA 5.4	ETH. 2.6	OTHER AFRICA 12.6	SOV. U. 3.3	ALL OTHER 2.4

ASIA — NORTH AMERICA — AFRICA

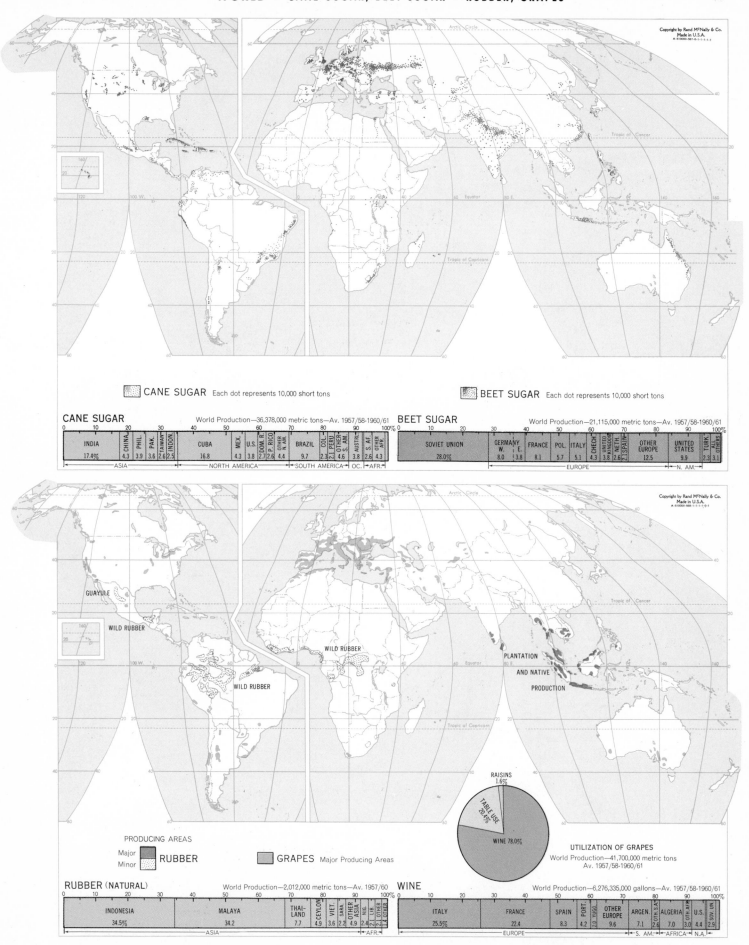

Copyright by Rand McNally & Co.
Made in U.S.A.
A-510000-567-0-1-1-1-1-1

CANE SUGAR Each dot represents 10,000 short tons

BEET SUGAR Each dot represents 10,000 short tons

CANE SUGAR

World Production—36,378,000 metric tons—Av. 1957/58-1960/61

INDIA 17.4%	CHINA 4.3	PHIL. 3.9	PAK. 3.6	TAIWAN 2.6	INDON. 2.5	CUBA 16.8	MEX. 4.3	U.S. 3.8	DOM. R. 2.7	P. RICO 2.6	OTHER N. AM. 4.4	BRAZIL 9.7	COL. 2.3	PERU 2.1

— ASIA — — NORTH AMERICA — — SOUTH AMERICA — OC. AFR.

(OTHER S. AM. 4.6 / AUSTRL. 3.8 / S. AF. 2.6 / OTHER AFR. 4.3)

BEET SUGAR

World Production—21,115,000 metric tons—Av. 1957/58-1960/61

SOVIET UNION 28.0%	GERMANY W. 8.0	E. 3.8	FRANCE 8.1	POL. 5.7	ITALY 5.1	CZECH. 4.3	UNITED KINGDOM 3.8	NETH. 2.6	SPAIN 2.1	OTHER EUROPE 12.5	UNITED STATES 9.9	TURK. 2.3	ALL OTHERS 3.1

— EUROPE — — N. AM. —

GUAYULE

WILD RUBBER

WILD RUBBER

WILD RUBBER

WILD RUBBER

PLANTATION

AND NATIVE

PRODUCTION

Copyright by Rand McNally & Co.
Made in U.S.A.
A-510000-568-1-1-1-1-0-1

PRODUCING AREAS
Major
Minor **RUBBER**

GRAPES Major Producing Areas

RAISINS 1.6%

TABLE USE 20%

WINE 78.0%

UTILIZATION OF GRAPES
World Production—41,700,000 metric tons
Av. 1957/58-1960/61

RUBBER (NATURAL)

World Production—2,012,000 metric tons—Av. 1957/60

INDONESIA 34.5%	MALAYA 34.2	THAI-LAND 7.7	CEYLON 4.9	VIET. 3.6	SARA. 2.2	OTHER ASIA 4.9	NIG. 2.4	LIB.	OTHER	OTHER

— ASIA — AFR.

WINE

World Production—6,276,335,000 gallons—Av. 1957/58-1960/61

ITALY 25.5%	FRANCE 22.4	SPAIN 8.3	PORT. 4.2	YUGO. 2.0	OTHER EUROPE 9.6	ARGEN. 7.1	OTH. S.A. 2.6	ALGERIA 7.0	OTH. AFR. 3.0	U.S. 4.4	SOV. UN. 2.9

— EUROPE — — S. AM. — — AFRICA — N.A.

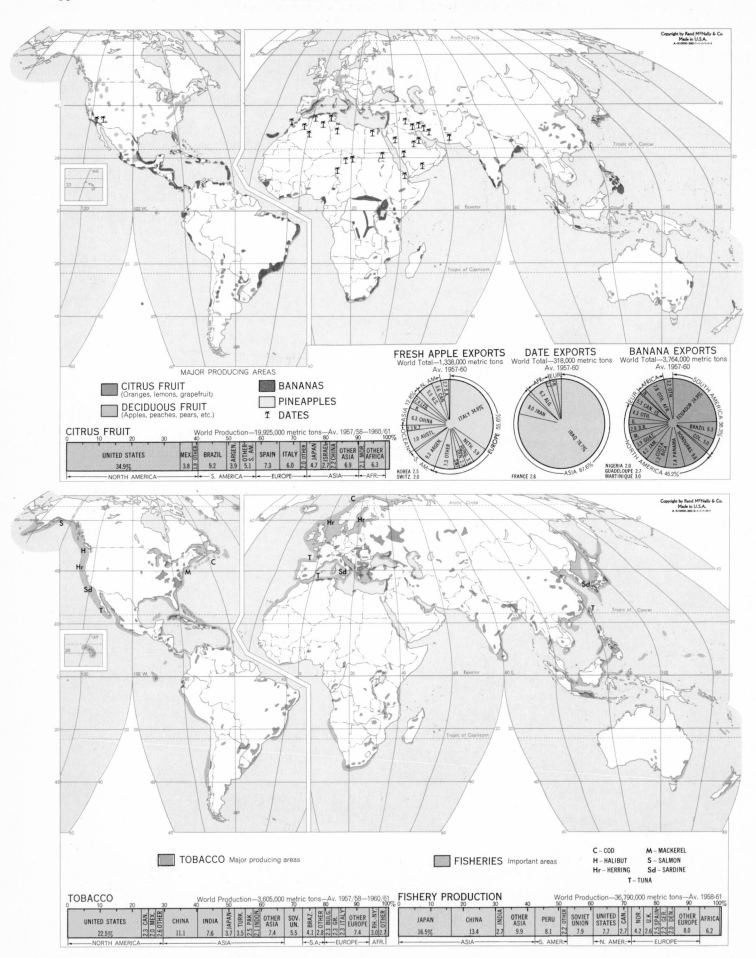

MAJOR PRODUCING AREAS

CITRUS FRUIT
(Oranges, lemons, grapefruit)

DECIDUOUS FRUIT
(Apples, peaches, pears, etc.)

BANANAS

PINEAPPLES

DATES

FRESH APPLE EXPORTS
World Total—1,338,000 metric tons
Av. 1957-60

ASIA 12.8% · N. AM. · EUR.
2.7 S.A.
3.6 CAN.
5.5 U.S.
6.3 CHINA
ITALY 34.6%
2.3 N.Z.
7.0 AUSTL.
9.3 OTHER
S. AM.
7.3 OTHER
NETH. 5.9
HUNG.
2.1
FR.
2.1
EUROPE 55.6%
KOREA 2.5
SWITZ. 2.0

DATE EXPORTS
World Total—318,000 metric tons
Av. 1957-60

AFR. · EUR.
6.2 ALG.
8.0 IRAN
IRAQ 78.9%
ASIA 81.6%
FRANCE 2.6

BANANA EXPORTS
World Total—3,764,000 metric tons
Av. 1957-60

EUR. · AFRICA
3.2 OTH.
7.8 OTR. AFR.
3.3 CAN. IS.
4.3 OTH.
SOUTH AMERICA 36.3%
ECUADOR 24.9%
2.8 D.R.
G.
3.0 GUAT.
M.
4.2 JAM.
BRAZIL 6.3
COL. 5.0
7.3 COSTA
RICA
7.4 PANAMA
HONDURAS 9.6
NORTH AMERICA 45.2%
NIGERIA 2.0
GUADELOUPE 2.7
MARTINIQUE 3.0

CITRUS FRUIT
World Production—19,925,000 metric tons—Av. 1957/58—1960/61

0	10	20	30	40	50	60	70	80	90	100%				
UNITED STATES 34.9%			MEX. 3.8	OTHER 1.9	BRAZIL 9.2	ARGEN. 3.9	OTHER S. AM. 5.1	SPAIN 7.3	ITALY 6.0	OTHER 2.0	JAPAN 4.7	ISRAEL 2.7	OTHER ASIA 6.9	MOR. 2.1 · OTHER AFRICA 6.3
◄—————NORTH AMERICA—————►					◄———S. AMERICA———►			◄———EUROPE———►		◄———————ASIA———————►				◄—AFR.—►

TOBACCO Major producing areas

FISHERIES Important areas

C — COD
H — HALIBUT
Hr — HERRING
M — MACKEREL
S — SALMON
Sd — SARDINE
T — TUNA

TOBACCO
World Production—3,605,000 metric tons—Av. 1957/58—1960/61

0	10	20	30	40	50	60	70	80	90	100%										
UNITED STATES 22.5%		CAN. 2.3	MEX. 2.0	OTHER 2.6	CHINA 11.1	INDIA 7.6	JAPAN 3.7	TURK. 3.5	PAK. 2.5	INDON. 2.1	OTHER ASIA 7.4	SOV. UN. 5.5	BRAZ. 4.1	OTHER 2.8	BULG. 2.3	GR. 2.3	ITALY 2.3	OTHER EUROPE 7.4	RH.-NY. 3.0 · OTHER 2.7
◄———NORTH AMERICA———►					◄——————————ASIA——————————►								◄S.A.►	◄————EUROPE————►					◄AFR.►

FISHERY PRODUCTION
World Production—36,790,000 metric tons—Av. 1958-61

0	10	20	30	40	50	60	70	80	90	100%									
JAPAN 16.5%		CHINA 13.4	INDIA 2.7	OTHER ASIA 9.9	PERU 8.1	OTHER 2.2	SOVIET UNION 7.9	UNITED STATES 7.7	CAN. 2.7	NOR. 4.2	U.K. 2.5	SPAIN 2.2	GER. 2.0	DEN. 2.0	OTHER EUROPE 8.0	AFRICA 6.2
◄—————————ASIA—————————►				◄S. AMER.►		◄—N. AMER.—►			◄——————————EUROPE——————————►						

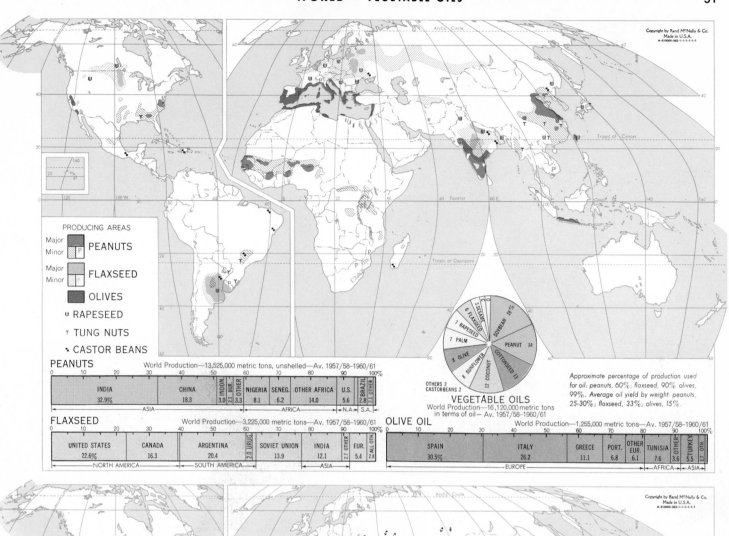

PRODUCING AREAS

Major / Minor [P] PEANUTS
Major / Minor [F] FLAXSEED
OLIVES
ꟺ RAPESEED
т TUNG NUTS
❧ CASTOR BEANS

VEGETABLE OILS
World Production—16,120,000 metric tons
in terms of oil—Av. 1957/58–1960/61

Pie chart: SOYBEAN 18%, PEANUT 14, COTTONSEED 13, COCONUT 12, SUNFLOWER 8, OLIVE 8, PALM 7, RAPESEED 7, FLAXSEED 6, SESAME 3, OTHERS 2, CASTORBEANS 2

Approximate percentage of production used
for oil: peanuts, 60%; flaxseed, 90% olives,
99%. Average oil yield by weight: peanuts,
25-30%; flaxseed, 33%; olives, 15%.

PEANUTS
World Production—13,525,000 metric tons, unshelled—Av. 1957/58–1960/61

INDIA 32.9%	CHINA 18.3	INDON. 3.0	BUR. 2.1	OTHER 3.3	NIGERIA 8.1	SENEG. 6.2	OTHER AFRICA 14.0	U.S. 5.6	BRAZIL 2.8	OTHER 2.1
← ASIA →					← AFRICA →			N.A.	S.A.	

FLAXSEED
World Production—3,225,000 metric tons—Av. 1957/58–1960/61

UNITED STATES 22.6%	CANADA 16.3	ARGENTINA 20.4	URUG. 2.0	SOVIET UNION 13.9	INDIA 12.1	OTHER 2.7	EUR. 5.4	ALL OTH. 2.8
← NORTH AMERICA →		← SOUTH AMERICA →		← ASIA →				

OLIVE OIL
World Production—1,255,000 metric tons—Av. 1957/58–1960/61

SPAIN 30.5%	ITALY 26.2	GREECE 11.1	PORT. 6.8	OTHER EUR. 6.1	TUNISIA 7.6	OTHER AFRICA 3.6	TURKEY 5.5	OTH. 1.7
← EUROPE →					← AFRICA →		← ASIA →	

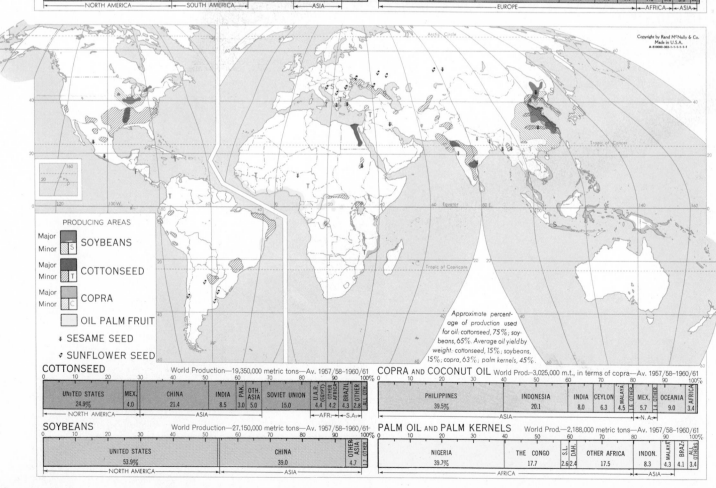

PRODUCING AREAS

Major / Minor [S] SOYBEANS
Major / Minor [T] COTTONSEED
Major / Minor [C] COPRA
OIL PALM FRUIT
ꕔ SESAME SEED
❧ SUNFLOWER SEED

Approximate percent-
age of production used
for oil: cottonseed, 75%; soybeans, 65%. Average oil yield by
weight: cottonseed, 15%; soybeans,
15%; copra, 63%; palm kernels, 45%.

COTTONSEED
World Production—19,350,000 metric tons—Av. 1957/58–1960/61

UNITED STATES 24.9%	MEX. 4.0	CHINA 21.4	INDIA 8.5	PAK. 3.0	OTH. ASIA 5.0	SOVIET UNION 15.0	U.A.R. (EGYPT) 4.4	OTHER AFRICA 4.2	BRAZIL 4.3	OTHER 2.8
← NORTH AMERICA →		← ASIA →					AFR.		S.A.	

COPRA AND COCONUT OIL
World Prod.—3,025,000 m.t., in terms of copra—Av. 1957/58–1960/61

PHILIPPINES 39.5%	INDONESIA 20.1	INDIA 8.0	CEYLON 6.3	MALAYA 4.5	OTHER 1.3	MEX. 5.7	OTHER 1.4	OCEANIA 9.0	AFRICA 3.4
← ASIA →						← N.A. →			

SOYBEANS
World Production—27,150,000 metric tons—Av. 1957/58–1960/61

UNITED STATES 53.9%	CHINA 39.0	OTHER ASIA 4.7	ALL OTHER 1.7
← NORTH AMERICA →	← ASIA →		

PALM OIL AND PALM KERNELS
World Prod.—2,188,000 metric tons—Av. 1957/58–1960/61

NIGERIA 39.7%	THE CONGO 17.7	S.L. 2.6	DAH. 2.4	OTHER AFRICA 17.5	INDON. 8.3	MALAYA 4.3	BRAZ. 4.1	ALL OTHERS 3.4
← AFRICA →					← ASIA →			

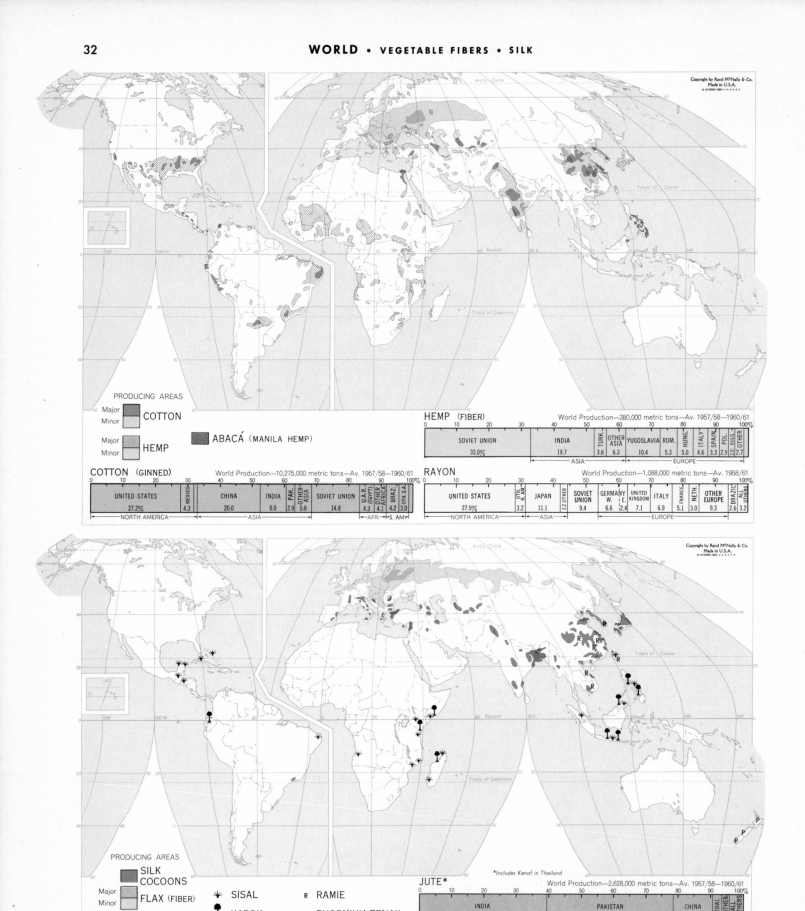

PRODUCING AREAS

Major / Minor **COTTON**

Major / Minor **HEMP**

ABACÁ (MANILA HEMP)

HEMP (FIBER)
World Production—380,000 metric tons—Av. 1957/58—1960/61

SOVIET UNION 33.0%	INDIA 19.7	TURK. 3.6	OTHER ASIA 6.3	YUGOSLAVIA 10.4	ROM. 5.3	HUNG. 5.0	ITALY 4.6	SPAIN 3.3	POL. 2.9	BULG. 2.0	OTHER 2.7

ASIA / EUROPE

COTTON (GINNED)
World Production—10,275,000 metric tons—Av. 1957/58—1960/61

UNITED STATES 27.2%	MEXICO 4.3	CHINA 20.0	INDIA 8.0	PAK. 2.9	OTHER ASIA 5.0	SOVIET UNION 14.8	U.A.R. (EGYPT) 4.3	OTHER AFRICA 4.1	BRAZ. 4.2	OTH. S.A. 3.0

NORTH AMERICA / ASIA / AFR.–S. AM

RAYON
World Production—1,088,000 metric tons—Av. 1958/61

UNITED STATES 27.9%	OTH. N. AM. 3.2	JAPAN 11.1	OTHER 2.2	SOVIET UNION 9.4	GERMANY W. 6.6 E. 2.4	UNITED KINGDOM 7.1	ITALY 6.9	FRANCE 5.1	NETH. 3.0	OTHER EUROPE 9.3	BRAZIL 2.6	ALL OTHERS 3.2

NORTH AMERICA / ASIA / EUROPE

PRODUCING AREAS

SILK COCOONS

Major / Minor **FLAX** (FIBER)

JUTE

★ **SISAL**

KAPOK

R **RAMIE**

P **PHORMIUM TENAX**

*Includes Kenaf in Thailand

JUTE*
World Production—2,628,000 metric tons—Av. 1957/58—1960/61

INDIA 39.5%	PAKISTAN 39.2	CHINA 12.2	THAI. 2.8	OTHER 2.3	ALL OTHERS 4.0

ASIA

FLAX (FIBER)
World Production—615,000 metric tons—Av. 1957/58—1960/61

SOVIET UNION 67.8%	POLAND 6.6	BEL. 4.6	FR. 4.6	NETH. 3.9	CZECH 3.0	OTHER EUR. 6.4	ASIA 2.1

EUROPE

SILK (RAW)
World Production—30,875 metric tons—Av. 1957/60

JAPAN 61.6%	CHINA 19.2	INDIA 3.7	OTHER ASIA 3.5	SOVIET UNION 7.4	ITALY 2.8	OTH. 1.8

ASIA

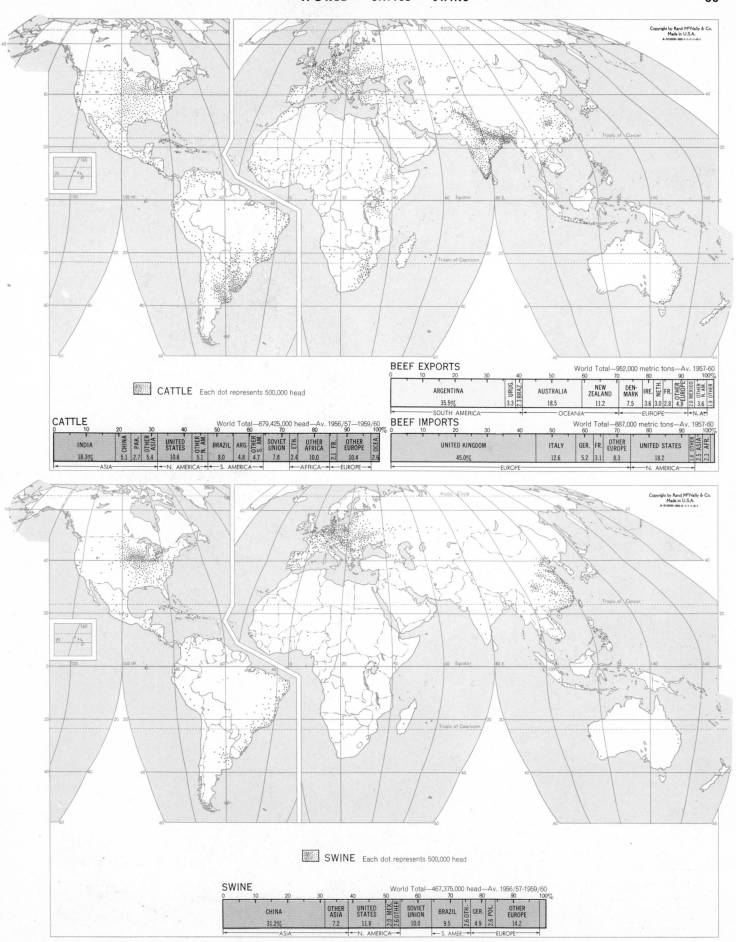

CATTLE Each dot represents 500,000 head

CATTLE World Total—879,425,000 head—Av. 1956/57–1959/60

0	10	20	30	40	50	60	70	80	90	100%				
INDIA 18.3%		CHINA 5.1	PAK. 2.7	OTHER ASIA 5.4	UNITED STATES 10.6	OTHER N. AM. 5.1	BRAZIL 8.0	ARG. 4.8	OTHER S. AM. 4.7	SOVIET UNION 7.8	ETH. 2.4	OTHER AFRICA 10.0	FR. 2.1	OTHER EUROPE 10.4	OCEA. 2.6
←————— ASIA —————→					←— N. AMERICA —→		←— S. AMERICA —→				←—AFRICA—→		←—EUROPE—→		

BEEF EXPORTS World Total—952,000 metric tons—Av. 1957-60

0	10	20	30	40	50	60	70	80	90	100%
ARGENTINA 35.5%				URUG. 3.3	BRAZ. 2.3	AUSTRALIA 18.5	NEW ZEALAND 11.2	DEN-MARK 7.5	IRE. 3.6	NETH. 3.0	FR. 2.8	OTHER EUROPE 4.8	MEXICO 2.0	OTHER N. AM. 3.6	OTHER 1.9
←——————— SOUTH AMERICA ———————→					←———— OCEANIA ————→		←———— EUROPE ————→				←— N. A. —→		

BEEF IMPORTS World Total—887,000 metric tons—Av. 1957-60

0	10	20	30	40	50	60	70	80	90	100%
UNITED KINGDOM 45.0%					ITALY 12.6	GER. 5.2	FR. 3.1	OTHER EUROPE 8.3	UNITED STATES 18.2	OTHER N. AM. 1.8	ASIA 2.5	AFR. 2.3
←——————————— EUROPE ———————————→									←— N. AMERICA —→		

SWINE Each dot represents 500,000 head

SWINE World Total—467,375,000 head—Av. 1956/57–1959/60

0	10	20	30	40	50	60	70	80	90	100%
CHINA 31.2%			OTHER ASIA 7.2	UNITED STATES 11.8	MEX. 2.0	OTHER 2.6	SOVIET UNION 10.0	BRAZIL 9.5	OTH. 2.6	GER. 4.9	POL. 2.6	OTHER EUROPE 14.2
←————— ASIA —————→			←—— N. AMERICA ——→			←— S. AMER —→		←———— EUROPE ————→		

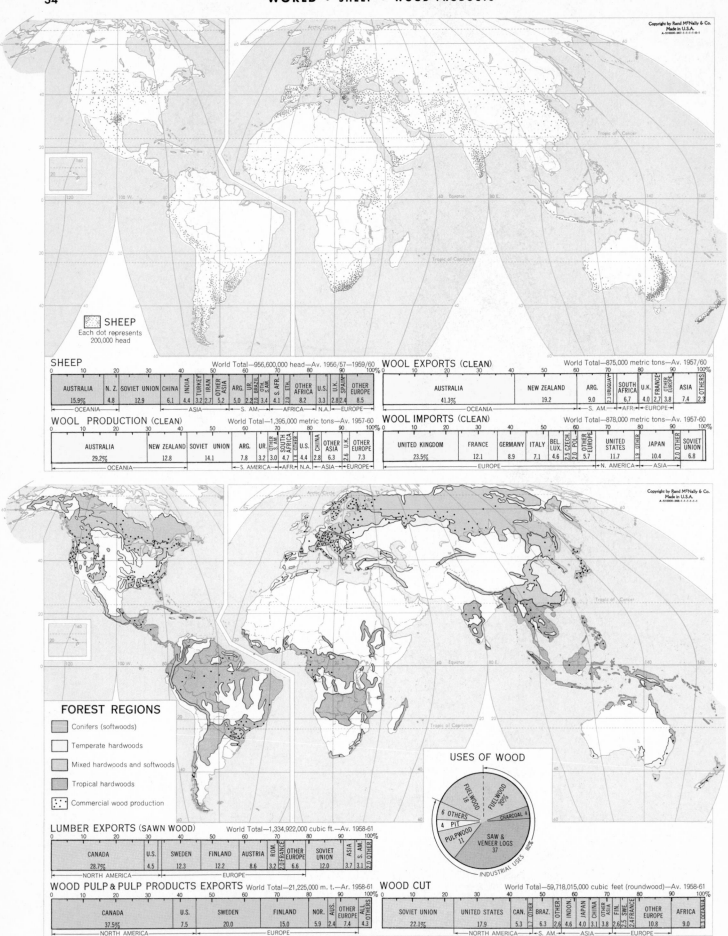

SHEEP
Each dot represents
200,000 head

SHEEP
World Total—956,600,000 head—Av. 1956/57—1959/60

0	10	20	30	40	50	60	70	80	90	100%
AUSTRALIA 15.9%	N.Z. 4.8	SOVIET UNION 12.9	CHINA 6.1	INDIA 4.4	TURKEY 3.2	IRAN 2.7	OTHER ASIA 5.2	ARG. 5.0	UR. 2.2	BRAZIL 3.4	OTH. S.AM.	S. AFR. 4.1	ETH. 2.0	OTHER AFRICA 8.2	U.S. 3.3	U.K. 2.8	SPAIN 2.4	OTHER EUROPE 8.5

OCEANIA — ASIA — S. AM. — AFRICA — N.A. — EUROPE

WOOL EXPORTS (CLEAN)
World Total—875,000 metric tons—Av. 1957/60

| AUSTRALIA 41.3% | NEW ZEALAND 19.2 | ARG. 9.0 | URUGUAY 2.3 | SOUTH AFRICA 6.7 | U.K. 4.0 | FRANCE 2.7 | OTHER EUROPE 3.8 | ASIA 7.4 | OTHERS 2.3 |

OCEANIA — S. AM. — AFR. — EUROPE

WOOL PRODUCTION (CLEAN)
World Total—1,395,000 metric tons—Av. 1957-60

| AUSTRALIA 29.2% | NEW ZEALAND 12.8 | SOVIET UNION 14.1 | ARG. 7.8 | UR. 3.2 | OTHER S. AM. 3.0 | SOUTH AFRICA 4.7 | OTHER 1.3 | U.S. 4.4 | CHINA 2.8 | OTHER ASIA 6.3 | U.K. 2.6 | OTHER EUROPE 7.3 |

OCEANIA — S. AMERICA — AFR. — N.A. — ASIA — EUROPE

WOOL IMPORTS (CLEAN)
World Total—878,000 metric tons—Av. 1957-60

| UNITED KINGDOM 23.5% | FRANCE 12.1 | GERMANY 8.9 | ITALY 7.1 | BEL. LUX. 4.6 | CZECH. 2.5 | POL. 2.0 | OTHER EUROPE 5.7 | UNITED STATES 11.7 | OTHER 1.9 | JAPAN 10.4 | OTHER 2.0 | SOVIET UNION 6.8 |

EUROPE — N. AMERICA — ASIA

FOREST REGIONS

- Conifers (softwoods)
- Temperate hardwoods
- Mixed hardwoods and softwoods
- Tropical hardwoods
- Commercial wood production

USES OF WOOD

FUELWOOD 18
FUELWOOD 20%
CHARCOAL 4
6 OTHERS
4 PIT
PULPWOOD 11
SAW & VENEER LOGS 37
INDUSTRIAL USES 80%

LUMBER EXPORTS (SAWN WOOD)
World Total—1,334,922,000 cubic ft.—Av. 1958-61

0	10	20	30	40	50	60	70	80	90	100%
CANADA 28.7%	U.S. 4.5	SWEDEN 12.3	FINLAND 12.2	AUSTRIA 8.6	ROM. 3.2	FRANCE 2.0	OTHER EUROPE 6.6	SOVIET UNION 12.0	ASIA 3.7	S.AM. 3.1	OTHER

NORTH AMERICA — EUROPE

WOOD PULP & PULP PRODUCTS EXPORTS
World Total—21,225,000 m. t.—Ar. 1958-61

0	10	20	30	40	50	60	70	80	90	100%
CANADA 37.5%	U.S. 7.5	SWEDEN 20.0	FINLAND 15.0	NOR. 5.9	AUS. 2.4	OTHER EUROPE 7.4	ALL OTHERS 4.3

NORTH AMERICA — EUROPE

WOOD CUT
World Total—59,718,015,000 cubic feet (roundwood)—Av. 1958-61

0	10	20	30	40	50	60	70	80	90	100%
SOVIET UNION 22.1%	UNITED STATES 17.9	CAN. 5.3	OTHER 1.7	BRAZ. 6.3	INDON. 2.6	JAPAN 4.6	CHINA 4.0	OTHER ASIA 3.1	FIN. 3.8	SWE. 2.6	FRANCE 2.4	OTHER EUROPE 10.8	AFRICA 9.0	OCEANIA 1.3

NORTH AMERICA — S. AM. — ASIA — EUROPE

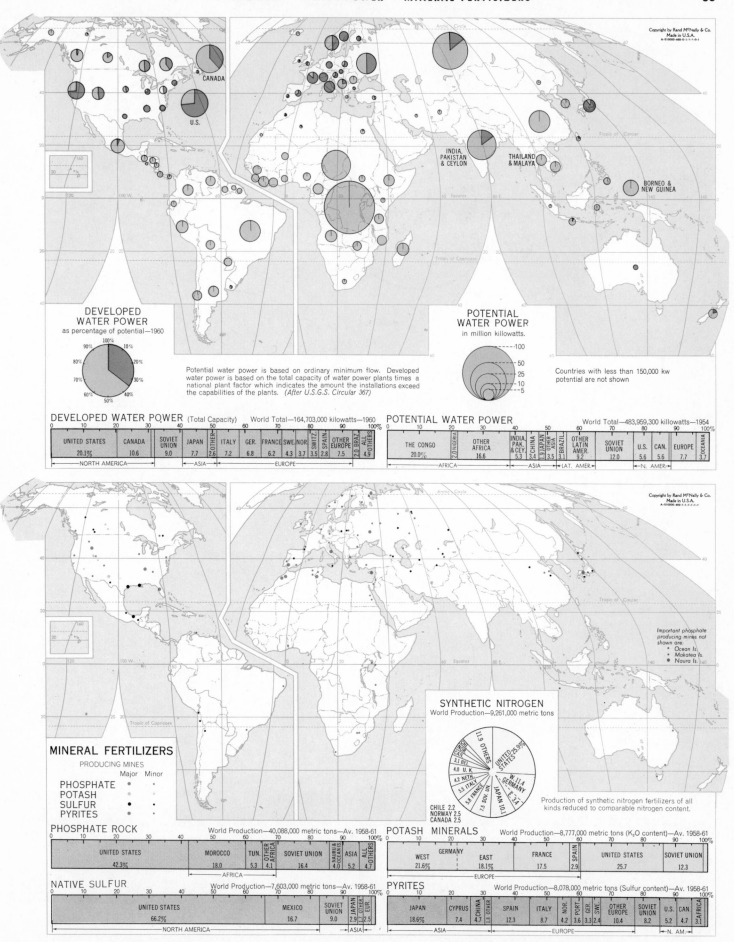

CANADA

U.S.

INDIA, PAKISTAN & CEYLON

THAILAND & MALAYA

BORNEO & NEW GUINEA

DEVELOPED WATER POWER
as percentage of potential—1960

100% 10%
90%   20%
80%   30%
70%   40%
60%   50%

Potential water power is based on ordinary minimum flow. Developed water power is based on the total capacity of water power plants times a national plant factor which indicates the amount the installations exceed the capabilities of the plants. (After U.S.G.S. Circular 367)

POTENTIAL WATER POWER
in million killowatts.

------100
-----50
----25
---10
--5

Countries with less than 150,000 kw potential are not shown

DEVELOPED WATER POWER (Total Capacity)   World Total—164,703,000 kilowatts-1960

UNITED STATES 20.1%	CANADA 10.6	SOVIET UNION 9.0	JAPAN 7.7	OTHER 2.6	ITALY 7.2	GER. 6.8	FRANCE 6.2	SWE. 4.3	NOR.	SWITZ. 3.5	SPAIN 2.8	OTHER EUROPE 7.5	BRAZ. 2.0	ALL OTHERS 4.9
←——— NORTH AMERICA ———→			←— ASIA —→		←————————— EUROPE —————————→									

POTENTIAL WATER POWER   World Total—483,959,300 killowatts-1954

THE CONGO 20.0%	NIGERIA 2.0	OTHER AFRICA 16.6	INDIA, PAK. & CEY. 5.3	CHINA 3.4	JAPAN 1.9	OTHER ASIA 3.5	BRAZIL 3.1	OTHER LATIN AMER. 9.2	SOVIET UNION 12.0	U.S. 5.6
←————————— AFRICA —————————→			←——— ASIA ———→				←LAT. AMER.→		←— N. AMER.→	

(continued columns: CAN. 5.6 | EUROPE 7.7 | OCEANIA 3.7)

Important phosphate producing mines not shown are:
• Ocean Is.
• Makatea Is.
• Naura Is.

SYNTHETIC NITROGEN
World Production—9,261,000 metric tons

UNITED STATES 25.9%
W. 11.4 GERMANY
JAPAN 10.1
7.3 SOV. UN.
5.8 FRANCE
E. 3.4
5.5 ITALY
4.2 NETH.
4.0 U.K.
3.1 BEL.
11.9 OTHERS

CHILE 2.2
NORWAY 2.5
CANADA 2.5

Production of synthetic nitrogen fertilizers of all kinds reduced to comparable nitrogen content.

MINERAL FERTILIZERS
PRODUCING MINES

	Major	Minor
PHOSPHATE	•	•
POTASH	•	•
SULFUR	•	•
PYRITES	•	•

PHOSPHATE ROCK   World Production—40,088,000 metric tons—Av. 1958-61

UNITED STATES 42.3%	MOROCCO 18.0	TUN. 5.3	OTHER AFRICA 4.1	SOVIET UNION 16.4	MAURIT. & OCEANIS. 4.0	ASIA 5.2	ALL OTHERS 4.7
	←——————— AFRICA ———————→						

NATIVE SULFUR   World Production—7,603,000 metric tons—Av. 1958-61

UNITED STATES 66.2%	MEXICO 16.7	SOVIET UNION 9.0	JAPAN 2.9	OTHER EUR. 2.5
←——————— NORTH AMERICA ———————→			←— ASIA —→	

POTASH MINERALS   World Production—8,777,000 metric tons (K₂O content)—Av. 1958-61

WEST GERMANY 21.6%	EAST 18.1%	FRANCE 17.5	SPAIN 2.9	UNITED STATES 25.7	SOVIET UNION 12.3
←————————— EUROPE —————————→					

PYRITES   World Production—8,078,000 metric tons (Sulfur content)—Av. 1958-61

JAPAN 18.6%	CYPRUS 7.4	CHINA 4.7	OTHER 1.8	SPAIN 12.3	ITALY 8.7	NOR. 4.2	PORT. 3.6	GER. 3.3	SWE. 2.4	OTHER EUROPE 10.4	SOVIET UNION 8.2	U.S. 5.2
←————— ASIA —————→				←————————— EUROPE —————————→								←N. AM.→

(continued: CAN. 4.7 | AFRICA 3.1)

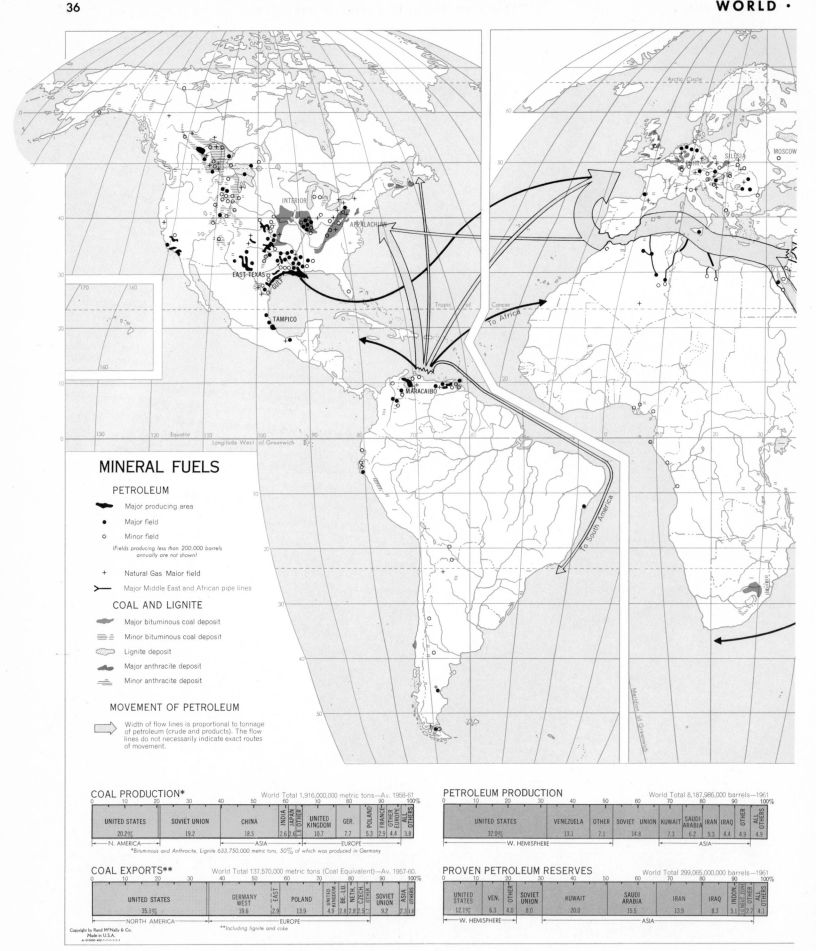

MINERAL FUELS

PETROLEUM

- ⬤ Major producing area
- ● Major field
- ○ Minor field

  (Fields producing less than 200,000 barrels annually are not shown)

- + Natural Gas Major field
- ⤙ Major Middle East and African pipe lines

COAL AND LIGNITE

- Major bituminous coal deposit
- Minor bituminous coal deposit
- Lignite deposit
- Major anthracite deposit
- Minor anthracite deposit

MOVEMENT OF PETROLEUM

⮕ Width of flow lines is proportional to tonnage of petroleum (crude and products). The flow lines do not necessarily indicate exact routes of movement.

COAL PRODUCTION*

World Total 1,916,000,000 metric tons—Av. 1958-61

| 0 | 10 | 20 | 30 | 40 | 50 | 60 | 70 | 80 | 90 | 100% |

| UNITED STATES 20.2% | SOVIET UNION 19.2 | CHINA 18.5 | INDIA 2.6 | JAPAN 2.6 | OTHER 1.6 | UNITED KINGDOM 10.7 | GER. 7.7 | POLAND 5.3 | FRANCE 2.9 | OTHER EUROPE 4.4 | ALL OTHERS 3.8 |

N. AMERICA — ASIA — EUROPE

Bituminous and Anthracite, Lignite 633,750,000 metric tons, 50% of which was produced in Germany.

COAL EXPORTS**

World Total 137,570,000 metric tons (Coal Equivalent)—Av. 1957-60

| 0 | 10 | 20 | 30 | 40 | 50 | 60 | 70 | 80 | 90 | 100% |

| UNITED STATES 35.1% | GERMANY WEST 19.6 | EAST 2.9 | POLAND 13.9 | UNITED KINGDOM 4.9 | BE.-LU. 2.8 | NETH. 2.8 | CZECH 2.5 | OTHER | SOVIET UNION 9.2 | ASIA 2.3 | OTHERS 1.8 |

NORTH AMERICA — EUROPE

**Including lignite and coke*

PETROLEUM PRODUCTION

World Total 8,187,986,000 barrels—1961

| 0 | 10 | 20 | 30 | 40 | 50 | 60 | 70 | 80 | 90 | 100% |

| UNITED STATES 32.0% | VENEZUELA 13.1 | OTHER 7.1 | SOVIET UNION 14.8 | KUWAIT 7.3 | SAUDI ARABIA 6.2 | IRAN 4.4 | IRAQ 4.9 | OTHER 4.9 | ALL OTHERS |

W. HEMISPHERE — ASIA

PROVEN PETROLEUM RESERVES

World Total 299,065,000,000 barrels—1961

| 0 | 10 | 20 | 30 | 40 | 50 | 60 | 70 | 80 | 90 | 100% |

| UNITED STATES 12.1% | VEN. 6.3 | OTHER 4.0 | SOVIET UNION 8.0 | KUWAIT 20.0 | SAUDI ARABIA 15.5 | IRAN 13.9 | IRAQ 8.3 | INDON. 3.1 | NEUT. ZONE 2.7 | OTHER | ALL OTHERS 4.1 |

W. HEMISPHERE — ASIA

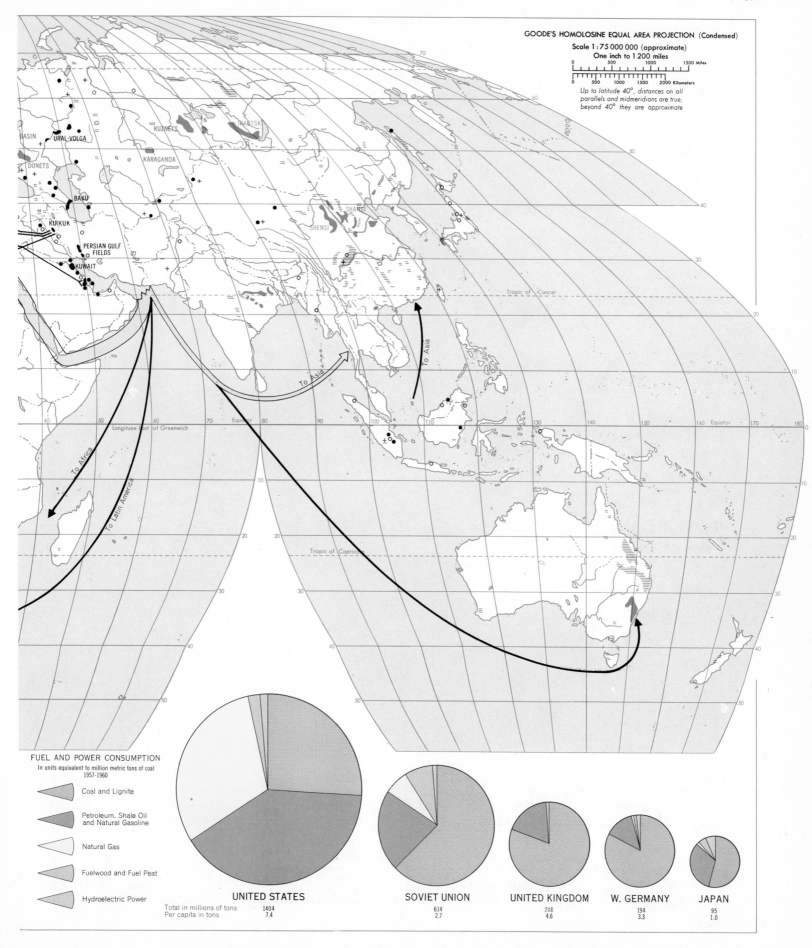

GOODE'S HOMOLOSINE EQUAL AREA PROJECTION (Condensed)
Scale 1:75 000 000 (approximate)
One inch to 1 200 miles

*Up to latitude 40°, distances on all
parallels and midmeridians are true;
beyond 40° they are approximate*

FUEL AND POWER CONSUMPTION
In units equivalent to million metric tons of coal
1957-1960

Coal and Lignite

Petroleum, Shale Oil
and Natural Gasoline

Natural Gas

Fuelwood and Fuel Peat

Hydroelectric Power

	UNITED STATES	SOVIET UNION	UNITED KINGDOM	W. GERMANY	JAPAN
Total in millions of tons	1404	614	248	194	95
Per capita in tons	7.4	2.7	4.6	3.3	1.0

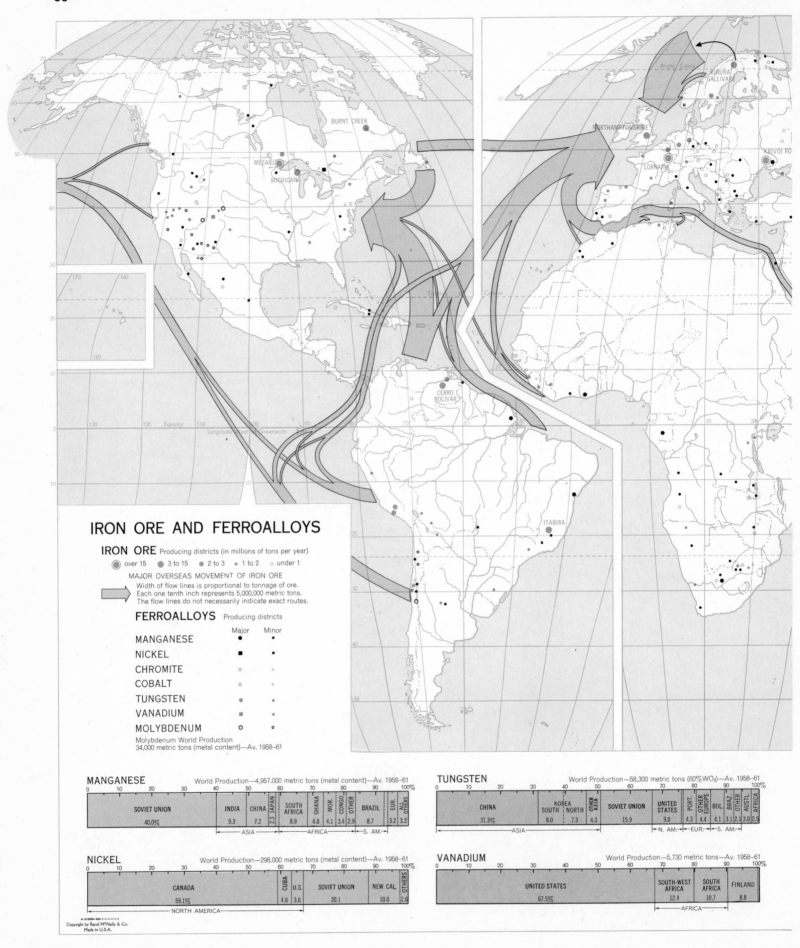

IRON ORE AND FERROALLOYS

IRON ORE Producing districts (in millions of tons per year)

⦿ over 15   ● 3 to 15   ● 2 to 3   • 1 to 2   ○ under 1

MAJOR OVERSEAS MOVEMENT OF IRON ORE

➤ Width of flow lines is proportional to tonnage of ore.
Each one tenth inch represents 5,000,000 metric tons.
The flow lines do not necessarily indicate exact routes.

FERROALLOYS Producing districts

	Major	Minor
MANGANESE	●	•
NICKEL	■	▪
CHROMITE	●	•
COBALT	▪	▪
TUNGSTEN	●	•
VANADIUM	▪	▪
MOLYBDENUM	○	○

Molybdenum World Production
34,000 metric tons (metal content)—Av. 1958–61

Map labels: BURNT CREEK, MESABI, MICHIGAN, CERRO BOLIVAR, ITABIRA, KIRUNA, GALLIVARE, NORTHAMPTONSHIRE, LORRAINE, KRIVOI ROG, Arctic Circle, Equator, Tropic of Cancer, Longitude West from Greenwich

MANGANESE
World Production—4,957,000 metric tons (metal content)—Av. 1958–61

SOVIET UNION 40.0%	INDIA 9.3	CHINA 7.2	JAPAN 2.3	SOUTH AFRICA 8.9	GHANA 4.8	MOR. 4.1	CONGO 3.4	OTHER 2.9	BRAZIL 8.7	EUR. 3.2	ALL OTHERS 3.2

ASIA — AFRICA — S. AM.

TUNGSTEN
World Production—58,300 metric tons (60%WO₃)—Av. 1958–61

CHINA 31.3%	KOREA SOUTH 8.0	NORTH 7.3	OTHER ASIA 4.3	SOVIET UNION 15.9	UNITED STATES 9.0	PORT. 4.3	OTHER EUROPE 4.4	BOL. 3.1	BRAZ. 2.1	OTHER 3.0	AUSTL. AFRICA 2.5

ASIA — N. AM. — EUR. — S. AM.

NICKEL
World Production—298,000 metric tons (metal content)—Av. 1958–61

CANADA 59.1%	CUBA 4.6	U.S. 3.6	SOVIET UNION 20.1	NEW CAL. 10.0	OTHERS 2.6

NORTH AMERICA

VANADIUM
World Production—5,730 metric tons—Av. 1958–61

UNITED STATES 67.5%	SOUTH-WEST AFRICA 12.4	SOUTH AFRICA 10.7	FINLAND 8.8

AFRICA

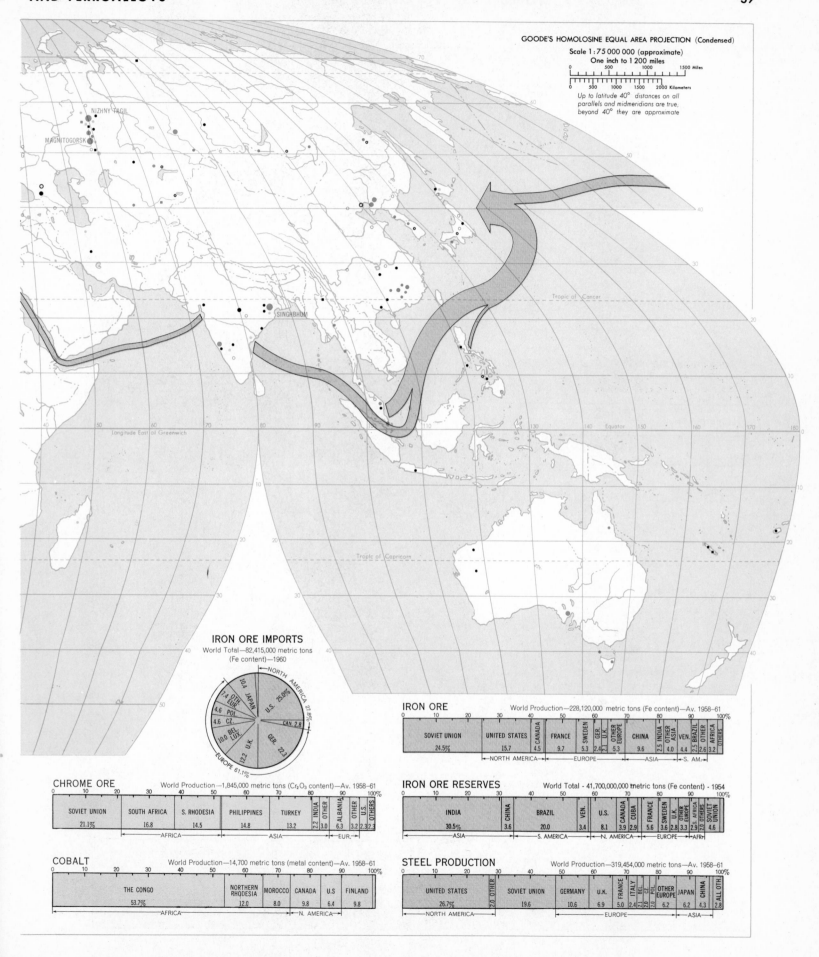

GOODE'S HOMOLOSINE EQUAL AREA PROJECTION (Condensed)

Scale 1:75 000 000 (approximate)
One inch to 1 200 miles

Up to latitude 40° distances on all
parallels and midmeridians are true;
beyond 40° they are approximate

NIZHNY TAGIL

MAGNITOGORSK

SINGHBHUM

Tropic of Cancer

Longitude East of Greenwich

Equator

Tropic of Capricorn

IRON ORE IMPORTS

World Total—82,415,000 metric tons
(Fe content)—1960

NORTH AMERICA 27.8%

U.S. 25.0%	
CAN. 2.8	
GER. 22.2	
12.2 U.K.	
10.0 BEL. LUX.	
4.6 CZ.	
4.6 POL.	
7.4 OTH. EUR.	
10.4 JAPAN	

EUROPE 61.1%

IRON ORE
World Production—228,120,000 metric tons (Fe content)—Av. 1958–61

0	10	20	30	40	50	60	70	80	90	100%

SOVIET UNION	UNITED STATES	CANADA	FRANCE	SWEDEN	GER.	OTHER EUROPE	CHINA	INDIA	OTHER ASIA	VEN.	BRAZIL	OTHER	AFRICA	OTHERS
24.5%	15.7	4.5	9.7	5.3	2.4 U.K.	5.3	9.6	2.5	4.0	4.4	2.5	2.6	3.2	

NORTH AMERICA — EUROPE — ASIA — S. AM.

CHROME ORE
World Production—1,845,000 metric tons (Cr₂O₃ content)—Av. 1958–61

0	10	20	30	40	50	60	70	80	90	100%

SOVIET UNION	SOUTH AFRICA	S. RHODESIA	PHILIPPINES	TURKEY	INDIA	OTHER	ALBANIA	OTHER	U.S.	OTHERS
21.1%	16.8	14.5	14.8	13.2	2.2	3.0	6.3	3.2	2.3	2.3

AFRICA — ASIA — EUR.

IRON ORE RESERVES
World Total - 41,700,000,000 metric tons (Fe content) - 1954

0	10	20	30	40	50	60	70	80	90	100%

INDIA	CHINA	BRAZIL	VEN.	U.S.	CANADA	CUBA	FRANCE	SWEDEN	U.K.	OTHER EUROPE	S. AFRICA	OTHERS	SOVIET UNION
30.5%	3.6	20.0	3.4	8.1	3.9	2.9	5.6	3.6	2.8	3.3	2.0	2.9	4.6

ASIA — S. AMERICA — N. AMERICA — EUROPE — AFR.

COBALT
World Production—14,700 metric tons (metal content)—Av. 1958–61

0	10	20	30	40	50	60	70	80	90	100%

THE CONGO	NORTHERN RHODESIA	MOROCCO	CANADA	U.S	FINLAND
53.7%	12.0	8.0	9.8	6.4	9.8

AFRICA — N. AMERICA

STEEL PRODUCTION
World Production—319,454,000 metric tons—Av. 1958–61

0	10	20	30	40	50	60	70	80	90	100%

UNITED STATES	OTHER	SOVIET UNION	GERMANY	U.K.	FRANCE	ITALY	BEL	CZ	POL	OTHER EUROPE	JAPAN	CHINA	ALL OTH.
26.7%	2.0	19.6	10.6	6.9	5.0	2.4	2.1	2.0		6.2	6.2	4.3	2.8

NORTH AMERICA — EUROPE — ASIA

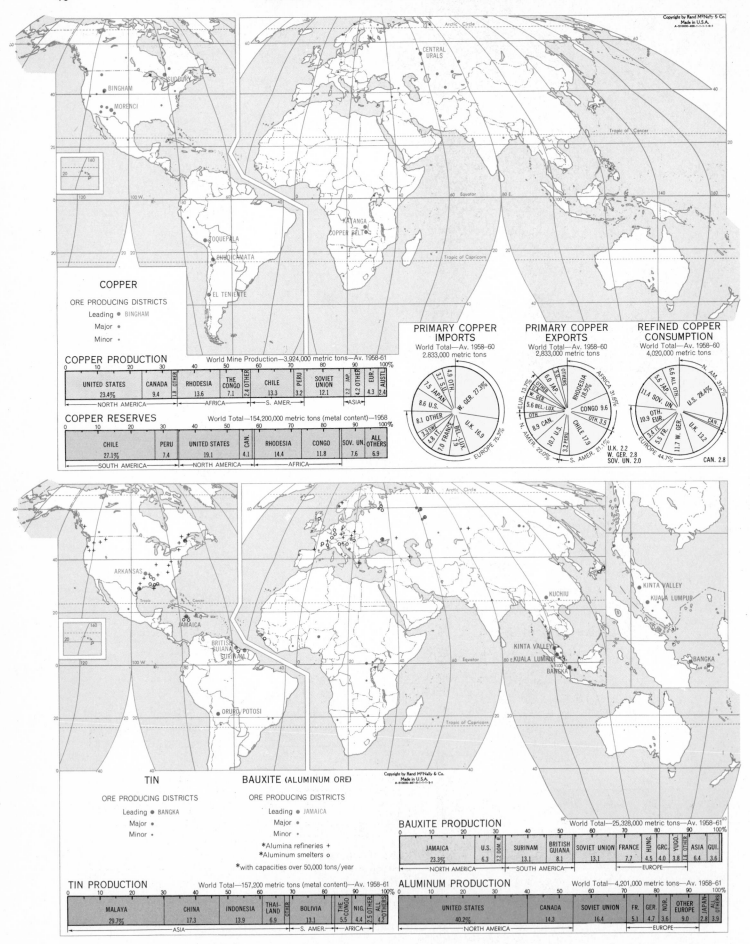

COPPER

ORE PRODUCING DISTRICTS

Leading ● BINGHAM

Major ●

Minor ·

COPPER PRODUCTION
World Mine Production—3,924,000 metric tons—Av. 1958-61

0	10	20	30	40	50	60	70	80	90	100%
UNITED STATES 23.4%	CANADA 9.4	OTHER 1.8	RHODESIA 13.6	THE CONGO 7.1	OTHER 2.4	CHILE 13.3	PERU 3.2	SOVIET UNION 12.1	JAP. 2.2	OTHER 4.2	EUR. 4.3	AUSTL. 2.4

NORTH AMERICA — AFRICA — S. AMER. — ASIA

COPPER RESERVES
World Total—154,200,000 metric tons (metal content)—1958

0	10	20	30	40	50	60	70	80	90	100%
CHILE 27.1%	PERU 7.4	UNITED STATES 19.1	CAN. 4.1	RHODESIA 14.4	CONGO 11.8	SOV. UN. 7.6	ALL OTHERS 6.9

SOUTH AMERICA — NORTH AMERICA — AFRICA

PRIMARY COPPER IMPORTS
World Total—Av. 1958-60
2,833,000 metric tons

W. GER. 27.3%
U.K. 16.9
FRANCE 7.9
BEL.-LUX.
S.W. 3.3
OTH. 4.8
8.1 Other
8.6 U.S.
7.5 JAPAN
3.7 S.U.
4.9 OTH.
EUROPE 75.3%

PRIMARY COPPER EXPORTS
World Total—Av. 1958-60
2,833,000 metric tons

AFRICA 31.6%
RHODESIA 18.5%
CONGO 9.6
OTH. 3.5
CHILE 17.9
PERU 3.2
CAN. 10.7
N. AMER. 22.0%
S. AMER. 21.1%
BEL.-LUX. 5.6
W. GER. 6.0
JAP. 6.0
OTHERS 13.7%
OTH.
EUR.

REFINED COPPER CONSUMPTION
World Total—Av. 1958-60
4,020,000 metric tons

N. AM. 31.7%
U.S. 28.4%
CAN.
U.K. 13.2
W. GER. 11.7
FR. 5.5
W. GER. 3.4
OTH. EUR. 10.9
SOV. UN. 11.4
JAP. 5.6
ALL OTH. 6.6
EUROPE 44.7%
U.K. 2.2
W. GER. 2.8
SOV. UN. 2.0
CAN. 2.8

TIN

ORE PRODUCING DISTRICTS

Leading ● BANGKA

Major ●

Minor ·

BAUXITE (ALUMINUM ORE)

ORE PRODUCING DISTRICTS

Leading ● JAMAICA

Major ●

Minor ·

*Alumina refineries +
*Aluminum smelters o

*with capacities over 50,000 tons/year

BAUXITE PRODUCTION
World Total—25,328,000 metric tons—Av. 1958-61

0	10	20	30	40	50	60	70	80	90	100%
JAMAICA 23.3%	U.S. 6.3	DOM. R. 2.2	SURINAM 13.1	BRITISH GUIANA 8.1	SOVIET UNION 13.1	FRANCE 7.7	HUNG. 4.5	GRC. 4.0	YUGO. 3.8	OTH. 1.8	ASIA 6.4	GUI. 3.6

NORTH AMERICA — SOUTH AMERICA — EUROPE

TIN PRODUCTION
World Total—157,200 metric tons (metal content)—Av. 1958-61

0	10	20	30	40	50	60	70	80	90	100%
MALAYA 29.7%	CHINA 17.3	INDONESIA 13.9	THAILAND 6.9	OTHER	BOLIVIA 13.1	THE CONGO 5.5	NIG. 4.4	OTHER 2.5	ALL OTHERS 4.7

ASIA — S. AMER. — AFRICA

ALUMINUM PRODUCTION
World Total—4,201,000 metric tons—Av. 1958-61

0	10	20	30	40	50	60	70	80	90	100%
UNITED STATES 40.2%	CANADA 14.3	SOVIET UNION 16.4	FR. 5.1	GER. 4.7	NOR. 3.6	OTHER EUROPE 9.0	JAPAN 2.8	ALL OTHERS 3.9

NORTH AMERICA — EUROPE

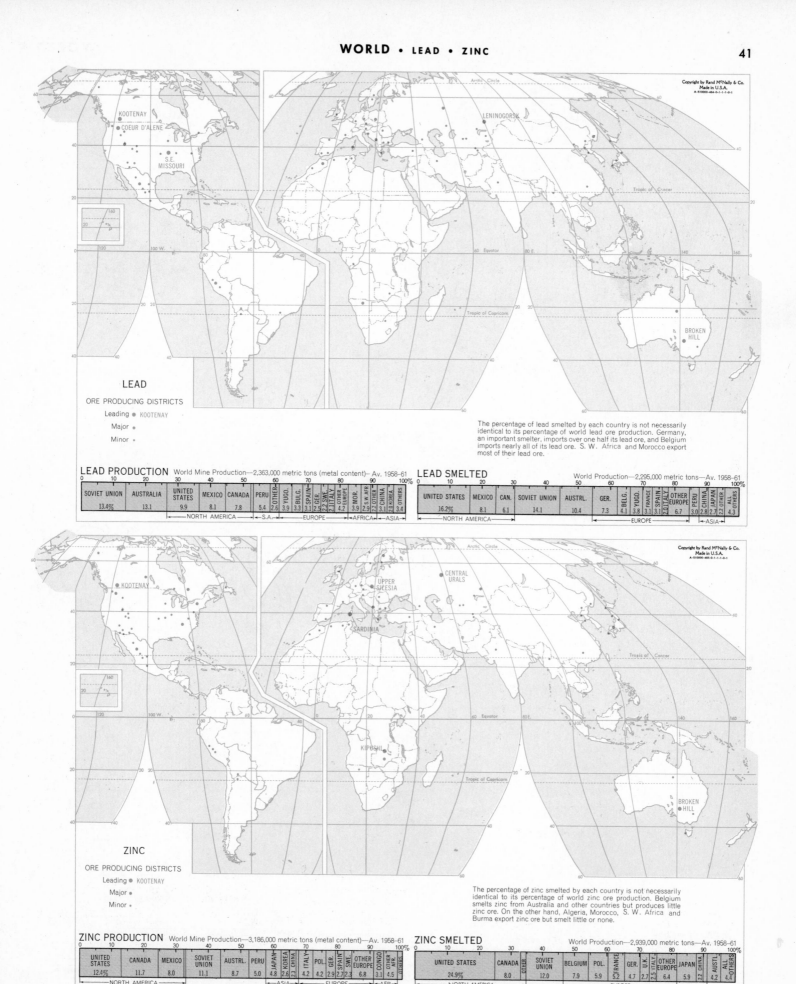

LEAD

ORE PRODUCING DISTRICTS

Leading ● KOOTENAY

Major ●

Minor ·

The percentage of lead smelted by each country is not necessarily identical to its percentage of world lead ore production. Germany, an important smelter, imports over one half its lead ore, and Belgium imports nearly all of its lead ore. S. W. Africa and Morocco export most of their lead ore.

LEAD PRODUCTION — World Mine Production—2,363,000 metric tons (metal content)— Av. 1958–61

SOVIET UNION	AUSTRALIA	UNITED STATES	MEXICO	CANADA	PERU	OTHER	YUGO.	BULG.	SPAIN	GER.	SWE.	ITALY	OTHER EUROPE	MOR.	S W AFR	OTHER	CHINA	KOREA	OTHERS
13.4%	13.1	9.9	8.1	7.8	5.4	2.6	3.9	3.3	3.1	2.5	2.2	2.1	4.2	3.9	2.9	2.2	3.1	2.0	3.4

NORTH AMERICA — S.A. — EUROPE — AFRICA — ASIA

LEAD SMELTED — World Production—2,295,000 metric tons— Av. 1958–61

UNITED STATES	MEXICO	CAN.	SOVIET UNION	AUSTRL.	GER.	BELG.	YUGO.	FRANCE	SPAIN-	ITALY	OTHER EUROPE	PERU	CHINA	OTHER	ALL OTHERS
16.2%	8.1	6.1	14.1	10.4	7.3	4.1	3.8	3.1	2.7	2.5	6.7	3.0	2.8	2.2	4.3

NORTH AMERICA — EUROPE — ASIA

ZINC

ORE PRODUCING DISTRICTS

Leading ● KOOTENAY

Major ●

Minor ·

The percentage of zinc smelted by each country is not necessarily identical to its percentage of world zinc ore production. Belgium smelts zinc from Australia and other countries but produces little zinc ore. On the other hand, Algeria, Morocco, S. W. Africa and Burma export zinc ore but smelt little or none.

ZINC PRODUCTION — World Mine Production—3,186,000 metric tons (metal content)— Av. 1958–61

UNITED STATES	CANADA	MEXICO	SOVIET UNION	AUSTRL.	PERU	JAPAN	KOREA	CHINA	ITALY	POL.	GER.	SPAIN	SWE.	OTHER EUROPE	CONGO	OTHER AFR.	OTHERS
12.4%	11.7	8.0	11.1	8.7	5.0	4.8	2.6	2.3	4.2	4.2	2.9	2.7	2.3	6.8	3.1		4.5

NORTH AMERICA — ASIA — EUROPE — AFR.

ZINC SMELTED — World Production—2,939,000 metric tons— Av. 1958–61

UNITED STATES	CANADA	OTHER	SOVIET UNION	BELGIUM	POL.	FRANCE	GER.	U.K.	ITALY	OTHER EUROPE	JAPAN	CHINA	AUSTL.	ALL OTHERS
24.9%	8.0		12.0	7.9	5.9	5.2	4.6	2.7	2.5	6.4	5.9	2.2	4.2	4.4

NORTH AMERICA — EUROPE — ASIA

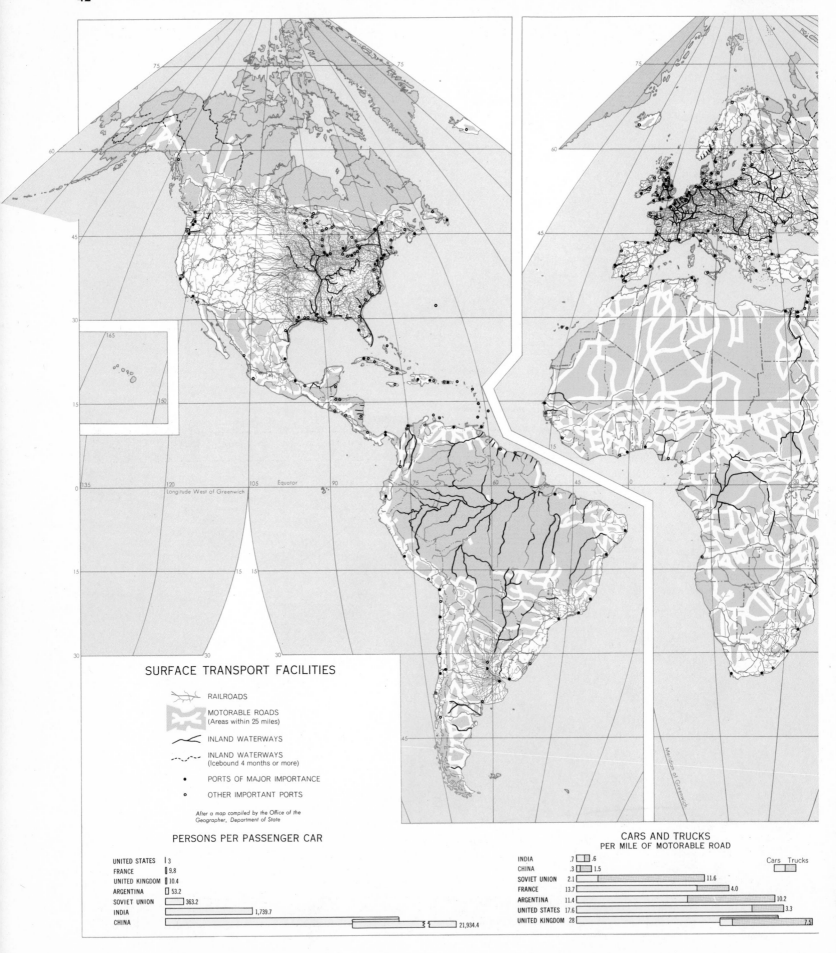

SURFACE TRANSPORT FACILITIES

RAILROADS

MOTORABLE ROADS
(Areas within 25 miles)

INLAND WATERWAYS

INLAND WATERWAYS
(Icebound 4 months or more)

● PORTS OF MAJOR IMPORTANCE

○ OTHER IMPORTANT PORTS

*After a map compiled by the Office of the
Geographer, Department of State*

PERSONS PER PASSENGER CAR

UNITED STATES	3
FRANCE	9.8
UNITED KINGDOM	10.4
ARGENTINA	53.2
SOVIET UNION	363.2
INDIA	1,739.7
CHINA	21,934.4

CARS AND TRUCKS
PER MILE OF MOTORABLE ROAD

	Cars	Trucks
INDIA	.7	.6
CHINA	.3	1.5
SOVIET UNION	2.1	11.6
FRANCE	13.7	4.0
ARGENTINA	11.4	10.2
UNITED STATES	17.6	3.3
UNITED KINGDOM	28	7.5

Longitude West of Greenwich

Equator

Meridian of Greenwich

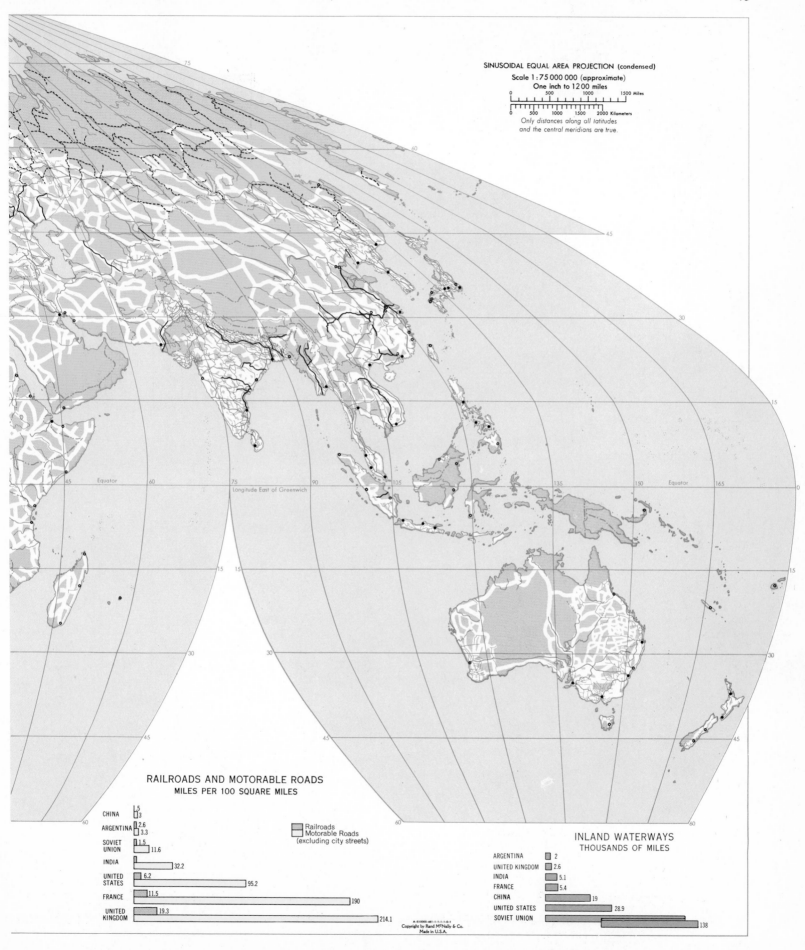

SINUSOIDAL EQUAL AREA PROJECTION (condensed)

Scale 1 : 75 000 000 (approximate)

One inch to 12 00 miles

Only distances along all latitudes
and the central meridians are true.

Equator

Longitude East of Greenwich

RAILROADS AND MOTORABLE ROADS
MILES PER 100 SQUARE MILES

	Railroads	Motorable Roads
CHINA	.5	3
ARGENTINA	2.6	3.3
SOVIET UNION	1.5	11.6
INDIA		32.2
UNITED STATES	6.2	95.2
FRANCE	11.5	190
UNITED KINGDOM	19.3	214.1

Railroads
Motorable Roads
(excluding city streets)

INLAND WATERWAYS
THOUSANDS OF MILES

ARGENTINA	2
UNITED KINGDOM	2.6
INDIA	5.1
FRANCE	5.4
CHINA	19
UNITED STATES	28.9
SOVIET UNION	138

A-510000-481-1-1-1-1-0-1
Copyright by Rand McNally & Co.
Made in U.S.A.

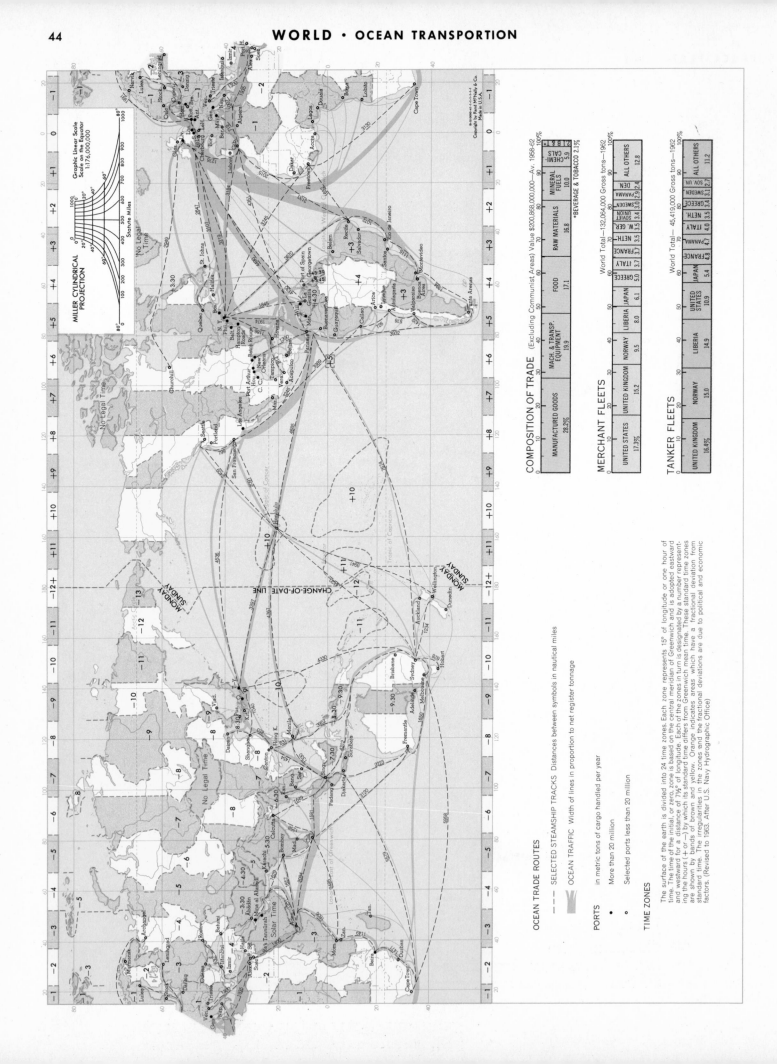

OCEAN TRADE ROUTES

– – – SELECTED STEAMSHIP TRACKS Distances between symbols in nautical miles

     OCEAN TRAFFIC Width of lines in proportion to net register tonnage

PORTS in metric tons of cargo handled per year

•   More than 20 million

○   Selected ports less than 20 million

TIME ZONES

The surface of the earth is divided into 24 time zones. Each zone represents 15° of longitude or one hour of time. The time of the initial, or zero, zone is based on the central meridian of Greenwich and is adopted eastward and westward for a distance of 7½° of longitude. Each of the zones in turn is designated by a number representing the hours (+ or –) by which its standard time differs from Greenwich mean time. These standard time zones are shown by bands of brown and yellow. Orange indicates areas which have a fractional deviation from standard time. The irregularities in the zones and the fractional deviations are due to political and economic factors. (Revised to 1963. After U.S. Navy Hydrographic Office)

COMPOSITION OF TRADE (Excluding Communist Areas) Value $200,868,000,000—Av. 1958-62

MANUFACTURED GOODS 28.2%	MACH. & TRANSP. EQUIPMENT 19.9	FOOD 17.1	RAW MATERIALS 16.8	MINERAL FUELS 10.0	CHEMI-CALS 5.9	*B.&T. 2.1%

*BEVERAGE & TOBACCO 2.1%

MERCHANT FLEETS

World Total—132,064,000 Gross tons—1962

UNITED STATES 17.3%	UNITED KINGDOM 15.2	NORWAY 9.5	LIBERIA 8.0	JAPAN 6.1	GREECE 5.0	ITALY 3.7	FRANCE 3.7	NETH. 3.5	W. GER. 3.5	SOVIET UNION 3.4	SWEDEN 3.0	DEN. 2.9	PANAMA 2.4	ALL OTHERS 12.8

TANKER FLEETS

World Total— 45,419,000 Gross tons—1962

UNITED KINGDOM 16.4%	NORWAY 15.0	LIBERIA 14.9	UNITED STATES 10.9	JAPAN 5.4	ITALY 4.8	FRANCE 4.7	PANAMA 4.0	NETH. 3.5	GREECE 3.4	SWEDEN 3.1	SOV. UN. 2.7	ALL OTHERS 11.2

MILLER CYLINDRICAL PROJECTION

Graphic Linear Scale
Scale on the Equator
1:176,000,000

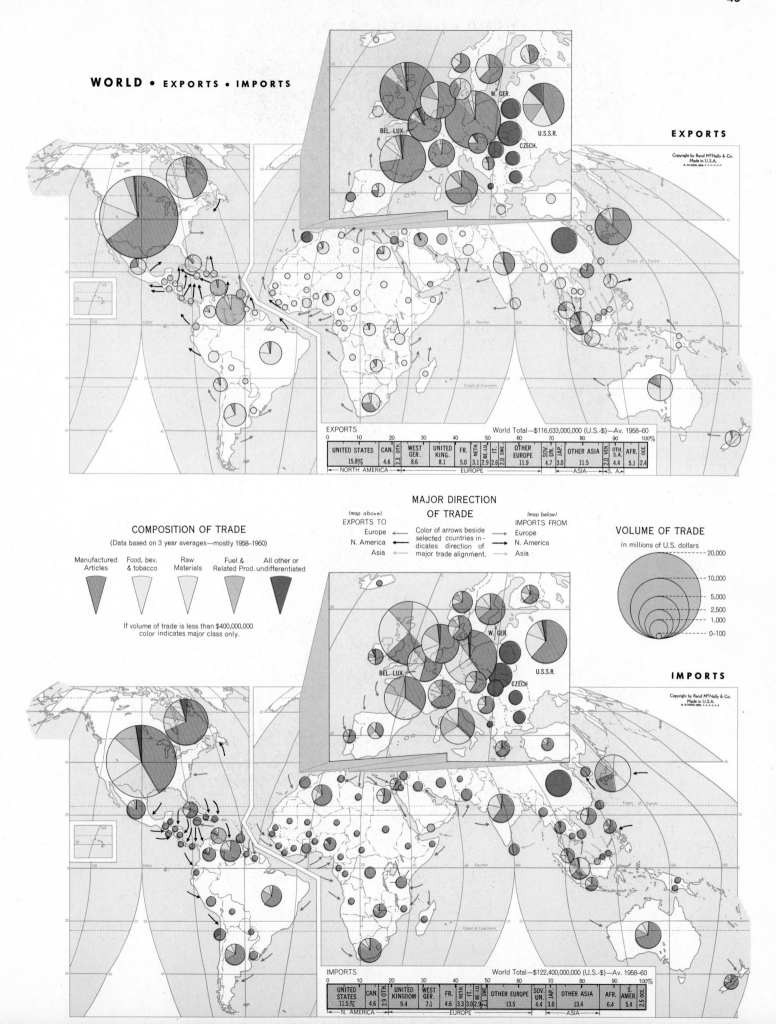

WORLD • EXPORTS • IMPORTS

EXPORTS

Copyright by Rand McNally & Co.
Made in U.S.A.
A-510000-964-1-1-1-1-1-1

EXPORTS											World Total—$116,633,000,000 (U.S.-$)—Av. 1958-60							
0	10		20		30		40		50		60	70		80		90	100%
UNITED STATES 15.8%	CAN. 4.6	OTH. 2.3	WEST GER. 8.6	UNITED KING. 8.1	FR. 5.0	NETH. 3.1	BE.-LU. 2.9	IT. 2.6	SWE. 2.0	OTHER EUROPE 11.9	SOV. UN. 4.7	JAP. 3.0	OTHER ASIA 11.5	VEN. 2.0	OTH. S.A. 4.4	AFR. 5.1	OCE. 2.4
←—— NORTH AMERICA ——→			←———————— EUROPE ————————→									←———— ASIA ————→		←— S. A. —→			

COMPOSITION OF TRADE

(Data based on 3 year averages—mostly 1958–1960)

Manufactured Articles

Food, bev. & tobacco

Raw Materials

Fuel & Related Prod.

All other or undifferentiated

If volume of trade is less than $400,000,000 color indicates major class only.

MAJOR DIRECTION OF TRADE

(map above) EXPORTS TO		(map below) IMPORTS FROM
Europe ←	Color of arrows beside selected countries indicates direction of major trade alignment.	→ Europe
N. America ←		→ N. America
Asia ←		→ Asia

VOLUME OF TRADE

in millions of U.S. dollars

- 20,000
- 10,000
- 5,000
- 2,500
- 1,000
- 0–100

IMPORTS

Copyright by Rand McNally & Co.
Made in U.S.A.
A-510000-965-1-1-1-1-1-1

IMPORTS											World Total—$122,400,000,000 (U.S.-$)—Av. 1958-60							
0	10		20		30		40		50		60	70		80		90	100%
UNITED STATES 11.5%	CAN. 4.6	OTH. 2.9	UNITED KINGDOM 9.4	WEST GER. 7.1	FR. 4.6	NETH. 3.3	IT. 3.0	BE.-LU. 2.9	SWE. 2.2	OTHER EUROPE 13.5	SOV. UN. 4.4	JAP. 3.0	OTHER ASIA 13.4	AFR. 6.4	S. AMER. 5.4	OCE. 2.5	
←— N. AMERICA —→			←———————— EUROPE ————————→									←———— ASIA ————→					

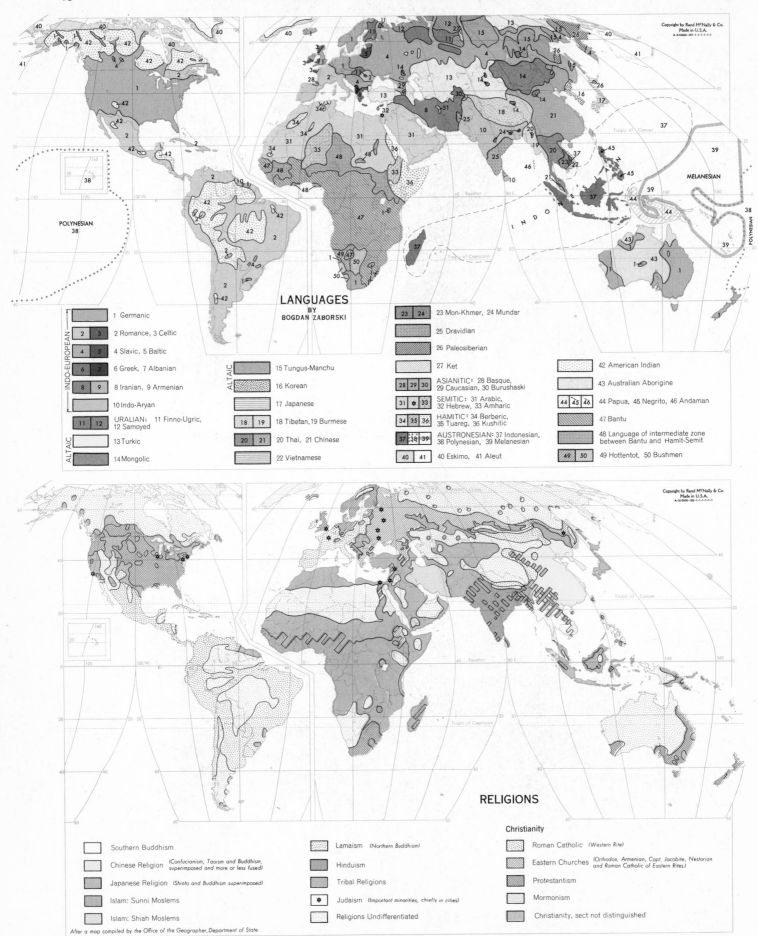

LANGUAGES
BY
BOGDAN ZABORSKI

INDO-EUROPEAN
1 Germanic
2 Romance, 3 Celtic
4 Slavic, 5 Baltic
6 Greek, 7 Albanian
8 Iranian, 9 Armenian
10 Indo-Aryan

URALIAN: 11 Finno-Ugric, 12 Samoyed

ALTAIC
13 Turkic
14 Mongolic
15 Tungus-Manchu
16 Korean
17 Japanese
18 Tibetan, 19 Burmese
20 Thai, 21 Chinese
22 Vietnamese

23 Mon-Khmer, 24 Mundar
25 Dravidian
26 Paleosiberian
27 Ket
ASIANITIC: 28 Basque, 29 Caucasian, 30 Burushaski
SEMITIC: 31 Arabic, 32 Hebrew, 33 Amharic
HAMITIC: 34 Berberic, 35 Tuareg, 36 Kushitic
AUSTRONESIAN: 37 Indonesian, 38 Polynesian, 39 Melanesian
40 Eskimo, 41 Aleut

42 American Indian
43 Australian Aborigine
44 Papua, 45 Negrito, 46 Andaman
47 Bantu
48 Language of intermediate zone between Bantu and Hamit-Semit
49 Hottentot, 50 Bushmen

RELIGIONS

Southern Buddhism

Chinese Religion *(Confucianism, Taoism and Buddhism, superimposed and more or less fused)*

Japanese Religion *(Shinto and Buddhism superimposed)*

Islam: Sunni Moslems

Islam: Shiah Moslems

Lamaism *(Northern Buddhism)*

Hinduism

Tribal Religions

Judaism *(Important minorities, chiefly in cities)*

Religions Undifferentiated

Christianity

Roman Catholic *(Western Rite)*

Eastern Churches *(Orthodox, Armenian, Copt, Jacobite, Nestorian and Roman Catholic of Eastern Rites.)*

Protestantism

Mormonism

Christianity, sect not distinguished

After a map compiled by the Office of the Geographer, Department of State

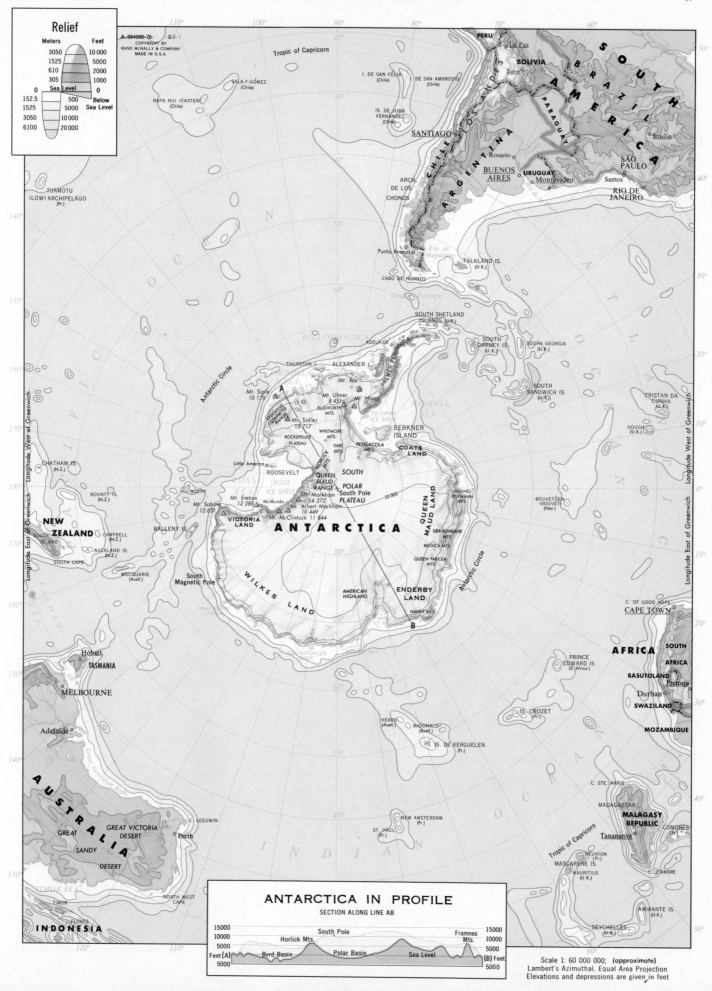

Relief

Meters		Feet
3050		10 000
1525		5000
610		2000
305		1000
	Sea Level	
0		0
152.5		500	Below
1525		5000	Sea Level
3050		10 000
6100		20 000

A-594000-76   2-2-2
COPYRIGHT BY
RAND McNALLY & COMPANY
MADE IN U.S.A.

ANTARCTICA IN PROFILE
SECTION ALONG LINE AB

Scale 1: 60 000 000;   (approximate)
Lambert's Azimuthal, Equal Area Projection
Elevations and depressions are given in feet

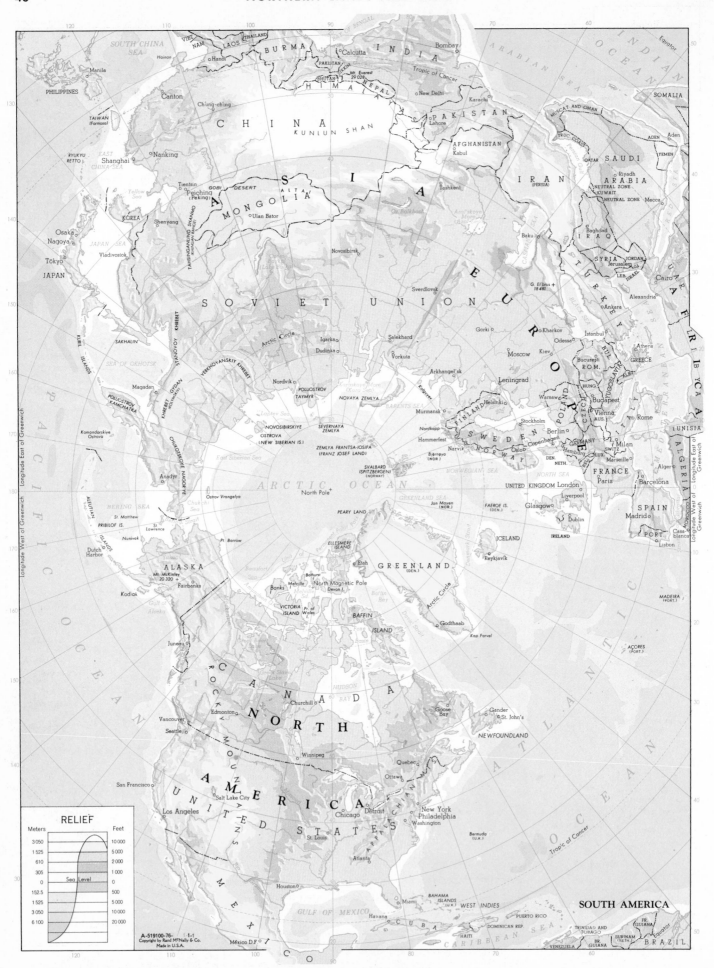

RELIEF

Meters		Feet
3050		10 000
1525		5000
610		2000
305		1000
0	Sea Level	0
152.5		500
1525		5000
3050		10 000
6100		20 000

A-519100-76- 1-1
Copyright by Rand McNally & Co.
Made in U.S.A.

Elevations and depressions are given in feet
LAMBERT AZIMUTHAL EQUAL-AREA PROJECTION
Scale 1:60,000,000 (approximate)

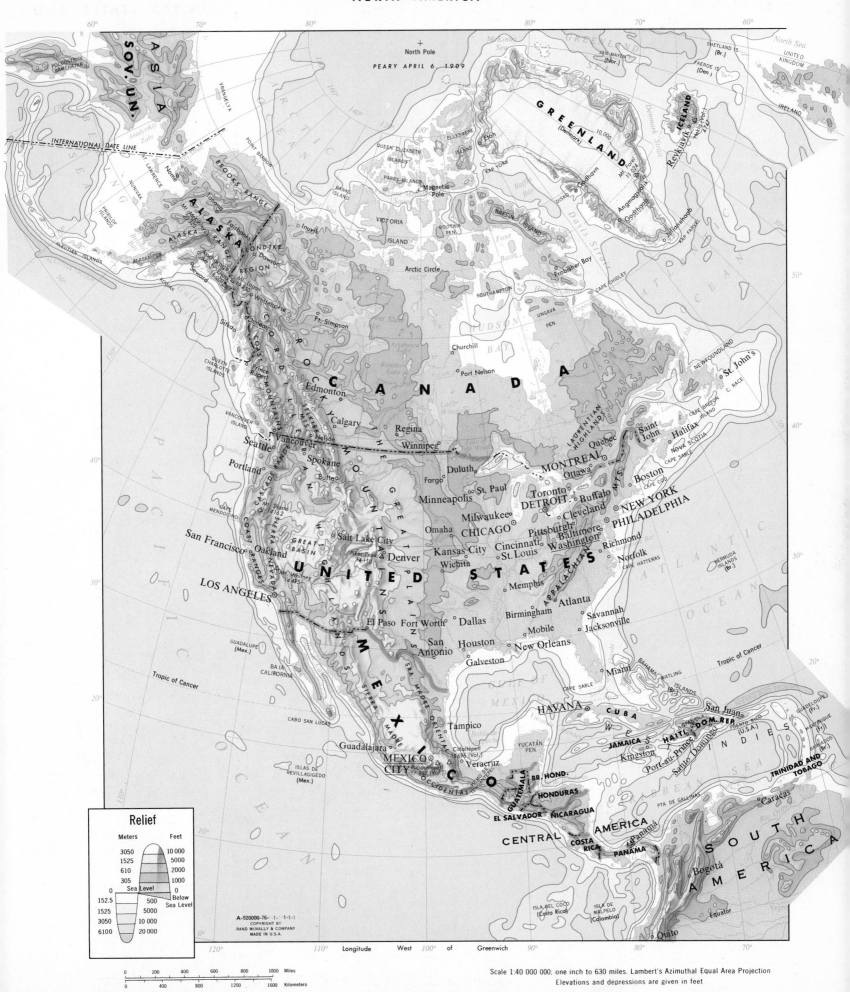

Relief

Meters		Feet
3050		10 000
1525		5000
610		2000
305		1000
0	Sea Level	0
152.5		500
1525	Below Sea Level	5000
3050		10 000
6100		20 000

A-520000-76- 1- 1-1-1
COPYRIGHT BY
RAND McNALLY & COMPANY
MADE IN U.S.A.

Longitude   West   of   Greenwich

0   200   400   600   800   1000 Miles
0   400   800   1200   1600 Kilometers

Scale 1:40 000 000; one inch to 630 miles. Lambert's Azimuthal Equal Area Projection
Elevations and depressions are given in feet

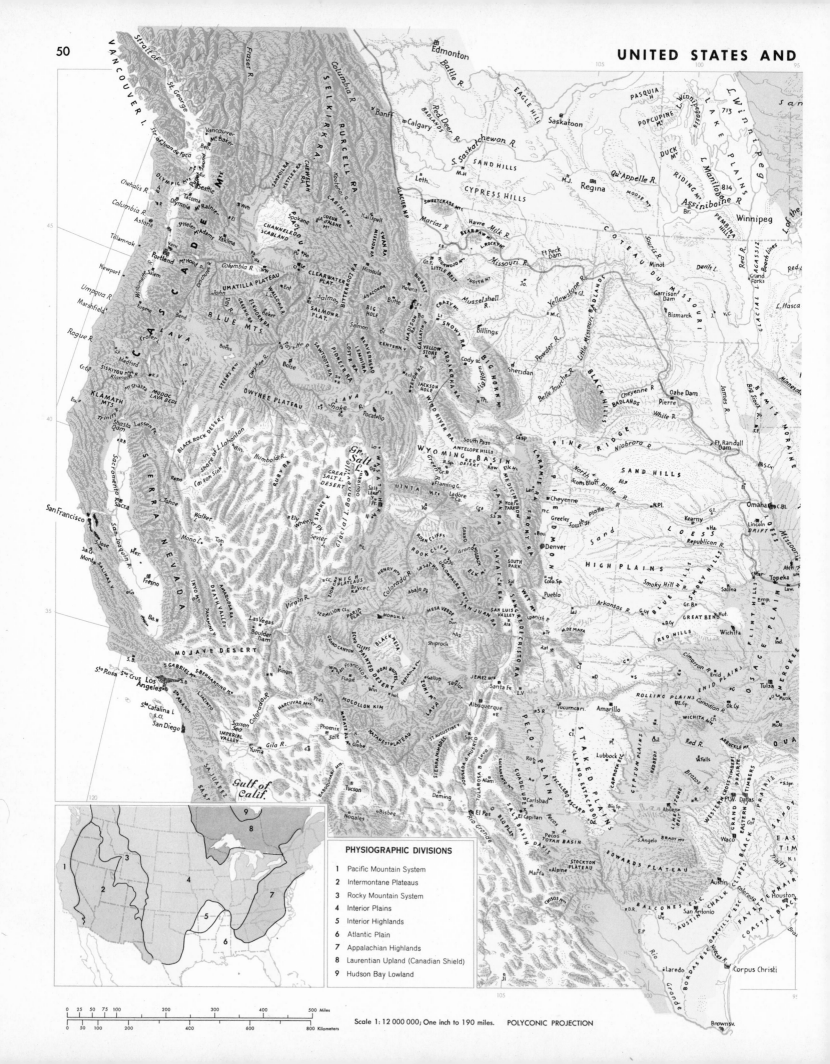

PHYSIOGRAPHIC DIVISIONS

1 Pacific Mountain System
2 Intermontane Plateaus
3 Rocky Mountain System
4 Interior Plains
5 Interior Highlands
6 Atlantic Plain
7 Appalachian Highlands
8 Laurentian Upland (Canadian Shield)
9 Hudson Bay Lowland

Scale 1: 12 000 000; One inch to 190 miles.   POLYCONIC PROJECTION

```
0  25 50 75 100      200        300        400        500 Miles

0   50   100        200        400                    600        800 Kilometers
```

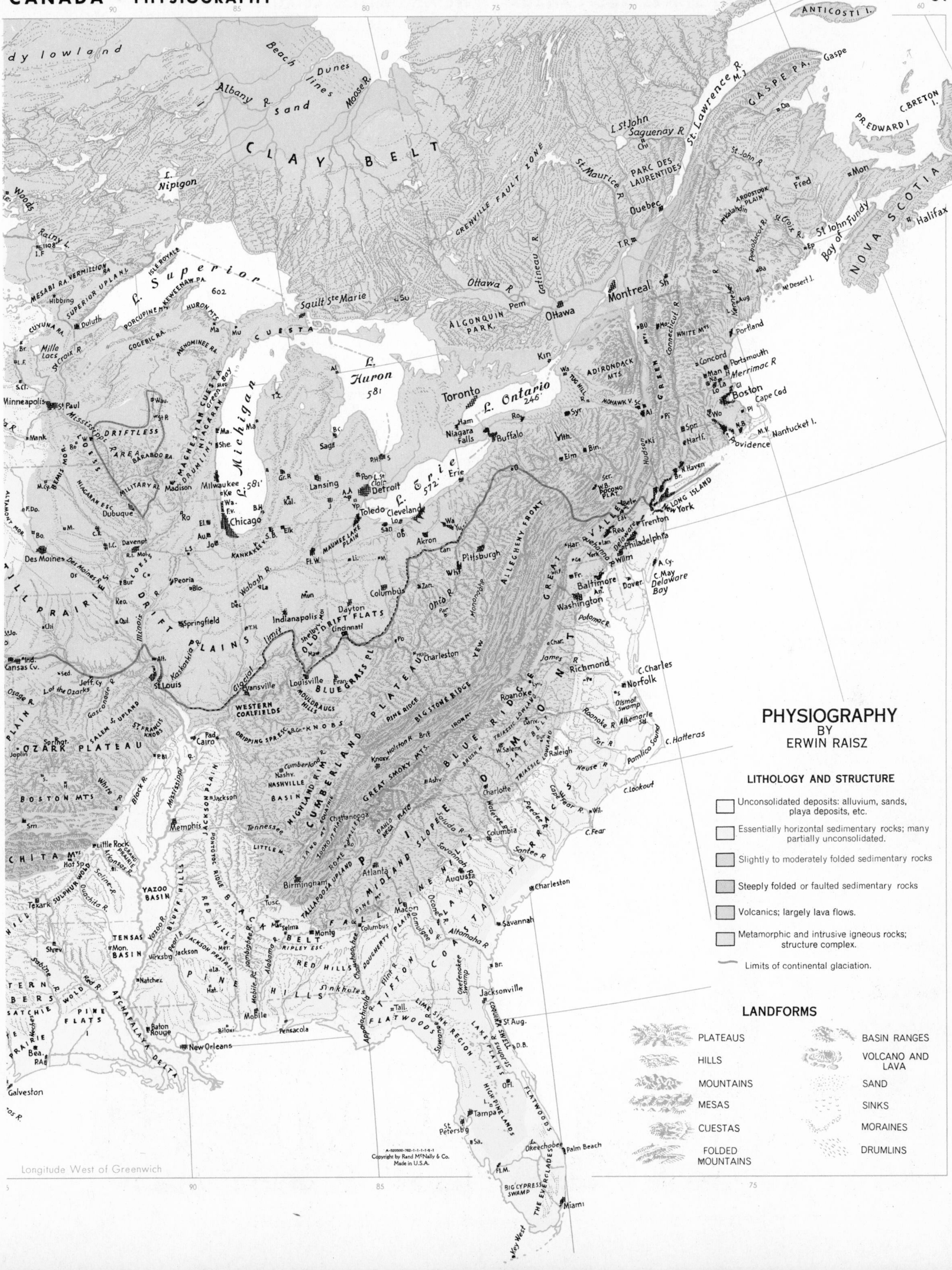

CLAY BELT

dy lowland
Albany R. sand
Moose R.
Beach lines Dunes

L. Nipigon

ANTICOSTI I.

Gaspe
GASPE P.A.
PR. EDWARD I.
C. BRETON I.

St. Lawrence R.
L. St. John
Saguenay R.
PARC DES LAURENTIDES
Quebec
St. Maurice R.
St. John R.
ABOOSTOOK PLAIN
Fred
Mon.
NOVA SCOTIA
Bay of Fundy
St. John
Halifax

GRENVILLE FAULT ZONE
Ottawa R.
Gatineau R.
ALGONQUIN PARK
Montreal
WHITE MTS.
Concord
Portland
Portsmouth
Man. Merrimac R.
Boston
Cape Cod

MESABI RA. VERMILION
Hibbing
Duluth
SUPERIOR UPLAND
ISLE ROYALE
L. Superior
602
Sault Ste Marie
PORCUPINE MTS. KEWEENAW PA.
HURON MTS.
CUYUNA RA.
GOGEBIC RA.
MENOMINEE RA.

Rainy L. 1108
Mille Lacs
St. Croix R.
DRIFTLESS AREA
BARABOO RA.
MAGNESIAN CUESTA
NIAGARA CUESTA
DRUMLINS
Green Bay

L. Huron 581
ADIRONDACK MTS.
MOHAWK V.
Syr.
Hudson R.
GREEN MTS.
Providence
Nantucket I.
LONG ISLAND
New York

Minneapolis
St. Paul
Madison
Milwaukee
L. Michigan 581
Chicago
Lansing
Toronto
L. Ontario 246
Hamilton
Niagara Falls
Buffalo
L. Erie 572
Erie
Cleveland
Toledo
Detroit
MAUMEE LAKE PLAIN
Akron
Pittsburgh
ALLEGHENY FRONT
W. POCONO PLAT.
Trenton
Philadelphia
Wilm.
Delaware
C. May
Delaware Bay

Dubuque
Davenport
Des Moines R.
TILL PRAIRIE
LOESS
OLD DRIFT FLATS
Springfield
Indianapolis
Dayton
Cincinnati
Columbus
Ohio R.
Charleston
GREAT VALLEY
BLUE RIDGE
Washington
Baltimore
Dover
Richmond
C. Charles
Norfolk
C. Hatteras

St. Louis
Evansville
Louisville
BLUEGRASS PL.
OLD DRIFT PLAINS
Glacial Limit
WESTERN COALFIELDS
MOULDRAUGS HILLS
DRIPPING SPRG.
KNOBS
CUMBERLAND PLATEAU
HIGHLAND PLATEAU
PINE RIDGE
BIG STONE RIDGE
Roanoke R.
PIEDMONT
Raleigh
TRIASSIC LOWLAND
Pamlico Sound
C. Lookout

OZARK PLATEAU
BOSTON MTS.
SALEM UPLAND
ST. FRANCIS KNOBS
Cairo
Memphis
Knoxville
Cumberland R.
Nashville
NASHVILLE BASIN
Chattanooga
GREAT SMOKY MTS.
Tennessee R.
Columbia
Charlotte
Augusta
Charleston
Savannah

OUACHITA MTS.
Hot Spgs.
Little Rock
GRAND PRAIRIE
JACKSON PLAIN
Jackson
YAZOO BASIN
BLACK BELT
Birmingham
Atlanta
TALLAPOOSA UPLAND
FALL LINE HILLS
DOUGHERTY PLAIN
MIDLAND SLOPE
Macon
COASTAL PLAIN
Savannah R.

Texark.
Shrev.
Red R.
PINE HILLS
TENSAS BASIN
Natchez
RED HILLS
Selma
Montg.
RIPLEY ESC.
RED HILLS
Columbus
FLINT SINK REGION
Okefenokee Swamp
Jacksonville

Baton Rouge
New Orleans
Biloxi
Mobile
Pensacola
TIFTON FLATWOODS
LIME SINK REGION
LAKE FLATWOODS
St. Aug.
Tampa
St. Petersburg
HIGH PINE LANDS
Palm Beach
Okeechobee
BIG CYPRESS SWAMP
THE EVERGLADES
Miami
Key West

Galveston

ATCHAFALAYA DELTA

PHYSIOGRAPHY
BY ERWIN RAISZ

LITHOLOGY AND STRUCTURE

- Unconsolidated deposits: alluvium, sands, playa deposits, etc.
- Essentially horizontal sedimentary rocks; many partially unconsolidated.
- Slightly to moderately folded sedimentary rocks
- Steeply folded or faulted sedimentary rocks
- Volcanics; largely lava flows.
- Metamorphic and intrusive igneous rocks; structure complex.
- Limits of continental glaciation.

LANDFORMS

PLATEAUS	BASIN RANGES
HILLS	VOLCANO AND LAVA
MOUNTAINS	SAND
MESAS	SINKS
CUESTAS	MORAINES
FOLDED MOUNTAINS	DRUMLINS

Longitude West of Greenwich

A-520500-782-1-1-1-1-9-1
Copyright by Rand McNally & Co.
Made in U.S.A.

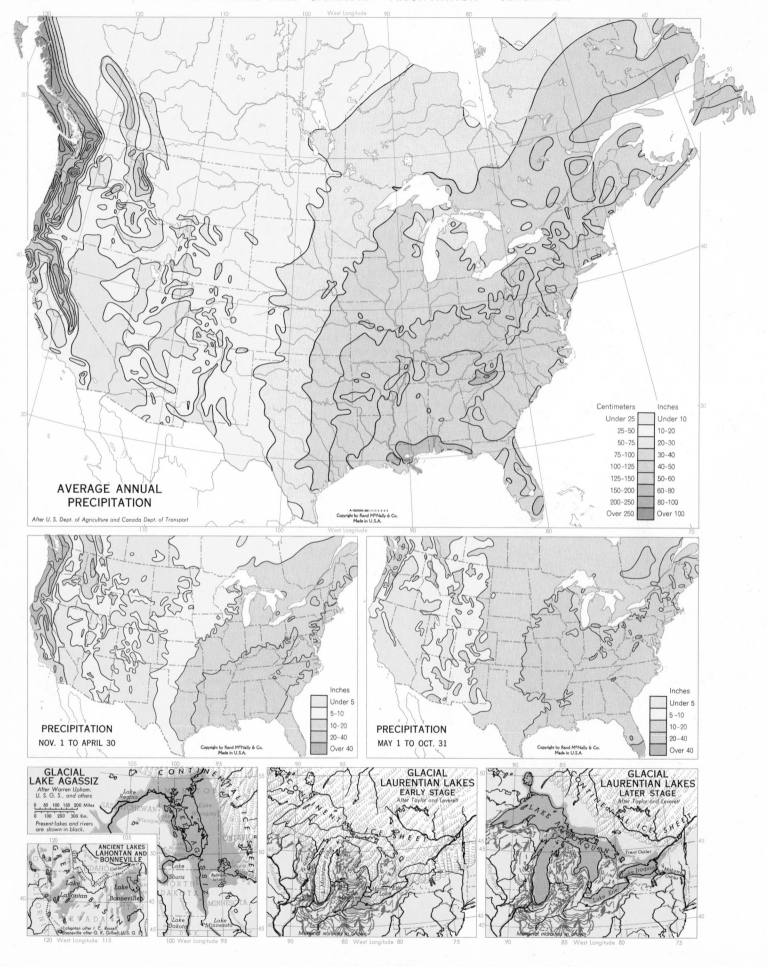

AVERAGE ANNUAL PRECIPITATION

After U. S. Dept. of Agriculture and Canada Dept. of Transport

A-520500-961-1-1-1-1-1-1
Copyright by Rand McNally & Co.
Made in U.S.A.

Centimeters		Inches
Under 25		Under 10
25–50		10–20
50–75		20–30
75–100		30–40
100–125		40–50
125–150		50–60
150–200		60–80
200–250		80–100
Over 250		Over 100

PRECIPITATION

NOV. 1 TO APRIL 30

Copyright by Rand McNally & Co.
Made in U.S.A.

Inches
Under 5
5–10
10–20
20–40
Over 40

PRECIPITATION

MAY 1 TO OCT. 31

Copyright by Rand McNally & Co.
Made in U.S.A.

Inches
Under 5
5–10
10–20
20–40
Over 40

GLACIAL LAKE AGASSIZ

*After Warren Upham.
U. S. G. S., and others*

0 50 100 150 200 Miles
0 100 200 300 Km.
*Present lakes and rivers
are shown in black.*

ANCIENT LAKES LAHONTAN AND BONNEVILLE

*Lahontan after I. C. Russell
Bonneville after G. K. Gilbert, U. S. G. S.*

GLACIAL LAURENTIAN LAKES

EARLY STAGE

After Taylor and Leverett

Marginal moraines in brown

GLACIAL LAURENTIAN LAKES

LATER STAGE

After Taylor and Leverett

Marginal moraines in brown

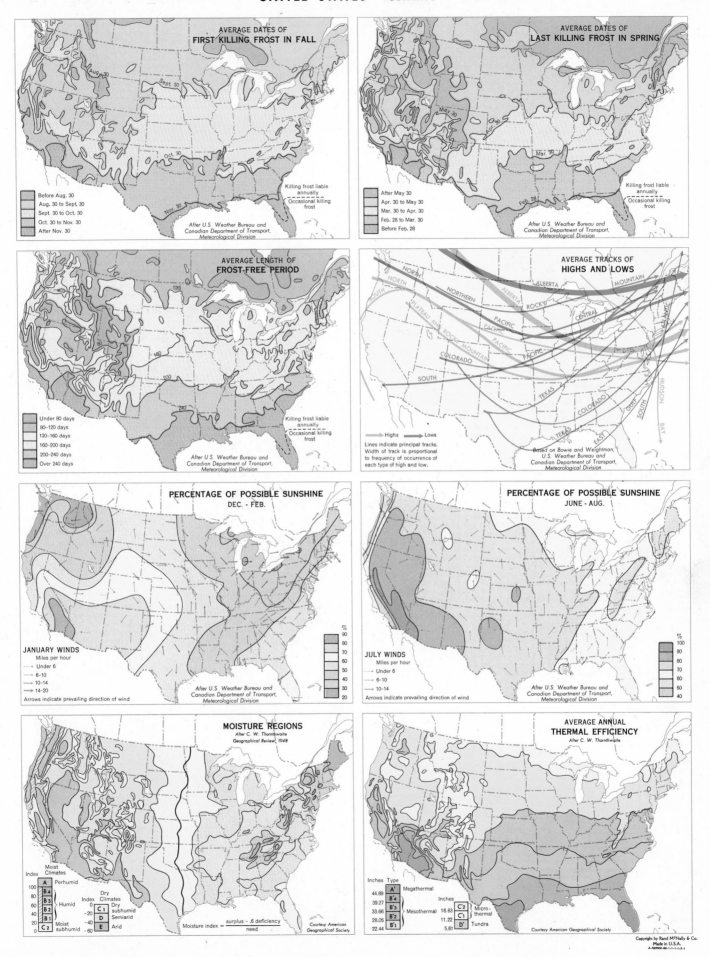

AVERAGE DATES OF FIRST KILLING FROST IN FALL

Before Aug. 30
Aug. 30 to Sept. 30
Sept. 30 to Oct. 30
Oct. 30 to Nov. 30
After Nov. 30

Killing frost liable annually
Occasional killing frost

After U.S. Weather Bureau and Canadian Department of Transport, Meteorological Division

AVERAGE DATES OF LAST KILLING FROST IN SPRING

After May 30
Apr. 30 to May 30
Mar. 30 to Apr. 30
Feb. 28 to Mar. 30
Before Feb. 28

Killing frost liable annually
Occasional killing frost

After U.S. Weather Bureau and Canadian Department of Transport, Meteorological Division

AVERAGE LENGTH OF FROST-FREE PERIOD

Under 80 days
80–120 days
120–160 days
160–200 days
200–240 days
Over 240 days

Killing frost liable annually
Occasional killing frost

After U.S. Weather Bureau and Canadian Department of Transport, Meteorological Division

AVERAGE TRACKS OF HIGHS AND LOWS

→ Highs   → Lows

Lines indicate principal tracks. Width of track is proportional to frequency of occurrence of each type of high and low.

Based on Bowie and Weightman, U.S. Weather Bureau and Canadian Department of Transport, Meteorological Division

PERCENTAGE OF POSSIBLE SUNSHINE DEC. - FEB.

%
90
80
70
60
50
40
30
20

JANUARY WINDS
Miles per hour
---- Under 6
→ 6–10
→ 10–14
→ 14–20
Arrows indicate prevailing direction of wind

PERCENTAGE OF POSSIBLE SUNSHINE JUNE - AUG.

%
100
90
80
70
60
50
40

JULY WINDS
Miles per hour
---- Under 6
→ 6–10
→ 10–14
Arrows indicate prevailing direction of wind

After U.S. Weather Bureau and Canadian Department of Transport, Meteorological Division

MOISTURE REGIONS
After C. W. Thornthwaite
Geographical Review, 1948

Index	Moist Climates	
100	A	Perhumid
80	B4	
60	B3	Humid
40	B2	
20	B1	Moist
0	C2	subhumid

Index	Dry Climates	
0	C1	Dry subhumid
-20	D	Semiarid
-40		
-60	E	Arid

Moisture index = (surplus − .6 deficiency) / need

Courtesy American Geographical Society

AVERAGE ANNUAL THERMAL EFFICIENCY
After C. W. Thornthwaite

Inches	Type	
44.88	A'	Megathermal
39.27	B'4	
33.66	B'3	Mesothermal
28.05	B'2	
22.44	B'1	

Inches		
16.83	C'2	Micro-
11.22	C'1	thermal
5.61	D'	Tundra

Courtesy American Geographical Society

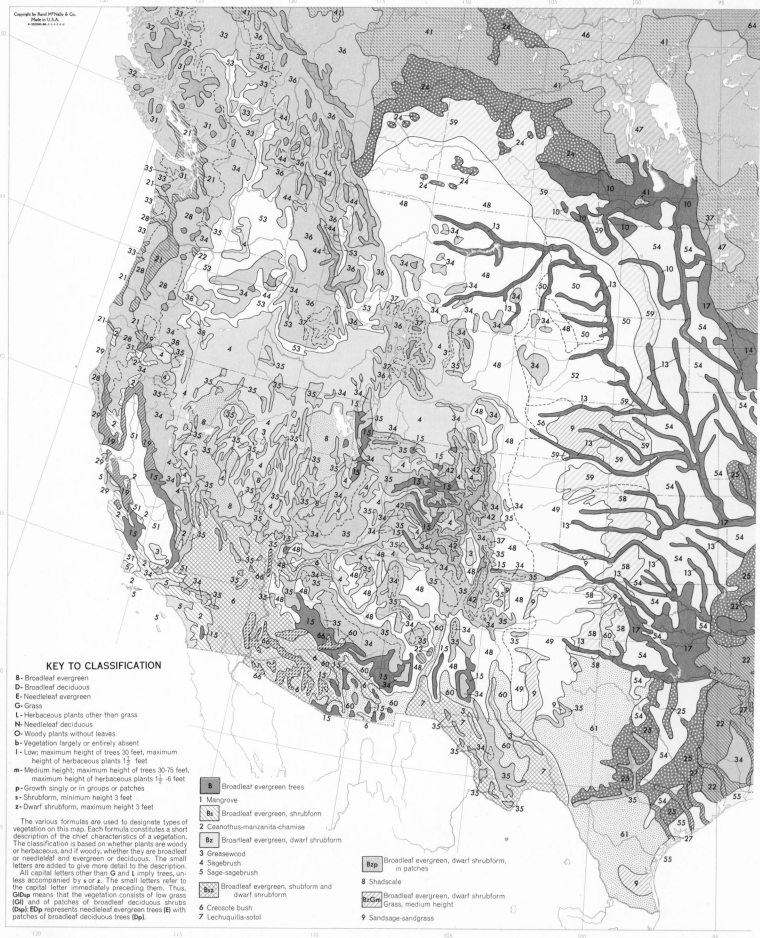

Copyright by Rand McNally & Co.
Made in U.S.A.
A-520500-96-1-1-1-1-1

KEY TO CLASSIFICATION

B - Broadleaf evergreen
D - Broadleaf deciduous
E - Needleleaf evergreen
G - Grass
L - Herbaceous plants other than grass
N - Needleleaf deciduous
O - Woody plants without leaves
b - Vegetation largely or entirely absent
l - Low; maximum height of trees 30 feet, maximum
　　height of herbaceous plants 1½ feet
m - Medium height; maximum height of trees 30-75 feet,
　　maximum height of herbaceous plants 1½ -6 feet
p - Growth singly or in groups or patches
s - Shrubform, minimum height 3 feet
z - Dwarf shrubform, maximum height 3 feet

　　The various formulas are used to designate types of
vegetation on this map. Each formula constitutes a short
description of the chief characteristics of a vegetation.
The classification is based on whether plants are woody
or herbaceous, and if woody, whether they are broadleaf
or needleleaf and evergreen or deciduous. The small
letters are added to give more detail to the description.
　　All capital letters other than G and L imply trees, unless accompanied by s or z. The small letters refer to
the capital letter immediately preceding them. Thus,
GlDsp means that the vegetation consists of low grass
(Gl) and of patches of broadleaf deciduous shrubs
(Dsp); EDp represents needleleaf evergreen trees (E) with
patches of broadleaf deciduous trees (Dp).

B　Broadleaf evergreen trees

1 Mangrove

Bs　Broadleaf evergreen, shrubform

2 Ceanothus-manzanita-chamise

Bz　Broadleaf evergreen, dwarf shrubform

3 Greasewood
4 Sagebrush
5 Sage-sagebrush

Bsz　Broadleaf evergreen, shubform and
　　　　dwarf shrubform

6 Creosote bush
7 Lechuquilla-sotol

Bzp　Broadleaf evergreen, dwarf shrubform,
　　　　in patches

8 Shadscale

BzGm　Broadleaf evergreen, dwarf shrubform
　　　　　Grass, medium height

9 Sandsage-sandgrass

Scale 1:14 000 000;　One inch to 220 miles.

0　25　50　75　100　　200　　　300　　　400　　　500 Miles

0　50　100　　200　　　400　　　600　　　800 Kilometers

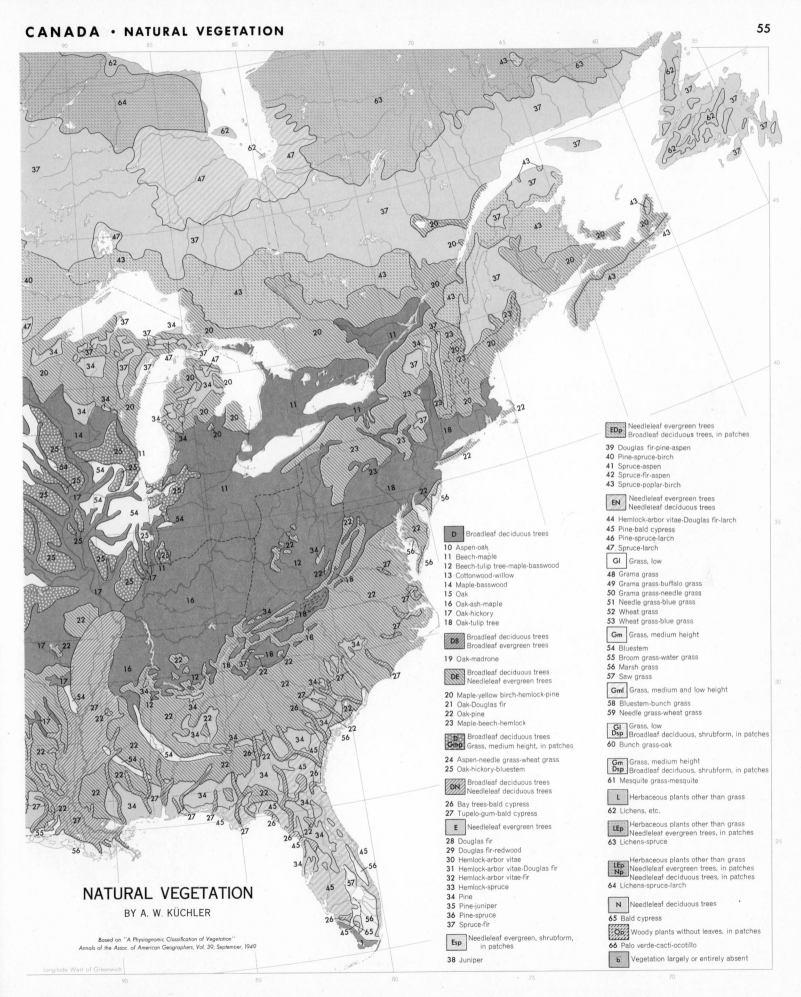

NATURAL VEGETATION

BY A. W. KÜCHLER

Based on "A Physiognomic Classification of Vegetation"
Annals of the Assoc. of American Geographers, Vol. 39, September, 1949

D Broadleaf deciduous trees

10 Aspen-oak
11 Beech-maple
12 Beech-tulip tree-maple-basswood
13 Cottonwood-willow
14 Maple-basswood
15 Oak
16 Oak-ash-maple
17 Oak-hickory
18 Oak-tulip tree

DB Broadleaf deciduous trees
Broadleaf evergreen trees

19 Oak-madrone

DE Broadleaf deciduous trees
Needleleaf evergreen trees

20 Maple-yellow birch-hemlock-pine
21 Oak-Douglas fir
22 Oak-pine
23 Maple-beech-hemlock

D-Gmp Broadleaf deciduous trees
Grass, medium height, in patches

24 Aspen-needle grass-wheat grass
25 Oak-hickory-bluestem

DN Broadleaf deciduous trees
Needleleaf deciduous trees

26 Bay trees-bald cypress
27 Tupelo-gum-bald cypress

E Needleleaf evergreen trees

28 Douglas fir
29 Douglas fir-redwood
30 Hemlock-arbor vitae
31 Hemlock-arbor vitae-Douglas fir
32 Hemlock-arbor vitae-fir
33 Hemlock-spruce
34 Pine
35 Pine-juniper
36 Pine-spruce
37 Spruce-fir

Esp Needleleaf evergreen, shrubform,
in patches

38 Juniper

EDp Needleleaf evergreen trees
Broadleaf deciduous trees, in patches

39 Douglas fir-pine-aspen
40 Pine-spruce-birch
41 Spruce-aspen
42 Spruce-fir-aspen
43 Spruce-poplar-birch

EN Needleleaf evergreen trees
Needleleaf deciduous trees

44 Hemlock-arbor vitae-Douglas fir-larch
45 Pine-bald cypress
46 Pine-spruce-larch
47 Spruce-larch

Gl Grass, low

48 Grama grass
49 Grama grass-buffalo grass
50 Grama grass-needle grass
51 Needle grass-blue grass
52 Wheat grass
53 Wheat grass-blue grass

Gm Grass, medium height

54 Bluestem
55 Broom grass-water grass
56 Marsh grass
57 Saw grass

Gml Grass, medium and low height

58 Bluestem-bunch grass
59 Needle grass-wheat grass

Gl-Dsp Grass, low
Broadleaf deciduous, shrubform, in patches

60 Bunch grass-oak

Gm-Dsp Grass, medium height
Broadleaf deciduous, shrubform, in patches

61 Mesquite grass-mesquite

L Herbaceous plants other than grass

62 Lichens, etc.

LEp Herbaceous plants other than grass
Needleleaf evergreen trees, in patches

63 Lichens-spruce

LEp-Np Herbaceous plants other than grass
Needleleaf evergreen trees, in patches
Needleleaf deciduous trees, in patches

64 Lichens-spruce-larch

N Needleleaf deciduous trees

65 Bald cypress

Op Woody plants without leaves, in patches

66 Palo verde-cacti-ocotillo

b Vegetation largely or entirely absent

Longitude West of Greenwich

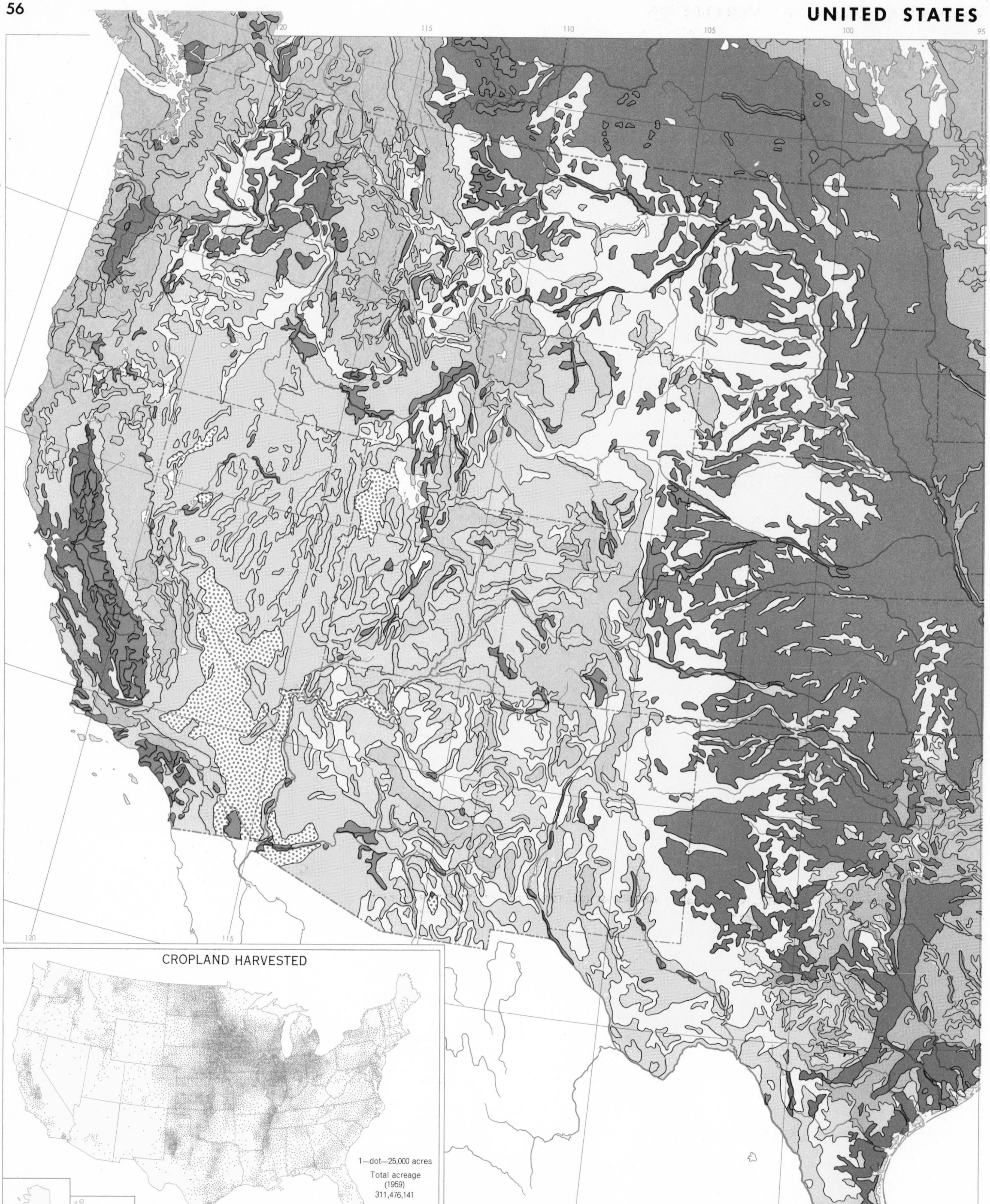

120
115
110
105
100
95
45
40
35
30
120
115
105
100
95
A-520500-361-1-1-1-1-1-1
Copyright by Rand McNally & Co.
Made in U.S.A.
CROPLAND HARVESTED
1—dot—25,000 acres
Total acreage
(1959)
311,476,141
U. S. Dept. of Commerce
Bureau of Census

0 25 50 75 100 200 300 400 500 Miles
0 50 100 200 400 600 800 Kilometers

Scale: 1:12 000 000; One inch to 190 miles.

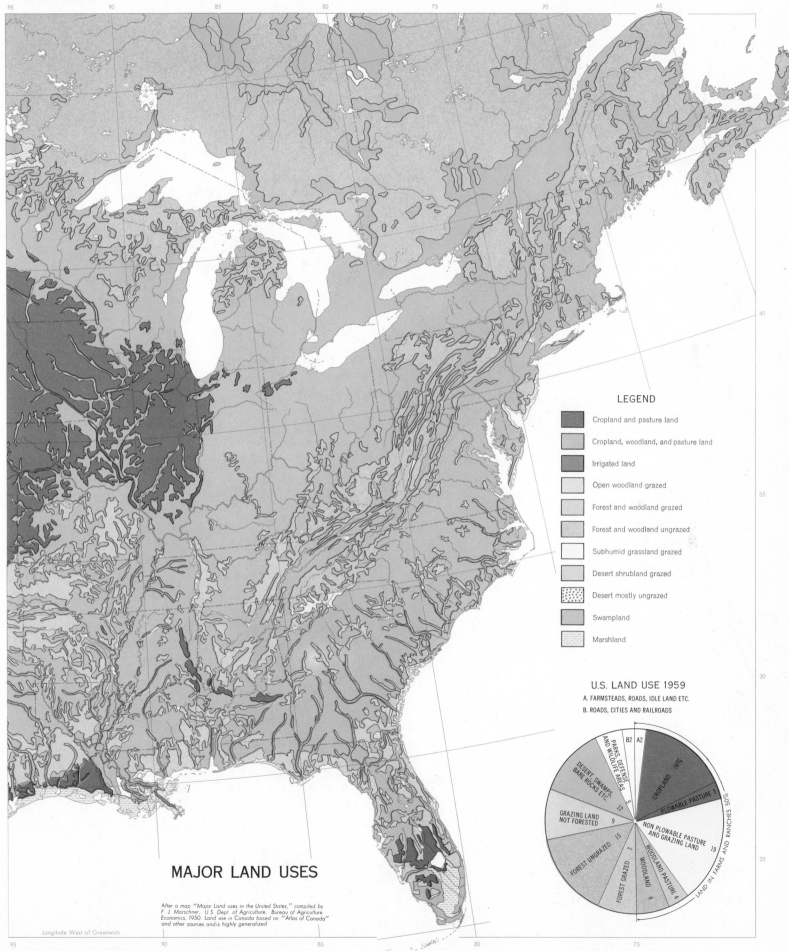

LEGEND

Cropland and pasture land

Cropland, woodland, and pasture land

Irrigated land

Open woodland grazed

Forest and woodland grazed

Forest and woodland ungrazed

Subhumid grassland grazed

Desert shrubland grazed

Desert mostly ungrazed

Swampland

Marshland

U.S. LAND USE 1959

A. FARMSTEADS, ROADS, IDLE LAND ETC.
B. ROADS, CITIES AND RAILROADS

PARKS, DEFENSE AND WILDLIFE AREAS
DESERT, SWAMPS, BARE ROCKS ETC. 12
GRAZING LAND NOT FORESTED 9
FOREST UNGRAZED 15
FOREST GRAZED 7
WOODLAND 6
WOODLAND PASTURE 4
NON PLOWABLE PASTURE AND GRAZING LAND 19
PLOWABLE PASTURE 3
CROPLAND 16%
B2 A2 5
LAND IN FARMS AND RANCHES 50%

MAJOR LAND USES

After a map "Major Land uses in the United States," compiled by
F. J. Marschner, U.S. Dept. of Agriculture. Bureau of Agriculture
Economics, 1950. Land use in Canada based on "Atlas of Canada"
and other sources and is highly generalized

Longitude West of Greenwich

LAMBERT CONFORMAL CONIC PROJECTION

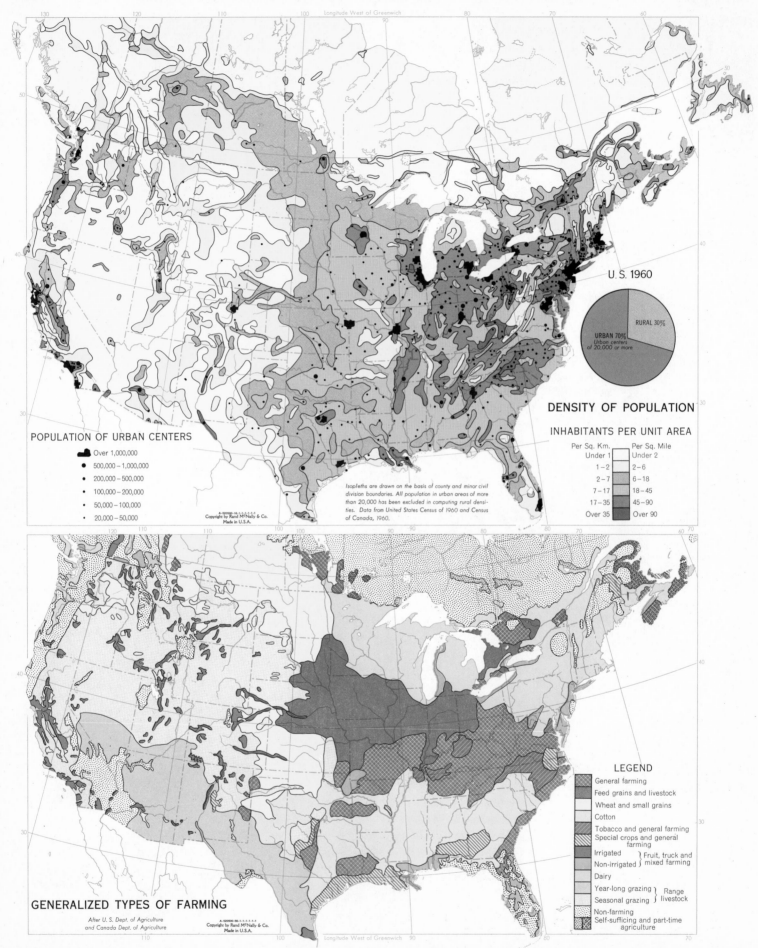

U. S. 1960

RURAL 30%

URBAN 70%
*Urban centers
of 20,000 or more*

POPULATION OF URBAN CENTERS

⬛ Over 1,000,000

● 500,000 – 1,000,000

● 200,000 – 500,000

• 100,000 – 200,000

• 50,000 – 100,000

• 20,000 – 50,000

*Isopleths are drawn on the basis of county and minor civil
division boundaries. All population in urban areas of more
than 20,000 has been excluded in computing rural densities. Data from United States Census of 1960 and Census
of Canada, 1960.*

Copyright by Rand McNally & Co.
Made in U.S.A.

DENSITY OF POPULATION

INHABITANTS PER UNIT AREA

Per Sq. Km.	Per Sq. Mile
Under 1	Under 2
1 – 2	2 – 6
2 – 7	6 – 18
7 – 17	18 – 45
17 – 35	45 – 90
Over 35	Over 90

GENERALIZED TYPES OF FARMING

*After U. S. Dept. of Agriculture
and Canada Dept. of Agriculture*

Copyright by Rand McNally & Co.
Made in U.S.A.

LEGEND

General farming

Feed grains and livestock

Wheat and small grains

Cotton

Tobacco and general farming

Special crops and general
farming

Irrigated } Fruit, truck and
Non-irrigated } mixed farming

Dairy

Year-long grazing } Range
Seasonal grazing } livestock

Non-farming

Self-sufficing and part-time
agriculture

Scale 1: 28 000 000; One inch to 440 miles.   LAMBERT CONFORMAL CONIC PROJECTION

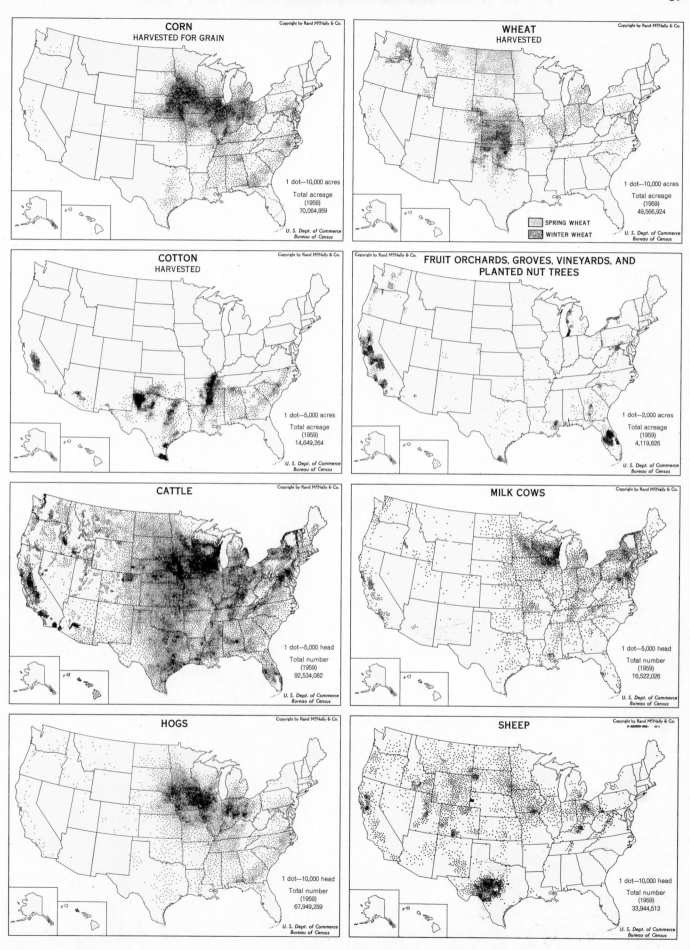

CORN
HARVESTED FOR GRAIN

Copyright by Rand McNally & Co.

1 dot—10,000 acres

Total acreage
(1959)
70,064,959

U. S. Dept. of Commerce
Bureau of Census

WHEAT
HARVESTED

Copyright by Rand McNally & Co.

1 dot—10,000 acres

Total acreage
(1959)
49,566,924

SPRING WHEAT
WINTER WHEAT

U. S. Dept. of Commerce
Bureau of Census

COTTON
HARVESTED

Copyright by Rand McNally & Co.

1 dot—5,000 acres

Total acreage
(1959)
14,649,264

U. S. Dept. of Commerce
Bureau of Census

**FRUIT ORCHARDS, GROVES, VINEYARDS, AND
PLANTED NUT TREES**

Copyright by Rand McNally & Co.

1 dot—2,000 acres

Total acreage
(1959)
4,119,826

U. S. Dept. of Commerce
Bureau of Census

CATTLE

Copyright by Rand McNally & Co.

1 dot—5,000 head

Total number
(1959)
92,534,082

U. S. Dept. of Commerce
Bureau of Census

MILK COWS

Copyright by Rand McNally & Co.

1 dot—5,000 head

Total number
(1959)
16,522,026

U. S. Dept. of Commerce
Bureau of Census

HOGS

Copyright by Rand McNally & Co.

1 dot—10,000 head

Total number
(1959)
67,949,259

U. S. Dept. of Commerce
Bureau of Census

SHEEP

Copyright by Rand McNally & Co.
A-520500-962-   -0-1

1 dot—10,000 head

Total number
(1959)
33,944,513

U. S. Dept. of Commerce
Bureau of Census

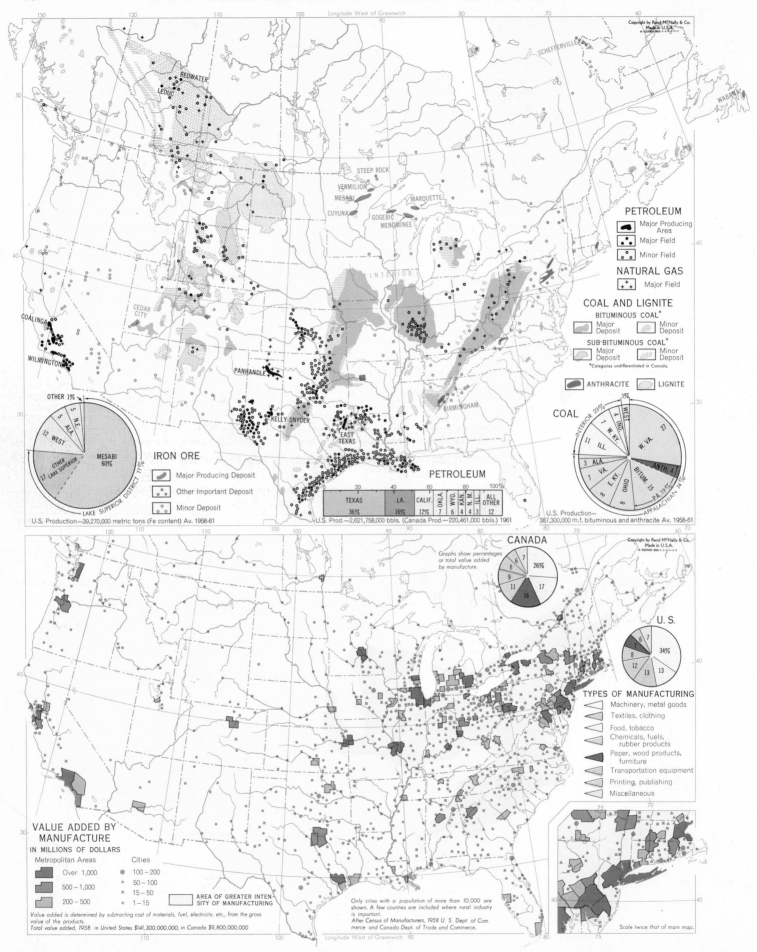

PETROLEUM
- Major Producing Area
- Major Field
- Minor Field

NATURAL GAS
- Major Field

COAL AND LIGNITE

BITUMINOUS COAL*
- Major Deposit
- Minor Deposit

SUB-BITUMINOUS COAL*
- Major Deposit
- Minor Deposit

*Categories undifferentiated in Canada.

- ANTHRACITE
- LIGNITE

COAL

INTERIOR 23% — WEST 3% — W. IND. 4 — W. KY. 7 — W. VA. 27 — ILL. 11 — ALA. 3 — VA. — E. KY. 7 — OHIO 8 — PA. 19% — ANTH. 4 — BITUM. 15 — APPALACHIAN 74%

U.S. Production— 387,300,000 m.t. bituminous and anthracite Av. 1958-61

IRON ORE
- Major Producing Deposit
- Other Important Deposit
- Minor Deposit

Other 1% — 5 ALA. — 5 N.E. — 12 WEST — MESABI 60% — 17 OTHER LAKE SUPERIOR — LAKE SUPERIOR DISTRICT 77%

U.S. Production—39,270,000 metric tons (Fe content) Av. 1958-61

PETROLEUM

TEXAS	LA.	CALIF.	OKLA.	WYO.	KAN.	N.M.	ILL.	ALL OTHER
36%	16%	12%	7	6	4	4	3	12

U.S. Prod.—2,621,758,000 bbls. (Canada Prod.—220,461,000 bbls.) 1961

CANADA

Graphs show percentages or total value added by manufacture.

7 — 6 — 26% — 8 — 17 — 9 — 11 — 16

U.S.

6 — 7 — 7 — 34% — 8 — 13 — 12 — 13

TYPES OF MANUFACTURING
- Machinery, metal goods
- Textiles, clothing
- Food, tobacco
- Chemicals, fuels, rubber products
- Paper, wood products, furniture
- Transportation equipment
- Printing, publishing
- Miscellaneous

VALUE ADDED BY MANUFACTURE

IN MILLIONS OF DOLLARS

Metropolitan Areas
- Over 1,000
- 500 – 1,000
- 200 – 500

Cities
- 100 – 200
- 50 – 100
- 15 – 50
- 1 – 15

- AREA OF GREATER INTENSITY OF MANUFACTURING

Value added is determined by subtracting cost of materials, fuel, electricity, etc., from the gross value of the products.
Total value added, 1958: in United States $141,300,000,000; in Canada $9,800,000,000

Only cities with a population of more than 10,000 are shown. A few counties are included where rural industry is important.
After Census of Manufacturers, 1958 U. S. Dept. of Commerce and Canada Dept. of Trade and Commerce.

Scale twice that of main map.

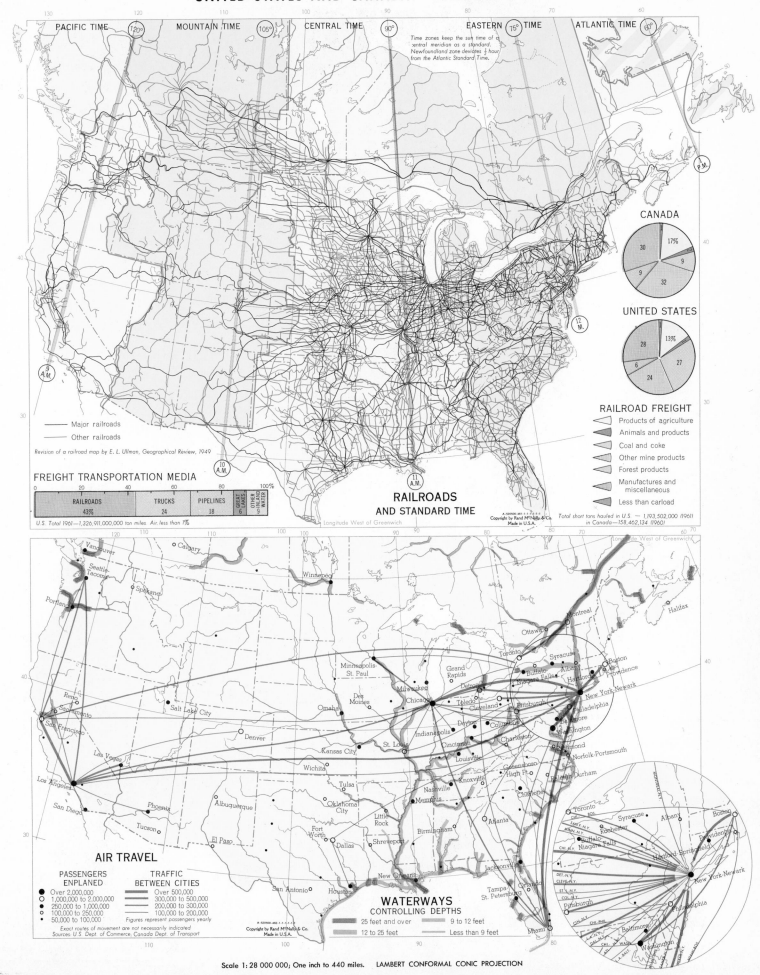

PACIFIC TIME | MOUNTAIN TIME | CENTRAL TIME | EASTERN TIME | ATLANTIC TIME

Time zones keep the sun time of a central meridian as a standard. Newfoundland zone deviates ½ hour from the Atlantic Standard Time.

CANADA

17%
30
9
9
32

UNITED STATES

13%
28
27
6
24

RAILROAD FREIGHT

Products of agriculture
Animals and products
Coal and coke
Other mine products
Forest products
Manufactures and miscellaneous
Less than carload

— Major railroads
— Other railroads

Revision of a railroad map by E. L. Ullman, Geographical Review, 1949

FREIGHT TRANSPORTATION MEDIA

| RAILROADS 43% | TRUCKS 24 | PIPELINES 18 | GREAT LAKES | OTHER INLAND WATER 6 |

U.S. Total 1961—1,326,911,000,000 ton miles. Air, less than 1%

RAILROADS
AND STANDARD TIME

Longitude West of Greenwich

A-520500-461-1-1-1-1-1-1-1
Copyright by Rand McNally & Co.
Made in U.S.A.

Total short tons hauled in U.S. — 1,193,502,000 (1961) in Canada—158,462,134 (1960)

AIR TRAVEL

PASSENGERS ENPLANED
● Over 2,000,000
○ 1,000,000 to 2,000,000
○ 250,000 to 1,000,000
○ 100,000 to 250,000
• 50,000 to 100,000

TRAFFIC BETWEEN CITIES
Over 500,000
300,000 to 500,000
200,000 to 300,000
100,000 to 200,000
Figures represent passengers yearly

Exact routes of movement are not necessarily indicated
Sources: U.S. Dept. of Commerce, Canada Dept. of Transport

WATERWAYS
CONTROLLING DEPTHS
25 feet and over   9 to 12 feet
12 to 25 feet   Less than 9 feet

A-520500-462-1-1-1-1-1-1-1
Copyright by Rand McNally & Co.
Made in U.S.A.

Scale 1: 28 000 000; One inch to 440 miles.   LAMBERT CONFORMAL CONIC PROJECTION

Continued on pages 86–87

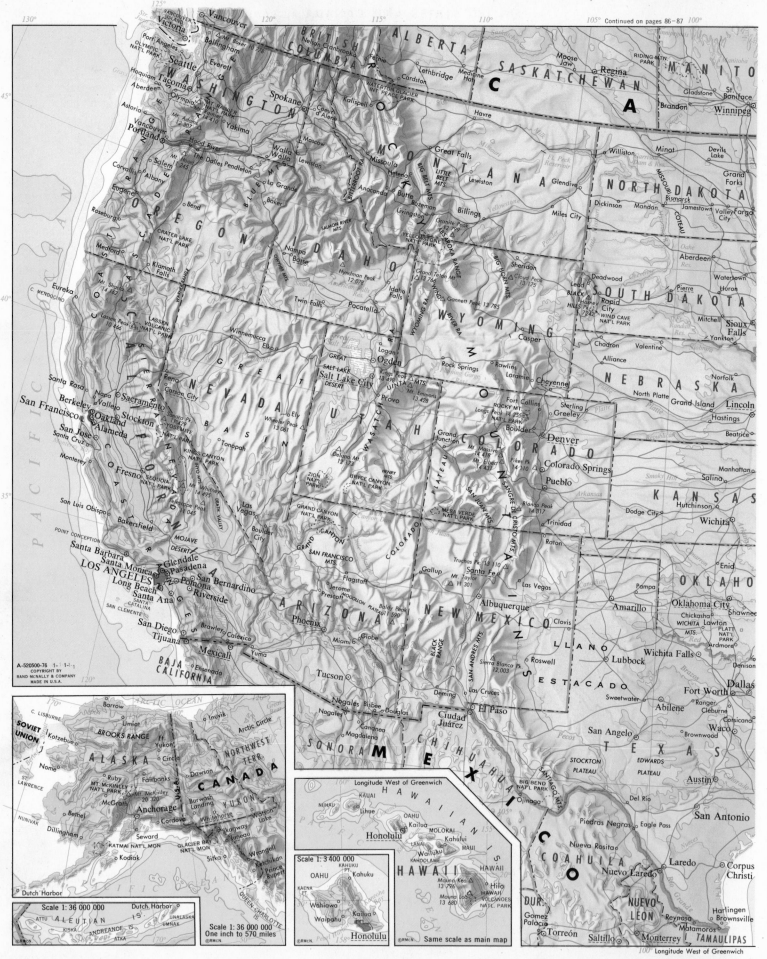

Scale 1:12 000 000; one inch to 190 miles. Polyconic Projection
Elevations and depressions are given in feet

Scale 1:36 000 000   Dutch Harbor
One inch to 570 miles

Scale 1:3 400 000

Same scale as main map

Longitude West of Greenwich

STATE OF ALASKA

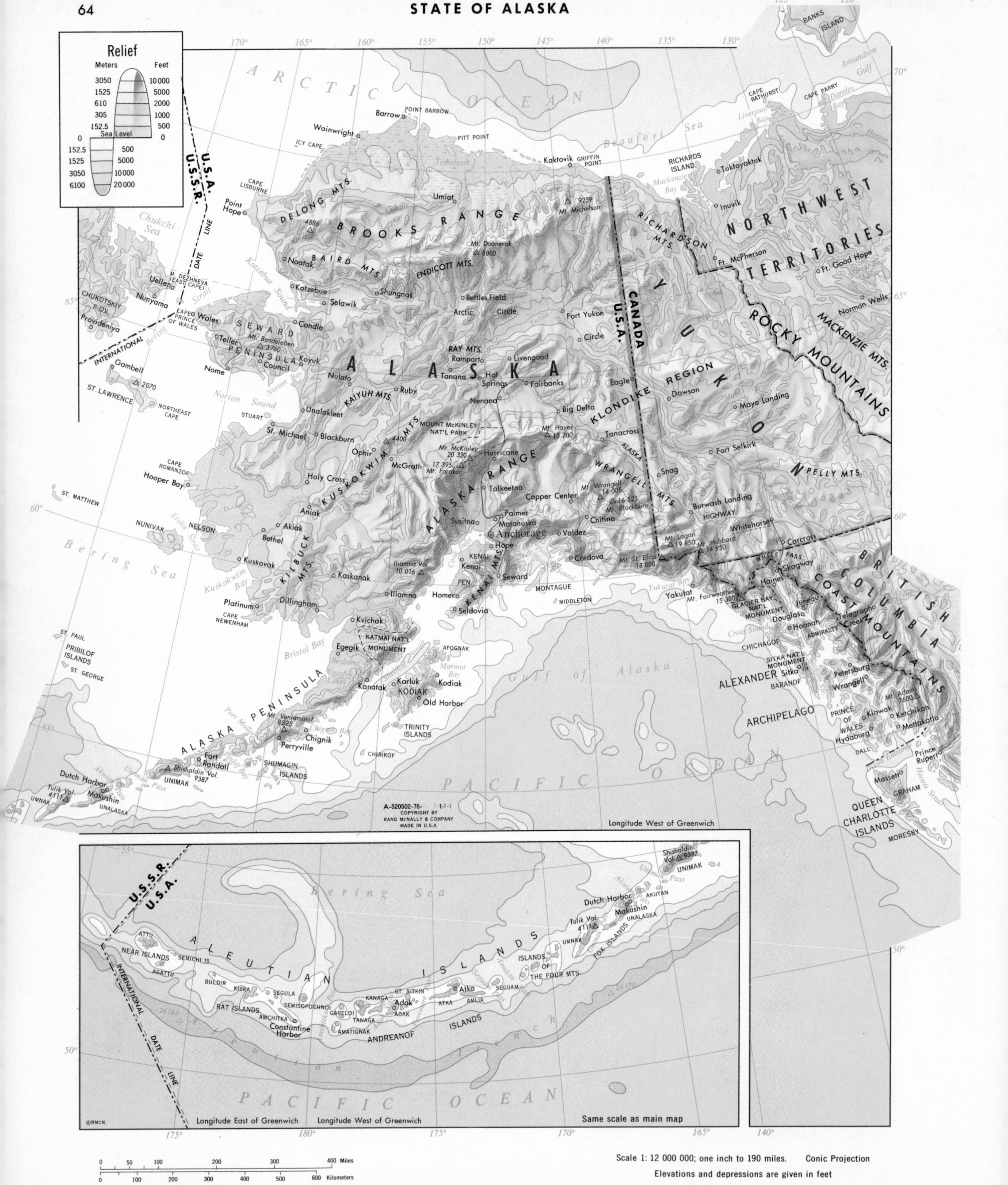

Relief

Meters	Feet
3050	10 000
1525	5000
610	2000
305	1000
152.5	500
0 Sea Level	0
152.5	500
1525	5000
3050	10 000
6100	20 000

ARCTIC OCEAN

U.S.A.
U.S.S.R.

DATE LINE

INTERNATIONAL

Chukchi Sea

Beaufort Sea

Point Barrow
Barrow
Wainwright
ICY CAPE
PITT POINT
Kaktovik
GRIFFIN POINT
RICHARDS ISLAND
CAPE BATHURST
CAPE PARRY
Amundsen Gulf
BANKS ISLAND
Liverpool Bay
Darnley Bay
Tuktoyaktuk
Mackenzie Bay
Inuvik
CAPE LISBURNE
Point Hope
Umiat
9239
Mt. Michelson
RICHARDSON MTS.
Ft. McPherson
Ft. Good Hope
NORTHWEST TERRITORIES
DELONG MTS.
4886
BROOKS RANGE
Mt. Doonerak 8800
BAIRD MTS.
ENDICOTT MTS.
Noatak
Norman Wells
Kotzebue
Shungnak
Bettles Field
Arctic Circle
Fort Yukon
Selawik
CANADA U.S.A.
ROCKY MOUNTAINS
MACKENZIE MTS.
M. DEZHNEVA (EAST CAPE)
Uelleh
CHUKOTSKIY P.OV.
Nunyama
CAPE PRINCE OF WALES
Wales
Teller
SEWARD PENINSULA
Mt. Bendeleben 3760
Candle
Koyuk
Council
Circle
Eagle
YUKON
Dawson
Providenya
Bering Strait
Nome
Nulato
Tanana
Hot Springs
Livengood
Fairbanks
KLONDIKE REGION
Mayo Landing
PELLY MTS.
Gambell
2070
NORTHEAST CAPE
ST. LAWRENCE
STUART
Ruby
Nenana
Big Delta
Mt. Hayes 13,700
Tanacross
ALASKA
KAIYUH MTS.
RAY MTS.
Rampart
Fort Selkirk
Norton Sound
Unalakleet
MOUNT McKINLEY NAT'L PARK
WRANGELL MTS.
Snag
ST. MICHAEL
St. Michael
Blackburn
4400
KUSKOKWIM MTS.
Mt. McKinley 20,320
17,395 Mt. Foraker
Hurricane
Mt. Wrangell 14,005
16,523 Mt. Blackburn
Burwash Landing
HIGHWAY
Whitehorse
CAPE ROMANZOF
Hooper Bay
Ophir
McGrath
Talkeetna
Copper Center
Chitina
Mt. Logan 19,850
Mt. Hubbard 14,950
Carcross
ST. MATTHEW
Holy Cross
ALASKA RANGE
Susitna
Palmer
Matanuska
Anchorage
Valdez
Mt. St. Elias 18,008
WHITE PASS
Skagway
Haines
BRITISH COLUMBIA
NELSON
NUNIVAK
Aniak
Akiak
Bethel
Iliamna Vol. 10,016
Hope
KENAI
Cordova
Yakutat
Mt. Fairweather 15,300
GLACIER BAY NAT'L MONUMENT
Juneau
Douglas
Telegraph Creek
COAST MOUNTAINS
Kuskokvak
Kaskanak
Iliamna
Homer
KENAI MTS.
Kenai
Seward
MONTAGUE
Yakutat Bay
Cross Sound
Hoonah
ADMIRALTY
Bering Sea
Platinum
Dillingham
CAPE NEWENHAM
Seldovia
MIDDLETON
CHICHAGOF
SITKA NAT'L MONUMENT
Sitka
Petersburg
Wrangell
Mt. Adams 7600
ST. PAUL
PRIBILOF ISLANDS
ST. GEORGE
Kvichak
KATMAI NAT'L MONUMENT
Egegik
Gulf of Alaska
ALEXANDER
BARANOF
ARCHIPELAGO
PRINCE OF WALES
Klawak
Ketchikan
Metlakatla
Bristol Bay
AFOGNAK
Marmot Bay
Kanatak
Karluk
KODIAK
Kodiak
Old Harbor
Hydaburg
DALL
ALASKA PENINSULA
Chignik
Perryville
TRINITY ISLANDS
CHIRIKOF
PACIFIC OCEAN
Masset
GRAHAM
Prince Rupert
Mt. Veniaminof 8225
Fort Randall
Shishaldin Vol. 9387
SHUMAGIN ISLANDS
QUEEN CHARLOTTE ISLANDS
MORESBY
Dutch Harbor
Tulik Vol. 4111
Makushin
UNIMAK
UNALASKA
UNMAK

A-520502-76- -1-J-1
COPYRIGHT BY
RAND McNALLY & COMPANY
MADE IN U.S.A.

Longitude West of Greenwich

Inset map:

U.S.S.R.
U.S.A.
INTERNATIONAL DATE LINE
Bering Sea
ALEUTIAN ISLANDS
Shishaldin Vol. 9387
UNIMAK PASS
Dutch Harbor
Makushin
AKUTAN
Tulik Vol. 4111
UNMAK
FOX ISLANDS
ATTU
NEAR ISLANDS
SEMICHI IS.
AGATTU
BULDIR
KISKA
SEGULA
SEMISOPOCHNOI
25,184
RAT ISLANDS
AMCHITKA
Constantine Harbor
GARELOI
TANAGA
AMATIGNAK
KANAGA
GT. SITKIN
Adak
ATKA
AMLIA
SEGUAM
Atka
ISLANDS OF THE FOUR MTS.
ANDREANOF ISLANDS
24,170
Aleutian Trench
PACIFIC OCEAN

Longitude East of Greenwich   Longitude West of Greenwich   Same scale as main map

Scale 1: 12 000 000; one inch to 190 miles.   Conic Projection

Elevations and depressions are given in feet

0 50 100 200 300 400 Miles
0 100 200 300 400 500 600 Kilometers

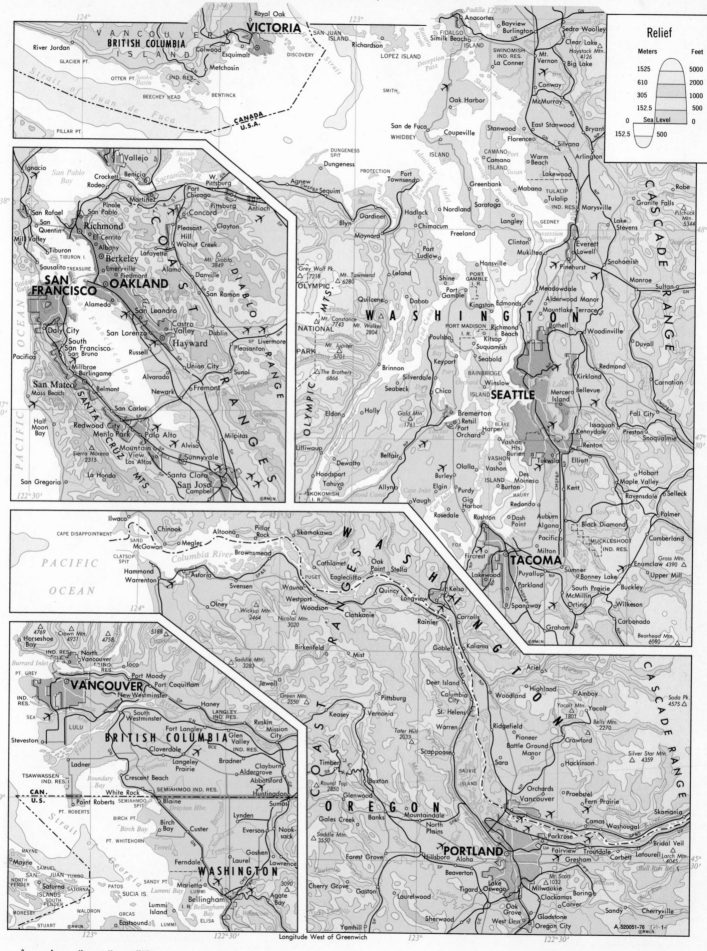

Scale 1:1 000 000; one inch to 16 miles.
Elevations and depressions are given in feet.

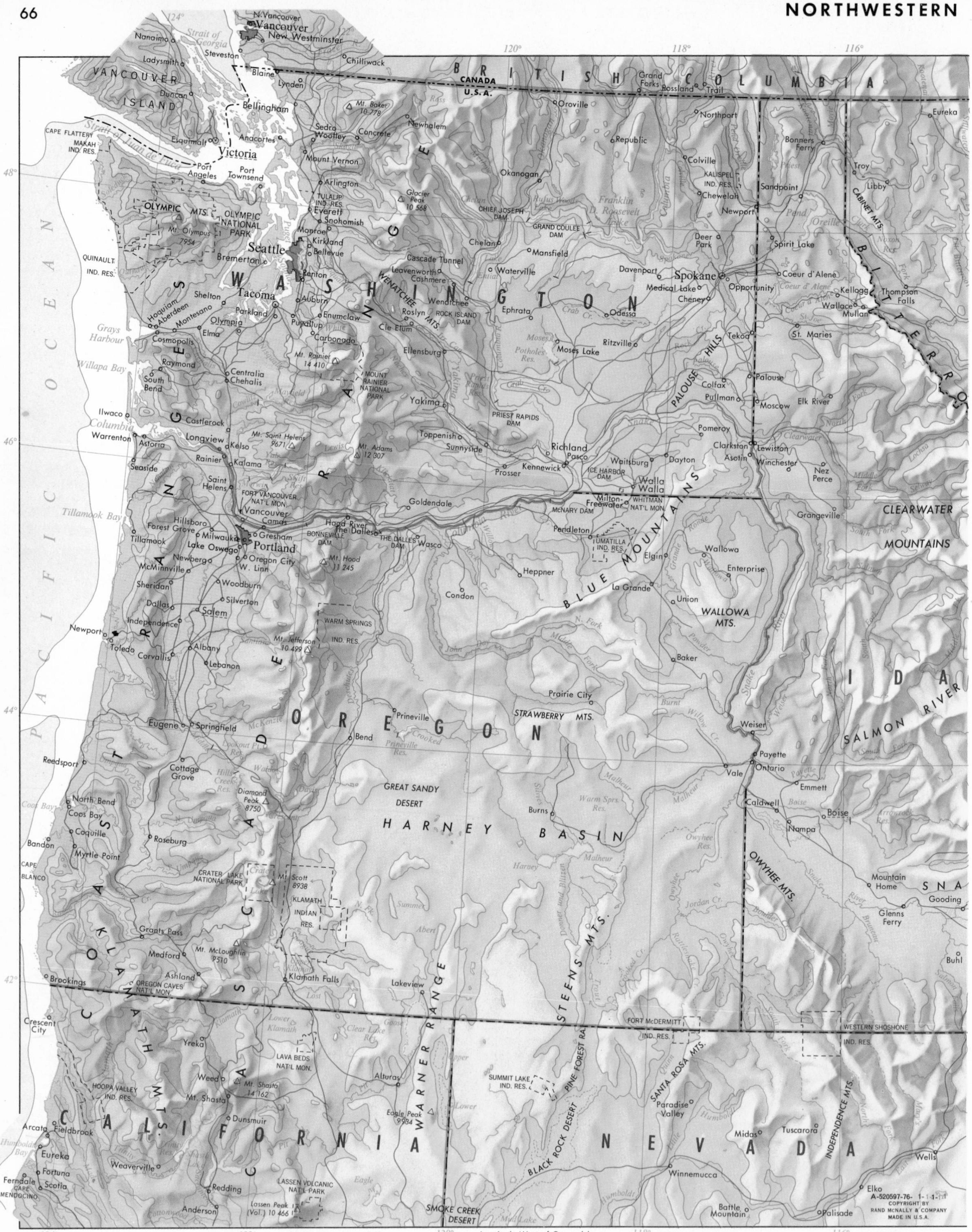

124° 122° 120° 118° 116°

BRITISH COLUMBIA
CANADA
U.S.A.

Grand Forks Rossland Trail Eureka

Nanaimo N. Vancouver Vancouver New Westminster Steveston Chilliwack

Ladysmith Blaine Lynden Mt. Baker 10,778 Newhalem Oroville Republic Northport Bonners Ferry Troy Libby

VANCOUVER ISLAND Duncan Bellingham Sedro Woolley Concrete Colville Kalispel Ind. Res. Chewelah Sandpoint CABINET MTS.

Esquimalt Anacortes Mount Vernon Newport

CAPE FLATTERY MAKAH IND. RES. Victoria Port Townsend Arlington Glacier Peak 10,568 Chelan Deer Park Spirit Lake

48° Strait of Juan de Fuca Port Angeles Tulalip Ind. Res. Everett CHIEF JOSEPH DAM GRAND COULEE DAM Noxon Res.

OLYMPIC MTS. OLYMPIC NATIONAL PARK Snohomish Okanogan Spokane Coeur d'Alene

Mt. Olympus 7954 Monroe Mansfield Davenport Medical Lake Opportunity Kellogg Thompson Falls

Seattle Kirkland Bellevue WASHINGTON Waterville Cheney Wallace Mullan

Bremerton Renton Cascade Tunnel St. Maries

QUINAULT IND. RES. Shelton Auburn Leavenworth Cashmere Ephrata Odessa Tekoa

Tacoma Parkland Enumclaw Roslyn Cle Elum Wenatchee ROCK ISLAND DAM Ritzville Moses Lake Colfax Palouse

Hoquiam Aberdeen Montesano Olympia Puyallup Garbonado Potholes Res. PALOUSE HILLS Pullman Moscow Elk River

Grays Harbour Cosmopolis Elma Mt. Rainier 14,410 Ellensburg Crab Cr.

Raymond Centralia MOUNT RAINIER NATIONAL PARK Yakima PRIEST RAPIDS DAM Pomeroy Clearwater

South Bend Chehalis Toppenish Richland Pasco Waitsburg Dayton Clarkston Lewiston Winchester

Willapa Bay Castlerock Sunnyside Prosser Kennewick ICE HARBOR DAM Asotin Nez Perce

46° Ilwaco Longview Mt. St. Helens 9671 Mt. Adams 12,307 Walla Walla WHITMAN NAT'L MON.

Columbia R. Warrenton Astoria Kelso McNARY DAM Milton-Freewater Grangeville CLEARWATER MOUNTAINS

Seaside Rainier Kalama Goldendale UMATILLA IND. RES. Pendleton Elgin

Saint Helens FORT VANCOUVER NAT'L MON. Hood River The Dalles THE DALLES DAM Wasco BLUE MOUNTAINS Wallowa

Tillamook Bay Hillsboro Vancouver Camas BONNEVILLE DAM Heppner Enterprise WALLOWA MTS.

Forest Grove Milwaukie Gresham Mt. Hood 11,245 Condon La Grande Union Baker

Tillamook Lake Oswego Portland W. Linn Oregon City McMinnville Newberg Woodburn

Sheridan Silverton OREGON

Dallas Salem WARM SPRINGS IND. RES. Prairie City STRAWBERRY MTS.

Newport Independence Albany Mt. Jefferson 10,499 SALMON RIVER

Toledo Corvallis Lebanon

44° PACIFIC OCEAN Eugene Springfield Prineville Bend Payette

Reedsport Cottage Grove Prineville Res. Vale Ontario Emmett Boise

North Bend Diamond Peak 8750 GREAT SANDY DESERT Burns Caldwell Nampa

Coos Bay Coquille Roseburg HARNEY BASIN Warm Sprs. Res. Owyhee Res.

Bandon Myrtle Point Owyhee R.

CAPE BLANCO CRATER LAKE NATIONAL PARK Mt. Scott 8938 Harney OWYHEE MTS. Mountain Home

Grants Pass KLAMATH INDIAN RES. Glenns Ferry

Medford Mt. McLoughlin 9510 SNAKE

42° Brookings Ashland OREGON CAVES NAT'L MON. Klamath Falls Lakeview FORT McDERMITT IND. RES. WESTERN SHOSHONE IND. RES. Buhl

Crescent City Yreka WARNER RANGE STEENS MTS.

LAVA BEDS NAT'L MON. PINE FOREST RA. SANTA ROSA MTS.

Arcata Fieldbrook Weed Alturas SUMMIT LAKE IND. RES. BLACK ROCK DESERT Paradise Valley

Eureka Fortuna Scotia Mt. Shasta 14,162 Eagle Peak 9934 INDEPENDENCE MTS. Wells

CAPE MENDOCINO Ferndale Dunsmuir CALIFORNIA NEVADA Midas Tuscarora

HOOPA VALLEY IND. RES. Weaverville SMOKE CREEK DESERT Winnemucca Elko

Redding LASSEN VOLCANIC NAT'L PARK Anderson Lassen Peak 10,466 Battle Mountain Palisade

A-520597-76- 1-11-
COPYRIGHT BY
RAND McNALLY & COMPANY
MADE IN U.S.A.

124° 122° 120° 118° 116°

Continued on pages 68-69 Longitude West of Greenwich

Scale 1: 4 000 000; one inch to 64 miles. Conic Projection
Elevations and depressions are given in feet

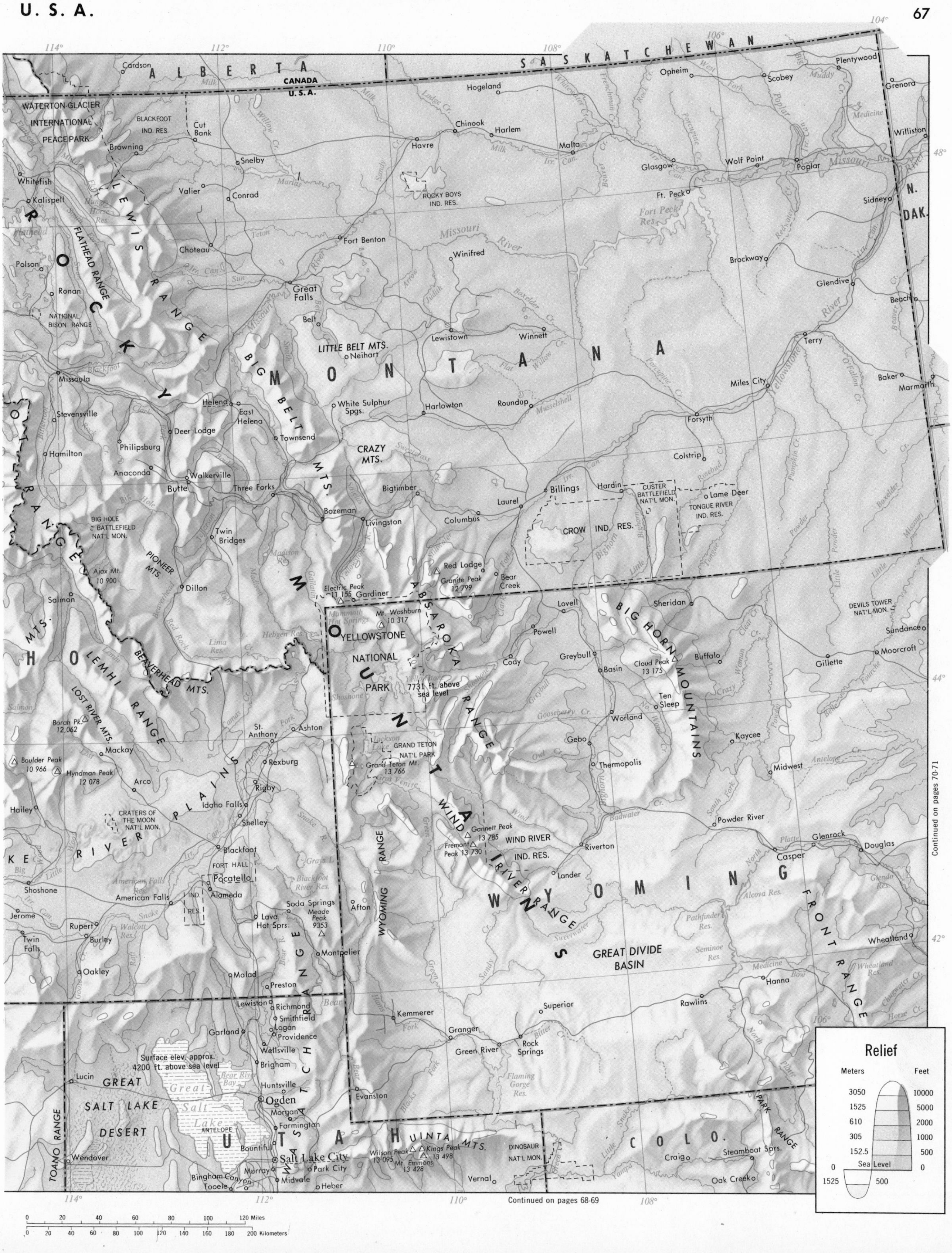

ALBERTA   SASKATCHEWAN

CANADA
U.S.A.

104°
106°
108°
110°
112°
114°

Cardson
Plentywood
Opheim
Scobey
Grenora
Hogeland
Chinook
Harlem
Malta
Wolf Point
Poplar
Williston
Glasgow
Ft. Peck
Sidney
48°

WATERTON-GLACIER
INTERNATIONAL
PEACE PARK
Browning
BLACKFOOT
IND. RES.
Cut Bank
Snelby
Valier
Conrad
Choteau

Whitefish
Kalispell
Polson
Ronan

ROCKY
LEWIS RANGE
FLATHEAD RANGE
BIG BELT MTS.
LITTLE BELT MTS.
Neihart

NATIONAL
BISON RANGE

Missoula
Helena
East Helena
Townsend
White Sulphur Spgs.
Harlowton
Lewistown
Winnett
Roundup

ROCKY BOYS
IND. RES.

Fort Benton
Winifred

Great Falls
Belt

Missouri River

MONTANA

Fort Peck Res.
Brockway
Glendive
Beach
N. DAK.
46°

Terry
Baker
Marmarth
Miles City
Forsyth
Colstrip

Stevensville
Deer Lodge
Philipsburg
Hamilton
Anaconda
Butte
Walkerville
Three Forks
Bigtimber
Billings
Hardin
Laurel
Columbus

CRAZY MTS.
Bozeman
Livingston

CUSTER
BATTLEFIELD
NAT'L MON.
Lame Deer
TONGUE RIVER
IND. RES.
CROW IND. RES.

BIG HOLE
BATTLEFIELD
NAT'L MON.
PIONEER MTS.
Twin Bridges
Dillon
Ajax Mt. 10 900

Red Lodge
Granite Peak 12 799
Bear Creek
Electric Peak 11 155
Gardiner

ABSAROKA RANGE

Lovell
Sheridan
DEVILS TOWER
NAT'L MON.
Sundance
Moorcroft
Gillette

Salmon
BEAVERHEAD MTS.
LEMHI RANGE
LOST RIVER MTS.
Mt. Washburn 10 317
YELLOWSTONE
NATIONAL
PARK
7731 ft. above sea level
Mammoth Hot Springs
Powell
Cody
Greybull
Basin
Buffalo
Cloud Peak 13 175
BIG HORN MOUNTAINS

44°

Borah Pk. 12,062
Boulder Peak 10 966
Hyndman Peak 12 078
Mackay
Arco
St. Anthony
Ashton
Rexburg
Rigby
GRAND TETON NAT'L PARK
Grand Teton Mt. 13 766
JACKSON Lake

WIND RIVER RANGE
Worland
Ten Sleep
Gebo
Thermopolis
Kaycee
Midwest

Hailey
SNAKE RIVER PLAINS
Idaho Falls
Shelley
CRATERS OF THE MOON NAT'L MON.
Blackfoot

Gannett Peak 13 785
Fremont Peak 13 730
WIND RIVER IND. RES.
Powder River

Shoshone
Jerome
FORT HALL IND. RES.
Pocatello
Alameda
American Falls
Soda Springs
Meade Peak 9353
Afton

Riverton
Lander

MOUNTAINS

WYOMING RANGE
SALT RIVER RANGE

Glenrock
Casper
Douglas

42°

Rupert
Burley
Twin Falls
Oakley
Lava Hot Sprs.
Montpelier

GREAT DIVIDE BASIN
Pathfinder Res.
Alcova Res.
Seminoe Res.
Hanna
Wheatland

Malad
Preston
Lewiston
Richmond
Smithfield
Logan
Providence
Wellsville
Brigham

Kemmerer
Granger
Green River
Rock Springs
Superior
Rawlins

FRONT RANGE

Lucin
Garland
Huntsville
Morgan
Farmington

Surface elev. approx. 4200 ft. above sea level
GREAT SALT LAKE DESERT
Great Salt Lake
ANTELOPE
Ogden
Bountiful

Flaming Gorge Res.
Evanston

WYOMING

PARK RANGE
106°

TOANO RANGE
Wendover
Salt Lake City
Murray
Bingham Canyon
Tooele
Midvale
Heber
Park City
Wilson Peak 13 095
Kings Peak 13 498
Mt. Emmons 13 428

UINTA MTS.
DINOSAUR NAT'L MON.

UTAH
COLO.

Vernal
Craig
Steamboat Sprs.
Oak Creek

WASATCH RANGE

Continued on pages 70-71

42°
44°
46°
48°

Relief

Meters		Feet
3050		10000
1525		5000
610		2000
305		1000
152.5		500
0	Sea Level	0
1525		500

Continued on pages 68-69

0 20 40 60 80 100 120 Miles
0 20 40 60 80 100 120 140 160 200 Kilometers

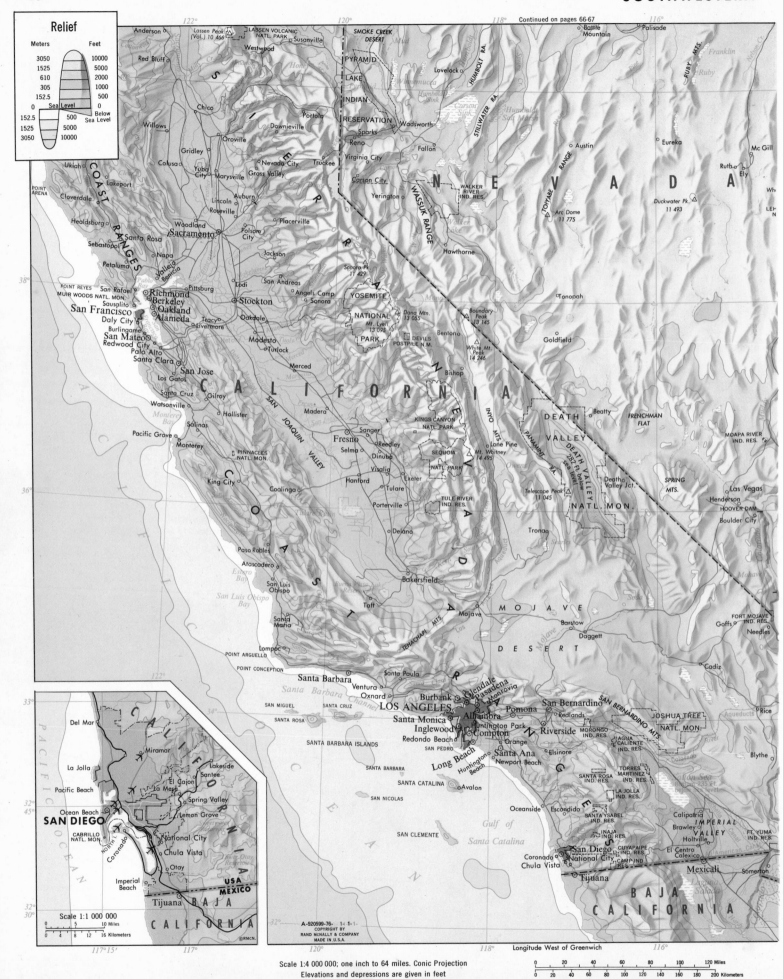

Continued on pages 66-67

Relief

Meters		Feet
3050		10000
1525		5000
610		2000
305		1000
152.5		500
0	Sea Level	0
		Below
	Sea Level	
152.5		500
1525		5000
3050		10000

Scale 1:1 000 000

Scale 0 5 10 Miles

0 4 8 12 16 Kilometers

©RMCN.

SAN DIEGO

A-520599-76- 1- 1- 1-
COPYRIGHT BY
RAND McNALLY & COMPANY
MADE IN U.S.A.

Longitude West of Greenwich

Scale 1:4 000 000; one inch to 64 miles. Conic Projection
Elevations and depressions are given in feet

0 20 40 60 80 100 120 Miles

0 20 40 60 80 100 120 140 160 180 200 Kilometers

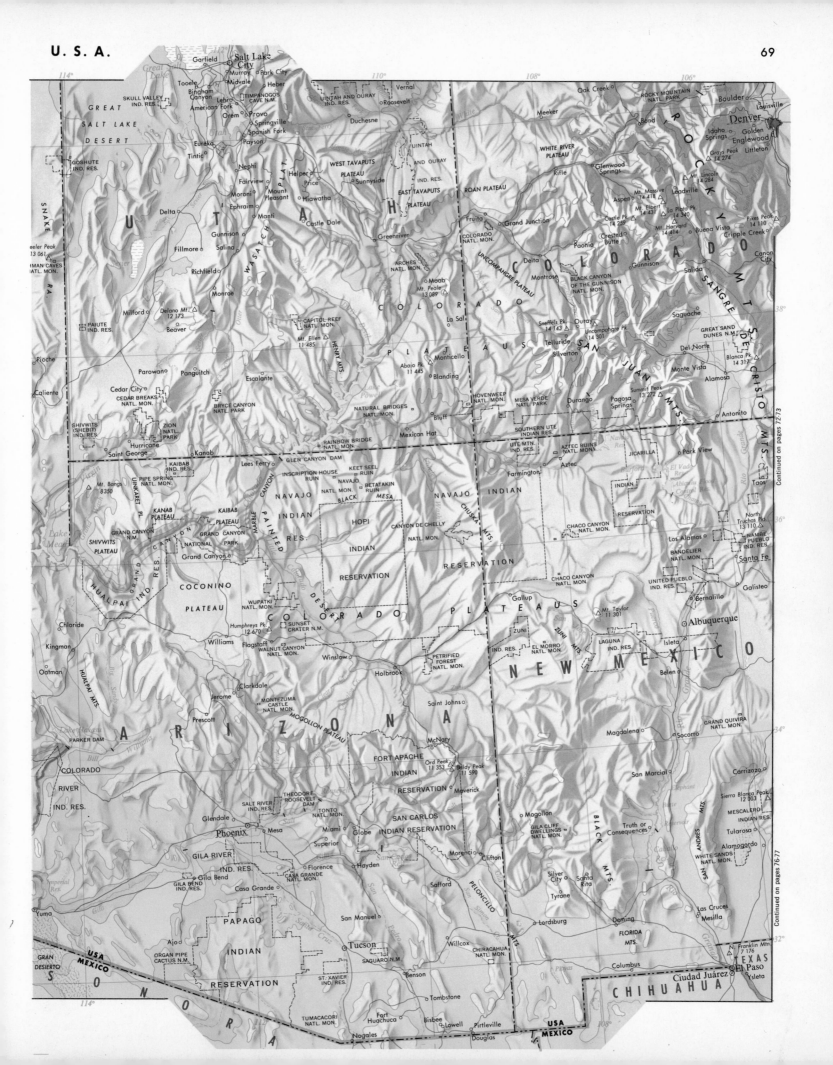

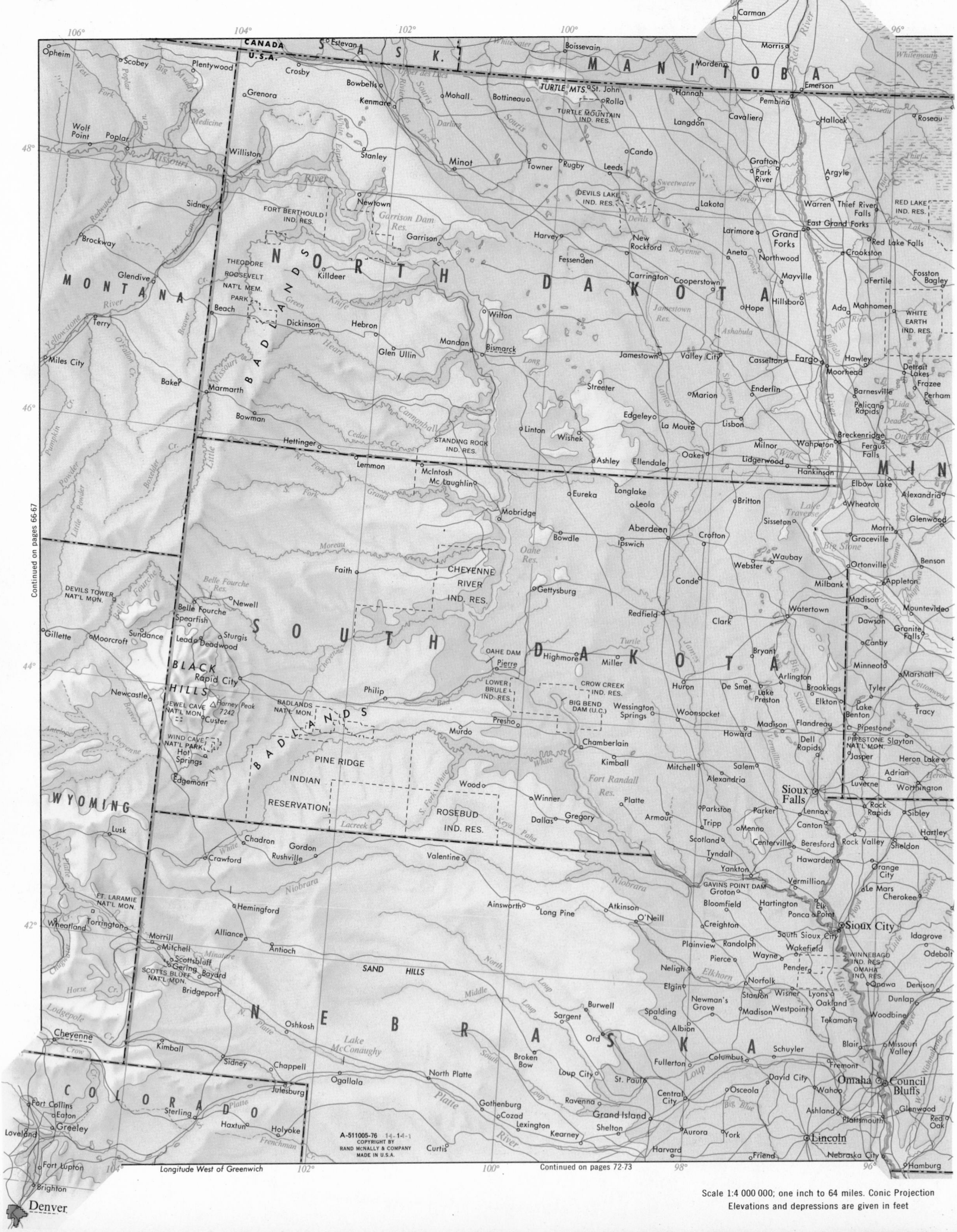

CANADA
U.S.A.

SASK. | MANITOBA

MONTANA

NORTH DAKOTA

SOUTH DAKOTA

WYOMING

NEBRASKA

COLORADO

MINN

Winnipeg
St. Boniface
Carman
Morris
Emerson
Pembina

Opheim
Scobey
Plentywood
Estevan
Crosby
Bowbells
Grenora
Kenmare
Mohall
Bottineau
TURTLE MTS.
St. John
Rolla
Hannah
Morden
Boissevain
Whitewater
Roseau

Wolf Point
Poplar
Williston
Stanley
Minot
Towner
Rugby
Leeds
Cando
Langdon
Cavalier
Hallock
Roseau

Sidney
Newtown
FORT BERTHOULD IND. RES.
Garrison
Garrison Dam Res.
Harvey
Fessenden
New Rockford
DEVILS LAKE IND. RES.
Lakota
Larimore
Grand Forks
East Grand Forks
Warren
Thief River Falls
RED LAKE IND. RES.

Brockway
Glendive
THEODORE ROOSEVELT NAT'L MEM. PARK
Beach
Killdeer
Dickinson
Hebron
Wilton
Carrington
Cooperstown
Aneta
Northwood
Mayville
Hillsboro
Crookston
Red Lake Falls
Fosston
Bagley

Terry
Marmarth
Glen Ullin
Mandan
Bismarck
Jamestown
Valley City
Casselton
Fargo
Moorhead
Hawley
Detroit Lakes
Frazee
Perham
WHITE EARTH IND. RES.

Miles City
Baker
Bowman
Hettinger
STANDING ROCK IND. RES.
Streeter
Edgeley
La Moure
Lisbon
Breckenridge
Pelican Rapids
Barnesville
Fergus Falls

Lemmon
McIntosh
McLaughlin
Eureka
Longlake
Leola
Ashley
Ellendale
Oakes
Lidgerwood
Hankinson
Wahpeton
Milnor
Elbow Lake
Alexandria
Glenwood

Mobridge
Bowdle
Ipswich
Aberdeen
Britton
Sisseton
Graceville
Morris
Benson

DEVILS TOWER NAT'L MON.
Newell
Belle Fourche
Spearfish
Faith
CHEYENNE RIVER IND. RES.
Gettysburg
Redfield
Conde
Webster
Waubay
Ortonville
Appleton

Gillette
Moorcroft
Sundance
Lead
Deadwood
Sturgis
BLACK HILLS
Rapid City
Philip
Highmore
Pierre
OAHE DAM
Miller
Huron
De Smet
Clark
Watertown
Madison
Montevideo

Newcastle
JEWEL CAVE NAT'L MON.
Harney Peak 7242
Custer
BADLANDS NAT'L MON.
LOWER BRULE IND. RES.
CROW CREEK IND. RES.
Wessington Springs
Woonsocket
Howard
Madison
Flandreau
PIPESTONE NAT'L MON.
Slayton

WIND CAVE NAT'L PARK
Hot Springs
Edgemont
BADLANDS
PINE RIDGE INDIAN RESERVATION
Murdo
Presho
BIG BEND DAM (U.C.)
Chamberlain
Kimball
Mitchell
Salem
Alexandria
Dell Rapids
Pipestone
Jasper
Heron Lake

ROSEBUD IND. RES.
Wood
Winner
Dallas
Gregory
Platte
Armour
Tripp
Parkston
Parker
Menno
Canton
Lennox
Rock Rapids
Sibley

Lusk
Chadron
Gordon
Rushville
Valentine
Scotland
Centerville
Beresford
Rock Valley
Sheldon
Hartley

Crawford
FORT RANDALL RES.
Tyndall
Hawarden
Yankton
Vermillion
Orange City
Le Mars

FT. LARAMIE NAT'L MON.
Wheatland
Torrington
Morrill
Mitchell
Scottsbluff
SCOTTS BLUFF NAT'L MON.
Gerling
Bayard
Bridgeport
Alliance
Antioch
Hemingford
Ainsworth
Long Pine
Atkinson
O'Neill
GAVINS POINT DAM
Groton
Bloomfield
Hartington
Elk Point
Ponca
Sioux City
Creighton
Plainview
Randolph
South Sioux City
Wakefield
WINNEBAGO IND. RES.
OMAHA IND. RES.
Idgrove
Cherokee

SAND HILLS
Oshkosh
Kimball
Sidney
Chappell
North Platte
Burwell
Spalding
Albion
Sargent
Broken Bow
Loup City
St. Paul
Fullerton
Columbus
Wisner
Norfolk
Elgin
Newman's Grove
Stanton
Madison
Westpoint
Pender
Lyons
Oakland
Tekamah
Woodbine

Cheyenne
Ogallala
Lake McConaughy
Gothenburg
Cozad
Lexington
Kearney
Shelton
Grand Island
Aurora
York
Ravenna
Central City
Osceola
David City
Wahoo
Ashland
Schuyler
Fremont
Omaha
Council Bluffs
Glenwood
Red Oak

Fort Collins
Eaton
Greeley
Loveland
Fort Lupton
Brighton
Denver
Sterling
Julesburg
Holyoke
Haxtun
Curtis
Harvard
Friend
Lincoln
Nebraska City
Hamburg

A-511005-76 14-14-1
COPYRIGHT BY
RAND McNALLY & COMPANY
MADE IN U.S.A.

Continued on pages 66-67

Continued on pages 72-73

Longitude West of Greenwich

Scale 1:4 000 000; one inch to 64 miles. Conic Projection
Elevations and depressions are given in feet

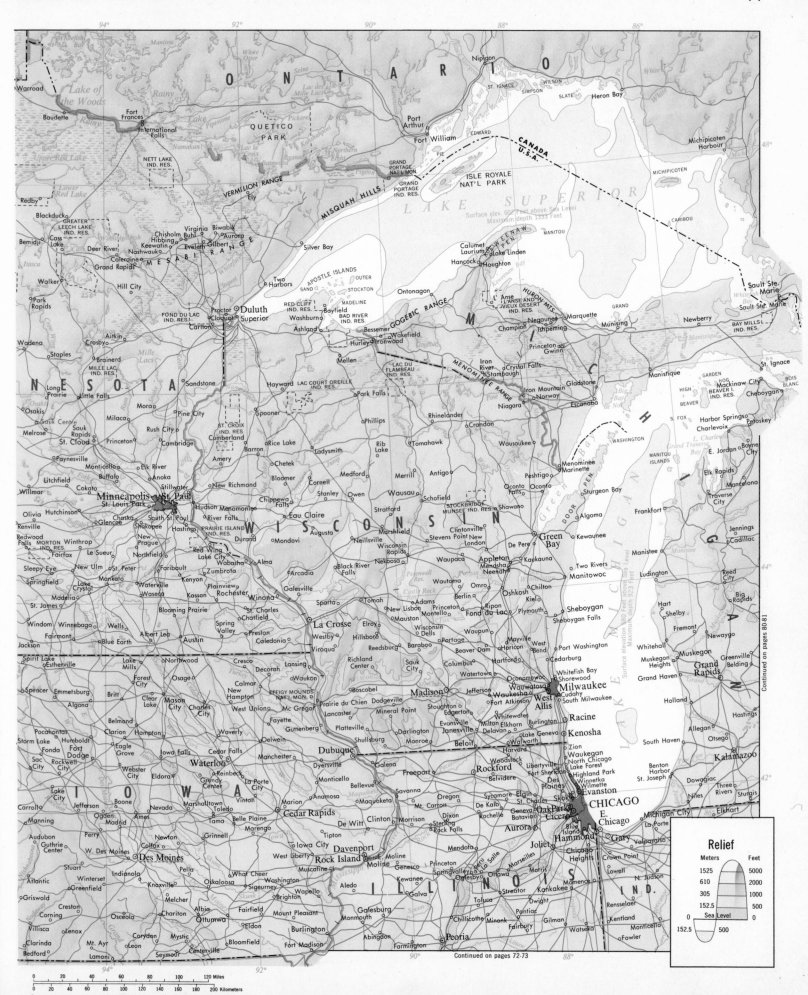

Continued on pages 80-81

Continued on pages 72-73

Relief

Meters		Feet
1525		5000
610		2000
305		1000
152.5		500
0	Sea Level	0
152.5		500

0 20 40 60 80 100 120 Miles

0 20 40 60 80 100 120 140 160 180 200 Kilometers

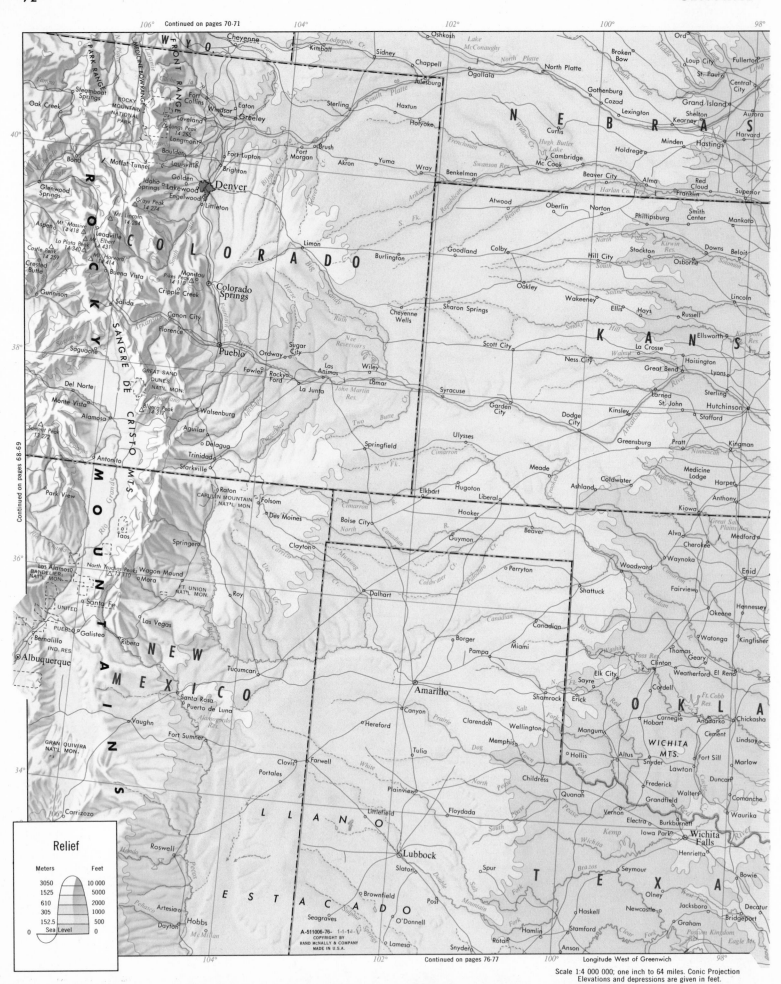

Continued on pages 70-71

Continued on pages 68-69

Continued on pages 76-77

Relief

Meters	Feet
3050	10 000
1525	5000
610	2000
305	1000
152.5	500
Sea Level	0
0	0

A-511006-76- 1-1-1-4
COPYRIGHT BY
RAND McNALLY & COMPANY
MADE IN U.S.A.

Longitude West of Greenwich

Scale 1:4 000 000; one inch to 64 miles. Conic Projection
Elevations and depressions are given in feet.

Continued on pages 70-71 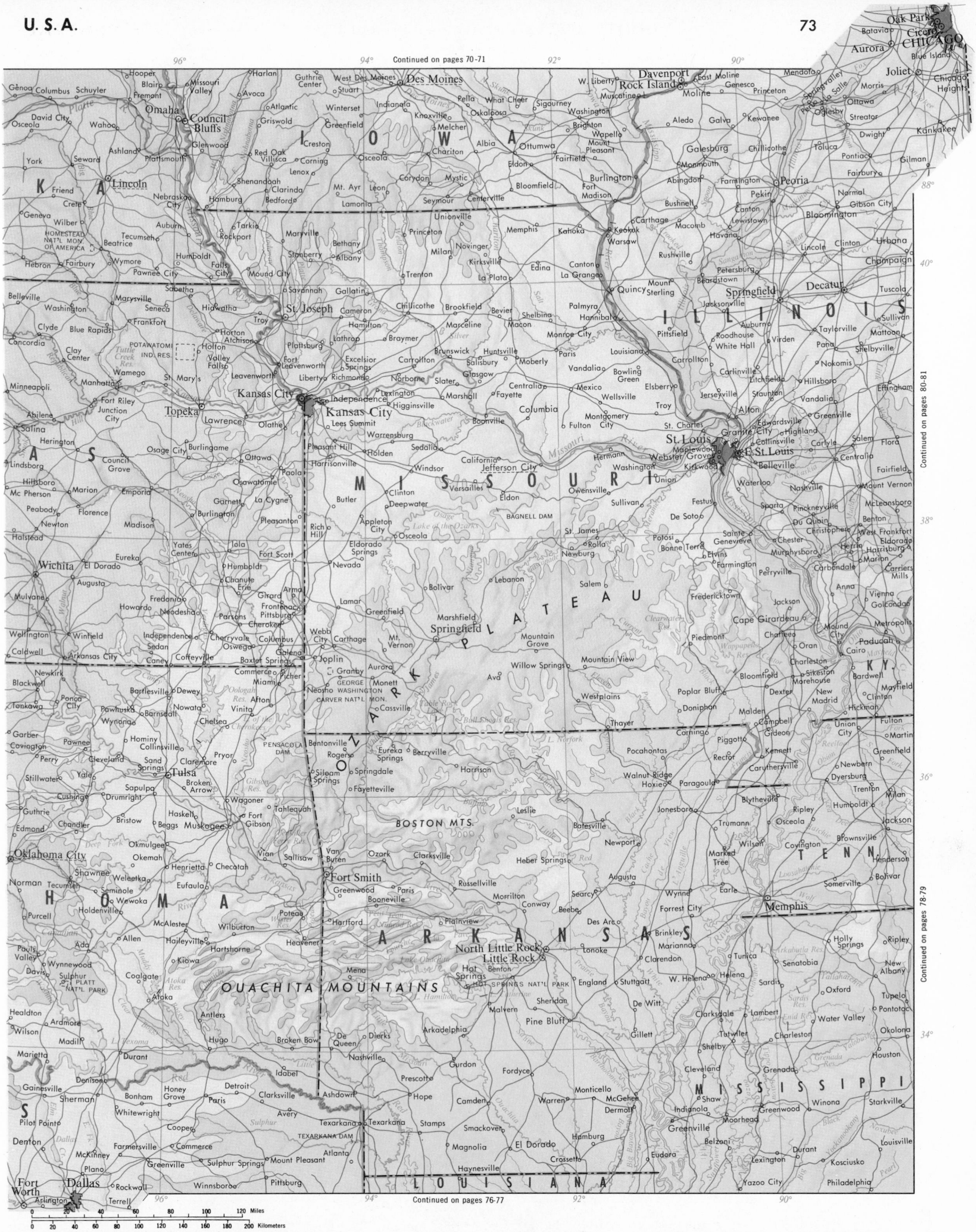
Continued on pages 80-81
Continued on pages 78-79
Continued on pages 76-77

96°   94°   92°   90°   88°   40°   38°   36°   34°

States: IOWA, ILLINOIS, KANSAS, MISSOURI, OKLAHOMA, ARKANSAS, TENN., MISSISSIPPI, LOUISIANA, KY.

Physical features: OZARK PLATEAU, BOSTON MTS., OUACHITA MOUNTAINS, Lake of the Ozarks, Bull Shoals Res., L. Norfork, BAGNELL DAM, PENSACOLA DAM, TEXARKANA DAM, GEORGE WASHINGTON CARVER NAT'L. MON., HOT SPRINGS NAT'L PARK, PLATT NAT'L PARK, HOMESTEAD NAT'L MON. OF AMERICA, POTAWATOMI IND. RES., Tuttle Creek Res., Oologah Res., Gibson Res.

Cities (selection):
CHICAGO, Oak Park, Cicero, Aurora, Batavia, Blue Island, Joliet, Chicago Heights, Kankakee, Davenport, Rock Island, East Moline, Moline, Geneseo, Princeton, Mendota, La Salle, Ottawa, Streator, Dwight, Pontiac, Gilman, Peoria, Pekin, Canton, Lewistown, Havana, Normal, Bloomington, Gibson City, Champaign, Urbana, Tuscola, Decatur, Springfield, Jacksonville, Auburn, Taylorville, Pana, Shelbyville, Mattoon, Effingham, Vandalia, Greenville, Carlyle, Salem, Flora, Fairfield, Mt. Vernon, Centralia, Belleville, Nashville, Sparta, Pinckneyville, Du Quoin, Benton, Christopher, West Frankfort, Eldorado, Harrisburg, Marion, Carbondale, Chester, Murphysboro, Carriers Mills, Metropolis, Cairo, Mound City, Charleston, Sikeston, New Madrid, Hickman, Fulton, Mayfield, Clinton, Bardwell, Paducah

Omaha, Council Bluffs, Des Moines, Davenport, Galesburg, Monmouth, Abingdon, Bushnell, Macomb, Carthage, Keokuk, Warsaw, Hamilton, Quincy, Hannibal, Louisiana, Pittsfield, Roodhouse, White Hall, Carrollton, Jerseyville, Alton, Granite City, Edwardsville, St. Louis, E. St. Louis, Kirkwood, Webster Groves, Maplewood, Collinsville, Highland, Waterloo, Festus, De Soto, Potosi, Bonne Terre, Farmington, Perryville, Cape Girardeau, Chaffee, Oran

St. Joseph, Kansas City, Independence, Lees Summit, Topeka, Lawrence, Olathe, Ottawa, Warrensburg, Sedalia, Jefferson City, Columbia, Fulton, Mexico, Moberly, Marshall, Boonville, Fayette, Montgomery City, Washington, Union, Hermann, Rolla, Newburg, Salem, Lebanon, Bolivar, Springfield, Marshfield, Mountain Grove, Mountain View, West Plains, Thayer, Poplar Bluff, Doniphan, Malden, Campbell, Gideon, Caruthersville, Kennett, Paragould, Walnut Ridge, Hoxie, Pocahontas, Corning, Piggott, Rector

Lincoln, York, Seward, Wahoo, Ashland, Plattsmouth, Beatrice, Wymore, Fairbury, Hebron, Belleville, Concordia, Clay Center, Minneapolis, Salina, Abilene, Junction City, Fort Riley, Manhattan, Marysville, Seneca, Frankfort, Blue Rapids, Clyde, Washington, Hiawatha, Horton, Atchison, Leavenworth, Lawrence, Emporia, Council Grove, Burlington, Garnett, Iola, Chanute, Fort Scott, Nevada, Eldorado Springs, Lamar, Carthage, Joplin, Webb City, Neosho, Monett, Cassville, Aurora

Wichita, El Dorado, Augusta, Newton, Hutchinson, McPherson, Marion, Florence, Peabody, Halstead, Mulvane, Wellington, Winfield, Arkansas City, Newkirk, Blackwell, Ponca City, Tonkawa, Caldwell, Sedan, Independence, Coffeyville, Bartlesville, Dewey, Nowata, Vinita, Afton, Miami, Picher, Commerce, Columbus, Oswego, Parsons, Pittsburg, Girard, Cherokee

Tulsa, Broken Arrow, Sapulpa, Sand Springs, Claremore, Pryor, Wagoner, Muskogee, Fort Gibson, Tahlequah, Checotah, Eufaula, Okmulgee, Henryetta, Okemah, Seminole, Shawnee, Oklahoma City, Norman, Purcell, Chandler, Stillwater, Cushing, Drumright, Bristow, Perry, Guthrie, Edmond

Fort Smith, Van Buren, Greenwood, Booneville, Paris, Ozark, Clarksville, Russellville, Morrilton, Conway, Searcy, Heber Springs, Batesville, Newport, Augusta, Beebe, North Little Rock, Little Rock, Benton, Hot Springs, Malvern, Arkadelphia, Mena, Benton, De Queen, Nashville, Hope, Prescott, Gurdon, Camden, El Dorado, Magnolia, Fordyce, Warren, Monticello, McGehee, Dermott, Stuttgart, De Witt, Clarendon, Helena, W. Helena, Marianna, Forrest City, Wynne, Earle, Memphis

Sheridan, Pine Bluff, Star City, England, Lonoke, Des Arc, Brinkley, Clarksdale, Lambert, Tutwiler, Charleston, Greenwood, Indianola, Moorhead, Belzoni, Yazoo City, Greenville, Leland, Shelby, Cleveland, Shaw, Winona, Grenada, Water Valley, Oxford, Pontotoc, Tupelo, New Albany, Holly Springs, Senatobia, Sardis, Batesville

Dallas, Fort Worth, Arlington, Denton, Sherman, Denison, Bonham, Paris, Clarksville, Texarkana, Durant, Ardmore, Madill, Marietta, Gainesville, Whitewright, Greenville, McKinney, Plano

Scale: 0 20 40 60 80 100 120 Miles; 0 20 40 60 80 100 120 140 160 180 200 Kilometers

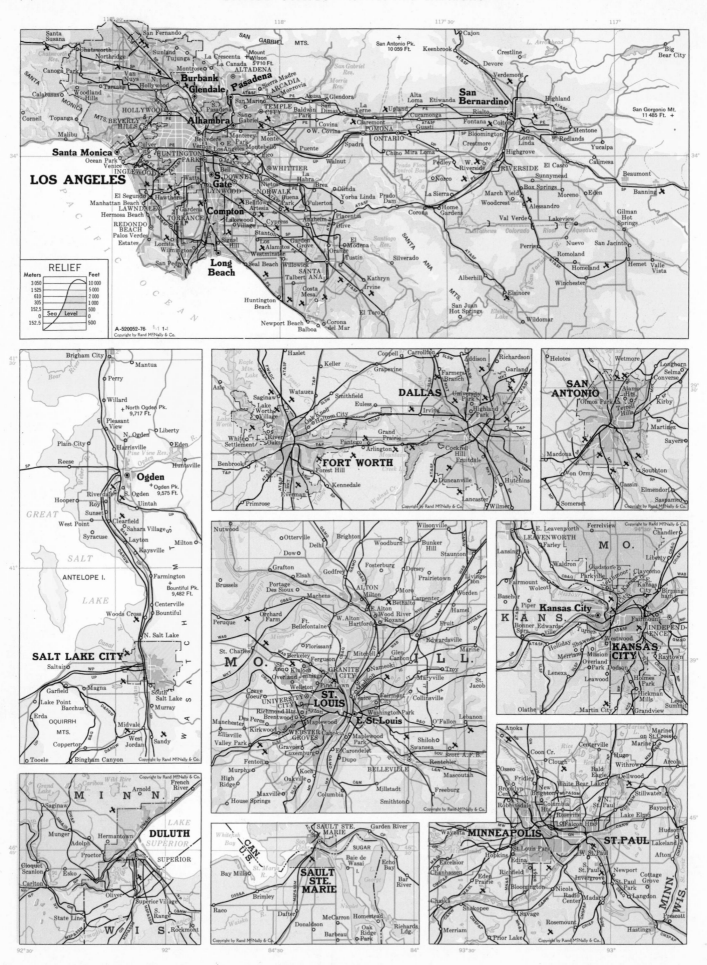

Scale 1:1 000 000; One inch to 16 miles.
Elevations and depressions are given in feet.

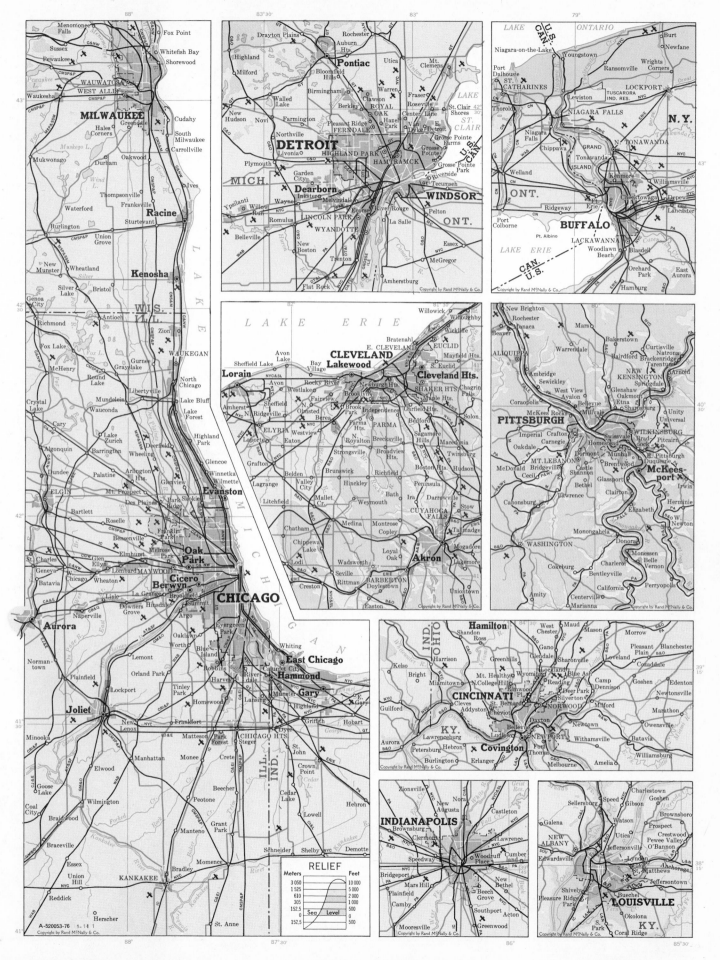

RELIEF

Meters		Feet
3 050		10 000
1 525		5 000
610		2 000
305		1 000
152.5		500
0	Sea Level	
152.5		500

0 2 4 6 8 10 12 14 16 18 20 22 24 Miles

0 4 8 12 16 20 24 28 32 36 40 Kilometers

Scale 1:1 000 000; One inch to 16 miles
Elevations and depressions are given in feet

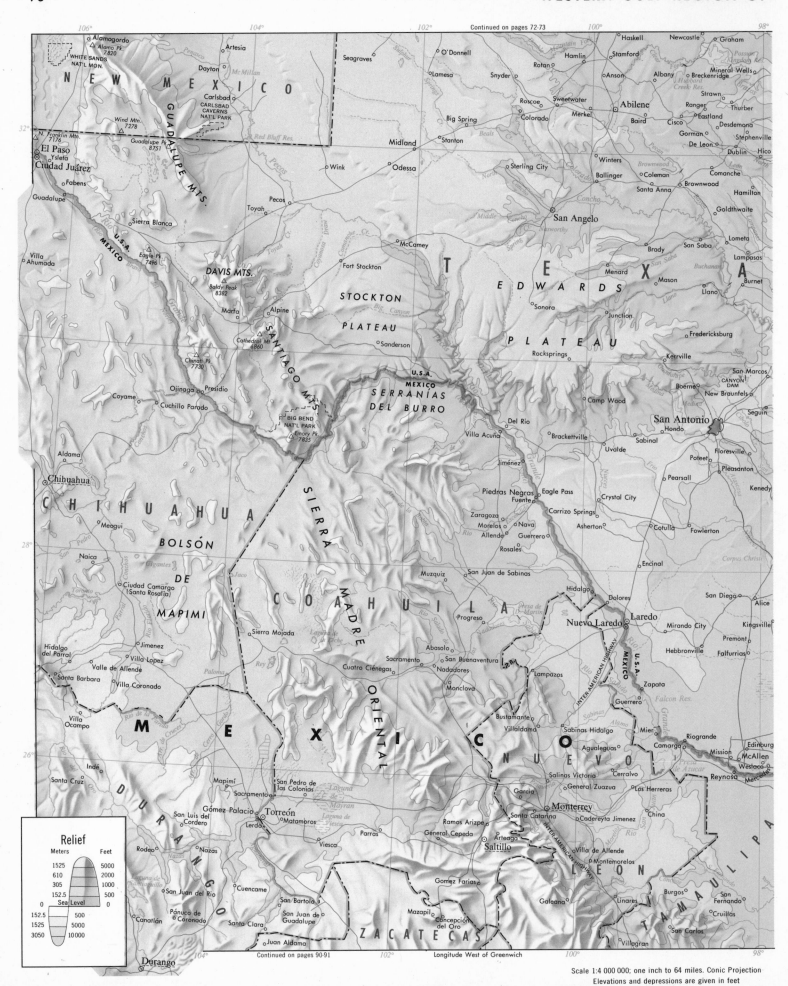

Continued on pages 72-73

NEW MEXICO

Alamogordo
Alamo Pk. 7820
WHITE SANDS NAT'L MON.

Artesia

Dayton
McMillan

Carlsbad
CARLSBAD CAVERNS NAT'L PARK

Seagraves

O'Donnell

Haskell   Newcastle   Graham

Hamlin   Stamford

Lamesa   Snyder   Rotan   Anson   Albany   Breckenridge   Mineral Wells

Wind Mtn. 7278

N. Franklin Mtn. 7176
El Paso
Ysleta
Ciudad Juárez
Fabens

Guadalupe Pk. 8751

GUADALUPE MTS.

Red Bluff Res.

Penasco

Pecos

Sierra Blanca

Toyah

Wink   Odessa

Midland

Stanton

Big Spring

Roscoe   Sweetwater   Merkel   Abilene   Baird   Cisco   Eastland   Desdemona

Colorado   Gorman   De Leon   Stephenville

Strawn   Ranger   Thurber   Dublin   Hico

TEXAS

Sterling City   Winters   Coleman   Comanche

Ballinger   Santa Anna   Brownwood   Hamilton

Guadalupe

Villa Ahumada

U.S.A.
MEXICO

Pecos

Toyah

DAVIS MTS.
Baldy Peak 8382

Eagle Pk. 7496

Marfa   Alpine

STOCKTON
PLATEAU

Fort Stockton

Sanderson

McCamey

San Angelo

Brady   San Saba   Lampasas

Menard   Mason   Llano   Burnet

EDWARDS

Sonora   Junction

PLATEAU

Fredericksburg

Rocksprings   Kerrville

Goldthwaite

Lometa

Cathedral Mt 6860

Chinati Pk. 7730

SANTIAGO MTS.

Presidio

Ojinaga

Coyame

Cuchillo Parado

BIG BEND NAT'L PARK
Emory Pk. 7835

U.S.A.
MEXICO

SERRANÍAS
DEL BURRO

Del Rio

Villa Acuña

Camp Wood

Boerne   New Braunfels

San Marcos
CANYON DAM

Chihuahua

Aldama

Meogui

Naica

CHIHUAHUA

BOLSÓN

DE

MAPIMI

SIERRA

MADRE

San Pedro

Toronto

Gigantes

Jaco

Brackettville

Jiménez

Piedras Negras
Fuente

Zaragoza   Morelos   Nava
Allende   Guerrero

Rosales

Muzquiz   San Juan de Sabinas

Eagle Pass

Carrizo Springs

Crystal City

Asherton

Hondo   Seguin

San Antonio

Uvalde   Sabinal   Floresville   Poteet   Pleasanton   Kenedy

Pearsall

Cotulla   Fowlerton

Encinal

Corpus Christi

Ciudad Camargo
(Santa Rosalia)

COAHUILA

Sierra Mojada

Laguna de Leche

San Diego   Alice

Hidalgo   Dolores
Progreso
Presa de Martin

Nuevo Laredo   Laredo

Mirando City   Kingsville

Premont

Jimenez
Hidalgo del Parral
Villa Lopez
Santa Barbara   Valle de Allende   Villa Coronado

Paloma

Rey

Cuatro Ciénegas

Sacramento   Abasolo
Nadadores   San Buenaventura

Monclova

ORIENTAL

Lampazos

Bustamante
Villaldama

Hebbronville   Falfurrias

Zapata

Guerrero

Falcon Res.

Villa Ocampo

MEXICO

Rio de la Parila

Cerro Gordo

Rio de las Cruces

Mapimí
Sacramento

San Pedro de las Colonias

Laguna de Mayran

Sabinas Hidalgo

Aguageguas

Villagran

Mier   Camargo   Riogrande   Edinburg   McAllen

Mission

Westaco   Mercedes

Reynosa

Santa Cruz   Inde

San Luis del Cordero

DURANGO

Rodeo   Nazas

Gómez Palacio   Torreón
Matambros
Lerdo

Parras

Laguna de Viesca

Viesca

General Zuazua   Los Herreras
Garcia
Salinas Victoria   Cerralvo   China

NUEVO

Ramos Arizpe   Monterrey   Cadereyta Jimenez

Santa Catarina

Canatlán

Pánuco de Coronado

San Juan del Rio

Cuencame

San Bartolo

San Juan de Guadalupe

Mazapil

Concepción del Oro

ZACATECAS

Gomez Farias

Galeana

Linares

Burgos

San Fernando

Cuillas

San Carlos

TAMAULIPA

LEON

Saltillo

Arteaga   Villa de Allende
General Cepeda   Montemorelos

INTER-AMERICAN HIGHWAY

Relief

Meters   Feet
1525   5000
610   2000
305   1000
152.5   500
0   Sea Level   0
152.5   500
1525   5000
3050   10000

Durango

Longitude West of Greenwich

Scale 1:4 000 000; one inch to 64 miles. Conic Projection
Elevations and depressions are given in feet

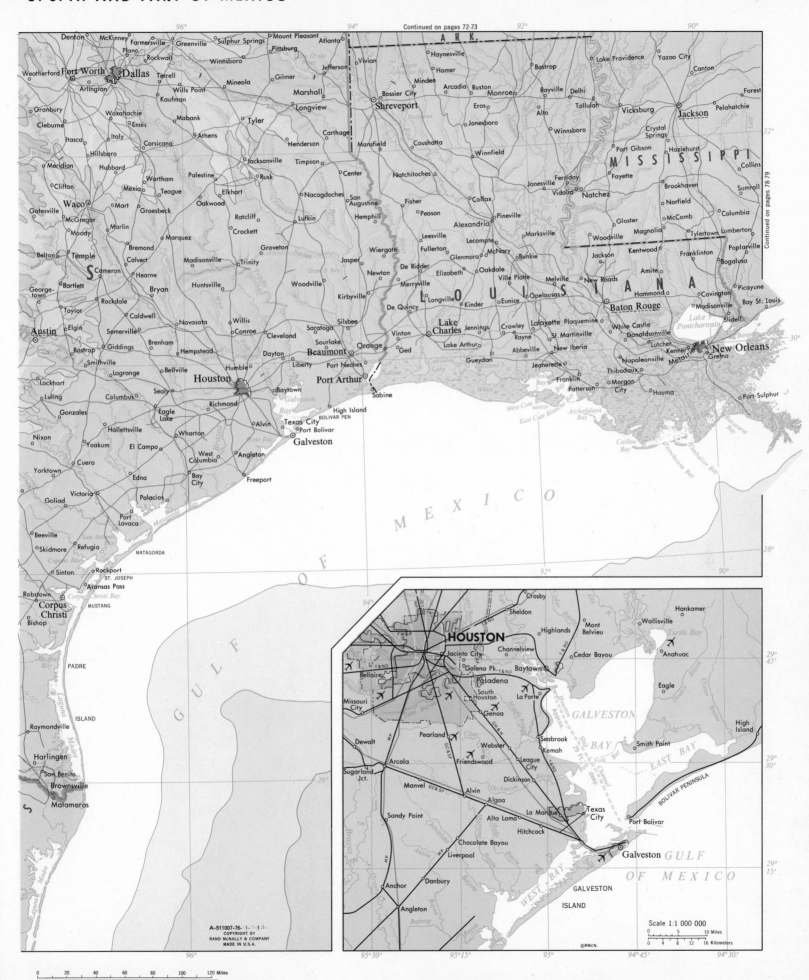

Continued on pages 72-73

Continued on pages 78-79

A-511007-76- 1- 1-1-
COPYRIGHT BY
RAND McNALLY & COMPANY
MADE IN U.S.A.

Scale 1:1 000 000

0   5   10 Miles

0 4 8 12 16 Kilometers

®RMcN.

0   20   40   60   80   100   120 Miles

0   20   40   60   80   100   120   140   160   180   200 Kilometers

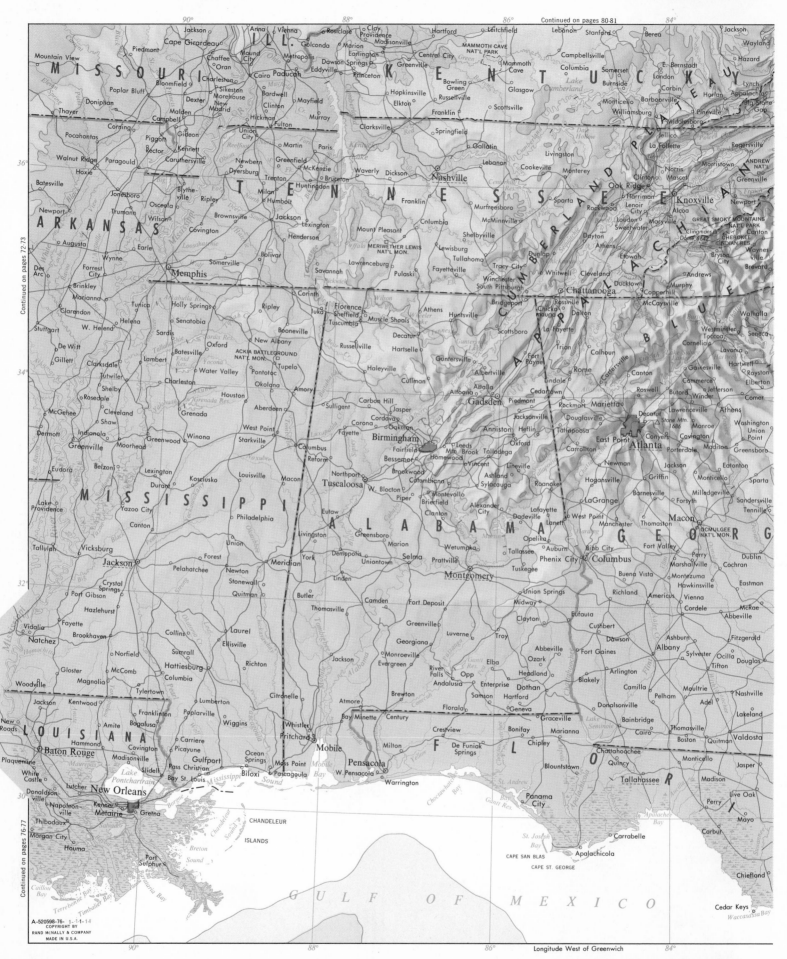

Continued on pages 80-81

Continued on pages 72-73

Continued on pages 76-77

Longitude West of Greenwich

A-520598-76- 1-11-14
COPYRIGHT BY
RAND McNALLY & COMPANY
MADE IN U.S.A.

Scale 1:4 000 000; one inch to 64 miles. Conic Projection
Elevations and depressions are given in feet

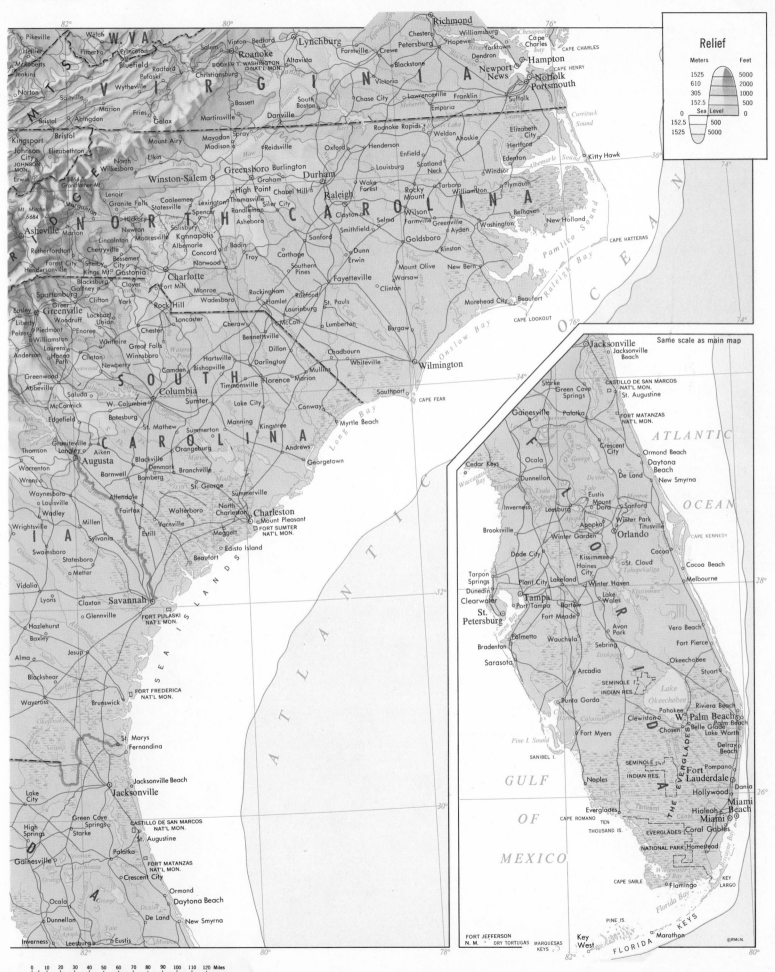

Relief

Meters		Feet
1525		5000
610		2000
305		1000
152.5		500
0	Sea Level	0
152.5		500
1525		5000

Same scale as main map

@RMcN.

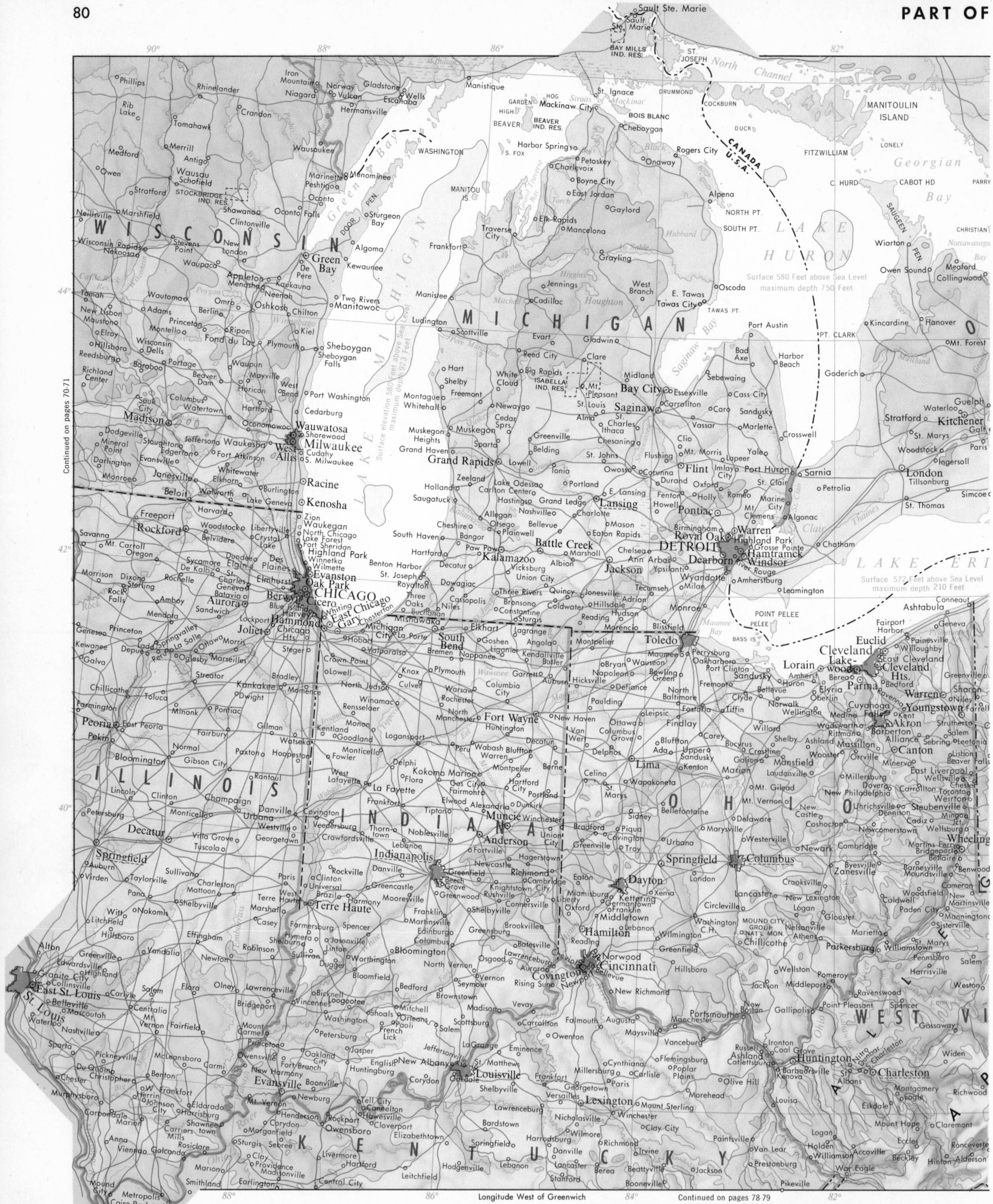

90° 88° 86° 82°

Sault Ste. Marie
Sault Ste. Marie
BAY MILLS IND. RES.
ST JOSEPH
North Channel
DRUMMOND
COCKBURN
CANADA
U.S.A.
FITZWILLIAM
MANITOULIN ISLAND
LONELY
Georgian Bay

Phillips
Rhinelander
Iron Mountain
Norway
Vulcan
Gladstone
Escanaba
Wells
Manistique
St. Ignace
Mackinaw City
BOIS BLANC
Cheboygan
C. HURD
CABOT HD
PARRY

Rib Lake
Medford
Antigo
Crandon
Niagara
Hermansville
HOG
HIGH
BEAVER
GARDEN
BEAVER IND. RES.
Harbor Springs
S. FOX
Petoskey
Onaway
Rogers City
Black
DUCK
SAUGEEN

Tomahawk
Merrill
Wausaukee
Marinette
Peshtigo
Menominee
WASHINGTON
Charlevoix
Boyne City
East Jordan
Gaylord
Alpena
NORTH PT.
SOUTH PT.
WIARTON
PEN
Owen Sound
CHRISTIAN
Nottawasaga Bay

Neillsville
Wausau
Schofield
STOCKBRIDGE IND. RES.
Shawano
Clintonville
Oconto Falls
Oconto
MANITOU IS.
Traverse City
Elk Rapids
Mancelona
Torch
Hubbard
C. HURD
Meaford
Collingwood

WISCONSIN
Marshfield
Wisconsin Rapids
Nekoosa
Stevens Point
New London
Waupaca
Green Bay
De Pere
Kewaunee
Algoma
Sturgeon Bay
DOOR
Frankfort
Grayling
West Branch
E. Tawas
Tawas City
TAWAS PT.
Oscoda
LAKE HURON
Kincardine
Hanover
O

44° Tomah
New Lisbon
Mauston
Adams
Berlin
Omro
Oshkosh
Neenah
Menasha
Appleton
Kaukauna
Chilton
Two Rivers
Manitowoc
Manistee
Jennings
Cadillac
Houghton
Reed City
Ludington
Scottville
Evart
Gladwin
Port Austin
Bad Axe
Harbor Beach
Surface 580 Feet above Sea Level maximum depth 750 Feet
Goderich
Mt. Forest

New Richmond
Princeton
Ripon
Fond du Lac
Kiel
Sheboygan
Sheboygan Falls
Plymouth
Hart
Shelby
White Cloud
Big Rapids
ISABELLA IND. RES.
Mt. Pleasant
St. Louis
Alma
Midland
Bay City
Essexville
Cass City
Caro
Sebewaing
Sandusky
Waterloo
Guelph
Kitchener

Richland Center
Reedsburg
Baraboo
Portage
Beaver Dam
Horicon
Mayville
West Bend
Cedarburg
Port Washington
Montague
Whitehall
Newaygo
Cedar Sprs.
Greenville
St. Louis
Ithaca
St. Charles
Chesaning
Saginaw
Carrollton
Vassar
Clio
Marlette
Crosswell
Stratford
Woodstock
Paris
Ingersoll

Madison
Dodgeville
Mineral Point
Evansville
Edgerton
Fort Atkinson
Oconomowoc
Hartford
Wauwatosa
Shorewood
Milwaukee
West Allis
S. Milwaukee
Muskegon Heights
Muskegon
Grand Haven
Sparta
Belding
St. Johns
Ionia
Owosso
Corunna
Durand
Flushing
Flint
Lapeer
St. Morris
Yale
Port Huron
St. Clair
Sarnia
London
Tillsonburg
Woodstock
St. Marys

Darlington
Monroe
Janesville
Whitewater
Elkhorn
Waukesha
Jefferson
Racine
Kenosha
Holland
Zeeland
Grand Rapids
Lowell
Portland
Grand Ledge
Lansing
E. Lansing
Fenton
Holly
Pontiac
Romeo
Oxford
Imlay City
Marine City
Algonac
St. Thomas
Simcoe

42° Beloit
Rockford
Harvard
Woodstock
Lake Geneva
Burlington
Zion
Waukegan
North Chicago
Saugatuck
Allegan
Otsego
Plainwell
Hastings
Charlotte
Nashville
Bellevue
Eaton Rapids
Mason
Howell
Birmingham
Royal Oak
Warren
Highland Park
Grosse Pointe
Chatham
LAKE ERIE

Freeport
Mt. Carroll
Oregon
Belvidere
Crystal Lake
Libertyville
Fort Sheridan
Highland Park
Winnetka
Wilmette
South Haven
Hartford
Bangor
Paw Paw
Battle Creek
Marshall
Albion
Chelsea
Ann Arbor
Jackson
Ypsilanti
DETROIT
Dearborn
Hamtramck
Windsor
Wyandotte
River Rouge
Amherstburg
Leamington
Surface 572 Feet above Sea Level maximum depth 210 Feet

Savanna
Dixon
Sycamore
De Kalb
Elgin
St. Charles
Batavia
Geneva
Des Plaines
Evanston
Oak Park
Berwyn
CHICAGO
Cicero
Whiting
East Chicago
Gary
Decatur
Dowagiac
Vicksburg
Union City
Three Rivers
Quincy
Jonesville
Hillsdale
Adrian
Tecumseh
Milan
Monroe
POINT PELEE
PELEE
Ashtabula
Conneaut
Geneva

Morrison
Rock Falls
Sterling
Rochelle
Aurora
Joliet
Lockport
Harvey
Hammond
Chicago Hts.
Steger
Michigan City
La Porte
South Bend
Mishawaka
Elkhart
Goshen
Lagrange
Angola
Reading
Hudson
Morencio
Blissfield
Maumee Bay
BASS IS.
Fairport Harbor
Painesville
Willoughby
Cleveland
Euclid
Lake-wood
East Cleveland
Cleveland Hts.

Geneseo
Princeton
Kewanee
Depue
La Salle
Peru
Ottawa
Morris
Marseilles
Streator
Crown Point
Hobart
Valparaiso
Lowell
Knox
North Judson
Culver
Plymouth
Bremen
Nappanee
Ligonier
Kendallville
Butler
Bryan
Wauseon
Napoleon
Defiance
Bowling Green
Perrysburg
Toledo
Oakharbor
Port Clinton
Sandusky
Huron
Amherst
Berea
Elyria
Oberlin
Parma
Bedford
Warren
Niles
Youngstown
Farrell

Galva
Farmington
Peoria
East Peoria
Pekin
Chillicothe
Toluca
Minonk
Pontiac
Bradley
Kankakee
Dwight
Momence
Watseka
Gilman
Winamac
Monon
Rensselaer
Rochester
Warsaw
Columbia City
Garrett
Auburn
Hicksville
Paulding
Ottawa
Leipsic
North Baltimore
Fostoria
Findlay
Tiffin
Clyde
Bellevue
Norwalk
Wellington
Medina
Wadsworth
Rittman
Orrville
Wooster
Ashland
Loudonville
Mansfield
Crestline
Shelby
Willard
Akron
Barberton
Massillon
Canton
Alliance
Sebring
Salem
Leetonia
Lisbon
East Liverpool
Wellsville
Chester

Normal
Bloomington
Gibson City
Paxton
Hoopeston
Fowler
West Lafayette
La Fayette
Delphi
Flora
Peru
Wabash
Bluffton
Montpelier
Berne
Celina
St. Marys
Wapakoneta
Lima
Ada
Kenton
Upper Sandusky
Carey
Bucyrus
Marion
Gallion
Mt. Gilead
Marysville
Delaware
Mt. Vernon
Millersburg
New Philadelphia
Dover
Carrollton
Minerva
Toronto
Steubenville
Mingo
Cadiz
Uhrichsville
Dennison
Newcomerstown

40° Lincoln
Clinton
Champaign
Urbana
Danville
Covington
Veedersburg
Crawfordsville
Frankfort
Kokomo
Marion
Tipton
Elwood
Alexandria
Dunkirk
Hartford City
Portland
Sidney
Bellefontaine
Piqua
Troy
Urbana
Springfield
Columbus
Westerville
Newark
Zanesville
Cambridge
Byesville
Barnesville
Woodsfield
Cameron
L O

Petersburg
Decatur
Monticello
Villa Grove
Tuscola
Georgetown
Westville
Lebanon
Noblesville
Anderson
Muncie
Winchester
Union City
Bradford
Covington
Greenville
Tray
ILLINOIS
INDIANA
OHIO
Wheeling
Benwood

Springfield
Auburn
Virden
Taylorville
Sullivan
Charleston
Mattoon
Paris
Rockville
Danville
Indianapolis
Greenfield
Beech Grove
Newcastle
Hagerstown
Richmond
Eaton
Miamisburg
Dayton
Kettering
Germantown
Franklin
Xenia
London
Circleville
Lancaster
New Lexington
Logan
Glouster
Crooksville
Nelsonville
Athens
Marietta
Williamstown
Parkersburg

Pana
Nokomis
Shelbyville
Clinton
Universal
Brazil
Terre Haute
West Terre Haute
Paris
Greencastle
Mooresville
Franklin
Shelbyville
Connersville
Liberty
Oxford
Middletown
Hamilton
Reading
Wilmington
Washington C.H.
MOUND CITY GROUP NAT'L MON.
Chillicothe
Greenfield
Caldwell
Martinsville
Paden City
Sistersville

Witt
Litchfield
Hillsboro
Pana
Casey
Marshall
Spencer
Farmersburg
Sullivan
Jasonville
Linton
Worthington
Bloomfield
Bedford
Martinsville
Edinburg
Columbus
Greensburg
Brookville
Batesville
Lawrenceburg
Osgood
North Vernon
Seymour
Brownstown
Madison
Aurora
Rising Sun
Norwood
Cincinnati
Covington
Newport
New Richmond
Hillsboro
Greenfield
Wellston
Pomeroy
Middleport
Ravenswood
Spencer
WEST VIRGINIA

Alton
Edwardsville
Granite City
Collinsville
St. Louis
East St. Louis
Belleville
Waterloo
Nashville
Sparta
Pinckneyville
Du Quoin
Christopher
Chester
Murphysboro
Carbondale
Marion
Greenville
Highland
Carlyle
Salem
Flora
Olney
Lawrenceville
Bicknell
Vincennes
Oolitic
Dugger
Mitchell
Orleans
Paoli
French Lick
Salem
Scottsburg
Carrollton
Owenton
Falmouth
Augusta
Maysville
Vanceburg
New Boston
Gallipolis
Point Pleasant
Jackson
Ironton
Ashland
Catlettsburg
Huntington
Barboursville
Kenova
Ceredo
Charleston
Nitro
St. Albans
Montgomery
Eagle
Richwood

88° 86°
Longitude West of Greenwich 84° 82°

Continued on pages 70-71
Continued on pages 78-79

Scale 1:4 000 000; one inch to 64 miles. Conic Projection
Elevations and depressions are given in feet

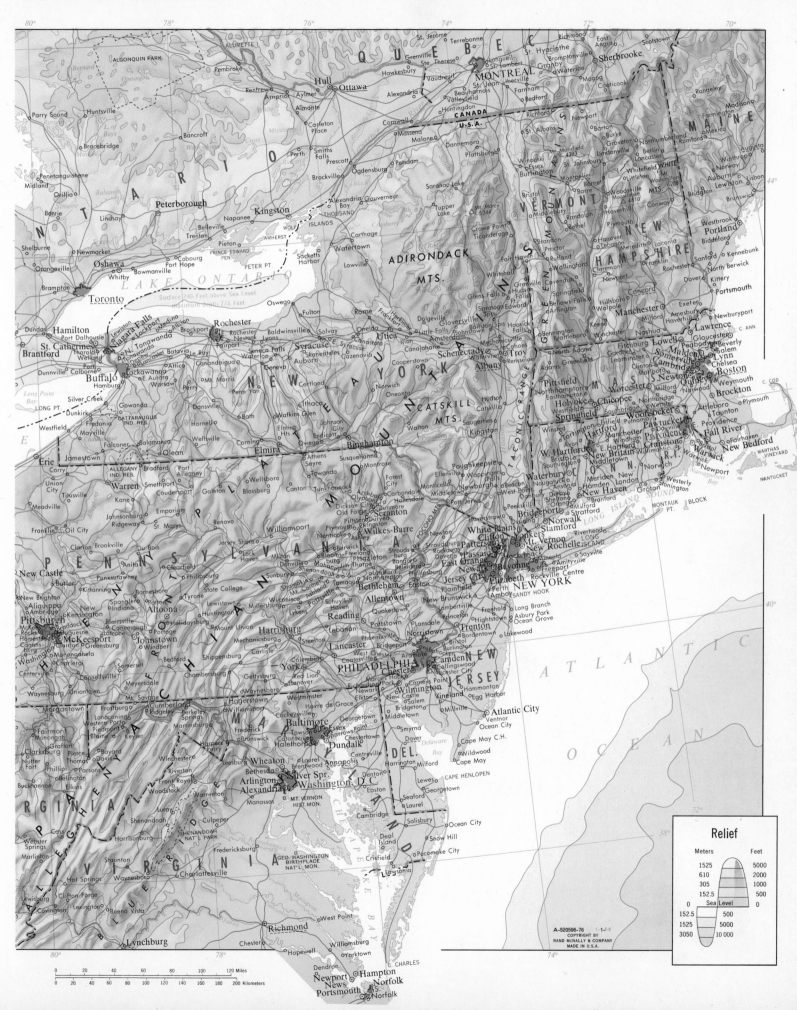

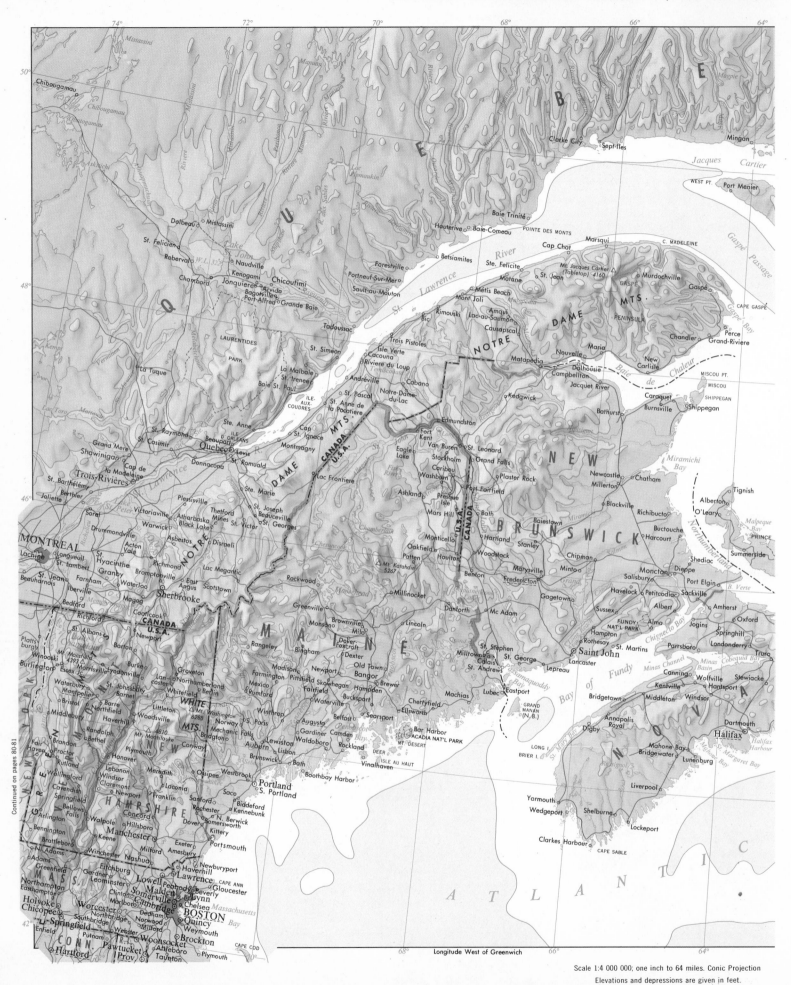

Scale 1:4 000 000; one inch to 64 miles. Conic Projection
Elevations and depressions are given in feet.

Longitude West of Greenwich

Continued on pages 80-81

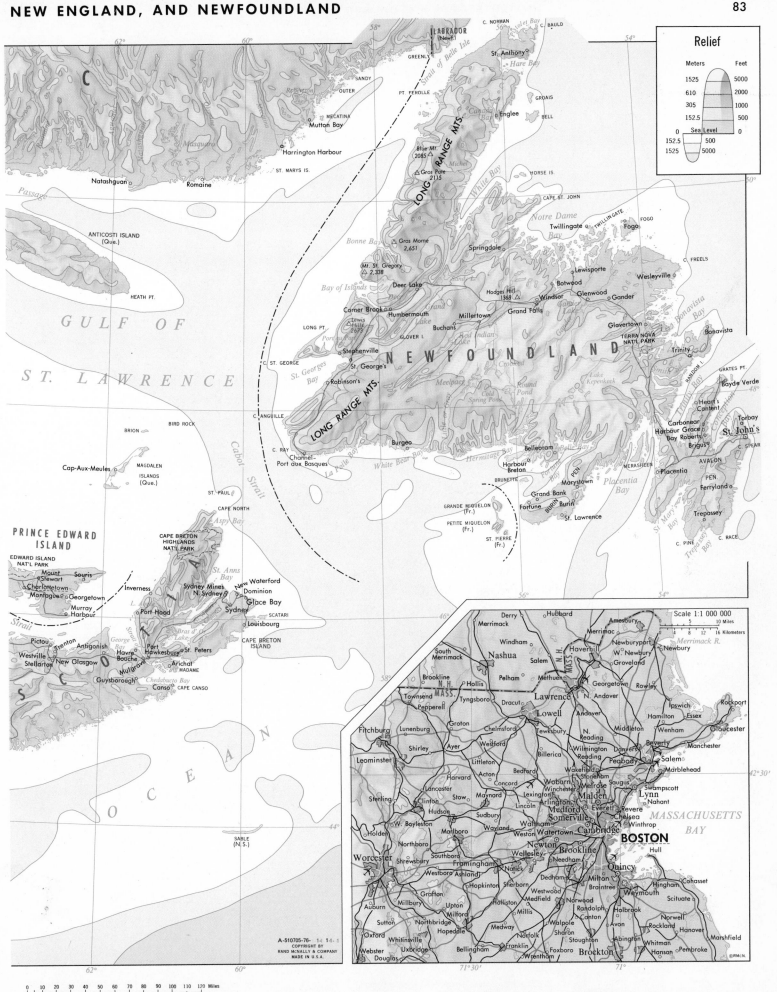

Relief

Meters		Feet
1525		5000
610		2000
305		1000
152.5		500
0	Sea Level	0
152.5		500
1525		5000

C. NORMAN

LABRADOR (Newf.)

Inlet Bay   C. BAULD

GREENLY   Strait of Belle Isle

St. Anthony

SANDY   PT. FEROLLE   Hare Bay

OUTER   GROAIS

MECATINA   Canada Bay   BELL

Mutton Bay   Englee

Harrington Harbour   Blue Mt. 2085

ST. MARYS IS.   △Gros Pate 2115   HORSE IS.

C

Robertson   CAPE ST. JOHN

Natashquan   Romaine   Notre Dame Bay   FOGO

Passage   Twillingate   Fogo
TWILLINGATE

Masquaro   Gros Morne 2,651   Springdale   C FREELS

ANTICOSTI ISLAND (Que.)   Bonne Bay   Lewisporte   Wesleyville

Mt. St. Gregory △2,338   Botwood

Jupiter   Deer Lake   Windsor   Glenwood   Gander

HEATH PT.   Hodges Hill 1368△   Bonavista Bay

GULF OF   Corner Brook   Humbermouth   Grand Falls   Glovertown

LONG PT.   Lewis Hills 2673   Millertown   Bonavista

Buchans   TERRA NOVA NAT'L PARK   Trinity

ST. LAWRENCE   Stephenville   GLOVER I.   Grand Lake   RANDOM I.

C. ST. GEORGE   St. George's   NEWFOUNDLAND   GRATES PT.

St. Georges Bay   Robinson's   Meelpaeg   Lake Kepenkeck   Bayde Verde

BRION   BIRD ROCK   C. ANGUILLE   Cold Spring Pond   Round Pond   Heart's Content

MAGDALEN   Carbonear   Torbay

Cap-Aux-Meules   ISLANDS (Que.)   C. RAY   Burgeo   Harbour Grace   St. John's

LONG RANGE MTS.   Bay Roberts   Brigus

ST. PAUL   Channel-Port aux Basques   Belleoram   AVALON

La Belle Baie   White Bear Bay   Placentia   C. SPEAR

CAPE NORTH   Harbour Breton   Marysheen   PEN.   Placentia

Aspy Bay   GRANDE MIQUELON (Fr.)   Marystown   Ferryland

PRINCE EDWARD ISLAND   CAPE BRETON HIGHLANDS NAT'L PARK   PETITE MIQUELON (Fr.)   Grand Bank   BURIN   Trepassey

EDWARD ISLAND NAT'L PARK   ST. PIERRE (Fr.)   Fortune   Burin   St. Lawrence   C. PINE   C. RACE

Mount Stewart   Souris   St. Anns Bay   Trepassey Bay

Charlottetown   Inverness   Sydney Mines   New Waterford

Montague   Georgetown   N. Sydney   Dominion   Glace Bay

Murray Harbour   Port Hood   Sydney   SCATARI

Strait   Bras d'Or Lake   Louisbourg   CAPE BRETON ISLAND

Pictou   Trenton   Antigonish   George Bay   St. Peters

Westville   Havre Bouche   Port Hawkesbury   St. Peters

Stellarton   New Glasgow   Mulgrave   Arichat MADAME

Guysborough   Chedabucto Bay   Canso   CAPE CANSO

O C E A N   SABLE (N.S.)

Boston inset:

Scale 1:1 000 000

Derry   Hubbard   Amesbury   Merrimack R.

Merrimack   Merrimac   Newburyport   W. Newbury   Newbury

Windham   N.H.   Salem   Haverhill

South Merrimack   Nashua   MASS.   Groveland

Brookline   Pelham   Methuen   Georgetown   Rowley   Rockport

N.H.   Hollis   Lawrence   N. Andover

Townsend   MASS.   Tyngsboro   Dracut   Andover   Ipswich   Essex

Pepperell   Hamilton   Gloucester

Fitchburg   Lunenburg   Groton   Chelmsford   Tewksbury   Wilmington   Middleton   Wenham

Shirley   Ayer   Westford   Reading   Danvers   Beverly   Manchester

Leominster   Littleton   Billerica   N. Reading   Peabody   Salem

Bedford   Wakefield   Stoneham   Marblehead

Sterling   Harvard   Acton   Concord   Woburn   Saugus   Swampscott

Lancaster   Stow   Maynard   Lexington   Winchester   Melrose   Lynn

Clinton   Hudson   Lincoln   Arlington   Malden   Nahant

Holden   Sudbury   Waltham   Medford   Everett   Revere

W. Boylston   Marlboro   Wayland   Somerville   Chelsea   Winthrop

Worcester   Northboro   Weston   Watertown   Cambridge   MASSACHUSETTS BAY

Shrewsbury   Southboro   Framingham   Newton   Brookline   BOSTON   Hull

Westboro   Ashland   Natick   Wellesley   Needham   Milton   Quincy   Cohasset

Grafton   Upton   Hopkinton   Sherborn   Dedham   Braintree   Weymouth   Hingham

Auburn   Millbury   Milford   Holliston   Medfield   Westwood   Norwood   Randolph   Scituate

Sutton   Northbridge   Hopedale   Millis   Canton   Holbrook   Norwell

Oxford   Whitinsville   Medway   Norfolk   Sharon   Stoughton   Avon   Rockland   Hanover

Webster   Uxbridge   Bellingham   Franklin   Foxboro   Brockton   Whitman   Hanson   Marshfield

Douglas   Wrentham   Abington   Pembroke

0 10 20 30 40 50 60 70 80 90 100 110 120 Miles

0 20 40 60 80 100 120 140 160 180 200 Kilometers

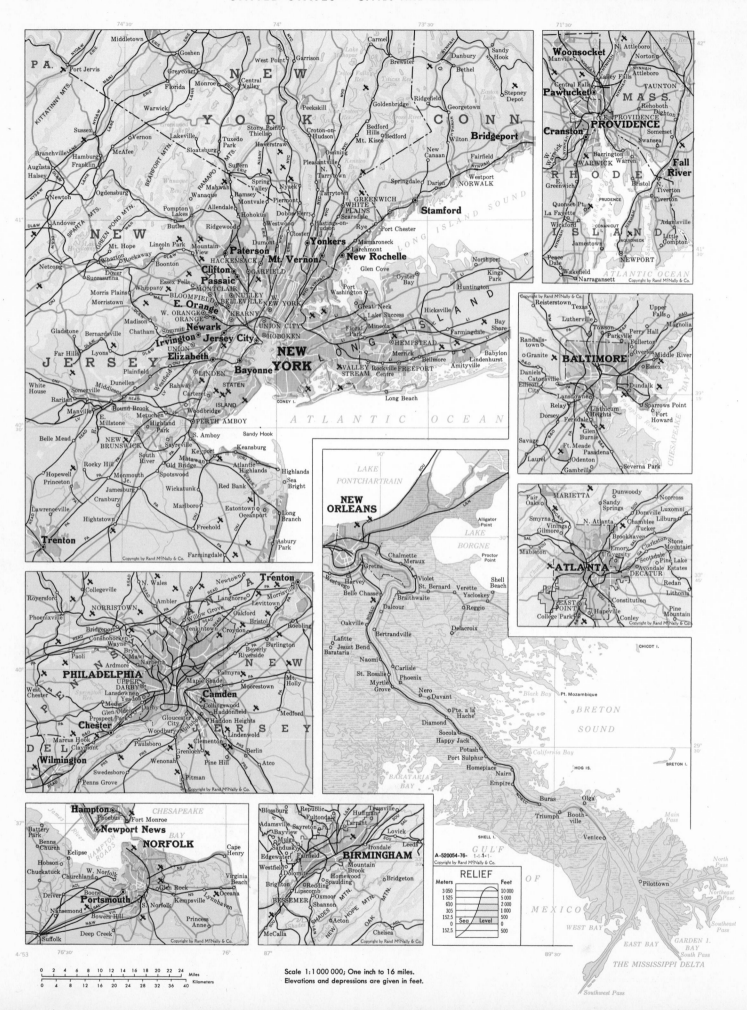

Scale 1:1 000 000; One inch to 16 miles.
Elevations and depressions are given in feet.

RELIEF

Meters		Feet
3 050		10 000
1 525		5 000
610		2 000
305		1 000
152.5		500
0	Sea Level	0
152.5		500

A-520054-76-
Copyright by Rand McNally & Co.

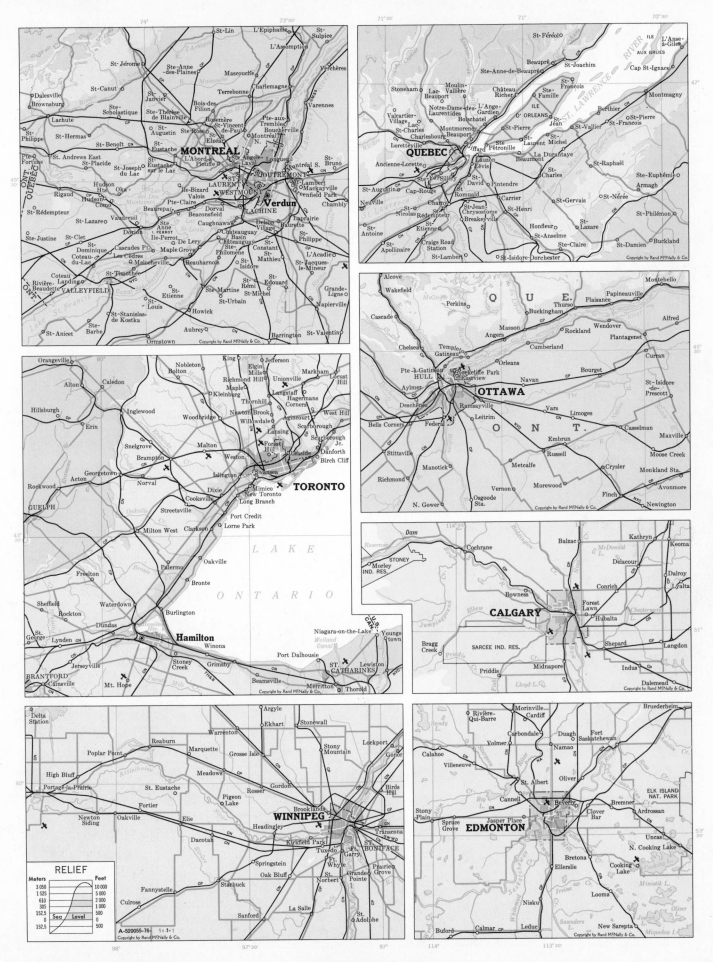

Scale 1:1 000 000; One inch to 16 miles.
Elevations and depressions are given in feet.

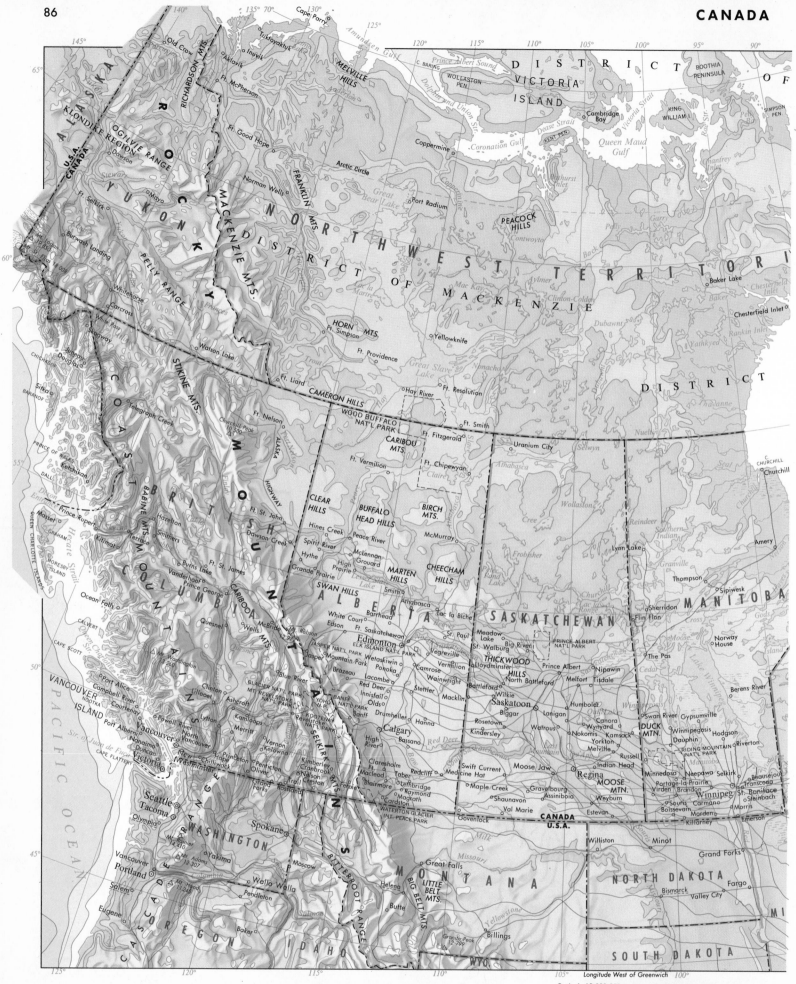

Scale 1: 12 000 000; one inch to 190 miles. Conic Projection
Elevations and depressions are given in feet

Longitude West of Greenwich

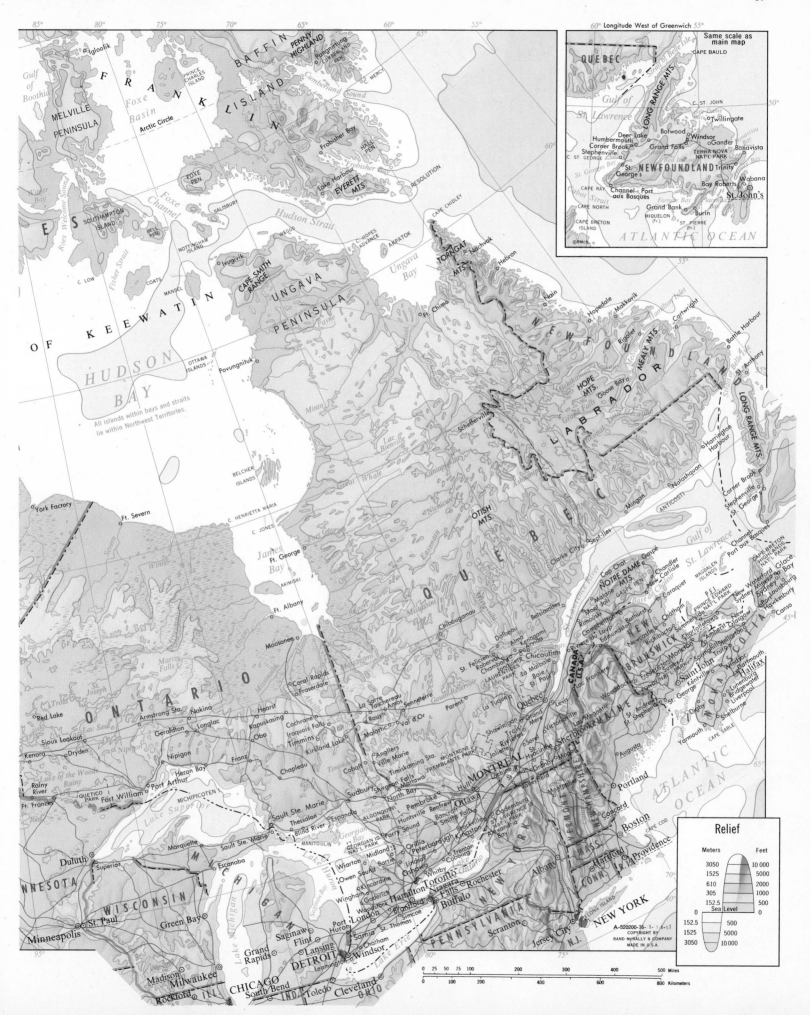

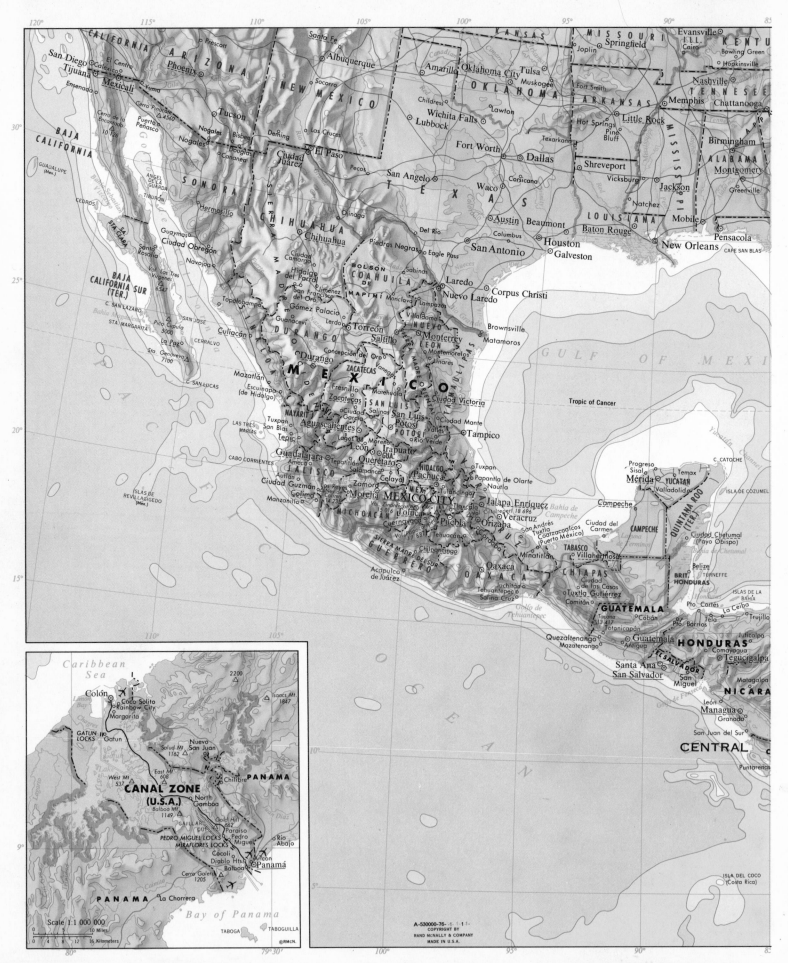

Scale 1:16 000 000; one inch to 250 miles. Polyconic Projection
Elevations and depressions are given in feet

Scale 1:1 000 000

A-530000-76- -1- -1- 1 1-
COPYRIGHT BY
RAND McNALLY & COMPANY
MADE IN U.S.A.

CKY
W.VIRGINIA
Richmond
VIRGINIA
Roanoke
Norfolk
Knoxville
Raleigh
NORTH CAROLINA
Mt. Mitchell
6684
Charlotte
CAPE HATTERAS
SOUTH
Atlanta
Columbia
CAROLINA
Wilmington
CAPE FEAR
Augusta
Charleston
GEORGIA
Savannah
Tallahassee
Jacksonville
St. Augustine
Ocala
Tampa
FLORIDA
W. Palm
Beach
Tampa Bay
Miami
CAPE SABLE
Key West

ATLANTIC OCEAN
San Juan
Arecibo
Aguadilla
Bayamón
CABEZAS DE
SAN JUAN
ST. THOMAS
(U.S.A.)
TORTOLA
(Br.)
PTA. HIGUERO
Utuado
PUERTO RICO
(U.S.A.)
CULEBRA
Charlotte
Amalie
ST. JOHN
(U.S.A.)
Mayagüez
Caguas
Cayey
Vieques (St. Thomas)
Coamo
Humacao
VIEQUES
18°
CABO ROJO
Ponce
Salinas
Guayama
CARIBBEAN SEA
Christiansted
SAINT CROIX
(U.S.A.)
Scale 1:4 000 000
0 10 20 30 40 Miles
0 10 20 30 40 50 60 Kilometers

64°50'
65°
LITTLE
HANS LOLLICK
OUTER BRASS
HANS LOLLICK
INNER BRASS
PICARA PT.
GRASS
CAY
STORMY PT.
ST. THOMAS
THATCH CAY
Crown Mt. (U.S.A.)
18°
1558
Charlotte Amalie
20'
(St. Thomas)
WATER
Nadir
FLAMINGO PT.
St. Thomas
Harbor
Scale 1:500 000

ATLANTIC OCEAN
BERMUDA
(Br.)
NORTH AMERICAN
BASIN
BAHAMA ISLANDS
GRAND
BAHAMA
GREAT ABACO
Nassau
ELEUTHERA
ANDROS
CAT
LONG
SAN SALVADOR (WATLING)
HAVANA
Guanabacoa
Matanzas
Marianao
Cárdenas
Pinar del Rio
Santa Clara
C U B A
Cienfuegos
Sancti Spíritus
ACKLINS
Trinidad
Ciego
Camagüey
Nuevitas
de Avila
CAICOS
BANK
ISLA DE
PINOS
Holguín
PTA. SEBANA
Manzanillo
Guantánamo
PUNTA
MAISI
Milwaukee
Depth
PUERTO RICO TROUGH
SIERRA MAESTRA
Cap-Haïtien
Puerto Plata
Santiago de los
30,246
GRAND CAYMAN
Santiago
Gonaïves
Caballeros
SAMANA
W E S T
de Cuba
Sánchez
Mayagüez
San Juan
C. CRUZ
Montego Bay
Mt. Denham
ILE DE LA
DOMINICAN
Ponce
Charlotte Amalie
3236
Port Antonio
GONAVE
HAITI
REPUBLIC
ST. THOMAS
VIRGIN IS.
Spanish Town
Mte. Mijo
PUERTO RICO
ST. JOHN
BARBUDA
(Br.)
JAMAICA
Kingston
7434
Santo Domingo
(U.S.A.)
SAINT CROIX
ST.
ANTIGUA
Port-au-Prince
(U.S.A.)
CHRISTOPHER
HISPANIOLA
(Br.)
Pointe-à-Pitre
V. Soufrière
GUADELOUPE
4869
(Fr.)
Basse-Terre
DOMINICA
MARTINIQUE (Fr.)
Fort-de-France

CARIBBEAN SEA
ST. LUCIA
(Br.)
ST. VINCENT
BARBADOS
(Br.)
(Br.)
Kingstown
Bridgetown
GRENADA
(Br.)
LESSER ANTILLES
TOBAGO
GUA
PUNTA DE GALLINAS
ARUBA
(Neth.)
CURAÇAO BONAIRE
(Neth.) (Neth.)
ISLA LA
ISLA DE
TRINIDAD AND TOBAGO
Bluefields
PENÍNSULA
SAN ROMAN
TORTUGA
MARGARITA
Port of Spain
DE GUAJIRA
PEN. DE
Willemstad
Santa Marta
Golfo de
PARAGUANA
Carúpano
Barranquilla
Venezuela
Coro
Puerto
La Guaira
TRINIDAD
AMERICA
Ciénaga
Cabello
CARACAS
Cumaná
OSTA
CANAL
Cartagena
San Felipe
Puerto
San José
ZONE
Soledad
Maracaibo
Maracay
la Cruz
Limón
(U.S.A.)
Cabimas
Barquisimeto
Valencia
Maturín
RICA
Colón
Lorica
Sincelejo
Mompós
Lago de
PANAMA
Portobello
Maracaibo
Trujillo
El Tigre
Panamá
Magangué
Calabozo
Morawhanna
Antón
Montería
Guanare
Santiago
Valera
Puerto de
Puerto Ordaz
PEN. DE
Gulf of
Ocaña
Mérida
Nutrias
AZUERO
Panama
Ciudad Bolívar
Cerro Bolívar
David
San Fernando
COIBA
Cúcuta
de Apure
VENEZUELA
Cerro Icutú
San Cristóbal
7800
BRITISH
ISLA DE
Barrancabermeja
GUIANA
MALPELO
Pamplona
(Colombia)
Bucaramanga
Medellín
Tunja
Relief
COLOMBIA
Meters
Feet
Manizales
3050
10000
Pereira
1525
5000
San Fernando
Armenia
de Atabapo
610
2000
Ibagué
Bogotá
305
1000
Buenaventura
Girardot
Villavicencio
152.5
500
Cali
Palmira
0
Sea Level
0
SERRA PACARAIMA
152.5
500
1525
5000
BRAZIL
3050
10000
6100
20000
Longitude West of Greenwich

0 50 100   200   300   400   500 Miles
0 100 200 400 600 800 Kilometers

Continued on pages 76-77

Relief

Meters	Feet
3050	10000
1525	5000
610	2000
305	1000
152.5	500
Sea Level	0
152.5	500
1525	5000
3050	10000

A-531695-76- 1-·1·1-·1
COPYRIGHT BY
RAND McNALLY & COMPANY
MADE IN U.S.A.

Longitude West of Greenwich

Scale 1:4 000 000; one inch to 64 miles. Conic Projection
Elevations and depressions are given in feet

MEXICO CITY inset map (Scale 1:1 000 000)

MÉXICO

Morelos
Nicolás Romero
Cahuacán
Cuautitlán
Tutitlán
Teotihuacán
Otumba
▲ Pyramid of Teotihuacán
Chiconautla
Acolman

HIDALGO
Calpulalpan

San Bartolo
Ixtlahuaca
Jiquipilco
Cerro La Catedral 13 000 △
Atizapán
Tlalnepantla
Mazatla
Tulpetlac
Tepetlaoxtoc
Texcoco
San Jerónimo
Nanacamilpa

TLAXCALA

Temoaya
Mimiapan
Chimalpa
Atzcapotzalco
Naucalpan
Gustavo A. Madero
Lago de Texcoco
Coatlinchán

Toluca
Cuajimalpa
Villa Obregón
Ixtacalco
MEXICO CITY
Chicoloapan

Lerma
Huixquilucan
Contreras
Coyoacán
Ixtapalapa
Los Reyes
Ayotla INTER-AMERICAN
Río Frío HY

Capultitlán
Metepec Mexicalcingo
Tlálpan
Xochimilco
Tláhuac
Ixtapaluca
Texmelucan

PUEBLA

Nevado de Toluca (Zinántecatl)
Almoloya
Cerro Muneco 12 655 △
San Andrés
Tecómitl
Tlalmanalco
Ixtacíhuatl 17 343 △

DISTRITO FEDERAL
Ajusco △
Cerro Ajusco 12 850 △
Topilejo
Milpa Alta
Oxtotepec
Tenango
Amecameca

Coatepec
Tenango
Tres Cumbres
Ozumba
Popocatépetl 17 883 △

Scale 1:1 000 000
0   5   10 Miles
0 4 8 12 16 Kilometers

Huitzilac
Tepoztlán
Tlalnepantla

MORELOS

©RMCN
Cuernavaca
Tlayacapan

Main map

Tropic of Cancer

PTA. JEREZ

Laguna Almagre

Laguna de San Andrés

Altamira
Ciudad Madero
Tampico
Villa Cuauhtémoc
Tampico Alto

Ozuluama

Laguna Tamiahua

CABO ROJO
ARRECIFE BLANQUILLA
ISLA DE LOBOS

Tancoco
Tamiahua
Alamo
Túxpan
ARRECIFE TANQUIJO
ARRECIFE TÚXPAN

GULF OF MEXICO

Mecapalapa
Tihuatlán
Poza Rica
Tecolutla
Gutiérrez Zamora
Furbero
Coyutla
Nautla
Coxquihui
Hueytlalpan
Cuetzalan del Progreso
Tlapacoyan
Vega de Alatorre
Zacatlán
Atempan
Jalacingo
Misantla
Zacapoaxtla
Teziutlán
Altotonga
Las Vigas
Naolinco
Perote
△ 14 048
Jalapa Enríquez
Libres
Nauchampatepetl
Coatepec
PUNTA ZEMPOALA

BAHÍA DE CAMPECHE

Huamantla
Teocelo
Antigua Veracruz
C. Matlalcueyetl
San Juan Ixtenco
Veracruz Llave
ARRECIFE CABEZA
Huatusco
Ciudad Serdán
18 696 △ Citlaltépetl (Vol.)
Coscomatepec
Tepeaca
Orizaba
Córdoba
Medellín
Tlalixcoyan
Acatzingo de Hidalgo
Nogales
Omealca
Cotaxtla
Atoyatempan
Maltrata
Tlacotepec
Tierra Blanca
San Martín (Vol.) △ 6000
PTA. ZAPOTITLÁN

YUCATÁN
Progreso
Sisal
Hunucmá
Mérida
Umán
Maxcanú
Halachó
Becal
Calkini
Dzitbalché
Hecelchakán

Lerma
Campeche
Seybaplaya
Champotón
Pustunich

CAMPECHE
Sabancuy
ISLA DEL CARMEN
Chicbul
Mamantel

Tehuacan
San Gabriel Chilac
Ajalpan
Zoquitlán
Santiago Tuxtla
Catemaco
San Andrés Tuxtla
Pajápan
Cosamaloapan
Chacaltianguis
Coatzacoalcos (Puerto México)
San Pedro
Frontera
Ciudad del Carmen
PUNTA FONTERA
Laguna de Términos
Palizada

Zinacatepec
Huatla de Jiménez
Ojitlán (S. Lucas)
Tuxtepec
Soteapan
Paraíso
Comalcalco
Allende
Jonuta
Balancán

Perfalcingo
S. Miguel
Teotitlán del Camino
Jalapa de Díaz (San Felipe)
Acayucan
Jaltipan
Cosoleacaque
Minatitlán
Cárdenas
Jalpa
Cunduacán
TABASCO
Emiliano Zapata
MÉXICO GUATEMALA

Huajuapan de León
Tepelmeme
Coixtlahuaca
Cuicatlán
Playa Vicente
San Juan Evangelista
Soyula
Texistepec
Villahermosa
Huimanguillo
San Carlos
Tacotalpa
Teapa
Palenque
Tenosique

Tamazulapan del Progreso
Tejúpan (Santiago)
Jesús Carranza
Puebla Viejo
Pichucalco
Chapultenango
Yajalán

Teposcolula (San Pedro y San Pablo)
Nochixtlán (Asunción)
Ixtlán de Juárez
Villa Alta (San Ildefonso)
ISTMO
Tecpatán
Pantepec
Simojovel
Bachajón

Tlaxiaco
Sta. María Asunción
Hidalgo Yalalag
Zacatepec (Santiago)
DE
Compainalá
Jitotol
Ocosingo

Putla de Guerrero
Chalcatongo
Yosonotú (Sta. Catarina)
Zaachila
Zimatlán de Alvarez
Oaxaca de Juárez
Mazatlán (San Juan)
Guichicovi (San Juan)
Berriozabal
Tuxtla Gutiérrez
9400
Cancuc
Oxchuc
MESETA DE AGUA ESCONDIDA

Itundujia Sta. Cruz
San Mateo (Etlatongo)
Tlacolula de Matamoros
Ocotlán de Morelos
CA
Ocozocoautla
Chiapa de Corzo
Bohom
Ciudad de las Casas
Acala
Amatenango

Sola de Vega (S. Miguel)
Táviche INTER-AMERICAN HY
Ejutla de Crespo
Jalapa del Marqués
Ixtepec
Ixtaltepec (Asunción)
Zanatepec (Sto. Domingo)
Unión Hidalgo
CHIAPAS
Suchiapa
Teopisca
Las Rosas
Comitán

OAXACA DEL SUR
Miahuatlán
Las Vacas
Tehuantepec (Sto. Domingo)
Juchitán de Zaragoza
Tapanatepec
Ixhuatán (San Francisco)
8202 △
Venustiano Carranza
Socoltenango
Trinitaria

SIERRA
Huazolotitlán (Sta. María)
Jamiltepec
Loxicha (Sta. Catarina)
Pluma Hidalgo
Salina Cruz
Arriaga
Tonalá
Villa Flores
La Concordia
SIERRA CUCHUMATANES

Pochutla (San Pedro)
SIERRA DE OAXACA
Golfo de Tehuantepec
COR. DE CHIAPAS
Cuauhtémoc
Jacatenango
GUATEMALA

Puerto Ángel
Puerto Ángel

Mapastepec
Escuintla
Huixtla
Pijijiapan

0   20   40   60   80   100   120 Miles
0 20 40 60 80 100 120 140 160 180 200 Kilometers

Continued on pages 92-93

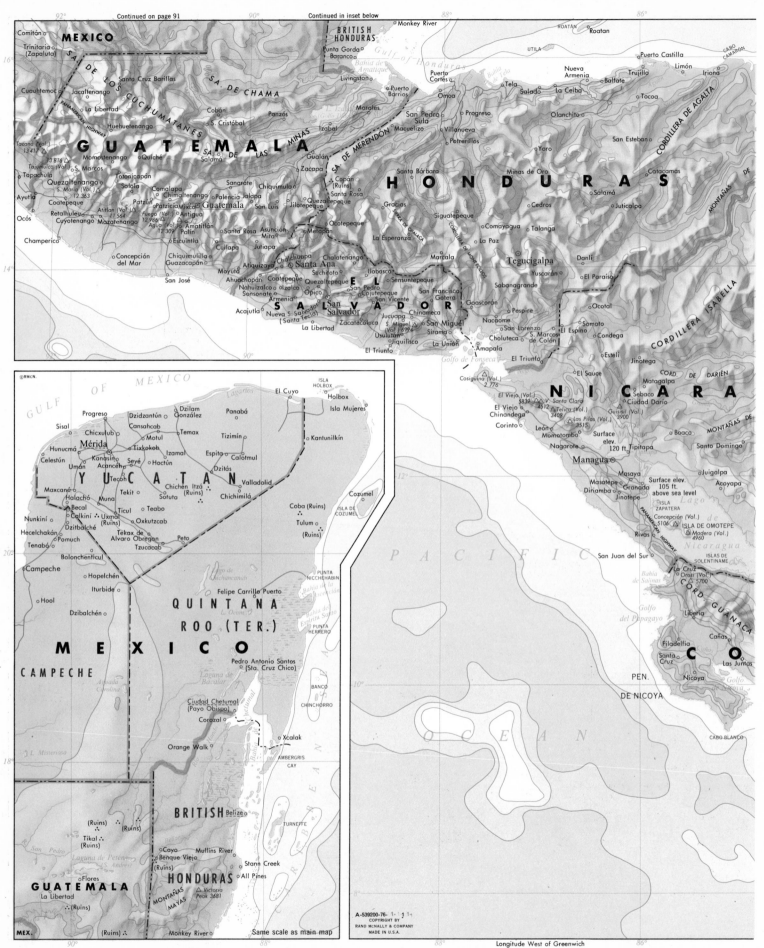

Continued on page 91   Continued in inset below

Longitude West of Greenwich

Scale 1:4 000 000; one inch to 64 miles. Sinusoidal Projection

Elevations and depressions are given in feet

A-539200-76-
COPYRIGHT BY
RAND McNALLY & COMPANY
MADE IN U.S.A.

Same scale as main map

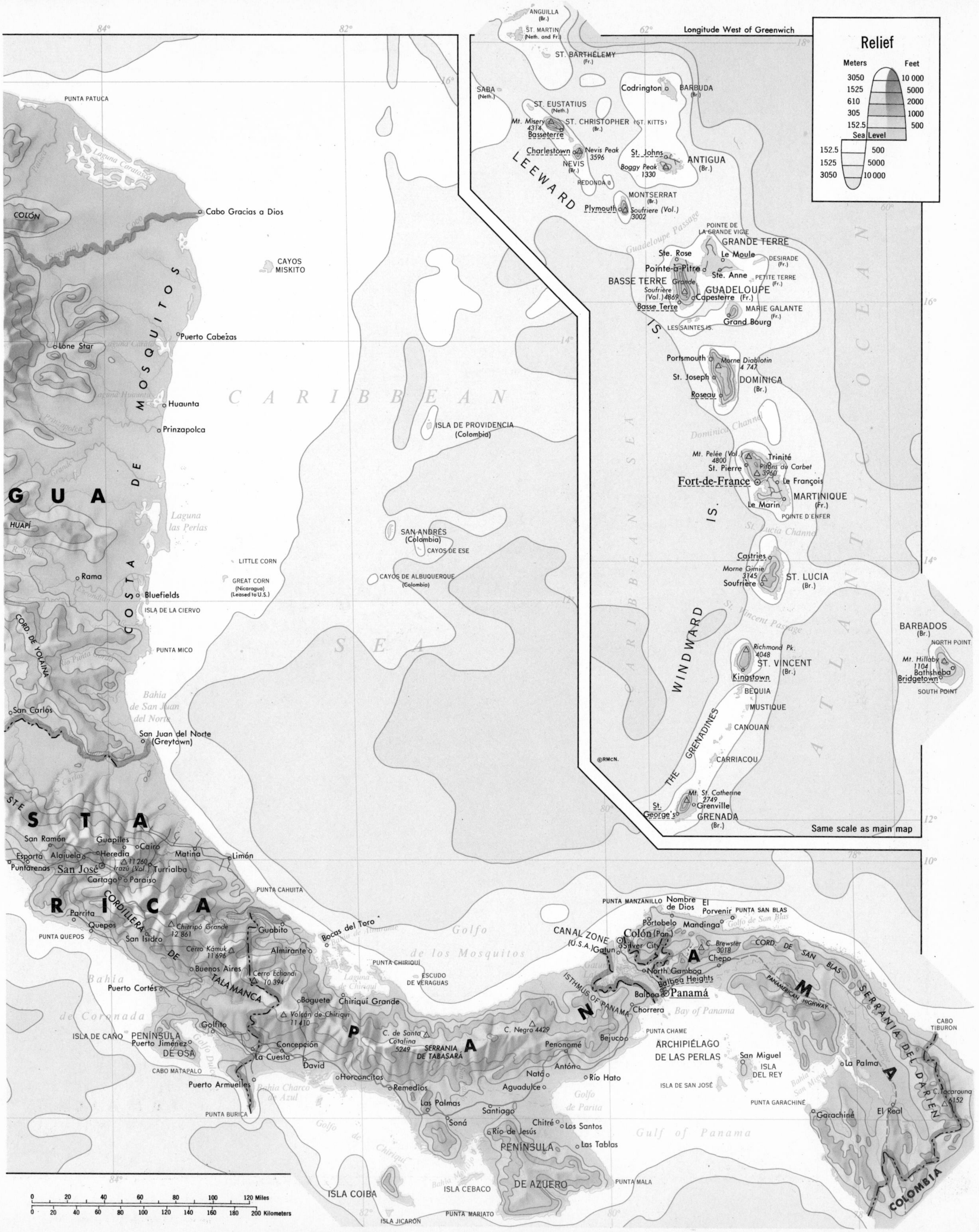

ANGUILLA (Br.)

ST. MARTIN (Neth. and Fr.)

Longitude West of Greenwich

ST. BARTHÉLEMY (Fr.)

Relief

Meters		Feet
3050		10 000
1525		5000
610		2000
305		1000
152.5		500
	Sea Level	
152.5		500
1525		5000
3050		10 000

SABA (Neth.)

Codrington ○ BARBUDA (Br.)

ST. EUSTATIUS (Neth.)

Mt. Misery 4314 ST. CHRISTOPHER (ST. KITTS) (Br.)
Basseterre

Charlestown Nevis Peak 3596
NEVIS (Br.)

St. Johns ANTIGUA (Br.)
Boggy Peak 1330

REDONDA ●

MONTSERRAT (Br.)
Plymouth ○ Soufrière (Vol.) 3002

PUNTA PATUCA

COLÓN

Cabo Gracias a Dios ○

CAYOS MISKITO

LEEWARD IS.

Guadeloupe Passage

POINTE DE LA GRANDE VIGIE
GRANDE TERRE
Ste. Rose Le Moule
Pointe-à-Pitre DÉSIRADE (Fr.)
Ste. Anne PETITE TERRE (Fr.)
BASSE TERRE Grande Soufrière (Vol.) 4869 GUADELOUPE
Capesterre (Fr.)
Basse Terre MARIE GALANTE
LES SAINTES IS. Grand Bourg (Fr.)

○ Puerto Cabezas

○ Lone Star

M O S Q U I T O S

C A R I B B E A N

Portsmouth ○ Morne Diablotin 4 747
St. Joseph ○ DOMINICA (Br.)
Roseau ○

Dominica Channel

○ Huaunta

○ Prinzapolca

ISLA DE PROVIDENCIA (Colombia)

N I C A R A G U A

HUAPÍ

Laguna las Perlas

SAN ANDRÉS (Colombia)
CAYOS DE ESE

Mt. Pelée (Vol.) 4800 Trinité
St. Pierre Pitons du Carbet 3960
Fort-de-France Le François
MARTINIQUE (Fr.)
Le Marin
POINTE D'ENFER

○ Rama

○ Bluefields

ISLA DE LA CIERVO

LITTLE CORN

GREAT CORN (Nicaragua) (Leased to U.S.)

CAYOS DE ALBUQUERQUE (Colombia)

St. Lucia Channel

Castries
Morne Gimie 3145 ST. LUCIA
Soufrière (Br.)

C O S T A

PUNTA MICO

S E A

St. Vincent Passage

C A R I B B E A N   S E A

BARBADOS (Br.)
NORTH POINT

Bahía de San Juan del Norte

○ San Carlos

San Juan del Norte (Greytown)

W I N D W A R D   I S.

Richmond Pk. 4048
ST. VINCENT (Br.)
Kingstown
BEQUIA

Mt. Hillaby 1104
Bathsheba
Bridgetown ○
SOUTH POINT

MUSTIQUE

San Ramón ○
Guápiles Cairo
Heredia ○ 11 260
Alajuela Irazú (Vol.) Turrialba
Esparta Puntarenas San José Cartago ○ Paraíso

CANOUAN

THE GRENADINES

CARRIACOU

R I C A

○ Limón

PUNTA CAHUITA

©RMcN.

Mt. St. Catherine 2749
St. George's ○ Grenville
GRENADA (Br.)

Same scale as main map

CORDILLERA

Parrita ○
Quepos ○
PUNTA QUEPOS
San Isidro ○

Chirripó Grande 12 861

Cerro Kámuk 11 696

Guábito ○

Bocas del Toro ○

Almirante ○

Golfo de los Mosquitos

PUNTA MANZANILLO Nombre de Dios
El Porvenir PUNTA SAN BLAS
Pórtobelo Mandinga Golfo de San Blas
CANAL ZONE (U.S.A.) Colón (Pan.)
Gatun Silver City C. Brewster 3018
Chepo
North Gamboa
Balboa Heights
Balboa Panamá
Chorrera

DE TALAMANCA

Buenos Aires ○

Cerro Echandi 10 394

Punta Chiriquí

ESCUDO DE VERAGUAS

Puerto Cortés ○
del Coronado

Golfito ○
ISLA DE CAÑO
PENÍNSULA Puerto Jiménez
DE OSA
La Cuesta ○

Boquete ○ Chiriquí Grande

Volcán de Chiriquí 11 410

Concepción ○
David ○

C. de Santa Catalina 5249
SERRANÍA DE TABASARÁ

P A N A M Á

ISTHMUS OF PANAMA

Bay of Panama

PUNTA CHAME

ARCHIPIÉLAGO DE LAS PERLAS

San Miguel
ISLA DEL REY

CORD. DE SAN BLAS

SERRANÍA DEL DARIÉN

CABO TIBURÓN

La Palma ○

CABO MATAPALO

Bahía Charco Azul

Horconcitos ○

Remedios ○

Puerto Armuelles ○

PUNTA BURICA

Las Palmas ○
Santiago ○
Soná ○

Nata ○
Antón ○
Aguadulce ○

ISLA DE SAN JOSÉ

San Miguel
Bahía San Miguel

El Real ○

Tacarcuna 6152

Garachiné ○

PUNTA GARACHINÉ

Río de Jesús ○ Chitré Los Santos ○
Las Tablas ○

Gulf of Panama

Golfo de Parita

PENÍNSULA DE AZUERO

PUNTA MALA

Golfo de Montijo

ISLA COIBA

ISLA CEBACO

COLOMBIA

PUNTA MARIATO

ISLA JICARÓN

0	20	40	60	80	100	120 Miles
0	20	40	60	80	100	120	140	160	180	200 Kilometers

WEST INDIES

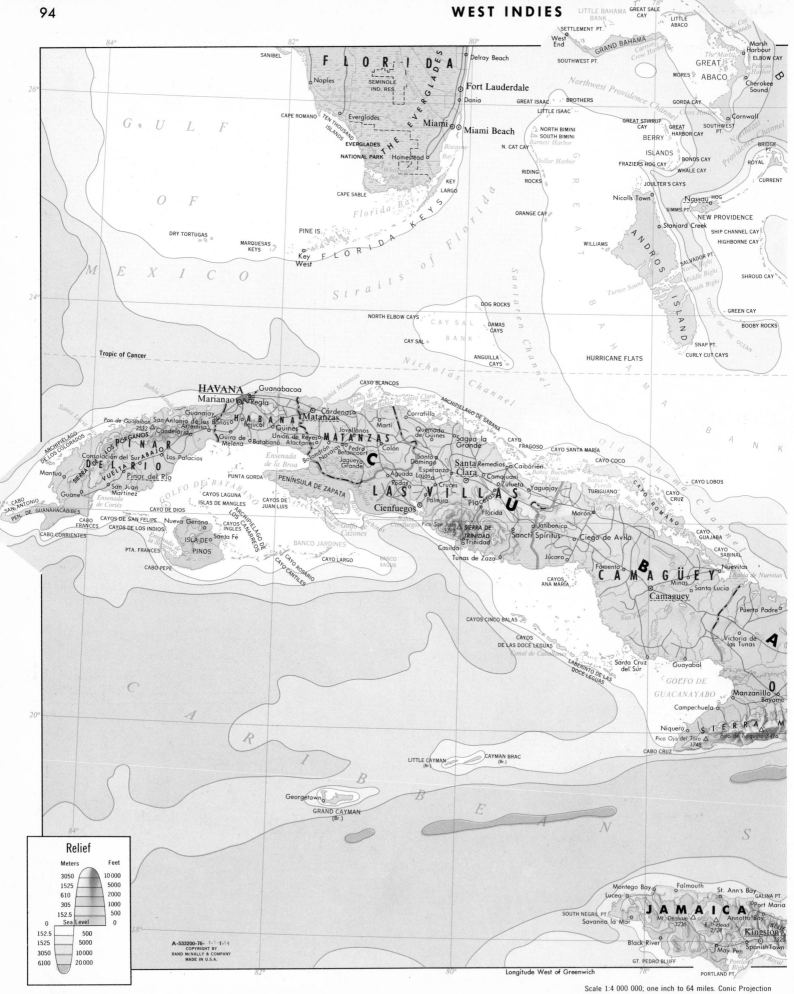

Relief

Meters	Feet
3050	10 000
1525	5000
610	2000
305	1000
152.5	500
0 Sea Level	0
152.5	500
1525	5000
3050	10 000
6100	20 000

A-533200-76- 1-1-1-14
COPYRIGHT BY
RAND McNALLY & COMPANY
MADE IN U.S.A.

Longitude West of Greenwich

Scale 1:4 000 000; one inch to 64 miles. Conic Projection
Elevations and depressions are given in feet.

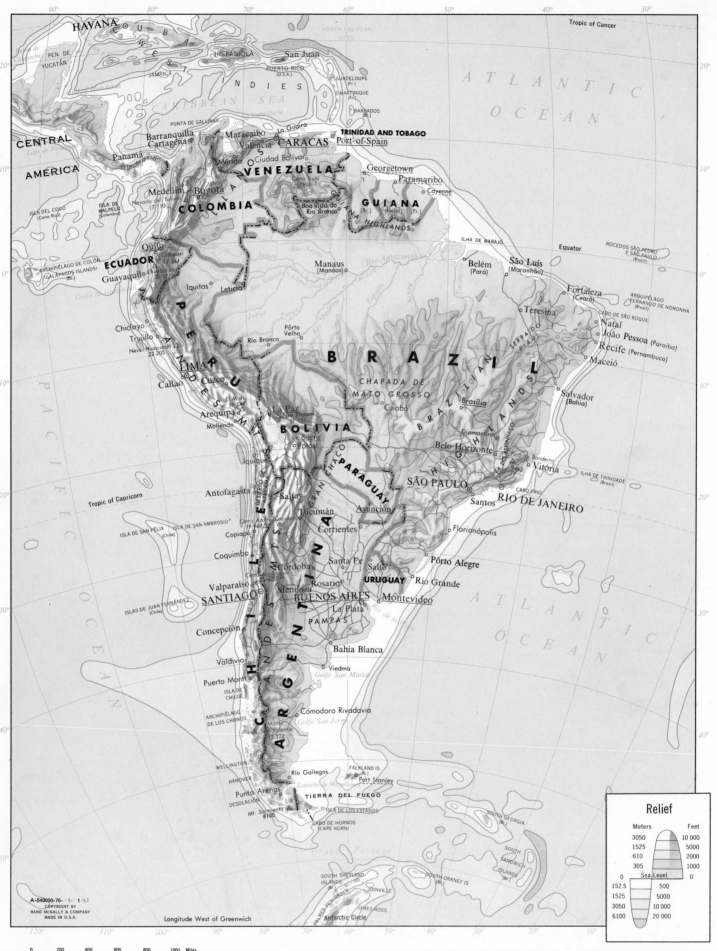

SOUTH AMERICA

90° 80° 70° 60° 50° 40° 30°

Tropic of Cancer

HAVANA
CUBA
PEN. DE YUCATÁN
CENTRAL AMÉRICA
Isla de Nicaragua
Panamá
ISLA DEL COCO (Costa Rica)
ISLA DE MALPELO (Colombia)
ARCHIPIÉLAGO DE COLÓN (GALÁPAGOS ISLANDS) (Ec.)

HISPANIOLA
San Juan
PUERTO RICO (U.S.A.)
JAMAICA
GUADELOUPE (Fr.)
MARTINIQUE (Fr.)
BARBADOS (Br.)

CARIBBEAN SEA
WEST INDIES

ATLANTIC OCEAN

PUNTA DE GALLINAS
Barranquilla
Cartagena
Maracaibo
Valencia
Mérida
La Guaira
CARACAS
Ciudad Bolívar
Cerro Icutú

TRINIDAD AND TOBAGO
Port-of-Spain
Georgetown
Paramaribo
Cayenne

Medellín
Bogotá
Nevado del Tolima 17 110
COLOMBIA
VENEZUELA
Boa Vista do Rio Branco
GUIANA
GUIANA HIGHLANDS

Quito
ECUADOR
Cotopaxi 19 344
Guayaquil
Chimborazo 20 577
Iquitos
Leticia
Manaus (Manáos)
Río Amazonas
Belém (Pará)
São Luís (Maranhão)
ILHA DE MARAJÓ
Equator
ROCEDOS SÃO PEDRO E SÃO PAULO (Brazil)

Chiclayo
Trujillo
Nevs. Huascarán 22 205
PERU
Río Branco
Pôrto Velho
Teresina
Fortaleza (Ceará)
ARQUIPÉLAGO FERNANDO DE NORONHA

BRAZIL
CABO DE SÃO ROQUE
Natal
João Pessoa (Paraíba)
Recife (Pernambuco)
Maceió

LIMA
Callao
Cuzco
El Misti 19 144
CHAPADA DE MATO GROSSO
Cuiabá
Brasília

Arequipa
Mollendo
La Paz
Nev. Illimani 21 151
BOLIVIA
Sucre
Potosí
Diamantina
Belo Horizonte
Pico da Bandeira 9 462
Salvador (Bahia)

Iquique
GRAN CHACO
CHACO
PARAGUAY
SÃO PAULO
Vitória
ILHA DE TRINIDADE (Brazil)

Antofagasta
Salta
Tucumán
Asunción
Santos
RIO DE JANEIRO
CABO FRIO

Tropic of Capricorn
ISLA DE SAN FÉLIX (Chile)
ISLA DE SAN AMBROSIO (Chile)
Cerro Azufre (Copiapó) 19 947
Copiapó
Corrientes
Florianópolis

Coquimbo
Córdoba
Santa Fe
Salto
URUGUAY
Pôrto Alegre
Rio Grande

Valparaíso
ISLAS DE JUAN FERNÁNDEZ (Chile)
SANTIAGO
Cerro Aconcagua 22 835
Mendoza
Rosario
BUENOS AIRES
Montevideo
La Plata
PAMPAS

Concepción
ARGENTINA
Bahía Blanca

Valdivia
Viedma
Golfo San Matías

Puerto Montt
ISLA DE CHILOÉ
ARCHIPIÉLAGO DE LOS CHONOS
Monte San Valentín 13 314
Comodoro Rivadavia
Golfo San Jorge

WELLINGTON
HANOVER
Río Gallegos
FALKLAND IS. (Br.)
Port Stanley

Punta Arenas
DESOLACIÓN
Mt. Sarmiento 8100
TIERRA DEL FUEGO
ISLA DE LOS ESTADOS
CABO DE HORNOS (CAPE HORN)
Estrecho de Magallanes
SOUTH GEORGIA (Br.)

PACIFIC OCEAN

ATLANTIC OCEAN

SOUTH SHETLAND ISLANDS
SOUTH ORKNEY IS.
JOINVILLE
SOUTH SANDWICH ISLANDS (Br.)
PALMER PENINSULA
JAMES ROSS
Antarctic Circle

Longitude West of Greenwich

120° 110° 100° 90° 80° 70° 60° 50° 40° 30° 20° 10°

A-540000-76- 1- 1-1
COPYRIGHT BY
RAND MCNALLY & COMPANY
MADE IN U.S.A.

Relief		
Meters		Feet
3050		10 000
1525		5000
610		2000
305		1000
0	Sea Level	0
152.5		500
1525		5000
3050		10 000
6100		20 000

0   200   400   600   800   1000 Miles
0   400   800   1200   1600 Kilometers

Scale 1:40 000 000; one inch to 630 miles. Lambert's Azimuthal, Equal Area Projection
Elevations and depressions are given in feet

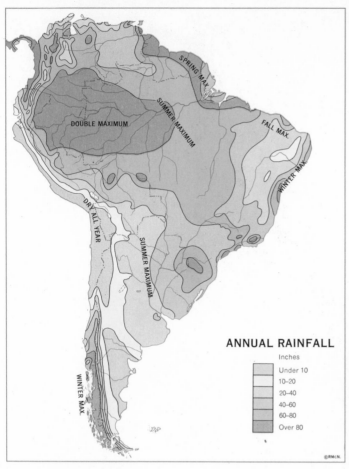

SPRING MAX.

SUMMER MAXIMUM

DOUBLE MAXIMUM

FALL MAX.

WINTER MAX.

DRY ALL YEAR

SUMMER MAXIMUM

WINTER MAX.

ANNUAL RAINFALL

Inches

- Under 10
- 10–20
- 20–40
- 40–60
- 60–80
- Over 80

©RMcN.

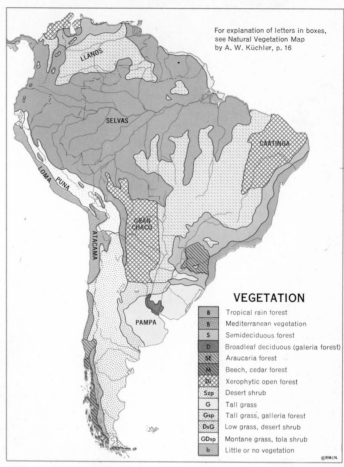

For explanation of letters in boxes,
see Natural Vegetation Map
by A. W. Küchler, p. 16

LLANOS

SELVAS

CAATINGA

LOMA

PUNA

ATACAMA

GRAN CHACO

PAMPA

VEGETATION

B	Tropical rain forest
B'	Mediterranean vegetation
S	Semideciduous forest
D	Broadleaf deciduous (galeria forest)
SE	Araucaria forest
M	Beech, cedar forest
Di	Xerophytic open forest
Szp	Desert shrub
G	Tall grass
Gsp	Tall grass, galleria forest
DsG	Low grass, desert shrub
GDsp	Montane grass, tola shrub
b	Little or no vegetation

©RMcN.

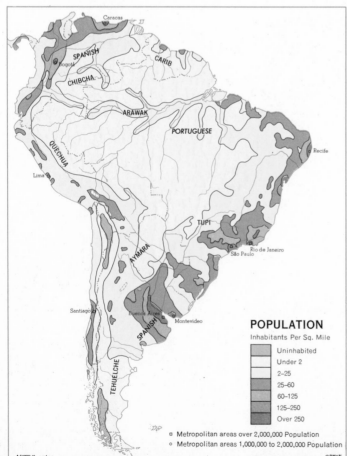

Caracas

SPANISH

CARIB

CHIBCHA

Bogotá

ARAWAK

PORTUGUESE

QUECHUA

Lima

Recife

TUPI

AYMARA

Rio de Janeiro
São Paulo

Santiago

Buenos Aires
Montevideo

SPANISH

TEHUELCHE

POPULATION

Inhabitants Per Sq. Mile

- Uninhabited
- Under 2
- 2–25
- 25–60
- 60–125
- 125–250
- Over 250

□ Metropolitan areas over 2,000,000 Population
○ Metropolitan areas 1,000,000 to 2,000,000 Population

A-840000-16

©RMcN.

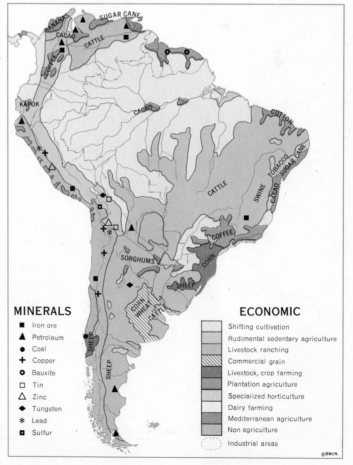

BANANAS
CACAO
SUGAR CANE
COFFEE
CATTLE

KAPOK

CACAO

COTTON

CATTLE
SWINE
TOBACCO
CACAO
SUGAR CANE

COFFEE
CORN

SORGHUMS

SHEEP

CORN
WHEAT
CATTLE

SHEEP

SHEEP

MINERALS

- ■ Iron ore
- ▲ Petroleum
- ● Coal
- ✚ Copper
- ◉ Bauxite
- □ Tin
- △ Zinc
- ◆ Tungsten
- ✶ Lead
- ▣ Sulfur

ECONOMIC

- Shifting cultivation
- Rudimental sedentary agriculture
- Livestock ranching
- Commercial grain
- Livestock, crop farming
- Plantation agriculture
- Specialized horticulture
- Dairy farming
- Mediterranean agriculture
- Non agriculture
- Industrial areas

©RMcN.

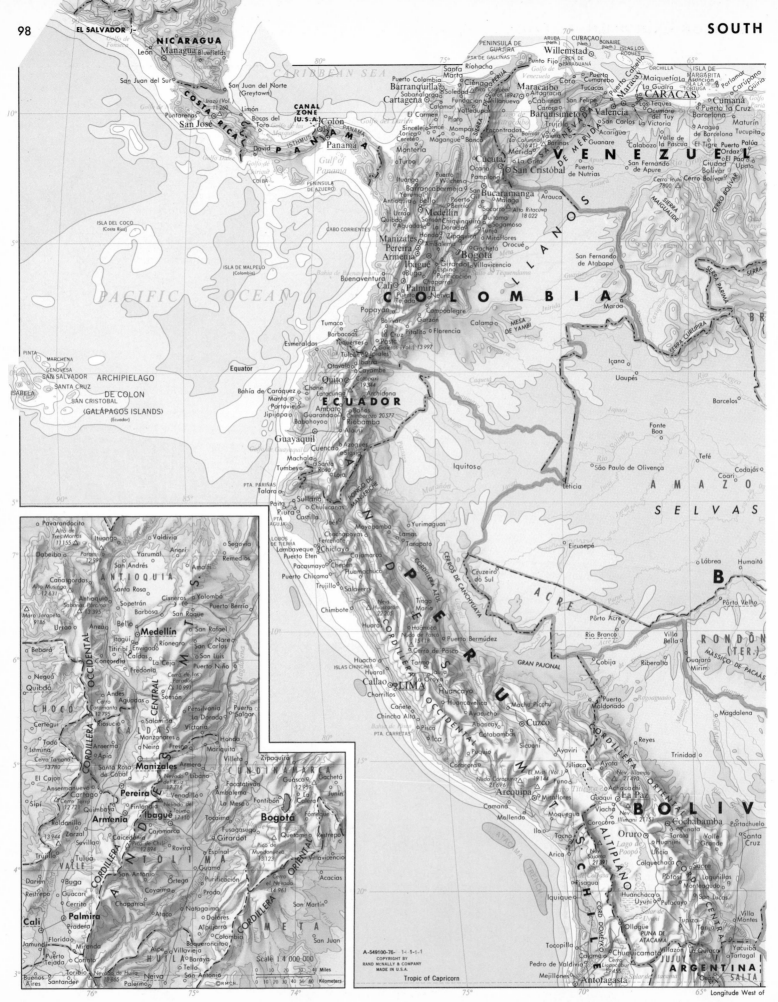

EL SALVADOR

NICARAGUA
León
Managua
Bluefields

CARIBBEAN SEA

PENINSULA DE GUAJIRA
ARUBA (Neth.) CURAÇAO (Neth.) BONAIRE (Neth.) ISLAS LOS ROQUES
Willemstad
ORCHILLA
ISLA DE TORTUGA
PTA DE GALLINAS

San Juan del Sur
San Juan del Norte (Greytown)

Puerto Colombia
Santa Marta
Riohacha
Punto Fijo
Golfo de Venezuela
Coro
Maiquetía La Guaira
Asunción
Porlamar
ISLA DE MARGARITA
Cumaná
Carúpano
Güiria

COSTA RICA
Irazú (Vol.) 11,260
Limón
Puntarenas
San José
Bocas del Toro
David
PANAMA
CANAL ZONE (U.S.A.)
Colón
Panamá

Barranquilla
Cartagena
Calamar
El Carmen
Plato
Magangué
Banco
Montería
Turbo

Maracaibo
Altagracia
Cabimas
Carora
Trujillo
San Felipe
Barquisimeto
Valencia
CARACAS
Los Teques
Ocumare del Tuy
La Victoria
Barcelona
Puerto la Cruz
Maturín
Tucupita

VENEZUELA
SIERRA MARGUALIDE

COBA
PENINSULA DE AZUERO

CABO CORRIENTES

ISLA DEL COCO (Costa Rica)

ISLA DE MALPELO (Colombia)

PACIFIC OCEAN

Equator

PINTA
MARCHENA
GENOVESA
SAN SALVADOR
SANTA CRUZ
SAN CRISTOBAL
ISABELA
ARCHIPIELAGO DE COLON (GALÁPAGOS ISLANDS) (Ecuador)

COLOMBIA
Medellín
Manizales
Pereira
Armenia
Ibagué
Cali
Palmira
Buenaventura
Popayán
Bolívar
Tumaco
Barbacoas
Esmeraldas

Cúcuta
San Cristóbal
Bucaramanga
Arauca
Barrancabermeja
Bello
Bogotá
Villavicencio

LLANOS

Maroa

ECUADOR
Quito
Guayaquil
Cuenca
Loja

PERU
LIMA
Callao
Cuzco

BOLIVIA
La Paz
Oruro
Sucre
Potosí

ARGENTINA

Scale 1:16 000 000; one inch to 250 miles. Sinusoidal Projection
Elevations and depressions are given in feet

A-549100-76- 14 1-1-1
COPYRIGHT BY
RAND McNALLY & COMPANY
MADE IN U.S.A.

Scale 1:4 000 000
0 10 20 30 40 Miles
0 10 20 30 40 50 60 Kilometers

Tropic of Capricorn

Longitude West of

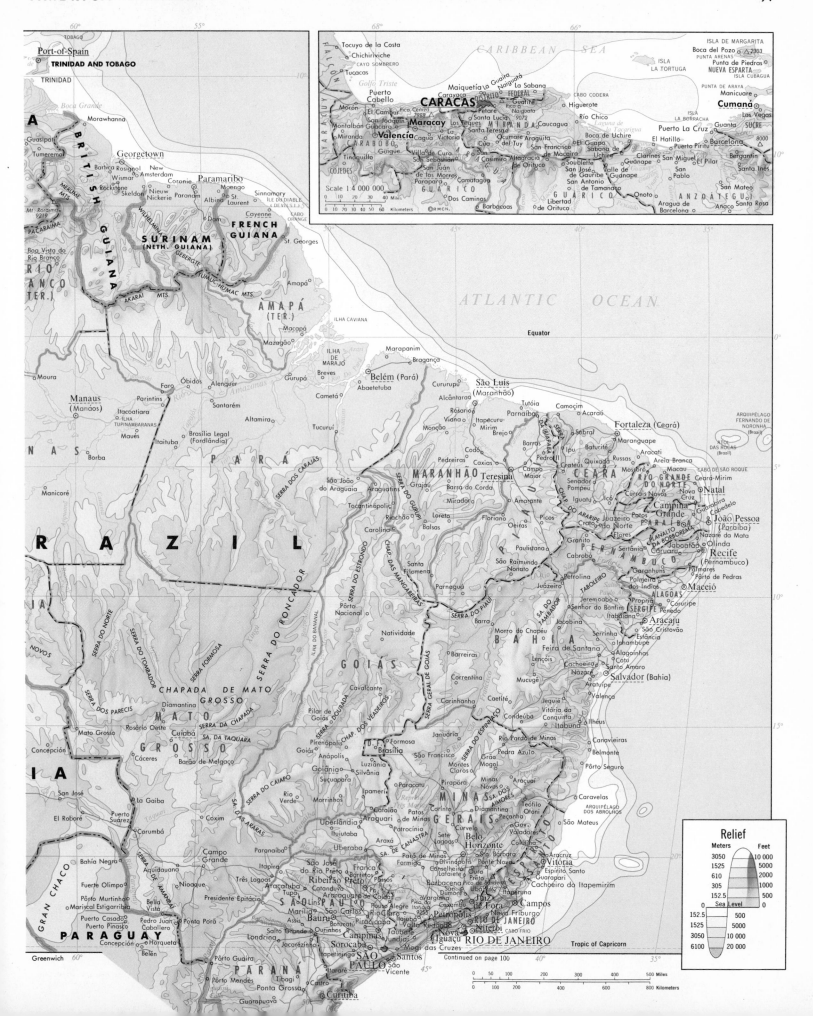

Continued on page 100

Continued on pages 98-99

BUENOS AIRES

Scale 1:1 000 000

0   4   8   12   16 Kilometers

RIO DE JANEIRO

Scale 1:1 000 000

0   5   10 Miles

0   4   8   12   16 Kilometers

Relief

Meters	Feet
3050	10 000
1525	5000
610	2000
305	1000
152.5	500
Sea Level	Sea Level
152.5	500
1525	5000
3050	10 000
6100	20 000
	Below Sea Level

A-549200-76- 1- 1-1-1
COPYRIGHT BY
RAND McNALLY & COMPANY
MADE IN U.S.A.

Longitude West of Greenwich

0   50   100   200   300   400   500 Miles

0   100   200   400   600   800 Kilometers

Scale 1:16 000 000; one inch to 250 miles. Sinusoidal Projection
Elevations and depressions are given in feet

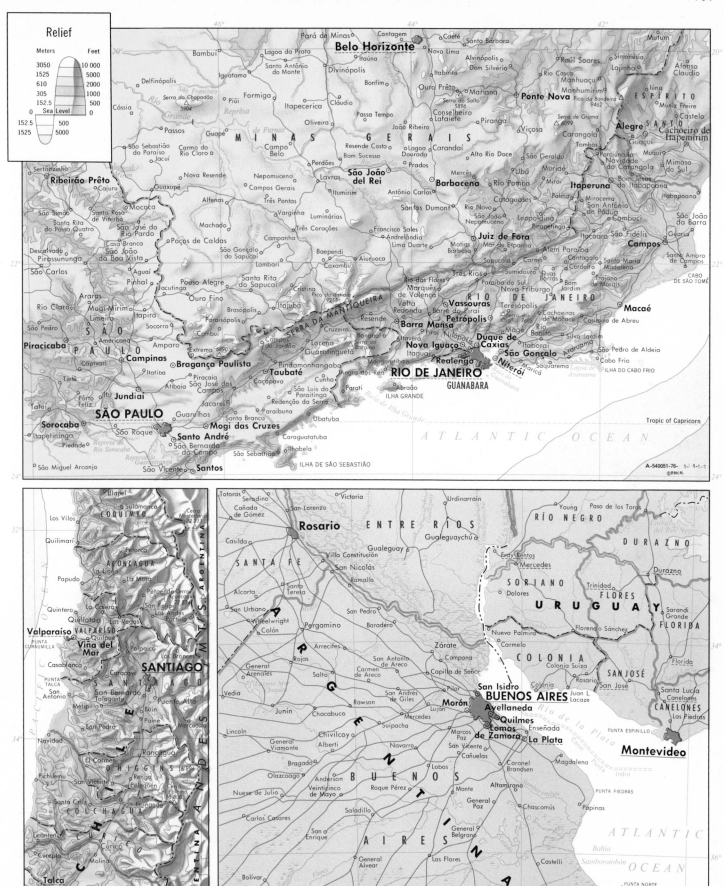

Relief

Meters		Feet
3050		10 000
1525		5000
610		2000
305		1000
152.5		500
0	Sea Level	0
152.5		Below Sea Level
1525		5000
3050		10 000

Longitude West of Greenwich   Longitude East of Greenwich

Continued on pages 164-165

Scale 1: 16 000 000; one inch to 250 miles. Conic Projection
Elevations and depressions are given in feet

| 0 | 50 | 100 | 200 | 300 | 400 | 500 Miles |

| 0 | 100 | 200 | 400 | 600 | 800 Kilometers |

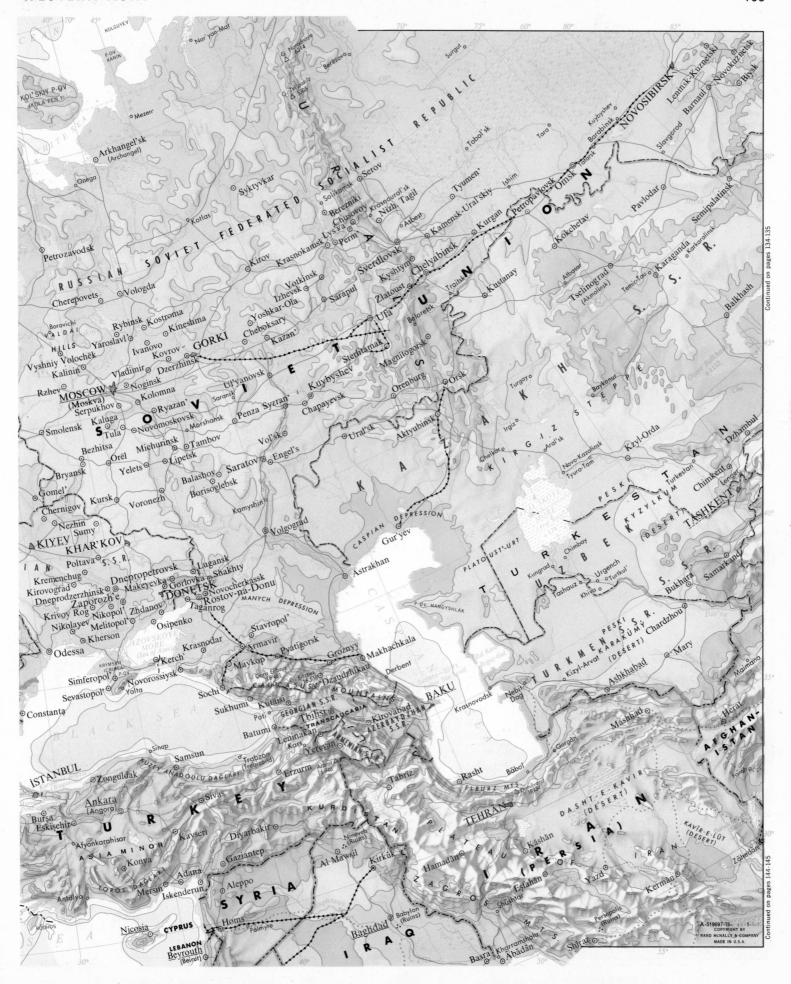

Continued on pages 134-135

Continued on pages 144-145

A-519697-76—
COPYRIGHT BY
RAND McNALLY & COMPANY
MADE IN U.S.A.

Scale 1:16 000 000; one inch to 250 miles. Conic Projection
Elevations and depressions are given in feet.

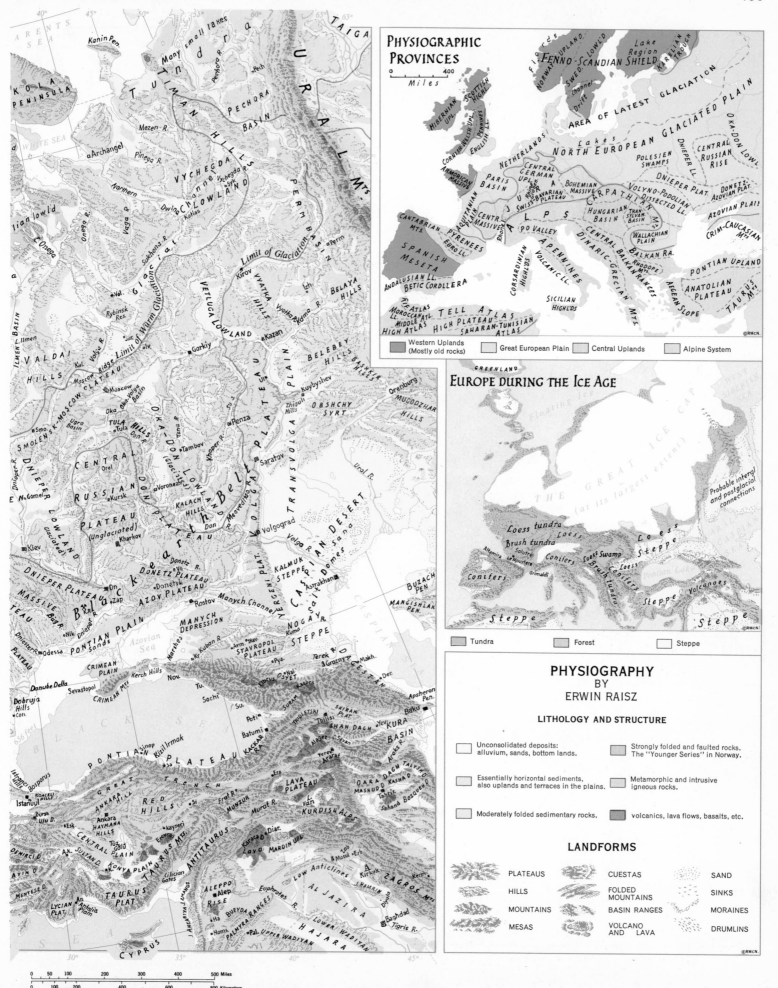

MAJOR LAND USES

Cropland-wheat important	Oases and important cotton areas
Cropland-rye important	Chiefly pasture land (meadow, alpine pastures) with some cropland
Cropland-corn important	Sparse pasture land (heath, maquis, steppe)
Cropland-oats and barley important	Sparse grass, desert shrub; seasonally grazed
Cropland and pasture with some woodland	Tundra; seasonally grazed
Intensive grape culture for wine	Forest and woodland
Mediterranean agriculture (including olives, grapes, grains and specialized vegetables)	Waste and unproductive areas

0   100   200   300   400   500   600 Miles
0   200   400   600   800   1000 Kilometers

Scale 1:20,000,000; one inch to 315 miles Conic Projection

COPYRIGHT BY
RAND McNALLY & COMPANY
MADE IN U.S.A.

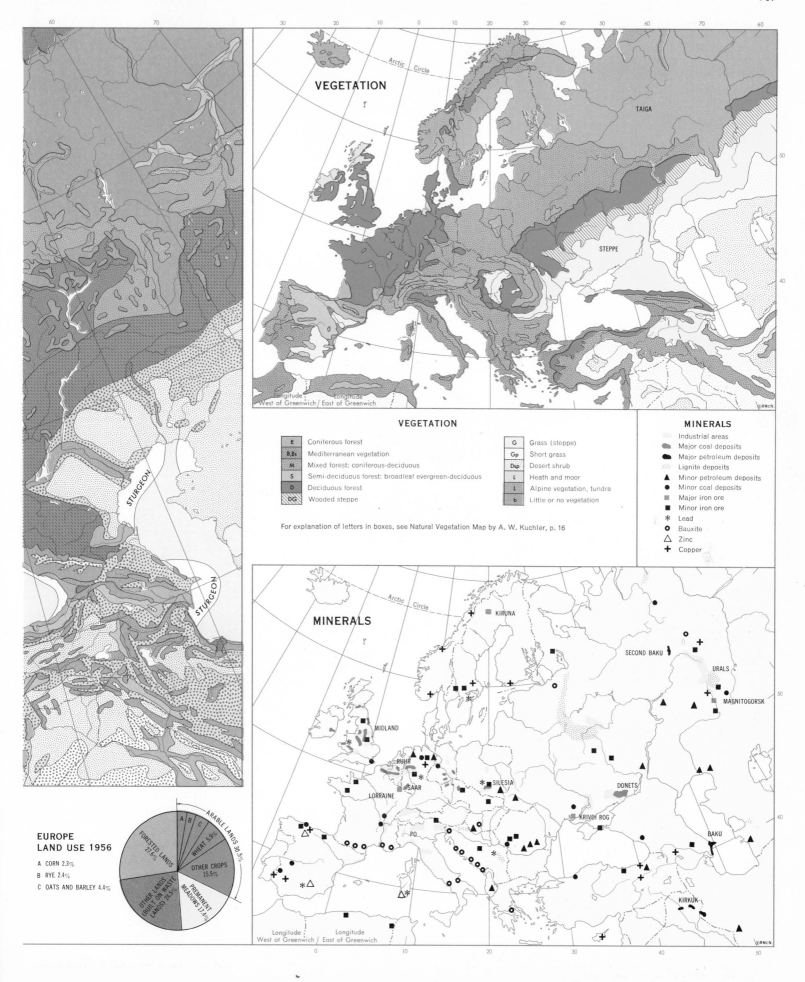

VEGETATION

TAIGA

STEPPE

STURGEON

STURGEON

Longitude Longitude
West of Greenwich / East of Greenwich
©RMcN.

VEGETATION

E	Coniferous forest
B,Bs	Mediterranean vegetation
M	Mixed forest: coniferous-deciduous
S	Semi-deciduous forest: broadleaf evergreen-deciduous
D	Deciduous forest
DG	Wooded steppe

G	Grass (steppe)
Gp	Short grass
Dsp	Desert shrub
L	Heath and moor
L	Alpine vegetation, tundra
b	Little or no vegetation

For explanation of letters in boxes, see Natural Vegetation Map by A. W. Kuchler, p. 16

MINERALS

	Industrial areas
	Major coal deposits
	Major petroleum deposits
	Lignite deposits
▲	Minor petroleum deposits
●	Minor coal deposits
■	Major iron ore
■	Minor iron ore
✳	Lead
◉	Bauxite
△	Zinc
✛	Copper

MINERALS

KIRUNA

SECOND BAKU

URALS

MAGNITOGORSK

MIDLAND

RUHR

SILESIA

DONETS

SAAR

LORRAINE

KRIVOI ROG

BAKU

PO

KIRKUK

Longitude Longitude
West of Greenwich / East of Greenwich
©RMcN.

EUROPE
LAND USE 1956

A CORN 2.3%
B RYE 2.4%
C OATS AND BARLEY 4.4%

A B C
ARABLE LANDS 30.5%
FORESTED LANDS 27.6%
WHEAT 5.9%
OTHER CROPS 15.5%
OTHER LANDS (BUILT ON WASTE LANDS) 24.3%
PREMANENT MEADOWS 17.4%

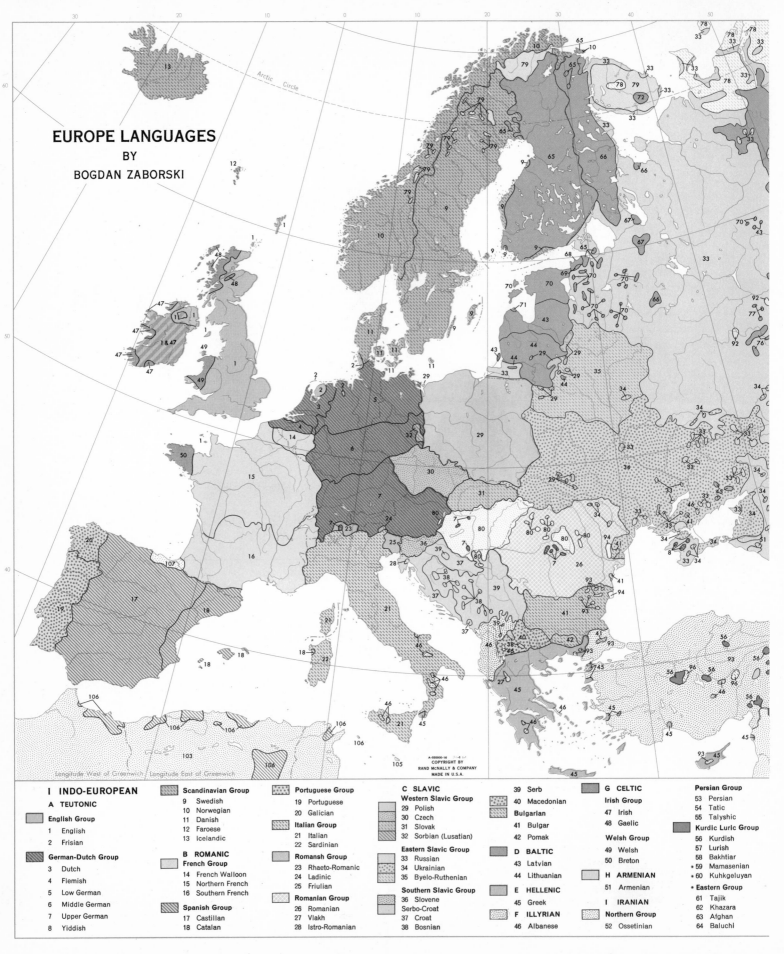

EUROPE LANGUAGES
BY
BOGDAN ZABORSKI

A-550000-16
COPYRIGHT BY
RAND McNALLY & COMPANY
MADE IN U.S.A.

I INDO-EUROPEAN	Scandinavian Group	Portuguese Group	C SLAVIC	39 Serb	G CELTIC	Persian Group
A TEUTONIC	9 Swedish	19 Portuguese	Western Slavic Group	40 Macedonian	Irish Group	53 Persian
	10 Norwegian	20 Galician	29 Polish	Bulgarian	47 Irish	54 Tatic
English Group	11 Danish		30 Czech	41 Bulgar	48 Gaelic	55 Talyshic
1 English	12 Faroese	Italian Group	31 Slovak	42 Pomak		Kurdic Luric Group
2 Frisian	13 Icelandic	21 Italian	32 Sorbian (Lusatian)		Welsh Group	56 Kurdish
		22 Sardinian		D BALTIC	49 Welsh	57 Lurish
German-Dutch Group	B ROMANIC		Eastern Slavic Group	43 Latvian	50 Breton	58 Bakhtiar
3 Dutch	French Group	Romansh Group	33 Russian	44 Lithuanian		*59 Mamasenian
4 Flemish	14 French Walloon	23 Rhaeto-Romanic	34 Ukrainian		H ARMENIAN	*60 Kuhkgeluyan
5 Low German	15 Northern French	24 Ladinic	35 Byelo-Ruthenian	E HELLENIC	51 Armenian	*Eastern Group
6 Middle German	16 Southern French	25 Friulian		45 Greek		61 Tajik
7 Upper German			Southern Slavic Group		I IRANIAN	62 Khazara
8 Yiddish	Spanish Group	Romanian Group	36 Slovene	F ILLYRIAN	Northern Group	63 Afghan
	17 Castillan	26 Romanian	Serbo-Croat	46 Albanese	52 Ossetinian	64 Baluchi
	18 Catalan	27 Vlakh	37 Croat			
		28 Istro-Romanian	38 Bosnian			

0   100   200   300   400   500   600 Miles

0   200   400   600   800   1000 Kilometers

Scale 1:20,000,000; one inch to 315 miles Conic Projection

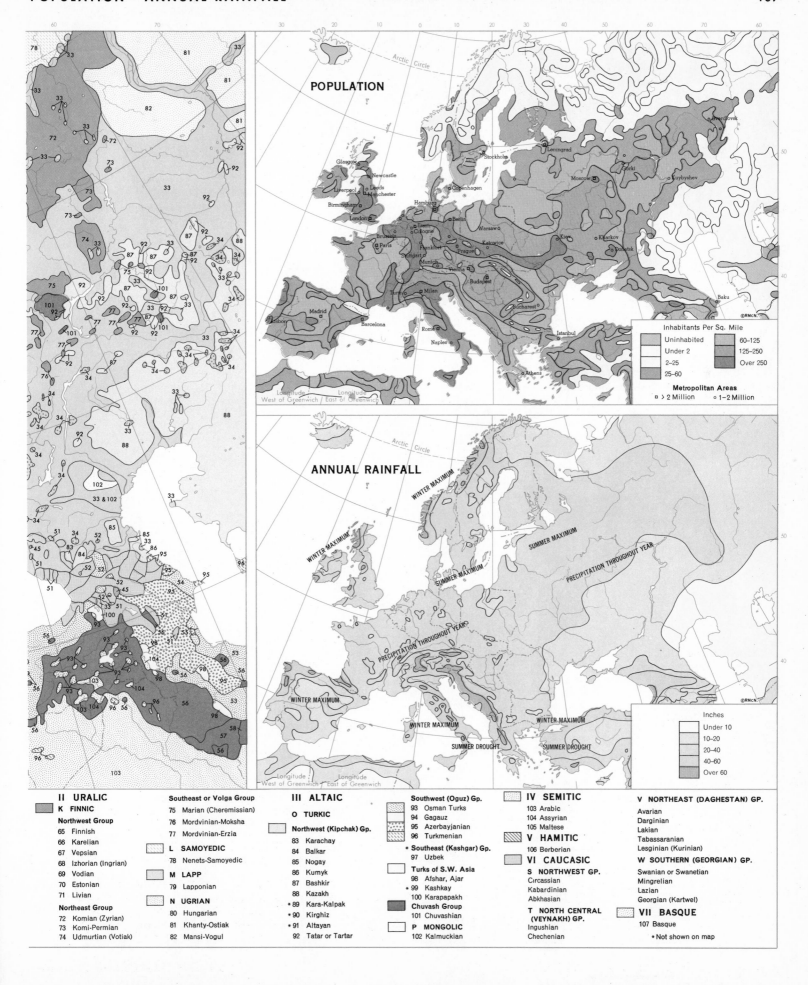

POPULATION

Inhabitants Per Sq. Mile
Uninhabited
Under 2
2–25
25–60
60–125
125–250
Over 250

Metropolitan Areas
□ > 2 Million   ○ 1–2 Million

ANNUAL RAINFALL

WINTER MAXIMUM
WINTER MAXIMUM
SUMMER MAXIMUM
SUMMER MAXIMUM
PRECIPITATION THROUGHOUT YEAR
PRECIPITATION THROUGHOUT YEAR
PRECIPITATION THROUGHOUT YEAR
WINTER MAXIMUM
WINTER MAXIMUM
WINTER MAXIMUM
SUMMER DROUGHT
SUMMER DROUGHT

Longitude West of Greenwich / Longitude East of Greenwich

Inches
Under 10
10–20
20–40
40–60
Over 60

II URALIC

K FINNIC

Northwest Group
65 Finnish
66 Karelian
67 Vepsian
68 Izhorian (Ingrian)
69 Vodian
70 Estonian
71 Livian

Northeast Group
72 Komian (Zyrian)
73 Komi-Permian
74 Udmurtian (Votiak)

Southeast or Volga Group
75 Marian (Cheremissian)
76 Mordvinian-Moksha
77 Mordvinian-Erzia

L SAMOYEDIC
78 Nenets-Samoyedic

M LAPP
79 Lapponian

N UGRIAN
80 Hungarian
81 Khanty-Ostiak
82 Mansi-Vogul

III ALTAIC

O TURKIC

Northwest (Kipchak) Gp.
83 Karachay
84 Balkar
85 Nogay
86 Kumyk
87 Bashkir
88 Kazakh
*89 Kara-Kalpak
*90 Kirghiz
*91 Altayan
92 Tatar or Tartar

Southwest (Oguz) Gp.
93 Osman Turks
94 Gagauz
95 Azerbayjanian
96 Turkmenian

Southeast (Kashgar) Gp.
97 Uzbek

Turks of S.W. Asia
98 Afshar, Ajar
*99 Kashkay
100 Karapapakh

Chuvash Group
101 Chuvashian

P MONGOLIC
102 Kalmuckian

IV SEMITIC
103 Arabic
104 Assyrian
105 Maltese

V HAMITIC
106 Berberian

VI CAUCASIC

S NORTHWEST GP.
Circassian
Kabardinian
Abkhasian

T NORTH CENTRAL (VEYNAKH) GP.
Ingushian
Chechenian

V NORTHEAST (DAGHESTAN) GP.
Avarian
Darginian
Lakian
Tabassaranian
Lesginian (Kurinian)

W SOUTHERN (GEORGIAN) GP.
Swanian or Swanetian
Mingrelian
Lazian
Georgian (Kartwel)

VII BASQUE
107 Basque

* Not shown on map

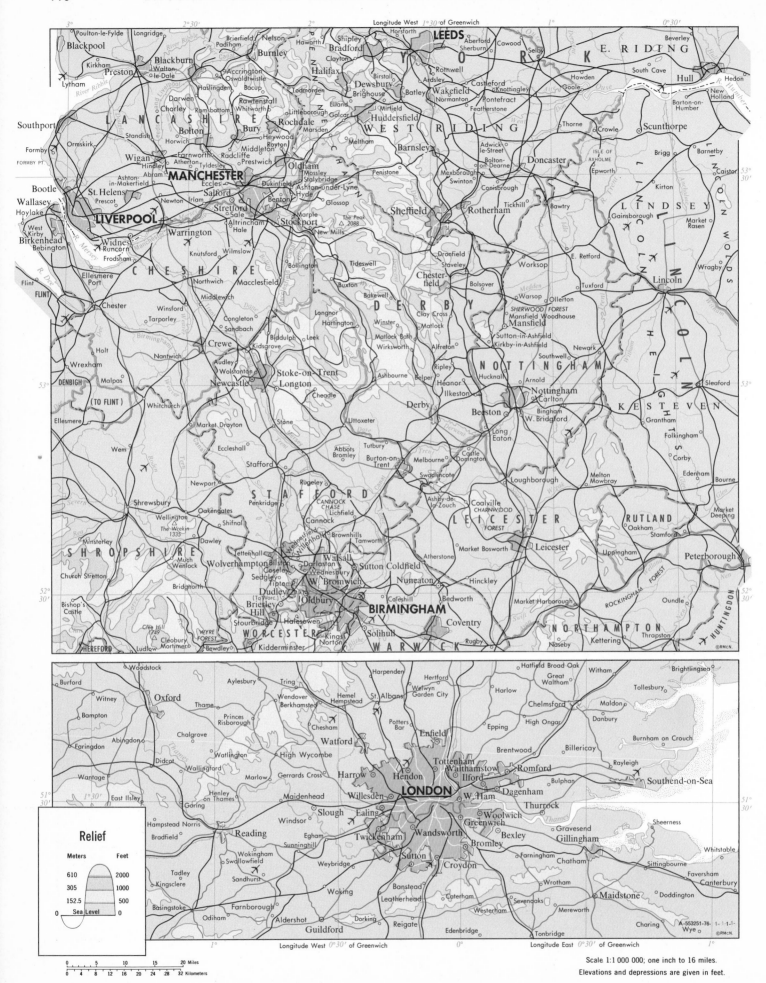

Relief

Meters	Feet	
610	2000	
305	1000	
152.5	500	
0	Sea Level	0

Scale 1:1 000 000; one inch to 16 miles.
Elevations and depressions are given in feet.

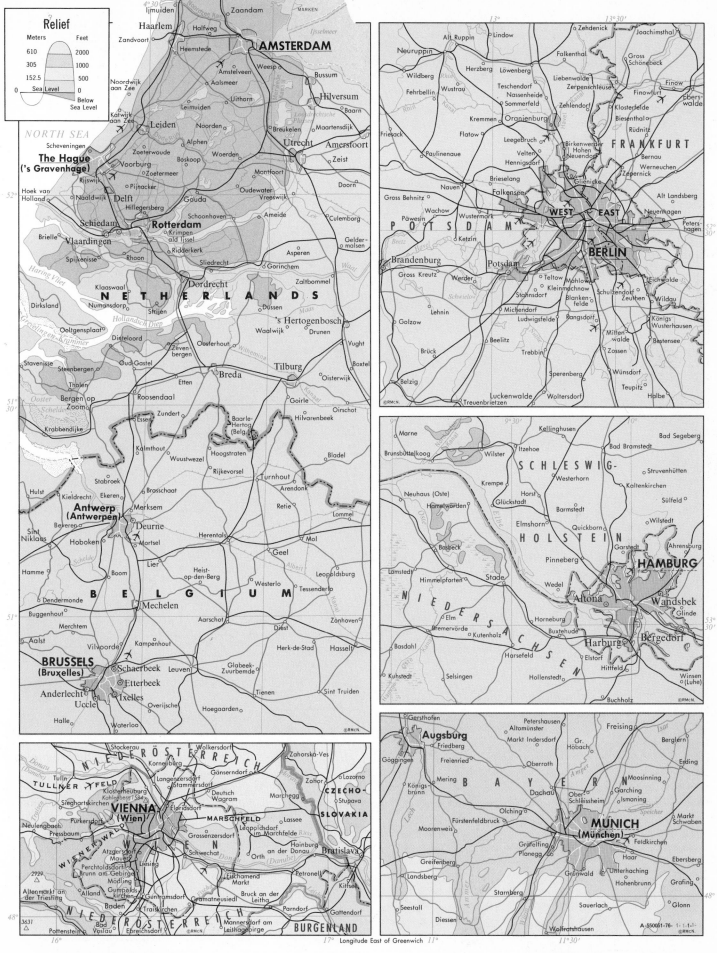

Relief

Meters	Feet
610	2000
305	1000
152.5	500
0 Sea Level	0
	Below Sea Level

NORTH SEA

Ijmuiden
Zaandam
MARKEN
Haarlem
Noordzee Kan
Halfweg
Zandvoort
Heemstede
AMSTERDAM
Ijsselmeer
Amstelveen
Weesp
Bussum
Aalsmeer
Noordwijk aan Zee
Leimuiden
Uithorn
Hilversum
Katwijk aan Zee
Noorden
Baarn
Scheveningen
Leiden
Alphen
Breukelen
Maartensdijk
The Hague
('s Gravenhage)
Zoeterwoude
Woerden
Utrecht
Amersfoort
Voorburg
Boskoop
Zeist
Rijswijk
Zoetermeer
Gouda
Montfoort
Doorn
Naaldwijk
Delft
Hillegersberg
Schoonhoven
Oudewater
Vreeswijk
Pijnacker
Ameide
Culemborg
Schiedam
Rotterdam
Krimpen
ald Ijssel
Gelder-malsen
Vlaardingen
Ridderkerk
Asperen
Brielle
Rhoon
Gorinchem
Waal
Spijkenisse
Sliedrecht
Zaltbommel
Haring Vliet
Klaaswaal
Dordrecht
NETHERLANDS
Dirksland
Numansdorp
Strijen
Dussen
's Hertogenbosch
Ooltgensplaat
Waalwijk
Drunen
Vught
Greelingen-Krammer
Dinteloord
Oosterhout
Withemina
Boxtel
Stavenisse
Zevenbergen
Tilburg
Oisterwijk
Steenbergen
Oud-Gastel
Oirschot
Tholen
Breda
Ooster
Bergen op Zoom
Roosendaal
Etten
Goirle
Krabbendijke
Zundert
Hilvarenbeek
Bladel
Essen
Baarle-Hertog (Belg.)
Hulst
Kalmthout
Hoogstraten
Wuustwezel
Turnhout
Kieldrecht
Rijkevorsel
Arendonk
Stabroek
Ekeren
Brasschaat
Retie
Lommel
Sint Niklaas
Merksem
Antwerp
(Antwerpen)
Deurne
Herentals
Mol
Beveren
Mortsel
Geel
Hoboken
Lier
Westerlo
Leopoldsburg
Hamme
Boom
Heist-op-den-Berg
Tessenderlo
Dendermonde
BELGIUM
Zonhoven
Buggenhout
Mechelen
Aarschot
Diest
Merchtem
Herk-de-Stad
Hasselt
Aalst
Kampenhout
BRUSSELS
(Bruxelles)
Schaerbeek
Leuven
Glabbeek-Zuurbemde
Vilvoorde
Tienen
Sint Truiden
Anderlecht
Etterbeek
Uccle
Ixelles
Overijse
Hoegaarden
Halle
Waterloo

Scale 1:1 000 000; one inch to 16 miles.
Elevations and depressions are given in feet.

Neuruppin
Alt Ruppin
Lindow
Zehdenick
Joachimsthal
Wildberg
Herzberg
Löwenberg
Falkenthal
Gross Schönebeck
Fehrbellin
Wustrau
Teschendorf
Liebenwalde
Finow
Finowfurt
Nassenheide
Zerpenschleuse
Eberswalde
Friesack
Kremmen
Sommerfeld
FRANKFURT
Flatow
Oranienburg
Zehlendorf
Klosterfelde
Paulinenaue
Leegebruch
Biesenthal
Rüdnitz
Birkenwerder
Velten
Hohen Neuendorf
Bernau
Nauen
Brieselang
Hennigsdorf
Werneuchen
Gross Behnitz
Wachow
Glienicke
Zepernick
Päwesin
Wustermark
WEST **EAST**
Alt Landsberg
Falkensee
Neuenhagen
POTSDAM
Naven
Petershagen
Beetz
Ketzin
Havel
Teltow
Mahlow
Eichwalde
Brandenburg
Gross Kreutz
Potsdam
Kleinmachnow
Schulzendorf
BERLIN
Werder
Stahnsdorf
Zeuthen
Wildau
Gross Kreutz
Blankenfelde
Königs Wusterhausen
Lehnin
Michendorf
Rangsdorf
Golzow
Ludwigsfelde
Mitten-walde
Bestensee
Brück
Zossen
Beelitz
Trebbin
Belzig
Sperenberg
Wünsdorf
Teupitz
Luckenwalde
Woltersdorf
Halbe
Treuenbrietzen

SCHLESWIG-
Marne
Kellinghusen
Bad Segeberg
Brunsbüttelkoog
Wilster
Itzehoe
Bad Bramstedt
Struvenhütten
Westerhorn
Kaltenkirchen
Krempe
Horst
Sülfeld
Neuhaus (Oste)
Glückstadt
Barmstedt
Quickborn
Wilstedt
Hamelwörden
Elmshorn
Pinneberg
Garstedt
Ahrensburg
HOLSTEIN
Basbeck
HAMBURG
Lamstedt
Himmelpforten
Stade
Wedel
Wandsbek
Glinde
NIEDERSACHSEN
Elm
Altona
Horneburg
Buxtehude
Bremervörde
Kutenholz
Harburg
Bergedorf
Basdahl
Harsefeld
Elstorf
Hittfeld
Kuhstedt
Selsingen
Hollenstedt
Winsen (Luhe)
Buchholz

Stockerau
Wolkersdorf
NIEDERÖSTERREICH
Korneuburg
Zahorská-Ves
Donau (Danube)
Tulln
Langenzersdorf
Gänserndorf
TULLNER FELD
Stammersdorf
Deutsch Wagram
Lozorno
Klosterneuburg
Kahlenberg 1584
Marchegg
Stupava
Sieghartskirchen
Floridsdorf
CZECHO-
VIENNA
MARSCHFELD
(Wien)
Lassee
SLOVAKIA
Pressbaum
Purkersdorf
Grossenzersdorf
Leopoldsdorf im Marchfelde
Russ
Neulengbach
WIEN
Hainburg an der Donau
Bratislava
Atzgersdorf
Mauer
Schwechat
Orth
Donau (Danube)
2929
Liesing
Fischamend Markt
Petronell
Perchtoldsdorf
Brunn am Gebirge
Mödling
Kittsee
Altenmarkt an der Triesting
Alland
Gumpolds-kirchen
Bruck an der Leitha
Parndorf
Gattendorf
Baden
Traiskirchen
3631
Gramatneusiedl
Bad Vöslau
Mannersdorf am Leithagebirge
BURGENLAND
Pottenstein
Ebreichsdorf
NIEDERÖSTERREICH

16° **17°** Longitude East of Greenwich

Gersthofen
Petershausen
Freising
Augsburg
Altomünster
Gr. Höbach
Berglern
Göggingen
Friedberg
Markt Indersdorf
Erding
Freienried
Oberroth
Isar
Mering
Ober Schleissheim
Moosinning
Königs-brunn
BAYERN
Dachau
Garching
Ismaning
Fürstenfeldbruck
Olching
Amper
Moorenweis
Speicher
MUNICH
Markt Schwaben
Greifenberg
(München)
Feldkirchen
Landsberg
Gräfelfing
Planegg
Haar
Ebersberg
Grünwald
Unterhaching
Grafing
Starnberg
Hohenbrunn
48°
Seestall
Diessen
Sauerlach
Glonn
Wolfratshausen
A-550061-76- 1-1-1-1

11° **11°30'**

Scale bar:
0 5 10 15 20 Miles
0 4 8 12 16 20 24 28 32 Kilometers

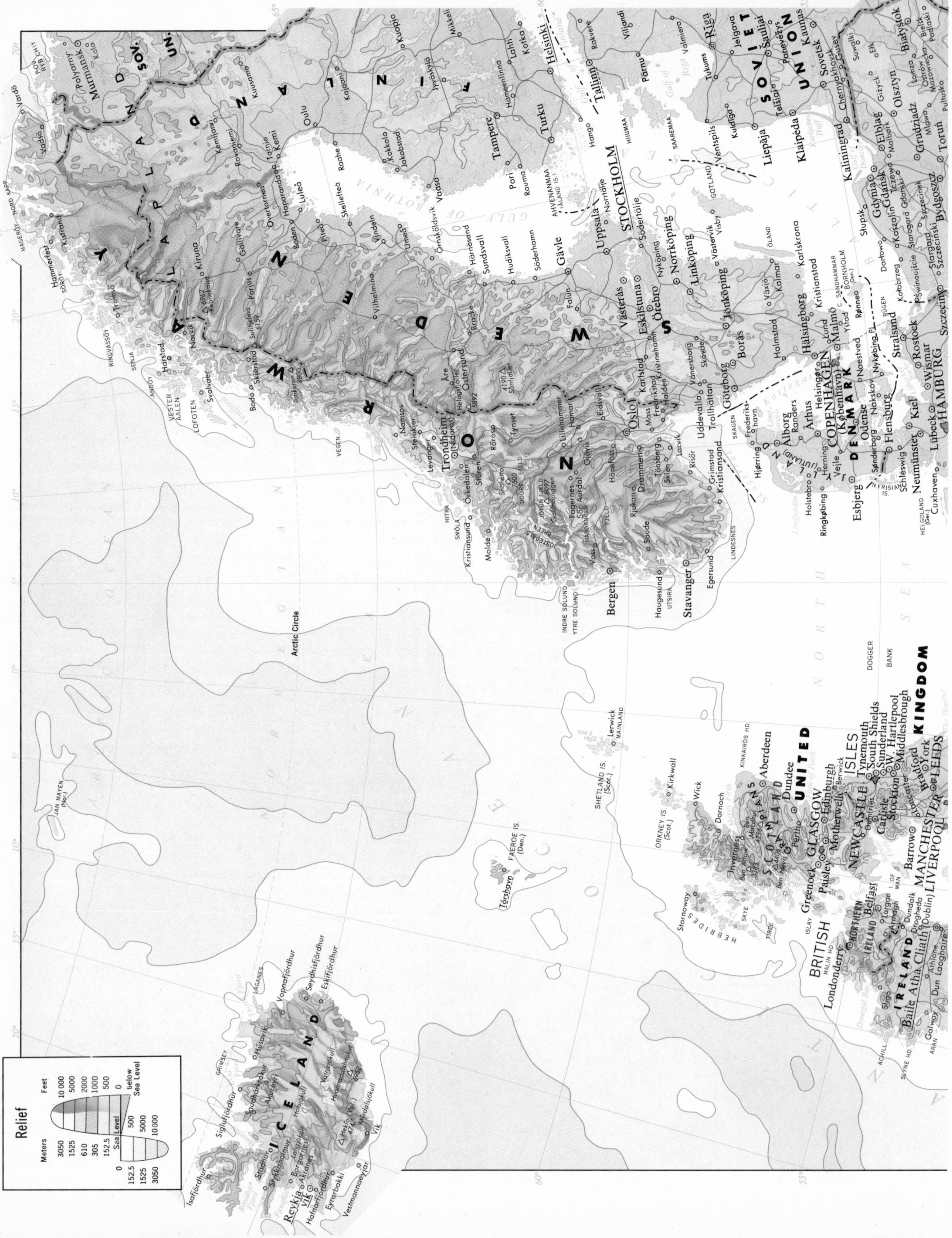

SOVIET UNION

FINLAND

NORWAY

SWEDEN

DENMARK

HAMBURG

UNITED KINGDOM

BRITISH ISLES

SCOTLAND

IRELAND

NORTHERN IRELAND

ICELAND

GULF OF BOTHNIA

NORTH SEA

NORWEGIAN SEA

ATLANTIC OCEAN

Arctic Circle

STOCKHOLM
COPENHAGEN
OSLO
Helsinki
Bergen
Stavanger
Trondheim
Göteborg
Malmö
Glasgow
Edinburgh
Newcastle
Manchester
Liverpool
Leeds
Belfast
Londonderry
Baile Átha Cliath (Dublin)

Murmansk
Polyarny
Kola
Vardö
Vadsö
Hammerfest
Tromsö
Narvik
Kiruna
Luleå
Oulu
Tampere
Turku
Riga
Tallinn
Kaliningrad
Gdynia
Gdańsk
Szczecin
Rostock
Kiel
Lübeck
Flensburg
Esbjerg
Ålborg
Århus
Odense
Helsingborg
Uppsala
Västerås
Örebro
Norrköping
Linköping
Jönköping
Borås
Halmstad
Kalmar
Visby
Gävle
Sundsvall
Östersund
Umeå
Skellefteå
Piteå
Boden
Vaasa
Pori
Rauma
Kokkola
Jakobstad

Scale 1 : 10 000 000; one inch to 160 miles. Conic Projection

Elevations and depressions are given in feet

A-559400-76- T: 1-1-1

COPYRIGHT BY
RAND McNALLY & COMPANY
MADE IN U.S.A.

Longitude East of Greenwich

Longitude West of Greenwich

POLAND

WARSAW

CZECHOSLOVAKIA

GERMANY

NETHERLANDS

BERLIN

BELGIUM

BRUSSELS

LONDON

ENGLAND

PARIS

FRANCE

SWITZERLAND

AUSTRIA

VIENNA

HUNGARY

BUDAPEST

ROMANIA

YUGOSLAVIA

BELGRADE

ALBANIA

TIRANË

ITALY

ROME

NAPLES

MILAN

MONACO

SARDINIA

CORSICA (Fr.)

SICILY

TUNISIA

ALGERIA

MOROCCO

SPAIN

MADRID

BARCELONA

VALENCIA

PORTUGAL

LISBON

ADRIATIC SEA

IONIAN SEA

TYRRHENIAN SEA

LIGURIAN SEA

MEDITERRANEAN SEA

ENGLISH CHANNEL

BAY OF BISCAY

BALEARES (Sp.)

MUNICH

FRANKFURT

STUTTGART

COLOGNE

DÜSSELDORF

ESSEN

HAMBURG

BREMEN

HANNOVER

LEIPZIG

DRESDEN

PRAGUE

BRATISLAVA

ZAGREB

SARAJEVO

MILES

KILOMETERS

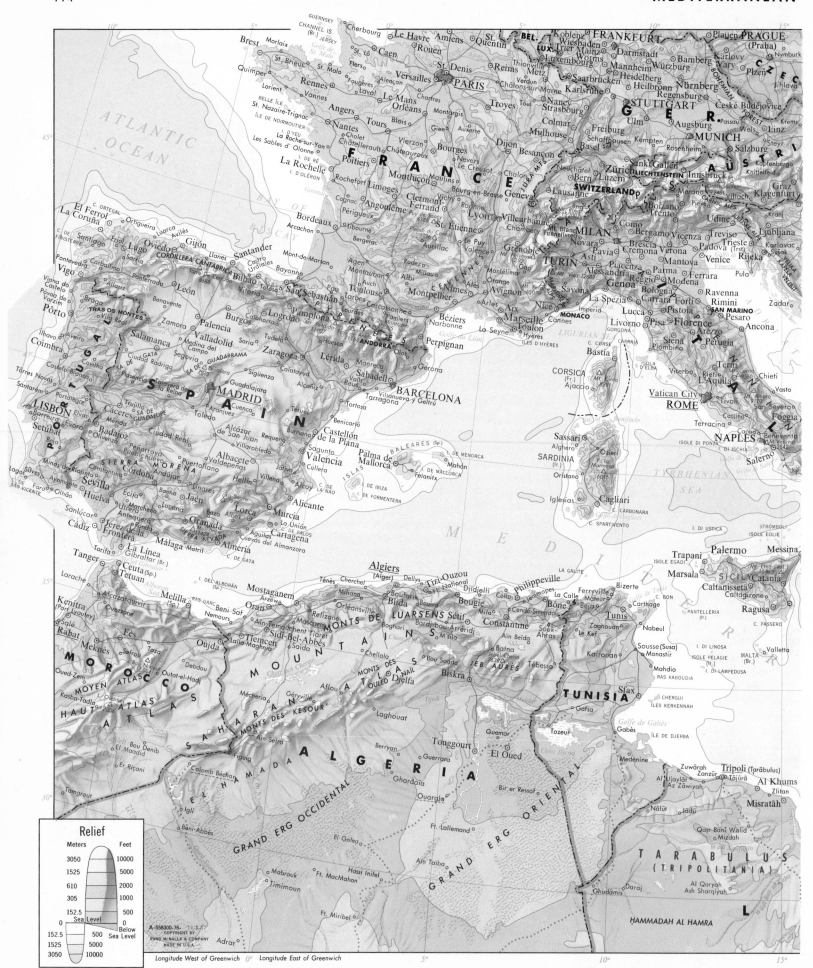

Relief

Meters	Feet
3050	10000
1525	5000
610	2000
305	1000
152.5	500
0 Sea Level	Sea Level
152.5	Below 500
1525	5000
3050	10000

A-558300-76-
COPYRIGHT BY
RAND McNALLY & COMPANY
MADE IN U.S.A.

Longitude West of Greenwich   Longitude East of Greenwich

Scale 1: 10 000 000; one inch to 160 miles. Bonne's Projection
Elevations and depressions are given in feet

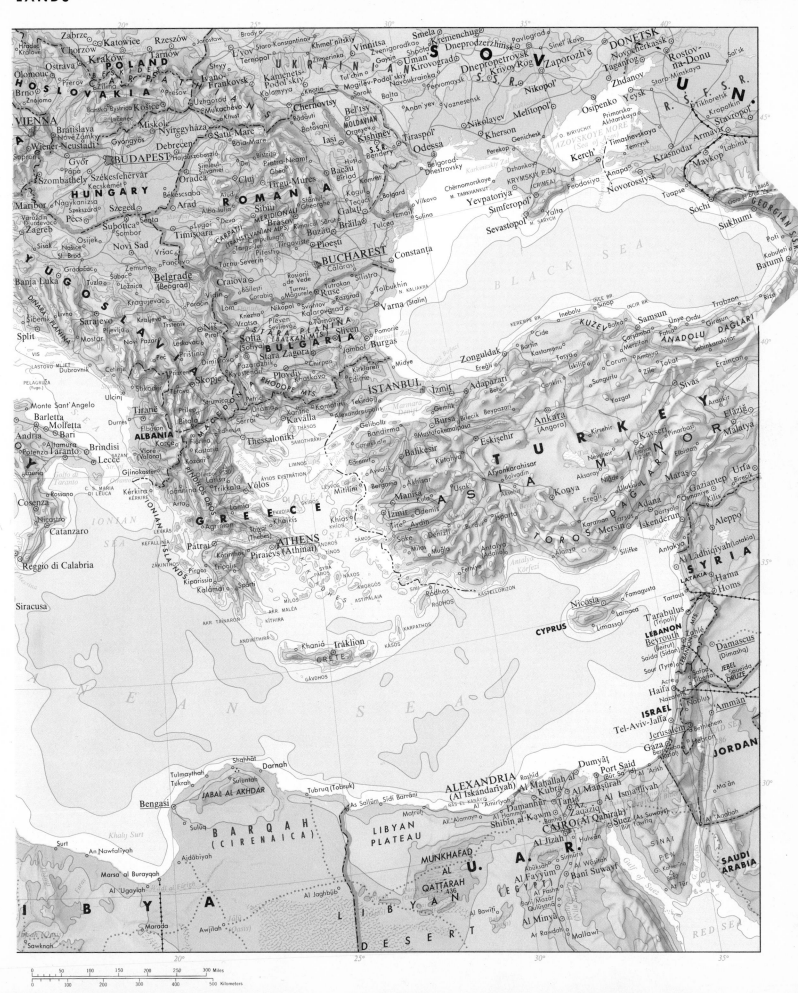

Same scale as main map

ATLANTIC

OCEAN

HERMA NESS
UNST
YELL
SHETLAND
ISLANDS
(Br.)
MAINLAND
Lerwick
FOULA

FAIR

WESTRAY
ROUSAY
N. RONALDSAY
SANDAY
STRONSAY
ORKNEY
Kirkwall
MAINLAND
ISLANDS
(Br.)
HOY
S. RONALDSAY
Pentland Firth
Thurso
DUNCANSBY HD.
SCOTLAND
©RMCN.

ATLANTIC

OCEAN

Relief

Meters	Feet
610	2000
305	1000
152.5	500
0 Sea Level	0
	Below
152.5	500 Sea Level
1525	5000

A-559700-76 -1 1-1-1
COPYRIGHT BY
RAND McNALLY & COMPANY
MADE IN U.S.A.

Longitude West of Greenwich

Scale 1: 4 000 000; one inch to 64 miles. Conic Projection
Elevations and depressions are given in feet

NORWAY

SWEDEN

Egersund
Sogndal
Flekkefjord
Farsund
Kristiansand
Mandal
LINDESNES
Arendal
Grimstad
Lillesand

Kungälv
Göteborg Borås
Mölndal
Alingsås
Ulricehamn

Skagen SKAGEN
Varberg
Falkenberg
Oskarström

Hjørring
Brønderslev
Frederikshavn
LAESØ
Halmstad
Laholm

DENMARK

JYLLAND

Thisted
Løgstør
Nykøbing
Skive
Struer
Holstebro
Silkeborg
Ålborg Limfjorden
Hobro Mariager
Viborg Randers
Aarhus
Skanderborg
Grenå

Ångelholm
Hälsingborg
Helsingør Landskrona
Hillerød
COPENHAGEN (København)
Lund
Malmö

Rinkøbing
Herning
Horsens
Nykøbing S
SAMSØ
Holbaek
SJAELLAND
Ringsted
Roskilde
Køge
Trälleborg

Varde
Vejle
Fredericia
Kalundborg
Slagelse
Korsør
Naestved

Ringkøbing
Fjord

BLÅVANDS HUK
Esbjerg Kolding
Ribe
Haderslev
FANØ
Odense
Assens
Nyborg
Svendborg Vordingborg
Rudkøbing
MØN

RØMØ
Åbenrå
ALS
Nakskov
FALSTER
Nykøbing Fl.
SYLT
Tønder Sønderborg
AERØ LANGELAND
Maribo
LOLLAND

FÖHR
Flensburg
SCHLESWIG
Schleswig
Husum
FEHMARN (Ger.)
Kiel Bay

NORTH FRISIAN IS.

HELGOLAND (Ger.)

Eckernförde
Rendsburg
Tönning
Heide
Neustadt
Kiel
Lübeck
Wismar
Güstrow

HOLSTEIN
Itzehoe
Neumünster
Bad Oldesloe
Elmshorn
Ratzeburg
Schwerin
Teterow

Cuxhaven

ISLANDS
NORDERNEY LANGEOOG
JUIST
BORKUM
Norden
Bremerhaven Stade
HAMBURG
Bergedorf
Lüneburg
Ludwigslust
Pritzwalk
MECKLENBURG N Y

FRISIAN
TERSCHELLING
AMELAND
Delfzijl
Emden
Leer
Wilhelmshaven

VLIELAND
Harlingen
Leeuwarden
Groningen
Oldenburg
Papenburg
Delmenhorst
Bremen
LÜNEBURGER
HEIDE
Soltau
Verden
Ülzen
Salzwedel
Perleberg
Wittenberge

TEXEL
Den Helder
Emmen
Meppen
Lingen
Nordhorn
Rheine
Nienburg
Minden
Celle
Gardelegen
Tangermünde
Stendal

Alkmaar
Zwolle
Almelo
NIEDERSACHSEN
Hannover
Braunschweig
Nevhaldensleben
Helmstedt
Schönebeck

NETHERLANDS
Zaandam
AMSTERDAM
Haarlem
Apeldoorn
Deventer
Enschede
Gronau
Osnabrück
Herford
Bielefeld
Hameln
Hildesheim
Wolfenbüttel
Goslar
Magdeburg
Halberstadt
Stassfurt
Bernburg

Kings Lynn
Norwich
Great Yarmouth
Lowestoft

The Hague ('s Gravenhage)
Delft
Leiden
Utrecht
Rheden
Arnhem
Münster
Coesfeld
Ahlen
WEST
GERMANY
Gütersloh
Paderborn
Lippstadt
Detmold
Northeim
Einbeck
Quedlinburg
Blankenburg
Aschersleben
Eisleben

Ely
Bury St. Edmunds
Ipswich
Colchester
Harwich
Chelmsford

Vlaardingen
Rotterdam
Dordrecht
Nijmegen
Kleve
Wesel
Bochum Hamm
Soest
Arnsberg
Kassel
Göttingen
Nordhausen
Heiligenstadt
Mühlhausen
Sangerhausen
Merseburg
Halle

Bergen op Zoom
Breda
Tilburg
Helmond
Hertogenbosch
Gelsenkirchen
Oberhausen
ESSEN
Mülheim
Dortmund
Hagen
Iserlohn
Lüdenscheid
Eschwege
THÜRINGEN
Mühlhausen
Sondershausen
Weimar

Ham Grave-send
Southend-on-Sea
Margate
NORTH FORELAND
Ramsgate
Vlissingen
Zeebrügge
Turnhout
Antwerp
Weert
Mönchengladbach
Eindhoven
DÜSSELDORF
Wuppertal
Solingen
Remscheid
Gummersbach
Siegen
NORDRHEIN-WESTFALEN
Marburg
Giessen
Fulda
Bad Hersfeld
Eisenach
Gotha
Erfurt
Jena
Arnstadt
Rudolstadt
Saalfeld

Maidstone
Chatham Canterbury
Gillingham
Sheerness
Dover
Oostende
Brugge Gent
Mechelen
Maastricht
Heerlen
Herstal
Aachen
Eupen
Bonn
Siegburg
Ahrweiler
Andernach
Neuwied
Koblenz
WESTERWALD
TAUNUS
Bad Homburg
Höchst
Hanau
FRANKFURT AM MAIN
Offenbach
Bad Kissingen
Schweinfurt
Schmalkalden
Meiningen
Suhl
Hildburghausen
Sonneberg
Coburg
Kulmbach

Hastings
Bexhill
Eastbourne
Folkestone
DOWNS
Calais
FLANDERS
Ieper
Torhout
Roeselare
St. Omer
Kortrijk
Tourcoing
Armentières
Lille
Roubaix
BELGIUM
BRUSSELS
Anderlecht
Aalst
Leuven
Nivelles
Jumet
Namur
Charleroi
Liège
Seraing
Verviers
Spa
Malmédy
Mayen
ARDENNES
EIFEL
Mayen
HUNSRÜCK
Wittlich
Bad Kreuznach
Kirn
Bingen
Wiesbaden
Boppard
Mainz
Bad Homburg
SPESSART
Aschaffenburg
Würzburg
Kitzingen
Forchheim
Erlangen
Bamberg
Bayreuth

FRANCE
St. Valéry
Le Tréport
Crécy
Abbeville
Hesdin
Étaples
Béthune
Douai
Arras
Cambrai
Denain
Valenciennes
Maubeuge
Haumont
Dinant
Givet
Fourmies
Bastogne
LUX.

Boulogne-sur-Mer

DOGGER
BANK
60—120 Ft.

NORTH

SEA

Skagerrak
Jammerbugt
Limfjorden
Mors
Nissum Fjord
Limfjorden
KATTEGAT
ANHOLT
SAMSØ
Kiel Bay
Lübecker Bucht
BALTIC SEA
FALSTER
LOLLAND

The Wash
The Nene
The Ouse
The Stour
R. Thames
Strait of Dover
CHANNEL
The Waveney

Longitude East of Greenwich

0 10 20 30 40 50 60 70 80 90 100 110 120 Miles
0 20 40 60 80 100 120 140 160 180 200 Kilometers

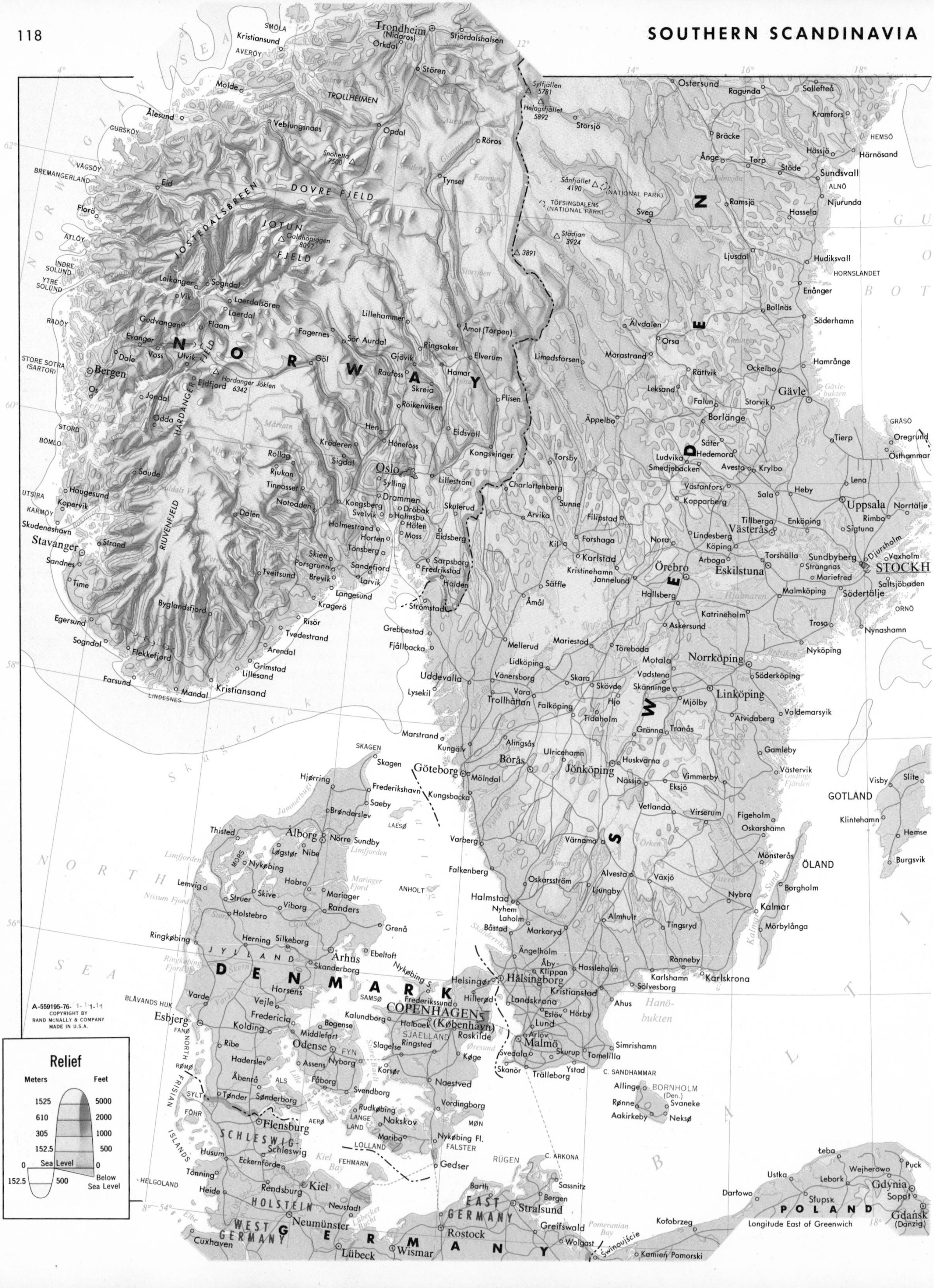

NORWAY

SWEDEN

DENMARK

WEST GERMANY

EAST GERMANY

POLAND

Trondheim (Nidaros)
Kristiansund
Smøla
Averøy
Molde
Ålesund
Gurskøy
Bremangerland
Vågsøy
Floro
Eid
Atløy
Indre Solund
Ytre Solund
Store Sotra (Sartor)
Bergen
Os
Radøy
Bømlo
Stord
Utsira
Karmøy
Kopervik
Skudeneshavn
Haugesund
Stavanger
Sandnes
Time
Egersund
Sogndal
Flekkefjord
Farsund
Mandal
Kristiansand
Lillesand
Grimstad
Arendal
Tvedestrand
Risør
Kragerø
Langesund
Brevik
Larvik
Sandefjord
Tønsberg
Horten
Holmestrand
Moss
Drøbak
Hølen
Skien
Porsgrunn
Notodden
Kongsberg
Svelvik
Drammen
Sylling
Oslo
Hønefoss
Lillestrøm
Kongsvinger
Eidsvoll
Hamar
Elverum
Flisen
Gjøvik
Lillehammer
Fagernes
Sør Aurdal
Ringsaker
Åmot (Torpen)
Røros
Tynset
Opdal
Stören
Orkdal
Stjørdalshalsen

DOVRE FJELD
JOTUN FJELD
TROLLHEIMEN
JOSTEDALSBREEN
HARDANGER FJELD
RJUVENFJELD
Snøhetta 7500
Galdhøpiggen 8097
Hardanger Jøklen 6342

NORWEGIAN SEA

Ostersund
Ragunda
Solleftea
Kramfors
Hemsö
Härnösand
Sundsvall
Alnö
Njurunda
Hassela
Enånger
Hudiksvall
Hornslandet
Söderhamn
Bollnäs
Ljusdal
Sveg
Ånge
Ramsjö
Torp
Stöde
Hässjö
Bräcke
Storsjö
Helagsfjället 5892
Sylfjällen 5781
Sånfjället 4190 (National Park)
Töfsingdalens (National Park)
Städjan 3924
3891

Älvdalen
Orsa
Mora
Rättvik
Leksand
Falun
Borlänge
Ludvika
Smedjebäcken
Säter
Hedemora
Avesta
Krylbo
Gävle
Storvik
Ockelbo
Hamrånge
Tierp
Oregrund
Östhammar
Gräsö
Uppsala
Norrtälje
Rimbo
Sigtuna
Enköping
Västerås
Köping
Arboga
Eskilstuna
Strängnäs
Mariefred
Södertälje
STOCKHOLM
Saltsjöbaden
Vaxholm
Djursholm
Sundbyberg
Torshälla
Örebro
Hallsberg
Askersund
Motala
Vadstena
Skänninge
Mjölby
Linköping
Norrköping
Söderköping
Nyköping
Trosa
Nynäshamn
Oxelösund
Valdemarsvik
Gamleby
Västervik
Vimmerby
Figeholm
Oskarshamn
Mönsterås
ÖLAND
Borgholm
Mörbylånga
Kalmar
Nybro
GOTLAND
Visby
Slite
Hemse
Burgsvik
Klintehamn
Gränna
Tranås
Atvidaberg
Huskvarna
Jönköping
Nässjö
Eksjö
Vetlanda
Virserum
Växjö
Alvesta
Ljungby
Almhult
Tingsryd
Värnamo
Ronneby
Karlskrona
Karlshamn
Sölvesborg
Ahus
Kristianstad
Hässleholm
Klippan
Åby
Ängelholm
Hälsingborg
Landskrona
Eslöv
Hörby
Lund
Malmö
Arlöv
Svedala
Skurup
Tomelilla
Simrishamn
Ystad
Trälleborg
Skanör
C. Sandhammar
Hanöbukten
BORNHOLM (Den.)
Allinge
Rønne
Svaneke
Neksø
Aakirkeby

Helsingør
Hillerød
Frederikssund
COPENHAGEN (København)
Roskilde
Holbæk
Ringsted
Slagelse
Korsør
SJÆLLAND
Køge
Næstved
Vordingborg
MØN
Nykøbing Fl. FALSTER
LOLLAND
Nakskov
Maribo
Gedser
Rødbyhavn
LANGELAND
Rudkøbing
Svendborg
Fåborg
FYN
Nyborg
Odense
Assens
Middelfart
Bogense
Kerteminde
AERØ
ALS
Sønderborg
Åbenrå
Haderslev
Kolding
Vejle
Fredericia
Horsens
Skanderborg
Århus
Ebeltoft
Grenå
Randers
Mariager
Hobro
Viborg
Skive
Struer
Holstebro
Herning
Silkeborg
Ikast
Ringkøbing
Skjern
Varde
Esbjerg
Ribe
Tønder
FANØ
RØMØ
SYLT
FÖHR
FRISIAN ISLANDS
Husum
Schleswig
Flensburg
Eckernförde
Kiel
Rendsburg
Neumünster
Neustadt
Lübeck
Wismar
Rostock
Stralsund
Greifswald
RÜGEN
C. ARKONA
Sassnitz
Barth
Wolgast
Świnoujście
Kamień Pomorski
Kołobrzeg
Darłowo
Słupsk
Ustka
Lębork
Wejherowo
Puck
Gdynia
Sopot
Gdańsk (Danzig)
Łeba
SCHLESWIG
HOLSTEIN
Cuxhaven
Helgoland
Heide
Tönning
Blåvands Huk

JYLLAND
Thisted
Hjørring
Frederikshavn
Skagen
Sæby
Brønderslev
Ålborg
Nørre Sundby
Nibe
Aars
Løgstør
Nykøbing
MORS
Lemvig
LÆSØ
ANHOLT
Läsö
Kattegat
Skagerrak
North Sea
Limfjorden
Mariager Fjord
Nissum Fjord
Ringkøbing Fjord

SKAGEN
Skagen
Göteborg
Mölndal
Kungsbacka
Varberg
Falkenberg
Oskarsström
Halmstad
Laholm
Båstad
Markaryd
Nyhem
Kungälv
Marstrand
Lysekil
Uddevalla
Fjällbacka
Grebbestad
Strömstad
Mellerud
Vänersborg
Trollhättan
Lidköping
Vara
Falköping
Skövde
Skara
Tidaholm
Hjo
Mariestad
Töreboda
Skänninge
Alingsås
Ulricehamn
Borås
Jönköping

Faemund
Faemunden
Storsjön
Hjälmaren
Vänern
Vättern
Mälaren
Öresund
Gulf of Bothnia

BALTIC SEA

Relief

Meters		Feet
1525		5000
610		2000
305		1000
152.5		500
0	Sea Level	Sea Level
152.5		500
		Below Sea Level

Longitude East of Greenwich

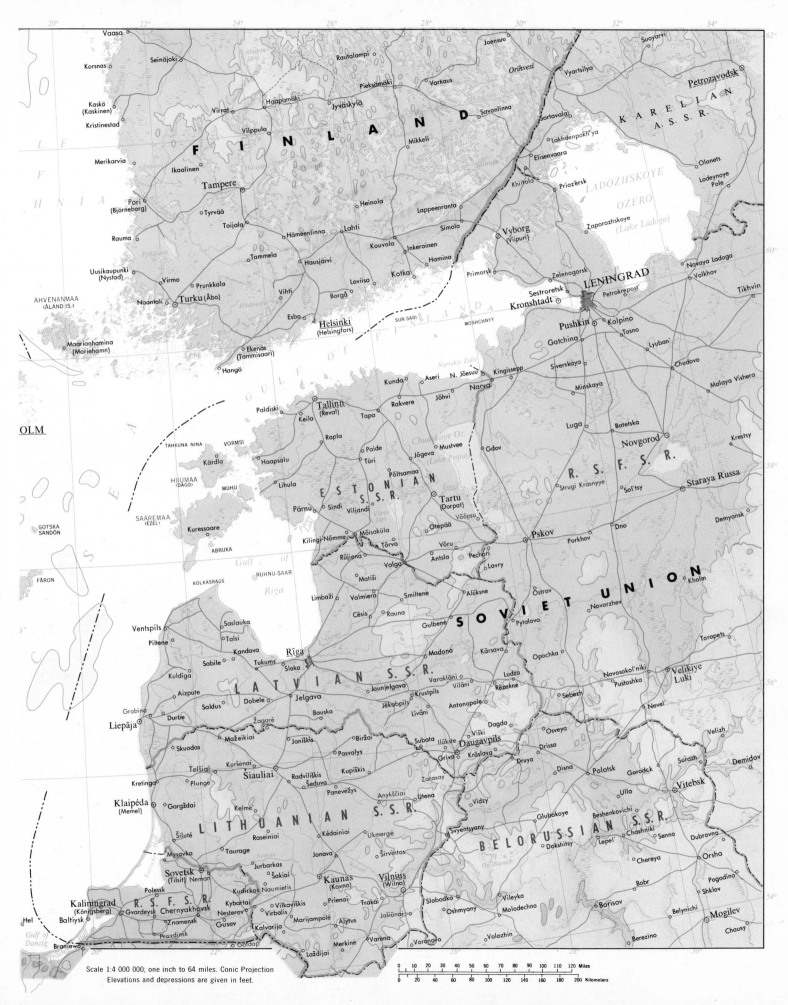

Scale 1:4 000 000; one inch to 64 miles. Conic Projection
Elevations and depressions are given in feet.

Continued on pp. 122-123

Continued on pp. 126 127

Longitude East of Greenwich

Scale 1:4 000 000; one inch to 64 miles. Conic Projection
Elevations and depressions are given in feet.

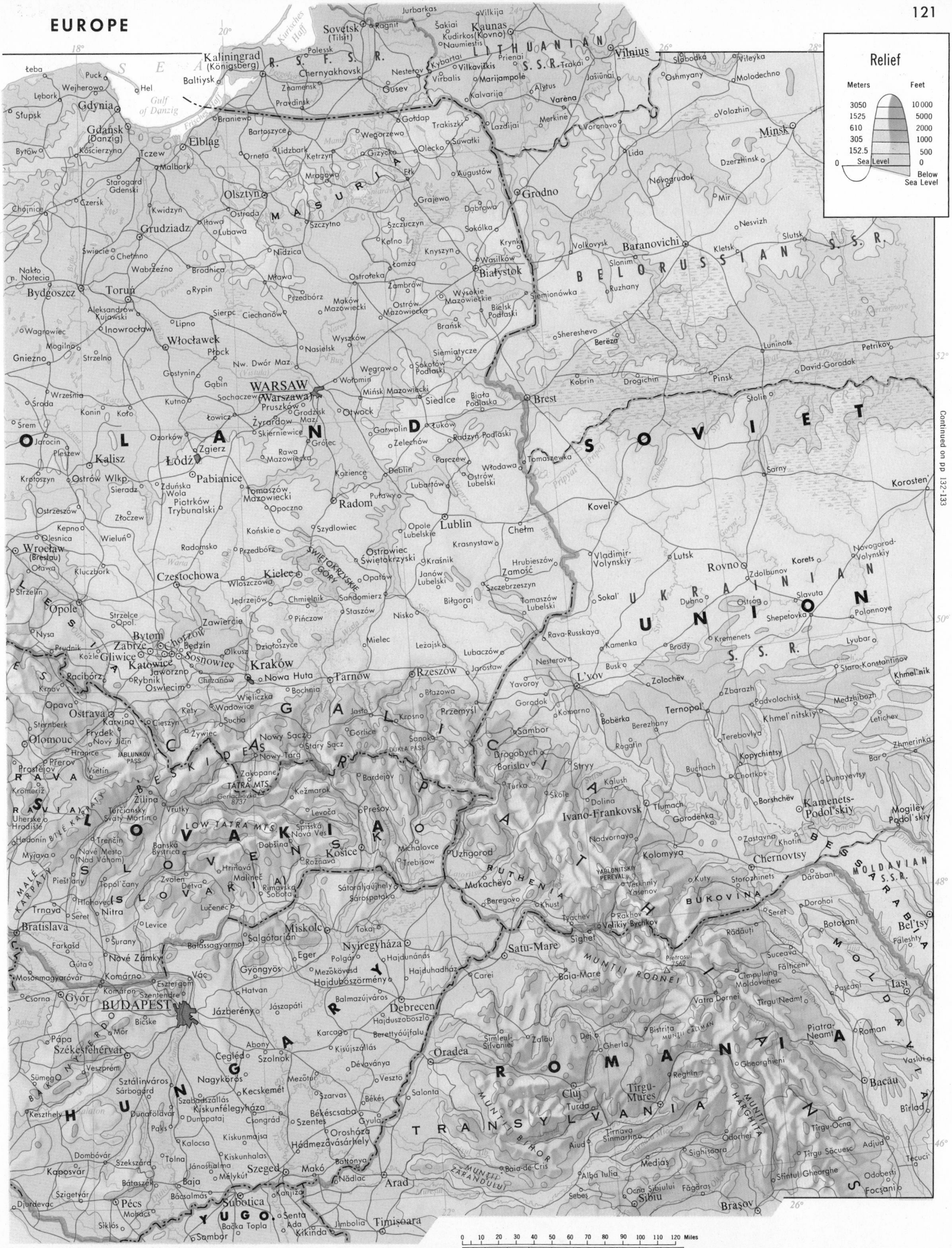

Relief

Meters	Feet
3050	10 000
1525	5000
610	2000
305	1000
152.5	500
0	Sea Level
	Below Sea Level

Continued on pp 132-133

POLAND

WARSAW (Warszawa)

SOVIET

R.S.F.S.R.

LITHUANIAN S.S.R.

BELORUSSIAN S.S.R.

UKRAINIAN UNION S.S.R.

MOLDAVIAN A.S.S.R.

CZECHOSLOVAKIA

SLOVAKIA

SLOVENSKO

HUNGARY

ROMANIA

TRANSYLVANIA

BUKOVINA

BESSARABIA

MOLDAVIA

RUTHENIA

GALICIA

CARPATHIANS

BESKIDS

TATRA MTS.

LOW TATRA MTS.

MASURIA

SILESIA

YUGO

SEA

Gulf of Danzig

BUDAPEST

Kaliningrad (Königsberg)

Gdańsk (Danzig)

Gdynia

Vilnius

Kaunas (Kovno)

Minsk

Brest

Białystok

Grodno

Olsztyn

Toruń

Bydgoszcz

Łódź

Kraków

Lublin

L'vov

Wrocław (Breslau)

Opole

Katowice

Ostrava

Olomouc

Bratislava

Košice

Uzhgorod

Ivano-Frankovsk

Chernovtsy

Kamenets-Podol'skiy

Mogilev-Podol'skiy

Ternopol

Rovno

Lutsk

Kovel'

Pinsk

Baranovichi

Iaşi

Cluj

Tirgu-Mures

Sibiu

Braşov

Arad

Timişoara

Oradea

Debrecen

Miskolc

Szeged

Pécs

Győr

Székesfehérvár

Subotica

Scale 1:4 000 000; one inch to 64 miles. Conic Projection
Elevations and depressions are given in feet

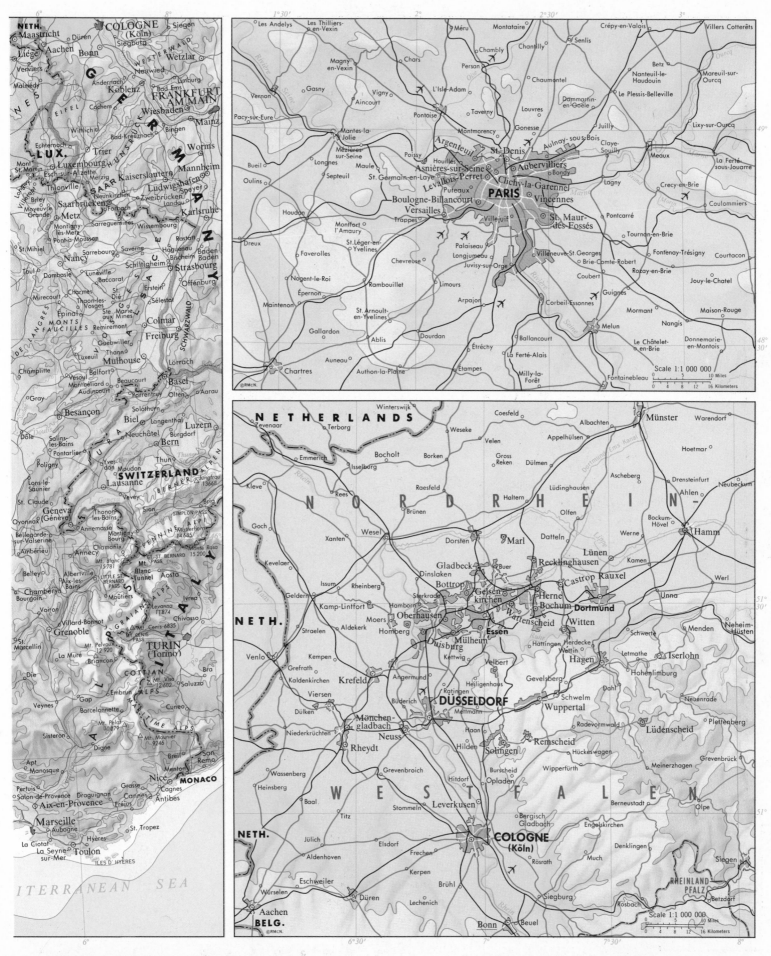

NETH.
Maastricht
Liège
Aachen
Verviers
Malmédy

COLOGNE
(Köln)
Düren
Siegen
Siegburg
Bonn
Wetzlar
Neuwied
Limburg
Andernach
Koblenz
Cochem
Bad Ems
FRANKFURT
AM MAIN
Wiesbaden
Mainz
Wittlich
Bingen
Bad Kreuznach
Worms

LUX.
Echternach
Trier
Luxembourg
Esch-sur-Alzette
Merzig
Saarbrücken
Metz
Neunkirchen
Forbach
Zweibrücken
Landau
Mannheim
Ludwigshafen
Speyer
Karlsruhe
Kaiserslautern

St. Martin
Longwy
Thionville
Briey
Moyeuvre-Grande
Montigny-lès-Metz
Pont-à-Mousson
Sarreguemines
Wissembourg
Rastatt
Baden Baden

Toul
Nancy
Dombasle
Lunéville
Baccarat
Sarrebourg
Saverne
Haguenau
Bischeim
Strasbourg
Schiltigheim
Erstein
Offenburg

Mirecourt
Charmes
Thaon-les-Vosges
St. Dié
Ste. Marie aux Mines
Sélestat
Epinal
Remiremont
Guebwiller
Thann
Colmar
Freiburg
Luxeuil
Mulhouse
Lörrach
Champlitte
Vesoul
Beaucourt
Basel
Montbéliard
Audincourt
Porrentruy
Olten
Aarau
Gray
Doubs
Besançon
Salins-les-Bains
Solothurn
Dôle
Biel
Langenthal
Luzern
Poligny
Neuchâtel
Burgdorf
Pontarlier
Bern
Lons-le-Saunier
Yverdon
Moudon
Thun
Jungfrau 13668
St. Claude
SWITZERLAND
Lausanne
Vevey
Geneva (Genève)
Thonon-les-Bains
Sion
Brig
Oyonnax
Annemasse
Martigny-Bourg
SIMPLON PASS
Bellegarde-sur-Valserine
Bourg
Chamonix
Matterhorn 14685
Ambérieu
Annecy
Mt. Blanc 15781
Monte Rosa 15200
Belley
Albertville
Mt. Blanc Tunnel
Aosta
Voiron
Moûtiers
Ivrea
Chambéry
Levanna 11874
Chivasso
Bourgoin
Villard-Bonnot
Mt. Cenis 6835
Grenoble
St. Denis PASS
La Mure
Mt. Pelvoux 12920
Briançon
TURIN (Torino)
Die
Embrun
Mt. Viso 12602
Saluzzo
Veynes
Gap
Cuneo
Barcelonnette
Sisteron
Digne
Mt. Pelat 10079
Mt. Mounier 9246
Bra
Apt
Manosque
Breil
San Remo
Menton
Grasse
Nice
Salon-de-Provence
Draguignan
Cannes
MONACO
Aix-en-Provence
Fréjus
Antibes
Marseille
Aubagne
St. Tropez
La Ciotat
La Seyne-sur-Mer
Toulon
Hyères
ILES D'HYÈRES

ITERRANEAN SEA

Scale 1:1 000 000

Les Andelys
Les Thilliers-en-Vexin
Méru
Montataire
Crépy-en-Valois
Villers Cotterêts
Magny-en-Vexin
Chambly
Chantilly
Senlis
Betz
Nanteuil-le-Haudouin
Mareuil-sur-Ourcq
Vernon
Gasny
Chars
Persan
Chaumontel
Dammartin-en-Goële
Le Plessis-Belleville
Lixy-sur-Ourcq
Pacy-sur-Eure
Vigny
Aincourt
L'Isle-Adam
Louvres
Juilly
Mantes-la-Jolie
Pontoise
Montmorency
Gonesse
Claye-Souilly
Meaux
La Ferté-sous-Jouarre
Bueil
Longnes
Poissy
Argenteuil
St.-Denis
Aulnay-sous-Bois
Houilles
Bondy
Oulins
Septeuil
Maule
St. Germain-en-Laye
Asnières-sur-Seine
Levallois-Perret
Puteaux
Clichy-la-Garenne
Lagny
Crécy-en-Brie
Houdan
Boulogne-Billancourt
PARIS
Vincennes
Coulommiers
Versailles
Villejuif
St. Maur-des-Fossés
Pontcarré
Trappes
Palaiseau
Villeneuve-St-Georges
Brie-Comte-Robert
Courtacon
Dreux
St. Léger-en-Yvelines
Longjumeau
Juvisy-sur-Orge
Fontenay-Trésigny
Faverolles
Chevreuse
Coubert
Rozay-en-Brie
Jouy-le-Chatel
Nogent-le-Roi
Limours
Arpajon
Guignes
Épernon
Rambouillet
Corbeil-Essonnes
Mormant
Maison-Rouge
Maintenon
St. Arnoult-en-Yvelines
Melun
Nangis
Gallardon
Dourdan
Ballancourt
Le Châtelet-en-Brie
Donnemarie-en-Montois
Ablis
Étréchy
La Ferté-Alais
Auneau
Étampes
Milly-la-Forêt
Auihon-la-Plaine
Chartres
Fontainebleau

Scale 1:1 000 000

NETHERLANDS
Winterswijk
Coesfeld
Albachten
Münster
Warendorf
Zevenaar
Terborg
Weseke
Appelhülsen
Hoetmar
Emmerich
Bocholt
Borken
Gross Reken
Dülmen
Ascheberg
Drensteinfurt
Neubeckum
Kleve
Isselburg
Raesfeld
Lüdinghausen
Ahlen
Rees
Haltern
Olfen
Werne
Bockum-Hövel
Hamm
Goch
Brünen
Datteln
Xanten
Wesel
Dorsten
Marl
Lünen
Kamen
Werl
Kevelaer
Buer
Recklinghausen
Gladbeck
Castrop Rauxel
Werne
Unna
Issum
Rheinberg
Dinslaken
Bottrop
Gelsenkirchen
Herne
Bochum
Dortmund
Geldern
Kamp-Lintfort
Hamborn
Sterkrade
Oberhausen
Wattenscheid
Witten
Straelen
Moers
Homberg
Essen
Venlo
Kempen
Aldekerk
Duisburg
Mülheim
Hattingen
Herdecke
Schwerte
Menden
Neheim-Hüsten
Grefrath
Kettwig
Velbert
Hagen
Letmathe
Iserlohn
Kaldenkirchen
Krefeld
Angermund
Heiligenhaus
Gevelsberg
Dahl
Hohenlimburg
Viersen
Büderich
Ratingen
Schwelm
Neuenrade
Dülken
DÜSSELDORF
Mettmann
Wuppertal
Mönchengladbach
Haan
Radevormwald
Lüdenscheid
Niederkrüchten
Neuss
Hilden
Solingen
Remscheid
Plettenberg
Rheydt
Hückeswagen
Grevenbrück
Wassenberg
Grevenbroich
Burscheid
Wipperfürth
Meinerzhagen
Heinsberg
Hitdorf
Opladen
WESTFALEN
Baal
Titz
Stommeln
Leverkusen
Bergisch Gladbach
Engelskirchen
Berneustadt
Olpe
Jülich
Elsdorf
Frechen
COLOGNE (Köln)
Much
Denklingen
Aldenhoven
Kerpen
Rösrath
Siegen
Würselen
Eschweiler
Brühl
Siegburg
RHEINLAND-PFALZ
Düren
Lechenich
Rosbach
Betzdorf
Aachen
BELG.
Bonn
Beuel

Scale 1:1 000 000

0 10 20 30 40 50 60 70 80 90 100 110 120 Miles
0 20 40 60 80 100 120 140 160 180 200 Kilometers

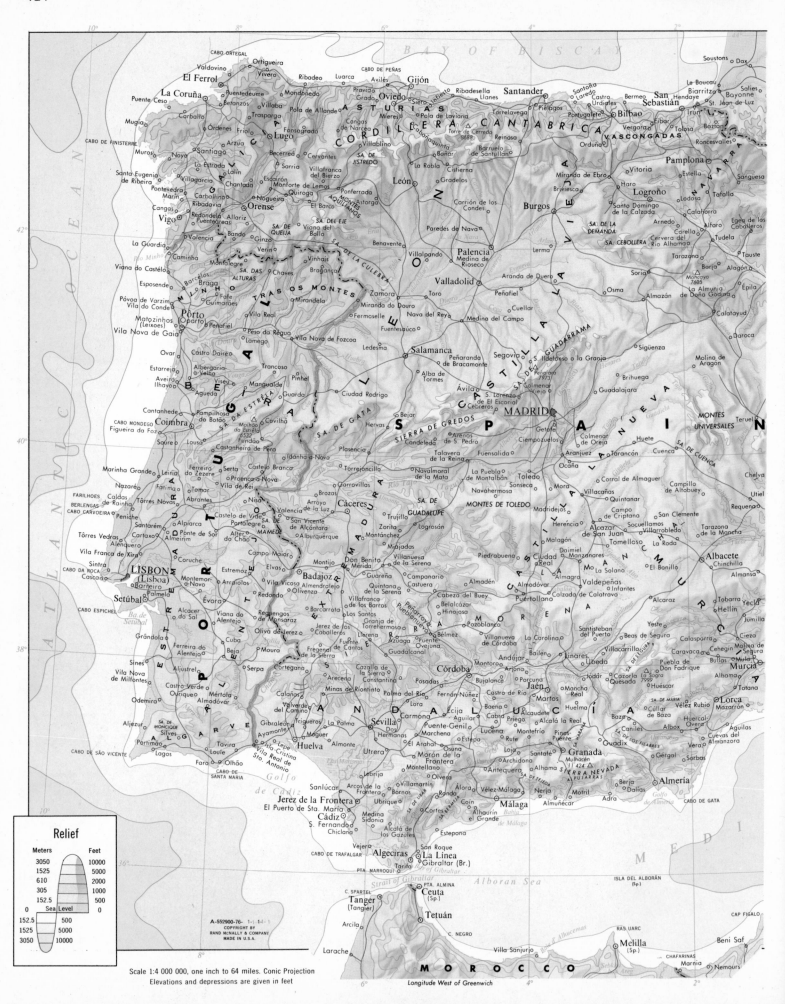

Relief

Meters		Feet
3050		10000
1525		5000
610		2000
305		1000
152.5		500
0	Sea Level	0
152.5		500
1525		5000
3050		10000

A-552900-76- 1-1-1-1-1
COPYRIGHT BY
RAND McNALLY & COMPANY
MADE IN U.S.A.

Scale 1:4 000 000, one inch to 64 miles. Conic Projection
Elevations and depressions are given in feet

Longitude West of Greenwich

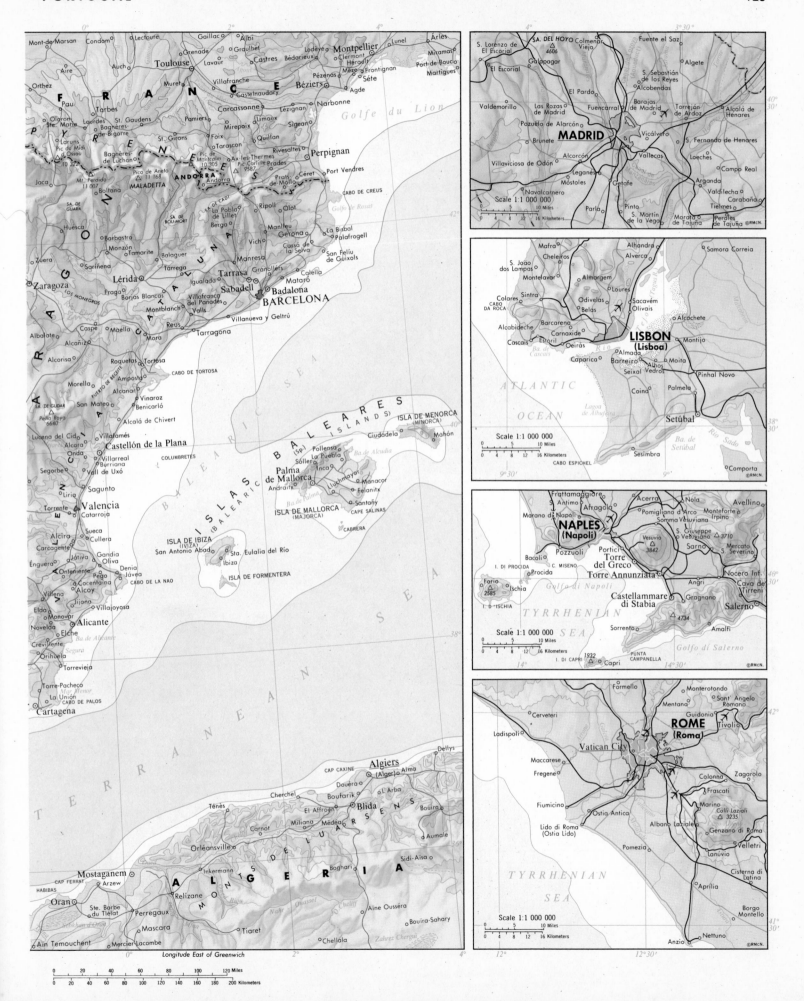

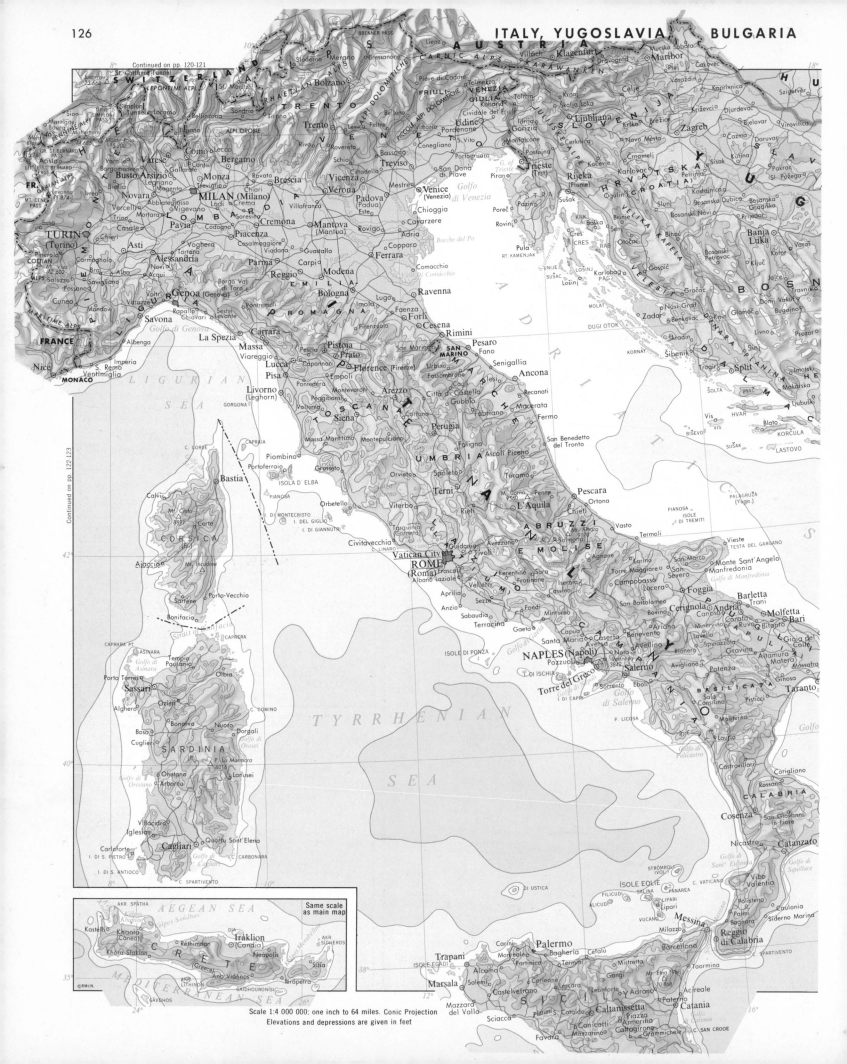

Continued on pp. 120-121

Continued on pp. 122-123

Scale 1:4 000 000; one inch to 64 miles. Conic Projection
Elevations and depressions are given in feet

Relief

Feet					
5000	2000	1000	500	0	
				Sea Level	500

Meters					
1525	610	305	152.5	0	
				152.5	

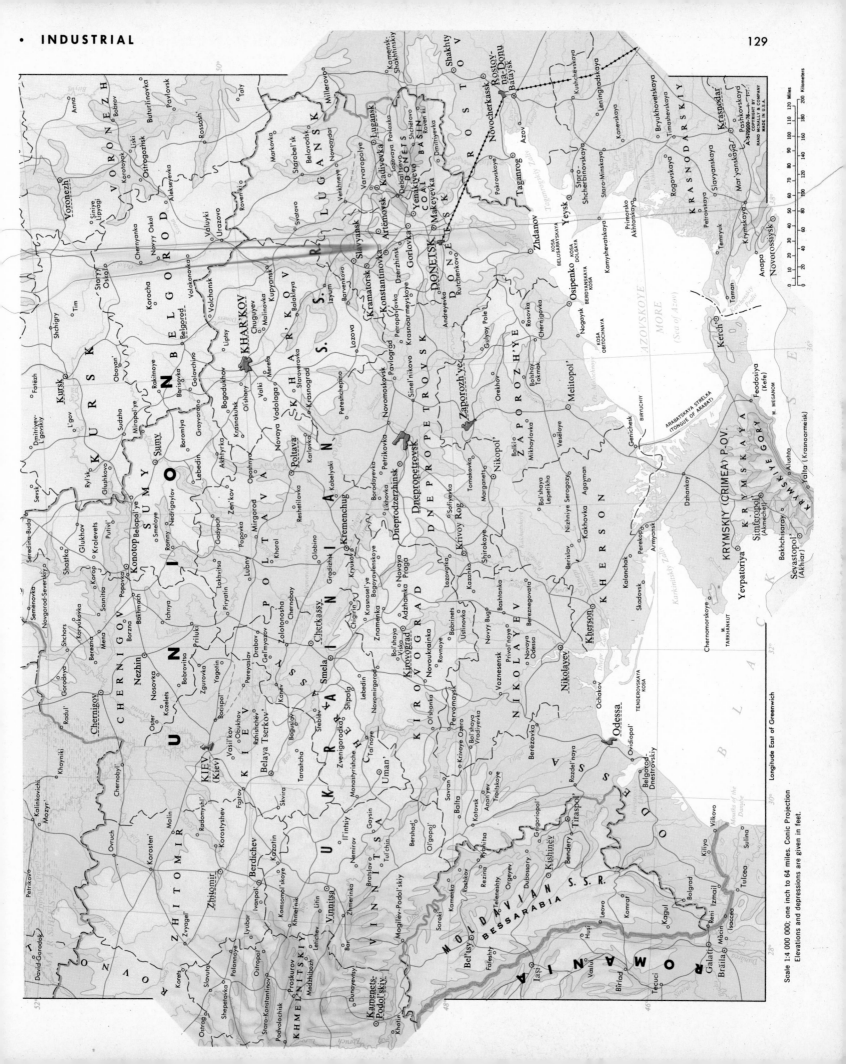

Scale 1:4 000 000; one inch to 64 miles. Conic Projection
Elevations and depressions are given in feet.

Longitude East of Greenwich

COPYRIGHT BY
RAND M℠NALLY & COMPANY
MADE IN U.S.A.
A-57900-76
Pochkovskaya

Scale 1:20 000 000; one inch to 315 miles.
Lambert's Azimuthal, Equal Area Projection
Elevations and depressions are given in feet

Relief

Meters		Feet
3050		10 000
1525		5000
610		2000
305		1000
152.5		500
Sea Level		0
152.5	Below Sea Level	500
1525		5000
3050		10 000

SEVERNAYA ZEMLYA
(NORTHERN LAND)

M. CHELYUSKIN

P-OV
GORY TAYMYR
BYRRANGA

BOL'SHOY BEGICHEV

DE-LONGA

NOVOSIBIRSKIYE O-VA
(NEW SIBERIAN ISLANDS)

FADDEYA   NOVAYA SIBIR'

KOTEL'NYY

MALYY LYAKHOVSKIY
LYAKHOVSKIY

M. SVYATOY NOS

M. BILOR-KHAYA

LAPTEV SEA

EAST SIBERIAN SEA

VRANGELYA
(WRANGEL)

M. SHELAGSKIY

AYON

Mys Arbachik
Nizhne-Kolymsk
Srednei-Kolymsk
Zyryanka
Zashiversk

M. MEDVEZH'I

Anadyr'

CHUKOTSKOYE NAGORYE

KHREBET GYDAN (KOLYMSKIY)

KORYAKSKIY KHREBET

Markovo
Penzhino

Arctic Circle

Nordvik
Ust'-Olenek

Tiksi
Bulun

Kazach'ye
Abyy
Verkhoyansk

KHREBET CHERSKOGO

A. S. S. R.

Gora Chen
10 171

Zhigansk

Oymyakon

Magadan

Okhotsk

Olyutorskiy
Palana

P-OV KAMCHATKA

Ust'-Kamchatsk

KOMANDORSKIE OSTROVA

KARAGINSKIY

Khatanga

Noril'sk

GORY PUTORANA

Igarka

Turukhansk

VILYUYSKIYE GORY

YAKUT

VERKHOYANSKIY KHREBET

Vilyuysk

Yakutsk

Amga   Ust'-Maya

Aldanskoye

Nel'kan

Ayan

Chumikan

Nikolayevsk-na-Amure

M. ALEVINA

Verkhne-Kamchatsk

Kyo-Nevskoye (vol.)
15 912

Petropavlovsk-Kamchatskiy

Ust'-Bol'sheretsk

M. LOPATKA

SEA OF OKHOTSK

SHANTAR

M. VELIZAVETY
Okha
M. TERPENIYA

SAKHALIN (Sov. Union)

Aleksandrovsk-Sakhalinskiy

Poronaysk
Uglegorsk

M. TERPENIYA

KURIL ISLANDS

ONEKOTAN

Baykit

Yartsevo

G. Polkan
3543

Yeniseysk

FEDERATED SOCIALIST REPUBLIC

Mukhtuya

Peleduy
Vitim

G. Golets Purpula
5377

PATOM PLATEAU

Bodaybo

Golets-Skalistyy
9186

Suntar

Olekminsk

Aldan

Tommot

STANOVOY KHREBET

DZHUGDZHUR KHREBET

Tyndinskiy

Zeya

KHREBET BUREINSKIY

Komsomol'sk na-Amure

Sovetskaya Gavan'

Yuzhno-Sakhalinsk

Kholmsk
Korsakov

KUNASHIRI

ITURUP

Kirensk

Ilimsk

NETSK   Krasnoyarsk

Bogotol

Kansk

Balakhta

Kuznetskiy

SIN

Nizhneudinsk

G. Piramida
10 801

Tulun

Tayshet

Bratsk

Zhigalovo

Kachugo

Nizhne-Angarsk

BURYAT

BAYKAL'SKIY KHREBET

Barguzin

A. S. S. R.

Ulan-Ude

Sretensk

Chita

Nerchinsk
Nerchinskiy Zavod

Skovorodino

Svobodnyy

Belogorsk

Ust' Tyrma

Bureya

Birobidzhan

Khabarovsk

KHREBET SIKHOTE ALIN'

Iman

Spassk
Dal'niy

Ussuriysk

Vladivostok

Minusinsk

Abakan

SAYAN KHREBET

Munku Sardyk
12 821

Kutuliko

Cheremkhovo

Angarsk

Irkutsk

Kyren

Gorodok

Petrovsk-Zabaykal'skiy

Kyakhta

YABLONOVYY KHREBET

Aginskoye

Borzya

NERCHINSKIY KHREBET

Nerchinskiy Zavod

GREATER KHINGAN MTS.

Blagoveshchensk

Nench'eng

LESSER KHINGAN MTS.

Suihua

Ch'ich'ihaerh
(Tsitsihar)   Hailun

Pok'ot'u

Kyzyl

TANNU-OLA

Aksha

TSASATA

HANGAYN NURUU
(KHANGAI MTS.)

Jirgalanta   Jibholanta

Tsasata Bogda Uula
13 865

Ulaan Baator

Oridor Haan

MONGOLIA

Sayr Usa

GOBI OR SHAMO
(DESERT)

Wench'üan

T'aonan

Lupei

Fuyü

HAERHPIN (Harbin)

Mutanchiang

CH'ANGCH'UN

Liaoyüan

Tunhua

MANCHURIA

Chilin

Najin

Chŏngjin

Hunch'un

Suchan
Nakhodka

Arsen'yev

Ol'ga

Spassk

P'oli

Dal'niy

P'yongyang

KOREA

SEOUL

Ch'ihfeng

INNER MONGOLIAN AUT. REG.

CHINA

Che'ngte

MUKDEN (Shenyang)

FUSHUN

Weich'ang

Changchiak'ou

Fengchen

PEKING (Peiching)

TIENTSIN (Tienching)

LÜTA

Kaesong
Andong

Taegu

PUSAN

P'o Hai

SHANTUNG PANTAO

YELLOW SEA

Ch'ingyüan

Korea Bay

HOKKAIDO

Otaru   Sapporo

Wakkanai

Esashi   Hakodate

Aomori

HONSHŪ

Akita

Sakata

Nagaoka   Sendai

JAPAN

Matsue   Tottori   KŌBE   KYŌTO

TŌKYŌ

Kanazawa

NAGOYA

Hiroshima   Okayama   OSAKA

Kōchi

KITAKYUSHŪ

Fukuoka

Nagaoka

A-570000-76
COPYRIGHT BY
RAND McNALLY & COMPANY
MADE IN U.S.A.

Longitude East of Greenwich

| 0 | 100 | 200 | 300 | 400 | 500 | 600 Miles |
| 0 | 200 | 400 | 600 | 800 | 1000 Kilometers |

Relief

Meters	Feet	
3050	10000	
1525	5000	
610	2000	
305	1000	
152.5	500	
0	Sea Level	
	0	
152.5	500	
1525	5000	
3050	10000	Below Sea Level

Continued on pages 112-113

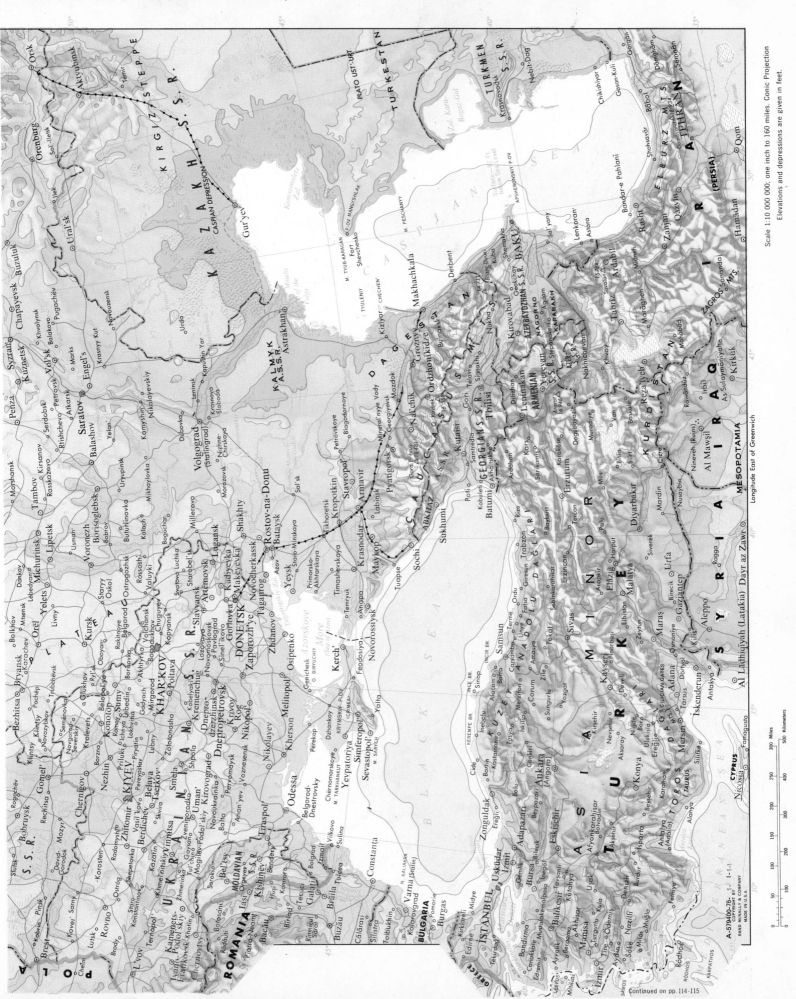

Scale 1:10 000 000; one inch to 160 miles. Conic Projection
Elevations and depressions are given in feet.

Longitude East of Greenwich

Continued on pp. 114-115

A-579400-76-1 1-1-1
COPYRIGHT BY
RAND M^cNALLY & COMPANY
MADE IN U.S.A.

Scale 1:16 000 000; one inch to 250 miles Conic Projection
Elevations and depressions are given in feet.

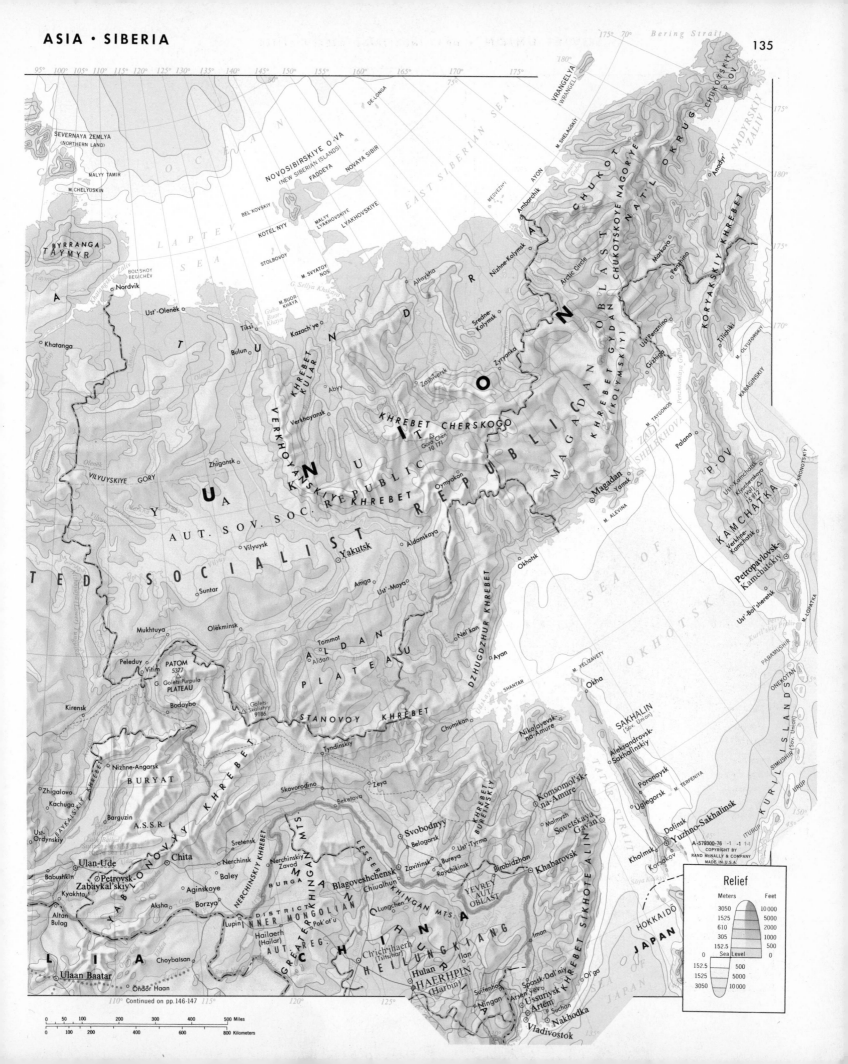

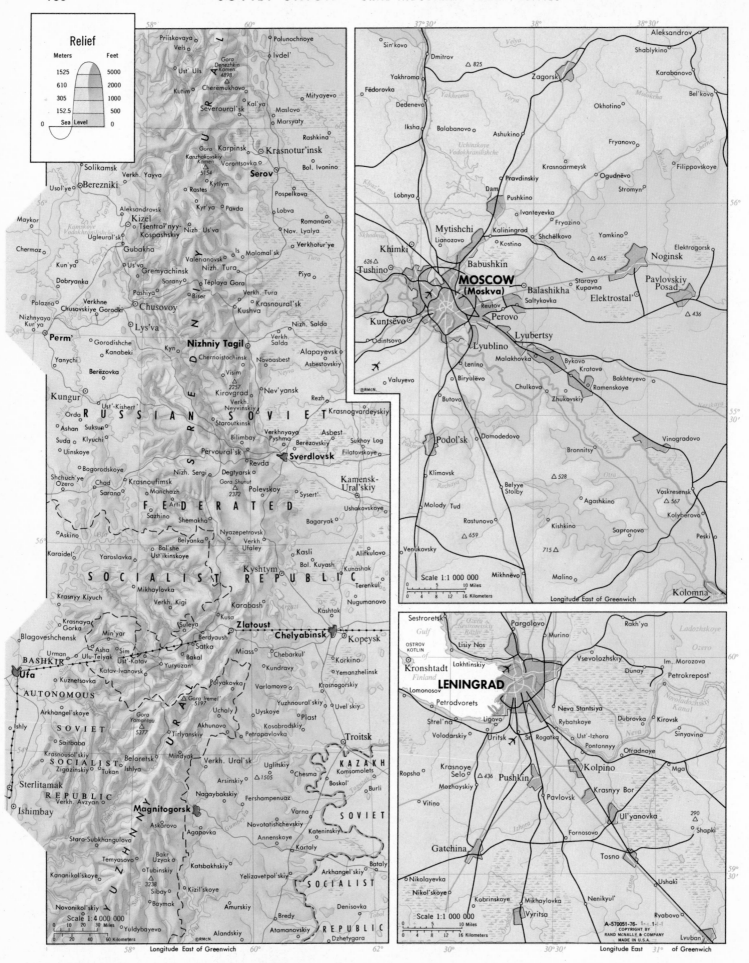

Relief

Meters		Feet
1525		5000
610		2000
305		1000
152.5		500
0	Sea Level	0

Scale 1:4 000 000

Scale 1:1 000 000

Scale 1:1 000 000

Longitude East of Greenwich

Longitude East of Greenwich

A-570051-76-
COPYRIGHT BY
RAND McNALLY & COMPANY
MADE IN U.S.A.

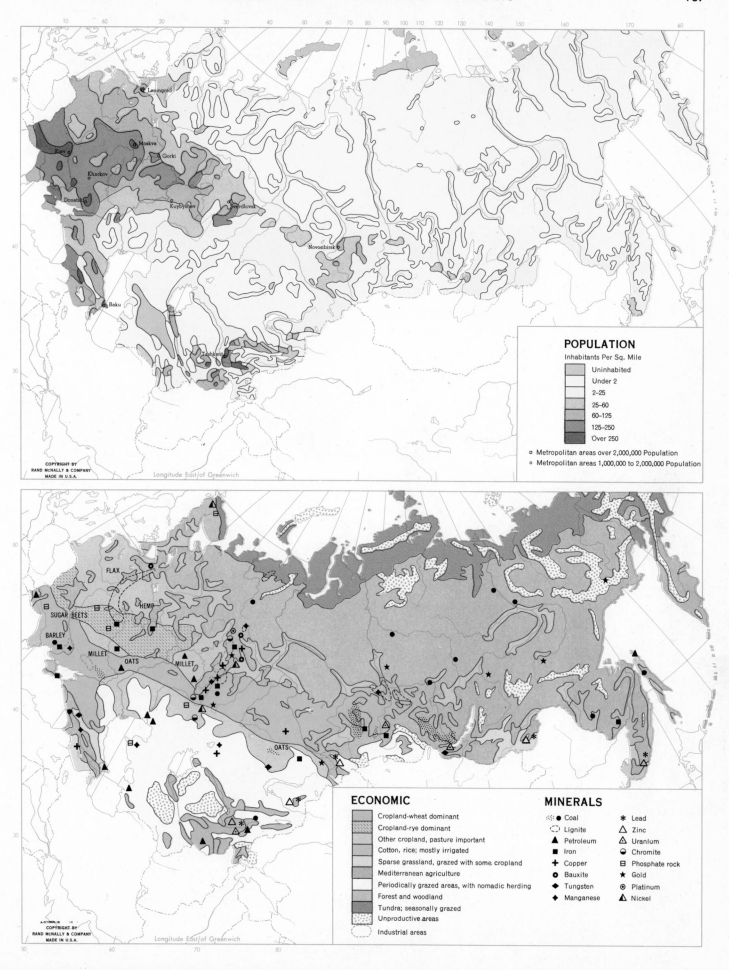

POPULATION

Inhabitants Per Sq. Mile

- Uninhabited
- Under 2
- 2–25
- 25–60
- 60–125
- 125–250
- Over 250

□ Metropolitan areas over 2,000,000 Population
○ Metropolitan areas 1,000,000 to 2,000,000 Population

COPYRIGHT BY
RAND MCNALLY & COMPANY
MADE IN U.S.A.

Longitude East of Greenwich

ECONOMIC

- Cropland-wheat dominant
- Cropland-rye dominant
- Other cropland, pasture important
- Cotton, rice; mostly irrigated
- Sparse grassland, grazed with some cropland
- Mediterranean agriculture
- Periodically grazed areas, with nomadic herding
- Forest and woodland
- Tundra; seasonally grazed
- Unproductive areas
- Industrial areas

MINERALS

- ● Coal
- Lignite
- ▲ Petroleum
- ■ Iron
- ✚ Copper
- ◉ Bauxite
- ◆ Tungsten
- ◆ Manganese
- ✳ Lead
- △ Zinc
- △ Uranium
- ◌ Chromite
- ⊟ Phosphate rock
- ★ Gold
- ⊙ Platinum
- △ Nickel

COPYRIGHT BY
RAND MCNALLY & COMPANY
MADE IN U.S.A.

Longitude East of Greenwich

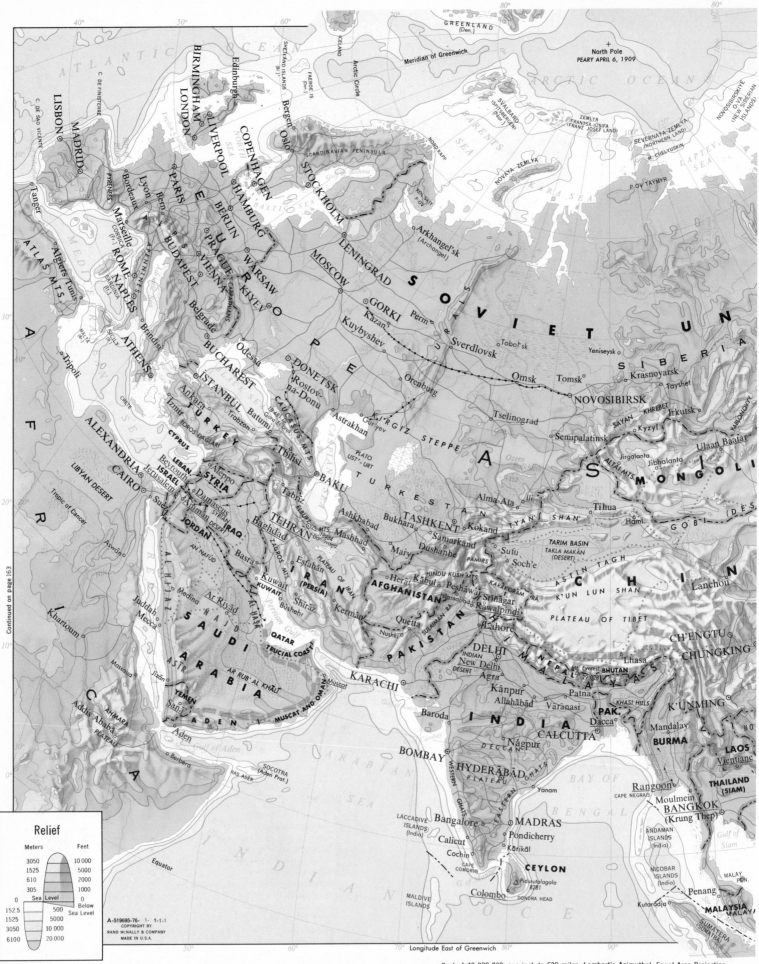

Scale 1:40 000 000; one inch to 630 miles. Lambert's Azimuthal, Equal Area Projection
Elevations and depressions are given in feet

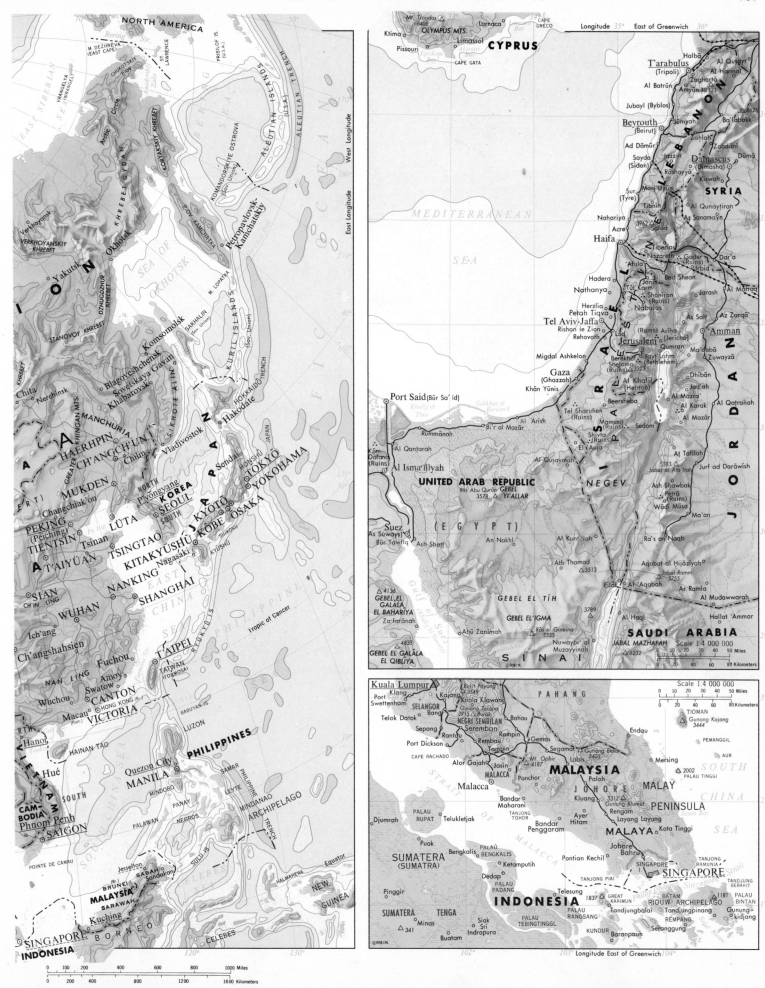

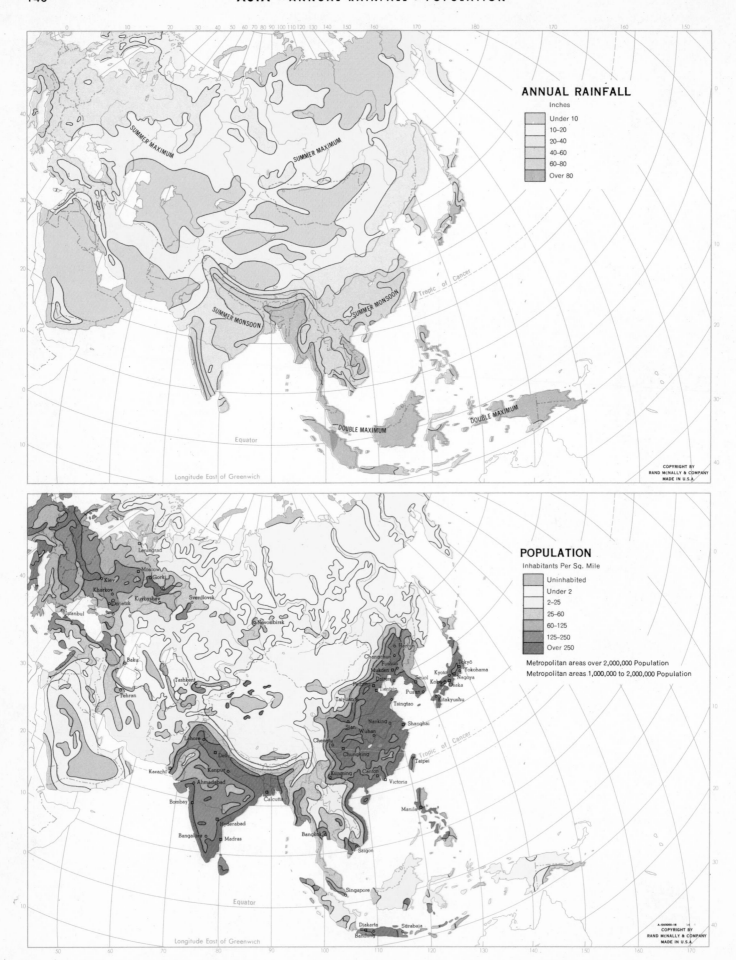

ANNUAL RAINFALL

Inches

Under 10
10–20
20–40
40–60
60–80
Over 80

SUMMER MAXIMUM

SUMMER MAXIMUM

SUMMER MAXIMUM

SUMMER MONSOON

SUMMER MONSOON

SUMMER MONSOON

Tropic of Cancer

DOUBLE MAXIMUM

DOUBLE MAXIMUM

Equator

Longitude East of Greenwich

POPULATION

Inhabitants Per Sq. Mile

Uninhabited
Under 2
2–25
25–60
60–125
125–250
Over 250

Metropolitan areas over 2,000,000 Population
Metropolitan areas 1,000,000 to 2,000,000 Population

Leningrad
Moscow
Kiev
Gorki
Kharkov
Donetsk
Kuybyshev
Sverdlovsk
Istanbul
Novosibirsk
Baku
Tashkent
Tehran
Harbin
Changchun
Fushun
Mukden
Kyoto
Tōkyō
Yokohama
Dairen
Seoul
Nagoya
Kobe
Osaka
Tientsin
Pusan
Taiyuan
Kitakyushu
Tsingtao
Nanking
Shanghai
Sian
Wuhan
Chengtu
Chungking
Taipei
Lahore
Delhi
Kunming
Canton
Kanpur
Victoria
Karachi
Ahmadabad
Calcutta
Bombay
Hyderabad
Manila
Bangalore
Madras
Bangkok
Saigon
Tropic of Cancer
Singapore
Equator
Longitude East of Greenwich
Djakarta
Surabaja
Bandung

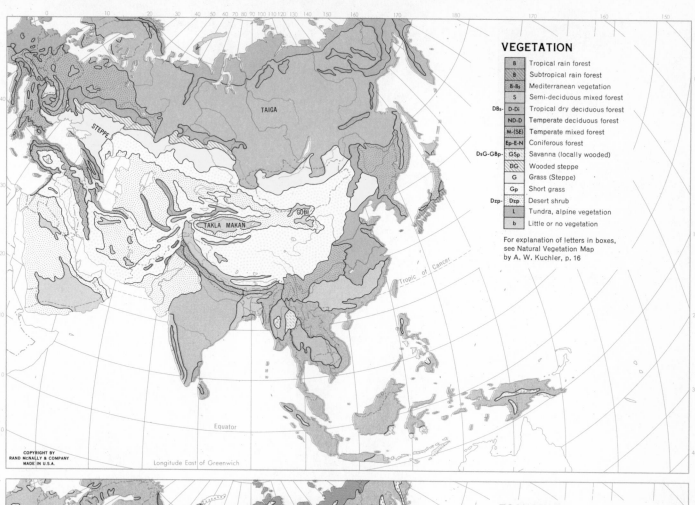

VEGETATION

B	Tropical rain forest
B	Subtropical rain forest
B-Bs	Mediterranean vegetation
S	Semi-deciduous mixed forest
DBs- D-Di	Tropical dry deciduous forest
ND-D	Temperate deciduous forest
M-(SE)	Temperate mixed forest
Ep-E-N	Coniferous forest
DsG-GBp- GSp	Savanna (locally wooded)
DG	Wooded steppe
G	Grass (Steppe)
Gp	Short grass
Dzp- Dzp	Desert shrub
L	Tundra, alpine vegetation
b	Little or no vegetation

For explanation of letters in boxes,
see Natural Vegetation Map
by A. W. Kuchler, p. 16

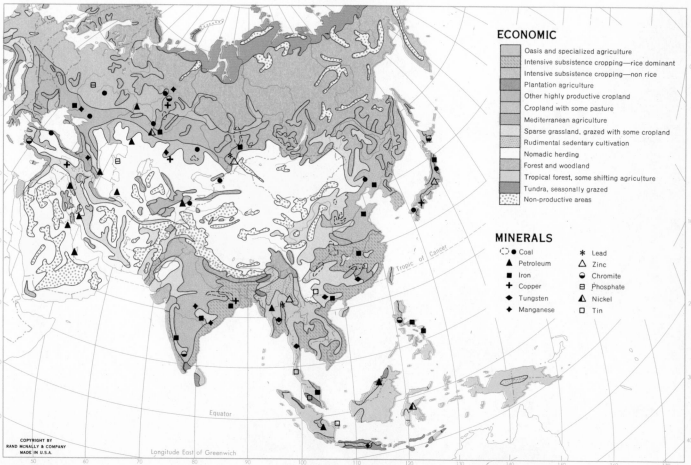

ECONOMIC

	Oasis and specialized agriculture
	Intensive subsistence cropping—rice dominant
	Intensive subsistence cropping—non rice
	Plantation agriculture
	Other highly productive cropland
	Cropland with some pasture
	Mediterranean agriculture
	Sparse grassland, grazed with some cropland
	Rudimental sedentary cultivation
	Nomadic herding
	Forest and woodland
	Tropical forest, some shifting agriculture
	Tundra, seasonally grazed
	Non-productive areas

MINERALS

⬡ ●	Coal	✳	Lead
▲	Petroleum	△	Zinc
■	Iron	◖	Chromite
✚	Copper	⊟	Phosphate
◆	Tungsten	◬	Nickel
◆	Manganese	▢	Tin

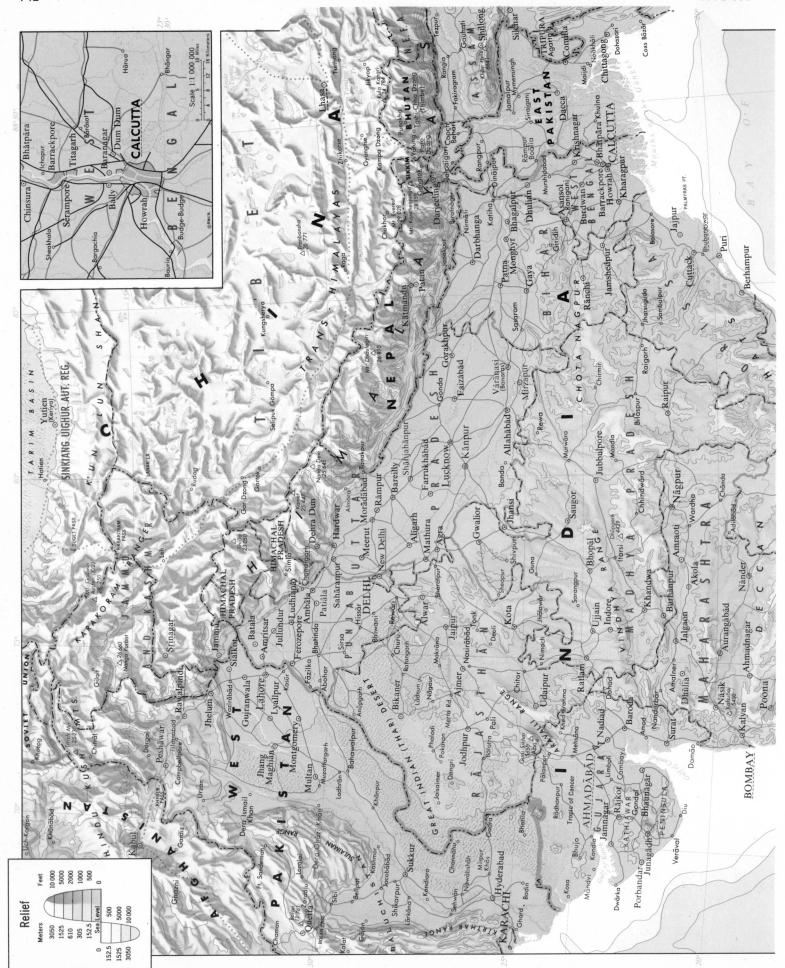

Scale 1:1 000 000

CALCUTTA

WEST BENGAL

Chinsura
Bhātpāra
Ichapore
Barrackpore
Serampore
Titagarh
Sheakhala
Bally
Bargachia
Howrah
Bauria
Budge-Budge
Dum Dum
Baranagar
Barāsat
Hārua
Bhāngar

Relief

Meters	Feet
3050	10 000
1525	5000
610	2000
305	1000
152.5	500
0	Sea Level
152.5	500
1525	5000
3050	10 000

BOMBAY

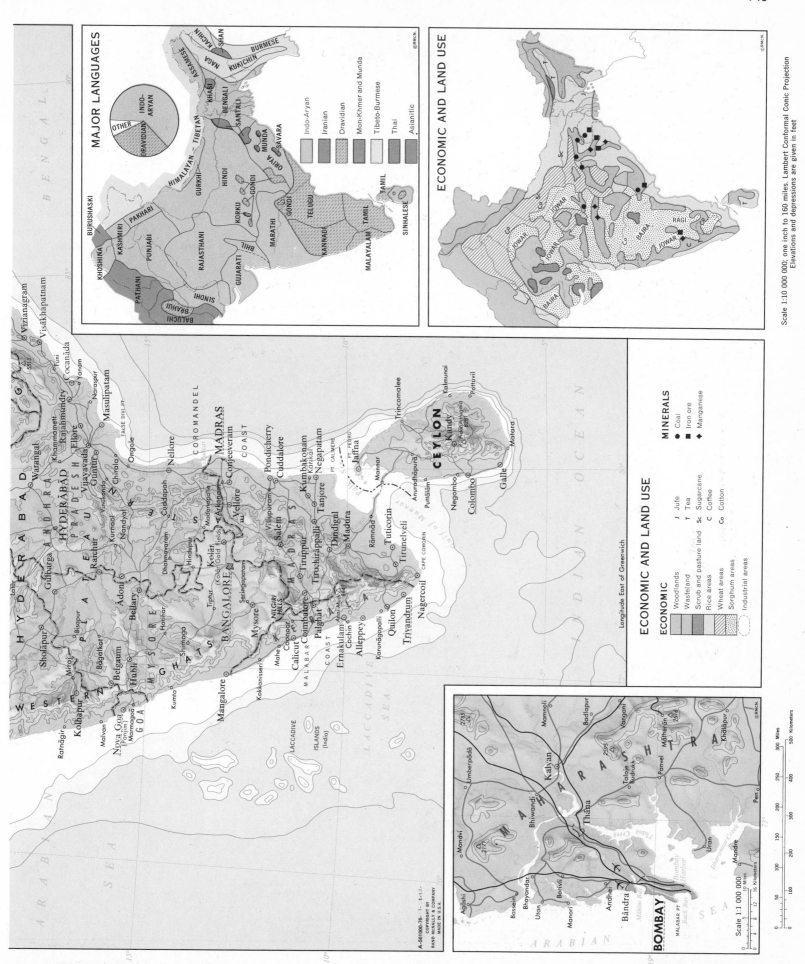

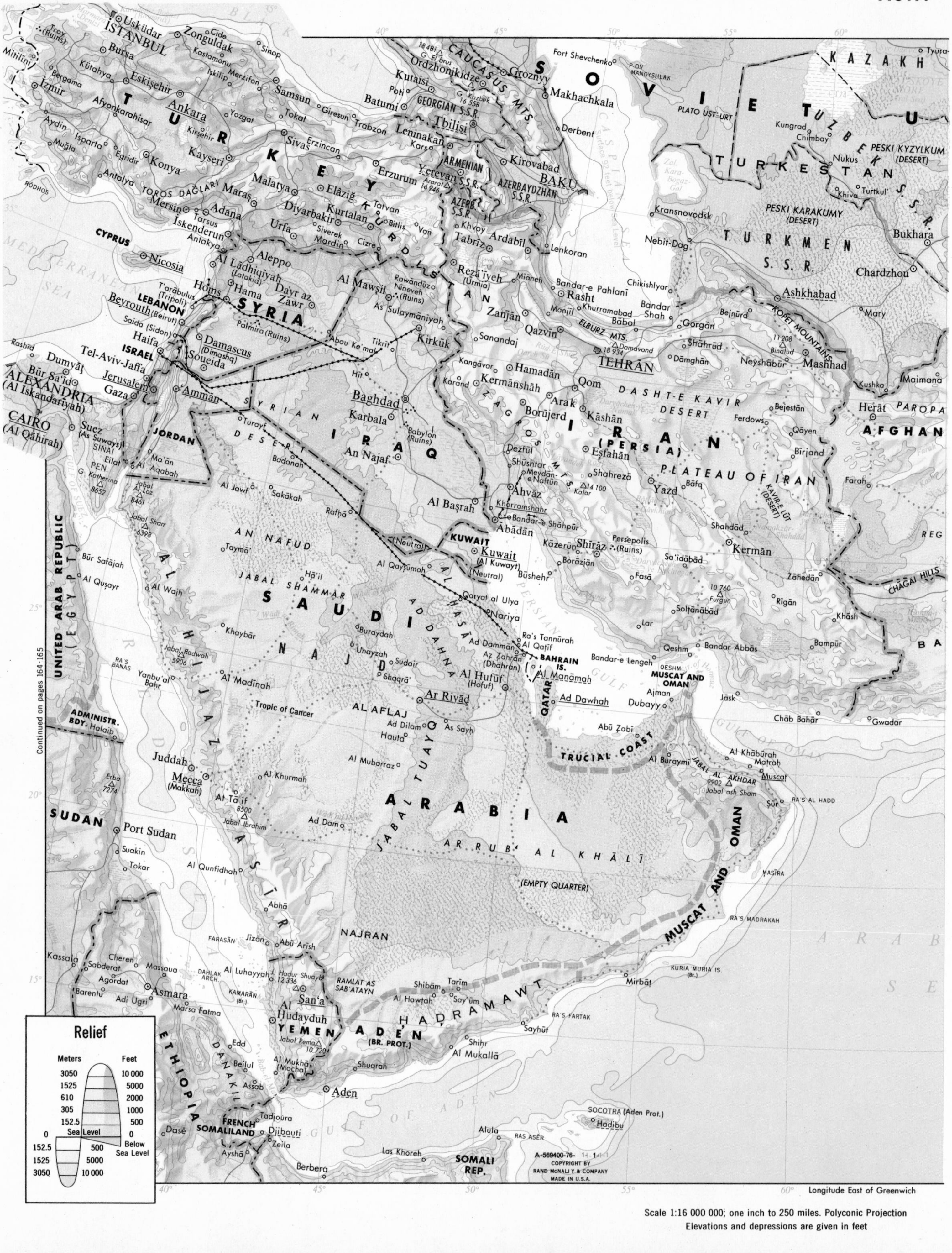

Üsküdar
ISTANBUL
Troy (Ruins)
Mitilini
Bergama
İzmir
Bursa
Kütahya
Eskişehir
Ankara
Afyonkarahisar
Aydın
Isparta
Eğridir
Muğla
Antalya
Konya
Kayseri
Kırşehir
TURKEY
TOROS DAĞLARI
Adana
Tarsus
Mersin
İskenderun
Antakya
RODHOS
Zonguldak
Kastamonu
Merzifon
İskilip
Cide
Sinop
Samsun
Giresun
Trabzon
Tokat
Sivas
Erzincan
Malatya
Maraş
Elâzığ
Diyarbakır
Urfa
Siverek
Mardin
Cizre
Kurtalan
BLACK SEA
CAUCASUS MTS.
Groznyy
Fort Shevchenko
Makhachkala
Ordzhonikidze
Kutaisi
Poti
Batumi
GEORGIAN S.S.R.
Tbilisi
Leninakan
Kars
Kirovabad
Derbent
ARMENIAN S.S.R.
Yerevan
Ararat
16 946
AZERBAYDZHAN S.S.R.
BAKU
AZERB. S.S.R.
Erzurum
Ağrı
Tatvan
Bitlis
Van
Khvoy
Ardabil
Tabriz
Rawandūz
Nineveh (Ruins)
Rezā'īyeh (Urmia)
Mīāneh
Bandar-e Pahlavi
Lenkoran
SOVIET
KAZAKH
Fort Shevchenko
P-OV MANGYSHLAK
PLATO UST-URT
KUNGRAD
Chimbay
Nukus
TUZBEK
TURKESTAN
PESKI KYZYLKUM (DESERT)
Khiva
Turtkul' S.S.R.
Bukhara
Kransnovodsk
Nebit-Dag
TURKMEN S.S.R.
PESKI KARAKUMY (DESERT)
Chardzhou
Ashkhabad
Mary
Kushko
Maimana
CYPRUS
Nicosia
MEDITERRANEAN SEA
Aleppo
Al Lādhiqīyah (Latakia)
Homs
Hama
Ţarābulus (Tripoli)
LEBANON
Beyrouth (Beirut)
Saida (Sidon)
Haifa
Tel-Aviv-Jaffa
ISRAEL
Jerusalem
Gaza
Rashīd
Dumyāţ
Bur Sa'īd
ALEXANDRIA (Al Iskandarīyah)
CAIRO (Al Qāhirah)
Suez (As Suways)
SINAI PEN.
G. Katherina
Jabal Katrina 8652
Amman
JORDAN
SYRIA
Dayr az Zawr
Palmira (Ruins)
Damascus (Dimashq)
Soueida
Abou Ke'mal
Tikrīt
Al Mawşil
As Sulaymānīyah
Kirkūk
Hīt
Baghdad
Karbalā
An Najaf
Babylon (Ruins)
IRAQ
Turayf
SYRIAN DESERT
Badanah
Al Jawf
Sakākah
Rafhā
Ma'ān
Al 'Aqabah
Elat
Jabal Sharr 8398
Taymā
AN NAFUD
Al Wajh
Khaybar
Jabal Radwah 5906
Yanbu' al Baḩr
Al Madīnah
SAUDI
NAJD
JABAL SHAMMAR
Ḩā'il
Buraydah
'Unayzah
Sudair
Shaqrā
Ad Dilam
Hauta
As Sayh
AL AFLAJ
Ar Riyāḑ
Al Kharmah
Al Mubarraz
Al Quşayr
Būr Safājah
Al Qunfidhah
Erba 7274
Juddah
Mecca (Makkah)
Aţ Ţā'if 8500
Jabal Ibrāhīm
Ad Dam
Ṭurayf
Rawandūz
Zanjān
Qazvīn
Sanandaj
Hamadān
Kermānshāh
Kangāvar
Karand
Qom
Arāk
Borūjerd
Kāshān
TEHRĀN
Damāvand 18 934
Bābol
Gorgān
Shāhrūd
Dāmghān
Neyshābūr
Mashhad
Bejnūrd
KOPET MOUNTAINS
11 208
Binalūd
IRAN (PERSIA)
Eşfahān
Shahreẕā
Yazd
PLATEAU OF IRAN
Bāfq
Ferdows
Qāyen
Bīrjand
Farah
HERĀT
AFGHAN
PAROPA
ZAGROS MTS.
Deẕfūl
Shūshtar
Meydān-e Naftūn
Kalar 14 100
Ahvāz
Khorramshahr
Bandar-e Shāhpūr
Ābādān
Al Başrah
KUWAIT
Kuwait (Al Kuwayt)
(Neutral)
Al Qayşūmah
Qaryat al Ulyā
Nariya
Ad Dammam
Al Qaţīf
Az Zahrān (Dhahran)
BAHRAIN IS.
Al Manāmah
Al Ḩufūf (Hofuf)
QATAR
Ad Dawhah
Abū Zabī
Persepolis (Ruins)
Kāzerūn
Shīrāz
Borāzjān
Būshehr
Fasā
Lar
Sa'īdābād
10 760
Furgun
Kermān
Shahdād
KAVIR-E LŪT (DESERT)
DASHT-E KAVIR DESERT
Zāhedān
Solţānābād
Rīgān
Khāsh
Bampūr
Bandar-e Lengeh
Qeshm
Bandar Abbās
Jāsk
Chāb Bahār
Gwadar
BA
CHAGAI HILLS
REG
MUSCAT AND OMAN
Ajman
Dubayy
Al Buraymī
JABAL AL AKHDAR
9902
Jabal ash Sham
Al Khābūrah
Matrah
Muscat
Sūr
RA'S AL HADD
TRUCIAL COAST
SUDAN
Port Sudan
Suakin
Tokar
Kassala
Cheren
Massaua
Sabderat
Agordat
Barentu
Asmara
Adi Ugri
Marsa Fatma
DAHLAK ARCH.
DANAKIL
ETHIOPIA
FRENCH SOMALILAND
Tadjoura
Djibouti
Zeila
Aysha
Dasē
Beilul
Edd
Assab
Al Ḩudaydah
San'a
Jabal Remā 10 720
Al Mukhā (Mocha)
YEMEN
Shuqrah
Al Luḩayyah
Jīzān
Abū Arīsh
FARASĀN
KAMARĀN (Br.)
Hodur Shuayb 12 336
RAMLAT AS SAB'ATAYN
Al Ḩawţah
Say'ūm
Shibām
Tarīm
HADRAMAWT
ADEN (BR. PROT.)
Aden
Shihr
Al Mukallā
Mirbāt
Sayhūt
RA'S FARTAK
GULF OF ADEN
SOCOTRA (Aden Prot.)
Hadibu
Alula
RAS ASER
Las Khoreh
Berbera
SOMALI REP.
SOMALI
ARABIA
AR RUB' AL KHĀLĪ
(EMPTY QUARTER)
AL HASĀ
ADDAHNA
JABAL TUWAYQ
AL HIJAZ
'ASĪR
NAJRAN
Abhā
AD DAHNA
Tropic of Cancer
MUSCAT AND OMAN
MAŞĪRA
RA'S MADRAKAH
KURIA MURIA IS. (Br.)
PERSIAN GULF
GULF OF OMAN
ARAB SEA
UNITED ARAB REPUBLIC (EGYPT)
RED SEA
RA'S BANAS
ADMINISTR. BDY. Halaib
AL HASĀ

Continued on pages 164-165

Relief

Meters		Feet
3050		10 000
1525		5000
610		2000
305		1000
152.5		500
0	Sea Level	0
152.5		500 Below
1525		5000 Sea Level
3050		10 000

A-569400-76- 14- 1-
COPYRIGHT BY
RAND McNALLY & COMPANY
MADE IN U.S.A.

Longitude East of Greenwich

Scale 1:16 000 000; one inch to 250 miles. Polyconic Projection
Elevations and depressions are given in feet

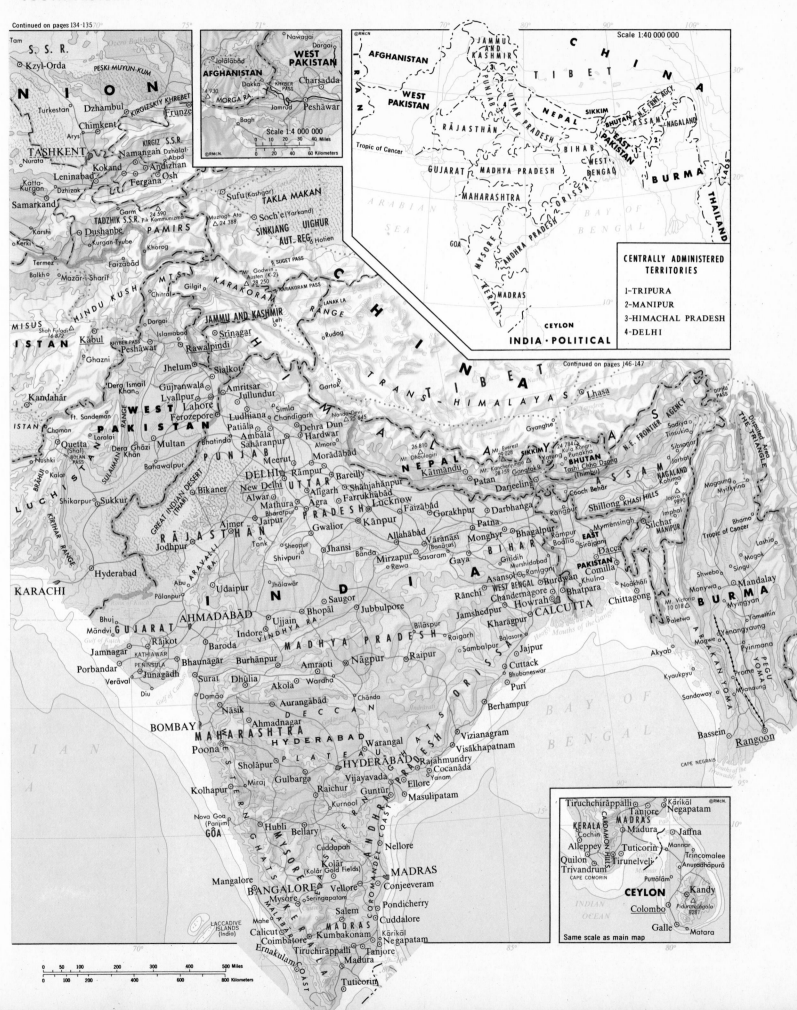

Continued on pages 134-135

Continued on pages 146-147

AFGHANISTAN

Scale 1:4 000 000

WEST PAKISTAN

CENTRALLY ADMINISTERED TERRITORIES

1-TRIPURA
2-MANIPUR
3-HIMACHAL PRADESH
4-DELHI

Scale 1:40 000 000

INDIA · POLITICAL

CEYLON

Same scale as main map

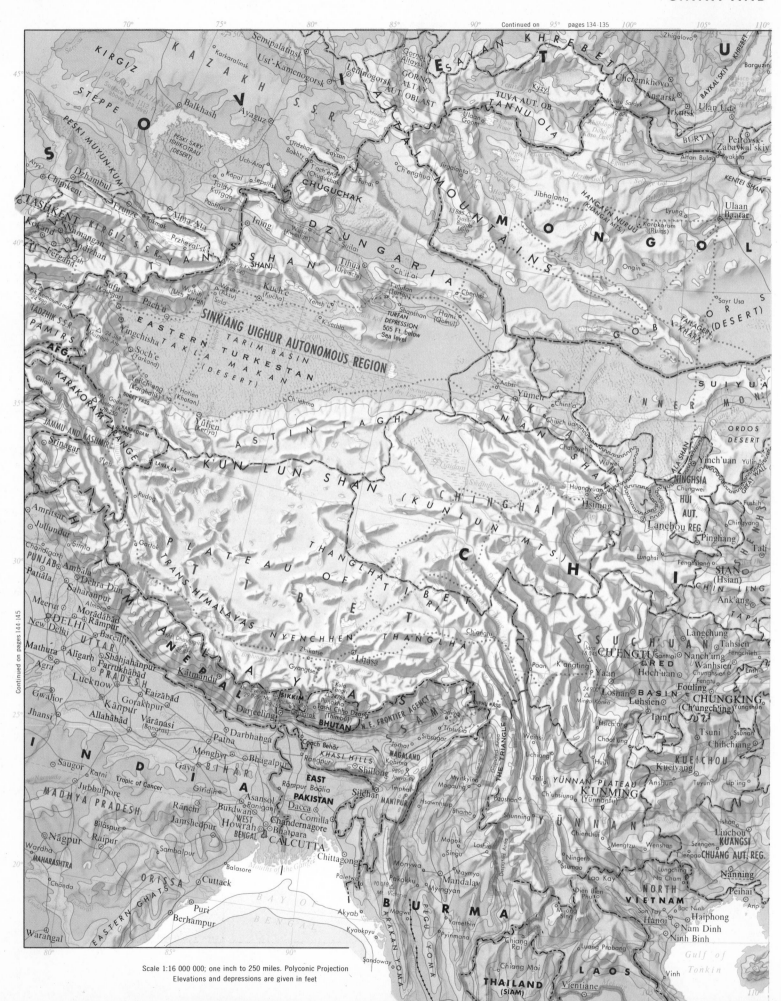

Continued on pages 134-135

Continued on pages 144-145

Scale 1:16 000 000; one inch to 250 miles. Polyconic Projection
Elevations and depressions are given in feet

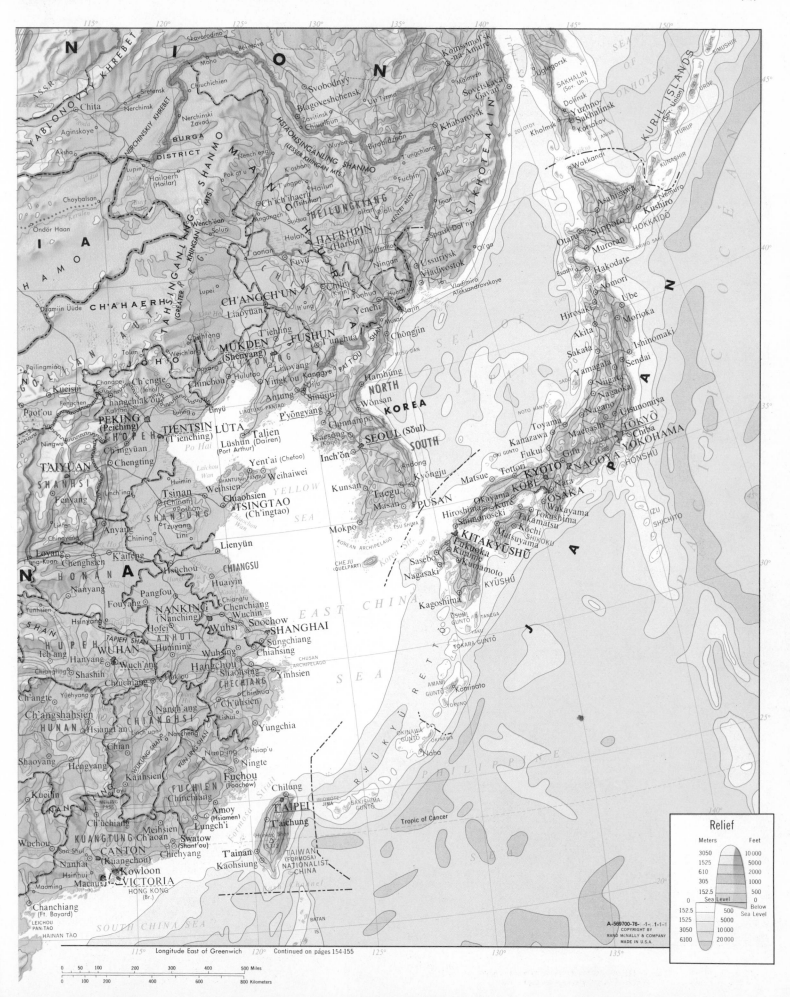

Continued on pages 154-155

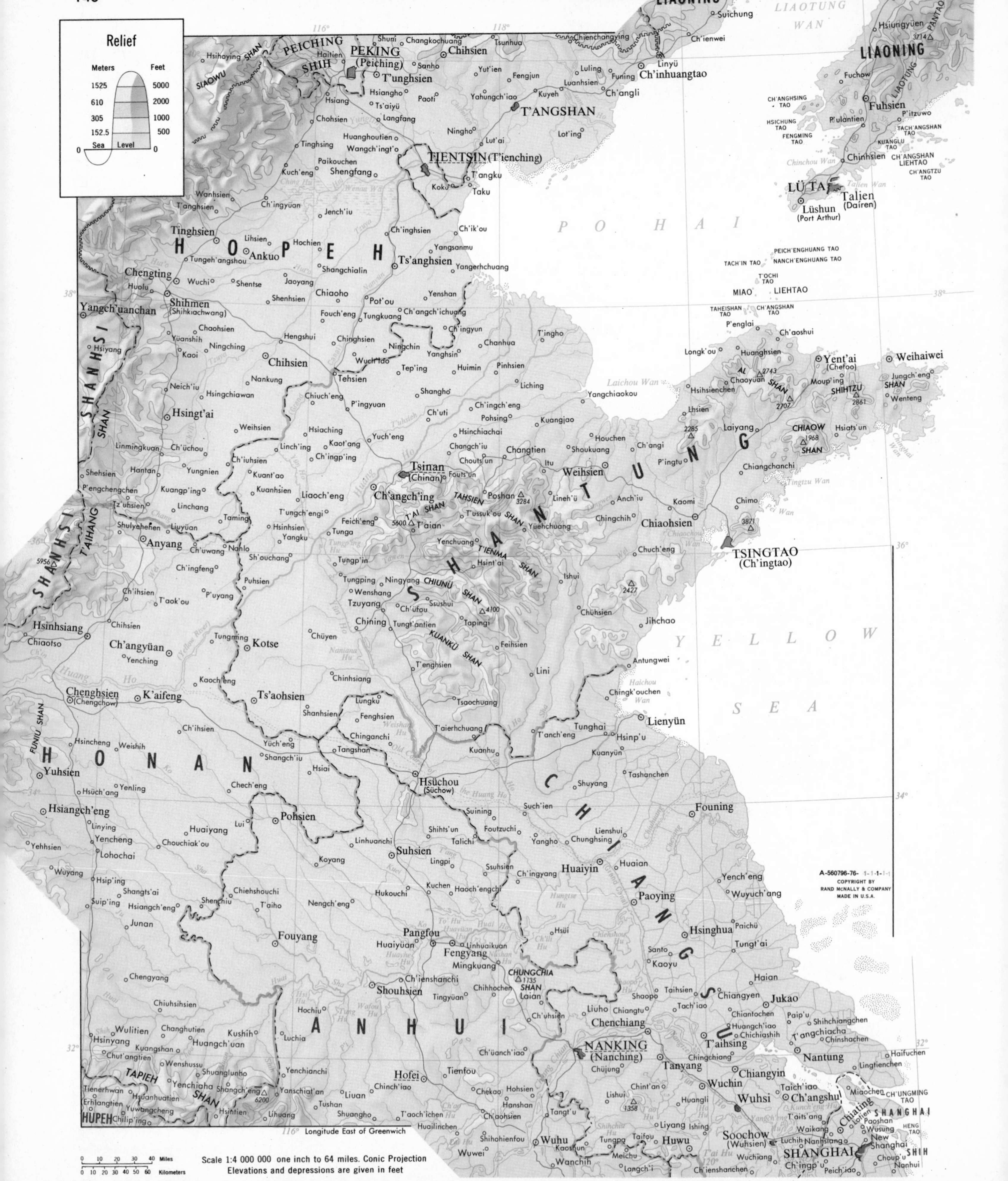

Relief

Meters	Feet
1525	5000
610	2000
305	1000
152.5	500
Sea Level	0

Scale 1:4 000 000 one inch to 64 miles. Conic Projection
Elevations and depressions are given in feet

0 10 20 30 40 Miles
0 10 20 30 40 50 60 Kilometers

Longitude East of Greenwich

A-560796-76- 1-1-1-1-1
COPYRIGHT BY
RAND McNALLY & COMPANY
MADE IN U.S.A.

LIAONING
LIAOTUNG WAN
POHAI
YELLOW SEA
HOPEH
HONAN
SHANTUNG
SHANSI
ANHUI
CHIANGSU
SHANGHAI
KIANGSU

PEKING (Peiching)
TIENTSIN (T'ienching)
T'ANGSHAN
Tsinan (Chinan)
TSINGTAO (Ch'ingtao)
Weihaiwei
Yent'ai (Chefoo)
NANKING (Nanching)
SHANGHAI
Soochow (Wuhsien)
Hsüchou (Süchow)
K'aifeng
Chenghsien (Chengchow)
Anyang
Hsinhsiang
Chiaotso
Yuhsien
Hsiangch'eng
Hofei
Pangfou
Fengyang
Shouhsien
Wuhu
Wuhsi
Ch'angshu
Nantung
Lü Tai
Talien (Dairen)
Lüshun (Port Arthur)
Fuhsien
Fuchow
Kaip'ing
Suichung
Ch'inhuangtao
Lienyün
Haichou Wan
Huaiyin
Paoying
Hsinghua
Tungt'ai
Haian
Jukao
T'aihsing
Chinkiang
Yangchow
Taichou

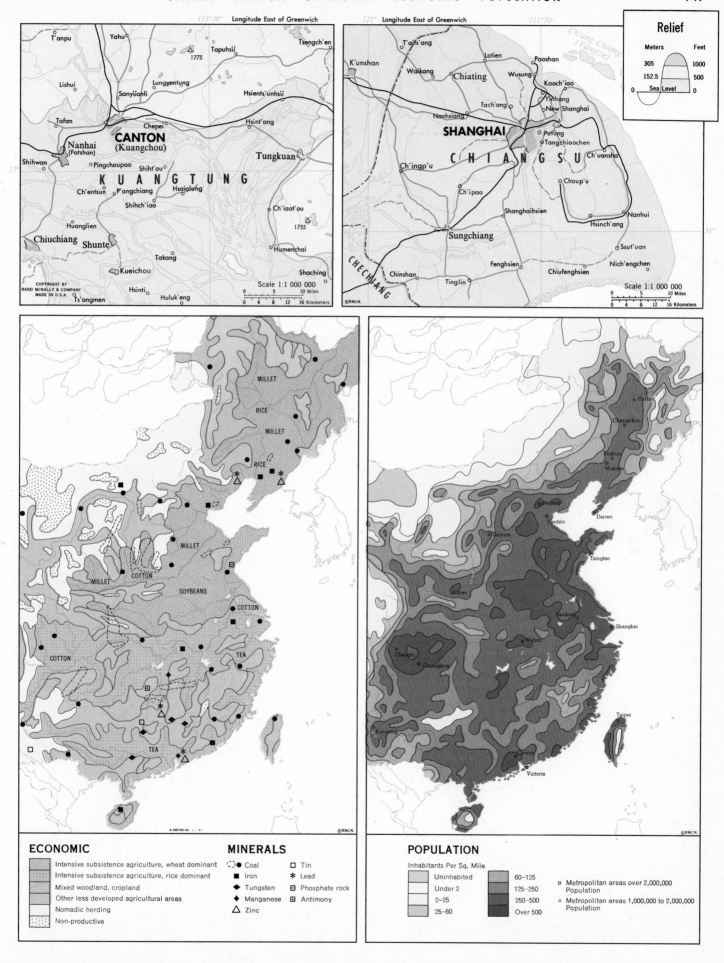

Canton map (upper left):

Longitude East of Greenwich 113°30'

T'anpu · Yahu · Tapuhsü · Tsengch'en · Lishui · Lungyentung · Hsients'unhsü · Sanyüanli · Hsint'ang · Tafan · Chepei · **CANTON (Kuangchou)** · **Nanhai (Fatshan)** · Tungkuan · Shihwan · Pingchoupao · Shiht'ou · **KUANGTUNG** · Ch'entsun · P'angchiang · Hsaiolung · Shihch'iao · Ch'iaot'ou · Huanglien · Chiuchiang · Shunte · Takang · Humenchai · Kueichou · Shaching · Hsinti · Huluk'eng · Ts'angmen

1775 · 1755

Scale 1:1 000 000
0 5 10 Miles
0 4 8 12 16 Kilometers

COPYRIGHT BY RAND McNALLY & COMPANY MADE IN U.S.A.

Shanghai map (upper right):

Longitude East of Greenwich 121° · 121°30'

T'aits'ang · Lotien · Paoshan · Ch'ang Chiang (Yangtze) · K'unshan · Waikang · Chiating · Wusung · Kaoch'iao · Yinhang · Tach'ang · New Shanghai · Nanhsiang · **SHANGHAI** · Putung · Tangchiaochen · Ch'uansha · **CHIANGSU** · Ch'ingp'u · Choup'u · Ch'ipao · Shanghaihsien · Nanhui · Hsinch'ang · Sungchiang · Ssut'uan · Nich'engchen · **CHECHIANG** · Chinshan · Fenghsien · Chiufenghsien · Tinglin

Scale 1:1 000 000
0 5 10 Miles
0 4 8 12 16 Kilometers

Relief

Meters		Feet
305		1000
152.5		500
0	Sea Level	0

Economic map (lower left):

MILLET · RICE · MILLET · RICE · MILLET · COTTON · MILLET · SOYBEANS · COTTON · COTTON · TEA · COTTON · TEA

ECONOMIC

- Intensive subsistence agriculture, wheat dominant
- Intensive subsistence agriculture, rice dominant
- Mixed woodland, cropland
- Other less developed agricultural areas
- Nomadic herding
- Non-productive

MINERALS

- ● Coal
- ■ Iron
- ◆ Tungsten
- ◆ Manganese
- △ Zinc
- □ Tin
- ✳ Lead
- ⊟ Phosphate rock
- ⊞ Antimony

Population map (lower right):

Harbin · Changchun · Fushun · Mukden · Peiping · Dairen · Tientsin · Taiyuan · Tsingtao · Sian · Nanking · Shanghai · Wuhan · Chengtu · Chungking · Kunming · Canton · Taipei · Victoria

POPULATION

Inhabitants Per Sq. Mile

- Uninhabited
- Under 2
- 2–25
- 25–60
- 60–125
- 125–250
- 250–500
- Over 500

- □ Metropolitan areas over 2,000,000 Population
- ○ Metropolitan areas 1,000,000 to 2,000,000 Population

©RMCN.

Continued on page 152

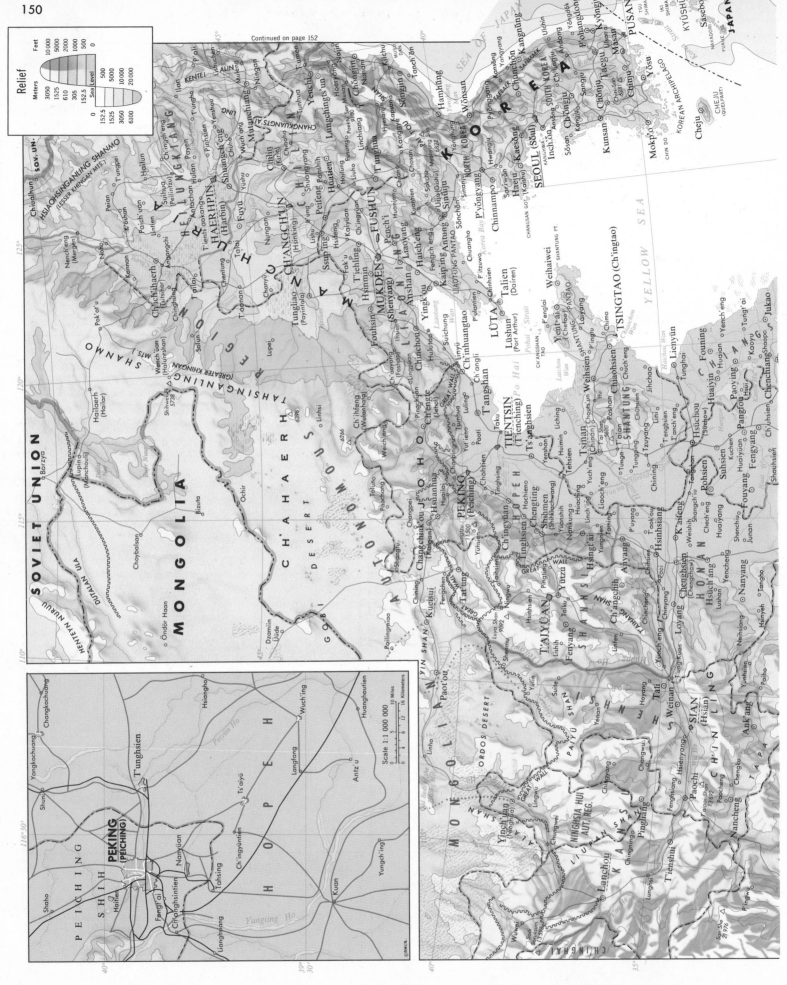

Scale 1:10 000 000; one inch to 160 miles, Lambert Conformal Conic Projection
Elevations and depressions are given in feet

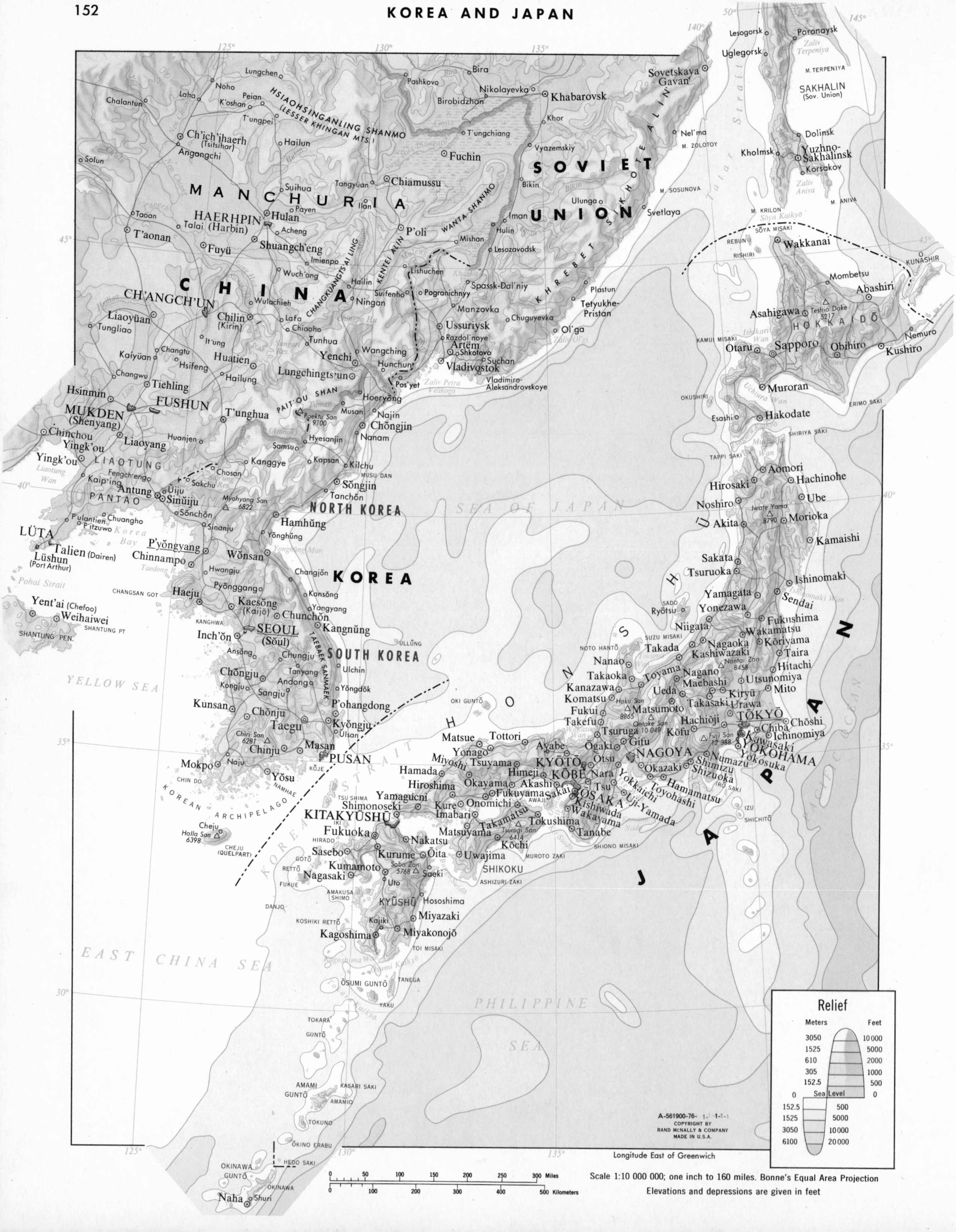

MANCHURIA

SOVIET UNION

CHINA

HSIAOHSINGANLING SHANMO (LESSER KHINGAN MTS)

SAKHALIN (Sov. Union)

HOKKAIDŌ

NORTH KOREA

KOREA

SEA OF JAPAN

SOUTH KOREA

SEOUL (Sŏul)

PʻYŎNGYANG

TŌKYŌ

YOKOHAMA

NAGOYA

KYŌTO

ŌSAKA

KŌBE

HONSHŪ

SHIKOKU

KYŪSHŪ

KITAKYŪSHŪ

PUSAN

YELLOW SEA

EAST CHINA SEA

PHILIPPINE SEA

J A P A N

MUKDEN (Shenyang)

LÜTA

Talien (Dairen)

Lüshun (Port Arthur)

Relief

Meters		Feet
3050		10 000
1525		5000
610		2000
305		1000
152.5		500
0	Sea Level	0
152.5		500
1525		5000
3050		10 000
6100		20 000

A-561900-76-
COPYRIGHT BY
RAND McNALLY & COMPANY
MADE IN U.S.A.

Longitude East of Greenwich

Scale 1:10 000 000; one inch to 160 miles. Bonne's Equal Area Projection
Elevations and depressions are given in feet

0　50　100　150　200　250　300 Miles
0　100　200　300　400　500 Kilometers

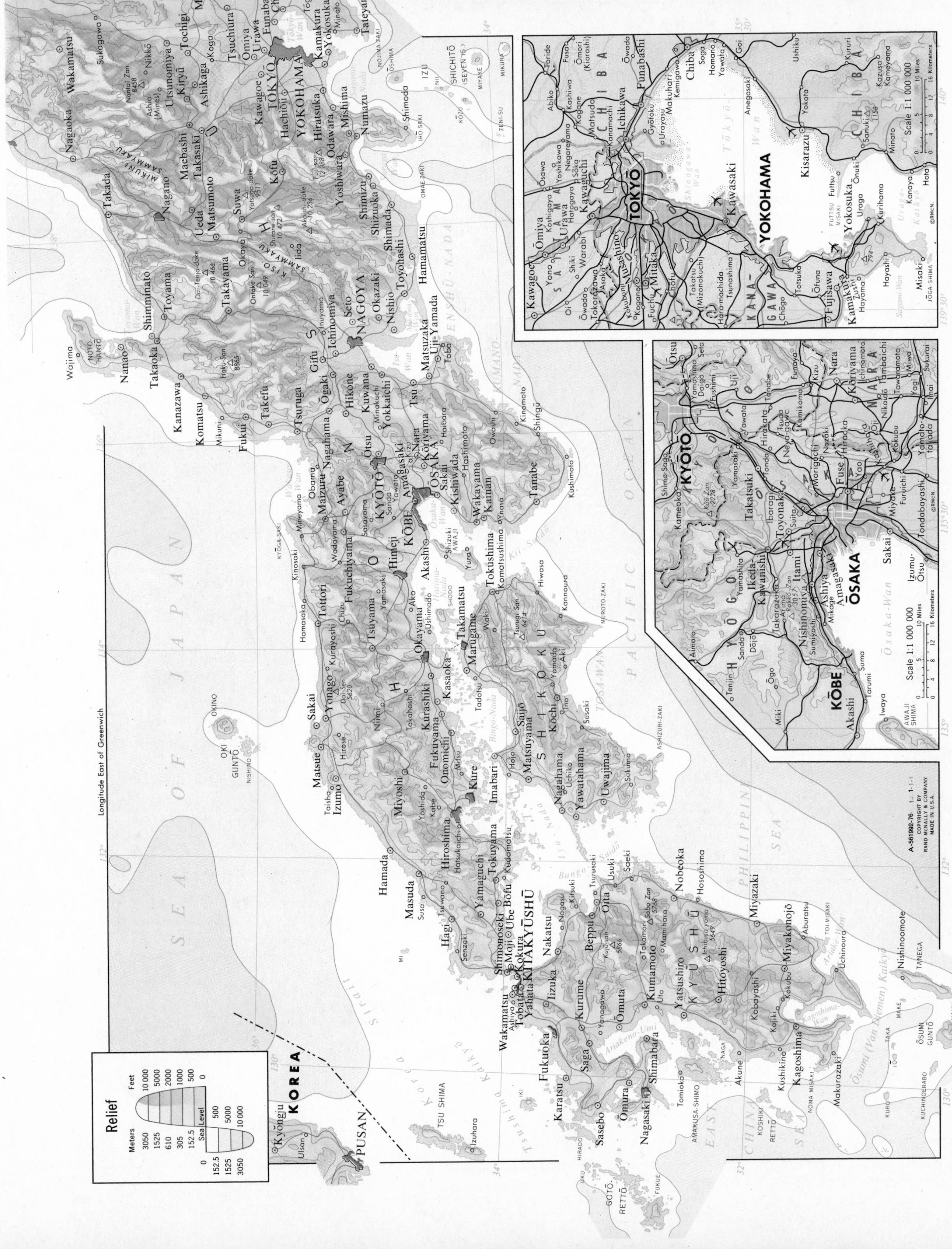

SOUTHERN JAPAN

Scale 1:4 000 000: one inch to 64 miles. Conic Projection
Elevations and depressions are given in feet.

TOKYO — YOKOHAMA Scale 1:1 000 000

KYOTO — OSAKA — KOBE Scale 1:1 000 000

Relief

Feet	Meters
10 000	3050
5000	1525
2000	610
1000	305
500	152.5
0	Sea Level
500	152.5
5000	1525
10 000	3050

A-561902-76 1:-1-1-1 COPYRIGHT BY RAND McNALLY & COMPANY MADE IN U.S.A.

SEA OF JAPAN

PACIFIC OCEAN

PHILIPPINE SEA

EAST CHINA SEA

KOREA

PUSAN

TOKYO YOKOHAMA NAGOYA KYOTO OSAKA KOBE
KYUSHU SHIKOKU HONSHU KITAKYUSHU

Fukuoka Nagasaki Kumamoto Kagoshima Miyazaki Oita Beppu
Hiroshima Okayama Kure Matsuyama Kochi Takamatsu Tokushima
Tottori Matsue Yamaguchi Shimonoseki Kitakyushu
Kanazawa Fukui Toyama Takaoka Nagano Matsumoto Takada
Shizuoka Hamamatsu Gifu Tsu Wakayama Nara Otsu

154

Relief

Meters	Feet
3050	10 000
1525	5000
610	2000
305	1000
152.5	500

Sea Level

152.5	500
1525	5000
3050	10 000
6100	20 000

A-569800-76- 1-1- 1-1-1
COPYRIGHT BY
RAND M⸱NALLY & COMPANY
MADE IN U.S.A.

Longitude East of Greenwich

Scale 1:16 000 000; one inch to 250 miles. Polyconic Projection
Elevations and depressions are given in feet

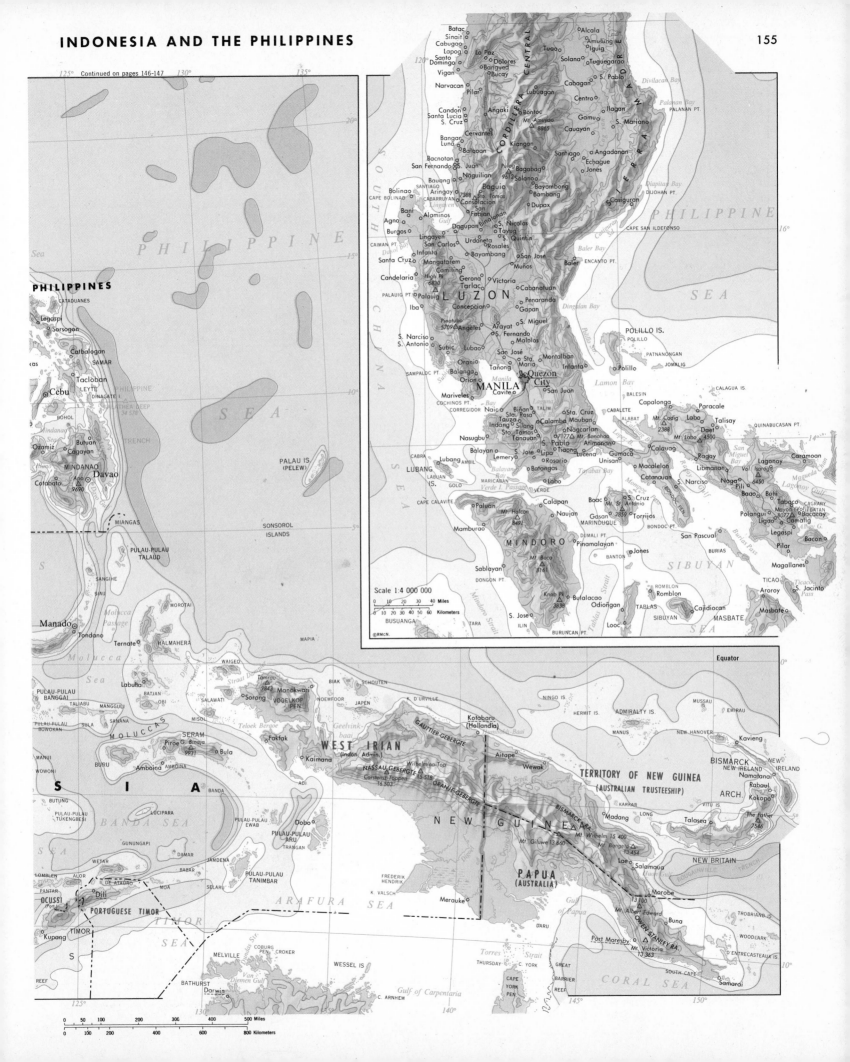

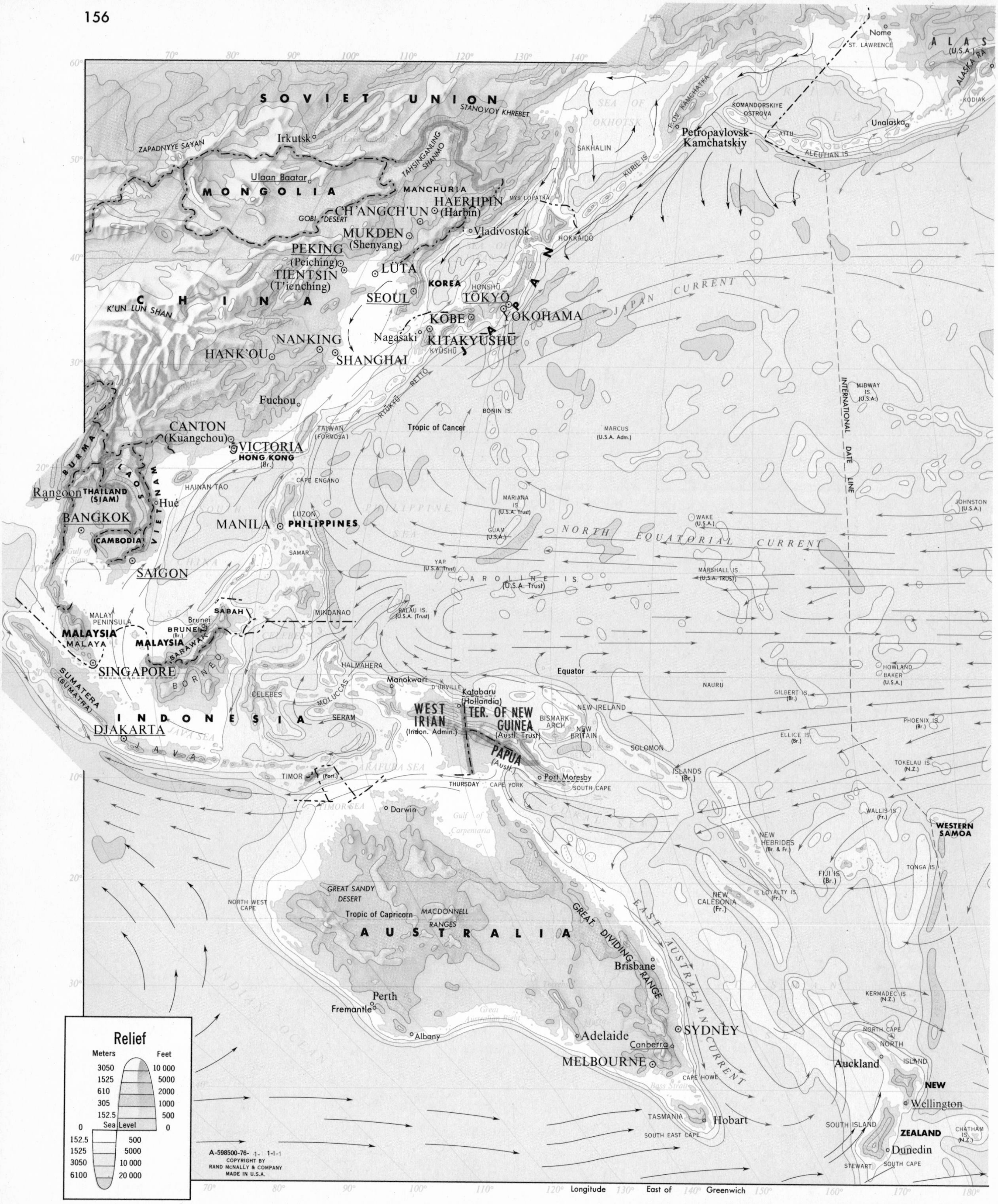

SOVIET UNION

STANOVOY KHREBET

ZAPADNYYE SAYAN

Irkutsk

Ulaan Baatar

MONGOLIA

GOBI DESERT

TAHSINGANLING SHANNO

MANCHURIA

CH'ANGCH'UN

HAERHPIN (Harbin)

MUKDEN (Shenyang)

Vladivostok

PEKING (Peiching)

LÜTA

TIENTSIN (T'ienching)

KOREA

SEOUL

CHINA

K'UN LUN SHAN

HONSHŪ

TŌKYŌ

KŌBE

YOKOHAMA

Nagasaki

KITAKYŪSHŪ

KYŪSHŪ

NANKING

SHANGHAI

HANK'OU

Fuchou

CANTON (Kuangchou)

VICTORIA

HONG KONG (Br.)

TAIWAN (FORMOSA)

RYŪKYŪ RETTO

HAINAN TAO

CAPE ENGAÑO

Tropic of Cancer

BONIN IS.

MARCUS (U.S.A. Adm.)

BURMA

LAOS

Rangoon

THAILAND (SIAM)

Hué

VIETNAM

BANGKOK

CAMBODIA

SAIGON

MANILA

PHILIPPINES

LUZON

SAMAR

MARIANA IS. (U.S.A. Trust)

GUAM (U.S.A.)

YAP (U.S.A. Trust)

WAKE (U.S.A.)

JOHNSTON (U.S.A.)

NORTH EQUATORIAL CURRENT

MALAY PENINSULA

MALAYSIA

MALAYA

SABAH

BRUNEI (Br.)

SARAWAK

MALAYSIA

SINGAPORE

SUMATERA (SUMATRA)

BORNEO

MINDANAO

PALAU IS. (U.S.A. Trust)

CAROLINE IS. (U.S.A. Trust)

MARSHALL IS. (U.S.A. Trust)

CELEBES

MOLUCCAS

HALMAHERA

Manokwari

D'URVILLE

Kotabaru (Hollandia)

Equator

NAURU

GILBERT IS. (Br.)

HOWLAND BAKER (U.S.A.)

INDONESIA

DJAKARTA

SERAM

WEST IRIAN (Indon. Admin.)

TER. OF NEW GUINEA (Austl. Trust)

BISMARK ARCH.

NEW IRELAND

NEW BRITAIN

SOLOMON

ISLANDS (Br.)

ELLICE IS. (Br.)

PHOENIX IS. (Br.)

JAVA SEA

JAVA

PAPUA (Austl.)

Port Moresby

TOKELAU IS. (N.Z.)

TIMOR (Port.)

ARAFURA SEA

THURSDAY

CAPE YORK

SOUTH CAPE

WALLIS IS. (Fr.)

TIMOR SEA

Darwin

Gulf of Carpentaria

NEW HEBRIDES (Br. & Fr.)

WESTERN SAMOA

NORTH WEST CAPE

GREAT SANDY DESERT

Tropic of Capricorn

MACDONNELL RANGES

AUSTRALIA

GREAT DIVIDING RANGE

FIJI IS. (Br.)

NEW CALEDONIA (Fr.)

LOYALTY IS. (Fr.)

TONGA IS.

EAST AUSTRALIAN CURRENT

Brisbane

Perth

Fremantle

Albany

Great Australian Bight

Adelaide

Canberra

SYDNEY

KERMADEC IS. (N.Z.)

NORTH CAPE

NORTH ISLAND

Auckland

MELBOURNE

CAPE HOWE

NEW

Wellington

TASMANIA

Hobart

Bass Strait

SOUTH EAST CAPE

SOUTH ISLAND

ZEALAND

CHATHAM IS. (N.Z.)

Dunedin

Stewart

SOUTH CAPE

Nome

ST. LAWRENCE

ALAS (U.S.A.)

RA

ALASKA RA

KODIAK

SEA OF OKHOTSK

P. OV KAMCHATKA

KOMANDORSKIYE OSTROVA

Unalaska

Petropavlovsk-Kamchatskiy

SAKHALIN

KURILE IS.

MYS LOPATKA

HOKKAIDO

ATTU

ALEUTIAN IS.

JAPAN CURRENT

MIDWAY IS. (U.S.A.)

INTERNATIONAL DATE LINE

Gulf of Siam

PHILIPPINE SEA

SOUTH CHINA SEA

INDIAN OCEAN

Relief

Meters		Feet
3050		10 000
1525		5000
610		2000
305		1000
152.5		500
0	Sea Level	0
152.5		500
1525		5000
3050		10 000
6100		20 000

A-598500-76- 1- 1-1-1

COPYRIGHT BY
RAND McNALLY & COMPANY
MADE IN U.S.A.

Longitude   East of   Greenwich

Warm ocean currents

Cold ocean currents

Scale 1:50 000 000; one inch to 800 miles. Goode's Homolosine Equal Area Projection
Elevations and depressions are given in feet

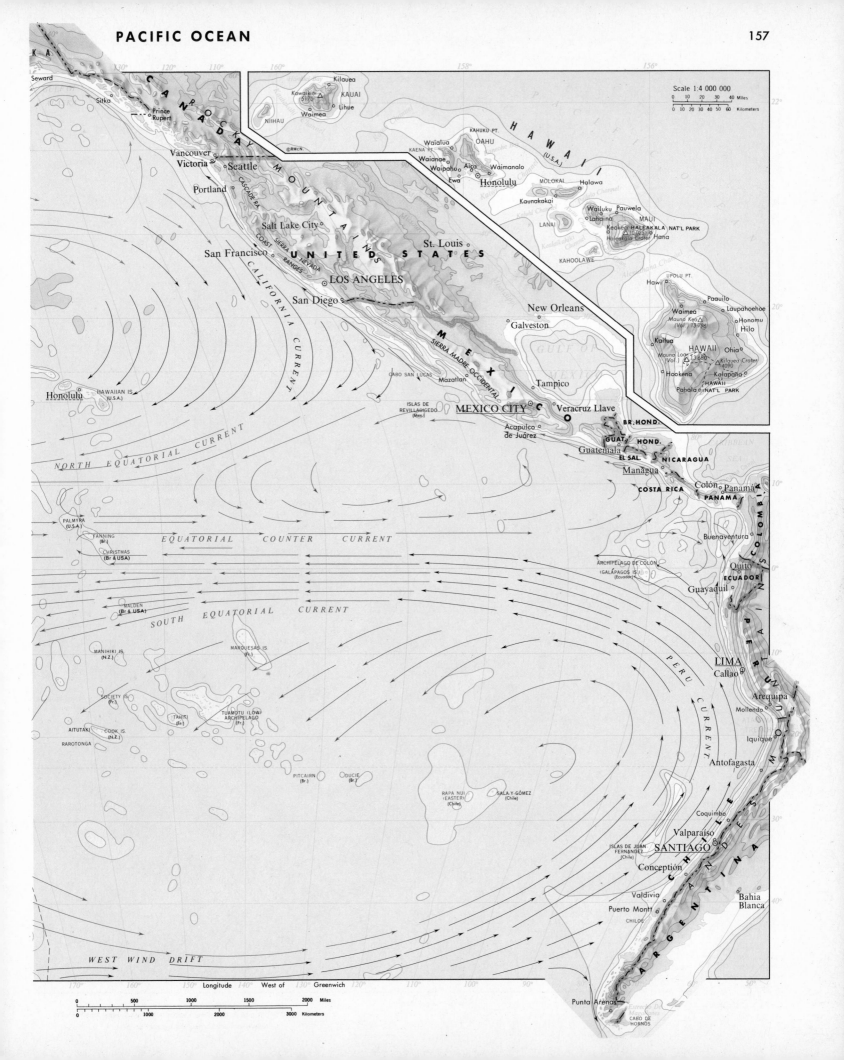

Seward

CANADA

ROCKY

Sitka

Prince Rupert

Vancouver
Victoria
Seattle

Portland

CASCADE RANGE

MOUNTAINS

Salt Lake City

San Francisco

SIERRA NEVADA

COAST RANGES

UNITED STATES

St. Louis

LOS ANGELES

San Diego

CALIFORNIA CURRENT

M E X I C O

SIERRA MADRE OCCIDENTAL

New Orleans

Galveston

GULF OF MEXICO

Honolulu

HAWAIIAN IS.
(U.S.A.)

CABO SAN LUCAS

Mazatlan

Tampico

ISLAS DE
REVILLAGIGEDO
(Mex.)

MEXICO CITY

Veracruz Llave

BR. HOND.

Acapulco
de Juárez

GUAT.

HOND.

NORTH   EQUATORIAL   CURRENT

Guatemala

EL SAL.

NICARAGUA

Managua

COSTA RICA

Colón

Panamá

PANAMA

PALMYRA
(U.S.A.)

FANNING
(Br.)

CHRISTMAS
(Br & USA)

EQUATORIAL   COUNTER   CURRENT

Buenaventura

COLOMBIA

ARCHIPELAGO DE COLÓN
(GALÁPAGOS IS.)
(Ecuador)

Quito

ECUADOR

Guayaquil

MALDEN
(Br & USA)

SOUTH   EQUATORIAL   CURRENT

MANIHIKI IS.
(N.Z.)

MARQUESAS IS.
(Fr.)

LIMA

Callao

PERU

Arequipa

SOCIETY IS.
(Fr.)

Mollendo

AITUTAKI
(N.Z.)

COOK IS.
(N.Z.)

TAHITI
(Fr.)

TUAMOTU (LOW)
ARCHIPELAGO
(Fr.)

Iquique

PERU CURRENT

RAROTONGA

Antofagasta

PITCAIRN
(Br.)

DUCIE
(Br.)

RAPA NUI
(EASTER)
(Chile)

SALA-Y-GÓMEZ
(Chile)

CHILE

ANDES

Coquimbo

Valparaíso

ISLAS DE JUAN
FERNANDEZ
(Chile)

SANTIAGO

Conceptión

ARGENTINA

Valdivia

Puerto Montt

Bahia
Blanca

CHILOE

WEST   WIND   DRIFT

Punta Arenas

CABO DE
HORNOS

Hawaii inset

HAWAII
(U.S.A.)

Kilauea

KAUAI

Kawaikini
(5170)

Lihue

NIIHAU

Waimea

KAHUKU PT.

OAHU

Waialua

KAENA PT.

Waianae

Aiea

Waimanalo

Waipahu

Ewa

Honolulu

MOLOKAI

Halawa

Kaunakakai

LANAI

Wailuku

Pauwela

Lahaina

Keokea

MAUI

HALEAKALA NAT'L PARK

HALEAKALA
10,025

Hana

Haleakala Crater

KAHOOLAWE

UPOLU PT.

Hawi

Paauilo

Waimea

Laupahoehoe

Mauna Kea
(Vol.) 13,796

Honomu

Kailua

Ohia

Hilo

HAWAII

Mauna Loa
(Vol.) 13,680

Kilauea Crater
4090

Hookena

Kalapana

HAWAII
NAT'L PARK

Pahala

Scale 1:4 000 000

Scale 1:4 000 000
0 10 20 30   40 Miles
0 10 20 30 40 50 60 Kilometers

Lower scale bars

0   500   1000   1500   2000 Miles
0   1000   2000   3000 Kilometers

Continued on pages 154-155

Relief

Meters		Feet
3050		10 000
1525		5000
610		2000
305		1000
152.5		500
0	Sea Level	0
		Below
152.5		500	Sea Level
1525		5000
3050		10 000
6100		20 000

A-590200-76- 1-1-1- -1
COPYRIGHT BY
RAND McNALLY & COMPANY
MADE IN U.S.A.

Longitude 115° East of Greenwich

Scale 1:16 000 000; one inch to 250 miles. Lambert's Azimuthal, Equal Area Projection
Elevations and depressions are given in feet

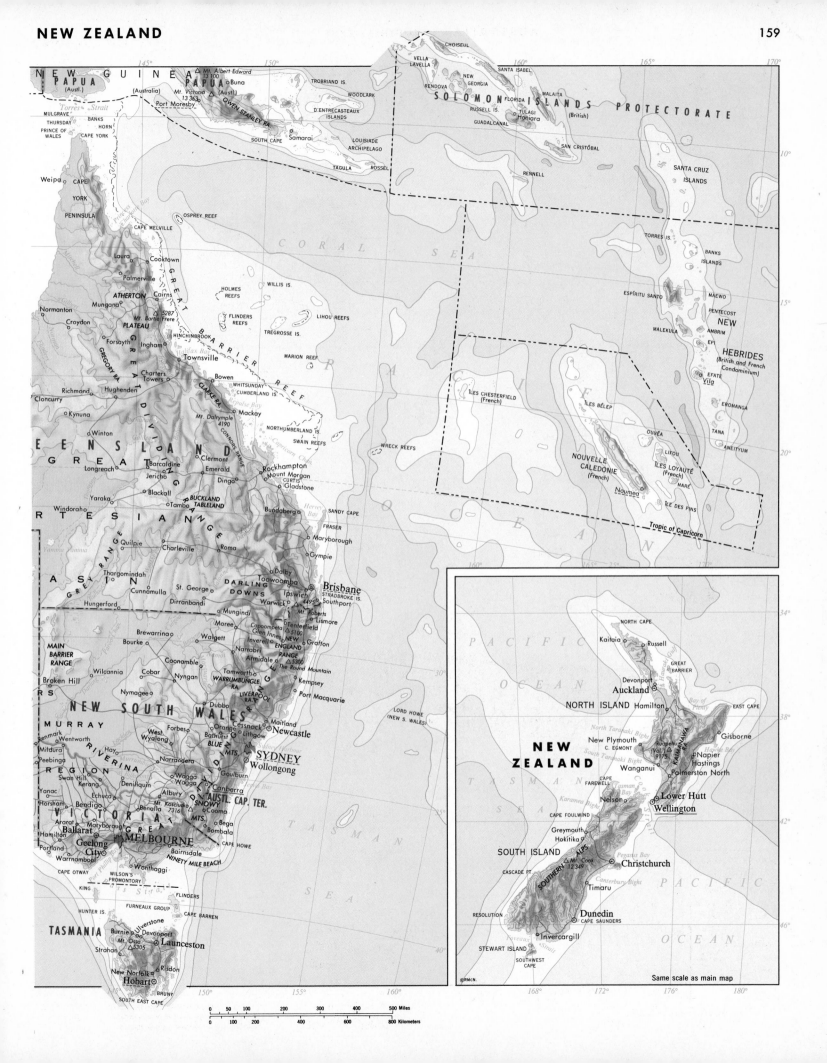

NEW GUINEA

PAPUA
(Austl.)

PAPUA
(Australia)

Mt. Albert Edward
13 100

△ Mt. Victoria
13 363
Port Moresby

Buna

TROBRIAND IS.

WOODLARK

CHOISEUL

VELLA
LAVELLA

NEW
GEORGIA

SANTA ISABEL

SOLOMON ISLANDS PROTECTORATE

RENDOVA

FLORIDA
RUSSELL IS.

MALAITA
(British)

MULGRAVE

THURSDAY
BANKS
PRINCE OF
WALES

HORN

Port Moresby

D'ENTRECASTEAUX
ISLANDS

Samarai

LOUISIADE
ARCHIPELAGO

TAGULA   ROSSEL

TULAGI
Honiara

GUADALCANAL

SAN CRISTÓBAL

SANTA CRUZ
ISLANDS

Torres   Strait

CAPE YORK

Weipa

CAPE
YORK

RENNELL

TORRES IS.

BANKS
ISLANDS

PENINSULA

OSPREY REEF

CORAL   SEA

ESPÍRITU SANTO

MAEWO

NEW

AMBRIM

Normanton

CAPE MELVILLE

HOLMES
REEFS

WILLIS IS.

LIHOU REEFS

PENTECOST

MALEKULA

HEBRIDES
(British and French
Condominium)

Laura

Cooktown

Palmerville

FLINDERS
REEFS

TREGROSSE IS.

EPI

EFATE
Vila

EROMANGA

ATHERTON

Cairns

Mungana

△ 5287
Mt. Bartle Frere

PLATEAU

Forsayth

Ingham

HINCHINBROOK

MARION REEF

ÎLES CHESTERFIELD
(French)

ÎLES BÉLEP

TANA

ANEITYUM

Croydon

Townsville

Richmond

Hughenden

Charters
Towers

CLARKE RA.

Halifax Bay

Bowen

WHITSUNDAY
CUMBERLAND IS.

WRECK REEFS

OUVÉA

LIFOU

ÎLES LOYAUTÉ
(French)

Cloncurry

Kynuna

GREGORY RA.

Repulse Bay

Mackay

NORTHUMBERLAND IS.
SWAIN REEFS

NOUVELLE
CALEDONIE
(French)

MARÉ

Winton

EENSLAND

Mt. Dalrymple
4190

CONNORS RANGE

Noumea

ÎLE DES PINS

Barcaldine

Longreach

Jericho

Clermont

Emerald

Dingo

Rockhampton
Mount Morgan

CURTIS

Capricorn Chan.

GREAT

Blackall

Yaraka

BUCKLAND
TABLELAND
Tambo

Gladstone

Bundaberg

Hervey Bay

SANDY CAPE

Tropic of Capricorn

RTESIANRANGE

Windorah

FRASER

Maryborough

O   C   E   A   N

Quilpie

Charleville

Roma

Gympie

ASIN

DARLING
DOWNS

Thargomindah

Cunnamulla

St. George

Dalby
Toowoomba

Ipswich

Brisbane

STRADBROKE IS.
Southport

Hungerford

GREATRANGE

Dirranbandi

Warwick   △ 4495
Mt. Roberts

Lismore

Mungindi

Moree

Capoompeta △ 5100
Glen Innes

Tenterfield

NEW
ENGLAND
RANGE

Grafton

Brewarrina

Walgett

Inverell

Narrabri

Armidale   △ 5300
The Round Mountain

MAIN
BARRIER
RANGE

Bourke

Coonamble

WARRUMBUNGLE
RA.

Tamworth

Kempsey

Wilcannia

Cobar

Nyngan

LIVERPOOL
RA.

Port Macquarie

Broken Hill

Nymagee

Dubbo

NEW SOUTH WALES

MURRAY

Forbes

Orange

Lithgow

Maitland

Newcastle

RS

West
Wyalong

Bathurst
BLUE
MTS.

Cessnock

Narrandera

Wagga
Wagga

Goulburn

SYDNEY
Wollongong

RIVERINA
REGION

Hay

Deniliquin

Albury

Benalla

Mt. Kosciusko
7316

Canberra

AUSTL. CAP. TER.

Swan Hill

Kerang

Echuca

SNOWY

Cooma

MTS.

Bega

Bombala

CAPE HOWE

Yanac

Horsham

Bendigo

Maryborough

VICTORIA

GREAT

Bairnsdale

Ararat

Ballarat

MELBOURNE

NINETY MILE BEACH

Hamilton

Portland

Geelong
City

Warrnambool

Wonthaggi

CAPE OTWAY

WILSON'S
PROMONTORY

KING

FURNEAUX GROUP

FLINDERS

CAPE BARREN

Bass   Strait

HUNTER IS.

TASMANIA

Burnie   Ulverstone
Devonport

Launceston

Strahan   Mt. Ossa
△5305

New Norfolk   Risdon

Hobart

BRUNY

SOUTH EAST CAPE

T   A   S   M   A   N

S   E   A

LORD HOWE
(NEW S. WALES)

PACIFIC

OCEAN

PACIFIC
OCEAN

NORTH CAPE

Kaitaia

Russell

GREAT
BARRIER

Devonport

Auckland

NORTH ISLAND   Hamilton

EAST CAPE

NEW
ZEALAND

New Plymouth
C. EGMONT

Ruapehu
Vol.) △
9 175

KAIMANAWA RA.

Gisborne

Napier

Hastings

CAPE
FAREWELL

Wanganui

Palmerston North

Nelson

Lower Hutt
Wellington

SOUTH ISLAND

Greymouth
Hokitika

SOUTHERN ALPS

Mt. Cook △
12 349

Christchurch

CASCADE PT

Timaru

TASMAN
SEA

RESOLUTION

Dunedin
CAPE SAUNDERS

Invercargill

STEWART ISLAND

SOUTHWEST
CAPE

PACIFIC

OCEAN

Same scale as main map

150°   155°   160°   165°   170°

10°

15°

20°

25°

30°

34°

38°

42°

46°

0   50   100   200   300   400   500 Miles
0   100   200   400   600   800 Kilometers

168°   172°   176°   180°

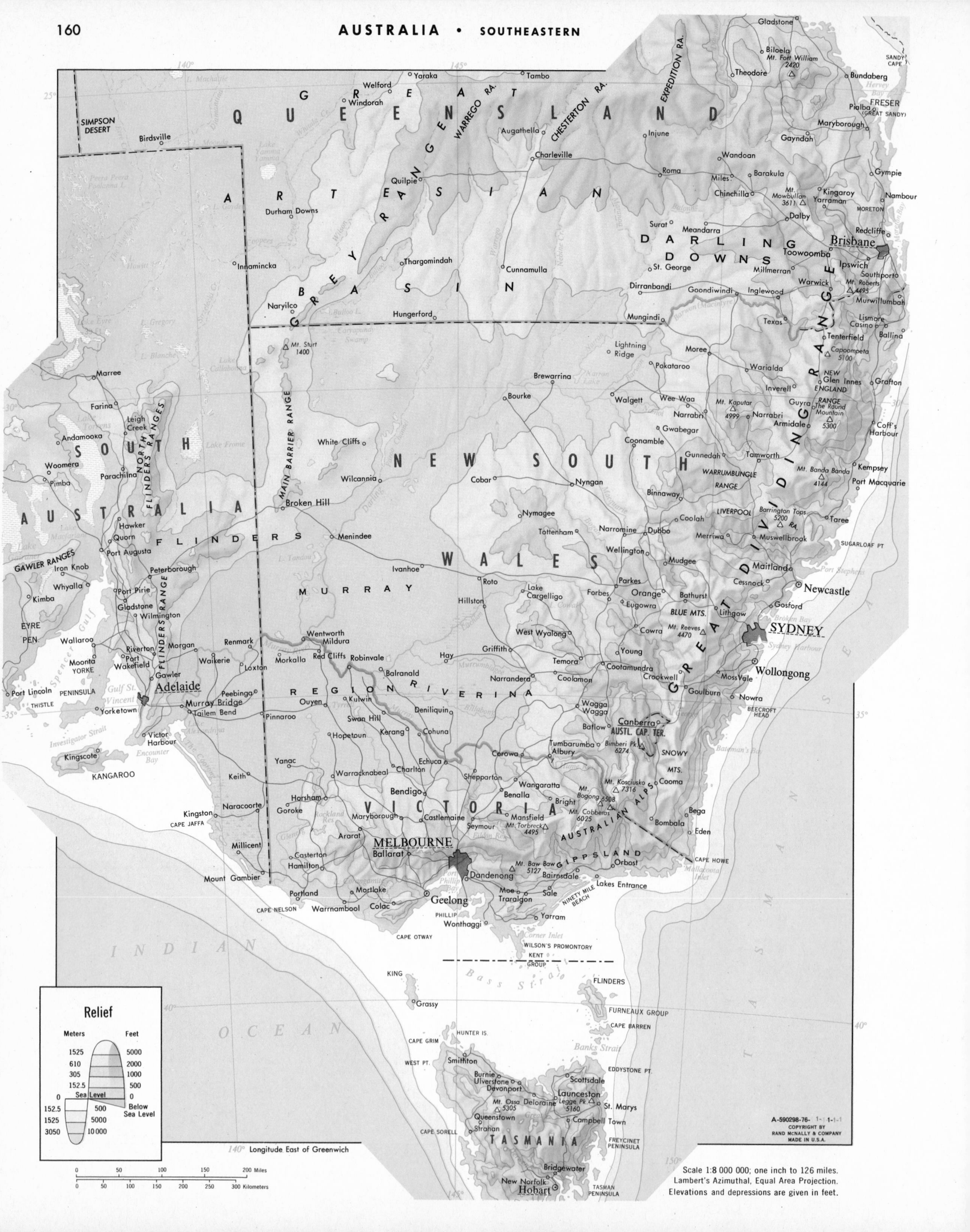

QUEENSLAND
GREAT ARTESIAN BASIN
GREY RANGE
WARREGO RA.
CHESTERTON RA.
EXPEDITION RA.
SIMPSON DESERT
Birdsville
Windorah
Welford
Yaraka
Tambo
Augathella
Charleville
Injune
Quilpie
Durham Downs
Innamincka
Thargomindah
Cunnamulla
Naryilco
Hungerford
Gladstone
Biloela
Mt. Fort William 2420
Theodore
Bundaberg
Hervey Bay
SANDY CAPE
FRESER (GREAT SANDY)
Pialba
Maryborough
Gayndah
Gympie
Nambour
Wandoan
Roma
Miles
Barakula
Chinchilla
Mt. Mowbullan 3611
Kingaroy
Yarraman
Dalby
MORETON
Redcliffe
Brisbane
Surat
Meandarra
DARLING DOWNS
Toowoomba
Ipswich
Millmerran
St. George
Warwick
Southport
Mt. Roberts 4495
Murwillumbah
Dirranbandi
Goondiwindi
Inglewood
Mungindi
Texas
Lismore
Casino
Tenterfield
Ballina
Mt. Sturt 1400
SOUTH AUSTRALIA
NORTHERN RANGES
FLINDERS RANGES
FLINDERS
Marree
Farina
Leigh Creek
Andamooka
Woomera
Pimba
Parachilna
Lake Torrens
Lake Frome
Lake Eyre
L. Gregory
L. Blanche
Lake Callabonna
Hawker
Quorn
Port Augusta
GAWLER RANGES
Iron Knob
Whyalla
Kimba
Peterborough
Port Pirie
Gladstone
Wilmington
EYRE PEN.
Wallaroo
Moonta
YORKE PENINSULA
Port Lincoln
THISTLE
Riverton
Port Wakefield
Morgan
Waikerie
Renmark
Loxton
Gawler
Adelaide
Gulf St. Vincent
Spencer Gulf
Peebinga
Murray Bridge
Tailem Bend
Yorketown
Investigator Strait
Victor Harbour
Kingscote
KANGAROO
Encounter Bay
Keith
Kingston
CAPE JAFFA
Naracoorte
Millicent
Mount Gambier
MAIN BARRIER RANGE
NEW SOUTH WALES
White Cliffs
Wilcannia
Broken Hill
Menindee
Ivanhoe
MURRAY
Roto
Hillston
Lake Cargelligo
Bourke
Brewarrina
Lightning Ridge
Walgett
Wee Waa
Narrabri
Pokataroo
Moree
Warialda
Inverell
Glen Innes
NEW ENGLAND RANGE
Grafton
Mt. Kaputar 4999
Guyra
The Round Mountain 5300
Armidale
Coff's Harbour
Capoompeta 5100
Gwabegar
Coonamble
Gunnedah
Tamworth
Mt. Banda Banda 4144
Kempsey
Port Macquarie
Cobar
Nyngan
WARRUMBUNGLE RANGE
Binnaway
LIVERPOOL RA.
Barrington Tops 5200
Taree
Coolah
Nymagee
Tottenham
Narromine
Dubbo
Merriwa
Muswellbrook
SUGARLOAF PT
Wellington
Mudgee
Maitland
Port Stephens
Cessnock
Newcastle
Parkes
Forbes
Orange
Eugowra
Bathurst
BLUE MTS.
Lithgow
Gosford
Broken Bay
Mt. Reeves 4470
SYDNEY
Sydney Harbour
West Wyalong
Cowra
Young
Griffith
Hay
Temora
Cootamundra
Crookwell
Goulburn
Moss Vale
Wollongong
Nowra
BEECROFT HEAD
Narrandera
Coolamon
WALES
GREAT DIVIDING RANGE
Wentworth
Mildura
Morkalla
Red Cliffs
Robinvale
Balranald
REGION RIVERINA
Ouyen
Kulwin
Swan Hill
Deniliquin
Pinnaroo
Hopetoun
Kerang
Cohuna
Wagga Wagga
Canberra
AUSTL. CAP. TER.
Batlow
Tumbarumba
Bimberi Pk. 6274
SNOWY MTS.
Corowa
Albury
Echuca
Yanac
Warracknabeal
Charlton
Shepparton
Wangaratta
Mt. Kosciusko 7316
Cooma
Bendigo
Benalla
Bright
Mt. Bogong 6508
Horsham
Goroke
Maryborough
Castlemaine
VICTORIA
Mansfield
Mt. Cobberas 6025
AUSTRALIAN ALPS
Bega
Bombala
Eden
Seymour
Mt. Torbreck 4495
Ararat
MELBOURNE
Ballarat
Casterton
Hamilton
GIPPSLAND
Orbost
CAPE HOWE
Mt. Baw Baw 5127
Bairnsdale
Dandenong
Port Phillip Bay
Portland
Mortlake
Geelong
Moe
Traralgon
Sale
Lakes Entrance
NINETY MILE BEACH
CAPE NELSON
Warrnambool
Colac
PHILLIP
Wonthaggi
Yarram
CAPE OTWAY
Corner Inlet
WILSON'S PROMONTORY
KENT GROUP
INDIAN OCEAN
Bass Strait
KING
Grassy
FLINDERS
FURNEAUX GROUP
CAPE BARREN
HUNTER IS.
CAPE GRIM
Banks Strait
WEST PT.
Smithton
EDDYSTONE PT.
Burnie
Ulverstone
Devonport
Scottsdale
Launceston
Mt. Ossa 5305
Deloraine
Legge Pk 5160
St. Marys
Queenstown
Campbell Town
Strahan
CAPE SORELL
TASMANIA
FREYCINET PENINSULA
Bridgewater
New Norfolk
Hobart
TASMAN PENINSULA
TASMAN SEA
Relief
Meters
Feet
1525 5000
610 2000
305 1000
152.5 500
0 Sea Level 0
152.5 500
1525 5000
3050 10000
Below Sea Level
140° Longitude East of Greenwich
0 50 100 150 200 Miles
0 50 100 150 200 250 300 Kilometers
A-590298-76-
COPYRIGHT BY RAND McNALLY & COMPANY MADE IN U.S.A.
Scale 1:8 000 000; one inch to 126 miles.
Lambert's Azimuthal, Equal Area Projection.
Elevations and depressions are given in feet.

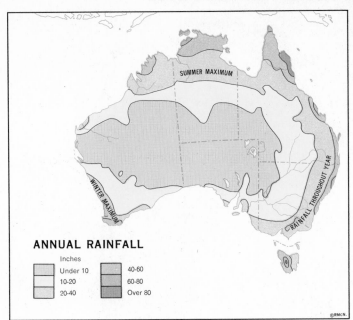

ANNUAL RAINFALL

Inches

Under 10
10-20
20-40

40-60
60-80
Over 80

©RMcN.

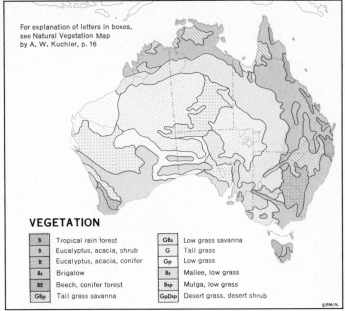

For explanation of letters in boxes,
see Natural Vegetation Map
by A. W. Kuchler, p. 16

VEGETATION

B	Tropical rain forest	
B	Eucalyptus, acacia, shrub	
B	Eucalyptus, acacia, conifer	
Bs	Brigalow	
BE	Beech, conifer forest	
GBp	Tall grass savanna	

GBs	Low grass savanna
G	Tall grass
Gp	Low grass
Bs	Mallee, low grass
Bsp	Mulga, low grass
GpDsp	Desert grass, desert shrub

©RMcN.

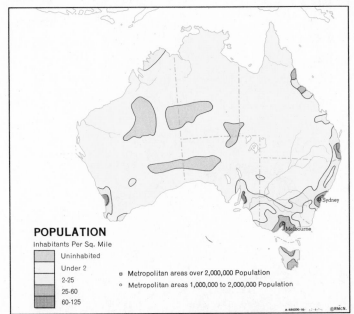

POPULATION

Inhabitants Per Sq. Mile

Uninhabited
Under 2
2-25
25-60
60-125

□ Metropolitan areas over 2,000,000 Population

○ Metropolitan areas 1,000,000 to 2,000,000 Population

A-590200-16-   ©RMcN.

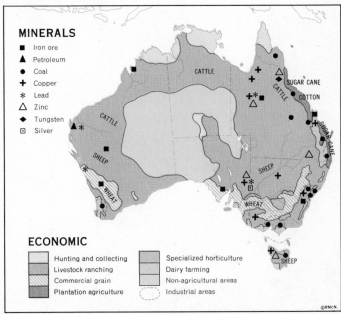

MINERALS

■ Iron ore
▲ Petroleum
● Coal
+ Copper
✶ Lead
△ Zinc
◆ Tungsten
⊡ Silver

ECONOMIC

Hunting and collecting	Specialized horticulture
Livestock ranching	Dairy farming
Commercial grain	Non-agricultural areas
Plantation agriculture	Industrial areas

©RMcN.

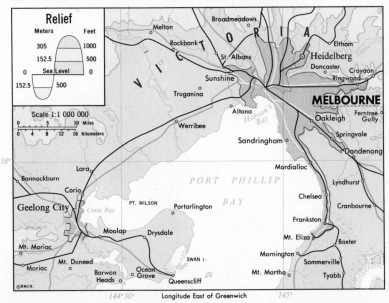

Relief

Meters	Feet
305	1000
152.5	500
0	Sea Level 0
152.5	500

Scale 1:1 000 000

0   5   10 Miles
0 4 8 12 16 Kilometers

©RMcN.

144°30'   Longitude East of Greenwich   145°

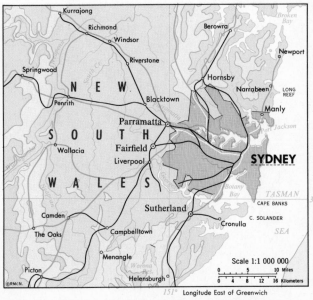

Scale 1:1 000 000

0   5   10 Miles
0 4 8 12 16 Kilometers

©RMcN.   151°   Longitude East of Greenwich

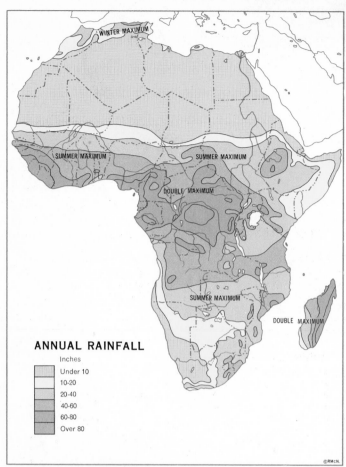

ANNUAL RAINFALL

Inches

- Under 10
- 10-20
- 20-40
- 40-60
- 60-80
- Over 80

©RMCN.

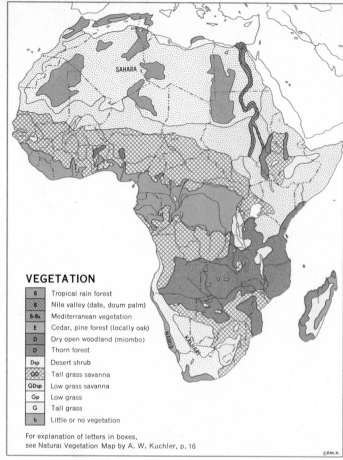

VEGETATION

B	Tropical rain forest
B	Nile valley (date, doum palm)
B-Bs	Mediterranean vegetation
E	Cedar, pine forest (locally oak)
D	Dry open woodland (miombo)
D	Thorn forest
Dsp	Desert shrub
GD	Tall grass savanna
GDsp	Low grass savanna
Gp	Low grass
G	Tall grass
b	Little or no vegetation

For explanation of letters in boxes,
see Natural Vegetation Map by A. W. Kuchler, p. 16

©RMCN.

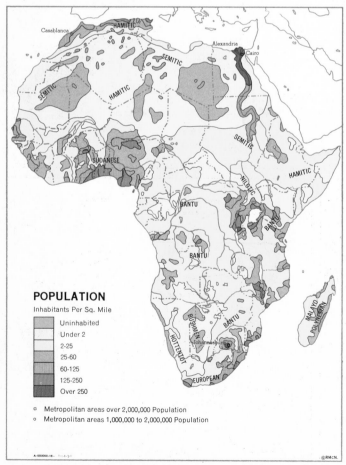

POPULATION

Inhabitants Per Sq. Mile

- Uninhabited
- Under 2
- 2-25
- 25-60
- 60-125
- 125-250
- Over 250

□   Metropolitan areas over 2,000,000 Population
○   Metropolitan areas 1,000,000 to 2,000,000 Population

A-580000-16 - 7-7-5-7

©RMCN.

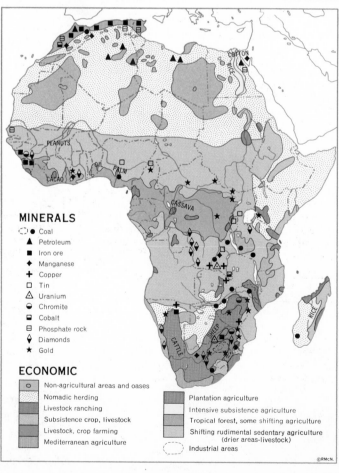

MINERALS

- ◌● Coal
- ▲ Petroleum
- ■ Iron ore
- ◆ Manganese
- ✚ Copper
- □ Tin
- △ Uranium
- ◔ Chromite
- ▭ Cobalt
- ⊟ Phosphate rock
- ◈ Diamonds
- ★ Gold

ECONOMIC

- Non-agricultural areas and oases
- Nomadic herding
- Livestock ranching
- Subsistence crop, livestock
- Livestock, crop farming
- Mediterranean agriculture
- Plantation agriculture
- Intensive subsistence agriculture
- Tropical forest, some shifting agriculture
- Shifting rudimental sedentary agriculture (drier areas-livestock)
- Industrial areas

©RMCN.

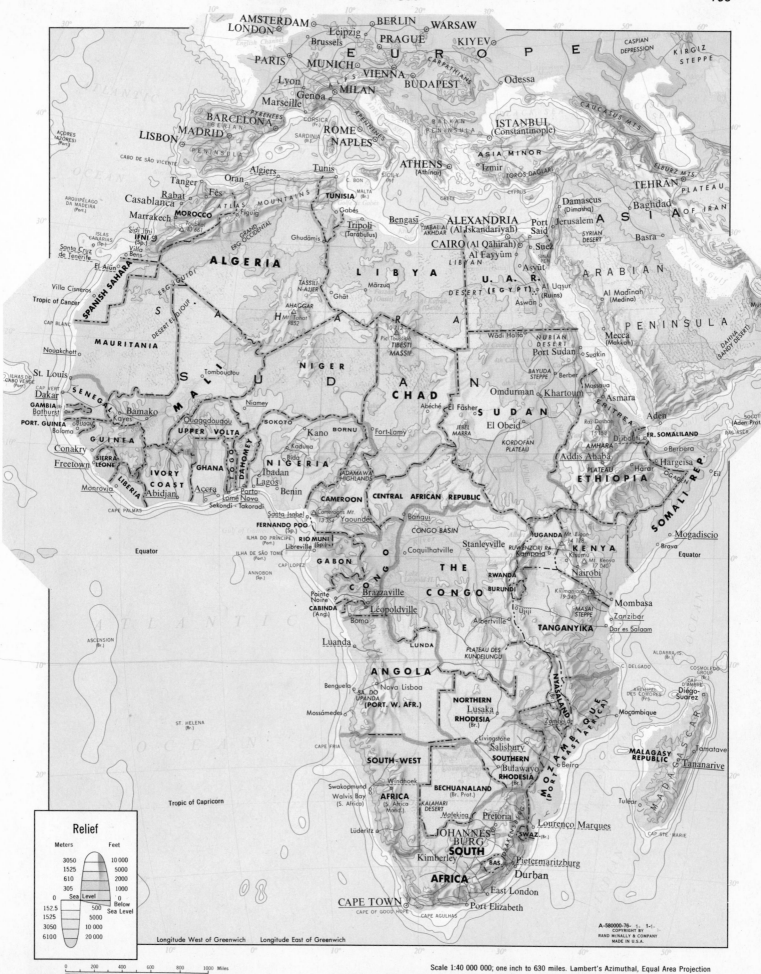

AMSTERDAM
LONDON
BERLIN WARSAW
Leipzig
Brussels PRAGUE KIYEV
PARIS MUNICH E U R O P E
Lyon VIENNA BUDAPEST
Marseille Genoa MILAN
BARCELONA ROME NAPLES
LISBON MADRID
CABO DE SÃO VICENTE
AÇORES (AZORES) (Port.)
ARQUIPÉLAGO DA MADEIRA (Port.)
Tanger ISTANBUL (Constantinople)
Algiers Tunis ATHENS (Athinai)
Oran
Rabat Fès CASPIAN DEPRESSION
Casablanca KIRGIZ STEPPE
Marrakech MOROCCO CAUCASUS MTS.
Izmir TOROS DAGLARI
ASIA MINOR
TEHRAN PLATEAU
ELBURZ MTS. OF IRAN
Damascus (Dimashq)
Baghdad
SYRIAN DESERT Basra
ALEXANDRIA (Al Iskandariyah)
Bengasi JABAL AL AKHDAR
ALGERIA LIBYA Port Said
Tripoli (Tarabulus) CAIRO (Al Qāhirah) Suez
Ghudámis U.A.R. (EGYPT) ARABIAN
ISLAS CANARIAS (Sp.) TASSILI-N-AJJER Al Fayyūm Al Madinah (Medina)
Sidi Ifni IFNI (Sp.) Ghat Märzuq LIBYAN Al Uqşur (Ruins) Mecca (Makkah) PENINSULA
Villa Bens AHAGGAR DESERT Aswan DAHNA (SANDY DESERT)
El Aiún SPANISH SAHARA Mt. Tahat 9852 Muscat
Villa Cisneros Pic Toussidé TIBESTI MASSIF Wādi Halfa SOCOTRA (Aden Prot.)
MAURITANIA NUBIAN DESERT Port Sudan Mecca
Nouakchott S A H A R A Tombouctou N I G E R Berber BAYUDA STEPPE Massaua
St. Louis Omdurman Khartoum Asmara Aden
Dakar M A L I CHAD SUDAN ERITREA
SENEGAL Niamey Abéché El Fāsher FR. SOMALILAND
GAMBIA Bamako SOKOTO Kano BORNU Fort-Lamy JEBEL MARRA El Obeid Djibouti Berbera
PORT. GUINEA Kayes UPPER VOLTA Ouagadougou KORDOFAN PLATEAU Addis Ababa Hargeisa
GUINEA Bissau Bolama Kaduna NIGERIA AMHARA SOMALI REP.
Conakry SIERRA LEONE Bida ADAMAWA HIGHLANDS ETHIOPIA Harar Ogadén
Freetown IVORY COAST GHANA DAHOMEY Ibadan Lagos Benin CAMEROON CENTRAL AFRICAN REPUBLIC PLATEAU
LIBERIA Abidjan Accra Porto Novo Cameroons Mt. 13 354 Yaoundé Bangui Mogadiscio
Monrovia Lomé Novo Santa Isabel FERNANDO POO (Sp.) CONGO BASIN UGANDA Mt. Elgon KENYA Brava
CAPE PALMAS Sekondi-Takoradi RIO MUNI (Sp.) Libreville Coquilhatville Stanleyville RUWENZORI RA. Kampala Mt. Kenya Equator
Equator ILHA DO PRÍNCIPE (Port.) GABON THE Kisumu Nairobi
ILHA DE SÃO TOMÉ (Port.) CONGO RWANDA Mombasa
ANNOBON (Sp.) Brazzaville BURUNDI Kilimanjaro Zanzibar
Pointe Noire Léopoldville Ujiji MASAI STEPPE Dar es Salaam
CABINDA (Ang.) Boma Albertville TANGANYIKA
ASCENSION (Br.) Luanda LUNDA
A T L A N T I C Benguela ANGOLA PLATEAU DES KUNDELUNGU CAP DELGADO
Nova Lisboa COSMOLEDO GROUP
ST. HELENA (Br.) SA. DO UPANDA (PORT. W. AFR.) NORTHERN Lusaka NYASALAND ALDABRA IS. (Br.) Diégo-Suarez
Mossámedes RHODESIA (Br.) CAP D'AMBRE MALAGASY REPUBLIC
O C E A N Livingstone Zomba Tamatave
CAPE FRIA Salisbury MOZAMBIQUE (PORT. EAST AFRICA) Beira
SOUTH-WEST Bulawayo SOUTHERN Moçambique
Swakopmund Windhoek AFRICA (S. Africa Mand.) RHODESIA (Br.) MADAGASCAR
Walvis Bay BECHUANALAND (Br. Prot.) Tuléar
Tropic of Capricorn KALAHARI DESERT Mafeking Pretoria SWAZ.(Br.) Lourenço Marques CAP STE. MARIE
Lüderitz JOHANNESBURG SOUTH Kimberley BAS. Pietermaritzburg
AFRICA Durban
CAPE TOWN East London
CAPE OF GOOD HOPE CAPE AGULHAS Port Elizabeth

Equator

Tropic of Cancer

CAP BLANC

CAP VERT

ILHAS DO CABO VERDE (Port.)

A-580000-76- 1- 1-1-
COPYRIGHT BY
RAND McNALLY & COMPANY
MADE IN U.S.A.

Longitude West of Greenwich   Longitude East of Greenwich

Scale 1:40 000 000; one inch to 630 miles. Lambert's Azimuthal, Equal Area Projection
Elevations and depressions are given in feet.

Relief

Meters		Feet
3050		10 000
1525		5000
610		2000
305		1000
0	Sea Level	0
		Below
152.5		500 Sea Level
1525		5000
3050		10 000
6100		20 000

0	200	400	600	800	1000 Miles
0	400	800	1200	1600 Kilometers

ACORES (AZORES)
(Port.)
Same scale as main map

FAIAL
GRACIOSA
PICO
SÃO JORGE
TERCEIRA
São Miguel
Ponta Delgada
STA. MARIA

SPAIN · AFRICA —

ATLANTIC OCEAN

ARQUIPÉLAGO
ILHA DE PORTO SANTO
ILHA DA MADEIRA
DA MADEIRA
(Port.)
Funchal

Cádiz
Gibraltar (Br.)
Tanger
Ceuta (Sp.)
Tetuán
Larache
Ouezzane
Rabat
Salé
Casablanca
Azemmour
El Jadida
Settat
Safi
(Asfi)
Kasba-Tadla
Essaouira
Demnate
Marrakech
Agadir
Taroudant
Taza
Fès
Meknès
Oued Zem
Oujda
Melilla
(Sp.)
Oran
Mostaganem
Relizane
Mascara
Sidi-bel-Abbès
Saïda
Tlemcen
Nemours

Algiers
(Alger)
Blida
Médéa
Orléansville
M'sila
Aflou
Laghouat
Djelfa
Aïn-Sefra
Colomb-Béchar
Figuig
Béni-Abbès
Igli

Bougie
Dellys
Tizi-
Ouzou
Sétif
Aïn Beïda
Batna
Biskra
El Oued
Touggourt
Ouargla
Haoud el
Hamra
Ft. Lallemand
El-Goléa
Ft. MacMahon
Hassi Inifel
GRAND ERG OCCIDENTAL

Philippeville
Collo
Constantine
Guelma
Souk Ahras
Tébessa
Gafsa
TUNISIA
Sfax
Gabès
Nalüt
HAMMADAH
Ghudāmis
Daraj
GRAND ERG ORIENTAL
Ft. Flatters
ERG EDEYEN
In Amenas
Ft. Polignac

Bizerte
Carthage
Tunis
Nabeul
Sousse
Kairouan
Zaghouan
Mila

ATLAS MOUNTAINS

MOROCCO

Sidi Ifni
IFNI
(Sp.)
Tiznit
JEBEL BANI
CAP DRA
CAP JUBY
Villa Bens

ISLAS CANARIAS
(Sp.)
LA PALMA
TENERIFE
Sta. Cruz
de Tenerife
San Sebastián
GOMERA
HIERRO
LANZAROTE
FUERTEVENTURA
GRAN CANARIA
Las Palmas

ALGERIA

Tindouf
Adrar
Taourirt
Chenachane
(Oasis)
Tropic of Cancer
Tarhmanant
(Well)

PLATEAU
DU TADEMAÏT
In-Salah
TOUAT
TIDIKELT
TANEZROUFT
Ouallène
In Zize
(Oasis)
Bidon Cinq
Mt. Tahat
9852
Djanet (Ft. Charlet)
Ghāt
TASSILI-N-AJJER

EL HANK
ERG CHECH
S A H A R A

El Aiún
SAGUIA EL
HAMRA
SPANISH SAHARA
CABO BOJADOR
RIO DE ORO
Villa Cisneros

ERG IGUIDI

Taoudenni
(Oasis)
DÉSERT EL DJOUF
Taoudenni
AHAGGAR
Ft. Laperrine
(Tamanrasset)
Timmissao

Port-Étienne
CAP BLANC
CAP D'ARGUIN
Atar
Chinguetti
OUARANE
Ft. Gouraud
El Memrhar
CAP TIMIRIS
Akjoujt
EL MERÉIÉ
Mabrouk
Araouane
Kidal
ADRAR DES IFORAS
In Azaoua
(Oasis)
Aguellal
Iferouane
5906
Monts Tamgak
AÏR (AZBINE)
Monts Baguezane
4593
TUAREG

MAURITANIA

Tidjikdja
Kiffa
Néma
Oualata
Tombouctou
Goundam
Bamba
Bourem
Gao
Agadès
VALLÉE DU TILEMSI
TÉNÉRÉ

Nouakchott
Boutilimit
Aleg
M'Bout
Nioro
Nara
Sokolo
NIGER

St. Louis
Podor
Dagama
Diorbivol
Matam
Bakel
Kaédi
Louga
Rufisque
Diourbel
Thiès
CAP
VERT
Dakar
Kaolack
Bathurst
GAMBIA
(Br.)
Ziguinchor
Casamance

SENEGAL

Linguere
Sélibaby
Goumbou
Tahoua
Madaoua
Tessaoua
Zinder
Gouré
Nguru
Geidam

Kayes
Tambacounda
Bafoulabé
Kita
Koulikoro
Ségou
Djenné
San
Mopti
Bandiagara
Dori
Tillabéri
Niamey
Say
Dosso
Sokoto
Maradi
Kaure Namoda
Katsina
Gumel
Hadejia
Komadugu Yobe
Potiskum

PORTUGUESE
GUINEA
Bissau
Bolama
Buba
ARQUIPÉLAGO
DOS BIJAGÓS
Boffao
Boké
Kindia
Boffao

M. du Tamgué
4970
FOUTA DJALON
Labé
Satadougou
Bamako
Koutiala
Dédougou
Ouagadougou
Koudougou
Tenkodogo
Fada
N' Gourma
Birnin Kebbi
Gusau
Zaria
Kano
Gaya

UPPER VOLTA

S O U D

GUINEA
Timbo
Kouroussa
Kankan
Siguiri
Bougouni
Sikasso
Bobo-
Dioulasso
Gambaga
Sansanné-Mango
Kandi
Kontagora
Bussa
Zúngeru
Minna
Bauchi
Gombe

NORTHERN REGION
NIGERIA

Conakry
Forécariah
Kabala
Faranah
Kissidougou
Beyla
Odienné
Korhogo
Kong
Bouna
Yendi
Sokodé
Atakpamé
Ilo
Jos
Karimama
BOR

SIERRA LEONE
Freetown
Moyamba
Banthe
Pandembu
Kolahun
Kabala
Kamabai
Dabakala
Bondoukou
Kintampo
Tamale
Bole
Salaga
Bimbilla
WESTERN REGION
Iseyin
Oyo
Ogbomosho
Oshogbo
Ilorin
Ilesha
Ife
Keffi
Baro
Ibi
Makurdi
Yola
ADAMAWA
SHEBSHI
GOTEL MTS.

Mt. Nimba
5760
Logoualé
Séguéla
Bouaké
Bouaflé
KONG
IVORY COAST
Naama
Taoula
Bopóro
Bomi Hills
Robertsport
Buchanan
River Cess
Greenville
Harper
CAPE PALMAS
Tabou

Monrovia
LIBERIA

GHANA
Kumasi
Koforidua
Tarkwa
Sekondi
Takoradi
Cape Coast
Winneba
Accra
Tema
Ada
Keta
Lomé
TOGO
DAHOMEY
Abomey
Allada
Porto-Novo
Cotonou
Ouidah
Grand-Popo
Lagos
Abeokuta
Ijebu Ode
Ibadan
Iwo
Benin
Sapele
Warri
Forcados
Brass
Bonny
Onitsha
Enugu
Owerri
Aba
Port
Harcourt
Calabar
Kumba
Mamfe
Foumban
Dschang
BAMBUTO
MTS.
13 354
CAMEROO

GULF OF GUINEA
Bight of Benin
Bight of Biafra
FERNANDO POO
(Sp.)
Santa Isabel
ILHA DO PRINCIPE
(Port.)
ILHA DE SÃO TOMÉ
(Port.)
São Tomé
Victoria
Douala
Kribi
Edéa
Eséka
Yaoundé
Campo
Ebolowa
RIO
MUNI
(Sp.)
Bata
Oyem
Makokou
Libreville
GABO

ATLANTIC OCEAN

SANTO ANTÃO
Pto. Grande
SÃO VICENTE
SÃO NICOLAU
SAL
BOA VISTA
ILHAS DO
CABO VERDE
(Port.)
Same scale as main map
SÃO TIAGO
MAIO
Praia
FOGO

A-589100-76   1-1-1 13
COPYRIGHT BY
RAND MCNALLY & COMPANY
MADE IN U.S.A.

Longitude West of Greenwich
Longitude East of Greenwich

Scale 1:16 000 000; one inch to 250 miles. Sinusoidal Projection
Elevations and depressions are given in feet

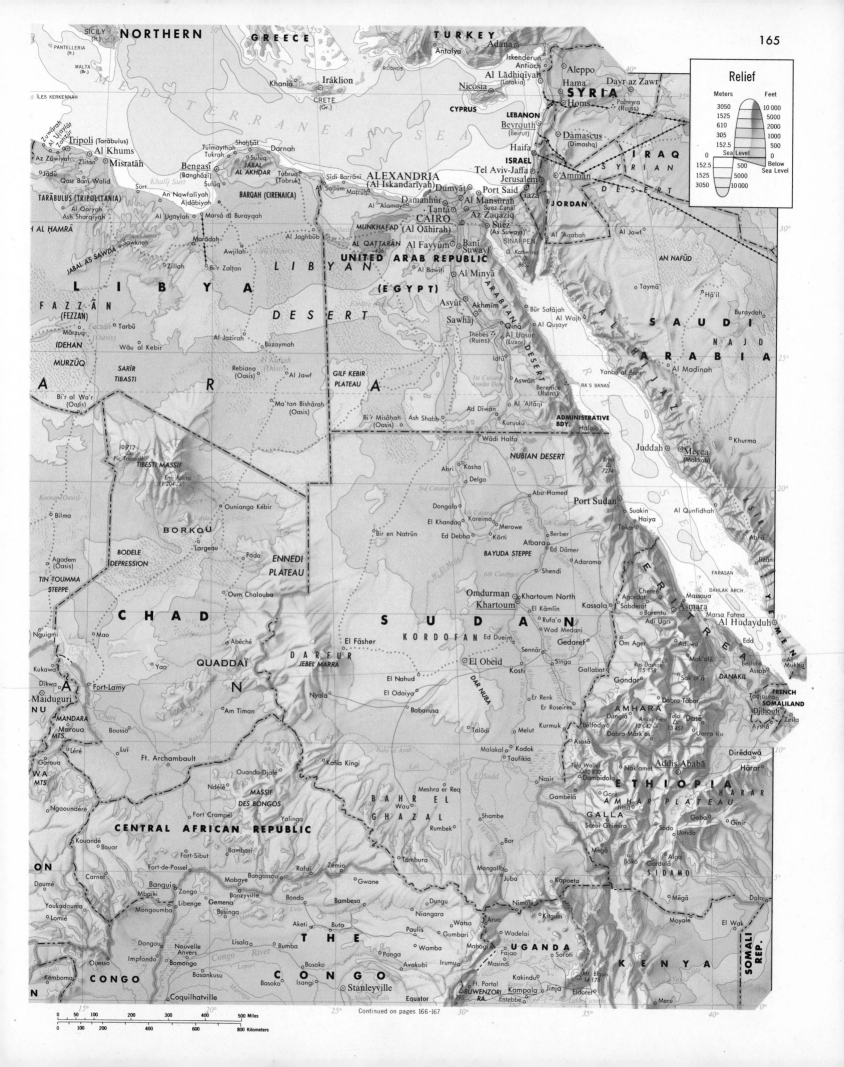

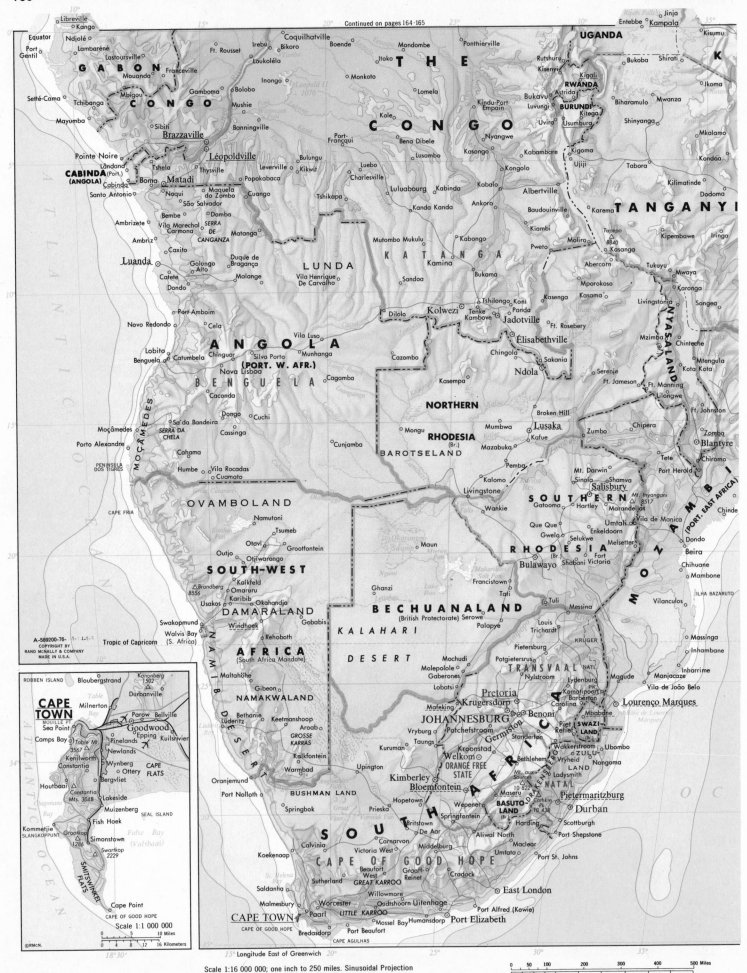

Continued on pages 164·165

Scale 1:16 000 000; one inch to 250 miles. Sinusoidal Projection
Elevations and depressions are given in feet

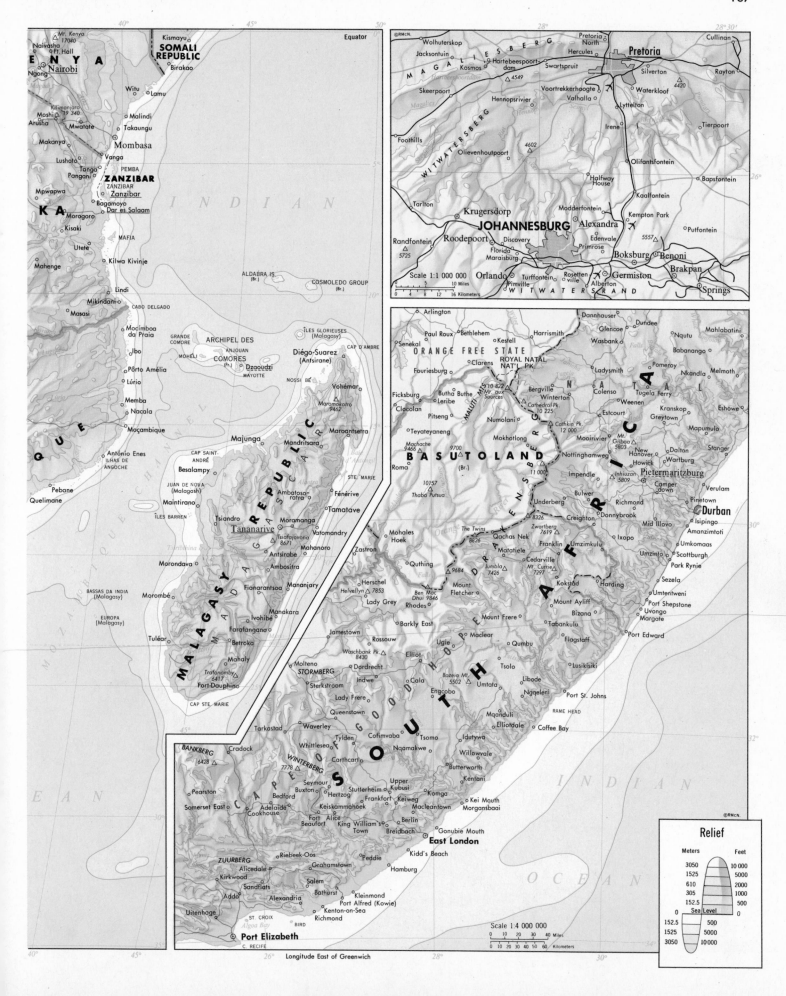

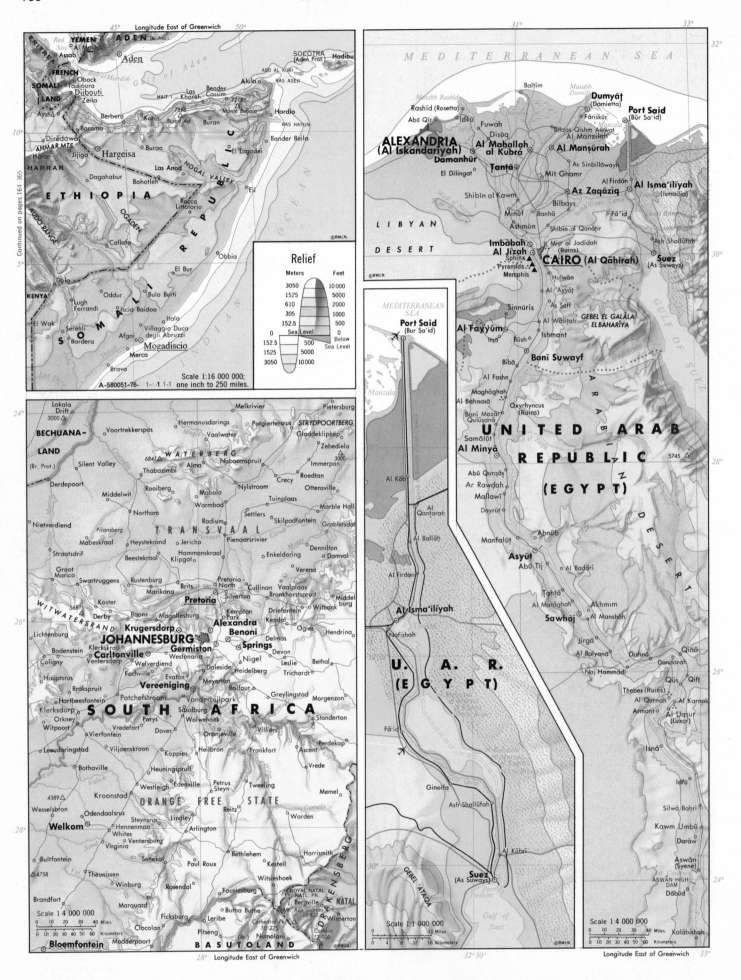

WORLD COMPARISONS

General Information

Equatorial diameter of the earth, 7,926.68 miles
Polar diameter of the earth, 7,899.99 miles
Diameter of the mean sphere of the earth, 7,917.78 miles
Equatorial circumference of the earth, 24,902.45 miles
Polar circumference of the earth, 24,818.60 miles
Mean distance from the earth to the sun, 92,900,000 miles
Mean distance from the earth to the moon, 238,857 miles
Total area of the earth, 196,940,400 square miles

Highest elevation on the earth's surface, Mt. Everest, Asia, 29,028 feet
Lowest elevation on the earth's land surface, shores of the Dead Sea, Asia,—1,286 feet.
Greatest known depth of the ocean, south of the Mariana Islands, Pacific Ocean, 36,198 feet
Total land area of the earth, including inland water and Antarctica, 57,280,000 square miles

Area of Africa, 11,685,000 square miles
Area of Antarctica, 5,100,000 square miles
Area of Asia, 17,085,000 square miles
Area of Europe, 3,825,000 square miles
Area of North America, 9,420,000 square miles
Area of Oceania, incl. Australia, 3,295,000 square miles
Area of South America, 6,870,000 square miles
Population of the earth (est. 1/1/1964), 3,193,000,000

Principal Islands and Their Areas

Island	Area Sq. Miles
Baffin, Arctic Region	183,810
Banks, Arctic Region	23,230
Borneo, Asia	286,967
Bougainville, Oceania	3,880
Celebes, Indonesia	72,986
Ceylon, Indian Ocean	25,332
Corsica, Mediterranean Sea	3,367
Crete, Mediterranean Sea	3,238
Cuba, West Indies	44,217
Cyprus, Mediterranean Sea	3,572
Devon, Arctic Region	20,861
Ellesmere, Arctic Region	82,119
Formosa, China Sea	13,885
Great Britain, Europe	88,756
Greenland, Arctic Region	840,000
Hainan Tao, South China Sea	13,127
Hawaii, Oceania	4,030
Hispaniola, West Indies	29,530
Hokkaidō, Japan	29,950
Honshū, Japan	88,930
Iceland, Arctic Region	39,800
Ireland, Europe	32,596
Jamaica, West Indies	4,411
Java, Indonesia	50,745
Kyūshū, Japan	16,215
Luzon, Philippines	40,814
Madagascar, Indian Ocean	227,800
Melville, Arctic Region	16,141
Mindanao, Philippines	36,906
Mindoro, Philippines	3,794
Negros, Philippines	4,903
New Britain, Oceania	14,592
Newfoundland, Canada	42,734
New Guinea, Oceania	316,856
North East Land, Arctic Region	6,350
North Island (New Zealand), Oceania	44,281
Nouvelle Caledonie, Oceania	5,671
Novaya Zemlya, Arctic Region	31,390
Palawan, Philippines	4,500
Panay, Philippines	4,448
Prince of Wales, Arctic Region	12,830
Puerto Rico, West Indies	3,435
Sakhalin, Soviet Union	29,344
Samar, Philippines	5,124
Sardinia, Mediterranean Sea	9,301
Seram, Indonesia	6,046
Sicily, Mediterranean Sea	9,926
Shikoku, Japan	7,245
Somerset, Arctic Region	9,370
Southampton, Hudson Bay	15,700
South Island (New Zealand) Oceania	58,093
Sumatra, Indonesia	182,859
Tasmania, Australia	26,215
Tierra del Fuego, S.A.	18,600
Timor, Asia	13,094
Vancouver, Canada	12,408
Victoria, Arctic Region	81,930
Vrangelya, Arctic Region	2,819
West Spitsbergen, Arctic Region	15,260

Principal Lakes, Oceans, Seas, and Their Areas

Lake Country	Area Sq. Miles
Aral'skoye More (Aral Sea) Sov. Un.	26,518
Arctic O.	5,427,000
Athabasca, L., Can.	3,120
Atlantic O.	31,744,000
Balkhash, Ozero (L.), Sov. Un.	6,678
Baltic Sea, Eur.	163,000
Baykal, Ozero (L.), Sov. Un.	12,159
Bering Sea, Asia-N.A.	876,000
Black Sea, Eur.-Asia	178,000
Caribbean Sea, N.A.-S.A.	750,000
Caspian Sea, Sov. Un.	152,084
Chad, L., Chad	6,300
Ch'ing Hai (Koko Nor) (L.), China	1,650
East China Sea, Asia	482,000
Erie, L., U. S.-Can.	9,940
Eyre, L., Austl.	3,700
Gairdner, L., Austl.	1,500
Great Bear L., Can.	12,275
Great Salt L., U. S.	1,700
Great Slave L., Can.	10,980
Hudson Bay, Can.	476,000
Huron, L., U. S.-Can.	23,010
Indian O.	28,371,000
Japan, Sea of, Asia	389,000
Ladozhskoye Ozero (Lake Ladoga), Sov. Un.	7,092
Leopold II, L., Con. L.	1,700
Manitoba, L., Can.	1,817
Mediterranean Sea, Eur.-Afr.-Asia	967,000
Mexico, G. of, N. A.	596,000
Michigan, L., U. S.	22,400
Nicaragua, Lago de (L.), Nic.	2,972
North Sea, Eur.	222,000
Nyasa, L., Afr.	10,900
Okhotsk, Sea of, Pac. O.	590,000
Onezhskoye Ozero (Lake Onega), Sov. Un.	3,821
Ontario, L., U. S.-Can.	7,540
Pacific O.	63,855,000
Red Sea, Afr.-Asia	169,000
Rudolf, L., Ken.-Eth.	2,473
Superior, L., U. S.-Can.	31,820
Tanganyika, L., Tan.-Con. L.	10,965
Titicaca, Lago (L.), Bol.-Peru	3,500
Torrens, L., Austl.	2,200
Vänern, L., Swe.	2,156
Van Gölü (L.), Tur.	1,470
Victoria, L., Tan.	26,828
Winnipeg, L., Can.	9,465
Winnipegosis, L., Can.	2,103
Yellow Sea, China	480,000

Principal Mountains and Their Heights

Mountain Country	Height in Feet
Aconcagua, Argentina	22,834
Albert Edward, Papua	13,100
Altar, Ecuador	17,457
Annapurna, Nepal	26,504
Antisana, Ecuador	18,714
Antofalla, Argentina	21,129
Apo, Philippines	9,690
Ararat, Turkey	16,946
Azufre (Copiapó), Chile	19,947
Balbi, Solomon I.	9,000
Bandeira, Brazil	9,462
Barriere Juliana, West Irian	15,420
Bejeda, Ethiopia	15,158
Belukha, Soviet Union	15,157
Blanc, France-Italy	15,781
Blanca, Colorado, U. S.	14,317
Bolívar (La Columna), Venezuela	16,411
Bona, Alaska, U. S.	16,421
Borah, Idaho, U. S.	12,662
Cameroons, Cam.	13,353
Cano, Cape Verde Is.	9,760
Carstensz-Toppen, West Irian	16,503
Cayambe, Ecuador	19,170
Chimborazo, Ecuador	20,577
Citlaltépetl, Mexico	18,696
Colima, Mexico	14,235
Cook, New Zealand	12,349
Cotopaxi, Ecuador	19,344
Cristobal Colón, Colombia	18,947
Damavand, Iran	18,934
Dhaulagiri, Nepal	28,810
Dos Conos, Argentina	22,507
Dykh-Tau, Soviet Union	17,054
Elbert, Colorado, U. S.	14,431
El'brus, Soviet Union	18,468
Elgon, Kenya	14,178
El Misti, Peru	19,144
Emi Koussi, Chad	11,204
Erebus, Antarctica	12,280
Etna, Italy	10,868
Everest, Nepal-China	29,028
Finsteraarhorn, Switzerland	14,026
Foraker, Alaska, U. S.	17,395
Fuji-san, Japan	12,388
Galdhöpiggen, Norway	8,400
Gasherbrum, India	26,470
Godwin Austen (K-2), Pak.	28,250
Gosainthan, China	26,291
Gran Paradiso, Italy	13,323
Gunnbjörn, Greenland	12,139
Gurla Mandhata, China	25,355
Hekla, Iceland	4,747
Hood, Oregon, U. S.	11,245
Hsinkao Shan, Taiwan	13,113
Huascarán, Peru	22,205
Huila, Colombia	18,865
Hvannadalshnukur, Iceland	6,952
Illampu, Bolivia	21,490
Illimani, Bolivia	21,151
Incahuasi, Argentina-Chile	21,719
Ixtacihuatl, Mexico	17,343
Jabal Al Loz, Saudi Arabia	8,461
Jabal Razih, Saudi Arabia	11,999
Jungfrau, Switzerland	13,668
Kailas, China (Tibet)	22,028
Kāmet, India	25,447
Kanchenjunga, Nepal-Sikkim	28,159
Karisimbi, Con. L.	14,787
Kazbek, Soviet Union	16,558
Kenya, Kenya	17,040
Kerintji, Indonesia	12,484
Kilimanjaro, Tanganyika	19,340
Kinabalu, Malaysia	13,455
Klyuchevskaya, Soviet Union	15,912
Kommunizma, Soviet Union	24,590
Korab, Albania	9,068
Kosciusko, Australia	7,316
Krakatoa (Rakata), Indonesia	2,667
Kwanmo, Korea	8,336
Lassen, California, U. S.	10,466
Lenina, Soviet Union	23,382
Leuser, Indonesia	11,178
Llullaillaco, Argentina-Chile	22,146
Logan, Canada	19,850
McKinley, Alaska, U. S.	20,320
Makalu, China-Nepal	27,790
Markham, Antarctica	15,100
Maromokotro, Malagasy	9,462
Matterhorn, Switz.-Italy	14,685
Mauna Kea, Hawaii, U. S.	13,796
Mauna Loa, Hawaii, U. S.	13,680
Mercedario, Argentina-Chile	22,211
Minya Konka, China	24,900
Mitchell, North Carolina, U. S.	6,684
Musala, Bulgaria	9,592
Muztagh Ata, China	24,388
Namcha Barwa, China	25,445
Nanda Devi, India	25,645
Nanga Parbat, Pak.	26,660
Negoi, Romania	8,344
Neiges, Piton des, Reunion	10,069
Ojos del Salado, Argentina-Chile	22,590
Ólimbos, Greece	9,550
Orohena, Tahiti	7,618
Paricutín, Mexico	9,100
Pelée, Martinique	4,800
Pic du Midi d'Ossau, France	10,322
Pidurutalagala, Ceylon	8,281
Pikes Peak, Colorado, U. S.	14,110
Pissis, Argentina	22,546
Pobeda, China-Soviet Union	24,409
Popocatépetl, Mexico	17,883
Pulog, Philippines	9,612
Qurnet es Sa'uda, Lebanon	10,131
Rainier, Washington, U. S.	14,410
Rakaposhi, India	25,551
Rindjani, Indonesia	12,225
Rosa, Monte, Italy-Switzerland	15,200
Ruapehu, New Zealand	9,175
Ruwenzori, Con. L.-Uganda	16,821
St. Elias, U.S.-Canada	18,008
Sajama, Bolivia	21,391
Sanford, Alaska, U. S.	16,208
Sangay, Ecuador	17,749
Semeroe, Indonesia	12,060
Shasta, California, U. S.	14,162
Shkhara, Soviet Union	17,059
Sources, Mt. aux, Basutoland-S. Afr.	10,822
Tengri Khan, Soviet Union	22,940
Thabantshonyana, Basutoland	11,425
Tina, Dominican Republic	9,285
Tirich Mir, Pak.	25,426
Tocorpuri, Bolivia-Chile	22,162
Toubkal, Morocco	13,661
Tupungato, Argentina-Chile	22,310
Ulugh Muztagh, China	25,340
Vesuvio (Vesuvius), Italy	3,842
Victoria, Papua	13,363
Vinson Massif, Ant.	16,864
Weisshorn, Switzerland	14,803
Whitney, California, U. S.	14,495
Wilhelmina-Top, West Irian	15,518
Wrangell, Alaska, U. S.	14,005
Yerupaja, Peru	21,758

Principal Rivers and Their Lengths

River Continent	Length in Miles
Albany, North America	610
Aldan, Asia	1,392
Amazonas, South America	3,900
Amu Dar'ya (Oxus), Asia	1,628
Amur, Asia	2,802
Araguaia, South America	1,630
Arkansas, North America	1,450
Athabasca, North America	765
Back, North America	605
Brahmaputra, Asia	1,800
Branco, South America	580
Brazos, North America	870
Canadian, North America	906
Churchill, North America	1,000
Colorado, North America	1,450
Columbia, North America	1,214
Congo, Africa	2,900
Cumberland, North America	687
Danube, Europe	1,770
Darling, Australia	1,750
Dnepr (Dnieper), Europe	1,420
Dnestr (Dniester), Europe	876
Don, Europe	1,224
Donets, Europe	735
Elbe, Europe	720
Euphrates, Asia	1,675
Fraser, North America	850
Gambia, Africa	680
Ganges, Asia	1,550
Gila, North America	630
Godāvari, Asia	930
Hsi Chiang, Asia	1,590
Hwang Ho (Yellow), Asia	2,903
Indus, Asia	1,980
Irrawaddy, Asia	1,425
Japurá, South America	1,400
Juruá, South America	1,200
Kama, Europe	1,261
Kolyma, Asia	1,615
Lena, Asia	2,653
Loire, Europe	625
Mackenzie, North America	2,635
Madeira, South America	2,060
Magdalena, South America	950
Marañón, South America	1,000
Mekong, Asia	2,600
Meuse, Europe	575
Mississippi, North America	2,348
Mississippi-Missouri-Red Rock, N. A.	3,860
Missouri-Red Rock, N. A.	2,683
Murray, Australia	1,600
Negro, South America	1,305
Nelson, North America	1,600
Neman, Eur.	582
Niger, Africa	2,590
Nile, Africa	4,132
Obitsu-Irtysh, Asia	3,461
Oder, Europe	565
Ohio, N. A.	981
Oka, Europe	920
Orange, Africa	1,155
Orinoco, South America	1,800
Ottawa, North America	696
Paraguay, South America	1,290
Paraná, South America	2,450
Parnaíba, South America	850
Peace, North America	1,195
Pechora, Europe	1,118
Pecos, North America	735
Pilcomayo, South America	1,550
Plata-Paraguay, S. America	2,300
Purús, South America	1,900
Red, North America	1,018
Rhein, Europe	820
Rhône, Europe	500
Rio Grande, North America	1,885
Roosevelt, South America	950
St. Lawrence, North America	1,900
Salado, South America	870
Salween, Asia	1,730
São Francisco, South America	1,800
Saskatchewan, North America	1,205
Sava, Europe	585
Senegal, Africa	1,000
Snake, North America	1,038
Sung Hua (Sungari), Asia	1,140
Syr Dar'ya, Asia	1,653
Tajo (Tagus), Europe	625
Tennessee, N. A.	652
Tigris, Asia	1,150
Tisza, Europe	607
Tobol, Asia	1,093
Tocantins, South America	1,640
Ucayali, South America	1,220
Ural, Europe	1,522
Uruguay, South America	1,025
Verkhnyaya Tunguska (Angara), Asia	1,549
Vilyuy, Asia	1,513
Volga, Europe	2,293
White, North America	690
Wisla (Vistula), Europe	630
Xingú, South America	1,230
Yangtze, Asia	3,430
Yellowstone, North America	671
Yenisey, Asia	2,566
Yukon, North America	1,800
Zambezi, Africa	1,659

PRINCIPAL COUNTRIES AND REGIONS OF THE WORLD

Political Division or Region	Area in sq. miles	Population 1/1/64 est.	Pop. per sq. mi.
Aden (U.K.)	111,100	1,250,000	11
Afghanistan	251,000	15,000,000	60
Africa	11,685,000	278,000,000	24
Alabama (U.S.)	51,609	3,414,000	66
Alaska (U.S.)	586,400	256,000	0.4
Albania	11,099	1,800,000	162
Alberta (Can.)	255,285	1,422,000	5.6
Algeria	917,537	11,200,000	12
American Samoa (U.S.)	76	22,000	289
Andorra	175	11,000	63
Angola (Port.)	481,351	5,050,000	10
Antarctica	5,100,000	....	....
Antigua (incl. Barbuda) (U.K.)	171	58,000	339
Argentina	1,072,070	21,800,000	20
Arizona (U.S.)	113,909	1,598,000	14
Arkansas (U.S.)	53,104	1,834,000	35
Asia	17,085,000	1,860,500,000	109
Australia (Br. Comm.)	2,971,081	11,065,000	3.7
Austria	32,374	7,175,000	222
Azores Is. (Port.)	894	331,000	370
Bahama Is. (U.K.)	4,375	116,000	27
Bahrain	231	162,000	701
Barbados (U.K.)	166	235,000	1,416
Basutoland (U.K.)	11,716	725,000	62
Bechuanaland (U.K.)	275,000	365,000	1.3
Belgium	11,778	9,300,000	790
Bermuda (U.K.)	21	58,000	2,762
Bhutan	19,300	710,000	37
Bolivia	424,163	3,650,000	8.6
Bonin Is. (U.S. Admin.)	40	200	5.0
Brazil	3,286,478	78,700,000	24
British Columbia (Can.)	366,255	1,710,000	4.7
Br. Comm. of Nations	11,177,751	777,440,000	70
British Guiana (U.K.)	83,000	620,000	7.5
British Honduras (U.K.)	8,866	100,000	11
Brunei (U.K.)	2,226	95,000	43
Bulgaria	42,729	8,100,000	190
Burma	261,789	23,000,000	88
Burundi (Urundi)	10,747	2,600,000	242
California (U.S.)	158,693	17,947,000	113
Cambodia	66,606	5,900,000	89
Cameroon	183,569	4,650,000	25
Canada (Br. Comm.)	3,851,809	19,100,000	5.0
Canal Zone (U.S.)	553	47,000	85
Canary Is. (Sp.)	2,808	990,000	353
Cape Verde Is. (Port.)	1,552	218,000	140
Cayman Is. (U.K.)	100	8,000	80
Central African Republic	238,200	1,275,000	5.4
Central America	200,412	13,247,000	66
Ceylon (Br. Comm.)	25,332	10,850,000	428
Chad	495,800	2,850,000	5.7
Channel Is. (U.K.)	75	109,000	1,453
Chile	286,397	8,050,000	28
China (excl. Taiwan)	3,691,500	710,000,000	192
Colombia	439,513	15,300,000	35
Colorado (U.S.)	104,247	1,978,000	19
Congo (Republic of Congo; capital Brazzaville)	132,000	850,000	6.4
Congo, The (Republic of the Congo; capital Léopoldville)	905,565	15,200,000	17
Connecticut (U.S.)	5,009	2,683,000	536
Cook Is. (N.Z.)	90	19,000	211
Costa Rica	19,600	1,350,000	69
Cuba	44,217	7,000,000	158
Cyprus	3,572	590,000	165
Czechoslovakia	49,367	14,000,000	284
Dahomey	44,696	2,200,000	49
Delaware (U.S.)	2,057	485,000	236
Denmark	16,619	4,710,000	283
Denmark and Possessions	857,159	4,783,000	5.6
Dist. of Columbia (U.S.)	69	785,000	11,377
Dominica (U.K.)	305	62,000	203
Dominican Republic	18,704	3,400,000	182
Ecuador	104,506	4,800,000	46
El Salvador	8,260	2,725,000	330
England & Wales (U.K.)	58,344	47,500,000	814
Ethiopia	457,267	21,000,000	46
Europe	3,825,000	595,800,000	156
Faeroe Is. (Den.)	540	36,000	67
Falkland Is. (excl. Deps.) (U.K.)	4,618	2,100	0.5
Fernando Poo (Sp.)	785	68,000	87
Fiji (U.K.)	7,040	441,000	63
Finland	130,119	4,565,000	35
Florida (U.S.)	58,560	5,751,000	98
France	212,822	48,000,000	226
France and Possessions	276,238	49,500,000	179
French Guiana (Fr.)	35,100	36,000	1.0
French Polynesia (Fr.)	1,550	80,000	52
French Somaliland (Fr.)	8,500	70,000	8.2
Gabon	103,100	475,000	4.6
Gambia (U.K.)	4,008	320,000	80
Georgia (U.S.)	58,876	4,180,000	71
Germany (Entire)	137,743	74,950,000	544
Germany, East	41,815	17,100,000	409
Germany, West (incl. West Berlin)	95,928	57,850,000	603
Ghana (Br. Comm.)	91,843	7,450,000	81
Gibraltar (U.K.)	2	28,000	14,000
Gilbert & Ellice Is. (U.K.)	369	50,000	136
Greece	50,547	8,450,000	167
Greenland (Den.)	840,000	37,000	0.04
Grenada (U.K.)	133	91,000	684
Guadeloupe (Fr.)	687	298,000	434
Guam (U.S.)	212	66,000	311
Guatemala	42,042	4,150,000	99
Guinea	94,925	3,300,000	35
Haiti	10,714	4,500,000	420
Hawaii (U.S.)	6,424	715,000	111
Honduras	43,277	2,040,000	47
Hong Kong (U.K.)	398	3,675,000	9,234
Hungary	35,919	10,110 000	281
Iceland	39,800	190,000	4.8
Idaho (U.S.)	83,557	700,000	8.4
Ifni (Sp.)	580	52,000	90
Illinois (U.S.)	56,400	10,457,000	185
India (incl. part of Kashmir) (Br. Comm.)	1,227,275	467,700,000	381
Indiana (U.S.)	36,291	4,825,000	133
Indonesia	574,670	101,000,000	176
Iowa (U.S.)	56,290	2,806,000	50
Iran	636,300	22,500,000	35
Iraq	171,599	7,700,000	45
Ireland	27,136	2,825,000	104
Isle of Man (U.K.)	227	48,000	211
Israel	7,815	2,435,000	312
Italy	116,303	50,650,000	436
Ivory Coast	124,503	3,500,000	28
Jamaica (Br. Comm.)	4,411	1,685,000	382
Japan	142,726	96,200,000	674
Jordan	37,301	1,825,000	49
Kansas (U.S.)	82,264	2,244,000	27
Kentucky (U.S.)	40,395	3,073,000	76
Kenya (Br. Comm.)	224,960	8,950,000	40
Korea (Entire)	85,255	37,500,000	440
Korea, North	47,255	10,300,000	218
Korea, South	38,000	27,200,000	716
Kuwait	6,000	350,000	58
Laos	91,400	1,950,000	21
Lebanon	4,000	1,940,000	485
Liberia	43,000	1,360,000	32
Libya	679,360	1,275,000	1.9
Liechtenstein	61	18,000	295
Louisiana (U.S.)	48,523	3,394,000	70
Luxembourg	998	325,000	326
Macao (Port.)	6	175,000	29,167
Madeira Is. (Port.)	308	269,000	873
Maine (U.S.)	33,215	1,003,000	30
Malagasy Republic (Madagascar)	227,800	5,950,000	26
Malaysia (Br. Comm.)	128,522	10,815,000	84
Maldive Is.	115	93,000	809
Mali	464,874	4,450,000	9.6
Malta (U.K.)	122	330,000	2,705
Manitoba (Can.)	251,000	960,000	3.8
Martinique (Fr.)	425	305,000	718
Maryland (U.S.)	10,577	3,300,000	312
Massachusetts (U.S.)	8,257	5,301,000	642
Mauritania	419,230	800,000	1.9
Mauritius (incl. Deps.) (U.K.)	808	735,000	910
Mexico	761,602	39,000,000	51
Michigan (U.S.)	58,216	8,133,000	140
Midway Is. (U.S.)	2	2,500	1,250
Minnesota (U.S.)	84,068	3,557,000	42
Mississippi (U.S.)	47,716	2,261,000	47
Missouri (U.S.)	69,686	4,402,000	63
Monaco	0.8	22,000	27,500
Mongolia	592,700	1,050,000	1.8
Montana (U.S.)	147,138	711,000	4.8
Montserrat (U.K.)	32	13,000	406
Morocco	171,305	12,700,000	74
Mozambique (Port.)	297,846	6,900,000	23
Muscat & Oman	82,000	575,000	7.0
Nauru (Austl.)	8	5,000	625
Nebraska (U.S.)	77,227	1,483,000	19
Nepal	54,362	9,800,000	180
Netherlands	12,978	12,050,000	928
Netherlands and Poss.	68,492	12,620,000	184
Neth. Antilles (Neth.)	371	204,000	550
Nevada (U.S.)	110,540	388,000	3.5
New Brunswick (Can.)	28,354	618,000	22
New Caledonia (incl. Deps.) (Fr.)	6,531	82,000	13
Newfoundland (Can.)	156,185	489,000	3.1
New Guinea Ter. (Austl.)	94,430	1,535,000	16
New Hampshire (U.S.)	9,304	643,000	69
New Hebrides (Fr.-U.K.)	5,700	65,000	11
New Jersey (U.S.)	7,836	6,430,000	821
New Mexico (U.S.)	121,666	1,029,000	8.5
New York (U.S.)	49,576	17,676,000	357
New Zealand (Br. Comm.)	103,736	2,575,000	25
Nicaragua	48,600	1,650,000	34
Niger	458,995	3,250,000	7.1
Nigeria (Br. Comm.)	356,669	37,600,000	105
Niue (N.Z.)	100	5,000	50
Norfolk I. (Austl.)	13	900	69
North America	9,420,000	283,900,000	30
North Carolina (U.S.)	52,712	4,771,000	91
North Dakota (U.S.)	70,665	644,000	9.1
Northern Ireland (U.K.)	5,459	1,450,000	266
Northern Rhodesia (U.K.)	288,130	3,550,000	12
Northwest Ters. (Can.)	1,304,903	24,000	0.02
Norway	125,064	3,685,000	29
Nova Scotia (Can.)	21,425	766,000	36
Nyasaland (U.K.)	45,747	3,200,000	70
Oceania	3,295,000	17,000,000	5.2
Ohio (U.S.)	41,222	10,369,000	252
Oklahoma (U.S.)	69,919	2,477,000	35
Ontario (Can.)	412,582	6,525,000	16
Oregon (U.S.)	96,981	1,887,000	19
Pacific Is. Tr. Ter. (U.S.)	672	85,000	126
Pakistan (incl. part of Kashmir) (Br. Comm.)	399,373	100,600,000	252
Panama	29,209	1,185,000	41
Papua (excl. N. Gui. Ter.) (Austl.)	90,600	560,000	6.2
Paraguay	157,047	1,875,000	12
Pennsylvania (U.S.)	45,333	11,504,000	254
Peru	496,223	11,900,000	24
Philippines	115,707	31,200,000	270
Pitcairn (excl. Deps.) (U.K.)	2	130	65
Poland	120,348	30,850,000	256
Portugal	35,340	9,025,000	255
Portugal and Possessions	837,733	22,523,000	27
Portuguese Guinea (Port.)	13,948	555,000	40
Portuguese Timor (Port.)	7,332	535,000	73
Prince Edward I. (Can.)	2,184	107,000	49
Puerto Rico (U.S.)	3,435	2,564,000	746
Qatar	8,500	65,000	7.6
Quebec (Can.)	594,860	5,525,000	9.3
Reunion (Fr.)	969	360,000	372
Rhode Island (U.S.)	1,214	878,000	723
Rio Muni (Sp.)	10,045	192,000	19
Romania	91,698	18,875,000	206
Rwanda (Ruanda)	10,169	2,875,000	283
St. Helena (incl. Deps.) (U.K.)	160	5,350	33
St. Kitts-Nevis-Anguilla (U.K.)	153	62,000	405
St. Lucia (U.K.)	238	92,000	387
St. Pierre & Miquelon (Fr.)	93	5,000	54
St. Vincent (U.K.)	150	84,000	560
San Marino	23	17,000	739
Sao Tome & Principe (Port.)	372	65,000	175
Saskatchewan (Can.)	251,700	938,000	3.7
Saudia Arabia	617,800	7,000,000	11
Scotland (U.K.)	30,411	5,250,000	173
Senegal	76,124	3,300,000	43
Seychelles (U.K.)	156	45,000	288
Sierra Leone (Br. Comm.)	27,925	2,600,000	93
Sikkim	2,744	170,000	62
Solomon Is. (Austl.)	4,320	60,000	14
Solomon Is., British (U.K.)	11,500	135,000	12
Somali Republic	246,202	2,000,000	8.1
South Africa	472,926	17,300,000	36
South America	6,870,000	157,800,000	23
South Carolina (U.S.)	31,055	2,458,000	79
South Dakota (U.S.)	77,047	709,000	9.2
Southern Rhodesia (U.K.)	150,333	4,080,000	27
S. W. Africa (S. Afr.)	317,887	565,000	1.8
Soviet Union	8,599,300	227,000,000	26
Spain	194,345	31,200,000	161
Spain and Possessions	308,540	31,695,000	103
Spanish Sahara (Sp.)	102,703	27,000	0.3
Sudan	967,500	13,000,000	13
Surinam (Neth.)	55,143	366,000	6.6
Svalbard (Nor.)	24,101	4,000 (winter only)	...
Swaziland (U.K.)	6,705	290,000	43
Sweden	173,666	7,620,000	44
Switzerland	15,941	5,825,000	365
Syria	71,498	5,000,000	70
Taiwan (Formosa) (Nationalist China)	13,884	11,900,000	857
Tanganyika (Br. Comm.)	361,800	9,800,000	27
Tennessee (U.S.)	42,244	3,668,000	87
Texas (U.S.)	267,339	10,313,000	39
Thailand	198,500	29,200,000	147
Tibet (China)	471,660	1,300,000	2.8
Togo	21,850	1,580,000	72
Tokelau (Union) Is. (N.Z.)	4	2,000	500
Tonga (U.K.)	270	70,000	260
Trinidad & Tobago (Br. Comm.)	1,980	925,000	467
Trucial Coast	32,300	115,000	3.6
Tunisia	48,332	4,400,000	91
Turkey	301,381	30,300,000	101
Turks & Caicos Is. (U.K.)	166	6,000	36
Uganda (Br. Comm.)	92,525	7,250,000	78
United Arab Republic (Egypt)	386,000	28,300,000	73
United Kingdom	94,214	54,200,000	575
United Kingdom and Poss.	1,118,573	75,427,000	67
United States	3,675,633	190,700,000	52
United States and Poss.	3,680,757	193,525,000	53
Upper Volta	105,869	4,600,000	43
Uruguay	72,172	2,450,000	34
Utah (U.S.)	84,916	985,000	12
Vatican City	0.2	1,000	5,000
Venezuela	352,143	8,250,000	23
Vermont (U.S.)	9,609	393,000	41
Vietnam (Entire)	125,881	33,000,000	262
Vietnam, North	59,933	17,500,000	292
Vietnam, South	65,948	15,500,000	235
Virgin Is. (U.S.-U.K.)	192	45,000	234
Virginia (U.S.)	40,815	4,237,000	104
Wales (incl. Monmouthshire) (U.K.)	8,017	2,655,000	331
Washington (U.S.)	68,192	3,030,000	44
Western Samoa	1,130	120,000	106
West Irian (Indon. Admin.)	160,600	775,000	4.8
West Virginia (U.S.)	24,181	1,748,000	72
Wisconsin (U.S.)	56,154	4,136,000	74
World	57,280,000	3,193,000,000	56
Wyoming (U.S.)	97,914	351,000	3.6
Yemen	75,300	5,000,000	66
Yugoslavia	98,766	19,200,000	194
Yukon (Can.)	207,076	16,000	0.08
Zanzibar (Br. Comm.)	1,020	327,000	321

GLOSSARY OF FOREIGN GEOGRAPHICAL TERMS

Annam ..... Annamese
Arab ..... Arabic
Bantu ..... Bantu
Bur ..... Burmese
Camb ..... Cambodian
Celt ..... Celtic
Chn ..... Chinese
Czech ..... Czech
Dan ..... Danish
Du ..... Dutch
Fin ..... Finnish
Fr ..... French
Ger ..... German
Gr ..... Greek
Hung ..... Hungarian
Ice ..... Icelandic
India ..... India
Indian ..... American Indian
Indon ..... Indonesian
It ..... Italian
Jap ..... Japanese
Kor ..... Korean
Mal ..... Malayan
Mong ..... Mongolian
Nor ..... Norwegian
Per ..... Persian
Pol ..... Polish
Port ..... Portuguese
Rom ..... Romanian
Rus ..... Russian
Siam ..... Siamese
So. Slav ... Southern Slavonic
Sp ..... Spanish
Swe ..... Swedish
Tib ..... Tibetan
Tur ..... Turkish
Yugo ..... Yugoslav

å, *Nor., Swe* ..... brook, river
aa, *Dan., Nor* ..... brook
aas, *Dan., Nor* ..... ridge
ab, *Per* ..... water, river
abad, *India, Per* ..... town, city
ada, *Tur* ..... island
adrar, *Arab* ..... mountain
air, *Indon* ..... stream
akrotírion, *Gr* ..... cape
älf, *Swe* ..... river
alp, *Ger* ..... mountain
altipiano, *It* ..... plateau
alto, *Sp* ..... height
archipel, *Fr* ..... archipelago
archipiélago, *Sp* ..... archipelago
arquipélago, *Port* ..... archipelago
arroyo, *Sp* ..... brook, stream
ås, *Nor., Swe* ..... ridge
austral, *Sp* ..... southern
baai, *Du* ..... bay
bab, *Arab* ..... gate, port
bach, *Ger* ..... brook, stream
backe, *Swe* ..... hill
bad, *Ger* ..... bath, spa
bahía, *Sp* ..... bay, gulf
bahr, *Arab* ..... sea, lake
baia, *It* ..... bay, gulf
baía, *Port* ..... bay
baie, *Fr* ..... bay, gulf
bajo, *Sp* ..... depression
bak, *Indon* ..... stream
bakke, *Dan., Nor* ..... hill
balkan, *Tur* ..... mountain range
bana, *Jap* ..... point, cape
banco, *Sp* ..... bank
bandar, *Mal., Per.* ..... town, port, harbor
bang, *Siam* ..... village
bassin, *Fr* ..... basin
batang, *Indon., Mal* ..... river
ben, *Celt* ..... mountain, summit
bender, *Arab* ..... harbor, port
bereg, *Rus* ..... coast, shore
berg, *Du., Ger., Nor., Swe.* ..... mountain, hill
bir, *Arab* ..... well
birket, *Arab* ..... pond, pool
bit, *Arab* ..... house
bjaerg, *Dan., Nor* ..... mountain
bocche, *It* ..... mouth
bogaz, *Tur* ..... strait
bois, *Fr* ..... forest, wood
boloto, *Rus* ..... marsh
bolsón, *Sp* flat-floored desert valley
boreal, *Sp* ..... northern
borg, *Dan., Nor., Swe* ..... castle, town
borgo, *It* ..... town, suburb
bosch, *Du* ..... forest, wood
bouche, *Fr* ..... river mouth
bourg, *Fr* ..... town, borough
bro, *Dan., Nor., Swe* ..... bridge
brücke, *Ger* ..... bridge
bucht, *Ger* ..... bay, bight
bugt, *Dan., Nor., Swe* ... bay, gulf
bulu, *Indon* ..... mountain
burg, *Du., Ger* ..... castle, town
buri, *Siam* ..... town
burun, burnu, *Tur* ..... cape
by, *Dan., Nor., Swe* ..... village
caatinga, *Port. (Brazil)* ..... open brushland
cabezo, *Sp* ..... summit
cabo, *Port., Sp* ..... cape
campo, *It., Port., Sp* ..... field
campos, *Port. (Brazil)* ..... plains
cañon, *Sp* ..... canyon
cap, *Fr* ..... cape
capo, *It* ..... cape
casa, *It., Port., Sp* ..... house
castello, *It., Port* ..... castle, fort
castillo, *Sp* ..... castle
càte, *Fr* ..... hill
çay, *Tur* ..... stream, river
cayo, *Sp* ..... rock, shoal, islet
cerro, *Sp* ..... hill
champ, *Fr* ..... field
chang, *Chn* ..... village, middle
château, *Fr* ..... castle
chen, *Chn* ..... market town
chiang, *Chn* ..... river
chott, *Arab* ..... salt lake
chou, *Chn* capital of district; island
chu, *Tib* ..... water, stream
cidade, *Port* ..... town, city
cima, *Sp* ..... summit, peak
città, *It* ..... town, city
ciudad, *Sp* ..... town, city
cochilha, *Port* ..... ridge
col, *Fr* ..... pass
colina, *Sp* ..... hill
cordillera, *Sp* ..... mountain chain
costa, *It., Port., Sp* ..... coast
côte, *Fr* ..... coast
cuchilla, *Sp* ..... mountain ridge
dag, *Tur* ..... mountain
dake, *Jap* ..... peak, summit
dal, *Dan., Du., Nor., Swe* ... valley
dan, *Kor* ..... point, cape
danau, *Indon* ..... lake
dar, *Arab* ... house, abode, country
darya, *Per* ..... river, sea
dasht, *Per* ..... plain, desert
deniz, *Tur* ..... sea
désert, *Fr* ..... desert
deserto, *It* ..... desert
desierto, *Sp* ..... desert
détroit, *Fr* ..... strait
dijk, *Du* ..... dam, dike
djebel, *Arab* ..... mountain
do, *Kor* ..... island
dorf, *Ger* ..... village
dorp, *Du* ..... village
duin, *Du* ..... dune
dzong, *Tib.* ..... fort, administrative capital
eau, *Fr* ..... water
ecuador, *Sp* ..... equator
eiland, *Du* ..... island
elv, *Dan., Nor* ..... river, stream
embalse, *Sp* ..... reservoir
erg, *Arab* ..... dune, sandy desert
est, *Fr., It* ..... east
estado, *Sp* ..... state
este, *Port., Sp* ..... east
estrecho, *Sp* ..... strait
étang, *Fr* ..... pond, lake
état, *Fr* ..... state
eyjar, *Ice* ..... islands
feld, *Ger* ..... field, plain
festung, *Ger* ..... fortress
fiume, *It* ..... river
fjäll, *Swe* ..... mountain
fjärd, *Swe* ..... bay, inlet
fjeld, *Nor* ..... mountain, hill
fjord, *Dan., Nor* ..... fiord, inlet
fjördur, *Ice* ..... fiord, inlet
fleuve, *Fr* ..... river
flod, *Dan., Swe* ..... river
flói, *Ice* ..... bay, marshland
fluss, *Ger* ..... river
foce, *It* ..... river mouth
fontein, *Du* ..... a spring
forêt, *Fr* ..... forest
fors, *Swe* ..... waterfall
forst, *Ger* ..... forest
fos, *Dan., Nor* ..... waterfall
fu, *Chn* ..... town, residence
fuente, *Sp* ..... spring, fountain
fuerte, *Sp* ..... fort
furt, *Ger* ..... ford
gang, *Kor* ..... stream, river
gangri, *Tib* ..... mountain
gat, *Dan., Nor* ..... channel
gàve, *Fr* ..... stream
gawa, *Jap* ..... river
gebergte, *Du* ..... mountain range
gebiet, *Ger* ..... district, territory
gebirge, *Ger* ..... mountains
ghat, *India* ... pass, mountain range
gobi, *Mong* ..... desert
goenoeng, *Mal* ..... mountain
gol, *Mong* ..... river
göl, gölü, *Tur* ..... lake
golf, *Du., Ger* ..... gulf, bay
golfe, *Fr* ..... gulf, bay
golfo, *It., Port., Sp* ..... gulf, bay
gomba, gompa, *Tib* ..... monastery
gora, *Rus., So. Slav* ..... mountain
góra, *Pol* ..... mountain
gorod, *Rus* ..... town
grad, *Rus., So. Slav* ..... town
guba, *Rus* ..... bay, gulf
gundung, *Indon* ..... mountain
guntō, *Jap* ..... archipelago
haf, *Swe* ..... sea, ocean
hafen, *Ger* ..... port, harbor
haff, *Ger* ..... gulf, inland sea
hai, *Chn* ..... sea, lake
hama, *Jap* ..... beach, shore
hamada, *Arab* ..... rocky plateau
hamn, *Swe* ..... harbor
hamun, *Per* ..... swampy lake, plain
hantō, *Jap* ..... peninsula
hassi, *Arab* ..... well, spring
haus, *Ger* ..... house
haut, *Fr* ..... summit, top
hav, *Dan., Nor* ..... sea, ocean
havn, *Dan., Nor* ..... harbor, port
havre, *Fr* ..... harbor, port
háza, *Hung* ..... house, dwelling of
heim, *Ger* ..... hamlet, home
hem, *Swe* ..... hamlet, home
higashi, *Jap* ..... east
hisar, *Tur* ..... fortress
hissar, *Arab* ..... fort
ho, *Chn* ..... river
hoek, *Du* ..... cape
hof, *Ger* ..... court, farm house
höfn, *Ice* ..... harbor
hoku, *Jap* ..... north
holm, *Dan., Nor., Swe* ..... island
hora, *Czech* ..... mountain
horn, *Ger* ..... peak
hoved, *Dan., Nor* ..... cape
hsien, *Chn* district, district capital
hu, *Chn* ..... lake
hügel, *Ger* ..... hill
huk, *Dan., Swe* ..... point
hus, *Dan., Nor., Swe* ..... house
île, *Fr* ..... island
ilha, *Port* ..... island
indsö, *Dan., Nor* ..... lake
insel, *Ger* ..... island
insjö, *Swe* ..... lake
irmak, irmagi, *Tur* ..... river
isla, *Sp* ..... island
isola, *It* ..... island
istmo, *It., Sp* ..... isthmus
istrova, *Rus* ..... islands
järvi, jaur, *Fin* ..... lake
jebel, *Arab* ..... mountain
jima, *Jap* ..... island
jökel, *Nor* ..... glacier
joki, *Fin* ..... river
jökull, *Ice* ... ice-covered mountain
kaap, *Du* ..... cape
kai, *Jap* ..... bay, gulf, sea
kaikyō, *Jap* ..... channel, strait
kalat, *Per* ..... castle, fortress
kale, *Tur* ..... fort
kali, *Mal* ..... river
kand, *Per* ..... village
kang, *Chn* mountain ridge; village
kap, *Dan., Ger* ..... cape
kapp, *Nor., Swe* ..... cape
kasr, *Arab* ..... fort, castle
kawa, *Jap* ..... river
kefr, *Arab* ..... village
kei, *Jap* ..... creek, river
ken, *Jap* ..... prefecture
khor, *Arab* ..... bay, inlet
khrebet, *Rus* ..... mountain range
kiang, *Chn* ..... large river
king, *Chn* ..... capital city, town
kita, *Jap* ..... north
ko, *Jap* ..... lake
köbstad, *Dan* ..... market-town
kol, *Mong* ..... lake
kólpos, *Gr* ..... gulf
kong, *Chn* ..... river
kopf, *Ger* ..... head, summit, peak
köpstad, *Swe* ..... market-town
korfezi, *Tur* ..... gulf
kosa, *Rus* ..... cape
kou, *Chn* ..... river mouth
köy, *Tur* ..... village
kraal, *Du. (Africa)* ... native village
ksar, *Arab* ..... fortified village
kuala, *Mal* ..... river mouth
kuh, *Per* ..... mountain
kum, *Tur* ..... sand
kuppe, *Ger* ..... summit
küste, *Ger* ..... coast
kyo, *Jap* ..... town, capital
la, *Tib* ..... mountain pass
labuan, *Mal* ..... anchorage, port
lac, *Fr* ..... lake
lago, *It., Port., Sp* ..... lake
lagoa, *Port* ..... lake, marsh
laguna, *It., Port., Sp* ... lagoon, lake
lahti, *Fin* ..... bay, gulf
län, *Swe* ..... county
landsby, *Dan., Nor* ..... village
liehtao, *Chn* ..... archipelago
liman, *Tur* ..... bay, port
ling, *Chn* ..... pass, ridge, mountain
llanos, *Sp* ..... plains
loch, *Celt. (Scotland)* ..... lake, bay
loma, *Sp* ..... long, low hill
lough, *Celt. (Ireland)* ..... lake, bay
machi, *Jap* ..... town
man, *Kor* ..... bay
mar, *Port., Sp* ..... sea
mare, *It., Rom* ..... sea
marisma, *Sp* ..... marsh, swamp
mark, *Ger* ..... boundary, limit
massif, *Fr* ..... block of mountains
mato, *Port* ..... forest, thicket
me, *Siam* ..... river
meer, *Du., Ger* ..... lake, sea
mer, *Fr* ..... sea
mesa, *Sp* ..... flat-topped mountain
meseta, *Sp* ..... plateau
mina, *Port., Sp* ..... mine
minami, *Jap* ..... south
minato, *Jap* ..... harbor, haven
misaki, *Jap* ..... cape, headland
mont, *Fr* ..... mount, mountain
montagna, *It* ..... mountain
montagne, *Fr* ..... mountain
montaña, *Sp* ..... mountain
monte, *It., Port., Sp.* ..... mount, mountain
more, *Rus., So. Slav* ..... sea
morro, *Port., Sp* ..... hill, bluff
mühle, *Ger* ..... mill
mund, *Ger* ..... mouth, opening
mündung, *Ger* ..... river mouth
mura, *Jap* ..... township
myit, *Bur* ..... river
mys, *Rus* ..... cape
nada, *Jap* ..... sea
nadi, *India* ..... river, creek
naes, *Dan., Nor* ..... cape
nafud, *Arab* ... desert of sand dunes
nagar, *India* ..... town, city
nahr, *Arab* ..... river
nam, *Siam* ..... river, water
nan, *Chn., Jap* ..... south
näs, *Nor., Swe* ..... cape
nez, *Fr* ..... point, cape
nishi, nisi, *Jap* ..... west
njarga, *Fin* ..... peninsula
nong, *Siam* ..... marsh
noord, *Du* ..... north
nor, *Mong* ..... lake
nord, *Dan., Fr., Ger., It., Nor., Swe* ..... north
norte, *Port., Sp* ..... north
nos, *Rus* ..... cape
nyasa, *Bantu* ..... lake
ö, *Dan., Nor., Swe* ..... island
occidental, *Sp* ..... western
ocna, *Rom* ..... salt mine
odde, *Dan., Nor* ..... point, cape
oedjoeng, *Mal* ..... point, cape
oeste, *Port., Sp* ..... west
oka, *Jap* ..... hill
oost, *Du* ..... east
oriental, *Sp* ..... eastern
óros, *Gr* ..... mountain
ost, *Ger., Swe* ..... east
öster, *Dan., Nor., Swe* ..... eastern
ostrov, *Rus* ..... island
oued, *Arab* ..... river, stream
ouest, *Fr* ..... west
ozero, *Rus* ..... lake
pää, *Fin* ..... mountain
padang, *Mal* ..... plain, field
pampas, *Sp. (Argentina)* ..... grassy plains
pará, *Indian (Brazil)* ..... river
pas, *Fr* ..... channel, passage
paso, *Sp* ..... passage
passo, *It., Port* ..... passage, strait
patam, *India* ..... city, town
pei, *Chn* ..... north
pélagos, *Gr* ..... open sea
pegunungan, *Indon* ..... mountains
peña, *Sp* ..... rock
peresheyek, *Rus* ..... isthmus
pertuis, *Fr* ..... strait
peski, *Rus* ..... desert
pic, *Fr* ..... mountain peak
pico, *Port., Sp* ..... mountain peak
piedra, *Sp* ..... stone, rock
ping, *Chn* ..... plain, flat
planalto, *Port* ..... plateau
planina, *Yugo* ..... mountains
playa, *Sp* ..... shore, beach
pnom, *Camb* ..... mountain
poelau, *Mal* ..... island
pointe, *Fr* ..... point
polder, *Du., Ger* ... reclaimed marsh
polje, *So. Slav* ..... field
poluostrov, *Rus* ..... peninsula
pont, *Fr* ..... bridge
ponta, *Port* ..... point, headland
ponte, *It., Port* ..... bridge
pore, *India* ..... city, town
porthmós, *Gr* ..... strait
porto, *It., Port* ..... port, harbor
potamós, *Gr* ..... river
p'ov, *Rus* ..... peninsula
prado, *Sp* ..... field, meadow
presqu'île, *Fr* ..... peninsula
proliv, *Rus* ..... strait
pu, *Chn* ..... commercial village
pueblo, *Sp* ..... town, village
puerto, *Sp* ..... port, harbor
pulau, *Mal* ..... island
punkt, *Ger* ..... point
punt, *Du* ..... point
punta, *It., Sp* ..... point
pur, *India* ..... city, town
puy, *Fr* ..... peak
qal'a, qal'at, *Arab* ..... fort, village
qasr, *Arab* ..... fort, castle
rann, *India* ..... wasteland
ras, *Arab* ..... cape, head
reka, *Rus., So. Slav* ..... river
represa, *Port* ..... reservoir
rettō, *Jap* ..... island chain
ría, *Sp* ..... estuary
ribeira, *Port* ..... stream
riberão, *Port* ..... river
rio, *It., Port* ..... stream, river
río, *Sp* ..... river
rivière, *Fr* ..... river
roca, *Sp* ..... rock
rt, *Yugo* ..... cape
rud, *Per* ..... river
saari, *Fin* ..... island
sable, *Fr* ..... sand
sahara, *Arab* ..... desert, plain
saki, *Jap* ..... cape
sal, *Sp* ..... salt
salar, *Sp* ..... salt flat, salt lake
salto, *Sp* ..... waterfall
san, *Jap., Kor* ..... mountain, hill
sat, satul, *Rom* ..... village
schloss, *Ger* ..... castle
sebkha, *Arab* ..... salt marsh
see, *Ger* ..... lake, sea
şehir, *Tur* ..... town, city
selat, *Indon* ..... stream
selvas, *Port. (Brazil)* ..... tropical rain forests
seno, *Sp* ..... bay
serra, *Port* ..... mountain chain
serranía, *Sp* ..... mountain ridge
seto, *Jap* ..... strait
severnaya, *Rus* ..... northern
shahr, *Per* ..... town, city
shan, *Chn* ... mountain, hill, island
shatt, *Arab* ..... river
shi, *Jap* ..... city
shima, *Jap* ..... island
shōtō, *Jap* ..... archipelago
si, *Chn* ..... west, western
sierra, *Sp* ..... mountain range
sjö, *Nor., Swe* ..... lake, sea
sö, *Dan., Nor* ..... lake, sea
söder, södra, *Swe* ..... south
soengai, soengei, *Mal* ..... river
song, *Annam* ..... river
sopka, *Rus* ..... peak, volcano
source, *Fr* ..... a spring
spitze, *Ger* ..... summit, point
staat, *Ger* ..... state
stad, *Dan., Du., Nor., Swe.* ..... city, town
stadt, *Ger* ..... city, town
stato, *It* ..... state
step, *Rus* ..... treeless plain, steppe
straat, *Du* ..... strait
strand, *Dan., Du., Ger., Nor., Swe* ..... shore, beach
stretto, *It* ..... strait
strom, *Ger* ..... river, stream
ström, *Dan., Nor., Swe* stream, river
stroom, *Du* ..... stream, river
su, suyu, *Tur* ..... water, river
sud, *Fr., Sp* ..... south
süd, *Ger* ..... south
suidō, *Jap* ..... channel
sul, *Port* ..... south
sund, *Dan., Nor., Swe* ..... sound
sungai, sungei, *Indon., Mal* ... river
sur, *Sp* ..... south
syd, *Dan., Nor., Swe* ..... south
tafelland, *Ger* ..... plateau
take, *Jap* ..... peak, summit
tal, *Ger* ..... valley
tandjoeng, tanjong, *Mal* ..... cape
tao, *Chn* ..... island
târg, târgul, *Rom* ..... market, town
tell, *Arab* ..... hill
teluk, *Indon* ..... bay, gulf
terra, *It* ..... land
terre, *Fr* ..... earth, land
thal, *Ger* ..... valley
tierra, *Sp* ..... earth, land
tō, *Jap* ..... east; island
tonle, *Camb* ..... river, lake
top, *Du* ..... peak
torp, *Swe* ..... hamlet, cottage
tsangpo, *Tib* ..... river
tsi, *Chn* ..... village, borough
tso, *Tib* ..... lake
tsu, *Jap* ..... harbor, port
tundra, *Rus* ... treeless arctic plains
tung, *Chn* ..... east
tuz, *Tur* ..... salt
udde, *Swe* ..... cape
ufer, *Ger* ..... shore, river bank
umi, *Jap* ..... sea, gulf
ura, *Jap* ..... bay, coast, creek
ust'ye, *Rus* ..... river mouth
valle, *It., Port., Sp* ..... valley
vallée, *Fr* ..... valley
valli, *It* ..... lake
vár, *Hung* ..... fortress
város, *Hung* ..... town
varoš, *So. Slav* ..... town
veld, *Du* ..... open plain, field
verkh, *Rus* ..... top, summit
ves, *Czech* ..... village
vest, *Dan., Nor., Swe* ..... west
vik, *Swe* ..... cove, bay
vila, *Port* ..... town
villa, *Sp* ..... town
villar, *Sp* ..... village, hamlet
ville, *Fr* ..... town, city
vostok, *Rus* ..... east
wad, wadi, *Arab.* ..... intermittent stream
wald, *Ger* ..... forest, woodland
wan, *Chn., Jap* ..... bay, gulf
weiler, *Ger* ..... hamlet, village
westersch, *Du* ..... western
wüste, *Ger* ..... desert
yama, *Jap* ..... mountain
yarimada, *Tur* ..... peninsula
yug, *Rus* ..... south
zaki, *Jap* ..... cape
zaliv, *Rus* ..... bay, gulf
zapad, *Rus* ..... west
zee, *Du* ..... sea
zemlya, *Rus* ..... land
zuid, *Du* ..... south

ABBREVIATIONS OF
GEOGRAPHICAL NAMES AND TERMS

Afg	Afghanistan
Afr	Africa
Ala	Alabama
Alb	Albania
Alg	Algeria
And	Andorra
Ang	Angola
Ant	Antarctica
Arc. O	Arctic Ocean
Arch	Archipelago
Arg	Argentina
Ariz	Arizona
Ark	Arkansas
A. S. S. R.	Autonomous Soviet Socialist Republic
Atl. O	Atlantic Ocean
Aus	Austria
Austl	Australia
Aut	Autonomous
B	Bay, Bahia
Ba. Is	Bahama Is.
Barb	Barbados
Bas	Basutoland
Bdy	Boundary
Bech	Bechuanaland
Bel	Belgium
Bg	Berg
Bhu	Bhutan
Bk	Bank
Bol	Bolivia
Br	British
Braz	Brazil
Br. Comm.	British Commonwealth of Nations
Br. Gu	British Guiana
Br. Hond	British Honduras
Brit. Prot	British Protectorate
Bru	Brunei
Bul	Bulgaria
Bur	Burma
C	Cerro, Cape
Calif	California
Cam	Cameroun
Camb	Cambodia
Can	Canal, Canada
Can. Is	Canary Is.
Cen. Afr. Rep.	Central African Republic
Cen. Am	Central America
C. H	Court House
Chan	Channel
Co	County
Col	Colombia
Colo	Colorado
Con. B.	Congo; capital Brazzaville
Con. L	Congo, The; capital; Léopoldville
Conn	Connecticut
Cor	Corsica
C. R	Costa Rica
Cr	Creek
C. V. Is	Cape Verde Is.
C. Z	Canal Zone
Czech	Czechoslovakia
D. C	District of Columbia
Del	Delaware
Den	Denmark
Dept	Department
Des	Desert
D. F	Distrito Federal
Dist	District
Div	Division
Dom. Rep.	Dominican Republic
E	East
Ec	Ecuador
Elec	Electric
Eng	England
E. Pak	East Pakistan
Eth	Ethiopia
Eur	Europe
Faer	Faeroe Is.
Falk. Is	Falkland Is.
Fd	Fjord
Fin	Finland
Fk	Fork
Fla	Florida
For	Forest
Fr	France
Fr. Gu	French Guiana
Fr. Som	French Somaliland
Ft	Fort
G	Gulf
Ga	Georgia
Gam	Gambia
Ger	Germany
Gib	Gibraltar
Grc	Greece
Grnld	Greenland
Gt	Great
Gt. Brit	Great Britain
Guad	Guadeloupe

Guat	Guatemala
Gui	Guinea
Hai	Haiti
Har., Hbr	Harbor
Hd	Head
Hond	Honduras
Hts	Heights
Hung	Hungary
I	Island
Ice	Iceland
Ill	Illinois
In	Inset
Ind	Indiana
Ind. O	Indian Ocean
Indon	Indonesia
Ind. Res	Indian Reservation
Int., Intl	International
Ire	Ireland
Is	Islands
Isr	Israel
Isth	Isthmus
It	Italy
Jam	Jamaica
Jap	Japan
Jc	Junction
Kans	Kansas
Ken	Kenya
Km	Kilometer, Kilometers
Kor	Korea
Kur. Is	Kuril Is.
Kuw	Kuwait
Ky	Kentucky
L	Lake, Loch, Lough
La	Louisiana
Lat	Latitude
Leb	Lebanon
Le. Is	Leeward Is.
Lib	Liberia
Liech	Liechtenstein
Long	Longitude
Lux	Luxembourg
M	Mile, Miles
Mad. Is	Madeira Islands
Mala	Malaysia
Malag. Rep.	Malagasy Republic
Mand	Mandate
Mart	Martinique
Mass	Massachusetts
Max	Maximum
Max. surf. elev.	Maximum surface elevation
Md	Maryland
Medit	Mediterranean
Mex	Mexico
Mi	Mile, Miles
Mich	Michigan
Minn	Minnesota
Miss	Mississippi
Mo	Missouri
Mong	Mongolia
Mont	Montana
Mor	Morocco
Moz	Mozambique
Mt	Mount
Mtn	Mountain
Mts	Mountains
Mus. & Om	Muscat & Oman
N	North
N. A	North America
Natl	National
Natl. Mon.	National Monument
N. C	North Carolina
N. Cal	New Caledonia
N. D	North Dakota
Nebr	Nebraska
Nep	Nepal
Neth	Netherlands
Nev	Nevada
New Hebr	New Hebrides
N. Gui. Ter	New Guinea Ter.
N. H	New Hampshire
Nic	Nicaragua
Nig	Nigeria
N. Ire	Northern Ireland
N. J	New Jersey
N. Mex	New Mexico
Nor	Norway
N. Rh	Northern Rhodesia
N. Y	New York
Nya	Nyasaland
N. Z	New Zealand
O	Ocean
Obs	Observatory
Okla	Oklahoma
Ore	Oregon
P	Pass
Pa	Pennsylvania
Pac. O	Pacific Ocean
Pan	Panama

Pap	Papua
Par	Paraguay
Pass	Passage
Pen	Peninsula
Phil	Philippines
Pk	Peak, Park
Plat	Plateau
Pln	Plain
Pol	Poland
Port	Portugal
Port. Gui	Portuguese Guinea
Port. Tim	Portuguese Timor
Poss	Possession
P. R	Puerto Rico
Prot	Protectorate
Prov	Province
Pt	Point
Pta	Punta
Pte	Pointe
R	River, Rio, Rivière
Ra	Range, Ranges
Reg	Region
Rep	Republic
Res	Reservation, Reservoir
Rf	Reef
R. I	Rhode Island
Rom	Romania
R. R	Railroad
R. S. F. S. R	Russian Soviet Federated Socialist Republic
Rw	Rwanda
Ry	Railway
Rys	Railways
S	San, Santo, South
Sa	Serra, Sierra
S. A	South America
Sal	Salvador
Sard	Sardinia
Sau. Ar	Saudi Arabia
S. C	South Carolina
Scot	Scotland
S. D	South Dakota
Sd	Sound
S. L	Sierra Leone
Sol. Is	Solomon Is.
Som	Somali Republic
Sov. Un	Soviet Union
Sp	Spain
Sp. Gui	Spanish Guinea
Spr., Sprs	Spring, Springs
Sp. Sah	Spanish Sahara
S. Rh	Southern Rhodesia
S. S. R	Soviet Socialist Republic
St	Saint
Sta	Santa
Ste	Sainte
Str	Strait
Strm	Stream
Sud	Sudan
Sur	Surinam
S. Afr	South Africa
S. W. Afr	South-West Africa
Swaz	Swaziland
Swe	Sweden
Switz	Switzerland
Swp	Swamp
Syr	Syria
Tan	Tanganyika
Tas	Tasmania
Tenn	Tennessee
Ter	Territory
Tex	Texas
Thai	Thailand
Trin	Trinidad and Tobago
Tr. Coast	Trucial Coast
Tun	Tunisia
Tur	Turkey
U. A. R.	United Arab Republic
Ug	Uganda
U. K	United Kingdom of Gt. Brit. and N. Ire.
Ur	Uruguay
U. S., U. S. A.	United States of America
Va	Virginia
Val	Valley
Ven	Venezuela
Viet	Vietnam
Vir. Is	Virgin Is.
Vol	Volcano
Vt	Vermont
W	West
Wash	Washington
W. I	West Indies
Wind. Is	Windward Islands
W. Irian	West Irian
Wis	Wisconsin
W. Pak	West Pakistan
W. Sam	Western Samoa
W. Va	West Virginia
Wyo	Wyoming
Yugo	Yugoslavia
Zan	Zanzibar

PRONUNCIATION OF
GEOGRAPHICAL NAMES

Key to the Sound Values of Letters and Symbols
Used in the Index to Indicate Pronunciation

ă—ăt, căt, băttle
ȧ—ȧppeal, finȧl
ā—rāte, elāte
â—inanimâte, senâte
a—cȧlm, ȧrm
a—ȧsk, bȧth
a—mȧrine, sofȧ (short neutral or indeterminate sound)
â—fâre, prepâre
ch—church, choose
dh—as th in other, either
ē—bē, ēve
ê—crête, êvent
ĕ—bĕt, ĕnd
ē—recĕnt (short neutral or indeterminate sound)
ē—cratēr, cindēr
g—gō, gāme
gh—guttural g
ĭ—wĭll, bĭt
ĭ—short neutral or indeterminate sound
ī—rīde, bīte
к—guttural k as ch in German ich
ng—sing
ŋ—baŋk, liŋger
N—indicates nasalized preceding vowel
ŏ—nŏd, ŏdd
ȯ—cȯmmit, cȯnnect
ō—ōld, bōld
ô—ôbey, hôtel
ô—ôrder, nôrth
oi—boil
ōō—fōōd, rōōt
ŏŏ—fŏŏt, wŏŏd
ou—thou, out
s—as in soft, so, sane
sh—dish, finish
th—thin, thick
ū—pūre, cūre
û—ûnite, ûsurp
û—ûrn, fûr
ŭ—stŭd, ŭp
ü—as in French tu or as "y" in study
u̇—circŭs, sŭbmit
zh—as z in azure
'—indeterminate vowel sound

In many cases the spelling of foreign geographic names does not even remotely indicate the pronunciation to an American, i. e., Slupca in Poland is pronounced swōōp'tsȧ; Jujuy in Argentina is pronounced hōō-hwē'; Spezia in Italy is spāt'sē-ä.

This condition is hardly surprising, however, when we consider that in our own language Worcester, Massachusetts, is pronounced wŏŏs'tēr; Sioux City, Iowa, sōō sĭ'tĭ; Schuylkill Haven, Pennsylvania, skōōl'kĭl; Poughkeepsie, New York, pô-kĭp'sē.

The indication of pronunciation of geographic names presents several peculiar problems:

(1) Many foreign tongues use sounds that are not present in the English language and which an American cannot normally articulate. Thus, though the nearest English equivalent sound has been indicated, only approximate results are possible.

(2) There are several dialects in each foreign tongue which cause variation in the local pronunciation of names. This also occurs in identical names in the various divisions of a great language group, as the Slavic or the Latin.

(3) Within the United States there are marked differences in pronunciation, not only of local geographic names, but also of common words, indicating that the sound and tone values for letters as well as the placing of the emphasis vary considerably from one part of the country to another.

(4) A number of different letter and diacritical combinations could be used to indicate essentially the same or approximate pronunciations.

Some variation in pronunciation other than that indicated in this index may be encountered, but such a difference does not necessarily indicate that either is in error, and in many cases it is a matter of individual choice as to which is preferred. In fact, an exact indication of pronunciation of many foreign names using English letters and diacritical marks is extremely difficult and sometimes impossible.

A PRONOUNCING INDEX

of over 30,000 Geographical Names

This universal index includes in a single alphabetical list all important names that appear on the reference maps. Each place name is preceded by the page number of the map on which it appears. Place names are followed by the pronunciation of the name (see facing page for an explanation of the pronunciation system); the location; and the approximate geographic coordinates.

State locations are listed for all places in the United States. All other place name entries show only country locations. When a name is only shown on an inset map the name of the inset on which it appears is listed.

All minor political divisions are followed by a descriptive term (Dist., Reg., Prov., State, etc.) and by the country in which they are located.

The names of physical features and points of interest that are shown on the maps are listed in the index. Each entry is followed by a descriptive term (Bay, Hill, Mtn., Is., Plat., etc.) to indicate its nature.

The system of alphabetizing used in the index is standard. When more than one name with the same spelling is shown, including both political and physical names, the order of precedence is as follows: *first*, place names, *second*, political divisions, and *third*, physical features.

Local official names are used on the maps for nearly all cities and towns, with the exception of about fifty major world cities for which Anglicized conventional names have been preferred. For these exceptions the index gives a cross reference to the official local name.

Page	Name Pronunciation Region	Lat. °′	Long. °′
123	Aachen (ä'kĕn)...Ger. (Ruhr In.)	50·46 N	6·07 E
118	Aakirkeby (ô-kĭr'kĕ-bü).....Den.	55·04 N	15·00 E
120	Aalen (ä'lĕn)...............Ger.	48·49 N	10·08 E
111	Aalsmeer..Neth. (Amsterdam In.)	52·16 N	4·44 E
111	Aalst..........Bel. (Brussels In.)	50·58 N	4·00 E
120	Aarau (är'ou).............Switz.	47·22 N	8·03 E
111	Aarschot......Bel. (Brussels In.)	50·59 N	4·51 E
164	Aba.......................Nig.	5·13 N	7·14 E
144	Ābādān (ä-bŭ-dän').........Iran	30·15 N	48·30 E
99	Abaetetuba (ä'băĕ-tĕ-tōō'bȧ) Braz.	1·44 s	48·45 w
69	Abajo Pk. (ä-bȧ'-hŏ)........Utah	38·50 N	109·35 w
134	Abakan (ŭ-bȧ-kän').....Sov. Un.	53·43 N	91·28 E
134	Abakan (R.)...........Sov. Un.	53·00 N	91·06 E
98	Abancay (ä-bän-kä'ê).......Peru	13·44 s	72·46 w
152	Abashiri (ä-bä-shē'rê)........Jap.	44·00 N	144·13 E
90	Abasolo (ä-bä-sō'lô)........Mex.	24·05 N	98·24 w
76	Abasolo..................Mex.	27·13 N	101·25 w
165	Abaya L. (ȧ-bä'yȧ).........Eth.	6·24 N	38·22 E
165	Abbai R. (ȧ-bä'ê)...........Eth.	9·45 N	37·23 E
78	Abbeville (ăb'ê-vĭl)..........Ala.	31·35 N	85·15 w
122	Abbeville (ȧb-vēl')...........Fr.	50·08 N	1·49 E
78	Abbeville (ăb'ê-vĭl)..........Ga.	31·53 N	83·23 w
77	Abbeville...................La.	29·59 N	92·07 w
79	Abbeville.................S. C.	34·09 N	82·25 w
126	Abbiategrasso (äb-byä'tȧ-gräs'sō) It.	45·23 N	8·52 E
110	Abbots Bromley (ăb'ŭts brŭm'lê).Eng.	52·49 N	1·52 w
65	Abbotsford (ăb'ŭts-fērd) Can. (Vancouver In.)	49·03 N	122·17 w
168	Abd Al Kuri I. (ăbd-ĕl-kōō'rê) Som. (Horn of Afr. In.)	12·21 N	51·00 E
132	Abdulino (äb-dōō-lē'nō)..Sov. Un.	53·40 N	53·45 E
165	Abéché (ȧ-bĕ-shā').........Chad	13·48 N	20·39 E
118	Åbenrå (ô'bĕn-rô)..........Den.	55·03 N	9·20 E
164	Abeokuta (ä-bȧ-ô-kōō'tȧ)....Nig.	7·14 N	3·19 E
166	Abercorn (ăb'ēr-kôrn).....N. Rh.	8·45 s	31·23 E
116	Aberdare (ăb-ēr-dâr').......Wales	51·45 N	3·35 w
116	Aberdeen (ăb-ēr-dēn')......Scot.	57·10 N	2·05 w
78	Aberdeen.................Miss.	33·49 N	88·33 w
70	Aberdeen.................S. D.	45·28 N	98·29 w
66	Aberdeen................Wash.	47·00 N	123·48 w
110	Aberford (ăb'ēr-fērd)........Eng.	53·49 N	1·21 w
116	Abergavenny (ăb'ēr-gȧ-vĕn'ĭ) Wales	51·45 N	3·05 w
66	Abert L. (ā'bērt)............Ore.	42·39 N	120·24 w
116	Aberystwyth (ȧ-bēr-ĭst'wĭth) Wales	52·25 N	4·04 w
136	Abestovskiy (ä-bĕs'tôv-skĭ) Sov. Un. (Urals In.)	57·46 N	61·23 E
144	Abhā..................Sau. Ar.	17·47 N	42·29 E
164	Abidjan (ä-bêd-zhäɴ').Ivory Coast	5·26 N	4·06 w
153	Abiko (ä-bē-kō).Jap. (Tōkyō In.)	35·53 N	140·01 E
73	Abilene (ăb'ĭ-lēn)..........Kans.	38·54 N	97·12 w
76	Abilene...................Tex.	32·25 N	99·45 w
110	Abingdon......Eng. (London In.)	51·38 N	1·17 w
71	Abingdon (ăb'ĭng-dŭn)........Ill.	40·48 N	90·21 w
79	Abingdon..................Va.	36·42 N	81·57 w
83	Abington (ăb'ĭng-tŭn) Mass. (Boston In.)	42·07 N	70·57 w
69	Abiquiu Res.............N. Mex.	36·26 N	106·42 w
87	Abitibi (L.) (ăb-ĭ-tĭb'ĭ)......Can.	48·27 N	80·20 w
87	Abitibi (R.)...............Can.	49·30 N	81·10 w
133	Abkhaz A.S.S.R.........Sov. Un.	43·10 N	40·45 E
123	Ablis (ȧ-blē')......Fr. (Paris In.)	48·31 N	1·50 E
168	Abnūb (ȧb-nōōb') U. A. R. (Nile In.)	27·18 N	31·11 E
	Åbo, see Turku		
142	Abohar..................India	30·12 N	74·13 E
164	Abomey (ȧb-ô-mā').....Dahomey	7·13 N	2·04 E
121	Abony (ŏ'bô-ny')..........Hung.	47·12 N	20·00 E
144	Abou Kemal (ä'bōō kĕ'mȧl) U. A. R.	34·27 N	40·46 E
155	Abra (R.) (ä'brä) Phil. (Manila In.)	17·16 N	120·38 E
101	Abraão (äbrȧ-ouɴ') Braz. (Rio de Janeiro In.)	23·10 s	44·10 w
95	Abraham's B.............Ba. Is.	22·20 N	73·50 w
110	Abram (ā'brăm)............Eng.	53·31 N	2·36 w
124	Abrantes (ȧ-brän'tĕs).......Port.	39·28 N	8·13 w
165	Abri.......................Sud.	20·36 N	29·57 E
99	Abrolhos, Arquipélago dos (Arch.) (ä-rōōê-pĕ'lä-gô-dôs-ä-brô'l-yōs) Braz.	17·58 s	38·40 w
119	Abruka (I.) (ȧ-brōō'kȧ)..Sov. Un.	58·09 N	22·30 E
126	Abruzzi and Molise (Reg.) (ä-brōōt'sē, mô'lê-zā)........It.	42·10 N	13·55 E
67	Absaroka Ra. (Mts.) (ȧb-sȧ-rō'kȧ).Wyo.	44·50 N	109·47 w
142	Abu (ȧ'bōō)...............India	24·38 N	72·45 E
144	Abū Arīsh (ä'bōō ȧ-rēsh').Sau. Ar.	16·48 N	43·00 E
165	Abu Hamed (ä'bōō hä'mĕd)..Sud.	19·37 N	33·21 E
115	Abūksāh................U. A. R.	29·29 N	30·40 E
98	Abunã (R.) (ȧ-bōō-nä').Bol-Braz..	10·25 s	67·00 w
168	Abū Qīr (ä'bōō kēr') U. A. R. (Nile In.)	31·18 N	30·06 E
168	Abū Qurqāṣ (ä'bōō kōōr-käs') U. A. R. (Nile In.)	27·57 N	30·51 E
139	Abu Qurûn, Ras (Mt.) U. A. R. (Palestine In.)	30·22 N	33·32 E
153	Aburatsu (ä'bōō-rät'sōō).....Jap.	31·33 N	131·20 E
168	Abū Tīj.......U. A. R. (Nile In.)	27·03 N	31·19 E
144	Abū Zabī...............Sau. Ar.	24·15 N	54·28 E
139	Abū Zanīmah U. A. R. (Palestine In.)	29·03 N	33·08 E
139	Abyad (R.).Jordan (Palestine In.)	30·07 N	36·01 E
118	Åby-Klippan (ô'bü klĭp'pȧn).Swe.	56·08 N	13·09 E
135	Abyy...................Sov. Un.	68·24 N	145·08 E
98	Acacias (ȧ-kȧ'sēäs).....Col. (In.)	3·59 N	73·44 w
82	Acadia Natl. Park (ȧ-kā'dĭ-ȧ) Maine	44·19 N	68·01 w
92	Acajutla (ä-kä-hōōt'lä).......Sal.	13·37 N	89·50 w
91	Acala (ä-kä'-lä)...........Mex.	16·38 N	92·49 w
90	Acàmbaro (ä-käm'bä-rō)....Mex.	20·03 N	100·42 w
92	Acancéh (ä-kän-sĕ') Mex. (Yucatan In.)	20·50 N	89·27 w
90	Acapetlahuaya (ä-kä-pĕt'lä-hwä'yä).Mex.	18·24 N	100·04 w
90	Acaponeta (ä-kä-pô-nā'tȧ)...Mex.	22·31 N	105·25 w
90	Acaponeta (R.)............Mex.	22·47 N	105·23 w
90	Acapulco de Juárez (ä-kä-pōōl'kō-dĕ-ĸwä'-rāz).Mex.	16·49 N	99·57 w
99	Acaraú (ä-kȧrhȧ-ōō').......Braz.	2·55 s	40·04 w
98	Acarigua (äkȧ-rē'gwä).......Ven.	9·29 N	69·11 w
90	Acatlán de Osorio (ä-kät-län'dā ô-sō'rē-ō).Mex.	18·11 N	98·04 w
91	Acatzingo de Hidalgo (ä-kät-zĭŋ'gō dā ê-dhăl'gō).Mex.	18·58 N	97·47 w
91	Acayucan (ä-kä-yōō'kän)....Mex.	17·56 N	94·55 w
80	Accoville (äk'kô-vĭl)......W. Va.	37·45 N	81·50 w
164	Accra (ă'krȧ).............Ghana	5·40 N	0·15 w
110	Accrington (ăk'rĭng-tŭn).....Eng.	53·45 N	2·22 w
125	Acerra (ä-chĕ'r-rä).It. (Naples In.)	40·42 N	14·22 E
98	Achacachi (ä-chä-kä'chê).....Bol.	16·11 s	68·32 w
152	Acheng (ä'chĕng')..........China	45·32 N	126·59 E
116	Achill (ă-chĭl')..............Ire.	53·55 N	10·05 w
134	Achinsk (ȧ-chênsk').....Sov. Un.	56·13 N	90·32 E
126	Acireale (ä-chê-rā-ä'lā)........It.	37·37 N	15·12 E
78	Ackia Battle Ground Natl. Mon. (ă-ĸyŭ').Miss.	34·22 N	89·05 w
95	Acklins (I.) (ăk'lĭns)......Ba. Is.	22·30 N	73·55 w
95	Acklins, The Bight of (B.).Ba. Is.	22·35 N	74·20 w
91	Acolman (ä-kôl-mȧ'n) Mex. (Mexico City In.)	19·38 N	98·56 w
101	Aconcagua (ä-kôn-kä'gwä) (Prov.) Chile (Santiago In.)	32·20 s	71·00 w
101	Aconcagua, Cerro (Mtn.) Arg. (Santiago In.)	32·38 s	70·00 w
101	Aconcagua (R.) Chile (Santiago In.)	32·43 s	70·53 w
164	Açores (Azores) Is. (ȧ-zōrz') (ä-zô'rês).Atl. O.	37·44 N	29·25 w
92	Acoyapa (ä-kô-yä'pä)........Nic.	11·54 N	85·11 w
126	Acqui (äk'kwē)...............It.	44·41 N	8·22 w
139	Acre (ä'kēr)...Isr. (Palestine In.)	32·56 N	35·05 E
98	Acre (State) (ä'krā)........Braz.	8·40 s	70·45 w
98	Acre (R.)..................Braz.	10·33 s	68·34 w
84	Acton (ăk'tŭn) Ala. (Birmingham In.)	33·21 N	86·49 w
85	Acton........Can. (Toronto In.)	43·38 N	80·02 w
75	Acton.....Ind. (Indianapolis In.)	39·39 N	85·58 w
83	Acton........Mass. (Boston In.)	42·29 N	71·26 w
82	Acton Vale................Can.	45·39 N	72·33 w
90	Actopan (äk-tô-pän').......Mex.	20·16 N	98·57 w
91	Actópan (R.) (äk-tŏ'pän)....Mex.	19·25 N	96·31 w
90	Acuitzio del Canje (ä-kwēt'zê-ō dĕl kän'hȧ).Mex.	19·28 N	101·21 w
95	Acul, Baie de l' (B.) (ä-kōōl').Hai.	19·55 N	72·20 w
164	Ada (ä'dä)...............Ghana	5·57 N	0·31 E
70	Ada (ā'dŭ)...............Minn.	47·17 N	96·32 w
80	Ada......................Ohio	40·45 N	83·45 w
73	Ada......................Okla.	34·45 N	96·43 w
127	Ada (ä'dä)................Yugo.	45·48 N	20·06 E
64	Adak (ă-dăk')............Alaska	56·50 N	176·48 w
64	Adak (I.)................Alaska	51·40 N	176·28 w
64	Adak Str.................Alaska	51·42 N	177·16 w
	Adalia, see Antalya		
164	Adamawa (Reg.) (ä-dä-mä'wä) Nig.-Cam.	8·39 N	11·58 E
81	Adams (ăd'ămz)...........Mass.	42·35 N	73·10 w
71	Adams....................Wis.	43·55 N	89·48 w
64	Adams, Mt...............Alaska	55·40 N	130·25 w
66	Adams, Mt...............Wash.	46·15 N	121·19 w
84	Adamsville (ăd'ămz-vĭl) Ala. (Birmingham In.)	33·36 N	86·57 w
84	Adamsville.....Ga. (Atlanta In.)	33·45 N	84·31 w
84	Adamsville, R. I. (Providence In.)	41·33 N	71·04 w
133	Adana (ä'dä-nä)............Tur.	37·05 N	35·20 E
133	Adapazari (ä-dä-pä-zä'rê)....Tur.	40·45 N	30·20 E
165	Adarama (ä-dä-rä'mä).......Sud.	17·11 N	34·56 E
126	Adda (R.) (äd'dä)............It.	45·43 N	9·31 E
144	Ad Dahna (Des.).........Sau. Ar.	26·05 N	47·15 E
144	Ad Dam (äd däm')......Sau. Ar.	20·45 N	44·12 E
144	Ad Dammān............Sau. Ar.	26·27 N	49·59 E
139	Ad Damur....Leb. (Palestine In.)	33·44 N	35·27 E
144	Ad Dawhah............Sau. Ar.	20·02 N	51·28 E
144	Ad Dilam...............Sau. Ar.	23·47 N	47·03 E
165	Addis Ababā...............Eth.	9·00 N	38·44 E
74	Addison (ă'dĭ-sŭn) Tex. (Dallas, Fort Worth In.)	32·58 N	96·50 w
165	Ad Dīwān.............U. A. R.	22·44 N	32·15 E
167	Addo (ădō)....S. Afr. (Natal In.)	33·33 s	25·43 E
75	Addyston (ăd'ê-stŭn) Ohio (Cincinnati In.)	39·09 N	84·42 w
78	Adel (ā-dĕl')................Ga.	31·08 N	83·55 w
167	Adelaide (ăd-ĕl'ād) S. Afr. (Natal In.)	32·41 s	26·07 E
160	Adelaide (ăd'ê-lād)........Austl.	34·46 s	139·08 E
47	Adelaide I.................Ant.	67·15 s	68·40 w
144	Aden (ä'dĕn)..............Aden	12·48 N	45·00 E
138	Aden.....................Asia	14·35 N	47·45 E
144	Aden, G. of...............Aden	11·45 N	45·45 E
155	Adi (I.) (ä'dē)..........W. Irian	4·25 s	133·52 E
114	Adige R. (ä'dê-jā).....Aus.-Switz.	46·34 N	10·51 E
126	Adige, Fiume (R.) (fyōō'mĕ-ä'dê-jā).It.	46·38 N	10·43 E
142	Ādilābād (ŭ-dĭl-ä-bäd').....India	19·47 N	78·30 E
143	Adini.....................India	15·42 N	77·18 E
81	Adirondack, Mts. (ăd-ĭ-rŏn'dăk) N. Y.	43·45 N	74·40 w
165	Adi Ugri (ä-dē ōō'grē).......Eth.	14·54 N	38·52 E
121	Adjud (äd'zhōōd)..........Rom.	46·05 N	27·12 E
64	Admiralty (I.)............Alaska	57·50 N	133·50 w
65	Admiralty Inlet (ăd'mĭrȧl-tê) Wash. (Seattle In.)	48·10 N	122·45 w
155	Admiralty Is........N. Gui. Ter.	1·40 s	146·45 E
74	Adolph (ā'dolf) Minn. (Duluth In.)	46·47 N	92·17 w
122	Adour (R.) (ȧ-dōōr').........Fr.	43·43 N	0·38 w
124	Adra (ä'drä)................Sp.	36·45 N	3·02 w
126	Adrano (ä-drä'nō)............It.	37·42 N	14·52 E
164	Adrar des Iforas (Reg.) (ä-drär') Alg.	20·22 N	1·44 E
126	Adria (ä'drê-ä)............. It.	45·03 N	12·01 E
80	Adrian (ā'drĭ-ăn)..........Mich.	41·55 N	84·00 w
70	Adrian..................Minn.	43·39 N	95·56 w
	Adrianople, see Edirne		
126	Adriatic Sea...............Eur.	41·30 N	14·27 E
164	Adrir......................Alg.	27·53 N	0·15 w
100	Adrogué (ȧdrō-gā')....Arg. (In.)	34·33 s	58·24 w
165	Aduwā....................Eth.	14·02 N	38·58 E
110	Adwick-le-Street (ăd'wĭk-lê-strēt') Eng.	53·35 N	1·11 w
135	Adycha (R.) (ä'dĭ-chȧ)..Sov. Un.	66·11 N	136·45 E
129	Adzhamka (ȧd-zhäm'kȧ).Sov. Un.	48·33 N	32·28 E
132	Adz'va (R.) (ädz'vȧ)....Sov. Un.	67·00 N	59·20 E
115	Aegean Sea (ê-jē'ăn)....Eur.-Asia	39·04 N	24·56 E
118	Aerø (I.) (âr'ö)............Den.	54·52 N	10·22 E
138	Afghanistan (ăf-găn-ĭ-stăn')..Asia	33·00 N	63·00 E
168	Afgoi (äf-gô'ĭ) Som. (Horn of Afr. In.)	2·08 N	45·08 E
164	Aflou (ä-flōō')..............Alg.	33·59 N	2·04 E
64	Afognak (I.) (ä-fŏg-nȧk')..Alaska	58·28 N	151·35 w
125	Afragola (ä-frȧ'gō-lä) It. (Naples In.)	40·40 N	14·19 E
7	Africa (ăf'rĭ-kȧ)		
74	Afton (ăf'tŭn)............Minn. (Minneapolis, St. Paul In.)	44·54 N	92·47 w

174 Afton–Alcaudete PRONOUNCING INDEX

Page	Name Pronunciation Region	Lat. °′	Long. °′
73	Afton . . . Okla.	36·42 N	94·56 W
67	Afton . . . Wyo.	42·42 N	110·52 W
139	'Afula (ä-fōō'lȧ) Isr. (Palestine In.)	32·36 N	35·17 E
133	Afyonkarahisar (ä-fē-ōn-kä-rȧ-hē-sär') . Tur.	38·45 N	30·20 E
165	Agadem (Oasis) (ä'gȧ-dĕm) . Niger	16·50 N	13·15 E
164	Agadès (ä'gȧ-dĕs) . . . Niger	17·01 N	7·55 E
164	Agadir (ä-gȧ-dēr) . . . Mor.	30·30 N	9·37 W
92	Agalta, Cord. de (Mts.) (kôr-dēl-yĕ'rä-dĕ-ä-gä'l-tä) . . . Hond.	15·15 N	85·42 W
136	Agapovka (ä-gä-pôv'kä) Sov. Un. (Urals In.)	53·18 N	59·10 E
142	Agartala . . . India	23·53 N	91·22 E
143	Agāshi . . . India (Bombay In.)	19·28 N	72·46 E
136	Agashkino (ȧ-gäsh'kĭ-nô) Sov. Un. (Moscow In.)	55·18 N	38·13 E
65	Agate Bay (ăg'ĭt) (ăg'ȧt) Wash. (Vancouver In.)	48·45 N	122·20 W
64	Agattu (I.) (ȧ'gä-tōō) . . . Alaska	52·14 N	173·40 E
129	Agayman (ä-gä-ē-män') . . Sov. Un.	46·39 N	34·20 E
133	Agdam (äg'dȧm) . . . Sov. Un.	40·00 N	47·00 E
122	Agde (ägd) . . . Fr.	43·19 N	3·30 E
122	Agen (ȧ-zhäN') . . . Fr.	44·13 N	0·31 E
85	Agincourt (ä'zhĕN-kōōr') Can. (Toronto In.)	43·47 N	79·16 W
135	Aginskoye (ä-hĭn'skô-yĕ) . Sov. Un.	51·15 N	113·15 E
65	Agnew (ăg'nū) . Wash. (Seattle In.)	48·06 N	123·15 W
155	Agno (äg'nō) . . . Phil. (Manila In.)	16·07 N	119·49 E
155	Agno (R.) . . . Phil. (Manila In.)	15·42 N	120·28 E
126	Agnone (än-yō'nā) . . . It.	41·49 N	14·23 E
165	Agordat (ä-gōr'dät) . . . Eth.	15·34 N	37·54 E
142	Agra (ä'grä) . . . India	27·18 N	78·00 E
126	Agri (R.) (ä'grē) . . . It.	40·15 N	16·21 E
127	Agrínion (à-grē'nyôn) . . . Grc.	38·38 N	21·06 E
92	Agua (Vol.) (ä'gwä) . . . Guat.	14·28 N	90·43 W
90	Agua Blanca, Río (R.) (rē'ō-ä-gwä-blä'n-kä) . Mex.	21·46 N	102·54 W
90	Agua Brava, Laguna de (L.) (lä-gōō'nä-dĕ-ä'gwä-brä'vä) . . . Mex.	22·04 N	105·40 W
68	Agua Caliente Ind. Res. (ä'gwä kal-yĕn'tä) . Calif.	33·50 N	116·24 W
94	Aguada (ä-gwä'dȧ) . . . Cuba	22·25 N	80·50 W
92	Aguada L. . . . Mex. (Yucatan In.)	18·46 N	89·40 W
98	Aguadas (ä-gwä'-dàs) . . . Col. (In.)	5·37 N	75·27 W
89	Aguadilla (ä-gwä-dēl'yä) P. R. (Puerto Rico In.)	18·27 N	67·10 W
93	Aguadulce (ä-gwä-dōōl'sä) . . . Pan.	8·15 N	80·33 W
91	Agua Escondida, Meseta de (Plat.) (mĕ-sĕ'tä-dĕ-ä'gwä-ĕs-kôn-dē'dä) . Mex.	16·54 N	91·35 W
101	Aguai (ägwä-ē') Braz. (Rio de Janeiro In.)	22·04 S	46·57 W
76	Agualeguas (ä-gwä-lä'gwäs) . Mex.	26·19 N	99·33 W
76	Aguanaval, R. (ä-guä-nä-väl') . Mex.	25·12 N	103·28 W
92	Aguán R. (ä-gwä'n) . . . Hond.	15·22 N	87·00 W
83	Aguanus (R.) (ä-gwä'nŭs) . . . Can.	50·45 N	62·03 W
90	Aguascalientes (ä'gwäs-käl-yĕn'täs) . Mex.	21·52 N	102·17 W
124	Agueda (ä-gwā'dȧ) . . . Port.	40·36 N	8·26 W
124	Agueda (R.) (ä-gĕ-dä) . . . Sp.	40·50 N	6·44 W
164	Aguellal (ä-gĕl-yäl) . . . Niger	19·05 N	8·10 E
72	Aguilar (ä-gē-lär') . . . Colo.	37·24 N	104·38 W
124	Aguilar . . . Sp.	37·32 N	4·39 W
124	Aguilas (ä'gē-läs) . . . Sp.	37·26 N	1·35 W
90	Aguililla (ä-gē-lēl-yä) . . . Mex.	18·44 N	102·44 W
98	Aguja, Pta. (Pt.) (pŭn'tä ȧ-gōō' hä) . Peru	6·00 S	81·15 W
166	Agulhas, C. (ä-gōōl'yäs) . . . S. Afr.	34·47 S	20·00 E
154	Agung, Gunung (Mtn.) (ä-gōōng') . Indon.	8·41 S	115·07 E
155	Agusan (R.) (ä-gōō'sän) . . . Phil.	8·12 N	126·07 E
164	Ahaggar (Mts.) (ȧ-hȧ-gär') . . . Alg.	23·14 N	6·00 E
123	Ahlen (ä'lĕn) . . . Ger. (Ruhr In.)	51·45 N	7·52 E
142	Ahmadābād (ŭ-mĕd-ä-bäd') . India	23·04 N	72·38 E
142	Ahmadnagar (ä'mŭd-nŭ-gûr) . India	19·09 N	74·45 E
168	Ahmar Mts. Eth. (Horn of Afr. In.)	9·22 N	42·00 E
165	Ahmara Plat. . . . Eth.	10·09 N	37·21 E
79	Ahoskie (ä-hŏs'kē) . . . N. C.	36·15 N	77·00 W
111	Ahrensburg (ä'rĕns-bōōrg) Ger. (Hamburg In.)	53·40 N	10·14 E
120	Ahrweiler (är'vī-lĕr) . . . Ger.	50·34 N	7·05 E
119	Ahtärin-järvi (L.) . . . Fin.	62·46 N	24·25 E
90	Ahuacatlán (ä-wä-kät-län') . . Mex.	21·05 N	104·28 W
92	Ahuachapan (ä-wä-chä-pän') . . Sal.	13·57 N	89·53 W
90	Ahualulco (ä-wä-lōōl'kō) . . . Mex.	20·43 N	103·57 W
90	Ahuatempan (ä-wä-tĕm-pän) . Mex.	18·11 N	98·02 W
118	Ahus (ô'hōōs) . . . Swe.	55·56 N	14·19 E
144	Ahvāz . . . Iran	31·15 N	48·54 E
118	Ahvenanma (Åland Is.) (ä'vĕ-nán-mô) (ô'länd) . Fin.	60·36 N	19·55 E
157	Aica . . . Hawaii (In.)	21·18 N	157·52 W
79	Aiken (ā'kĕn) . . . S. C.	33·32 N	81·43 W
99	Aimorés, Serra dos (Mts.) (sĕ'r-rä-dōs-ī-mō-rĕ's) . Braz.	17·40 S	42·38 W
153	Aimoto (ī-mô-tō) . Jap. (Ōsaka In.)	34·59 N	135·09 E
164	Aïn Beida (ä'ēn bā-dä') . . . Alg.	35·57 N	7·25 E
123	Aincourt (ăN-kōō'r) . Fr. (Paris In.)	49·04 N	1·47 E
125	Aïne Ousséra (ĕn ōō-sā-rä) . . . Alg.	35·25 N	2·50 E
164	Aïn Sefra (ä'ēn sĕf'rä) . . . Alg.	32·49 N	0·39 W
83	Ainsle, L. (ān'slē) . . . Can.	46·08 N	61·23 W
70	Ainsworth (ānz'wûrth) . . . Nebr.	42·32 N	99·51 W
114	Aïn Taïba (ä'ēn tä'ē-bä) . . . Alg.	30·20 N	5·30 E
113	Aïn-Temouchent (ä'ēntĕ-mōō-shaN') . Alg.	35·20 N	1·23 W
98	Aipe (ī'-pĕ) . . . Col. (In.)	3·13 N	75·15 W
122	Aire (âr) . . . Fr.	43·42 N	0·17 W
110	Aire (R.) . . . Eng.	53·42 N	1·00 W
139	Airhitam, Selat (Str.) Indon. (Singapore In.)	0·58 N	102·38 E
164	Aïr ou Azbine (Mts.) . . . Niger	18·28 N	7·51 E
122	Aisne (R.) (ĕn) . . . Fr.	49·28 N	3·32 E
155	Aitape (ä-ē-tä'pä) . . . N. Gui. Ter.	3·00 S	142 10 E
71	Aitkin (āt'kĭn) . . . Minn.	46·32 N	93·43 W

Page	Name Pronunciation Region	Lat. °′	Long. °′
127	Aitolikón (ȧ-tō'lĭ-kôn) . . . Grc.	38·27 N	21·21 E
127	Aitos (ä-ē'tōs) . . . Bul.	42·42 N	27·17 E
157	Aitutaki (I.) (ī-tōō-tä'kē) . Cook Is.	19·00 S	162·00 W
121	Aiud (ä'ē-ōōd) . . . Rom.	46·19 N	23·40 E
101	Aiuruoca (äē'ōō-rōōō'-kȧ) Braz. (Rio de Janeiro In.)	21·57 S	44·36 W
101	Aiuruoca (R.) Braz. (Rio de Janeiro In.)	22·11 S	44·35 W
122	Aix-en-Provence (ĕks-prô-vȧNs) Fr. (Marseille In.)	43·32 N	5·27 E
123	Aix-les-Bains (ĕks'-lā-baN') . . . Fr.	45·42 N	5·56 E
127	Aiyien . . . Grc.	37·37 N	22·12 E
127	Aíyina (I.) . . . Grc.	37·43 N	23·35 E
127	Aíyion . . . Grc.	38·13 N	22·04 E
119	Aizpute (ä'ēz-pōō-tĕ) . . . Sov. Un.	56·44 N	21·37 E
126	Ajaccio (ä-yät'chō) . . . Fr.	41·55 N	8·42 E
91	Ajalpan (ä-häl'pän) . . . Mex.	18·21 N	97·14 W
158	Ajana (āj-än'ēr) . . . Austl.	28·00 S	114·45 E
67	Ajax Mt. (ā'jăks) . . . Mont.	45·19 N	113·43 W
165	Ajdabiyah . . . Libya	30·56 N	20·16 E
144	Ajman . . . Tr. Coast	25·15 N	54·30 E
142	Ajmer (ŭj-mēr') . . . India	26·26 N	74·42 E
69	Ajo (ä'hō) . . . Ariz.	32·20 N	112·55 W
90	Ajuchitlán del Progreso (ä-hōō-chet-lân) . Mex.	18·11 N	100·32 W
91	Ajusco (ä-hōō's-kō) Mex. (Mexico City In.)	19·13 N	99·12 W
91	Ajusco, Cerro (sĕ'r-rô-ä-hōō's-kō) Mex. (Mexico City In.)	19·12 N	99·16 W
153	Akaishi-dake (Mtn.) (ä-kī-shē dä'kä) . Jap.	5·30 N	138·00 E
99	Akarai Mts. (ä'kä-rä'ē) . Braz.-Sur.	1·30 N	57·40 W
153	Akashi (ä'kä-shē) . Jap. (Ōsaka In.)	34·38 N	134·59 E
165	Aketi (ä-kâ-tē) . . . Con. L.	2·58 N	23·57 E
133	Akhaltsikhe (äkä'l-tsĭ-kĕ) Sov. Un.	41·40 N	42·50 E
165	Akhdar, Jabal al (Mts.) . . . Libya	32·45 N	21·52 E
144	Akhdar, Jabal al (Mts.) Mus. & Om.-Sau. Ar.	23·30 N	56·43 E
127	Akhelóös (R.) (ä-hĕ'lō-ōs) . . . Grc.	38·45 N	21·26 E
133	Akhisar (äk-hĭs-sär') . . . Tur.	38·58 N	27·58 E
129	Akhtarskaya, Bukhta (B.) (bōōk'tä äK-tär'skä-yä) . Sov. Un.	45·53 N	38·22 E
127	Akhtopol (äK'tô-pōl) . . . Bul.	42·08 N	27·54 E
129	Akhtyrka (äK-tür'kä) . Sov. Un.	50·18 N	34·53 E
136	Akhunovo (ä-kŭ'nô-vô) Sov. Un. (Urals In.)	54·13 N	59·36 E
153	Aki (ä'kē) . . . Jap.	33·31 N	133·51 E
64	Akiak (äk'yȧk) . . . Alaska	61·00 N	161·02 W
87	Akimiski (I.) (ä-kĭ-mĭ'skĭ) . . . Can.	52·54 N	80·22 W
152	Akita (ä'kē-tä) . . . Jap.	39·40 N	140·12 E
164	Akjoujt . . . Mauritania	19·45 N	14·30 W
86	Aklavik (äk'lä-vĭk) . . . Can.	68·28 N	135·26 W
153	Ako (ä'kō) . . . Jap.	34·44 N	134·22 E
142	Akola (ȧ-kô'lä) . . . India	20·47 N	77·00 E
87	Akpatok (I.) (äk'pȧ-tŏk) . . . Can.	60·30 N	67·10 W
112	Akranes . . . Ice.	64·18 N	21·40 W
127	Akrítas, Akr. (C.) . . . Grc.	37·45 N	23·53 E
72	Akron (ăk'rŭn) . . . Colo.	40·09 N	103·14 W
75	Akron . . . Ohio (Cleveland In.)	41·05 N	81·30 W
139	Akrotiri B. . Cyprus (Palestine In.)	34·38 N	33·18 E
133	Aksaray (äk-sȧ-rī') . . . Tur.	38·30 N	34·05 E
133	Akşehir (äk'shȧ-hēr) . . . Tur.	38·20 N	31·20 E
133	Aksehir (L.) . . . Tur.	38·40 N	31·30 E
135	Aksha (äk'shȧ) . . . Sov. Un.	50·28 N	113·00 E
	Aksu, see Wensu		
146	Ak Su (R.) . . . China	40·34 N	77·15 E
133	Aktyubinsk (äk'työō-bĕnsk) Sov. Un.	50·20 N	57·00 E
153	Akune (ä'kōō-nā) . . . Jap.	32·03 N	130·16 E
112	Akureyri (ä-kōō-rä'rē) . . . Ice.	65·39 N	18·01 W
64	Akutan (I.) (ä-kōō-tän') . . Alaska	53·58 N	169·54 W
63	Alabama (State) (ăl-ȧ-băm'ȧ) . U. S.	32·50 N	87·30 W
78	Alabama (R.) . . . Ala.	31·20 N	87·39 W
155	Alabat (I.) (ä-lä-bät') Phil. (Manila In.)	14·14 N	122·05 E
155	Alaca (ä-lä-kä) . Phil. (Manila In.)	17·56 N	121·39 E
133	Alacam (ä-lä-chäm') . . . Tur.	41·30 N	35·40 E
94	Alacranes (ä-lä-krä'nȧs) . . . Cuba	22·45 N	81·35 W
144	Alaflau (Des.) . . . Sau. Ar.	24·00 N	44·47 E
99	Alagôas (ä-lä-gō'äzh) . . . Braz.	9·50 S	36·33 W
99	Alagoinhas (ä-lä-gō-ēn'yäzh) . Braz.	12·13 S	38·12 W
124	Alagón (ä-lä-gōn') . . . Sp.	41·46 N	1·07 W
124	Alagón (R.) . . . Sp.	39·53 N	6·42 W
90	Alahuatán (R.) (ä-lä-wä-tà'n) . Mex.	18·30 N	100·00 W
93	Alajuela (ä-lä-hwa'lä) . . . C.R.	10·01 N	84·14 W
134	Alakol (L.) . . . Sov. Un.	45·45 N	81·13 E
157	Alalakeiki Chan. (ä-lä-lä-kā'kē) Hawaii (In.)	20·40 N	156·30 W
165	Al 'Alamayn . . . U. A. R.	30·53 N	28·52 E
165	Al 'Allāqī . . . U. A. R.	23·06 N	32·47 E
65	Alameda (ăl-ȧ-mā'dȧ) Calif. (San Francisco In.)	37·46 N	122·15 W
67	Alameda . . . Idaho	42·51 N	112·29 W
65	Alameda (R.) Calif. (San Francisco In.)	37·36 N	122·02 W
155	Alaminos (ä-lä-mē'nōs) Phil. (Manila In.)	16·09 N	119·58 E
115	Al 'Āmirīyah . . . U. A. R.	31·01 N	29·52 E
65	Alamo (ă'lȧ-mō) Calif. (San Francisco In.)	37·51 N	122·02 W
91	Alamo (ä'lä-mô) . . . Mex.	21·07 N	99·35 W
76	Alamo, R. (ä'lä-mô) . . . Mex.	26·33 N	99·35 W
69	Alamogordo (ăl-ȧ-mō-gôr'dō) N. Mex.	32·55 N	106·00 W
74	Alamo Heights (ă'lȧ-mō) Tex. (San Antonio In.)	29·28 N	98·27 W
76	Alamo Pk. (ă'lȧ-mō pēk) . N. Mex.	32·50 N	105·55 W
69	Alamosa (ăl-ȧ-mō'sȧ) . . . Colo.	37·25 N	105·50 W
136	Alandskiy (ä-länt'skĭ) Sov. Un. (Urals In.)	52·14 N	59·48 E
133	Alanya . . . Tur.	36·40 N	32·10 E
167	Alaotra (L.) (ä-lä-ō'trȧ) Malag. Rep.	17·15 S	48·17 E
136	Alapayevsk (ä-lä-pä'yĕfsk) Sov. Un. (Urals In.)	57·50 N	61·35 E

Page	Name Pronunciation Region	Lat. °′	Long. °′
139	Al Aqabah. Jordan (Palestine In.)	29·32 N	35·00 E
90	Alaquines (ä-lä-kē'nȧs) . . . Mex.	22·07 N	99·35 W
139	Al 'Arīsh (a-rēsh') U. A. R. (Palestine In.)	31·08 N	33·48 E
150	Ala Shan (Mtns.) (ä'lä-shän') China	38·02 N	105·20 E
62	Alaska (State) (ȧ-lăs'kȧ) . . . U. S.	65·00 N	158·00 W
64	Alaska, G. of . . . Alaska	57·42 N	147·40 W
64	Alaska Hy. . . . Alaska	63·00 N	142·00 W
64	Alaska Pen. . . . Alaska	55·50 N	162·10 W
64	Alaska Ra. . . . Alaska	62·00 N	152·18 W
132	Alatyr' (ä'lä-tür) . . . Sov. Un.	54·55 N	46·30 E
98	Alausí (à-lou-sē') . . . Ec.	2·15 S	78·45 W
168	Al 'Ayyāţ (ä-ē-yăt') U. A. R. (Nile In.)	29·38 N	31·18 E
126	Alba (äl'bä) . . . It.	44·41 N	8·02 E
124	Albacete (äl-bä-thā'tä) . . . Sp.	39·00 N	1·49 W
123	Albachten (äl-bä'K-tĕn) Ger. (Ruhr In.)	51·55 N	7·31 E
168	Al Badārī . . . U. A. R. (Nile In.)	26·59 N	31·29 E
124	Alba de Tormes (äl-bȧ dā tôr'mās) Sp.	40·48 N	5·28 W
168	Al Bahnasā . . . U. A. R. (Nile In.)	28·35 N	30·30 E
121	Alba Iulia (äl-bä yōō'lyà) . . . Rom.	46·05 N	23·32 E
125	Albalate (äl-bä-lä'tä) . . . Sp.	41·07 N	0·34 W
168	Al Ballāḩ (bà'lä) U. A. R. (Suez In.)	30·46 N	32·20 E
168	Al Balyanā . . . U. A. R. (Nile In.)	26·12 N	32·00 E
102	Albania (ăl-bā'nĭ-ȧ) . . . Eur.	41·45 N	20·00 E
125	Albano, Lago (L.) (lä'-gō-äl-bä'nō) It. (Rome In.)	41·45 N	12·44 E
125	Albano Laziale (äl-bä'nō lät-zē-ä'lä) . It. (Rome In.)	41·44 N	12·43 E
158	Albany (ôl'bȧ-nĭ) . . . Austl.	35·00 S	118·00 E
65	Albany . Calif. (San Francisco In.)	37·54 N	122·18 W
78	Albany . . . Ga.	31·35 N	84·10 W
73	Albany . . . Mo.	40·14 N	94·18 W
81	Albany . . . N. Y.	42·40 N	73·50 W
66	Albany . . . Ore.	44·38 N	123·06 W
76	Albany . . . Tex.	32·43 N	99·17 W
87	Albany (R.) . . . Can.	51·45 N	83·30 W
144	A'l Basrah . . . Iraq	30·27 N	47·52 E
139	Al Batrūn (bȧ-trōōn') Leb. (Palestine In.)	34·16 N	35·39 E
165	Al Bawīţī . . . U. A. R.	28·19 N	29·00 E
155	Albay G. (äl-bä'ē) Phil. (Manila In.)	13·09 N	123·52 E
79	Albemarle (ăl'bē-märl) . . . N. C.	35·24 N	80·36 W
79	Albemarle Sd. . . . N. C.	36·00 N	76·17 W
126	Albenga (äl-bĕn'gä) . . . It.	44·04 N	8·13 E
124	Alberche (R.) (äl-bĕr'chå) . . . Sp.	40·08 N	4·19 W
158	Alberga, The (R.) (ăl-bŭr'gȧ) Austl.	27·15 S	135·00 E
124	Albergaria a-Velha (äl-bĕr-gȧ-rē'-ȧ-ä-väl'yȧ) . Port.	40·47 N	8·31 W
74	Alberhill (ăl'bĕr-hĭl) Calif. (Los Angeles In.)	33·43 N	117·23 W
82	Albert (ăl'bĕrt) . . . Can.	45·44 N	64·46 W
122	Albert (äl-bâr') . . . Fr.	50·00 N	2·49 E
86	Alberta (Prov.) (ăl-bûr'tȧ) . . . Can.	54·33 N	117·10 W
155	Albert Edward, Mt. (ăl'bĕrt ĕd'wĕrd) . Austl.	8·25 S	147·25 E
101	Alberti (äl-bĕ'r-tē) Arg. (Buenos Aires In.)	35·01 S	60·16 W
111	Albert Kanal (can.) Bel. (Brussels In.)	51·07 N	5·07 E
165	Albert L. (ăl'bĕrt) (äl-bâr') Con. L.-Ug.	2·00 N	30·16 E
71	Albert Lea (ăl'bĕrt lē') . . . Minn.	43·38 N	93·24 W
82	Alberton (ăl'bĕr-tŭn) . . . Can.	46·50 N	64·02 W
167	Alberton . . . S. Afr. (Johannesburg & Pretoria In.)	26·16 S	28·08 E
78	Albertville (ăl'bĕrt-vĭl) . . . Ala.	34·15 N	86·10 W
166	Albertville (äl-bĕr-vēl') . . . Con. L.	5·59 S	29·12 E
123	Albertville . . . Fr.	45·42 N	6·25 E
122	Albi (äl-bē') . . . Fr.	43·54 N	2·07 E
71	Albia (ăl bĭ-ȧ) . . . Iowa	41·01 N	92·44 W
99	Albina (äl-bē'nä) . . . Fr. Gu.	5·30 N	54·33 W
75	Albino, Pt. (äl-bē'nō) Can. (Buffalo In.)	42·50 N	79·05 W
80	Albion (ăl'bĭ-ŭn) . . . Mich.	42·15 N	84·50 W
70	Albion . . . Nebr.	41·42 N	99·00 W
81	Albion . . . N. Y.	43·15 N	78·10 W
124	Alboran, Isla del (I.) (ē's-lä-dĕl-äl-bō-rä'n) . Sp.	35·58 N	3·02 W
124	Alboran Sea . . . Medit.	35·54 N	4·26 W
118	Ålborg (ôl'bŏr) . . . Den.	57·02 N	9·55 E
124	Albox (äl-bōk') . . . Sp.	37·23 N	2·08 W
69	Albuquerque (ăl-bŭ-kûr'kē) N. Mex.	35·05 N	106·40 W
93	Albuquerque, Cayus de (I.) (ăl-bŭ-kûr'kē) . Col.	12·12 N	81·24 W
144	Al Buraymī . . . Sau. Ar.	23·45 N	55·39 E
124	Alburquerque (äl-bōōr-kĕr'kä) . Sp.	39·13 N	6·58 W
160	Albury (ôl'bĕr-ē) . . . Austl.	36·00 S	147·00 E
125	Alcabideche (äl-kȧ-bē-dā'chå) Port. (Lisbon In.)	38·43 N	9·24 W
124	Alcacer do Sal (äl-kä'sĕr dōō säl') Port.	38·24 N	8·33 W
125	Alcalá de Chivert (äl-kä-lä'dä chē-vĕrt') . Sp.	40·18 N	0·12 E
125	Alcalá de Henares (äl-kä-lä' dä ä nä'räs). Sp. (Madrid In.)	40·29 N	3·22 W
124	Alcalá de los Gazules (äl-kä-lä' dä lōs gä-thōō'läs) . Sp.	36·29 N	5·44 W
124	Alcalá la Real (äl-kä-lä'lä rā-äl') . Sp.	37·27 N	3·57 W
126	Alcamo (äl'kä-mō) . . . It.	37·58 N	13·03 E
125	Alcanadre (R.) (äl-kä-nä'drā) . Sp.	41·41 N	0·18 W
125	Alcanar (äl-kä-när') . . . Sp.	40·35 N	0·27 E
125	Alcañiz (äl-kän-yēth') . . . Sp.	41·03 N	0·08 W
99	Alcântara (äl-kän'tȧ-rȧ) . . . Braz.	2·17 S	44·29 W
124	Alcaraz (äl-kä-räth') . . . Sp.	38·39 N	2·28 W
124	Alcaudete (äl-kou-dhā'tä) . . . Sp.	37·38 N	4·05 W

ăt; finăl; rate; senâte; ärm; àsk; sofȧ; fâre; ch-choose; dh-as th in other; bē; ēvent; bĕt; recĕnt; cratẽr; g-go; gh-guttural g; bĭt; ĭ-short neutral; rīde; K-guttural k as ch in German ich;

PRONOUNCING INDEX   Alcazar de San Juan–Alta Gracia   175

Page	Name Pronunciation Region	Lat. °′	Long. °′
124	Alcázar de San Juan (äl-kä'thär dā sän hwän') Sp.	39·22 N	3·12 W
114	Alcazarquivir Mor.	35·01 N	5·48 W
125	Alcira (ä-thē'rä) Sp.	39·09 N	0·26 W
78	Alcoa (ăl-kō'à) Tenn.	35·45 N	84 00 W
125	Alcobendas (äl-kō-běn'däs) Sp. (Madrid In.)	40·32 N	3·39 W
125	Alcochete (äl-kō-chā'ta) Port. (Lisbon In.)	38·45 N	8·58 W
125	Alcora (äl-kō'rä) Sp.	40·05 N	0·12 W
125	Alcorisa (äl-kō-rē'sä) Sp.	40·53 N	0·20 W
125	Alcorón (äl-kô-rô'n) Sp. (Madrid In.)	40·22 N	3·50 W
101	Alcorta (àl-kôr'tä) Arg. (Buenos Aires In.)	33·32 S	61·08 W
67	Alcova Res. (ăl-kō'và) Wyo.	42·31 N	106·33 W
85	Alcove (ăl-kōv') Can. (Ottawa In.)	45·41 N	75·55 W
125	Alcoy (äl-koi') Sp.	38·42 N	0·30 W
125	Alcudia, Ba. de (B.) (bä-ē'ä-dě-äl-kōō-dhē'à) Sp.	39·48 N	3·20 E
167	Aldabra Is. (äl-dä'brä) Afr.	9·16 S	46·17 E
90	Aldama (äl-dä'mä) Mex.	22·54 N	98·04 W
76	Aldama Mex.	28·50 N	105·54 W
135	Aldan Sov. Un.	58·46 N	125·19 E
135	Aldan (R.) Sov. Un.	63·30 N	132·14 E
135	Aldan Plat Sov. Un.	57·42 N	130·28 E
135	Aldanskaya Sov. Un.	61·52 N	135·29 E
123	Aldekerk (äl'dĕ-kĕ'rk) Ger. (Ruhr In.)	51·26 N	6·26 E
123	Aldenhoven (äl'děn-hō'věn) Ger. (Ruhr In.)	50·54 N	6·18 E
65	Aldergrove (ôl'dēr-grōv) Can. (Vancouver In.)	49·03 N	122·28 W
122	Alderney (I.) (ôl'dēr-nĭ) Chan. Is.	49·43 N	2·11 W
110	Aldershot (ôl'dēr-shŏt) Eng. (London In.)	51·14 N	0·46 W
80	Alderson (ôl-dēr-sŭn) W. Va.	37·40 N	80·40 W
65	Alderwood Manor (ôl'dēr-wŏŏd măn'ŏr) Wash. (Seattle In.)	47·49 N	122·18 W
73	Aledo (à-le'dō) Ill.	41·12 N	90·47 W
164	Aleg Mauritania	17·10 N	13·57 W
101	Alegre (àlĕ'-grĕ) Braz. (Rio de Janeiro In.)	20·41 S	41·32 W
100	Alegre (R.) Braz. (In.)	22·22 S	43·34 W
100	Alegrete (ä-lå-grā'tā) Braz.	29·46 S	55·44 W
136	Aleksandrov (ä-lyĕk-sän' drôf) Sov. Un. (Moscow In.)	56·24 N	38·45 E
136	Aleksandrovsk (ä-lyĕk-sän'drôfsk) Sov. Un. (Urals In.)	59·11 N	57·36 E
135	Aleksandrovsk-Sakhalinskiy (ä-lyěk-sän'drôfsk-sŭ-kŭ-lyēn'skē) Sov. Un.	51·02 N	142·21 E
121	Aleksandrow Kujawski (ä-lěk-säh'drōov kōō-yav'skē) Pol.	52·54 N	18·45 E
129	Alekseyevka (ä-lyěk-sā-yěf'kà) Sov. Un.	50·39 N	38·40 E
128	Aleksin (ä-lyěk-sēn) Sov. Un.	54·31 N	37·07 E
127	Aleksinac (à-lyěk-sē-nák') Yugo.	43·33 N	21·42 E
101	Alem Paraíba (ä-lě'm-pà-räē'bà) Braz. (Rio de Janeiro In.)	21·54 S	42·40 W
122	Alençon (ä-läN-sôN') Fr.	48·26 N	0·08 E
99	Alenquer (ä-lěŋ-kěr') Braz.	1·58 S	54·44 W
124	Alenquer Port.	39·04 N	9·01 W
124	Alentjo (Reg.) (ä-lěŋ-tā'zhōō) Port.	38·05 N	7·45 W
157	Alenuihaha Chan. (ä'lâ-nōō-ē-hä'hä) Hawaii (In.)	20·20 N	156·05 W
115	Aleppo (à-lěp-ō) Syria	36·10 N	37·18 E
122	Alès (ä-lěs') Fr.	44·07 N	4·06 E
126	Alessandria (ä-lěs-sän'drê-ä) It.	44·53 N	8·35 E
74	Alessandro (ä-lěs-san'drō) Calif. (Los Angeles In.)	33·52 N	117·16 W
	Alessio, see Lesh		
118	Ålesund (ô'lě-sōōn') Nor.	62·28 N	6·14 E
64	Aleutian Is. (à-lu'shăn) Alaska	52·40 N	177·30 E
64	Aleutian Trench Alaska	50·40 N	177·10 E
135	Alevina, Mys (C.) Sov. Un.	58·49 N	151·44 E
64	Alexander Arch. (ăl-ĕg-zăn'dēr) Alaska	57·05 N	138·10 W
78	Alexander City Ala.	32·55 N	85·55 W
47	Alexander I Ant.	71·00 S	71·00 W
167	Alexandra (äl-ex-än'-drà) S. Afr. (Johannesburg & Pretoria In.)	26·07 S	28·07 E
158	Alexandria (ăl-ĕg-zăn'drĭ-à) Austl.	19·00 S	136·56 E
81	Alexandria Can.	45·50 N	74·35 W
80	Alexandria Ind.	40·20 N	85·20 W
77	Alexandria La.	31·18 N	92·28 W
70	Alexandria Minn.	45·53 N	95·23 W
127	Alexandria Rom.	43·55 N	25·21 E
70	Alexandria S. D.	43·39 N	97·45 W
167	Alexandria (ăl-ĕx-ăn-drĭ-ä) S. Afr. (Natal In.)	33·40 S	26·26 E
81	Alexandria (ăl-ĕg-zăn'drĭ-à) Va.	38·50 N	77·05 W
	Alexandria, see Al Iskandarīyah		
81	Alexandria Bay N. Y.	44·20 N	75·55 W
127	Alexandroúpolis (Dedeagats) (ä-lěk-sän-drōō'pō-lĭs) (dě'dě-ä-gäts) Grc.	40·51 N	25·51 E
124	Alfaro (äl-färō) Sp.	42·08 N	1·43 W
168	Al Fashn U. A. R. (Nile In.)	28·47 N	30·53 E
165	Al Fayyūm U. A. R.	29·14 N	30·48 E
101	Alfenas (äl-fě'nàs) Braz. (Rio de Janeiro In.)	21·26 S	45·55 W
127	Alfiós (R.) Grc.	37·33 N	21·50 E
168	Al Firdān (fer-dän') U. A. R. (Nile In.)	30·43 N	32·20 E
101	Alfonso Claudio (äl-fōn'sô-klou'dēō) Braz. (Rio de Janeiro In.)	20·05 S	41·05 W
85	Alfred (ăl'frěd) Can. (Ottawa In.)	45·34 N	74·52 W
110	Alfreton (ăl'fēr-tŭn) Eng.	53·06 N	1·23 W
165	Alga Eth.	5·56 N	38·09 E
124	Algarve (Reg.) (äl-gär'vě) Port	37·15 N	8·12 W
124	Algeciras (äl-hä-thē'räs) Sp.	36·08 N	5·25 W
164	Alger (Algiers) (àl-zhā') (ăl-jēr) Alg.	36·51 N	2·56 E
163	Algeria (ăl-gē'rĭ-à) Afr.	34·58 N	2·00 E
125	Algete (äl-hä'tā) Sp. (Madrid In.)	40·36 N	3·30 W
126	Alghero (äl-gâ'rō) It.	40·32 N	8·22 E
	Algiers, see Alger		
77	Algoa (ăl-gō'à) Tex. (In.)	29·24 N	95·11 W
167	Algoa B. (ăl'gōà) S. Afr. (Natal In.)	33·51 S	24·50 E
65	Algoma Wash. (Seattle In.)	47·17 N	122·15 W
71	Algoma Wis.	44·38 N	87·29 W
71	Algona Iowa	43·04 N	94·11 W
80	Algonac (ăl'gô-năk) Mich.	42·35 N	82·30 W
75	Algonquin (ăl-gŏŋ'kwĭn) Ill. (Chicago In.)	42·10 N	88·17 W
81	Algonquin Park Can.	45·50 N	78·20 W
124	Alhama (äl-hä'mä) Sp.	37·00 N	3·59 W
124	Alhama Sp.	37·50 N	1·24 W
74	Alhambra (ăl-hăm'brà) Calif. (Los Angeles In.)	34·05 N	118·08 W
115	Al Ḩammām U. A. R.	30·46 N	29·42 E
125	Alhandra (äl-yän'drà) Port. (Lisbon In.)	38·55 N	9·01 W
139	Al Haql Sau. Ar. (Palestine In.)	29·15 N	34·57 E
139	Al Harmal Leb. (Palestine In.)	34·23 N	36·22 E
144	Al Hasā (Plain) Sau. Ar.	27·00 N	47·48 E
124	Alhaurín el Grande (ä-lou-rēn'ěl-grä'n-dě) Sp.	36·40 N	4·40 W
144	Al Hijaz (Reg.) Sau. Ar.	23·45 N	39·08 E
125	Alhos Vedros (äl'yōs-vā'drōs) Port. (Lisbon In.)	38·39 N	9·02 W
124	Alhucemas, Baie d' (B.) Mor.	35·18 N	5·50 W
144	Al Hudayduh Yemen	14·43 N	43·03 E
144	Al Hufūf (Hofuf) (hô-fōōf') Sau. Ar.	25·15 N	49·43 E
127	Aliákmon (R.) (äl-ê-ăk'-mōn) Grc.	40·26 N	22·17 E
125	Alicante (ä-lê-kän'tā) Sp.	38·20 N	0·30 W
125	Alicante, Bahia de (B.) (bä-ē'ä-dě-ä-lê-kän'tā) Sp.	38·12 N	0·22 W
76	Alice (ăl'ĭs) Tex.	27·45 N	98·04 W
167	Alice (ăl-ĭs) S. Afr. (Natal In.)	32·47 S	26·51 E
167	Alicedale (ăl'ĭs-dāl) S. Afr. (Natal In.)	33·18 S	26·04 E
158	Alice Springs (ăl'ĭs) Austl.	23·38 S	133·56 E
126	Alicudi (I.) (ä-lē-kōō'dē) It.	38·34 N	14·21 E
136	Alifkulovo (ä-lĭf-kŭ'lô-vô) Sov. Un. (Urals In.)	55·57 N	62·06 E
142	Aligarh (ä-lê-gŭr') India	27·58 N	78·08 E
118	Alingsås (å'lĭŋ-sôs) Swe.	57·57 N	12·30 E
75	Aliquippa (ăl-ĭ-kwĭp'à) Pa. (Pittsburgh In.)	40·37 N	80·15 W
168	Al Iskandarīyah (Alexandria) U. A. R. (Nile In.)	31·12 N	29·58 E
168	Al Ismā'īlīyah (Ismailia) (ēs-mä-ěl'ē-à) U. A. R. (Suez In.)	30·35 N	32·17 E
166	Aliwal North (ä-lê-wäl') S. Afr.	31·09 S	28·26 E
139	Al Jafr (L.) Jordan (Palestine In.)	30·17 N	36·20 E
165	Al Jaghbūb Libya	29·46 N	24·32 E
165	Al Jawf Libya	24·14 N	23·15 E
144	Al Jawf Sau. Ar.	29·45 N	39·30 E
165	Al Jazirah Libya	25·47 N	21·25 E
124	Aljezur (äl-zhä-zōōr') Port.	37·18 N	8·52 W
168	Al Jīzah U. A. R. (Nile In.)	30·01 N	31·12 E
165	Al Jufrah (Oasis) Libya	29·30 N	15·16 E
124	Aljustrel (äl-zhōō-strěl') Port.	37·44 N	8·23 W
168	Al Kāb U. A. R. (Suez In.)	30·56 N	32·19 E
139	Al Karak (kě-räk') Jordan (Palestine In.)	31·11 N	35·42 E
168	Al Karnak (kär'nak) U. A. R. (Nile In.)	25·42 N	32·43 E
144	Al Khābūrah Mus. & Om.	23·45 N	57·30 E
139	Al Khalīl (Hebron) Jordan (Palestine In.)	31·31 N	35·07 E
165	Al Khums Libya	32·35 N	14·10 E
144	Al Khurmah Sau. Ar.	21·37 N	41·44 E
117	Alkmaar (älk-mär') Neth.	52·39 N	4·42 E
168	Al Kūbrī (kōō'brê) U. A. R. (Suez In.)	30·01 N	32·35 E
165	Al Kufrah (Oasis) Libya	24·45 N	22·45 E
139	Al Kuntillah U. A. R. (Palestine In.)	29·59 N	34·42 E
144	Al Kuwayt (Kuwait) (koō-wit) Kuwait	29·04 N	47·59 E
164	Allada (äl-lä'dä) Dahomey	6·44 N	2·08 E
115	Al Lādhiqīyah (Latakia) Syr.	35·32 N	35·51 E
82	Allagash (R.) (ăl'à-găsh) Maine	46·50 N	69·24 W
142	Allahābād (ŭl-ŭ-hä-bäd') India	25·32 N	81·53 E
68	All American can. (âl à-měr'ĭ-kăn) Calif.	32·43 N	115·12 W
111	Alland Aus. (Vienna In.)	48·04 N	16·05 E
124	Allariz (äl-yä-rēth') Sp.	42·10 N	7·48 W
78	Allatoona (R.) (ăl'à-tōōn'à) Ga.	34·05 N	84·57 W
122	Allauch (ä-lě'ōō) Fr. (Marseille In.)	43·21 N	5·30 E
135	Allaykha (ä-lī'kà) Sov. Un.	70·32 N	148·53 E
80	Allegan (ăl'ê-găn) Mich.	42·30 N	85·55 W
81	Allegany Ind. Res. (ăl-ê-gā'nĭ) N. Y.	42·05 N	78·55 W
81	Allegheny (R.) Pa.	41·10 N	79·20 W
63	Allegheny Mts U. S.	37·35 N	81·55 W
80	Allegheny Plat U. S.	39·00 N	81·15 W
81	Allegheny Front (Mts.) U. S.	38·12 N	80·03 W
73	Allen (ăl'ěn) Okla.	34·51 N	96·26 W
116	Allen, Lough (B.) (lŏk ăl'ěn) Ire.	54·07 N	8·09 W
84	Allendale (ăl'ěn-dāl) N. J. (New York In.)	41·02 N	74·08 W
79	Allendale S. C.	33·00 N	81·19 W
91	Allende (äl-yěn'dā) Mex.	18·23 N	92·49 W
76	Allende Mex.	28·20 N	100·50 W
81	Allentown (ăl'en-toun) Pa.	40·35 N	75·30 W
143	Alleppey (à-lěp'ē) India	9·33 N	76·22 E
120	Aller R. (äl'ěr) Ger.	52·43 N	9·50 E
70	Alliance (à-lī'ăns) Nebr.	42·06 N	102·53 W
80	Alliance Ohio	40·55 N	81·10 W
122	Allier (R.) (à-lyā') Fr.	46·43 N	3·03 E
84	Alligator Pt. (al'ĭ-gā-tēr) La. (New Orleans In.)	30·57 N	89·41 W
118	Allinge (äl'ĭŋ-ě) Den.	55·16 N	14·48 E
92	All Pines (ôl pīnz) Br. Hond. (Yucatan In.)	16·55 N	88·15 W
144	Al Luhayyah Yemen	15·58 N	42·48 E
65	Allyn (ăl'ĭn) Wash. (Seattle In.)	47·23 N	122·51 W
125	Alma (ä-mà) Alg.	36·44 N	1·27 E
82	Alma (ăl'mà) Can.	45·36 N	65·01 W
79	Alma Ga.	31·33 N	82·31 W
80	Alma Mich.	43·25 N	84·40 W
72	Alma Nebr.	40·08 N	99·21 W
87	Alma Can.	48·29 N	71·42 W
168	Alma S. Afr. (Johannesburg & Pretoria In.)	24·30 S	28·05 E
71	Alma Wis.	44·21 N	91·57 W
134	Alma-Ata (àl'mà à'tà) Sov. Un.	43·19 N	77·08 E
125	Almada (äl-mä'dä) Port. (Lisbon In.)	38·40 N	9·09 W
124	Almadén (äl-mà-dhän') Sp.	38·47 N	4·50 W
144	Al Madīnah Sau. Ar.	24·26 N	39·42 E
139	Al Mafraq Jordan (Palestine In.)	32·21 N	36·13 E
91	Almagre, Laguna (L.) (lä-gōō'nä-äl-mä'grě) Mex.	22·48 N	97·45 W
124	Almagro (äl-mä'grō) Sp.	38·52 N	3·41 W
168	Al Mahallah al Kubrá U. A. R. (Nile In.)	31·00 N	31·10 E
144	Al Manāmah Bahrain	26·01 N	50·33 E
68	Almanor (R.) (ăl-măn'ôr) Calif.	40·11 N	121·20 W
124	Almansa (äl-män'sä) Sp.	38·52 N	1·09 W
168	Al Manshāh U. A. R. (Nile In.)	26·31 N	31·46 E
124	Almansor (R.) (äl-män-sôr) Port.	38·41 N	8·27 W
168	Al Manşūrah U. A. R. (Nile In.)	31·02 N	31·25 W
168	Al Manzilah (män'za-la) U. A. R. (Nile In.)	31·09 N	32·05 E
124	Almanzora (R.) (äl-män-thō'rä) Sp.	37·20 N	2·25 W
168	Al Marāghah U. A. R. (Nile In.)	26·41 N	31·35 E
125	Almargem (äl-mär-zhěN) Port. (Lisbon In.)	38·51 N	9·16 W
144	Al Mawsil Iraq	36·00 N	42·53 E
124	Almazán (äl-mä-thän') Sp.	41·30 N	2·33 W
139	Al Mazār Jordan (Palestine In.)	31·04 N	35·41 E
139	Al Mazra' Jordan (Palestine In.)	31·17 N	35·33 E
124	Almeirim (äl-māĭ-rěN') Port.	39·13 N	8·31 W
117	Almelo (äl'mē-lō) Neth.	52·20 N	6·42 E
124	Almendralejo (äl-män-drä-lā'hō) Sp.	38·43 N	6·24 W
124	Almería (äl-mā-rē'ä) Sp.	36·52 N	2·28 W
124	Almeria, Golfo de (G.) (gôl-fô-dě-äl-māĭ-reN') Sp.	36·45 N	2·26 W
124	Almería (R.) Sp.	37·00 N	2·40 W
118	Almhult (älm'hōōlt) Swe.	56·35 N	14·08 E
124	Almina, Pta. (äl-mē'nä) Mor.	35·58 N	5·17 W
168	Al Minyā U. A. R. (Nile In.)	28·04 N	30·45 E
93	Almirante (äl-mē-rän'tā) Pan.	9·18 N	82·24 W
93	Almirante, Bahia de (B.) (bä-ē'ä-dě-äl-mē-rän'tā) Pan.	9·22 N	82·07 W
127	Almirós Grc.	39·13 N	22·47 E
124	Almodóvar (äl-mō-dhō'vär) Sp.	38·43 N	4·10 W
142	Almoi India	29·41 N	79·42 E
90	Almoloya (äl-mō-lō'yä) Mex.	19·32 N	99·44 W
91	Almoloya Mex. (Mexico City In.)	19·11 N	99·28 W
81	Almonte (ăl-mŏn'tê) Can.	45·15 N	76·15 W
124	Almonte (äl-mōn'tā) Sp.	37·16 N	6·32 W
124	Almonte (R.) Sp.	39·35 N	5·50 W
142	Almora India	29·20 N	79·40 E
144	Al Mubarraz Sau. Ar.	22·31 N	46·27 E
139	Al Mudawwarah Jordan (Palestine In.)	29·20 N	36·01 E
144	Al Mukallā Aden	14·27 N	49·05 E
144	Al Mukhā Yemen	13·43 N	43·27 E
124	Almuñécar (äl-mōōn-yä'kär) Sp.	36·44 N	3·43 W
118	Alnö (I.) Swe.	62·20 N	17·39 E
65	Aloha (ä'lō-hä) Ore. (Portland In.)	45·29 N	122·52 W
155	Alor (I.) (ä'lôr) Indon.	8·07 S	125·00 E
124	Álora (ä'lō-rä) Sp.	36·49 N	4·42 W
139	Alor Gajah Mala (Singapore In.)	2·23 N	102·13 E
154	Alor Star (ä'lôr stär) Mala.	6·24 N	100·08 E
65	Alouette (R.) (ä-lōō-ět') Can. (Vancouver In.)	49·16 N	122·32 W
80	Alpena (ăl-pē'nà) Mich.	45·05 N	83·30 W
111	Alphen Neth. (Amsterdam In.)	52·07 N	4·38 E
124	Alpiarca (äl-pyär'sà) Port.	39·38 N	8·37 W
76	Alpine (ăl'pīn) Tex.	30·21 N	103·41 W
114	Alps (Mts.) (ălps) Eur.	46·18 N	8·42 E
98	Alpujarra (äl-pōō-kä'r'rä) Col. (In.)	3·23 N	74·56 W
124	Alpujarras (Mts.) (äl-pōō-här'räs) Sp.	36·55 N	3·25 W
168	Al Qāhirah (Cairo) U. A. R. (Nile In.)	30·03 N	31·17 E
168	Al Qanţarah U. A. R. (Suez In.)	30·51 N	32·20 E
165	Al Qaryah ash Shargiyah Libya	30·36 N	13·13 E
144	Al Qatif Sau. Ar.	26·30 N	50·00 E
139	Al Qaţranah Jordan (Palestine In.)	31·15 N	36·04 E
144	Al Qaysumah Sau. Ar.	28·30 N	46·27 E
139	Al Quarayyah Sau. Ar. (Palestine In.)	28·43 N	36·11 E
139	Al Qunaytirah Syr. (Palestine In.)	33·09 N	35·49 E
144	Al Qunfidhah Sau. Ar.	18·48 N	41·20 E
168	Al Qurnah (kōōr'na) U. A. R. (Nile In.)	25·44 N	32·39 E
139	Al Quşaymah U. A. R. (Palestine In.)	30·40 N	34·23 E
165	Al Quşayr U. A. R.	26·14 N	34·11 E
139	Al Qusayr U. A. R. (Palestine In.)	34·32 N	36·33 E
118	Als (äls) Den.	55·06 N	9·40 E
123	Alsace (Reg.) (äl-sà's) Fr.	48·25 N	7·24 E
148	Al Shan (Mts.) (äī'shän) China	37·27 N	120·35 E
118	Alsterån (R.) Swe.	56·54 N	15·50 E
74	Altadena (ăl-tà-dē'nà) Calif. (Los Angeles In.)	34·12 N	118·08 W
100	Alta Gracia (äl'tä grä'sê-à) Arg.	31·41 S	64·19 W

ng-sing; ŋ-baŋk; N-nasalized n; nŏd; cŏmmit; ōld; ôbey; ôrder; fōōd; fŏŏt; ou-out; s-soft; sh-dish; th-thin; pūre; ûnite; ûrn; stŭd; circŭs; ü-as "y" in study; '-indeterminate vowel.

176 Altagracia–Angaki PRONOUNCING INDEX

Page	Name Pronunciation Region	Lat. °'	Long. °'
98	Altagracia Ven.	10·42 N	71·34 W
99	Altagracia de Orituco (ä'l-tà-grà' sēà-dě-ôrē-tōō'kô). Ven. (In.)	9·53 N	66·22 W
134	Altai Ter. Sov. Un.	53·39 N	78·52 E
146	Altai Mts. (äl'tī') Asia	49·11 N	87·15 E
74	Alta Loma (ăl'tă lō'mä) Calif. (Los Angeles In.)	34·07 N	117·35 W
77	Alta Loma (ăl'tȧ lō-mȧ) Tex. (In.)	29·22 N	95·05 W
79	Altamaha (R.) (ôl-tȧ-mȧ-hô'). Ga.	31·50 N	82·00 W
99	Altamira (äl-tä-mē'rä) Braz.	3·13 S	52·14 W
91	Altamira Mex.	22·25 N	97·55 W
100	Altamirano (äl-tä-mê-rā'nō). Arg.	35·26 S	58·12 W
126	Altamura (äl-tä-mōō'rä) It.	40·40 N	16·35 E
135	Altan Bulag Mong.	50·18 N	106·31 E
79	Altavista (ăl-tä-vēs'tȧ) Va.	37·08 N	79·14 W
112	Alten (R.) (äl'tĕn) Nor.	69·40 N	24·09 E
120	Altenburg (äl-tĕn-bŏŏrgh) Ger.	50·59 N	12·27 E
111	Altenmarkt an der Triesting Aus. (Vienna In.)	48·02 N	16·00 E
124	Alter do Chão (äl-tĕr'dŏŏ shäN'ōN). Port.	39·13 N	7·38 W
90	Altiplanicie Mexicana (Plat.) (äl-tē-plä-nē'syĕ-mĕ-Kē-kȧ-nä) Mex.	22·38 N	102·33 W
98	Altiplano (Plat.) (äl-tē-plȧ'nō) Bol.	18·38 S	68·20 W
111	Alt Landsberg (ält länts'bĕrgh) Ger. (Berlin In.)	52·34 N	13·44 E
77	Alto (ăl'tō) La.	32·21 N	91·52 W
98	Alto Marañón, Rio (R.) (rê'ō-ȧl'tô-mä-rän-yŏ'n). Peru	8·18 S	77·13 W
111	Altomünster (äl'tō-mün'stĕr) Ger. (Munich In.)	48·24 N	11·16 E
85	Alton (ôl'tŭn). Can. (Toronto In.)	43·52 N	80·05 W
74	Alton Ill. (St. Louis In.)	38·53 N	90·11 W
161	Altona Austl. (Melbourne In.)	37·52 S	144·50 E
111	Altona (äl'tō-nȧ) Ger. (Hamburg In).	53·33 N	9·54 E
78	Altoona (ăl-tōō'nȧ) Ala.	34·01 N	86·15 W
81	Altoona Pa.	40·25 N	78·25 W
65	Altoona Wash. (Portland In.)	46·16 N	123·39 W
101	Alto Rio Doce (äl'tô-rē'ô-dō'sĕ) Braz. (Rio de Janeiro In.)	21·02 S	43·23 W
95	Alto Songo (äl-fō-sôŋ'gō) Cuba	20·10 N	75·45 W
91	Altotonga (ȧl-tō-tôŋ'gä) Mex.	19·44 N	97·13 W
95	Alto Velo (I.) (äl-tô-vĕ'lō) Dom. Rep.	17·30 N	71·35 W
110	Altrincham (ôl'trĭng-ăm) Eng.	53·18 N	2·21 W
111	Alt Ruppin (ält rōō'ppēn) Ger. (Berlin In.)	54·56 N	12·48 E
66	Alturas (ăl-tōō'rȧs) Calif.	41·29 N	120·33 W
72	Altus (ăl'tŭs) Okla.	34·38 N	99·20 W
165	Al 'Ugaylah Libya	30·15 N	19·07 E
165	Al Ujaylāt Libya	32·45 N	12·27 E
128	Alūksne (ä'lŏŏks-nĕ) Sov. Un.	57·24 N	27·04 E
168	Alula (ä-lōō'lä) Som. (Horn of Afr. In.)	11·53 N	50·40 E
81	Alumette I. (ȧ-lü-mĕt') Can.	45·50 N	77·00 W
168	Al Uqşur (Luxor) U. A. R. (Nile In.)	25·38 N	32·59 E
129	Alushta (ä'lŏŏsh-tȧ) Sov. Un.	44·39 N	34·23 E
72	Alva (ăl'vȧ) Okla.	36·46 N	98·41 W
65	Alvarado (ăl-vȧ-rā'dō) Calif (San Francisco In.)	37·35 N	122·05 W
91	Alvarado (äl-vä-rä'dhō) Mex.	18·48 N	95·45 W
91	Alvarado, Luguna de (L.) (lä-gŏŏ'nä-dĕ-äl-vä-rȧ'dô). Mex.	18·44 N	96·45 W
118	Älvdalen (ĕlv'dä-lĕn) Swe.	61·14 N	14·04 E
125	Alverca (al-vĕr'kȧ) Port. (Lisbon In.)	38·53 N	9·02 W
118	Alvesta (äl-vĕs'tä) Swe.	56·55 N	14·29 E
77	Alvin (ăl'vĭn) Tex. (In.)	29·25 N	95·14 W
101	Alvinópolis (äl-vēnō'pō-lês) Braz. (Rio de Janeiro In.)	20·07 S	43·03 W
65	Alviso (ăl-vī'sō) Calif. (San Francisco In.)	37·26 N	121·59 W
144	Al Wajh Sau. Ar.	26·15 N	36·32 E
142	Alwar (ŭl'wŭr) India	27·39 N	76·39 E
168	Al Wāsiţah U. A. R. (Nile In.)	29·21 N	31·15 E
119	Alytus (ä'lê-tŏŏs) Sov. Un.	54·25 N	24·05 E
118	Åmå (ô'môl) Swe.	59·05 N	12·40 E
90	Amacuzac (R.) (ä-mä-kōō-zȧk) Mex.	18·00 N	99·03 W
158	Amadeus, (L.) (ăm-ȧ-dē'ŭs). Austl.	24·30 S	131·25 E
87	Amadjuak (L.) (ä-mädj'wäk). Can.	64·50 N	69·20 W
153	Amagasaki (ä'mä-gä-sä'kê) Jap. (Osaka In.)	34·43 N	135·25 E
153	Amakusa-Shimo (I.) (ämä-kōō'sä shē-mō). Jap.	32·24 N	129·35 E
98	Amalfi (ä'mȧ'l-fē) Col. (In.)	6·55 N	75·04 W
125	Amalfi (ä-mä'l-fê). It. (Naples In.)	40·23 N	14·36 E
127	Amaliás (ȧ-mäl'yȧs) Grc.	37·48 N	21·23 E
142	Amalner India	21·07 N	75·06 E
99	Amambay, Cordillera de (Mts.) Braz.	20·06 S	57·08 W
152	Amami Guntō (Is.) (ä'mä'mē gŏŏn'tō'). Jap.	28·25 N	129·00 E
152	Amamio (I.) (ä-mä'mē-ō) Jap.	28·10 N	129·55 E
167	Amanzimtoti S. Afr. (Natal In.)	30·02 S	30·54 E
99	Amapá (ä-mä-pȧ') Braz.	2·14 N	50·48 W
99	Amapá (Ter.) Braz.	1·15 N	52·15 W
92	Amapala (ä-mä-pä'lä) Hond.	13·16 N	87·39 W
99	Amarante (ä-mä-rän'tā) Braz.	6·17 S	42·43 W
68	Amargosa (R.) (ȧ'mär-gō'sȧ) Calif.	35·55 N	116·45 W
72	Amarillo (ăm-ȧ-rĭl'ō) Tex.	35·14 N	101·49 W
126	Amaro, Mt. (ä-mä'rō) It.	42·07 N	14·07 E
133	Amasya (ä-mä'sê-ȧ) Tur.	40·40 N	35·50 E
91	Amatenango (ä-mä-tā-naŋ'gō) Mex.	16·30 N	92·29 W
64	Amatignak (I.) (ä-mȧ'tê-näk) Alaska	51·12 N	178·30 W
92	Amatique, Bahía de (B.) (bä-ē'ä-dĕ-ä-mä-tē'kā). Guat.-Br. Hond.	15·58 N	88·50 W
92	Amatitlán (ä-mä-tê-tlän'). Guat.	14·27 N	90·39 W
90	Amatlán de Cañas (ä-mät-län'dā kän-yäs). Mex.	20·50 N	104·22 W
98	Amazonas Selvas (Reg.) (ä-mä-thō'näs). Braz.	4·15 S	64·30 W
99	Amazonas, Rio (R.) (rē'ō-ä-mä-thō'näs). Braz.	2·03 S	53·18 W
142	Ambala (ŭm-bä'lŭ) India	30·31 N	76·48 E
98	Ambalema (äm-bä-lā'mä) Col. (In.)	4·47 N	74·45 W
135	Ambarchik (ŭm-bär'chĭk) Sov. Un.	69·39 N	162·18 E
98	Ambato (äm-bä'tō) Ec.	1·15 S	78·44 W
167	Ambatosoratra (ämbä'tōō-sōōr-ä'trŭ). Malag. Rep.	17·44 S	48·41 E
120	Amberg (äm'bĕrgh) Ger.	49·26 N	11·51 E
95	Ambergris Cays (Is.) (ăm'bēr-grēs kāz) Caicos	21·20 N	71·40 W
92	Ambergris I. Br. Hond. (Yucatan In.)	18·04 N	87·43 W
123	Ambérieu (äN-bā-rê-û') Fr.	45·57 N	5·21 E
122	Ambert (äN-bĕr') Fr.	45·32 N	3·41 E
155	Ambil (I.) (äm'bēl) Phil. (Manila In.)	13·51 N	120·25 E
84	Ambler (ăm'blĕr) Pa. (Philadelphia In.)	40·09 N	75·13 W
155	Amboina (ăm-boi'nȧ) Indon.	3·45 S	128·17 E
155	Amboina (I.) Indon.	4·50 S	128·45 E
122	Amboise (äN-bwăz') Fr.	47·25 N	0·56 E
167	Ambositra (äN-bô-sē'trä) Malag. Rep.	20·31 S	47·28 E
80	Amboy (ăm'boi) Ill.	41·41 N	89·15 W
65	Amboy Wash. (Portland In.)	45·55 N	122·27 W
167	Ambre, Cap d' (C.). Malag. Rep.	12·06 S	49·15 E
75	Ambridge (ăm'brĭdj) Pa. (Pittsburgh In.)	40·36 N	80·13 W
159	Ambrim (I.) New Heb.	16·28 S	158·17 E
166	Ambriz Ang.	7·50 S	15·10 E
166	Ambrizete Ang.	7·15 S	12·50 E
64	Amchitka P. (ăm-chĭt'kȧ). Alaska	51·30 N	179·36 W
90	Amealco (ä-mā-äl'kō) Mex.	20·12 N	100·08 W
90	Ameca (ä-mĕ'kä) Mex.	20·34 N	104·02 W
91	Amecameca (ä-mȧ-kä-mā'kä) Mex. (Mexico City In.)	19·06 N	98·46 W
111	Ameide Neth. (Amsterdam In.)	51·57 N	4·57 E
117	Ameland (I.) Neth.	53·29 N	5·54 E
75	Amelia (ȧ-mēl'yȧ) Ohio (Cincinnati In.)	39·01 N	84·12 W
68	American (R.) (ȧ-mĕr'ĭ-kăn) Calif.	38·37 N	121·19 W
101	Americana (ä-mĕ-rê-kȧ'nȧ) Braz. (Rio de Janeiro In.)	22·46 S	47·19 W
67	American Falls (ȧ-mĕr-ĭ-kăn). Idaho	42·45 N	112·53 W
67	American Falls Res. Idaho	42·56 N	113·18 W
69	American Fork Utah	40·20 N	111·50 W
47	American Highland Ant.	72·00 S	79·00 E
78	Americus (ȧ-mĕr'ĭ-kŭs) Ga.	32·04 N	84·15 W
111	Amersfoort (ä'mĕrz-fōrt) Neth. (Amsterdam In.)	52·08 N	5·23 E
86	Amery (ā'mēr-ê) Can.	56·32 N	93·58 W
71	Amery Wis.	45·19 N	92·24 W
71	Ames (āmz) Iowa	42·00 N	93·36 W
83	Amesbury (āmz'bēr-ê) Mass. (Boston In.)	42·51 N	70·56 W
127	Ámfissa (ȧm-fĭ'sȧ) Grc.	38·32 N	22·26 E
135	Amga (ŭm-gä') Sov. Un.	61·08 N	132·09 E
135	Amga (R.) Sov. Un.	61·41 N	133·11 E
135	Amgun (R.) Sov. Un.	53·33 N	137·57 E
165	Amhara (Prov.) (äm-hä'rä). Eth.	11·30 N	36·45 E
82	Amherst (ăm'hērst) Can.	45·49 N	64·14 W
75	Amherst Ohio (Cleveland In.)	41·24 N	82·13 W
81	Amherst (I.) Can.	44·10 N	76·40 W
122	Amiens (ä-myäN') Fr.	49·54 N	2·18 E
142	Amio Tsönag Tsho (L.) China	31·38 N	91·18 E
47	Amirante Is. Ind. O.	6·02 S	52·30 E
77	Amite (ă-mēt') La.	30·43 N	90·32 W
77	Amite R. La.	30·45 N	90·48 W
75	Amity (ăm'ĭ-tĭ) Pa. (Pittsburgh In.)	40·02 N	80·11 W
84	Amityville (ăm'ĭ-tĭ-vĭl) N. Y. (New York In.)	40·41 N	73·24 W
64	Amlia (I.) (ȧ'm-lêä) Alaska	52·00 N	173·28 W
139	'Ammān (äm' mȧn) Jordan (Palestine In.)	31·57 N	35·57 E
111	Ammer L. (äm'mĕr) Ger. (Munich In.)	48·00 N	11·08 E
74	Amnicon R. (ăm'nė-kŏn) Wis. (Duluth In.)	46·35 N	91·56 W
	Amnok, see Yalu		
	Amnok, see Yalu (R.)		
142	Amod India	21·47 N	72·58 E
127	Amorgós (I.) (ä-môr'gōs) Grc.	36·47 N	25·47 E
78	Amory (ām'o-rē) Miss.	33·58 N	88·27 W
87	Amos (ā'mŭs) Can.	48·31 N	78·04 W
118	Åmot (Torpen) (ô'mōt) (tôr'pĕn) Nor.	61·08 N	11·17 E
	Amoy, see Hsiamen		
101	Amparo (äm-pȧ'-rô) Braz. (Rio de Janeiro In.)	22·43 S	46·44 W
111	Amper R. (äm'pĕr) Ger. (Munich In.)	48·18 N	11·32 E
125	Amposta (äm-pōs'tä) Sp.	40·42 N	0·34 E
82	Amqui Can.	48·27 N	67·27 W
142	Amraoti (ŭm-rŭ-ŏ'tê) India	20·58 N	77·47 E
142	Amritsar (ŭm-rĭt'sŭr) India	31·43 N	74·52 E
111	Amstelveen Neth. (Amsterdam In.)	52·18 N	4·51 E
111	Amsterdam (äm-stēr-däm') Neth. (Amsterdam In.)	52·21 N	4·52 E
81	Amsterdam (ăm'stēr-dăm). N. Y.	42·55 N	74·10 W
47	Amsterdam (I.) Ind. O.	37·52 S	77·32 E
120	Amstetten (äm'stĕt-ĕn) Aus.	48·09 N	14·53 E
165	Am Timan (äm'tê-män') Chad	11·18 N	20·30 E
144	Amu Dar'ya (Oxus) (R.) (ä-mŏŏ-dä'rēä). Asia	40·40 N	62·47 E
142	Amu Dar'ye (R.) (ä-mōō dä'rēä) Afg.-Sov. Un.	36·50 N	66·58 E
64	Amukta P. (ä-mōōk'tȧ) Alaska	52·30 N	172·00 W
155	Amulung (ä'mōō'lōōng) Phil. (Manila In.)	17·51 N	121·43 E
86	Amundsen G. (ä'mŭn-sĕn) Can.	70·17 N	23·28 W
47	Amundsen Sea Ant.	72·00 S	110·00 W
118	Amungen (L.) Swe.	61·07 N	16·00 E
150	Amur R. (ä-mŏŏr') China and Sov. Un.	49·38 N	127·25 E
136	Amurskiy (ä-mûr'skĭ) Sov. Un. (Urals In.)	52·35 N	59·36 E
152	Amurskiy, Zaliv (B.) (zä'lĭf ä-mŏŏr'skĭ). Sov. Un.	43·20 N	131·40 E
90	Amusgos (San Pedro) (ä-mōō's-gôs) (sän-pĕ'drō). Mex.	16·39 N	98·09 W
155	Amuyao, Mt. (ä-mōō-yä'ō) Phil. (Manila In.)	17·04 N	121·09 E
127	Amvrakikos Kólpos (G.) Grc.	39·00 N	21·00 E
139	Amyun Leb. (Palestine In.)	34·18 N	35·48 E
135	Anabar (R.) (ăn-ȧ-bär'). Sov. Un.	71·15 N	113·00 E
99	Anaco (ä-nȧ'kô) Ven. (In.)	9·29 N	64·27 W
67	Anaconda (ăn-ȧ-kŏn'dȧ) Mont.	46·07 N	112·55 W
65	Anacortes (ăn-ȧ-kôr'tĕz) Wash. (Seattle In.)	48·30 N	122·37 W
72	Anadarko (ăn-ȧ-där'kō) Okla.	35·05 N	98·14 W
135	Anadyr (ŭ-nȧ-dĭr') Sov. Un.	64·47 N	177·01 E
135	Anadyr (R.) Sov. Un.	65·30 N	172·45 E
139	Anadyrskiy Zaliv (B.) Sov. Un.	64·10 N	178·00 W
74	Anaheim (ăn'ȧ-hīm) Calif. (Los Angeles In.)	33·50 N	117·55 W
77	Anahuac (ä-nä'wäk) Tex. (In.)	29·46 N	94·41 W
143	Anai Mudi Mt. India	15·28 N	77·10 E
94	Ana María, Cayos (Is.) (kä'yōs-ä'nȧ mȧ-rē'ȧ). Cuba	21·55 N	78·50 W
154	Anambas, Pulau-Pulau (Is.) (ä-näm-bäs). Indon.	2·41 N	106·38 E
71	Anamosa (ăn-ȧ-mō'sȧ) Iowa	42·06 N	91·18 W
129	Anan'yev (ȧ-nä'nyĕf) Sov. Un.	47·43 N	29·59 E
129	Anapa (ȧ-nä'pä) Sov. Un.	44·54 N	37·19 E
99	Anápolis (ä-nȧ'pō-lês) Braz.	16·17 S	48·47 W
100	Añatuya (ȧ-nyä-tōō'yȧ) Arg.	28·22 S	62·45 W
122	Ancenis (äN-sē-nē') Fr.	47·24 N	1·12 W
100	Anchieta (ȧn-chyĕ'tä). Braz. (In.)	22·49 S	43·24 W
64	Anchitka (I.) (än-chĕ't-kä). Alaska	51·25 N	178·10 E
148	Anch' iu (än'chê) China	36·26 N	119·12 E
110	Ancholme (R.) (ăn'chŭm). Eng.	53·28 N	0·27 W
77	Anchor (ăŋ'kēr) Tex. (In.)	29·13 N	95·28 W
64	Anchorage (ăŋ'kēr-ȧj) Alaska	61·12 N	149·48 W
75	Anchorage Ky. (Louisville In.)	38·16 N	85·32 W
85	Ancienne-Lorette (äN-syĕn' lō-rĕt'). Can. (Quebec In.)	46·48 N	71·21 W
88	Ancon (äŋ-kōn') C. Z. (Panama Canal In.)	8·55 N	79·32 W
126	Ancona (än-kō'nä) It.	43·37 N	13·32 E
100	Ancud (äŋ-kōōdh') Chile	41·52 S	73·45 W
100	Ancud, G. de (gôl-fô-dĕ-äŋ-kōōdh'). Chile	41·15 S	73·00 W
100	Andalgalá (ȧ'n-däl-gȧ-lȧ') Arg.	27·35 S	66·14 W
124	Andalucia (Reg.) (än-dä-lōō-sê'ä). Sp.	37·35 N	5·40 W
78	Andalusia (ăn-dȧ-lōō'zhĭȧ) Ala.	31·19 N	86·19 W
154	Andaman Is. (ăn-dȧ-măn'). India	11·38 N	92·17 E
154	Andaman Sea Asia	12·44 N	95·45 E
111	Anderlecht (än'dēr-lĕkt) Bel. (Brussels In.)	50·49 N	4·16 E
120	Andernach (än'dĕr-näK) Ger.	50·25 N	7·23 E
101	Anderson (ȧ'n-dĕr-sōn) Arg. (Buenos Aires In.)	35·15 S	60·15 W
66	Anderson (ăn'dēr-sŭn) Calif.	40·28 N	122·19 W
80	Anderson Ind.	40·05 N	85·50 W
79	Anderson S. C.	34·30 N	82·40 W
86	Anderson (R.) Can.	68·32 N	125·12 W
98	Andes (ăn'dēz) (än'dās). Col. (In.)	5·40 N	75·54 W
96	Andes Mts. S. A.	13·00 S	75·00 W
143	Andhei India (Bombay In.)	19·08 N	72·50 E
143	Andhra Pradesh (State) India	22·00 N	78·50 E
115	Andikíthira (I.) Grc.	35·50 N	23·20 E
134	Andizhan (än-dê-zhän'). Sov. Un.	40·51 N	72·39 E
152	Andong (än'dŭng') Kor.	36·31 N	128·42 E
125	Andorra (än-dôr'rä) And.	42·38 N	1·30 E
125	Andorra Eur.	42·32 N	1·18 E
83	Andover (ăn'dô-vēr) Mass. (Boston In.)	42·39 N	71·08 W
84	Andover N. J. (New York In.)	40·59 N	74·45 W
112	Andöy (I.) (änd-ûê) Nor.	69·12 N	14·58 E
125	Andraitx (än-drȧ-ĭtsh') Sp.	39·34 N	2·25 E
64	Andreanof Is. (än-drȧ-ä'nôf) Alaska	51·10 N	177·00 W
101	Andrelândia (än-drĕ-lȧ'n-dyȧ) Braz. (Rio de Janeiro In.)	21·45 S	44·18 W
82	Andréville Can.	47·40 N	69·44 W
78	Andrew Johnson Natl Mon. (ăn'drōō jŏn'sŭn). Tenn.	36·15 N	82·55 W
78	Andrews (ăn'drōōz) N. C.	35·12 N	83·48 W
79	Andrews S. C.	33·25 N	79·32 W
129	Andreyevka (än-drȧ-yĕf'kȧ) Sov. Un.	48·03 N	37·03 E
126	Andria (än'drê-ä) It.	41·17 N	15·55 E
127	Andros (ȧn'dhrôs) Grc.	37·50 N	24·54 E
94	Andros I. (ăn'drŏs) Ba. Is.	24·30 N	78·00 W
127	Andrós (I.) (ȧn'dhrôs) Grc.	37·59 N	24·55 E
82	Androscoggin (R.) (ăn-drŭs-kŏg'ĭn). Maine	44·25 N	70·45 W
124	Andújar (än-dōō'här) Sp.	38·04 N	4·03 W
164	Anécho (ȧ-nā'chō) Togo	6·25 N	1·36 E
153	Anegasaki (ä'mȧ-gä-sä'kê) Jap. (Tōkyō In.)	35·29 N	140·02 E
159	Aneityum (I.) (ä-nȧ-ē'tê-ŭm) New Hebr.	20·15 S	169·49 E
70	Aneta (ă-nē'tȧ) N. D.	47·41 N	97·57 W
155	Angadanan (äŋ-gȧ-dä'nȧn) Phil. (Manila In.)	16·45 N	121·45 E
155	Angaki (än-gä'kê) Phil. (Manila In.)	17·10 N	120·40 E

ăt: finăl; rāte; senâte; ärm; ȧsk; sofȧ; fâre; ch-choose; dh-as th in other; bē; êvent; bĕt; recĕnt; cratēr; g-go; gh-guttural g; bĭt; ĭ-short neutral; rīde; K-guttural k as ch in German ich;

ng-sing; ŋ-baŋk; N-nasalized n; nŏd; cŏmmit; ōld; ôbey; ôrder; fōōd; fŏŏt; ou-out; s-soft; sh-dish; th-thin; pūre; ûnite; ûrn; stŭd; circŭs; ū-as "y" in study; ′-indeterminate vowel.

Page	Name Pronunciation Region	Lat. °'	Long. °'
127	Arda (R.) (är'dȧ) ... Bul.	41·36 N	25·18 E
144	Ardabīl ... Iran	38 15 N	48·00 E
133	Ardahan (är-dȧ-hän') ... Tur.	41·10 N	42·40 E
118	Ardals Fd. (är-däls) ... Nor.	58·53 N	7·55 E
132	Ardatov (är-dȧ-tôf') ... Sov. Un.	54·58 N	46·10 E
117	Ardennes (Mts.) (ȧr-dĕn') ... Bel.	50·01 N	5·12 E
124	Ardila (R.) (är-dē'lȧ) ... Port.	38·12 N	9·20 W
73	Ardmore (ärd'mōr) ... Okla.	34·10 N	97·08 W
84	Ardmore ... Pa. (Philadelphia In.)	40·01 N	75·18 W
85	Ardrossan (är-drŏs'ăn) Can. (Edmonton In.)	53·33 N	113·08 W
110	Ardsley (ärdz'lē) ... Eng.	53·43 N	1·33 W
112	Åre ... Swe.	63·12 N	13·12 E
124	Arecena (ä-rĕ-sĕ'nä) ... Sp.	37·53 N	6·34 W
89	Arecibo (ä-rȧ-sē'bō) P. R. (Puerto Rico In.)	18·28 N	66·45 W
99	Areia Branca (ä-rĕ'yä-brä'n-kä) Braz.	4·58 S	37·02 W
68	Arena, Pt. (ä-rā'nȧ) ... Calif.	38·57 N	123·40 W
99	Arenas, Punta (Pt.) (pōō'n-tä-rĕ'näs) . Ven. (In.)	10·57 N	64·24 W
124	Arenas de San Pedro (ä-rā'nȧs dā sän pā'drō) . Sp.	40·12 N	5·04 W
118	Arendal (ä'rĕn-däl) ... Nor.	58·29 N	8·44 E
111	Arendonk ... Bel. (Brussels In.)	51·19 N	5·07 E
98	Arequipa (ä-rȧ-kē'pä) ... Peru	16·27 S	71·30 W
126	Arezzo (ä-rĕt'sō) ... It.	43·28 N	11·54 E
124	Arga (R.) (är'gä) ... Sp.	42·35 N	1·55 W
125	Arganda (är-gän'dä) Sp. (Madrid In.)	40·18 N	3·27 W
136	Argazi L. (är'gä-zĭ) Sov. Un. (Urals In.)	55·24 N	60·37 E
136	Argazi R. ... Sov. Un. (Urals In.)	55·33 N	57·30 E
122	Argentan (ȧr-zhäN-täN') ... Fr.	48·45 N	0·01 W
122	Argentat (ȧr-zhäN-tä') ... Fr.	45·07 N	1·57 E
123	Argenteuil (är-zhäN-tû'y') Fr. (Paris In.)	48·56 N	2·15 E
96	Argentina (är-jĕn-tē'nȧ) ... S. A.	35·30 S	67·00 W
100	Argentino (L.) (är-kĕn-tē'nō) . Arg.	50·15 S	72·45 W
122	Argenton-sur-Creuse (är-zhäN'tôN-sür-krôs) . Fr.	46·34 N	1·28 E
127	Arges (R.) (är'zhĕsh) ... Rom.	44·27 N	25·22 E
75	Argo (är'gō) ... Ill. (Chicago In.)	41·47 N	87·49 W
127	Argolikos Kólpos (G.) ... Grc.	37·20 N	23·00 E
122	Argonne (Mts.) (ä'r-gôn) ... Fr.	49·21 N	5·54 E
127	Argos (är'gŏs) ... Grc.	37·38 N	22·45 E
127	Argostólion (är-gŏs-tŏ'lē-ōn) . Grc.	38·10 N	20·30 E
68	Arguello, Pt. (är-gwāl'yō) . Calif.	34·35 N	120·40 W
135	Argun R. (ȧr-gōōn') Sov. Un.-China	50·15 N	118·45 E
85	Argyle (är'gīl) Can. (Winnipeg In.)	50·11 N	97·27 W
70	Argyle ... Minn.	48·21 N	96·48 W
118	Århus (ôr'hōōs) ... Den.	56·09 N	10·10 E
153	Ariakeno-Uni (Sea) (ä-rē'ä-kä'nō ōō'nē) . Jap.	33·03 N	130·18 E
153	Ariake-Wan (B.) (ä'rē-ä'kȧ wän) Jap.	31·18 N	131·15 E
126	Ariano (ä-rē-ä'nō) ... It.	41·09 N	15·11 E
98	Ariari (ä-ryä'rē) (R.) ... Col. (In.)	3·34 N	73·42 W
98	Arica (ä-rē'kä) ... Chile	18·34 S	70·14 W
83	Arichat (ä-rĭ-shät') ... Can.	45·33 N	61·03 W
122	Ariège (R.) (ä-rê-ĕzh') ... Fr.	43·26 N	1·29 E
65	Ariel (ā'rĭ-ĕl) Wash. (Portland In.)	45·57 N	122·34 W
121	Ariesul R. (ä-rê-ä'shōōl) ... Rom.	46·25 N	23·15 E
95	Ariguanabo, L. de (lä'gō-dĕ-ä-rē-gwä-nä'bō) Cuba (Havana In.)	22·17 N	82·33 W
139	Arīhā (Jericho) Jordan (Palestine In.)	31·51 N	35·28 E
72	Arikaree (R.) (ă-rĭ-kȧ-rē') ... Colo.	39·51 N	102·18 W
153	Arima (ä'rē-mä') Jap. (Ōsaka In.)	34·17 N	135·16 E
155	Aringay (ä-rĭŋ-gä'ē) Phil. (Manila In.)	16·25 N	120·20 E
99	Arinos (R.) (ä-rē'nōzsh) ... Braz.	12·09 S	56·49 W
99	Aripuanã (R.) (ȧ-rē-pwän'yȧ) Braz.	7·06 S	60·29 W
139	Arish (R.) (ȧ-rēsh') U. A. R. (Palistine In.)	29·53 N	33·39 E
62	Arizona (State) (ăr-ĭ-zō'nȧ) . U. S.	34·00 N	113·00 W
124	Arjona (är-hō'nä) ... Sp.	37·58 N	4·03 W
135	Arka (R.) ... Sov. Un.	60·12 N	142·30 E
78	Arkabutla Res. (är-kȧ-bŭt'lȧ) Miss.	34·48 N	88·53 W
73	Arkadelphia (är-kȧ-dĕl'fĭ-ȧ) . Ark.	34·06 N	93·05 W
63	Arkansas (State) (är'kăn-sô) (är-kăn'sȧs) . U. S.	34·50 N	93·40 W
73	Arkansas City ... Kans.	37·04 N	97·02 W
73	Arkansas R. ... Okla.	35·20 N	94·56 W
132	Arkhangel'sk (Archangel) (är-käN'gĕlsk) . Sov. Un.	64·30 N	40·25 E
136	Arkhangel'skiy (är-kän-gĕl'skĭ) Sov. Un. (Urals In.)	52·52 N	61·53 E
136	Arkhangel'skoye (är-kän-gĕl'skō-yĕ) . Sov. Un. (Urals In.)	54·25 N	56·48 E
116	Arklow (ärk'lō) ... Ire.	52·47 N	6·10 W
118	Arkona, C. (är'kō-nä) ... Ger.	54·43 N	13·43 E
143	Arkonam (är-kō-näm') ... India	13·05 N	79·43 E
124	Arlanza (R.) (är-län-thä') ... Sp.	42·08 N	3·45 W
124	Arlanzón (R.) (är-län-thōn') ... Sp.	42·12 N	3·58 W
120	Arlberg Tun. (ärl'bĕrgh) ... Aus.	47·05 N	10·15 E
122	Arles (ärl) ... Fr.	43·42 N	4·38 E
78	Arlington (är'lĭng-tŭn') ... Ga.	31·25 N	84·42 W
83	Arlington ... Mass. (Boston In.)	42·26 N	71·13 W
70	Arlington (är'-lĕng-tŭn) ... S. D.	44·23 N	97·09 W
74	Arlington (är'lĭng-tŭn) Tex. (Dallas, Fort Worth In.)	32·44 N	97·07 W
168	Arlington . S. Afr. (Johannesburg & Pretoria In.)	28·02 S	27·52 E
81	Arlington ... Vt.	43·05 N	73·05 W
81	Arlington ... Va.	38·55 N	77·10 W
65	Arlington ... Wash. (Seattle In.)	48·11 N	122·08 W
75	Arlington Heights (är-lĭng-tŭn-hī'ts) . Ill. (Chicago In.)	42·05 N	87·59 W
118	Arlöv (är'lûf) ... Swe.	55·38 N	13·05 E
158	Arltunga (ärl-tōōŋ'gȧ) ... Austl.	23·19 S	134·45 E
73	Arma (är'mȧ) ... Kans.	37·34 N	94·43 W
85	Armagh (är-mä') (är-mäK') Can. (Quebec In.)	46·45 N	70·36 W
116	Armagh ... N. Ire.	54·21 N	6·25 W
168	Armant (är-mänt') U. A. R. (Nile In.)	25·37 N	32·32 E
98	Armaro (är-mȧ'rō) ... Col. (In.)	4·58 N	74·54 W
133	Armavir (är-mȧ-vĭr') ... Sov. Un.	45·00 N	41·00 E
98	Arm'enia (är-mĕ'nēȧ) ... Col. (In.)	4·33 N	75·40 W
92	Armenia (är-mā'nē-ä) ... Sal.	13·44 N	89·31 W
130	Armenian, S. S. R. ... Sov. Un.	41·00 N	44·39 E
122	Armentières (är-mäN-tyâr') ... Fr.	50·43 N	2·53 E
90	Armeria, Rio de (R.) (rē'ō-dĕ-är-mȧ-rē'ä) . Mex.	19·36 N	104·10 W
75	Armherstburg (ärm'hĕrst-bōōrgh) Can. (Detroit In.)	42·06 N	83·06 W
160	Armidale (är'mĭ-dāl) ... Austl.	30·27 S	151·50 E
70	Armour (är'mēr) ... S. D.	43·18 N	98·21 W
87	Armstrong Station (ärm'strŏng) . Can.	50·21 N	89·00 W
129	Armyansk (ärm'yänsk) . . Sov. Un.	46·06 N	33·42 E
124	Arnedo (är-nā'dō) ... Sp.	42·12 N	2·03 W
117	Arnhem (ärn'hĕm) ... Neth.	51·58 N	5·56 E
158	Arnhem, C. ... Austl.	12·15 S	137·00 E
158	Arnhem Land, (Reg.) (ärn'hĕm-lănd) . Austl.	13·15 S	133·00 E
126	Arno (R.) (ä'r-nō) ... It.	43·45 N	10·42 E
110	Arnold (är'nŭld) ... Eng.	53·00 N	1·08 W
74	Arnold (ȧr'nŭld) Minn. (Duluth In.)	46·53 N	92·06 W
75	Arnold ... Pa. (Pittsburgh In.)	40·35 N	79·45 W
81	Arnprior (ärn-prī'ēr) ... Can.	45·25 N	76·20 W
117	Arnsberg (ärns'bĕrgh) ... Ger.	51·25 N	8·02 E
120	Arnstadt (ärn'shtät) ... Ger.	50·51 N	10·57 E
166	Aroab (är'ō-ȧb) ... S. W. Afr.	25·40 S	19·45 E
82	Aroostook (ȧ-rōōs'tōōk) ... Maine	46·44 N	68·15 W
155	Aroroy (ä-rô-rō'ē) Phil. (Manila In.)	12·30 N	123·24 E
123	Arpajon (ăr-pä-jô'n) Fr. (Paris In.)	48·35 N	2·15 E
100	Arpoador, Ponta do (Pt.) (pô'n-tä-dō-är'pôä-dō'r) . Braz. (In.)	22·59 S	43·11 W
124	Arraiolos (är-rī-ō'lōzh) ... Port.	38·47 N	7·59 W
139	Ar Ramta . Jordan (Palestine In.)	29·31 N	35·57 E
116	Arran (I.) (ă'rȧn) ... Scot.	55·39 N	5·30 W
122	Arras (ȧ-räs') ... Fr.	50·21 N	2·40 E
168	Ar Rawḍah ... U. A. R. (Nile In.)	27·47 N	30·52 E
101	Arrecifes (är-rȧ-sē'fäs) Arg. (Buenos Aires In.)	34·03 S	60·05 W
101	Arrecifes (R.) Arg. (Buenos Aires In.)	34·07 S	59·50 W
122	Arrée, Mts. d' (är-rā') ... Fr.	48·27 N	4·00 W
91	Arriaga (är-rêä'gä) ... Mex.	16·15 N	95·00 W
144	Ar Riyāḍ ... Sau. Ar.	24·31 N	46·47 E
125	Arrone (R.) ... It. (Rome In.)	41·57 N	12·17 E
74	Arrowhead, L. (lăk ăr'ōhĕd) Calif. (Los Angeles In.)	34·17 N	117·13 W
67	Arrow R. (ăr'ō) ... Mont.	47·29 N	109·53 W
66	Arrowrock Res. (ăr'ō-rŏk) . Idaho	43·40 N	115·30 W
95	Arroya Arena (är-rō'yä-rĕ'nä) Cuba (Havana In.)	23·01 N	82·30 W
91	Arroy Caribe (R.) (är-rō'ĭ-kä-rē'bĕ) . Mex.	18·18 N	90·38 W
124	Arroyo de la Luz (är-rō'yō-dĕ-lä-lōō'z) . Sp.	39·39 N	6·46 W
90	Arroyo Grande (R.) (är-rô'yō-grä'n-dĕ) . Mex.	23·30 N	98·45 W
90	Arroyo Seco (är-rō'yō sä'kō) . Mex.	21·31 N	99·44 W
144	Ar Rub Al Khālī (Empty Quarter) (Des.) . Sau. Ar.	20·30 N	51·45 E
135	Arsen'yev ... Sov. Un.	44·13 N	133·32 E
136	Arsinskiy (är-sĭn'skĭ) Sov. Un. (Urals In.)	53·46 N	59·54 E
127	Árta (är'tä) ... Grc.	39·08 N	21·02 E
76	Arteaga (är-tä-ä'gä) ... Mex.	25·28 N	100·50 W
135	Artëm (ȧr-tyôm') ... Sov. Un.	43·28 N	132·29 E
94	Artemisa (är-tȧ-mē'sä) ... Cuba	22·50 N	82·45 W
129	Artëmovsk (ȧr-työm'ŏfsk) Sov. Un.	48·37 N	38·00 E
72	Artesia (är-tē'sĭ-ȧ) ... N. Mex.	32·44 N	104·23 W
160	Artesian Basin, The (är-tē'zhăn) . Austl.	26·45 S	141·40 E
95	Arthur's Town ... Ba. Is.	24·40 N	74·30 W
136	Arti (är'tĭ) ... Sov. Un. (Urals In.)	56·20 N	58·38 E
95	Artibonite (R.) (är-tē-bô-nē'tā) Hai.	19·00 N	72·25 W
100	Artigas (är-tē'gäs) ... Ur.	32·33 S	53·29 W
155	Aru, Pulau-Pulau (Is.) ... Indon.	6·20 S	133·00 E
165	Arua (ä'rōō-ä) ... Ug.	3·04 N	31·01 E
98	Aruba (ä-rōō'bȧ) (I.) Neth. Antilles	12·29 N	70·00 W
167	Arusha (ȧ-rōō'shȧ) ... Tan.	3·18 S	36·43 E
165	Aruwimi R. (ä-rōō-wē'mē) Con. L.	1·04 N	28·31 E
82	Arvida ... Can.	48·25 N	71·11 W
118	Arvika (är-vē'kȧ) ... Swe.	59·41 N	12·35 E
132	Arzamas (är-zä-mäs') ... Sov. Un.	55·20 N	43·52 E
125	Arzew (är-zȧ-ōō') ... Alg.	35·50 N	0·20 W
124	Arzua (är-thōō'ä) ... Sp.	42·54 N	8·19 W
120	As (ăsh') ... Czech.	50·12 N	12·13 E
152	Asahigawa (ä-sä'hē-gä'wä) . . Jap.	43·50 N	142·09 E
153	Asahi-Gawa (Strm.) (ä-sä'hē-gä'wä) . Jap.	35·01 N	133·40 E
153	Asaka (ä-sä'kä) . Jap. (Tōkyō In.)	35·47 N	139·36 E
136	Asbest (äs- bĕst') Sov. Un. (Urals In.)	57·02 N	61·28 E
82	Asbestos (ăs bĕs'tōs) ... Can.	45·49 N	71·52 W
84	Asbury Park (ăz'bĕr-ĭ) N. J. (New York In.)	40·13 N	74·01 W
92	Ascencion, Bahía de la (B.) (bä-ē'ä-dĕ-lä-äs-sĕn-sē-ōn') Mex. (Yucatan In.)	19·39 N	87·30 W
90	Ascensión (äs-sĕn-sē-ōn') ... Mex.	24·21 N	99·54 W
163	Ascension (I.) (ȧ-sĕn'shŭn) . Atl. O.	8·00 S	13·00 W
168	Ascent (ăs-ĕnt') ... S. Afr. (Johannesburg & Pretoria In.)	27·14 S	29·06 E
120	Aschaffenburg (ä-shäf'ĕn-bōōrgh) Ger.	49·58 N	9·12 E
123	Ascheberg (ä'shĕ-bĕrg) Ger. (Ruhr In.)	51·47 N	7·38 E
120	Aschersleben (äsh'ĕrs-lā-bĕn) . Ger.	51·46 N	11·28 E
126	Ascoli Piceno (äs'kō-lēpē-chā'nō) It.	42·50 N	13·55 E
127	Asenovgrad ... Bul.	42·00 N	24·49 E
168	Aser, Ras (C.) Som. (Horn of Afr. In.)	11·55 N	51·30 E
128	Aseri (ȧ'sĕ-rĭ) ... Sov. Un.	59·26 N	26·58 E
	Asfi, see Safi		
136	Asha (ä'shȧ) . Sov. Un. (Urals In.)	55·01 N	57·17 E
70	Ashabula (L.) (ăsh'ȧ-bū-lă) . . N. D.	47·07 N	97·51 W
136	Ashan (ä'shän) Sov. Un. (Urals In.)	57·08 N	56·25 E
110	Ashbourne (ăsh'bŭrn) ... Eng.	53·01 N	1·44 W
78	Ashburn (ăsh'bŭrn) ... Ga.	31·42 N	83·42 W
158	Ashburton (R.) (ăsh'bûr-tŭn) Austl.	22·30 S	115·30 E
110	Ashby-de-la-Zouch (ăsh'bĭ-dē-lȧ zōōsh') . Eng.	52·44 N	1·23 W
86	Ashcroft ... Can.	50·47 N	121·02 W
73	Ashdown (ăsh'doun) ... Ark.	33·41 N	94·07 W
79	Asheboro (ăsh'bŭr-ō) ... N. C.	35·41 N	79·50 W
76	Asherton (ăsh'ēr-tŭn) ... Tex.	28·26 N	99·45 W
79	Asheville (ăsh'vĭl) ... N. C.	35·35 N	82·35 W
153	Ashikaga (ä'shē-kä'gȧ) ... Jap.	36·22 N	139·26 E
153	Ashiya (ä'shē-yä') ... Jap.	33·54 N	130·40 E
153	Ashiya ... Jap. (Osaka In.)	34·44 N	135·18 E
153	Ashizuri-Zaki (Pt.) (ä-shē-zōō-rē zä-kē) . Jap.	32·43 N	133·04 E
103	Ashkhabad (ŭsh-kä-bät') . Sov. Un.	39·45 N	58·13 E
78	Ashland (ăsh'lănd) ... Ala.	33·15 N	85·50 W
72	Ashland ... Kans.	37·11 N	99·46 W
80	Ashland ... Ky.	38·25 N	82·40 W
82	Ashland ... Maine	46·37 N	68·26 W
83	Ashland ... Mass. (Boston In.)	42 16 N	71·28 W
70	Ashland ... Nebr.	41·02 N	96·23 W
80	Ashland ... Ohio	40·50 N	82·15 W
66	Ashland ... Ore.	42·12 N	122·42 W
81	Ashland ... Pa.	40·45 N	76·20 W
71	Ashland ... Wis.	46·34 N	90·55 W
70	Ashley (ăsh'lē) ... N. D.	46·03 N	99·23 W
81	Ashley ... Pa.	41·15 N	75·55 W
154	Ashmore Ref. (ăsh'mōr) ... Indon.	12·08 S	122·45 E
168	Ashmūn (ȧsh-mōōn') U. A. R. (Nile In.)	30·19 N	30·57 E
165	Ash Shabb (Shĕb) ... U. A. R.	22·34 N	29·52 E
168	Ash Shallūfah (Shăl'lōō-fȧ) U. A. R. (Suez In.)	30·09 N	32·33 E
139	Ash Shaṭṭ U. A. R. (Palestine In.)	29·58 N	32·36 E
139	Ash Shawbak Jordan (Palestine In.)	30·31 N	35·35 E
139	Ash Shīdīyah (R.) Jordan (Palestine In.)	29·53 N	36·49 E
80	Ashtabula (ăsh-tȧ-bū'lȧ) ... Ohio	41·55 N	80·50 W
67	Ashton (ăsh'tŭn) ... Idaho	44·04 N	111·28 W
110	Ashton-in-Makerfield (ăsh'tŭn-ĭn-māk'ēr-fēld) . Eng.	53·29 N	2·39 W
110	Ashton-under-Lyne (ăsh'tŭn-ŭn-dēr-līn') . Eng.	53·29 N	2·04 W
87	Ashuanipi (L.) (ăsh-wȧ-nĭp'ĭ) . Can.	52·40 N	67·42 W
82	Ashuapmuchuan (R.) (ăsh-wăp-mōō-chwän') . Can.	49·10 N	73·10 W
136	Ashukino (ȧ-shōō'kĭ-nô) Sov. Un. (Moscow In.)	56·10 N	37·57 E
7	Asia (ā'zhȧ)		
103	Asia Minor (ā'zhȧ) ... Asia	38·18 N	31·18 E
90	Asientos (ä-sē-ĕn'tōs) ... Mex.	22·13 N	102·05 W
126	Asinara, Golfo di (G.) (gôl'fō-dē-ä-sē-nä'rä) . . It.	40·58 N	8·28 E
126	Asinara (I.) (ä-sē-nä'rä) ... It.	41·02 N	8·22 E
144	Asīr (Reg.) (ä-sēr') ... Sau. Ar.	19·30 N	21·27 E
136	Askarovo (äs-kä-rô'vô) Sov. Un. (Urals In.)	53·21 N	58·32 E
118	Askersund (äs'kĕr-sōōnd) ... Swe.	58·43 N	14·53 E
136	Askino (äs'kĭ-nô) Sov. Un. (Urals In.)	56·06 N	56·29 E
82	Askitichi (L.) (äs-kĭ-tĭ'chĭ) ... Can.	49·15 N	73·55 W
165	Asmara (äs-mä'rä) ... Eth.	15·17 N	38·56 E
123	Asnières-sur-Seine (ä-nyâr'-sür-sĕ'n) . Fr. (Paris In.)	48·55 N	2·18 E
165	Asosā ... Eth.	10·13 N	34·28 E
66	Asotin (ȧ-sō'tĭn) ... Wash.	46·19 N	117·01 W
69	Aspen (ăs'pĕn) ... Colo.	39·15 N	106·55 W
111	Asperen ... Neth. (Amsterdam In.)	51·52 N	5·07 E
83	Aspy B. (ăs'pē) ... Can.	46·26 N	60·17 W
168	Assab (ȧs-säb') Eth. (Horn of Afr. In.)	12·52 N	42·39 E
168	Aş Şaff ... U. A. R. (Nile In.)	29·33 N	31·23 E
165	As Sallūm ... U. A. R.	31·34 N	25·09 E
139	As Salt ... Jordan (Palestine In.)	32·02 N	35·44 E
142	Assam (State) (ăs-săm') ... India	30·45 N	90·55 E
144	As Sayh ... Sau. Ar.	24·00 N	47·45 E
118	Assens (äs'sĕns) ... Den.	55·16 N	9·54 E
168	As Sinbillāwayn U. A. R. (Nile In.)	30·53 N	31·37 E
86	Assiniboia ... Can.	49·36 N	106·10 W
85	Assiniboine R. (ă-sĭn'ĭ-boin) Can. (Winnipeg In.)	50·02 N	97·56 W
164	Assinie (ȧ-sē-nē') ... Ivory Coast	4·52 N	3·16 W
99	Assis (ä-sĕ's) ... Braz.	22·39 S	50·21 W
144	As Sulaymānīyah ... Iraq	35·47 N	45·23 E
168	As Suways (Suez) U.A.R. (Suez In.)	29·58 N	32·34 E
127	Astakós (äs'tä-kôs) ... Grc.	38·42 N	21·00 E
133	Astara ... Sov. Un.	38·30 N	48·50 E
126	Asti (äs'tē) ... It.	44·54 N	8·12 E
146	Astin Tagh (Mts.) ... China	36·58 N	85·09 E
115	Astipálaia (I.) ... Grc.	36·31 N	26·19 E
124	Astorga (äs-tôr'gä) ... Sp.	42·28 N	6·03 W
65	Astoria (ăs-tō'rĭ-ȧ) Ore. (Portland In.)	46·11 N	123·51 W

ăt; finȧl; rāte; senāte; ärm; ȧsk: sofȧ; fâre; ch-choose; dh-as th in other; bē; ėvent; bĕt; recĕnt; cratēr; g-go; gh-guttural g; bĭt; ĭ-short neutral; rīde; K-guttural k as ch in German ich;

Page	Name Pronunciation Region	Lat. °′	Long. °′
85	Astotin Cr. (äs-tō-těN′) Can. (Edmonton In.)	53·43 N	113·00 W
133	Astrakhan' (äs-trȧ-kän′) .Sov. Un.	46·15 N	48·00 E
166	Astrida (äs-trē′dȧ) . . . . Rw.	2·37 S	29·48 E
124	Asturias (Reg.) (äs-tōō′ryäs) . . Sp.	43·21 N	6·00 W
100	Asunción (ä-sōōn-syōn′) . . . . . . Par.	25·25 S	57·30 W
	Asuncion, see Ixtaltepec		
	Asunción, see Nochixtlán		
92	Asuncion Mita (ȧ-sōōn-syŏ′n-mē′tȧ) . . Guat.	14·19 N	89·43 W
117	Åsunden (L.) (ô′sōōn-dĕn) . . . Swe.	57·46 N	13·16 E
168	Aswān (Syene) (ä-swän′) (sê-ā′nĕ) . U. A. R. (Nile In.)	24·05 N	32·57 E
165	Aswān Dam . . . . U. A. R.	23·50 N	31·30 E
168	Aswān High Dam U. A. R. (Nile In.)	23·58 N	32·53 E
168	Asyūt (ä-syōōt′) U. A. R. (Nile In.)	27·10 N	31·10 E
100	Atacama, Puna de (Reg.) (pōō′nä-dĕ-ȧtä-kȧ′mä) . Chile	23·15 S	68·45 W
98	Atacama, Puna de (Plat.) (pōō′nä-dĕ-ä-tä-kȧ′mä) . Bol.	21·35 S	66·58 W
96	Atacama, Desierto de (Des.) (dĕ-syĕ′r-tô-dĕ-ä-tä-kȧ′mä) Chile-Peru	23·50 S	69·00 W
100	Atacama, Salar de (L.) (sȧ-lȧr′dĕ-ȧtä-kȧ′mä) . Chile	23·38 S	68·15 W
98	Ataco (ä-tȧ′kŏ) . . . . Col. (In.)	3·36 N	75·22 W
139	‘Ata‘Itah, Jabal al (Mts.) Jordan (Palestine In.)	30·48 N	35·19 E
164	Atakpamé (ä′tȧk-pȧ-mā′) . . . Togo	7·37 N	1·09 E
136	Atamanovskiy (ä-tä-mä′nôv-skĭ) Sov. Un. (Urals In.)	52·15 N	60·47 E
168	Ataqa Gebel (Plat.) U. A. R. (Suez In.)	29·59 N	32·20 E
164	Atar (ä-tär′) . . . . Mauritania	20·45 N	13·16 W
68	Atascadero (ăt-ăs-kȧ-dâ′rō) . Calif.	35·29 N	120·40 W
76	Atascosa R. (ăt-ăs-kō′sȧ) . . . . Tex.	28·50 N	98·17 W
165	Atbara (ät′bȧ-rä) . . . . Sud.	17·45 N	30·01 E
165	Atbara R . . . . Sud.	17·14 N	34·27 E
134	Atbasar (ät′bä-sär′) . . . . . Sov. Un.	51·42 N	68·28 E
77	Atchafalaya B. (ăch-ȧ-fȧ-lī′ȧ) . La.	29·25 N	91·30 W
77	Atchafalaya R . . . . La.	30·53 N	91·51 W
73	Atchison (ăch′ĭ-sŭn) . . . . Kans.	39·33 N	95·08 W
84	Atco (ăt′kō) N. J. (Philadelphia In.)	39·46 N	74·53 W
91	Atempan (ä-tĕm-pȧ′n) . . . . . . Mex.	19·49 N	97·25 W
90	Atenguillo (R.) (ä-tĕn-gē′l-yô) Mex.	20·18 N	104·35 W
86	Athabasca (ăth-ȧ-băs′kȧ) . . . . Can.	54·41 N	113·11 W
86	Athabasca (L.) . . . . Can.	59·04 N	109·10 W
86	Athabasca (R.) . . . . Can.	57·21 N	112·02 W
82	Atharbaska (ăth-ȧr-băs′kȧ) . . Can.	46·03 N	71·54 W
78	Athens (ăth′ĕnz) . . . . Ala.	34·47 N	86·58 W
78	Athens . . . . Ga.	33·55 N	83·24 W
80	Athens . . . . Ohio	39·20 N	82·10 W
81	Athens . . . . Pa.	42·00 N	76·30 W
78	Athens . . . . Tenn.	35·26 N	84·36 W
77	Athens . . . . Tex.	32·13 N	95·51 W
	Athens, see Athínai		
110	Atherstone (ăth′ēr-stŭn) . . . . . Eng.	52·34 N	1·33 W
110	Atherton (ăth′ēr-tŭn) . . . . Eng.	53·32 N	2·29 W
159	Atherton Plat. (ădh-ĕr-tŏn) . Austl.	17·00 S	144·30 E
167	Athi (R.) (ä′tê) . . . . Ken.	2·31 S	35·28 E
127	Athínai (Athens) (ä-thē′nĕ) . . . Grc.	38·00 N	23·38 E
116	Athlone (ăth-lōn′) . . . . Ire.	53·24 N	7·30 W
127	Athos (Mtn.) (ăth′ŏs) . . . . Grc.	40·10 N	24·15 E
139	Ath Thamad U. A. R. (Palestine In.)	29·41 N	34·17 E
116	Athy (ȧ-thī) . . . . Ire.	52·59 N	7·08 W
101	Atibaia (ä-tē-bȧ′yȧ) Braz. (Rio de Janeiro In.)	23·08 S	46·32 W
87	Atikonak (L.) . . . . Can.	52·34 N	63·49 W
85	Atim Cr . . . . Can. (Edmonton In.)	53·34 N	113·59 W
155	Atimonan (ä-tê-mō′nän) Phil. (Manila In.)	13·59 N	121·56 E
92	Atiquizaya (ä′tê-kê-zä′yä) . . . . Sal.	14·00 N	89·42 W
92	Atitlan (Vol.) (ä-tê-tlän′) . . . Guat.	14·35 N	91·11 W
92	Atitlan L. (ä-tê-tlän′) . . . . . . Guat.	14·38 N	91·23 W
91	Atizapán (ä′tê-zȧ-pän′) Mex. (Mexico City In.)	19·33 N	99·16 W
64	Atka (ăt′kȧ) . . . . Alaska	52·18 N	174·18 W
64	Atka (I.) . . . . Alaska	51·58 N	174·30 W
133	Atkarsk (ȧt-kärsk′) . . . . . . Sov. Un.	51·50 N	45·00 E
70	Atkinson (ăt′kĭn-sŭn) . . . . Nebr.	42·32 N	98·58 W
84	Atlanta (ăt-lăn′tȧ) Ga. (Atlanta In.)	33·45 N	84·23 W
73	Atlanta . . . . Tex.	33·09 N	94·09 W
71	Atlantic (ăt-lăn′tĭk) . . . . Iowa	41·23 N	94·58 W
84	Atlantic Highlands N. J. (New York In.)	40·25 N	74·04 W
81	Atlantic City . . . . N. J.	39·20 N	74·30 W
6	Atlantic Ocean		
164	Atlas Mts. (ăt′lăs) . . . . . Alg.-Mor.	31·22 N	4·57 W
90	Atliaca (ät-lê-ä′kä) . . . . Mex.	17·38 N	99·24 W
86	Atlin (L.) (ăt′lĭn) . . . . Can.	59·34 N	133·20 W
90	Atlixco (ät-lēz′kō) . . . . Mex.	18·52 N	98·27 W
118	Atlöy (I.) (ät-lûê) . . . . Nor.	61·24 N	4·46 E
78	Atmore (ȧt′mōr) . . . . Ala.	31·01 N	87·31 W
73	Atoka (ȧ-tō′kȧ) . . . . Okla.	34·23 N	96·07 W
73	Atoka Res . . . . Okla.	34·30 N	96·05 W
90	Atotonilco el Alto (ä′tô-tô-nēl′kō ĕl ȧl′tō) . Mex.	20·35 N	102·32 W
90	Atotonilco el Grande (ä′tô-tô-nēl-kō ĕl grän′dā) Mex.	20·17 N	98·41 W
164	Atoui R. (ȧ-tōō-ē′) Mauritania-Sp. Sah.	21·00 N	15·32 W
90	Atoyac (ä-tô-yäk′) . . . . Mex.	20·01 N	103·28 W
91	Atoyac (R.) . . . . Mex.	16·27 N	97·28 W
90	Atoyac (R.) . . . . Mex.	18·35 N	98·16 W
90	Atoyac de Alvarez (ä-tô-yäk′dā äl′vä-rāz) . Mex.	17·13 N	100·29 W
91	Atoyatempan (ä-tō′yȧ-tĕm-pän′) Mex.	18·47 N	97·54 W
144	Atrak, Rud-e (R.) . . . . Iran	37·42 N	55·30 E
118	Atran (R.) . . . . Swe.	57·02 N	12·43 E
99	Atrato, Rio (R.) (rê′ō-ä-trä′tō) . Col.	7·00 N	77·12 W
98	Atrato (R.) (ä-trä′tō) . . . Col. (In.)	5·48 N	76·19 W
139	Aţ Tafīlah (tä-fē′la) Jordan (Palestine In.)	30·50 N	35·36 E
144	At Tāif . . . . Sau. Ar.	21·03 N	41·00 E
78	Attalla (ȧ-tȧl′yȧ) . . . . Ala.	34·01 N	86·05 W
87	Attawapiskat (R.) (ăt′ȧ-wȧ-pĭs′kăt) . Can.	52·31 N	86·22 W
120	Atter See (L.) (Kammer) . . . . Aus.	47·57 N	13·25 E
81	Attica (ăt′ĭ-kȧ) . . . . N. Y.	42·55 N	78·15 W
84	Attleboro (ăt′′l-bŭr-ô) Mass. (Providence In.)	41·56 N	71·15 W
116	Attow, Ben (Mtn.) (bĕn ăt′tô) Scot.	57·15 N	5·25 W
77	Attoyac Bay (ă-toi′yăk) . . . . . Tex.	31·45 N	94·23 W
64	Attu (I.) (ät-tōō′) . . . . Alaska	53·08 N	173·18 E
115	Aţ Ţūr . . . . U. A. R.	28·09 N	33·47 E
118	Atvidaberg (ôt-vē′dȧ-bĕrgh) . . Swe.	58·12 N	15·55 E
72	Atwood (ăt′wŏŏd) . . . . Kans.	39·48 N	101·06 W
91	Atzcapotzalco (ät′zkä-pô-tzäl′kō) Mex. (Mexico City In.)	19·29 N	99·11 W
111	Atzgersdorf . . . . . Aus. (Vienna In.)	48·10 N	16·17 E
157	Auau Chan (ä′ŏŏ-ä′ŏŏ) Hawaii (In.)	20·55 N	156·50 W
123	Aubagne (ō-bän′y′) . . . . Fr.	43·18 N	5·34 E
122	Aube (R.) (ōb) . . . . Fr.	48·42 N	3·49 E
122	Aubenas (ōb′-nä′) Fr.	44·37 N	4·22 E
123	Aubervilliers (ō-bĕr-vē-yā′) Fr. (Paris In.)	48·54 N	2·23 E
122	Aubin (ō-băN′) . . . . Fr.	44·29 N	2·12 E
85	Aubrey (ô-brē′) Can. (Montreal In.)	45·08 N	73·47 W
78	Auburn (ô′bŭrn) . . . . Ala.	32·35 N	85·26 W
68	Auburn . . . . Calif.	38·52 N	121·05 W
73	Auburn . . . . Ill.	39·36 N	89·46 W
80	Auburn . . . . Ind.	41·20 N	85·05 W
82	Auburn . . . . Maine	44·04 N	70·24 W
83	Auburn . . . . Mass. (Boston In.)	42·11 N	71·51 W
73	Auburn . . . . Nebr.	40·23 N	95·50 W
81	Auburn . . . . N. Y.	42·55 N	76·35 W
65	Auburn . . . . Wash. (Seattle In.)	47·18 N	122·14 W
75	Auburn Hts . . . Mich. (Detroit In.)	42·37 N	83·13 W
122	Aubusson (ō-bü-sôN′) . . . . Fr.	45·57 N	2·10 E
122	Auch (ōsh) . . . . Fr.	43·38 N	0·35 E
78	Aucilla (R.) (ô-sĭl′ȧ) . . . . . Fla.-Ga.	30·15 N	83·55 W
159	Auckland (ôk′lănd) . . . . N. Z. (In.)	37·43 S	174·53 E
47	Auckland Is . . . . N. Z.	50·30 S	166·30 E
122	Aude (ōd) . . . . Fr.	42·55 N	2·08 E
122	Audierne (ō-dyĕrn′) . . . . Fr.	48·02 N	4·31 W
123	Audincourt (ō-dăn-kōōr′) . . . . . . Fr.	47·30 N	6·49 W
110	Audley (ôd′lî) . . . . Eng.	53·03 N	2·18 W
168	Audo Ra . . Eth. (Horn of Afr. In.)	6·58 N	41·18 E
71	Audubon (ô′dŏŏ-bŏn) . . . . Iowa	41·43 N	94·57 W
84	Audubon . N. J. (Philadelphia In.)	39·54 N	75·04 W
120	Aue (ou′ē) . . . . Ger.	50·35 N	12·44 E
160	Augathella (ôr′gȧ′thĕ-lȧ) . . . . Austl.	25·49 S	146·40 E
166	Aughrabies Falls (ô-grä′bês) S. Afr.	28·30 S	20·00 E
111	Augsburg (ouks′bŏŏrgh) Ger. (Munich In.)	48·23 N	10·55 E
73	Augusta (ô-gŭs′tȧ) . . . . Ark.	35·16 N	91·21 W
79	Augusta . . . . Ga.	33·26 N	82·00 W
73	Augusta . . . . Kans.	37·41 N	96·58 W
80	Augusta . . . . Ky.	38·45 N	84·00 W
82	Augusta . . . . Maine	44·19 N	69·42 W
84	Augusta . . . . N. J. (New York In.)	41·07 N	74·44 W
71	Augusta . . . . Wis.	44·40 N	91·09 W
121	Augustow (ou-gŏŏs′tŏŏf) . . . . . Pol.	53·52 N	23·00 E
123	Aulnay-sous-Bois (ō-nĕ′sōō-bwä′) Fr. (Paris In.)	48·56 N	2·30 E
122	Aulne (R.) (ōn) . . . . Fr.	48·08 N	3·53 W
125	Aumale (ô-mäl′) . . . . Alg.	36·05 N	3·40 E
123	Auneau (ō-nĕü) . . . . Fr. (Paris In.)	48·28 N	1·45 E
166	Auob (R.) (ä′wŏb) . . . . . S. W. Afr.	25·00 S	19·00 E
139	Aur (I.) . . . . Mala. (Singapore In.)	2·27 N	104·51 E
142	Aurangābād (ou-rŭŋ-gä-bäd′) India	19·56 N	75·19 E
122	Auray (ō-rĕ′) . . . . Fr.	47·42 N	3·00 W
122	Aurillac (ō-rē-yȧk′) . . . . Fr.	44·57 N	2·27 E
75	Aurora (ô-rō′rȧ) . Ill. (Chicago In.)	41·45 N	88·18 W
75	Aurora . . . . . Ind. (Cincinnati In.)	39·04 N	84·55 W
71	Aurora . . . . Minn.	47·31 N	92·17 W
73	Aurora . . . . Mo.	36·58 N	93·42 W
72	Aurora . . . . Nebr.	40·54 N	98·01 W
118	Aursunden (L.) (äûr-sûndĕn) . Nor.	62·42 N	11·10 E
80	Au Sable (R.) (ô-sā′b′l) . . . . . Mich.	44·40 N	84·25 W
81	Ausable (R.) . . . . N. Y.	44·25 N	73·50 W
	Aussig, see Usti nad Labem		
71	Austin (ôs′tĭn) . . . . Minn.	43·40 N	92·58 W
68	Austin . . . . Nev.	39·30 N	117·05 W
77	Austin . . . . Tex.	30·15 N	97·42 W
158	Austin (L.) . . . . Austl.	27·45 S	117·30 E
77	Austin Bay (ôs′tĭn bī-ōō′) Tex. (In.)	29·17 N	95·21 W
7	Australia (ôs-trā′lĭ-ȧ)		
160	Australian Alps (Mts.) . . . . . Austl.	37·10 S	147·55 E
160	Australian Capital Ter. (ôs-trā′lĭ-ăn) . Austl.	35·30 S	148·40 E
102	Austria (ôs′trĭ-ȧ) . . . . Eur.	47·15 N	11·53 E
123	Authon-la-Plaine (ō-tô′N-lă-plĕ′n) Fr. (Paris In.)	48·27 N	1·58 E
90	Autlán (ä-ōōt-län′) . . . . Mex.	19·47 N	104·24 W
122	Autun (ō-tŭN′) . . . . Fr.	46·58 N	4·14 E
122	Auvergne (Mts.) (ō-vĕrn′y′) . . . Fr.	45·12 N	2·31 E
122	Auxerre (ō-sâr′) . . . . Fr.	47·48 N	3·32 E
85	Aux Grues, Ile (I.) (ō grü) Can. (Quebec In.)	47·05 N	70·32 W
73	Ava (ā′vȧ) . . . . Mo.	36·56 N	92·40 W
165	Avakubi (ä-vȧ-kōō′bê) . . . . Con. L.	1·19 N	27·32 E
122	Avallon (ȧ-vȧ-lôN′) . . . . Fr.	47·30 N	3·58 E
75	Avalon (ăv′ȧ-lŏn) Pa. (Pittsburgh In.)	40·31 N	80·05 W
68	Avalon . . . . Calif.	33·21 N	118·22 W
83	Avalon Pen . . . . Can.	47·23 N	53·10 W
124	Aveiro (ä-vā′rŏŏ) . . . . Port.	40·38 N	8·38 W
100	Avelar (ä′vĕ-lȧ′r) . . . . . . Braz. (In.)	22·20 S	43·25 W
100	Avellaneda (ä-vĕl-yä-nā′dhä) Arg. (In.)	34·25 S	58·23 W
125	Avellino (ä-vĕl-lē′nō) It. (Naples In.)	40·40 N	14·46 E
118	Averöy (I.) (ävĕr-ûê) . . . . Nor.	63·40 N	7·16 E
126	Aversa (ä-vĕr′sä) . . . . It.	40·58 N	14·13 E
73	Avery (ā′vēr-ĭ) . . . . Tex.	33·34 N	94·46 W
118	Avesta (ä-vĕs′tä) . . . . Swe.	60·16 N	16·09 E
122	Aveyron (R.) (ä-vâ-rôN) . . . . Fr.	44·07 N	1·45 E
126	Avezzano (ä-vȧt-sä′nō) . . . . It.	42·03 N	13·27 E
126	Avigliano (ä-vēl-yä′nō) . . . . It.	40·45 N	15·44 E
122	Avignon (ȧ-vē-nyôN′) . . . . Fr.	43·55 N	4·50 E
124	Avila (ä-vê-lä) . . . . Sp.	40·39 N	4·42 W
124	Avilés (ä-vê-lās′) . . . . Sp.	43·33 N	5·55 W
73	Avoca (ȧ-vō′kȧ) . . . . Iowa	41·29 N	95·16 W
81	Avon (ā′vŏn) . . . . Conn.	41·40 N	72·50 W
116	Avon (R.) (ā′vŭn) . . . . Eng.	52·05 N	1·55 W
83	Avon (ā′vŏn) . . Mass. (Boston In.)	42·08 N	71·03 W
75	Avon . . . . Ohio (Cleveland In.)	41·27 N	82·02 W
84	Avondale . . . . Ga. (Atlanta In.)	33·47 N	84·16 W
75	Avon Lake . . Ohio (Cleveland In.)	41·31 N	82·01 W
85	Avonmore (ä′vōN-mōr) Can. (Ottawa In.)	45·11 N	74·58 W
79	Avon Park (ā′vŏn pärk′) . Fla. (In.)	27·35 N	81·29 W
122	Avranches (ȧ-vräNsh′) . . . . Fr.	48·43 N	1·34 W
153	Awaji (ä′wä-jê) . . . . Jap.	34·23 N	135·00 E
153	Awaji-Shima (I.) (ä′wä-jê shē-mä) Jap. (Osaka In.)	34·32 N	135·02 E
165	Awash R. (ȧ-wäsh′) . . . . Eth.	9·19 N	40·30 E
116	Awe, Loch (L.) (lŏK ôr) . . . . . Scot.	56·22 N	5·04 W
165	Awjilah . . . . Libya	29·07 N	21·21 E
122	Ax-les-Thermes (äks′lā tĕrm′) . . Fr.	42·43 N	1·50 E
90	Axochiapan (äks-ō-chyä′pän) . Mex.	18·29 N	98·49 W
122	Ay (ȧ′ê) . . . . Fr.	49·05 N	3·58 E
132	Ay (R.) . . . . Sov. Un.	55·55 N	57·55 E
153	Ayabe (ä′yä-bĕ) . . . . Jap.	35·16 N	135·17 E
100	Ayacucho (ä-yä-kōō′chō) . . . . . Arg.	37·05 S	58·30 W
98	Ayacucho . . . . Peru	12·12 S	74·03 W
134	Ayaguz (ä-yȧ-gōōz′) . . . . . Sov. Un.	48·00 N	80·12 E
124	Ayamonte (ä-yä-mô′n-tĕ) . . . . . Sp.	37·14 N	7·28 W
135	Ayan (ȧ-yän′) . . . . Sov. Un.	56·26 N	138·18 E
98	Ayata (ä-yä′tä) . . . . Bol.	15·17 S	68·43 W
98	Ayaviri (ä-yä-vē′rē) . . . . Peru	14·46 S	70·38 W
129	Aydar (R.) (ī-där′) . . . . . . Sov. Un.	49·15 N	38·48 E
79	Ayden (ā′dĕn) . . . . N. C.	35·27 N	77·25 W
133	Aydin (ȧ′ĭ-dĭn) . . . . Tur.	37·40 N	27·40 E
83	Ayer (âr) . . . . . Mass. (Boston In.)	42·33 N	71·36 W
139	Ayer Hitam . Mala. (Singapore In.)	1·55 N	103·11 E
127	Ayiá (ā-yē′ȧ) . . . . Grc.	39·42 N	22·47 E
127	Ayiassos . . . . Grc.	39·06 N	26·25 E
127	Áyion Óros (Mount Athos) (Reg.) Grc.	40·20 N	24·15 E
127	Áyios Evstrátion (I.) . . . . Grc.	39·30 N	24·58 E
110	Aylesbury (ālz′bēr-ĭ) Eng. (London In.)	51·47 N	0·49 W
85	Aylmer (āl′mēr) Can. (Ottawa In.)	45·24 N	75·50 W
86	Aylmer (L.) . . . . Can.	64·27 N	108·22 W
90	Ayo el Chico (ä′yô el chē′kō) . Mex.	20·31 N	102·21 W
135	Ayon (I.) (ī-ôn′) . . . . Sov. Un.	70·04 N	168·33 E
91	Ayotla (ä-yōt′lä) Mex. (Mexico City In.)	19·18 N	98·55 W
116	Ayr (âr) . . . . Scot.	55·27 N	4·40 W
116	Ayr (L.) . . . . Scot.	55·25 N	4·20 W
168	Ayshā . . . . Eth. (Horn of Afr. In.)	10·48 N	42·32 E
92	Ayutla (ȧ-yōōt′lä) . . . . Guat.	14·44 N	92·11 W
90	Ayutla . . . . Mex.	16·50 N	99·16 W
90	Ayutla . . . . Mex.	20·09 N	104·20 W
154	Ayutthaya (ȧ-yōōt′hē′ä) . . . . Thai.	14·16 N	100·37 E
127	Ayvalik (ȧĭ-vä′lêk) . . . . Tur.	39·19 N	26·40 E
164	Azemmour (ȧ-zē-mōōr′) . . . . . Mor.	33·20 N	8·21 W
130	Azerbaydzhan (Azerbaijan) (S. S. R.) (ä′zēr-bä-ê-jän′). Sov. Un.	40·38 N	47·25 E
82	Aziscoos (L.) (ăz′ĭ kōōs′) . . . Maine	45·03 N	70·50 W
74	Azle (ȧz′lē) Tex. (Dallas, Fort Worth In.)	35·54 N	97·33 W
98	Azogues (ä-sō′gās) . . . . Ec.	2·47 S	78·45 W
129	Azov (ȧ-zôf′) (ä′zôf) . . . . . Sov. Un.	47·07 N	39·19 E
	Azov, Sea of, see Azovskoye More		
129	Azovskoye More (Sea of Azov) (ȧ-zôf′skô-yĕ mô′rĕ) . Sov. Un.	46·00 N	36·20 E
90	Azoyú (ä-zô-yōō′) . . . . Mex.	16·42 N	98·46 W
69	Aztec (ăz′tĕk) . . . . N. Mex.	36·40 N	108·00 W
69	Aztec Ruins Natl. Mon . . N. Mex.	36·50 N	108·00 W
95	Azua (ä′swä) . . . . Dom. Rep.	18·30 N	70·45 W
124	Azuaga (ä-thwä′gä) . . . . Sp.	38·15 N	5·42 W
93	Azuero, Peninsula de (Pen.) (ä-swā′rō) . Pan.	7·30 N	80·34 W
76	Azucar, Presa de (Res.) (prĕ′sä-dĕ-ä-zōō′kär) . Mex.	26·06 N	98·44 W
100	Azufre, Cerro (Copiapó) (Vol.) (sĕr′rō ä-sōō′frā) (kō-pê-äpō′) Chile	26·10 S	69·00 W
101	Azul (ä-sōōl′) Arg. (Buenos Aires In.)	36·46 S	59·51 W
90	Azul, Sierra (Mts.) (sē-ĕ′r-rä-zōō′l) Mex.	23·20 N	98·28 W
98	Azul, Cordillera (Mts.) (kô′r-dē-lyĕ′rä-zōō′l) . Peru	7·15 S	75·30 W
74	Azusa (ȧ-zōō′sȧ) Calif. (Los Angeles In.)	34·08 N	117·55 W
144	Az Zahrān (Dhahran) (dä-rän′) Sau. Ar.	26·13 N	50·00 E
168	Az Zaqāzīq . . . . U. A. R. (Nile In.)	30·36 N	31·36 E
139	Az Zarqā′ . . Jordan (Palestine In.)	32·03 N	36·07 E
165	Az Zawiyah . . . . Libya	32·28 N	11·55 E
123	Baal (bäl) . . . . Ger. (Ruhr In.)	51·02 N	6·17 E
155	Baao (bä′ō) . . . . Phil. (Manila In.)	13·27 N	123·22 E
111	Baarle-Hertog . . . Bel. (Brussels In.)	51·26 N	4·57 E
111	Baarn . . . . Neth. (Amsterdam In.)	52·12 N	5·18 E
127	Babaeski (bä′bä-ĕs′kĭ) . . . . Tur.	41·25 N	27·05 E
98	Babahoyo (bä-bä-ō′yō) . . . . Ec.	1·56 S	79·24 W
167	Babanango . . . . S. Afr. (Natal In.)	28·24 S	31·11 E
165	Babanusa . . . . Sud.	11·30 N	27·55 E
155	Babar (I.) (bä′bär) . . . . Indon.	7·50 S	129·15 E

ng-sing; ŋ-baŋk; N-nasalized n; nŏd; cŏmmit; ōld; ôbey; ôrder; fōōd; fŏŏt; ou-out; s-soft; sh-dish; th-thin; pūre; ûnite; ûrn; stŭd; circŭs; ü-as "y" in study; ′-indeterminate vowel.

ăt; fīnăl; rāte; senâte; ârm; àsk; sofȧ; fâre; ch-choose; dh-as th in other; bē; ēvent; bĕt; recĕnt; cratēr; g-go; gh-guttural g; bĭt; ĭ-short neutral; rīde; κ-guttural k as ch in German ich;

PRONOUNCING INDEX Bandelier–Bathsheba 181

Page	Name Pronunciation Region	Lat. °′	Long. °′
69	Bandelier Natl. Mon. (băn-dĕ-lēr') N. Mex.	35·50 N	106·45 W
90	Banderas, Bahía de (B.) (bä-ē'ä-dĕ-bän-dĕ'räs). Mex.	20·38 N	103·25 W
168	Bander Beila Som. (Horn of Afr. In.)	9·40 N	50·45 E
164	Bandiagara (bän-dê-à-gä'rä). Mali	14·19 N	3·39 W
133	Bandirma (bän-dĭr'mà) Tur.	40·25 N	27·50 E
154	Bandjermasin (bän-jĕr-mä'sên) Indon.	3·18 S	114·32 E
124	Bando (bä'n-dô) Sp.	42·02 N	7·58 W
66	Bandon (băn'dŭn) Ore.	43·06 N	124·25 W
143	Bāndra India (Bombay In.)	19·04 N	72·49 E
154	Bandung Indon.	7·00 S	107·22 E
95	Banes (bä'näs) Cuba	21·00 N	75·45 W
86	Banff (bănf) Can.	51·17 N	115·30 W
116	Banff Scot.	57·39 N	2·37 W
86	Banff Natl. Park Can.	51·45 N	116·04 W
100	Bánfield (bà'n-fyĕ'ld) Arg. (In.)	34·30 S	58·24 W
143	Bangalore (băŋ'gà'lôr) India	13·03 N	77·39 E
155	Bangar (bäŋ-gär') Phil. (Manila In.)	16·54 N	120·24 E
165	Bangassou (bäN-gà-sōō') Cen. Afr. Rep.	4·47 N	22·49 E
155	Bangeta, Mt. N. Gui. Ter.	6·20 S	147·00 E
155	Banggai, Pulau-Palau (Is.) (bäng-gī') Indon.	1·05 S	123·45 E
154	Banggi (I.) Mala.	7·12 N	117·10 E
165	Banghāzī (Bengasi) (bĕn-gä'zē) Libya	32·08 N	20·06 E
139	Bangi Mala. (Singapore In.)	2·54 N	101·48 E
154	Bangka (I.) (bäŋ'kà) Indon.	2·24 S	106·55 E
154	Bangkalan (bäng-kà-län') Indon.	6·07 S	112·50 E
	Bangkok, see Krung Thep		
82	Bangor (băn'gẽr) Maine	44·47 N	68·47 W
80	Bangor Mich.	42·20 N	86·05 W
81	Bangor Pa.	40·55 N	75·10 W
116	Bangor (băŋ'ẽr) (băŋ'ôr) Wales	53·13 N	4·05 W
69	Bangs, Mt. (băngs) Ariz.	36·45 N	113·50 W
155	Bangued (bän-gād') Phil. (Manila In.)	17·36 N	120·38 E
165	Bangui (bäN-gē') Cen. Afr. Rep.	4·28 N	18·35 E
166	Bangweulu, L. (băng-wê-ōō'lōō) N. Rh.	10·30 S	30·15 E
168	Banhā U. A. R. (Nile In.)	30·24 N	31·11 E
95	Bani (bä'-nê) Dom. Rep.	18·15 N	70·25 W
155	Bani (bä'nē) Phil. (Manila In.)	16·11 N	119·51 E
164	Bani (R.) Mali	13·00 N	5·36 W
164	Bani, Jebel (Mts.) (jĕb'ĕl bä'nê) Mor.	28·39 N	9·33 W
95	Bánica (bä'-nē-kä) Dom. Rep.	19·00 N	71·35 W
168	Banī Mazār U. A. R. (Nile In.)	28·29 N	30·48 E
168	Banī Suwayf U. A. R. (Nile In.)	29·05 N	31·06 E
126	Banja Luka (bän-yä-lōō'kà) Yugo.	44·45 N	17·11 E
154	Banjuwangi (bän-jōō-wäŋ'gê) Indon.	8·15 S	114·15 E
154	Ban Kantang (bän-kän'täng') Thai.	7·26 N	99·28 E
167	Bankberg (Mts.) (bàŋk'bûrg) S. Afr. (Natal In.)	32·10 S	25·11 E
65	Banks (bănks) Ore. (Portland In.)	45·37 N	123·07 W
159	Banks (Is.) Austl.	10·10 S	143·08 E
161	Banks, C. Austl. (Sydney In.)	34·01 S	151·17 E
49	Banks I. Can.	73·00 N	123·00 W
159	Banks Is. New Hebr.	13·38 S	168·23 E
160	Banks Str. Austl.	40·45 S	148·00 E
154	Ban Kui Nua Thai.	12·04 N	99·50 E
116	Bann (R.) (băn) N. Ire.	54·50 N	6·29 W
74	Banning (băn'ĭng) Calif. (Los Angeles In.)	33·56 N	116·53 W
166	Banningville Con. L.	3·19 S	17·28 E
79	Bannister (R.) (băn'ĭs-tẽr) Va.	36·45 N	79·17 W
161	Bannockburn Austl. (Melbourne In.)	38·03 S	144·11 E
98	Baños (bä'-nyôs) Ec.	1·30 S	78·22 W
121	Banská Bystrica (bän'skä bê'strê-tzà). Czech.	48·46 N	19·10 E
127	Bansko (bän'skō) Bul.	41·51 N	23·33 E
110	Banstead (băn'stĕd) Eng. (London In.)	51·18 N	0·09 W
164	Banthe (băn'thĕ) S. L.	7·36 N	12·34 W
155	Banton (bän-tōn') Phil. (Manila In.)	12·54 N	121·55 E
116	Bantry (băn'trĭ) Ire.	51·39 N	9·30 W
116	Bantry B. Ire.	51·25 N	10·09 W
165	Banzyville (bäN-zê-vēl') Con. L.	4·14 N	21·11 E
164	Baoule R. (bà-ōō-lā') Mali	14·00 N	9·08 W
167	Bapsfontein (băps-fŏn-tān') S. Afr. (Johannesburg & Pretoria In.)	26·01 S	28·26 E
98	Baqueroncito (bä-kĕ-rô'n-sē-tô) Col. (In.)	3·18 N	74·40 W
129	Bar (bär) Sov. Un.	49·02 N	27·44 E
127	Bar Yugo.	42·05 N	19·09 E
134	Barabinsk (bá'rà-bĭnsk) Sov. Un.	55·18 N	78·00 E
71	Baraboo (bâr'à-bōō) Wis.	43·29 N	89·44 W
95	Baracoa (bä-rä-kō'ä) Cuba	20·20 N	74·25 W
95	Baracoa Cuba (Havana In.)	23·03 N	82·34 W
101	Baradeo (bä-rä-dĕ'ō) Arg. (Buenos Aires In.)	33·50 S	59·30 W
95	Baradères, Baie des (B.) (bä-rä-dâr') Hai.	18·35 N	73·35 W
95	Barahona (bä-rä-ô'nä) Dom. Rep.	18·15 N	71·10 W
125	Barajas de Madrid (bä-rä'häs dā mä-drēdh') Sp. (Madrid In.)	40·28 N	3·35 W
165	Baraka R. (bà-rä'kä) Eth.	16·44 N	37·34 E
142	Baranagar India (Calcutta In.)	22·38 N	88·25 E
92	Baranco (bä-räŋ'kō) Br. Hond.	16·01 N	88·55 W
64	Baranof (I.) (bä-rä'nôf) Alaska	56·48 N	136·08 W
121	Baranovichi (bä'rä-nô-vē'chê) Sov. Un.	53·08 N	25·59 E
139	Baranpauh Indon. (Singapore In.)	0·40 N	103·28 E
100	Barão de Juperanã (bà-rouN-dĕ-zhōō-pe-rä'nà) Braz. (In.)	22·21 S	43·41 W
99	Barão de Melgaço (bä-rouN-dĕ-mĕl-gä'sô) Braz.	16·12 S	55·48 W
142	Bārāsat India (Calcutta In.)	22·42 N	88·29 E
84	Barataria (bä-rà-tä'rê-à) La. (New Orleans In.)	29·44 N	90·08 W
77	Barataria B. La.	29·13 N	89·90 W
98	Baraya (bä-rá'yä) Col. (In.)	3·10 N	75·04 W
101	Barbacena (bär-bä-sā'nà) Braz. (Rio de Janeiro In.)	21·15 S	43·46 W
98	Barbacoas (bär-bä-kō'äs) Col.	1·39 N	78·12 W
99	Barbacoas (bär-bä-kô'ás) Ven. (In.)	9·30 N	66·58 W
93	Barbados I. (bär-bā'dōz) N. A. (Le. & Wind. Is. In.)	13·30 N	59·48 W
125	Barbastro (bär-bäs'trō) Sp.	42·05 N	0·05 E
74	Barbeau (bär-bō') Mich. (Sault Ste. Marie In.)	46·17 N	84·16 W
75	Barberton (bär'bẽr-tŭn) Ohio (Cleveland In.)	41·01 N	81·37 W
166	Barberton S. Afr.	25·48 S	31·04 E
122	Barbezieux (bärb'zyû') Fr.	45·30 N	0·11 W
78	Barboorville (bär'bẽr-vĭl) Ky.	36·52 N	83·58 W
98	Barbosa (bär-bô'-sà) Col. (In.)	6·26 N	75·19 W
80	Barboursville (bär'bẽrs-vĭl) W. Va.	38·20 N	82·20 W
93	Barbuda I. (bär-bōō'dà) Barbados (Le. & Wind. Is. In.)	17·40 N	61·37 W
159	Barcaldine (bär'kôl-dĭn) Austl.	28·30 S	145·43 E
125	Barcarena (bär-kä-rĕ'-nä) Port. (Lisbon In.)	38·29 N	9·17 W
124	Barcarrota (bär-kär-rō'tä) Sp.	38·31 N	6·50 W
126	Barcellona (bär-chĕl-lō'nä) It.	38·07 N	15·15 E
125	Barcelona (bär-thâ-lō'nä) Sp.	41·25 N	2·08 E
99	Barcelona (bär-sä-lō'nä) Ven. (In.)	10·09 N	64·41 W
123	Barcelonnette (bär-sĕ-lô-nĕt') Fr.	44·24 N	6·42 E
98	Barcelos (bär-sĕ'lôs) Braz.	1·04 S	63·00 W
124	Barcélos (bär-thâ'lōs) Port.	41·34 N	8·39 W
144	Bardar-e Pahlant Iran	37·16 N	49·15 E
139	Bardawīl, Sabkhat al (B.) U. A. R. (Palestine In.)	31·20 N	33·24 E
121	Bardejov (bär'dyĕ-yôf) Czech.	49·18 N	21·18 E
168	Bardera (bär-dā'rä) Som. (Horn of Afr. In.)	2·13 N	42·24 E
116	Bardsey (I.) (bärd'sê) Wales	52·45 N	4·50 W
80	Bardstown (bärds'toun) Ky.	37·50 N	85·30 W
78	Bardwell (bärd'wĕl) Ky.	36·51 N	88·57 W
130	Barents Sea (bä'rĕnts) Sov. Un.	72·14 N	37·28 E
165	Barentu (bä-rĕn'tōō) Eth.	15·06 N	37·39 E
122	Barfleur, Pte. de (Pt.) (bàr-flûr') Fr	49·43 N	1·17 W
142	Bargāchia India (Calcutta In.)	22·39 N	88·07 E
135	Barguzin (bär'gōō-zĭn) Sov. Un.	53·44 N	109·28 E
82	Bar Harbor (bär här'bẽr) Maine	44·22 N	68·13 W
126	Bari (bä'rē) It.	41·08 N	16·53 E
98	Barinas (bä-rē'näs) Ven.	8·36 N	70·14 W
86	Baring, C. (bâr'ĭng) Can.	70·07 N	119·48 W
154	Barisan, Pegunungan (Mts.) (bä-rê-sän') Indon.	2·38 S	101·45 E
154	Barito (Strm.) (bä-rē'tō) Indon.	2·10 S	114·38 E
167	Barkly East (bärk'lē ēst) S. Afr. (Natal In.)	30·58 S	27·37 E
158	Barkly Tableland (Reg.) (bär'klê) Austl.	18·15 S	145·55 E
122	Bar-le-Duc (băr-lē-dük') Fr.	48·47 N	5·05 E
158	Barlee (L.) (bär-lē') Austl.	29·45 S	119·00 E
126	Barletta (bär-lĕt'tä) It.	41·19 N	16·20 E
111	Barmstedt (bärm'shtĕt) Ger. (Hamburg In.)	53·47 N	9·46 E
134	Barnaul (bär-nä-ōōl') Sov. Un.	53·18 N	83·23 E
81	Barnesboro (bärnz'bẽr-ô) Pa.	40·45 N	78·50 W
78	Barnesville (bärnz'vĭl) Ga.	33·03 N	84·10 W
70	Barnesville Minn.	46·38 N	96·25 W
80	Barnesville Ohio	39·55 N	81·10 W
81	Barnet (bär'nĕt) Vt.	44·20 N	72·00 W
110	Barnetby (bär'nĕt-bĭ) Eng.	53·34 N	0·26 W
94	Barnett Hbr Ba. Is.	25·40 N	79·20 W
73	Barnsdall (bärnz'dôl) Okla.	36·38 N	96·14 W
110	Barnsley (bärnz'lĭ) Eng.	53·33 N	1·29 W
116	Barnstaple (bärn'stā-p'l) Eng.	51·06 N	4·05 W
79	Barnwell (bärn'wĕl) S. C.	33·14 N	81·23 W
164	Baro (bä'rô) Nig.	8·34 N	6·25 E
142	Baroda (bä-rō'dä) India	22·21 N	73·12 E
165	Baro R. Eth.	7·40 N	34·17 E
166	Barotseland (Reg.) (bà-rŏt'sĕ-lănd) N. Rh.	16·00 S	22·52 E
165	Barqah (Cirenaica) (Prov.) Libya	31·09 N	21·45 E
98	Barquisimeto (bär-kē-sê-mā'tō) Ven.	10·04 N	69·16 W
99	Barra (băr'rä) Braz.	11·04 S	43·11 W
142	Barrackpore India (Calcutta In.)	22·46 N	88·22 E
99	Barra do Corda (bär'rä dōō cōr-dä) Braz.	5·33 S	45·13 W
116	Barra Is. (băr'rà) Scot.	56·57 N	6·85 W
101	Barra Mansa (bär'rä män'sä) Braz. (Rio de Janeiro In.)	22·35 S	44·09 W
98	Barrancabermeja (bär-räŋ'kä-bĕr-mā'hä) Col.	7·06 N	73·49 W
98	Barranquilla (bär-rän-kēl'yä) Col.	10·57 N	75·00 W
99	Barras (bä'r-räs) Braz.	4·13 S	42·14 W
81	Barre (băr'ê) Vt.	44·15 N	72·30 W
101	Barre do Piraí (bär'rĕ-dô-pē'rä-ē') Braz. (Rio de Janeiro In.)	22·30 S	43·49 W
99	Barreiras (bär-rā'-räs) Braz.	12·13 S	44·59 W
125	Barreiro (bär-rĕ'ê-rōō) Port. (Lisbon In.)	38·39 N	9·05 W
160	Barren, C. (băr'ĕn) Austl.	40·20 S	149·00 E
167	Barren, Îles (Is.) Malag. Rep.	18·18 S	43·57 E
78	Barren (R.) Ky.	37·00 N	86·20 W
99	Barretos (bär-rā'tōs) Braz.	20·40 S	48·36 W
86	Barrhead (băr-hĕd) (bär'ĭd) Can.	54·10 N	114·20 W
81	Barrie (băr'ĭ) Can.	44·25 N	79·45 W
85	Barrington (bă-rēng-tŏn) Can. (Montreal In.)	45·07 N	73·35 W
75	Barrington Ill. (Chicago In.)	42·09 N	88·08 W
84	Barrington R. I. (Providence In.)	41·44 N	71·16 W
160	Barrington Tops (Mtn.) Austl.	32·00 S	151·25 E
74	Bar River (bär) Can. (Sault Ste. Marie In.)	46·27 N	84·02 W
71	Barron (băr'ŭn) Wis.	45·24 N	91·51 W
64	Barrow (băr'ō) Alaska	71·20 N	156·00 W
116	Barrow Eng.	54·10 N	3·15 W
158	Barrow (I.) Austl.	21·05 S	11·30 E
64	Barrow, Pt. Alaska	71·20 N	156·00 W
158	Barrow Creek Austl.	21 23 S	133·55 E
116	Barrow R. (bă-rô) Ire.	52·35 N	7·05 W
124	Barruelo de Santullán (bär-rōō-ā-lō dā sän-tōō-lyän') Sp.	42·55 N	4·19 W
74	Barry (băr'ĭ) Mo. (Kansas City In.)	39·14 N	94·36 W
68	Barstow (bär'stō) Calif.	34·53 N	117·03 W
120	Barth (bärt) Ger.	54·20 N	12·43 E
73	Bartholomew Bay. (bär-thŏl'ô-mū bī-ōō') Ark.	33·53 N	91·45 W
82	Barthurst (băr-thŭrst') Can.	47·38 N	65·40 W
99	Bartica (bär'tĭ-kä) Br. Gu.	6·23 N	58·32 W
133	Bartin (bär'tĭn) Tur.	41·35 N	32·12 E
159	Bartle Frere, Mt. (bärt''l frēr') Austl.	17·30 S	145·46 E
73	Bartlesville (bär'tlz-vĭl) Okla.	36·44 N	95·58 W
75	Bartlett (bärt'lĕt) Ill. (Chicago In.)	41·59 N	88·11 W
77	Bartlett Tex.	30·48 N	97·25 W
81	Barton (bär'tŭn) Vt.	44·45 N	72·05 W
110	Barton-on-Humber (bär'tŭn-ŏn-hŭm'bẽr) Eng.	53·41 N	0·26 W
121	Bartoszyce (bär-tô-shĭ'tsä) Pol.	54·15 N	20·50 E
79	Bartow (bär'tō) Fla. (In.)	27·51 N	81·50 W
129	Barvenkovo (bär'vĕn-kô'vô) Sov. Un.	48·55 N	36·59 E
160	Barwon (R.) (bär'wŭn) Austl.	29·45 S	148·25 E
161	Barwon Heads Austl. (Melbourne In.)	38·17 S	144·59 E
120	Barycz R. (bä'rĭch) Pol.	51·30 N	16·38 E
165	Basankusu (bä-sän-kōō'sōō) Con. L.	1·14 N	19·45 E
111	Basbeck (bäs'bĕk) Ger. (Hamburg In.)	53·40 N	9·11 E
111	Basdahl (bäs'däl) Ger. (Hamburg In.)	53·27 N	9·00 E
74	Basehor (bās'hôr) Kans. (Kansas City In.)	39·08 N	94·55 W
120	Basel (bä'z'l) Switz.	47·32 N	7·35 E
167	Bashee (R.) (bă-shē') S. Afr. (Natal In.)	31·47 S	28·25 E
151	Bashi Chan (bäsh'ê) Phil.	21·20 N	120·22 E
132	Bashkir (A.S.S.R.) (básh-kēr') Sov. Un.	54·12 N	57·15 E
129	Bashtanka (básh-tän'kà) Sov. Un.	47·32 N	32·31 E
154	Basilan (I.) Phil.	6·37 N	122·07 E
126	Basilicata (Reg.) (bä-zē-lê-kä'tä) It.	40·30 N	15·55 E
67	Basin (bā'sĭn) Wyo.	44·22 N	108·02 W
110	Basingstoke (bā'zĭng-stōk) Eng. (London In.)	51·14 N	1·06 W
126	Baška (bäsh'kà) Yugo.	44·58 N	14·44 E
133	Baskale (bäsh-kä'lĕ) Tur.	38·10 N	44·00 E
133	Baskunchak (L.) Sov. Un.	48·20 N	46·40 E
165	Basoko (ná-sō'kō) Con. L.	0·52 N	23·50 E
165	Basoko Con. L.	1·22 N	23·40 E
86	Bassano (băs-săn'ō) Can.	50·44 N	112·35 W
126	Bassano It.	45·46 N	11·44 E
167	Bassas da India (I.) (bäs'säs dä ēn'dê-à) Malag. Rep.	21·23 S	39·42 E
154	Bassein (bŭ-sēn') Bur.	16·46 N	94·47 E
143	Bassein India (Bombay In.)	19·20 N	72·47 E
79	Basset (băs'sĕt) Va.	36·45 N	81·58 W
93	Basse Terre (bäs' târ') Basse Terre (Le. & Wind. Is. In.)	16·00 N	61·43 W
93	Basseterre St. Kitts-Nevis-Anguilla (Le. & Wind. Is. In.)	17·20 N	62·42 W
93	Basse Terre I. Guad. (Le. & Wind. Is. In.)	16·10 N	62·14 W
80	Bass Is. (băs) Ohio	41·40 N	82·50 W
160	Bass Str. Austl.	39·40 S	145·40 E
71	Basswood (L.) (băs'wŏŏd) Can.-Minn.	48·10 N	91·36 W
118	Båstad (bô'stät) Swe.	56·26 N	12·46 E
126	Bastia (bäs'tē-ä) Fr.	42·43 N	9·27 E
117	Bastogne (bås-tôn'y') Bel.	50·02 N	5·45 E
77	Bastrop (băs'trŭp) La.	32·47 N	91·55 W
77	Bastrop Tex.	30·08 N	97·18 W
77	Bastrop Bay Tex. (In.)	29·07 N	95·22 W
166	Basutoland (bà-sōō'tō-lănd) Afr.	29·45 S	28·07 E
164	Bata (bä'tä) Rio Muni	1·53 N	9·48 E
94	Batabanó (bä-tä-bä-nō') Cuba	22·45 N	82·20 W
94	Batabano, Golfo de (G.) (gōl-fô-dĕ-bä-tä-bä'nô) Cuba	22·10 N	83·05 W
155	Batac Phil. (Manila In.)	17·56 N	120·29 E
142	Batala India	31·54 N	75·18 E
136	Bataly (bá-tä'lĭ) Sov. Un. (Urals In.)	52·51 N	62·03 E
139	Batam I. (bä-täm') Indon. (Singapore In.)	1·03 N	104·00 E
155	Batan (bä-tän') Phil. (Manila In.)	13·20 N	124·00 E
151	Batan Is. Phil.	20·58 N	122·20 E
151	Batangan, C. Viet.	15·18 N	109·10 E
155	Batangas (bä-tän'gäs) Phil. (Manila In.)	13·45 N	121·04 E
121	Bataszék (bä'tà-sĕk) Hung.	46·07 N	18·40 E
75	Batavia (bà-tā'vĭ-à) Ill. (Chicago In.)	41·51 N	88·18 W
81	Batavia N. Y.	43·00 N	78·15 W
75	Batavia Ohio (Cincinnati In.)	39·05 N	84·10 W
129	Bataysk (bà-tīsk') Sov. Un.	47·08 N	39·44 E
79	Batesburg (bāts'bûrg) S. C.	33·53 N	81·34 W
73	Batesville (bāts'vĭl) Ark.	35·46 N	91·39 W
80	Batesville Ind.	39·15 N	85·15 W
78	Batesville Miss.	34·17 N	89·55 W
128	Batetska (bà-tĕ'tskà) Sov. Un.	58·36 N	30·21 E
82	Bath (bàth) Can.	46·31 N	67·36 W
116	Bath Eng.	51·24 N	2·20 W
82	Bath Maine	43·54 N	69·50 W
81	Bath N. Y.	42·25 N	77·20 W
75	Bath Ohio (Cleveland In.)	41·11 N	81·38 W
93	Bathsheba Barbados (Le. & Wind. Is. In.)	13·13 N	60·30 W

ng-sing; ŋ-baŋk; N-nasalized n; nŏd; cŏmmit; ōld; ôbey; ôrder; fōōd; fŏŏt; ou-out; s-soft; sh-dish; th-thin; pūre; ûnite; ûrn; stŭd; circŭs; ü-as "y" in study; '-indeterminate vowel.

182 Bathurst–Bellingham PRONOUNCING INDEX

Page	Name Pronunciation Region	Lat. °'	Long. °'
159	Bathurst (bàth'ŭrst)...Aust.	33·28 s	149·30 E
164	Bathurst...Gam.	13·23 N	16·45 W
167	Bathurst (băt-hûrst) S. Afr. (Natal In.)	33·26 s	26·53 E
64	Bathurst, C. (bàth'ŭrst)...Can.	70·33 N	127·55 W
158	Bathurst (I.)...Austl.	11·19 s	130·13 E
86	Bathurst Inlet...Can.	67·25 N	106·50 W
155	Batian (I.)...Indon.	1·07 s	127·52 E
144	Batin, Wādī al (R.)...Sau. Ar.	27·17 N	44·13 E
155	Batjan (I.) (bät-jän')...Indon.	1·07 s	127.52 E
144	Bātlaq-E Gāvkhūn (L.)...Iran	31·40 N	52·48 E
110	Batley (băt'lĭ)...Eng.	53·43 N	1·37 W
164	Batna (bät'nä)...Alg.	35·41 N	6·12 E
77	Baton Rouge (băt'ŭn ro͞ozh')..La.	30·28 N	91·10 W
154	Battambang (bàt-tàm-băng') Camb.	13·14 N	103·15 E
84	Battery Park (băt'ēr-ĭ) Va. (Norfolk In.)	36·59 N	76·36 W
80	Battle Creek (băt''l krēk')..Mich.	42·20 N	85·15 W
86	Battleford (băt''l-fērd)...Can.	52·44 N	108·30 W
65	Battle Ground (băt''l ground) Wash. (Portland In.)	45·47 N	122·32 W
87	Battle Harbour (băt''l här'bēr) Can.	52·17 N	55·33 W
66	Battle Mountain...Nev.	40·40 N	116·56 W
121	Battonya (bät-tô'nyä)...Hung.	46·17 N	21·00 E
154	Batu (I.) (bä'to͞o)...Indon.	0·10 s	99·55 E
133	Batumi (bŭ-to͞o'mē)...Sov. Un.	41·40 N	41·30 E
99	Baturité (bä-to͞o-rē-tā')...Braz.	4·16 s	38·47 W
155	Bauang (bä'wäng) Phil. (Manila In.)	16·31 N	120·19 E
164	Bauchi (bà-o͞o'chē)...Nig.	10·19 N	9·51 E
166	Baudouinville (bō-dwăN-vēl') Con. L.	7·12 s	29·39 E
83	Bauld, C...Can.	51·38 N	55·10 W
85	Baurette (bō-rĕt') Can. (Montreal In.)	45·24 N	73·32 W
142	Bāuria...India (Calcutta In.)	22·29 N	88·08 E
99	Bauru (bou-ro͞o')...Braz.	22·21 s	48·57 W
119	Bauska (bou'skà)...Sov. Un.	56·24 N	24·12 E
95	Bauta (bä'o͞o-tä) Cuba (Havana In.)	22·14 N	82·33 W
120	Bautzen (bout'sĕn)...Ger.	51·11 N	14·27 E
	Bavaria, see Bayern		
160	Baw Baw, Mt. (bà-bà)...Austl.	37·50 s	146·17 E
154	Bawean (I.) (bà'vē-än)...Indon.	5·50 s	112·40 E
110	Bawtry (bô'trĭ)...Eng.	53·26 N	1·01 W
79	Baxley (băks'lĭ)...Ga.	31·47 N	82·22 W
161	Baxter (băks'tēr) Austl. (Melbourne In.)	38·12 s	145·10 E
73	Baxter Springs (băks'tēr sprĭngs') Kans.	37·01 N	94·44 W
95	Bayaguana (bä-yä-gwä'nä) Dom. Rep.	18·45 N	69·40 W
114	Bay al Kabīr Wadi (R.)...Libya	29·52 N	14·28 E
155	Bayambang (bä-yäm-băng') Phil. (Manila In.)	15·50 N	120·26 E
94	Bayamo (bä-yä'mō)...Cuba	20·25 N	76·35 W
89	Bayamón . P. R. (Puerto Rico In.)	18·27 N	66·13 W
134	Bayan-Aul (bä'yän-oul').Sov. Un.	50·43 N	75·37 E
70	Bayard (bā'ērd)...Nebr.	41·45 N	103·20 W
81	Bayard...W. Va.	39·15 N	79·20 W
133	Bayburt (bä'ĭ-bo͝ort)...Tur.	40·15 N	40·10 E
80	Bay City (bā)...Mich.	43·35 N	83·55 W
77	Bay City...Tex.	28·59 N	95·58 W
146	Baydarag Gol (R.)...Mong.	46·09 N	98·52 E
132	Baydaratskaya Guba (B.) Sov. Un.	69·20 N	66·10 E
83	Bayde Verde...Can.	48·06 N	52·50 W
120	Bayern (Bavaria) (State) (bī'ērn) (bȧ-vâ-rĭ-ȧ).Ger.	49·00 N	11·16 E
122	Bayeux (bà-yû')...Fr.	49·19 N	0·41 W
71	Bayfield (bā'fēld)...Wis.	46·48 N	90·51 W
135	Baykal, Ozero (Baikal, L.) (bī'käl') (bī'kôl).Sov. Un.	53·00 N	109·28 E
135	Baykals'kiy Khrebet (Baikal Mts.).Sov. Un.	53·30 N	102·00 E
134	Baykit (bī-kēt')...Sov. Un.	61·43 N	96·39 E
134	Baykonur (bī-kô-no͞or')..Sov. Un.	47·46 N	66·11 E
136	Baymak (bày'mäk) Sov. Un. (Urals In.)	52·35 N	58·21 E
78	Bay Minette (bā'mĭn-ĕt')...Ala.	30·52 N	87·44 W
74	Bay Mills (bā mĭlls) Mich. (Sault Ste. Marie In.)	46·27 N	84·36 W
71	Bay Mills Ind. Res...Mich.	46·19 N	85·03 W
155	Bayombong (bä-yôm-bŏng') Phil. (Manila In.)	16·28 N	121·09 E
122	Bayonne (bà-yôn')...Fr.	43·28 N	1·30 W
84	Bayonne (bā-yōn') N. J. (New York In.)	40·40 N	74·07 W
77	Bayou Bodcau Res. (bī'yo͞o bŏd'kō).La.	32·49 N	93·22 W
74	Bayport (bā'pōrt) Minn. (Minneapolis, St. Paul In.)	45·02 N	92·46 W
127	Bayramiç...Tur.	39·48 N	26·35 E
120	Bayreuth (bī-roit')...Ger.	49·56 N	11·35 E
83	Bay Roberts (bā rŏb'ērts)...Can.	47·36 N	53·12 W
81	Bays, L. of (bās)...Can.	45·15 N	79·00 W
78	Bay St. Louis (bā' sânt lo͞o'ĭs) Miss.	30·19 N	89·20 W
84	Bay Shore (bā' shôr) N. Y. (New York In.)	40·44 N	73·15 W
139	Bayt Lahm (Bethlehem) (bĕth'lē-hĕm).Jordan (Palestine In.)	31·42 N	35·13 E
77	Baytown (bā'town)...Tex. (In.)	29·44 N	95·01 W
165	Bayuda Steppe (bä-yo͞o'dä)..Sud.	17·27 N	31·43 E
84	Bayview (bā'vū) Ala. (Birmingham In.)	33·34 N	86·59 W
65	Bayview...Wash. (Seattle In.)	48·29 N	122·28 W
75	Bay Village (bā) Ohio (Cleveland In.)	41·29 N	81·56 W
124	Baza (bä'thä)...Sp.	37·29 N	2·46 W
133	Bazar-Dyuzi, Gora (Mt.) (bä'zår-dyo͞oz'ĭ).Sov. Un.	41·20 N	47·40 E
166	Bazaruto, Ilha (I.) (ē'lä-bä-zä-ro͞o'tō).Moz.	21·42 s	36·10 E
167	Bazeia Mt. (bä-zēȧ) S. Afr. (Natal In.)	31·33 s	28·23 E
124	Baztán (bäth-tän')...Sp.	43·12 N	1·30 W
70	Beach (bēch)...N. D.	46·55 N	104·00 W
81	Beacon (bē'kŭn)...N. Y.	41·30 N	73·55 W
85	Beaconsfield (bē'kŭnz-fēld) Can. (Montreal In.)	45·26 N	73·51 W
84	Beafort Mtn. (bē'fōrt) N. J. (New York In.)	41·08 N	74·23 W
76	Beals Cr. (bēls)...Tex.	32·10 N	101·14 W
85	Beamsville...Can. (Toronto In.)	43·10 N	79·29 W
67	Bear Creek (bâr krēk)...Mont.	45·11 N	109·07 W
78	Bear Cr. (bâr)...Ala.	34·27 N	88·00 W
74	Bear Cr. Tex. (Dallas, Fort Worth In.)	32·56 N	97·09 W
81	Bear Cr. Flood Control Res...Pa.	41·07 N	75·45 W
73	Beardstown (bērds'toun)...Ill.	40·01 N	90·26 W
65	Bearhead Mtn. (bâr'hĕd) Wash. (Seattle In.)	47·01 N	121·49 W
67	Bear L...Idaho-Utah	41·56 N	111·10 W
67	Bear R...Idaho	42·17 N	111·42 W
74	Bear R.Utah (Salt Lake City In.)	41·28 N	112·10 W
67	Bear River B...Utah	41·25 N	112·20 W
124	Beas de Segura (bā'äs dā sä-go͞o'rä) Sp.	38·16 N	2·53 W
95	Beata (I.) (bĕ-ä'tä)...Dom. Rep.	17·40 N	71·40 W
95	Beata, Cabo (C.) (kà'bō-bĕ-ä'tä) Dom. Rep.	17·40 N	71·20 W
73	Beatrice (bē'ȧ-trĭs)...Nebr.	40·16 N	96·45 W
68	Beatty (bĕt'ē)...Nev.	36·58 N	116·48 W
80	Beattyville (bĕt'ē-vĭl)...Ky.	37·35 N	83·40 W
122	Beaucaire (bō-kâr')...Fr.	43·49 N	4·37 E
82	Beauceville (bōs'vĕl)...Can.	46·12 N	70·46 W
123	Beaucourt (bō-ko͞or')...Fr.	47·30 N	6·54 E
79	Beaufort (bō'fērt)...N. C.	34·43 N	76·40 W
79	Beaufort...S. C.	32·25 N	80·40 W
64	Beaufort Sea...Alaska	70·30 N	138·40 W
166	Beaufort West...S. Afr.	32·20 s	22·45 E
85	Beauharnois (bō-är-nwä') Can. (Montreal In.)	45·23 N	73·52 W
74	Beaumont (bō'mŏnt) Calif. (Los Angeles In.)	33·57 N	116·57 W
85	Beaumont...Can. (Quebec In.)	46·50 N	71·01 W
77	Beaumont...Tex.	30·05 N	94·06 W
122	Beaune (bōn)...Fr.	47·02 N	4·49 E
85	Beauport (bō-pôr') Can. (Quebec In.)	46·52 N	71·11 W
85	Beaupré (bō-prā') Can. (Quebec In.)	47·03 N	70·53 W
85	Beaurepaire (bōr-pĕr') Can. (Montreal In.)	45·25 N	73·53 W
86	Beausejour...Can.	50·07 N	96·39 W
122	Beauvais (bō-vĕ')...Fr.	49·25 N	2·05 E
72	Beaver (bē'vēr)...Okla.	36·46 N	100·31 W
75	Beaver...Pa. (Pittsburgh In.)	40·42 N	80·18 W
69	Beaver...Utah	38·15 N	112·40 W
80	Beaver (I.)...Mich.	45·40 N	85·30 W
86	Beaver (R.)...Can.	54·21 N	111·50 W
72	Beaver City...Nebr.	40·08 N	99·52 W
72	Beaver Cr...Colo.	39·42 N	103·37 W
72	Beaver Cr...Kans.	39·44 N	101·05 W
70	Beaver Cr...Mont.	46·45 N	104·18 W
67	Beaver Cr...Wyo.	43·46 N	104·25 W
71	Beaver Dam...Wis.	43·29 N	88·50 W
67	Beaverhead Mts. (bē'vēr-hĕd) Mont.	44·33 N	112·59 W
67	Beaverhead R...Mont.	45·05 N	112·50 W
80	Beaver Ind. Res...Mich.	45·40 N	85·30 W
65	Beaverton (bē'vēr-tŭn) Ore. (Portland In.)	45·29 N	122·49 W
98	Bebara' (bĕ-bä-rä')...Col. (In.)	6·07 N	76·39 W
110	Bebington (bē'bĭng-tŭn)...Eng.	53·20 N	2·59 W
91	Becal (bā-käl')...Mex.	20·25 N	90·04 W
127	Bečej (bĕ'chā)...Yugo.	45·36 N	20·03 E
124	Becerreá (bā-thā'rē-ä)...Sp.	42·49 N	7·12 W
64	Becharof (bĕk à rôf)..Alaska	57·58 N	156·58 W
65	Becher B. (bēch'ēr) Can. (Seattle In.)	48·18 N	123·37 W
163	Bechuanaland (bĕch-o͞o-ä'nȧ-lănd).Afr.	22·10 s	23·13 E
80	Beckley (bĕk'lĭ)...W. Va.	37·40 N	81·15 W
122	Bédarieux (bā-dà-ryû')...Fr.	43·36 N	3·11 E
85	Beddington Cr. (bĕd'ĕng tŭn) Can. (Calgary In.)	51·14 N	114·13 W
81	Bedford (bĕd'fērd)...Can.	45·10 N	73·00 W
116	Bedford...Eng.	52·10 N	0·25 W
80	Bedford...Ind.	38·50 N	86·30 W
71	Bedford...Iowa	40·40 N	94·41 W
83	Bedford...Mass. (Boston In.)	42·30 N	71·17 W
84	Bedford...N. Y. (New York In.)	41·12 N	73·38 W
75	Bedford...Ohio (Cleveland In.)	41·23 N	81·32 W
81	Bedford...Pa.	40·05 N	78·20 W
167	Bedford...S. Afr. (Natal In.)	32·43 s	26·19 E
79	Bedford...Va.	37·19 N	79·27 W
84	Bedford Hill N. Y. (New York In.)	41·14 N	73·41 W
110	Bedworth (bĕd'wērth)...Eng.	52·29 N	1·28 W
121	Bedzin (bäN-jēn')...Pol.	50·19 N	19·10 W
73	Beebe (bē'bē)...Ark.	35·04 N	91·54 W
75	Beecher (bē'chŭr) Ill. (Chicago In.)	41·20 N	87·38 W
65	Beechey Hd. (bē'chĭ hĕd) Can. (Seattle In.)	48·19 N	123·40 W
75	Beech Grove (bēch grōv) Ind. (Indianapolis In.)	39·43 N	86·05 W
160	Beecroft Hd. (bē'krŭft)...Austl.	35·03 s	151·15 E
111	Beelitz (bĕ'lētz)..Ger. (Berlin In.)	52·14 N	12·59 E
139	Beer (R.)...Isr. (Palestine In.)	31·23 N	34·30 E
139	Beersheba (bēr-shē'bà) Isr. (Palestine In.)	31·15 N	34·48 E
168	Beestekraal...S. Afr. (Johannes-burg & Pretoria In.)	25·22 s	27·34 E
110	Beeston (bēs't'n)...Eng.	52·55 N	1·11 W
111	Beetz R. (bĕtz)..Ger. (Berlin In.)	52·28 N	12·37 E
77	Beeville (bē'vĭl)...Tex.	28·24 N	97·44 W
160	Bega (bā'gȧ)...Austl.	36·50 s	149·49 E
73	Beggs (bĕgz)...Okla.	35·46 N	96·06 W
122	Bégles (bĕ'gl')...Fr.	44·47 N	0·34 W
142	Behampur...India	20·19 N	85·53 E
165	Beilul...Eth.	13·15 N	42·21 E
166	Beira (bā'rȧ)...Moz.	19·46 s	34·58 E
124	Beira (Reg.) (bĕ'y-rä)...Port.	40·38 N	8·00 W
	Beirut, see Beyrouth		
139	Beit Shean...Isr. (Palestine In.)	32·30 N	35·30 E
124	Beja (bā'zhä)...Port.	38·03 N	7·53 W
124	Bejar...Sp.	40·25 N	5·43 W
144	Bejestān...Iran	34·30 N	58·22 E
144	Bejnurd...Iran	37·29 N	57·13 E
95	Bejucal (bā-ho͞o-käl') Cuba (Havana In.)	22·08 N	82·23 W
93	Bejuco (bĕ-ko͞o'kō)...Pan.	8·37 N	79·54 W
121	Békés (bā'kāsh)...Hung.	46·45 N	21·08 E
121	Békéscsaba (bā'kāsh-chô'bô) Hung.	46·39 N	21·06 E
147	Beketova (bĕk'e-to'và)..Sov. Un.	53·23 N	125·21 E
127	Bela Crkva (bĕ'lä tsĕrk'vä).Yugo.	44·53 N	21·25 E
124	Belalcázar (bāl-äl-kä'thär)...Sp.	38·35 N	5·12 W
125	Belas (bĕ'-läs).Port. (Lisbon In.)	38·47 N	9·16 W
127	Bela-Slatina (byä'la slä'tēnä).Bul.	43·26 N	23·56 E
154	Belawan (bå-lä'wån)...Indon.	3·43 N	98·43 E
132	Belaya (R.) (byĕ'lĭ-yà).Sov. Un.	52·45 N	61·15 E
129	Belaya Tserkov' (byĕ'lĭ-yà tsĕr'kôf).Sov. Un.	49·48 N	30·09 E
87	Belcher Is. (bĕl'chēr)...Can.	56·20 N	80·40 W
75	Belden (bĕl'dĕn) Ohio (Cleveland In.)	41·14 N	82·01 W
80	Belding (bĕl'dĭng)...Mich.	43·05 N	85·25 W
132	Belebey (byĕ'lĕ-bā'ĭ)...Sov. Un.	54·00 N	54·10 E
159	Belef, Isles...N. Cal.	19·30 s	160·32 E
99	Belém (Pará) (bå-lĕN') (pä-rä') Braz.	1·18 s	48·27 W
69	Belen (bĕ-lân')...N. Mex.	34·40 N	106·45 W
100	Belén (bā-lān')...Par.	23·30 s	57·09 W
128	Belëv (byĕl'yĕf)...Sov. Un.	53·49 N	36·06 E
65	Belfair (bĕl'fâr) Wash. (Seattle In.)	47·27 N	122·50 W
116	Belfast (bĕl'fást)...N. Ire.	54·36 N	5·45 W
82	Belfast...Maine	44·25 N	69·01 W
116	Belfast, Lough (B.) (lŏk bĕl'fást) Ire.	54·45 N	7·40 W
165	Bēlfodiyo...Eth.	10·45 N	39·27 E
123	Belfort (bā-fôr')...Fr.	47·40 N	7·50 E
143	Belgaum...India	15·57 N	74·32 E
102	Belgium (bĕl'jĭ-ŭm)...Eur.	51·00 N	2·52 E
129	Belgorod (byĕl'gŭ-rut)...Sov. Un.	50·36 N	36·32 E
129	Belgorod (Oblast)...Sov. Un.	50·40 N	36·42 E
129	Belgorod Dnestrovskiy (byĕl'gŭ-rud nyĕs-trôf'skē).Sov. Un.	46·09 N	30·19 E
	Belgrade, see Beograd		
79	Belhaven (bĕl'hā-vĕn)...N. C.	35·33 N	76·37 W
81	Belington (bĕl'ĭng-tŭn)...W. Va.	39·00 N	79·55 W
127	Beli Timok (R.) (Bĕ'lĕ Tē'môk) Yugo.	43·35 N	22·13 E
154	Belitung (I.)...Indon.	3·30 s	107·30 E
92	Belize (bĕ-lēz') Br. Hond. (Yucatan In.)	17·31 N	88·10 W
92	Belize R.Br. Hond. (Yucatan In.)	17·16 N	88·56 W
136	Bel'kovo (byĕl'kô-vô) Sov. Un. (Moscow In.)	56·15 N	38·49 E
135	Bel'kovskiy (I.) (byĕl-kôf'skĭ) Sov. Un.	75·52 N	133·00 E
74	Bell (bĕl). Calif. (Los Angeles In.)	33·59 N	118·11 W
83	Bell (I.)...Can.	50·45 N	55·35 W
80	Bellaire (bĕl-âr')...Ohio	40·00 N	80·45 W
77	Bellaire...Tex. (In.)	29·43 N	95·28 W
143	Bellary (bĕl-lä'rē)...India	15·15 N	76·56 E
100	Bella Union (bĕ'l-yä-o͞o-nyô'n).Ur.	30·18 s	57·26 W
100	Bella Vista (bā'lyä vēs'tä)...Arg.	27·07 s	65·14 W
100	Bella Vista...Arg.	28·35 s	58·53 W
100	Bella Vista...Arg. (In.)	34·18 s	58·41 W
99	Bella Vista...Braz.	22·16 s	56·14 W
83	Belle B. (bĕl)...Can.	47·35 N	55·15 W
84	Belle Chasse (bĕl shäs') La. (New Orleans In.)	29·52 N	90·00 W
80	Bellefontaine (bĕl-fŏn'tān).. Ohio	40·25 N	83·50 W
70	Belle Fourche (bĕl' fo͞orsh')..S. D.	44·28 N	103·50 W
70	Belle Fourche (R.)...Wyo.	44·29 N	104·40 W
70	Belle Fourche Res...S. D.	44·51 N	103·44 W
123	Bellegarde-sur-Valserine (bĕl-gärd'sür-väl-så-rēn').Fr.	46·06 N	6 50 E
79	Belle Glade (bĕl glād)...Fla. (In.)	26·39 N	80·37 W
122	Belle Île (I.) (bĕl-ēl')...Fr.	47·15 N	3·30 W
87	Belle Isle, Str. of...Can.	51·21 N	55·56 W
84	Belle Mead (bĕl mēd) N. J. (New York In.)	40·28 N	74·40 W
83	Belleoram...Can.	47·29 N	55·50 W
71	Belle Plaine (bĕl plān')...Iowa	41·52 N	92·19 W
75	Belle Vernon (bĕl vŭr'nŭn) Pa. (Pittsburgh In.)	40·08 N	79·52 W
81	Belleville (bĕl'vĭl)...Can.	44·15 N	77·25 W
74	Belleville...Ill. (St. Louis In.)	38·31 N	89·59 W
73	Belleville...Kans.	39·49 N	97·37 W
75	Belleville...Mich. (Detroit In.)	42·12 N	83·29 W
84	Belleville...N. J. (New York In.)	40·47 N	74·09 W
71	Bellevue (bĕl'vū)...Iowa	42·14 N	90·26 W
75	Bellevue...Ky. (Cincinnati In.)	39·06 N	84·29 W
80	Bellevue...Mich.	42·30 N	85·00 W
80	Bellevue...Ohio	41·15 N	82·45 W
75	Bellevue...Pa. (Pittsburgh In.)	40·30 N	80·04 W
65	Bellevue...Wash. (Seattle In.)	47·37 N	122·12 W
123	Belley (bĕ-lē')...Fr.	45·46 N	5·41 E
74	Bellflower (bĕl-flou'ēr) Calif. (Los Angeles In.)	33·53 N	118·08 W
83	Bellingham (bĕl'ĭng-hăm) Mass. (Boston In.)	42·05 N	71·28 W
65	Bellingham Wash. (Vancouver In.)	48·46 N	122·29 W
65	Bellingham B. Wash. (Vancouver In.)	48·44 N	122·34 W

ăt; finȧl; rāte; senâte; ärm; ȧsk; sofȧ; fâre; ch-choose; dh-as th in other; bē; ėvent; bĕt; recĕnt; cratẽr; g-go; gh-guttural g; bĭt; ĭ-short neutral; rīde: K-guttural k as ch in German ich;

PRONOUNCING INDEX

Bellingshausen–Biafra 183

Page	Name Pronunciation Region	Lat. °′	Long. °′
47	Bellingshausen Sea (bĕl'ĭngz houz'n). Ant.	72·00 S	80·30 W
126	Bellinzona (bĕl-ĭn-tsō'nä)... Switz.	46·10 N	9·09 E
84	Bellmore (bĕl-mōr) N. Y. (New York In.)	40·40 N	73·31 W
98	Bello (bĕ'l-yō) Col. (In.)	6·20 N	75·33 W
81	Bellows Falls (bĕl'ōz fôls) Vt.	43·10 N	72·30 W
142	Bellpat W. Pak.	29·08 N	68·00 E
87	Bell Pen. Can.	63·50 N	81·16 W
85	Bells Corners . Can. (Ottawa In.)	45·20 N	75·49 W
65	Bells Mtn. (bĕls) Wash. (Portland In.)	45·50 N	122·21 W
126	Belluno (bĕl-lōō'nō) It.	46·08 N	12·14 E
100	Bell Ville (bĕl vēl') Arg.	32·33 S	62·36 W
166	Bellville S. Afr. (Cape Town In.)	33·54 S	18·38 E
77	Bellville (bĕl'vĭl) Tex.	29·57 N	96·15 W
124	Bélmez (bĕl'mĕth) Sp.	38·17 N	5·17 W
71	Belmond (bĕl'mŏnd) Iowa	42·49 N	93·37 W
65	Belmont . Calif. (San Francisco In.)	37·34 N	122·18 W
99	Belmonte (bĕl-mōn'tä) Braz.	15·58 S	38·47 W
135	Belogorsk Sov. Un.	51·09 N	128·32 E
101	Belo Horizonte (bĕ'lô-re-sô'n-tĕ) Braz. (Rio de Janeiro In.)	19·54 S	43·56 W
72	Beloit (bē-loit') Kans.	39·26 N	98·06 W
71	Beloit Wis.	42·31 N	89·04 W
132	Belomorsk (byĕl-ō-môrsk') Sov. Un.	64·30 N	34·42 E
129	Belopol'ye (byĕ'lô-pôl'yĕ) . Sov. Un.	51·10 N	34·19 E
136	Beloretsk (byĕ'lō-rĕtsk) Sov. Un. (Urals In.)	53·58 N	58·25 E
130	Belorussian (S. S. R.) Sov. Un.	53·30 N	25·33 E
129	Belosarayskaya, Kosa (C.) (kô-sä' byĕ'lô-sä-räy'skä'yä) Sov. Un.	46·43 N	37·18 E
134	Belovo (byĕ'lŭ-vû) Sov. Un.	54·17 N	86·23 E
129	Belovodsk (byĕ-lŭ-vôdsk') Sov. Un.	49·12 N	39·36 E
132	Beloye (L.) Sov. Un.	60·10 N	38·05 E
132	Belozersk (byĕ-lŭ-zyôrsk') . Sov. Un.	60·00 N	38·00 E
110	Belper (bĕl'pēr) Eng.	53·01 N	1·28 W
67	Belt (bĕlt) Mont.	47·11 N	110·58 W
67	Belt Cr. Mont.	47·19 N	110·58 W
77	Belton (bĕl'tŭn) Tex.	31·04 N	97·27 W
77	Belton L. Tex.	31·15 N	97·35 W
129	Bel'tsy (bĕl'tsē) Sov. Un.	47·47 N	27·57 E
134	Belukha, Gol'tsy (Mtn.) . Sov. Un.	49·47 N	86·23 E
74	Belvedere (bĕl-vĕ-dēr') Calif. (Los Angeles In.)	34·02 N	118·11 W
71	Belvidere Ill.	42·14 N	88·52 W
81	Belvidere Pa.	40·50 N	75·05 W
159	Belyando (R.) (bĕl-yän'dō) . Austl.	22·09 S	146·48 E
136	Belyanka (byĕl'yän-kȧ) Sov. Un. (Urals In.)	56·04 N	59·16 E
128	Belynichi (byĕl-ĭ-nĭ'chĭ) . Sov. Un.	54·02 N	29·42 E
128	Belyy (byĕ'lē) Sov. Un.	55·52 N	32·58 E
134	Belyy (I.) Sov. Un.	73·19 N	72·00 E
136	Belyye Stolby (byĕ'lĭ-ye stôl'bĭ) Sov. Un. (Moscow In.)	55·20 N	37·52 E
111	Belzig (bĕl'tsēg) . . Ger. (Berlin In.)	52·08 N	12·35 E
78	Belzoni (bĕl-zō'nē) Miss.	33·09 N	90·30 W
166	Bembe (bĕn'bĕ) Ang.	7·00 S	14·20 E
124	Bembezar (R.) (bĕm-bä-thär') . Sp.	38·00 N	5·18 W
71	Bemidji (bē-mĭj'ĭ) Minn.	47·28 N	94·54 W
166	Bena Dibele (bĕn'ȧ dē-bĕ'lĕ) Con. L.	4·00 S	22·49 E
160	Benalla (bĕn-ăl'ȧ) Austl.	36·30 S	14·600 E
124	Benavente (bā-nä-vĕn'tä) Sp.	42·01 N	5·43 W
74	Benbrook (bĕn'brŏŏk) Tex. (Dallas, Fort Worth In.)	32·41 N	97·27 W
66	Bend (bĕnd) Ore.	44·04 N	121·17 W
64	Bendeleben, Mt. (bĕn-dĕl-bĕn) Alaska	65·18 N	163·45 W
168	Bender Cassim Som. (Horn of Afr. In.)	11·19 N	49·10 E
129	Bendery (bĕn-dyĕ're) Sov. Un.	46·49 N	29·29 E
160	Bendigo (bĕn'dĭ-gō) Austl.	36·39 S	144·20 E
120	Benešov (bĕn'ĕ-shôf) Czech.	49·48 N	14·40 E
126	Benevento (bā-nā-vĕn'tō) It.	41·08 N	14·46 E
138	Bengal, B. of (bĕn-gôl') Asia	17·30 N	87·00 E
	Bengasi, see Banghāzī		
139	Bengkalis (bĕng-kä'lĭs) Indon. (Singapore In.)	1·29 N	102·06 E
154	Bengkulu Indon.	3·46 S	102·18 E
166	Benguela (bĕn-gĕl'ȧ) Ang.	12·35 S	13·28 E
166	Benguela (Reg.) Ang.	13·13 S	16·00 E
116	Ben Hope (Mtn.) (bĕn hōp) . Scot.	58·25 N	4·25 W
84	Ben Hill (bĕn hĭl) Ga. (Atlanta In.)	33·42 N	84·31 W
98	Beni (R.) (bā'nē) Bol.	13·41 S	67·30 W
164	Beni-Abbés (bā'nē ȧ-bĕs') . . Alg.	30·11 N	2·13 W
125	Benicarló (bā-nē-kär-lō') Sp.	40·26 N	0·25 E
65	Benicia (bē-nĭsh'ĭ-ȧ) Calif. (San Francisco In.)	38·03 N	122·09 W
164	Benin (bĕn-ēn') Nig.	6·21 N	5·34 E
164	Benin, Bight of Afr.	5·09 N	2·19 E
164	Beni Saf (bā'nē säf') Alg.	35·23 N	1·20 W
72	Benkelman (bĕn-kĕl-mȧn) . Nebr.	40·05 N	101·35 W
126	Benkovac (bĕn'kō-vȧts) Yugo.	44·02 N	15·41 E
167	Ben Mac Dhui (Mtn.) (bĕn măk-dōō'ē) . Bas. (Natal In.)	30·38 S	27·54 E
79	Bennettsville (bĕn'ĕts vĭl) . . S. C.	34·35 N	79·41 W
81	Bennington (bĕn'ĭng-tŭn) Vt.	42·55 N	73·15 W
84	Benns Church (bĕnz' chûrch') Va. (Norfolk In.)	36·47 N	76·35 W
167	Benoni (bĕ-nō'nī) S. Afr. (Johannesburg & Pretoria In.)	26·11 S	28·19 E
92	Benque Viejo (bĕn-kĕ bĭĕ'hō) Br. Hond. (Yucatan In.)	17·07 N	89·07 W
75	Bensenville (bĕn'sĕn-vĭl) Ill. (Chicago In.)	41·57 N	87·56 W
120	Bensheim (bĕns-hīm) Ger.	49·42 N	8·38 E
69	Benson (bĕn-sŭn) Ariz.	32·00 N	110·20 W
70	Benson Minn.	45·18 N	95·36 W
75	Bentleyville (bent'lē vĭl) Pa. (Pittsburgh In.)	40·07 N	80·01 W
82	Benton (bĕn'tŭn) Can.	45·59 N	67·36 W
73	Benton Ark.	34·34 N	92·34 W
68	Benton Calif.	37·44 N	118·22 W
110	Benton Eng.	53·27 N	2·07 W
80	Benton Ill.	38·00 N	88·55 W
80	Benton Harbor (bĕn'tŭn här'bēr) Mich.	42·05 N	86·30 W
73	Bentonville (bĕn'tŭn-vĭl) Ark.	36·22 N	94·11 W
164	Benue R. (bā'nōō-ā) Nig.	7·49 N	7·54 E
139	Benut (R.) . Mala. (Singapore In.)	1·43 N	103·20 E
80	Benwood (bĕn-wŏŏd) W. Va.	39·55 N	80·45 W
127	Beograd (Belgrade) (bĕ-ō'gräd) (bĕl'grād) . Yugo.	44·48 N	20·32 E
153	Beppu (bĕ'pōō) Jap.	33·16 N	131·30 E
93	Bequia I. (bĕk-ē'ä) N. A. (Le. & Wind. Is. In.)	13·00 N	61·08 W
155	Beraoe, Teloek (B.) W. Irian	2·22 S	131·40 E
127	Berat (bĕ-rät') Alb.	40·43 N	19·59 E
100	Berazategui (bĕ-rä-zá'tĕ-gē) Arg. (In.)	34·31 S	58·12 W
165	Berber (bûr'bĕr) Sud.	18·11 N	34·00 E
168	Berbera (bûr'bûr-ȧ) Som. (Horn of Afr. In.)	10·25 N	45·05 E
122	Berck (bĕrk) Fr.	50·26 N	1·36 E
129	Berdichev (bĕ-dē'chĕf) . . Sov. Un.	49·53 N	28·32 E
129	Berdyanskaya, Kosa (C.) (kô-sä' bĕr-dyän'skä-yä) . Sov. Un.	46·38 N	36·42 E
136	Berdyaush (bĕr'dyâûsh) Sov. Un. (Urals In.)	55·10 N	59·12 E
78	Berea (bê-rē'ȧ) Ky.	37·30 N	84·19 W
75	Berea Ohio (Cleveland In.)	41·22 N	81·51 W
121	Beregovo (bĕ'rĕ-gô-vô) . . Sov. Un.	48·13 N	22·40 E
139	Berekhot Shelmo (Mt) Jordan (Palestine In.)	31·35 N	35·07 E
165	Berenice (Ruins) (bĕr-ê-nī'sê) U. A. R.	23·56 N	35·18 E
86	Berens River (bĕr'ĕnz) Can.	52·28 N	97·11 W
70	Beresford (bĕr'ĕs-fērd) S. D.	43·05 N	96·46 W
121	Berettyóújfalu (bĕ'rĕt-tyō-ōō'y'fô-lōō) . Hung.	47·14 N	21·33 E
121	Berëza (bĕ-rā'zȧ) Sov. Un.	52·29 N	24·59 E
121	Berezhany (bĕr-yĕ'zhä-nē) Sov. Un.	49·25 N	24·58 E
128	Berezina (R.) (bĕr-yĕ'zē-nä) Sov. Un.	53·20 N	29·05 E
128	Berezino (bĕr-yä'zē-nô) . . Sov. Un.	53·51 N	28·54 E
129	Berezna (bĕr-yôz'nȧ) Sov. Un.	51·32 N	31·47 E
129	Bereznegovata Sov. Un.	47·19 N	32·58 E
136	Berezniki (bĕr-yôz'nyē-kē) Sov. Un. (Urals In.)	59·25 N	56·46 E
129	Berezovka (bĕr-yôz'ôf-kȧ) Sov. Un.	47·12 N	30·56 E
136	Berëzovka . . . Sov. Un. (Urals In.)	57·35 N	57·19 E
132	Berëzovo (bĭr-yô'zē-vû) Sov. Un.	64·10 N	65·10 E
136	Berëzovskiy (bĕr-yô'zôf-skĭ) Sov. Un. (Urals In.)	56·54 N	60·47 E
125	Berga (bĕr'gä) Sp.	42·05 N	1·52 E
127	Bergama (bĕr'gä-mä) Tur.	39·08 N	27·09 E
126	Bergamo (bĕr'gä-mō) It.	45·43 N	9·41 E
99	Bergantín (bĕr-gän-tē'n) Ven. (In.)	10·04 N	64·23 W
111	Bergedorf (bĕr'gĕ-dôrf) Ger. (Hamburg In.)	53·29 N	10·12 E
120	Bergen (bĕr'gĕn) Ger.	54·26 N	13·26 E
118	Bergen Nor.	60·24 N	5·20 E
111	Bergen op Zoom Neth. (Amsterdam In.)	51·29 N	3·16 E
122	Bergerac (bĕr-zhē-räk') Fr.	44·49 N	0·28 E
123	Bergisch Gladbach (bĕrg'ĭsh-glät'bäk) . Ger. (Ruhr In.)	50·59 N	7·08 E
111	Berglern (bĕrgh'lĕrn) Ger. (Munich In.)	48·24 N	11·55 E
74	Bergs (bûrgs) Tex. (San Antonio In.)	29·19 N	98·26 W
167	Bergville (bĕrg'vĭl) S. Afr. (Natal In.)	28·46 S	29·22 E
166	Bergvliet . S. Afr. (Cape Town In.)	34·03 S	18·27 E
49	Bering Sea (bē'rĭng) . . . Asia-N. A.	58·00 N	175·00 W
64	Bering Str. Alaska	64·50 N	169·50 W
129	Berislav (byĕr'ĭ-släf) Sov. Un.	46·49 N	33·24 E
124	Berja (bĕr'hä) Sp.	36·50 N	2·56 W
65	Berkeley (bûrk'lĭ) Calif. (San Francisco In.)	37·52 N	122·17 W
74	Berkeley Mo. (St. Louis In.)	38·45 N	90·20 W
81	Berkeley Springs (bûrk'lĭ sprĭngz) W. Va.	39·40 N	78·10 W
110	Berkhamsted (bĕrk'hăm'stĕd) Eng. (London In.)	51·44 N	0·34 W
75	Berkley (bûrk'lĭ) Mich. (Detroit In.)	42·30 N	83·10 W
127	Berkovitsa (bĕ-kō'vē-tsȧ) Bul.	43·14 N	23·08 E
124	Berlengas (Is.) (bĕr-lĕn'gäzh) . Port.	39·25 N	9·33 W
111	Berlin (bĕr-lēn') . . Ger. (Berlin In.)	52·27 N	13·26 E
81	Berlin (bûr-lĭn) N. H.	44·25 N	71·10 W
84	Berlin N. J. (Philadelphia In.)	39·47 N	74·56 W
167	Berlin (bĕr-lĭn) . S. Afr. (Natal In.)	32·53 S	27·36 E
71	Berlin (bûr-lĭn') Wis.	43·58 N	88·58 W
124	Bermeja, Sierra (Mts.) (sē-ĕ'r-rä-bĕr-mĕ'hä) . Sp.	36·35 N	5·03 W
100	Bermejo (R.) (bĕr-mā'hō) Arg.	25·05 S	61·00 W
124	Bermeo (bĕr-mā'yō) Sp.	43·23 N	2·43 W
89	Bermuda (I.) N. A.	32·20 N	65·45 W
120	Bern (bĕrn) Switz.	46·55 N	7·25 E
100	Bernal (bĕr-näl') Arg. (In.)	34·27 S	58·17 W
69	Bernalillo (bĕr-nä-lē'yō) . . N. Mex.	35·20 N	106·30 W
81	Bernard (L.) (bēr-närd') Can.	45·45 N	79·25 W
84	Bernardsville (bûr nârds'vĭl) N. J. (New York In.)	40·43 N	74·34 W
111	Bernau (bĕr'nou) . Ger. (Berlin In.)	52·40 N	13·35 E
120	Bernburg (bĕrn'bŏŏrgh) Ger.	51·48 N	11·43 E
120	Berndorf (bĕrn'dôrf) Aus.	47·57 N	16·05 E
80	Berne (bûrn) Ind.	40·40 N	84·55 W
120	Berner Alpen (Mts.) Switz.	46·29 N	7·30 E
123	Berneustadt (bĕr'noi'shtät) Ger. (Ruhr In.)	51·01 N	7·39 E
158	Bernier (I.) (bĕr-nēr') Austl.	24·58 S	113·15 E
120	Bernina Pizzo (Pk.) Switz.	46·23 N	9·58 E
120	Beroun (bā'rōn) Czech.	49·57 N	14·03 E
120	Berounka R. (bĕ-rōn'kȧ) . . . Czech.	49·53 N	13·40 E
161	Berowra Austl. (Sydney In.)	33·36 S	151·10 E
122	Berre, Étang de (L.) (ā-tôn' dĕ bâr') . Fr. (Marseille In.)	43·27 N	5·07 E
122	Berre-l' Étang (bâr'lā-tôn') Fr. (Marseille In.)	43·28 N	5·11 E
91	Berriozabal (bā'rēō-zä-bäl') . . Mex.	16·47 N	93·16 W
114	Berryan (bĕr-ē-än') Alg.	32·50 N	3·49 E
68	Berryessa (R.) (bĕ'rĭ ĕs'ȧ) . . . Calif.	38·35 N	122·33 W
94	Berry Is. Ba. Is.	25·35 N	3·49 E
73	Berryville (bĕr'ē-vĭl) Ark.	36·21 N	93·34 W
129	Bershad' (byĕr'shät) Sov. Un.	48·22 N	29·31 E
82	Berthier (bĕr-tyā') Can.	46·04 N	73·14 W
85	Berthier Can. (Quebec In.)	46·56 N	70·44 W
65	Bertrand (R.) (bûr'trănd) Wash. (Vancouver In.)	48·58 N	122·31 W
84	Bertrandville (bûr'trănd-vĭl) La. (New Orleans In.)	29·47 N	90·01 W
116	Berwick (bûr'ĭk) Scot.	55·45 N	2·01 W
81	Berwick (bûr'wĭk) Pa.	41·05 N	76·10 W
75	Berwyn (bûr'wĭn) Ill (Chicago In.)	41·49 N	87·47 W
116	Berwyn Ra. Wales	52·45 N	3·41 W
167	Besalampy (bĕz-ȧ-lȧm-pē') Malag. Rep.	16·48 S	40·40 E
123	Besançon (bē-sän-sôn) Fr.	47·14 N	6·02 E
139	Besar, Gunong (Mt.) Mala. (Singapore In.)	2·31 N	103·09 E
128	Besed (R.) (byĕ'syĕt) . Sov. Un.	52·58 N	31·36 E
128	Beshenkovichi (byĕ'shĕn-kō vē'chĭ) . Sov. Un.	55·04 N	29·29 E
121	Beskides (Mts.) (bĕs'kēdz') Czech.-Pol.	49·23 N	19·00 E
122	Bessèges (bĕ-sĕzh') Fr.	44·20 N	4·07 E
84	Bessemer (bĕs'ē-mēr) Ala. (Birmingham In.)	33·24 N	86·58 W
71	Bessemer Mich.	46·29 N	90·04 W
79	Bessemer City N. C.	35·16 N	81·17 W
111	Bestensee (bĕs'tĕn-zā) Ger. (Berlin In.)	52·15 N	13·39 E
124	Betanzos (bĕ-tän'thōs) Sp.	43·18 N	8·14 W
69	Betatakin Ruin (bĕt-ȧ-täk'ĭn) Ariz.	36·40 N	110·29 W
168	Bethal (bĕth'ăl) . S. Afr. (Johannesburg & Pretoria In.)	26·27 S	29·28 E
74	Bethalto (bȧ-thâl'tō) Ill. (St. Louis In.)	38·54 N	90·03 W
166	Bethanie (bĕth'ȧ-nĭ) . . . S. W. Afr.	26·20 S	16·10 E
73	Bethany Mo.	40·15 N	94·04 W
64	Bethel (bĕth'ĕl) Alaska	60·50 N	161·50 W
84	Bethel Conn. (New York In.)	41·22 N	73·24 W
75	Bethel Pa. (Pittsburgh In.)	40·19 N	80·02 W
81	Bethel Vt.	43·50 N	72·40 W
81	Bethesda (bĕ-thĕs'dȧ) Md.	39·00 N	77·10 W
81	Bethlehem (bĕth'lē-hĕm) Pa.	40·40 N	75·25 W
168	Bethlehem . S. Afr. (Johannesburg & Pretoria In.)	28·14 S	28·18 E
	Bethlehem, see Bayt Lahm		
122	Béthune (bā-tün') Fr.	50·32 N	2·37 E
167	Betroka (bĕ-trōk'ȧ) . . Malag. Rep.	23·13 S	46·17 E
82	Betsiamites Can.	48·55 N	68·39 W
82	Betsiamites, R. Can.	49·10 N	69·15 W
167	Betsiboka (R.) (bĕt-sĭ-bō'kȧ) Malag. Rep.	16·47 S	46·45 E
164	Bettié (bĕt-tyā') Ivory Coast	6·04 N	3·32 W
64	Bettles Field (bĕt'tŭls) Alaska	66·58 N	151·48 W
142	Betwa (R.) (bĕt'wȧ) India	23·56 N	77·37 E
123	Betz (bĕ) Fr. (Paris In.)	49·09 N	2·58 E
123	Betzdorf (bĕtz'dōrf) Ger. (Ruhr In.)	50·47 N	7·53 E
123	Beuel (boi'ĕl) . . . Ger. (Ruhr In.)	50·44 N	7·08 E
111	Beveren Bel. (Brussels In.)	51·13 N	4·14 E
85	Beverly (bĕv'ĕr-lĭ) Can. (Edmonton In.)	53·34 N	113·23 W
110	Beverly Eng.	53·50 N	0·25 W
83	Beverly Mass. (Boston In.)	42·34 N	70·53 W
84	Beverly N. J. (Philadelphia In.)	40·03 N	74·56 W
74	Beverly Hills Calif. (Los Angeles In.)	34·05 N	118·24 W
73	Bevier (bē-vēr') Mo.	39·44 N	92·36 W
110	Bewdley (būd'lĭ) Eng.	52·22 N	2·19 W
117	Bexhill (bĕks'hĭl) Eng.	50·49 N	0·25 E
110	Bexley (bĕks'ly) Eng. (London In.)	51·26 N	0·09 E
164	Beyla (bā'lä) Gui.	8·38 N	8·39 W
133	Beypazari (bā-pȧ-zä'rĭ) Tur.	40·10 N	31·40 E
139	Beyrouth (Beirut) (bā-rōōt') Leb. (Palestine In.)	33·53 N	35·30 E
133	Beyşehir (bā-shĕ'h'r) Tur.	38·00 N	31·45 E
133	Beyşehir Gölü (L.) Tur.	38·00 N	31·30 E
129	Beysugskiy, Liman (B.) (lĭ-män' bĕy-sōōg'skĭ) . Sov. Un.	46·07 N	38·35 E
128	Bezhetsk (byĕ-zhĕtsk') . . . Sov. Un.	57·46 N	36·40 E
128	Bezhitsa (byĕ-zhĭ'tsȧ) . . . Sov. Un.	53·19 N	34·18 E
122	Béziers (bā-zyā') Fr.	43·21 N	3·12 E
142	Bhagalpur (bä'gŭl-pōōr) India	25·15 N	86·59 E
146	Bhamo (bŭ-mō') Bur.	24·22 N	97·13 E
142	Bhāngar India (Calcutta In.)	22·30 N	88·36 E
142	Bharatpur (bĕrt'pōōr) India	27·21 N	77·33 E
142	Bhatinda (bŭ-tĭn-dä) India	30·19 N	74·56 E
142	Bhātpāra (bŭt-pä'rä) India (Calcutta In.)	22·58 N	88·30 E
142	Bhaunāgār (bäv-nŭg'ŭr) . . . India	21·45 N	72·58 E
143	Bhayandar . . . India (Bombay In.)	19·20 N	72·50 E
142	Bhima (R.) (bē'mȧ) India	17·44 N	75·28 E
142	Bhiwani India	28·53 N	76·08 E
143	Bhiwandi India (Bombay In.)	19·18 N	73·03 E
142	Bhopāl (bō-päl) India	23·20 N	77·25 E
142	Bhorila W. Pak.	24·48 N	70·11 E
142	Bhubaneswar (bōō-bû-näsh'vûr) India	20·21 N	85·53 E
142	Bhuj (bōōj) India	23·22 N	69·39 E
138	Bhutan (bōō-tän') Asia	28·00 N	90·00 E
164	Biafra, Bight of Cam.	2·52 N	9·01 E

Page	Name	Pronunciation	Region	Lat. °'	Long. °'
155	Biak (I.)	(bē'ăk)	W. Irian	0·45 s	135·00 e
121	Biała Podlaska				
		(byä'wä pŏd-läs'kä)	Pol.	52·01 n	23·08 e
120	Białogard	(byä-wō'gärd)	Pol.	54·00 n	16·01 e
121	Białystok	(byä-wĭs'tŏk)	Pol.	53·08 n	23·12 e
122	Biarritz	(byä-rēts')	Fr.	43·27 n	1·39 w
168	Bibā	(bē'bä)	U. A. R. (Nile In.)	28·54 n	30·59 e
78	Bibb City	(bĭb' sĭ'tē)	Ga.	32·31 n	84·56 w
120	Biberach	(bē'bĕräk)	Ger.	48·06 n	9·49 e
82	Bic	(bĭk)	Can.	48·21 n	68·44 w
80	Bicknell	(bĭk'nĕl)	Ind.	38·45 n	87·20 w
121	Bicske	(bĭsh'kĕ)	Hung.	47·29 n	18·38 e
164	Bida	(bē'dä)	Nig.	9·05 n	6·04 e
82	Biddeford	(bĭd'ê-fêrd)	Maine	43·29 n	70·29 w
110	Biddulph	(bĭd'ŭlf)	Eng.	53·07 n	2·10 w
164	Bidon Cing		Alg.	22·22 n	0·33 e
121	Biebrza R.	(byĕb'zhä)	Pol.	53·18 n	22·25 e
120	Biel	(bēl)	Switz.	47·09 n	7·12 e
120	Bielefeld	(bē'lĕ-fĕlt)	Ger.	52·01 n	8·35 e
127	Bieljina	(byĕ'lyĕ-nä)	Yugo.	44·44 n	19·15 e
126	Biella	(byĕl'lä)	It.	45·34 n	8·05 e
121	Bielsk Podlaski	(byĕlsk pŭd-lä'skĭ)			
			Pol.	52·47 n	23·14 e
87	Bienville, Lac (L.)		Can.	55·32 n	72·45 w
111	Biesenthal	(bē'sĕn-täl)			
			Ger. (Berlin In.)	52·46 n	13·38 e
126	Biferno (R.)	(bē-fĕr'nō)	It.	41·49 n	14·46 e
82	Big (L.)	(bĭg)	Can.	45·06 n	67·43 w
65	Big (L.)	(bĭg)	Wash. (Seattle In.)	48·23 n	122·14 w
78	Big (R.)		Ark.	33·55 n	90·10 w
127	Biğa	(bē'ghä)	Tur.	40·13 n	27·14 e
73	Big Bay	(bĭg' bī'yōō)	Ark.	33·04 n	91·28 w
71	Big Bay de Noc	(bĭg bā dê nok')			
			Mich.	45·48 n	86·41 w
74	Big Bear City	(bĭg bâr)			
			Calif. (Los Angeles In.)	34·16 n	116·51 w
74	Big Bear Lake	(bĭg bâr lāk)			
			Calif. (Los Angeles In.)	34·14 n	116·54 w
67	Big Belt Mts.	(bĭg bĕlt)	Mont.	46·53 n	111·43 w
70	Big Bend Dam	(bĭg bĕnd)	S. D.	44·11 n	99·33 w
76	Big Bend Natl. Park		Tex.	29·15 n	103·15 w
78	Big Black (R.)	(bĭg blăk)	Miss.	32·05 n	90·49 w
73	Big Blue (R.)	(bĭg blōō)	Nebr.	40·53 n	97·00 w
76	Big Canyon	(bĭg kăn'yŭn)	Tex.	30·27 n	102·19 w
79	Big Cypress Swp.	(bĭg sĭ'prĕs)			
			Fla. (In.)	26·02 n	81·20 w
64	Big Delta	(bĭg dĕl'tà)	Alaska	64·08 n	145·48 w
71	Big Fork (R.)	(bĭg fôrk)	Minn.	48·08 n	93·47 w
86	Biggar		Can.	52·09 n	108·10 w
67	Big Hole R.	(bĭg 'hōl)	Mont.	45·53 n	113·15 w
67	Big Hole Battlefield Natl. Mon.				
		(bĭg hŏl băt'l-fēld)	Mont.	45·44 n	113·35 w
67	Big Horn Mts.	(bĭg hôrn)	Wyo.	44·47 n	107·40 w
67	Bighorn R		Mont.	45·17 n	107·53 w
65	Big Lake	(bĭg lāk)			
			Wash. (Seattle In.)	48·24 n	122·14 w
85	Big L.	(bĭg lāk)			
			Can. (Edmonton In.)	53·35 n	113·47 w
80	Big Muddy (R.)		Ill.	37·55 n	89·10 w
67	Big Muddy Cr.	(bĭg mud'ĭ)	Mont.	48·53 n	105·02 w
80	Big Rapids	(bĭg răp'ĭdz)	Mich.	43·40 n	85·30 w
86	Big River		Can.	53·50 n	107·20 w
	Big Sandy, see Fraser I.				
69	Big Sandy (R.)	(bĭg sănd'ê)	Ariz.	34·59 n	113·36 w
80	Big Sandy (R.)		Ky.-W. Va.	38·15 n	82·35 w
72	Big Sandy Cr.		Colo.	39·08 n	103·36 w
70	Big Sioux (R.)	(bĭg sōō)	S. D.	44·34 n	97·00 w
76	Big Spring	(bĭg spring)	Tex.	32·15 n	101·28 w
70	Big Stone (L.)	(bĭg stōn)			
			Minn.-S. Dak.	45·29 n	96·40 w
78	Big Stone Gap		Va.	36·50 n	82·50 w
67	Bigtimber	(bĭg'tĭm-bêr)	Mont.	45·50 n	109·57 w
67	Big Wood R.	(bĭg wŏŏd)	Idaho	43·02 n	114·30 w
126	Bihać	(bē'häch)	Yugo.	44·48 n	15·52 e
142	Bihar (State)	(bē-här')	India	23·48 n	84·57 e
166	Biharamulo	(bē-hä-rä-mōō'lô)			
			Tan.	2·38 s	31·39 e
121	Bihor, Muntii (Mts.)	(bē'hôr)			
			Rom.	46·37 n	22·37 e
164	Bijagós, Arquipelago dos (Is.)				
		(är-kē-pä'lä-gō dôs bē-zhä-gôs')			
			Port. Gui.	10·58 n	16·39 w
143	Bijapur		India	16·53 n	75·42 e
127	Bijelo Polje	(bē'yĕ'lô pô'lyĕ)			
			Yugo.	43·02 n	19·48 e
72	Bijou Cr.	(bē'zhōō)	Colo.	39·41 n	104·13 w
142	Bikaner	(bĭ-kä'nûr)	India	28·07 n	73·19 e
152	Bikin	(bĭ-kēn')	Sov. Un.	46·41 n	134·29 e
152	Bikin (R.)		Sov. Un.	46·37 n	135·55 e
166	Bikoro	(bē-kō'rô)	Con. L.	0·45 s	18·51 e
142	Bilāspur	(bē-läs'pōŏr)	India	22·08 n	82·12 e
154	Bilauktaung Ra.		Thai.	14·27 n	98·53 e
124	Bilbao	(bĭl-bä'ō)	Sp.	43·12 n	2·48 w
168	Bilbays		U. A. R. (Nile In.)	30·26 n	31·37 e
127	Bileća	(bē-lĕ-chä)	Yugo.	42·52 n	18·26 e
133	Bilecik	(bē-lĕd-zhĕk')	Tur.	40·10 n	29·58 e
121	Bílé Karpaty (Mts.)		Czech.	48·53 n	17·35 e
121	Biłgoraj	(bēw-gō'rī)	Pol.	50·31 n	22·43 e
136	Bilimbay	(bē'lĭm-bày)			
			Sov. Un. (Urals In.)	56·59 n	59·53 e
160	Billabong (R.)	(bĭl'à-bŏng)	Austl.	35·15 s	145·20 e
83	Billerica	(bĭl'rĭk-à)			
			Mass. (Boston In.)	42·33 n	71·46 w
110	Billericay		Eng. (London In.)	51·38 n	0·26 e
67	Billings	(bĭl'ĭngz)	Mont.	45·47 n	108·29 w
69	Bill Williams (L.)	(bĭl-wĭl'yumz)			
			Ariz.	34·10 n	113·50 w
165	Bilma	(bēl'mä)	Niger.	18·41 n	13·20 e
78	Biloxi	(bĭ-lŏk'sĭ)	Miss.	30·24 n	88·50 w
168	Bilqas Qishm Awwal				
			U. A. R. (Nile In.)	31·14 n	31·25 e
110	Bilston	(bĭl'stŭn)	Eng.	52·34 n	2·04 w
160	Bimberi Pk.	(bĭm'bĕrĭ)	Austl.	35·45 s	148·50 e
155	Binaja, Gunung (Mtn.)		Indon.	3·07 s	129·25 e
155	Binalonan	(bē-nä-lô'nän)			
			Phil. (Manila In.)	16·03 n	120·35 e

Page	Name	Pronunciation	Region	Lat. °'	Long. °'
144	Binalud (Mtn.)		Iran	36·32 n	58·34 e
155	Biñan	(bē'nän)	Phil. (Manila In.)	14·20 n	121·06 e
120	Bingen	(bĭn'gĕn)	Ger.	49·57 n	7·54 e
164	Bingerville	(băn-zhä-vēl')			
			Ivory Coast	5·24 n	3·56 w
110	Bingham	(bĭng'ăm)	Eng.	52·57 n	0·57 w
82	Bingham		Maine	45·03 n	69·51 w
74	Bingham Canyon				
			Utah (Salt Lake City In.)	40·33 n	112·09 w
81	Binghamton	(bĭng'ăm-tŭn)	N. Y.	42·05 n	75·55 w
153	Bingo-Nada (Sea)	(bĭn'gō nä-dä)			
			Jap.	34·06 n	133·14 e
154	Binh Dinh	(bĭng'dĭng')	Viet.	13·55 n	109·00 e
160	Binnaway	(bĭn'ă-wä)	Austl.	31·42 s	149·22 e
139	Bintan, Palau (I.)	(bĭn'tän)			
			Indon. (Singapore In.)	1·09 n	104·43 e
154	Bintulu	(bĕn'tōō-lōō)	Mala.	3·07 n	113·06 e
152	Bira	(bē'rá)	Sov. Un.	49·00 n	133·18 e
152	Bira (R.)		Sov. Un.	48·55 n	132·25 e
167	Birakao		Som.	1·14 s	41·47 e
139	Bi'r al Mazār				
			U. A. R. (Palestine In.)	31·03 n	33·24 e
165	Bi'r al Wa'r (Oasis)		Libya	22·51 n	14·22 e
142	Biratnagar	(bĭ-rät'nŭ-gŭr)	Nep.	26·35 n	87·18 e
65	Birch Bay. Wash.	(Vancouver In.)		48·55 n	122·45 w
65	Birch B.	(bûrch)			
			Wash. (Vancouver In.)	48·55 n	122·52 w
85	Birch Cliff	(bêrch klĭf)			
			Can. (Toronto In.)	43·41 n	79·16 w
86	Birch Mts.		Can.	57·36 n	113·10 w
65	Birch Pt.	Wash.	(Vancouver In.)		48·57 n	122·50 w
167	Bird (I.)	(bêrd)			
			S. Afr. (Natal In.)	33·51 s	26·21 e
95	Bird Rock (I.)	(bûrd)	Ba. Is.	22·50 n	74·20 w
83	Bird Rock (I.)		Can.	47·53 n	61·00 w
85	Birds Hill	(bûrds)			
			Can. (Winnipeg In.)	49·58 n	97·00 w
160	Birdsville	(bûrdz'vĭl)	Aust.	22·50 s	139·31 e
158	Birdum	(bûrd'ŭm)	Austl.	15·45 s	133·25 e
133	Birecik	(bē-rĕd-zhĕk')	Tur.	37·10 n	37·50 e
165	Bir en Natrūn		Sud.	18·13 n	26·44 e
114	Bir er Ressof	(bēr-ĕr-rĕ-sôf')	Alg.	32·19 n	7·58 e
144	Bīrjand	(bēr'jänd)	Iran	32·53 n	59·16 e
65	Birkenfeld	Ore.	(Portland In.)		45·59 n	123·20 w
110	Birkenhead	(bûr'kĕn-hĕd)	Eng.	53·23 n	3·02 w
111	Birkenwerder	(bēr'kĕn-vĕr-dêr)			
			Ger. (Berlin In.)	52·41 n	13·22 e
121	Bîrlad		Rom.	46·15 n	27·43 e
84	Birmingham	(bûr'mĭng-hăm)			
			Ala. (Birmingham In.)	33·31 n	86·49 w
110	Birmingham		Eng.	52·29 n	1·53 w
75	Birmingham	Mich.	(Detroit In.)		42·32 n	83·13 w
74	Birmingham				
			Mo. (Kansas City In.)	39·10 n	94·22 w
165	Birmingham, Can.	Eng.			53·07 n	2·40 w
165	Bi'r Misāḥah (Oasis)		U. A. R.	22·16 n	28·04 e
164	Birnin Kebbi		Nig.	12·26 n	4·04 e
135	Birobidzhan	(bē'rô-bē-jän')			
			Sov. Un.	48·42 n	133·28 e
132	Birsk	(bĭrsk)	Sov. Un.	55·25 n	55·30 e
110	Birstall	(bûr'stôl)	Eng.	53·44 n	1·39 w
129	Biryuchiy (I.)	(bĭr-yōō'chĭ)			
			Sov. Un.	46·07 n	35·12 e
136	Biryulëvo	(bēr-yōōl'yô-vô)			
			Sov. Un. (Moscow In.)	55·35 n	37·39 e
134	Biryusa (R.)	(bēr-yōō'sá)	Sov. Un.	56·43 n	97·30 e
118	Biržai	(bēr-zhä'ê)	Sov. Un.	56·11 n	24·45 e
165	Bi'r Zaltan		Libya	28·20 n	19·40 e
69	Bisbee	(bĭz'bē)	Ariz.	31·30 n	109·55 w
113	Biscay, B. of	(bĭs'kā')	Eur.	45·19 n	3·51 w
79	Biscayne B.	(bĭs-kān')	Fla. (In.)	25·22 n	80·15 w
123	Bischeim	(bĭsh'hĭm)	Fr.	48·40 n	7·48 e
136	Biser	(bē'sĕr)	Sov. Un. (Urals In.)	58·24 n	58·54 e
126	Biševo (Is.)	(bē'shĕ-vô)	Yugo.	43·58 n	15·41 e
68	Bishop	(bĭsh'ŭp)	Calif.	37·22 n	118·25 w
77	Bishop		Tex.	27·35 n	97·46 w
110	Bishop's Castle	(bĭsh'ŏps käs'l)			
			Eng.	52·29 n	2·57 w
79	Bishopville	(bĭsh'ŭp-vĭl)	S. C.	34·11 n	80·13 w
164	Biskra	(bĕs'krä)	Alg.	34·52 n	5·39 e
70	Bismarck	(bĭz'märk)	N. D.	46·48 n	100·46 w
155	Bismarck Arch		N. Gui. Ter.	3·15 s	150·45 e
155	Bismarck Ra		N. Gui. Ter.	5·15 s	144·15 e
164	Bissau	(bē-sä'ōō)	Port. Gui.	11·52 n	15·47 w
77	Bistineau L.	(bĭs-tĭ-nō')	La.	32·19 n	93·45 w
121	Bistrita	(bĭs'trĭt-sä)	Rom.	47·09 n	24·29 e
121	Bistrita R		Rom.	47·08 n	25·47 e
133	Bitlis	(bĭt-lēs')	Tur.	38·30 n	42·00 e
127	Bitola (Monastir)	(bē'tô-lä)			
			(mô'nä-stēr) Yugo.	41·02 n	21·22 e
126	Bitonto	(bē-tôn'tō)	It.	41·08 n	16·42 e
67	Bitter Cr.	(bĭt'êr)	Wyo.	41·36 n	108·29 w
120	Bitterfeld	(bĭt'êr-fĕlt)	Ger.	51·39 n	12·19 e
66	Bitterroot Ra.	(bĭt'êr-ōōt)	Mont.	45·15 n	115·13 w
67	Bitterroot R.		Mont.	46·28 n	114·10 w
129	Bityug (R.)	(bĭt'yōōg)	Sov. Un.	51·23 n	40·33 e
71	Biwabik	(bĭ-wä'bĭk)	Minn.	47·32 n	92·24 w
153	Biwa-ko (L.)	(bē-wä'kō)			
			Jap. (Ōsaka In.)	35·03 n	135·51 e
134	Biya (R.)	(bĭ'yä)	Sov. Un.	52·22 n	87·28 e
134	Biysk	(bēsk)	Sov. Un.	52·32 n	85·28 e
167	Bizana	(bĭz-änä)			
			S. Afr. (Natal In.)	30·51 s	29·54 e
164	Bizerte	(bē-zĕrt')	Tun.	37·23 n	9·52 e
150	Bizuta		Mong.	41·28 n	115·10 e
126	Bjelovar	(byĕ-lô'vär)	Yugo.	45·54 n	16·53 e
	Bjorneborg, see Pori				
118	Bjorne Fd.	(byūr'nĕ fyôrd)	Nor.	60·11 n	5·26 e
80	Black (L.)	(blăk)	Mich.	45·25 n	84·15 w
81	Black (L.)		N. Y.	44·30 n	75·35 w
73	Black (R.)		Ark.	35·47 n	91·22 w
81	Black (R.)		N. Y.	43·45 n	75·20 w
79	Black (R.)		S. C.	33·55 n	80·08 w
71	Black (R.)		Wis.	44·07 n	90·56 w
159	Blackall	(blăk'ŭl)	Austl.	24·23 s	145·37 e
71	Black B.	(blăk)	Can.	48·36 n	88·32 w

Page	Name	Pronunciation	Region	Lat. °'	Long. °'
84	Black B.. La.	(New Orleans In.)		29·38 n	89·33 w
64	Blackburn	(blăk'bûrn)	Alaska	63·20 n	159·45 w
110	Blackburn		Eng.	53·45 n	2·28 w
64	Blackburn, Mt.		Alaska	61·50 n	143·12 w
69	Black Canyon of the Gunnison				
		Natl. Mon. (blăk kăn'yŭn)	Colo.	38·35 n	107·45 w
65	Black Diamond	(dī'mŭnd)			
			Wash. (Seattle In.)	47·19 n	122·00 w
116	Blackdown Hills	(blăk'doun)	Eng.	50·58 n	3·19 w
71	Blackduck	(blăk'dŭk)	Minn.	47·41 n	94·33 w
67	Blackfoot	(blăk'fŏŏt)	Idaho	43·11 n	112·23 w
67	Blackfoot Ind. Res.		Mont.	48·49 n	112·53 w
67	Blackfoot R.		Mont.	46·53 n	113·33 w
67	Blackfoot River Res.		Idaho	42·53 n	111·23 w
70	Black Hills (Reg.)		S. D.	44·08 n	103·47 w
82	Black Lake		Can.	46·02 n	71·24 w
69	Black Mesa	(blăk mäsà)	Ariz.	36·33 n	110·40 w
69	Black Mts.		N. Mex.	33·15 n	107·55 w
85	Blackmud Cr.	(blăk'mŭd)			
			Can. (Edmonton In.)	53·28 n	113·34 w
110	Blackpool	(blăk'pōōl)	Eng.	53·49 n	3·02 w
94	Black River	(blăk)	Jam.	18·00 n	77·50 w
75	Black R.	Ohio	(Cleveland In.)		41·26 n	82·08 w
151	Black R.		Viet.	20·56 n	104·30 e
71	Black River Falls		Wis.	44·18 n	90·51 w
66	Black Rock Des.	(rŏk)	Nev.	40·55 n	119·00 w
79	Blacksburg	(blăks'bûrg)	S. C.	35·09 n	81·30 w
103	Black Sea		Eur.-Asia	43·01 n	32·16 e
79	Blackshear	(blăk'shĭr)	Ga.	31·20 n	82·15 w
79	Blackstone	(blăk'stôn)	Va.	37·04 n	78·00 w
71	Black Sturgeon (R.)	(stŭ'jŭn)	Can.	49·12 n	88·41 w
161	Blacktown	(blăk'toun)			
			Austl. (Sydney In.)	33·47 s	150·55 e
82	Blackville	(blăk'vĭl)	Can.	46·44 n	65·50 w
79	Blackville		S. C.	33·21 n	81·19 w
164	Black Volta R.	(vōl'tá)			
			Upper Volta	11·21 n	4·21 w
78	Black Warrior (R.)	(blăk wŏr'ĭ-êr)			
			Ala.	32·37 n	87·42 w
78	Black Warrior (R.), Locust Fk.				
			Ala.	34·06 n	86·27 w
78	Black Warrior (R.), Mulberry Fk.				
			Ala.	34·06 n	86·32 w
116	Blackwater	(blăk-wô'tēr)	Ire.	52·05 n	9·02 w
73	Blackwater (R.)		Mo.	38·53 n	93·22 w
79	Blackwater (R.)		Va.	37·07 n	77·10 w
73	Blackwell	(blăk'wĕl)	Okla.	36·47 n	97·19 w
111	Bladel	Neth.	(Amsterdam In.)		51·22 n	5·15 e
133	Blagodarnoye	(blä'gô-där-nô'yĕ)			
			Sov. Un.	45·00 n	43·30 e
127	Blagoevgrad (Gorna Dzhumaya)				
			Bul.	42·01 n	23·06 e
135	Blagoveshchensk	(blä'gŏ-vyĕsh'-			
		chĕnsk) Sov. Un.	50·16 n	127·47 e
136	Blagoveshchensk				
			Sov. Un. (Urals In.)	55·03 n	56·00 e
65	Blaine	(blān)			
			Wash. (Vancouver In.)	48·59 n	122·49 w
81	Blaine		W. Va.	39·25 n	79·10 w
70	Blair	(blâr)	Nebr.	41·33 n	96·09 w
86	Blairmore	(blâr-mōr)	Can.	49·38 n	114·20 w
81	Blairsville	(blârs'vĭl)	Pa.	40·30 n	79·40 w
65	Blake (I.)	(blāk)	Wash. (Seattle In.)	47·37 n	122·28 w
78	Blakely	(blāk'lê)	Ga.	31·22 n	84·55 w
164	Blanc, Cap (C.)		Mauritania	20·39 n	18·08 w
123	Blanc, Mt.	(môn blän)	Fr.-It.	45·50 n	6·53 e
100	Blanca, Bahia (B.)				
		(bä-ē'ä-blän'kä) .Arg.	39·30 s	61·00 w
72	Blanca Pk.	(blăn'kä)	Colo.	37·36 n	105·22 w
160	Blanch, L.	(blănch)	Austl.	29·20 s	139·12 e
85	Blanche, R.	Can.	(Ottawa In.)		45·34 n	75·38 w
75	Blanchester	(blăn'chĕs-tēr)			
			Ohio (Cincinnati In.)	39·18 n	83·58 w
100	Blanco, C.	(blän'kô)	Arg.	47·08 s	65·47 w
92	Blanco, Cabo (C.)	(kä'bô-blän'kô)			
			C. R.	9·29 n	85·15 w
66	Blanco, C.	(blăn'kō)	Ore.	42·53 n	124·38 w
91	Blanco (R.)		Mex.	18·42 n	96·03 w
90	Blanco (R.)		Mex.	24·05 n	99·21 w
94	Blancos, Cayo (I.)				
		(kä'yô-blän'kōs) .Cuba	23·15 n	80·55 w
69	Blanding		Utah	37·40 n	109·31 w
117	Blankenburg	(blän'kĕn-bōŏrgh)			
			Ger.	51·45 n	13·07 e
111	Blankenfelde	(blän'kĕn-fĕl-dĕ)			
			Ger. (Berlin In.)	52·20 n	13·24 e
91	Blanquilla, Arrecife (Reef)	(är-rĕ-			
		sē'fĕ-blän-kē'l-yä) .Mex.	21·32 n	97·14 w
166	Blantyre	(blän-tîr')	Nya.	15·48 s	35·07 e
75	Blasdell	(blăz'dĕl)			
			N. Y. (Buffalo In.)	42·48 n	78·51 w
126	Blato	(blä'tō)	Yugo.	42·55 n	16·47 e
118	Blåvands Huk (cape)	(blô'väns-hŏk)			
			Den.	55·36 n	7·35 e
122	Blaye-et-Ste. Luce				
		(blä'ā-sănt-lüs') .Fr.	45·08 n	0·40 w
121	Błazowa	(bwä-zhô'và)	Pol.	49·51 n	22·05 e
164	Blida		Alg.	36·33 n	2·45 e
87	Blind River (blind)		Can.	46·10 n	83·09 w
80	Blissfield	(blĭs-fĕld)	Mich.	41·50 n	83·50 w
110	Blithe (R.)	(blĭth)	Eng.	52·52 n	1·49 w
81	Block (I.)	(blŏk)	R. I.	41·05 n	71·35 w
168	Bloemfontein	(blōōm'fōn-tān)			
			S. Afr. (Johannesburg & Pretoria In.)	29·09 s	26·16 e
122	Blois	(blwä)	Fr.	47·36 n	1·21 e
71	Bloomer	(blōōm'ēr)	Wis.	45·07 n	91·30 w
80	Bloomfield	(blōōm'fēld)	Ind.	39·00 n	86·55 w
71	Bloomfield		Iowa	40·44 n	92·21 w
73	Bloomfield		Mo.	36·54 n	89·55 w
70	Bloomfield		Nebr.	42·36 n	97·40 w
84	Bloomfield. N. J.	(New York In.)		40·48 n	74·12 w
75	Bloomfield Hills				
			Mich. (Detroit In.)	42·35 n	83·15 w
71	Blooming Prairie	(blōōm'ĭng prä'rĭ) .Minn.		43·52 n	93·04 w

PRONOUNCING INDEX
Bloomington–Borujerd 185

Page	Name Pronunciation Region	Lat. °′	Long. °′
74	Bloomington (blōōm′ĭng-tŭn) Calif. (Los Angeles In.)	34·04 N	117·24 W
80	Bloomington . . . Ill.	40·30 N	89·00 W
80	Bloomington . . . Ind.	39·10 N	86·35 W
74	Bloomington Minn. (Minneapolis, St. Paul In.)	44·50 N	93·18 W
81	Bloomsburg (blōōmz′bûrg) . . . Pa.	41·00 N	76·25 W
84	Blossburg (blŏs′bûrg) Ala. (Birmingham In.)	33·38 N	86·57 W
81	Blossburg . . . Pa.	41·45 N	77·00 W
166	Bloubergstrand S. Afr. (Cape Town In.)	33·48 S	18·28 E
78	Blountstown (blŭnts′tun) . . . Fla.	30·24 N	85·02 W
120	Bludenz (blōō-dĕnts′) . . . Aus.	47·09 N	9·50 E
83	Blue, Mt . . . Can.	50·28 N	57·11 W
75	Blue Ash (blōō ăsh) Ohio (Cincinnati In.)	39·14 N	84·23 W
71	Blue Earth (blōō ûrth) . . . Minn.	43·38 N	94·05 W
71	Blue Earth (R.) . . . Minn.	43·55 N	94·16 W
79	Bluefield (blōō′fēld) . . . W. Va.	37·15 N	81·11 W
93	Bluefields (blōō′fēldz) . . . Nic.	12·03 N	83·45 W
75	Blue Island . . . Ill. (Chicago In.)	41·39 N	87·41 W
160	Blue Mts. . . . Austl.	33·35 S	149·00 E
94	Blue Mts. . . . Jam.	18·05 N	76·35 W
66	Blue Mts. . . . Ore.	45·15 N	118·50 W
158	Blue Mud B. (blōō mŭd) . . . Austl.	13·20 S	136·45 E
	Blue Nile, see El Azraq, Bahr		
73	Blue Rapids (blōō răp′ĭdz) . . Kans.	39·40 N	96·41 W
63	Blue Ridge (Mts.) (blōō rĭj) . U. S.	35·30 N	82·50 W
86	Blue River . . . Can.	52·09 N	119·21 W
74	Blue R. . . . Mo. (Kansas City In.)	38·55 N	94·33 W
69	Bluff . . . Utah	37·18 N	109·34 W
80	Bluffton (blŭf-tŭn) . . . Ind.	40·40 N	85·15 W
80	Bluffton (blŭf-tŭn) . . . Ohio	40·50 N	83·55 W
100	Blumenau (blōō′mĕn-ou) . . . Braz.	26·53 S	48·58 W
139	Blumut, Gunong (Mt.) Mala. (Singapore In.)	2·03 N	103·34 E
65	Blyn (blĕn) . . . Wash. (Seattle In.)	48·01 N	123·00 W
116	Blyth (blīth) . . . Eng.	55·03 N	1·34 W
68	Blythe . . . Calif.	33·37 N	114·37 W
73	Blytheville (blīth′vĭl) . . . Ark.	35·55 N	89·51 W
155	Boac . . . Phil. (Manila In.)	13·26 N	121·50 E
92	Boaco (bō-ä′kō) . . . Nic.	12·24 N	85·41 W
99	Boa Vista do Rio Branco (bō′ä vēsh′tä dŏŏ rē′ŏŏ brän′kŏŏ) . Braz.	2·46 N	60·45 W
164	Boa Vista I. (bō-ä-vēsh′tȧ) C. V. Is. (In.)	16·01 N	23·52 W
121	Boberka (bō′bĕr-kȧ) . . . Sov. Un.	49·36 N	24·18 E
164	Bobo-Dioulasso (bō′bō-dyōō-lȧs-sō′) . Upper Volta	11·13 N	4·13 W
128	Bobr (bô′b′r) . . . Sov. Un.	54·19 N	29·11 E
129	Bobrinets (bô′brē-nyĭts) . Sov. Un.	48·04 N	32·10 E
120	Bobr R. (bŭ′br) . . . Pol.	51·44 N	15·13 E
129	Bobrov (bŭb-rôf′) . . . Sov. Un.	51·07 N	40·01 E
129	Bobrovitsa (bŭb-rô′vê-tsȧ) Sov. Un.	50·43 N	31·27 E
128	Bobruysk (bŏ-brōō′ĭsk) . Sov. Un.	53·07 N	29·13 E
99	Boca del Pozo (bô-kä-dĕl-pô′zŏ) Ven. (In.)	11·00 N	64·21 W
99	Boca de Uchire (bô-kä-dĕ-ōō-chē′rĕ) . Ven. (In.)	10·09 N	65·27 W
101	Bocaina, Serra da (Mtn.) (sĕ′r-rä-dȧ-bô-kä′ē-nä) . Braz. (Rio de Janeiro In.)	22·47 S	44·39 W
90	Bocas (bō′käs) . . . Mex.	22·29 N	101·03 W
93	Bocas del Toro (bō′käs dĕl tō′rō) Pan.	9·24 N	82·15 W
121	Bochnia (bōĸ′nyä) . . . Pol.	49·58 N	20·28 E
123	Bocholt (bō′ĸōlt) . Ger. (Ruhr In.)	51·50 N	6·37 E
123	Bochum (bō′ĸŏŏm) Ger. (Ruhr In.)	51·29 N	7·13 E
123	Bockum-Hövel (bō′ĸŏŏm-hû′fĕl) Ger. (Ruhr In.)	51·41 N	7·45 E
135	Bodaybo (bō-dī′bō) . . . Sov. Un.	57·12 N	114·46 E
165	Bodele Depression (bō-dȧ-lā′) Chad	17·21 N	16·38 E
112	Boden . . . Swe.	65·51 N	21·29 E
120	Boden See (L.) (bō′dĕn zā) . . . Ger.	47·48 N	9·22 E
168	Bodenstein (bō′dĕn-stān) S. Afr. (Johannesburg & Pretoria In.)	26·20 S	26·27 E
116	Boderg (bō′dûrg) . . . Ire.	53·51 N	8·06 W
116	Bodmin (bŏd′mĭn) . . . Eng.	50·29 N	4·45 W
116	Bodmin Moor (bŏd′mĭn mŏŏr) Eng.	50·36 N	4·43 W
112	Bodö (bôd′û) . . . Nor.	67·13 N	14·19 E
166	Boende (bō-ĕn′dȧ) . . . Con. L.	0·21 S	21·06 E
76	Boerne (bō′ĕrn) . . . Tex.	29·49 N	98·44 W
77	Boeuf R. (bĕf) . . . La.	32·23 N	91·57 W
164	Boffa (bôf′ȧ) . . . Gui.	10·13 N	14·06 W
153	Bōfu (bō′fōō) . . . Jap.	34·03 N	131·35 E
77	Bogalusa (bō-gȧ-lōō′sȧ) . . . La.	30·48 N	82·52 W
160	Bogan (R.) (bō′gĕn) . . . Austl.	32·10 S	147·40 E
118	Bogense (bō′gĕn-sĕ) . . . Den.	55·34 N	10·09 E
93	Boggy Pk. (bŏg′ĭ-pēk) Antigua (Le. & Wind. Is. In.)	17·03 N	61·50 W
125	Boghari (bō-gȧ-rē′) (bō-gä′rê) . Alg.	35·50 N	2·48 E
129	Bogodukhov (bŏ-gŏ-dōō′ĸôf) Sov. Un.	50·10 N	35·31 E
160	Bogong, Mt . . . Austl.	36·50 S	147·15 E
154	Bogor . . . Indon.	6·45 S	106·45 E
128	Bogoroditsk (bŏ-gŏ′rô-dĭtsk) Sov. Un.	53·48 N	38·06 E
132	Bogorodsk . . . Sov. Un.	56·02 N	43·40 E
136	Bogorodskoye (bô-gô-rôd′skô-yĕ) Sov. Un. (Urals In.)	56·43 N	56·53 E
98	Bogotá (bō-gō-tä′) . . . Col. (In.)	4·38 N	74·06 W
98	Bogotá, Rio (R.) (rê′ō-bō-gō-tä′) Col. (In.)	4·27 N	74·38 W
134	Bogotol (bŏ′gô-tŏl) . . . Sov. Un.	56·13 N	89·13 E
129	Bogoyavlenskoye (bŏ′gô-yäf′lĕn-skō′yĕ) . Sov. Un	48·46 N	33·19 E
133	Boguchar (bō′gŏŏ-chär) . . Sov. Un.	49·40 N	41·00 E
93	Boguete (bô-gĕ′tĕ) . . . Pan.	8·54 N	82·29 W
129	Boguslav (bō′gŏŏ-släf) . . . Sov. Un.	49·34 N	30·51 E
122	Bohain-en-Vermandois (bô-ăɴ-ŏɴ-vâr-mäɴ-dwä′) . Fr.	49·58 N	3·22 E
	Bohemia, see Ceske		
120	Bohemian For. (bô-hē′mĭ-ăn) . Ger.	49·35 N	12·27 E
155	Bohol (I.) (bô-hôl′) . . . Phil.	9·28 N	124·35 E
91	Bohom (bŏ-ô′m) . . . Mex.	16·47 N	92·42 W
168	Bohotleh (bô-hŏt′lĕ) Som. (Horn of Afr. In.)	8·15 N	46·20 E
82	Boiestown (boiz′toun) . . . Can.	46·27 N	66·25 W
127	Boin (R.) (bô′ên) . . . Yugo.	44·19 N	17·54 E
80	Bois Blanc (I.) (boi′ blăŋk) . Mich.	45·45 N	84·30 W
85	Boischatel (bwä-shä-tĕl′) Can. (Quebec In.)	46·54 N	71·08 W
85	Bois-des-Filion (bōō-ä′dĕ-fē-yōɴ′) Can. (Montreal In.)	45·40 N	73·46 W
66	Boise (boi′zē) . . . Idaho	43·38 N	116·12 W
72	Boise City . . . Okla.	36·42 N	102·30 W
66	Boise R. . . . Idaho	43·43 N	116·30 W
86	Boissevain (bois′vān) . . . Can.	49·11 N	100·01 W
145	Boizabād . . . Afg.	37·13 N	70·38 E
164	Bojador, Cabo (C.) (kȧ′bô-bō-hä-dōr′) (bŏj-ȧ-dōr′) . Sp. Sah.	26·21 N	16·08 W
164	Boké (bō-kā′) . . . Gui.	10·58 N	14·15 W
118	Bokn Fd. (bôk′′n fyôrd) . . . Nor.	59·12 N	5·37 E
167	Boksburg (bŏĸs′bûrgh) . . . S. Afr. (Johannesburg & Pretoria In.)	26·13 S	28·15 E
164	Bolama (bô-lä′mä) . . . Port. Gui.	11·34 N	15·41 W
142	Bolan Mt. (bô-län′) . . . W. Pak.	35·13 N	67·09 E
90	Bolaños (bō-län′yôs) . . . Mex.	21·40 N	103·48 W
90	Bolaños (R.) . . . Mex.	21·26 N	103·54 W
142	Bolan P. . . . W. Pak.	34·50 N	67·10 E
122	Bolbec (bôl-bĕk′) . . . Fr.	49·37 N	0·26 E
164	Bole (bō′lȧ) . . . Ghana	9·02 N	2·28 W
120	Boleslawiec (bō-lĕ-slä′vyĕts) . . Pol.	51·15 N	15·35 E
129	Bolgrad (bŏl-grȧt) . . . Sov. Un.	45·41 N	28·38 E
155	Bolinao (bō-lê-nä′ô) Phil. (Manila In.)	16·24 N	119·53 E
155	Bolinao, C. . . . Phil. (Manila In.)	16·24 N	119·42 E
101	Bolívar (bô-lē′vär) Arg. (Buenos Aires In.)	36·15 S	61·05 W
98	Bolívar . . . Col.	1·46 N	76·58 W
73	Bolivar (bŏl′ĭ-vȧr) . . . Mo.	37·37 N	93·22 W
78	Bolivar . . . Tenn.	35·14 N	88·56 W
98	Bolívar, Cerro (Mts.) (sĕr-rô-bô-lē′vär) . Ven.	6·25 N	64·52 W
98	Bolívar (La Columna) (Mtn.) (bô-lē′vär) (lä-kô-lōō′m-nä) . Ven.	8·44 N	70·54 W
77	Bolivar Pen. (bŏl′ĭ-vȧr) . Tex. (In.)	29·25 N	94·40 W
96	Bolivia (bô-lĭv′ĭ-ȧ) . . . S. A.	17·00 S	64·00 W
128	Bolkhov (bŏl-ĸôf′) . . . Sov. Un.	53·27 N	35·59 E
110	Bollin (R.) (bŏl′ĭn) . . . Eng.	53·18 N	2·11 W
110	Bollington (bôl′ĭng-tŭn) . . . Eng.	53·18 N	2·06 W
118	Bollnäs (bôl′nĕs) . . . Swe.	61·22 N	16·20 E
118	Bolmen (L.) (bôl′mĕn) . . . Swe.	56·58 N	13·25 E
166	Bolobo (bō′lô-bô) . . . Con. L.	2·14 S	16·18 E
126	Bologna (bô-lōn′yä) . . . It.	44·30 N	11·18 E
128	Bologoye (bŏ-lŏ-gô′yĕ) . . . Sov. Un.	57·52 N	34·02 E
92	Bolonchenticul (bô-lôn-chĕn-tē-kōō′l) . Mex. (Yucatan In.)	20·03 N	89·47 W
94	Bolondrón (bô-lôn-drōn′) . . . Cuba	22·45 N	81·25 W
126	Bolseno, Lago di (L.) (lä′gō-dē-bôl-sā′nô) . It.	42·35 N	11·40 E
132	Bol'shaya Kinel' (R.) . . . Sov. Un.	53·20 N	52·40 E
129	Bol'shaya Lepetikha (bŏl-shȧ′ yȧ lyĕ′pyĕ-tē′ĸȧ) . Sov. Un.	47·11 N	33·58 E
129	Bol'shaya Viska (vĭs-kä′) . Sov. Un.	48·34 N	31·54 E
129	Bol'shaya Vradiyevka (vrȧ-dyĕf′kȧ) . Sov. Un.	47·51 N	30·38 E
136	Bol'she Ust'ikinskoye (bôl′she ŏŏs-tyĭ-kēn′skô-yĕ) Sov. Un. (Urals In.)	55·58 N	58·18 E
135	Bolshoy Anyuy (R.) . . . Sov. Un.	67·58 N	161·15 E
135	Bol'shoy Begichëv (I.) . . . Sov. Un.	74·30 N	114·40 E
135	Bolshoy Chuva (R.) . . . Sov. Un.	58·15 N	111·13 E
136	Bol'shoye Ivonino (ĭ-vô′nĭ-nô) Sov. Un. (Urals In.)	59·41 N	61·12 E
136	Bol'shoy Kuyash (bôl′-shôy kōō′yȧsh) . Sov. Un. (Urals In.)	55·52 N	61·07 E
129	Bolshoy Tokmak (bŏl-shôy′ tôk-mäk′) . Sov. Un.	47·17 N	35·48 E
76	Bolson de Mapimi (bôl-sŏ′n-dĕ-mä-pē′mē) . Mex.	28·07 N	104·30 W
110	Bolsover (bōl′zô-vĕr) . . . Eng.	53·14 N	1·17 W
125	Boltana (bôl-tä′nä) . . . Sp.	42·28 N	0·03 E
85	Bolton (bōl′tŭn) . Can. (Toronto In.)	43·53 N	79·44 W
110	Bolton . . . Eng.	53·35 N	2·26 W
110	Bolton-on-Dearne (bōl′tŭn-ŏn-dûrn) . Eng.	53·31 N	1·19 W
133	Bolu (bō′lōō) . . . Tur.	40·45 N	31·45 E
128	Bolva (R.) (bôl′vä) . . . Sov. Un.	53·30 N	34·30 E
133	Bolvadin (bŏl-vä-dēn′) . . . Tur.	38·50 N	30·50 E
126	Bolzano (bôl-tsä′nō) . . . It.	46·29 N	9·22 E
166	Boma (bō′mä) . . . Con. L.	5·45 S	13·05 E
160	Bombala (bŭm-bä′lă) . . . Austl.	36·55 S	149·07 E
143	Bombay (bŏm-bā′) India (Bombay In.)	18·58 N	72·50 E
142	Bombay (State) . . . India	27·20 N	72·56 E
143	Bombay Hbr . India (Bombay In.)	18·55 N	72·52 E
164	Bomi Hills . . . Lib.	7·00 N	11·00 W
101	Bom Jardim (bôn zhär-dēɴ′) Braz. (Rio de Janeiro In.)	22·10 S	42·25 W
101	Bom Jesus do Itabapoana (bôɴ-zhĕ-sōō′s-dô-ē-tȧ′bä-pô-ȧ′nä) Braz. (Rio de Janeiro In.)	21·08 S	41·51 W
118	Bömlo (I.) (bûmlô) . . . Nor.	59·47 N	4·57 E
165	Bomongo . . . Con. L.	1·35 N	18·20 E
101	Bom Sucesso (bôɴ-sōō-sĕ′sŏ) Braz. (Rio de Janeiro In.)	21·02 S	44·44 W
113	Bon, C. (bôɴ) . . . Tun.	37·04 N	11·13 E
98	Bonaire (I.) (bô-nâr′) Neth. Antilles	12·10 N	68·15 W
124	Boñar (bō-nyär′) . . . Sp.	42·53 N	5·18 W
83	Bonavista (bŏ-nȧ-vĭs′tȧ) . . . Can.	48·38 N	53·09 W
83	Bonavista B . . . Can.	48·48 N	53·20 W
72	Bond (bŏnd) . . . Colo.	39·53 N	106·40 W
165	Bondo (bôn′dô) . . . Con. L.	3·49 N	23·43 E
155	Bondoc Pen. (bôn-dŏk′) Phil. (Manila In.)	13·24 N	122·30 E
155	Bondoc Pt . . . Phil. (Manila In.)	13·11 N	122·20 E
164	Bondoukou (bŏn-dōō′kōō) Ivory Coast	8·06 N	3·47 W
94	Bonds Cay (I.) (bŏnds kē) . Ba. Is.	25·30 N	77·45 W
164	Bone (bōn) . . . Alg.	36·57 N	7·39 E
154	Bonė, Teluk (L.) . . . Indon.	4·09 S	121·00 E
101	Bonfim (bôɴ-fē′ɴ) Braz. (Rio de Janeiro In.)	20·20 S	44·15 W
165	Bongos, Massif des (Mts.) Cen. Afr. Rep.	8·04 N	21·59 E
151	Bong Son . . . Viet.	14·20 N	109·10 E
73	Bonham (bŏn′ăm) . . . Tex.	33·35 N	96·09 W
95	Bonhomme, Pic (Pk.) . . . Hai.	19·10 N	72·20 W
126	Bonifacio (bō-nê-fä′chō) . . . Fr.	41·23 N	9·10 E
126	Bonifacio, Str. of . . . Eur.	41·14 N	9·02 E
78	Bonifay (bŏn-ĭ-fā′) . . . Fla.	30·46 N	85·40 W
156	Bonin Is. (bō′nĭn) . . . Asia	26·30 N	141·00 E
123	Bonn (bôn) . . . Ger. (Ruhr In.)	50·44 N	7·06 E
66	Bonners Ferry (bon′erz fĕr′ĭ) Idaho	48·41 N	116·19 W
74	Bonner Springs (bŏn′ēr sprĭngz) Kans. (Kansas City In.)	39·04 N	94·52 W
73	Bonne Terre (bŏn târ′) . . . Mo.	37·55 N	90·32 W
66	Bonneville Dam (bôn′ê-vĭl) Wash.-Ore.	45·37 N	121·57 W
83	Bonnie B. (bôn′ê) . . . Can.	49·38 N	58·15 W
164	Bonny (bŏn′ê) . . . Nig.	4·29 N	7·13 E
65	Bonny Lake (bŏn′ê lăk) Wash. (Seattle In.)	47·11 N	122·11 W
126	Bonorva (bô-nôr′vä) . . . It.	40·26 N	8·46 E
154	Bonthain (bôn-tīn′) . . . Indon.	5·30 S	119·52 E
155	Bontoc (bôn-tŏk′) Phil. (Manila In.)	17·10 N	121·01 E
94	Booby Rocks (I.) (bōō′bĭ rŏks) Ba. Is.	25·55 N	77·00 W
79	Booker T. Washington Natl. Mon. (bŏŏk′ĕr tē wŏsh′ĭng-tŭn) . Va.	37·07 N	79·45 W
111	Boom . . . Bel. (Brussels In.)	51·05 N	4·22 E
71	Boone (bōōn) . . . Iowa	42·04 N	93·51 W
84	Boone . . . Va. (Norfolk In.)	36·50 N	76·26 W
73	Booneville (bōōn′vĭl) . . . Ark.	35·09 N	93·54 W
80	Booneville . . . Ky.	37·25 N	83·40 W
78	Booneville . . . Miss.	34·37 N	88·35 W
168	Boons . . . S. Afr. (Johannesburg & Pretoria In.)	25·59 S	27·15 E
84	Boonton (bōōn′tŭn) N. J. (New York In.)	40·54 N	74·24 W
80	Boonville . . . Ind.	38·00 N	87·15 W
73	Boonville . . . Mo.	38·57 N	92·44 W
82	Boothbay Harbor (bōōth′bā här′bĕr) . Maine	43·51 N	69·39 W
87	Boothia, G. of (bōō′thĭ-ȧ) . . . Can.	69·04 N	86·04 W
49	Boothia Pen . . . Can.	73·30 N	95·00 W
84	Boothville (bōōth′vĭl) La. (New Orleans In.)	29·21 N	89·25 W
110	Bootle (bōōt′l) . . . Eng.	53·29 N	3·02 W
164	Boporo (bô-pō′rō) . . . Lib.	7·13 N	10·47 W
120	Boppard (bôp′ärt) . . . Ger.	50·14 N	7·35 E
165	Bor (bôr) . . . Sud.	6·13 N	31·35 E
133	Bor (bōr) . . . Tur.	37·50 N	34·40 E
67	Borah Pk. (bō′rä) . . . Idaho	44·12 N	113·47 W
168	Borama (bôr-á-mă) Som. (Horn of Afr. In.)	10·05 N	43·08 E
118	Borås (bŏŏ′rōs) . . . Swe.	57·43 N	12·55 E
144	Borāzjān (bō-räz-jän′) . . . Iran	29·13 N	51·13 E
99	Borba (bôr′bä) . . . Braz.	4·23 S	59·31 W
99	Borborema, Planalto da (Plat.) (plä-nȧl′tô-dä-bôr-bō-rĕ′mä) Braz.	7·35 S	36·40 W
122	Bordeaux (bôr-dō′) . . . Fr.	44·50 N	0·37 W
81	Bordentown (bôr′dĕn-toun) . . N. J.	40·05 N	74·40 W
113	Bordj-bou-Arréridj (bôrj-bōō-ȧ-rā-rēj′) . Alg.	36·03 N	4·48 E
119	Borgå (bôr′gō) . . . Fin.	60·26 N	25·41 E
112	Borgarnes . . . Ice.	64·31 N	21·40 W
72	Borger (bôr′gĕr) . . . Tex.	35·40 N	101·23 W
118	Borgholm (bôrg-hŏlm′) . . . Swe.	56·52 N	16·40 E
77	Borgne L. (bôrn′y′) . . . La.	30·03 N	89·36 W
126	Borgomanero (bôr′gō-mă-nâ′rō) . It.	45·40 N	8·28 E
125	Borgo Montello (bô′r-zhō-môn-tĕ′lō) It. (Rome In.)	41·31 N	12·48 E
126	Borgo Val di Taro (bô′r-zhō-väl-dē-tȧ′rō) . It.	44·29 N	9·44 E
65	Boring (bōr ĭng) Ore. (Portland In.)	45·26 N	122·22 W
121	Borislav (bô′rĭs-lôf) . . . Sov. Un.	49·17 N	23·24 E
133	Borisoglebsk (bŏ-rē sô-glyĕpsk′) Sov. Un.	51·20 N	42·00 E
128	Borisov (bŏ-rē′sôf) . . . Sov. Un.	54·16 N	28·33 E
129	Borisovka (bŏ-rē-sôf′kȧ) . Sov. Un.	50·38 N	36·00 E
129	Borispol' (bo-rĭs′pol) . . . Sov. Un.	50·17 N	30·54 E
143	Borivli . . . India (Bombay In.)	19·15 N	72·48 E
124	Borja (bôr′hä) . . . Sp.	41·50 N	1·33 W
125	Borjas Blancas (bô′r-ĸäs-blä′n-käs) . Sp.	41·29 N	0·53 E
123	Borken (bōr′kĕn) . Ger. (Ruhr In.)	51·50 N	6·51 E
165	Borkou (Reg.) (bôr-kōō′) . . . Chad.	18·11 N	18·28 E
120	Borkum I. (bōr′kōōm) . . . Ger.	53·31 N	6·50 E
118	Borlänge (bôr-lĕŋ′gĕ) . . . Swe.	60·30 N	15·24 E
154	Borneo (I.) (bôr′nê-ō) . . . Asia	0·25 N	112·39 E
118	Bornholm (I.) (bôrn-hôlm) . . . Den.	55·16 N	15·15 E
124	Bornos (bôr′nōs) . . . Sp.	36·48 N	5·45 W
164	Bornu (Reg.) . . . Nig.	11·13 N	12·15 E
129	Borodayevka . . . Sov. Un.	48·44 N	34·09 E
129	Boromlya (bŏ-rôm′′l-yä) . Sov. Un.	50·36 N	34·58 E
127	Borovan (bŏ-rô-vän′) . . . Bul.	43·24 N	23·47 E
128	Borovichi (bŏ-rô-vē′chê) . Sov. Un.	58·22 N	33·56 E
128	Borovsk (bô′rŏvsk) . . . Sov. Un.	55·13 N	36·26 E
99	Borracha, Isla la (I.) (ê′s-lä-lȧ-bôr-rȧ′chä) . Ven. (In.)	10·18 N	64·44 W
158	Borroloola (bŏr-rô-lōō′lȧ) . . . Austl.	16·15 S	136·19 E
121	Borshchëv (bôrsh-chyôf′) . Sov. Un.	48·47 N	26·04 E
122	Bort-les-Orgues (bôr-lā-zôrg) . . . Fr.	45·26 N	2·26 E
144	Borūjerd . . . Iran	33·45 N	48·53 E

ng-sing; ŋ-baŋk; ɴ-nasalized n; nŏd; cŏmmit; ōld; ôbey; ôrder; fōōd; fŏŏt; ou-out; s-soft; sh-dish; th-thin; pūre; ûnite; ûrn; stŭd; circŭs; ü-as "y" in study; ′-indeterminate vowel.

Page	Name Pronunciation Region	Lat. °′	Long. °′
129	Borzna (bôrz'nȧ) Sov. Un.	51·15 N	32·26 E
135	Borzya (bôrz'yȧ) Sov. Un.	50·37 N	116·53 E
126	Bosa (bō'sä) It.	40·18 N	8·34 E
126	Bosanska Dubica (bō'sän-skä dōō'bĭt-sä) Yugo.	45·10 N	16·49 E
126	Bosanska Gradiška (bō'sän-skä grä-dĭsh'kä) Yugo.	45·08 N	17·15 E
126	Bosanski Novi (bō's sän-skĭ nō'vē) Yugo.	45·00 N	16·22 E
126	Bosanski Petrovac (bō'sän-skĭ pĕt'rō-väts) Yugo.	44·33 N	16·23 E
127	Bosanski Šamac (bō'sän-skĭ shä'mȧts) Yugo.	45·03 N	18·30 E
71	Boscobel (bŏs'kō-bĕl) Wis.	43·08 N	90·44 W
136	Boskol' (bàs-kôl') Sov. Un. (Urals In.)	53·45 N	61·17 E
111	Boskoop Neth. (Amsterdam In.)	52·04 N	4·39 E
120	Boskovice (bŏs'kō-vē-tsĕ) Czech.	49·26 N	16·37 E
127	Bosnia (Reg.) (bŏs'nĭ-ȧ) Yugo.	44·17 N	16·58 E
	Bosporous, see Karadeniz Boğazi		
77	Bossier City (bŏsh'ēr) La.	32·31 N	93·42 W
78	Boston (bôs'tŭn) Ga.	30·47 N	83·47 W
83	Boston Mass. (Boston In.)	42·15 N	71·07 W
75	Boston Heights Ohio (Cleveland In.)	41·15 N	81·30 W
73	Boston Mts. Ark.	35·46 N	93·32 W
161	Botany B. (bŏt'ȧ-nĭ) Austl. (Sydney In.)	33·58 S	151·11 E
127	Botevgrad Bul.	42·54 N	23·41 E
168	Bothaville (bō'tä-vĭl) S. Afr. (Johannesburg & Pretoria In.)	27·24 S	26·38 E
65	Bothell (bŏth'ĕl) Wash. (Seattle In.)	47·46 N	122·12 W
112	Bothnia, G. of (bŏth'nĭ-ȧ) Eur.	61·45 N	19·45 E
121	Botosani (bō-tō-shàn'ĭ) Rom.	47·46 N	26·40 E
70	Bottineau (bŏt-ĭ-nō') N. D.	48·48 N	100·28 W
123	Bottrop (bŏt'trōp) Ger. (Ruhr In.)	51·31 N	6·56 E
99	Botucatú (bô-tōō-kä-tōō') Braz.	22·50 S	48·23 W
83	Botwood (bŏt'wŏŏd) Can.	49·10 N	55·23 W
164	Bouaflé (bōō-ȧ-flā') Ivory Coast	7·23 N	5·32 W
164	Bouaké (bōō-ȧ-kā') Ivory Coast	7·45 N	5·08 W
165	Bouar (bōō-är) Cen. Afr. Rep.	6·04 N	15·34 E
83	Bouche Can.	45·37 N	61·25 W
85	Boucherville (bōō-shā-vēl') Can. (Montreal In.)	45·37 N	73·27 W
164	Bou Denib (bōō-dĕ-nēb') Mor.	32·14 N	3·04 W
71	Boudette (bōō-dĕt) Minn.	48·42 N	94·34 W
113	Bou Dia, C. (bōō dē'ȧ) Tun.	35·18 N	11·17 E
125	Boufarik (bōō-fȧ-rēk') Alg.	36·35 N	2·55 E
156	Bougainville Trench (bōō-găN-vēl') Oceania	7·00 S	152·00 E
164	Bougie (bōō-zhē') Alg.	36·46 N	5·00 E
164	Bougouni (bōō-gōō-nē') Mali	11·27 N	7·30 W
114	Bouira (boo-ē'rȧ) Alg.	36·25 N	3·55 W
125	Bouïra-Sahary (bwē-rȧ sȧ'ȧ-rē) Alg.	35·16 N	3·23 E
158	Boulder (bōl'dēr) Austl.	31·00 S	121·40 E
72	Boulder Colo.	40·02 N	105·19 W
68	Boulder City Nev.	35 57 N	114·50 W
66	Boulder Cr. Idaho	42·53 N	116·49 W
67	Boulder Pk. Idaho	43·53 N	114·33 W
67	Boulder R. Mont.	46·10 N	112·07 W
164	Boulé R. (bōō-lā') Mali	10·53 N	7·30 W
123	Boulogne-Billancourt (bōō-lôn'y'-bē-yäN-kōōr') Fr. (Paris In.)	48·50 N	2·14 E
122	Boulogne-sur-Mer (bōō-lôn'y-sür-mâr') Fr.	50·44 N	1·37 E
125	Bou-Mort, Sierra de (Mts.) (sē-ĕ'r-rä-dĕ-bō-ōō-mō'rt) Sp.	42·11 N	1·05 E
164	Bouna (bōō-nä') Ivory Coast	9·14 N	3·56 W
65	Boundary B. (boun'dȧ-rĭ) Can. (Vancouver In.)	49·03 N	122·59 W
68	Boundary Pk. Nev.	37·52 N	118·20 W
84	Bound Brook (bound brŏŏk) N. J. (New York In.)	40·34 N	74·32 W
74	Bountiful (boun'tĭ-fŏŏl) Utah (Salt Lake City In.)	40·55 N	111·53 W
75	Bountiful Pk. (boun'tĭ-fŏŏl) Utah (Salt Lake City In.)	40·58 N	111·49 W
47	Bounty Is. N. Z.	47·42 S	179·05 E
164	Bourem (bōō-rĕm') Mali	16·43 N	0·15 W
122	Bourg-en-Bresse (bōōr-gĕN-brĕs') Fr.	46·12 N	5·13 E
122	Bourges (bōōrzh) Fr.	47·06 N	2·22 E
85	Bourget (bōōr-zhĕ') Can. (Ottawa In.)	45·26 N	75·09 W
123	Bourgoin (bōōr-gwăN') Fr.	45·46 N	5·17 E
160	Bourke (bûrk) Austl.	30·10 S	146·00 E
135	Bour Khaya, Guba (B.) Sov. Un.	71·45 N	131·00 E
110	Bourne (bôrn) Eng.	52·46 N	0·22 W
116	Bournemouth (bôrn'mŭth) Eng.	50·44 N	1·55 W
114	Bou Saada (bōō-sä'dä) Alg.	35·13 N	4·17 E
165	Bousso (bōō-sō') Chad	10·33 N	16·45 E
164	Boutilimit (bōō-tē-lē-mē') Mauritania	17·30 N	14·54 W
	Bouvet (I.), see Bouvetøya		
47	Bouvetøya (Bouvet) (I.) Atl. O.	54·26 S	3·24 E
126	Bovino (bō-vē'nō) It.	41·14 N	15·21 E
86	Bow (R.) (bō) Can.	50·33 N	112·25 W
70	Bowbells (bō'bĕls) N. D.	48·50 N	102·16 W
70	Bowdle (bōd''l) S. D.	45·28 N	99·42 W
159	Bowen (bō'ĕn) Austl.	20·02 S	148·14 E
84	Bowers Hill (bou'ērs) Va. (Norfolk In.)	36·47 N	76·25 W
72	Bowie (bōō'ĭ) (bō'ē) Tex.	33·34 N	97·50 W
78	Bowling Green (bōlĭng grēn) Ky.	37·00 N	86·26 W
73	Bowling Green Mo.	39·19 N	91·09 W
80	Bowling Green Ohio	41·25 N	83·40 W
70	Bowman (bō'măn) N. D.	46·11 N	103·23 W
81	Bowmanville (bō'măn-vĭl) Can.	43·50 N	78·40 W
85	Bowness Can. (Calgary In.)	51·06 N	114·13 W
155	Bowokan, Pulau-Pulau (Is.) Indon.	2·20 S	123·45 E
70	Boxelder Cr. (bŏks'ĕl-dēr) Mont.	45·35 N	104·28 W
67	Boxelder Cr. Mont.	47·17 N	108·37 W
74	Box Springs (bŏks sprĭngz) Calif (Los Angeles In.)	33·55 N	117·17 W
111	Boxtel Neth. (Amsterdam In.)	51·40 N	5·21 E
85	Boyer, R. (boi'ēr) Can. (Quebec In.)	46·46 N	70·56 W
70	Boyer (R.) Iowa	41·45 N	95·36 W
116	Boyle (boil) Ire.	53·59 N	8·15 W
80	Boyne City Mich.	45·15 N	85·05 W
116	Boyne R. (boin) Ire.	53·40 N	6·40 W
127	Bozcaada (Tenedos) (bōz-cä'dä) (tĕ'nĕ-dŏs) Tur.	39·50 N	26·05 E
127	Bozcaada (I.) (bōz-cä'dä) Tur.	39·50 N	26·00 E
67	Bozemen (bōz'măn) Mont.	45·41 N	111·00 W
126	Bra (brä) It.	44·41 N	7·52 E
126	Brač (I.) (bräch) Yugo.	43·18 N	16·36 E
126	Bracciano, Lago di (L.) (lä'gō-dē-brä-chä'nō) It.	42·05 N	12·00 E
81	Bracebridge (brās'brĭj) Can.	45·05 N	79·20 W
75	Braceville (brās'vĭl) Ill. (Chicago In.)	41·13 N	88·16 W
118	Bräcke (brĕk'kĕ) Swe.	62·44 N	15·28 E
75	Brackenridge (brăk'ĕn-rĭj) Pa. (Pittsburgh In.)	40·37 N	79·44 W
76	Brackettville (brăk'ĕt-vĭl) Tex.	29·19 N	100·24 W
99	Braço Maior (R.) Braz.	11·00 S	51·00 W
99	Braço Menor (R.) (brä'zō-mĕ-nō'r) Braz.	11·38 S	50·00 W
126	Brádano (R.) (brä-dä'nō) It.	40·43 N	16·22 E
75	Braddock (brăd'ŭk) Pa. (Pittsburgh In.)	40·24 N	79·52 W
79	Bradenton (brā'dĕn-tŭn) Fla. (In.)	27·28 N	82·35 W
110	Bradfield (brăd-fēld) Eng. (London In.)	51·25 N	1·08 W
110	Bradford (brăd'fērd) Eng.	53·47 N	1·44 W
80	Bradford Ohio	40·10 N	84·30 W
81	Bradford Pa.	42·00 N	78·40 W
75	Bradley (brăd'lĭ) Ill. (Chicago In.)	41·09 N	87·52 W
65	Bradner (brăd'nēr) Can. (Vancouver In.)	49·05 N	122·26 W
76	Brady (brā'dĭ) Tex.	31·09 N	99·21 W
124	Braga (brä'gä) Port.	41·20 N	8·25 W
101	Bragado (brä-gä'dō) Arg. (Buenos Aires In.)	35·07 S	60·28 W
99	Bragança (brä-gän'sä) Braz.	1·02 S	46·50 W
124	Bragança Port.	41·48 N	6·46 W
101	Bragança Paulista (brä-gän'sä-pä'ōō-lē's-tà) Braz. (Rio de Janeiro In.)	22·58 S	46·31 W
85	Bragg Creek (brăg) Can. (Calgary In.)	50·57 N	114·35 W
145	Brahmaputra (R.) (brä'mȧ-pōō'trȧ) India	26·45 N	92·45 E
145	Brahui (Reg.) W. Pak.	28·32 N	66·15 E
75	Braidwood (brād'wŏŏd) Ill. (Chicago In.)	41·16 N	88·13 W
129	Brăila (brē'ēlà) Rom.	45·15 N	27·58 E
71	Brainerd (brān'ērd) Minn.	46·20 N	94·09 W
83	Braintree (brān'trē) Mass. (Boston In.)	42·14 N	71·00 W
84	Braithwaite (brīth'wĭt) La. (New Orleans In.)	29·52 N	89·57 W
167	Brakpan (brăk'păn) S. Afr. (Johannesburg & Pretoria In.)	26·15 S	28·22 E
168	Brakspruit S. Afr. (Johannesburg & Pretoria In.)	26·41 S	26·3[illegible] E
85	Brampton (brămp'tŭn) Can. (Toronto In.)	43·41 N	79·46 W
100	Branca, Pedra (Mtn.) (pĕ'drä-brä'N-kä) Braz. (In.)	22·55 S	43·28 W
84	Branchville (brănch'vĭl) N. J. (New York In.)	41·09 N	74·44 W
79	Branchville S. C.	33·17 N	80·48 W
99	Branco (R.) (brăŋ'kō) Braz.	2·21 N	60·38 W
166	Brandberg (Mtn.) S. W. Afr.	21·15 S	14·15 E
111	Brandenburg (brän'dĕn-bōōrgh) Ger. (Berlin In.)	52·25 N	12·33 E
120	Brandenburg (Reg.) Ger.	52·12 N	13·31 E
168	Brandfort (brănd-fôrt) S. Afr. (Johannesburg & Pretoria In.)	28·42 S	26·29 E
86	Brandon (brăn'dŭn) Can.	49·42 N	99·53 W
81	Brandon Vt.	43·45 N	73·05 W
116	Brandon Hill (brăn-dŏn) Ire.	52·15 N	10·12 W
81	Branford (brăn'fērd) Conn.	41·15 N	72·50 W
121	Braniewo (brä-nyĕ'vō) Pol.	54·23 N	19·50 E
168	Brankhorstspruit S. Afr. (Johannesburg & Pretoria In.)	24·47 S	28·45 E
121	Brańsk (brän' sk) Pol.	52·44 N	22·51 E
85	Brantford (brănt'fērd) Can. (Toronto In.)	43·09 N	80·17 W
83	Bras d'Or L. (brä-dôr') Can.	45·53 N	60·47 W
99	Brasília (brä-sē'lyä) Braz.	15·49 S	47·39 W
99	Brasilia Legal (Fordlândia) (brä-sē'lyä-lĕ-gäl) (fō'rd-län-dyä) Braz.	3·45 S	55·46 W
101	Brasópolis (brä-sô'pō-lēs) Braz. (Rio de Janeiro In.)	22·30 S	45·36 W
127	Brașov (Orașul-Stalin) Rom.	45·39 N	25·35 E
164	Brass (brăs) Nig.	4·28 N	6·28 E
111	Brasschaat (bräs'kät) Bel. (Brussels In.)	51·19 N	5·30 E
75	Bratenahl (bră'tĕn-ôl) Ohio (Cleveland In.)	41·34 N	81·36 W
111	Bratislava (brä'tĭs-lä-vä) Czech (Vienna In.)	48·09 N	17·07 E
134	Bratsk (brätsk) Sov. Un.	56·10 N	102·04 E
129	Bratslav (brät'slàf) Sov. Un.	48·48 N	28·59 E
81	Brattleboro (brăt''l-bŭr-ō) Vt.	42·50 N	72·35 W
120	Braunau (brou'nou) Aus.	48·15 N	13·05 E
120	Braunschweig (broun'shvīgh) Ger.	52·16 N	10·32 E
168	Brava (brä'vä) Som. (Horn of Afr. In.)	1·20 N	44·00 E
118	Bråviken (R.) Swe.	58·40 N	16·40 E
	Bravo del Norte, Rio, see Grande, Rio		
68	Brawley (brô'lĭ) Calif.	32·59 N	115·32 W
116	Bray (brā) Ire.	53·10 N	6·05 W
73	Braymer (brā'mēr) Mo.	39·34 N	93·47 W
77	Brays Bay. (brās'bī'yōō) Tex. (In.)	29·41 N	95.33 W
86	Brazeau Can.	52·31 N	116·00 W
80	Brazil (brȧ-zĭl') Ind.	39·30 N	87·00 W
96	Brazil S. A.	9·00 S	53·00 W
96	Brazilian Highlands (Mts.) (brȧ zĭl yȧn hī-lăndz) Braz.	14·00 S	48·00 W
62	Brazos (R.) (brä'zōs) U. S.	33·10 N	98·50 W
76	Brazos (R.), Clear Fk. Tex.	32·56 N	99·14 W
72	Brazos (R.), Double Mountain Fk. Tex.	33·23 N	101·21 W
72	Brazos (R.), Salt Fk. (sôlt fôrk) Tex.	33·20 N	100·57 E
166	Brazzaville (brȧ-zȧ-vēl') Con. B.	4·10 S	15·18 E
127	Brčko (bĕrch'kō) Yugo.	44·54 N	18·46 E
121	Brda R. (bĕr-dä') Pol.	53·18 N	17·55 E
74	Brea (brē'ȧ) Calif. (Los Angeles In.)	33·55 N	117·54 W
85	Breakeyville Can. (Quebec In.)	46·40 N	71·13 W
70	Breckenridge (brĕk'ĕn-rĭj) Minn.	46·17 N	96·35 W
76	Breckenridge Tex.	32·46 N	98·53 W
75	Brecksville (brĕks'vĭl) Ohio (Cleveland In.)	41·19 N	81·38 W
120	Breclav (brzhĕl'làf) Czech.	48·46 N	16·54 E
116	Brecon Beacons (brĕk'ŭn bē kŭns) Wales	52·00 N	3·55 W
111	Breda (brā-dä') Neth. (Amsterdam In.)	51·35 N	4·47 E
166	Bredasdorp (brā'das-dôrp) S. Afr.	34·15 S	20·00 E
136	Bredy (brĕ'dĭ) Sov. Un. (Urals In.)	52·25 N	60·23 E
120	Bregenz (brā'gĕnts) Aus.	47·30 N	9·46 E
127	Bregovo (brĕ'gō-vō) Yugo.	44·07 N	22·45 E
167	Breidbach (brĕd'băk) S. Afr. (Natal In.)	32·54 S	27·26 E
112	Breidha Fd. (brā'dĭ) Ice.	65·15 N	22·50 W
123	Breil (brĕ'y') Fr.	43·57 N	7·36 E
99	Brejo (brâ'zhŏŏ) Braz.	3·33 S	42·46 W
118	Bremangerland (I.) (brĕ-măngĕr-lănd) Nor.	61·51 N	4·25 E
120	Bremen (brā-mĕn) Ger.	53·05 N	8·50 E
80	Bremen (brē'mĕn) Ind.	41·25 N	86·05 W
120	Bremerhaven (brām-ĕr-hä'fĕn) Ger.	53·33 N	8·38 E
65	Bremerton (brĕm'ēr-tŭn) Wash. (Seattle In.)	47·34 N	122·38 W
111	Bremervörde (brĕ'mĕr-fûr-dĕ) Ger. (Hamburg In.)	53·29 N	9·09 E
85	Bremner (brĕm'nēr) Can (Edmonton In.)	53·34 N	113·14 W
77	Bremond (brĕm'ŭnd) Tex.	31·11 N	96·40 W
77	Brenham (brĕn'ăm) Tex.	30·10 N	96·24 W
120	Brenner P. (brĕn'ēr) Aus.-It.	47·00 N	11·30 E
110	Brentwood (brĕnt'wŏŏd) Eng. (London In.)	51·37 N	0·18 E
81	Brentwood Md.	39·00 N	76·55 W
74	Brentwood Mo. (St. Louis In.)	38·37 N	90·21 W
75	Brentwood Pa. (Pittsburgh In.)	40·22 N	79·59 W
126	Brescia (brā'shä) It.	45·33 N	10·15 E
	Breslau, see Wrocław		
126	Bressanone (brĕs-sä-nō'nā) It.	46·42 N	11·40 E
122	Bressuire (brĕ-swēr') Fr.	46·49 N	0·14 W
122	Brest (brĕst) Fr.	48·24 N	4·30 W
121	Brest Sov. Un.	52·06 N	23·43 E
128	Brest (Oblast) Sov. Un.	52·30 N	26·50 E
122	Bretagne, Monts de (Mts.) (mŏN-dĕ-brĕ-tăN'yĕ) Fr.	48·25 N	3·36 W
122	Breton, Pertvis (Str.) (pâr-twĕ'brĕ-tôN') Fr.	46·18 N	1·43 W
84	Breton I. (brĕt'ŭn) La. (New Orleans In.)	29·27 N	89·10 W
77	Breton Sd. (brĕt'ŭn) La.	29·38 N	89·15 W
85	Bretona (brĕ-tō'nä) Can. (Edmonton In.)	53·27 N	113·20 W
111	Breukelen Neth. (Amsterdam In.)	52·09 N	5·00 E
78	Brevard (brē-värd') N. C.	35·14 N	82·45 W
99	Breves (brā'vĕzh) Braz.	1·32 S	50·13 W
118	Brevik (brĕ'vĕk) Nor.	59·04 N	9·39 E
160	Brewarrina (brōō-ēr-rē'nȧ) Austl.	29·54 S	146·50 E
82	Brewer (brōō'ēr) Maine	44·46 N	68·46 W
84	Brewster (brōō'stēr) N. Y. (New York In.)	41·23 N	73·38 W
93	Brewster, Cerro (Mt.) (sĕ'r-rō-brōō'stēr) Pan.	9·19 N	79·15 W
78	Brewton (brōō'tŭn) Ala.	31·06 N	87·04 W
126	Brežice (brĕ'zhē-tsĕ) Yugo.	45·55 N	15·37 E
127	Breznik (brĕs'nĕk) Bul.	42·44 N	22·55 E
123	Briancon (brē-än-sôN') Fr.	44·54 N	6·39 E
122	Briare (brē-är') Fr.	47·40 N	2·46 E
65	Bridal Veil (brīd'ăl vāl) Ore. (Portland In.)	45·33 N	122·10 W
94	Bridge Pt. (brĭj) Ba. Is.	25·35 N	76·40 W
78	Bridgeport (brĭj'pôrt) Ala.	34·55 N	85·42 W
84	Bridgeport Conn. (New York In.)	41·12 N	73·12 W
80	Bridgeport Ill.	38·40 N	87·45 W
75	Bridgeport Ind. (Indianapolis In.)	39·44 N	86·18 W
70	Bridgeport Nebr.	41·40 N	103·06 W
80	Bridgeport Ohio	40·00 N	80·45 W
84	Bridgeport Pa. (Philadelphia In.)	40·06 N	75·21 W
72	Bridgeport Tex.	33·13 N	97·46 W
84	Bridgeton (brĭj'tŭn) Ala. (Birmingham In.)	33·27 N	86·39 W
81	Bridgeton N. J.	39·30 N	75·15 W
82	Bridgetown Can.	44·51 N	65·21 W
93	Bridgetown (brĭj' toun) Barbados (Le. & Wind. Is. In.)	13·08 N	59·37 W
75	Bridgeville (brĭj'vĭl) Pa. (Pittsburgh In.)	40·22 N	80·07 W
160	Bridgewater (brĭj'wô-tēr) Austl.	42·50 S	147·28 E
82	Bridgewater Can.	44·24 N	64·34 W
110	Bridgnorth (brĭj'nôrth) Eng.	52·32 N	2·25 W
82	Bridgton (brĭj'tŭn) Maine	44·04 N	70·45 W
116	Bridlington (brĭd'lĭng-tŭn) Eng.	54·06 N	0·10 W

ăt; finăl; rāte; senâte; ärm; àsk; sofȧ; fâre; ch-choose; dh-as th in other; bē; ēvent; bĕt; recĕnt; cratēr; g-go; gh-guttural g; bĭt; ĭ-short neutral; rīde; K-guttural k as ch in German ich;

PRONOUNCING INDEX Brie-Comte-Robert–Burdur 187

Page	Name Pronunciation Region	Lat. °′	Long. °′
123	Brie-Comte-Robert (brē-kôNt-ĕ-rō-bâr′) . Fr. (Paris In.)	48·42 N	2·37 E
111	Brielle . . . . Neth. (Amsterdam In.)	51·54 N	4·08 E
82	Brier (I.) (brī′ẽr) . . . . Can.	44·16 N	66·24 W
78	Brierfield (brī′ẽr-fēld) . . . . Ala.	33·01 N	86·55 W
110	Brierfield (brī′ẽr fēld) . . . . Eng.	53·49 N	2·14 W
110	Brierley Hill (brī′ẽr-lē hĭl) . . . . Eng.	52·28 N	2·07 W
111	Brieselang (brē′zĕ-läng) Ger. (Berlin In.)	52·36 N	12·59 E
123	Briey (brē-ĕ′) . . . . Fr.	49·15 N	5·57 E
120	Brig (brēg) . . . . Switz.	46·17 N	7·59 E
110	Brigg (brĭg) . . . . Eng.	53·33 N	0·29 W
74	Brigham City (brĭg′ăm) Utah (Salt Lake City In.)	41·31 N	112·01 W
110	Brighouse (brĭg′hous) . . . . Eng.	53·42 N	1·47 W
160	Bright (brīt) . . . . Austl.	36·43 S	147·00 E
75	Bright (brīt) . Ind. (Cincinnati In.)	39·13 N	84·51 W
110	Brightlingsea (brī′t-lĭng-sē) Eng. (London In.)	51·50 N	1·00 E
84	Brighton (brīt′ŭn) Ala. (Birmingham In.)	33·27 N	86·56 W
72	Brighton . . . . Colo.	39·58 N	104·49 W
116	Brighton . . . . Eng.	50·47 N	0·07 W
74	Brighton . . . . Ill. (St. Louis In.)	39·03 N	90·08 W
71	Brighton . . . . Iowa	41·11 N	91·47 W
83	Brigus (brĭg′ŭs) . . . . Can.	47·31 N	53·11 W
124	Brihuega (brē-wä′gä) . . . . Sp.	40·32 N	2·52 W
74	Brimley (brĭm lē) Mich. (Sault Ste. Marie In.)	46·24 N	84·34 W
127	Brindisi (brēn′dē-zē) . . . . It.	40·38 N	17·57 E
126	Brinje (brēn′yĕ) . . . . Yugo.	45·00 N	15·08 E
73	Brinkley (brĭŋk′lĭ) . . . . Ark.	34·52 N	91·12 W
65	Brinnon (brĭn′ŭn) Wash. (Seattle In.)	47·41 N	122·54 W
83	Brion (brē-ôN′) . . . . Can.	47·47 N	61·26 W
122	Brioude (brē-ōōd′) . . . . Fr.	45·18 N	3·22 E
160	Brisbane (brĭz′ bȧn) . . . . Austl.	27·30 S	153·10 E
81	Bristol (brĭs′ tŭl) . . . . Conn.	41·40 N	72·55 W
116	Bristol . . . . Eng.	51·29 N	2·39 W
84	Bristol . . . . . Pa. (Philadelphia In.)	40·06 N	74·51 W
84	Bristol . . . . . . R.I. (Providence In.)	41·41 N	71·14 W
79	Bristol . . . . Tenn.	36·35 N	82·10 W
81	Bristol . . . . Vt.	44·10 N	73·00 W
79	Bristol . . . . Va.	36·36 N	82·12 W
75	Bristol . . . . . . Wis. (Milwaukee In.)	42·32 N	88·04 W
64	Bristol B. . . . . Alaska	58·08 N	158·54 W
116	Bristol Chan . . . . Eng.	51·20 N	3·47 E
73	Bristow (brĭs′tō) . . . . Okla.	35·50 N	96·25 W
86	British Columbia (Prov.) (brĭt′ĭsh kŏl′ŭm-bĭ-ȧ) . Can.	56·00 N	124·53 W
99	British Guiana (gē-ä′nȧ) . . . . . S. A.	7·00 N	59·40 W
88	British Honduras (hŏn-dōō′rȧs) N. A.	17·00 N	88·40 W
168	Brits . . S. Afr. (Johannesburg & Pretoria In.)	25·39 S	27·47 E
166	Britstown (brĭts′toun) . . . . . S. Afr.	30·30 S	23·40 E
71	Britt (brĭt) . . . . Iowa	43·05 N	93·47 W
70	Britton (brĭt′ŭn) . . . . S. D.	45·47 N	97·44 W
122	Brive-la-Gaillarde (brēv-lä-gī-yärd′ĕ) . Fr.	45·10 N	1·31 E
124	Briviesca (brē-vyās′kȧ) . . . . Sp.	42·34 N	3·21 W
120	Brno (b′r′nô) . . . . Czech.	49·18 N	16·37 E
94	Broa, Ensenada de la (B.) (ĕn-sĕ-nä′-dä-dĕ-lä-brō′ä) . Cuba	22·30 N	82·00 W
78	Broad (R.) (brôd) . . . . Ga.	34·15 N	83·14 W
79	Broad (R.) . . . . N. C.	35·38 N	82·40 W
161	Broadmeadows (brôd′mĕd-ōz) Austl. (Melbourne In.)	37·40 S	144·53 E
75	Broadview Heights (brôd′vū) Ohio (Cleveland In.)	41·18 N	81·41 W
81	Brockport (brŏk′pōrt) . . . . . . N. Y.	43·15 N	77·55 W
83	Brockton (brŏk′tŭn) Mass. (Boston In.)	42·04 N	71·01 W
81	Brockville (brŏk′vĭl) . . . . Can.	44·35 N	75·40 W
67	Brockway (brŏk′wā) . . . . Mont.	47·24 N	105·41 W
121	Brodnica (brôd′nĭt-sȧ) . . . . Pol.	53·16 N	19·26 E
121	Brody (brô′dĭ) . . . . Sov. Un.	50·05 N	25·10 E
73	Broken Arrow (brō′kĕn ăr′ō) . Okla.	36·03 N	95·48 W
161	Broken B. . . . . Austl. (Sydney In.)	33·34 S	151·20 E
70	Broken Bow (brō′kĕn bō) . . . Nebr.	41·24 N	99·37 W
73	Broken Bow . . . . Okla.	34·02 N	94·43 W
160	Broken Hill (brōk′ĕn) . . . . . . Austl.	31·55 S	141·35 E
166	Broken Hill . . . . N. Rh.	14·18 S	28·28 E
110	Bromley (brŭm′lĭ) Eng. (London In.)	51·23 N	0·01 E
81	Bromptonville (brŭmp′tŭn-vĭl) Can.	45·30 N	72·00 W
118	Brønderslev (brûn′dẽr-slĕv) . . Den.	57·15 N	9·56 E
136	Bronnitsy (brô-nyĭ′tsĭ) Sov. Un. (Moscow In.)	55·26 N	38·16 E
80	Bronson (brŏn′sŭn) . . . . Mich.	41·55 N	85·15 W
85	Bronte (brŏNt) Can. (Toronto In.)	43·24 N	79·43 W
85	Bronte Cr . . . . . Can. (Toronto In.)	43·25 N	79·53 W
79	Brood (R.) (brōōd) . . . . S. C.	34·46 N	81·25 W
85	Brook, The (R.) Can. (Ottawa In.)	45·25 N	75·09 W
75	Brookfield (brŏŏk′fēld) Ill. (Chicago In.)	41·49 N	87·51 W
73	Brookfield . . . . Mo.	39·45 N	93·04 W
84	Brookhaven (brŏŏk′hāv′n) Ga. (Atlanta In.)	33·52 N	84·21 W
78	Brookhaven . . . . Miss.	31·35 N	90·26 W
66	Brookings (brŏŏk′ĭngs) . . . . Ore.	42·04 N	124·16 W
70	Brookings . . . . S. D.	44·18 N	96·47 W
85	Brooklands (brŏŏk′lăndz) Can. (Winnipeg In.)	49·56 N	97·12 W
83	Brookline (brŏŏk′lĭn) Mass. (Boston In.)	42·20 N	71·08 W
83	Brookline . . . . . N. H. (Boston In.)	42·44 N	71·37 W
75	Brooklyn (brŏŏk′lĭn) Ohio (Cleveland In.)	41·26 N	81·44 W
74	Brooklyn Center Minn. (Minneapolis, St. Paul In.)	45·05 N	93·21 W
75	Brook Park (brŏŏk) Ohio (Cleveland In.)	41·24 N	81·50 W
64	Brooks Range (brŏŏks) . . . . Alaska	68·20 N	159·00 W
79	Brooksville (brŏŏks′vĭl) . Fla. (In.)	28·32 N	82·28 W
80	Brookville (brŏŏk′vĭl) . . . . Ind.	39·20 N	85 00 W
81	Brookville . . . . Pa.	41·10 N	79·00 W
78	Brookwood (brŏŏk′wŏŏd) . . . . . Ala.	33·15 N	87·17 W
116	Broom (L.) (brōōm) . . . . Scot.	57·59 N	5·32 W
158	Broome (brōōm) . . . . Austl.	18·00 S	122·15 E
94	Brothers (Is.) (brŭd′hẽrs) . . Ba. Is.	26·05 N	79·00 W
120	Broumov (brōō′môf) . . . . . . Czech.	50·33 N	15·55 E
95	Brown Bk . . . . Ba. Is.	21·30 N	74·35 W
72	Brownfield (broun′fēld) . . . . . . Tex.	33·11 N	102·16 W
110	Brownhills (broun′hĭlz) . . . . . . Eng.	52·38 N	1·55 W
67	Browning (broun′ĭng) . . . . Mont.	48·37 N	113·05 W
75	Brownsboro (brounz′bô-rô) Ky. (Louisville In.)	38·22 N	85·30 W
85	Brownsburg (brouns′bûrg) Can. (Montreal In.)	45·40 N	74·24 W
75	Brownsburg Ind. (Indianapolis In.)	39·51 N	86·23 W
65	Brownsmead (brounz′-mĕd) Ore. (Portland In.)	46·13 N	123·33 W
80	Brownstown (brounz′toun) . . . Ind.	38·50 N	86·00 W
78	Brownsville (brounz′vĭl) . . . . Tenn.	35·35 N	89·15 W
77	Brownsville . . . . Tex.	25·55 N	97·30 W
82	Brownville (broun′vĭl) . . . . . Maine	45·20 N	69·04 W
76	Brownwood (broun′wŏŏd) . . . . Tex.	31·44 N	98·58 W
76	Brownwood L. . . . . Tex.	31·55 N	99·15 W
124	Brozas (brō′thäs) . . . . Sp.	39·37 N	6·44 W
158	Bruce, Mt. (brōōs) . . . . Austl.	22·35 S	118·15 E
78	Bruceton (brōōs′tŭn) . . . . Tenn.	36·02 N	88·14 W
120	Bruchsal (brŏŏk′zäl) . . . . Ger.	49·08 N	8·34 E
120	Bruck (brŏŏk) . . . . Aus.	47·25 N	15·14 E
111	Brück (brük) . . . . Ger. (Berlin In.)	52·12 N	12·45 E
111	Bruck an der Leitha Aus. (Vienna In.)	48·01 N	16·47 E
85	Bruederheim (brōō′dẽr-hīm) Can. (Edmonton In.)	53·47 N	113·56 W
117	Brugge . . . . Bel.	51·13 N	3·05 E
123	Brühl (brül) . . . . . . Ger. (Ruhr In.)	50·49 N	6·54 E
66	Bruneau R. (brōō-nō′) . . . . . . Idaho	42·47 N	115·43 W
154	Brunei . . . . Asia	4·52 N	113·38 E
154	Brunei (brōō-nī′) . . . . Bru.	5·00 N	114·59 E
123	Brünen (brü′nĕn) . Ger. (Ruhr In.)	51·43 N	6·41 E
125	Brunete (brōō-nā′tā) Sp. (Madrid In.)	40·24 N	4·00 W
83	Brunette (I.) (brōō-nĕt′) . . . . . Can.	47·17 N	55·55 W
111	Brunn am Gebirge (brōōn′äm gĕ-bĭr′gĕ) Aus. (Vienna In.)	48·07 N	16·18 E
111	Brunsbüttelkoog (brōōns′büt-tĕl-kōg) . Ger. (Hamburg In.)	53·58 N	9·10 E
79	Brunswick (brŭnz′wĭk) . . . . Ga.	31·08 N	81·30 W
82	Brunswick . . . . Maine	43·54 N	69·57 W
81	Brunswick . . . . Md.	39·20 N	77·35 W
73	Brunswick . . . . Mo.	39·25 N	93·07 W
175	Brunswick . . . Ohio (Cleveland In.)	41·14 N	81·50 W
100	Brunswick, Pen. de . . . . Chile	53·25 S	71·15 W
59	Bruny (I.) (brōō′nē) . . . . Austl.	43·30 S	47·50 E
72	Brush (brŭsh) . . . . Colo.	40·14 N	103·40 W
100	Brusque (brōō′s-kōōĕ) . . . . . . Braz.	27·15 S	48·45 W
74	Brussels (brŭs′ĕls) Ill. (St. Louis In.)	38·57 N	90·36 W
	Brussels, see Bruxelles		
111	Bruxelles (Brussels) (brü-sĕl′) (brŭs′ĕls) . Bel. (Brussels In.)	50·51 N	4·21 E
80	Bryan (brī′ăn) . . . . Ohio	41·25 N	84·30 W
77	Bryan . . . . Tex.	30·40 N	96·22 W
128	Bryansk (b′r-yänsk′) . . . . Sov. Un.	53·12 N	34·23 E
128	Bryansk (Oblast) . . . . Sov. Un.	52·43 N	32·25 E
70	Bryant (brī′ănt) . . . . S. D.	44·35 N	97·29 E
65	Bryant . . . . Wash. (Seattle In.)	48·14 N	122·10 W
69	Bryce Canyon Natl. Park (brīs) Utah	37·35 N	112·15 W
84	Bryn Mawr (brĭn mâr′) Pa. (Philadelphia In.)	40·02 N	75·20 W
78	Bryson City (brīs′ŭn) . . . . N. C.	35·25 N	83·25 W
129	Bryukhovetskaya (b′ryŭk′ô-vyĕt-skä′yä) . Sov. Un.	45·56 N	38·58 E
139	Buatam . . . . Indon. (Singapore In.)	0·45 N	101·49 E
164	Buba (bōō′bȧ) . . . . Port. Gui.	11·39 N	14·58 W
98	Bucaramanga (bōō-kä′rä-mäŋ′gä) Col.	7·12 N	73·14 W
155	Bucay (bōō-ki′) . Phil. (Manila In.)	17·32 N	120·42 E
158	Buccaneer Arch. (bŭk-ȧ-nēr′) Austl.	16·05 S	122·00 E
121	Buchach (bŏŏ′chȧch) . . . . Sov. Un.	49·04 N	25·25 E
164	Buchanan (bû-kăn′ăn) . . . . Lib.	6·05 N	10·10 W
80	Buchanan . . . . Mich.	41·50 N	86·25 W
159	Buchanan (L.) (bû-kăn′nŏn) . Austl.	21·45 S	21·02 E
76	Buchanan L. (bû-kăn′ăn) . . . . Tex.	30·55 N	98·40 W
83	Buchans . . . . Can.	48·49 N	56·54 W
	Bucharest, see București		
111	Buchholtz (bŏŏk′hōltz) Ger. (Hamburg In.)	53·19 N	9·53 E
75	Buck Cr. (bŭk) Ind. (Indianapolis In.)	39·43 N	85·58 W
81	Buckhannon (bŭk-hăn′ŭn) W. Va.	39·00 N	80·10 W
116	Buckhaven (bŭk-hā′v′n) . . . . Scot.	56·10 N	3·10 W
116	Buckie (bŭk′ĭ) . . . . Scot.	57·40 N	2·50 W
85	Buckingham (bŭk′ĭng-ăm) Can. (Ottawa In.)	45·35 N	75·25 W
142	Buckingham (R.) (bŭk′ĭng-ăm) India	15·18 N	79·50 E
85	Buckland (bŭk′lănd) Can. (Quebec In.)	46·37 N	70·33 W
159	Buckland Tableland, (Reg.) Austl.	24·31 S	148·00 E
65	Buckley (buk′lē) Wash. (Seattle In.)	47·10 N	122·02 W
82	Bucksport (bŭks′pôrt) . . . . . Maine	44·35 N	68·47 W
82	Buctouche (bük-tōōsh′) . . . . . . Can.	46·30 N	64·42 W
127	București (Bucharest) (bōō-kōō-rĕsh′tĭ) (bōō-kȧ-rĕst′) . Rom.	44·23 N	26·10 E
80	Bucyrus (bû-sī′rŭs) . . . . Ohio	40·50 N	82·55 W
121	Budapest (bōō′dȧ-pĕsht′) . . . Hung.	47·30 N	19·05 E
123	Büderich (bü′dĕ-rēĸ) Ger. (Ruhr In.)	51·15 N	6·41 E
142	Budge-Budge . India (Calcutta In.)	22·28 N	88·08 E
75	Buechel (bĕ-chûl′) Ky. (Louisville In.)	38·12 N	85·38 W
123	Bueil (bwā′) . . . . Fr. (Paris In.)	48·55 N	1·27 E
74	Buena Park (bwā′nȧ pärk) Calif. (Los Angeles In.)	33·52 N	118·00 W
98	Buenaventura (bwā′nä-vĕn-tōō′rȧ) Col.	3·46 N	77·09 W
95	Buenaventura Cuba (Havana In.)	22·08 N	82·22 W
98	Buenaventura, Bahía de (B.) (bä-ē′ä-dĕ-bwā′nä-vĕn-tōō′rȧ) Col.	3·45 N	79·23 W
72	Buena Vista (bū′nȧ vĭs′tȧ) . . Colo.	38·51 N	106·07 W
78	Buena Vista . . . . Ga.	32·15 N	84·30 W
81	Buena Vista . . . . Va.	37·45 N	79·20 W
94	Buena Vista, Bahía (B.) (bä-ē′ä-bwĕ-nä-vē′s-tä) . Cuba	22·30 N	79·10 W
68	Buena Vista Lake Res. (bū′nȧ vĭs′tȧ) Calif.	35·14 N	119·17 W
100	Buenos Aires (bwā′nōs ī′rās) Arg. (In.)	34·20 S	58·30 W
98	Buenos Aires . . . . Col. (In.)	3·01 N	76·34 W
93	Buenos Aires . . . . C. R.	9·10 N	83·21 W
100	Buenos Aires (Prov.) . . . . Arg.	36·15 S	61·45 W
100	Buenos Aires (L.) . . . . . . Arg.-Chile	46·30 S	72·15 W
123	Buer (bür) . . . . Ger. (Ruhr In.)	51·35 N	7·03 E
71	Buffalo (buf′ȧ lō) . . . . Minn.	45·10 N	93·50 W
75	Buffalo . . . . N. Y. (Buffalo In.)	42·54 N	78·51 W
67	Buffalo . . . . Wyo.	44·19 N	106·42 W
73	Buffalo (R.) . . . . Ark.	35·56 N	92·58 W
167	Buffalo (R.) . . . . S. Afr. (Natal In.)	28·35 S	30·27 E
78	Buffalo (R.) . . . . Tenn.	35·24 N	87·10 W
77	Buffalo Bay . . . . Tex. (In.)	29·46 N	95·32 W
71	Buffalo Cr. . . . . Minn.	44·46 N	94·28 W
86	Buffalo Head Hills . . . . Can.	57·16 N	116·18 W
85	Buford (bū′fûrd) Can. (Edmonton In.)	53·15 N	113·55 W
78	Buford (bū′fērd) . . . . Ga.	34·05 N	84·00 W
69	Buford (L.) . . . . N. Mex.	36·37 N	107·12 W
129	Bug (R.) (bŏŏk) . . . . Sov. Un.	48·12 N	30·13 E
98	Buga (bōō′gä) . . . . Col. (In.)	3·54 N	76·17 W
111	Buggenhout . . . . Bel. (Brussels In.)	51·01 N	4·10 E
126	Bugojno (bōō-gô ĭ nô) . . . . . . Yugo.	44·03 N	17·28 E
121	Bug R. (bōōg) . . . . Pol.	52·29 N	21·20 E
132	Bugul′ma (bōō-gōōl′mȧ) . Sov. Un.	54·40 N	52·40 E
132	Buguruslan (bōō-gōō-rōōs-lān′) Sov. Un.	53·30 N	52·32 E
155	Buhi (bōō′ē) . . . . Phil. (Manila In.)	13·26 N	123·31 E
66	Buhl (būl) . . . . Idaho	42·36 N	114·45 W
71	Buhl . . . . Minn.	47·28 N	92·49 W
101	Buin (bōō-ēn′) Chile (Santiago In.)	33·44 S	70·44 W
133	Buinaksk (bōō′ē-näksk) . . Sov. Un.	42·40 N	47·20 E
124	Bujalance (bōō-hä-län′thā) . . . . Sp.	37·54 N	4·22 W
166	Bukama (bōō-kä′mä) . . . . . Con. L.	9·08 S	26·00 E
166	Bukavu . . . . Con. L.	2·39 S	28·50 E
103	Bukhara (bōō-kä′rä) . . . . . Sov. Un.	39·31 N	64·22 E
154	Bukittinggi . . . . Indon.	0·25 S	100·28 E
166	Bukoba . . . . Tan.	1·19 S	31·49 E
121	Bukovina (Reg.) (bōō-kô′vĭ-nȧ) Sov. Un.	48·06 N	25·20 E
155	Bula (bōō′lä) . . . . Indon.	3·17 S	130·27 E
155	Bulalacao (bōō-lä-lä′kä-ô) Phil. (Manila In.)	12·32 N	121·25 E
166	Bulawayo (bōō-lȧ-wā′yō) . . . S. Rh.	20·12 S	28·43 E
64	Buldir (I.) (bŭl dĭr) . . . . Alaska	52·22 N	175·50 E
102	Bulgaria (bŏŏl-gā′rĭ-ă) . . . . Eur.	42·12 N	24·13 E
124	Bullaque (R.) (bōō-lä′kȧ) . . . . . Sp.	39·15 N	4·13 W
124	Bullas (bōōl′yäs) . . . . Sp.	38·07 N	1·48 W
69	Bulldog Cr. (bŭl′dŏg′) . . . . . . Utah	37·45 N	110·55 W
94	Bull Head (Mtn.) . . . . Jam.	18·10 N	77·15 W
159	Bulloo (R.) (bŭ-lōō′) . . . . Austl.	25·23 S	143·30 E
65	Bull Run (R.) (bŏŏl) Ore. (Portland In.)	45·26 N	122·11 W
65	Bull Run Res. (bŏŏl) Ore. (Portland In.)	45·29 N	122·11 W
73	Bull Shoals Res. (bŏŏl shōlz) Ark.-Mo.	36·35 N	92·57 W
168	Bulo Burti (bōō′lō bŏŏr′tĭ) Som. (Horn of Afr. In.)	3·53 N	45·30 E
110	Bulphan (bŏŏl′făn) Eng. (London In.)	51·33 N	0·21 E
168	Bultfontein (bŏŏlt′fŏn-tān′) S. Afr. (Johannesburg & Pretoria In.)	28·18 S	26·10 E
135	Bulun (bōō-lōōn′) . . . . . . Sov. Un.	70·48 N	127·27 E
166	Bulungu (bōō-lōōŋ′gōō) . . . Con. L.	4·58 S	18·57 E
167	Bulwer (bŏŏl-wẽr) S. Afr. (Natal In.)	29·49 S	29·48 E
165	Bumba (bŏŏm′bȧ) . . . . Con. L.	2·15 N	22·32 E
155	Buna (bōō′nȧ) . . . . Pap.	8·58 S	148·38 E
158	Bunbury (bŭn′bŭrĭ) . . . . Austl.	33·25 S	115·45 E
160	Bundaberg (bŭn′dȧ-bûrg) . . . Austl.	24·45 S	152·18 E
153	Bungo-Suidō (Chan.) (bŏŏŋ′gō sōō-ē′dō) . Jap.	33·26 N	131·54 E
74	Bunker Hill (bŭnk′ẽr hĭl) Ill. (St. Louis In.)	39·03 N	89·57 W
77	Bunkie (bŭŋ′kĭ) . . . . La.	30·55 N	92·10 W
135	Buor Khaya, Mys (C.) . . Sov. Un.	71·47 N	133·22 E
168	Buran (bûr′ăn) Som. (Horn of Afr. In.)	10·38 N	48·30 E
168	Burao . . . . Som. (Horn of Afr. In.)	9·20 N	45·45 E
84	Buras (bûr′ȧs) La. (New Orleans In.)	29·22 N	89·33 W
144	Buraydah . . . . Sau. Ar.	26·23 N	44·14 E
74	Burbank (bûr′bănk) Calif. (Los Angeles In.)	34·11 N	118·19 W
159	Burdekin (R.) (bûr′dē-kĭn) . Austl.	19·22 S	145·07 E
133	Burdur (bōōr-dōōr′) . . . . Tur.	37·50 N	30·15 E

ng-sing; ŋ-baŋk; N-nasalized n; nŏd; cŏmmit; ōld; ôbey; ôrder; fōōd; fŏŏt; ou-out; s-soft; sh-dish; th-thin; pūre; ûnite; ûrn; stŭd; circŭs; ü-as "y" in study; ′-indeterminate vowel.

Page	Name	Pronunciation	Region	Lat. °'	Long. °'
142	Burdwan	(boord-wän')	India	23·29 N	87·53 E
100	Burdwood, Banco (Bk.)		Atl. O.	54·00 s	60·45 w
135	Bureinskiy, Khrebet (Mts.)		Sov. Un.	51·15 N	133·30 E
135	Bureya	(boora'a)	Sov. Un.	49·55 N	130·00 E
135	Bureya (R.)	(boo-rā'yä)	Sov. Un.	51·00 N	130·14 E
110	Burford	(bur-ferd)	Eng. (London In.)	51·46 N	1·38 w
147	Burga Dist.		China	50·31 N	120·30 E
127	Burgas	(boor-gäs')	Bul.	42·29 N	27·30 E
127	Burgaski Zaliv (G.)		Bul.	42·30 N	27·40 E
79	Burgaw	(bur'gô)	N. C.	34·31 N	77·56 w
120	Burgdorf	(boorg'dôrf)	Switz.	47·04 N	7·37 E
111	Burgenland (State)		Aus. (Vienna In.)	47·58 N	16·57 E
83	Burgeo		Can.	47·36 N	57·39 w
76	Burgos	(boor'gōs)	Mex.	24·57 N	98·47 w
155	Burgos		Phil. (Manila In.)	16·03 N	119·52 E
124	Burgos	(boor'r-gôs)	Sp.	42·20 N	3·44 E
118	Burgsvik	(boorgs'vik)	Swe.	57·04 N	18·18 E
142	Burhänpur	(boor'hän-poor)	India	21·26 N	76·08 E
155	Burias I.	(boo'rē-äs)	Phil. (Manila In.)	12·56 N	122·56 E
155	Burias Pass	(boo'rē-äs)	Phil. (Manila In.)	13·04 N	123·11 E
93	Burica, Punta (Pt.)	(poo'n-tä-boo'rē-kä)	Pan.	8·02 N	83·12 w
65	Burien	(bu'rĭ-ĕn)	Wash. (Seattle In.)	47·28 N	122·20 w
83	Burin	(bur'in)	Can.	47·03 N	55·33 w
83	Burin Pen.		Can.	47·00 N	55·14 w
72	Burkburnett	(burk-bur'nĕt)	Tex.	34·04 N	98·35 w
81	Burke	(burk)	Idaho	47·40 N	72·00 w
158	Burketown	(burk'toun)	Austl.	17·50 s	139·30 E
67	Burley	(bur'lĭ)	Idaho	42·31 N	113·48 w
65	Burley		Wash. (Seattle In.)	47·25 N	122·38 w
136	Burli		Sov. Un. (Urals In.)	53·36 N	61·55 E
65	Burlingame	(bur'lĭn-gām)	Calif. (San Francisco In.)	37·35 N	122·22 w
73	Burlingame		Kans.	38·45 N	95·49 w
85	Burlington	(bur'lĭng-tŭn)	Can. (Toronto In.)	43·19 N	79·48 w
72	Burlington		Colo.	39·17 N	102·26 w
71	Burlington		Iowa	40·48 N	91·05 w
73	Burlington		Kans.	38·10 N	95·46 w
75	Burlington		Ky. (Cincinnati In.)	39·01 N	84·44 w
84	Burlington		N. J. (Philadelphia In.)	40·04 N	74·52 w
79	Burlington		N. C.	36·05 N	79·26 w
81	Burlington		Vt.	44·30 N	73·15 w
65	Burlington		Wash. (Seattle In.)	48·28 N	122·20 w
75	Burlington		Wis. (Milwaukee In.)	42·41 N	88·16 w
138	Burma	(bur'mä)	Asia	21·00 N	95·15 E
76	Burnet	(bur'nĕt)	Tex.	30·46 N	98·14 w
110	Burnham on Crouch	(burn'äm-ŏn-krouch)	Eng. (London In.)	51·38 N	0·48 E
160	Burnie	(bur'nē)	Austl.	41·15 s	146·05 E
110	Burnley	(burn'lĭ)	Eng.	53·47 N	2·19 w
66	Burns	(burnz)	Ore.	43·35 N	119·05 w
78	Burnside	(burn'sĭd)	Ky.	36·57 N	84·33 w
86	Burns Lake	(burnz lāk)	Can.	54·12 N	125·38 w
82	Burnsville	(burnz'vĭl)	Can.	47·44 N	65·07 w
66	Burnt R.	(burnt)	Ore.	44·26 N	117·53 w
65	Burrard Inlet	(bur'ärd)	Can. (Vancouver In.)	49·19 N	123·15 w
125	Burriana	(boor-rē-ä'nä)	Sp.	39·53 N	0·05 w
133	Bursa	(boor'sä)	Tur.	40·10 N	28·10 E
165	Bür Safäjah		U. A. R.	26·57 N	33·56 E
168	Bür Sa'id (Port Said)		U. A. R. (Suez In.)	31·15 N	32·19 E
123	Burscheid	(boor'shīd)	Ger. (Ruhr In.)	51·05 N	7·07 E
75	Burt	(burt)	N. Y. (Buffalo In.)	43·19 N	78·45 w
80	Burt (L.)	(burt)	Mich.	45·25 N	84·45 w
139	Bür Tawfiq		U. A. R. (Palestine In.)	29·58 N	32·33 E
65	Burton	(bur'tŭn)	Wash. (Seattle In.)	47·24 N	122·28 w
110	Burton-on-Trent	(bur'tŭn-ŏn-trĕnt)	Eng.	52·48 N	1·37 w
78	Burton Res.		Ga.	34·46 N	83·40 w
155	Buru (I.)		Indon.	3·30 s	126·30 E
168	Burullus L.		U. A. R. (Nile In.)	31·20 N	30·58 E
155	Buruncan Pt.		Phil. (Manila In.)	12·11 N	121·23 E
166	Burundi		Afr.	3·00 s	29·30 E
86	Burwash Landing	(bur wäsh)	Can.	61·20 N	139·12 w
70	Burwell	(bur'wĕl)	Nebr.	41·46 N	99·08 w
110	Bury	(bĕr'ĭ)	Eng.	53·36 N	2·17 w
135	Buryat A.S.S.R.		Sov. Un.	54·15 N	111·22 E
117	Bury St. Edmunds	(bĕr'ĭ-sänt ĕd'mŭndz)	Eng.	52·14 N	0·44 E
100	Burzaco	(boor-zä'kō)	Arg. (In.)	34·35 s	58·23 w
168	Büsh	(boosh)	U. A. R. (Nile In.)	29·13 N	31·08 E
144	Büshehr		Iran	28·48 N	50·53 E
166	Bushman Land (Reg.)	(boosh-män länd)	S. Afr.	29·15 s	18·45 E
167	Bushmans (R.)		S. Afr. (Natal In.)	33·29 s	26·09 E
73	Bushnell	(boosh'nĕl)	Ill.	40·33 N	90·28 w
165	Businga	(boo-sin'gä)	Con. L.	3·14 N	20·33 E
121	Busk	(boo'sk)	Sov. Un.	49·58 N	24·39 E
164	Bussa	(boo'sä)	Nig.	10·11 N	4·20 E
158	Busselton	(bus"l-tŭn)	Austl.	33·40 s	115·30 E
111	Bussum		Neth. (Amsterdam In.)	52·16 N	5·10 E
76	Bustamante	(boos-tä-män'tä)	Mex.	26·34 N	100·30 w
126	Busto Arsizio	(boos'tō är-sēd'zē-ō)	It.	45·47 N	8·51 E
155	Busuanga (I.)	(boo-swän'gä)	Phil.	12·20 N	119·43 E
165	Buta	(boo'tä)	Con. L.	2·47 N	24·46 E
167	Butha Buthe	(boo-thä-boo'thä)	Bas. (Natal In.)	28·49 s	28·16 E
78	Butler	(bŭt'lēr)	Ala.	32·05 N	88·10 w
80	Butler		Ind.	41·25 N	84·50 w
73	Butler		Mo.	38·16 N	94·19 w
84	Butler		N. J. (New York In.)	41·00 N	74·20 w
81	Butler		Pa.	40·50 N	79·55 w
136	Butovo	(boo-tô'vô)	Sov. Un. (Moscow In.)	55·33 N	37·36 E
78	Buttahatchie (R.)	(but-ä-häch'ē)	Ala.-Miss.	34·02 N	88·05 w
67	Butte	(būt)	Mont.	46·00 N	112·31 w
167	Butterworth	(bu ter'wurth)	S. Afr. (Natal In.)	32·20 s	28·09 E
116	Butt of Lewis (C.)	(but ŏv lu'ĭs)	Scot.	58·34 N	6·15 w
155	Butuan	(boo-too'än)	Phil.	8·40 N	125·33 E
155	Butung (I.)		Indon.	5·15 s	124·15 E
129	Buturlinovka	(boo-too'lē-nôf'ka)	Sov. Un.	50·47 N	40·35 E
111	Buxtehude	(books-tĕ-hoo'dĕ)	Ger. (Hamburg In.)	53·29 N	9·42 E
110	Buxton	(buks't'n)	Eng.	53·15 N	1·55 w
65	Buxton		Ore. (Portland In.)	45·41 N	123·11 w
167	Buxton		S. Afr. (Natal In.)	32·36 s	26·39 E
132	Buy	(bwē)	Sov. Un.	58·30 N	41·48 E
150	Buyr Nuur	(boo'yer nôr)	Mong.	47·50 N	117·00 E
127	Buzău	(boo-zǔ'oo)	Rom.	45·09 N	26·51 E
129	Buzău (R.)		Rom.	45·17 N	27·22 E
133	Buzuluk	(boo-zoo-look')	Sov. Un.	52·50 N	52·10 E
127	Byala		Bul.	43·26 N	25·44 E
	Byblos, see Jubayl				
121	Bydgoszcz	(bĭd'gôshch)	Pol.	53·07 N	18·00 E
80	Byesville	(bīz-vĭl)	Ohio	39·55 N	81·35 w
118	Bygdin	(bügh-dēn')	Nor.	61·24 N	8·31 E
118	Byglandsfjord	(bügh'länds-fyôr)	Nor.	58·40 N	7·49 E
128	Bykhovo	(bĭ-kô'vô)	Sov. Un.	53·32 N	30·15 E
136	Bykovo	(bĭ-kô'vô)	Sov. Un. (Moscow In.)	55·38 N	38·05 E
134	Byrranga, Gory (Mts.)		Sov. Un.	74·15 N	94·28 E
135	Bytantay (R.)	(byän'tāy)	Sov. Un.	68·15 N	132·15 E
121	Bytom	(bǐ'tŭm)	Pol.	50·21 N	18·55 E
128	Bytosh'	(bī-tôsh')	Sov. Un.	53·48 N	34·06 E
121	Bytow	(bǐ'tŭf)	Pol.	54·10 N	17·30 E
127	Buziu (R.)		Rom.	45·18 N	26·29 E
100	Caazapa'	(kä-zä-pä')	Par.	26·14 s	56·18 w
155	Cabagan	(kä-bä-gän')	Phil. (Manila In.)	17·27 N	12·46 E
155	Cabalete (I.)	(kä-bä-lä'tä)	Phil. (Manila In.)	14·19 N	122·00 E
94	Caballones, Canal de (Chan.)	(kä-näl'-dĕ-kä-bäl-yô'nĕs)	Cuba	20·45 N	79·20 w
69	Caballo Res.	(kä-bä-lyô')	N. Mex.	33·00 N	107·20 w
124	Cabañaquinta	(kä-bän-yä-kē'n-tä)	Sp.	43·10 N	5·37 w
155	Cabanatuan	(kä-bä-nä-twän')	Phil. (Manila In.)	15·30 N	120·56 E
82	Cabano	(kä-bä-nō')	Can.	47·41 N	68·55 w
160	Cabar	(kä'bĕr)	Austl.	31·28 s	145·50 E
155	Cabarruyan (I.)	(kä-bä-roo'yän)	Phil. (Manila In.)	16·21 N	120·10 E
99	Cabedelo	(kä-bē-dā'loo)	Braz.	6·58 s	34·49 w
91	Cabeza, Arrecife (Reef)	(är-rē-sē'fē-kä-bĕ-zä)	Mex.	19·07 N	95·52 w
124	Cabeza del Buey	(kä-bä'thä dĕl bwä')	Sp.	38·43 N	5·18 w
98	Cabimas	(kä-bē'mäs)	Ven.	10·21 N	71·27 w
166	Cabinda	(kä-bĭn'dä)	Ang.	5·45 s	12·10 E
163	Cabinda	(kä-bĭn'dä)	Afr.	5·00 s	10·00 E
66	Cabinet Mts.	(kăb'ĭ-nĕt)	Mont.	48·13 N	115·52 w
101	Cabo Frio	(kä'bô-frē'ô)	Braz. (Rio de Janeiro In.)	22·53 s	42·02 w
101	Cabo Frio, Ilha do	(ē'lä-dô-kä'bô frē'ô)	Braz. (Rio de Janeiro In.)	23·01 s	42·00 w
80	Cabot Hd.	(kăb'ŭt)	Can.	45·15 N	81·20 w
83	Cabot Str.	(kăb'ŭt)	Can.	47·35 N	60·00 w
164	Cabo Verde, Ilhas do		Afr. (In.)	15·08 N	26·02 w
124	Cabra	(käb'rä)	Sp.	37·28 N	4·29 w
155	Cabra (I.)		Phil. (Manila In.)	13·55 N	119·55 E
125	Cabrera (I.)	(kä-brā'rä)	Sp.	39·08 N	2·57 E
124	Cabriel (R.)	(kä-brē-ĕl')	Sp.	39·41 N	1·32 w
68	Cabrillo Natl. Mon.	(kä-brēl'yō)	Calif. (San Diego In.)	32·41 N	117·03 w
99	Cabrobo'	(kä-brō-bô')	Braz.	8·34 s	39·13 w
100	Cabuçu (R.)	(kä-boo'-soo)	Braz. (In.)	22·57 s	43·36 w
155	Cabugao	(kä-boo'gä-ô)	Phil. (Manila In.)	17·48 N	120·28 E
127	Čačak	(chä'chàk)	Yugo.	43·51 N	20·22 E
101	Caçapava	(ká'sä-pá'vä)	Braz. (Rio de Janeiro In.)	23·05 s	45·42 w
99	Cáceres	(kä'sĕ-rĕs)	Braz.	16·11 s	57·32 w
124	Cáceres	(kä'thä-räs)	Sp.	39·28 N	6·20 w
101	Cachapoal (R.)	(kä-chä-pô-ä'l)	Chile (Santiago In.)	34·23 s	70·19 w
101	Cachari'	(kä-chä-rē')	Arg. (Buenos Aires In.)	36·23 s	59·29 w
73	Cache (R.)	(kàsh)	Ark.	35·24 N	91·12 w
68	Cache Cr.	(kàsh)	Calif.	38·53 N	122·24 w
72	Cache la Poudre (R.)	(kàsh lä pood'r')	Colo.	40·43 N	105·39 w
100	Cachi, Nevados de (Pk.)	(nĕ-vä'dôs-dĕ-kä'chē)	Arg.	24·35 s	65·59 w
100	Cachinal	(kä-chē-näl')	Chile	24·57 s	69·33 w
99	Cachoeira	(kä-shô-ā'rä)	Braz.	12·32 s	38·47 w
100	Cachoeira do Sul	(kä-shô-ā'rä-dô-soo'l)	Braz.	30·02 s	52·49 w
101	Cachoeiras de Macacu	(kä-shô-ā'räs-dĕ-mä-kä'koo)	Braz. (Rio de Janeiro In.)	22·28 s	42·39 w
101	Cachoeiro de Itapemirim	(kä-shô-ā'rô-dĕ-ē'tä-pĕmē-rē'N)	Braz. (Rio de Janeiro In.)	20·51 s	41 06 w
166	Cacconda	(kä-kôn'dä)	Ang.	13·40 s	15·05 E
77	Caddo L.	(kăd'ō)	La.-Tex.	32·37 N	94·15 w
90	Cadereyta	(kä-dā-rā'tä)	Mex.	20·42 N	99·47 w
76	Cadereyta Jimenez	(kä-dä-rā'tä hē-mā'näz)	Mex.	25·36 N	99·59 w
125	Cadi, Sierra de (Mts.)	(sē-ĕ'r-rä-dĕ-kä'dē)	Sp.	42·17 N	1·34 E
155	Cadig, Mt.	(kä'dĕg)	Phil. (Manila In.)	14·11 N	122·26 E
80	Cadillac	(kăd'ĭ-lăk)	Mich.	44·15 N	85·25 w
68	Cadiz	(kä'dĭz)	Calif.	34·33 N	115·30 w
80	Cadiz		Ohio	40·15 N	81·00 w
124	Cádiz	(kä'dēz)	Sp.	36·34 N	6·20 w
124	Cádiz, Golfo de (G.)	(gôl-fô-dĕ-kä'dēz)	Sp.	36·50 N	7·00 w
122	Caen	(kän)	Fr.	49·13 N	0·22 w
101	Caeté	(kä-ĕ-tĕ')	Braz. (Rio de Janeiro In.)	19·53 s	43·41 w
99	Caetité	(kä-ā-tē-tā')	Braz.	14·02 s	42·14 w
166	Cagamba	(kä-gä'm-bä)	Ang.	13·20 s	19·55 E
155	Cagayan	(kä-gä-yän')	Phil.	8·13 N	124·30 E
154	Cagayan (R.)		Phil.	16·45 N	121·55 E
154	Cagayan Is.		Phil.	9·40 N	120·30 E
154	Cagayan Sulu (I.)	(kä-gä-yän soo'loo)	Phil.	7·00 N	118·30 E
126	Cagli	(käl'yē)	It.	42·33 N	12·38 E
126	Cagliari	(käl'yä-rē)	It.	39·16 N	9·08 E
126	Cagliari, Golfo di (G.)	(gôl-fô-dē-käl'yä-rē)	It.	39·08 N	9·12 E
123	Cagnes	(kän'y')	Fr.	43·40 N	7·14 E
99	Cagua	(kä'gwä)	Ven. (In.)	10·12 N	67·27 w
89	Caguas	(kä'gwäs)	P. R. (Puerto Rico In.)	18·12 N	66·01 w
78	Cahaba (R.)	(kä hä-bä)	Ala.	32·50 N	87·15 w
166	Cahama	(kä-ä'mä)	Ang.	16·15 s	14·15 E
74	Cahokia	(kä-hō'kĭ-à)	Ill. (St. Louis In.)	38·34 N	90·11 w
122	Cahors	(kä-ôr')	Fr.	44·27 N	1·27 E
91	Cahuacán	(kä-wä-kä'n)	Mex. (Mexico City In.)	19·38 N	99·25 w
93	Cahuita, Punta (Pt.)	(poo'n-tä-kä-wē'tá)	C. R.	9·47 N	82·41 w
99	Caiapó, Serra do (Mts.)	(sē'r-rä-dô-kä-yä-pô')	Braz.	17·52 s	52·37 w
94	Caibarién	(kī-bä-rē-ĕn')	Cuba	22·35 N	79·30 w
98	Caicedonia	(kī-sĕ-dô-nēä)	Col. (In.)	4·21 N	75·48 w
95	Caicos Bk.	(kī'kōs)	Ba. Is.	21·35 N	72·00 w
95	Caicos Is.		Turks & Caicos Is.	21·45 N	71·50 w
95	Caicos Passage (Str.)		Ba. Is.	21·55 N	72·45 w
77	Caillou B.	(kä-yoo')	La.	29·07 N	91·00 w
95	Caimanera	(kī-mä-nä'rä)	Cuba	20·00 N	75·10 w
90	Caimanere, Laguna del	(lä-goo'nä-dĕl-kä-ē-mä-nĕ-rĕ-kä)	Mex.	22·57 N	106·07 w
155	Caiman Pt.	(kī'män)	Phil. (Manila In.)	15·56 N	119·33 E
88	Caimito, (R.)	(kä-ē-mē'tô)	Pan. (Panama Canal In.)	8·50 N	79·45 w
95	Caimito del Guayabal	(kä-ē-mē'tō-dĕl-gwä-yä-bä'l)	Cuba (Havana In.)	22·12 N	82·36 w
85	Cainsville	(kānz'vĭl)	Can. (Toronto In.)	43·09 N	80·13 w
159	Cairns	(kârnz)	Austl.	17·02 s	145·49 E
93	Cairo	(kī'-rô)	C. R.	10·06 N	83·47 w
78	Cairo	(kā'rō)	Ga.	30·48 N	84·12 w
73	Cairo		Ill.	36·59 N	89·11 w
	Cairo, see Al Qāhirah				
110	Caistor	(kâs'tēr)	Eng.	53·30 N	0·20 w
98	Cajamarca	(kä-ä-mä'r-kä)	Col. (In.)	4·25 N	75·25 w
98	Cajamarca	(kä-hä-mär'kä)	Peru	7·16 s	78·30 w
155	Cajidiocan	(kä-hē-dyô'kän)	Phil. (Manila In.)	12·22 N	122·41 E
127	Čajniče	(chī'nĭ-chĕ)	Yugo.	43·32 N	19·04 E
74	Cajon	(kä-hōn')	Calif. (Los Angeles In.)	34·18 N	117·28 w
101	Cajuru	(kä-zhoo'-roo)	Braz. (Rio de Janeiro In.)	21·17 s	47·17 w
126	Čakovec	(chä'kō-vĕts)	Yugo.	46·23 N	16·27 E
167	Cala	(cä-là)	S. Afr. (Natal In.)	31·33 s	27·41 E
164	Calabar	(kăl-à-bär')	Nig.	4·58 N	8·21 E
74	Calabasas	(kä-lä-bäs'äs)	Calif. (Los Angeles In.)	34·09 N	118·39 w
95	Calabazar	(kä-lä-bä-zä'r)	Cuba (Havana In.)	23·02 N	82·25 w
98	Calabozo	(kä-lä-bō'zō)	Ven.	8·48 N	67·27 w
126	Calabria (Reg.)	(kä-lä'brē-ä)	It.	39·26 N	16·23 E
127	Calafat	(kä-lä-fät')	Rom.	43·59 N	22·56 E
155	Calagua Is.	(kä-läg'wä)	Phil. (Manila In.)	14·30 N	123·06 E
85	Calahoo	(kä-lä-hoo')	Can. (Edmonton In.)	53·42 N	113·58 w
124	Calahorra	(kä-lä-ôr'rä)	Sp.	42·18 N	1·58 w
82	Calais	(kä-lĕ')	Can.	45·11 N	67·15 w
122	Calais	(kä-lĕ')	Fr.	50·56 N	1·51 E
100	Calama	(kä-lä'mä)	Chile	22·17 s	68·58 w
98	Calama	(kä-lä'mä)	Col.	1·55 N	72·33 w
98	Calamar	(kä-lä-mär')	Col.	10·24 N	75·00 w
155	Calamba	(kä-läm'bä)	Phil. (Manila In.)	14·12 N	121·10 E
154	Calamian Group (Is.)	(kä-lä-myän')	Phil.	12·14 N	118·38 E
124	Calañas	(kä-län'yäs)	Sp.	37·41 N	6·52 w
155	Calapan	(kä-lä-pän')	Phil. (Manila In.)	13·25 N	121·11 E
115	Călărasi	(kŭ-lŭ-räsh'ĭ)	Rom.	44·09 N	27·20 E
114	Calasparra	(kä-lä-spär'rä)	Sp.	38·13 N	1·40 w
124	Calatayud	(kä-lä-tä-yoodh')	Sp.	41·23 N	1·37 w
155	Calauag	(kä-lä-wäg')	Phil. (Manila In.)	13·56 N	122·16 E
155	Calauag B.		Phil. (Manila In.)	14·07 N	122·10 E
65	Calaveras Res.	(kăl-à-vĕr'äs)	Calif. (San Francisco In.)	37·29 N	121·47 w
155	Calavite, C.	(kä-lä-vē'tä)	Phil. (Manila In.)	13·29 N	120·00 E
77	Calcasieu L.	(kăl'kä-shū)	La.	29·58 N	93·08 w
77	Calcasieu R.		La.	30·22 N	93·08 w

PRONOUNCING INDEX Calcutta–Cape Flats 189

Page	Name Pronunciation Region	Lat. °'	Long. °'
142	Calcutta (kăl-kŭt'ȧ) India (Calcutta In.)	22·32 N	88·22 E
98	Caldas (kȧ'l-däs) Col. (In.)	6·06 N	75·38 W
98	Caldas (Dept.) Col. (In.)	5·20 N	75·38 W
124	Caldas de Rainha (kăl'däs dä rĭn'yȧ) Port.	39·25 N	9·08 W
110	Calder (R.) (kôl'dẽr) Eng.	53·39 N	1·30 W
110	Calder (R.) Eng.	53·48 N	2·25 W
100	Caldera (käl-dā'rä) Chile	27·02 S	70·53 W
66	Caldwell (kôld'wĕl) Idaho	43·40 N	116·43 W
73	Caldwell Kans.	37·04 N	97·36 W
80	Caldwell Ohio	39·40 N	81·30 W
77	Caldwell Tex.	30·30 N	96·40 W
85	Caledon (kăl'ē-dŏn) Can. (Toronto In.)	43·52 N	79·59 W
71	Caledonia (kăl-ē-dō'nĭ-ȧ) Minn.	43·38 N	91·31 W
116	Caledonian Can. (kăl-ē-dō'nĭ-ăn) Scot.	56·58 N	4·05 W
125	Calella (kä-lĕl'yä) Sp.	41·37 N	2·39 E
90	Calera Victor Rosales (kä-lā'rä-vē'k-tôr-rô-sä'lĕs) Mex.	22·57 N	102·42 W
68	Calexico (kȧ-lĕk'sĭ-kō) Calif.	32·41 N	115·30 W
85	Calgary (kăl'gȧ-rĭ) Can. (Calgary In.)	51·03 N	114·05 W
78	Calhoun (kăl-hōōn') Ga.	34·30 N	84·56 W
98	Cali (kä'lē) Col. (In.)	3·26 N	76·30 W
143	Calicut (kăl'ĭ-kŭt) India	11·19 N	75·49 E
69	Caliente (kăl-yĕn'tä) Nev.	37·38 N	114·30 W
73	California (kăl-ĭ-fôr'nĭ-ȧ) Mo.	38·38 N	92·38 W
75	California Pa. (Pittsburgh In.)	40·03 N	79·53 W
62	California (State) U. S.	38·10 N	121·20 W
88	California, Golfo de (G.) (gôl-fô-dĕ-kä-lē-fôr-nyä) Mex.	30·30 N	113·45 W
84	California B. La. (New Orleans In.)	29·29 N	89·32 W
121	Căliman, Muntii (Mts.) Rom.	47·05 N	24·47 E
143	Calimere, Pt. India	15·25 N	80·05 E
74	Calimesa (kă-lĭ-mā'sȧ) Calif. (Los Angeles In.)	34·00 N	117·04 W
68	Calipatria (kăl-ĭ-pȧt'rĭ-ȧ) Calif.	33·03 N	115·30 W
91	Calkini (käl-kē-nē') Mex.	20·21 N	90·06 W
160	Callabonna, L. (călă'bŏnȧ) Austl.	29·35 S	140·28 E
168	Callafo Eth. (Horn of Afr. In.)	5·40 N	44·00 E
98	Callao (käl-yä'ō) Peru	12·80 S	77·07 W
85	Calmar (kăl'mär) Can. (Edmonton In.)	53·16 N	113·49 W
71	Calmar Iowa	43·12 N	91·54 W
90	Calnali (käl-nä-lē') Mex.	20·53 N	98·34 W
79	Calooshatchee (R.) (kȧ-loo-sȧ-hăch'ē) Fla. (In.)	26·45 N	81·41 W
92	Calotmul (kä-lôt-mōōl) Mex. (Yucatan In.)	20·58 N	88·11 W
90	Calpulalpan (käl-pōō-läl'pän) Mex.	19·35 N	98·33 W
126	Caltagirone (käl-tä-jē-rō'nä) It.	37·14 N	14·32 E
126	Caltanissetta (käl-tä-nē-sĕt'tä) It.	37·30 N	14·02 E
71	Calumet (kă-lū-mĕt') Mich.	47·15 S	88·29 W
75	Calumet, L. Ill. (Chicago In.)	41·43 N	87·36 W
75	Calumet City Ill. (Chicago In.)	41·37 N	87·33 W
77	Calvert (kăl'vẽrt) Tex.	30·59 N	96·41 W
86	Calvert (I.) Can.	51·40 N	129·02 W
126	Calvi (käl'vē) Fr.	42·33 N	8·35 E
90	Calvillo (käl-vēl'yō) Mex.	21·51 N	102·44 W
166	Calvinia (kăl-vĭn'ĭ-ȧ) S. Afr.	31·20 S	19·50 E
124	Calzada de Calatrava (käl-zä'dä-dĕ-kä-lä-trä'vä) Sp.	38·42 N	3·44 W
116	Cam (R.) (kăm) Eng.	52·15 N	0·05 E
94	Camaguey (kä-mä-gwā') Cuba	21·25 N	78·00 W
94	Camaguey (State) Cuba	21·30 N	78·10 W
94	Camajuani (kä-mä-hwä'nē) Cuba	22·25 N	79·50 W
155	Camalig (kä-mä'lēg) Phil. (Manila In.)	13·11 N	123·36 E
98	Camaná (kä-mä'nä) Peru	16·37 S	72·33 W
65	Camano (kȧ-mä'no) Wash. (Seattle In.)	48·10 N	122·32 W
65	Camano I. Wash. (Seattle In.)	48·11 N	122·29 W
76	Camargo (kä-mär'gō) Mex.	26·19 N	98·49 W
92	Camaron, Cabo (C.) (kȧ'bô-kä-mä-rōn') Hond.	16·06 N	85·05 W
65	Camas (kăm'ȧs) Wash. (Portland In.)	45·35 N	122·54 W
67	Camas Cr. Idaho	44·10 N	112·09 W
99	Camatagua (kä-mä-tä'gwä) Ven. (In.)	9·49 N	66·55 W
154	Ca Mau, Pte de Viet.	8·42 N	103·11 E
142	Cambay (kăm-bā') India	22·22 N	72·39 E
142	Cambay, G. of India	21·05 N	71·58 E
64	Cambell (kămbĕl') Alaska	63·48 N	171·58 W
139	Cambodia (kăm-bō'dĭ-ȧ) Asia	14·00 N	105·45 E
116	Camborne (kăm'bôrn) Eng.	50·15 N	5·28 W
122	Cambrai (käN-brĕ') Fr.	50·10 N	3·15 E
116	Cambrian (Mts.) (kăm'brĭ-ăn) Wales	52·05 N	4·05 W
116	Cambridge (kām'brĭj) Eng.	52·12 N	0·11 E
81	Cambridge Md.	38·35 N	76·10 W
83	Cambridge Mass. (Boston In.)	42·23 N	71·07 W
71	Cambridge Minn.	45·35 N	93·14 W
72	Cambridge Nebr.	40·17 N	100·10 W
80	Cambridge Ohio	40·00 N	81·35 W
86	Cambridge Bay Can.	69·15 N	105·00 W
80	Cambridge City Ind.	39·45 N	85·15 W
101	Cambuci (käm-bōō'sē) Braz. (Rio de Janeiro In.)	21·35 S	41·54 W
101	Cambuí (käm-bōō-ē') Braz. (Rio de Janeiro In.)	22·38 S	46·02 W
75	Camby (kăm'bē) Ind. (Indianapolis In.)	39·40 N	86·19 W
78	Camden (kăm'dĕn) Ala.	31·58 N	87·15 W
73	Camden Ark.	33·36 N	92·49 W
161	Camden Austl. (Sydney In.)	34·03 S	150·42 E
82	Camden Maine	44·11 N	69·05 W
84	Camden N. J. (Philadelphia In.)	39·56 N	75·06 W
79	Camden S. C.	34·14 N	80·37 W
73	Cameron (kăm'ẽr-ŭn) Mo.	39·44 N	94·14 W
77	Cameron Tex.	30·52 N	96·57 W
80	Cameron W. Va.	39·40 N	80·35 W
86	Camerons Hills Can.	60·13 N	120·20 W
163	Cameroon Afr.	5·48 N	11·00 E
164	Cameroons Mt. Cam.	4·15 N	9·01 E
99	Cametá (kä-mȧ-tä') Braz.	1·14 S	49·30 W
155	Camiling (kä-mē-lĭng') Phil. (Manila In.)	15·42 N	120·24 E
78	Camilla (kȧ-mĭl'ȧ) Ga.	31·13 N	84·12 W
124	Caminha (kä-mĭn'yȧ) Port.	41·52 N	8·44 W
99	Camoçim (kä-mô-sēN') Braz.	2·56 S	40·55 W
158	Camooweal Austl.	20·00 S	138·13 E
101	Campana (käm-pä'nä) Arg. (Buenos Aires In.)	34·10 S	58·58 W
100	Campana (I.) (käm-pän'yä) Chile	48·20 S	75·15 W
124	Campanario (käm-pä-nä'rē-ō) Sp.	38·51 N	5·36 W
125	Campanella, Punta (C.) (pōō'n-tä-käm-pä-nĕ'lä) It. (Naples In.)	40·20 N	14·21 E
101	Campanha (käm-pän-yäN') Braz. (Rio de Janeiro In.)	21·51 S	45·24 W
126	Campania (Reg.) (käm-pän'yä) It.	43·00 N	14·40 E
65	Campbell (kăm'bĕl) Calif. (San Francisco In.)	37·17 N	121·57 W
73	Campbell Mo.	36·29 N	90·04 W
47	Campbell Is. N. Z.	52·30 S	169·00 E
142	Campbellpore W. Pak.	33·49 N	72·24 E
86	Campbell River Can.	50·00 N	125·24 W
78	Campbellsville (kăm'bĕlz-vĭl) Ky.	37·19 N	85·20 W
82	Campbellton (kăm'bĕl-tŭn) Can.	48·00 N	66·43 W
161	Campbelltown (kăm'bĕl-toun) Austl. (Sydney In.)	34·04 S	150·49 E
116	Campbeltown (kăm'b'l-toun) Scot.	55·25 N	5·50 W
75	Camp Dennison (dĕ'nĭ-sŏn) Ohio (Cincinnati In.)	39·12 N	84·17 W
91	Campeche (käm-pā'chā) Mex.	19·51 N	90·32 W
88	Campeche (State) Mex.	18·55 N	90·20 W
88	Campeche, Bahía de (B.) (bä-ē'ä-dĕ-käm-pā'chā) Mex.	19·30 N	93·40 W
94	Campechuela (käm-pā-chwā'lä) Cuba	20·15 N	77·15 W
167	Camperdown (kăm'pẽr-doun) S. Afr. (Natal In.)	29·14 S	30·33 E
124	Campillo de Altobuey (käm-pēl'yō dä äl-tō-bōō'ā) Sp.	39·37 N	1·50 W
99	Campina Grande (käm-pē'nä grän'dĕ) Braz.	7·15 S	35·49 W
101	Campinas (käm-pē'näzh) Braz. (Rio de Janeiro In.)	22·53 S	47·03 W
68	Camp Ind. Res. (kămp) Calif.	32·39 N	116·26 W
164	Campo (käm'pō) Cam.	2·32 N	9·54 E
98	Campoalegre (kăm'pô-ălĕ'grĕ) Col.	2·34 N	75·20 W
126	Campobasso (käm'pô-bäs'sō) It.	41·35 N	14·39 E
100	Campo Belo (kä'm-pô-bĕ'lō) Braz. (In.)	22·54 S	43·33 W
101	Campo Belo Braz. (Rio de Janeiro In.)	20·52 S	45·15 W
124	Campo de Criptana (käm'pō dä krēp-tä'nä) Sp.	39·24 N	3·09 W
95	Campo Florido (kä'm-pō flô-rē'dō) Cuba (Havana In.)	23.07 N	82.07 W
99	Campo Grande (käm-pōō grän'dĕ) Braz.	20·28 S	54·32 W
99	Campo Maior (käm-pōō mä-yôr') Braz.	4·48 S	42·12 W
124	Campo Maior Port.	39·03 N	7·06 W
125	Campo Real (käm'pô rå-äl') Sp. (Madrid In.)	40·21 N	3·23 W
164	Campo R. Cam.	2·23 N	11·07 E
101	Campos (kȧ'm-pôs) Braz. (Rio de Janeiro In.)	21·46 S	41·19 W
101	Campos do Jordão (kȧ'm-pôs-dô-zhôr-dou'N) Braz. (Rio de Janeiro In.)	22·45 S	45·35 W
101	Campos Gerais (kȧ'm-pôs-zhĕ-rȧ'es) Braz. (Rio de Janeiro In.)	21·17 S	45·43 W
166	Camps Bay (kămps) S. Afr. (Cape Town In.)	33·57 S	18·22 E
76	Camp Wood (kămp wŏŏd) Tex.	29·39 N	100·02 W
86	Camrose (kăm-rōz) Can.	53·08 N	112·50 W
95	Camu (R.) (kä'mōō) Dom. Rep.	19·05 N	70·15 W
82	Canaan (R.) (kā'năn) Can.	45·55 N	65·45 W
49	Canada (kăn'ȧ-dȧ) N. A.	50·00 N	100·00 W
83	Canada B. Can.	50·51 N	56·22 W
101	Cañada de Gomez (kä-nyä'dä-dĕ-gô'mĕz) Arg. (Buenos Aires In.)	32·49 S	61·24 W
72	Canadian (kȧ-nā'dĭ-ăn) Tex.	35·54 N	100·24 W
73	Canadian R. Okla.	34·53 N	97·06 W
81	Canajoharie (kăn-ȧ-jō-hăr'ē) N. Y.	42·55 N	74·35 W
127	Çanakkale (chä-näk-kä'lĕ) Tur.	40·10 N	26·26 E
127	Çanakkale Boğazi (Dardanelles) (Str.) (chä-näk-kä'lĕ) (där-dȧ-nĕlz') Tur.	40·05 N	25·50 E
88	Canal Zone N. A. (Panama Canal In.)	9·08 N	80·30 W
81	Canandaigua (kăn-ăn-dā'gwȧ) N. Y.	42·55 N	77·20 W
81	Canandaigua (L.) N. Y.	42·45 N	77·20 W
88	Cananea (kä-nä-nĕ'ä) Mex.	31·00 N	110·20 W
75	Canard R. Can. (Detroit In.)	42·10 N	83·04 W
164	Canarias, Islas (Is.) (ē's-läs-kä-nä'ryäs) Sp.	20·09 N	17·30 W
94	Canarreos, Arch. de los (Is.) (är-chē-pyĕ'lä-gô-dĕ-lôs-kä-när-rĕ'ōs) Cuba	21·35 N	82·20 W
92	Cañas (kä'-nyäs) C. R.	10·26 N	85·06 W
98	Cañasgordas (kä'nyäs-gô'r-däs) Col. (In.)	6·44 N	76·01 W
92	Cañas R. C. R.	10·20 N	85·21 W
81	Canastota (kăn-ȧs-tō'tȧ) N. Y.	43·05 N	75·45 W
99	Canastra, Serra de (Mts.) (sĕ'r-rȧ-dĕ-kȧ-nȧ's-trȧ) Braz.	19·53 S	46·57 W
76	Canatlán (kä-nät-län') Mex.	24·30 N	104·45 W
	Canaveral, C., see Kennedy, C.		
99	Canavieiras (kä-nȧ-vē-ā'räs) Braz.	15·40 S	38·49 W
160	Canberra (kăn'bĕr-ȧ) Austl.	35·21 S	149·10 E
70	Canby (kăn'bĭ) Minn.	44·43 N	96·15 W
98	Canchuaya, Cerros de (Mts.) (sĕ'r-rôs-dĕ-kän-chōō-ȧ'ïä) Peru	7·30 S	74·30 W
91	Cancuc (kän-kōōk) Mex.	16·58 N	92·17 W
94	Candelaria (kän-dĕ-lä'ryä) Cuba	22·45 N	82·55 W
155	Candelaria (kän-dȧ-lä'rē-ä) Phil. (Manila In.)	15·39 N	119·55 E
91	Candelaria (R.) (kän-dĕ-lä-ryä) Mex.	18·25 N	91·21 W
124	Candeleda (kän-dhâ-lā'dhä) Sp.	40·09 N	5·18 W
	Candia, see Kráklion		
64	Candle (kăn'd'l) Alaska	65·00 N	162·04 W
70	Cando (kăn'dō) N. D.	48·27 N	99·13 W
155	Candon (kän-dōn') Phil. (Manila In.)	17·13 N	120·26 E
	Canea, see Khaniá		
101	Canelones (kä-nĕ-lô-nĕs) Ur. (Buenos Aires In.)	34·32 S	56·19 W
101	Canelones (Dept.) Ur. (Buenos Aires In.)	34·34 S	56·15 W
98	Cañete (kän-yā'tȧ) Peru	13·06 S	76·17 W
95	Caney (kä-nā') (kā'nĭ) Cuba	20·05 N	75·45 W
73	Caney (kā'nĭ) Kans.	37·00 N	95·57 W
78	Caney (R.) Tenn.	36·10 N	85·50 W
166	Canganza, Sierra de (Mts.) (sĕr'rȧ dä kän-gän'zȧ) Ang.	7·35 S	15·30 E
124	Cangas (kän'gäs) Sp.	42·15 N	8·43 W
124	Cangas de Narcea (kä'n-gäs-dĕ-när-sĕ-ä) Sp.	43·08 N	6·36 W
126	Canicatti (kä-nē-kät'tē) It.	37·18 N	13·58 E
124	Caniles (kä-nē'läs) Sp.	37·26 N	2·43 W
90	Cañitas (kän-yē'täs) Mex.	23·38 N	102·44 W
133	Cankiri (chän-kē'rē) Tur.	40·40 N	33·40 E
85	Cannell Can. (Edmonton In.)	53·35 N	113·38 W
80	Cannelton (kăn'ĕl-tŭn) Ind.	37·55 N	86·45 W
123	Cannes (kän) Fr.	43·34 N	7·05 E
82	Canning (kăn'ĭng) Can.	45·11 N	64·26 W
110	Cannock (kăn'ŭk) Eng.	52·41 N	2·02 W
110	Cannock Chase (Reg.) (kăn'ŭk chās) Eng.	52·43 N	1·54 W
71	Cannon (R.) (kăn'ŭn) Minn.	44·18 N	93·24 W
70	Cannonball (R.) (kăn'ŭn-băl) N. D.	46·17 N	101·35 W
93	Caño, Isla de (I.) (ē's-lä-dĕ-kä'nō) C. R.	8·38 N	84·00 W
74	Canoga Park (kȧ-nō'gȧ) Calif. (Los Angeles In.)	34·07 N	118·36 W
72	Canon City (kăn'yŭn) Colo.	38·27 N	105·16 W
75	Canonsburg (kăn'ŭnz-bûrg) Pa. (Pittsburgh In.)	40·16 N	80·11 W
79	Canoochee (R.) (kȧ-nōō'chē) Ga.	32·25 N	82·11 W
86	Canora (kȧ-nōrȧ) Can.	51·43 N	102·32 W
126	Canosa (kä-nō'sä) It.	41·14 N	16·03 E
93	Canouan I. N. A. (Le. & Wind. Is. In.)	12·44 N	61·10 W
92	Cansaheab (kän-sä-ĕ-äb) Mex. (Yucatan In.)	21·11 N	89·05 W
83	Canso (kăn'sō) Can.	45·23 N	60·59 W
83	Canso, C. Can.	45·21 N	60·46 W
83	Canso, Str. of Can.	45·50 N	61·35 W
101	Cantagalo (kän-tä-gȧ'lo) Braz. (Rio de Janeiro In.)	21·59 S	42·22 W
124	Cantanhede (kän-täN-yā'dȧ) Port.	40·22 N	8·35 W
110	Canterbury (kăn'tẽr-bĕr-ē) Eng. (London In.)	51·17 N	1·06 E
159	Canterbury Bght. N. Z. (In.)	44·17 S	172·38 E
94	Cantiles, Cayo (I.) (kȳ-ō-kän-tē'lās) Cuba	21·40 N	82·00 W
	Canton, see Kuangchou		
78	Canton Ga.	34·13 N	84·29 W
73	Canton Ill.	40·34 N	90·02 W
83	Canton Mass. (Boston In.)	42·09 N	71·09 W
78	Canton Miss.	32·36 N	90·01 W
73	Canton Mo.	40·08 N	91·33 W
78	Canton N. C.	35·32 N	82·50 W
80	Canton Ohio	40·50 N	81·25 W
81	Canton Pa.	41·50 N	76·45 W
70	Canton S. D.	43·17 N	96·37 W
126	Cantu (kän-tōō') It.	45·43 N	9·09 E
101	Cañuelas (kä-nyōōĕ'-läs) Arg. (Buenos Aires In.)	35·03 S	58·45 W
99	Canumã (R.) (kä-nōō-mä') Braz.	6·20 S	58·57 W
72	Canyon (kăn'yŭn) Tex.	34·59 N	101·57 W
65	Canyon (R.) Wash. (Seattle In.)	48·09 N	121·48 W
76	Canyon Dam Tex.	29·51 N	98·20 W
69	Canyon De Chelly Natl. Mon. Ariz.	36·14 N	110·00 W
155	Capalonga (kä-pä-lôŋ'gä) Phil. (Manila In.)	14·20 N	122·30 E
126	Capannori (kä-pän'nô-rē) It.	43·50 N	10·30 E
125	Caparica (kä-pä-rē'kä) Port. (Lisbon In.)	38·40 N	9·12 W
83	Cap-Aux-Meules Can.	47·25 N	61·51 W
99	Capaya (R.) (kä-pä-ïä) Ven. (In.)	10·28 N	66·15 W
82	Cap Chat (kȧp shä') Can.	49·07 N	66·42 W
82	Cap de la Madeleine (kȧp dē lȧ mȧ-d'lĕn') Can.	46·23 N	72·30 W
83	Cape Breton (I.) (kāp brĕt'ŭn) Can.	45·48 N	59·53 W
83	Cape Breton Highlands Natl. Park Can.	46·45 N	61·05 W
79	Cape Charles (kāp chärlz) Va.	37·13 N	76·02 W
164	Cape Coast Ghana	5·14 N	1·19 W
81	Cape Cod B. (kāp kŏd) Mass.	41·50 N	70·20 W
79	Cape Fear (R.) (kāp fēr) N. C.	34·43 N	78·41 W
166	Cape Flats (kāp flăts) S. Afr. (Cape Town In.)	34·01 S	18·37 E

ng-sing; ŋ-baŋk; N-nasalized n; nŏd; cŏmmit; ōld; ôbey; ôrder; fōōd; fŏŏt; ou-out; s-soft; sh-dish; th-thin; pūre; ûnite; ûrn; stŭd; circŭs; ü-as "y" in study; '-indeterminate vowel.

190 Cape Girardeau–Castellammare di Stabia PRONOUNCING INDEX

Page	Name Pronunciation Region	Lat. °′	Long. °′
73	Cape Girardeau (jē-rär-dō′) . . Mo.	37·17 N	89·32 W
84	Cape Henry (hĕn′rē) Va. (Norfolk In.)	36·55 N	76·00 W
81	Cape May (kāp mā) . . . . N. J.	38·55 N	74·50 W
81	Cape May C. H. (kāp mā) . . N. J.	39·05 N	75·00 W
166	Cape of Good Hope (Prov.) (kāp ŏv gŏŏd hōp) . S. Afr.	31·50 S	21·15 E
86	Cape Parry (kāp păr′rē) . . . . . Can.	70·29 N	127·41 W
166	Cape Point.S. Afr. (Cape Town In.)	34·21 S	18·29 E
87	Cape Smith Ra. (kāp smĭth) . Can.	61·23 N	76·32 W
93	Capesterre Basse Terre (Le. & Wind Is. In.)	16·02 N	61·37 W
166	Cape Town (kāp toun) S. Afr. (Cape Town In.)	33·48 S	18·28 E
159	Cape York Pen. (kāp yôrk) . Austl.	12·30 S	142·35 E
95	Cap-Haitian (kȧp ȧ-ē-syăn′) . . Hai.	19·45 N	72·15 W
101	Capilla de Señor (kä-pēl′yä dā sän-yôr′) . Arg. (Buenos Aires In.)	34·18 S	59·07 W
69	Capitol Reef Natl. Mon. (kăp′ĭ-tŏl) . Utah	38·15 N	111·10 W
101	Capivari (kä-pē-vȧ′rē) Braz. (Rio de Janeiro In.)	22·59 S	47·29 W
100	Capivari . . . . Braz. (In.)	22·39 S	43·19 W
160	Capoompeta (Mtn.) (kȧ-pōōm-pē′tȧ) . Austl.	29·15 S	152·12 E
126	Caporetto (kä-pô-rĕt′tō) . . . Yugo.	46·15 N	13·34 E
126	Capraia (I.) (kä-prä′yä) . . . . It.	43·02 N	9·51 E
126	Caprara Pt. (kä-prä′rä) . . . . It.	41·08 N	8·20 E
126	Caprera (I.) (kä-prā′rä) . . . . It.	41·12 N	9·28 E
125	Capri . . . . It. (Naples In.)	40·18 N	14·16 E
125	Capri, I. di (ē′-sō-lä-dē-kä′prē) It. (Naples In.)	40·19 N	14·10 E
159	Capricorn Chan. (kăp′rĭ-kôrn) Austl.	22·27 S	151·24 E
85	Cap-Rouge (kȧp rōōzh′) Can. (Quebec In.)	46·45 N	71·21 W
85	Cap St. Ignace (kĭp săɴ-tē-nyȧs′) Can. (Quebec In.)	47·02 N	70·27 W
126	Capua (kä′pwä) . . . . It.	41·07 N	14·14 E
90	Capulhuac (kä-pōōl-hwăk′) . . Mex.	19·33 N	99·43 W
72	Capulin Mountain Natl. Mon. (kȧ-pū′lĭn) . N. Mex.	36·15 N	103·58 W
91	Capultitlán (kä-pōō′l-tē-tlà′n) Mex. (Mexico City In.)	19·15 N	99·40 W
98	Caquetá (R.) (kä-kä-tä′) . . . . . Col.	0·23 S	73·22 W
125	Carabaña (kä-rä-bän′yä) Sp. (Madrid In.)	40·16 N	3·15 W
99	Carabobo (State) (kä-rä-bô′-bô) Ven. (In.)	10·07 N	68·06 W
127	Caracal (kȧ-rȧ-kȧl′) . . . . Rom.	44·06 N	24·22 E
99	Caracas (kä-rä′käs) . . . . Ven. (In.)	10·30 N	66·58 W
90	Carácuaro de Morelos (kä-rä′kwä-rō-dĕ-mô-rĕ-lôs) . Mex.	18·44 N	101·04 W
101	Caraguatatuba (kä-rä-gwä-tȧ-tōō′bȧ) . Braz. (Rio de Janeiro In.)	23·37 S	45·26 W
99	Carajás, Serra dos (Mts.) (sĕ′r-rä-dôs-kä-rä-zhà′s) . Braz.	5·58 S	51·45 W
98	Caramanta, Cerro (Mtn.) (sĕ′r-rô-kä-rä-mà′n-tä) . Col. (In.)	5·29 N	76·01 W
100	Caramarca (kä-rä-mà′r-kä) . . . Arg.	28·29 S	65·45 W
155	Caramoan (kä-rä-mō′än) Phil. (Manila In.)	13·46 N	123·52 E
101	Carandaí (kä-rän-dȧē′) Braz. (Rio de Janeiro In.)	20·57 S	43·47 W
101	Carangola (kä-ràn′gŏ′lä) Braz. (Rio de Janeiro In.)	20·46 S	42·02 W
127	Caransebes (kȧ-rȧn-sā′bĕsh) . Rom.	45·24 N	22·13 E
100	Carapeguá (kä-rä-pȧ-gwä′) . . . Arg.	26·01 S	58·13 W
82	Caraquet (kȧ-rȧ-kĕt′) . . . . Can.	47·47 N	64·56 W
93	Carata, Laguna (L.) (lä-gōō′nä-kä-rä′tä) . Nic.	13·59 N	83·41 W
93	Caratasca, Laguna (L.) (lä-gōō′nä-kä-rä-täs′kä) . Hond.	15·20 N	83·45 W
124	Caravaca (kä-rä-vä′kä) . . . . Sp.	38·05 N	1·51 W
99	Caravelas (kȧ-rä-vĕl′äzh) . . . . Braz.	17·46 S	39·06 W
99	Carayaca (kä-rä-ïä′kä) . . Ven. (In.)	10·32 N	67·07 W
100	Caràzinho (kä-rȧ′zē-nyŏ) . . . . Braz.	28·22 S	52·33 W
124	Carballino (kär-bäl-yē′nō) . . . . Sp.	42·26 N	8·04 W
124	Carballo (kär-bäl′yō) . . . . Sp.	43·13 N	8·40 W
65	Carbon (R.) (kär′bŏn) Wash. (Seattle In.)	47·06 N	122·08 W
65	Carbonado (kȧr-bō-nä′dō) Wash. (Seattle In.)	47·05 N	122·03 W
126	Carbonara, C. (kär-bō-nä′rä) . . It.	39·08 N	9·33 E
85	Carbondale (kär′bŏn-dāl) Can. (Edmonton In.)	53·45 N	113·32 W
73	Carbondale . . . . Ill.	37·42 N	89·12 W
81	Carbondale . . . . Pa.	41·35 N	75·30 W
83	Carbonear (kär-bō-nēr′) . . . . . Can.	47·43 N	53·16 W
78	Carbon Hill (kär′bŏn hĭl) . . . . . Ala.	33·53 N	87·34 W
78	Carbur (kär′bûr) . . . . Fla.	29·55 N	83·25 W
125	Carcagente (kär-kä-hĕn′tä) . . . . Sp.	39·09 N	0·29 W
122	Carcans, Étang de (L.) (ā-taɴ-dĕ-kär-kȧɴ) . Fr.	45·12 N	1·00 W
122	Carcassonne (kȧr-kȧ-sŏn′) . . . . . Fr.	43·12 N	2·23 E
86	Carcross (kär′krŏs) . . . . Can.	60·18 N	134·54 W
145	Cardamon Hills (kär′dȧ-mŭm) Ceylon (In.)	9·45 N	77·28 E
94	Cárdenas (kär′dȧ-näs) . . . . . . Cuba	23·00 N	81·10 W
91	Cárdenas (kà′r-dĕ-näs) . . . . . . Mex.	17·59 N	93·23 W
90	Cárdenas . . . . Mex.	22·01 N	99·38 W
95	Cardenas, Bahía de (B.) (bä-ē′ä-dĕ-kär′dȧ-näs) . Cuba	23·10 N	81·10 W
85	Cardiff (kär′dĭf) Can. (Edmonton In.)	53·46 N	113·36 W
116	Cardiff . . . . Wales	51·30 N	3·18 W
116	Cardigan (kär′dĭ-găn) . . . . . . Wales	52·05 N	4·40 W
116	Cardigan B . . . . Wales	52·35 N	4·40 W
86	Cardston (kärds′tŭn) . . . . Can.	49·14 N	113·23 W
121	Carei (kä-rē′) . . . . Rom.	47·42 N	22·28 E
122	Carentan (kä-rôɴ-täɴ′) . . . . Fr.	49·19 N	1·14 W
80	Carey (kā′rē) . . . . Ohio	40·55 N	83·25 W
158	Carey (I.) (kâr′ē) . . . . Austl.	29·20 S	123·35 E
122	Carhaix (kär-ĕ′) . . . . Fr.	48·17 N	3·37 W
89	Caribbean Sea (kăr-ĭ-bē′ăn) N. A.-S. A.	14·30 N	75·30 W
86	Cariboo Mts. (kă′rĭ-bōō) . . . . Can.	53·51 N	122·13 W
82	Caribou . . . . Maine	46·51 N	68·01 W
71	Caribou (I.) . . . . Can.	47·22 N	85·42 W
74	Caribou L. . . . . Minn. (Duluth In.)	46·54 N	92·16 W
86	Caribou Mts. . . . . Can.	59·20 N	115·30 W
99	Carinhanha (kä-rĭ-nyăn′yä) . Braz.	14·14 S	43·44 W
126	Carini (kä-rē′nē) . . . . It.	38·09 N	13·10 E
	Carinthia, See Kärnten		
81	Carleton Place (kärl′tŭn) . . . . Can.	45·15 N	76·10 W
73	Carlinville (kär′lĭn-vĭl) . . . . Ill.	39·16 N	89·52 W
116	Carlisle (kär-līl′) . . . . Eng.	54·54 N	3·03 W
80	Carlisle . . . . Ky.	38·20 N	84·00 W
84	Carlisle . . . . La. (New Orleans In.)	29·41 N	89·57 W
81	Carlisle . . . . Pa.	40·10 N	77·15 W
122	Carlitte, Pic (Pk.) (pēk′-kär-lēt′) Fr.	42·33 N	1·56 E
126	Carloforte (kär′lō-fôr-tȧ) . . . . . . It.	39·11 N	8·18 E
101	Carlos Casares (kär-lôs-kä-sȧ′rĕs) Arg. (Buenos Aires In.)	35·38 S	61·17 W
116	Carlow (kär′lō) . . . . Ire.	52·50 N	7·00 W
76	Carlsbad (kärlz′băd) . . . . . N. Mex.	32·24 N	104·12 W
76	Carlsbad Caverns Natl. Park N. Mex.	32·08 N	104·30 W
110	Carlton (kärl′tŭn) . . . . Eng.	52·58 N	1·05 W
74	Carlton . . . . Minn. (Duluth In.)	46·40 N	92·26 W
80	Carlton Center (kärl′tŭn sĕn′tēr) Mich.	42·45 N	85·20 W
168	Carltonville S. Afr. (Johannesburg & Pretoria In.)	26·20 S	27·23 E
73	Carlyle (kär-līl′) . . . . Ill.	38·37 N	89·23 W
126	Carmagnola (kär-mä-nyô′lä) . . . It.	44·52 N	7·48 E
86	Carman (kär′mȧn) . . . . Can.	49·30 N	98·02 W
116	Carmarthen (kär-mär′thĕn) . Wales	51·50 N	4·20 W
116	Carmarthen B. (kär-mär′thĕn) Wales	51·33 N	4·50 W
122	Carmaux (kȧr-mō′) . . . . Fr.	44·05 N	2·09 E
84	Carmel (kär′mĕl) N. Y. (New York In.)	41·25 N	73·42 W
101	Carmelo (kär-mĕ′lo) Ur. (Buenos Aires In.)	33·59 S	58·15 W
90	Carmen, Isla del (I.) (ē′s-lä-dĕl-kà′r-mĕn) . Mex.	18·43 N	91·40 W
91	Carmen, Laguna del (L.) (lä-gŏŏ′nä-dĕl-kà′r-mĕn) . Mex.	18·15 N	93·26 W
101	Carmen de Areco (kär′mĕn′ dā ä-rā′kō) . Arg. (Buenos Aires In.)	34·21 S	59·50 W
100	Carmen de Patagones (kȧ′r-mĕn-dĕ-pä-tä-gô′-nĕs) . Arg.	40·47 S	62·56 W
80	Carmi (kär′mī) . . . . Ill.	38·05 N	88·10 W
101	Carmo (kȧ′r-mô) Braz. (Rio de Janeiro In.)	21·57 S	42·06 W
101	Carmo do Rio Clara (kȧ′r-mô-dō-rē′ô-klȧ′-rä) Braz. (Rio de Janeiro In.)	20·57 S	46·04 W
124	Carmona (kär-mō′nä) . . . . Sp.	37·28 N	5·38 W
158	Carnarvon (kär-när′vŭn) . . . Austl.	24·45 S	113·45 E
166	Carnarvon . . . . S. Afr.	31·00 S	22·15 E
116	Carnarvon . . . . Wales	53·08 N	4·17 W
116	Carnarvon Bay . . . . Wales	53·09 N	4·56 W
65	Carnation (kär-nā′shŭn) Wash. (Seattle In.)	47·39 N	121·55 W
125	Carnaxide (kär-nä-shē′dĕ) Port. (Lisbon In.)	38·44 N	9·15 W
116	Carndonagh (kärn-dō-nä′) . . . . Ire.	54·75 N	6·75 W
72	Carnegie (kär-nĕg′ĭ) . . . . Okla.	35·06 N	98·38 W
75	Carnegie . . . . Pa. (Pittsburgh In.)	40·24 N	80·06 W
81	Carneys Point (kär′nês) . . . . . N. J.	39·45 N	75·25 W
120	Carnic Alps (Mts.) . . . . . . Aus.-It.	46·43 N	12·38 E
125	Carnot (kär nō′) . . . . Alg.	36·15 N	1·40 E
165	Carnot . . . . Cen. Afr. Rep.	4·56 N	16·00 E
116	Carnsore Pt. (kärn′sôr) . . . . . . Ire.	52·10 N	6·16 W
80	Caro (kâ′rō) . . . . Mich.	43·30 N	83·25 W
99	Carolina (kä-rô-lē′nä) . . . . Braz.	7·26 S	47·16 W
166	Carolina (kăr-ô-lī′nȧ) . . . . . . S. Afr.	26·07 S	30·09 E
92	Carolina L. (kä-rŏ-lē′-nä) Mex. (Yucatan In.)	18·41 N	89·40 W
156	Caroline Is. (kăr′ô-līn) Pac. Is. Trust Ter.	9·30 N	143·00 E
98	Caroni (R.) (kä-rō′nē) . . . . Ven.	5·49 N	62·57 W
98	Carora (kä-rō′rä) . . . . Ven.	10·09 N	70·12 W
115	Carpathians Mts. (kär-pā′thĭ-ăn) Eur.	49·23 N	20·14 E
127	Carpatii Meridionali (Transyl-vanian Alps) (Mts.) . Rom.	45·30 N	23·30 E
158	Capentaria, G. of (kär-pĕn-târ′ĭȧ) . Austl.	14·45 S	138·50 E
74	Carpenter (kär′pĕn-tēr) Ill. (St. Louis In.)	38·54 N	89·54 W
122	Carpentras (kär-päɴ-träs′) . . . . Fr.	44·04 N	5·01 E
126	Carpi . . . . It.	44·48 N	10·54 E
78	Carrabelle (kăr′ȧ-bĕl) . . . . Fla.	29·50 N	84·40 W
116	Carrantuohill (kă-rǎn-tōō′ĭl) . Ire.	52·01 N	9·48 W
126	Carrara (kä-rä′rä) . . . . It.	44·05 N	10·05 E
98	Carretas, Punta (Pt.) (pōō′n-tä-kär-rĕ′tȧs) . Peru	13·50 S	76·24 W
93	Carriacou I. (kăr-ē-ȧ-kōō′) N. A. (Le. & Wind. Is. In.)	12·28 N	61·20 W
116	Carrick (kăr′ĭk) . . . . Ire.	52·20 N	7·35 W
85	Carrier (kăr′ĭ-ēr) Can. (Quebec In.)	46·43 N	71·05 W
78	Carriere (kȧ-rēr′) . . . . Miss.	30·37 N	89·37 W
80	Carriers Mills (kăr′ĭ-ērs) . . . . . . Ill.	37·40 N	88·40 W
70	Carrington (kăr′ĭng-tŭn) . . . . N. D.	47·26 N	99·06 W
65	Carr Inlet (kär ĭn′lĕt) Wash. (Seattle In.)	47·20 N	122·42 W
124	Carrion (kär-rê-ōn′) . . . . Sp.	42·36 N	6·42 W
94	Carrion Crow Hbr. (kăr′ĭŭn krō) Ba. Is.	26·35 N	77·55 W
124	Carrión de los Condes (kär-rê-ōn′ dā lōs kōn′dâs) . Sp.	42·20 N	4·35 W
72	Carrizo Cr. (kär-rē′zō) . . . N. Mex.	36·22 N	103·39 W
76	Carrizo Springs . . . . Tex.	28·32 N	99·51 W
69	Carrizozo (kär-rē-zō′zō) . . N. Mex.	33·40 N	105·55 W
71	Carroll (kăr′ŭl) . . . . Iowa	42·03 N	94·51 W
78	Carrollton (kăr-ŭl-tŭn) . . . . Ga.	33·35 N	84·05 W
73	Carrollton . . . . Ill.	39·18 N	90·22 W
80	Carrollton . . . . Ky.	38·45 N	85·15 W
80	Carrollton . . . . Mich.	43·30 N	83·55 W
73	Carrollton . . . . Mo.	39·21 N	93·29 W
80	Carrollton . . . . Ohio	40·35 N	81·10 W
74	Carrollton Tex. (Dallas, Fort Worth In.)	32·58 N	96·53 W
75	Carrollville (kăr′ŭl vĭl) Wis. (Milwaukee In.)	42·53 N	87·52 W
65	Carrols (kăr′ŭlz) Wash. (Portland In.)	46·05 N	122·51 W
116	Carron (L.) (kȧ′rŭn) . . . . Scot.	57·25 N	5·25 W
122	Carry-le-Rouet (kä-rē′lĕ-rōō-ā′) Fr. (Marseille In.)	43·20 N	5·10 E
133	Çarşamba (chär-shäm′bä) . . . . Tur.	41·05 N	36·40 E
68	Carson (R.) (kär′sŭn) . . . . Nev.	39·15 N	119·25 W
68	Carson City . . . . Nev.	39·10 N	119·45 W
68	Carson Sink . . . . Nev.	39·51 N	118·25 W
155	Carstensz-Toppen (Pk.) (kärs′tĕns) W. Irian	4·00 S	137·10 E
98	Cartagena (kär-tä-hā′nä) . . . . . Col.	10·30 N	75·40 W
125	Cartagena (kär-tä-kĕ′nä) . . . . . . Sp.	37·46 N	1·00 W
98	Cartago (kär-tä′gō) . . . . . Col. (In.)	4·44 N	75·54 W
93	Cartago . . . . C. R.	9·52 N	83·56 W
124	Cartaxo (kär-tä′shō) . . . . Port.	39·10 N	8·48 W
84	Carteret (kär′tē-rĕt) N. J. (New York In.)	40·35 N	74·13 W
78	Cartersville (kär′tērs-vĭl) . . . . . Ga.	34·09 N	84·47 W
73	Carthage (kär′thāj) . . . . Ill.	40·27 N	91·09 W
73	Carthage . . . . Mo.	37·10 N	94·18 W
81	Carthage . . . . N. Y.	44·00 N	75·45 W
79	Carthage . . . . N. C.	35·22 N	79·25 W
77	Carthage . . . . Tex.	32·09 N	94·20 W
164	Carthage . . . . Tun.	37·04 N	10·18 E
167	Carthcart (cärth-cȧ′t) S. Afr. (Natal In.)	32·18 S	27·11 E
87	Cartwright (kärt′rīt) . . . . Can.	53·36 N	57·00 W
99	Caruaru (kä-rōō-ȧ-rōō′) . . . . . Braz.	8·19 S	35·52 W
98	Carúpano (kä-rōō′pä-nō) . . . . . Ven.	10·45 N	63·21 W
73	Caruthersville (kȧ-rŭdh′ērz-vĭl) Mo	36·09 N	89·41 W
65	Carver (kärv′ēr) Ore. (Portland In.)	45·24 N	122·30 W
124	Carvoeira, Cabo (C.) (kȧ′bō-kär-vô-ĕ′y-rä) . Port.	39·22 N	9·24 W
75	Cary (kā′rē) . . . . Ill. (Chicago In.)	42·13 N	88·14 W
101	Casablanca (kä-sä-blăŋ′kä) Chile (Santiago In.)	33·19 S	71·24 W
164	Casablanca . . . . Mor.	33·32 N	7·41 W
101	Casa Branca (kȧ′sȧ-brȧ′ɴ-kȧ) Braz. (Rio de Janeiro In.)	21·47 S	47·04 W
69	Casa Grande (kä′sä grän′dā) . Ariz.	32·50 N	111·45 W
69	Casa Grande Natl. Mon. . . . . Ariz.	33·00 N	111·33 W
126	Casale (kä-sä′lä) . . . . It.	45·08 N	8·26 E
126	Casalmaggiore (kä-säl-mȧd-jō′rä) . It.	45·00 N	10·24 E
164	Casamance R. (kä-sȧ-mȧɴs′) Senegal	12·58 N	15·15 W
85	Cascade (kăs-kād′) Can. (Ottawa In.)	45·35 N	75·51 W
159	Cascade Pt. . . . . N. Z. (In.)	43·59 S	168·23 E
62	Cascade Ra . . . . U. S.	42·50 N	122·20 W
85	Cascades Point (kăs-kādz′) Can. (Montreal In.)	45·19 N	73·58 W
66	Cascade Tun. . . . . Wash.	47·41 N	120·53 W
125	Cascais (käs-kȧ-ēzh) Port. (Lisbon In.)	38·42 N	9·25 W
125	Cascais, Ba. de (B.) (bä-ē′ä-dĕ-käs-kī′s) Port. (Lisbon In.)	38·41 N	9·24 W
65	Case Inlet (kās) Wash. (Seattle In.)	47·22 N	122·47 W
100	Caseros (kä-sā′rôs) . . . . . Arg. (In.)	34·21 S	58·34 W
126	Caserta (kä-zĕr′tä) . . . . It.	41·04 N	14·21 E
80	Casey (kā′sĭ) . . . . Ill.	39·20 N	88·00 W
66	Cashmere (kăsh′mĭr) . . . . Wash.	47·30 N	120·28 W
155	Casiguran (kä-sē-gōō′rän) Phil. (Manila In.)	16·15 N	122·10 E
155	Casiguran Sd. . . Phil. (Manila In.)	16·02 N	121·51 E
101	Casilda (kä-sē′l-dä) Arg. (Buenos Aires In.)	33·02 S	61·11 W
94	Casilda . . . . Cuba	21·50 N	80·00 W
101	Casimiro de Abreu (kä′sē-mē′ro-dĕ-ȧ-brĕ′ōō) . Braz. (Rio de Janeiro In.)	22·30 S	42·11 W
160	Casino (kȧ-sē′nō) . . . . Austl.	28·35 S	153·10 E
98	Casiquiare (R.) (kä-sê-kyä′rä) Ven.	2·11 N	66·15 W
125	Caspe (käs′pȧ) . . . . Sp.	41·18 N	0·02 W
67	Casper (kăs′pēr) . . . . Wyo.	42·51 N	106·18 W
132	Caspian Dep. (kăs′pĭ-ăn) . Sov. Un.	47·40 N	51·40 E
130	Caspian Sea . . . . Sov. Un.	39·30 N	52·00 E
81	Cass (kăs) . . . . W. Va.	38·25 N	79·55 W
71	Cass (L.) . . . . Minn.	47·23 N	94·28 W
125	Cassá de la Selva (käs-sä′dĕ-lä-sĕl-vä) . Sp.	41·52 N	2·52 E
166	Cassai (R.) (kä-sä′ē) . . . . Ang.	11·15 S	21·00 E
80	Cass City (kăs) . . . . Mich.	43·35 N	83·10 W
85	Casselman (kăs′′l-mȧn) Can. (Ottawa In.)	45·18 N	75·05 W
70	Casselton (kăs′′l-tŭn) . . . . N. D.	46·53 N	97·14 W
101	Cássia (kȧ′syä) Braz. (Rio de Janeiro In.)	20·36 S	46·53 W
74	Cassin (kăs′ĭn) Tex. (San Antonio In.)	29·16 N	98·29 W
166	Cassinga (kä-sĭŋ′gä) . . . . Ang.	15·05 S	16·15 E
126	Cassino (käs-sē′nō) . . . . It.	41·30 N	13·50 E
71	Cass Lake (kăs) . . . . Minn.	47·23 N	94·37 W
80	Cassopolis (kăs-ŏ′pō-lĭs) . . . . Mich.	41·55 N	86·00 W
73	Cassville (kăs′vĭl) . . . . Mo.	36·41 N	93·52 W
124	Castanheira de Pêra (käs-tän-yā′rä-dĕ-pĕ′rä) . Port.	40·00 N	8·07 W
122	Casteljaloux (käs-tĕl-zhä-lōō′) . Fr.	44·20 N	0·04 E
125	Castellammare di Stabia (käs-tĕl-läm-mä′rä-dē-stä′byä) It. (Naples In.)	40·26 N	14·29 E

ăt; finăl; rāte; senâte; ärm; ȧsk; sofȧ; fâre; ch-choose; dh-as th in other; bē; ēvent; bĕt; recĕnt; cratēr; g-go; gh-guttural g; bĭt; ĭ-short neutral: rīde; ĸ-guttural k as ch in German ich;

ng-sing; ŋ-baŋk; ɴ-nasalized n; nŏd; cŏmmit; ōld; ōbey; ôrder; fōōd; fŏŏt; ou-out; s-soft; sh-dish; th-thin; pūre; ûnite; ûrn; stŭd; circŭs; ü-as "y" in study; '-indeterminate vowel.

192 Chalon-sur-Saone–Chepo PRONOUNCING INDEX

Page	Name Pronunciation Region	Lat. °′	Long. °′
122	Châlon-sur-Saône Fr.	46·47 N	4·54 E
100	Chaltel, Cerro (Mtn.) (sĕ'r-rô-chäl'tĕl). Arg.-Chile	48·10 S	73·18 W
69	Chama (R.) (chä'mä) N. Mex.	36·19 N	106·31 W
92	Chama, Sierra de (Mts.) (sē-ĕ'r-rä-dĕ-chä-mä). Guat.	15·48 N	90·20 W
122	Chamalières (shä-mä-lyâr') Fr.	45·45 N	2·59 E
142	Chaman (chŭm,-än') W. Pak.	30·58 N	66·21 E
142	Chambal (R.) (chŭm-bäl') India	26·05 N	76·37 E
70	Chamberlain (chām'bĕr-lĭn) S. D.	43·48 N	99·21 W
82	Chamberlain (L.) Maine	46·15 N	67·05 W
81	Chambersburg (chām'bĕrz-bûrg) Pa.	40·00 N	77·40 W
123	Chambéry (shäm-bā-rē') Fr.	45·35 N	5·54 E
84	Chamblee (chăm-blē') Ga. (Atlanta In.)	33·53 N	84·18 W
85	Chambly (shäN-blē') Can. (Montreal In.)	45·27 N	73·17 W
123	Chambly Fr. (Paris In.)	49·11 N	2·14 E
87	Chambord Can.	48·22 N	72·01 W
93	Chame, Punta (Pt.) (po͞o'n-tä-chä'mȧ). Pan.	8·41 N	79·27 W
92	Chamelecón R. (chä-mĕ-lĕ-kŏ'n) Hond.	15·09 N	88·42 W
165	Chamo L. (chä'mō) Eth.	5·58 N	37·00 E
123	Chamonix (shȧ-mô-nē') Fr.	45·55 N	6·50 E
122	Champagne (Reg.) (shäm-pän'-yē). Fr.	48·53 N	4·48 E
80	Champaign (shăm-pān') Ill.	40·10 N	88·15 W
92	Champerico (chăm-pȧ-rē'kō) Guat.	14·18 N	91·55 W
71	Champion (chăm'pĭ-ŭn) Mich.	46·30 N	87·59 W
81	Champlain, L. (shăm-plān') N. Y.-Vt.	44·45 N	73·20 W
123	Champlitte (shäN-plēt') Fr.	47·38 N	5·28 E
91	Champotón (chäm-pō-tōn') Mex.	19·21 N	90·43 W
91	Champotón (R.) Mex.	19·19 N	90·15 W
100	Chañaral (chän-yä-räl') Chile	26·20 S	70·46 W
124	Chanca (R.) (chäŋ'kä) Sp.-Port.	38·15 N	7·22 W
151	Chanchiang (Fort Bayard) China	21·20 N	110·28 E
142	Chanda (chăn'dŭ) India	19·58 N	79·21 E
78	Chandeleur Is. (shăn-dē-lo͞or'). La.	29·53 N	88·35 W
78	Chandeleur Sd. La.	29·47 N	89·08 W
142	Chandīgarh India	30·51 N	77·13 E
82	Chandler (chăn'dlēr) Can.	48·24 N	64·40 W
74	Chandler Mo. (Kansas City In.)	39·18 N	94·24 W
73	Chandler Okla.	35·42 N	96·52 W
148	Chang (R.) (jäng) China	36·17 N	114·31 E
166	Changane (R.) Moz.	22·42 S	32·46 E
148	Ch'angch'ichuang (chäng'chē'zho͝oäng). China	37·59 N	116·57 E
150	Ch'angchih China	35·58 N	112·58 E
148	Ch'angch'ing (chäng'chĭng). China	36·33 N	116·42 E
148	Changch'iu (zhängchĭu) China	36·50 N	117·29 E
150	Ch'angch'un (Hsinking) (chäng'cho͞on') (hsĭn'kĭng) China	43·55 N	125·25 E
148	Ch'anghsing Tao (I.) (chängsĭng dou). China	39·38 N	121·10 E
150	Ch'anghsintien China (Peking In.)	39·49 N	116·12 E
151	Changhua (chäng'hwä') Taiwan	24·02 N	120·32 E
148	Changhutien (jang'ho͞o'dĭan) China	32·07 N	114·44 E
148	Ch'angi (jäng'yē) China	36·51 N	119·23 E
152	Changjŏn (chäng'jŭn') Kor.	38·38 N	128·02 E
150	Changkochuang China (Peking In.)	40·09 N	116·56 E
150	Changkuangts'ai Ling (Mts.) China	43·50 N	127·55 E
148	Ch'angli (chäng'lē') China	39·46 N	119·10 E
150	Changpei (chäng'pē') China	41·12 N	114·50 E
152	Changsan Cot (I.) Kor.	38·06 N	124·50 E
148	Ch'angshan Liehtao (Is.) (chäng'shän' lĭĕdou). China	39·08 N	122·26 E
148	Ch'angshan Tao (I.) (chäng'shän' dou). China	37·56 N	120·42 E
148	Ch'angshu (chäng'sho͞o') China	31·40 N	120·45 E
151	Ch'angte (chäng'tĕ') China	29·00 N	111·38 E
148	Changtien (jäng'dĭan) China	36·48 N	118·04 E
151	Changting China	25·50 N	116·18 E
146	Ch'angtu (chäng'to͞o') China	31·06 N	96·30 E
152	Changtu China	43·00 N	124·02 E
148	Ch'angtzu Tao (I.) (chäng'zho͞o dou). China	39·02 N	122·44 E
150	Changwu (chäng'wo͞o') China	35·12 N	107·45 E
152	Changwu China	42·21 N	123·00 E
146	Changyeh China	38·46 N	101·00 E
148	Ch'angyüan (chäng'yü-än'). China	35·10 N	114·41 E
74	Chanhassen (shăn'hăs-sĕn) Minn. (Minneapolis, St. Paul In.)	44·52 N	93·32 W
148	Chanhua (jän'ho͞oä) China	37·42 N	117·49 E
122	Channel Is. (chăn'ĕl) Eur.	49·20 N	2·40 W
83	Channel-Port aux Basques (pôr'tō bȧsk). Can.	47·36 N	59·09 W
77	Channelview (chăn'ĕlvū) Tex. (In.)	29·46 N	95·07 W
150	Chanping China	40·12 N	116·10 E
124	Chantada (chän-tä'dä) Sp.	42·38 N	7·36 W
154	Chanthaburi Thai.	12·37 N	102·04 E
123	Chantilly (shäN-tē-yē') Fr. (Paris In.)	49·12 N	2·30 E
86	Chantrey Inlet (chăn-trē) Can.	67·49 N	94·30 W
73	Chanute (shȧ-no͞ot') Kans.	37·41 N	95·27 W
134	Chany (L.) (chä'nê) Sov. Un.	54·15 N	77·31 E
150	Chanyü China	44·30 N	122·30 E
151	Ch'aoan (chä'ō-än') China	23·48 N	117·10 E
148	Ch'aohsien (chou'sĭan) China	31·37 N	117·50 E
148	Chaohsien China	37·46 N	114·48 E
154	Chao Phraya, Mae Nam (R.) Thai.	16·13 N	99·33 E
148	Ch'aoshui (jĭousōōĭ) China	37·43 N	120·56 E
151	Chaot'ung (chä'ō-to͞ong) China	27·18 N	103·50 E
151	Ch'aoyang (chä'ō-yäng') China	23·18 N	116 32 E
150	Ch'aoyang (Foshan) China	41·32 N	120·20 E
148	Chaoyüan (chä'ō-yü-än') China	37·22 N	120·23 E
99	Chapada, Serra da (Mts.) (sĕ'r-rä-dä-shä-pá'dä). Braz.	14·57 S	54·34 W
101	Chapadão, Serra do (Mtn.) (sĕ'r-rä-dô-shä-pä-dou'N) Braz. (Rio de Janeiro In.)	20·31 S	46·20 W
90	Chapala, Lago de (L.) (lä'gô-dĕ-chä-pä'lä). Mex.	20·14 N	103·02 W
90	Chapalagana (R.) (chä-pä-lä-gȧ'nä). Mex.	22·11 N	104·09 W
98	Chaparral (chä-pär-rȧ'l). Col. (In.)	3·44 N	75·28 W
90	Chapata (chä-pä'tä) Mex.	20·18 N	103·10 W
133	Chapayevsk (chȧ-pī'ĕfsk). Sov. Un.	53·00 N	49·30 E
79	Chapel Hill (chăp''l hĭl) N. C.	35·55 N	79·05 W
65	Chaplain (L.) (chăp'lĭn) Wash. (Seattle In.)	47·58 N	121·50 W
87	Chapleau (chăp-lō') Can.	47·43 N	83·28 W
166	Chapmans B. (chăp'mȧns bă) S. Afr. (Cape Town In.)	34·06 S	18·17 E
70	Chappell (chă-pĕl') Nebr.	41·06 N	102·29 W
91	Chapultenango (chä-po͞ol-tē-näŋ'gō). Mex.	17·19 N	93·08 W
90	Charcas (chär'käs) Mex.	23·09 N	101·09 W
93	Charco de Azul, Bahia (B.) (bä-ē'ä-chä'r-kō-dĕ-ä-zo͞o'l). Pan.	8·14 N	82·45 W
103	Chardzhou (chēr-jô'o͞o) Sov. Un.	38·52 N	63·37 E
122	Charente (shȧ-räNt') Fr.	45·48 N	0·28 W
165	Chari (R.) (shä-rē') Chad	11·02 N	15·46 E
110	Charing (chă'rĭng) Eng. (London In.)	51·13 N	0·49 E
71	Chariton (chăr'ĭ-tŭn) Iowa	41·02 N	93·16 W
73	Chariton (R.) Mo.	40·24 N	92·38 W
85	Charlemagne (shärl-māny') Can. (Montreal In.)	45·43 N	73·29 W
117	Charleroi (shȧr-lē-rwä') Bel.	50·25 N	4·35 E
75	Charleroi (shär'lē-roi) Pa. (Pittsburgh In.)	40·08 N	79·54 W
79	Charles, C. (chärlz) Va.	37·05 N	75·48 W
85	Charlesbourg (shȧrl-bo͞or') Can. (Quebec In.)	46·51 N	71·16 W
71	Charles City (chärlz) Iowa	43·03 N	92·40 W
80	Charleston (chärlz'tŭn) Ill.	39·30 N	88·10 W
78	Charleston Miss.	34·00 N	90·02 W
73	Charleston Mo.	36·53 N	89·20 W
79	Charleston S. C.	32·47 N	79·56 W
80	Charleston W. Va.	38·20 N	81·35 W
75	Charlestown (chärlz'toun) Ind. (Louisville In.)	38·46 N	85·39 W
93	Charlestown St. Kitts-Nevis-Anguilla (Le. & Wind. Is. In.)	17·10 N	62·32 W
166	Charlesville Con. L.	5·19 S	30·59 E
160	Charleville (chär'lē-vĭl) Austl.	26·16 S	146·28 E
122	Charleville (shärl-vēl') Fr.	49·48 N	4·41 E
80	Charlevoix (shär'lē-voi) Mich.	45·20 N	86·15 W
71	Charlevoix, L. Mich.	45·17 N	85 43 W
80	Charlotte (shär'lŏt) Mich.	42·35 N	84·50 W
79	Charlotte N. C.	35·15 N	80·50 W
89	Charlotte Amalie (St. Thomas) (shär-lŏt'ĕ ä-mä'lĭ-ȧ). Virgin Is. (U. S. A.) (St. Thomas In.)	18·21 N	64·54 W
79	Charlotte Hbr. Fla. (In.)	26·47 N	81·58 W
118	Charlottenberg (shär-lŭt'ĕn-bĕrg) Swe.	59·53 N	12·17 E
81	Charlottesville (shär'lŏtz-vĭl) Va.	38·00 N	78·25 W
83	Charlottetown (shär'lŏt-toun) Can.	46·14 N	63·08 W
158	Charlotte Waters (shär'lŏt). Austl.	26·00 S	134·50 E
123	Charmes (shärm) Fr.	48·23 N	6·19 E
110	Charnwood Forest (chärn'wo͝od) Eng.	52·42 N	1·15 W
85	Charny (shär-nē') Can. (Quebec In.)	46·43 N	71·16 W
142	Charol Tsho (L.) China	34·00 N	81·47 E
123	Chars (shär) Fr. (Paris In.)	49·09 N	1·57 E
145	Charsadda (chŭr-sä'dä) W. Pak. (Khyber Pass In.)	34·17 N	71·43 E
159	Charters Towers (chär'tērz) Austl.	20·03 S	146·20 E
123	Chartres (shärt'r'). Fr. (Paris In.)	48·26 N	1·29 E
101	Chascomús (chäs-kō-mo͞os') Arg. (Buenos Aires In.)	35·32 S	58·01 W
79	Chase City (chās) Va.	36·45 N	78·27 W
128	Chashniki (chäsh'nyē-kē). Sov. Un.	54·51 N	29·08 E
74	Chaska (chăs'kȧ) Minn. (Minneapolis, St. Paul In.)	44·48 N	93·36 W
122	Châteaubriant (shȧ-tō-brē-äN'). Fr.	47·43 N	1·23 W
122	Châteaudun (shȧ-tō-dăN') Fr.	48·04 N	1·23 E
122	Château-Gontier (shȧ-tō' gôN' tyā'). Fr.	47·48 N	0·43 W
85	Chateauguay (shȧ-tō-gā') Can. (Montreal In.)	45·22 N	73·45 W
85	Châteauguay, R. Can. (Montreal In.)	45·13 N	73·51 W
85	Chateauguay Basin Can. (Montreal In.)	45·22 N	73·44 W
122	Chateauneuf-les-Martigues (shȧ-tō-nûf'lā-mär-tēg'ĕ) Fr. (Marseille In.)	43·23 N	5·11 E
122	Château-Renault (shȧ-tō-rē-nō') Fr.	47·36 N	0·57 E
85	Château-Richer (shȧ-tō'rē-shā') Can. (Quebec In.)	46·58 N	71·01 W
122	Châteauroux (shȧ-tō-ro͞o') Fr.	46·47 N	1·39 E
122	Château-Thierry (shȧ-tō'tyĕr-rē') Fr.	49·03 N	3·22 E
122	Châtellerault (shä-tĕl-rō') Fr.	46·48 N	0·31 E
71	Chatfield (chăt'fēld) Minn.	43·50 N	92·10 W
80	Chatham (chăt'ȧm) Can.	42·25 N	82·10 W
82	Chatham Can.	47·01 N	65·28 W
110	Chatham (chăt'ŭm) Eng. (London In.)	51·21 N	0·27 E
84	Chatham (chăt'ȧm) N. J. (New York In.)	40·44 N	74·23 W
75	Chatham Ohio (Cleveland In.)	41·06 N	82·01 W
156	Chatham Is. N. Z.	44·00 S	178·00 W
64	Chatham Str. Alaska	57·00 N	134·40 W
74	Chatsworth (chătz'wûrth) Calif. (Los Angeles In.)	34·16 N	118·36 W
74	Chatsworth Res. Calif. (Los Angeles In.)	34·15 N	118·41 W
78	Chattahoochee (chăt-tȧ-ho͞o' chēē) Fla.	30·42 N	84·47 W
78	Chattahoochee (R.) Ala.-Ga.	31·17 N	85·10 W
78	Chattanooga (chăt-ȧ-no͞o'gȧ) Tenn.	35·01 N	85·15 W
78	Chattooga (R.) (chȧ-to͞o'gȧ) Ga.-S. C.	34·47 N	83·13 W
82	Chaudiere (R.) (shō-dyĕr') Can.	46·26 N	71·10 W
154	Chau Doc (shō-dôk') Camb.	10·49 N	104·57 E
122	Chaumont (shō-môN') Fr.	48·08 N	5·07 E
123	Chaumontel (shō-mŏN-tĕl') Fr. (Paris In.)	49·07 N	2·26 E
135	Chaunskaya Guba (B.) Sov. Un.	69·15 N	170·00 E
122	Chauny (shō-nē') Fr.	49·40 N	3·09 E
128	Chausy (chou'sĭ) Sov. Un.	53·57 N	30·58 E
81	Chautauqua (L.) (shȧ-tô'kwȧ) N. Y.	42·10 N	79·25 W
132	Chavaniga Sov. Un.	66·02 N	37·50 E
124	Chaves (chä'vĕzh) Port.	41·44 N	7·30 W
90	Chavinda (chä-vē'n-dä) Mex.	20·01 N	102·27 W
91	Chazumba (chä-zo͞om'bä) Mex.	18·11 N	97·41 W
110	Cheadle (chē'd'l) Eng.	52·59 N	1·59 W
81	Cheat (R.) (chēt) W. Va.	39·35 N	79·40 W
120	Cheb (κĕb) Czech.	50·05 N	12·23 E
136	Chebarkul (chĕ-bȧr-kûl') Sov. Un. (Urals In.)	54·59 N	60·22 E
132	Cheboksary (chyĕ-bôk-sä'rê) Sov. Un.	56·00 N	47·20 E
80	Cheboygan (shê-boi'gȧn) Mich.	45·40 N	84·30 W
164	Chech, Erg (Dune) Alg.	24·45 N	2·07 W
133	Chechen' (I.) (chyĕch'ĕn). Sov. Un.	44·00 N	48·10 E
148	Chech'eng (jĭucheng) China	34·05 N	115·19 E
147	Chechiang (Chekiang) (Prov.) China	29·28 N	119·33 E
73	Checotah (chê-kō'tȧ) Okla.	35·27 N	95·32 W
83	Chedabucto B. (chĕd-ȧ-bŭk-tō) Can.	45·25 N	61·05 W
154	Cheduba (I.) Bur.	18·45 N	93·01 E
86	Cheecham Hills (chēē'hăm) Can.	55·56 N	112·06 W
75	Cheektowaga (chēk-tō-wä'gȧ) N. Y. (Buffalo In.)	42·54 N	78·46 W
	Chefoo, see Yent'ai		
66	Chehalis (chê-hā'lĭs) Wash.	46·39 N	122·58 W
66	Chehalis R. Wash.	46·47 N	123·17 W
152	Cheju (chĕ'jo͞o') Kor.	33·29 N	126·40 E
152	Cheju (Quelpart) (I.) Kor.	33·20 N	126·25 E
128	Chekalin (chĕ-kä'lĭn) Sov. Un.	54·05 N	36·13 E
148	Chekao (jĭugou) China	31·47 N	117·44 E
	Chekiang, see Chechiang		
166	Chela, Serrada (Mts.) (sĕr'rȧ dä shä'lȧ). Ang.	15·30 S	13·30 E
66	Chelan (chê-lăn') Wash.	47·51 N	119·59 W
151	Chelang Chiao (Pt.) China	22·38 N	116·00 E
66	Chelan R. Wash.	48·09 N	120·20 W
125	Cheleiros (shĕ-la'rōzh) Port. (Lisbon In.)	38·54 N	9·19 W
113	Chelic (Mt.) (shĕl-ĭk) Alg.	35·22 N	6·47 E
125	Chéliff, Oued (R.) (o͞o-ĕd shä-lēf) Alg.	36·17 N	1·22 E
134	Chelkar (chyĕl'kär) Sov. Un.	47·52 N	59·41 E
133	Chelkar (L.) Sov. Un.	50·30 N	51·30 E
134	Chelkar Tengiz (L.) (chyĕl'kär tĕn'yēz). Sov. Un.	47·42 N	61·45 E
125	Chellala (chĕl-ȧ'lä) Alg.	35·12 N	2·20 E
121	Chełm (κĕlm) Pol.	51·08 N	23·30 E
121	Chełmno (κĕlm'nō) Pol.	53·20 N	18·25 E
110	Chelmsford (chĕlm's-fērd) Eng. (London In.)	51·44 N	0·28 E
83	Chelmsford Mass. (Boston In.)	42·36 N	71·21 W
84	Chelsea (chĕl'sê) Ala. (Birmingham In.)	33·20 N	86·38 W
161	Chelsea Austl. (Melbourne In.)	38·05 S	145·08 E
85	Chelsea Can. (Ottawa In.)	45·30 N	75·46 W
83	Chelsea Mass. (Boston In.)	42·23 N	71·02 W
80	Chelsea Mich.	42·20 N	84·00 W
73	Chelsea Okla.	36·32 N	95·23 W
116	Cheltenham (chĕlt''nȧm) Eng.	51·57 N	2·06 W
125	Chelva (chĕl'vä) Sp.	39·43 N	1·00 W
136	Chelyabinsk (chĕl-yä-bênsk') Sov. Un. (Urals In.)	55·10 N	61·25 E
135	Chelyuskin, Mys (C.) (chĕl-yo͞os'-kĭn). Sov. Un.	77·45 N	104·45 E
122	Chemillé (shĕ-mê-yā') Fr.	47·13 N	0·46 W
	Chemnitz, see Karl-Marx-Stadt		
81	Chemung (R.) (shê-mŭng) N. Y.	42·20 N	77·25 W
135	Chĕn, Gora (Mtn.) Sov. Un.	65·13 N	142·12 E
142	Chenāb (R.) (chê-näb) W. Pak.	31·33 N	72·28 E
164	Chenachane (Oasis) (shē-nȧ-shän') Alg.	26·14 N	4·14 W
148	Chenchiang (jienjäng) China	32·13 N	119·24 E
66	Cheney (chē'nȧ) Wash.	47·29 N	117·34 W
	Chengchow, see Chenghsien		
151	Ch'enghai China	23·22 N	116·40 E
148	Chenghsien (Chengchow) (jĕngsĭen) (jĕngjō). China	34·46 N	113·42 E
146	Ch'enghua China	47·52 N	87·50 E
151	Chengku China	33·05 N	107·25 E
150	Ch'engte (Jehol) (chĕng'tĕ') (rē-hōl'). China	40·50 N	117·50 E
148	Chengting (chengding) China	38·10 N	114·35 E
151	Ch'engtu (chĕng'to͞o') China	30·30 N	104·10 E
148	Chengyang (chĕn'yäng') China	32·34 N	114·22 E
146	Chenhsi China	43·43 N	92·50 E
151	Ch'enshien China	25·40 N	113·00 E
149	Ch'entsun China (Canton In.)	22·58 N	113·14 E
150	Chentung China	45·28 N	123·42 E
151	Chenyüan (chĕn'yü-an') China	27·08 N	108·30 E
149	Chepei China (Canton In.)	23·07 N	113·23 E
98	Chepén (chĕ-pĕ'n) Peru	7·17 S	79·24 W
93	Chepo (chä'pō) Pan.	9·12 N	79·06 W

ăt; finȧl; rāte; senȧte; ärm; ȧsk; sofȧ; fâre; ch-choose; dh-as th in other; bē; ēvent; bĕt; recĕnt; cratēr; g-go; gh-guttural g; bĭt; ĭ-short neutral; rīde; κ-guttural k as ch in German ich;

PRONOUNCING INDEX Chepo–Chinhsiang 193

Page	Name	Pronunciation	Region	Lat. °′	Long. °′
93	Chepo R.		Pan.	9·10 N	78·36 W
122	Cher (R.)	(shâr)	Fr.	47·14 N	1·34 E
90	Cheran	(chā-rän')	Mex.	19·41 N	101·54 W
79	Cheraw	(chē'rô)	S. C.	34·40 N	79·52 W
122	Cherbourg	(shär-bōōr')	Fr.	49·39 N	1·43 W
164	Cherchel	(shĕr-shĕl')	Alg.	36·38 N	2·09 E
146	Cherchen (R.)	(chĕr-chĕn')	China	39·00 N	87·19 E
132	Cherdyn'	(chĕr-dyēn')	Sov. Un.	60·25 N	56·32 E
134	Cheremkhovo	(chĕr'yĕm-kô-vō)	Sov. Un.	52·58 N	103·18 E
136	Cherëmukhovo	(chĕr-yĕ-mû-kô-vô)	Sov. Un. (Urals In.)	60·20 N	60·00 E
165	Cheren	(chĕr'ĕn)	Eth.	15·46 N	38·28 E
134	Cherepanovo	(chĕr'yĕ pä-nô'vō)	Sov. Un.	54·13 N	83·18 E
128	Cherepovets	(chĕr-yĕ-pô'vyĕtz)	Sov. Un.	59·08 N	35·54 E
128	Chereya	(chĕr-ā'yä)	Sov. Un.	54·38 N	29·16 E
114	Chergui, Chott ech (L.)	(chĕr gē)	Alg.	34·12 N	0·10 W
114	Chergui I.		Tun.	34·48 N	11·41 E
128	Cherikov	(chĕ'rē-kôf)	Sov. Un.	53·34 N	31·22 E
129	Cherkassy	(chĕr-kä'sĭ)	Sov. Un.	49·26 N	32·03 E
129	Cherkassy (Oblast)		Sov. Un.	48·58 N	30·55 E
134	Cherlak	(chĭr-läk')	Sov. Un.	54·04 N	74·28 E
136	Chermoz	(chĕr-môz')	Sov. Un. (Urals In.)	58·47 N	56·08 E
128	Chern'	(chĕrn)	Sov. Un.	53·28 N	36·49 E
129	Chërnaya Kalitva (R.)	(chôr'nȧ yȧ kȧ-lēt'vȧ)	Sov. Un.	50·15 N	39·16 E
129	Chernigov	(chĕr-nē'gôf)	Sov. Un.	51·28 N	31·18 E
129	Chernigov (Oblast)	(chĕr-nē'gôf)	Sov. Un.	51·23 N	31·15 E
129	Chernobay	(chĕr-nō-bī')	Sov. Un.	49·41 N	32·24 E
129	Chernobyl'	(chĕr-nō-bĭl')	Sov. Un.	51·17 N	30·14 E
134	Chernogorsk	(chĕr-nŏ-gôrsk')	Sov. Un.	54·01 N	91·07 E
129	Chernogovka	(chĕr-nô-gôf'kȧ)	Sov. Un.	47·08 N	36·20 E
136	Chernoistochinsk	(chĕr-nôy-stô'chĭnsk)	Sov. Un. (Urals In.)	57·44 N	59·55 E
129	Chërnomorskoye	(chĕr-nô-môr'skô-yĕ)	Sov. Un.	45·29 N	32·43 E
121	Chernovtsy (Cernăuti)	(chĭr-nôf'tsē) (chĕr-nou'tsĕ)	Sov. Un.	48·18 N	25·56 E
119	Chernyakhovsk	(chĕr-nyä'kôfsk)	Sov. Un.	55·38 N	21·17 E
129	Chernyanka	(chĕrn-yäŋ'kȧ)	Sov. Un.	50·56 N	37·48 E
70	Cherokee	(chĕr-ô-kē')	Iowa	42·43 N	95·33 W
73	Cherokee		Kans.	37·21 N	94·50 W
72	Cherokee		Okla.	36·44 N	98·22 W
78	Cherokee (R.)		Tenn.	36·22 N	83·22 W
78	Cherokee Indian Res.		N. C.	35·33 N	83·12 W
94	Cherokee Sd.		Ba. Is.	26·15 N	76·55 W
73	Cherokees, L. of the	(chĕr-ô-kēz')	Okla.	36·32 N	95·14 W
82	Cherryfield	(chĕr'ĭ-fēld)	Maine	44·37 N	67·56 W
65	Cherry Grove		Ore. (Portland In.)	45·27 N	123·15 W
73	Cherryvale		Kans.	37·16 N	95·33 W
79	Cherryville	(chĕr'ĭ-vĭl)	N. C.	35·32 N	81·22 W
65	Cherryville		Ore. (Portland In.)	45·22 N	122·08 W
135	Cherskogo, Khrebet (Mts.)		Sov. Un.	66·15 N	138·30 E
128	Cherven'	(chĕr'vyĕn)	Sov. Un.	53·43 N	28·26 E
128	Chervonoye (L.)	(chĕr-vô'nô-yĕ)	Sov. Un.	52·24 N	28·12 E
80	Chesaning	(chĕs'ȧ-nĭng)	Mich.	43·10 N	84·10 W
81	Chesapeake B.	(chĕs'ȧ-pēk bā)	Md.	38·20 N	76·15 W
110	Chesham	(chĕsh'ŭm)	Eng. (London In.)	51·41 N	0·37 W
80	Cheshire	(chĕsh'ĭr)	Mich.	42·25 N	86·00 W
110	Cheshire (Co.)		Eng.	53·16 N	2·30 W
132	Chëshskaya Guba (B.)		Sov. Un.	67·25 N	46·00 E
136	Chesma	(chĕs'mȧ)	Sov. Un. (Urals In.)	53·50 N	60·42 E
134	Chesnokovka	(chĕs-nŏ-kôf'kȧ)	Sov. Un.	53·28 N	83·41 E
110	Chester	(chĕs'tẽr)	Eng.	53·12 N	2·53 W
73	Chester		Ill.	37·54 N	89·48 W
84	Chester		Pa. (Philadelphia In.)	39·51 N	75·22 W
79	Chester		S. C.	34·42 N	81·11 W
79	Chester		Va.	37·20 N	77·24 W
80	Chester		W. Va.	40·35 N	80·30 W
110	Chesterfield	(chĕs'tẽr-fēld)	Eng.	53·14 N	1·26 W
159	Chesterfield, Isles		N. Cal.	19·38 S	160·08 E
86	Chesterfield (Inlet)		Can.	63·59 N	92·09 W
86	Chesterfield Inlet		Can.	63·19 N	91·11 W
85	Chestermere L.	(chĕs'tẽr-mēr)	Can. (Calgary In.)	51·03 N	113·45 W
80	Chesterton	(chĕs'tẽr-tŭn)	Ind.	41·35 N	87·05 W
81	Chestertown	(chĕs'tẽr-toun)	Md.	39·15 N	76·05 W
82	Chesuncook	(chĕs'ŭn-kŏŏk)	Maine	46·03 N	69·40 W
71	Chetek	(chĕ'tĕk)	Wis.	45·18 N	91·41 W
92	Chetumal, Bahia de (B.)	(bä-ē-ä dĕ chĕt-ōō-mäl')	Br. Hond. (Yucatan In.)	18·07 N	88·05 W
69	Chevalon Cr.	(shĕv'ȧ-lŏn)	Ariz.	34·35 N	111·00 W
75	Cheviot	(shĕv'ĭ-ŭt)	Ohio (Cincinnati In.)	39·10 N	84·37 W
116	Cheviot Hills		Scot., Eng.	55·20 N	2·40 W
123	Chevreuse	(shĕ-vrûz')	Fr. (Paris In.)	48·42 N	2·02 E
66	Chewelah	(chē-wē'lä)	Wash.	48·17 N	117·42 W
148	Cheyang (R.) (Sïyang)		China	33·42 N	119·40 E
70	Cheyenne	(shī-ĕn')	Wyo.	41·10 N	104·49 W
70	Cheyenne (R.)		S. D.	44·20 N	102 15 W
70	Cheyenne River Ind. Res.		S. D.	45·07 N	100·46 W
72	Cheyenne Wells		Colo.	38·46 N	102·21 W
151	Chiachi		China	19·10 N	110·28 E
151	Chiahsing		China	30·45 N	120·50 E
151	Chiai	(chï'ï')	Taiwan	23·28 N	120·28 E
151	Chialing (R.)		China	30·30 N	106·20 E
151	Chian		China	27·12 N	115·10 E

Page	Name	Pronunciation	Region	Lat. °′	Long. °′
150	Chian		China	41·00 N	126·04 E
148	Chiangchanchi		China	36·39 N	120·31 E
83	Chianghsi (Kiangsi) (Prov.)		China	28·16 N	115·34 E
151	Chiangling		China	30·30 N	112·10 E
146	Chiang Mai		Thai.	18·38 N	98·44 E
154	Chiang Rai		Thai.	19·53 N	99·48 E
147	Chiangsu (Kiangsu) (Prov.)		China	33·51 N	120·09 E
148	Chiangtu	(jiang'dōō)	China	32·24 N	119·24 E
148	Chiangyen	(jĭäng'yĭn)	China	32·33 N	120·07 E
148	Chiangyin	(jĭäng'ĭn)	China	31·54 N	120·15 E
148	Chiantochen	(jĭäng'tō'jĕn)	China	32·23 N	120·14 E
148	Chiaochou Wan (B.)	(jĭou'zhēō wän)	China	36·10 N	119·55 E
148	Chiaoho	(jēou'hŭ)	China	38·03 N	116·18 E
150	Chiaoho		China	43·40 N	127·20 E
148	Chiaohsien	(jēou'sĭän)	China	36·18 N	120·01 E
149	Ch'iaot'ou		China (Canton In.)	22·55 N	113·39 E
148	Chiaotso	(jēou'zhōŏŭ)	China	35·17 N	113·11 E
148	Chiaow Shan (Mts.)	(jēou shän)	China	36·59 N	121·15 E
92	Chiapa, Rio de (R.)	(rē-ô-dĕ-chê-ä'pä)	Mex.	16·00 N	92·20 W
91	Chiapa de Corzo	(chê-ä'pä dä kôr'zō)	Mex.	16·44 N	93·01 W
88	Chiapas (State)	(chê-ä'päs)	Mex.	17·10 N	93·00 W
91	Chiapas, Cordilla de (Mts.)	(kôr-dēl-yĕ'rä-dĕ-chyä'räs)	Mex.	15·55 N	93·15 W
126	Chiari	(kyä'rē)	It.	45·31 N	9·57 E
120	Chiasso		Switz.	45·50 N	8·57 E
149	Chiating		China (Shanghai In.)	31·23 N	121·15 E
90	Chiautla	(chyä-ōōt'lä)	Mex.	18·16 N	98·37 W
126	Chiavari	(kyä-vä'rē)	It.	44·18 N	9·21 E
151	Chiayü		China	33·00 N	114·00 E
153	Chiba	(chē'bȧ)	Jap. (Tōkyō In.)	35·37 N	140·08 E
153	Chiba (Pref.)		Jap. (Tōkyō In.)	35·47 N	140·02 E
87	Chibougamau	(chē-bōō'gȧ-mou)	Can.	49·57 N	74·23 W
75	Chicago	(shĭ-kô-gō) (chĭ-kȧ'gō)	Ill. (Chicago In.)	41·49 N	87·37 W
75	Chicago Heights	(shĭ-kô'gō) (chĭ-kä'gō)	Ill. (Chicago In.)	41·30 N	87·38 W
166	Chicapa (R.)	(chē-kä'pȧ)	Ang.	8·15 S	20·15 E
91	Chicbul	(chēk-bōō'l)	Mex.	18·45 N	90·56 W
64	Chichagof (I.)	(chê-chä'gôf)	Alaska	57·50 N	137·00 W
92	Chichâncanab, Lago de (L.)	(lä'-gô-dĕ-chē-chän-kä-nä'b)	Mex. (Yucatan In.)	19·50 N	88·28 W
92	Chichen Itzá (Ruins)	(chē-chĕ'n-ē-tsä')	Mex. (Yucatan In.)	20·38 N	88·35 W
116	Chichester	(chĭch'ĕs-tẽr)	Eng.	50·50 N	0·55 W
151	Chichiang		China	29·05 N	106·40 E
148	Chichiashih	(jï'jïä'shē)	China	32·10 N	120·17 E
150	Ch'ich'ihaerh (Tsitsihar)		China	47·18 N	124·00 E
92	Chichimila	(chē-chē-mê'lä)	Mex. (Yucatan In.)	20·36 N	88·14 W
99	Chichiriviche	(chē-chē-rē-vē-chĕ)	Ven. (In.)	10·56 N	68·17 W
78	Chickamauga	(chĭk-ȧ-mô'gȧ)	Ga.	34·50 N	85·15 W
79	Chickamauga, (R.)		Tenn.	35·18 N	85·22 W
78	Chickasawhay (R.)	(chĭk-ȧ-sô'wā)	Miss.	31·45 N	88·45 W
72	Chickasha	(chĭk'ȧ-shā)	Okla.	35·04 N	97·56 W
124	Chiclana	(chê-klä'nä)	Sp.	36·25 N	6·09 W
98	Chiclayo	(chê-klä'yō)	Peru	6·46 S	79·50 W
68	Chico	(chē'kō)	Calif.	39·43 N	121·51 W
65	Chico		Wash. (Seattle In.)	47·37 N	122·43 W
100	Chico (R.)		Arg.	44·30 S	66·00 W
100	Chico (R.)		Arg.	49·15 S	69·30 W
155	Chico (R.)		Phil. (Manila In.)	17·33 N	121·24 E
91	Chicoloapan	(chê-kō-lwä'pän)	Mex. (Mexico City In.)	19·24 N	98·54 W
91	Chiconautla	(chê-kō-nä-ōō'tlä)	Mex. (Mexico City In.)	19·39 N	99·01 W
90	Chicontepec	(chê-kōn'tĕ-pĕk')	Mex.	20·58 N	98·08 W
81	Chicopee	(chĭk'ô-pē)	Mass.	42·10 N	72·35 W
84	Chicot I.	(shē-kō')	La. (New Orleans In.)	29·44 N	89·15 W
82	Chicoutimi	(shē-kōō'tē-mē')	Can.	48·27 N	71·03 W
92	Chicxulub	(chēk-sōō-lōō'b)	Mex. (Yucatan In.)	21·10 N	89·30 W
87	Chidley, C.	(chĭd'lĭ)	Can.	60·32 N	63·56 W
66	Chief Joseph Dam		Wash.	48·00 N	119·39 W
78	Chiefland	(chēf'lănd)	Fla.	29·30 N	82·50 W
146	Ch'iehmo		China	38·02 N	85·16 E
148	Chiehshou Hu (L.)	(jĭeh'shō hōō)	China	32·59 N	119·04 E
151	Chiehyang		China	23·38 N	116·20 E
120	Chiem See (L.)	(Kēm zā)	Ger.	47·58 N	12·20 E
148	Chienchangying	(jĭan'chang'yĭng)	China	40·09 N	118·47 E
148	Chienkan (R.)	(jĭan'gän)	China	39·35 N	117·34 E
151	Chienli		China	29·50 N	112·52 E
151	Chienning		China	26·50 N	116·55 E
151	Chienou		China	27·10 N	118·18 E
148	Ch'ienshanchen	(chĭan'shän'jen)	China	31·05 N	120·24 E
148	Ch'ienshanchi	(chĭan'shan'jï)	China	32·38 N	117·02 E
151	Chienshih		China	30·40 N	109·45 E
151	Chienshui		China	23·32 N	102·50 E
148	Ch'ienwei	(chĭän'wä)	China	40·11 N	120·05 E
126	Chieri	(kyâ'rē)	It.	45·03 N	7·48 E
126	Chieti	(kyĕ'tē)	It.	42·22 N	14·22 E
129	Chigirin	(chê-gē'rĕn)	Sov. Un.	49·02 N	32·39 E
90	Chignanuapan	(chē'g-nä-nwä-pä'n)	Mex.	19·49 N	98 02 W
82	Chignecto B.	(shĭg-nĕk'tō)	Can.	45·33 N	64·50 W
64	Chignik	(chĭg'nĭk)	Alaska	56·14 N	158·12 W
64	Chignik B.		Alaska	56·18 N	157·22 W
151	Chihchiang		China	27·25 N	109·45 E
150	Ch'ihfeng	(chï'fûng)	China	42·18 N	118·52 E
148	Chihhochen	(zhï'hŭ'jen)	China	32·32 N	117·57 E
148	Ch'ihsien	(chï'hsyĕn')	China	34·33 N	114·47 E

Page	Name	Pronunciation	Region	Lat. °′	Long. °′
148	Chihsien		China	35·25 N	114·03 E
148	Ch'ihsien		China	35·36 N	114·13 E
148	Chihsien		China	37·37 N	115·33 E
148	Chihsien		China	40·03 N	117·25 E
76	Chihuahua	(chê-wä'wä)	Mex.	28·37 N	106·06 W
88	Chihuahua (State)		Mex.	29·00 N	107·30 W
166	Chihuane	(chē-wä'nȧ)	Moz.	20·43 S	34·57 E
133	Chikishlyar	(chê-kêsh-lyär')	Sov. Un.	37·40 N	53·50 E
148	Ch'ik'ou	(chē'kō)	China	38·37 N	117·33 E
90	Chilapa	(chê-lä'pä)	Mex.	17·34 N	99·14 W
90	Chilchota	(chêl-chō'tä)	Mex.	19·40 N	102·04 W
72	Childress	(chīld'rĕs)	Tex.	34·26 N	100·11 W
96	Chile	(chē'lā)	S.A.	53·24 N	2·53 W
100	Chilecito	(chê-lȧ-sē'tō)	Arg.	29·06 S	67·25 W
98	Chilí, Pico de (Pk.)	(pē'kô-dĕ chē-lê')	Col. (In.)	4·14 N	75·38 W
88	Chilibre	(chē-lê'brĕ)	Pan. (Panama Canal In.)	9·09 N	79·37 W
148	Ch'ili Hu (L.)	(chē'lē hōō)	China	32·57 N	118·26 E
150	Chilin (Kirin)	(chĭl'ĭn') (kĭr'ĭn)	China	43·58 N	126·40 E
147	Chilin (Prov.)		China	44·36 N	124·23 E
148	Chilip'ing	(chē'lē'pĭng)	China	31·28 N	114·41 E
142	Chilka (L.)		India	19·26 N	85·42 E
100	Chillán	(chēl-yän')	Chile	36·44 S	72·06 W
80	Chillicothe	(chĭl-ĭ-kŏth'ē)	Ill.	41·55 N	89·30 W
73	Chillicothe		Mo.	39·46 N	93·32 W
80	Chillicothe		Ohio	39·20 N	83·00 W
86	Chilliwack	(chĭl'ĭ-wăk)	Can.	49·09 N	121·59 W
100	Chiloé, Isla de (I.)	(ē's-lä-dĕ-chē-lô-ā')	Chile	43·00 S	76·30 W
90	Chilpancingo	(chēl-pän-sēŋ'gō)	Mex.	17·32 N	97·30 W
71	Chilton	(chĭl'tŭn)	Wis.	44·00 N	88·12 W
151	Chilung (Kirin)	(chĭ'lŭng')	Taiwan	25·02 N	121·48 E
65	Chimacum	(chĭm'ä-kŭm)	Wash. (Seattle In.)	48·01 N	122·47 W
91	Chimalpa	(chē-mäl'pä)	Mex. (Mexico City In.)	19·26 N	99·22 W
92	Chimaltenango	(chê-mäl-tȧ-näŋ'gō)	Guat.	14·39 N	90·48 W
90	Chimaltitan	(chêmäl-tē-tän')	Mex.	21·36 N	103·50 W
103	Chimbay	(chĭm-bī')	Sov. Un.	43·00 N	59·44 E
98	Chimborazo (Mtn.)	(chêm-bô-rä'zō)	Ec.	1·35 S	78·45 W
98	Chimbote	(chêm-bō'tȧ)	Peru	9·02 S	78·33 W
134	Chimkent	(chĭm-kĕnt)	Sov. Un.	42·17 N	69·42 E
148	Chimo	(gē'mŭ)	China	36·22 N	120·28 E
138	China	(chī'nȧ)	Asia	36·45 N	93·00 E
76	China	(chē'nä)	Mex.	25·43 N	99·13 W
92	Chinameca	(chĕ-nä-mā'kā)	Sal.	13·31 N	88·18 W
	Chinan, see Tsinan				
92	Chinandega	(chē-nän-dā'gä)	Nic.	12·38 N	87·08 W
76	Chinati Pk.	(chĭ-nā'tē)	Tex.	92·56 N	104·29 W
145	Chinawin (R.)		Bur.	23·30 N	94·30 E
98	Chincha Alta	(chĭn'chä äl'tä)	Peru	13·24 S	76·04 W
98	Chinchas, Islas (Is.)	(ē's-läs-chē'n-chäs)	Peru	11·27 S	79·05 W
150	Chincheng		China	35·30 N	112·50 E
151	Chinchiang		China	24·58 N	118·40 E
148	Chinch'iao	(jĭnchĭou)	China	31·46 N	116·46 E
160	Chinchilla	(chĭn-chĭl'ȧ)	Austl.	26·44 S	150·36 E
124	Chinchilla	(chên-chē'lyä)	Sp.	38·54 N	1·43 W
92	Chinchorro, Banco (Bk.)	(bä'n-kô-chēn-chô'r-rō)	Mex. (Yucatan In.)	18·43 N	87·25 W
150	Chinchou		China	41·00 N	121·00 E
148	Chinchou Wan (B.)	(jĭn'zhō wän)	China	39·07 N	121·17 E
166	Chinde	(shēn'dĕ)	Moz.	17·39 S	36·34 E
152	Chin Do (I.)		Kor.	34·30 N	125·43 E
142	Chindwara		India	22·08 N	78·57 E
146	Chindwin R.	(chĭn-dwĭn)	Bur.	23·30 N	94·34 E
148	Chinganchi	(jing'än'jï)	China	34·30 N	116·55 E
148	Ch'ingcheng	(chĭng'cheng)	China	37·12 N	117·43 E
150	Ch'ingch'eng		China	46·50 N	127·30 E
151	Chingchiang	(jĭng'jĭang)	China	28·00 N	115·30 E
148	Chingchiang		China	32·02 N	120·15 E
148	Chingchih	(jĭng'jĕ)	China	36·19 N	119·23 E
148	Ch'ingfeng	(chingfeng)	China	35·52 N	115·05 E
146	Chinghai (Tsinghai) (Prov.)		China	36·14 N	95·30 E
146	Ch'ing Hai (Koko Nor) (L.)	(kō'kō nor)	China	37·26 N	98·30 E
148	Chinghai Wan (B.)	(jĭng'häĭ wän)	China	36·47 N	122·10 E
150	Ching Ho (R.)	(chĭng'hō')	China	34·40 N	108·20 E
151	Chinghsien	(jĭng'sĭan)	China	26·32 N	109·45 E
148	Chinghsien		China	37·43 N	116·17 E
148	Ch'inghsien	(chingsĭan)	China	38·37 N	116·48 E
150	Chinghsing		China	47·00 N	123·00 E
148	Ching Hu (L.)	(chĭng hōō)	China	39·00 N	115·45 E
148	Chingk'ouchen	(chĭng'kō'jĕn)	China	34·52 N	119·07 E
151	Chingliu		China	26·15 N	116·50 E
150	Chingning		China	35·28 N	105·50 E
166	Chingola	(chĭng-gōlä)	N. Rh.	12·32 S	27·35 E
148	Ch'ingp'ing	(chĭng'pĭng)	China	36·46 N	116·03 E
150	Chingpo Hu (L.)		China	44·10 N	129·00 E
149	Ch'ingp'u		China (Shanghai In.)	31·08 N	121·06 E
148	Ch'ingtao (Tsingtao)	(tsĭng'dou)	China	36·05 N	120·10 E
166	Chinguar	(chĭng-gär)	Ang.	12·35 S	16·15 E
164	Chinguetti	(chēŋ-gĕt'ē)	Mauritania	20·34 N	12·34 W
148	Ch'ingyang	(chĭng'yäng)	China	33·25 N	118·13 E
150	Chingyang		China	36·02 N	107·42 E
148	Ch'ingyüan	(chĭng'yōōän)	China	38·52 N	115·31 E
150	Ch'ingyüan		China	42·04 N	125·00 E
151	Ch'ingyüang		China	23·43 N	113·10 E
148	Ch'ingyun	(chĭng'yōōn)	China	37·52 N	117·26 E
150	Ch'ingyütien		China (Peking In.)	39·41 N	116·31 E
148	Chinhsiang	(jĭn'sĭäng)	China	35·03 N	116·20 E

ng-sing; ŋ-baŋk; N-nasalized n; nŏd; cŏmmit; ōld; ôbey; ôrder; fōōd; fŏŏt; ou-out; s-soft; sh-dish; th-thin; pūre; ûnite; ûrn; stŭd; circŭs; ü-as "y" in study; '-indeterminate vowel.

194 Chinhsien–Ciudad Hidalgo PRONOUNCING INDEX

Page	Name Pronunciation Region	Lat. °′	Long. °′
148	Chinhsien (jĭn'sĭän) China	37·08 N	121·43 E
151	Ch'inhsien China	22·00 N	108·35 E
151	Chinhua China	29·10 N	119·42 E
148	Ch'inhuangtao (chĭnhōōäng'dou) China	39·57 N	119·34 E
148	Chining (jē'nĭng) China	35·26 N	116·34 E
150	Chining China	41·00 N	113·10 E
152	Chinju (chĭn'jōō) Kor.	35·13 N	128·10 E
151	Chinkiang (chĭn'kyäng') China	32·05 N	119·25 E
151	Chinmen China	24·42 N	118·05 E
	Chinmen, see Quemoy		
151	Chinmen (I.) China	24·40 N	118·38 E
151	Chinmu Chiao (Pt.) China	18·10 N	109·40 E
152	Chinnampo (chĭn-nàm'pō) Kor.	38·47 N	125·28 E
74	Chino (chē'nō) Calif. (Los Angeles In.)	34·01 N	117·42 W
122	Chinon (shē-nôɴ') Fr.	47·09 N	0·13 E
67	Chinook (shĭn-ŏŏk') Mont.	48·35 N	109·15 W
65	Chinook (shĭn-ŏŏk') Wash. (Portland In.)	46·17 N	123·57 W
148	Chinshachen (jĭn'shä'jĕn) China	32·08 N	121·06 E
149	Chinshan...China (Shanghai In.)	30·53 N	121·09 E
142	Chinsura.....India (Calcutta In.)	22·53 N	88·24 E
146	Chint'a China	40·11 N	98·45 E
148	Chint'an (jĭn'tän) China	31·47 N	119·34 E
166	Chinteche (chĭn-tĕ'chĕ) Nya.	11·48 S	34·14 E
150	Chinyang (chĭn'yäng') China	35·00 N	112·55 E
151	Chinyüh China	28·40 N	120·08 E
126	Chioggia (kyôd'jä) It.	45·12 N	12·17 E
149	Ch'ipao.....China (Shanghai In.)	31·06 N	121·16 E
166	Chipera (zhē-pĕ'rä) Moz.	15·16 S	32·30 E
78	Chipley (chĭp'lĭ) Fla.	30·45 N	85·33 W
82	Chipman (chĭp'mǎn) Can.	46·11 N	65·53 W
78	Chipola (R.) (chĭ-pō'lȧ) Fla.	30·40 N	85·14 W
75	Chippawa (chĭp'ê-wâ) Can. (Buffalo In.)	43·03 N	79·03 W
70	Chippewa (R.) (chĭp'ê-wä) Minn.	45·07 N	95·41 W
71	Chippewa (R.) Wis.	45·07 N	91·19 W
71	Chippewa Falls Wis.	44·55 N	91·26 W
75	Chippewa Lake Ohio (Cleveland In.)	41·04 N	81·54 W
82	Chiputneticook (L.) (chĭ-pōōt-nĕt'ĭ-kŏŏk) Can.	45·47 N	67·35 W
92	Chiquimula (chē-kê-mōō'lä) Guat.	14·47 N	89·31 W
92	Chiquimulilla (chē-kē-mōō-lē'l-yä) Guat.	14·08 N	90·23 W
98	Chiquinquira (chê-kēŋ'kê-rä') Col.	5·33 N	73·49 W
101	Chiquíta, Laguna Mar (L.) (lä-gōō'nä-mär-chê-kē'tä) Arg. (Buenos Aires In.)	34·25 S	61·10 W
69	Chiracahua Natl. Mon. (chĭ-rä-cä'hwä) Ariz.	32·02 N	109·18 W
143	Chirald India	15·52 N	80·22 E
134	Chirchik (chĭr-chĕk') Sov. Un.	41·28 N	69·18 E
64	Chirikof (I.) (chĭ'rĭ-kôf) Alaska	55·50 N	155·35 W
93	Chiriquí, Golfo de (G.) (gôl-fô-dĕ-chē-rê-kē') Pan.	7·56 N	82·18 W
93	Chiriquí, Laguna de (L.) (lä-gōō'nä-dĕ-chē-rê-kē') Pan.	9·06 N	82·02 W
93	Chiriquí, Punta (Pt.) (pōō'n-tä-chē-rê-kē') Pan.	9·13 N	81·39 W
93	Chiriquí, Volcán de (Vol.) (vôl-kà'n-dĕ-chē-rê-kē') Pan.	8·48 N	82·37 W
93	Chiriquí Grande (chē-rê-kē' grän'dā) Pan.	8·57 N	82·08 W
152	Chiri San (Mt.) (chĭ'rĭ-sän') Kor.	35·20 N	127·39 E
142	Chirmir India	23·10 N	82·20 E
166	Chiromo Nya.	16·34 S	35·13 E
127	Chirpan Bul.	42·12 N	25·19 E
93	Chirripo, R. (chêr-rē'pō) C. R.	9·50 N	83·20 W
93	Chirripo Grande (Mt.) (chêr-rē'pō grän'dā) C. R.	9·30 N	83·31 W
71	Chisholm (chĭz'ŭm) Minn.	47·28 N	92·53 W
132	Chistopol' (chĭs-tô'pôl-y') Sov. Un.	55·18 N	50·30 E
135	Chita (chê-tà') Sov. Un.	52·09 N	113·39 E
146	Ch'it'ai China	44·07 N	89·04 E
64	Chitina (chĭ-tē'nȧ) Alaska	61·28 N	144·35 W
142	Chitor India	24·59 N	74·42 E
142	Chitrāl (chē-träl') W. Pak.	35·58 N	71·48 E
93	Chitré (chē'trâ) Pan.	7·59 N	80·26 W
142	Chittagong (chĭt-á-gông') E. Pak.	22·26 N	90·51 E
150	Chiualhun China	49·59 N	127·15 E
148	Chiuch'eng (jĭō'chĕng) China	37·14 N	116·03 E
146	Chiuch'ian China	39·46 N	98·26 E
151	Chiuchiang China	29·43 N	116·00 E
149	Chiuchiang...China (Canton In.)	23·50 N	113·02 E
147	Chiuchichien China	52·23 N	121·04 E
149	Chiufenghsien China (Shanghai In.)	30·55 N	121·38 E
148	Ch'iuhsien (chĭō'sĭän) China	36·43 N	115·13 E
148	Chiuhsihsien (jĭo'sē'sĭän) China	32·20 N	114·42 E
148	Chiuhuang (R.) (jĭō'hooäng) China	33·48 N	119·30 E
166	Chiumbe (R.) (chê-ōōm'bâ) Ang.	10·00 S	21·00 E
151	Ch'iungshan China	20·00 N	110·20 E
148	Chiunü Shan (Mts.) (jĭō'nü'shän) China	35·47 N	117·23 E
126	Chivasso (kê-väs'sō) It.	45·13 N	7·52 E
101	Chivilcoy (chē-vēl-koi') Arg. (Buenos Aires In.)	34·51 S	60·03 W
92	Chixoy R. (chē-ĸoi') Guat.	15·40 N	90·35 W
151	Chiyang China	26·40 N	112·00 E
151	Ch'iyao Shan (Mtn.) China	30·00 N	108·50 E
153	Chizu (chê-zōō') Jap.	35·16 N	134·15 E
69	Chloride (klō'rīd) Ariz.	35·25 N	114·15 W
121	Chmielnik (ĸmyĕl'nēĸ) Pol.	50·36 N	20·46 E
101	Choapa (chô-à'pä) (R.) Chile (Santiago In.)	31·56 S	70·48 W
98	Chocó (chô-kô') (Dept.) Col. (In.)	5·33 N	76·28 W
77	Chocolate Bay (chŏ'ô-lĭt) (chŏk'lĭt) Tex. (In.)	29·21 N	95·19 W
78	Choctawhatchee, B. (chôk-tô-hăch'ê) Fla.	30·15 N	86·32 W
78	Choctawhatchee, R. Fla.-Ga.	30·37 N	85·56 W
120	Chodziez (ĸōj'yĕsh) Pol.	52·59 N	16·55 E
100	Choele Choel (chô-ĕ'lĕ-chôĕ'l) Arg.	39·14 S	66·46 W
153	Chōfu (chō'fōō') Jap. (Tōkyō In.)	35·39 N	139·33 E
153	Chōgo (chō-gō) Jap. (Tōkyō In.)	35·25 N	139·28 E
148	Chohsien (jōōŭ'sĭän) China	39·30 N	115·59 E
159	Choiseul, (I.) (shwä-zûl') Sol. Is.	7·30 S	157·30 E
121	Chojnice (ĸoĭ-nē-tsĕ) Pol.	53·41 N	17·34 E
122	Cholet (shô-lĕ') Fr.	47·06 N	0·54 W
150	Ch'olo (R.) China	47·20 N	121·40 E
90	Cholua (chō-lōō'lä) Mex.	19·04 N	98·19 W
92	Choluteca (chō-lōō-tā'kä) Hond.	13·18 N	87·12 W
92	Choluteco R. Hond.	13·34 N	86·59 W
120	Chomutov (kō'mōō-tôf) Czech.	50·27 N	13·23 E
135	Chona (R.) (chō'nä) Sov. Un.	60·45 N	109·15 E
98	Chone (chô'nĕ) Ec.	0·48 S	80·06 W
152	Chŏngjin (chŭng-jĭn') Kor.	41·48 N	129·46 E
152	Chŏngju (chŭng-jōō') Kor.	36·35 N	127·30 E
152	Chŏnju (chŭn-jōō') Kor.	35·48 N	127·08 E
110	Chorley (chôr'lĭ) Eng.	53·40 N	2·38 W
98	Chorrillos (chôr-rē'l-yōs) Peru	12·17 S	76·55 W
121	Chortkov (chôrt'kôf) Sov. Un.	49·01 N	25·48 E
121	Chorzów (kô-zhōōf') Pol.	50·17 N	19·00 E
152	Chosan (chō-sän') Kor.	40·44 N	125·48 E
79	Chosen (chō'z'n) Fla. (In.)	26·41 N	80·41 W
153	Chōshi (chō'shē) Jap.	35·40 N	140·55 E
120	Choszczno (chôsh'chnô) Pol.	53·10 N	15·25 E
142	Chota Nagpur (Reg.) India	28·20 N	81·40 E
67	Choteau (shō'tō) Mont.	47·51 N	112·10 W
113	Chott el Hodna (L.) Alg.	35·20 N	3·27 E
148	Chou (R.) (jēō) China	31·59 N	114·57 E
148	Chouchiak'ou (jēō'jĭä'kō) China	33·39 N	114·40 E
149	Choup'u...China (Shanghai In.)	31·07 N	121·33 E
148	Chouts'un (jēō'tsōōn) China	36·49 N	117·52 E
79	Chowan (R.) (chô-wän') N. C.	36·13 N	76·46 W
150	Choybalsan Mong.	47·50 N	114·15 E
159	Christchurch (krīst'chûrch) N. Z. (In.)	43·30 S	172·38 E
80	Christian (I.) (krĭs'chǎn) Can.	44·50 N	80·00 W
79	Christiansburg (krĭs'chǎnz-bûrg) Va.	37·08 N	80·25 W
89	Christiansted Vir. Is. (U. S. A.) (Puerto Rico In.)	17·45 N	64·44 W
154	Christmas (I.) Ind. O.	10·35 S	105·40 E
157	Christmas (I.) Gilbert & Ellice Is.	2·20 N	157·40 W
73	Christopher (krĭs'tô-fēr) Ill.	37·58 N	89·04 W
120	Chrudim (ĸrōō'dyĕm) Czech.	49·57 N	15·46 E
121	Chrzanów (ĸzhá'nōōf) Pol.	50·08 N	19·24 E
148	Ch'üanch'iao (chüän'jĭou) China	32·06 N	118·17 E
150	Chuangho China	39·40 N	123·00 E
151	Ch'üanhsien China	25·58 N	111·02 E
149	Ch'uansha...China (Shanghai In.)	31·12 N	121·41 E
100	Chubut (Prov.) (chōō-bōōt') Arg.	44·00 S	69·15 W
100	Chubut (chōō-bōōt') (R.) Arg.	43·05 S	69·00 W
148	Chuch'eng (chōō'chĕng') China	36·01 N	119·24 E
151	Chuchi China	29·58 N	120·10 E
151	Ch'üchiang China	24·58 N	113·42 E
149	Chu Chiang (Pearl R.) China (Canton In.)	23·04 N	113·28 E
148	Ch'üchou (chü'jēō) China	36·47 N	114·58 E
84	Chuckatuck (chŭck à-tŭck) Va. (Norfolk In.)	36·51 N	76·35 W
93	Chucunague, R. (chōō-kōō-nä'kä) Pan.	8·36 N	77·48 W
128	Chudovo (chōō'dô-vô) Sov. Un.	59·03 N	31·56 S
128	Chudskoye Oz. (Peipus, L.) (chōōt'skô-yĕ) Sov. Un.	58·43 N	26·45 E
148	Ch'üfou (chü'fōō) China	35·37 N	116·59 E
	Chuguchak, see T'ach'eng		
146	Chuguchak (Reg.) (chōō'gōō-chäk') China	46·09 N	83·58 E
129	Chuguyev (chōō'gōō-yĕf) Sov. Un.	49·52 N	36·40 E
152	Chuguyevka (chōō-gōō'yĕf-kȧ) Sov. Un.	43·58 N	133·49 E
70	Chugwater Cr. (chŭg'wô-tēr) Wyo.	41·43 N	104·54 W
150	Chuho China	45·18 N	127·52 E
151	Ch'ühsien China	28·58 N	118·58 E
148	Ch'ühsien (chōō'sĭän) China	32·19 N	118·19 E
148	Chühsien (jü'sĭän) China	35·35 N	118·50 E
146	Ch'uhsiung China	25·19 N	101·34 E
148	Chühua Tao (I.) (jü'hōōä dou) China	40·30 N	120·47 E
148	Chüjung (jü'rōōng) China	31·58 N	119·12 E
142	Chukhor China	28·22 N	87·28 E
135	Chukot Natl. Okrug (Reg.) Sov. Un.	68·15 N	170·00 E
135	Chukotskiy (Chukot) P-Ov (Pen.) Sov. Un.	66·12 N	174·35 E
135	Chukotskoye Nagor'ye (Mts.) Sov. Un.	66·00 N	166·00 E
68	Chula Vista (chōō'lȧ vĭs'tȧ) Calif. (San Diego In.)	32·38 N	117·05 W
136	Chulkovo (chōōl-kô vô) Sov. Un. (Moscow In.)	55·33 N	38·04 E
98	Chulucanas (chōō-lōō-kä'näs) Peru	5·13 S	80·13 W
134	Chulum (R.) Sov. Un.	57·52 N	84·45 E
148	Chüma (R.) (jü'mä) China	39·37 N	115·45 E
135	Chumikan (chōō-mē-kän') Sov. Un.	54·47 N	135·09 E
152	Chunchŏn (chōōn-chŭn') Kor.	37·51 N	127·46 E
148	Chungchia Shan (Mts.) (jōōng'jĭä shän) China	32·42 N	118·19 E
151	Ch'ungch'ing (Chungking) (ch'ungch'ing) (chōōng'kĭng') China	29·38 N	107·30 E
151	Chunghsien China	30·20 N	108·00 E
148	Chunghsing (jōōng'sĭng) China	33·43 N	118·42 E
152	Chungju (chŭng'jōō') Kor.	37·00 N	128·19 E
	Chungking, see Ch'ungch'ing		
151	Ch'ungming Tao (I.) China	31·40 N	122·30 E
150	Chungwei (chōōng'wä) China	37·32 N	105·10 E
134	Chunya (R.) (chōōn'yä') Sov. Un.	61·45 N	101·28 E
100	Chuquicamata (chōō-kê-kä-mä'tä) Chile	22·08 S	68·57 W
120	Chur (kōōr) Switz.	46·51 N	9·32 E
86	Churchill (chûrch'ĭl) Can.	58·48 N	94·10 W
86	Churchill, C. Can.	59·07 N	93·50 W
86	Churchill (R.) Can.	57·00 N	95·21 W
86	Churchill Pk. Can.	58·10 N	125·14 W
84	Churchland (chûrch-lǎnd) Va. (Norfolk In.)	36·52 N	76·24 W
110	Church Stretton (chûrch strĕt'ŭn) Eng.	52·32 N	2·49 W
142	Churu India	28·22 N	75·00 E
90	Churumuco (chōō-rōō-mōō'kō) Mex.	18·39 N	101·40 W
151	Chusan Archipelago (Is.) China	30·00 N	123·00 E
151	Ch'ushien China	30·40 N	106·48 E
69	Chuska, Mts. (chŭs-kȧ) Ariz.-N. Mex.	36·21 N	109·11 W
136	Chusovaya R. (chōō-sô-vä'yȧ) Sov. Un. (Urals In.)	58·08 N	58·35 E
136	Chusovoy (chōō-sô-vôy') Sov. Un. (Urals In.)	58·18 N	57·50 E
134	Chust (chōōst) Sov. Un.	41·05 N	71·28 E
148	Chut'angtien (jō'däng'dĭän) China	31·59 N	114·13 E
148	Ch'uti (chü'tē) China	37·07 N	117·17 E
132	Chuvash (A. S. S. R.) (chōō'vàsh) Sov. Un.	55·45 N	46·00 E
76	Chuviscar R. (chōō-vēs-kär') Mex.	28·34 N	105·36 W
148	Ch'uwang (chōō'wäng) China	36·08 N	114·53 E
154	Chu Yang Sin (Pk.) Viet.	12·22 N	108·20 E
148	Chüyen (jü'yĕ) China	35·24 N	116·05 E
	Cibao Mts., see Central, Cordillera		
76	Cibolo Cr. (sē'bô-lō) Tex.	29·28 N	98·13 W
75	Cicero (sĭs'ēr-ō) Ill. (Chicago In.)	41·50 N	87·46 W
133	Cide (jē'dĕ) Tur.	41·50 N	33·00 E
121	Ciechanów (tsyĕ-kä'nōōf) Pol.	52·52 N	20·39 E
94	Ciego de Avila (syā'gō dā ä'vê-lä) Cuba	21·50 N	78·45 W
124	Ciempozuelos (thyĕm-pô-thwā'lōs) Sp.	40·09 N	3·36 W
98	Ciénaga (syā'nä-gä) Col.	11·01 N	74·15 W
94	Cienfuegos (syĕn-fwā'gōs) Cuba	22·10 N	80·30 W
94	Cienfuegos, Bahía (B.) (bä-ē'ä-syĕn-fwā'gōs) Cuba	22·00 N	80·35 W
93	Ciervo, Isla de la (I.) (ē's-lä-dĕ-lä-syĕ'r-vô) Nic.	11·56 N	83·20 W
121	Cieszyn (tsyĕ'shēn) Pol.	49·47 N	18·45 E
124	Cieza (thyā'thä) Sp.	38·13 N	1·25 W
90	Cihuatlán (sē-wä-tlä'n) Mex.	19·13 N	104·36 W
90	Cihuatlán (R.) Mex.	19·11 N	104·30 W
133	Cilician Gates (P.) Tur.	37·30 N	35·30 E
116	Cill Mantainn (Wicklow) (kĭl män'tän) (wĭk'lō) Ire.	52·59 N	6·06 W
72	Cimarron (R.), North Fk. Colo.	37·13 N	102·30 W
72	Cimarron R. (sĭm-ȧ-rōn') Okla.	36·26 N	98·47 W
127	Cîmpina Rom.	45·08 N	25·47 E
127	Cîmpulung Rom.	45·15 N	25·03 E
121	Cîmpulung Moldovenesc Rom.	47·31 N	25·36 E
125	Cinca (R.) (thēŋ'kä) Sp.	42·09 N	0·08 E
75	Cincinnati (sĭn-sĭ-nät'ĭ) Ohio (Cincinnati In.)	39·08 N	84·30 W
94	Cinco Balas, Cayos (Is.) (kä'yōs-thēŋ'kō bä'läs) Cuba	21·05 N	79·25 W
91	Cintalapa (sēn-tä-lä'pä) Mex.	16·41 N	93·44 W
91	Cintalapa (R.) Mex.	16·46 N	93·36 W
126	Cinto, Mt. (chēn'tō) Fr.	42·24 N	8·54 E
64	Circle (sûr'k'l) Alaska	65·49 N	144·22 W
80	Circleville (sûr'k'lvĭl) Ohio	39·35 N	83·00 W
	Cirenica, see Bargah		
76	Cisco (sĭs'kō) Tex.	32·23 N	98·57 W
98	Cisneros (sēs-nĕ'rōs) Col. (In.)	5.33 N	75·05 W
125	Cisterna di Latina (chēs-tĕ'r-nä-dē-lä-tē'nä) It. (Rome In.)	41·36 N	12·53 E
124	Cistierna (thês-tyĕr'nä) Sp.	42·48 N	5·08 W
91	Citlaltépetl (Vol.) (sē-tlàl-tĕ'pĕtl) Mex.	19·04 N	97·14 W
78	Citronelle (cĭt-rô'nĕl) Ala.	3·04 N	88·12 W
126	Cittadella (chēt-tä-dĕl'lä) It.	45·39 N	11·51 E
126	Città di Castello (chĕt-tä'dē käs-tĕl'lō) It.	43·27 N	12·17 E
90	Ciudad Altamirano (syōō-dä'd-äl-tä-mē-rä'nô) Mex.	18·24 N	100·38 W
98	Ciudad Bolívar (syōō-dhädh' bô-lē'vär) Ven.	8·07 N	63·41 W
76	Ciudad Camargo (Santa Rosalia) (syōō-dhädh' kä-mär'gō) (sän'tä rō-sä'lēä) Mex.	27·42 N	105·10 W
92	Ciudad Chetumal (Payo Obispo) (syōō-dhädh' chĕt-ōō-mäl) (pä'yō ō-bēs'pō) Mex. (Yucatan In.)	18·30 N	88·17 W
92	Ciudad Dario (syōō-dhädh'dä'rê-ō) Nic.	12·44 N	86·08 W
91	Ciudad de las Casas (syōō-dä'd-dĕ-läs-kä'säs) Mex.	16·44 N	92·39 W
91	Ciudad del Carmen (syōō-dä'd-dĕl-kä'r-mĕn) Mex.	18·39 N	91·49 W
90	Ciudad del Maíz (syōō-dhädh'del mä-ēz') Mex.	22·24 N	99·37 W
90	Ciudad de Valles (syōō-dhädh'dā vä'lyās) Mex.	21·59 N	99·02 W
125	Ciudadela (thyōō-dhä-dhā'lä) Sp.	40·00 N	3·52 E
90	Ciudad Fernández (syōō-dhädh'fĕr-nän'dĕz) Mex.	21·56 N	100·03 W
90	Ciudad Garcia (syōō-dhädh'gär-sē'ä) Mex.	22·39 N	103·02 W
90	Ciudad Guzmán (syōō-dhädh'gōōz-män') Mex.	19·40 N	103·29 W
90	Ciudad Hidalgo (syōō-dä'd-ê-dä'l-gô) Mex.	19·41 N	100·35 W

ăt; finǎl; rāte; senâte; ärm; àsk; sofȧ; fâre; ch-choose; dh-as th in other; bē; êvent; bĕt; recĕnt; cratēr; g-go; gh-guttural g; bĭt; ĭ-short neutral; rīde; ĸ-guttural k as ch in German ich;

PRONOUNCING INDEX Ciudad Juarez–Coldwater 195

Page	Name Pronunciation Region	Lat. °′	Long. °′
76	Ciudad Juárez (syōō-dhädh hwä'räz) . Mex.	31·44 N	106·28 W
91	Ciudad Madero (syōō-dä'd-mä-dě'-rô) . Mex.	22·16 N	97·52 W
90	Ciudad Mante (syōō-dä'd-män'tě) . Mex.	22·34 N	98·58 W
90	Ciudad Manuel Doblado (syōō-dä'd-män-wäl' dō-blä'dō) Mex.	20·43 N	101·57 W
88	Ciudad Obregon (syōō-dhädh-ô-brě-gô'n) . Mex.	27·40 N	109·58 W
124	Ciudad Real (thyōō-dhädh'rä-äl') . Sp.	38·59 N	3·55 W
124	Ciudad Rodrigo (thyōō-dhädh'rô-drē'gō) . Sp.	40·38 N	6·34 W
91	Ciudad Serdán (syōō-dä'd-sěr-dà'n) . Mex.	18·58 N	97·26 W
90	Ciudad Victoria (syōō-dhädh'vêk-tō'rê-ä) . Mex.	23·43 N	99·09 W
126	Civadale del Friuli (chē-vê-dä'lä-děl-frē-ōō'lē) . It.	46·06 N	13·24 E
126	Civitavecchia (chē'vê-tä-věk'kyä) It.	42·06 N	11·49 E
65	Clackamas (klăc-kȧ'măs) Ore. (Portland In.)	42·25 N	122·34 W
86	Claire (L.) (klâr) . . . Can.	58·33 N	113·16 W
75	Clairton (klârtŭn) Pa. (Pittsburgh In.)	40·17 N	79·53 W
78	Clanton (klăn'tŭn) . . . Ala.	32·50 N	86·38 W
80	Clare (klâr) . . . Mich.	43·50 N	84·45 W
116	Clare (I.) . . . Ire.	53·46 N	9·60 W
74	Claremont (klâr'mŏnt) Calif. (Los Angeles In.)	34·06 N	117·43 W
81	Claremont (klâr'mŏnt) . . . N. H.	43·20 N	72·20 W
80	Claremont . . . W. Va.	37·55 N	81·00 W
73	Claremore (klâr'mōr) . . . Okla.	36·16 N	95·37 W
116	Claremorris (klâr-mŏr'ĭs) . . . Ire.	53·46 N	9·05 W
158	Clarence Str. (klăr'ĕns) . . . Austl.	12·15 S	130·05 E
95	Clarence Town . . . Ba. Is.	23·05 N	75·00 W
73	Clarendon (klâr'ĕn-dŭn) . . . Ark.	34·42 N	91·17 W
72	Clarendon . . . Tex.	34·55 N	100·52 W
167	Clarens (clâ-rěns) S. Afr. (Natal In.)	28·34 S	28·26 E
86	Claresholm (klâr'ěs-hōlm) . . . Can.	50·01 N	113·30 W
71	Clarinda (klȧ-rĭn'dȧ) . . . Iowa	40·42 N	95·00 W
99	Clarines (klä-rē'něs) . . . Ven. (In.)	9·57 N	65·10 W
71	Clarion (klăr'ĭ-ŭn) . . . Iowa	42·43 N	93·45 W
81	Clarion . . . Pa.	41·10 N	79·25 W
70	Clark (klärk) . . . S. D.	44·52 N	97·45 W
80	Clark, Pt. . . . Can.	44·05 N	81·50 W
82	Clark City . . . Can.	50·12 N	66·38 W
69	Clarkdale (klärk-dāl) . . . Ariz.	34·45 N	112·05 W
159	Clarke Ra. . . . Austl.	20·30 S	148·00 E
82	Clarkes Harbour (klärks) . . . Can.	43·28 N	65·37 W
67	Clark Fork R. . . . Mont.	47·50 N	115·35 W
79	Clark Hill Res. (klärk-hĭl) Ga.-S. C.	33·50 N	82·35 W
81	Clarksburg (klärkz'bûrg) . . W. Va.	39·15 N	80·20 W
78	Clarksdale (klärks-dāl) . . . Miss.	34·10 N	90·31 W
85	Clarkson . . . Can. (Toronto In.)	43·31 N	79·38 W
84	Clarkston (klärks'-tŭn) Ga. (Atlanta In.)	33·49 N	84·15 W
66	Clarkston . . . Wash.	46·24 N	117·01 W
73	Clarksville (klärks-vĭl) . . . Ark.	35·28 N	93·26 W
78	Clarksville . . . Tenn.	36·30 N	87·23 W
73	Clarksville . . . Tex.	33·37 N	95·02 W
65	Clatskanie . . . Oreg. (Portland In.)	46·06 N	123·11 W
65	Clatskanie (R.) (klăt-skā'nê) Ore. (Portland In.)	46·06 N	123·11 W
65	Clatsop Spit (klăt-sŏp) Ore. (Portland In.)	46·13 N	124·04 W
101	Cláudio (klou'-dēō) Braz. (Rio de Janeiro In.)	20·26 S	44·44 W
151	Claveria (klä-vä-rē'ä) . . . Phil.	18·38 N	121·08 E
75	Clawson (klô's'n) Mich. (Detroit In.)	42·32 N	83·09 W
79	Claxton (klăks'tŭn) . . . Ga.	32·07 N	81·54 W
78	Clay (klā) . . . Ky.	37·28 N	87·50 W
65	Clayburn (klā'bûrn) Can. (Vancouver In.)	49·05 N	122·17 W
73	Clay Center (klā sěn'tēr) . . . Kans.	39·23 N	97·08 W
80	Clay City (klā sĭ'tĭ) . . . Ky.	37·50 N	83·55 W
74	Claycomo (kla-kō'mo) Mo. (Kansas City In.)	39·12 N	94·30 W
110	Clay Cross (klā krŏs) . . . Eng.	53·10 N	1·25 W
123	Claye-Souilly (klě-sōō-yē') Fr. (Paris In.)	48·56 N	2·43 E
84	Claymont (klā-mŏnt) Del. (Philadelphia In.)	39·48 N	75·28 W
78	Clayton (klā'tŭn) . . . Ala.	31·52 N	85·25 W
65	Clayton . Calif. (San Francisco In.)	37·56 N	122·56 W
110	Clayton . . . Eng.	53·47 N	1·49 W
74	Clayton . . . Mo. (St. Louis In.)	38·39 N	90·20 W
72	Clayton . . . N. Mex.	36·26 N	103·12 W
79	Clayton . . . N. C.	35·40 N	78·27 W
68	Clear, (L.) . . . Calif.	39·05 N	122·50 W
116	Clear, C. (klēr) . . . Ire.	51·24 N	9·15 W
73	Clear Boggy Cr. (klēr bŏg'ĭ krēk) Okla.	34·21 N	96·22 W
69	Clear Cr. . . . Ariz.	34·40 N	111·05 W
67	Clear Cr. . . . Wyo.	44·35 N	106·20 W
81	Clearfield (klēr-fēld) . . . Pa.	41·00 N	78·25 W
74	Clearfield Utah (Salt Lake City In.)	41·07 N	112·01 W
86	Clear Hills . . . Can.	57·11 N	119·20 W
71	Clear Lake . . . Iowa	43·09 N	93·23 W
65	Clear Lake . . . Wash. (Seattle In.)	48·27 N	122·14 W
66	Clear Lake Res. . . . Calif.	41·53 N	121·00 W
77	Clear R. . . . Tex. (In.)	29·34 N	95·13 W
79	Clearwater (klēr-wô'tēr) . Fla. (In.)	27·43 N	82·45 W
66	Clearwater Mts. . . . Idaho	45·56 N	115·15 W
73	Clearwater Res. . . . Mo.	37·20 N	91·04 W
66	Clearwater R. . . . Idaho	46·27 N	116·33 W
66	Clearwater R., Middle Fork . Idaho	46·10 N	115·48 W
66	Clearwater R., North Fork . . Idaho	46·34 N	116·08 W
66	Clearwater R., South Fork . . Idaho	45·46 N	115·53 W
77	Cleburne (klē'bŭrn) . . . Tex.	32·21 N	97·23 W
110	Clee Hill (klē) . . . Eng.	52·24 N	2·37 W
66	Cle Elum (klē ĕl'ŭm) . . . Wash.	47·12 N	120·55 W
84	Clementon (klē'měn-tŭn) N. J. (Philadelphia In.)	39·49 N	75·00 W
110	Cleobury Mortimer (klē'ō-bēr'ĭ môr'tĭ-měr) . Eng.	52·22 N	2·29 W
159	Clermont (klēr'mŏnt) . . . Austl.	23·02 S	147·46 E
75	Clermont . . Ind. (Indianapolis In.)	39·48 N	86·19 W
122	Clermont-Ferrand (klěr-môn'fěr-răn') . Fr.	45·47 N	3·03 E
122	Clermont l'Herault (klěr-mŏn' lā-rō') . Fr.	43·38 N	3·22 E
78	Cleveland (klēv'lănd) . . . Miss.	33·45 N	90·42 W
75	Cleveland . . . Ohio (Cleveland In.)	41·30 N	81·42 W
73	Cleveland . . . Okla.	36·18 N	96·28 W
78	Cleveland . . . Tenn.	35·09 N	84·52 W
77	Cleveland . . . Tex.	30·18 N	95·05 W
75	Cleveland Heights Ohio (Cleveland In.)	41·30 N	81·35 W
75	Cleves (klē'věs) Ohio (Cincinnati In.)	39·10 N	84·45 W
116	Clew (B.) (klōō) . . . Ire.	53·47 N	9·45 W
79	Clewiston (klē'wĭs-tŭn) . . Fla. (In.)	26·44 N	80·55 W
123	Clichy-la-Garennel (klē-shē'-lä-gä-rě-něl') Fr. (Paris In.)	48·54 N	2·18 E
116	Clifden (klĭf'děn) . . . Ire.	53·31 N	10·04 W
69	Clifton (klĭf'tŭn) . . . Ariz.	33·05 N	109·20 W
84	Clifton . . . N. J. (New York In.)	40·35 N	74·09 W
79	Clifton . . . S. C.	35·00 N	81·47 W
77	Clifton . . . Tex.	31·45 N	97·31 W
81	Clifton Forge . . . Va.	37·50 N	79·50 W
78	Clinch Res. (klĭnch) . . . Tenn.-Va.	36·30 N	83·19 W
78	Clingmans Dome, (Mtn.) (klĭng'măns dōm) . N. C.	35·37 N	83·26 W
86	Clinton (klĭn-tŭn) . . . Can.	51·09 N	121·40 W
80	Clinton . . . Ill.	40·10 N	88·55 W
80	Clinton . . . Ind.	39·40 N	87·25 W
71	Clinton . . . Iowa	41·50 N	90·13 W
78	Clinton . . . Ky.	36·39 N	88·56 W
83	Clinton . . . Mass. (Boston In.)	42·25 N	71·41 W
73	Clinton . . . Mo.	38·23 N	93·46 W
79	Clinton . . . N. C.	35·58 N	78·20 W
72	Clinton . . . Okla.	35·31 N	98·56 W
79	Clinton . . . S. C.	34·27 N	81·53 W
78	Clinton . . . Tenn.	36·05 N	84·08 W
65	Clinton . . . Wash. (Seattle In.)	47·59 N	122·22 W
86	Clinton-Colden (L.) . . . Can.	63·58 N	106·34 W
75	Clinton R. . . . Mich. (Detroit In.)	42·36 N	83·00 W
71	Clintonville (klĭn'tŭn-vĭl) . . . Wis.	44·37 N	88·46 W
80	Clio (klē'ō) . . . Mich.	43·10 N	83·45 W
158	Cloates, Pt. (klōts) . . . Austl.	22·47 S	113·45 E
168	Clocolan S. Afr. (Johannesburg & Pretoria In.)	28·56 S	27·35 E
116	Clonakilty B. (klŏn-ȧ-kĭltē) . . . Ire.	51·30 N	8·50 W
158	Cloncurry (klŏn-kŭr'ê) . . . Austl.	20·58 S	140·42 E
116	Clonmel (klŏn-měl) . . . Ire.	52·21 N	7·45 W
74	Cloquet (klô-kā') Minn. (Duluth In.)	46·28 N	92·28 W
71	Cloquet (R.) . . . Minn.	47·02 N	92·17 W
84	Closter (clōs'tēr) N. J. (New York In.)	40·58 N	74·57 W
67	Cloud Pk. (kloud) . . . Wyo.	44·23 N	107·11 W
74	Clough (klou'h) Minn. (Minneapolis, St. Paul In.)	45·08 N	93·14 W
79	Clover (klō'vēr) . . . S. C.	35·08 N	81·08 W
85	Clover Bar (klō'vēr bär) Can. (Edmonton In.)	53·34 N	113·20 W
68	Cloverdale (klō'vēr-dāl) . . . Calif.	38·47 N	123·03 W
65	Cloverdale . . Can. (Vancouver In.)	49·06 N	122·44 W
80	Cloverport (klō'vēr pōrt) . . . Ky.	37·50 N	86·35 W
72	Clovis (klō'vĭs) . . . N. Mex.	34·24 N	103·11 W
121	Cluj (klōōzh) . . . Rom.	46·46 N	23·34 E
110	Clun (R.) (klŭn) . . . Eng.	52·25 N	2·56 W
122	Cluny (klü-nē') . . . Fr.	46·27 N	4·40 E
159	Clutha (R.) (klōō'thȧ) . N. Z. (In.)	45·26 S	169·15 E
73	Clyde (klīd) . . . Kans.	39·34 N	97·23 W
80	Clyde . . . Ohio	41·15 N	83·00 W
116	Clyde (L.) . . . Scot.	55·35 N	3·50 W
116	Clyde, Firth of (fûrth ŏv klīd) Scot.	55·28 N	5·01 W
116	Clydebank . . . Scot.	55·56 N	4·20 W
124	Côa (R.) (kô'ä) . . . Port.	40·28 N	6·55 W
91	Coacalco (kō-ä-käl'kō) Mex. (Mexico City In.)	19·37 N	99·06 W
68	Coachella, Can. (kō'chěl-lȧ) . . Calif.	30·10 N	115·23 W
90	Coahuayana, Rio de (R.) (rê'ō-dě-kō-ä-wä-yä'nä) . Mex.	19·00 N	103·33 W
90	Coahuayutla (kō-ä-wē'lä) . . . Mex.	18·19 N	101·44 W
88	Coahuila (State) (kō-ä-wē'lä) Mex.	27·30 N	103·00 W
75	Coal City (kōl sĭ'tĭ) Ill. (Chicago In.)	41·17 N	88·17 W
90	Coalcomán, Sierra de (Mts.) (syěr'rä dä kō-äl-kō-män') . Mex.	18·30 N	102·45 W
90	Coalcomán, Rio de (R.) (rê'ō-dě-kō-äl-kō-män') . Mex.	18·30 N	102·48 W
90	Coalcomán de Matamoros (kō-äl-kō-män' dā mä-tä-mō'rôs) Mex.	18·46 N	103·10 W
73	Coalgate (kōl'gāt) . . . Okla.	34·33 N	96·13 W
80	Coal Grove (kōl grōv) . . . Ohio	38·20 N	82·40 W
68	Coalinga (kō-ȧ-lĭŋ'gȧ) . . . Calif.	36·09 N	120·23 W
110	Coalville (kōl'vĭl) . . . Eng.	52·43 N	1·21 W
89	Coamo (kō-ä'mō) P. R. (Puerto Rico In.)	18·05 N	66·21 W
98	Coari (kō-är'ê) . . . Braz.	4·06 S	63·10 W
86	Coast Mts. (kōst) . . . Can.	57·10 N	131·05 W
62	Coast Ranges, (Mts.) . . . U. S.	41·28 N	123·30 W
90	Coatepec (kō-ä-tä-pěk) . . . Mex.	19·23 N	98·44 W
91	Coatepec . . . Mex.	19·26 N	96·56 W
91	Coatepec . Mex. (Mexico City In.)	19·08 N	99·25 W
92	Coatepeque (kō-ä-tà-pā'kå) . Guat.	14·40 N	91·52 W
92	Coatepeque . . . Sal.	13·56 N	89·30 W
81	Coatesville (kōts'vĭl) . . . Pa.	40·00 N	75·50 W
90	Coatetelco (kō-ä-tà-těl'kō) . . . Mex.	18·43 N	99·47 W
81	Coaticook (kō'tĭ-kŏŏk) . . . Can.	45·10 N	71·55 W
91	Coatlinchán (kô-ä-tlē'n-chä'n) Mex. (Mexico City In.)	19·26 N	98·52 W
87	Coats (I.) (kōts) . . . Can.	62·23 N	82·11 W
47	Coats Land (Reg.) . . . Ant.	74·00 S	12·00 W
91	Coatzacoalcos (Puerto Mexico) kō-ät'zä-kō-äl'kōs) (pwě'r-tô-mě'-kē-kô) Mex.	18·09 N	94·26 W
91	Coatzacoalcos (R.) . . . Mex.	17·40 N	94·41 W
92	Coba (Ruins) (kô'bä) Mex. (Yucatan In.)	20·23 N	87·23 W
87	Cobalt (kō'bôlt) . . . Can.	47·21 N	79·40 W
92	Cobán (kō-bän') . . . Guat.	15·28 N	90·19 W
160	Cobberas, Mt. (cŏ-bēr-ăs) . . Austl.	36·45 S	148·15 E
82	Cobequid B. (kŏb'ê-kwĭd) . . . Can.	45·22 N	63·50 W
116	Cobh (kôv) . . . Ire.	51·52 N	8·09 W
98	Cobija (kô-bē'hä) . . . Bol.	11·12 S	68·49 W
81	Cobourg (kō'bōōrgh) . . . Can.	43·55 N	78·05 W
94	Cobre (R.) (kō'brā) . . . Jam.	18·05 N	77·00 W
120	Coburg (kō'bōōrg) . . . Ger.	50·16 N	10·57 E
143	Cocanāda (kō-kō-nā'dȧ) . . . India	16·58 N	82·18 E
125	Cocentaina (kō-thân-tä-ē'nȧ) . . Sp.	38·44 N	0·27 W
98	Cochabamba (kō-chä-bäm'bä) . Bol.	17·28 S	65·43 W
123	Cochem (kō'kěm) . . . Ger.	50·10 N	7·06 E
143	Cochin (kō-chĭn') . . . India	9·58 N	76·19 E
154	Cochin (Reg.) . . . Viet.	9·45 N	107·20 E
94	Cochinos, Bahia (B.) (bä-ē'ä-kô-chê'nōs) . Cuba	22·05 N	81·10 W
95	Cochinos Bks. . . . Ba. Is.	22·20 N	76·15 W
155	Cochinos Pt. (kô-chē'-nôs) Phil. (Manila In.)	14·25 N	120·15 E
78	Cochran (kŏk'răn) . . . Ga.	32·23 N	83·23 W
87	Cochrane (kŏk'răn) . . . Can.	49·01 N	81·06 W
85	Cochrane . . . Can. (Calgary In.)	51·11 N	114·28 W
80	Cockburn (I.) (kŏk-bûrn) . . . Can.	45·55 N	83·25 W
81	Cockeysville (kŏk'ĭz-vĭl) . . . Md.	39·30 N	76·40 W
74	Cockrell Hill (kŏk'rĕl) Tex. (Dallas, Fort Worth In.)	32·44 N	96·53 W
98	Coco, Isla del (I.) (ê's-lä-děl-kô-kô) C. R.	5·33 N	87·02 W
94	Coco, Cayo (I.) (kä'yō-kô'kō) Cuba	22·30 N	78·30 W
79	Cocoa (kō'kō) . . . Fla. (In.)	28·21 N	80·44 W
79	Cocoa Beach . . . Fla. (In.)	28·09 N	80·37 W
88	Cocoli (kô-kô'lē) C. Z. (Panama Canal In.)	8·58 N	79·36 W
69	Coconino, Plat. (kō kō nê'nō) . Ariz.	35·45 N	112·28 W
93	Coco R. (Segovia) (kô-kô) (sě-gô'vyä) . Hond.	14·55 N	83·45 W
7	Cocos (Keeling) (kō'kôs) (kē'lĭng) Is. Oceania	11·50 S	90·50 E
88	Coco Solito (kô-kô-sŏ-lē'tŏ) C. Z. (Panama Canal In.)	9·21 N	79·53 W
82	Cocouna . . . Can.	47·54 N	69·31 W
90	Cocula (kō-kōō'lä) . . . Mex.	20·23 N	103·47 W
90	Cocula (R.) . . . Mex.	18·17 N	99·11 W
98	Codajás (kō-dä-häzh') . . . Braz.	3·44 S	62·09 W
99	Codera, Cabo (C.) (kȧ'bô-kō-dě'rä) . Ven. (In.)	10·35 N	66·06 W
99	Codó (kō'dō) . . . Braz.	4·21 S	43·52 W
126	Codogno (kô-dō'nyō) . . . It.	45·08 N	9·43 E
93	Codrington (kŏd'rĭng-tŭn) Barbuda (Le. & Wind. Is. In.)	17·39 N	61·49 W
67	Cody (kō'dĭ) . . . Wyo.	44·31 N	109·02 W
123	Coesfeld (kûs'fěld) Ger. (Ruhr In.)	51·56 N	7·10 E
66	Coeur d' Alene (kûr dȧ-lān') Idaho	47·43 N	116·35 W
66	Coeur d' Alene L. . . . Idaho	47·32 N	116·39 W
66	Coeur d' Alene R. . . . Idaho	47·26 N	116·35 W
167	Coffee Bay (cŏfē bā) S. Afr. (Natal In.)	31·58 S	29·10 E
73	Coffeyville (kŏf'ĭ-vĭl) . . . Kans.	37·01 N	95·38 W
160	Coff's Harbour . . . Austl.	30·20 S	153·10 E
167	Cofimvaba (cäfĭm'vä-bȧ) S. Afr. (Natal In.)	32·01 S	27·37 E
126	Coghinas (R.) (kō'gē-nȧs) . . . It.	40·31 N	9·00 E
122	Cognac (kôn-yak') . . . Fr.	45·41 N	0·22 W
83	Cohasset (kô-hăs'ět) Mass. (Boston In.)	42·14 N	70·48 W
81	Cohoes (kô-hōz') . . . N. Y.	42·50 N	73·40 W
100	Coig (kô'ěk) (R.) . . . Arg.	51·15 S	71·00 W
143	Coimbatore (kô-ēm-bȧ-tōr') . India	11·03 N	76·56 E
124	Coimbra (kô-ēm'brä) . . . Port.	40·14 N	8·23 W
124	Coín (kô-ēn') . . . Sp.	36·40 N	4·45 W
125	Coina (kô-ē'nȧ) . Port. (Lisbon In.)	38·35 N	9·03 W
125	Coina (R.) (kô'y-nä) Port. (Lisbon In.)	38·35 N	9·02 W
98	Coipasa, Salar de (Salt Flat) (sä-lä'r-dě-koi-pä'-sä) . Chile	19·12 S	69·13 W
91	Coixtlahuaca (kō-ēks'tlä-wä'kä) Mex.	17·42 N	97·17 W
99	Cojedes (State) (kô-kě'děs) Ven. (In.)	9·50 N	68·21 W
95	Cojimar (kō-hê-mär') Cuba (Havana In.)	23·10 N	82·19 W
92	Cojutepeque (kô-hōō-tě-pā'kå) Sal.	13·45 N	88·50 W
71	Cokato (kô-kā'tō) . . . Minn.	45·03 N	94·11 W
75	Cokeburg (kōk bûgh) Pa. (Pittsburgh In.)	40·06 N	80·03 W
160	Colac (kŏ'låc) . . . Austl.	38·25 S	143·40 E
125	Colares (kô-lä'rěs) Port. (Lisbon In.)	38·47 N	9·27 W
99	Colatina (kô-lä-tē'nä) . . . Braz.	19·33 S	40·42 W
72	Colby (kōl'bĭ) . . . Kans.	39·23 N	101·04 W
101	Colchagua (Prov.) (kōl-chä'gwä) Chile (Santiago In.)	36·42 S	71·24 W
117	Colchester (kōl'chěs-tēr) . . . Eng.	51·52 N	0·50 E
83	Cold Spring Pd. (kōld) . . . Can.	48·08 N	56·25 W
72	Coldwater (kōld'wô-tēr) . . . Kans.	37·14 N	99·21 W
80	Coldwater . . . Mich.	41·55 N	85·00 W
78	Coldwater (R.) . . . Miss.	34·25 N	90·12 W
72	Coldwater Cr. . . . Tex.	36·10 N	101·45 W

n-sing ŋ-baŋk; ɴ-nasalized n; nŏd; cŏmmit; ōld; ôbey; ôrder; fōōd; fŏŏt; ou-out; s-soft; sh-dish; th-thin; pūre; ûnite; ûrn; stŭd; circŭs; ü-as "y" in study; '-indeterminate vowel.

PRONOUNCING INDEX Coracora–Crisul Alb 197

Page	Name Pronunciation Region	Lat. °′	Long. °′
98	Coracora (kō'rä-kō'rä) Peru	15·12 s	73·42 w
79	Coral Gables Fla. (In.)	25·43 N	80·14 w
94	Coralillo (kô-rä-lē-yō) Cuba	73·00 N	80·40 w
87	Coral Rapids (kŏr'ăl) Can.	50·18 N	81·49 w
75	Coral Ridge (kŏr'ăl) Ky. (Louisville In.)	38·05 N	85·42 w
156	Coral Sea (kŏr'ăl) Oceania	13·30 s	150·00 E
160	Corangamite, L. (cōr-ăŋg'ȧ-mĭt) Austl.	38·05 s	142·55 E
75	Coraopolis (kō-rä-ŏp'ō-lĭs) Pa. (Pittsburgh In.)	40·31 N	80·10 w
126	Corato (kô'rä-tô) It.	41·08 N	16·28 E
123	Corbeil-Essonnes (kôr-bâ'yĕ-sŏn') Fr. (Paris In.)	48·31 N	2·29 E
65	Corbett (kôr'bĕt) Ore. (Portland In.)	45·31 N	122·17 w
122	Corbie (kôr-bē') Fr.	49·55 N	2·27 E
78	Corbin (kôr'bĭn) Ky.	36·55 N	84·06 w
110	Corby (kôr'bĭ) Eng.	52·50 N	0·32 w
100	Corcovado (Mtn.) (kôr-kô-vä'dōō) Braz. (In.)	22·57 s	43·13 w
100	Corcovado, Golfo (G.) (kôr-kô-vä'dhō). Chile	43·40 s	75·00 w
101	Cordeiro (kôr-dā'rō) Braz. (Rio de Janeiro In.)	22·03 s	42·22 w
78	Cordele (kôr-dēl') Ga.	31·55 N	83·50 w
72	Cordell (kôr-dĕl') Okla.	35·19 N	98·58 w
124	Cordillera Cantabrica (Mts.) (kôr-dēl-yĕ'rä-kän-tä'brē-kä). Sp.	43·05 N	6·05 w
155	Cordillera Central (Mts.) (kôr-dēl-yĕ'rä-sĕn'träl) Phil. (Manila In.)	17·05 N	120·55 E
49	Cordilleran Highlands (Reg.) (kōr dĭl'lŭr ȧn). N. A.	55·00 N	125·00 w
100	Córdoba (kôr'dô-vä) Arg.	30·20 s	64·03 w
91	Cordoba (kô'r-dô-bä) Mex.	18·53 N	96·54 w
124	Córdoba (kô'r-dô-bä) Sp.	37·55 N	4·45 w
100	Córdoba (Prov.) (kôr'dô-vä). Arg.	32·00 s	64·00 w
100	Córdoba, Sa. de (Mts.) Arg.	31·15 s	64·30 w
78	Cordova (kôr'dô-vȧ) Ala.	33·45 N	86·11 w
64	Cordova (kôr'dô-vȧ) Alaska	60·34 N	145·38 w
124	Corella (kô-rĕl-yä) Sp.	42·07 N	1·48 w
126	Corigliano (kō-rē-lyä'nō) It.	39·35 N	16·30 E
78	Corinth (kŏr'ĭnth) Miss.	34·55 N	88·30 w
	Corinth, see Korinthos		
99	Corinto (kô-rē'n-tō) Braz.	18·20 s	44·16 w
98	Corinto Col. (In.)	3·09 N	76·12 w
92	Corinto (kŏr-ĭn'to) Nic.	12·30 N	87·12 w
161	Corio Austl. (Melbourne In.)	38·05 s	144·22 E
161	Corio B. Austl. (Melbourne In.)	38·07 s	144·25 E
116	Cork (kôrk) Ire.	51·54 N	8·25 w
116	Cork Hbr. Ire.	51·44 N	8·15 w
126	Corleone (kôr-lâ-ō'nā) It.	37·48 N	13·18 E
127	Corlu (chôr'lōō) Tur.	41·09 N	27·48 E
78	Cornelia (kôr-nē'lyȧ) Ga.	34·31 N	83·30 w
168	Cornelis R. (kôr-nē'lĭs) S. Afr. (Johannesburg & Pretoria In.)	27·48 s	29·15 E
74	Cornell (kôr-nĕl') Calif. (Los Angeles In.)	34·06 N	118·46 w
71	Cornell Wis.	45·10 N	91·10 w
83	Corner Brook (kôr'nẽr) Can.	48·58 N	57·49 w
160	Corner Inlet Austl.	38·55 s	146·45 E
	Corneta, see Targuinia		
73	Corning (kôr'nĭng) Ark.	36·26 N	90·35 w
71	Corning Iowa	40·58 N	94·40 w
81	Corning N. Y.	42·10 N	77·05 w
126	Corno, M. (Mtn.) (kôr'nō) It.	42·28 N	13·37 E
94	Cornwall Ba. Is.	25·55 N	77·15 w
81	Cornwall (kôrn'wôl) Can.	45·05 N	74·35 w
116	Cornwall Pen. (kôrn'wăl) Eng.	50·25 N	5·04 w
98	Coro (kō'rō) Ven.	11·22 N	69·43 w
98	Corocoro (kō-rō-kō'rō) Bol.	17·15 s	68·21 w
143	Coromandel Coast (kŏr-ô-man'dĕl) India	17·50 N	80·14 E
78	Corona (kô-rō'nȧ) Ala.	33·42 N	87·28 w
74	Corona Calif. (Los Angeles In.)	33·52 N	117·34 w
93	Coronada, Bahia de (B.) (bä-ē'ä-dĕ-kô-rô-nä'dō). C.R.	8·47 N	84·04 w
74	Corona del Mar (kô-rō'nȧ dēl mär) Calif. (Los Angeles In.)	33·36 N	117·53 w
68	Coronado (kŏr-ô-nä'dō) Calif. (San Diego In.)	32·42 N	117·12 w
86	Coronation G. (kŏr-ô-nā'shŭn) Can.	68·07 N	112·50 w
100	Coronel (kō-rō-nĕl') Chile	37·00 s	73·10 w
101	Coronel Brandsen (kō-rô-nĕl-brä'nd-sĕn) Arg. (Buenos Aires In.)	35·09 s	58·15 w
100	Coronel Dorrego (kŏ-rô-nĕl-dôr-rĕ'gô). Arg.	38·43 s	61·16 w
100	Coronel Oviedo (kŏ-rô-nĕl-ô-vēĕ'dô). Par.	25·28 s	56·22 w
100	Coronel Pringles (kŏ-rô-nĕl-prēn'glĕs). Arg.	37·54 s	61·22 w
100	Coronel Suárez (kŏ-rô-nĕl-swä'rās). Arg.	37·24 s	66·49 w
99	Coronie Sur.	5·51 N	56·17 w
160	Corowa (cŏr-ôwȧ) Austl.	36·02 s	146·23 E
92	Corozal (cŏr-ŏth-äl') Br. Hond. (Yucatan In.)	18·25 N	88·23 w
77	Corpus Christi (kôr'pŭs krĭs'tē) Tex.	27·48 N	97·24 w
77	Corpus Christi B. Tex.	27·47 N	97·14 w
76	Corpus Christi L. Tex.	28·08 N	98·20 w
100	Corral (kô-räl') Chile	39·57 s	73·15 w
124	Corral de Almaguer (kô-räl'dä äl-mä-gär'). Sp.	39·45 N	3·10 w
155	Corregidor (I.) (kô-rä-hē-dōr') Phil. (Manila In.)	14·21 N	120·25 E
99	Correntina (kô-rĕn-tē-nȧ) Braz.	13·18 s	44·33 w
116	Corrib, Lough (B.) (lŏk kŏr'ĭb) Ire.	53·56 N	9·19 w
100	Corrientes (kō-ryĕn'tās) Arg.	27·25 s	58·39 w
100	Corrientes (Prov.) Arg.	28·45 s	58·00 w
98	Corrientes, Cabo (kä'bô-kō-ryĕn'tās). Col.	5·34 N	77·35 w
94	Corrientes, Cabo (C.) (kä'bô-kôr-rē-ĕn'tĕs). Cuba	21·50 N	84·25 w
94	Corrientes, Ensenada de (B.) (ĕn-sĕ-nä-dä-dĕ-kō-ryĕn'tās) Cuba	21·45 N	84·45 w
90	Corrientes, Cabo (C.) Mex.	20·25 N	105·41 w
81	Cory (kŏr'ĭ) Pa.	41·55 N	79·40 w
126	Corse, C. (kôrs) Fr.	42·59 N	9·19 E
126	Corsica (I.) (kô'r-sē-kä) Fr.	42·10 N	8·55 E
77	Corsicana (kôr-sĭ-kăn'ȧ) Tex.	32·06 N	96·28 w
90	Cortazar (kôr-tä-zär') Mex.	20·30 N	100·57 w
126	Corte (kôr'tā) Fr.	42·18 N	9·10 E
124	Cortegana (kôr-tå-gä'nä) Sp.	37·54 N	6·48 w
124	Cortes (kôr-tās') Sp.	36·38 N	5·20 w
94	Cortés, Ensenada de (B.) (ĕn-sĕ-nä-dä-dĕ-kôr-tās'). Cuba	22·05 N	83·45 w
81	Cortland (kôrt'lȧnd) N. Y.	42·35 N	76·10 w
126	Cortona (kôr-tō'nä) It.	43·16 N	12·00 E
124	Coruche (kô-rōō'she) Port.	38·58 N	8·34 w
133	Coruh (R.) (chō-rōōk') Tur.	40·30 N	41·10 E
133	Corum (chô-rōōm') Tur.	39·30 N	34·50 E
99	Corumbá (kō-rōōm-bä') Braz.	19·01 s	57·28 w
80	Corunna (kô-rŭn'ȧ) Mich.	43·00 N	84·05 w
99	Coruripe (kō-rōō-rē'pĭ) Braz.	10·09 s	36·13 w
66	Corvallis (kŏr-văl'ĭs) Ore.	44·34 N	123·17 w
110	Corve (R.) (kôr'vê) Eng.	52·28 N	2·43 w
80	Corydon (kŏr'ĭ-dŭn) Ind.	38·10 N	86·05 w
71	Corydon Iowa	40·45 N	93·20 w
80	Corydon Ky.	37·45 N	87·40 w
91	Cosamaloápan (kô-sä-mä-lwä'pän) Mex.	18·21 N	95·48 w
91	Coscomatepec (kôs'kōmä-tĕ-pĕk') Mex.	19·04 N	97·03 w
110	Coseley (kôs'lē) Eng.	52·33 N	2·10 w
126	Cosenza (kô-zĕnt'sä) It.	39·18 N	16·15 E
80	Coshocton (kô-shŏk'tŭn) Ohio	40·15 N	81·55 w
92	Cosigüina (Vol.) Nic.	12·59 N	83·35 w
167	Cosmoledo Group (Is.) (kŏs-mô-lā'dō). Afr.	9·42 s	47·45 E
66	Cosmopolis (kŏz-mŏp'ô-lĭs). Wash.	46·58 N	123·47 w
122	Cosne-sur-Loire (kōn-sür-lwär') Fr.	47·25 N	2·57 E
91	Cosoleacaque (kō sō lā-ä-kä'kē) Mex.	18·01 N	94·38 w
74	Costa Mesa (kŏs'tȧ mā'sȧ) Calif. (Los Angeles In.)	33·39 N	118·54 w
89	Costa Rica (kŏs'tȧ rē'kȧ) N. A.	10·30 N	84·30 w
68	Cosumnes (R.) (kô-sŭm'nĕz). Calif.	38·21 N	121·17 w
98	Cotabambas (kô-tä-bäm'bäs) Peru	13·49 s	72·17 w
155	Cotabato (kō-tä-bä'tō) Phil.	7·06 N	124·13 E
91	Cotaxtla (kō-täs'tlä) Mex.	18·49 N	96·22 w
91	Cotaxtla (R.) Mex.	18·54 N	96·21 w
85	Coteau-du-Lac (cō-tō'dü-lăk) Can. (Montreal In.)	45·17 N	74·11 w
85	Coteau Landing Can. (Montreal In.)	45·15 N	74·13 w
95	Coteaux Hai.	18·15 N	74·05 w
122	Côte d'Or (hill) (kōt-dŏr') Fr.	47·02 N	4·35 E
90	Cotija de la Paz (kô-tē'-kä-dĕ-lä-pá'z). Mex.	19·46 N	102·43 w
164	Cotonou (kô-tô-nōō') Dahomey	6·26 N	2·19 E
98	Cotopaxi (Mtn.) (kō-tô-păk'sē) Ec.	0·40 s	78·26 w
95	Cotorro (kô-tôr-rō) Cuba (Havana In.)	23·03 N	82·17 w
116	Cotswold Hills (kŏtz'wōld) Eng.	51·35 N	2·16 w
74	Cottage Grove (kŏt'ăj grōv) Minn. (Minneapolis, St. Paul In.)	44·50 N	92·52 w
66	Cottage Grove Ore.	43·48 N	123·04 w
120	Cottbus (kōtt'bōōs) Ger.	51·47 N	14·20 E
123	Cottian Alps (Mts.) (kŏ'tē-ŭn-ălps). Fr.-It.	44·46 N	7·02 E
70	Cottonwood (R.) (kŏt'ŭn-wŏŏd) Minn.	44·25 N	95·35 w
66	Cottonwood Cr. Calif.	40·24 N	122·50 w
95	Cotui (kô-tōō'-ē) Dom. Rep.	19·05 N	70·10 w
76	Cotulla (kŏ-tŭl'lȧ) Tex.	28·26 N	99·14 w
123	Coubert (kōō-bâr'). Fr. (Paris In.)	48·40 N	2·43 E
81	Coudersport (koŭ'dẽrz-port) Pa.	41·45 N	78·00 w
82	Coudres, Ile-aux Can.	47·25 N	70·25 w
122	Couéron (kōō-â-rôN') Fr.	47·16 N	1·45 w
123	Coulommiers (kōō-lô-myā') Fr. (Paris In.)	48·49 N	3·05 E
100	Coulto, Serra do (Mts.) (sĕ'r-rä-dô-kô-ōō'tô). Braz. (In.)	22·33 s	43·27 w
64	Council (koun'sĭl) Alaska	64·55 N	163·40 w
70	Council Bluffs (koun'sĭl blŭf) Iowa	41·16 N	95·53 w
73	Council Grove (koun'sĭl grōv) Kans.	38·39 N	96·30 w
65	Coupeville (kōōp'vĭl) Wash. (Seattle In.)	48·13 N	122·41 w
99	Courantyne (R.) (kôr'ȧntīn) Br. Gu.-Sur.	4·28 N	57·42 w
86	Courtenay (cōōrt-nā') Can.	49·51 N	125·07 w
77	Coushatta (kou-shăt'ȧ) La.	32·02 N	93·21 w
122	Coutras (kōō-trä') Fr.	45·02 N	0·07 w
110	Coventry (kŭv'ĕn-trĭ) Eng.	52·25 N	1·29 w
124	Covilhã (kō-vēl'yăN) Port.	40·18 N	7·29 w
74	Covina (kô-vē'nȧ) Calif. (Los Angeles In.)	34·06 N	117·54 w
78	Covington (kŭv'ĭng-tŭn) Ga.	33·36 N	83·50 w
80	Covington Ind.	40·10 N	87·15 w
75	Covington Ky. (Cincinnati In.)	39·05 N	84·31 w
77	Covington La.	30·30 N	90·06 w
80	Covington Ohio	40·10 N	84·20 w
73	Covington Okla.	36·18 N	97·32 w
78	Covington Tenn.	35·33 N	89·40 w
81	Covington Va.	37·50 N	80·00 w
160	Cowal, L. (kou'ăl) Austl.	33·30 s	147·10 E
158	Cowan, (L.) (kou'ȧn) Austl.	32·00 s	122·30 E
66	Cow Cr. (kou) Ore.	42·45 N	123·35 w
116	Cowes (kouz) Eng.	50·43 N	1·25 w
66	Cowlitz R. (kou'lĭts) Wash.	46·30 N	122·45 w
160	Cowra (kou'rȧ) Austl.	33·50 s	148·33 E
99	Coxim (kō-shēN') Braz.	18·32 s	54·43 w
91	Coxquihui (kōz-kē-wē') Mex.	20·10 N	97·34 w
142	Coxs Bazar E. Pak.	21·32 N	92·00 E
98	Coyaima (kō-yàē'-mä). Col. (In.)	3·48 N	75·11 w
76	Coyame (kō-yä'mä) Mex.	29·26 N	105·05 w
76	Coyanosa Draw (kō yȧ-nō'sȧ). Tex.	30·55 N	103·07 w
91	Coyoacàn (kô-yô-ȧ-kän') Mex. (Mexico City In.)	19·21 N	99·10 w
65	Coyote (R.) (kī'ōt) Calif. (San Francisco In.)	37·27 N	121·57 w
90	Coyuca de Benítez (kō-yōō'kä dā bā-nē'tāz). Mex.	17·04 N	100·06 w
90	Coyuca de Catalán (kō-yōō'kä dā kä-tä-län'). Mex.	18·19 N	100·41 w
91	Coyutla (kō-yōō'tlä) Mex.	20·13 N	97·40 w
72	Cozad (kō'zăd) Nebr.	40·53 N	99·59 w
75	Cozaddale (kō-zăd-dāl) Ohio (Cincinnati In.)	39·16 N	84·09 w
90	Cozoyoapan (kô-zō-yô-ä-pä'n) Mex.	16·45 N	98·17 w
92	Cozumel (kŏ-zōō-mĕ'l) Mex. (Yucatan In.)	20·31 N	86·55 w
92	Cozumel, Isla de (I.) (ē's-lä-dĕ-kŏ-zōō-mĕ'l) Mex. (Yucatan In.)	20·26 N	87·10 w
66	Crab Cr. (krăb) Wash.	46·47 N	119·43 w
66	Crab Cr. Wash.	47·21 N	119·09 w
167	Cradock (kră'dŭk) S. Afr. (Natal In.)	32·12 s	25·38 E
75	Crafton (krăf'tŭn) Pa. (Pittsburgh In.)	40·26 N	80·04 w
67	Craig (krāg) Colo.	40·32 N	107·31 w
85	Craigs Road Station (krāgz) Can. (Quebec In.)	46·37 N	71·22 w
127	Craiova (krȧ-yō'vȧ) Rom.	44·18 N	23·50 E
81	Cranberry (L.) (krăn'bĕr-ĭ). N. Y.	44·10 N	74·50 w
161	Cranbourne Austl. (Melbourne In.)	38·07 s	145·16 E
86	Cranbrook (krăn'brŏŏk) Can.	49·43 N	115·47 w
84	Cranbury (krăn'bē-rĭ) N. J. (New York In.)	40·19 N	74·31 w
71	Crandon (krăn'dŭn) Wis.	45·35 N	88·55 w
122	Cransac (krāN-zàk') Fr.	44·28 N	2·19 E
84	Cranston (krăns'tŭn) R. I. (Providence In.)	41·46 N	71·25 w
66	Crater L. (krā'tẽr) Ore.	43·00 N	122·08 w
66	Crater Lake Natl. Park Ore.	4258· N	122·40 w
67	Craters of the Moon Natl. Park (krā'tẽr). Idaho	43·28 N	113·15 w
99	Crateús (krä-tȧ-ōōzh') Braz.	5·09 s	40·35 w
99	Crato (krä'tōō) Braz.	7·19 s	39·13 w
70	Crawford (krô'fẽrd) Nebr.	42·41 N	103·25 w
65	Crawford Wash. (Portland In.)	45·49 N	122·24 w
80	Crawfordsville (krô'fẽrdz-vĭl). Ind.	40·00 N	86·55 w
67	Crazy Mts. (krā'zĭ) Mont.	46·11 N	110·25 w
67	Crazy Woman Cr. Wyo.	44·08 N	106·40 w
122	Crécy (krā-sē') Fr.	50·13 N	1·48 E
168	Crecy (krĕ-sē) S. Afr. (Johannesburg & Pretoria In.)	24·38 s	28·52 E
123	Crecy-en-Brie (krā-sē'-ĕN-brē') Fr. (Paris In.)	48·52 N	2·55 E
85	Credit R. Can. (Toronto In.)	43·41 N	79·55 w
86	Cree (L.) (krē) Can.	57·35 N	107·52 w
70	Creighton (krā'tŭn) Nebr.	42·27 N	97·54 w
167	Creighton (cre-tŏn) S. Afr. (Natal In.)	30·02 s	29·52 E
122	Creil (krĕ'y') Fr.	49·18 N	2·28 E
126	Crema (krā'mä) It.	45·21 N	9·53 E
126	Cremona (krā-mō'nä) It.	45·09 N	10·02 E
126	Crépy-en-Valois (krā-pē'-ĕN-vä-lwä') Fr. (Paris In.)	49·14 N	2·53 E
126	Cres (Tsrĕs) Yugo.	44·58 N	14·21 E
126	Cres (I.) Yugo.	44·50 N	14·31 E
79	Crescent (R.) (krĕs'ĕnt) Fla.	29·33 N	81·30 w
85	Crescent Beach Can. (Vancouver In.)	49·03 N	122·58 w
79	Crescent City Fla.	29·26 N	81·35 w
66	Crescent L. Ore.	43·25 N	121·58 w
71	Cresco (krĕs'kō) Iowa	43·23 N	92·07 w
66	Cresent City (krĕs'ĕnt) Calif.	41·46 N	124·13 w
69	Crested Butte (krĕst'ĕd būt). Colo.	38·50 N	107·00 w
74	Crestline (krĕst-līn) Calif. (Los Angeles In.)	34·15 N	117·17 w
80	Crestline Ohio	40·50 N	82·40 w
74	Crestmore (krĕst'môr) Calif. (Los Angeles In.)	34·02 N	117·23 w
86	Creston (krĕs'tŭn) Can.	49·09 N	116·32 w
71	Creston Iowa	41·04 N	94·22 w
75	Creston Ohio (Cleveland In.)	40·59 N	81·54 w
78	Crestview (krĕst'vū) Fla.	30·44 N	86·35 w
75	Crestwood (krĕst'wŏŏd) Ky. (Louisville In.)	38·20 N	85·28 w
75	Crete (krēt) Ill. (Chicago In.)	41·26 N	87·38 w
73	Crete Nebr.	40·38 N	96·56 w
126	Crete (I.) Grc. (Inset)	35·15 N	24·30 E
125	Creus, Cabo de (C.) (kä'-bô-dĕ-krĕ-ōōs). Sp.	42·16 N	3·18 E
122	Creuse (krûz) Fr.	46·51 N	0·49 E
74	Creve Coeur (krēv kōōr) Mo. (St. Louis In.)	38·40 N	90·27 w
125	Crevillente (krä-vē-lyĕn'tå) Sp.	38·12 N	0·48 w
110	Crewe (krōō) Eng.	53·06 N	2·27 w
79	Crewe Va.	37·09 N	78·08 w
	Crimea Poluostrov (Pen.), see Krymskiy		
120	Crimmitschau (krĭm'ĭt-shou). Ger.	50·49 N	12·22 E
72	Cripple Creek (krĭp''l) Colo.	38·44 N	105·12 w
81	Crisfield (krĭs-fēld) Md.	38·00 N	78·50 w
101	Cristina (krēs-tē'-nä) Braz. (Rio de Janeiro In.)	22·13 s	45·15 w
98	Cristobal Colón, Pico (Pk.) (pē'kô-krēs-tô'bäl-kō-lōn'). Col.	11·00 N	74·00 w
121	Crisul Alb R. (krē'shōōl ălb) Rom.	46·20 N	22·15 E

ng-sing; ŋ-baŋk; N-nasalized n; nŏd; cŏmmit; ōld; ôbey; ôrder; fōōd; fŏŏt; ou-out; s-soft; sh-dish; th-thin; pūre; ûnite; ûrn; stŭd; circŭs; ü-as "y" in study; '-indeterminate vowel.

ăt; fin*ȧ*l; rāte; senāte; ärm; ȧsk; sof*ȧ*; fâre; ch-choose; dh-as th in other; bē; êvent; bĕt; recĕnt; cratēr; g-go; gh-guttural g; bĭt; ɨ-short neutral; rīde; ĸ-guttural k as ch in German ich;

PRONOUNCING INDEX Daley–Dem'yanka 199

Page	Name Pronunciation Region	Lat. °′	Long. °′
158	Daley (L.) (dā'lĭ) Austl.	14·15 S	131·15 E
158	Daley Waters (dā-lē) Austl.	16·15 S	133·30 E
72	Dalhart (dăl'härt) Tex.	36·04 N	102·32 W
82	Dalhousie (dăl-hōō'zē) Can.	48·03 N	66·24 W
124	Dalías (dä-lē'äs) Sp.	36·49 N	2·50 W
64	Dall (I.) (dăl) Alaska	54·50 N	133·10 W
66	Dallas (dăl'lås) Ore.	44·55 N	123·20 W
70	Dallas S. D.	43·13 N	99·34 W
74	Dallas Tex. (Dallas Fort Worth In.)	32·45 N	96·48 W
73	Dallas (L.) Tex.	33·16 N	96·54 W
66	Dalles Dam Ore.	45·36 N	121·08 W
126	Dalmacija (Reg.) (däl-mä'tsē-yä) Yugo.	43·25 N	16·37 E
85	Dalroy (dăl'roi) Can. (Calgary In.)	51·08 N	113·40 W
159	Dalrymple, Mt. (dăl'rĭm-p'l) Austl.	21·14 S	148·46 E
78	Dalton (dôl't*ŭ*n) Ga.	34·46 N	84·58 W
167	Dalton (dŏl'tŏn) S. Afr. (Natal In.)	29·21 S	30·41 E
65	Daly City (dā'lē) Calif. (San Francisco In.)	37·42 N	122·27 W
99	Dam (däm) Sur.	4·36 N	54·54 W
168	Damanhūr (dä-män-hōōr') U. A. R. (Nile In.)	30·59 N	30·31 E
142	Damão Asia	20·32 N	75·52 E
155	Damar (I.) Indon.	7·15 S	129·15 E
166	Damaraland (Reg.) (dä'm*å*-r*å*-lănd) S. W. Afr.	22·15 S	16·15 E
94	Damas Cays (Is.) (dä'mäs) Ba. Is.	23·50 N	79·50 W
	Damascus, see Dimashq		
133	Damavand (Mtn.) Iran	36·05 N	52·05 E
166	Damba (däm'bä) Ang.	6·50 S	15·20 E
165	Dambidolo Eth.	8·46 N	34·46 E
77	Dam B Res. (dăm) Tex.	30·52 N	94·30 W
95	Dame Marie, Cap (C.) (däm mȧrē') Hai.	18·35 N	74·50 W
144	Dāmghān (dām-gān') Iran	35·50 N	54·15 E
	Damietta, see Dumyāṭ		
123	Dammartin-en-Goële (däɴ-mär-tăɴ-äɴ-gô-ĕl') Fr. (Paris In.)	49·03 N	2·40 E
155	Dampier, Straat (Str.) (däm'pēr) W. Irian	0·40 N	131·15 E
158	Dampier Arch. (däɴ-pyâr') Austl.	20·15 S	116·25 E
79	Dan (R.) (dăn) N. C.	36·26 N	79·40 W
165	Danakil Des. Eth.	12·45 N	41·01 E
154	Danau (R.) Indon.	4·17 S	105·00 E
84	Danbury (dăn'bĕr-ĭ) Conn. (New York In.)	41·23 N	73·27 W
110	Danbury Eng. (London In.)	51·42 N	0·34 E
77	Danbury Tex. (In.)	29·14 N	95·22 W
168	Dandarah (dĕn'dȧ-rȧ) U. A. R. (Nile In.)	26·08 N	32·42 E
161	Dandenong (dăn'dē-nông) Austl. (Melbourne In.)	37·59 S	145·13 E
110	Dane (R.) (dān) Eng.	53·11 N	2·14 W
85	Danforth (dăn'fûrth) Can. (Toronto In.)	43·42 N	79·15 W
82	Danforth Maine	45·38 N	67·53 W
165	Dānglā Eth.	11·17 N	36·69 E
142	Dangri India	26·43 N	71·32 E
79	Dania (dā'nĭ-ȧ) Fla. (In.)	26·01 N	80·10 W
84	Daniels (dă-nĭ-*ĕ*ls) Md. (Baltimore In.)	39·19 N	76·49 W
128	Danilov (dä'nē-lôf) Sov. Un.	58·12 N	40·08 E
127	Danilov Grad (dä'nē-lôf'gräd) Yugo.	42·31 N	19·08 E
128	Dankov (däŋ'kôf) Sov. Un.	53·17 N	39·09 E
92	Danlí (dän'lē) Hond.	14·02 N	86·35 W
81	Dannemora (dăn-ē-mō'r*å*) N. Y.	44·45 N	73·45 W
167	Dannhauser (dän'hou-zēr) S. Afr. (Natal In.)	28·07 S	30·04 E
81	Dansville (dănz'vĭl) N. Y.	42·30 N	77·40 W
129	Danube, Mouths of the (dăn'ub) Rom.	45·13 N	29·37 E
115	Danube R. Eur.	43·41 N	23·35 E
83	Danvers (dăn'vērz) Mass. (Boston In.)	42·34 N	70·57 W
65	Danville (dăn'vĭl) Calif. (San Francisco In.)	37·49 N	122·00 W
80	Danville Ill.	40·10 N	87·35 W
80	Danville Ind.	39·45 N	86·30 W
80	Danville Ky.	37·35 N	84·50 W
81	Danville Pa.	41·00 N	76·35 W
79	Danville Va.	36·35 N	79·24 W
	Danzig, see Gdańsk		
112	Danzig, G. of (dan'tsĭk) Pol.	54·41 N	19·01 E
139	Dar'a Syria (Palestine In.)	32·37 N	36·07 E
121	Dărăbani (dă-ră-băn'ĭ) Rom.	48·13 N	26·38 E
164	Daraj Libya	30·12 N	10·14 E
168	Darāw (dȧ-rä'ōō) U. A. R. (Nile In.)	24·24 N	32·56 E
142	Darbhanga (dŭr-bŭŋ'gä) India	26·03 N	85·09 E
84	Darby (där'bĭ) Pa. (Philadelphia In.)	39·55 N	75·16 W
95	Darby (I.) Ba. Is.	23·50 N	76·20 W
	Dardanelles (Str.), see Çanakkale Boğazi		
167	Dar es Salaam (där ĕs sȧ-läm') Tan.	6·58 S	39·13 E
165	Darfur (Prov.) (där-fōōr') Sud.	13·21 N	23·46 E
145	Dargai (dŭr-gä'ē) W. Pak. (Khyber Pass In.)	34·32 N	71·55 E
164	D'Arguin, Cap (C.) Mauritania	20·28 N	17·46 W
98	Darien (dā-rĭ-ĕn') Col. (In.)	3·56 N	76·30 W
84	Darien (dâ-rē-ĕn') Conn. (New York In.)	41·04 N	73·28 W
	Daíren, see Talien		
92	Darien, Cordillera de (Mts.) Nic.	13·00 N	85·42 W
98	Darien, Golfo del (G.) (gôl-fô-dĕl-dā-rĭ-ĕn') N. A.-S. A.	9·36 N	77·54 W
93	Darien, Serrania del (Ra.) (sĕr-ä-nē'ä dĕl dä-rē-ĕn') Pan.	8·13 N	77·28 W
142	Darjeeling (dŭr-jē'lĭng) India	27·05 N	88·16 E
110	Darlaston (där'lȧs-t*ŭ*n) Eng.	52·34 N	2·02 W
70	Darling (L.) (där'lĭng) N. D.	48·35 N	101·25 W
160	Darling (R.) Austl.	31·50 S	143·20 E
160	Darling Downs (Reg.) Austl.	27·22 S	150·50 E
158	Darling Ra. Austl.	30·30 S	115·45 E
116	Darlington (där'lĭng-t*ŭ*n) Eng.	54·32 N	1·35 W
79	Darlington S. C.	34·15 N	79·52 W
71	Darlington Wis.	42·41 N	90·06 W
120	Darlowo (där-lô'vô) Pol.	24·25 N	16·21 E
120	Darmstadt (därm'shtät) Ger.	49·53 N	8·40 E
165	Darnah Libya	32·44 N	22·41 E
64	Darnley B. (därn'lē) Alaska	70·00 N	124·00 W
165	Dar Nuba (Reg.) Sud.	12·22 N	30·39 E
124	Daroca (dä-rō-kä) Sp.	41·08 N	1·24 W
75	Darrowville (dăr'rō-vĭl) Ohio (Cleveland In.)	41·12 N	81·27 W
116	Dartmoor (därt'mōōr) Eng.	50·35 N	4·05 W
82	Dartmouth (därt'm*ŭ*th) Can.	44·41 N	63·36 W
116	Dartmouth Eng.	50·33 N	3·28 W
155	Daru (I.) (dä'rōō) Pap.	9·17 S	143·13 E
126	Daruvar (där'rōō-vär) Yugo.	45·37 N	17·16 E
154	Darvel B. (där'vĕl) Mala.	4·50 N	118·40 E
110	Darwen (där'wĕn) Eng.	53·42 N	2·28 W
158	Darwin (där'wĭn) Austl.	12·25 S	131·00 E
100	Darwin, Cordillera (Mts.) (kôr-dēl-yĕ'rä-där'wĕn) Chile-Arg.	54·40 S	69·30 W
144	Daryācheh-ye Rezācheh (L.) Iran	38·07 N	45·17 E
124	Das Alturas, Serra (Mts.) (sĕ'r-rä-däs-äl-tōō'räs) Port.	40·43 N	7·48 W
165	Dasē Eth.	11·00 N	39·51 E
65	Dash Point (dăsh) Wash. (Seattle In.)	47·19 N	122·25 W
144	Dasht (R.) (dŭsht) W. Pak.	25·47 N	63·01 E
144	Dasht-E Kavir Des. (dŭsht-ē-ka-vēr') Iran	34·43 N	53·30 E
155	Dasol B. (dä-sōl') Phil. (Manila In.)	15·53 N	119·40 E
123	Datteln (dät'tĕln) Ger. (Ruhr In.)	51·39 N	7·20 E
154	Datu, Tandjung (C.) Indon.	2·08 N	110·15 E
165	Daua R. (dä'wä) Eth.	4·34 N	41·34 E
128	Daugavpils (dä'ōō-gäv-pēls) Sov. Un.	55·52 N	25·32 E
86	Dauphin (dô'fĭn) Can.	51·09 N	100·01 W
84	Davant (dă'vănt) La. (New Orleans In.)	29·36 N	89·51 W
155	Davao (dä'vä-ô) Phil.	7·05 N	125·30 E
71	Davenport (dăv'ĕn-pōrt) Iowa	41 34 N	90·38 W
159	Davenport N. Z. (In.)	37·29 S	174·47 E
66	Davenport Wash.	47·39 N	118·07 W
93	David (dȧ-vēdh') Pan.	8·27 N	82·27 W
70	David City (dā'vĭd) Nebr.	41·15 N	97·10 W
121	David-Gorodok (dȧ-vēt' gō-rō'dôk) Sov. Un.	52·02 N	27·14 E
73	Davis (dā'vĭs) Okla.	34·34 N	97·08 W
81	Davis W. Va.	39·15 N	79·25 W
66	Davis L. Ore.	43·38 N	121·43 W
76	Davis Mts. Tex.	30·45 N	104·17 W
47	Davis Sea Ant.	66·00 S	92·00 E
49	Davis Str. Can.	66·00 N	60·00 W
155	Davo G. (dä'-vô) Phil.	6·30 N	125·45 E
120	Davos (dä'vōs) Switz.	46·47 N	9·50 E
144	Dawāsir, Wādī ad (R.) Sau. Ar.	20·48 N	44·07 E
110	Dawley (dô'lĭ) Eng.	52·38 N	2·28 W
154	Dawna Ra. (dô'nȧ) Bur.	17·02 N	98·01 E
86	Dawson (dô's*ŭ*n) Can.	64·04 N	139·22 W
78	Dawson Ga.	31·45 N	84·29 W
70	Dawson Minn.	44·54 N	96·03 W
160	Dawson (R.) Austl.	24·20 S	149·45 E
86	Dawson Creek Can.	55·49 N	120·21 W
78	Dawson Springs Ky.	37·10 N	87·40 W
122	Dax (dȧks) Fr.	43·42 N	1·06 W
144	Dayr az Zawr (dȧ-ēr'ez-zōr') Syr.	35·15 N	40·01 E
168	Dayrūṭ U. A. R. (Nile In.)	27·33 N	30·48 E
75	Dayton (dā't*ŭ*n) Ky. (Cincinnati In.)	39·07 N	84·28 W
72	Dayton N. Mex.	32·44 N	104·23 W
80	Dayton Ohio	39·45 N	84·15 W
78	Dayton Tenn.	35·30 N	85·00 W
77	Dayton Tex.	30·03 N	94·53 W
66	Dayton Wash.	46·18 N	117·59 W
79	Daytona Beach (dā-tō'n*å*) Fla.	29·11 N	81·02 W
81	Dayville (dā'vĭl) Conn.	41·50 N	71·55 W
166	De Aar (dē-är') S. Afr.	30·45 S	24·05 E
70	Dead (L.) (dĕd) Minn.	46·28 N	96·00 W
70	Deadwood (dĕd'wŏŏd) S. D.	44·23 N	103·43 W
81	Deal Island (dēl-ī'l*ă*nd) Md.	38·10 N	75·55 W
100	Deán Funes (dĕ-ä'n-fōō-nĕs) Arg.	30·26 S	64·12 W
75	Dearborn (dēr'bûrn) Mich. (Detroit In.)	42·18 N	83·15 W
116	Dearg, Ben (Mtn.) (bĕn dŭrg) Scot.	57·48 N	4·59 W
86	Dease Str. (dēz) Can.	68·50 N	108·20 W
155	De Atauro (I.) (dĕ-ä-tä'ōō-rô) Port. Timor	8·20 S	126·15 E
68	Death Valley Calif.-Nev.	36·55 N	117·12 W
68	Death Valley Junction Calif.	36·18 N	116·26 W
68	Death Valley Natl. Mon. Calif.	36·34 N	117·00 W
129	Debal'tsevo (dyĕb'äl-tsyĕ'vô) Sov. Un.	48·23 N	38·29 E
127	Debar (Dibra) (dĕ'bär) (dā'brä) Yugo.	41·31 N	20·32 E
114	Debdou (dĕb-dōō') Mor.	34·01 N	2·50 W
121	Deblin (dăN'blĭn) Pol.	51·34 N	21·49 E
121	Debno (dĕb-nô') Sov. Un.	50·24 N	25·44 E
164	Debo Swp. (dā'bō) Mali	15·33 N	3·28 W
121	Debrecen (dĕ'brĕ-tsĕn) Hung.	47·32 N	21·40 E
78	Decatur (dē-kā't*ŭ*r) Ala.	34·35 N	87·00 W
84	Decatur Ga. (Atlanta In.)	33·47 N	84·18 W
73	Decatur Ill.	39·50 N	88·59 W
80	Decatur Ind.	40·50 N	84·55 W
80	Decatur Mich.	42·10 N	86·00 W
72	Decatur Tex.	33·14 N	97·33 W
122	Decazeville (dē-käz'vēl') Fr.	44·33 N	2·16 E
143	Decean Plat. (dĕk'ăn) India	26·36 N	76 35 E
65	Deception P. (dē-sĕp'sh*ŭ*n) Wash. (Seattle In.)	48·24 N	122·44 W
120	Decin (dyĕ'chĕn) Czech.	50·47 N	14·14 E
71	Decorah (dē-kō'r*å*) Iowa	43·18 N	91·48 W
139	Dedap Indon. (Singapore In.)	1·19 N	102·22 E
	Dedeagats, see Alexandroupolis		
136	Dedenevo (dyĕ-dyĕ'nyĕ-vô) Sov. Un. (Moscow In.)	56·14 N	37·31 E
83	Dedham (dĕd'ăm) Mass. (Boston In.)	42·15 N	71·11 W
100	Dedo do Deus (Mt.) (dĕ-dô-dô-dĕ'ōōs) Braz. (In.)	22·30 S	43·02 W
164	Dédougou (dā-dōō-gōō') Upper Volta	12·28 N	3·21 W
116	Dee (R.) Wales	53·00 N	3·10 W
116	Dee (R.) Scot.	57·05 N	2·25 W
79	Deep (R.) (dēp) N. C.	35·36 N	79·32 W
84	Deep Creek Va. (Norfolk In.)	36·44 N	76·22 W
73	Deep Fk. (R.) Okla.	35·35 N	96·42 W
73	Deepwater (dep-wô-tēr) Mo.	38·15 N	93·46 W
83	Deer (dēr) Can.	49·06 N	57·45 W
82	Deer Maine	44·07 N	68·38 W
75	Deerfield (dēr'fēld) Ill. (Chicago In.)	42·10 N	87·51 W
65	Deer Island Ore. (Portland In.)	45·56 N	122·51 W
83	Deer Lake Can.	49·09 N	57·26 W
67	Deer Lodge (dēr lŏj) Mont.	46·23 N	112·42 W
75	Deer Park Ohio (Cincinnati In.)	39·12 N	84·24 W
66	Deer Park Wash.	47·58 N	117·28 W
71	Deer River Minn.	47·20 N	93·49 W
80	Defiance (dē-fī'*ă*ns) Ohio	41·15 N	84·20 W
78	DeFuniak Springs (dē fū'nĭ-ăk) Fla.	30·42 N	86·06 W
120	Deggendorf (dĕ'ghĕn-dôrf) Ger.	48·50 N	12·59 E
90	Degollado (dā-gō-lyä'dō) Mex.	20·27 N	102·11 W
158	DeGrey (R.) (dē grā') Austl.	20·20 S	119·25 E
136	Degtyarsk (dĕg-ty'arsk) Sov. Un. (Urals In.)	56·42 N	60·05 E
142	Dehra Dun (dā'rŭ) India	30·09 N	78·07 E
121	Dej (dāzh) Rom.	47·09 N	23·53 E
71	De Kalb (dē kălb') Ill.	41·54 N	88·46 W
85	Delacour (dĕ-lä-kōōr') Can. (Calgary In.)	51·09 N	113·45 W
84	Delacroix (dĕl *å*-krō') La. (New Orleans In.)	29·46 N	89·47 W
72	Delagua (dĕl-ä'gwä) Colo.	37·19 N	104·42 W
79	De Land (dē lănd') Fla.	29·00 N	81·19 W
68	Delano (dĕl'*å*-nō) Calif.	35·47 N	119·15 W
69	Delano, Mt. Utah	38·25 N	112·25 W
71	Delavan (dĕl'*å*-văn) Wis.	42·39 N	88·38 W
80	Delaware (dĕl'*å*-wâr) Ohio	40·15 N	83·05 W
63	Delaware (State) U. S.	38·40 N	75·30 W
73	Delaware (R.) Kans.	39·45 N	95·47 W
81	Delaware (R.) N. J.-Pa.	41·50 N	75·20 W
81	Delaware B. Del.-N. J.	39·05 N	75·10 W
80	Delaware Res. Ohio	40·30 N	83·05 W
124	Del Eje, Sierra (Mts.) (sē-ĕ'r-rä-dĕl-ĕ'ĸĕ) Sp.	42·15 N	6·45 W
120	Delemont (dē-lā-mōɴ') Switz.	47·21 N	7·18 E
76	De Leon (dē lē-ŏn') Tex.	32·06 N	98·33 W
85	De Léry (dā lā-rī') Can. (Montreal In.)	45·21 N	73·49 W
101	Delfínópolis (dĕl-fē'nō'pō-lēs) Braz. (Rio de Janeiro In.)	20·20 S	46·50 W
111	Delft (dĕlft) Neth. (Amsterdam In.)	52·01 N	4·20 E
117	Delfzijl Neth.	53·20 N	6·50 E
100	Delgada Pta. (Pt.) (pōō'n-tä-dĕl-gä'dä) Arg.	43·46 S	63·46 W
167	Delgado, Cabo (C.) (kä'bō-dĕl-gä'dō) Moz.	10·30 S	41·00 E
165	Delgo (dĕl'gô) Sud.	20·07 N	30·41 E
74	Delhi (dĕl'hī) Ill. (St. Louis In.)	39·03 N	90·16 W
142	Delhi India	28·54 N	77·13 E
77	Delhi La.	32·26 N	91·29 W
125	Del Hoyo, Sierra (Mtn.) (sē-ĕ'r-rä-dĕl-ô'yô) Sp. (Madrid In.)	40·39 N	3·56 W
120	Delitzsch (dā'lĭch) Ger.	51·32 N	12·18 E
127	Dell Alice, Pt. (dĕl-ä-lē'chĕ) It.	39·23 N	17·10 E
70	Dell Rapids (dĕl) S. D.	43·50 N	96·43 W
74	Dellwood (dĕl'wŏŏd) Minn. (Minneapolis, St. Paul In.)	45·05 N	92·58 W
164	Dellys (dĕ'lēs') Alg.	36·59 N	3·40 E
68	Del Mar (dĕl mär') Calif. (San Diego In.)	32·57 N	117·16 W
168	Delmas (dĕl'm*ȧ*s) S. Afr. (Johannesburg & Pretoria In.)	26·08 S	28·43 E
120	Delmenhorst (dĕl'mĕn-hôrst) Ger.	53·03 N	8·38 E
69	Del Norte (dĕl nôrt') Colo.	37·40 N	106·25 W
135	De-Longa (I.) Sov. Un.	76·58 N	157·39 E
64	Delong Mts. (dē'lŏng) Alaska	68·30 N	163·25 W
160	Deloraine (dĕ-l*ŭ*-rān') Austl.	41·30 S	146·40 E
80	Delphi (dĕl'fī) Ind.	40·35 N	86·40 W
80	Delphos (dĕl'fŏs) Ohio	40·50 N	84·20 W
79	Delray Beach (dĕl-rā') Fla. (In.)	26·27 N	80·05 W
76	Del Rio (dĕl rē'ō) Tex.	29·21 N	100·52 W
85	Delson Village (dĕl's*ŭ*n) Can. (Montreal In.)	45·24 N	73·32 W
69	Delta Colo.	38·45 N	108·05 W
69	Delta Utah	39·20 N	112·35 W
68	Delta Mendota can. Calif.	37·10 N	121·02 W
85	Delta Station Can. (Winnipeg In.)	50·10 N	98·20 W
127	Delvine (dĕl'vē-nȧ) Alb.	39·58 N	20·10 E
132	Dēma (R.) (dyĕm'ä) Sov. Un.	53·40 N	54·30 E
128	Demidov (dzyĕ'mē-dô'f) Sov. Un.	55·16 N	31·32 E
69	Deming (dĕm'ĭng) N. Mex.	32·15 N	107·45 W
120	Demmin (dĕm'mēn) Ger.	53·54 N	13·04 E
164	Demnate (dĕm-nät) Mor.	31·58 N	7·03 W
78	Demopolis (dē-mŏp'ō-lĭs) Ala	32·30 N	87·50 W
75	Demotte (dē'mŏt) Ind. (Chicago In.)	41·12 N	87·13 W
154	Dempo, Gunung (Vol.) (dĕm'pō) Indon.	4·04 S	103·11 E
134	Dem'yanka (R.) (dyĕm-yän'kä) Sov. Un.	59·07 N	72·58 E

ng-sing; ŋ-baŋk; ɴ-nasalized n; nŏd; cŏmmit; ōld; ôbey; ôrder; fōōd; fŏŏt; ou-out; s-soft; sh-dish; th-thin; pūre; ûnite; ûrn; stŭd; circ*ŭ*s; ü-as "y" in study; '-indeterminate vowel.

200 Demyansk–Dogubayazit PRONOUNCING INDEX

Page	Name Pronunciation	Region	Lat. °′	Long. °′
128	Demyansk (dyĕm-yänsk′)	Sov. Un.	57·39 N	32·26 E
122	Denain (dē-năN′)	Fr.	50·23 N	3·21 E
116	Denbigh (dĕn′bĭ)	Wales	53·15 N	3·25 W
110	Denbigh (Co.)	Wales	53·01 N	2·59 W
111	Dendermonde	Bel. (Brussels In.)	51·02 N	4·04 E
79	Dendron (dĕn′drŭn)	Va.	37·02 N	76·53 W
136	Denezhkin Kamen, Gora (Mtn.) (dzyĕ-ŋĕ′zhkĕn kămĭēŋ)	Sov. Un. (Urals In.)	60·26 N	59·35 E
93	D'Enfer, Pointe (Pt.)	Mart. (Le. & Wind. Is. In.)	14·21 N	60·48 W
94	Denham, Mt.	Jam.	18·20 N	77·30 W
117	Den Helder (dĕn hĕl′dĕr)	Neth.	52·55 N	5·45 E
125	Denia (dā′nyä)	Sp.	38·48 N	0·06 E
160	Deniliquin (dĕ-nĭl′ĭ-kwĭn)	Austl.	35·20 S	144·52 E
70	Denison (dĕn′ĭ-sŭn)	Iowa	42·01 N	95·22 W
73	Denison	Tex.	33·45 N	97·02 W
136	Denisovka (dĕ-nē′sof-kȧ)	Sov. Un. (Urals In.)	52·26 N	61·45 E
133	Denizli (dĕn-ĭz-lē′)	Tur.	37·40 N	29·10 E
123	Denklingen (dĕn′klēn-gĕn)	Ger. (Ruhr In.)	50·54 N	7·40 E
79	Denmark (dĕn′märk)	S. C.	33·18 N	81·09 W
102	Denmark	Eur.	56·14 N	8·30 E
49	Denmark Str.	Grnld.	66·30 N	27·00 W
168	Dennilton (dĕn-ĭl-tŭn)	S. Afr. (Johannesburg & Pretoria In.)	25·18 S	29·13 E
80	Dennison (dĕn′ĭ-sŭn)	Ohio	40·25 N	81·20 W
81	Denton (dĕn′tŭn)	Md.	38·55 N	75·50 W
73	Denton	Tex.	33·12 N	97·06 W
158	D'entrecasteaux, Pt. (däN-tr′kȧs-tō′)	Austl.	34·50 S	114·45 E
155	D'entrecasteaux Is. (dăN-tr′-kȧs-tō′)	Pap.	9·45 S	152·00 E
72	Denver (dĕn′vĕr)	Colo.	39·44 N	104·59 W
142	Deoli	India	25·52 N	75·23 E
71	De Pere (dē pēr′)	Wis.	44·25 N	88·04 W
75	Depew (dē-pū′)	N. Y. (Buffalo In.)	42·55 N	78·43 W
80	Depue (dē pū)	Ill.	41·15 N	89·55 W
73	De Queen (dē kwēn′)	Ark.	34·02 N	94·21 W
77	De Quincy (dē kwĭn′sĭ)	La.	30·27 N	93·27 W
142	Dera Ghāzi Khān (dā′rū gä-zē′ kän′)	W. Pak.	30·09 N	70·39 E
142	Dera Ismail Khan (dā′rŭ ĭs-mä-ēl′ kän′)	W. Pak.	31·55 N	70·51 E
133	Derbent (dĕr-bĕnt′)	Sov. Un.	42·00 N	48·10 E
158	Derby (där′bē) (dûr′bē)	Austl.	17·20 S	123·40 E
81	Derby (dûr′bē)	Conn.	41·20 N	73·05 W
110	Derby (där′bē)	Eng.	52·55 N	1·29 W
168	Derby (där′bĭ)	S. Afr. (Johannesburg & Pretoria In.)	25·55 S	27·02 E
110	Derby (Co.) (där′bē)	Eng.	53·11 N	1·30 W
168	Derdepoort	S. Afr. (Johannesburg & Pretoria In.)	24·39 S	26·21 E
116	Derg, Lough (B.) (lŏk dĕrg)	Ire.	53·00 N	8·09 W
77	De Ridder (dē rĭd′ĕr)	La.	30·50 N	93·18 W
73	Dermott (dûr′mŏt)	Ark.	33·32 N	91·24 W
83	Derry (dâr′ĭ)	N. H. (Boston In.)	45·52 N	71·22 W
127	Derventa (dĕr′ven-tȧ)	Yugo.	45·58 N	17·58 E
160	Derwent (R.) (dûr′wĕnt)	Austl.	42·21 S	146·30 E
110	Derwent (R.) (dĕr′wĕnt)	Eng.	52·54 N	1·24 W
73	Des Arc (dāz ärk′)	Ark.	34·59 N	91·31 W
101	Descalvado (dĕs-käl-vȧ-dō)	Braz. (Rio de Janeiro In.)	21·55 S	47·37 W
85	Deschenes	Can. (Ottawa In.)	45·23 N	75·47 W
85	Deschenes, L.	Can. (Ottawa In.)	54·25 N	75·53 W
66	Deschutes R. (dā-shōōt′)	Ore.	44·25 N	121·21 W
76	Desdemona (dĕz-dē-mō′nȧ)	Tex.	32·16 N	98·33 W
100	Deseado, Rio (R.) (rē′-ō-dā-sā-ä′dhō)	Arg.	46·50 S	67·45 W
93	Desirade I. (dā-zē-rȧs′)	N. A. (Le. & Wind. Is. In.)	16·21 N	60·51 W
70	De Smet (dē smĕt′)	S. D.	44·23 N	97·33 W
71	Des Moines (dē moin′)	Iowa	41·35 N	93·37 W
72	Des Moines	N. Mex.	36·42 N	103·48 W
65	Des Moines	Wash. (Seattle In.)	46·24 N	122·20 W
63	Des Moines (R.)	U. S.	43·45 N	94·20 W
129	Desna (R.) (dyĕs-nȧ′)	Sov. Un.	51·05 N	31·03 E
100	Desolación (dĕ-sō-lä-syō′n) (I.)	Chile	53·05 S	74·00 W
73	De Soto (dē sō′tō)	Mo.	38·07 N	90·32 W
74	Des Peres (dĕs pĕr′ĕs)	Mo. (St. Louis In.)	38·36 N	90·26 W
75	Des Plaines (dĕs plānz′)	Ill. (Chicago In.)	42·02 N	87·54 W
75	Des Plaines R.	Ill. (Chicago In.)	41·39 N	88·05 W
120	Dessau (dĕs′ou)	Ger.	51·50 N	12·15 E
120	Detmold (dĕt′mōld)	Ger.	51·57 N	8·55 E
75	Detroit (dē-troit′)	Mich. (Detroit In.)	42·22 N	83·10 W
73	Detroit	Tex.	33·41 N	95·16 W
70	Detroit Lakes (dē-troit′ lăkz)	Minn.	46·48 N	95·51 W
75	Detroit R.	U. S.-Can. (Detroit In.)	42·08 N	83·07 W
121	Detva (dyĕt′vä)	Czech.	48·32 N	19·21 E
111	Deurne	Bel. (Brussels In.)	51·13 N	4·27 E
111	Deutsch Wagram	Aus. (Vienna In.)	48·19 N	16·34 E
85	Deux Montagnes, Lac des (dû mōN-tăny′′)	Can. (Montreal In.)	45·28 N	74·00 W
127	Deva (dā′vä)	Rom.	45·52 N	22·52 E
121	Dévaványa (dā′vô-vän-yô)	Hung.	47·01 N	20·58 E
133	Develi (dĕ′vȧ-lē)	Tur.	38·20 N	35·10 E
117	Deventer (dĕv′ĕn-tĕr)	Neth.	52·14 N	6·07 E
70	Devils (L.) (dĕv′′lz)	N. D.	47·57 N	99·04 W
76	Devils (R.)	Tex.	29·55 N	101·10 W
	Devils I., see Diable, Ile du			
62	Devils Lake	N. D.	48·10 N	98·55 W
70	Devils Lake Ind. Res.	N. D.	48·08 N	99·40 W
68	Devils Postpile Natl. Mon.	Calif.	37·42 N	119·12 W
67	Devils Tower Natl. Mon.	Wyo.	44·38 N	105·07 W
127	Devoll (R.)	Alb.	40·55 N	20·10 E
168	Devon (dĕv′ŭn)	S. Afr. (Johannesburg & Pretoria In.)	26·23 S	28·47 E
160	Devonport (dĕv′ŭn-pôrt)	Austl.	41·20 S	146·30 E
74	Devore (dē-vôr′)	Calif. (Los Angeles In.)	34·13 N	117·24 W
77	Dewalt (dū′ȧlt)	Tex. (In.)	29·33 N	95·33 W
65	Dewatto (dē-wät′ō)	Wash. (Seattle In.)	47·27 N	123·04 W
73	Dewey (dū′ĭ)	Okla.	36·48 N	95·55 W
73	De Witt (dē wĭt′)	Ark.	34·17 N	91·22 W
71	De Witt	Iowa	41·46 N	90·34 W
110	Dewsbury (dūz′bēr-ĭ)	Eng.	53·42 N	1·39 W
82	Dexter (dĕks′tĕr)	Maine	45·01 N	69·19 W
73	Dexter	Mo.	36·46 N	89·56 W
79	Dexter (L.)	Fla.	29·07 N	81·24 W
144	Dezfūl	Iran	32·14 N	48·37 E
139	Dezhneva, Mys (East Cape) (dyĕzh′nyĭf)	Sov. Un.	68·00 N	172·00 W
	Dhahran, see AzZahrān			
143	Dharamtar Cr.	India (Bombay In.)	18·49 N	72·54 E
143	Dharmavaram	India	14·32 N	77·43 E
142	Dhaulagiri, Mt. (dou-lȧ-gē′rē)	Nep.	33·50 N	83·32 E
127	Dhenoúsa (I.)	Grc.	37·09 N	25·53 E
139	Dhibān	Jordan (Palestine In.)	31·30 N	35·46 E
127	Dhidhimótikhon	Grc.	41·20 N	26·27 E
127	Dhodhekánisos (Dodecanese) (Is.)	Grc.	38·00 N	26·10 E
142	Dhūlia (dōōl′yȧ)	India	20·58 N	74·43 E
142	Dhupgarth (Mt.)	India	27·30 N	78·27 E
126	Dia (I.) (dē′ä)	Grc. (Inset)	35·27 N	25·17 E
99	Diable, Île du (Devils I.)	Fr. Gu.	5·15 N	57·10 W
65	Diablo, Mt. (dyȧ′blō)	Calif. (San Francisco In.)	37·52 N	121·55 W
88	Diablo Heights (dyȧ′blō)	C. Z. (Panama Canal In.)	8·58 N	79·34 W
65	Diablo Range (Mts.)	Calif. (San Francisco In.)	37·47 N	121·50 W
99	Diamantina (dē-ȧ-män-tē′nȧ)	Braz.	14·22 S	56·23 W
99	Diamantina	Braz.	18·14 S	43·32 W
158	Diamantina (R.) (dī′man-tē′nȧ)	Austl.	25·38 S	139·53 E
84	Diamond (dī′ȧ-mŭnd)	La. (New Orleans In.)	29·34 N	89·48 W
66	Diamond Pk.	Ore.	43·32 N	122·08 W
154	Diamond Pt. (dī′mŭnd)	Indon.	5·30 N	96·45 E
95	Diana Bk. (dī′ăn′ȧ)	Ba. Is.	22·30 N	74·45 W
155	Diapitan B. (dyȧ-pē-tä′n)	Phil. (Manila In.)	16·28 N	122·25 E
	Dibra, see Debar			
70	Dickinson (dĭk′ĭn-sŭn)	N. D.	46·52 N	102·49 W
77	Dickinson (dĭk′ĭn-sŭn)	Tex. (In.)	29·28 N	95·02 W
77	Dickinson Bay	Tex. (In.)	29·26 N	95·08 W
78	Dickson (dĭk′sŭn)	Tenn.	36·03 N	87·24 W
81	Dickson City	Pa.	41·25 N	75·40 W
133	Dicle (R.) (dĭj′lȧ)	Tur.	37·50 N	40·40 E
110	Didcot (dĭd′cŏt)	Eng. (London In.)	51·35 N.	1·15 W
123	Die (dē)	Fr.	44·45 N	5·22 E
95	Diego de Ocampo, Pico (Pk.) (pē′-kō-dyĕ′gō-dĕ-ŏ-kä′m-pō)	Dom. Rep.	19·40 N	70·45 W
100	Diego Ramirez, Islas (Is.) (dē ä′gō rä-mē′räz)	Chile	56·15 S	70·15 W
167	Diégo-Suarez (Antsirane) (dē-ä′gō-swä′räz) (änt-sē-rän′)	Malag. Rep.	12·18 S	49·16 E
146	Dien Bien Phu	Viet.	21·38 N	102·49 E
82	Dieppe (dē-ĕp′)	Can.	46·08 N	64·45 W
122	Dieppe	Fr.	49·54 N	1·05 E
73	Dierks (dērks)	Ark.	34·06 N	94·02 W
111	Diessen (dēs′sĕn)	Ger. (Munich In.)	47·57 N	11·06 E
111	Diest	Bel. (Brussels In.)	50·59 N	5·05 E
82	Digby (dĭg′bĭ)	Can.	44·37 N	65·48 W
84	Dighton (dī-tŭn)	Mass. (Providence In.)	41·49 N	71·05 W
123	Digne (dēn′y′)	Fr.	44·07 N	6·16 E
155	Digoel (R.)	W. Irian	7.00 S	140·25 E
122	Digoin (dē-gwăN′)	Fr.	46·28 N	4·06 E
155	Dijohan Pt. (dē-kō-än)	Phil. (Manila In.)	16·24 N	122·25 E
122	Dijon (dē-zhōN′)	Fr.	47·21 N	5·02 E
134	Dikson (dĭk′sŏn)	Sov. Un.	72·47 N	79·20 E
165	Dikwa (dē′kwä)	Nig.	12·06 N	13·53 E
155	Dili (dĭl′ē)	Port. Timor	8·35 S	125·35 E
114	Di Linosa I. (dē-lē-nō′sä)	Medit. Sea	36·01 N	12·43 E
133	Dilizhan	Sov. Un.	40·45 N	45·00 E
64	Dillingham (dĭl′ĕng-häm)	Alaska	59·10 N	158·38 W
67	Dillon (dĭl′ŭn)	Mont.	45·12 N	112·40 W
79	Dillon	S. C.	34·24 N	79·28 W
166	Dilolo (dē-lō′lō)	Con. L.	10·19 S	22·23 E
139	Dimashq (Damascus) (dȧ-măs′kŭs)	Syria (Palestine In.)	33·31 N	36·18 E
127	Dimbovita (R.)	Rom.	44·43 N	25·41 E
127	Dimitrovo (Pernik) (pĕr-nēk′)	Bul.	42·36 N	23·04 E
155	Dinagate I. (dē-nä′gät)	Phil.	10·15 N	126·15 E
142	Dinājpur	India	25·38 N	87·39 E
122	Dinan (dē-năN′)	Fr.	48·27 N	2·03 W
117	Dinant (dē-năN′)	Bel.	50·17 N	4·50 E
126	Dinara Planina (Mts.) (dē′nä-rä plä′nē-nä)	Yugo.	43·50 N	16·15 E
143	Dindigul	India	10·25 N	78·03 E
155	Dingalan B. (dĭŋ-gä′län)	Phil. (Manila In.)	15·19 N	121·33 E
116	Dingle (dĭng′′l)	Ire.	52·10 N	10·13 W
116	Dingle B.	Ire.	52·02 N	10·15 W
159	Dingo (dĭŋ′gō)	Austl.	23·45 S	149·26 E
116	Dingwall (dĭng′wôl)	Scot.	57·37 N	4·23 W
67	Dinosaur Natl. Mon. (dī′nō-sôr)	Utah-Colo.	40·45 N	109·17 W
123	Dinslaken (dēns′lä-kĕn)	Ger. (Ruhr In.)	51·33 N	6·44 E
111	Dinterloord	Neth. (Amsterdam In.)	51·38 N	4·21 E
68	Dinuba (dĭ-nū′bȧ)	Calif.	36·33 N	119·29 W
164	Diorbivol (dē-ôr-bē-vôl′)	Senegal	16·07 N	13·52 W
94	Dios, Cayo de (I.) (kä′yō-dĕ-dē-ōs′)	Cuba	22·05 N	83·05 W
164	Diourbel (dē-ōōr-bĕl′)	Senegal	14·37 N	16·28 W
145	Diphu Pass (dĭ-pōō)	China	28·15 N	96·45 E
93	Diquis R. (dē-kēs′)	C. R.	8·59 N	83·24 W
168	Diredawa	Eth. (Horn of Afr. In.)	9·40 N	41·47 E
92	Diriamba (dēr-yäm′bä)	Nic.	11·52 N	86·15 W
158	Dirk Hartog (I.)	Austl.	26·25 S	113·15 E
111	Dirksland	Neth. (Amsterdam In.)	51·45 N	4·04 E
160	Dirranbandi (dĭ-rȧ-băn′dē)	Austl.	28·24 S	148·29 E
69	Dirty Devil (R.) (dûr′tĭ dĕv′′l)	Utah	38·20 N	110·30 W
158	Disappointment (L.)	Austl.	23·20 S	120·20 E
65	Disappointment, C. (dĭs′ȧ-point′ment)	Wash. (Portland In.)	46·16 N	124·11 W
125	D'Ischia, I. (dē′sh-kyä)	It. (Naples In.)	40·26 N	13·55 E
167	Discovery (dĭs-cŭv′ĕr-ĭ)	S. Afr. (Johannesburg & Pretoria In.)	26·10 S	27·53 E
65	Discovery Is. (dĭs-kŭv′ĕr-ē)	Can. (Seattle In.)	48·25 N	123·13 W
168	Dishnā (dēsh′nȧ)	U. A. R. (Nile In.)	26·08 N	32·27 E
49	Disko (dĭs′kō) (I.)	Grnld.	70·00 N	54·00 W
79	Dismal Swp. (dĭz′măl)	N. C.-Va.	36·35 N	76·34 W
128	Disna (dēs′nȧ)	Sov. Un.	55·34 N	28·15 E
82	Disraeli (dĭs-rā′lĭ)	Can.	45·53 N	71·23 W
81	District of Columbia	U. S.	38·50 N	77·00 W
91	Distrito Federal (Dist.) (dēs-trē′tō-fĕ-dĕ-rä′l)	Mex.	19·14 N	99·08 W
168	Disūq (dē-sōōk′)	U. A. R. (Nile In.)	31·07 N	30·41 E
142	Diu (dē′ōō)	Asia	20·48 N	70·58 E
122	Dives (dēv)	Fr.	49·18 N	0·05 W
155	Divilacan B. (dē-vē-lä′kän)	Phil.	17·26 N	122·25 E
101	Divinópolis (dē-vē-nô′pō-lēs)	Braz. (Rio de Janeiro In.)	20·10 S	44·53 W
85	Dixie (dĭk′sĭ)	Can. (Toronto In.)	43·36 N	79·35 W
71	Dixon (dĭks′ŭn)	Ill.	41·50 N	89·30 W
86	Dixon Ent.	Alaska-Can.	54·36 N	132·32 W
133	Diyarbakir (dē-yär-bĕk′ĭr)	Tur.	38·00 N	40·10 E
165	Dja R.	Cam.	2·40 N	14·11 E
155	Djailolo Pass	Indon.	0·05 S	129·08 E
154	Djakarta (yä-kär′tä)	Indon.	6·17 S	106·45 E
154	Djambi (jäm′bē)	Indon.	1·45 S	103·28 E
164	Djanet (Fort Charlet)	Alg.	24·29 N	9·26 E
114	Djedi R.	Alg.	34·18 N	4·39 E
164	Djelfa (jĕl′fä)	Alg.	34·40 N	3·17 E
164	Djenné (jĕnnā′)	Mali	13·55 N	4·26 W
114	Djerba, Ile de (I.)	Tun.	33·53 N	11·26 E
164	Djerid, Chott (L.) (jĕr′ĭd)	Tun.	33·15 N	8·29 E
168	Djibouti (jē-bōō-tē′)	Fr. Som. (Horn of Afr. In.)	11·34 N	43·00 E
113	Djidjelli (jē-jĕ-lē′)	Alg.	36·49 N	5·47 E
139	Djumrah	Indon. (Singapore In.)	1·48 N	101·04 E
126	Djurdevac (dūr′dyĕ-văts′)	Yugo.	46·03 N	17·03 E
118	Djursholm (djōōrs′hōlm)	Swe.	59·26 N	18·01 E
129	Dmitriyevka (d′mē-trē-yĕf′kȧ)	Sov. Un.	47·57 N	38·56 E
129	Dmitriyev L'govskiy (d′mē′trĭ-yĕf l′gôf′skĭ)	Sov. Un.	52·07 N	35·05 E
136	Dmitrov (d′mē′trôf)	Sov. Un. (Moscow In.)	56·21 N	37·32 E
128	Dmitrovsk (d′mē′trôfsk)	Sov. Un.	52·30 N	35·10 E
129	Dnepr (Dnieper) (R.) (nē′pĕr)	Sov. Un.	46·47 N	32·57 E
129	Dneprodzerzhinsk (d′nyĕp′rô-zĕr-shĭnsk)	Sov. Un.	48·32 N	34·38 E
129	Dnepropetrovsk (d′nyĕp′rô-pä-trôfsk)	Sov. Un.	48·23 N	34·10 E
129	Dnepropetrovsk (Oblast)	Sov. Un.	48·15 N	34·08 E
129	Dnepr Zaliv (B.) (dnyĕp′r zä′lĭf)	Sov. Un.	46·33 N	31·45 E
129	Dnestr (Dniester) (R.) (nēst′rōōl) (nēs′tĕr)	Sov. Un.	48·21 N	28·10 E
129	Dnestrovskiy Liman (B.)	Sov. Un.	46·13 N	29·50 E
	Dnieper (R.), see Dnepr			
	Dniester (R.), see Dnestr			
128	Dno (d′nô′)	Sov. Un.	57·49 N	29·59 E
84	Dobbs Ferry (dŏbz′ fĕ′rē)	N. Y. (New York In.)	41·01 N	73·53 W
158	Dobbyn (dôb′ĭn)	Austl.	19·45 S	140·02 E
119	Dobele (dō′bĕ-lĕ)	Sov. Un.	56·37 N	23·18 E
120	Döbeln (dû′bĕln)	Ger.	51·08 N	13·07 E
155	Dobo	Indon.	6·00 S	134·18 E
127	Doboj (dō′boi)	Yugo.	44·42 N	18·04 E
136	Dobryanka (dôb-ryän′kȧ)	Sov. Un. (Urals In.)	58·27 N	56·26 E
121	Dobšina (dôp′shē-nä)	Czech.	48·48 N	20·25 E
99	Doce (R.) (dō′sä)	Braz.	19·01 S	42·14 W
94	Doce Leguas, Cayos de las (Is.) (kä′yōs-dĕ-läs-dô-sĕ-lĕ′gwäs)	Cuba	20·55 N	79·05 W
90	Doctor Arroyo (dōk-tōr′ är-rō′yō)	Mex.	23·41 N	100·10 W
110	Doddington (dŏd′dĭng-tŏn)	Eng. (London In.)	51·17 N	0·47 E
	Dodecanese (Is.), see Dhodhekánisos			
72	Dodge City (dŏj)	Kans.	37·44 N	100·01 W
81	Dodgeville (dŏj′vĭl)	N. Y.	43·10 N	74·45 W
71	Dodgeville	Wis.	42·58 N	90·07 W
166	Dodoma (dō′dô-mȧ)	Tan.	6·13 S	35·36 E
74	Dodson (dŏd′s′n)	Mo. (Kansas City In.)	38·48 N	94·33 W
71	Dog (L.) (dŏg)	Can.	48·42 N	89·24 W
117	Dogger Bk. (dŏg′gĕr)	Eur.	55·07 N	2·25 E
94	Dog Rocks (I.)	Ba. Is.	24·05 N	79·50 W
133	Dogubayazit	Tur.	39·35 N	44·00 E

ăt; finȧl; rāte; senâte; ärm; ȧsk; sofȧ; fâre; ch-choose; dh-as th in other; bē; ēvent; bĕt; recĕnt; cratẽr; g-go; gh-guttural g; bĭt; ĭ-short neutral; rīde; K-guttural k as ch in German ich;

Page	Name Pronunciation Region	Lat. °′	Long. °′
142	Dohad India	22·52 N	74·18 E
127	Doiran (L.) Grc.	41·10 N	23·00 E
153	Dōjō (dō-jō) Jap. (Osaka In.)	34·51 N	135·14 E
128	Dokshitsy (dôk-shēts'ĕ) Sov. Un.	54·53 N	27·49 E
82	Dolbeau Can.	48·52 N	72·16 W
123	Dôle (dōl) Fr.	47·07 N	5·28 E
129	Dolgaya, Kosa (C.) (kô'sà dôl-gä'yă) Sov. Un.	46·42 N	37·42 E
132	Dolgiy (I.) Sov. Un.	69·20 N	59·20 E
121	Dolina (dô-lyē'nà) Sov. Un.	48·57 N	24·01 E
152	Dolinsk (då-lēnsk') Sov. Un.	47·29 N	142·31 E
94	Dollar Hbr. Ba. Is.	25·30 N	79·15 W
165	Dolo Som.	4·01 N	42·14 E
84	Dolomite (dŏl'ô-mīt) Ala. (Birmingham In.)	33·28 N	86·57 W
126	Dolomitiche, Alpi (Mts.) (äl-pē-dô-lō'mē-tē'chĕ) It.	46·16 N	11·43 E
101	Dolores (dô-lō'rĕs) Arg. (Buenos Aires In.)	36·20 S	57·42 W
98	Dolores Col. (In.)	3·33 N	74·54 W
155	Dolores (dô-lô-rĕs) Phil. (Manila In.)	17·40 N	120·43 E
76	Dolores (dô-lō'rĕs) Tex.	27·42 N	99·47 W
101	Dolores Ur. (Buenos Aires In.)	33·32 S	58·15 W
69	Dolores (R.) Colo.-Utah	38·35 N	108·50 W
90	Dolores Hidalgo (dô-lô'rĕs-ē-dăl'gō) Mex.	21·09 N	100·56 W
86	Dolphin and Union Str. (dŏl'fĭn ūn'yŭn) Can.	69·22 N	117·10 W
120	Domažlice (dō'mäzh-lē-tsĕ) Czech.	49·27 N	12·55 E
123	Dombasle (dôɴ-bäl') Fr.	48·38 N	6·18 E
121	Dombóvár (dōm'bō-vär) Hung.	46·22 N	18·08 E
122	Dôme, Puy de (Pk.) (pwē'dĕ-dôm') Fr.	45·47 N	2·54 E
98	Domeyko, Cordillera (Mts.) (kôr-dēl-yĕ'rä-dô-mā'kō) Chile	20·50 S	69·02 W
93	Dominica Chan. (dŏ-mĭ-nē'kȧ) N. A. (Le. & Wind. Is. In.)	15·00 N	61·30 W
93	Dominica I. N. A. (Le. & Wind. Is. In.)	15·24 N	61·05 W
88	Dominican Republic (dô-mĭn'ĭ-kăn) N. A.	18·59 N	70·40 W
83	Dominion (dô-mĭn'yŭn) Can.	46·13 N	60·01 W
136	Domodedovo (dô-mô-dyĕ'do-vô) Sov. Un. (Moscow In.)	55·27 N	37·45 E
101	Dom Silvério (doɴ-sēl-vĕ'ryō) Braz. (Rio de Janeiro In.)	20·09 S	42·57 W
110	Don (R.) (dŏn) Eng.	53·27 N	1·34 W
110	Don (R.) Eng.	53·39 N	0·58 W
116	Don (R.) Scot.	57·19 N	2·39 W
74	Donaldson (dŏn'ăl-sŭn) Mich. (Sault Ste. Marie In.)	46·19 N	84·22 W
77	Donaldsonville (dŏn'ăld-sŭn-vĭl) La.	30·05 N	90·58 W
78	Donalsonville Ga.	31·02 N	84·50 W
120	Donawitz (dō'nȧ-vĭts) Aus.	47·23 N	15·05 E
142	Donazari E. Pak.	22·18 N	91·52 E
124	Don Benito Mérida (dōn' bā-nē'tō-mĕ'rē-dä) Sp.	38·55 N	6·08 W
161	Doncaster (doŋ'kăs-tēr) Austl. (Melbourne In.)	37·47 S	145·08 E
110	Doncaster (doŋ'kăs-tēr) Eng.	53·32 N	1·07 W
166	Dondo (dōn'dō) Ang.	9·35 S	14·25 E
166	Dondo Moz.	19·33 S	34·47 E
116	Donegal (dŏn-ê-gôl') Ire.	54·44 N	8·05 W
116	Donegal, Mts. of (dŏn-ê-gôl') Ire.	54·44 N	8·10 W
116	Donegal Bay (dŏn-ê-gôl') N. Ire.	54·35 N	8·36 W
129	Donets (R.) (dō-nyĕts') Sov. Un.	48·48 N	38·42 E
129	Donets Coal Basin (Reg.) (dō-nyĕts') Sov. Un.	48·15 N	38·50 E
133	Donetsk (Stalino) (dō-nyĕts'k) (stä'lĭ-nō) Sov. Un.	48·00 N	37·35 E
158	Dongara (dôŋ-gă'rȧ) Austl.	29·15 S	115·00 E
154	Donggala (dôŋ-gä'lä) Indon.	0·45 S	119·32 E
151	Dong Hoi (dông-hō-ē') Viet.	17·25 N	106·42 E
166	Dongo (dôŋ'gō) Ang.	14·45 S	15·30 E
165	Dongola (dŏŋ'gō-lȧ) Sud.	19·21 N	30·19 E
155	Dongon Pt. (dōng-ôn') Phil. (Manila In.)	12·43 N	120·35 E
165	Dongou (dôŋ-gōō') Con. B.	2·12 N	18·08 E
73	Doniphan (dŏn'ĭ-făn) Mo.	36·37 N	90·50 W
126	Donji Vakuf (dōn'yĭ väk'ŏŏf) Yugo.	44·08 N	17·25 E
76	Don Martin, Presa de (Res.) (prĕ'sä-dĕ-dôn-mär-tē'n) Mex.	27·35 N	100·38 W
82	Donnacona Can.	46·40 N	71·46 W
123	Donnemarie-en-Montois (dôn-mä-rē'ĕɴ-môɴ-twä') Fr. (Paris In.)	48·29 N	3·09 E
66	Donner und Blitzen R. (dŏn'ēr ŏŏnt blĭ'tsĕn) Ore.	42·45 N	118·57 W
167	Donnybrook (dŏ-nĭ-brŏŏk) S. Afr. (Natal In.)	29·56 S	29·54 E
75	Donora (dŏ-nō'rȧ) Pa. (Pittsburgh In.)	40·10 N	79·51 W
64	Doonerak (dōō'nē-răk) Alaska	68·00 N	150·34 W
111	Doorn Neth. (Amsterdam In.)	52·02 N	5·21 E
71	Door Pen. (dōr) Wis.	44·40 N	87·36 W
126	Dora Baltea (dō'rä bäl'tä-ä) It.	45·40 N	7·34 E
84	Doraville (dō'rȧ-vĭ.) Ga. (Atlanta In.)	33·54 N	84·17 W
116	Dorchester (dôr'chĕs-tēr) Eng.	50·45 N	2·34 W
122	Dordogne (R.) (dôr-dôn'yĕ) Fr.	44·53 N	0·16 E
111	Dordrecht (dôr'drĕkt) Neth. (Amsterdam In.)	51·48 N	4·39 E
167	Dordrecht (dô'drĕkt) S. Afr. (Natal In.)	31·24 S	27·06 E
126	Dorgali (dôr'gä-lē) Sard.	40·18 N	9·37 E
164	Dori (dô-rē') Upper Volta	13·56 N	0·01 W
85	Dorion (dôr-yō) Can. (Montreal In.)	45·23 N	74·01 W
110	Dorking (dôr'kĭng) Eng. (London In.)	51·12 N	0·20 W
85	D'Orleans, Ile (I.) (dōr-lĕ-äɴ', yl) Can. (Quebec In.)	46·56 N	70·27 W

Page	Name Pronunciation Region	Lat. °′	Long. °′
75	Dormont (dôr'mŏnt) Pa. (Pittsburgh In.)	40·24 N	80·02 W
120	Dornbirn (dōrn'bĕrn) Aus.	47·24 N	9·45 E
116	Dornoch (dôr'nŏk) Scot.	57·55 N	4·01 W
116	Dornoch Firth (dôr'nŏk fûrth) Scot.	57·55 N	3·55 W
128	Dorogobuzh (dôrôgô'-bōō'zh) Sov. Un.	54·57 N	33·18 E
121	Dorohoi (dō-rô-hoi') Rom.	47·57 N	26·28 E
	Dorpat, see Tartu		
158	Dorre (I.) (dôr) Austl.	25·19 S	113·10 E
74	Dorsey (dôrsĭ) Ill. (St. Louis In.)	38·59 N	90·00 W
84	Dorsey Md. (Baltimore In.)	39·11 N	76·45 W
123	Dorsten (dōr'stĕn) Ger. (Ruhr In.)	51·40 N	6·58 E
123	Dortmund (dôrt'mŏŏnt) Ger. (Ruhr In.)	51·31 N	7·28 E
123	Dortmund-Ems Kanal (can.) (dōrt'mōōnd-ĕms' kä-näl') Ger. (Ruhr In.)	51·50 N	7·25 E
133	Dörtyal (dûrt'yôl) Tur.	36·50 N	36·20 E
85	Dorval (dôr-vål') Can. (Montreal In.)	45·26 N	73·44 W
99	Dos Caminos (dôs-kä-mē'nôs) Ven. (In.)	9·38 N	67·17 W
65	Dosewallips (R.) (dō'sê-wäl'lĭps) Wash. (Seattle In.)	47·45 N	123·04 W
124	Dos Hermanas (dōsĕr-mä'näs) Sp.	37·17 N	5·56 W
164	Dosso (dôs-ō') Niger	13·03 N	3·09 E
78	Dothan (dō'thăn) Ala.	31·13 N	85·23 W
122	Douai (dōō-ā') Fr.	50·23 N	3·04 E
164	Douala (dōō-ä'lä) Cam.	4·00 N	9·37 E
122	Douarnenez (dōō-är-nē-nĕs') Fr.	48·06 N	4·18 W
77	Double Bay. (dŭb''l bī'yōō) Tex. (In.)	29·40 N	94·38 W
125	Douéra (dōō-ā'rȧ) Alg.	36·40 N	2·55 E
64	Douglas (dŭg'lăs) Alaska	58·18 N	134·35 W
69	Douglas Ariz.	31·20 N	109·30 W
78	Douglas Ga.	31·30 N	82·53 W
116	Douglas (dŭg'lăs) Isle of Man	54·10 N	4·24 W
83	Douglas (dŭg'lăs) Mass. (Boston In.)	42·04 N	71·45 W
67	Douglas (dŭg'lăs) Wyo.	42·45 N	105·21 W
110	Douglas (R.) (dŭg'lăs) Eng.	53·38 N	2·48 W
78	Douglas (R.) (dŭg'lăs) Tenn.	36·00 N	83·35 W
78	Douglasville (dŭg'lăs-vĭl) Ga.	33·45 N	84·47 W
165	Doumé (dōō-mā') Cam.	4·14 N	13·26 E
99	Dourada, Serra (Mts.) (sĕ'r-rä-dōōō-rà'dä) Braz.	15·11 S	49·57 W
123	Dourdan (dōōr-däɴ') Fr. (Paris In.)	48·32 N	2·01 E
124	Douro, Rio (R.) (rē'ō-dô'ōō-rō) Port.	41·03 N	8·12 W
110	Dove (R.) (dŭv) Eng.	52·53 N	1·47 W
81	Dover (dō vēr) Del.	39·10 N	75·30 W
117	Dover Eng.	51·08 N	1·19 E
81	Dover N. H.	43·15 N	71·00 W
84	Dover N. J. (New York In.)	40·53 N	74·33 W
80	Dover Ohio	40·35 N	81·30 W
168	Dover S. Afr. (Johannesburg & Pretoria In.)	27·05 S	27·44 E
117	Dover, Str. of Eur.	50·50 N	1·15 W
82	Dover-Foxcroft (dō'vēr fôks'krôft) Maine	45·10 N	69·15 W
132	Dovlekanovo (dŏv'lyĕk-à-nô-vô) Sov. Un.	54·15 N	55·05 E
118	Dovre Fjeld (Plat.) (dŏv'rĕ fyĕl') Nor.	62·03 N	8·36 E
74	Dow (dou) Ill. (St. Louis In.)	39·01 N	90·20 W
166	Dow, L Bech.	21·22 S	24·52 E
80	Dowagiac (dô-wô'jăk) Mich.	42·00 N	86·05 W
75	Downers Grove (dou'nērz grōv) Ill. (Chicago In.)	41·48 N	88·00 W
74	Downey (dou'nĭ) Calif. (Los Angeles In.)	33·56 N	118·08 W
68	Downieville (dou'nĭ-vĭl) Calif.	39·35 N	120·48 W
72	Downs (dounz) Kans.	39·29 N	98·32 W
75	Doylestown (doilz'toun) Ohio (Cleveland In.)	40·58 N	81·43 W
124	Draa, C. (drà) Mor.	28·39 N	12·15 W
164	Draa, Wadi R. (wä-dĭ drä') Mor.	28·00 N	9·31 W
129	Drabov (drä'bôf) Sov. Un.	49·57 N	32·14 E
123	Drac (R.) (dräk) Fr.	44·50 N	5·47 E
83	Dracut (drä'kŭt) Mass. (Boston In.)	42·40 N	71·19 W
127	Draganovo (drä-gä-nō'vō) Bul.	43·13 N	25·45 E
127	Drăgăsani (drä-gà-shän'ĭ) Rom.	44·39 N	24·18 E
123	Draguignan (drä-gên-yäɴ') Fr.	43·35 N	6·28 E
166	Drakensberg (Mts.) (drä'kĕnz-bĕrgh) S. Afr.	29·15 S	29·07 E
96	Drake Passage (drāk păs'ĭj) S. A.-Ant.	57·00 S	65·00 W
127	Dráma (drä'mä) Grc.	41·09 N	24·10 E
118	Drammen (dräm'ĕn) Nor.	59·45 N	10·15 E
120	Drau R. (drou) Aus.	46·44 N	13·45 E
126	Drava (R.) (Drä'vä) Yugo.	46·37 N	15·17 E
126	Dravograd (Drä'vô-gräd') Yugo.	46·37 N	15·01 E
120	Drawsko Pomorskie (dräv'skô pō-mōr'skyĕ) Pol.	53·31 N	15·50 E
65	Drayton Hbr. (drā'tŭn) Wash. (Vancouver In.)	48·58 N	122·40 W
75	Drayton Plains Mich. (Detroit In.)	42·41 N	83·23 W
146	Dre Chu (R.) China	34·11 N	96·08 E
123	Drensteinfurt (drĕn'shtīn-fōōrt) Ger. (Ruhr In.)	51·47 N	7·44 E
120	Dresden (drās'dĕn) Ger.	51·05 N	13·45 E
123	Dreux (drû) Fr. (Paris In.)	48·44 N	1·24 E
168	Driefontein S. Afr. (Johannesburg & Pretoria In.)	25·53 S	29·10 E
127	Drin (R.) (drēn) Alb.	42·13 N	20·13 E
127	Drina (R.) (drē'nä) Yugo.	44·09 N	19·30 E
127	Drinit, Pellg I (Bght.) Alb.	41·42 N	19·17 E
128	Drissa (drĭs'sä) Sov. Un.	55·48 N	27·59 E
128	Drissa (R.) Sov. Un.	55·44 N	28·58 E

Page	Name Pronunciation Region	Lat. °′	Long. °′
84	Driver Va. (Norfolk In.)	36·50 N	76·30 W
118	Dröbak (drû'bäk) Nor.	59·40 N	10·35 E
116	Drogheda (drŏ'hē-dȧ) Ire.	53·43 N	6·15 W
121	Drogichin (drō-gē'chĭn) Sov. Un.	52·10 N	25·11 E
121	Drohobych (drô-hô'bĭch) Sov. Un.	49·21 N	23·31 E
122	Drôme (R.) (drōm) Fr.	44·42 N	4·53 E
110	Dronfield (drŏn'fēld) Eng.	53·18 N	1·28 W
86	Drumheller (drŭm-hĕl-ēr) Can.	51·30 N	112·42 W
80	Drummond (I.) (drŭm'ŭnd) Mich.	46·00 N	83·50 W
82	Drummondville (drŭm'ŭnd-vĭl) Can.	45·53 N	72·33 W
73	Drumright (drŭm'rīt) Okla.	35·59 N	96·37 W
111	Drunen Neth. (Amsterdam In.)	51·41 N	5·10 E
128	Drut' (R.) (drōōt) Sov. Un.	53·40 N	29·45 E
128	Druya (drōō'yà) Sov. Un.	55·45 N	27·26 E
115	Druze, Jebel (Mts.) Syria	32·40 N	36·58 E
121	Drweca R. (d'r-văn'tsȧ) Pol.	53·06 N	19·13 E
87	Dryden (drī-dĕn) Can.	49·50 N	92·47 W
161	Drysdale Austl. (Melbourne In.)	38·11 S	144·34 E
79	Dry Tortugas (I.) (tôr-tōō'gäz) Fla. (In.)	24·37 N	82·45 W
164	Dschang (dshäng) Cam.	5·34 N	10·09 E
85	Duagh Can. (Edmonton In.)	53·43 N	113·24 W
101	Duas Barras (dōō'äs-bà'r-räs) Braz. (Rio de Janeiro In.)	22·03 S	42·30 W
86	Dubawnt (L.) (dōō-bônt') Can.	63·27 N	103·30 W
86	Dubawnt (R.) Can.	61·30 N	103·49 W
144	Dubayy Tr. Coast	25·18 N	55·26 E
160	Dubbo (dŭb'ō) Austl.	32·20 S	148·42 E
65	Dublin (dŭb'lĭn) Calif. (San Francisco In.)	37·42 N	121·56 W
78	Dublin Ga.	32·33 N	82·55 W
76	Dublin Tex.	32·05 N	98·20 W
	Dublin, see Baile Atha Cliath		
121	Dubno (dōō'b nô) Sov. Un.	50·24 N	25·44 E
81	Du Bois (dōō-bois') Pa.	41·10 N	78·45 W
129	Dubossary (dōō-bô-sä'rĭ) Sov. Un.	47·16 N	29·11 E
133	Dubovka (dōō-bôf'kȧ) Sov. Un.	49·00 N	44·50 E
136	Dubrovka (dōō-brôf'kȧ) Sov. Un. (Leningrad In.)	59·51 N	30·56 E
127	Dubrovnik (Ragusa) (dōō'brôv-nēk) (rä-gōō'sä) Yugo.	42·40 N	18·10 E
128	Dubrovno (dōō-brôf'nō) Sov. Un.	54·39 N	30·54 E
71	Dubuque (dōō-būk') Iowa	42·30 N	90·43 W
69	Duchesne (dōō-shān') Utah	40·12 N	110·23 W
69	Duchesne (R.) Utah	40·20 N	110·50 W
158	Duchess (dŭch'ĕs) Austl.	21·30 S	139·55 E
157	Ducie I. (dü-sē') Oceania	25·30 S	126·20 W
80	Duck (I.) (dŭk) Can.	45·35 N	83·00 W
78	Duck (R.) Tenn.	35·55 N	87·40 W
65	Duckabush (R.) (dŭk'ȧ-bōōsh) Wash. (Seattle In.)	47·41 N	123·09 W
86	Duck Mtn. Can.	51·43 N	101·07 W
78	Ducktown (dŭk'toun) Tenn.	35·03 N	84·20 W
68	Duckwater Pk. (dŭk-wô-tēr) Nev.	39·00 N	115·31 W
98	Duda (dōō'dä) (R.) Col. (In.)	3·25 N	74·23 W
134	Dudinka (dōō-dĭn'kȧ) Sov. Un.	69·15 N	85·42 E
110	Dudley (dŭd'lĭ) Eng.	52·31 N	2·04 W
124	Duero (R.) (dwĕ'rō) Sp.	41·30 N	5·10 W
80	Dugger (dŭg'ēr) Ind.	39·00 N	87·10 W
126	Dugi Otok (I.) (dōō'gē O'tôk) Yugo.	44·03 N	14·40 E
123	Duisburg (dōō'ĭs-bŏŏrgh) Ger. (Ruhr In.)	51·26 N	6·46 E
98	Duitama (dōōē-tä'mä) Col.	5·48 N	73·09 W
128	Dukhovshchina (dōō-kôfsh'chēnä) Sov. Un.	55·13 N	32·26 E
110	Dukinfield (dŭk'ĭn-fēld) Eng.	53·28 N	2·05 W
121	Dukla P. (dōō'klä) Pol.	49·25 N	21·44 E
93	Dulce, Golfo (G.) (gōl'fô dōōl'sä) C. R.	8·25 N	83·13 W
	Dulcigno, see Ulčinj		
123	Dülken (dül'kĕn) Ger. (Ruhr In.)	51·15 N	6·21 E
123	Dülmen (dül'mĕn) Ger. (Ruhr In.)	51·50 N	7·17 E
74	Duluth (dōō·lōōth') Minn. (Duluth In.)	46·50 N	92·07 W
139	Dūmā Syria (Palestine In.)	33·34 N	36·17 E
155	Dumaguete City (dōō-mä-gä'tä) Phil.	9·14 N	123·15 E
168	Dumaît, Masabb (R. Mth.) U. A. R. (Nile In.)	31·36 N	31·45 E
155	Dumali Pt. (dōō-mä'lē) Phil. (Manila Pt.)	13·07 N	121·42 E
116	Dumbarton (dŭm'bär-tŭn) Scot.	56·00 N	4·35 W
142	Dum Dum India (Calcutta In.)	22·37 N	88·25 E
116	Dumfries (dŭm-frēs') Scot.	54·05 N	3·40 W
84	Dumont (dōō'mŏnt) N. J. (New York In.)	40·56 N	74·00 W
77	Dumont Tex. (In.)	29·40 N	95·14 W
168	Dumyāţ (Damietta) (dōōm-yät') (dăm-ĭ-ĕt'ȧ) U. A. R. (Nile In.)	31·22 N	31·50 E
121	Dunaföldvar (dōō'nô-fûld'vär) Hung.	46·48 N	18·55 E
121	Dunajec R. (dōō-nä'yĕts) Pol.	49·52 N	20·53 E
121	Dunapataj (doo'nô-pô-toi) Hung.	46·42 N	19·03 E
121	Duna R. (dōō'nä) Hung.	46·07 N	18·45 E
136	Dunay (dōō'nĭ) Sov. Un. (Leningrad In.)	59·59 N	30·57 E
129	Dunayevtsy (dōō-nä'yĕf-tsĭ) Sov. Un.	48·52 N	26·51 E
116	Dunbar (dŭn'bär) Scot.	56·00 N	2·25 W
80	Dunbar W. Va.	38·20 N	81·45 W
66	Duncan (dŭŋ'kăn) Can.	48·46 N	123·42 W
72	Duncan Okla.	34·29 N	97·56 W
116	Duncansby Hd. (dŭn'kănz-bĭ) Scot.	58·40 N	3·01 W
74	Duncanville (dŭn'kăn-vĭl) Tex. (Dallas, Fort Worth In.)	32·39 N	96·55 W
116	Dundalk (dŭn'dôk) Ire.	54·00 N	6·18 W
84	Dundalk Md. (Baltimore In.)	39·16 N	76·31 W
116	Dundalk B. (dŭn'dôk) Ire.	53·55 N	6·15 W

Page	Name Pronunciation Region	Lat. °′	Long. °′
85	Dundas (dŭn-dȧs') Can. (Toronto In.)	43·16 N	79·58 W
75	Dundee (dŭn-dē') Ill. (Chicago In.)	42·06 N	88·17 W
116	Dundee Scot.	56·30 N	2·55 W
167	Dundee S. Afr. (Natal In.)	28·14 S	30·16 E
158	Dundras (L.) (dŭn-drȧs) Austl.	32·15 S	132·00 E
158	Dundras Str. (dŭn'drȧs) Austl.	10·35 S	131·15 E
116	Dundrum B. (dŭn-drŭm') Ire.	54·13 N	5·47 W
79	Dunedin (dŭn-ē'dĭn) Fla. (In.)	28·00 N	82·43 W
159	Dunedin N. Z. (In.)	45·48 S	170·32 E
84	Dunellen (dŭn-ĕl'l'n) N. J. (New York In.)	40·36 N	74·28 W
116	Dunfermline (dŭn-fĕrm'lĭn) Scot.	56·05 N	3·30 W
116	Dungarvin (dŭn-gȧr'vȧn) Ire.	52·06 N	7·50 W
65	Dungeness (dŭnj-nĕs') Wash. (Seattle In.)	48·09 N	123·07 W
65	Dungeness (R.) Wash. (Seattle In.)	48·03 N	123·10 W
65	Dungeness Spit Wash. (Seattle In.)	48·11 N	123·03 W
165	Dungu (dōōŋ-gōō') Con. L.	3·48 N	28·32 E
122	Dunkerque (dŭn-kĕrk') Fr.	51·02 N	2·37 E
80	Dunkirk (dŭn'kûrk) Ind.	40·20 N	85·25 W
81	Dunkirk N. Y.	42·30 N	79·20 W
116	Dun Laoghaire (dŭn-lā'rĕ) Ire.	53·16 N	6·09 W
70	Dunlap (dŭn'lăp) Iowa	41·53 N	95·33 W
78	Dunlap Tenn.	35·23 N	85·23 W
81	Dunmore (dŭn'mōr) Pa.	41·25 N	75·30 W
79	Dunn (dŭn) N. C.	35·18 N	78·37 W
79	Dunnellon (dŭn-ĕl'ŏn) Fla.	29·02 N	82·28 W
81	Dunnville (dŭn'vĭl) Can.	42·55 N	79·40 W
66	Dunsmuir (dŭnz'mūr) Calif.	41·08 N	122·17 W
84	Dunwoody (dŭn-wŏŏd'ĭ) Ga. (Atlanta In.)	33·57 N	84·20 W
75	Du Page R. (dōō pāj) Ill. (Chicago In.)	41·41 N	88·11 W
75	Du Page R., E. Br. Ill. (Chicago In.)	41·49 N	88·05 W
75	Du Page R., W. Br. Ill. (Chicago In.)	41·48 N	88·10 W
155	Dupax (dōō'päks) Phil. (Manila In.)	16·16 N	121·06 E
127	Dupnitsa (dŏŏp'nē-tsȧ) Bul.	42·15 N	23·07 E
74	Dupo (dū'pō) Ill. (St. Louis In.)	38·31 N	90·12 W
166	Duque de Bragança (dōō'kȧ dȧ brä-gäN'sä) Ang.	8·55 S	16·10 E
100	Duque de Caxias (dōō'kĕ-dĕ-kȧ'shyȧs) Braz. (In.)	22·46 S	43·18 W
75	Duquesne (dŏŏ-kān') Pa. (Pittsburgh In.)	40·22 N	79·51 W
73	Du Quoin (dŏŏ-kwoin') Ill.	38·01 N	89·14 W
123	Durance (R.) (dü-räNs') Fr.	43·46 N	5·52 E
80	Durand (dŭ-rănd') Mich.	42·50 N	84·00 W
71	Durand Wis.	44·37 N	91·58 W
69	Durango (dŏŏ-răŋ'gō) Colo.	37·15 N	107·55 W
88	Durango (State) Mex.	25·00 N	106·00 W
78	Durant (dŭ-rănt') Miss.	33·05 N	89·50 W
73	Durant Okla.	33·59 N	96·23 W
124	Duratón (R.) (dōō-rä-tōn') Sp.	41·55 N	3·55 W
101	Durazno (dōō-räz'nō) Ur. (Buenos Aires In.)	33·21 S	56·31 W
101	Durazno (Dept.) Ur. (Buenos Aires In.)	33·00 S	56·35 W
167	Durban (dûr'băn) S. Afr. (Natal In.)	29·48 S	31·00 E
166	Durbanville (dûr-băn'vĭl) S. Afr. (Cape Town In.)	33·50 S	18·39 E
119	Durbe (dōōr'bĕ) Sov. Un.	56·36 N	21·24 E
123	Düren (dü'rĕn) Ger. (Ruhr In.)	50·48 N	6·30 E
116	Durham (dûr'ăm) Eng.	54·47 N	1·46 W
79	Durham N. C.	36·00 N	78·55 W
75	Durham Wis. (Milwaukee In.)	42·52 N	88·04 W
160	Durham Downs Austl.	27·30 S	141·55 E
127	Durrës (dōōr'ĕs) Alb.	41·19 N	19·27 E
155	D'urville, Kap (C.) (dûr'vĭl) W. Irian	1·20 S	138·45 E
81	Duryea (dōōr-yā') Pa.	41·20 N	75·50 W
144	Dushanbe Sov. Un.	38·41 N	68·43 E
123	Düsseldorf (düs'ĕl-dôrf) Ger. (Ruhr In.)	51·14 N	6·47 E
111	Dussen Neth. (Amsterdam In.)	51·43 N	4·58 E
150	Dutalan Ula (Mtn.) Mong.	49·25 N	112·40 E
64	Dutch Harbor (dŭch här'bĕr) Alaska	53·58 N	166·30 W
65	Duvall (dōō'vâl) Wash. (Seattle In.)	47·44 N	121·59 W
95	Duvergé (dōō-vĕr-hĕ') Dom. Rep.	18·20 N	71·20 W
65	Duwamish (dōō-wăm'ĭsh) Wash. (Seattle In.)	47·24 N	122·18 W
	Dvina, Western, R., see Zapadnaya Dvina		
132	Dvinskaya Guba (G.) Sov. Un.	65·10 N	38·40 E
120	Dvur Kralove nad Labem (dvōōr' krä'lô-vā) Czech.	50·28 N	15·43 E
142	Dwārka India	22·18 N	68·59 E
80	Dwight (dwīt) Ill.	41·00 N	88·20 W
128	Dyat'kovo (dyăt'kō-vō) Sov. Un.	53·36 N	34·19 E
75	Dyer (dī'ĕr) Ind. (Chicago In.)	41·30 N	87·31 W
78	Dyersburg (dī'ĕrz-bûrg) Tenn.	36·02 N	89·23 W
71	Dyersville (dī'ĕrz-vĭl) Iowa	42·28 N	91·09 W
65	Dyes Inlet (dīz) Wash. (Seattle In.)	47·37 N	122·45 W
146	Dzabhan Gol (R.) Mong.	48·19 N	94·08 E
150	Dzamiin Üüde Mong.	44·38 N	111·32 E
167	Dzaoudzi (dzou'dzĭ) Comores, Arch. des	12·44 S	45·15 E
103	Dzaudzhikau (dzou-jĭ-kou') Sov. Un.	48·00 N	44·52 E
129	Dzerzhinsk (dzhĕr-zhĭnsk') Sov. Un.	48·24 N	37·58 E
128	Dzerzhinsk Sov. Un.	53·41 N	27·14 E
132	Dzerzhinsk Sov. Un.	56·20 N	43·50 E
134	Dzhalal-Abad (jȧ-lăl'ȧ-băt') Sov. Un.	41·13 N	73·35 E
134	Dzhambul (dzhăm-bōōl') Sov. Un.	42·51 N	71·29 E
129	Dzhankoy (dzhăn'koi) Sov. Un.	45·43 N	34·22 E
136	Dzhetygara (dzhĕt'-gȧ'rȧ) Sov. Un. (Urals In.)	52·12 N	61·18 E
134	Dzhizak (dzhê'zăk) Sov. Un.	40·13 N	67·58 E
135	Dzhugdzhur Khrebet (Mts.) (jōōg-jōōr') Sov. Un.	56·15 N	137·00 E
121	Działoszyce (jyä-wō-shē'tsĕ) Pol.	50·21 N	20·22 E
92	Dzibalchén (zē-bäl-chĕ'n) Mex. (Yucatan In.)	19·25 N	89·39 W
92	Dzidzantún (zēd-zän-tōō'n) Mex. (Yucatan In.)	21·18 N	89·00 W
120	Dzierzoniów (dzyĕr-zhôn'yŭf) Pol.	50·44 N	16·38 E
92	Dzilam Gonzalez (zē-lä'm-gôn-zä'lĕz) Mex. (Yucatan In.)	21·21 N	88·53 W
92	Dzitás (zē-tà's) Mex. (Yucatan In.)	20·47 N	88·32 W
92	Dzitbalché (dzēt-bäl-chā') Mex. (Yucatan In.)	20·18 N	90·03 W
146	Dzungaria (Reg.) (dzōōŋ-gä'rĭ-ȧ) China	44·39 N	86·13 E
64	Eagle (ē'g'l) Alaska	64·42 N	141·20 W
77	Eagle Tex. (In.)	29·40 N	94·40 W
80	Eagle W. Va.	38·10 N	81·20 W
69	Eagle (R.) Colo.	39·32 N	106·28 W
65	Eaglecliff (ē'g'l-klĭf) Wash. (Portland In.)	46·10 N	123·13 W
75	Eagle Cr. Ind. (Indianapolis In.)	39·54 N	86·17 W
74	Eagle Ford (ē'g'l fērd) Tex. (Dallas, Fort Worth In.)	32·47 N	96·52 W
71	Eagle Grove Iowa	42·39 N	93·55 W
82	Eagle Lake Maine	47·03 N	68·38 W
77	Eagle Lake Tex.	29·37 N	96·20 W
66	Eagle L. Calif.	40·45 N	120·52 W
74	Eagle Mountain L. Tex. (Dallas, Fort Worth In.)	32·56 N	97·27 W
76	Eagle Pass Tex.	28·49 N	100·30 W
66	Eagle Pk. Calif.	41·18 N	120·11 W
110	Ealing (ē'lĭng) Eng. (London In.)	51·29 N	0·19 W
73	Earle (ûrl) Ark.	35·14 N	90·28 W
78	Earlington (ûr'lĭng-tŭn) S. C.	37·15 N	87·31 W
79	Easley (ēz'lĭ) S. C.	34·48 N	82·37 W
88	East, Mt. C. Z. (Panama Canal In.)	9·09 N	79·16 W
74	East Alton (ôl'tŭn) Ill. (St. Louis In.)	38·53 N	90·08 W
81	East Angus (ăŋ'gŭs) Can.	45·35 N	71·40 W
75	East Aurora (ô-rō'rȧ) N. Y. (Buffalo In.)	42·46 N	78·38 W
84	East B. La. (New Orleans In.)	29·03 N	89·16 W
77	East B. Tex. (In.)	29·30 N	94·41 W
111	East Berlin (bĕr-lēn') Ger. (Berlin In.)	52·31 N	13·28 E
78	East Bernstadt (bûrn'stăt) Ky.	37·09 N	84·08 W
65	Eastbound (ēst-bound) Wash. (Vancouver In.)	48·42 N	122·42 W
117	Eastbourne (ēst'bôrn) Eng.	50·48 N	0·16 E
95	East Caicos (I.) (kī'kōs) Caicos	21·40 N	71·35 W
159	East C. N. Z. (In.)	37·37 S	178·33 E
	East Cape, see Dezhneva, Mys		
74	East Carondelet (kȧ-rŏn'dĕ-lĕt) Ill. (St. Louis In.)	38·33 N	90·14 W
75	East Chicago (shĭ-kô'gō) Ind. (Chicago In.)	41·39 N	87·29 W
147	East China Sea Asia	30·28 N	125·52 E
75	East Cleveland (klēv'lănd) Ohio (Cleveland In.)	41·33 N	81·35 W
77	East Cote Blanche B. (kōt bläNsh') La.	29·30 N	92·07 W
71	East Des Moines (R.) (dē moin') Iowa	42·57 N	94·17 W
75	East Detroit (dē-troit') Mich. (Detroit In.)	42·28 N	82·57 W
	Easter (I.), see Rapa Nui		
120	Eastern Alps (Mts.) Aus.-Switz.	47·03 N	10·55 E
143	Eastern Ghats (Mts.) India	19·35 N	78·08 E
146	Eastern Turkestan (Reg.) (tōōr-kĕ-stän') (tûr-kĕ-stăn') China	38·23 N	80·41 E
75	East Gary (gā'rĭ) Ind. (Chicago In.)	41·34 N	87·15 W
70	East Grand Forks (grănd fôrks) Minn.	47·56 N	97·02 W
84	East Greenwich (grĭn'ĭj) R. I. (Providence In.)	41·40 N	71·27 W
81	Easthampton (ēst-hămp'tŭn) Mass.	42·15 N	72·45 W
81	East Hartford (härt'fērd) Conn.	41·45 N	72·35 W
67	East Helena (hĕ-lē'nȧ) Mont.	46·31 N	111·50 W
110	East Ilsley (ĭl'slē) Eng. (London In.)	51·30 N	1·18 W
80	East Jordan (jôr'dăn) Mich.	45·05 N	85·05 W
74	East Kansas City (kăn'zȧs) Mo. (Kansas City In.)	39·09 N	94·30 W
76	Eastland (ēst'lănd) Tex.	32·24 N	98·47 W
80	East Lansing (lăn'sĭng) Mich.	42·45 N	84·30 W
74	East Leavenworth (lĕv'ĕn-wûrth) Mo. (Kansas City In.)	39·18 N	94·50 W
80	East Liverpool (lĭv'ēr-pōōl) Ohio	40·40 N	80·35 W
167	East London (lŭn'dŭn) S. Afr. (Natal In.)	33·02 S	27·54 E
74	East Los Angeles (lōs ăŋ'hȧ-lās) Calif. (Los Angeles In.)	34·01 N	118·09 W
87	Eastmain (R.) (ēst'mān) Can.	52·12 N	73·19 W
78	Eastman (ēst-măn) Ga.	32·10 N	83·11 W
84	East Millstone (mĭl'stōn) N. J. (New York In.)	40·30 N	74·35 W
71	East Moline (mō-lēn') Ill.	41·31 N	90·28 W
73	East Nishnabotna (R.) (nĭsh-nȧ-bŏt'nȧ) Iowa	40·53 N	95·23 W
81	Easton (ēs'tŭn) Md.	72·45 N	76·05 W
75	Easton (ēst'ŭn) Ohio (Cleveland In.)	40·57 N	81·45 W
81	Easton Pa.	40·45 N	75·15 W
84	Easton L. Conn. (New York In.)	41·18 N	73·17 W
84	East Orange (ŏr'ĕnj) N. J. (New York In.)	40·46 N	74·12 W
80	East Peoria (pē-ō'rĭ-ȧ) Ill.	40·40 N	89·30 W
75	East Pittsburgh (pĭts'bûrg) Pa. (Pittsburgh In.)	40·24 N	79·50 W
84	East Point Ga. (Atlanta In.)	33·41 N	84·27 W
82	Eastport (ēst-pōrt) Can.	44·53 N	67·01 W
84	East Providence (prŏv'ĭ-dĕns) R. I. (Providence In.)	41·49 N	71·22 W
110	East Retford (rĕt'fērd) Eng.	53·19 N	0·56 W
110	East Riding (Co.) (rīd'ĭng) Eng.	53·47 N	0·36 W
81	East Rochester (rŏch'ĕs-tēr) N. Y.	43·10 N	77·30 W
74	East St. Louis (sānt lōō'ĭs) (lōō-ĭ) Ill. (St. Louis In.)	38·38 N	90·10 W
130	East Siberian Sea (sī-bĭr'y'n) Sov. Un.	73·00 N	153·28 E
65	East Stanwood (stăn'wŏŏd) Wash. (Seattle In.)	48·14 N	122·21 W
81	East Stroudsburg (stroudz'bûrg) Pa.	41·00 N	75·10 W
81	East Syracuse (sĭr'ȧ-kūs) N. Y.	43·05 N	76·00 W
69	East Tavaputs Plat. (tă-vă'-pŭts) Utah	39·25 N	109·45 W
80	East Tawas (tô'wȧs) Mich.	44·15 N	83·30 W
85	Eastview (ēst'vyōō) Can. (Ottawa In.)	45·27 N	75·39 W
68	East Walker (R.) (wôk'ēr) Nev.	38·36 N	119·02 W
75	Eaton (ē'tŭn) Colo.	40·31 N	104·42 W
80	Eaton Ohio	39·45 N	84·40 W
75	Eaton Ohio (Cleveland In.)	41·19 N	82·01 W
80	Eaton Rapids (răp'ĭdz) Mich.	42·30 N	84·40 W
78	Eatonton (ē'tŭn-tŭn) Ga.	33·20 N	83·24 W
84	Eatontown (ē'tŭn-toun) N. J. (New York In.)	40·18 N	74·04 W
71	Eau Claire (ō klâr') Wis.	44·47 N	91·32 W
118	Ebeltoft (ĕ'bĕl-tŭft) Den.	56·11 N	10·39 E
111	Ebersberg (ĕ'bĕrs-bĕrgh) Ger. (Munich In.)	48·05 N	11·58 E
120	Ebingen (ā'bĭng-ĕn) Ger.	48·13 N	9·04 E
146	Ebi Nuur (L.) (ā'bê) China	45·09 N	83·15 E
126	Eboli (ĕb'ō-lē) It.	40·38 N	15·04 E
164	Ebolowa Cam.	2·54 N	11·09 E
111	Ebreichsdorf Aus. (Vienna In.)	47·58 N	16·24 E
125	Ebro, Río (R.) (rê'-ô-ā'brō) Sp.	41·22 N	0·17 W
110	Eccles (ĕk''lz) Eng.	53·29 N	2·20 W
80	Eccles W. Va.	37·45 N	81·10 W
110	Eccleshall (ĕk''lz-hôl) Eng.	52·51 N	2·15 W
127	Eceabat (Maidos) Tur.	40·10 N	26·21 E
155	Echague (ā-chä'gwä) Phil. (Manila In.)	16·43 N	121·40 E
93	Echandi, Cerro (Mt.) (sĕ'r-rô-ĕ-chä'nd) Pan.	9·05 N	82·51 W
74	Echo Bay (ĕk'ō) Can. (Sault Ste. Marie In.)	46·29 N	84·04 W
123	Echternach (ĕk'tēr-näk) Lux.	49·48 N	6·25 E
160	Echuca (ê-chōō'kȧ) Austl.	36·10 S	144·47 E
124	Écija (ā'thê-hä) Sp.	37·20 N	5·07 W
120	Eckernförde Ger.	54·27 N	9·51 E
84	Eclipse (ê-klĭps') Va. (Norfolk In.)	36·55 N	76·29 W
75	Ecorse (ê-kôrs') Mich. (Detroit In.)	42·15 N	83·09 W
96	Ecuador (ĕk'wȧ-dôr) S. A.	0·00 N	78·30 W
165	Edd Eth.	13·57 N	41·37 E
165	Ed Dāmer (ĕd dä'mĕr) Sud.	17·38 N	33·57 E
165	Ed Debba (dĕb'ȧ) Sud.	18·04 N	30·58 E
165	Ed Dueim (dōō-ām') Sud.	13·56 N	32·22 E
78	Eddyville (ĕd'ĭ-vĭl) Ky.	37·03 N	88·03 W
164	Edéa (ĕ-dā'ä) Cam.	3·45 N	10·08 E
74	Eden (ē'd'n) Calif. (Los Angeles In.)	33·54 N	117·05 W
74	Eden Utah (Salt Lake City In.)	41·18 N	111·49 W
116	Eden (R.) (ē'dĕn) Eng.	54·40 N	2·35 W
110	Edenbridge (ē'dĕn-brĭj) Eng. (London In.)	51·11 N	0·05 E
110	Edenham (ē'd'n-ăm) Eng.	52·46 N	0·25 W
74	Eden Prairie (prâr'ĭ) Minn. (Minneapolis, St. Paul In.)	44·51 N	93·29 W
79	Edenton (ē'dĕn-tŭn) N. C.	36·02 N	76·37 W
75	Edenton Ohio (Cincinnati In.)	39·14 N	84·02 W
167	Edenvale (ĕd'ĕn-väl) S. Afr. (Johannesburg & Pretoria In.)	29·06 S	28·10 E
168	Edenville (ĕ'd'n-vĭl) S. Afr. (Johannesburg & Pretoria In.)	27·33 S	27·42 E
120	Eder R. (ā'dĕr) Ger.	51·05 N	8·52 E
164	Edeyen, Erg (Dunes) (ĕ-dā'yĕn) Alg.	27·30 N	7·30 E
79	Edgefield (ĕj'fēld) S. C.	33·52 N	81·55 W
70	Edgeley (ĕj'lĭ) N. D.	46·24 N	98·43 W
70	Edgemont (ĕj'mŏnt) S. D.	43·19 N	103·50 W
71	Edgerton (ĕj'ēr-tŭn) Wis.	42·49 N	89·06 W
84	Edgewater (ĕj-wô-tēr) Ala. (Birmingham In.)	33·31 N	86·52 W
127	Édhessa Grc.	40·48 N	22·04 E
74	Edina (ē-dī'nȧ) Minn. (Minneapolis, St. Paul In.)	44·55 N	93·20 W
73	Edina Mo.	40·10 N	92·11 W
80	Edinburg (ĕd''n-bûrg) Ind.	39·20 N	85·55 W
76	Edinburg Tex.	26·18 N	98·08 W
116	Edinburgh (ĕd''n-bŭr-ô) Scot.	55·57 N	3·10 W
127	Edirne (Adrianople) (ĕ-dĭr'nĕ) (ā-drĭ-ăn-ō'p'l) Tur.	41·41 N	26·35 E
79	Edisto, (R.) (ĕd'ĭs-tō) S. C.	33·10 N	80·50 W
79	Edisto (R.), North Fk. S. C.	33·42 N	81·24 W
79	Edisto (R.), South Fk. S. C.	33·43 N	81·35 W
79	Edisto Island S. C.	32·32 N	80·20 W
73	Edmond (ĕd'mŭnd) Okla.	35·39 N	97·29 W
65	Edmonds (ĕd'mŭndz) Wash. (Seattle In.)	47·49 N	122·23 W
85	Edmonton Can. (Edmonton In.)	53·30 N	113·45 W
82	Edmundston (ĕd'mŭn-stŭn) Can.	47·23 N	68·20 W
77	Edna (ĕd'nȧ) Tex.	28·59 N	96·39 W
127	Edremit (ĕd-rĕ-mēt') Tur.	39·35 N	27·00 E
127	Edremit Körfezi (G.) Tur.	39·28 N	26·35 E
86	Edson (ĕd'sŭn) Can.	53·40 N	116·40 W

ăt; finăl; rāte; senāte; ärm; ȧsk; sofȧ; fâre; ch-choose; dh-as th in other; bē; êvent; bĕt; recĕnt; cratēr; g-go; gh-guttural g; bĭt; ĭ-short neutral; rīde; K-guttural k as ch in German ich;

PRONOUNCING INDEX Edward–Ems-Weser 203

Page	Name Pronunciation Region	Lat. °′	Long. °′
71	Edward (I.) (ĕd'wẽrd) Can.	48·21 N	88·29 W
166	Edward (L.) Con. L.	0·15 S	28·32 E
74	Edwardsville (ĕd'wẽrdz-vĭl) Ill. (St. Louis In.)	38·49 N	89·58 W
75	Edwardsville . Ind. (Louisville In.)	38·17 N	85·53 W
74	Edwardsville Kans. (Kansas City In.)	39·04 N	94·49 W
66	Eel R. (ēl) Calif.	40·39 N	124·15 W
80	Eel (R.) Ind.	40·50 N	85·55 W
159	Efate (I.) (ā-fä'tā) New Hebr.	18·02 S	168·29 E
71	Effigy Mounds Natl. Mon. (ĕf'ĭ-jŭ mounds) . Iowa	43·04 N	91·15 W
80	Effingham (ĕf'ĭng-hăm) Ill.	39·05 N	88·30 W
124	Ega (R.) (ā'gä) Sp.	42·40 N	2·20 W
126	Egadi, Isole (Is.) (ē'sō-lĕ-ĕ'gä-dē) . It.	38·01 N	12·00 E
124	Egea de los Caballeros (ā-kā'ä dā lōs kä-băl-yā'rōs) . Sp.	42·07 N	1·05 W
64	Egegik (ĕg'ĕ-jĭt) Alaska	58·10 N	157·22 W
121	Eger (ĕ gĕr) Hung.	47·53 N	20·24 E
	Eger, see Ohre R.		
118	Egersund (ĕ'ghĕr-sōōn') Nor.	58·29 N	6·01 E
81	Egg Harbor (ĕg här'bẽr) N. J.	39·30 N	74·35 W
110	Egham (ĕg'ŭm) Eng. (London In.)	51·24 N	0·33 W
146	Egiin Gol (R.) (â-gēn') Mong.	49·41 N	100·40 E
159	Egmont, C. (ĕg'mŏnt) . N. Z. (In.)	39·18 S	173·49 E
133	Egridir Gölü (L.) (ā-rĭ-dĭr') . . Tur.	38·10 N	30·00 E
122	Eguilles (ĕ-gwē') Fr. (Marseille In.)	43·34 N	5·21 E
	Egypt, see United Arab Republic		
124	Eibar (ā'ē-bär) Sp.	43·12 N	2·20 W
120	Eichstätt (īk'shtät) Ger.	48·54 N	11·14 E
111	Eichwalde (īk'väl-dĕ) Ger. (Berlin In.)	52·22 N	13·37 E
118	Eid (īdh) Nor.	61·54 N	6·01 E
118	Eidsberg (īdhs'bĕrgh) Nor.	59·32 N	11·16 E
118	Eidsvoll (īdhs'vôl) Nor.	60·19 N	11·15 E
120	Eifel (Plat.) (ī'fĕl) Ger.	50·08 N	6·30 E
168	Eil Som. (Horn of Afr. In.)	7·53 N	49·45 E
139	Eilat Jordan (Palestine In.)	29·34 N	34·57 E
120	Eilenburg (ī'lĕn-bōōrgh) Ger.	51·27 N	12·38 E
167	Elliot S. Afr. (Natal In.)	31·19 S	27·52 E
120	Einbeck (īn'bĕk) Ger.	51·49 N	9·52 E
117	Eindhoven (īnd'hō-vĕn) Neth.	51·29 N	5·20 E
98	Eirunepé (ā-rōō-nĕ-pĕ') Braz.	6·37 S	69·58 W
120	Eisenach (ī'zĕn-äk) Ger.	50·58 N	10·18 E
120	Eisenhuttenstadt Ger.	52·08 N	14·40 E
120	Eisleben (īs'lā'bĕn) Ger.	51·31 N	11·33 E
118	Ejdfjord (ĕĭd'fyōr) Nor.	60·28 N	7·04 E
91	Ejutla de Crespo (ā-hōōt'lā dā krās'pō) . Mex.	16·34 N	96·44 W
119	Ekenäs (Tammisaari) (ĕ'kĕ-nâs) (tàm'ĭ-sä'rĭ) . Fin.	59·59 N	23·25 E
111	Ekeren Bel. (Brussels In.)	51·17 N	4·27 E
85	Ekhart (ĕk'ărt) Can. (Winnipeg In.)	50·08 N	97·26 W
118	Eksjö (ĕk'shû) Swe.	57·41 N	14·55 E
165	El Abyad, Bahr (R.) (White Nile) (bär ĕl ä-byäd') . Sud.	14·09 N	32·27 E
125	El Affroun (ĕl âf-froun') Alg	36·28 N	2·38 E
164	El Aiún (ĕl ä-ē-ōō'n) Sp. Sah.	26·45 N	13·15 W
167	Elands (R.) S. Afr. (Natal In.)	31·48 S	26·09 E
168	Elands R. (ē'lănds) S. Afr. (Johannesburg & Pretoria In.)	25·11 S	28·52 E
165	El Arab, Buhr (R.) Sud.	9·46 N	26·52 E
124	El Arahal (ĕl ä-rä-äl') Sp.	37·17 N	5·32 W
139	El 'Auja (ăl oujà) Isr.-U. A. R. (Palestine In.)	30·53 N	34·28 E
133	Elâzig (ĕl-ä'zêz) Tur.	38·30 N	39·10 E
165	El Azrag, Bahr (R.) (Blue Nile) (bär ĕläz-räk') . Sud.	13·59 N	33·45 E
78	Elba (ĕl'bȧ) Ala.	31·25 N	86·01 W
126	Elba, Isola di (I.) (ē-sō-lä-dē-ĕl'bȧ) . It.	42·42 N	10·25 E
124	El Barco (ĕl bär'kō) Sp.	42·26 N	6·58 W
127	Elbasan (ĕl-bä-sän'') Alb.	41·08 N	20·05 E
	Elbe, see Labe R.		
120	Elbe R. (ĕl'bĕ) Ger.	53·47 N	9·20 E
69	Elbert, Mt. (ĕl'bẽrt) Colo.	39·05 N	106·25 W
78	Elberton (ĕl'bẽr-tŭn) Ga.	34·05 N	82·53 W
122	Elbeuf (ĕl-bûf') Fr.	49·16 N	0·59 E
133	Elbistan (ĕl-bē-stän') Tur.	38·20 N	37·10 E
121	Elblag (ĕl'blăng) Pol.	54·11 N	19·25 E
124	El Bonillo (ĕl bō-nēl'yō) Sp.	38·56 N	2·31 W
94	Elbow Cay (I.) Ba. Is.	26·25 N	77·55 W
70	Elbow Lake Minn.	46·00 N	95·59 W
85	Elbow R. (ĕl'bō) Can. (Calgary In.)	51·03 N	114·24 W
133	El'brus, Gora (Mt.) (ĕl'brŏŏs') Sov. Un.	43·20 N	42·25 E
168	El Buheirat el Murrat el Kubra (Great Bitter) . U. A. R. (Suez In.)	30·24 N	32·27 E
168	El Buheirat el Murrat el Sughra (Little Bitter) . U. A. R. (Suez In.)	30·10 N	32·36 E
168	El Bur Som. (Horn of Afr. In.)	4·35 N	46·40 E
133	Elburz Mts. (ĕl'bŏŏrz') Iran	36·30 N	51·00 E
68	El Cajon Calif. (San Diego In.)	32·48 N	116·58 W
98	El Cajon (ĕl-kä-kô'n) Col. (In.)	4·50 N	76.35 W
99	El Cambur (käm-bōō'r) . Ven. (In.)	10·24 N	68·06 W
77	El Campo (kăm'pō) Tex.	29·13 N	96·17 W
101	El Carmen (kà'r-mĕn) Chile (Santiago In.)	34·14 S	71·23 W
98	El Carmen (kà'r-mĕn) Col.	9·54 N	75·12 W
74	El Casco (kăs'kō) Calif. (Los Angeles In.)	33·59 N	117·08 W
68	El Centro (sĕn'trō) Calif.	32·47 N	115·33 W
65	El Cerrito (sĕr-rē'tō) Calif. (San Francisco In.)	37·55 N	122·19 W
100	El Chaco (Prov.) (chä'kō) Arg.	26·00 S	60·45 W
125	Elche (ĕl'chā) Sp.	38·15 N	0·42 W
92	El Cuyo Mex. (Yucatan In.)	21·30 N	87·42 W
125	Elda (ĕl'dä) Sp.	38·28 N	0·44 W
120	Elde R. (ĕl'dĕ) Ger.	53·11 N	11·30 E
168	El Dilingat U. A. R. (Nile In.)	30·48 N	30·32 E
164	El Djouf (Des.) (ĕl djōōf) Mauritania	21·38 N	7·44 W
71	Eldon (ĕl-dŭn) Iowa	40·55 N	92·15 W
73	Eldon Mo.	38·21 N	92·36 W
65	Eldon Wash. (Seattle In.)	47·33 N	123·02 W
71	Eldora (ĕl-dō'rȧ) Iowa	42·21 N	93·08 W
73	El Dorado (ĕl dō-rā'dō) Ark.	33·13 N	92·39 W
80	Eldorado Ill.	37·50 N	88·30 W
73	El Dorado Kans.	37·49 N	96·51 W
73	Eldorado Springs (sprĭngz) Mo.	37·51 N	94·02 W
165	Eldoret (ĕl-dô-rĕt') Ken.	00·31 N	35·18 E
90	El Ebano (ā-bä'nō) Mex.	22·13 N	98·26 W
72	Electra (ē-lĕk'trȧ) Tex.	34·02 N	98·54 W
67	Electric Pk. (ē-lĕk'trĭk) Mont.	45·03 N	110·52 W
136	Elektrogorsk (ĕl-yĕk'trô-gôrsk) Sov. Un. (Moscow In.)	55·53 N	38·48 E
136	Elektrostal (ĕl-yĕk'trô-stál) Sov. Un. (Moscow In.)	55·47 N	38·27 E
69	Elephant Butte Res. (ĕl'ē-fănt būt) . N. Mex.	33·25 N	107·10 W
125	El Escorial (ĕl-ĕs-kô-ryä'l) Sp. (Madrid In.)	40·38 N	4·08 W
92	El Espino (ĕl-ĕs-pē'nō) Nic.	13·26 N	86·48 W
95	Eleuthera (I.) (ē-lū'thēr-ȧ) Ba. Is.	25·05 N	76·10 W
95	Eleuthera Pt. Ba. Is.	24·35 N	76·05 W
73	Eleven Point (R.) (ē-lĕv'ĕn) . Mo.	36·53 N	91·39 W
165	El Fasher (fä'shēr) Sud.	13·38 N	25·21 E
124	El Ferrol (fä-rōl') Sp.	43·30 N	8·12 W
75	Elgin (ĕl'jĭn) Ill. (Chicago In.)	42·03 N	88·16 W
70	Elgin Nebr.	41·58 N	98·04 W
66	Elgin Ore.	45·34 N	117·58 W
116	Elgin Scot.	57·40 N	3·30 W
77	Elgin Tex.	30·21 N	97·22 W
65	Elgin Wash. (Seattle In.)	47·23 N	122·42 W
85	Elgin Mills (mĭls) Can. (Toronto In.)	43·54 N	79·26 W
164	El Goléa (gō-lā-ä') Alg.	30·39 N	2·52 E
165	Elgon, Mt. (ĕl'gŏn) Ken.	1·07 N	34·37 E
90	El Grullo (grōōl-yō) Mex.	19·46 N	104·10 W
99	El Guapo (gwà'pô) Ven. (In.)	10·07 N	66·00 W
114	El Hamada (Plat.) (häm'ȧ-dä) Alg.	30·53 N	1·52 W
164	El Hank (Bluffs) Mauritania-Mali	23·44 N	6·45 W
99	El Hatillo (ä-tē'l-yō) Ven. (In.)	10·08 N	65·13 W
85	Elie (ē'lē) Can. (Winnipeg In.)	49·55 N	97·45 W
166	Elila (R.) (ĕ-lē'là) Con. L.	3·38 S	27·48 E
65	Elisa (I.) (ē-lī'sȧ) Wash. (Vancouver In.)	48·43 N	122·37 W
166	Élisabethville Con. L.	11·41 S	27·32 E
119	Elisenvaara (ā-lē'sĕn-vä'rä) Sov. Un.	61·25 N	29·46 E
77	Elizabeth (ē-lĭz'ȧ-bĕth) La.	30·50 N	92·47 W
84	Elizabeth N. J. (New York In.)	40·40 N	74·13 W
75	Elizabeth Pa. (Pittsburgh In.)	40·16 N	79·53 W
79	Elizabeth City N. C.	36·15 N	76·15 W
79	Elizabethton (ē-lĭz-ȧ-bĕth'tŭn) Tenn.	36·19 N	82·12 W
80	Elizabethtown (ē-lĭz'ȧ-bĕth-toun) Ky.	37·40 N	85·55 W
164	El Jadida Mor.	33·14 N	8·34 W
121	Ełk (ĕłk) Pol.	53·53 N	22·23 E
78	Elk (R.) Tenn.	35·05 N	86·36 W
80	Elk (R.) W. Va.	38·30 N	81·05 W
165	El Kāmlin (kăm-lēn') Sud.	15·09 N	33·06 E
72	Elk City (ĕlk) Okla.	35·23 N	99·23 W
165	El Khandaq (kän-däk') Sud.	18·38 N	30·29 E
80	Elkhart (ĕlk'härt) Ind.	41·40 N	86·00 W
72	Elkhart Kans.	37·00 N	101·54 W
77	Elkhart Tex.	31·38 N	95·35 W
71	Elkhorn (ĕlk'hôrn) Wis.	42·39 N	88·32 W
70	Elkhorn (R.) Nebr.	42·06 N	97·46 W
79	Elkin (ĕl'kĭn) N. C.	36·15 N	80·50 W
81	Elkins (ĕl'kĭnz) W. Va.	38·55 N	79·50 W
86	Elk Island Natl. Park (ĕlk ī'lănd) Can.	53·21 N	115·47 W
66	Elko (ĕl'kō) Nev.	40·51 N	115·46 W
70	Elk Point S. D.	42·41 N	96·41 W
80	Elk Rapids (răp'ĭdz) Mich.	44·55 N	85·25 W
66	Elk River (rĭv'ẽr) Idaho	46·47 N	116·11 W
71	Elk River Minn.	45·17 N	93·33 W
78	Elkton (ĕlk'tŭn) Ky.	36·47 N	87·08 W
81	Elkton Md.	39·35 N	75·50 W
70	Elkton S. D.	44·15 N	96·28 W
168	El Lagodei Som. (Horn of Afr. In.)	9·20 N	49·09 E
110	Elland (el'ănd) Eng.	53·41 N	1·50 W
69	Ellen, Mt. (ĕl'ĕn) Utah	38·05 N	110·50 W
70	Ellendale (ĕl'ĕn-dāl) N. D.	46·01 N	98·33 W
66	Ellensburg (ĕl'ĕnz-bûrg) Wash.	47·00 N	120·31 W
81	Ellenville (ĕl'ĕn-vĭl) N. Y.	41·40 N	74·25 W
85	Ellerslie (ĕl'ẽrz-lē) Can. (Edmonton In.)	53·25 N	113·30 W
110	Ellesmere (ĕlz'mēr) Eng.	52·55 N	2·54 W
49	Ellesmere I. Can.	81·00 N	80·00 W
110	Ellesmere Port Eng.	53·17 N	2·54 W
156	Ellice Is. (ĕl'ĭs) Oceania	5·20 S	174·00 E
84	Ellicott City (ĕl'ĭ-kŏt sĭ'tē) Md. (Baltimore In.)	39·16 N	76·48 W
75	Ellicott Cr. N. Y. (Buffalo In.)	43·00 N	78·46 W
167	Elliotdale (ĕl-ĭ-ŏt'dāl) S. Afr. (Natal In.)	31·58 S	28·42 E
65	Elliott (el'ĭ-ŭt) . Wash. (Seattle In.)	47·28 N	122·08 W
72	Ellis (ĕl'ĭs) Kans.	38·56 N	99·34 W
78	Ellisville (ĕl'ĭs-vĭl) Miss.	31·37 N	89·10 W
74	Ellisville Mo. (St. Louis In.)	38·35 N	90·35 W
143	Ellore (ĕl-lōr') India	16·44 N	80·09 E
72	Ellsworth (ĕlz'wûrth) Kans.	38·43 N	98·14 W
82	Ellsworth Maine	44·33 N	68·26 W
47	Ellsworth Highland Ant.	77·00 S	90·00 W
120	Ellwangen (ĕl'văŋ-gĕn) Ger.	48·57 N	10·08 E
111	Elm (ĕlm) Ger. (Hamburg In.)	53·31 N	9·13 E
70	Elm (R.) S. D.	45·47 N	98·28 W
80	Elm (R.) W. Va.	38·30 N	81·05 W
66	Elma (ĕl'mȧ) Wash.	47·02 N	123·20 W
114	El Maadid Mor.	31·32 N	4·30 W
73	Elm Cr. Tex.	33·34 N	97·03 W
164	El Memrhar Mauritania	19·30 N	16·18 W
74	Elmendorf (ĕl'mĕn-dôrf) Tex. (San Antonio In.)	29·16 N	98·20 W
164	El Meréié (Des.) Mauritania	19·45 N	8·00 W
74	Elm Fork (ĕlm fôrk) Tex. (Dallas, Fort Worth In.)	32·55 N	96·56 W
75	Elmhurst (ĕlm'hûrst) Ill. (Chicago In.)	41·54 N	87·56 W
81	Elmira (ĕl-mī'rȧ) N. Y.	42·05 N	76·50 W
81	Elmira Heights N. Y.	42·10 N	76·50 W
98	El Misti (Vol.) (mē's-tē) Peru	16·04 S	71·20 W
74	El Modena (mô-dē'nô) Calif. (Los Angeles In.)	33·47 N	117·48 W
74	El Monte (mōn'tā) Calif. (Los Angeles In.)	34·04 N	118·02 W
69	El Morro Natl. Mon. N. Mex.	35·05 N	108·20 W
111	Elmshorn (ĕlms'hōrn) Ger. (Hamburg In.)	53·45 N	9·39 E
75	Elmwood Pl. (ĕlm'wŏŏd plās) Ohio (Cincinnati In.)	39·11 N	84·30 W
165	El Nahud (nä'hōōd) Sud.	12·39 N	28·18 E
165	El Obeid (ô-bād') Sud.	13·15 N	30·15 E
165	El Odaiya (ô-dī'yȧ) Sud.	12·06 N	28·16 E
65	Elokomin (R.) (ē-lō'kō-mĭn) Wash. (Portland In.)	46·16 N	123·16 W
90	El Oro (ô-rô) Mex.	19·49 N	100·04 W
164	El Oued (wĕd') Alg.	33·23 N	6·49 E
98	El Pao (ĕl pà'ô) Ven.	8·08 N	62·37 W
92	El Paraíso (pä-rä-ē'sō) Hond.	13·55 N	86·35 W
125	El Pardo (pä'r-dô) Sp. (Madrid In.)	40·31 N	3·47 W
76	El Paso (pas'ō) Tex.	31·47 N	106·27 W
99	El Pilar (pē-lä'r) Ven. (In.)	9·56 N	64·48 W
93	El Porvenir (pôr-vä-nēr') Pan.	9·34 N	78·55 W
124	El Puerto de Sta. María (pwĕr tō dā sän tä mä-rē'ä) . Sp.	36·36 N	6·18 W
93	El Real (rā-äl) Pan.	8·07 N	77·43 W
72	El Reno (rē'nō) Okla.	35·31 N	97·57 W
99	El Roboré (rô-bō-rĕ') Bol.	18·23 S	59·43 W
71	Elroy (ĕl'roi) Wis.	43·44 N	90·17 W
74	Elsah (ĕl'zȧ) Ill. (St. Louis In.)	38·57 N	90·22 W
90	El Salto (säl'tō) Mex.	22·48 N	105·22 E
88	El Salvador N. A.	14·00 N	89·30 W
92	El Sauce (ĕl-sà'ōō-sĕ) Nic.	13·00 N	86·40 W
73	Elsberry (ĕlz'bĕr-ĭ) Mo.	39·09 N	90·44 W
123	Elsdorf (ĕls'dōrf) . Ger. (Ruhr In.)	50·56 N	6·35 E
74	El Segundo (sĕgŭn'dō) Calif. (Los Angeles In.)	33·55 N	118·24 W
74	Elsinore (ĕl'sĭ-nôr) Calif. (Los Angeles In.)	33·40 N	117·19 W
74	Elsinore L. Calif. (Los Angeles In.)	33·38 N	117·21 W
111	Elstorf (ĕls'tōrf) Ger. (Hamburg In.)	53·25 N	9·48 E
165	El Sudd (Swp.) Sud.	8·45 N	30·45 E
161	Eltham (ĕl'thăm) Austl. (Melbourne In.)	37·43 S	145·08 E
98	El Tigre (tē'grĕ) Ven.	8·49 N	64·15 W
133	El'ton (L.) Sov. Un.	49·10 N	47·00 E
74	El Toro (tō'rō) Calif. (Los Angeles In.)	33·37 N	117·42 W
92	El Triunfo (ĕl-trē-ōō'n-fô) . Hond.	13·06 N	87·00 W
92	El Triunfo Sal.	13·17 N	88·32 W
69	El Vado Res. N. Mex.	36·37 N	106·30 W
124	Elvas (ĕl'vāzh) Port.	38·53 N	7·11 W
118	Elverum (ĕl'vĕ-rōōm) Nor.	60·53 N	11·33 E
92	El Viego (ĕl-vyĕ'kō) Nic.	12·44 N	87·03 W
92	El Viejo (Vol.) Nic.	12·44 N	87·03 W
73	Elvins (ĕl'vĭnz) Mo.	37·49 N	90·31 W
165	El Wak (wăk') Ken.	3·00 N	41·00 E
75	Elwood (ĕl'wŏŏd) Ill. (Chicago In.)	41·24 N	88·07 W
80	Elwood Ind.	40·15 N	85·50 W
117	Ely (ē'lĭ) Eng.	52·25 N	0·17 E
71	Ely Minn.	47·54 N	91·53 W
68	Ely Nev.	39·16 N	114·53 W
75	Elyria (ē-lĭr'ĭ-ȧ) Ohio (Cleveland In.)	41·22 N	82·07 W
119	Ema (R.) (â'mà) Sov. Un.	58·25 N	27·00 E
118	Emån (R.) Swe.	57·15 N	15·46 E
133	Emba (R.) (yĕm'bà) Sov. Un.	46·50 N	54·10 E
80	Embarrass (R.) (ĕm-băr'ăs) Ill.	39·15 N	88·05 W
85	Embrun (ĕm'brŭn) Can. (Ottawa In.)	45·16 N	75·17 W
123	Embrun (äN-brûN') Fr.	44·35 N	6·32 E
120	Emden (ĕm'dĕn) Ger.	53·21 N	7·15 E
159	Emerald (ĕm'ẽr-ăld) Austl.	28·34 S	148·00 E
86	Emerson (ĕm'ẽr-sŭn) Can.	49·00 N	97·18 W
65	Emeryville (ĕm'ẽr-ĭ-vĭl) Calif. (San Francisco In.)	37·50 N	122·17 W
165	Emi Koussi (Mtn.) (ā'mē kōō-sē') Chad	19·50 N	18·30 E
126	Emilia (Reg.) (ā-mēl'yä) It.	44·35 N	10·48 E
91	Emiliano Zapata (ĕ-mē-lyà'nô-zä-pà'tà) . Mex.	17·45 N	91·46 W
80	Eminence (ĕm'ĭ-nĕns) Ky.	38·25 N	85·15 W
155	Emirau (I.) (ā-mē-rä'ōō) N. Gui. Ter.	1·40 S	150·28 E
117	Emmen (ĕm'ĕn) Neth.	52·48 N	6·55 E
123	Emmerich (ĕm'ẽr-ĭk) Ger. (Ruhr In.)	51·51 N	6·16 E
71	Emmetsburg (ĕm'ĕts-bûrg) Ia.	43·07 N	94·41 W
66	Emmett (ĕm'ĕt) Idaho	43·53 N	116·30 W
67	Emmons Mt. (ĕm'ŭnz) Utah	40·43 N	110·20 W
76	Emory Pk. (ĕ'mō-rē pēk) Tex.	29·13 N	103·20 W
84	Empire (ĕm'pīr) La. (New Orleans In.)	29·24 N	89·37 W
126	Empoli (ām'pô-lē) It.	43·43 N	10·55 E
73	Emporia (ĕm-pō'rĭ-ȧ) Kans.	38·24 N	96·11 W
79	Emporia Va.	37·40 N	77·34 W
81	Emporium (ĕm-pō'rĭ-ŭm) Pa.	41·30 N	78·15 W
	Empty Quarter, see Ar Al Khālī		
120	Ems R. (ĕms) Ger.	52·52 N	7·16 E
120	Ems-Weser (can.) (vä'zĕr) Ger.	52·23 N	8·11 E

Page	Name Pronunciation Region	Lat. °'	Long. °'
118	Enånger (ĕn-ôŋ'gĕr) Swe.	61·36 N	16·55 E
88	Encantada, Cerro de la (Mtn.) (sĕ'r-rô-dĕ-lä-ĕn-kän-tä'dä) Mex.	31·58 N	115·15 W
155	Encanto Pt. (ĕn-kän'tō) Phil. (Manila In.)	15·44 N	121·46 E
100	Encarnación (ĕn-kär-nä-syōn') Par.	27·26 S	55·52 W
90	Encarnación de Diaz (ĕn-kär-nä-syōn dä dē'äz) Mex.	21·34 N	102·15 W
76	Encinal (ĕn'sĭ-nôl) Tex.	28·02 N	99·22 W
98	Encontrados (ĕn-kōn-trä'dōs) Ven.	9·01 N	72·10 W
160	Encounter B. (ĕn-koun'tēr) Austl.	35·50 S	138·45 E
139	Endau Mala. (Singapore In.)	2·39 N	103·38 E
139	Endau (R.) Mala. (Singapore In.)	2·29 N	103·40 E
47	Enderby Land (Reg.) (ĕn'dĕr bĭ) Ant.	72·00 S	52·00 E
70	Enderlin (ĕn'dĕr-lĭn) N. D.	46·38 N	97·37 W
81	Endicott (ĕn'dĭ-kŏt) N. Y.	42·05 N	76·00 W
64	Endicott Mts. Alaska	67·30 N	153·45 W
127	Enez Tur.	40·42 N	26·05 E
81	Enfield (ĕn'fēld) Conn.	41·55 N	72·35 W
110	Enfield Eng. (London In.)	51·38 N	0·06 W
79	Enfield N. C.	36·10 N	77·41 W
95	Engano, Cabo (C.) (kä'-bô-ĕn-gä-nô) Dom. Rep.	18·40 N	68·30 W
154	Engaño, C. (ĕn-gän'yō) Phil.	18·40 N	122·45 E
165	Engare Vaso Nyiro R. (ĕn-gä'rä wä'sô nyē'rô) Ken.	0·59 N	37·47 E
167	Engcobo (ĕŋg-cô-bô) S. Afr. (Natal In.)	31·41 S	27·59 E
133	Engel's (ĕn'gĕls) Sov. Un.	51·20 N	45·40 E
123	Engelskirchen (ĕn'gĕls-kēr'kĕn) Ger. (Ruhr In.)	50·59 N	7·25 E
72	Engelwood (ĕn'g'l-wŏŏd) Colo.	39·39 N	105·00 W
154	Enggano (ĕng-gä'nō) Indon.	5·22 S	102·18 E
73	England (ĭŋ'glănd) Ark.	34·33 N	91·58 W
116	England (Reg.) (ĭŋ'glănd) U. K.	51·35 N	1·40 W
83	Englee (ĕn-glē) Can.	50·46 N	56·07 W
80	English (ĭn'glĭsh) Ind.	38·15 N	86·25 W
87	English (R.) Can.	50·31 N	94·12 W
113	English Chan. Eng.	49·45 N	3·06 W
125	Enguera (ān'gārä) Sp.	38·58 N	0·42 W
72	Enid (ē'nĭd) Okla.	36·25 N	97.52 W
78	Enid Res. Miss.	34·13 N	89·47 W
166	Enkeldoorn (ĕŋ'k'l-dōōrn) S. Rh.	19·59 S	30·58 E
168	Enkeldoring (ĕŋ'k'l-dôr-ĭng) S. Afr. (Johannesburg & Pretoria In.)	25·24 S	28·43 E
118	Enköping (ĕn'kû-pĭng) Swe.	59·39 N	17·05 E
165	Ennedi Plat. (ĕn-nĕd'ē) Chad.	17·15 N	22·45 E
116	Ennis (ĕn'ĭs) Ire.	52·54 N	9.05 W
77	Ennis Tex.	32·20 N	96·38 W
116	Enniscorthy (ĕn-ĭs-kôr'thĭ) Ire.	52·33 N	6·27 W
116	Enniskillen (ĕn-ĭs-kĭl'ĕn) N. Ire.	54·20 N	7·25 W
120	Enns R. (ĕns) Aus.	47·37 N	14·35 E
79	Enoree (ē-nō'rē) S. C.	34·43 N	81·58 W
79	Enoree, (R.) S. C.	34·35 N	81·55 W
95	Enriquillo (ĕn-rē-kē'l-yô) Dom. Rep.	17·55 N	71·15 W
95	Enriquillo, Lago (L.) (lä'gô-ĕn-rē-kē'l-yô) Dom. Rep.	18·35 N	71·35 W
117	Enschede (ĕns'kä-dĕ) Neth.	52·10 N	6·50 E
88	Ensenada (ĕn-sĕ-nä'dä) Mex.	32·00 N	116·30 W
101	Ensenada Arg. (Buenos Aires In.)	34·50 S	57·55 W
151	Enshih China	30·18 N	109·25 E
153	Enshū-Nada (Sea) (ĕn'shōō nä-dä) Jap.	34·25 N	137·14 E
165	Entebbe (ĕn-tĕb'ĕ) Ug.	0·01 N	32·29 E
78	Enterprise (ĕn'tēr-prīz) Ala.	31·20 N	85·50 W
66	Enterprise Ore.	45·25 N	117·16 W
66	Entiat, L. Wash.	45·43 N	120·11 W
122	Entraygues (ĕn-trĕg') Fr.	44·39 N	2·33 E
100	Entre Ríos (Prov.) (ĕn-trā rē'ōs) Arg.	31·30 S	59·00 W
164	Enugu (ĕ-nōō'gōō) Nig.	6·13 N	7·18 E
65	Enumclaw (ĕn'ŭm-klô) Wash. (Seattle In.)	47·12 N	121·59 W
98	Envigado (ĕn-vē-gä'dô) Col. (In.)	6·10 N	75·34 W
126	Eolie, Isole (Is.) (ē'sō-lĕ-ĕ-ô'lyĕ) It.	38·43 N	14·43 E
127	Epeirus (Reg.) Grc.	39·35 N	20·45 E
122	Epernay (ā-pĕr-nĕ') Fr.	49·02 N	3·54 E
123	Épernon (ā-pĕr-nôn') Fr. (Paris In.)	48·36 N	1·41 E
69	Ephraim (ē'frā-ĭm) Utah	39·20 N	111·40 W
66	Ephrata (ē frā'tȧ) Wash.	47·18 N	119·35 W
159	Epi (ā'pē) New Hebr.	16·59 S	168·29 E
124	Épila (ā'pē-lä) Sp.	41·38 N	1·15 W
123	Épinal (ā-pē-nál') Fr.	48·11 N	6·27 E
139	Episkopi B. Cyprus (Palestine In.)	34·34 N	32·41 E
110	Epping (ĕp'ĭng) Eng. (London In.)	51·41 N	0·06 E
166	Epping S. Afr. (Cape Town In.)	33·56 S	18·35 E
110	Epworth (ĕp'wûrth) Eng.	53·31 N	0·50 W
122	Equeurdreville (ā-kûr-dr'vēl') Fr.	49·38 N	1·42 W
85	Eramosa R. (ĕr-ȧ-mō'sȧ) Can. (Toronto In.)	43·39 N	80·08 W
165	Erba (Mt.) (ĕr'bȧ) Sud.	20·53 N	36·45 E
115	Erciyas (Mtn.) Tur.	38·30 N	35·36 E
74	Erda (ĕr'dä) Utah (Salt Lake City In.)	40·41 N	112·17 W
111	Erding (ĕr'dēng) Ger. (Munich In.)	48·19 N	11·54 E
100	Erechim (ĕ-rĕ-shē'n) Braz.	27·43 S	52·11 W
133	Ereğli (ĕ-rā'ĭ-le) Tur.	37·40 N	34·00 E
133	Ereğli Tur.	41·15 N	31·25 E
120	Erfurt (ĕr'fōōrt) Ger.	50·59 N	11·04 E
127	Ergene (R.) (ĕr'gĕ-nĕ) Tur.	41·17 N	26·50 E
124	Erges (R.) (ĕr'-zhĕs) Port. Sp.	39·45 N	7·01 W
148	Erhlangtien (ĕ'läng'diän) China	31·33 N	114·07 E
124	Eria (R.) (ā-rē'ä) Sp.	42·10 N	6·08 W
72	Erick (âr'ĭk) Okla.	35·14 N	99·51 W
73	Erie (ē'rĭ) Kans.	37·35 N	95·17 W
81	Erie Pa.	42·05 N	80·05 W
63	Erie, L. U. S.-Can.	42·15 N	81·25 W
152	Erimo Saki (C.) (ā'rē-mō sä-kē) Jap.	41·53 N	143·20 E
85	Erin (ĕ'rĭn) Can. (Toronto In.)	43·46 N	80·04 W
165	Eritrea (Reg.) (ā-rē-trā'á) Eth.	16·15 N	38·30 E
120	Erlangen (ĕr'läng-ĕn) Ger.	49·36 N	11·03 E
75	Erlanger (ēr'läng-ēr) Ky. (Cincinnati In.)	39·01 N	84·36 W
	Ermoúpolis, see Síros		
143	Ernakulam India	9·58 N	76·23 E
116	Erne, Upper, Lough (B.) (lŏk ûrn) N. Ire.	54·20 N	7·24 W
116	Erne, Lough (B.) N. Ire.	54·30 N	7·40 W
159	Eromanga (I.) New Hebr.	18·58 S	169·18 E
77	Eros (ē'rōs) La.	32·23 N	92·22 W
165	Er Renk (ĕr rĕnk') Sud.	11·45 N	32·53 E
114	Er Ricani Mor.	31·09 N	4·20 W
116	Errigal, Mt. (ĕr-ĭ-gôl') Ire.	54·60 N	8·13 W
165	Er Roseires (rô-sä'rĕs) Sud.	11·38 N	34·42 E
123	Erstein (ĕr'shtīn) Fr.	48·27 N	7·40 E
79	Erwin (ûr'wĭn) N. C.	35·16 N	78·40 W
79	Erwin Tenn.	36·07 N	82·25 W
120	Erzgebirge (Ore Mts.) (ĕrts'gĕ-bē'gĕ) Ger.	50·29 N	12·40 E
133	Erzincan (ĕr-zĭn-jän') Tur.	39·50 N	39·30 E
133	Erzurum (ĕrz'rōōm') Tur.	39·55 N	41·10 E
152	Esashi (ĕs'ä-shē) Jap.	41·50 N	140·10 E
118	Esbjerg (ĕs'byĕrgh) Den.	55·29 N	8·25 E
119	Esbo (ĕs'bô) Fin.	60·13 N	24·41 E
124	Escairón (ĕs-kī-rô'n) Sp.	42·34 N	7.40 W
69	Escalante (ĕs-kȧ-lăn'tē) Utah	37·50 N	111·40 W
69	Escalante (R.) Utah	37·40 N	111·20 W
78	Escambia (R.) (ĕs-kăm'bĭ-ȧ) Fla.	30·38 N	87·20 W
71	Escanaba (ĕs-kȧ-nô'bȧ) Mich.	45·44 N	87·05 W
71	Escanaba (R.) Mich.	46·10 N	87·22 W
123	Esch-sur-Alzette Lux.	49·32 N	6·21 E
120	Eschwege (ĕsh'vā-gē) Ger.	51·11 N	10·02 E
123	Eschweiler (ĕsh'vī-lēr) Ger. (Ruhr In.)	50·49 N	6·15 E
95	Escocesá, Bahia (B.) (bä-ē'ä-ĕs-kō-sĕ'sä) Dom. Rep.	19·25 N	69·40 W
68	Escondido (ĕs-kŏn-dē'dō) Calif.	33·07 N	117·07 W
76	Escondido, Rio (R.) (rê'ō-ĕs-kōn-dĕ'dô) Mex.	28·30 N	100·45 W
93	Escondido R. Nic.	12·04 N	84·09 W
93	Escudo de Veraguas I. (ĕs-kōō'dä dä vä-rä'gwäs) Pan.	9·07 N	81·25 W
90	Escuinapa (ĕs-kwē-nä'pä) Mex.	22·49 N	105·44 W
92	Escuintla (ĕs-kwēn'tlä) Guat.	14·16 N	90·47 W
91	Escuintla Mex.	15·20 N	92·45 W
93	Ese, Cayos de (I.) Col.	12·24 N	81·07 W
164	Eséka (ĕ-sā'kä) Cam.	3·40 N	11·08 E
144	Esfahān Iran	32·38 N	51·30 E
124	Esgueva (R.) (ĕs-gĕ'vä) Sp.	41·48 N	4·10 W
167	Eshowe (ĕsh'ô-wē) S. Afr. (Natal In.)	28·54 S	31·28 E
80	Eskdale (ĕsk'dāl) W. Va.	38·05 N	81·25 W
112	Eskifjördhur (ĕs'kē-fyûr'dōōr) Ice.	65·04 N	14·01 W
118	Eskilstuna (å'shĕl-stü-na) Swe.	59·23 N	16·28 E
86	Eskimo L. (es'kĭ-mō) Can.	69·29 N	129·57 W
133	Eskişehir (ĕs-kē-shĕ'h'r) Tur.	39·40 N	30·20 E
74	Esko (ĕs'kô) Minn. (Duluth In.)	46·27 N	92·22 W
124	Esla (R.) (ĕs-lä) Sp.	41·50 N	5·48 W
118	Eslöv (ĕs'lûv) Swe.	55·50 N	13·17 E
98	Esmeraldas (ĕs-mȧ-räl'däs) Ec.	0·58 N	79·45 W
95	Espada, Punta (Pt.) (pōō'n-tä-ĕs-pä'dä) Dom. Rep.	18·30 N	68·30 W
87	Espanola (ĕs-pȧ-nō'lȧ) Can.	46·11 N	81·59 W
93	Esparta (ĕs-pär'tä) C. R.	9·59 N	84·40 W
158	Esperance (ĕs'pē-rȧns) Austl.	33·45 S	122·07 E
94	Esperenza (ĕs-pĕ-rä'n-zä) Cuba	22·30 N	80·10 W
125	Espichel, Cabo (C.) (kä'bō-ĕs-pē-shĕl') Port. (Lisbon In.)	38·25 N	9·13 W
98	Espinal (ĕs-pē-näl') Col. (In.)	4·10 N	74·53 W
99	Espinhaço, Serra do (Mts.) (sĕ'r-rä-dô-ĕs-pē-nä-sô) Braz.	16·06 S	44·56 W
101	Espinillo, Punta (Pt.) (pōō'n-tä-ĕs-pē-nē'l-yô) Ur. (Buenos Aires In.)	34·49 S	56·27 W
99	Espirito Santo (ĕs-pē'rē-tô-sän'tô) Braz.	20·27 S	40·18 W
99	Espírito Santo (State) Braz.	19·57 S	40·58 W
92	Espíritu Santo, Bahia del (B.) (bä-ē'ä-dĕl-ĕs-pē'rē-tōō-sän'tô) Mex. (Yucatan In.)	19·25 N	87·28 W
159	Espiritu Santo (I.) (ĕs-pē'rē-tōō sän'tō) New Hebr.	15·45 S	166·50 E
92	Espita (ĕs-pē'tä) Mex. (Yucatan In.)	20·57 N	88·22 W
124	Esposende (ĕs-pō-zĕn'dä) Port.	41·33 N	8·45 W
100	Esquel (ĕs-kĕ'l) Arg.	42·47 S	71·22 W
65	Esquimalt (ĕs-kwī'mŏlt) Can. (Seattle In.)	48·26 N	123·25 W
164	Essaouira Mor.	31·34 N	9·44 W
111	Essen Bel. (Brussels In.)	51·28 N	4·27 E
123	Essen (ĕs'sĕn) Ger. (Ruhr In.)	51·26 N	6·59 E
99	Essequibo (R.) (ĕs-ä-kē'bō) Br. Gu.	4·26 N	58·17 W
75	Essex (ĕs'ĕks) Can. (Detroit In.)	42·10 N	82·50 W
75	Essex Ill. (Chicago In.)	41·11 N	88·11 W
84	Essex Md. (Baltimore In.)	39·19 N	76·29 W
83	Essex Mass. (Boston In.)	42·38 N	70·47 W
81	Essex Vt.	44·30 N	73·05 W
84	Essex Fells (ĕs'ĕks fĕlz) N. J. (New York In.)	40·50 N	74·16 W
80	Essexville (ĕs'ĕks-vĭl) Mich.	43·35 N	83·50 W
120	Esslingen (ĕs'slĕn-gĕn) Ger.	48·45 N	9·19 E
62	Estacado, Llano (Plain) (yä-nō ĕs-tȧ-cȧ-dō') U. S.	33·50 N	103·20 W
100	Estados, Isla de los S. A.	55·05 S	63·00 W
99	Estância (ĕs-tän'sĭ-ä) Braz.	11·17 S	37·18 W
124	Estarreja (ĕs-tär-rā'zhä) Port.	40·44 N	8·39 W
167	Estcourt (ĕst-coort) S. Afr. (Natal In.)	29·04 S	29·53 E
126	Este (ĕs'tā) It.	45·13 N	11·40 E
92	Estelí (ĕs-tä-lē') Nic.	13·10 N	86·23 W
124	Estella (ĕs-tāl'yä) Sp.	42·40 N	2·01 W
124	Estepa (ĕs-tā'pä) Sp.	37·18 N	4·54 W
124	Estepona (ĕs-tå-pō'nä) Sp.	36·26 N	5·08 W
68	Esteros, B. (ĕs-tā'rōs) Calif.	35·22 N	121·04 W
86	Estevan (ĕ-stē'vȧn) Can.	49·11 N	102·57 W
71	Estherville (ĕs'tēr-vĭl) Iowa	43·24 N	94·49 W
79	Estill (ĕs'tĭl) S. C.	32·46 N	81 15 W
130	Estonian S. S. R. (ĕs-tō'nĭ-ä) Sov. Un.	59·10 N	25·00 E
125	Estoril (ĕs-tô-rēl') Port. (Lisbon In.)	38·45 N	9·24 W
100	Estrêla (R.) (ĕs-trĕ'lȧ) Braz. (In.)	22·39 S	43·16 W
124	Estrêla, Serra da (Mts.) (sĕr'rȧ dȧ ĕs-trā'lȧ) Port.	40·25 N	7·45 W
124	Estremadura (Reg.) (ĕs-trā-mä-dōō'rȧ) Port.	41·35 N	8·36 W
124	Estremoz (ĕs-trā-mōzh') Port.	38·50 N	7·35 W
99	Estrondo, Serra do (Mts.) (sĕr'rȧ dōō ĕs-trôn'dōō) Braz.	9·52 S	48·56 W
121	Esztergom (ĕs'tēr-gōm) Hung.	47·46 N	18·45 E
49	Etah (ē'tȧ) Grnld.	78·20 N	72·42 W
123	Étampes (ā-tänp') Fr. (Paris In.)	48·26 N	2·09 E
122	Étaples (ā-täp'l') Fr.	50·32 N	1·38 E
85	Etchemin, R. (ĕch'ĕ-mĭn) Can. (Quebec In.)	46·39 N	71·03 W
163	Ethiopia (ē-thē-ō'pē-ȧ) Afr.	7·53 N	37·55 E
74	Etiwanda (ĕ-tĭ-wän'dȧ) Calif. (Los Angeles In.)	34·07 N	117·31 W
	Etlatongo, see San Mateo		
75	Etna (ĕt'nȧ) Pa. (Pittsburgh In.)	40·30 N	79·55 W
126	Etna, Mt. (Vol.) It.	37·48 N	15·00 E
85	Etobicoke Cr. Can. (Toronto In.)	43·44 N	79·48 W
64	Etolin Str. (ĕt ō lĭn) Alaska	60·35 S	165·40 W
166	Etosha Pan (ĕtō'shä) S. W. Afr.	19·07 S	15·30 E
78	Etowah (ĕt'ô-wä) Tenn.	35·18 N	84·31 W
78	Etowah (R.) Ga.	34·23 N	84·19 W
123	Étréchy (ā-trā-shē') Fr. (Paris In.)	48·29 N	2·12 E
111	Etten Neth. (Amsterdam In.)	51·34 N	4·38 E
111	Etterbeek (ĕt'ĕr-bāk) Bel. (Brussels In.)	50·51 N	4·24 E
90	Etzatlán (ĕt-zä-tlän') Mex.	20·44 N	104·04 W
158	Eucla (ū'klȧ) Austl.	31·45 S	128·50 E
75	Euclid (ū'klĭd) Ohio (Cleveland In.)	41·34 N	81·32 W
73	Eudora (u-dō'rȧ) Ark.	33·07 N	91·16 W
78	Eufaula (û-fô'lȧ) Ala.	31·53 N	85·09 W
73	Eufaula Okla.	35·16 N	95·35 W
66	Eugene (û-jēn') Ore.	44·02 N	123·06 W
74	Euless (ū'lĕs) Tex. (Dallas, Fort Worth In.)	32·50 N	97·05 W
77	Eunice (ū'nĭs) La.	30·30 N	92·25 W
117	Eupen (oi'pĕn) Bel.	50·39 N	6·05 E
144	Euphrates, R. (û-frā'tēz) Asia	35·52 N	39·53 E
122	Eure (R.) (ûr) Fr.	49·03 N	1·22 E
66	Eureka (û-rē'kȧ) Calif.	40·45 N	124·10 W
73	Eureka Kans.	37·48 N	96·17 W
66	Eureka Mont.	48·53 N	115·07 W
68	Eureka Nev.	39·33 N	115·58 W
70	Eureka S. D.	45·46 N	99·38 W
69	Eureka Utah	39·55 N	112·10 W
73	Eureka Springs Ark.	36·24 N	93·43 W
144	Eurgun (Mtn.) Iran	28·47 N	57·00 E
7	Europe (ū'rŭp)		
79	Eustis (ūs'tĭs) Fla.	28·50 N	81·41 W
78	Eutaw (ū-tȧ) Ala.	32·48 N	87·50 W
118	Evanger (ĕ-väŋ'gĕr) Nor.	60·40 N	6·06 E
75	Evanston (ĕv'ănz-tūn) Ill. (Chicago In.)	42·03 N	87·41 W
67	Evanston Wyo.	41·17 N	111·02 W
80	Evansville (ĕv'ănz-vĭl) Ind.	38·00 N	87·30 W
71	Evansville Wis.	42·46 N	89·19 W
80	Evart (ĕv'ĕrt) Mich.	43·55 N	85·10 W
168	Evaton (ĕv'ȧ-tŏn) S. Afr. (Johannesburg & Pretoria In.)	26·32 S	27·53 E
71	Eveleth (ĕv'ē-lĕth) Minn.	47·27 N	92·35 W
158	Everard (L.) (ĕv'ēr-ărd) Austl.	36·20 S	134·10 E
158	Everard Ra. Austl.	27·15 S	132·00 E
142	Everest, Mt. (ĕv'ēr-ĕst) Nep.-China	32·58 N	86·57 E
83	Everett (ĕv'ēr-ĕt) Mass. (Boston In.)	42·24 N	71·03 W
65	Everett (ĕv'ēr-ĕt) Wash. (Seattle In.)	47·59 N	122·11 W
87	Everett Mts. Can.	62·34 N	68·00 W
79	Everglades (ĕv'ēr-glădz) Fla. (In.)	25·50 N	81·25 W
94	Everglades, The (Swp.) Fla.	25·35 N	80·55 W
79	Everglades Natl. Park Fla. (In.)	25·39 N	80·57 W
78	Evergreen (ĕv'ēr-grēn) Ala.	31·25 N	87·56 W
75	Evergreen Park Ill. (Chicago In.)	41·44 N	87·42 W
74	Everman (ĕv'ēr-măn) Tex. (Dallas, Fort Worth In.)	32·38 N	97·17 W
65	Everson (ĕv'ēr-sŭn) Wash. (Vancouver In.)	48·55 N	122·21 W
124	Évora (ĕv'ô-rä) Port.	38·35 N	7·54 W
122	Évreux (ā-vrû') Fr.	49·02 N	1·11 E
127	Evrotas (R.) (ĕv-rō'tàs) Grc.	37·15 N	22·17 E
127	Evvoia (Pen.) Grc.	38·38 N	23·45 E
157	Ewa (ē'wä) Hawaii (In.)	21·17 N	158·03 E
155	Ewab, Palau-Palan Is. Indon.	5·55 S	131·30 E
74	Excelsior (ĕk-sel'sĭ-ŏr) Minn. (Minneapolis, St. Paul In.)	44·54 N	93·35 W
73	Excelsior Springs Mo.	39·20 N	94·13 W
116	Exe (R.) (ĕks) Eng.	50·57 N	3·37 W
68	Exeter (ĕk'sē-tēr) Calif.	36·18 N	119·09 W
116	Exeter Eng.	50·45 N	3·33 W
81	Exeter N. H.	43·00 N	71·00 W
116	Exmoor (ĕks'mōōr) Eng.	51·10 N	3·55 W
116	Exmouth (ĕks'mŭth) Eng.	50·40 N	3·20 W
158	Exmouth, G. Austl.	21·45 S	114·30 E
83	Exploits (R.) (ĕks-ploits') Can.	48·50 N	56·15 W
90	Extórrax (R.) (ĕx-tō'ráx) Mex.	21·04 N	99·39 W
101	Extrema (ĕsh-trĕ'mä) Braz. (Rio de Janeiro In.)	22·52 S	46·19 W

ăt; finăl; rāte; senåte; ärm; åsk; sofȧ; fâre; ch-choose; dh-as th in other; bē; ēvent; bĕt; recĕnt; cratēr; g-go; gh-guttural g; bĭt; ĭ-short neutral; rīde; K-guttural k as ch in German ich;

206 Findlay–Fort Portal PRONOUNCING INDEX

Page	Name Pronunciation Region	Lat. °′	Long. °′
80	Findlay (fĭnd'lȧ) Ohio	41·05 N	83·40 W
124	Finisterre, Cabo de (C.) (kä'bô-dĕ-fĭn-ĭs-târ'). Sp.	42·52 N	9·48 W
158	Finke (R.) (fĭŋ'kĕ) Austl.	25·25 S	134·30 E
102	Finland (fĭn'lănd) Eur.	62·45 N	26·13 E
119	Finland, G. of (fĭn'lănd) Eur.	59·35 N	23·35 E
98	Finlandia (fēn-lä'n-dēä). Col. (In.)	4·38 N	75·39 W
86	Finlay (R.) (fĭn'lā) Can.	56·57 N	124·40 W
111	Finofurt (fē'nō-fōōrt) Ger. (Berlin In.)	52·50 N	13·41 E
111	Finow (fē'nōv). Ger. (Berlin In.)	52·50 N	13·44 E
120	Finsterwalde (fĭn'stēr-väl-dĕ). Ger.	51·38 N	13·42 E
133	Firat (R.) (fē-rät') Tur.	39·40 N	38·30 E
65	Fircrest (fûr'krĕst) Wash. (Seattle In.)	47·14 N	122·31 W
126	Firenze (Florence) (fē-rĕnt'sä). It.	43·47 N	11·15 E
126	Firenzuola (fē-rĕnt-swô'lä) It.	44·08 N	11·21 E
165	First Cataract U. A. R.	24·00 N	32·52 E
111	Fischa (R.) Aus. (Vienna In.)	48·04 N	16·33 E
111	Fischamend Markt Aus. (Vienna In.)	48·07 N	16·37 E
95	Fish Cay (I.) Ba. Is.	22·30 N	74·20 W
85	Fish Cr. (fĭsh). Can. (Calgary In.)	50·52 N	114·21 W
77	Fisher (fĭsh'ēr) La.	31·28 N	93·30 W
87	Fisher Str. Can.	62·43 N	84·28 W
166	Fish Hoek (fĭsh'hōōk) S. Afr. (Cape Town In.)	34·13 S	18·26 E
83	Fitchburg (fĭch'bûrg) Mass. (Boston In.)	42·35 N	71·48 W
78	Fitzgerald (fĭts-jĕr'ăld) Ga.	31·42 N	83·17 W
158	Fitzroy (R.) (fĭts-roi') Austl.	18·00 S	124·05 E
159	Fitzroy (R.) Austl.	23·45 S	150·02 E
158	Fitzroy Crossing Austl.	18·08 S	126·00 E
80	Fitzwilliam (I.) (fĭts-wĭl'yŭm) Can.	45·30 N	81·45 W
	Fiume, see Rijeka		
125	Fiumicino (fyōō-mē-chē'nō) It. (Rome In.)	41·47 N	12·19 E
118	Fjällbacka (fyĕl'băk-ȧ) Swe.	58·37 N	11·17 E
118	Flaam (flôm) Nor.	60·51 N	7·01 E
69	Flagstaff (flăg-stȧf) Ariz.	35·15 N	111·40 W
167	Flagstaff (flăg'stäf) S. Afr. (Natal In.)	31·06 S	29·31 E
81	Flagstaff (L.) (flăg-stȧf) Maine	45·05 N	70·30 W
111	Flalow (flä'lōv). Ger. (Berlin In.)	52·44 N	12·58 E
71	Flambeau (R.) (flăm-bō') Wis.	45·32 N	91·05 W
67	Flaming Gorge Res. Wyo.	41·13 N	109·30 W
79	Flamingo (flȧ-mĭŋ'gō) Fla.	25·10 N	80·55 W
95	Flamingo Cay (I.) (flȧ-mĭŋ'gō) Ba. Is.	22·50 N	75·50 W
89	Flamingo Pt. Vir. Is. (U. S. A.) (St. Thomas In.)	18·19 N	65·00 W
117	Flanders (Reg.) Fr.	50·53 N	2·29 E
70	Flandreau (flăn'drō) S. D.	44·02 N	96·35 W
116	Flannan (Is.) (flăn'ăn) Scot.	58·13 N	8·14 W
67	Flathead L. (flăt'hĕd) Mont.	47·57 N	114·20 W
67	Flathead Ra. Mont.	47·50 N	113·40 W
67	Flathead R. Mont.	48·45 N	114·20 W
67	Flathead R., Middle Fork Mont.	48·30 N	113·47 W
67	Flathead R., South Fork Mont.	48·05 N	113·45 W
75	Flat Rock (flăt rŏk) Mich. (Detroit In.)	42·06 N	83·17 W
66	Flattery C. (flăt'ēr-ĭ) Wash.	48·22 N	125·10 W
67	Flat Willow Cr. (flat wĭl'ō). Mont.	46·45 N	108·47 W
118	Flekkefjord (flĕk'kē-fyôr) Nor.	58·19 N	6·38 E
80	Flemingsburg (flĕm'ĭngz-bûrg) Ky.	38·25 N	83·45 W
120	Flensburg (flĕns'bōōrgh) Ger.	54·48 N	9·27 E
122	Flers-del-l'Orne (flĕr-dĕ-lôrn'). Fr.	48·43 N	0·37 W
158	Flinders (Reg.) (flĭn'dērz) Austl.	32·15 S	138·45 E
160	Flinders (I.) Austl.	39·35 S	148·10 E
159	Flinders (R.) Austl.	18·48 S	141·07 E
160	Flinders Ra. Austl.	34·09 S	138·56 E
159	Flinders Rfs. Austl.	17·30 S	149·02 E
86	Flin Flon Can.	54·50 N	101·52 W
110	Flint Wales	53·15 N	3·07 W
80	Flint Mich.	43·00 N	83·45 W
110	Flint (Co.) Wales	53·13 N	3·06 W
78	Flint (R.) (flĭnt) Ga.	31·25 N	84·15 W
118	Flisen (flē'sĕn) Nor.	60·35 N	12·03 E
80	Flora (flō'rȧ) Ill.	38·40 N	88·25 W
80	Flora Ind.	40·25 N	86·30 W
78	Florala (flŏr-ăl'ȧ) Ala.	31·01 N	86·19 W
84	Floral Park (flôr'ăl pärk) N. Y. (New York In.)	40·42 N	73·42 W
78	Florence (flŏr'ĕns) Ala.	34·46 N	87·40 W
69	Florence Ariz.	33·00 N	111·25 W
72	Florence Colo.	38·23 N	105·08 W
73	Florence Kans.	38·14 N	96·56 W
79	Florence S. C.	34·10 N	79·45 W
65	Florence Wash. (Seattle In.)	48·13 N	122·21 W
	Florence, see Firenze		
98	Florencia (flō-rĕn'sē-ȧ) Col.	1·31 N	75·13 W
101	Florencio Sánchez (flō-rĕn-sēō-sä'n-chĕz). Ur. (Buenos Aires In.)	33.52 S	57·24 W
100	Florencio Varela (flō-rĕn'sē-o vä-rā'lä). Arg. (In.)	34·34 S	58·16 W
99	Flores (flō'rĕzh) Braz.	7·57 S	37·48 W
92	Flores Guat. (Yucatan In.)	16·53 N	89·54 W
101	Flores (Dept.) Ur. (Buenos Aires In.)	33·33 S	57·00 W
154	Flores (I.) Indon.	8·14 S	121·08 E
101	Flores (R.) Arg. (Buenos Aires In.)	36·13 S	60·28 W
154	Flores Sea Indon.	7·09 N	120·30 E
76	Floresville (flō'rĕs-vĭl) Tex.	29·10 N	98·08 W
99	Floriano (flō-rē-ä'nōō) Braz.	6·17 S	42·58 W
100	Florianópolis (flō-rē-ä-nō'pō-lēs) Braz.	27·30 S	48·30 W
98	Florida (flō-rē'-dä) Col. (In.)	3·20 N	76·12 W
94	Florida Cuba	22·10 N	79·50 W
84	Florida (flŏr'ĭ-dȧ) N. Y. (New York In.)	41·20 N	74·21 W
167	Florida S. Afr. (Johannesburg & Pretoria In.)	26·11 S	27·56 E
101	Florida (flō-rē-dhä) Ur. (Buenos Aires In.)	34·06 S	56·14 W
63	Florida (State) (flŏr'ĭ-dȧ) U. S.	30·30 N	84·40 W
101	Florida (Dept.) (flō-rē'dhä) Ur. (Buenos Aires In.)	33·48 S	56·15 W
159	Florida (I.) Sol. Is.	8·56 S	159·45 E
94	Florida, Strs. of N. A.	24·10 N	81·00 W
79	Florida B. (flŏr'ĭ-dȧ) Fla. (In.)	24·55 N	80·55 W
79	Florida Keys (Is.) Fla. (In.)	24·33 N	81·20 W
69	Florida Mts. N. Mex.	32·10 N	107·35 W
76	Florido, R. (flō-rē'dō) Mex.	27·21 N	104·48 W
111	Floridsdorf (flō'rĭds-dôrf) Aus. (Vienna In.)	48·16 N	16·25 E
127	Florina (flō-rē'nä) Grc.	40·48 N	21·24 E
74	Florissant (flŏr'ĭ-sănt) Mo. (St. Louis In.)	38·47 N	90·20 W
118	Florö (flôr'ü) Nor.	61·36 N	5·01 E
70	Floyd (R.) (floid) Iowa	42·38 N	96·15 W
72	Floydada (floi-dā'dȧ) Tex.	33·59 N	101·19 W
75	Floyds Fk. (R.) (floi-dz) Ky. (Louisville In.)	38·08 N	85·30 W
126	Flumendosa, R. (flōō-mĕn-dô'sä) It.	39·45 N	9·18 E
80	Flushing (flŭsh'ĭng) Mich.	43·05 N	83·50 W
155	Fly (R.) (flī) Austl.	8·00 S	141·45 E
127	Foča (fō'chä) Yugo.	43·29 N	18·48 E
168	Fochville (fŏk'vĭl) S. Afr. (Johannesburg & Pretoria In.)	26·29 S	27·29 E
121	Focsani (fōk-shä'nē) Rom.	45·41 N	27·17 E
126	Foggia (fôd'jä) It.	41·30 N	15·34 E
83	Fogo (fô'gō) Can.	49·43 N	54·14 W
83	Fogo (I.) Can.	49·44 N	53·53 W
164	Fogo I. C. V. Is. (In.)	14·46 N	24·51 W
120	Fohnsdorf (fōns'dôrf) Aus.	47·13 N	14·40 E
120	Föhr I. (fûr) Ger.	54·47 N	8·30 E
122	Foix (fwä) Fr.	42·58 N	1·34 E
151	Fokang China	23·50 N	113·35 E
126	Foligno (fō-lēn'yō) It.	42·58 N	12·41 E
110	Folkingham (fō'kĭng-ăm) Eng.	52·53 N	0·24 W
117	Folkstone (fōk'stŭn) Eng.	51·05 N	3·04 W
72	Folsom (fŏl'sŭm) N. Mex.	36·47 N	103·56 W
68	Folsom City Calif.	38·40 N	121·10 W
94	Fomento (fō-mĕ'n-tō) Cuba	21·35 N	78·20 W
98	Fómeque (fō'mĕ-kĕ) Col. (In.)	4·29 N	73·52 W
71	Fonda (fŏn'dȧ) Iowa	42·33 N	94·51 W
71	Fond du Lac (fŏn dū lăk') Wis.	43·47 N	88·29 W
71	Fond du Lac Ind. Res. Minn.	46·44 N	93·04 W
126	Fondi (fōn'dē) It.	41·23 N	13·25 E
124	Fonsagrada (fōn-sä-grä'dhä) Sp.	43·08 N	7·07 W
92	Fonseca, Golfo de (G.) (gôl-fô-dĕ-fôn-sā'kä). Hond.	13·09 N	87·55 W
123	Fontainebleau (fôN-tĕn-blō') Fr. (Paris In.)	48·24 N	2·42 E
74	Fontana (fŏn-tă'nȧ) Calif. (Los Angeles In.)	34·06 N	117·27 W
98	Fonte Boa (fōn'tā bō'ȧ) Braz.	2·32 S	66·05 W
122	Fontenay-le-Comte (fôNt-nĕ'lē-kôNt'). Fr.	46·28 N	0·53 W
123	Fontenay-Trésigny (fôN-tē-hā' tra-sēn-yē'). Fr. (Paris In.)	48·43 N	2·53 E
91	Fontera, Punta (Pt.) (pōō'n-tä-fôn-tĕ'rä). Mex.	18·36 N	92·43 W
98	Fontibón (fōn-tē-bôn'). Col. (In.)	4·42 N	74·09 W
	Foochow, see Fuchou		
167	Foothills (fōōt-hĭls) S. Afr. (Johannesburg & Pretoria In.)	25·55 S	27·36 E
64	Foraker, Mt. (fôr'ȧ-kēr) Alaska	62·40 N	152·40 W
123	Forbach (fôr'bäk) Fr.	49·12 N	6·54 E
160	Forbes (fôrbz) Austl.	33·24 S	148·05 E
164	Forcados (fôr-kä'dōs) Nig.	5·19 N	5·26 E
120	Forchheim (fôrk'hīm) Ger.	49·43 N	11·05 E
	Fordlândia, see Brasília Legal		
73	Fordyce (fôr'dīs) Ark.	33·48 N	92·24 W
164	Forecariah (fōr-kȧ-rē'ȧ') Gui.	9·31 N	13·14 W
49	Forel, Mt. Grnld.	65·50 N	37·41 W
78	Forest (fŏr'ĕst) Miss.	32·22 N	89·29 W
70	Forest (R.) N. D.	48·08 N	97·45 W
71	Forest City Iowa	43·14 N	93·40 W
79	Forest City N. C.	35·20 N	81·52 W
81	Forest City Pa.	41·35 N	75·30 W
65	Forest Grove (grōv) Ore. (Portland In.)	45·31 N	123·07 W
85	Forest Hill (hĭl) Can. (Toronto In.)	43·42 N	79·25 W
74	Forest Hill Tex. (Dallas, Fort Worth In.)	32·40 N	97·16 W
85	Forest Lawn (lôn) Can. (Calgary In.)	51·02 N	113·59 W
82	Forestville (fŏr'ĕst-vĭl) Can.	48·46 N	69·05 W
122	Forez, Mts. du (môN dü fô-rā'). Fr.	44·55 N	3·43 E
116	Forfar (fôr'fȧr) Scot.	57·10 N	2·55 W
125	Forio (Mtn.) (fô'ryō) It. (Naples In.)	40·29 N	13·55 E
75	Forked Cr. (fôrk'd) Ill. (Chicago In.)	41·16 N	88·01 W
78	Forked Deer (R.) Tenn.	35·53 N	89·29 W
126	Forli (fôr-lē') It.	44·13 N	12·03 E
110	Formby (fôrm'bē) Eng.	53·34 N	3·04 W
110	Formby Pt. Eng.	53·33 N	3·06 W
125	Formello (fôr-mĕ'lō) It. (Rome In.)	42·04 N	12·25 E
125	Formentera, Isla de (I.) (ē's-lä-dĕ-fôr-mĕn-tā'rä). Sp.	38·43 N	1·25 E
101	Formiga (fôr-mē'gȧ) Braz. (Rio de Janeiro In.)	20·27 S	45·25 W
95	Formigas Bk. (fōr-mē'gäs) N. A.	18·30 N	75·40 W
100	Formosa (fôr-mō'sä) Arg.	27·25 S	58·12 W
99	Formosa Braz.	15·32 S	47·10 W
100	Formosa (Prov.) Arg.	24·30 S	60·45 W
	Formosa, see Taiwan (I.)		
99	Formosa, Serra (Mts.) (sĕ'r-rä) Braz.	12·59 S	55·11 W
139	Formosa Str. (fŏr-mō'sȧ) Asia	24·30 N	120·00 E
136	Fornosovo (fôr-nô'sô vô) Sov. Un. (Leningrad In.)	59·35 N	30·34 E
73	Forrest City (for'ĕst sĭ'tĭ) Ark.	35·00 N	90·46 W
159	Forsayth (fôr-sīth') Austl.	18·33 S	143·42 E
118	Forshaga (fôrs'hä'gä) Swe.	59·34 N	13·25 E
201	Forst (fôrst) Ger.	51·45 N	14·38 E
78	Forsyth (fôr-sīth') Ga.	33·02 N	83·56 W
67	Forsyth Mont.	46·15 N	106·41 W
87	Fort Albany (fôrt ôl'bȧ nĭ) Can.	52·10 N	81·40 W
99	Fortaleza (Ceará) (fôr'tä-lā'zä) (sā-ä-rä'). Braz.	3·35 S	38·31 W
69	Fort Apache Ind. Res. (ȧ-păch'ē) Ariz.	34·02 N	110·27 W
165	Fort-Archambault (är-chaN-bō') Chad	9·04 N	18·17 E
71	Fort Atkinson (ăt'kĭn-sŭn) Wis.	42·55 N	88·46 W
	Fort Bayard, see Chanchiang		
167	Fort Beaufort (bō'fôrt) S. Afr. (Natal In.)	32·47 S	26·39 E
74	Fort Bellefontaine (bĕl-fōn-tān') Mo. (St. Louis In.)	38·50 N	90·15 W
67	Fort Benton (bĕn'tŭn) Mont.	47·51 N	110·40 W
70	Fort Berthould Ind. Res. (bĕrth'ôld). N. D.	47·47 N	103·28 W
80	Fort Branch (brănch) Ind.	38·15 N	87·35 W
	Fort Charlet, see Djanet		
87	Fort Chimo Can.	58·18 N	68·08 W
86	Fort Chipewyan Can.	58·46 N	111·15 W
72	Fort Cobb Res. Okla.	35·12 N	98·28 W
72	Fort Collins (kŏl'ĭns) Colo.	40·36 N	105·04 W
165	Fort Crampel (kräm-pĕl') Cen. Afr. Rep.	7·10 N	19·07 E
167	Fort-Dauphin (dō-făN') Malag. Rep.	24·59 S	46·58 E
93	Fort-de-France (dē fräNs) Mart. (Le. & Wind. Is. In.)	14·37 N	61·06 W
78	Fort Deposit (dē-pŏz'ĭt) Ala.	31·58 N	86·35 W
165	Fort de Possel (dē pô-sĕl') Cen. Afr. Rep.	5·03 N	19·11 E
71	Fort Dodge (dŏj) Iowa	42·31 N	94·10 W
81	Fort Edward (wērd) N. Y.	43·15 N	73·30 W
75	Fort Erie (ē'rĭ) Can. (Buffalo In.)	42·55 N	78·56 W
158	Fortescue (R.) (fôr'tĕs-kū). Austl.	21·25 S	116·50 E
82	Fort Fairfield (fâr'fēld) Maine	46·46 N	67·53 W
86	Fort Fitzgerald (fĭts-jĕr'ăld). Can.	59·48 N	111·50 W
164	Fort Flatters (flȧ-târ') Alg.	28·06 N	6·34 E
87	Fort Frances (frăn'sĕs) Can.	48·41 N	94·29 W
79	Fort Frederica Natl. Mon. (frĕd'ĕ-rĭ-kȧ). Ga.	31·12 N	85·25 W
78	Fort Gaines (gānz) Ga.	31·35 N	85·03 W
85	Fort Garry (gă'rē) Can. (Winnipeg In.)	49·50 N	97·09 W
87	Fort George (jôrj) Can.	53·40 N	78·58 W
87	Fort George (R.) Can.	53·50 N	78·34 W
73	Fort Gibson (gĭb'sŭn) Okla.	35·50 N	95·13 W
86	Fort Good Hope (gŏŏd hōp). Can.	66·19 N	128·52 W
164	Fort Gouraud Mauritania	22·45 N	12·38 W
116	Forth, Firth of (fûrth ôv fôrth) Scot.	56·04 N	3·03 W
167	Fort Hall (hôl) Ken.	0·47 S	37·13 E
67	Fort Hall Ind. Res. Idaho	43·02 N	112·21 W
84	Fort Howard (hou'ȧrd) Md. (Baltimore In.)	39·12 N	76·27 W
69	Fort Huachuca (wä-chōō'kä). Ariz.	31·30 N	110·25 W
85	Fortier (fôr-tyā') Can. (Winnipeg In.)	49·56 N	97·55 W
166	Fort Jameson (jām'sŭn) N. Rh.	13·35 S	32·43 E
79	Fort Jefferson Natl. Mon. (jĕf'ēr-sŭn). Fla. (In.)	24·42 N	83·02 W
166	Fort Johnston Nya.	14·16 S	35·14 E
82	Fort Kent (kĕnt) Maine	47·14 N	68·37 W
164	Fort Lallemand (lȧ-lē-mäN'). Alg.	31·17 N	6·13 E
165	Fort-Lamy (lȧ-mē') Chad	12·15 N	15·04 E
65	Fort Langley (lăng'lĭ) Can. (Vancouver In.)	49·10 N	122·35 W
164	Fort Laperrine (Tamanrasset) (fôr lȧ-pē-rēn'). Alg.	22·34 N	5·34 E
70	Fort Laramie Natl. Mon. (fôrt lăr'ȧ-mĭ). Wyo.	42·10 N	104·34 W
79	Fort Lauderdale (lô'dēr-dāl) Fla. (In.)	26·07 N	80·09 W
86	Fort Liard Can.	60·16 N	123·34 W
95	Fort Liberté (lē-bĕr-tā') Hai.	19·40 N	71·50 W
78	Fort Louden (R.) (fôrt lou'dĕn) Tenn.	35·52 N	84·10 W
72	Fort Lupton (lŭp'tŭn) Colo.	40·04 N	104·45 W
66	Fort McDermitt Ind. Res. (măk Dēr'mĭt). Ore.	42·04 N	118·07 W
86	Fort Macleod (mȧ-kloud') Can.	49·40 N	113·22 W
164	Fort MacMahon (mȧk mȧ-ôN') Alg.	29·55 N	1·49 E
86	Fort McPherson (mȧk-fŭr's'n) Can.	67·37 N	134·59 W
71	Fort Madison (măd'ĭ-sŭn) Iowa	40·40 N	91·17 W
166	Fort Manning (măn'ĭng) Nya.	13·42 S	33·00 E
79	Fort Matanzas (mä-tän'zäs). Fla.	29·39 N	81·17 W
79	Fort Meade (mēd) Fla. (In.)	27·45 N	81·48 W
84	Fort Meade. Md. (Baltimore In.)	39·06 N	76·44 W
79	Fort Mill (mĭl) S.C.	35·03 N	80·57 W
114	Fort Miribel (mē-rē-bĕl') Alg.	28·50 N	2·51 E
68	Fort Mojave Ind. Res. (mō-hä'vä) Calif.	34·59 N	115·02 W
84	Fort Monroe (mŏn-rō') Va. (Norfolk In.)	37·00 N	76·19 W
72	Fort Morgan (môr'gȧn) Colo.	40·14 N	103·49 W
79	Fort Myers (mī'ērz) Fla. (In.)	26·36 N	81·45 W
114	Fort National (fô nȧ-syō-nȧl') Alg.	36·45 N	4·15 E
86	Fort Nelson (nĕl'sŭn) Can.	58·57 N	122·30 W
86	Fort Nelson (R.) (nĕl'sŭn) Can.	58·44 N	122·20 W
78	Fort Payne (pān) Ala.	34·26 N	85·41 W
67	Fort Peck (pĕk) Mont.	47·58 N	106·30 W
67	Fort Peck Res. Mont.	47·52 N	106·59 W
79	Fort Pierce (pērs) Fla. (In.)	27·25 N	80·20 W
164	Fort Polignac (pō-lē-nyȧk') Alg.	26·35 N	8·24 E
165	Fort Portal (pôr'tȧl) Ug.	00·40 N	30·16 E

ăt; finȧl; rāte; senâte; ärm; ȧsk; sofȧ; fâre; ch-choose; dh-as th in other; bē; ēvent; bĕt; recĕnt; cratēr; g-go; gh-guttural g; bĭt; ĭ-short neutral; rīde; K-guttural k as ch in German ich;

PRONOUNCING INDEX Fort Providence–Fulda 207

Page	Name Pronunciation Region	Lat. °′	Long. °′
86	Fort Providence (prŏv'ĭ-dĕns) Can.	61·27 N	117·59 W
79	Fort Pulaski Natl. Mon. (pu-lăs'kĭ) . Ga.	31·59 N	80·56 W
64	Fort Randall (răn'd'l) . . . . . Alaska	55·12 N	162·38 W
62	Fort Randall Dam . . . . U. S.	43·05 N	100·15 W
70	Fort Randall Res. . . . . S. D.	43·35 N	99·12 W
86	Fort Resolution (rĕz'ō-lū'shŭn) Can.	61·08 N	113·42 W
73	Fort Riley (rī'lĭ) . . . . Kans.	39·05 N	96·46 W
166	Fort Rosebery (rōz'bēr-ĭ) . . N. Rh.	11·14 S	28·58 E
166	Fort Rousset (fôr rōō-sĕ') . . Con. B.	0·23 S	15·42 E
86	Fort St. James (fôrt sānt jāmz) Can.	54·28 N	124·19 W
86	Fort St. John (sānt jŏn) . . . . . Can.	56·28 N	120·57 W
142	Fort Sandeman (săn'da-măn) W. Pak.	31·28 N	69·29 E
85	Fort Saskatchewan (săs-kăt'chōō-ân) Can. (Edmonton In.)	53·42 N	113·14 W
73	Fort Scott (skŏt) . . . . Kans.	37·50 N	94·43 W
86	Fort Selkirk (sĕl-kûrk') . . . . . . Can.	62·43 N	137·40 W
87	Fort Severn (sĕv'ērn) . . . . Can.	56·58 N	87·50 W
133	Fort Shevchenko (shĕv-chĕn'kô) Sov. Un.	44·30 N	50·18 E
165	Fort Sibut (fôr sē-bü') Cen. Afr. Rep.	5·52 N	19·01 E
72	Fort Sill (fôrt sĭl) . . . . Okla.	34·41 N	98·25 W
86	Fort Simpson (sĭmp'sŭn) . . . . Can.	61·52 N	121·48 W
73	Fort Smith (smĭth) . . . . Ark.	35·23 N	94·24 W
86	Fort Smith . . . . Can.	60·09 N	112·08 W
76	Fort Stockton (stŏk'tŭn) . . . . . Tex.	30·54 N	102·51 W
72	Fort Sumner (sŭm'nēr) . . . N. Mex.	34·30 N	104·17 W
79	Fort Sumter Natl. Mon. (sŭm'tēr) . S. C.	32·43 N	79·54 W
75	Fort Thomas (tŏm'ăs) Ky. (Cincinnati In.)	39·05 N	84·27 W
66	Fortuna (fôr-tū'nȧ) . . . . Calif.	40·36 N	124·10 W
83	Fortune (fôr'tŭn) . . . . Can.	47·04 N	55·51 W
95	Fortune (I.) . . . . Ba. Is.	22·35 N	74·20 W
83	Fortune B . . . . Can.	47·25 N	55·30 W
72	Fort Union Natl. Mon. (ūn'yŭn) N. Mex.	35·51 N	104·57 W
78	Fort Valley (văl'ĭ) . . . . Ga.	32·33 N	83·53 W
66	Fort Vancouver Natl. Mon. (văn-kōō'vēr) . Wash.	45·50 N	122·36 W
86	Fort Vermilion (vēr-mĭl'yŭn) . Can.	58·23 N	115·50 W
166	Fort Victoria . . . . S. Rh.	20·07 S	30·47 E
80	Fortville (fôrt-vĭl) . . . . Ind.	40·00 N	85·50 W
80	Fort Wayne (wān) . . . . Ind.	41·00 N	85·10 W
85	Fort Whyte (whīt) Can. (Winnipeg In.)	49·49 N	97·13 W
87	Fort William (wĭl'yŭm) . . . . . . Can.	48·20 N	89·20 W
116	Fort William (wĭl'yŭm) . . . . . Scot.	56·50 N	3·00 W
160	Fort William, Mt. (wĭ 'ĭ-ăm) Austl.	24·45 S	151·15 E
74	Fort Worth (wûrth) Tex. (Dallas, Fort Worth In.)	32·45 N	97·20 W
64	Fort Yukon (yōō'kŏn) . . . . . Alaska	66·30 N	145·00 W
68	Fort Yuma Ind. Res. (yōō'mä) Calif.	32·54 N	114·47 W
122	Fos, Golfe de (G.) (gôlf'dĕ-fôs') Fr. (Marseille In.)	43·22 N	4·55 E
	Foshan, see Ch'aoyang		
126	Fossano (fôs-sä'nō) . . . . It.	44·34 N	7·42 E
74	Fossil Cr. (fŏs-ĭl) Tex. (Dallas, Fort Worth In.)	32·53 N	97·19 W
126	Fossombrone (fôs-sôm-brō'nä) . . It.	43·41 N	12·48 E
72	Foss Res. . . . . Okla.	35·38 N	99·11 W
70	Fosston (fôs'tŭn) . . . . Minn.	47·34 N	95·44 W
74	Fosterburg (fŏs'tēr-bûrg) Ill. (St. Louis In.)	38·58 N	90·04 W
80	Fostoria (fŏs-tō'rĭ-ȧ) . . . . Ohio	41·10 N	83·20 W
148	Fouch'eng (fōō'chĕng) . . . . . . China	37·53 N	116·08 E
122	Fougères (fōō-zhâr') . . . . Fr.	48·23 N	1·14 W
150	Fouhsin . . . . China	42·05 N	121·40 E
116	Foula (I.) (fou'lȧ) . . . . Scot.	60·08 N	2·04 W
151	Fouliang . . . . China	29·18 N	117·18 E
151	Fouling . . . . China	29·40 N	107·30 E
159	Foulwind, C. (foul'wĭnd) N. Z. (In.)	41·45 S	171·37 E
164	Foumban (fōōm-bän') . . . . . . Cam.	5·49 N	10·52 E
148	Founing (fōō'nĭng) . . . . China	33·55 N	119·54 E
72	Fountain Cr. (foun'tĭn) . . . . . Colo.	38·36 N	104·37 W
73	Fourche la Fave (R.) (fōōrsh lä fäv') . Ark.	34·46 N	93·45 W
168	Fouriesburg (fōō'rēz-bûrg) S. Afr. (Johannesburg & Pretoria In.)	28·38 S	28·13 E
122	Fourmies (fōōr-mē') . . . . Fr.	50·01 N	4·01 E
64	Four Mts., Is. of the (fōr) . . Alaska	52·58 N	170·40 W
165	Fourth Cataract . . . . Sud.	18·52 N	32·07 E
164	Fouta Djalon (Mts.) (fōō'tä jä-lôN) . Gui.	11·37 N	12·29 W
148	Fouts'un (fōō'tsōōn) . . . . China	36·38 N	117·26 E
148	Foutzuchi (fōō'tzĕ'jē) . . . . China	33·48 N	118·13 E
148	Fouyang (fōō'yäng) . . . . China	32·53 N	115·48 E
159	Foveaux Str. (fô-vō') . . N. Z. (In.)	46·30 S	167·43 E
72	Fowler (foul'ēr) . . . . Colo.	38·04 N	104·02 W
80	Fowler . . . . Ind.	40·35 N	87·20 W
158	Fowler, Pt. . . . . Austl.	32·05 S	132·30 E
76	Fowlerton (foul'ēr-tŭn) . . . . . . Tex.	28·26 N	98·48 W
65	Fox (I.) (fŏks) . Wash. (Seattle In.)	47·15 N	122·08 W
71	Fox (R.) . . . . Ill.	41·35 N	88·43 W
71	Fox (R.) . . . . Wis.	44·18 N	88·23 W
83	Foxboro (fŏks'bŭrô) Mass. (Boston In.)	42·04 N	71·15 W
86	Foxe Basin (fŏks) . . . . Can.	67·35 N	79·21 W
87	Foxe Chan . . . . Can.	64·30 N	79·23 W
87	Foxe Pen . . . . Can.	64·57 N	77·26 W
64	Fox Is. (fŏks) . . . . Alaska	53·04 N	167·30 W
75	Fox Lake (lăk) . . Ill. (Chicago In.)	42·24 N	88·11 W
75	Fox L . . . . Ill. (Chicago In.)	42·24 N	88·07 W
75	Fox Point . . . Wis. (Milwaukee In.)	43·10 N	87·54 W
116	Folye, Lough (B.) (lŏk foil') . . Ire.	54·69 N	6·75 W
125	Fraga (frä'gä) . . . . Sp.	41·31 N	0·20 E
94	Fragoso, Cayo (I.) (kä'yō-frȧ-gō'sô) . Cuba	22·45 N	79·30 W
127	Francavilla (frän-kä-vēl'lä) . . . . It.	40·32 N	17·37 E
99	France (frä'n-kä) . . . . Braz.	20·28 S	47·20 W
102	France (fråns) . . . . Eur.	46·39 N	0·47 E
86	Frances (L.) (frăn'sĭs) . . . . Can.	61·27 N	128·28 W
94	Frances, Cabo (C.) (kä'bô-frän-sĕ's) . Cuba	21·55 N	84·05 W
94	Frances, Punta (Pt.) (pōō'n-tä-frän-sĕ's) . Cuba	21·45 N	83·10 W
95	Frances Viejo, Cabo (C.) (kä'bô-frän'sås vyā'hō) Dom. Rep.	19·40 N	69·35 W
166	Franceville (fräNs-vēl') . . . . Gabon.	1·37 S	13·37 E
101	Francisco Sales (frän-sē's-kô-sä'lĕs) . Braz. (Rio de Janeiro In.)	21·42 S	44·26 W
166	Francistown (frăn'sĭs-toun) . . Bech.	21·17 S	27·28 E
75	Frankfort (frăŋk'fŭrt) Ill. (Chicago In.)	41·30 N	87·51 W
80	Frankfort . . . . Ind.	40·15 N	86·30 W
73	Frankfort . . . . Kans.	39·42 N	96·27 W
80	Frankfort . . . . Ky.	38·10 N	84·55 W
80	Frankfort . . . . Mich.	44·40 N	86·15 W
81	Frankfort . . . . N. Y.	43·05 N	75·05 W
168	Frankfort . S. Afr. (Johannesburg & Pretoria In.)	27·17 S	28·30 E
167	Frankfort (frănk'fŏrt) S. Afr. (Natal In.)	32·43 S	27·28 E
120	Frankfurt (fräŋk'fōōrt) . . . . . . Ger.	52·20 N	14·31 E
111	Frankfurt (Dist.) . Ger. (Berlin In.)	52·42 N	13·37 E
120	Frankfurt am Main . . . . Ger.	50·07 N	8·40 E
80	Franklin (frănk'lĭn) . . . . Ind.	39·25 N	86·00 W
78	Franklin . . . . Ky.	36·42 N	86·34 W
77	Franklin . . . . La.	29·47 N	91·31 W
83	Franklin . . . . . . Mass. (Boston In.)	42·05 N	71·24 W
72	Franklin . . . . Nebr.	40·06 N	99·01 W
81	Franklin . . . . N. H.	43·25 N	71·40 W
84	Franklin . . . . N. J. (New York In.)	41·08 N	74·35 W
80	Franklin . . . . Ohio	39·30 N	84·20 W
81	Franklin . . . . Pa.	41·25 N	79·50 W
78	Franklin . . . . Tenn.	35·54 N	86·54 W
167	Franklin . . . . . . S. Afr. (Natal In.)	30·19 S	29·28 E
79	Franklin . . . . Va.	36·41 N	76·57 W
86	Franklin, Dist. of . . . . Can.	70·46 N	105·22 W
68	Franklin (L.) . . . . Nev.	40·23 N	115·10 W
66	Franklin D. Roosevelt L . . . Wash.	48·12 N	118·43 W
86	Franklin Mts . . . . Can.	65·36 N	125·55 W
75	Franklin Park . . . Ill. (Chicago In.)	41·56 N	87·53 W
77	Franklinton (frăŋk'lĭn-tŭn) . . . . La.	30·49 N	90·09 W
161	Frankston . Austl. (Melbourne In.)	38·09 S	145·08 E
75	Franksville (frănkz'vĭl) Wis. (Milwaukee In.)	42·46 N	87·55 W
87	Franz (fránz) . . . . Can.	48·27 N	84·28 W
	Franz Josef Land (Is.), see Zemlya Frantsa Iosifa		
125	Frascati (fräs-kä'tē) It. (Rome In.)	41·49 N	12·45 E
75	Fraser (frā'zēr) Mich. (Detroit In.)	42·32 N	82·57 W
160	Fraser (Great Sandy) (I.) (frā'zēr) Austl.	25·12 S	153·00 E
86	Fraser (R.) . . . . Can.	51·41 N	122·19 W
116	Fraserburgh (frā'zēr-bûrg) . . . Scot.	57·40 N	2·01 W
87	Fraserdale (frā'zēr-dāl) . . . . . . Can.	49·51 N	81·40 W
125	Frattamaggiore (frät-tä-mäg-zhyō'rĕ) . It. (Naples In.)	40·41 N	14·16 E
101	Fray Bentos (frī bĕn'tōs) Ur. (Buenos Aires In.)	33·10 S	58·19 W
70	Frazee (frȧ-zē') . . . . Minn.	46·42 N	95·43 W
94	Fraziers Hog Cay (I.) . . . . . Ba. Is.	25·25 N	77·55 W
123	Frechen (frĕ'ĸĕn) . . Ger. (Ruhr In.)	50·54 N	6·49 E
118	Fredericia (frĕdh-ĕ-rē'tsē-ȧ) . . Den.	55·35 N	9·45 E
81	Frederick (frĕd'ēr-ĭk) . . . . Md.	39·25 N	77·25 W
72	Frederick . . . . Okla.	34·23 N	99·01 W
76	Fredericksburg (frĕd'ēr-ĭkz-bûrg) . Tex.	30·16 N	98·52 W
81	Fredericksburg . . . . Va.	38·20 N	77·30 W
73	Fredericktown (frĕd'ēr-ĭk-toun) . Mo.	37·32 N	90·16 W
82	Fredericton (frĕd'ēr-ĭk-tŭn) . . Can.	45·58 N	66·40 W
155	Frederik Hendrik (I.) (frĕd'ēr-ĭk hĕn'drēk) . W. Irian	7·45 S	137·30 E
118	Frederikshavn (frĕdh'ĕ-rĕks-houn) . Den.	57·27 N	10·31 E
118	Frederikssund (frĕdh'ĕ-rĕks-sōōn) Den.	55·51 N	12·04 E
98	Fredonia (frĕ-dō'nyä) . . . Col. (In.)	5·55 N	75·40 W
73	Fredonia (frē-dō'nĭ-ȧ) . . . . . . Kans.	36·31 N	95·50 W
81	Fredonia . . . . N. Y.	42·25 N	79·20 W
118	Fredrikstad (frådh'rĕks-städ) . Nor.	59·14 N	10·58 E
74	Freeburg (frē'bûrg) Ill. (St. Louis In.)	38·26 N	89·59 W
84	Freehold (frē'hōld) N. J. (New York In.)	40·15 N	74·16 W
81	Freeland (frē'lănd) . . . . Pa.	41·00 N	75·50 W
65	Freeland . . . . . . Wash. (Seattle In.)	48·01 N	122·32 W
83	Freels, C. (frēlz) . . . . Can.	49·18 N	53·10 W
85	Freelton (frēl'tŭn) Can. (Toronto In.)	43·24 N	80·02 W
71	Freeport (frē'pōrt) . . . . Ill.	42·19 N	89·30 W
84	Freeport . . . N. Y. (New York In.)	40·39 N	73·35 W
77	Freeport . . . . Tex.	28·56 N	95·21 W
164	Freetown (frē'toun) . . . . S. L.	8·29 N	13·16 W
124	Fregenal de la Sierra (frā-hȧ-näl' dā lä syĕr'rä) . Sp.	38·09 N	6·40 W
125	Fregene (frĕ-zhĕ'-nĕ) It. (Rome In.)	41·52 N	12·12 E
120	Freiberg (frī'bĕrgh) . . . . Ger.	50·54 N	13·18 E
111	Freienried (frī'ĕn-rēd) Ger. (Munich In.)	48·20 N	11·08 E
100	Freirina (frå-ĭ-rē'nä) . . . . Chile	28·35 S	71·26 W
111	Freising (frī'zĭng) Ger. (Munich In.)	48·25 N	11·45 E
123	Fréjus (frā-zhüs') . . . . Fr.	43·28 N	6·46 E
158	Fremantle (frē'măn-t'l) . . . . . Austl.	32·03 S	116·05 E
65	Fremont (frē-mŏnt') Calif. (San Francisco In.)	37·33 N	122·00 W
80	Fremont . . . . Mich.	43·25 N	85·55 W
70	Fremont . . . . Nebr.	41·26 N	96·30 W
80	Fremont . . . . Ohio	41·20 N	83·05 W
69	Fremont (R.) . . . . Utah	38·20 N	111·30 W
67	Fremont Pk . . . . Wyo.	43·05 N	109·35 W
	French, see Loyaute, Iles.		
78	French Broad (R.) (frĕnch brôd) Tenn.-N. C.	35·59 N	83·01 W
99	French Guiana (gē-ä'nä) . . . . S. A.	4·20 N	53·00 W
80	French Lick (frĕnch lĭk) . . . . . . Ind.	38·35 N	86·35 W
67	Frenchman Cr. (frĕnch-măn) Mont.	48·51 N	107·20 W
72	Frenchman Cr . . . . Nebr.	40·24 N	101·50 W
68	Frenchman F . . . . Nev.	36·55 N	116·11 W
74	French River . Minn. (Duluth In.)	46·54 N	91·54 W
	French, see Loyaute, Iles		
163	French Somaliland . . . . Afr.	11·35 N	45·08 E
90	Fresnillo (frås-nēl'yô) . . . . Mex.	23·10 N	102·52 W
68	Fresno (frĕz'nō) . . . . Calif.	36·43 N	119·47 W
98	Fresno (frĕs'-nô) . . . . Col. (In.)	5·10 N	75·01 W
68	Fresno (R.) (frĕz'nō) . . . . Calif.	37·00 N	120·24 W
68	Fresno Slough . . . . Calif.	36·39 N	120·12 W
120	Freudenstadt (froi'den-shtät) . Ger.	48·28 N	8·26 E
160	Freycinet Pen. (frā-sē-nĕ') . . Austl.	42·13 S	148·56 E
69	Fria (R.) (frē-ȧ) . . . . Ariz.	34·03 N	112·12 W
166	Fria, C. (frĭȧ) . . . . S. W. Afr.	18·15 S	12·10 E
100	Frias (frē-äs) . . . . Arg.	28·43 S	65·03 W
120	Fribourg (frē-bōōr') . . . . Switz.	46·48 N	7·07 E
74	Fridley (frĭd'lĭ) Minn. (Minneapolis, St. Paul In.)	45·05 N	93·16 W
120	Frieburg (frī'bōōrgh) . . . . Ger.	47·59 N	7·50 E
111	Friedberg (frēd'bĕrgh) Ger. (Munich In.)	48·22 N	11·00 E
120	Friedland (frēt'länt) . . . . Ger.	53·39 N	13·34 E
120	Friedrichshafen (frē-drēks-häf'ĕn) Ger.	47·39 N	9·28 E
73	Friend (frĕnd) . . . . Nebr.	40·40 N	97·16 W
77	Friendswood (frĕnds'-wōōd) Tex. (In.)	29·31 N	95·11 W
79	Fries (frēz) . . . . Va.	36·42 N	80·59 W
111	Friesack (frē'säk) Ger. (Berlin In.)	52·44 N	12·35 E
99	Frio, Cabo (C.) (kä'bō-frē'ō) Braz.	22·58 S	42·08 W
76	Frio R. Tex.	29·00 N	99·15 W
124	Friol (frē-ōl') . . . . Sp.	43·02 N	7·48 W
121	Frisches Haff B. (frĭsh'ĕs häf) . Pol.	54·22 N	19·38 E
117	Frisian (Is.) (frē'zhăn) . . . . . . Neth.	53·30 N	5·20 E
86	Frobisher (L.) (frŏb'ĭsh-ēr) . . . Can.	56·33 N	107·57 W
87	Frobisher Bay . . . . Can.	63·48 N	68·31 W
87	Frobisher B . . . . Can.	62·49 N	66·41 W
110	Frodsham (frŏdz'ăm) . . . . Eng.	53·18 N	2·48 W
160	Frome, L. (frōōm) . . . . Austl.	30·40 S	140·13 E
73	Frontenac (frŏn'tē-năk) . . . . Kans.	37·27 N	94·41 W
91	Frontera (frôn-tā'rä) . . . . Mex.	18·34 N	92·38 W
122	Frontignan (frôN-tē-nyäN') . . . . Fr.	43·26 N	3·45 E
67	Front Ra. (frŭnt) . . . . Wyo.	42·17 N	105·53 W
81	Front Royal (frŭnt) . . . . Va.	38·55 N	78·10 W
112	Fro Sea (frô) . . . . Nor.	63·49 N	9·12 E
126	Frosinone (frō-zē-nō'nȧ) . . . . It.	41·38 N	13·22 E
81	Frostburg (frôst'bûrg) . . . . Md.	39·40 N	78·55 W
74	Fruit (frōōt) . . . . Ill. (St. Louis In.)	38·50 N	89·51 W
69	Fruita (frōōt-ȧ) . . . . Colo.	39·10 N	108·45 W
74	Fruitdale (frōōt'dāl) Tex. (Dallas, Fort Worth In.)	32·43 N	96·46 W
134	Frunze (frōōn'zĕ) . . . . Sov. Un.	42·49 N	74·42 E
136	Fryanovo (f'ryä'nô-vô) Sov. Un. (Moscow In.)	56·08 N	38·28 E
136	Fryazino (f'ryä'zĭ-nô) Sov. Un. (Moscow In.)	55·58 N	38·05 E
121	Frydek (frē'dĕk) . . . . Czech.	49·43 N	18·22 E
120	Frydlant (frēd'länt) . . . . Czech.	50·56 N	15·05 E
147	Fuchien (Fukien) (Prov.) . . . China	25·39 N	117·21 E
147	Fuchin (fōō'chĭn') . . . . China	47·13 N	132·11 E
151	Fuchou (Foochow) (fōō'chó) China	26·02 N	119·18 E
148	Fuchow (fōō'chō') . . . . China	39·46 N	121·44 E
153	Fuchu (fōō'chōō) . Jap. (Tōkyō In.)	35·41 N	139·29 E
151	Fuch'un (R.) . . . . China	29·50 N	120·00 E
92	Fuego (Vol.) (fwā'gō) . . . . Guat.	14·29 N	90·52 W
125	Fuencarral (fuän-kär-räl') Sp. (Madrid In.)	40·29 N	3·42 W
124	Fuensalida (fwān-sä-lē'dä) . . . . Sp.	40·04 N	4·15 W
76	Fuente (fwĕ'n-tĕ) . . . . Mex.	28·39 N	100·34 W
124	Fuente de Cantos (fwĕn'tā dā kän'tōs) . Sp.	38·15 N	6·18 W
125	Fuente el Saz (fwĕn'tā ĕl säth') Sp. (Madrid In.)	40·39 N	3·30 W
124	Fuente-Ovejuna (fwĕn'tâ-ōvâ-hōō'nä) . Sp.	38·15 N	5·30 W
124	Fuentesaúco (fwĕn-tâ-sä-ōō'kō) Sp.	41·18 N	5·25 W
88	Fuerte, Rio del (R.) (rē'ō-dĕl-fōō-ĕ'r-tĕ) . Mex.	26·15 N	108·50 W
99	Fuerte Olimpo (fwĕr'tā ō-lēm-pō) Par.	21·10 S	57·49 W
164	Fuerteventura I. (fwĕr'tâ-vĕn-tōō'rä) . Can. Is.	28·24 N	13·21 W
146	Fuhai . . . . China	47·01 N	87·07 E
148	Fuhsien (fōō'siän) . . . . China	39·36 N	121·59 E
153	Fuji (R.) . . . . Jap.	35·20 N	138·23 E
153	Fuji-san (Mtn.) (fōō'jē sän) . . Jap.	35·23 N	138·44 E
153	Fujisawa (fōō'jē-sä'wa) Jap. (Tōkyō In.)	35·20 N	139·29 E
	Fukien (Prov.), see Fuchien		
153	Fukuchiyama (fōō'kōō-chē-yä'mä) . Jap.	35·18 N	135·07 E
153	Fukue (I.) (fōō-kōō'ā) . . . . Jap.	32·40 N	129·02 E
153	Fukui (fōō'kōō-ē) . . . . Jap.	36·05 N	136·14 E
153	Fukuoka (fōō'kōō-ō'kä) . . . . . . Jap.	33·35 N	130·23 E
152	Fukushima (fōō'kōō-shē'mä) . . Jap.	37·45 N	140·29 E
153	Fukuyama (fōō'kōō-yä'mä) . . . Jap.	34·31 N	133·21 E
120	Fulda R. (fōōl'dä) . . . . Ger.	51·05 N	9·40 E

208 Fullerton–Gemlik PRONOUNCING INDEX

Page	Name Pronunciation Region	Lat. °'	Long. °'
74	Fullerton (fo͞ol'ẽr-tŭn) Calif. (Los Angeles In.)	33·53 N	117·56 W
77	Fullerton La.	31·00 N	93·00 W
84	Fullerton Md. (Baltimore In.)	39·22 N	76·31 W
70	Fullerton Nebr.	41·21 N	97·59 W
78	Fulton (fo͝ol'tŭn) Ky.	36·30 N	88·53 W
73	Fulton Mo.	38·51 N	91·56 W
81	Fulton N. Y.	43·20 N	76·25 W
85	Fulton Cr. Can. (Edmonton In.)	53·30 N	113·24 W
84	Fultondale (fŭl'tŭn-dāl) Ala. (Birmingham In.)	33·37 N	86·48 W
153	Funabashi (fo͞o'nà-bä'shē) Jap. (Tōkyō In.)	35·43 N	139·59 E
153	Funaya (fo͞o-nä'yä) Jap. (Osaka In.)	34·45 N	135·52 E
164	Funchal (fo͝on-shäl') Mad. Is.	32·41 N	16·15 W
98	Fundacion (fo͞on-dä-syō'n) Col.	10·43 N	74·13 W
124	Fundão (fo͝on-douɴ') Port.	40·08 N	7·32 W
82	Fundy, B. of (fŭn'dĭ) Can.	44·50 N	66·05 W
82	Fundy Natl. Park Can.	45·38 N	65·25 W
148	Funing (fo͞o'nĭng') China	39·55 N	119·16 E
151	Funing Wan (B.) (fo͞o'nĭng') China	26·48 N	120·35 E
148	Funiu Shan (Mts.) (fo͞o'nēo shän) China	34·25 N	113·28 E
91	Furbero (fo͞or-bĕ'rô) Mex.	20·21 N	97·32 W
128	Furmanov (fûr-mä'nôf) Sov. Un.	57·14 N	41·11 E
101	Furnas, Represa de (Res.) Braz. (Rio de Janeiro In.)	21·00 S	46·00 W
159	Furneaux Group (Is.) (fûr'nō) Austl.	40·15 S	146·27 E
120	Fürstenfeld (für'stĕn-fĕlt) Aus.	47·02 N	16·03 E
111	Fürstenfeldbruck (fur'stĕn-fĕld' bro͝ok). Ger. (Munich In.)	48·11 N	11·16 E
120	Fürstenwalde (für'stĕn-väl-dĕ) Ger.	52·21 N	14·04 E
120	Fürth (fürt) Ger.	49·28 N	11·03 E
153	Furuichi (fo͞o'ro͞o-ē'chē) Jap. (Ōsaka In.)	34·33 N	135·37 E
153	Fusa (fo͞o'sä) Jap. (Tōkyō In.)	35·52 N	140·08 E
98	Fusagasugá (fo͞o-sä-gä-so͞o-gä') Col. (In.)	4·22 N	74·22 W
153	Fuse (fo͞o'sâ) Jap. (Ōsaka In.)	34·39 N	135·35 E
146	Fushih China	36·46 N	109·15 E
153	Fushimi (fo͞o'shē-mē) Jap. (Osaka In.)	34·57 N	135·47 E
150	Fushun (fo͞o'sho͞on') China	41·50 N	124·00 E
150	Fusung China	42·12 N	127·12 E
153	Futtsu (fo͞ot'tso͞o') Jap. (Tōkyō In.)	35·19 N	139·49 E
153	Futtsu Misaki (C.) (fo͞ot'tso͞o' mē-sä'kē). Jap. (Tōkyō In.)	35·19 N	139·46 E
168	Fuwah (fo͞o'wä). U. A. R. (Nile In.)	31·13 N	30·35 E
151	Fuyang China	30·10 N	119·58 E
150	Fuyü (fo͞o'yo͞o') China	45·20 N	125·00 E
118	Fyn (fü'n) Den.	55·24 N	10·33 E
116	Fyne (L.) (fīn) Scot.	56·14 N	5·10 W
118	Fyresdal Vand (L.) (fü'rĕs-däl vän). Nor.	59·04 N	7·55 E
166	Gaberones (gä-bē-rō'nēz) Bech.	24·28 S	25·59 E
164	Gabès (gä'bĕs) Tun.	33·51 N	10·04 E
164	Gabès, Golfe de (G.) Tun.	32·22 N	10·59 E
121	Gabin (gŏn'bēn) Pol.	52·23 N	19·47 E
163	Gabon (gà-bôɴ') Afr.	0·30 S	10·45 E
77	Gabriel R. (gā'brĭ-ĕl) Tex.	30·38 N	97·15 W
127	Gabrovo (gäb'rō-vō) Bul.	42·52 N	25·19 E
98	Gachetá (gä-chā'tä) Col (In.)	4·50 N	73·36 W
127	Gacko (gäts'kô) Yugo.	43·10 N	18·34 E
139	Gader Jordan (Palestine In.)	32·39 N	35·41 E
78	Gadsden (gădz'dĕn) Ala.	34·00 N	86·00 W
129	Gadyach (gäd-yäch') Sov. Un.	50·22 N	33·59 E
127	Gaesti (gä-yĕsh'tē) Rom.	44·43 N	25·21 E
126	Gaeta (gä-å'tä) It.	41·18 N	13·34 E
79	Gaffney (găf'nĭ) S. C.	35·04 N	81·47 W
164	Gafsa (gäf'sä) Tun.	34·16 N	8·37 E
82	Gagetown (gāj'toun) Can.	45·47 N	66·09 W
155	Gagrary (I.) (gä-grä-rē) Phil. (Manila In.)	13·23 N	123·58 E
126	Gaidhouronísi (I.) Grc. (Inset)	34·53 N	25·45 E
122	Gaillac-sur-Tarn (gà-yäk'sür-tärn'). Fr.	43·54 N	1·52 E
88	Gaillard Cut (gä-ēl-yä'rd) C. Z. (Panama Canal In.)	9·03 N	79·42 W
79	Gainesville (gānz'vĭl) Fla.	29·38 N	82·19 W
78	Gainesville Ga.	34·16 N	83·48 W
73	Gainesville Tex.	33·38 N	97·08 W
110	Gainsborough (gānz'bŭr-ô) Eng.	53·23 N	0·46 W
160	Gairdner, L. (gârd'nẽr) Austl.	32·20 S	136·30 E
142	Gajan W. Pak.	28·45 N	67·30 E
139	Galala, Gebel el (Mts.) U. A. R. (Palestine In.)	28·51 N	32·14 E
125	Galapagar (gä-lä-pä-gär') Sp. (Madrid In.)	40·36 N	4·00 W
	Galápagos Is., see Colon, Archip. de		
116	Galashiels (găl-à-shēlz) Scot.	55·40 N	2·57 W
129	Galati (gà-lätz'ĭ) Rom.	45·25 N	28·05 E
127	Galatina (gä-lä-tē'nä) It.	40·10 N	18·12 E
127	Galaxidhion Grc.	38·26 N	22·22 E
118	Galdhöpiggen (Mtn.) (gäld-hû-pĭggĕn). Nor.	61·39 N	8·12 E
76	Galeana (gä-lā-ä'nä) Mex.	24·50 N	100·04 W
71	Galena (gà-lē'nà) Ill.	42·26 N	90·27 W
75	Galena Ind. (Louisville In.)	38·21 N	85·55 W
73	Galena Kans.	37·06 N	94·39 W
77	Galena Pk. Tex. (In.)	29·44 N	95·14 W
88	Galera, Cerro (Mtn.) (sĕ'r-rō-gä-lĕ'rä) C. Z. (Panama Canal In.)	8·55 N	79·38 W
125	Galera (R.) (gä-lĕ'-rä) It. (Rome In.)	41·58 N	12·21 E
98	Galeras (Vol.) (gä-lĕ'räs) Col.	0·57 N	77·27 W
65	Gales (R.) (gālz) Ore. (Portland In.)	45·33 N	123·11 W
73	Galesburg (gālz'bûrg) Ill.	40·56 N	90·21 W
71	Galesville (gālz'vĭl) Wis.	44·04 N	91·22 W
81	Galeton (gāl'tŭn) Pa.	41·45 N	77·40 W
127	Galibolu (Gallipoli) (gĕ-lĭb'ô-lo͞o) (gà-lĭp'ô-lē). Tur.	40·25 N	26·40 E
132	Galich (gàl'ĭch) Sov. Un.	58·20 N	42·38 E
121	Galicia (Reg.) (gà-lĭsh'ĭ-à) Pol.-Sov. Un.	49·48 N	21·05 E
124	Galicia (Reg.) (gä-lē'thyä) Sp.	43·35 N	8·03 W
159	Galilee (L.) (găl'ĭ-lē) Austl.	22·23 S	145·09 E
139	Galilee, Sea of U. A. R. (Palestine In.)	32·53 N	35·45 E
94	Galina Pt. (gä-lē'nä) Jam.	18·25 N	76·50 W
80	Galion (găl'ĭ-ŭn) Ohio	40·45 N	82·50 W
69	Galisteo (gä-lĭs-tā'ō) N. Mex.	35·20 N	106·00 W
113	Galite, I. La (gä-lēt) Alg.	37·36 N	8·03 E
165	Galla (Prov.) (gäl'lä) Eth.	7·22 N	35·28 E
165	Gallabat (gäl'à-băt) Sud.	12·55 N	36·12 E
126	Gallarate (gäl-lä-rä'tä) It.	45·37 N	8·48 E
123	Gallardon (gä-lär-dôɴ') Fr. (Paris In.)	48·31 N	1·40 E
73	Gallatin (găl'à-tĭn) Mo.	39·55 N	93·58 W
78	Gallatin Tenn.	36·23 N	86·28 W
67	Gallatin R. Mont.	45·12 N	111·10 W
143	Galle (gäl) Ceylon	6·13 N	80·10 E
125	Gállego (R.) (gäl-yā'gō) Sp.	42·27 N	0·37 W
98	Gallinas, Pta. de (Pt.) (gä-lyē'näs) Col.	12·10 N	72·10 W
127	Gallipoli (gäl-lē'pô-lē) It.	40·03 N	17·58 E
	Gallipoli, see Galibolu		
80	Gallipolis (găl-ĭ-pô-lēs) Ohio	38·50 N	82·10 W
112	Gällivare (yĕl-ĭ-vär'ĕ) Swe.	68·06 N	20·29 E
124	Gallo (R.) (gäl'yō) Sp.	40·43 N	1·42 W
69	Gallup (găl'ŭp) N. Mex.	35·30 N	108·45 W
165	Galnale Doria R. Eth.	5·35 N	40·26 E
116	Galty Mts. Ire.	52·19 N	8·20 W
73	Galva (găl'và) Ill.	41·11 N	90·02 W
77	Galveston (găl'vĕs-tŭn). Tex. (In.)	29·18 N	94·48 W
77	Galveston B. Tex.	29·39 N	94·45 W
77	Galveston I. Tex. (In.)	29·12 N	94·53 W
116	Galway Ire.	53·16 N	9·05 W
116	Galway B. (gôl'wā) Ire.	53·10 N	9·47 W
164	Gambaga (găm-bä'gä) Ghana	10·37 N	0·20 W
165	Gambēlā (găm-bā'là) Eth.	8·15 N	34·33 E
163	Gambia (găm'bē-à) Afr.	13·38 N	19·38 W
164	Gambia R. Gam.-Senegal	12·58 N	12·58 W
166	Gamboma (găm-bō'mä) Con. B.	2·30 S	16·00 E
84	Gambrills (găm-brĭls) Md. (Baltimore In.)	39·04 N	76·38 W
118	Gamleby (gäm'lĕ-bü) Swe.	57·54 N	16·20 E
155	Gamu (gä-mo͞o'). Phil. (Manila In.)	17·05 N	121·50 E
142	Gandak (R.) India	26·37 N	84·22 E
83	Gander (găn'dẽr) Can.	48·59 N	54·32 W
83	Gander (R.) Can.	48·45 N	55·13 W
83	Gander L. Can.	48·57 N	55·10 W
125	Gandia (gän-dē'ä) Sp.	38·56 N	0·10 W
142	Ganges, Mouths of (găn'jēz). India	21·18 N	88·40 E
142	Ganges (R.) (găn'jēz) India	24·32 N	87·58 E
126	Gangi (gän'jē) It.	37·48 N	14·15 E
146	Gangtok Sikkim	27·15 N	88·30 E
67	Gannett Pk. (găn'ĕt) Wyo.	43·10 N	109·38 W
75	Gano (g'ĕ'nô). Ohio (Cincinnati In.)	39·18 N	84·24 W
111	Gänserndorf Aus. (Vienna In.)	48·21 N	16·43 E
164	Gao (gä'ō) Mali	16·17 N	0·00
164	Gaoua (gà-o͞o-ä') Upper Volta	10·21 N	3·11 W
123	Gap (gàp) Fr.	44·34 N	6·08 E
155	Gapan (gä-pän). Phil. (Manila In.)	15·18 N	120·56 E
93	Garachiné (gä-rä-chē'nā) Pan.	8·02 N	78·22 W
93	Garachiné, Punta (Pt.) (po͞o'n-tä-gä-rä-chē'nā). Pan.	8·08 N	78·35 W
99	Garanhuns (gä-rän-yo͞oɴsh'). Braz.	8·49 S	36·28 W
73	Garber (gär'bẽr) Okla.	36·28 N	97·35 W
111	Garching (gär'kĕng) Ger. (Munich In.)	48·15 N	11·39 E
76	Garcia (gär-sē'ä) Mex.	25·90 N	100·37 W
90	Garcia de la Cadena (dĕ-lä-kä-dĕ-nä). Mex.	21·14 N	103·26 W
126	Garda, Lago di (L.) (lä'gō-dē-gär'dä). It.	45·43 N	10·26 E
122	Gardanne (gär-dän') Fr. (Marseille In.)	43·28 N	5·29 E
120	Gardelegen (gär-dē-lā'ghĕn). Ger.	52·32 N	11·22 E
80	Garden (I.) (gär'd'n) Mich.	45·50 N	85·50 W
74	Gardena (gär-dē'nà) Calif. (Los Angeles In.)	33·53 N	118·19 W
75	Garden City. Mich. (Detroit In.)	42·20 N	83·21 W
72	Garden City Kan.	37·58 N	100·52 W
74	Garden Grove (gär'd'n grōv) Calif. (Los Angeles In.)	33·47 N	117·56 W
84	Garden Island B. La. (New Orleans In.)	29·03 N	89·07 W
74	Garden River Can. (Sault Ste. Marie In.)	46·33 N	84·10 W
82	Gardiner (gärd'nẽr) Maine	44·12 N	69·46 W
67	Gardiner Mont.	45·03 N	110·43 W
65	Gardiner Wash. (Seattle In.)	48·03 N	122·55 W
142	Gardiz Afg.	33·43 N	69·09 E
81	Gardner Mass.	42·35 N	72·00 W
165	Gardulā Eth.	5·43 N	37·40 E
142	Gar Dzong China	32·28 N	79·50 E
64	Gareloi (I.) (gär-lo͞o-ä') Alaska	51·40 N	178·48 W
84	Garfield (gär'fēld) N. J. (New York In.)	40·53 N	74·06 W
74	Garfield Utah (Salt Lake City In.)	40·45 N	112·10 W
75	Garfield Heights Ohio (Cleveland In.)	41·25 N	81·36 W
127	Gargaliánoi (gär-gä-lyä'nē) Grc.	37·07 N	21·50 E
119	Gargždai (gärgzh'dī) Sov. Un.	55·43 N	20·09 E
100	Garin (gä-rē'n) Arg. (In.)	34·10 S	58·44 W
74	Garland (gär'lănd) Tex. (Dallas, Fort Worth In.)	32·55 N	96·39 W
67	Garland Utah	41·45 N	112·10 W
134	Garm Sov. Un.	39·12 N	70·28 E
120	Garmisch-Partenkirchen (gär'mēsh pär'tĕn-kēr'kĕn). Ger.	47·38 N	11·10 E
73	Garnett (gär'nĕt) Kans.	38·16 N	95·15 W
122	Garonne Rivière (R.) (gà-rôn) Fr.	44·43 N	0·25 W
165	Garoua (gär'wä) Cam.	9·16 N	13·24 E
80	Garrett (găr'ĕt) Ind.	41·20 N	85·10 W
84	Garrison (găr'ĭ-sŭn) N. Y. (New York In.)	41·23 N	73·57 W
70	Garrison N. D.	47·38 N	101·24 W
70	Garrison Dam Res. N. D.	47·49 N	101·58 W
124	Garrovillas (gä-rō-vēl'yäs) Sp.	39·42 N	6·30 W
86	Garry (L.) (găr'ĭ) Can.	66·16 N	99·23 W
111	Garstedt (gär'shtĕt) Ger. (Hamburg In.)	53·40 N	9·58 E
142	Gartok (gär-tŏk') China	31·11 N	80·35 E
121	Garwolin (gär-vō'lĕn) Pol.	51·54 N	21·40 E
75	Gary (gā'rĭ) Ind. (Chicago In.)	41·35 N	87·21 W
98	Garzón (gär-thōn') Col.	2·13 N	75·44 W
155	Gasan (gä-sän'). Phil. (Manila In.)	13·19 N	121·52 E
133	Gasan-Kuli Sov. Un.	37·25 N	53·55 E
80	Gas City (găs) Ind.	40·30 N	85·40 W
122	Gascogne (Reg.) (gäs-kôn'yĕ). Fr.	43·45 N	1·49 W
73	Gasconade (R.) (găs-kô-nād'). Mo.	37·46 N	92·15 W
158	Gascoyne (R.) (găs-koin'). Austl.	25·15 S	117·00 E
74	Gashland (găsh'-lănd) Mo. (Kansas City In.)	39·15 N	94·35 W
123	Gasny (gäs-nē') Fr. (Paris In.)	49·05 N	1·36 E
82	Gaspé, C. Can.	48·44 N	64·00 W
82	Gaspe (I.) Can.	48·52 N	65·45 W
82	Gaspé B. (gas'pā) (găs-pā') Can.	48·40 N	64·07 W
82	Gaspé Passage Can.	49·21 N	64·16 W
82	Gaspé Pen. Can.	48·51 N	64·32 W
95	Gasper Hernandez (gäs-pär' ĕr-nän'dāth) Dom. Rep.	19·40 N	70·15 W
80	Gassaway (găs'à-wā) W. Va.	38·40 N	80·45 W
65	Gaston (găs'tŭn) Ore. (Portland In.)	45·26 N	123·08 W
79	Gastonia (găs-tô'nĭ-à) N. C.	35·15 N	81·14 W
100	Gastre (gäs-trĕ) Arg.	42·12 S	68·50 W
139	Gata, C. Cyprus (Palestine In.)	34·31 N	33·08 E
124	Gata, Cabo de (C.) (kà'bô-dĕ-gä'tä). Sp.	36·42 N	2·00 W
124	Gata, Sierra de (Mts.) (syĕr'rà dā gä'tä). Sp.	40·12 N	6·39 W
136	Gatchina (gä-chē'nà) Sov. Un. (Leningrad In.)	59·33 N	30·08 E
116	Gateshead (gāts'hĕd) Eng.	54·56 N	1·38 W
77	Gatesville (gāts'vĭl) Mex.	31·26 N	97·43 W
85	Gatineau (gà'tē-nō) Can. (Ottawa In.)	45·29 N	75·38 W
81	Gatineau (R.) Can.	45·45 N	75·50 W
166	Gatooma (gä-to͞o'mà) S. Rh.	18·14 S	29·46 E
111	Gattendorf Aus. (Vienna In.)	48·01 N	17·00 E
88	Gatun (gä-to͞on') C. Z. (Panama Canal In.)	9·16 N	79·25 W
88	Gatun, L. Pan.-C. Z. (Panama Canal In.)	9·13 N	79·24 W
88	Gatun (R.) Pan. (Panama Canal In.)	9·21 N	79·10 W
88	Gatun Locks C. Z. (Panama Canal In.)	9·16 N	79·27 W
142	Gauhati India	26·09 N	91·51 E
119	Gauja (R.) (gà'o͝o-yà) Sov. Un.	57·10 N	24·30 E
155	Gauttier-Gebergte (Mts.) (gō-tyā') W. Irian	2·30 S	138·45 E
126	Gávdhos (I.) (gäv'dôs). Grc. (In.)	34·48 N	24·08 E
70	Gavins Point Dam (gă'-vĭns) Nebr.	42·47 N	97·47 W
118	Gävle (yĕv'lĕ) Swe.	60·40 N	17·07 E
118	Gavle-bukten (B.) Swe.	60·45 N	17·30 E
128	Gavrilov Posad (gà'vrē-lôf'ka po-sàt). Sov. Un.	56·34 N	40·09 E
128	Gavrilov-Yam (gà'vrē-lôf yäm') Sov. Un.	57·17 N	39·49 E
160	Gawler (gô'lẽr) Austl.	34·35 S	138·47 E
160	Gawler Ra. Austl.	32·35 S	136·30 E
142	Gaya (gŭ'yä) (gī'à) India	24·53 N	85·04 E
164	Gaya (gä'yä) Nig.	11·58 N	9·05 E
80	Gaylord (gā'lôrd) Mich.	45·00 N	84·35 W
160	Gayndah (gān'dăh) Austl.	25·43 S	151·33 E
129	Gaysin Sov. Un.	48·46 N	29·22 E
	Gaza, see Ghazzah		
133	Gaziantep (gä-zē-än'tĕp) Tur.	37·10 N	37·30 E
121	Gdańsk (Danzig) (g'dänsk) (dän'tsĕg). Pol.	54·20 N	18·40 E
128	Gdov (g'dôf') Sov. Un.	58·44 N	27·51 E
121	Gdynia (g'dĕn'yä) Pol.	54·29 N	18·30 E
72	Geary (gē'rĭ) Okla.	35·36 N	98·19 W
168	Gebel el Galala el Bahariya (Plat.) U. A. R. (Nile In.)	29·23 N	31·50 E
67	Gebo (gĕb'ō) Wyo.	43·49 N	108·13 W
77	Ged (gĕd) La.	30·07 N	93·36 W
165	Gedaref Sud.	14·03 N	35·11 E
115	Gediz (R.) Tur.	38·44 N	28·45 E
65	Gedney (I.) (gĕd-nē) Wash. (Seattle In.)	48·01 N	122·18 W
120	Gedser Den.	54·35 N	12·08 E
111	Geel Bel. (Brussels In.)	51·09 N	5·01 E
161	Geelong (jē-lông') Austl. (Melbourne In.)	38·06 S	144·13 E
155	Geelvink-baai (B.) (gäl'vĭnk) W. Irian	2·20 S	135·30 E
164	Geidam Nig.	12·49 N	11·49 E
158	Geikie Ra. (gē'kē) Austl.	17·35 S	125·32 E
120	Geislingen (gis'lĭng-ĕn) Ger.	48·37 N	9·52 E
75	Geist Res. (gēst) Ind. (Indianapolis In.)	39·57 N	85·59 W
111	Geldermalsen Neth. (Amsterdam In.)	51·53 N	5·18 E
123	Geldern (gĕl'dĕrn) Ger. (Ruhr In.)	51·31 N	6·20 E
127	Gelibolu, Yarimada (Pen.) (gĕ-lĭb'ô-lo͞o). Tur.	40·23 N	25·10 E
129	Gel'myazov Sov. Un.	49·49 N	31·54 E
123	Gelsenkirchen (gĕl-zĕn-kĭrk-ĕn) Ger. (Ruhr In.)	51·31 N	7·05 E
139	Gemas (jĕm'ás) Mala. (Singapore In.)	2·35 N	102·37 E
165	Gemena Con. L.	4·00 N	19·53 E
133	Gemlik (gĕm'lĭk) Tur.	40·30 N	29·10 E

ăt; finăl; rāte; senâte; ärm; åsk; sofà; fâre; ch-choose; dh-as th in other; bē; ēvent; bĕt; recĕnt; cratẽr; g-go; gh-guttural g; bĭt; ĭ-short neutral; rīde; ᴋ-guttural k as ch in German ich;

PRONOUNCING INDEX

General Alvear–Goggingen 209

Page	Name Pronunciation Region	Lat. °′	Long. °′
101	General Alvear (gě-ně-rál'ál-vě-á'r) .Arg. (Buenos Aires In.)	36·04 s	60·02 w
101	General Arenales (á-rě-nä'lěs) Arg. (Buenos Aires In.)	34·19 s	61·16 w
101	General Belgrano (běl-grá'nô) Arg. (Buenos Aires In.)	35·45 s	58·32 w
76	General Cepeda (sě-pě'dä) Mex.	25·24 N	101·29 w
101	General Conesa (kô-ně'sä) Arg. (Buenos Aires In.)	36·30 s	57·19 w
101	General Guido (gē'dô) Arg. (Buenos Aires In.)	36·41 s	57·48 w
101	General Lavalle (lá-vá'l-yě) Arg. (Buenos Aires In.)	36·25 s	56·55 w
100	General Madariaga (män-dá-rêä'gä) .Arg.	36·59 s	57·14 w
101	General Paz (pá'z) Arg. (Buenos Aires In.)	35·30 s	58·20 w
90	General Pedro Antonio Santios (pě'drô-än-tô'nyô-sän-työs). Mex.	21·37 N	98·58 w
100	General Pico (pē'kô) Arg.	36·46 s	63·44 w
100	General Roca (rô-kä) Arg.	39·01 s	67·31 w
100	General San Martín (sän-mär-tē'n) Arg. (In.)	34·19 s	58·32 w
101	General Viamonte (vēá'môn-tě) Arg. (Buenos Aires In.)	35·01 s	60·59 w
76	General Zuazua (zwä'zwä) .Mex.	25·54 N	100·07 w
71	Genesco (jě-něs'cō) Ill.	41·28 N	90·11 w
81	Genesee (R.) (jěn-ê-sē') N. Y.	42·25 N	78·10 w
78	Geneva (jê-nē'vȧ) Ala.	31·03 N	85·50 w
75	Geneva Ill. (Chicago In.)	41·53 N	88·18 w
73	Geneva Nebr.	40·32 N	97·37 w
81	Geneva N. Y.	42·50 N	77·00 w
80	Geneva Ohio	41·45 N	80·55 w
	Geneva, see Génève		
120	Geneva, L Switz.	46·28 N	6·30 E
120	Génève (Geneva) (zhē-něv') .Switz.	46·14 N	6·04 E
129	Genichesk (gå'nê-chyěsk') Sov. Un.	46·11 N	34·47 E
124	Genil (R.) (hâ-nēl') Sp.	37·12 N	4·30 w
73	Genoa (jen'ô-ȧ) Nebr.	41·26 N	97·43 w
77	Genoa Tex. (In.)	29·37 N	95·11 w
	Genoa, see Genova		
75	Genoa City .Wis. (Milwaukee In.)	42·31 N	88·19 w
126	Genova (Genoa) (jěn'ō-vä) It.	44·23 N	9·52 E
126	Genova, Golfo di (G.) (gôl-fô-dē-jěn'ō-vä) .It.	44·10 N	8·45 E
98	Genovesa (I.) (ě's-lä-gě-nō-vě-sä) Ec.	0·08 N	90·15 w
117	Gent Bel.	51·05 N	3·40 E
120	Genthin (gěn-tēn') Ger.	52·24 N	12·10 E
125	Genzano di Roma (gzhěnt-zá'-nô-dē-rô'-mä) It. (Rome In.)	41·43 N	12·49 E
158	Geographe B. (jē-ô-grǎf') Austl.	33·00 s	114·00 E
158	Geographic Chan. (jēô'grǎ-fǐk) Austl.	24·15 s	112·50 E
133	Geokchay (gě-ôk'chī) Sov. Un.	40·40 N	47·40 E
79	George (L.) (jôr-ĭj) Fla.	29·10 N	81·50 w
81	George (L.) (jôrj) N. Y.	43·40 N	73·30 w
83	George B. (jôr-ĭj) Can.	45·46 N	61·45 w
74	George L. (jôrg) Can.-U. S. (Sault Ste. Marie In.)	46·26 N	84·09 w
75	George, L. Ind. (Chicago In.)	41·31 N	87·17 w
161	Georges (R.) Austl. (Sydney In.)	33·57 s	151·00 E
95	George Town Ba. Is.	23·30 N	75·50 w
99	Georgetown (jôrj'toun) Br. Gu.	7·45 N	58·04 w
83	Georgetown (jôr-ĭj-toun) Can.	46·09 N	62·32 w
85	Georgetown (jôrg-toun) Can. (Toronto In.)	43·39 N	79·56 w
84	Georgetown .Conn.(New York In.)	41·15 N	73·25 w
81	Georgetown Del.	38·40 N	75·20 w
94	Georgetown Cayman Is.	19·20 N	81·20 w
80	Georgetown Ill.	40·00 N	87·40 w
80	Georgetown Ky.	38·10 N	84·35 w
81	Georgetown Md.	39·25 N	75·55 w
83	Georgetown (jôrg-toun) Mass. (Boston In.)	42·43 N	71·00 w
79	Georgetown (jôr-ĭj-toun) S. C.	33·22 N	79·17 w
77	Georgetown (jôrg-toun) Tex.	30·37 N	97·40 w
81	George Washington Birthplace Natl. Mon. (jôrj wŏsh'ĭng-tŭn) Va.	38·10 N	77·00 w
73	George Washington Carver Natl. Mon. (jôrg wǎsh-ĭng-tŭn kär'-vēr) .Mo.	36·58 N	94·21 w
63	Georgia (State) (jôr'ji-ǎ) U. S.	32·40 N	83·50 w
65	Georgia, Str. of Wash. (Vancouver In.)	48·56 N	123·06 w
130	Georgian (S. S. R.) Sov. Un.	42·17 N	43·00 E
78	Georgiana (jôr-jē-ǎn'ǎ) Ala.	31·39 N	86·44 w
87	Georgian Is. Natl. Park (jôr'ji-ǎn) .Can.	45·15 N	81·10 w
158	Georgina (R.) (jôr-jē'nȧ) Austl.	22·00 s	138·15 E
133	Georgiyevsk (gyôr-gyěfsk') Sov. Un.	44·05 N	43·30 E
120	Gera (gā'rä) Ger.	50·52 N	12·06 E
100	Geral, Serra (Mts.) (sěr'rȧ zhä-räl') .Braz.	28·30 s	51·00 w
99	Geral de Goiás, Serra (Mts.) (zhä-räl'-dě-gô-yá's) .Braz.	14·22 s	45·40 w
158	Geraldton (jěr'ǎld-tŭn) Austl.	28·40 s	114·35 E
87	Geraldton Can.	49·43 N	87·00 w
124	Gérgal (gěr'gäl) Sp.	37·08 N	2·29 w
70	Gering (gē'rĭng) Nebr.	41·49 N	103·41 w
121	Gerlachovka Pk Czech.	49·12 N	20·05 E
80	Germantown (jûr'mǎn-toun) .Ohio	39·35 N	84·25 w
102	Germany (jûr'mȧ-nĭ) Eur.	51·44 N	8·46 E
167	Germiston (jûr'mĭs-tŭn) S. Afr. (Johannesburg & Pretoria In.)	26·19 s	28·11 E
155	Gerona (hä-rō'nä) Phil. (Manila In.)	15·36 N	120·36 E
124	Gerona (hě-rô'-nä) Sp.	41·55 N	2·48 E
110	Gerrards Cross (jěr'ǎrds krôs) Eng. (London In.)	51·34 N	0·33 w
125	Gers (R.) (zhěr) Fr.	43·25 N	0·30 E
111	Gersthofen (gěrst-hō'fěn) Ger. (Munich In.)	48·26 N	10·54 E
114	Géryville (zhā-rê-vēl') Alg.	33·42 N	1·06 E
168	Gestro R. .Eth. (Horn of Afr. In.)	5·18 N	41·50 E
125	Getafe (hä-tä'fâ) Sp. (Madrid In.)	40·19 N	3·44 w
81	Gettysburg (gět'ĭs-bûrg) Pa.	39·50 N	77 15 w
70	Gettysburg S. D.	45·01 N	99·59 w
123	Gevelsberg (gě-fěls'běrgh) Ger. (Ruhr In.)	51·18 N	7·20 E
142	Ghāghra (R.) India	27·19 N	81·22 E
163	Ghana (gän'ä) Afr.	8·00 N	2·00 w
166	Ghanzi (gän'zē) Bech.	21·30 s	22·00 E
142	Ghard W. Pak.	24·50 N	68·35 E
164	Ghardaïa (gär-dä'ē-ä) Alg.	32·29 N	3·38 E
164	Ghāt Libya	24·52 N	10·16 E
165	Ghazal, Bahr el (R.) (bär ěl ghä-zäl') .Sud.	9·11 N	29·37 E
142	Ghazni (gŭz'nē) Afg.	33·43 N	68·18 E
139	Ghazzah (Gaza) Gaza Area (Palestine In.)	31·30 N	34·29 E
121	Gheorghieni Rom.	46·48 N	25·30 E
121	Gherla (gěr'lä) Rom.	47·01 N	23·55 E
164	Ghugāmis Alg.	30·07 N	9·26 E
126	Giannutri, I. di (jän-nōō'trē) It.	42·15 N	11·06 E
95	Gibara (hē-bä'rä) Cuba	21·05 N	76·10 w
166	Gibeon (gĭb'ê-ŭn) S. W. Afr.	24·45 s	16·40 E
124	Gibraleón (hē-brä-lå-ōn') Sp.	37·24 N	7·00 w
124	Gibraltar (hê-bräl-tä'r) Eur.	36·08 N	5·22 w
124	Gibraltar, Bay of Sp.	35·04 N	5·10 w
124	Gibraltar, Strait of Afr.-Eur.	35·55 N	5·45 w
75	Gibson (gĭb'sŭn) Ind. (Louisville In.)	38·24 N	85·40 w
80	Gibson City Ill.	40·25 N	88·20 w
158	Gibson Des Austl.	24·45 s	123·15 E
73	Gibson Res Okla.	36·07 N	95·08 w
77	Giddings (gĭd'ĭngz) Tex.	30·11 N	96·55 w
73	Gideon (gĭd'ê-ŭn) Mo.	36·27 N	89·56 w
122	Gien (zhē-ǎN') Fr.	47·43 N	2·37 E
120	Giessen (gēs'sěn) Ger.	50·35 N	8·40 E
85	Giffard (zhē-färd') Can. (Quebec In.)	46·51 N	71·12 w
153	Gifu (gē'fōō) Jap.	35·25 N	136·45 E
65	Gig Harbor (gĭg) Wash. (Seattle In.)	47·20 N	122·36 w
126	Giglio, I. di (jēl'yō) It.	42·23 N	10·55 E
124	Gigüela (R.) (hē-gā'lä) Sp.	39·53 N	2·54 w
124	Gijón (hê-hōn') Sp.	43·33 N	5·37 w
69	Gila (R.) (hē'lȧ) Ariz.	32·41 N	113·50 w
69	Gila Bend Ariz.	32·59 N	112·41 w
69	Gila Bend Ind. Res. Ariz.	33·02 N	112·48 w
69	Gila Cliff Dwellings Natl. Mon. N. Mex.	33·15 N	108·20 w
69	Gila River Ind. Res Ariz.	33·11 N	112·38 w
71	Gilbert (gĭl'bērt) Minn.	47·27 N	92·29 w
159	Gilbert (R.) (gĭl'bērt) Austl.	17·15 s	142·09 E
156	Gilbert Is Oceania	1·30 s	173·00 E
167	Gilboa, Mt. (gĭl-bôȧ) S. Afr. (Natal In.)	29·13 s	30·17 E
165	Gilf Kebir Plat U. A. R.	24·09 N	25·29 E
142	Gilgit (gĭl'gĭt) Pak.	35·58 N	73·48 E
158	Gillen (I.) (jĭl'ěn) Austl.	26·15 s	125·15 E
73	Gillett (jĭ-lět') Ark.	34·07 N	91·22 w
67	Gillette Wyo.	44·17 N	105·30 w
110	Gillingham (gĭl'ĭng ǎm) Eng. (London In.)	51·23 N	0·33 E
80	Gilman (gĭl'mǎn) Ill.	40·45 N	87·55 w
74	Gilman Hot Springs Calif. (Los Angeles In.)	33·49 N	116·57 w
77	Gilmer (gĭl'mēr) Tex.	32·43 N	94·57 w
84	Gilmore (gĭl'môr) .Ga. (Atlanta In.)	33·51 N	84·29 w
68	Gilroy (gĭl-roi') Calif.	37·00 N	121·34 w
155	Giluwe, Mt N. Gui. Ter.	6·04 s	144·00 E
122	Gimone (R.) (zhē-mōn') Fr.	43·26 N	0·36 E
168	Gineifa (jê-nā'fȧ) U. A. R. (Suez In.)	30·11 N	32·26 E
139	Gineina, Ras el (Mt.) U. A. R. (Palestine In.)	29·02 N	33·58 E
165	Ginir Eth.	7·13 N	40·44 E
126	Ginosa (jê-nō'zä) It.	40·35 N	16·48 E
124	Ginzo (hēn-thō') Sp.	42·03 N	7·43 w
126	Gioja del Colle (jō'yä děl kôl'lā) It.	40·48 N	16·55 E
99	Gi-Paraná (R.) (zhē-pä-rä-nà') Braz.	9·33 s	61·35 w
139	Girâfi (R.) .U. A. R. (Palestine In.)	29·48 N	34·43 E
73	Girard (jĭ-rärd') Kans.	37·30 N	94·50 w
98	Girardot (hē-rär-dōt') Col. (In.)	4·19 N	75·47 w
133	Giresun (ghěr'ě-sōōn') Tur.	40·55 N	38·20 E
142	Giridih (jē'rê-dê) India	24·12 N	81·18 E
122	Gironde (Est.) (zhē-rôNd') Fr.	45·31 N	1·00 w
116	Girvan (gûr'vǎn) Scot.	55·15 N	5·01 w
159	Gisborne (gĭz'bŭrn) N. Z. (In.)	38·40 s	178·08 E
122	Gisors (zhē-zôr') Fr.	49·19 N	1·47 E
127	Giurgiu (jŏŏr'jŏŏ) Rom.	43·53 N	25·58 E
122	Givet (zhē-vě') Fr.	50·80 N	4·47 E
122	Givors (zhē-vôr') Fr.	45·35 N	4·46 E
135	Gizhiga (gē'zhi-gȧ) Sov. Un.	61·59 N	160·46 E
121	Gizycko (gē'zhĭ-kô) Pol.	54·03 N	21·48 E
127	Gjinokastër Alb.	40·04 N	20·10 E
118	Gjövik (gyû'vēk) Nor.	60·47 N	10·36 E
111	Glabeek-Zuurbemde Bel. (Brussels In.)	50·52 N	4·59 E
64	Glacier Bay Natl. Mon. (glā'shēr) Alaska	58·40 N	136·50 w
86	Glacier Natl. Park Can.	51·35 N	120·00 w
66	Glacier Pk Wash.	48·07 N	121·10 w
65	Glacier Pt Can. (Seattle In.)	48·24 N	123·59 w
123	Gladbeck (gläd'běk) Ger. (Ruhr In.)	51·35 N	6·59 E
168	Gladdeklipkop S. Afr. (Johannesburg & Pretoria In.)	24·17 s	29·36 E
160	Gladstone (glǎd'stōn) Austl.	23·45 s	150·00 E
160	Gladstone Austl.	33·15 s	138·20 E
62	Gladstone Can.	50·20 N	99·00 w
71	Gladstone Mich.	45·50 N	87·04 w
84	Gladstone N. J. (New York In.)	40·43 N	74·39 w
65	Gladstone Ore. (Portland In.)	45·23 N	122·36 w
80	Gladwin (glǎd'wĭn) Mich.	44·00 N	84·25 w
126	Glamoč (glǎm'ôch) Yugo.	44·03 N	16·51 E
120	Glarus (glä'rōōs) Switz.	47·02 N	9·03 E
116	Glasgow (glás'gō) Scot.	55·54 N	4·25 w
78	Glasgow Ky.	37·00 N	85·55 w
73	Glasgow Mo.	39·14 N	92·48 w
67	Glasgow Mont.	48·14 N	106·39 w
83	Glass B. (glás) Can.	46·12 N	59·57 w
75	Glassport (glás'pōrt) Pa. (Pittsburgh In.)	40·19 N	79·53 w
120	Glauchau (glou'ĸou) Ger.	50·51 N	12·28 E
132	Glazov (glä'zôf) Sov. Un.	58·05 N	52·52 E
120	Glda R. (g'l'dä) Pol.	53·27 N	16·52 E
110	Glen (R.) (glěn) Eng.	52·44 N	0·18 w
122	Glénans, Iles de (Is.) (ēl-dě-glā-näN') .Fr.	47·43 N	4·42 w
84	Glen Burnie (bûr'nê) Md. (Baltimore In.)	39·10 N	76·38 w
69	Glen Canyon Dam (glěn kǎn'yŭn) Ariz.	36·57 N	111·25 w
74	Glen Carbon (kär'bǒn) Ill. (St. Louis In.)	38·45 N	89·59 w
75	Glencoe Ill. (Chicago In.)	42·08 N	87·45 w
71	Glencoe (glěn'kō) Minn.	44·44 N	94·07 w
167	Glencoe (glěn-cô) S. Afr. (Natal In.)	28·14 s	30·09 E
84	Glen Cove (kōv) N. Y. (New York In.)	40·51 N	73·38 w
69	Glendale (glěn'dāl) Ariz.	33·30 N	112·15 w
74	Glendale Calif. (Los Angeles In.)	34·09 N	118·15 w
75	Glendale Ohio (Cincinnati In.)	31·16 N	84·22 w
67	Glendive (glěn'dīv) Mont.	47·08 N	104·41 w
67	Glendo Wyo.	42·32 N	104·54 w
74	Glendora (glěn-dō'rȧ) Calif. (Los Angeles In.)	34·08 N	117·52 w
160	Glenelg (R.) Austl.	37·20 s	141·30 E
75	Glen Ellyn (glěn ěl'-lěn) Ill. (Chicago In.)	41·53 N	88·04 w
160	Glen Innes (ĭn'ěs) Austl.	29·45 s	152·02 E
77	Glenmora (glěn-mō'rȧ) La.	30·58 N	92·36 w
66	Glenns Ferry (fěr'ĭ) Idaho	42·58 N	115·21 w
79	Glennville (glěn'vĭl) Ga.	31·55 N	81·56 w
84	Glen Olden (ōl'd'n) Pa. (Philadelphia In.)	39·54 N	75·17 w
84	Glen Rock (rǒk) .Va. (Norfolk In.)	36·50 N	76·13 w
67	Glenrock (glěn'rǒk) Wyo.	42·50 N	105·53 w
81	Glens Falls (glěnz fôlz) N. Y.	43·20 N	73·40 w
75	Glenshaw (glěn'shô) Pa. (Pittsburgh In.)	40·33 N	79·57 w
70	Glen Ullin (glěn'ŭl'ĭn) N. D.	46·47 N	101·49 w
65	Glen Valley .Can. (Vancouver In.)	49·09 N	122·30 w
75	Glenview (glěn'vū) Ill. (Chicago In.)	42·04 N	87·48 w
83	Glenwood (glěn-wŏŏd) Can.	48·59 N	54·51 w
70	Glenwood Iowa	41·03 N	95·44 w
70	Glenwood Minn.	45·39 N	95·23 w
69	Glenwood Springs Colo.	39·35 N	107·20 w
111	Glienicke (glē'nē-kě) Ger. (Berlin In.)	52·38 N	13·19 E
111	Glinde (glěn'dě) Ger. (Hamburg In.)	53·32 N	10·13 E
121	Gliwice (gwĭ-wĭt'sě) Pol.	50·18 N	18·40 E
69	Globe (glōb) Ariz.	33·20 N	110·50 w
129	Globino (glôb'ê-nô) Sov. Un.	49·22 N	33·17 E
120	Głogów Szprotawa (gwô'gōōv shprō-tä'vä) .Pol.	51·40 N	16·04 E
118	Glomma (R.) (glômmä) Nor.	61·22 N	11·02 E
118	Glommen (R.) (glôm'ěn) Nor.	60·03 N	11·15 E
111	Glonn (glônn) Ger. (Munich In.)	47·59 N	11·52 E
167	Glorieuses, Îles (Is.) Malag. Rep.	11·28 s	47·50 E
110	Glossop (glŏs'ŭp) Eng.	53·26 N	1·57 w
78	Gloster (glŏs'tēr) Miss.	31·10 N	91·00 w
116	Gloucester (glŏs'tēr) Eng.	51·54 N	2·11 w
83	Gloucester Mass. (Boston In.)	42·37 N	70·40 w
84	Gloucester City N. J. (Philadelphia In.)	39·53 N	75·08 w
80	Glouster (glŏs'tēr) Ohio	39·35 N	82·05 w
83	Glover I. (glŭv'ēr) Can.	48·41 N	57·30 w
81	Gloversville (glŭv'ērz-vĭl) N. Y.	43·05 N	74·20 w
83	Glovertown (glŭv'ēr-toun) Can.	48·42 N	54·01 w
128	Glubokoye (glōō-bô-kō'yě) Sov. Un.	55·08 N	27·44 E
111	Glückstadt(glük-shtät) Ger. (Hamburg In.)	53·47 N	9·25 E
129	Glukhov (glōō'kôf') Sov. Un.	51·42 N	33·52 E
129	Glushkovo (glōōsh'kô-vō) .Sov. Un.	51·21 N	34·43 E
120	Gmünden (g'mōōn'děn) Aus.	47·57 N	13·47 E
121	Gniezno (g'nyâz'nô) Pol.	52·32 N	17·34 E
127	Gnjilane (gnyě'lä-ně) Yugo.	42·28 N	21·27 E
143	Gôa (Ter.) (gō'ȧ) Asia	20·40 N	74·13 E
92	Goascorán (gō-äs'kō-rän') Hond.	13·37 N	87·43 w
165	Goba (gō'bä) Eth.	7·17 N	39·58 E
166	Gobabis (gō-bä'bĭs) S. W. Afr.	22·25 s	18·50 E
146	Gobi or Shamo (Des.) (gō'be) Mong.	43·29 N	103·15 E
65	Goble (gō'b'l) Ore. (Portland In.)	46·01 N	122·53 w
123	Goch (gōĸ) Ger. (Ruhr In.)	51·35 N	6·10 E
142	Godāvari (R.) (gō-dä'vŭ-rê) .India	17·42 N	81·15 E
158	Goddards Soak (Swp.) (gŏd'ǎrdz) Austl.	31·20 s	123·30 E
80	Goderich (gōd'rĭch) Can.	43·45 N	81·45 w
74	Godfrey (gŏd'frê) Ill. (St. Louis In.)	38·57 N	90·12 w
49	Godhavn (gōdh'hāvn) Grnld.	69·15 N	53·30 w
86	Gods (L.) (gŏdz) Can.	54·38 N	95·23 w
49	Godthaab (gŏt'hōōb) Grnld.	64·10 N	51·32 w
146	Godwin Austen, Mt. (gŏd wĭn ôs'těn) .Pak.	36·06 N	76·38 E
68	Goffs (gôfs) Calif.	34·57 N	115·06 w
71	Gogebic (L.) (gō-gē'bĭk) Mich.	46·24 N	89·25 w
71	Gogebic Ra. Mich.	46·37 N	89·48 w
111	Goggingen (gûg'gěn-gěn) Ger. (Munich In.)	48·21 N	10·53 E

Page	Name Pronunciation Region	Lat. °′	Long. °′
90	Gogorrón (gō-gô-rōn′) . . . . Mex.	21·51 N	100·54 W
153	Goi (gō′ē) . . . . Jap. (Tōkyō In.)	35·31 N	140·05 E
99	Goiânia (gô-yà′nyä) . . . . Braz.	16·41 S	48·57 W
99	Goiás (gô-yà′s) . . . . Braz.	15·57 S	50·10 W
99	Goiás (State) . . . . Braz.	12·35 S	48·38 W
111	Goirle . . . . Neth. (Amsterdam In.)	51·31 N	5·06 E
133	Göksu (R.) (gûk′sōō′) . . . . Tur.	36·40 N	33·30 E
118	Göl (gûl) . . . . Nor.	60·58 N	8·54 E
118	Göla älv (R.) . . . . Swe.	58·11 N	12·03 E
79	Golax (gō′lăks) . . . . Va.	36·41 N	80·56 W
110	Golcar (gŏl′kàr) . . . . Eng.	53·38 N	1·52 W
73	Golconda (gŏl-kŏn′dȧ) . . . . Ill.	37·21 N	88·32 W
121	Gołdap (gôl′dăp) . . . . Pol.	54·17 N	22·17 E
72	Golden . . . . Colo.	39·44 N	105·15 W
84	Goldenbridge (gōl′dĕn-brĭj) N. Y. (New York In.)	41·17 N	73·41 W
66	Goldendale (gōl′dĕn-dāl) . . . Wash.	45·49 N	120·48 W
65	Golden Gate (Str.) (gōl′dĕn gāt) Calif. (San Francisco In.)	37·48 N	122·32 W
68	Goldfield (gōld-fēld) . . . . Nev.	37·42 N	117·15 W
88	Gold Hill (Mtn.) C. Z. (Panama Canal In.)	9·03 N	79·08 W
65	Gold Mtn. (gōld) Wash. (Seattle In.)	47·33 N	122·48 W
79	Goldsboro (gōldz-bûr′ô) . . . . . N. C.	35·23 N	77·59 W
76	Goldthwaite (gōld′thwāt) . . . . Tex.	31·27 N	98·34 W
120	Goleniów (gô-lĕ-nyŭf′) . . . . Pol.	53·33 N	14·51 E
135	Golets-Purpula, Gol′tsy (Mtn.) Sov. Un.	59·08 N	115·22 E
93	Golfito (gôl-fē′tō) . . . . C. R.	8·40 N	83·12 W
	Golfo Dulce, see Izabal, L.		
77	Goliad (gō-lĭ-ăd′) . . . . Tex.	28·40 N	97·21 W
155	Golo (gō′lō) . . . . Phil. (Manila In.)	13·38 N	120·17 E
126	Golo (R.) . . . . Cor.	42·28 N	9·18 E
129	Golovchino (gō-lôf′chê-nō) Sov. Un.	50·34 N	35·52 E
166	Golungo Alto (gô-lōōŋ′gô àl′tō) Ang.	9·10 S	14·40 E
127	Golyamo Konare (gō′lȧ-mō-kō′nä-rĕ) . Bul.	42·16 N	24·33 E
111	Golzow (gōl′tsōv) Ger. (Berlin In.)	52·17 N	12·36 E
164	Gombe . . . . Nig.	10·23 N	11·08 E
128	Gomel′ (gô′mĕl′) . . . . Sov. Un.	52·20 N	31·03 E
128	Gomel′ (Oblast) . . . . Sov. Un.	52·18 N	29·00 E
164	Gomera I. (gô-mā′rä) . . . . Can. Is.	28·00 N	18·01 W
76	Gomez Farias (gō′māz fä-rē′ás) Mex.	24·59 N	101·02 W
76	Gómez Palacio (pä-lä′syō) . . . Mex.	25·35 N	103·30 W
95	Gonaïves (gō-nȧ-ēv′) . . . . Hai.	19·25 N	72·45 W
95	Gonaïves, Golfe des (G.) (gō-nȧ-ēv′) . Hai.	19·20 N	73·20 W
95	Gonâve, Ile De La (I.) (gô-nàv′) Hai.	18·50 N	73·30 W
142	Gonda . . . . India	27·13 N	82·00 E
142	Gondal . . . . India	22·02 N	70·47 E
165	Gondar (gŏn′dȧr) . . . . Eth.	12·39 N	37·30 E
123	Gonesse (gô-nĕs′) . . Fr. (Paris In.)	48·59 N	2·28 E
153	Gonō (R.) (gô′nō) . . . . Jap.	35·00 N	132·25 E
85	Gonor (gō′nŏr) Can. (Winnipeg In.)	50·04 N	96·57 W
167	Gonubie Mouth (gŏn′ōō-bē mouth) . S. Afr. (Natal In.)	32·56 S	28·02 E
90	Gonzales (gôn-zȧ′lĕs) . . . . Mex.	22·47 N	98·26 W
77	Gonzales (gŏn-zä′lĕz) . . . . Tex.	29·31 N	97·25 W
100	González Catán (gōn-zȧ′lĕz-kä-tȧ′n) . Arg. (In.)	34·31 S	58·39 W
166	Good Hope, C. of (kāp ov gŏŏd hôp) . S. Afr. (Cape Town In.)	34·21 S	18·29 E
66	Gooding (gŏŏd′ĭng) . . . . Idaho	42·55 N	114·43 W
80	Goodland (gŏŏd′lănd) . . . . Ind.	40·50 N	87·15 W
72	Goodland . . . . Kans.	39·19 N	101·43 W
166	Goodwood (gŏŏd′wŏŏd) S. Afr. (Cape Town In.)	33·54 S	18·33 E
110	Goole (gōōl) . . . . Eng.	53·42 N	0·52 W
70	Goose (R.) . . . . N. D.	47·40 N	97·41 W
87	Goose Bay . . . . Can.	53·19 N	60·33 W
67	Gooseberry Cr. (gōōs-bĕr′ĭ) . . Wyo.	44·04 N	108·35 W
67	Goose Cr. (gōōs) . . . . Idaho	42·07 N	113·53 W
75	Goose Lake (gōōs lāk) Ill. (Chicago In.)	41·21 N	88·18 W
66	Goose L . . . . Calif.	41·56 N	120·35 W
142	Gorakhpur (gō′rŭk-pōōr) . . . . India	26·45 N	82·39 E
94	Gorda, Punta (Pt.) (pōō′n-tä-gôr-dä) . Cuba	22·25 N	82·10 W
94	Gorda Cay (gôr′dä) . . . . Ba. Is.	26·05 N	77·30 W
85	Gordon (gôr′dŭn) Can. (Winnipeg In.)	50·00 N	97·20 W
70	Gordon . . . . Nebr.	42·47 N	102·14 W
165	Gorē (gō′rĕ) . . . . Eth.	8·12 N	35·34 E
144	Gorgān . . . . Iran	36·44 N	54·30 E
126	Gorgona (I.) (gôr-gō′nä) . . . . It.	43·27 N	9·55 E
133	Gori (gō′rê) . . . . Sov. Un.	42·00 N	44·08 E
111	Gorinchem (gō′rĭn-kĕm) Neth. (Amsterdam In.)	51·50 N	4·59 E
110	Goring (gôr′ĭng) Eng. (London In.)	51·30 N	1·08 W
126	Gorizia (gô-rê′tsê-yä) . . . . Yugo.	44·56 N	13·40 E
132	Gorki (gôr′kē) . . . . Sov. Un.	56·15 N	44·05 E
132	Gor′kovskoye . . . . Sov. Un.	56·38 N	43·40 E
128	Gor′kovskoye (Gorkov) (L.) (gôr′kôf-skô-yĕ) . Sov. Un.	57·38 N	41·18 E
121	Gorlice (gôr-lē′tsĕ) . . . . Pol.	49·38 N	21·11 E
120	Gorlitz (gŭr′lĭts) . . . . Ger.	51·10 N	15·01 E
129	Gorlovka (gôr′lôf-kȧ) . . . . Sov. Un.	48·17 N	38·03 E
76	Gorman (gôr′măn) . . . . Tex.	32·13 N	98·40 W
127	Gorna-Oryakhovitsa (gôr′nä-ôr-yĕk′ô-vē-tsȧ) . Bul.	43·08 N	25·40 E
127	Gornji Milanovac (gôrn′yē-mē′la-nô-väts) . Yugo.	44·02 N	20·29 E
134	Gorno-Altay Aut. Oblast . Sov. Un.	51·00 N	86·00 E
134	Gorno-Altaysk (gôr′nŭ-ŭl-tīsk′) Sov. Un.	52·28 N	82·45 E
121	Gorodënka (gō-rô-deŋ′kä) Sov. Un.	48·40 N	25·30 E
132	Gorodets (Res.) . . . . Sov. Un.	57·00 N	43·55 E
136	Gorodishche (gô-rô′dĭsh-chĕ) Sov. Un. (Urals In.)	57·57 N	57·03 E
129	Gorodnya (gô-rôd′′nyä) . . Sov. Un.	51·54 N	31·31 E
121	Gorodok (gô-rô-dôk′) . . . . Sov. Un.	49·37 N	23·40 E
134	Gorodok . . . . Sov. Un.	50·30 N	103·58 E
128	Gorodok . . . . Sov. Un.	55·27 N	29·58 E
154	Gorontalo (gō-rōn-tä′lo) . . . Indon.	0·40 N	123·04 E
121	Goryn′ R. (gō′rĕn′) . . . . . . Sov. Un.	50·55 N	26·07 E
120	Gorzow Wielkopolski (gō-zhōōv′vyĕl-ko-pōl′skē) . Pol.	53·44 N	15·15 E
80	Goshen (gō′shĕn) . . . . Ind.	41·35 N	85·50 W
75	Goshen . . . . Ky. (Louisville In.)	38·24 N	85·34 W
84	Goshen . . . . N. Y. (New York In.)	41·24 N	74·19 W
75	Goshen . . . . . Ohio (Cincinnati In.)	39·14 N	84·09 W
65	Goshen . . . . Wash. (Vancouver In.)	48·52 N	122·20 W
69	Goshute Ind. Res. (gō-shōōt′) Utah	39·50 N	114·00 W
120	Goslar (gôs′lär) . . . . Ger.	51·55 N	10·25 E
99	Gospa (R.) (gôs-pä) . . . . Ven. (In.)	9·43 N	64·23 W
126	Gospić (gôs′pĭch) . . . . Yugo.	44·31 N	15·03 E
127	Gostivar (gos′tê-vär) . . . . Yugo.	41·46 N	20·58 E
121	Gostynin (gôs-tē′nĭn) . . . . Pol.	52·24 N	19·30 E
118	Göta Can. (yû′tȧ) . . . . Swe.	58·35 N	15·24 E
118	Göteborg (yû′tĕ-bôrgh) . . . . . . Swe.	57·39 N	11·56 E
164	Gotel Mts . . . . Nig.-Cam.	7·04 N	11·28 E
92	Gotera (gō-tā′rä) . . . . Sal.	13·41 N	88·06 W
120	Gotha (gō′tȧ) . . . . Ger.	50·57 N	10·43 E
72	Gothenburg (gŏth′ĕn-bûrg) . Nebr.	40·57 N	100·08 W
118	Gotland (I.) . . . . Swe.	57·35 N	17·35 E
153	Gotō-Rettō (Is.) (gō′tō rĕt′tō) Jap.	33·06 N	128·54 E
119	Gotska Sandön (I.) . . . . Swe.	58·24 N	19·15 E
120	Göttingen (gût′ĭng-ĕn) . . . . Ger.	51·32 N	9·57 E
111	Gouda (gou′dä) Neth. (Amsterdam In.)	52·00 N	4·42 E
47	Gough (I.) (gŏf) . . . . Atl. O.	40·00 S	10·00 W
87	Gouin Res. . . . . Can.	77·12 N	75·34 W
160	Goulburn (gōl′bŭrn) . . . . Austl.	34·47 S	149·40 E
164	Goumbou (gōōm-bōō′) . . . . Mali	15·02 N	7·35 W
164	Goundam (gōōn-däɴ′) . . . . Mali	16·29 N	3·37 W
164	Gouré (gōō-rā′) . . . . Niger	13·53 N	10·44 E
81	Gouverneur (gŭv-ẽr-nōōr′) . . N. Y.	44·20 N	75·25 W
86	Govenlock (gŭvĕn-lŏk) . . . . . . Can.	49·09 N	109·42 W
100	Governador Ilhado (I.) (gô-vĕr-nä-dō′r-ē-lȧ′dô) . Braz. (In.)	22·48 S	43·13 W
100	Governador Portela (pōr-tĕ′lȧ) Braz. (In.)	22·28 S	43·30 W
99	Governador Valadares (vä-lä-dä′rĕs) . Braz.	18·47 S	41·45 W
95	Governor's Harbour . . . . Ba. Is.	25·15 N	76·15 W
81	Gowanda (gô-wŏn′dȧ) . . . . . . N. Y.	42·30 N	78·55 W
100	Goya (gō′yä) . . . . Arg.	29·06 S	59·12 W
110	Goyt (R.) (goit) . . . . Eng.	53·19 N	2·03 W
166	Graaff-Reinet (gräf′rī′nĕt) . . S. Afr.	32·10 S	24·40 E
126	Gračac (grä′chäts) . . . . Yugo.	44·16 N	15·50 E
127	Gračanica (grȧ-chän′′i-tsä) . Yugo.	44·42 N	18·19 E
78	Graceville (grās′vĭl) . . . . Fla.	30·57 N	85·30 W
70	Graceville . . . . Minn.	45·33 N	96·25 W
92	Gracias (grä′sê-äs) . . . . Hond.	14·35 N	88·37 W
93	Gracias a Dios, Cabo (C.) (kȧ′bô-grä-syäs-ä-dyô′s) . . Hond.	15·00 N	83·13 W
164	Graciosa I. (grä-syô′sä) Azores (In.)	39·07 N	27·30 W
127	Gradačac (gra-dä′chats) . . . . Yugo.	44·50 N	18·28 E
124	Gradelos (grä-dĕ-lôs) . . . . Sp.	42·38 N	5·15 W
129	Gradizhsk (grä-dēzhsk′) . Sov. Un.	49·12 N	33·06 E
124	Grado (grä′dō) . . . . Sp.	43·24 N	6·04 W
111	Grafelfing (grä′fĕl-fēng) Ger. (Munich In.)	48·07 N	11·27 E
111	Grafing (grä′fēng) Ger. (Munich In.)	48·03 N	11·58 E
160	Grafton (graf′tŭn) . . . . Austl.	29·38 S	153·05 E
74	Grafton . . . . Ill. (St. Louis In.)	38·58 N	90·26 W
83	Grafton . . . . Mass. (Boston In.)	42·13 N	71·41 W
70	Grafton . . . . N. D.	48·24 N	97·25 W
75	Grafton . . . . . Ohio (Cleveland In.)	41·16 N	82·04 W
81	Grafton . . . . W. Va.	39·20 N	80·00 W
125	Gragnano (grän-yä′nô) It. (Naples In.)	40·27 N	14·32 E
79	Graham (grā′ăm) . . . . N. C.	36·03 N	79·23 W
72	Graham . . . . Tex.	33·07 N	98·34 W
65	Graham . . . . . . Wash. (Seattle In.)	47·03 N	122·18 W
86	Graham (I.) . . . . Can.	53·37 N	131·47 W
167	Grahamstown (grā′ăms′toun) S. Afr. (Natal In.)	33·19 S	26·33 E
123	Graian Alps (Mts.) (grā′yăn) Fr.-It.	45·17 N	6·52 E
99	Grajaú (grȧ-zhȧ-ōō′) . . . . Braz.	5·59 S	46·03 W
99	Grajaú (R.) . . . . Braz.	4·24 S	46·04 W
121	Grajewo (grä-yā′vo) . . . . Pol.	53·38 N	22·28 E
101	Grama, Serra de (Mtn.) (sĕ′r-rä-dĕ-grȧ′mȧ) Braz. (Rio de Janeiro In.)	23·42 S	42·28 W
127	Gramada (grä′mä-dä) . . . . Bul.	43·46 N	22·41 E
111	Gramatneusiedl . Aus. (Vienna In.)	48·02 N	16·29 E
126	Grammichele (gräm-mê-kĕ′lā) . . It.	37·15 N	14·40 E
116	Grampian Mts. (grăm′pĭ-ăn) Scot.	56·30 N	4·55 W
92	Granada (grä-nä′dhä) . . . . Nic.	11·55 N	85·58 W
124	Granada (grä-nä′dä) . . . . Sp.	37·13 N	3·37 W
100	Gran Bajo (Pln.) (grȧn′bä′kō) Arg.	47·35 S	68·45 W
77	Granbury (grăn′bẽr-ĭ) . . . . Tex.	32·26 N	97·45 W
81	Granby (grăn′bĭ) . . . . Can.	45·30 N	72·40 W
73	Granby . . . . Mo.	36·54 N	94·15 W
72	Granby (L.) . . . . Colo.	40·07 N	105·40 W
164	Gran Canaria I. (grän′kä-nä′rê-ä) . Can. Is.	27·39 N	15·39 W
100	Gran Chaco (Reg.) (grȧn′chȧ′kŏ) Arg.-Par.	25·30 S	62·15 W
71	Grand (I.) . . . . Mich.	46·37 N	86·38 W
82	Grand (L.) . . . . Can.	45·17 N	67·42 W
82	Grand (L.) . . . . Can.	66·15 N	45·59 W
80	Grand (R.) . . . . Can.	43·45 N	80·20 W
80	Grand (R.) . . . . Mich.	42·58 N	85·13 W
73	Grand (R.) . . . . Mo.	39·50 N	93·52 W
70	Grand (R.) . . . . S. D.	45·40 N	101·55 W
70	Grand (R.), North Fork . . . . S. D.	45·52 N	102·49 W
70	Grand (R.), South Fork . . . . . S. D.	45·38 N	102·56 W
94	Grand Bahama (I.) . . . . Ba. Is.	26·35 N	78·30 W
83	Grand Bank (grănd băngk) . . Can.	47·05 N	55·44 W
164	Grand Bassam (gräɴ bȧ-säɴ′) Ivory Coast	5·14 N	3·51 W
93	Grand Bourg (gräɴ bōōr′) Marie Galante (Le. & Wind. Is. In.)	15·54 N	61·20 W
95	Grand Caicos (I.) (grănd kä-ē′kōs) . Caicos	21·45 N	71·50 W
116	Grand Canal . . . . Ire.	53·21 N	7·15 W
	Grand Canal, see Yün Ho		
69	Grand Canyon (grănd kăn′yŭn) Ariz.	36·05 N	112·10 W
69	Grand Canyon . . . . Ariz.	35·50 N	113·16 W
69	Grand Canyon Natl. Mon . . . Ariz.	36·18 N	113·26 W
69	Grand Canyon Natl. Park . . . Ariz.	36·15 N	112·20 W
94	Grand Cayman (I.) (kā′măn) Cayman Is.	19·15 N	81·15 W
66	Grand Coulee Dam (kōō′lē) . Wash.	47·58 N	119·28 W
100	Grande, Bahia (B.) (bä-ē′ä-grȧn′dĕ) . Arg.	50·45 S	68·00 W
100	Grande, Salinas (F.) (sä-lê′näs) Arg.	29·45 S	65·00 W
98	Grande, Rio (R.) . . . . Bol.	16·49 S	63·19 W
99	Grande, Rio (R.) . . . . Braz.	19·48 S	49·54 W
101	Grande, Ilha (I.) (grän′dĕ) Braz. (Rio de Janeiro In.)	23·11 S	44·14 W
99	Grande, Salto (Falls) (säl-tô) Braz.	16·18 S	39·38 W
101	Grande (R.) . . Chile (Santiago In.)	35·25 S	70·14 W
91	Grande (R.) . . . . Mex.	17·37 N	96·41 W
88	Grande, Ciri (R.) (sē′rē-grän′dĕ) Pan. (Panama Canal In.)	8·55 N	80·04 W
62	Grande, Rio (Bravo del Norte, Rio) (R.) (grän′dā) . . U. S.-Mex.	26·50 N	99·10 W
101	Grande (R.) . Ur. (Buenos Aires In.)	33·19 S	57·15 W
100	Grande, Cuchilla (Mts.) (kōō-chē′l-yä) . Ur.	33·00 S	55·15 W
99	Grande, Boca (Est.) (bŏ′kä-grä′n-dĕ) . Ven.	8·46 N	60·17 W
82	Grande Baie (gräɴd bā′) . . . . . Can.	48·17 N	70·53 W
95	Grande Cayemite, Ile (I.) . . . . Hai.	18·45 N	73·55 W
167	Grande Comore (grä′n-dĕ-kô-mô-rĕ) . Comores, Arch. des	11·44 S	42·38 E
92	Grande de Otoro (grän′dâ dā ô-tō′rô) . Hond.	14·42 N	88·21 W
164	Grande Erg Occidental (Dunes) Alg.	29·37 N	6·04 E
85	Grande-Ligne (lēn′y′) Can. (Montreal In.)	45·13 N	73·17 W
83	Grande Miquelon (I.) (mĭk-ē-lôn′) Can.	47·03 N	56·20 W
85	Grande Pointe (grănd point′) Can. (Winnipeg In.)	49·47 N	97·03 W
86	Grande Prairie (prâr′ĭ) . . . . . . Can.	55·09 N	118·48 W
93	Grande R. (grän′dĕ) . . . . Nic.	13·01 N	84·21 W
95	Grande Rivière du Nord (rē-vyâr′ dü nôr′) . Hai.	19·35 N	72·10 W
66	Grande Ronde R. (rônd′) . . . . Ore.	45·32 N	117·52 W
68	Gran Desierto (Des.) (grän-dĕ-syĕ′r-tô) . Mex.	32·14 N	114·28 W
93	Grande Terre I. (târ′) Guad. (Le. & Wind. Is. In.)	16·28 N	61·13 W
93	Grande Vigie, Pointe de la (Pt.) (gräɴd vē-gē′) Grande Terre (Le. & Wind. Is. In.)	16·32 N	61·25 W
82	Grand Falls (fôlz) . . . . Can.	47·02 N	67·46 W
87	Grand Falls . . . . Can.	53·34 N	64·23 W
79	Grandfather, Mt. (grănd-fä-thẽr) N. C.	36·07 N	81·48 W
72	Grandfield (grănd′fēld) . . . . . Okla.	34·13 N	98·39 W
86	Grand Forks (fôrks) . . . . Can.	49·00 N	118·27 W
70	Grand Forks . . . . N. D.	47·55 N	97·05 W
80	Grand Haven (hā′v′n) . . . . . . Mich.	43·05 N	86·15 W
72	Grand Island (ī′lȧnd) . . . . Nebr.	40·56 N	98·20 W
75	Grand I . . . . . . N. Y. (Buffalo In.)	43·03 N	78·58 W
69	Grand Junction (jŭngk′shŭn) Colo.	39·05 N	108·35 W
164	Grand Lahou (lȧ-ōō′) . Ivory Coast	5·08 N	5·06 W
83	Grand Lake (lāk) . . . . Can.	49·00 N	57·10 W
77	Grand L . . . . La.	29·57 N	91·25 W
74	Grand L . . . . . . Minn. (Duluth In.)	46·54 N	92·26 W
80	Grand Ledge (lĕj) . . . . Mich.	42·45 N	84·50 W
122	Grand-Lieu, L. de (gräɴ′-lyû) . Fr.	46·00 N	1·45 W
82	Grand Manan (I.) (mă-năn) . Can.	44·42 N	66·50 W
82	Grand′Mere (gräɴ mâr′) . . . . . Can.	46·36 N	72·43 W
123	Grand Morin (R.) (mô-ràɴ′) Fr. (Paris In.)	48·23 N	2·19 E
124	Grândola (grăɴ′dô-lȧ) . . . . Port.	38·10 N	8·36 W
164	Grand-Popo (pô-pô′) . . . . Dahomey	6·27 N	1·52 E
71	Grand Portage Ind. Res. (pōr′tĭj) Minn.	47·54 N	89·34 W
71	Grand Portage Nat′l Mon. . . Mich.	47·59 N	89·47 W
74	Grand Prairie (prĕ′rê) Tex. (Dallas, Fort Worth In.)	32·45 N	97·00 W
69	Grand Quivira Natl. Mon. (kē-vĕ′rȧ) . N. Mex.	34·10 N	106·05 W
80	Grand Rapids (răp′ĭdz) . . . . . Mich.	43·00 N	85·45 W
71	Grand Rapids . . . . Minn.	47·16 N	93·33 W
82	Grand-Riviere . . . . Can.	48·26 N	64·30 W
93	Grand Soufriere Vol. (sōō-frê-âr′) Guad. (Le. & Wind. Is. In.)	16·06 N	61·42 W
67	Grand Teton Mt. . . . . Wyo.	43·46 N	110·50 W
67	Grand Teton Natl. Park (tē′tŏn) Wyo.	43·54 N	110·15 W
80	Grand Traverse B. (trăv′ẽrs) Mich.	45·00 N	85·30 W
95	Grand Turk (I.) (tûrk) . . Turks Is.	21·30 N	71·10 W
74	Grandview (grănd′vyōō) Mo. (Kansas City In.)	38·53 N	94·32 W
69	Grand Wash (R.) (wŏsh) . . . . Ariz.	36·20 N	113·52 W
67	Granger (grān′jẽr) . . . . Wyo.	41·37 N	109·58 W
66	Grangeville (grānj′vĭl) . . . . . . Idaho	45·56 N	116·08 W

ăt; finăl; rāte; senâte; ārm; àsk; sofȧ; fâre; ch-choose; dh-as th in other; bē; êvent; bĕt; recĕnt; cratẽr; g-go; gh-guttural g; bĭt; ĭ-short neutral; rīde; K-guttural k as ch in German ich;

PRONOUNCING INDEX Granite–Grottaglie 211

Page	Name Pronunciation Region	Lat. °′	Long. °′
84	Granite (grăn'ĭt) Md. (Baltimore In.)	39·21 N	76·51 W
74	Granite City Ill. (St. Louis In.)	38·42 N	90·09 W
70	Granite Falls (fôlz) Minn.	44·46 N	95·34 W
79	Granite Falls N. C.	35·49 N	81·25 W
65	Granite Falls Wash. (Seattle In.)	48·05 N	121·59 W
67	Granite Pk. Mont.	45·13 N	109·48 W
79	Graniteville (grăn'ĭt-vĭl) S. C.	33·35 N	81·50 W
99	Granito (grä-nē'tō) Braz.	7·39 S	39·34 W
124	Granja de Torrehermosa (grän'hä dā tôr'rā-ĕr-mō'sä) Sp.	38·21 N	5·38 W
118	Gränna (grĕn'å) Swe.	58·02 N	14·28 E
125	Granollérs (grä-nôl-yĕrs') Sp.	41·36 N	2·19 E
98	Gran Pajonal (Marsh) (grä'n-pä-kô-näl') Peru	11·14 S	71·45 W
95	Gran Piedra (Mtn.) (grän-pyĕ'drä) Cuba	20·00 N	75·40 W
110	Grantham (grăn'tăm) Eng.	52·54 N	0·38 W
75	Grant Park (grănt pärk) Ill. (Chicago In.)	41·14 N	87·39 W
66	Grants Pass (grănts pås) Ore.	42·26 N	123·20 W
122	Granville (gräN-vēl') Fr.	48·52 N	1·35 W
81	Granville (grăn'vĭl) N. Y.	43·25 N	73·15 W
86	Granville (L.) Can.	56·18 N	99·39 W
99	Grão Mogol (grouN' mōō-gôl') Braz.	16·34 S	42·35 W
74	Grapevine (grāp'vīn) Tex. (Dallas, Fort Worth In.)	32·56 N	97·05 W
118	Gräsö (I.) Swe.	60·30 N	18·35 E
81	Grass (R.) N. Y.	44·45 N	75·10 W
89	Grass Cay (I.) Vir. Is. (U.S.A.) (St. Thomas In.)	18·22 N	64·50 W
123	Grasse (gräs) Fr.	43·39 N	6·57 E
65	Grass Mtn. (grås) Wash. (Seattle In.)	47·13 N	121·48 W
68	Grass Valley Calif.	39·12 N	121·04 W
83	Grates Pt. (grāts) Can.	48·14 N	52·45 W
122	Graulhet (grō-lĕ') Fr.	43·46 N	1·58 E
86	Gravelbourg (gråv'ĕl-bôrg) Can.	49·55 N	106·53 W
110	Gravesend (grāvz'ĕnd') Eng. (London In.)	51·26 N	0·22 E
126	Gravina (grä-vē'nä) It.	40·48 N	16·27 E
74	Gravois (grav'ois) Mo. (St. Louis In.)	38·33 N	90·20 W
95	Gravois, Pte. (grå-vwä') Hai.	18·00 N	74·20 W
123	Gray (grå) Fr.	47·26 N	5·35 E
80	Grayling (grā'lĭng) Mich.	44·40 N	84·40 W
75	Grayslake (grāz'lāk) Ill. (Chicago In.)	42·20 N	88·20 W
72	Grays Pk. (grāz) Colo.	39·29 N	105·52 W
129	Grayvoron (grå-ĕ'vô-rôn) Sov. Un.	50·28 N	35·41 E
120	Graz (gräts) Aus.	47·05 N	15·26 E
94	Great Abaco (I.) (ä'bä-kō) Ba. Is.	26·30 N	77·05 W
159	Great Artesian Basin (Reg.) (är-tēzh-ăn bā-sĭn) Austl.	23·16 S	143·37 E
158	Great Australian Bight (ôs-trā'-lĭ-ăn bĭt) Austl.	33·30 S	127·00 E
94	Great Bahama Bk. (bȧ-hā'mȧ) Ba. Is.	25·00 N	78·50 W
159	Great Barrier (I.) (băr'ĭ-ēr) N. Z. (In.)	37·00 S	175·31 E
159	Great Barrier Rf. (bȧ-rĭ-ēr rēf) Austl.	16·43 S	146·34 E
62	Great Basin (grāt bā's'n) U. S.	40·08 N	117·10 W
86	Great Bear L. (bâr) Can.	66·10 N	119·53 W
72	Great Bend (bĕnd) Kans.	38·41 N	98·46 W
	Great Bitter, see El Buheirat el Murrat el Kubra		
116	Great Blasket (Is.) (blăs'kĕt) Ire.	52·05 N	10·55 W
102	Great Britain (brĭt'n) U. K.	56·53 N	0·02 W
166	Great Cataract (Falls) (kăt'ȧ-răkt) Ang.-S. W. Afr.	17·25 S	14·20 E
93	Great Corn I. Nic.	12·10 N	82·54 W
67	Great Divide Basin (dĭ-vīd' bā's'n) Wyo.	42·10 N	108·10 W
159	Great Dividing Ra. (dĭ-vī-dĭng rānj) Austl.	35·16 S	146·38 E
	Greater Khingan Mts., see Tahsinganling Shanmo		
71	Greater Leech Ind. Res. (grāt'ēr lēch) Minn.	47·39 N	94·27 W
95	Great Exuma (I.) (ĕk-sōō'mä) Ba. Is.	23·35 N	76·00 W
83	Great Falls Can.	48·58 N	55·37 W
67	Great Falls (fôlz) Mont.	47·30 N	111·15 W
79	Great Falls S. C.	34·32 N	80·53 W
166	Great Fish (R.) (fĭsh) S. W. Afr.	28·00 S	17·45 E
167	Great Fish (R.) S. Afr. (Natal In.)	33·04 S	26·08 E
95	Great Guana Cay (I.) (gwä'nä) Ba. Is.	24·00 N	76·20 W
94	Great Harbor Cay (I.) (kē) Ba. Is.	25·45 N	77·50 W
95	Great Inagua (I.) (ê-nä'gwä) Ba. Is.	21·00 N	73·15 W
142	Great Indian (Thar) Des. (tŭr) India	32·04 N	70·25 E
94	Great Isaac (I.) (ī'zăk) Ba. Is.	26·05 N	79·05 W
139	Great Karimun (Is.) Indon. (Singapore In.)	1·11 N	103·12 E
166	Great Karroo (Mts.) (grāt kȧ'rōō) S. Afr.	32·45 S	22·00 E
167	Great Kei (R.) (kē) S. Afr. (Natal In.)	32·17 S	27·30 E
84	Great Neck (nĕk) N. Y. (New York In.)	40·48 N	73·44 W
154	Great Nicobar I. (nĭk-ô-bär') India	7·00 N	94·18 E
154	Great Paternoster Is. (pā'tēr-nŏs-tēr) Indon.	7·35 S	118·00 E
94	Great Pedro Bluff (Hd.) Jam.	17·50 N	78·05 W
49	Great Plains, The (Reg.) (plāns) N. A.	45·00 N	104·00 W
95	Great Ragged (I.) Ba. Is.	22·10 N	75·45 W
126	Great St. Bernard Pass (sănt bēr-närd') Switz.-It.	45·53 N	7·15 E
94	Great Sale Cay (I.) (sāl kē) Ba. Is.	27·00 N	78·15 W
67	Great Salt L. (sôlt lāk) Utah	41·19 N	112·48 W
62	Great Salt Lake Des. U. S.	41·00 N	113·30 W
72	Great Salt Plains Res. Okla.	36·56 N	98·14 W
72	Great Sand Dunes Natl. Mon. Colo.	37·56 N	105·25 W
158	Great Sandy Des. (săn'dē) Austl.	21·50 S	123·10 E
66	Great Sandy Des. (săn'dĭ) Ore.	43·43 N	120·44 W
64	Great Sitkin (I.) (sĭt-kĭn) Alaska	52·18 N	176·22 W
86	Great Slave (L.) (slāv) Can.	61·37 N	114·58 W
78	Great Smoky Mts. Natl. Park (smōk-ē) N. C.	35·43 N	83·20 W
94	Great Stirrup Cay (I.) (stĭr-ŭp) Ba. Is.	25·50 N	77·55 W
158	Great Victoria Des. (vĭk-tō'rĭ-ȧ) Austl.	29·45 S	124·30 E
110	Great Waltham (wôl'thŭm) Eng.	51·47 N	0·27 E
87	Great Whale (R.) (hwāl) Can.	54·57 N	75·51 W
117	Great Yarmouth (yär-mŭth) Eng.	52·35 N	1·45 E
118	Grebbestad (grĕb-bĕ-städh) Swe.	58·42 N	11·15 E
139	Greco, C. Cyprus (Palestine In.)	34·57 N	34·11 E
124	Gredos, Sierra de (Mts.) (syĕr'rä dā grā'dōs) Sp.	40·13 N	5·30 W
102	Greece (grēs) Eur.	39·00 N	21·30 E
72	Greeley (grē'lĭ) Colo.	40·25 N	104·41 W
78	Green (R.) Ky.	37·13 N	86.30 W
70	Green (R.) N. D.	47·05 N	103·05 W
62	Green (R.) (grēn) U. S.	38·30 N	110·10 W
65	Green (R.) Wash. (Seattle In.)	47·17 N	121·57 W
65	Greenbank (grēn'bănk) Wash. (Seattle In.)	48·06 N	122·35 W
77	Green Bay Tex. (In.)	29·53 N	95·13 W
71	Green Bay Wis.	44·30 N	88·04 W
63	Green B. U. S.	44·55 N	87·40 W
80	Greencastle (grēn-kås''l) Ind.	39·40 N	86·50 W
94	Green Cay (I.) Ba. Is.	24·05 N	77·10 W
79	Green Cove Springs (kōv) Fla.	29·56 N	81·42 W
75	Greendale (grēn'dāl) Wis. (Milwaukee In.)	42·56 N	87·59 W
80	Greenfield (grēn'fēld) Ind.	39·45 N	85·40 W
71	Greenfield Iowa	41·16 N	94·30 W
81	Greenfield Mass.	42·35 N	72·35 W
73	Greenfield Mo.	37·23 N	93·48 W
80	Greenfield Ohio	39·15 N	83·25 W
78	Greenfield Tenn.	36·08 N	88·45 W
85	Greenfield Park Can. (Montreal In.)	45·29 N	73·29 W
75	Greenhills (grēn-hĭls) Ohio (Cincinnati In.)	39·16 N	84·31 W
49	Greenland (grēn'lănd) N. A.	74·00 N	40·00 W
83	Greenly (I.) (grēn'lē) Can.	51·23 N	57·15 W
65	Green Mtn. Ore. (Portland In.)	45·52 N	123·24 W
69	Green Mountain Res. Colo.	39·50 N	106·20 W
81	Green Mts. Vt.	43·10 N	73·05 W
116	Greenock (grēn'ŭk) Scot.	55·55 N	4·45 W
84	Green Pond Mtn. (pŏnd) N. J. (New York In.)	41·00 N	74·32 W
69	Greenriver (grēn-rĭv'ēr) Utah	39·00 N	110·05 W
67	Green River Wyo.	41·32 N	109·26 W
67	Green R., Blacks Fk. Wyo.	41·08 N	110·27 W
67	Green R., Hams Fk. Wyo.	41·55 N	110·40 W
78	Greensboro (grēnz'bŭro) Ala.	32·42 N	87·36 W
78	Greensboro (grēns-bûr'ô) Ga.	33·34 N	83·11 W
79	Greensboro N. C.	36·04 N	79·45 W
80	Greensburg (grēnz'bûrg) Ind.	39·20 N	85·30 W
72	Greensburg (grēns-bûrg) Kans.	37·36 N	99·17 W
81	Greensburg Pa.	40·20 N	79·30 W
78	Greenville (grēn'vĭl) Ala.	31·49 N	86·39 W
73	Greenville Ill.	38·52 N	89·22 W
78	Greenville Ky.	37·11 N	87·11 W
164	Greenville Lib.	5·06 N	8·44 W
82	Greenville Maine	45·26 N	69·35 W
80	Greenville Mich.	43·10 N	85·25 W
78	Greenville Miss.	33·25 N	91·00 W
79	Greenville N. C.	35·35 N	77·22 W
80	Greenville Ohio	40·05 N	84·35 W
80	Greenville Pa.	41·20 N	80·25 W
79	Greenville S. C.	34·50 N	82·25 W
78	Greenville Tenn.	36·08 N	82·50 W
73	Greenville Tex.	33·09 N	96·07 W
84	Greenwich Conn. (New York In.)	41·01 N	73·37 W
110	Greenwich (grĭn'ĭj) Eng. (London In.)	51·28 N	0·00
73	Greenwood (grēn-wŏŏd) Ark.	35·13 N	94·15 W
75	Greenwood Ind. (Indianapolis In.)	39·37 N	86·07 W
78	Greenwood Miss.	33·30 N	90·09 W
79	Greenwood S. C.	34·10 N	82·10 W
79	Greenwood (R.) S. C.	34·17 N	81·55 W
84	Greenwood L. N. Y. (New York In.)	41·13 N	74·20 W
79	Greer (grēr) S. C.	34·55 N	81·56 W
123	Grefrath (grĕf'rät) Ger. (Ruhr In.)	51·20 N	6·21 E
70	Gregory (grĕg'ō-rĭ) S. D.	43·12 N	99·27 W
160	Gregory, L. (grĕg'ô-rê) Austl.	29·47 S	139·15 E
159	Gregory Ra. Austl.	19·23 S	143·45 E
111	Greifenberg (grī'fĕn-bĕrgh) Ger. (Munich In.)	48·04 N	11·06 E
120	Greifswald (grīfs'vält) Ger.	54·05 N	13·24 E
120	Greiz (grīts) Ger.	50·39 N	12·14 E
136	Gremyachinsk (grâ'myå-chĭnsk) Sov. Un. (Urals In.)	58·35 N	57·53 E
118	Grenå (grĕn'ô) Den.	56·25 N	10·51 E
78	Grenada (grê-nā'dȧ) Miss.	33·45 N	89·47 W
93	Grenada I. N. A. (Le. & Wind. Is. In.)	12·02 N	61·27 W
78	Grenada Res. Miss.	33·52 N	89·30 W
122	Grenade (grē-näd') Fr.	43·46 N	1·15 E
93	Grenadines, The (Is.) (grĕn'ȧ-dēnz) Grenada-St. Vincent (Le. & Wind. Is. In.)	12·37 N	61·35 W
84	Grenloch (grĕn-lŏk) N. J. (Philadelphia In.)	39·48 N	75·04 W
123	Grenoble (grē-nô'bl') Fr.	45·14 N	5·45 E
70	Grenora (grê-nō'rȧ) N. D.	48·38 N	103·55 W
81	Grenville (grĕn'vĭl) Can.	45·40 N	74·35 W
93	Grenville Grenada (Le. & Wind. Is. In.)	12·07 N	61·38 W
65	Gresham (grĕsh'ăm) Ore. (Portland In.)	45·30 N	122·25 W
84	Gretna (grĕt'nȧ) La. (New Orleans In.)	29·56 N	90·03 W
111	Grevelingen Krammer, R. Neth. (Amsterdam In.)	51·42 N	4·03 E
127	Grevená (grĕ'vä-nä) Grc.	40·02 N	21·30 E
123	Grevenbroich (grĕ'fĕn-broik) Ger. (Ruhr In.)	51·05 N	6·36 E
123	Grevenbrück (grĕ'fĕn-brük) Ger. (Ruhr In.)	51·08 N	8·01 E
65	Grey, Pt. (grā) Can. (Vancouver In.)	49·22 N	123·16 W
67	Greybull (grā'bŏŏl) Wyo.	44·28 N	108·05 W
67	Greybull R. Wyo.	44·13 N	108·43 W
84	Greycourt (grā-kōrt) N. Y. (New York In.)	41·22 N	74·16 W
168	Greylingstad (grā-lĭng'shtȧt) S. Afr. (Johannesburg & Pretoria In.)	26·40 S	29·13 E
159	Greymouth (grā'mouth) N. Z. (In.)	42·27 S	171·17 E
160	Grey Ra. Austl.	28·40 S	142·05 E
66	Greys Hbr. (grās) Wash.	46·55 N	124·23 W
167	Greytown (grā'toun) S. Afr. (Natal In.)	29·07 S	30·38 E
	Greytown, see San Juan del Norte		
65	Grey Wolf Pk. (grā wŏŏlf) Wash. (Seattle In.)	48·53 N	123·12 W
68	Gridley (grĭd'lĭ) Calif.	39·22 N	121·43 W
78	Griffin (grĭf'ĭn) Ga.	33·15 N	84·16 W
64	Griffin Pt. Alaska	70·05 N	143·21 W
160	Griffith (grĭf-ĭth) Austl.	34·16 S	146·10 E
75	Griffith Ind. (Chicago In.)	41·31 N	87·26 W
129	Grigoriopol' (grĭ'gor-i-ô'pôl) Sov. Un.	47·09 N	29·18 E
91	Grijalva (R.) (grē-häl'vä) Mex.	18·15 N	92·45 W
160	Grim, C. (grĭm) Austl.	40·43 S	144·30 E
120	Grimma (grĭm'å) Ger.	51·14 N	12·43 E
85	Grimsby (grĭmz'bĭ) Can. (Toronto In.)	43·11 N	79·33 W
112	Grimsey (I.) (grĭms'å) Ice.	66·30 N	17·50 W
118	Grimstad (grĭm-städh) Nor.	58·21 N	8·30 E
71	Grinnel (grĭ-nĕl') Iowa	41·44 N	92·44 W
71	Griswold (grĭz'wŭld) Iowa	41·11 N	95·05 W
128	Griva (grē'vå) Sov. Un.	55·51 N	26·31 E
83	Groais (I.) Can.	50·56 N	55·35 W
119	Grobina (grō'bĭnĭa) Sov. Un.	56·35 N	21·10 E
168	Groblersdal S. Afr. (Johannesburg & Pretoria In.)	25·11 S	29·25 E
121	Grodno (grôd'nō) Sov. Un.	53·40 N	23·49 E
121	Grodzisk Masowiecki (grō'jēsk mä-zō-vyĕts'ke) Pol.	52·06 N	20·40 E
120	Grodzisk Wielkopolski (grō'jēsk vyĕl-ko-pōl'skē) Pol.	52·14 N	16·22 E
77	Groesbeck (grōs'bĕk) Tex.	31·32 N	96·31 W
122	Groix, I. de (ēl dē grwä') Fr.	47·39 N	3·28 W
121	Grójec (grōō'yĕts) Pol.	51·53 N	20·52 E
120	Gronau (grō'nou) Ger.	52·12 N	7·05 E
117	Groningen (grō'nĭng-ĕn) Neth.	53·13 N	6·30 E
158	Groote Eyelandt (I.) (grō'tē ī'lănt) Austl.	13·50 S	137·30 E
166	Grootfontein (grōt'fōn-tān') S. W. Afr.	18·15 S	19·30 E
166	Grootkop (Mtn.) S. Afr. (Cape Town In.)	34·11 S	18·23 E
168	Groot Marico S. Afr. (Johannesburg & Pretoria In.)	25·36 S	26·23 E
168	Groot R. S. Afr. (Johannesburg & Pretoria In.)	25·13 S	26·20 E
166	Groot Vloer (L.) (grōt' vlōōr') S. Afr.	30·00 S	20·16 E
83	Gros Morne (Mtn.) (grō môrn') Can.	49·37 N	57·45 W
83	Gros Pate (Mtn.) Can.	50·16 N	57·25 W
111	Gross Behnitz (grōss bĕ'nētz) Ger. (Berlin In.)	52·35 N	12·45 E
75	Grosse I. (grōs) Mich. (Detroit In.)	42·08 N	83·09 W
85	Grosse Isle (īl') Can. (Winnipeg In.)	50·04 N	97·27 W
166	Grosse Karras (Mts.) S. W. Afr.	27·10 S	18·30 E
120	Grossenhain (grōs'ĕn-hīn) Ger.	51·17 N	13·33 E
111	Grossenzersdorf Aus. (Vienna In.)	48·13 N	16·33 E
75	Grosse Pointe (point') Mich. (Detroit In.)	42·23 N	82·54 W
75	Grosse Pointe Farms (färm) Mich. (Detroit In.)	42·25 N	82·53 W
75	Grosse Pointe Park (pärk) Mich. (Detroit In.)	42·23 N	82·55 W
126	Grosseto (grôs-sā'tō) It.	42·46 N	11·09 E
120	Grossglockner Pk. (glôk'nēr) Aus.	47·06 N	12·45 E
111	Gross Höbach (hû'bȧk) Ger. (Munich In.)	48·21 N	11·36 E
111	Gross Kreutz (kroitz) Ger. (Berlin In.)	52·24 N	12·47 E
123	Gross Reken (rĕ'kĕn) Ger. (Ruhr In.)	51·50 N	7·20 E
111	Gross Schonebeck (shō'nĕ-bĕk) Ger. (Berlin In.)	52·54 N	13·32 E
67	Gros Ventre R. (grōvĕn't'r) Wyo.	43·38 N	110·34 W
81	Groton (grôt'ŭn) Conn.	41·20 N	72·00 W
83	Groton Mass. (Boston In.)	42·37 N	71·34 W
70	Groton Nebr.	42·44 N	97·32 W
127	Grottaglie (grôt-täl'yä) It.	40·32 N	17·26 E

ng-sing; ŋ-baŋk; N-nasalized n; nŏd; cŏmmit; ōld; ôbey; ôrder; fōōd; fŏŏt; ou-out; s-soft; sh-dish; th-thin; pūre; ūnite; ûrn; stŭd; circŭs; ü-as "y" in study; '-indeterminate vowel.

212 Grouard–Haifeng PRONOUNCING INDEX

Page	Name Pronunciation Region	Lat. °′	Long. °′
86	Grouard Can.	55·35 N	116·11 W
83	Groveland (grōv'lănd) Mass. (Boston In.)	42·45 N	71·02 W
81	Groveton (grōv'tŭn) N. H.	44·35 N	71·30 W
77	Groveton Tex.	31·04 N	95·07 W
133	Groznyy (grôz'nĭ) Sov. Un.	43·20 N	45·40 E
121	Grudziadz (grōō'jyônts) Pol.	53·30 N	18·48 E
111	Grumpholds-Kirchen Aus. (Wien In.)	48·03 N	16·17 E
71	Grundy Center (grŭn'dĭ sĕn'tēr) Iowa	42·22 N	92·45 W
90	Gruñidora (grōō-nyē-dô'rō) Mex.	24·10 N	101·49 W
111	Grunwald (grōōn'väld) Ger. (Munich In.)	48·04 N	11·34 E
128	Gryazi (gryä'zĭ) Sov. Un.	52·31 N	39·59 E
128	Gryazovets (gryä'zô-vĕts) Sov. Un.	58·52 N	40·14 E
120	Gryfice (grĭ'fĭ-tsĕ) Pol.	53·55 N	15·11 E
120	Gryfino (grĭ'fē-nô) Pol.	53·16 N	14·30 E
93	Guabito (gwä-bē'tô) Pan.	9·30 N	82·33 W
94	Guacanayabo, Golfo de (G.) (gôl-fô-dĕ-gwä-kä-nä-yä'bō) Cuba	20·30 N	77·40 W
99	Guacara (gwä'-kä-rä) Ven. (In.)	10·16 N	67·48 W
98	Guacarí (gwä-kä-rē') Col. (In.)	3·45 N	76·20 W
101	Guaçuí (gwä'-sōō-ē') Braz. (Rio de Janeiro In.)	20·47 S	41·40 W
90	Guadalajara (gwä-dhä-lä-hä'rä) Mex.	20·41 N	103·21 W
124	Guadalajara (gwä-dä-lä-kä'-rä) Sp.	40·37 N	3·10 W
124	Guadalcanal (gwä-dhäl-kä-näl') Sp.	38·05 N	5·48 W
159	Guadalcanal (I.) Sol. Is.	9·48 S	158·43 E
90	Guadalcázar (gwä-dhäl-kä'zär) Mex.	22·38 N	100·24 W
124	Guadalete (R.) (gwä-dhä-lā'tā) Sp.	38·53 N	5·38 W
124	Guadalhorce (R.) (gwä-dhäl-ôr'thā) Sp.	37·05 N	4·50 W
124	Guadalimar (R.) (gwä-dhä-lē-mär') Sp.	38·29 N	2·53 W
125	Guadalope (R.) (gwä-dä-lô-pĕ) Sp.	40·48 N	0·10 W
124	Guadalquivir, Río (R.) (rē'-ō-gwä-dhäl-kē-vēr') Sp.	5·57 N	6·00 W
76	Guadalupe Mex.	31·23 N	106·06 W
124	Guadalupe, Sierra de (Mts.) (Syĕr'rä dä gwä-dhä-lōō'pä) Sp.	39·30 N	5·25 W
88	Guadalupe I. Mex.	29·00 N	118·45 W
76	Guadalupe Mts. N. Mex.-Tex.	32·00 N	104·55 W
76	Guadalupe Pk. Tex.	31·55 N	104·55 W
76	Guadalupe R. (gwä-dhä-lōō'pä) Tex.	29·54 N	99·03 W
124	Guadarrama, Sierra de (Mts.) (gwä-dhär-rä'mä) Sp.	41·00 N	3·40 W
125	Guadarrama (R.) (gwä-dhär-rä'mä) Sp. (Madrid In.)	40·34 N	3·58 W
93	Guadeloupe (Is.) (gwä-dē-lōōp') N. A. (Le. & Wind. Is. In.)	16·07 N	61·19 W
93	Guadeloupe Pass N. A. (Le. & Wind. Is. In.)	16·26 N	62·00 W
94	Guadiana, Bahía de (B.) (bä-ē'ä-dĕ-gwä-dhē-ä'nä) Cuba	22·10 N	84·35 W
124	Guadiana, Rio (R.) (rē'ō-gwä-dvä'nä) Port.	37·43 N	7·43 W
124	Guadiana Alto (R.) (äl'tō) Sp.	39·02 N	2·52 W
124	Guadiana Menor (R.) (mā'nôr) Sp.	37·43 N	2·45 W
124	Guadiaro (R.) (gwä-dhē-ä'rō) Sp.	37·38 N	5·25 W
125	Guadiato (R.) (gwä-dhē-ä'tō) Sp.	38·10 N	5·05 W
124	Guadiela (R.) (gwä-dhē-ā'lä) Sp.	40·23 N	2·23 W
124	Guadix (gwä-dhēsh') Sp.	37·18 N	3·09 W
99	Guaire (R.) (gwī'-rĕ) Ven. (In.)	10·25 N	66·43 W
94	Guajaba, Cayo (I.) (kä'yō-gwä-hä'bä) Cuba	21·50 N	77·35 W
98	Guajará Mirim (gwä-zhä-rä'mē-rēN') Braz.	10·58 S	65·12 W
98	Guajira, Pen. de (Pen.) (pĕ-nē'ng-sōō-lä-dĕ-gwä-κē'rä) Col.-Ven.	12·35 N	73·00 W
92	Gualán (gwä-län') Guat.	15·08 N	89·21 W
101	Gualeguay (gwä-lĕ-gwä'y) Arg. (Buenos Aires In.)	33·10 S	59·20 W
101	Gualeguay (R.) Arg. (Buenos Aires In.)	32·49 S	59·05 W
101	Gualeguaychú (gwä-lā-gwī-chōō') Arg. (Buenos Aires In.)	33·01 S	58·32 W
101	Gualeguaychú (R.) Arg. (Buenos Aires In.)	32·58 S	58·27 W
100	Gualicho, Salina (F.) (sä-lē'nä-gwä-lē'chō) Arg.	40·20 S	65·15 W
156	Guam (I.) (gwäm) Oceania	14·00 N	143·20 E
100	Guaminí (gwä-mē-nē') Arg.	37·02 S	62·21 W
98	Guamo (gwä'mō) Col. (In.)	4·02 N	74·58 W
95	Guanabacoa (gwä-nä-bä-kō'ä) Cuba (Havana In.)	23·08 N	82·19 W
100	Guanabara (gwä-nä-bä'rä) Braz.	23·03 N	43·32 W
100	Guanabara, Baia de (B.) Braz. (In.)	22·44 S	43·09 W
92	Guanacaste Cord. (Mts.) (kôr-dēl-yĕ'rä-gwä-nä-käs'tā) C. R.	10·54 N	85·27 W
88	Guanacevi (gwä-nä-sĕ-vē') Mex.	25·30 N	105·45 W
94	Guanahacabibes, Pen. de (pĕ-nēn-sōō-lä-dĕ-gwä-nä hä-kä-bē'bäs) Cuba	21·55 N	84·35 W
94	Guanajay (gwä-nä-hī') Cuba	22·55 N	82·40 W
90	Guanajuato (gwä-nä-hwä'tō) Mex.	21·01 N	101·16 W
88	Guanajuato (State) Mex.	21·00 N	101·00 W
99	Guanape (gwä-nä'pĕ) Ven. (In.)	9·55 N	65·32 W
99	Guanape (R.) Ven. (In.)	9·52 N	65·20 W
98	Guanare (gwä-nä'rä) Ven.	8·57 N	69·47 W
100	Guanduçu (R.) (gwä'n-dōō'sōō) Braz. (In.)	22·50 S	43·40 W
94	Guane (gwä'nå) Cuba	22·10 N	84·05 W
99	Guanta (gwän'tä) Ven. (In.)	10·15 N	64·35 W
95	Guantánamo (gwän-tä'nä-mō) Cuba	20·10 N	75·10 W
95	Guantanamo, Bahía de (B.) (bä-ē'ä-dĕ) Cuba	19·35 N	75·35 W
101	Guapé (gwä-pĕ') Braz. (Rio de Janeiro In.)	20·45 S	45·55 W
93	Guapiles (gwä-pē-lĕs) C. R.	10·05 N	83·54 W
100	Guapimirim (gwä-pē-mē-rē'N) Braz. (In.)	22·31 S	42·59 W
98	Guaporé (R.) (gwä-pô-rā') Bol.-Braz.	12·11 S	63·47 W
98	Guaqui (guä'kē) Bol.	16·42 S	68·47 W
125	Guara, Sierra de (Mts.) (sē-ĕ'r-rä-dĕ-gwä'rä) Sp.	42·24 N	0·15 W
99	Guarabira (gwä-rä-bē'rå) Braz.	6·49 S	35·27 W
98	Guaranda (gwä-rän'dä) Ec.	1·39 S	78·57 W
99	Guarapari (gwä-rä-pä'rē) Braz.	20·34 S	40·31 W
101	Guarapiranga, Represa do (Res.) (r'ĕ-prĕ-sä-dô-gwä'rä-pē-rä'n-gä) Braz. (Rio de Janeiro In.)	23·45 S	46·44 W
100	Guarapuava (gwä-rä-pwä'vå) Braz.	25·29 S	51·26 W
101	Guaratinguetá (guä-rä-tĭN-gå-tä') Braz. (Rio de Janeiro In.)	22·49 S	45·10 W
124	Guarda (gwär'dä) Port.	40·32 N	7·17 W
124	Guareña (gwä-rā'nyä) Sp.	38·52 N	6·08 W
99	Guaribe (R.) (gwä-rē'bĕ) Ven. (In.)	9·48 N	65·17 W
99	Guarico (State) Ven. (In.)	9·42 N	67·25 W
99	Guárico (R.) Ven. (In.)	9·50 N	67·07 W
101	Guarulhos (gwä-rōō'l-yôs) Braz. (Rio de Janeiro In.)	32·28 S	46·30 W
101	Guarus (gwä'rōōs) Braz. (Rio de Janeiro In.)	21·44 S	41·19 W
98	Guasca (gwäs'kä) Col. (In.)	4·52 N	73·52 W
99	Guasipati (gwä-sē-pä'tē) Ven.	7·26 N	61·57 W
126	Guastalla (gwäs-täl'lä) It.	44·53 N	10·39 E
74	Guasti (gwäs'tĭ) Calif. (Los Angeles In.)	34·04 N	117·35 W
92	Guatemala (guä-tå-mä'lä) Guat.	14·37 N	90·32 W
88	Guatemala N. A.	15·45 N	91·45 W
99	Guatire (gwä-tē'rĕ) Ven. (In.)	10·28 N	66·34 W
101	Guaxupé (gwä-shōō-pĕ') Braz. (Rio de Janeiro In.)	21·18 S	46·42 W
94	Guayabal (gwä-yä-bä'l) Cuba	20·40 N	77·40 W
90	Guayalejo (R.) (gwä-yä-lĕ'hō) Mex.	23·24 N	99·09 W
89	Guayama (gwä-yä'mä) P. R. (Puerto Rico In.)	18·00 N	66·08 W
95	Guayamouc (R.) Hai.	19·05 N	72·00 W
92	Guayape R. Hond.	14·39 N	86·37 W
98	Guayaquil (gwī-ä-kēl') Ec.	2·16 S	79·53 W
98	Guayaquil, Golfo de (G.) (gôl-fô-dĕ) Ec.	3·03 S	82·12 W
98	Guayiare (R.) (gwä-yä'rĕ) Col.	3·35 N	69·28 W
88	Guaymas (gwä'y-mäs) Mex.	27·49 N	110·58 W
95	Guayubin (gwä-yōō-bē'n) Dom. Rep.	19·40 N	71·25 W
92	Guazacapán (gwä-zä-kä-pän') Guat.	14·04 N	90·26 W
136	Gubakha (gōō-bä'kå) Sov. Un. (Urals In.)	58·53 N	57·35 E
126	Gubbio (gōōb'byô) It.	43·23 N	12·36 E
125	Gudar, Sierra de (Mts.) (syĕr'rä dä gōō'dhär) Sp.	40·28 N	0·47 W
118	Gudenaa (R.) Den.	56·20 N	9·47 E
118	Gudinge Fjärden (Fd.) Swe.	57·43 N	16·55 E
118	Gudvangen (gōōdh'văn-gĕn) Nor.	60·52 N	6·45 E
123	Guebwiller (gĕb-vē-lâr') Fr.	47·53 N	7·10 E
164	Guelma (gwĕl'mä) Alg.	36·32 N	7·17 E
85	Guelph (gwĕlf) Can. (Toronto In.)	43·33 N	80·15 W
114	Guemar (gē-mär') Alg.	33·32 N	6·42 E
99	Güere (gwĕ'rĕ) (R.) Ven. (In.)	9·39 N	65·00 W
122	Guéret (gā-rĕ') Fr.	46·09 N	1·52 E
122	Guernsey (I.) (gûrn'zĭ) Eur.	49·27 N	2·36 W
114	Guerrara (gĕr-rä'rä) Alg.	32·50 N	4·26 E
76	Guerrero (gĕr-rä'rō) Mex.	26·47 N	99·20 W
76	Guerrero Mex.	28·20 N	100·24 W
122	Gueugnon (gû-nyôN') Fr.	46·35 N	4·01 E
77	Gueydan (gā'dăn) La.	30·01 N	92·31 W
100	Guia de Pacobaíba (gwē'ä-dĕ-pä'kō-bī'bä) Braz. (In.)	22·42 S	43·10 W
96	Guiana Highlands (Mts.) Braz.	3·20 N	60·00 W
91	Guichicovi (San Juan) (gwē-chē-kō'vē) Mex.	16·58 N	95·10 W
125	Guidonia (gwē-dō'nyä) It. (Rome In.)	42·00 N	12·45 E
123	Guignes (gēN'yĕ) Fr. (Paris In.)	48·38 N	2·48 E
99	Güigüe (gwē'gwĕ) Ven. (In.)	10·05 N	67·48 W
92	Guija, L. (gē'hä) Sal.	14·16 N	89·21 W
110	Guildford (gĭl'fērd) Eng. (London In.)	51·13 N	0·34 W
75	Guilford (gĭl'fērd) Ind. (Cincinnati In.)	39·10 N	84·55 W
124	Guimarães (gē-mä-răNsh') Port.	41·27 N	8·22 W
163	Guinea (gĭn'ē) Afr.	10·48 N	12·28 W
163	Guinea, G. of Afr.	2·00 N	1·00 E
94	Güines (gwē'nās) Cuba	22·50 N	82·05 W
122	Guingamp (găN-găN') Fr.	48·35 N	3·10 W
94	Güira de Melena (gwē'rä dā må-lā'nä) Cuba	22·45 N	82·30 W
98	Güiria (gwē-rē'ä) Ven.	10·43 N	62·16 W
114	Guir R. Mor.-Alg.	31·55 N	2·48 W
123	Guise (guēz) Fr.	49·54 N	3·37 E
92	Guisisil (Vol.) (gē-sē-sēl') Nic.	12·40 N	86·11 W
142	Gujarat (State) India	22·54 N	79·00 E
142	Gujranwala (gōōj-rän'va-lå) W. Pak.	32·08 N	74·14 E
118	Gula (R.) (gōō'lå) Nor.	62·55 N	10·45 E
143	Gulbarga (gōōl-bûr'gå) India	17·25 N	76·52 E
128	Gulbene (gōōl-bā'nĕ) Sov. Un.	57·09 N	26·49 E
78	Gulfport (gŭlf'pōrt) Miss.	30·24 N	89·05 W
129	Gulyay Pole Sov. Un.	47·39 N	36·12 E
155	Gumaca (gōō-mä-kä') Phil. (Manila In.)	13·55 N	122·06 E
165	Gumbari (gōōm-bä-rē) Con. L.	2·45 N	29·00 E
136	Gumbeyka R. (gōōm-bĕy'kå) Sov. Un. (Urals In.)	53·20 N	59·42 E
164	Gumel Nig.	12·43 N	9·19 E
120	Gummersbach (gōōm'ĕrs-bäk) Ger.	51·02 N	7·34 E
111	Gumpoldskirchen Aus.	48·04 N	16·15 E
142	Guna India	24·44 N	77·17 E
160	Gunnedah (gŭ'nē-dä) Austl.	31·00 S	150·10 E
69	Gunnison (gŭn'ĭ-sŭn) Colo.	38·30 N	107·00 W
69	Gunnison Utah	39·10 N	111·50 W
69	Gunnison (R.) Colo.	38·50 N	107·55 W
78	Guntersville (gŭn'tērz-vĭl) Ala.	34·20 N	86·19 W
78	Guntersville L. Ala.	34·30 N	86·20 W
111	Guntramsdorf Aus. (Vienna In.)	48·04 N	16·19 E
143	Guntūr (gōōn'tōōr) India	16·22 N	80·29 E
155	Gunungapi (I.) (gōō'nōōng-ä'pē) Indon.	6·52 S	127·15 E
139	Gunungkidjang Indon. (Singapore In.)	0·55 N	104·39 E
73	Gurdon (gûr'dŭn) Ark.	33·56 N	93·10 W
99	Gurgucia (R.) (gōōr-gōō'syä) Braz.	8·12 S	43·49 W
75	Gurnee (gûr'nē) Ill. (Chicago In.)	42·22 N	87·55 W
118	Gurskōy (I.) (gōōrskûē) Nor.	62·18 N	5·20 E
99	Gurupá (gōō-rōō-pä') Braz.	1·28 S	51·32 W
99	Gurupi, Serra do (Mts.) (sĕ'r-rä-dô-gōō-rōō-pē') Braz.	5·32 S	47·02 W
99	Gurupí (R.) (gōō-rōō-pē') Braz.	2·37 S	46·45 W
142	Guru Sikhar Mt. India	29·42 N	72·50 E
133	Gur'yev (gōōr'yĕf) Sov. Un.	47·10 N	51·50 E
134	Gur'yevsk (gōōr-yĭfsk') Sov. Un.	54·14 N	86·07 E
164	Gusau (gōō-zä'ōō) Nig.	12·11 N	6·40 E
119	Gusev (gōō'sĕf) Sov. Un.	54·35 N	22·15 E
127	Gusinje (gōō-sēn'yĕ) Yugo.	42·34 N	19·54 E
128	Gus'-Khrustal'nyy (gōōs-κrōō-stäl'ny') Sov. Un.	55·39 N	40·41 E
91	Gustavo A. Madero (gōōs-tä'vô-ä-mä-dĕ'rô) Mex. (Mexico City In.)	19·29 N	99·07 W
120	Gustrow (güs'trō) Ger.	53·48 N	12·12 E
121	Gúta (gōō'tå) Czech.	47·54 N	17·59 E
120	Gütersloh (gü'tērs-lō) Ger.	51·54 N	8·22 E
73	Guthrie (gŭth'rĭ) Okla.	35·52 N	97·26 W
71	Guthrie Center Iowa	41·41 N	94·33 W
91	Gutiérrez Zamora (gōō-tĭ-âr'räz zä-mō'rä) Mex.	20·27 N	97·17 W
71	Guttenberg (gŭt'ĕn-bûrg) Iowa	42·48 N	91·09 W
72	Guymon (gī'mŏn) Okla.	36·41 N	101·29 W
83	Guysborough (gīz'bŭr-ō) Can.	45·25 N	61·30 W
119	Gvardeysk (gvär-dĕysk') Sov. Un.	54·39 N	21·11 E
144	Gwadar (gwä'dŭr) W. Pak.	25·15 N	62·29 E
165	Gwane (gwän) Con. L.	4·49 N	26·46 E
166	Gwelo (gwā'lō) S. Rh.	19·15 S	29·48 E
71	Gwinn (gwĭn) Mich.	46·15 N	87·30 W
146	Gyangtse (gyäng'tsĕ') China	29·00 N	89·28 E
142	Gyantse China	28·53 N	89·39 E
135	Gydan, Khrebet (Kolymskiy) (Mts.) Sov. Un.	61·45 N	155·00 E
134	Gydanskiy, P-Ov (Pen.) Sov. Un.	70·42 N	76·03 E
160	Gympie (gĭm'pē) Austl.	26·20 S	152·50 E
121	Gyöngyös (dyûn'dyûsh) Hung.	47·47 N	19·55 E
121	Györ (dyûr) Hung.	47·40 N	17·37 E
153	Gyōtoku (gyō'tō-kōō') Jap. (Tōkyō In.)	35·42 N	139·56 E
86	Gypsumville (jĭp'sŭm'vĭl) Can.	51·49 N	98·42 W
121	Gyula (dyōō'lä) Hung.	46·38 N	21·18 E
128	Gzhatsk (g'zhätsk) Sov. Un.	55·32 N	34·58 E
123	Haan (hän) Ger. (Ruhr In.)	51·12 N	7·00 E
119	Haapamäki (häp'ä-mĕ-kē) Fin.	62·16 N	24·20 E
119	Haapsalu (häp'sä-lōō) Sov. Un.	58·56 N	23·33 E
111	Haar (här) Ger. (Munich In.)	48·06 N	11·44 E
139	Ha'arava (R.) (Araba) Isr. (Palestine In.)	30·32 N	35·16 E
111	Haarlem (här'lĕm) Neth. (Amsterdam In.)	52·22 N	4·37 E
94	Habana (State) (hä-vä'nä) Cuba	22·55 N	82·15 W
125	Habibas (C.) (hä-bē'bàs) Alg.	35·50 N	0·45 W
152	Hachinohe (hä'chē-nō'hå) Jap.	40·29 N	141·40 E
153	Hachiōji (hä'chē-ō'jē) Jap.	35·39 N	139·18 E
84	Hackensack (hăk'ĕn-săk) N. J. (New York In.)	40·54 N	74·03 W
84	Haddonfield (hăd'ŭn-fēld) N. J. (Philadelphia In.)	39·53 N	75·02 W
84	Haddon Heights (hăd'ŭn hīts) N. J. (Philadelphia In.)	39·53 N	75·03 W
164	Hadejia (hä-dä'jä) Nig.	12·32 N	10·04 E
139	Hadera (κä-dĕ'rä) Isr. (Palestine In.)	32·26 N	34·55 E
118	Haderslev (hä'dhĕrs-lĕv) Den.	55·17 N	9·28 E
168	Hadibu Som. (Horn of Afr. In.)	12·40 N	53·50 E
65	Hadlock (hăd'lŏk) Wash. (Seattle In.)	48·02 N	122·46 W
144	Hadramawt (Reg.) Sau. Ar.-Aden	15·15 N	48·32 E
152	Haeju (hä'ĕ-jŭ) Kor.	38·03 N	125·42 E
150	Haerhpin (Harbin) (här-bēn') China	45·40 N	126·30 E
112	Hafnarfjördhur Ice.	64·02 N	21·32 W
168	Hafun, Ras (C.) (hä-fōōn') Som. (Horn of Afr. In.)	10·15 N	51·35 E
67	Hageland (hăge'lănd) Mont.	48·53 N	108·43 W
123	Hagen (hä'gĕn) Ger. (Ruhr In.)	51·21 N	7·29 E
85	Hagermans Corners (hăg'ĕr-măns kôr'nĕr) Can. (Toronto In.)	43·51 N	79·19 W
80	Hagerstown (hā'gĕrz-toun) Ind.	39·55 N	85·10 W
81	Hagerstown Md.	39·40 N	77·45 W
153	Hagi (hä'gĭ) Jap.	34·25 N	131·25 E
122	Hague, C. de la (dĕ lä äg') Fr.	49·44 N	1·55 W
	Hague, The, see 's Gravenhagen		
123	Haguenau (äg'nō') Fr.	48·47 N	7·48 E
148	Haian (hăī'äN) China	32·35 N	120·25 E
153	Haibara (hä'ē-bä'rä) Jap.	34·29 N	135·57 E
150	Haich'eng China	40·58 N	122·45 E
148	Haichou Wan (B.) (hăī'jō wän) China	34·58 N	119·27 E
139	Haifa (hä'ē-fä) Isr. (Palestine In.)	32·48 N	35·00 E
151	Haifeng (hä'ē-fĕng') China	23·00 N	115·20 E

ăt; finăl; rāte; senâte; ärm; àsk; sofȧ; fâre; ch-choose; dh-as th in other; bē; êvent; bĕt; recĕnt; cratēr; g-go; gh-guttural g; bĭt; ĭ-short neutral; rīde; κ-guttural k as ch in German ich;

Page	Name Pronunciation Region	Lat. °′	Long. °′
148	Haifuchen (hăī′fōō′jĕn) China	31·57 N	121·48 E
144	Ḥā'il (hāl) Sau. Ar.	27·30 N	41·57 E
150	Hailaerh (Hailar) (hä-ê-lär′) China	49·10 N	118·40 E
	Hailar, see Hailaerh		
67	Hailey (hā′lĭ) Idaho	43·31 N	114·19 W
73	Haileyville (hā′lĭ-vĭl) Okla.	34·51 N	95·34 W
152	Hailin (hä′ê-lĕn′) China	44·31 N	129·11 E
151	Hailing Tao (I.) China	21·30 N	112·15 E
150	Hailun (hä′ê-lōōn′) China	47·18 N	126·50 E
150	Hailung (hä′ê-lōōng′) China	42·32 N	125·52 E
151	Hainan Tao (I.) (hä′e-nän′dou) China	19·00 N	111·10 E
111	Hainburg an der Donau Aus. (Vienna In.)	48·09 N	16·57 E
64	Haines (hānz) Alaska	59·10 N	135·38 W
79	Haines City Fla. (In.)	28·05 N	81·38 W
151	Haiphong (hī′fông′) (hä′ēp-hông) Viet.	20·52 N	106·40 E
89	Haiti (hā′tĭ) N. A.	19·00 N	72·15 W
150	Haitien (hī′tyĕn′) China (Peking In.)	39·59 N	116·17 E
165	Haiya Sud.	18·40 N	37·45 E
121	Hajduböszörmeny (hô′ĭ′dōō-bû′sûr-mān′) Hung.	47·41 N	21·30 E
121	Hajduhadház (hô′ĭ-dōō-hôd′häz) Hung.	47·32 N	21·32 E
121	Hajdunánás (hô′ĭ-dōō-nä′näsh) Hung.	47·52 N	21·27 E
121	Hajduszoboszló (hô′ĭ-dōō-sô′bôs-lō) Hung.	47·24 N	21·25 E
152	Hakodate (hä-kō-dä′tå) Jap.	41·46 N	140·42 E
153	Haku-San (Mtn.) (hä′kōō-sän′) Jap.	36·11 N	136·45 E
91	Halachó (ä-lä-chō′) Mex.	20·28 N	90·06 W
165	Halaib (hä-lä′ĕb) U. A. R.	22·10 N	36·40 E
157	Halawa (hä-lä′wä) Hawaii (In.)	21·12 N	156·55 E
139	Halbā Leb. (Palestine In.)	34·33 N	36·03 E
111	Halbe (häl′bĕ) Ger. (Berlin In.)	52·07 N	13·43 E
120	Halberstadt (häl′bĕr-shtät) Ger.	51·54 N	11·07 E
155	Halcon, Mt. (häl-kōn′) Phil. (Manila In.)	13·19 N	120·55 E
118	Halden (häl′dĕn) Nor.	59·10 N	11·21 E
110	Hale (hāl) Eng.	53·22 N	2·20 W
157	Haleakala Crater (hä′lä-ä′kä-lä) Hawaii (In.)	20·44 N	156·15 W
157	Haleakala Natl. Park Hawaii (In.)	20·46 N	156·00 W
75	Hales Corners (hālz kôr′nērz) Wis. (Milwaukee In.)	42·56 N	88·03 W
110	Halesowen (hālz′ô-wĕn) Eng.	52·26 N	2·03 W
81	Halethorpe (hāl-thôrp) Md.	39·15 N	76·40 W
78	Haleyville (hā′lĭ-vĭl) Ala.	34·11 N	87·36 W
65	Half Moon Bay (häf′mōōn) Calif. (San Francisco In.)	37·28 N	122·26 W
167	Halfway House (häf-wā hous) S. Afr. (Johannesburg & Pretoria In.)	26·00 S	28·08 E
111	Halfweg Neth. (Amsterdam In.)	52·23 N	4·45 E
82	Halifax (hăl′ĭ-făks) Can.	44·40 N	63·36 W
110	Halifax Eng.	53·44 N	1·52 W
159	Halifax B. (hăl′ĭ-făx) Austl.	18·56 S	147·07 E
82	Halifax Hbr Can.	44·35 N	63·25 W
139	Halīlah (R.) Jordan (Palestine In.)	30·28 N	35·57 E
152	Halla San (Mt.) (häl′lä-sän) Kor.	33·20 N	126·37 E
139	Hallat 'Ammar Sau. Ar. (Palestine In.)	29·09 N	36·05 E
111	Halle (häl′lĕ) Bel. (Brussels In.)	50·45 N	4·13 E
120	Halle Ger.	51·30 N	11·59 E
77	Hallettsville (hăl′ĕts-vĭl) Tex.	29·26 N	96·55 W
70	Hallock (hăl′ŭk) Minn.	48·46 N	96·57 W
87	Hall Pen (hôl) Can.	63·14 N	65·40 W
77	Halls Bay Tex. (In.)	29·55 N	95·23 W
118	Hallsberg (häls′bĕrgh) Swe.	59·04 N	15·04 E
158	Halls Creek (hôlz) Austl.	18·15 S	127·45 E
82	Halls Strm. (hôls) Can.-Maine	45·07 N	71·34 W
155	Halmahera (I.) (häl-mä-hä′rä) Indon.	0·45 N	128·45 E
118	Halmstad (hälm′städ) Swe.	56·40 N	12·46 E
118	Halse Fd. (häl′sĕ fyôrd) Nor.	63·03 N	8·23 E
84	Halsey (hôl′zê) N. J. (New York In.)	41·06 N	74·45 W
118	Hälsingborg (hĕl′sĭng-bôrgh) Swe.	56·04 N	12·40 E
73	Halstead (hôl′stĕd) Kans.	38·02 N	97·36 W
151	Halt'an Tao (I.) China	25·40 N	119·45 E
123	Haltern (häl′tĕrn) Ger. (Ruhr In.)	51·45 N	7·10 E
74	Haltom City (hôl′tŏm) Tex. (Dallas, Fort Worth In.)	32·48 N	97·17 W
	Halunrshan, see Wenchüan		
111	Halvarenbeek Neth. (Amsterdam In.)	51·29 N	5·10 E
115	Hama (hä′mä) Syr.	35·08 N	36·53 E
144	Hamadān (hŭ-mŭ-dän′) Iran	34·45 N	48·07 E
153	Hamamatsu (hä′mä-mät′sōō) Jap.	34·41 N	137·43 E
118	Hamar (hä′mär) Nor.	60·49 N	11·05 E
153	Hamasaka (hä′mä-sä′kä) Jap.	35·37 N	134·27 E
123	Hamborn (häm′bōrn) Ger. (Ruhr In.)	51·30 N	6·43 E
73	Hamburg (hăm′bûrg) Ark.	33·15 N	91·49 W
111	Hamburg (häm′bŏŏrgh) Ger. (Hamburg In.)	53·34 N	10·02 E
70	Hamburg Iowa	40·39 N	95·40 W
84	Hamburg N. J. (New York In.)	41·09 N	74·35 W
75	Hamburg N. Y. (Buffalo In.)	42·44 N	78·51 W
167	Hamburg (hăm′bûrg) S. Afr. (Natal In.)	33·18 S	27·28 E
81	Hamden (hăm′dĕn) Conn.	41·20 N	72·55 W
119	Hämeenlinna (hĕ′mân-lĭn-nä) Fin.	61·00 N	24·29 E
74	Hamel (hăm′ĕl) Ill. (St. Louis In.)	38·53 N	89·51 W
120	Hameln (hä′mĕln) Ger.	52·06 N	9·23 E
111	Hamelwörden (hä′mĕl-vûr-dĕn) Ger. (Hamburg In.)	53·47 N	9·19 E
158	Hamersley Ra. (hăm′ērz-lê) Austl.	22·15 S	117·50 E
152	Hamhung (häm′hōōng′) Kor.	39·57 N	127·35 E
146	Hami (Qomul) (hä′mê) (kô-mōōl′) China	42·58 N	93·14 E
160	Hamilton (hăm′ĭl-tŭn) Austl.	37·50 S	142·10 E
85	Hamilton Can. (Toronto In.)	43·15 N	79·52 W
83	Hamilton Mass. (Boston In.)	42·37 N	70·52 W
73	Hamilton Mo.	39·43 N	93·59 W
67	Hamilton Mont.	46·15 N	114·09 W
159	Hamilton N. Z. (In.)	37·45 S	175·28 E
75	Hamilton Ohio (Cincinnati In.)	39·22 N	84·33 W
76	Hamilton Tex.	31·42 N	98·07 W
73	Hamilton, L Ark.	34·25 N	93·32 W
85	Hamilton Hbr. Can. (Toronto In.)	43·17 N	79·50 W
87	Hamilton Inlet Can.	54·20 N	56·57 W
119	Hamina (hä′mê-nä) Fin.	60·34 N	27·15 E
79	Hamlet (hăm′lĕt) N. C.	35·52 N	79·46 W
72	Hamlin (hăm′lĭn) Tex.	32·54 N	100·08 W
123	Hamm (häm) Ger. (Ruhr In.)	51·40 N	7·48 E
168	Hammanskraal (hä-mȧns-kräl′) S. Afr. (Johannesburg & Pretoria In.)	25·24 S	28·17 E
111	Hamme Bel. (Brussels In.)	51·06 N	4·07 E
111	Hamme-Oste Kanal (Can.) (hä′mĕ-ōs′tĕ kä-näl) Ger. (Hamburg In.)	53·20 N	8·59 E
112	Hammerfest (häm′mĕr-fĕst) Nor.	70·38 N	23·59 E
75	Hammond (hăm′ŭnd) Ind. (Chicago In.)	41·37 N	87·31 W
77	Hammond La.	30·30 N	90·28 W
65	Hammond Ore. (Portland In.)	46·12 N	123·57 W
81	Hammonton (hăm′ŭn-tŭn) N. J.	39·40 N	74·45 W
82	Hampden (hăm′dĕn) Maine	44·44 N	68·51 W
116	Hampshire Downs (hămp′shĭr dounz) Eng.	51·01 N	1·05 W
110	Hampstead Norris (hămp-stĕd nŏ′rĭs) Eng. (London In.)	51·27 N	1·14 W
82	Hampton (hămp′tŭn) Can.	45·34 N	65·50 W
71	Hampton Iowa	42·43 N	93·15 W
84	Hampton Va. (Norfolk In.)	37·02 N	76·21 W
84	Hampton Roads (Inlet) (Va. (Norfolk In.)	36·56 N	76·23 W
164	Ḥamrā, Ḥammādah al (Plat.) Libya	29·39 N	10·53 E
118	Hamrånge (häm′rông′ĕ) Swe.	60·56 N	17·00 E
75	Hamtramck (hăm-trăm′ĭk) Mich. (Detroit In.)	42·24 N	83·03 W
144	Hāmūn-l Māshkel (L.) (hä-mōōn′ē mäsh-kĕl′) W. Pak.	28·28 N	64·13 E
152	Han (R.) Kor.	37·10 N	127·40 E
157	Hana (hä′nä) Hawaii (In.)	20·43 N	155·59 W
94	Hanábana (R.) (hä-nä-bä′nä) Cuba	22·30 N	80·55 W
157	Hanalei B. (hä-nä-lä′ê) Hawaii (In.)	22·15 N	159·40 W
120	Hanau (hä′nou) Ger.	50·08 N	8·56 E
151	Han Chiang (R.) China	25·00 N	116·35 E
71	Hancock (hăn′kŏk) Mich.	47·08 N	88·37 W
65	Haney (hä-nê) Can. (Vancouver In.)	49·13 N	122·36 W
68	Hanford (hăn′fērd) Calif.	36·20 N	119·38 W
146	Hangayn Nuruu (Khangai Mts.) Mong.	48·03 N	99·45 E
151	Hangchou (hăng′chō′) China	30·17 N	120·12 E
151	Hangchou Wan (B.) (hăng′chō′) China	30·20 N	121·25 E
119	Hangö (häŋ′gû) Fin.	59·49 N	22·56 E
77	Hankamer (hăŋ′kȧ-mẽr) Tex. (In.)	29·52 N	94·42 W
151	Han Kiang (R.) (hän′kyäng′) China	31·40 N	112·04 E
70	Hankinson (hăŋ′kĭn-sŭn) N. D.	46·04 N	96·54 W
151	Hank'ou (hăn′kō′) China	30·42 N	114·22 E
158	Hann, Mt. (hän) Austl.	16·05 S	126·07 E
86	Hanna (hăn′ ȧ) Can.	51·36 N	111·58 W
67	Hanna Wyo.	41·51 N	106·34 W
70	Hannah N. D.	48·58 N	98·42 W
73	Hannibal (hăn′ĭ băl) Mo.	39·42 N	91·22 W
120	Hannover (hän-ō′vĕr) Ger.	52·22 N	9·45 E
118	Hanö-bukten (B.) Swe.	55·54 N	14·55 E
151	Hanoi (hä-noi′) Viet.	21·04 N	105·50 E
80	Hanover (hăn′ô-vēr) Can.	44·10 N	81·05 W
83	Hanover Mass. (Boston In.)	42·07 N	70·49 W
81	Hanover N. H.	43·45 N	72·15 W
81	Hanover Pa.	39·50 N	77·00 W
100	Hanover (I.) Chile	51·00 S	74·45 W
148	Hanshan (hän′shän′) China	31·43 N	118·06 E
89	Hans Lollick (I.) (häns′lŏl′ĭk) Vir. Is. (U. S. A.) (St. Thomas In.)	18·24 N	64·55 W
83	Hanson (hăn′sŭn) Mass. (Boston In.)	42·04 N	70·53 W
65	Hansville (hăns′-vĭl) Wash. (Seattle In.)	47·55 N	122·33 W
148	Hantan (hän′tän′) China	36·37 N	114·30 E
82	Hantsport (hănts′pōrt) Can.	45·05 N	64·12 W
151	Hanyang (han′yäng′) China	30·30 N	114·10 E
148	Haoch'engchi (hou′chĕng′jē) China	33·19 N	117·33 E
112	Haparanda (hä-pä-rän′dä) Swe.	65·54 N	23·57 E
84	Hapeville (hăp′vĭl) Ga. (Atlanta In.)	33·39 N	84·25 W
84	Happy Jack (hăp′ĭ jăk) La. (New Orleans In.)	29·31 N	89·44 W
153	Hara-machida (hä-rä mä-chê′dä) Jap. (Tōkyō In.)	35·32 N	139·28 E
124	Harana, Sierra (Mts.) (sē-ĕ′r-rä-rä′nä) Sp.	37·17 N	3·28 W
146	Hara Nuur (L.) Mong.	47·47 N	94·01 E
168	Hārar (hä-rär′) Eth. (Horn of Afr. In.)	9·43 N	42·10 E
165	Harar (Prov.) Eth.	8·15 N	41·00 E
146	Hara Usa (L.) Mong.	48·00 N	92·32 E
	Harbin, see Haerhpin		
80	Harbor Beach (här′bēr bēch) Mich.	43·50 N	82·40 W
80	Harbor Springs Mich.	45·25 N	85·05 W
83	Harbour Breton (brĕt′ŭn) (brē-tôɴ′) Can.	47·28 N	55·50 W
83	Harbour Grace (grās) Can.	47·39 N	53·15 W
111	Harburg (här-bŏŏrgh) Ger. (Hamburg In.)	53·28 N	9·58 E
82	Harcourt (här′côrt) (år-kōōr′) Can.	46·28 N	65·14 W
118	Hardanger Fd. (hăr-dăng′ēr fyôrd) Nor.	59·58 N	6·30 E
118	Hardanger Fjeld (Mts.) (fyĕl′) Nor.	60·15 N	6·56 E
118	Hardanger Jöklen (Mtn.) (yû′kōōl-ĕn) Nor.	60·33 N	7·23 E
67	Hardin (här′dĭn) Mont.	45·44 N	107·36 W
167	Harding (här′dĭng) S. Afr. (Natal In.)	30·34 S	29·54 E
78	Harding (L.) Ala.-Ga.	32·43 N	85·00 W
142	Hardwar (hŭr′dvär) India	29·56 N	78·06 E
68	Hardy (R.) (här′dĭ) Mex.	32·04 N	115·10 W
83	Hare B. (hâr) Can.	51·21 N	55·45 W
168	Hargeisa (här-gā′ê-sȧ) Som. (Horn of Afr. In.)	9·20 N	43·57 E
121	Harghita, Muntii (Mts.) Rom.	46·25 N	25·40 E
153	Harima-Nada (Sea) (hä′rê-mä nä-dä) Jap.	34·34 N	134·37 E
111	Haring Vliet (R.) Neth. (Amsterdam In.)	51·49 N	4·03 E
73	Harlan (här′lăn) Iowa	41·40 N	95·10 W
78	Harlan Ky.	36·50 N	83·19 W
72	Harlan Co. Res Nebr.	40·03 N	99·51 W
67	Harlem (här′lĕm) Mont.	48·33 N	108·50 W
143	Harlhar India	14·32 N	75·41 E
117	Harlingen (här′lĭng-ĕn) Neth.	53·10 N	5·24 E
77	Harlingen Tex.	26·12 N	97·42 W
110	Harlow (här′lō) Eng. (London In.)	51·46 N	0·08 E
67	Harlowton (här′lô-tŭn) Mont.	46·26 N	109·50 W
80	Harmony (här′mô-nĭ) Ind.	39·35 N	87·00 W
66	Harney Basin (här′nĭ) Ore.	43·26 N	120·19 W
66	Harney L Ore.	43·11 N	119·23 W
70	Harney Pk S. D.	43·52 N	103·32 W
118	Härnösand (hĕr-nû-sänd) Swe.	62·37 N	17·54 E
124	Haro (ä′rō) Sp.	42·35 N	2·49 W
65	Haro Str. (hă′rō) Can.-U. S.	48·27 N	123·11 W
110	Harpenden (här′pĕn-d′n) Eng. (London In.)	51·48 N	0·22 W
72	Harper (här′pēr) Kans.	37·17 N	98·02 W
164	Harper Lib.	4·28 N	7·52 W
65	Harper Wash. (Seattle In.)	47·31 N	122·32 W
81	Harpers Ferry (här′pērz) W. Va.	39·20 N	77·45 W
133	Harput (kär-pōōt′) Tur.	38·45 N	39·10 E
78	Harriman (hăr′ĭ-măn) Tenn.	35·55 N	84·34 W
81	Harrington (hăr′ĭng-tŭn) Del.	38·55 N	75·35 W
87	Harrington Harbour (här′bēr) Can.	50·30 N	59·19 W
144	Harri Rud (R.) Afg.	34·29 N	61·16 E
116	Harris (I.) (hăr′ĭs) Scot.	57·55 N	6·40 W
79	Harris (L.) Fla. (In.)	28·43 N	81·40 W
80	Harrisburg (hăr′ĭs-bûrg) Ill.	37·45 N	88·35 W
81	Harrisburg Pa.	40·15 N	76·50 W
168	Harrismith (hă-rĭs′mĭth) S. Afr. (Johannesburg & Pretoria In.)	28·17 S	29·08 E
73	Harrison (hăr′ĭ-sŭn) Ark.	36·13 N	93·06 W
75	Harrison Ohio (Cincinnati In.)	39·16 N	84·45 W
81	Harrisonburg (hăr′-ĭ-sŭn-bûrg) Va.	38·30 N	78·50 W
73	Harrisonville (hăr-ĭ-sŭn-vĭl) Mo.	38·39 N	94·21 W
74	Harrisville (hăr′ĭs-vĭl) Utah (Salt Lake City In.)	41·17 N	112·00 W
80	Harrisville W. Va.	39·10 N	81·05 W
80	Harrodsburg (hăr′ŭdz-bûrg) Ky.	37·45 N	84·50 W
75	Harrods Cr. (hăr′ŭdz) Ky. (Louisville In.)	38·24 N	35·33 W
110	Harrow (hăr′ō) Eng. (London In.)	51·34 N	0·21 W
111	Harsefeld (här′zĕ-fĕld′) Ger. (Hamburg In.)	53·27 N	9·30 E
112	Harstad (här′städh) Nor.	68·49 N	16·10 E
80	Hart (härt) Mich.	43·40 N	86·25 W
168	Hartbeesfontein S. Afr. (Johannesburg & Pretoria In.)	26·46 S	26·25 E
167	Hartbeespoortdam (L.) S. Afr. (Johannesburg & Pretoria In.)	25·47 S	27·43 E
167	Hartebeespoortdam S. Afr. (Johannesburg & Pretoria In.)	25·44 S	27·51 E
78	Hartford (härt′fērd) Ala.	31·05 N	85·42 W
73	Hartford Ark.	35·01 N	94·21 W
81	Hartford Conn.	41·45 N	72·40 W
74	Hartford Ill. (St. Louis In.)	38·50 N	90·06 W
78	Hartford Ky.	37·25 N	86·50 W
80	Hartford Mich.	42·15 N	86·15 W
71	Hartford Wis.	43·19 N	88·25 W
80	Hartford City Ind.	40·35 N	85·25 W
110	Hartington (härt′ĭng-tŭn) Eng.	53·08 N	1·48 W
70	Hartington Nebr.	42·37 N	97·18 W
82	Hartland (härt′lănd) Can.	46·19 N	67·32 W
116	Hartland Pt. Eng.	51·03 N	4·40 W
166	Hartley S. Rh.	18·11 S	30·08 E
70	Hartley (härt′lĭ) Iowa	43·12 N	95·29 W
78	Hartselle (härt′sĕl) Ala.	34·24 N	86·55 W
73	Hartshorne (härts′hôrn) Okla.	34·49 N	95·34 W
79	Hartsville (härts′vĭl) S. C.	34·20 N	80·04 W
78	Hartwell (härt′wĕl) Ga.	34·21 N	82·56 W
78	Hartwell Res. Ga.	34·30 N	83·00 W
142	Hārua India (Calcutta In.)	22·36 N	88·40 E
71	Harvard (här′vȧrd) Ill.	42·25 N	88·39 W
83	Harvard Mass. (Boston In.)	42·30 N	71·35 W
72	Harvard Nebr.	40·36 N	98·08 W
69	Harvard, Mt Colo.	38·55 N	106·20 W
67	Harve (här′vĭ) Mont.	48·34 N	109·42 W
75	Harvey Ill. (Chicago In.)	41·37 N	87·39 W
84	Harvey La. (New Orleans In.)	29·54 N	90·05 W
70	Harvey N. D.	47·46 N	99·55 W
117	Harwich (här′wĭch) Eng.	51·53 N	1·13 E
120	Harz Mts. (härts) Ger.	51·42 N	10·50 E
139	Hasa (R.) Jordan (Palestine In.)	30·57 N	35·51 E
153	Hashimoto (hä′shê-mō′tō) Jap.	34·19 N	135·37 E
119	Häsijärvi (L.) (hĕ′sē-yĕr′vē) Fin.	61·42 N	24·05 E

ng-sing; ŋ-baŋk; ɴ-nasalized n; nŏd; cŏmmit; ōld; ôbey; ôrder; fōōd; fŏŏt; ou-out; s-soft; sh-dish; th-thin; pūre; ůnite; ûrn; stŭd; circŭs; ü-as "y" in study; ′-indeterminate vowel.

214 Haskell–Highland Park PRONOUNCING INDEX

Page	Name Pronunciation Region	Lat. °′	Long. °′
73	Haskell (hăs'kĕl) Okla.	35·49 N	95·41 W
72	Haskell Tex.	33·09 N	99·43 W
74	Haslet (hăs'lĕt) Tex. (Dallas, Fort Worth In.)	32·58 N	97·21 W
110	Haslingden (hăz'lĭng dĕn) Eng.	53·43 N	2·19 W
118	Hassela (häs'ĕl-ô) Swe.	62·05 N	16·46 E
111	Hasselt (häs'ĕlt) Bel. (Brussels In.)	50·56 N	5·23 E
164	Hassi Inifel Alg.	29·54 N	3·47 E
118	Hässjö (hĕs'shû) Swe.	62·36 N	17·33 E
118	Hassleholm (häs'lĕ-hōlm) Swe.	56·10 N	13·44 E
117	Hastings (hās'tĭngz) Eng.	50·52 N	0·28 E
80	Hastings Mich.	42·40 N	85·20 W
74	Hastings Minn. (Minneapolis, St. Paul In.)	44·44 N	92·51 W
72	Hastings Nebr.	40·34 N	98·42 W
159	Hastings N. Z. (In.)	39·33 S	176·53 E
84	Hastings-on-Hudson (ōn-hŭd'sŭn) N. Y. (New York In.)	40·59 N	73·53 W
78	Hatchie (R.) (hăch'ē) Tenn.	35·28 N	89·14 W
127	Hateg (kät-säg') Rom.	45·35 N	22·57 E
110	Hatfield Broad Oak (hăt-fēld brôd ōk) Eng.	51·50 N	0·14 E
153	Hatogaya (hä'tō-gä-yä) Jap. (Tōkyō In.)	35·50 N	139·45 E
153	Hatsukaichi (hät'sōō-kä'ē-chē) Jap.	34·22 N	132·19 E
79	Hatteras, C. (hăt'ēr-ȧs) N. C.	35·15 N	75·24 W
78	Hattiesburg (hăt'ĭz-bûrg) Miss.	31·20 N	89·18 W
123	Hattingen (hä'tēn-gĕn) Ger. (Ruhr In.)	51·24 N	7·11 E
121	Hatvan (hôt'vôn) Hung.	47·39 N	19·44 E
118	Haugesund (hou'gē-soon') Nor.	59·26 N	5·20 E
119	Haukivesi (L.) (hou'kē-vĕ'sē) Fin.	62·02 N	29·02 E
168	Hauptsrus S. Afr. (Johannesburg & Pretoria In.)	26·35 S	26·16 E
159	Hauraki, G. (hä-ōō-rä'kē) N. Z. (In.)	36·44 S	175·15 E
119	Hausjärvi (hä'ōōs-yĕr'vē) Fin.	60·44 N	24·44 E
82	Haut, Isle au (hō) Maine	44·03 N	68·13 W
144	Hauta (hou'tä) Sau. Ar.	23·12 N	45·38 E
114	Haut Atlas (Mts.) Mor.	32·10 N	5·49 W
82	Hauterive Can.	49·12 N	68·15 W
122	Hautmont (ō-môɴ') Fr.	50·14 N	3·50 E
73	Havana (hȧ-vă'nȧ) Ill.	40·17 N	90·02 W
	Havana, see La Habana		
69	Havasu L. (hăv'ȧ-sōō) Ariz.	34·26 N	114·09 W
82	Havelock (hăv'lŏk) Can.	56·58 N	65·20 W
120	Havel R. (hä'fĕl) Ger.	53·09 N	13·10 E
81	Haven (hā-vĕn) Pa.	40·31 N	76·14 W
83	Haverhill (hā'vēr-hĭl) Mass. (Boston In.)	42·46 N	71·05 W
81	Haverhill N. H.	44·00 N	72·05 W
84	Haverstraw (hā'vēr-strô) N. Y. (New York In.)	41·11 N	73·58 W
83	Havre (hăv'rȧ) Can.	45·42 N	61·30 W
81	Havre de Grace (hăv'ēr dē gräs') Md.	39·35 N	76·05 W
79	Haw (R.) (hô) N. C.	36·17 N	79·46 W
62	Hawaii (State) U. S.	20·00 N	157·40 W
157	Hawaii (I.) Hawaii (In.)	19·35 N	155·30 W
62	Hawaiian Is. (hä-wī'ăn) Oceania	22·00 N	158·00 W
157	Hawaii Vol. Natl. Park (hä-wī'ē) Hawaii (In.)	19·15 N	155·20 W
70	Hawarden (hā'wär-dĕn) Iowa	43·00 N	96·28 W
157	Hawi (hä'wē) Hawaii (In.)	20·16 N	155·48 W
116	Hawick (hô'ĭk) Scot.	55·25 N	2·55 W
159	Hawke B. (hôk) N. Z. (In.)	39·17 S	177·58 E
160	Hawker (hô'kēr) Austl.	31·58 S	138·12 E
81	Hawkesbury (hôks'bĕr-ĭ) Can.	45·35 N	74·35 W
83	Hawkesbury, Port Can.	45·39 N	60·48 W
78	Hawkinsville (hô'kĭnz-vĭl) Ga.	32·15 N	83·30 W
95	Hawks Nest Pt. Ba. Is.	24·05 N	75·30 W
70	Hawley (hô'lĭ) Minn.	46·52 N	96·18 W
110	Haworth (hā'wûrth) Eng.	53·50 N	1·57 W
144	Hawtah Sau. Ar.	15·58 N	48·26 E
74	Hawthorne (hô'thôrn) Calif. (Los Angeles In.)	33·55 N	118·22 W
68	Hawthorne Nev.	38·33 N	118·39 W
72	Haxtun (hăks'tŭn) Colo.	40·39 N	102·38 W
158	Hay (R.) (hā) Austl.	123·00 S	136·45 E
86	Hay (R.) Can.	60·21 N	117·14 W
153	Hayama (hä-yä'mä) Jap. (Tōkyō In.)	35·16 N	139·35 E
153	Hayashi (hä-yä'shē) Jap. (Tōkyō In.)	35·13 N	139·38 E
69	Hayden (hā'dĕn) Ariz.	33·00 N	110·50 W
64	Hayes, Mt. (hāz) Alaska	63·32 N	146·40 W
86	Hayes (R.) Can.	55·30 N	94·00 W
77	Haynesville (hānz'vĭl) La.	32·55 N	93·08 W
127	Hayrabolu Tur.	41·14 N	27·05 E
86	Hay River Can.	60·50 N	115·53 W
72	Hays (hāz) Kans.	38·51 N	99·20 W
65	Haystack Mtn. (hā-stăk') Wash. (Seattle In.)	48·26 N	122·07 W
65	Hayward (hā'wērd) Calif. (San Francisco In.)	37·40 N	122·06 W
71	Hayward Wis.	46·01 N	91·31 W
78	Hazard (hăz'ȧrd) Ky.	37·13 N	83·10 W
79	Hazelhurst (hā'z'l-hûrst) Ga.	31·50 N	82·36 W
78	Hazelhurst Miss.	31·52 N	90·23 W
75	Hazel Park Mich. (Detroit In.)	42·28 N	83·06 W
86	Hazelton (hā'z'l-tŭn) Can.	55·18 N	127·11 W
81	Hazleton Pa.	41·00 N	76·00 W
85	Headingley (hĕd'ĭng-lĭ) Can. (Winnipeg In.)	49·53 N	97·25 W
78	Headland (hĕd'lănd) Ala.	31·22 N	85·20 W
68	Healdsburg (hēldz'bûrg) Calif.	38·37 N	122·52 W
73	Healdton (hēld'tŭn) Okla.	34·13 N	97·28 W
110	Heanor (hēn'ŏr) Eng.	53·01 N	1·22 W
47	Heard I. (hûrd) Ind. O.	53·10 S	74·35 E
77	Hearne (hûrn) Tex.	30·53 N	96·35 W
87	Hearst (hûrst) Can.	49·36 N	83·40 W
70	Heart (R.) (härt) N. D.	46·46 N	102·34 W
83	Heart's Content (härts kŏn'tĕnt) Can.	47·55 N	53·20 W
83	Heath Pt. (hēth) Can.	49·06 N	61·45 W
73	Heavener (hēv'nēr) Okla.	34·52 N	94·36 W
76	Hebbronville (hē'brŭn-vĭl) Tex.	27·18 N	98·40 W
69	Heber (hē'bēr) Utah	40·30 N	111·25 W
73	Heber Springs Ark.	35·28 N	91·59 W
67	Hebgen Res. (hĕb'gĕn) Mont.	44·47 N	111·38 W
116	Hebrides, Sea of Scot.	56·63 N	6·41 W
87	Hebron (hēb'rŭn) Can.	58·11 N	62·56 W
75	Hebron Ind. (Chicago In.)	41·19 N	87·13 W
75	Hebron Ky. (Cincinnati In.)	39·04 N	84·43 W
73	Hebron Nebr.	40·11 N	97·36 W
70	Hebron N. D.	46·54 N	102·04 W
	Hebron, see Al Khalil		
118	Heby (hĭ'bü) Swe.	59·56 N	16·48 E
86	Hecate Str. (hĕk'ȧ-tē) Can.	53·34 N	130·53 W
91	Hecelchakán (ā-sĕl-chä-kän') Mex.	20·10 N	90·09 W
118	Hedemora (hĭ-dĕ-mō'rä) Swe.	60·16 N	15·55 E
118	Hedesunda Fd. (hi-de-sōōn'dä) Swe.	60·22 N	16·50 E
110	Hedon (hĕdŭn) Eng.	53·44 N	0·12 W
152	Hedo Saki (C.) (hå'dō sä'kē) Jap.	26·48 N	128·40 E
111	Heemstede Neth. (Amsterdam In.)	52·20 N	4·36 E
117	Heerlen Bel.	50·55 N	5·58 E
78	Heflin (hĕf'lĭn) Ala.	33·40 N	85·33 W
120	Heide (hī'dē) Ger.	54·13 N	9·06 E
161	Heidelberg (hī'dĕl-bûrg) Austl. (Melbourne In.)	37·45 S	145·04 E
120	Heidelberg (hīdĕl-bĕrgh) Ger.	49·24 N	8·43 E
120	Heidenheim (hī'dĕn-hīm) Ger.	48·41 N	10·09 E
168	Heilbron (hĭl'brōn) S. Afr. (Johannesburg & Pretoria In.)	27·17 S	27·58 E
120	Heilbronn (hīl'brōn) Ger.	49·09 N	9·16 E
123	Heiligenhaus (hī'lē-gĕn-houz) Ger. (Ruhr In.)	51·19 N	6·58 E
120	Heiligenstadt (hī'lē-gĕn-shtät) Ger.	51·21 N	10·10 E
147	Heilungkiang (Prov.) (hå-lōōng' kyäng') China	46·36 N	128·07 E
119	Heinola (hå-nō'lä) Fin.	61·13 N	26·03 E
123	Heinsberg (hīnz'bĕrgh) Ger. (Ruhr In.)	51·04 N	6·07 E
139	Heisi (R.) U. A. R. (Palestine In.)	29·21 N	34·30 E
111	Heist-op-den-Berg Bel. (Brussels In.)	51·05 N	4·14 E
112	Hekla (Vol.) (hĕk'lȧ) Ice.	63·53 N	19·37 W
121	Hel (häl) Pol.	54·37 N	18·53 E
118	Helagsfjället (M.) Swe.	62·54 N	12·24 E
73	Helena (hē-lē'nȧ) Ark.	34·33 N	90·35 W
67	Helena (hĕ-lĕ'nȧ) Mont.	46·35 N	112·01 W
161	Helensburgh (hĕl'ĕnz-bŭr-ô) Austl. (Sydney In.)	34·11 S	150·59 E
116	Helensburgh Scot.	56·01 N	4·53 W
118	Helge (R.) (hĕl'gĕ) Swe.	56·31 N	13·47 E
120	Helgoland I. (hĕl'gō-länd) Ger.	54·13 N	7·30 E
79	Hellier (hĕl'yēr) Ky.	37·16 N	82·27 W
124	Hellín (ĕl-yēn') Sp.	38·30 N	1·40 W
144	Helmand (R.) (hĕl'mŭnd) Afg.	31·00 N	63·48 E
117	Helmond (hĕl'mōnt) (ĕl'môɴ') Neth.	51·35 N	5·04 E
120	Helmstedt (hĕlm'shtĕt) Ger.	52·14 N	11·03 E
74	Helotes (hē'-lōts) Tex. (San Antonio In.)	29·35 N	98·41 W
69	Helper (hĕlp'ēr) Utah	39·40 N	110·55 W
	Helsingfors, see Helsinki		
118	Helsingør (hĕl-sĭng-ûr') Den.	56·03 N	12·33 E
119	Helsinki (Helsingfors) (hĕl'sĕn-kē) (hĕl'sĭng-fôrs') Fin.	60·10 N	24·53 E
167	Helvellyn (Mts.) (hĕl-vĕl-lĭn) S. Afr. (Natal In.)	30·32 S	27·18 E
110	Hemel Hempstead (hĕm'ĕl hĕmp'stĕd) Eng. (London In.)	51·43 N	0·29 W
74	Hemet (hĕm'ĕt) Calif. (Los Angeles In.)	33·45 N	116·57 W
70	Hemingford (hĕm'ĭng-fērd) Nebr.	42·21 N	103·30 W
77	Hemphill (hĕmp'hĭl) Tex.	31·20 N	93·48 W
84	Hempstead (hĕmp'stĕd) N. Y. (New York In.)	40·42 N	73·37 W
77	Hempstead Tex.	30·07 N	96·05 W
118	Hemse (hĕm'sē) Swe.	57·15 N	18·25 E
118	Hemsö (I.) Swe.	62·43 N	18·22 E
118	Hen (hĭn) Nor.	60·14 N	10·10 E
124	Henares (R.) (å-nä'räs) Sp.	40·50 N	2·55 W
122	Hendaye (äɴ-dā') Fr.	43·20 N	1·46 W
80	Henderson (hĕn'dēr-sŭn) Ky.	37·50 N	87·30 W
68	Henderson Nev.	36·09 N	115·04 W
79	Henderson N. C.	36·18 N	78·24 W
78	Henderson Tenn.	35·25 N	88·40 W
77	Henderson Tex.	32·09 N	94·48 W
79	Hendersonville (hĕn'dēr-sŭn-vĭl) N. C.	35·17 N	82·28 W
110	Hendon (hĕn'dŭn) Eng. (London In.)	51·34 N	0·13 W
168	Hendrina (hĕn-drē'nȧ) S. Afr. (Johannesburg & Pretoria In.)	26·10 S	29·44 E
151	Hengch'un (hĕng'chŭn') Taiwan	22·00 N	120·42 E
117	Hengelo (hĕng'ĕ-lō) Neth.	52·20 N	6·45 E
151	Henghsien China	22·40 N	104·20 E
151	Hengshan (hĕng'shän') China	27·20 N	112·40 E
148	Hengshui (hĕng'shōō-ē') China	37·43 N	115·42 E
151	Hengyang China	26·58 N	112·30 E
110	Henley on Thames (hĕn'lē ŏn tĕmz) Eng. (London In.)	51·31 N	0·54 W
81	Henlopen, C. (hĕn-lō'pĕn) Del.	38·45 N	75·05 W
122	Hennebont (ĕn-bôɴ') Fr.	47·47 N	3·16 W
168	Hennenman S. Afr. (Johannesburg & Pretoria In.)	27·59 S	27·03 E
72	Hennessey (hĕn'ĕ-sĭ) Okla.	36·04 N	97·53 W
111	Hennigsdorf (hĕ'nĕngz-dōrf) Ger. (Berlin In.)	52·39 N	13·12 E
167	Hennops (R.) (hĕn'ŏps) S. Afr. (Johannesburg & Pretoria In.)	25·51 S	27·57 E
167	Hennopsrivier S. Afr. (Johannesburg & Pretoria In.)	25·50 S	27·59 E
73	Henrietta (hĕn-rĭ-ĕt'ȧ) Okla.	35·25 N	95·58 W
72	Henrietta (hen-rĭ-ĕ'tȧ) Tex.	33·47 N	98·11 W
87	Henrietta Maria, C. (hĕn-rĭ-ĕt'ȧ) Can.	55·10 N	82·20 W
69	Henry Mts. (hĕn'rĭ) Utah	38·55 N	110·45 W
150	Henteyn Nuruu (Mts.) Sov. Un.	49·40 N	111·00 E
66	Heppner (hĕp'nēr) Ore.	45·21 N	119·33 W
144	Herāt (hĕ-rät') Afg.	34·28 N	62·13 E
127	Hercegovina (Reg.) (hĕr-tsĕ-gô'vē-nä) Yugo.	43·23 N	17·52 E
167	Hercules (hĕr'ku-lēs) S. Afr. (Johannesburg & Pretoria In.)	25·43 S	28·10 E
123	Herdecke (hĕr'dĕ-kĕ) Ger. (Ruhr In.)	51·24 N	7·26 E
93	Heredia (ā-rā'dhē-ä) C. R.	10·04 N	84·06 W
116	Hereford (hĕrĕ'fērd) Eng.	52·05 N	2·44 W
110	Hereford (Co.) Eng.	52·22 N	2·52 W
72	Hereford (hĕr'ē-fērd) Tex.	34·47 N	102·25 W
139	Hereidin (R.) U. A. R. (Palestine In.)	31·02 N	34·03 E
124	Herencia (å-rān'thē-ä) Sp.	39·23 N	3·22 W
111	Herentals Bel. (Brussels In.)	51·10 N	4·51 E
120	Herford (hĕr'fôrt) Ger.	52·06 N	8·42 E
73	Herington (hĕr'ĭng-tŭn) Kans.	38·41 N	96·57 W
120	Herisau (hā'rē-zou) Switz.	47·23 N	9·18 E
111	Herk-de-Stad Bel. (Brussels In.)	50·56 N	5·13 E
81	Herkimer (hûr'kĭ-mēr) N. Y.	43·05 N	75·00 W
116	Herma Ness (Prom.) (hûr'mȧ nĕs) Scot.	60·50 N	1·10 W
73	Hermann (hûr'mȧn) Mo.	38·41 N	91·27 W
80	Hermansville (hûr'mȧns-vĭl) Mich.	45·40 N	87·35 W
74	Hermantown (hĕr'mȧn-toun) Minn. (Duluth In.)	46·46 N	92·12 W
168	Hermanusdorings S. Afr. (Johannesburg & Pretoria In.)	24·08 S	27·46 E
75	Herminie (hûr-mĭ'nē) Pa. (Pittsburgh In.)	40·16 N	79·45 W
83	Hermitage B. (hûr'mĭ-tĕj) Can.	47·31 N	56·30 W
155	Hermit Is. (hûr'mĭt) N. Gui. Ter.	1·48 S	144·55 E
74	Hermosa Beach (hĕr-mō'sȧ) Calif. (Los Angeles In.)	33·51 N	118·24 W
88	Hermosillo (ĕr-mô-sē'l-yō) Mex.	29·00 N	110·57 W
123	Herne (hĕr'nĕ) Ger. (Ruhr In.)	51·32 N	7·13 E
118	Herning (hĕr'nĭng) Den.	56·08 N	8·55 E
70	Heron (L.) (hĕr'ŭn) Minn.	43·42 N	95·23 W
87	Heron Bay Can.	48·32 N	86·20 W
70	Heron Lake Minn.	43·48 N	95·20 W
92	Herrero, Punta (pt.) (pōō'n-tä-ĕr-rĕ'rô) Mex. (Yucatan In.)	19·18 N	87·24 W
80	Herrin (hĕr'ĭn) Ill.	37·50 N	89·00 W
167	Herschel (hĕr'-shĕl) S. Afr. (Natal In.)	30·37 S	27·12 E
75	Herscher (hĕr'shēr) Ill. (Chicago In.)	41·03 N	88·06 W
117	Herstal (hĕr'stäl) Bel.	50·42 N	5·32 E
110	Hertford (hûrt'fērd) Eng.	51·46 N	0·05 W
79	Hertford N. C.	36·10 N	76·30 W
111	Hertzberg (hĕrtz'bĕrgh) Ger. (Berlin In.)	52·54 N	12·58 E
167	Hertzog (hĕrt'zŏg) S. Afr. (Natal In.)	32·36 S	26·46 E
139	Herzlia Isr. (Palestine In.)	32·10 N	34·49 E
122	Hesdin (ĕ-dăɴ') Fr.	50·24 N	1·59 E
120	Hessen (State) (hĕs'ĕn) Ger.	50·16 N	8·48 E
68	Hetch Hetchy Aqueduct (hĕtch hĕt'-chĭ ăk'wē-dŭkt) Calif.	37·27 N	120·54 W
70	Hettinger (hĕt'ĭn-jēr) N. D.	45·58 N	102·36 W
168	Heuningspruit S. Afr. (Johannesburg & Pretoria In.)	27·28 S	27·26 E
168	Heystekrand S. Afr. (Johannesburg & Pretoria In.)	25·16 S	27·14 E
110	Heywood (hā'wŏŏd) Eng.	53·36 N	2·12 W
79	Hialeah (hī-ȧ-lē'-ăh) Fla. (In.)	25·49 N	80·18 W
73	Hiawatha (hī-ȧ-wô'thȧ) Kans.	39·50 N	95·33 W
69	Hiawatha Utah	39·25 N	111·05 W
71	Hibbing (hĭb'ĭng) Minn.	47·26 N	92·58 W
78	Hickman (hĭk'mȧn) Ky.	34·33 N	89·10 W
74	Hickman Mills Mo. (Kansas City In.)	38·56 N	94·32 W
79	Hickory (hĭk'ō-rĭ) N. C.	35·43 N	81·21 W
84	Hicksville (hĭks'vĭl) N. Y. (New York In.)	40·47 N	73·25 W
80	Hicksville Ohio	41·15 N	84·45 W
76	Hico (hī'kō) Tex.	32·00 N	98·02 W
90	Hidalgo (ē-dhäl'gō) Mex.	24·14 N	99·25 W
76	Hidalgo Mex.	27·49 N	99·53 W
88	Hidalgo (State) Mex.	20·45 N	99·30 W
76	Hidalgo del Parral (ē-dä'l-gō-dĕl-pär-rä'l) Mex.	26·55 N	105·40 W
91	Hidalgo Yalalag (ē-dhäl'gō-yä-lä-läg) Mex.	17·12 N	96·11 W
168	Hiedelberg S. Afr. (Johannesburg & Pretoria In.)	26·32 S	28·22 E
164	Hierro I. (yĕ'r-rô) Can. Is.	27·37 N	18·29 W
80	Higgins (L.) (hĭg'ĭnz) Mich.	44·20 N	84·45 W
73	Higginsville (hĭg'ĭnz-vĭl) Mo.	39·05 N	93·44 W
80	High (I.) Mich.	45·45 N	85·45 W
85	High Bluff Can. (Winnipeg In.)	50·01 N	98·08 W
94	Highborne Cay (hī'bôrn kē) Ba. Is.	24·45 N	76·50 W
74	Highgrove (hī'grōv) Calif. (Los Angeles In.)	34·01 N	117·20 W
77	High Island Tex. (In.)	29·34 N	94·24 W
74	Highland (hī'lănd) Calif. (Los Angeles In.)	34·08 N	117·13 W
73	Highland Ill.	38·44 N	89·41 W
75	Highland Ind. (Chicago In.)	41·33 N	87·28 W
75	Highland Mich. (Detroit In.)	42·38 N	83·37 W
65	Highland Wash. (Portland In.)	45·55 N	122·37 W
75	Highland Park Ill. (Chicago In.)	42·11 N	87·47 W
75	Highland Park Mich. (Detroit In.)	42·24 N	83·06 W
84	Highland Park N. J. (New York In.)	40·30 N	74·25 W

PRONOUNCING INDEX

Highland Park–Horten 215

Page	Name Pronunciation Region	Lat. °′	Long. °′
74	Highland Park Tex. (Dallas, Fort Worth In.)	32·49 N	96·48 W
84	Highlands (hī-lǎndz) N. J. (New York In.)	40·24 N	73·59 W
77	Highlands Tex. (In.)	29·49 N	95·01 W
70	Highmore (hī'-mōr) S. D.	44·30 N	99·26 W
110	High Ongar (on'gēr) Eng. (London In.)	51·43 N	0·15 E
155	High Pk. Phil. (Manila In.)	15·38 N	120·05 E
79	High Point N. C.	35·55 N	80·00 W
86	High Prairie Can.	55·30 N	116·47 W
74	High Ridge Mo. (St. Louis In.)	38·27 N	90·32 W
86	High River Can.	50·40 N	113·47 W
79	Highrock (R.) (hī'-rŏk) N. C.	35·40 N	80·15 W
79	High Springs Fla.	29·48 N	82·38 W
84	Hightstown (hīts-toun) N. J. (New York In.)	40·16 N	74·32 W
110	High Wycombe (wĭ-kŭm) Eng. (London In.)	51·36 N	0·45 W
89	Higuero, Pta. (Pt.) P. R. (Puerto Rico In.)	18·21 N	67·11 W
99	Higuerote (ē-gĕ-rō'-tĕ) Ven. (In.)	10·29 N	66·06 W
95	Higüey (ê-gwĕ'y) Dom. Rep.	18·40 N	68·45 W
119	Hiiumaa (D'Ago) (hē'ōōm-ô) Sov. Un.	58·47 N	22·05 E
153	Hikone (hē'kô-nĕ) Jap.	35·15 N	136·15 E
120	Hildburghausen (hĭld'bōōrg hou-zĕn) Ger.	50·26 N	10·45 E
123	Hilden (hĕl'dĕn) Ger. (Ruhr In.)	51·10 N	6·56 E
120	Hildesheim (hĭl'dĕs-hīm) Ger.	52·08 N	9·56 E
93	Hillaby, Mt. (hĭl'ȧ-bĭ) Barb. (Le. & Wind. Is. In.)	13·15 N	59·35 W
72	Hill City (hĭl) Kans.	39·22 N	99·54 W
71	Hill City Minn.	46·58 N	93·38 W
111	Hillegersberg Neth. (Amsterdam In.)	51·57 N	4·29 E
118	Hillerød (hê'lĕ-rûdh) Den.	55·56 N	12·17 E
73	Hillsboro (hĭlz'bŭr-ō) Ill.	39·09 N	89·28 W
73	Hillsboro Kans.	38·22 N	97·11 W
81	Hillsboro N. H.	43·05 N	71·55 W
70	Hillsboro N. D.	47·23 N	97·05 W
80	Hillsboro Ohio	39·10 N	83·40 W
65	Hillsboro Ore. (Portland In.)	45·31 N	122·59 W
77	Hillsboro Tex.	32·01 N	97·06 W
71	Hillsboro Wis.	43·39 N	90·20 W
85	Hillsburgh (hĭlz'bûrg) Can. (Toronto In.)	43·48 N	80·09 W
66	Hills Creek Res. Ore.	43·41 N	122·26 W
80	Hillsdale (hĭls-dāl) Mich.	41·55 N	84·35 W
157	Hilo (hē'lō) Hawaii (In.)	19·44 N	155·01 W
111	Hilversum (hĭl'vēr-sŭm) Neth. (Amsterdam In.)	52·13 N	5·10 E
142	Himachal Pradesh (Ter.) India	36·03 N	77·41 E
145	Himalaya Mts. (hĭ-mä'lȧ-yȧ) Asia	29·30 N	85·02 E
153	Himeji (hē'mȧ-jē) Jap.	34·50 N	134·42 E
111	Himmelpforten (hē'mĕl-pfōr-tĕn) Ger. (Hamburg In.)	53·37 N	9·19 E
95	Hinche (hēn'chȧ) (ǎNsh) Hai.	19·10 N	72·05 W
159	Hinchinbrook (I.) (hĭn-chĭn-brŏŏk) Austl.	18·23 S	146·57 W
110	Hinckley (hĭnk'lĭ) Eng.	52·32 N	1·21 W
110	Hindley (hĭnd'lĭ) Eng.	53·32 N	2·35 W
145	Hindu Kush Mts. (hĭn'dōō kōōsh') Asia	35·15 N	68·44 E
143	Hindupur (hĭn'dōō-pōōr) India	13·52 N	77·34 E
86	Hines Creek (hīnz) Can.	56·15 N	118·33 W
83	Hingham (hĭng'ǎm) Mass. (Boston In.)	42·14 N	70·53 W
75	Hinkley (hĭnk'-lĭ) Ohio (Cleveland In.)	41·14 N	81·45 W
124	Hinojosa (ê-nô-kō'sä) Sp.	38·30 N	5·09 W
75	Hinsdale (hĭnz'dāl) Ill. (Chicago In.)	41·48 N	87·56 W
80	Hinton (hĭn'tŭn) W. Va.	37·40 N	80·55 W
153	Hirado (I.) (hē'rä-dō) Jap.	33·19 N	129·18 E
153	Hirakata (hē'rä-kä'tä) Jap. (Ōsaka In.)	34·49 N	135·40 E
153	Hiraoka (hē'rä-ō'kä) Jap. (Ōsaka In.)	34·40 N	135·39 E
153	Hiratsuka (hē-rät-sōō'kȧ) Jap.	35·20 N	139·19 E
146	Hirgis Nuur (L.) Mong.	49·18 N	94·21 E
152	Hirosaki (hē'rô-sä'kê) Jap.	40·31 N	140·38 E
153	Hirose (hē'rô-sä) Jap.	35·20 N	133·11 E
153	Hiroshima (hē-rô-shē'mȧ) Jap.	34·22 N	132·25 E
122	Hirson (ēr-sôN') Fr.	49·54 N	4·00 E
89	Hispaniola (I.) (hĭ'spăn-ĭ-ō-lȧ) N. A.	17·30 N	73·15 W
142	Hissar India	29·15 N	75·47 E
144	Hīt (hēt) Iraq	33·32 N	42·35 E
152	Hitachi (hē-tä'chē) Jap.	36·42 N	140·47 E
77	Hitchcock (hĭch'kŏk) Tex. (In.)	29·21 N	95·01 W
123	Hitdorf (hēt'dōrf) Ger. (Ruhr In.)	51·04 N	6·56 E
153	Hitoyoshi (hē'tô-yō'shê) Jap.	32·13 N	130·45 E
112	Hitra (I.) (hĭträ) Nor.	63·34 N	7·37 E
111	Hittefeld (hē'tĕ-fĕld) Ger. (Hamburg In.)	53·23 N	9·59 E
153	Hiwasa (hē'wȧ-sä) Jap.	33·44 N	134·31 E
78	Hiwassee (R.) (hī-wŏs'sē) Tenn.	35·10 N	84·35 W
118	Hjälmaren (L.) Swe.	59·07 N	16·05 E
118	Hjo (yō) Swe.	58·19 N	14·11 E
118	Hjørring (jûr'ĭng) Den.	57·27 N	9·59 E
121	Hlohovec (hlō'hô-vĕts) Czech.	48·24 N	17·49 E
160	Hobart (hō'bȧrt) Austl.	43·00 S	147·30 E
75	Hobart Ind. (Chicago In.)	41·31 N	87·15 W
72	Hobart Okla.	35·02 N	99·06 W
65	Hobart Wash. (Seattle In.)	47·25 N	121·58 W
72	Hobbs (hŏbs) N. Mex.	32·41 N	104·04 W
146	Hobdo Gol (R.) Mong.	49·06 N	91·16 E
111	Hoboken (hō'bō-kĕn) Bel. (Brussels In.)	51·11 N	4·20 E
84	Hoboken N. J. (New York In.)	40·43 N	74·03 W
118	Hobro (hô-brō') Den.	56·38 N	9·47 E
84	Hobson (hŏb'-sŭn) Va. (Norfolk In.)	36·54 N	76·31 W
161	Hobson's B. (hŏb'sŭnz) Austl. (Melbourne In.)	37·54 S	144·45 E
148	Hochien (hŭ'jĭän) China	38·28 N	116·05 E
148	Hochiu China	32·19 N	116·17 E
120	Höchst (hûKst) Ger.	50·06 N	8·37 E
151	Hoch'uan China	30·00 N	106·20 E
65	Hockinson (hŏk'-ĭn-sŭn) Wash. (Portland In.)	45·44 N	122·29 W
92	Hoctún (ôk-tōō'n) Mex. (Yucatan In.)	20·52 N	89·10 W
80	Hodgenville (hŏj'ĕn-vĭl) Ky.	37·35 N	85·45 W
83	Hodges Hill (hŏj'ĕz) Can.	49·03 N	55·54 W
86	Hodgson (hŏj-sŭn) Can.	51·16 N	97·40 W
121	Hódmezövásárhely (hōd'mĕ-zû-vô'shôr-hĕl-y') Hung.	46·24 N	20·21 E
121	Hodonin (hē'dô-nén) Czech.	48·50 N	17·06 E
111	Hoegaarden Bel. (Brussels In.)	50·46 N	4·55 E
111	Hoek van Holland Neth. (Amsterdam In.)	51·59 N	4·05 E
152	Hoeryŏng (hwĕr'yŭng) Kor.	42·28 N	129·39 E
123	Hoetmar (hût'mär) Ger. (Ruhr In.)	51·52 N	7·54 E
120	Hof (hōf) Ger.	50·19 N	11·55 E
148	Hofei (hŏ'fā) China	31·51 N	117·15 E
112	Hofsjökull (Gl.) (hôfs'yû'kōōl) Ice.	64·55 N	18·40 W
	Hofuf, see Al Hufūf		
94	Hog (I.) (hŏg) Ba. Is.	25·05 N	77·20 W
80	Hog (I.) Mich.	45·50 N	85·20 W
78	Hogansville (hō'gănz-vĭl) Ga.	33·10 N	84·54 W
95	Hog Cay (I.) Ba. Is.	23·35 N	75·30 W
95	Hogsty Rf. Ba. Is.	21·45 N	73·50 W
111	Hohenbrunn (hō'hĕn-brōōn) Ger. (Munich In.)	48·03 N	11·42 E
123	Hohenlimburg (hō'hĕn lĕm'bōōrg) Ger. (Ruhr In.)	51·20 N	7·35 E
111	Hohen Neuendorf (hō'hĕn noi'ĕn-dōrf) Ger. (Berlin In.)	52·40 N	13·22 E
120	Hohe Tauern (Mts.) (hō'ĕ tou'ērn) Aus.	47·11 N	12·12 E
84	Hohokus (hō-hō-kŭs) N. J. (New York In.)	41·01 N	74·08 W
151	Hohsien China	24·20 N	24·20 E
148	Hohsien (hō'syĕn') China	31·44 N	118·20 E
148	Ho Hu (L.) (hŭ'hoo) China	31·37 N	119·57 E
72	Hoisington (hoi'zĭng-tŭn) Kans.	38·30 N	98·46 W
153	Hojo (hō'jō) Jap.	33·58 N	132·50 E
159	Hokitika (hō-kĭ-tē'kä) N. Z. (In.)	42·43 S	171·12 E
152	Hokkaido (I.) (hŏk'kī-dō) Jap.	43·30 N	142·45 E
151	Hokou (hō'kō') China	29·58 N	116·20 E
118	Holbaek (hôl'bĕk) Den.	55·42 N	11·40 E
92	Holbox (ôl-bŏ'x) Mex. (Yucatan In.)	21·33 N	87·19 W
92	Holbox, Isla (I.) (ē's-lä-ôl-bŏ'x) Mex. (Yucatan In.)	21·40 N	87 21 W
69	Holbrook (hōl'brŏŏk) Ariz.	34·55 N	110·15 W
83	Holbrook Mass. (Boston In.)	42·10 N	71·01 W
83	Holden (hōl'dĕn) Mass. (Boston In.)	42·21 N	71·51 W
73	Holden Mo.	38·42 N	94·00 W
80	Holden W. Va.	37·45 N	82·05 W
73	Holdenville (hōl'dĕn-vĭl) Okla.	35·05 N	96·25 W
72	Holdrege (hōl'drĕj) Nebr.	40·25 N	99·28 W
118	Hölen (hûl'ĕn) Nor.	59·34 N	10·40 E
95	Holguín (ôl-gēn') Cuba	20·55 N	76·15 W
81	Holidaysburg (hŏl'ĭ-dāz-bûrg) Pa.	40·30 N	78·30 W
120	Hollabrunn Aus.	48·33 N	16·04 E
80	Holland (hŏl'ǎnd) Mich.	42·45 N	86·10 W
111	Hollandsch Diep (Chan.) Neth. (Amsterdam In.)	51·43 N	4·25 E
111	Hollenstedt (hō'lĕn-shtĕt) Ger. (Hamburg In.)	53·22 N	9·43 E
74	Holliday (hŏl'ĭ-dā) Mo. (Kansas City In.)	39·02 N	94·48 W
83	Hollis (hŏl'ĭs) N. H. (Boston In.)	42·30 N	71·29 W
72	Hollis Okla.	34·39 N	99·56 W
68	Hollister (hŏl'ĭs-tēr) Calif.	36·50 N	121·25 W
83	Holliston (hŏl'ĭs-tŭn) Mass. (Boston In.)	42·12 N	71·25 W
80	Holly (hŏl'ĭ) Mich.	42·45 N	83·30 W
65	Holly Wash. (Seattle In.)	47·34 N	122·58 W
78	Holly Springs (hŏl'ĭ sprĭngz) Miss.	34·45 N	89·28 W
74	Hollywood (hŏl'ê-wŏŏd) Calif. (Los Angeles In.)	34·06 N	118·20 W
79	Hollywood Fla. (In.)	26·00 N	80·11 W
74	Holmes Park Mo. (Kansas City In.)	38·57 N	94·33 W
159	Holmes Rfs. (hōmz) Austl.	16·33 S	148·43 E
118	Holmestrand (hôl'mĕ-strän) Nor.	59·29 N	10·17 E
118	Holmsbu (hôlms'bōō) Nor.	59·36 N	10·26 E
118	Holmsjön (L.) Swe.	62·23 N	15·43 E
118	Holstebro (hôl'stĕ-brô') Den.	56·22 N	8·39 E
78	Holston (R.) (hōl'stŭn) Tenn.	36·02 N	83·42 W
110	Holt (hōlt) Eng.	53·05 N	2·53 W
73	Holton (hōl'tŭn) Kans.	39·27 N	95·43 W
116	Holy (I.) (hō'lĭ) Wales	53·45 N	4·45 W
116	Holy (I.) Eng.	55·43 N	1·48 W
64	Holy Cross (hō'lĭ krôs) Alaska	62·10 N	159·40 W
116	Holyhead (hŏl'ē-hĕd) Wales	53·48 N	4·45 W
72	Holyoke (hōl'yōk) Colo.	40·36 N	102·18 W
81	Holyoke Mass.	42·10 N	72·40 W
153	Homano (hō-mä'nō) Jap. (Tōkyō In.)	35·33 N	140·08 E
123	Homberg (hōm'bĕrgh) Ger. (Ruhr In.)	51·27 N	6·42 E
74	Home Gardens (hōm gär'd'nz) Calif. (Los Angeles In.)	33·53 N	117·32 W
74	Homeland (hōm'lǎnd) Calif. (Los Angeles In.)	33·44 N	117·07 W
84	Homeplace (hōm-plās) La. (New Orleans In.)	29·27 N	89·40 W
64	Homer (hō'mēr) Alaska	59·42 N	151·30 W
77	Homer La.	32·46 N	93·05 W
79	Homestead (hōm'stĕd) Fla. (In.)	25·27 N	80·28 W
74	Homestead Mich. (Sault Ste. Marie In.)	46·20 N	84·07 W
75	Homestead Pa. (Pittsburgh In.)	40·29 N	79·55 W
73	Homestead Natl. Mon. of America Nebr.	40·16 N	96·51 W
84	Homewood (hōm'wŏŏd) Ala. (Birmingham In.)	33·28 N	86·48 W
75	Homewood Ill. (Chicago In.)	41·34 N	87·40 W
73	Hominy (hŏm'ĭ-nĭ) Okla.	36·25 N	96·24 W
78	Homochiho (R.) (hō-mō-chĭt'ō) Miss.	31·23 N	91·15 W
115	Homs (hōms) Syr.	34·42 N	36·52 E
147	Honan (Prov.) (hō'nän') China	33·58 N	112·33 E
98	Honda (hōn'dȧ) Col. (In.)	5·13 N	74·45 W
94	Honda, Bahía (B.) (bä-ē'ä-ô'n-dä) Cuba	23·10 N	83·20 W
76	Hondo Tex.	29·20 N	99·08 W
92	Hondo, Rio (R.) (hon-dō') Br. Hond. (Yucatan In.)	18·16 N	88·32 W
72	Hondo (R.) N. Mex.	33·22 N	105·06 W
88	Honduras (hŏn-dōō'rȧs) N. A.	14·30 N	88·00 W
88	Honduras, Gulf of N. A.	16·30 N	87·30 W
79	Honea Path (hŭn'ĭ păth S. C.	34·25 N	82·16 W
118	Hönefoss (hē'nē-fôs) Nor.	60·10 N	10·15 E
81	Honesdale (hōnz'dāl) Pa.	41·30 N	75·15 W
68	Honey (R.) (hŭn'ĭ) Calif.	40·11 N	120·34 W
73	Honey Grove (hŭn'ĭ grōv) Tex.	33·35 N	95·54 W
85	Honfleur (ôN-flûr') Can. (Quebec In.)	46·39 N	70·53 W
122	Honfleur (ôN-flûr') Fr.	49·26 N	0·13 E
151	Hon Gay Viet.	20·58 N	107·10 E
159	Honiara Austl.	9·15 S	159·45 E
116	Honiton (hŏn'ĭ-tŏn) Eng.	50·49 N	3·10 W
151	Hong Kong (I.) (hŏng' kŏng') Asia	22·15 N	114·40 E
157	Honolulu (hōn-ô-lōō'lōō) Hawaii (In.)	21·18 N	157·50 W
157	Honomu (hŏn'ô-mōō) Hawaii (In.)	19·50 N	155·04 W
152	Honshū (I.) (hŏn'shōō) Jap.	36·50 N	135·20 E
66	Hood, Mt. Ore.	45·20 N	121·43 W
65	Hood Can. (hŏŏd) Wash. (Seattle In.)	47·45 N	122·45 W
66	Hood River Ore.	45·42 N	121·30 W
65	Hoodsport (hŏŏdz'pōrt) Wash. (Seattle In.)	47·25 N	123·09 W
142	Hoogly (R.) (hōōg'lĭ) India	21·30 N	87·28 E
111	Hoogstraten Bel. (Brussels In.)	51·24 N	4·46 E
157	Hookena (hōō-kĕ-nä) Hawaii (In.)	19·23 N	155·51 W
72	Hooker (hŏŏk'ēr) Okla.	36·49 N	101·13 W
92	Hool (ōō'l) Mex. (Yucatan In.)	19·32 N	90·22 W
64	Hoonah (hōō'nä) Alaska	58·05 N	135·25 W
66	Hoopa Valley Ind. Res. (hōō'pȧ) Calif.	41·18 N	123·35 W
73	Hooper (hŏŏp'ēr) Nebr.	41·37 N	96·31 W
74	Hooper Utah (Salt Lake City In.)	41·10 N	112·08 W
64	Hooper Bay Alaska	61·32 N	166·02 W
80	Hoopeston (hōōps'tŭn) Ill.	40·35 N	87·40 W
81	Hoosick Falls (hōō'sĭk) N. Y.	42·55 N	73·15 W
68	Hoover Dam (hōō'vēr) Nev.	36·00 N	115·06 W
84	Hopatcong, L. (hō-păt'kong) N. J. (New York In.)	40·57 N	74·38 W
64	Hope (hōp) Alaska	60·54 N	149·48 W
73	Hope Ark.	33·41 N	93·35 W
86	Hope Can.	49·25 N	121·10 W
70	Hope N. D.	47·17 N	97·45 W
87	Hopedale (hōp'dāl) Can.	55·26 N	60·11 W
83	Hopedale (hōp'dāl) Mass. (Boston In.)	42·08 N	71·33 W
147	Hopeh (Prov.) China	39·09 N	115·22 E
92	Hopelchén (o-pĕl-chĕ'n) Mex. (Yucatan In.)	19·47 N	89·51 W
87	Hope Mts. Can.	53·58 N	62·29 W
87	Hopes Advance, C. (hōps ǎd-văns') Can.	61·00 N	69·12 W
158	Hopetoun (hōp'toun) Austl.	33·50 S	120·15 E
84	Hopewell (hōp'wĕl) N. J. (New York In.)	40·23 N	74·45 W
79	Hopewell Va.	37·14 N	77·15 W
166	Hopetown (hōp'toun) S. Afr.	29·35 S	24·10 E
69	Hopi Ind. Res. (hō'pē) Ariz.	36·20 N	110·30 W
74	Hopkins (hŏp'-kĭns) Minn. (Minneapolis, St. Paul In.)	44·55 N	93·24 W
78	Hopkinsville (hŏp'-kĭns-vĭl) Ky.	36·50 N	87·28 W
83	Hopkinton (hŏp'-kĭn-tŭn) Mass. (Boston In.)	42·14 N	71·31 W
151	Hop'u China	21·28 N	109·10 E
66	Hoquiam (hō'kwĭ-ǎm) Wash.	47·00 N	123·53 W
118	Horby (hûr'bü) Swe.	55·50 N	13·41 E
93	Horconcitos (ŏr-kŏn-sē'-tôs) Pan.	8·18 N	82·11 W
168	Hordio Som. (Horn of Afr. In.)	10·43 N	51·05 E
120	Horgen (hôr'gĕn) Switz.	47·16 N	8·35 E
71	Horicon (hŏr'ĭ-kŏn) Wis.	43·26 N	88·40 W
144	Hormuz, Str. of (hôr'mŭz') Asia	26·37 N	15·27 E
	Horn, C., see Hornos, Cabo de		
159	Horn (Is.) (hôrn) Austl.	10·30 S	143·30 E
112	Hornavan (L.) Swe.	65·54 N	16·17 E
111	Horneburg (hôr'nĕ-bōōrgh) Ger. (Hamburg In.)	53·30 N	9·35 E
81	Hornell (hôr-nĕl') N. Y.	42·10 N	77·40 W
86	Horn Mts. Can.	62·12 N	120·29 W
100	Hornos, C. de (Horn, C.) (kȧ'-bô-dĕ-ô'r-nôs) (kā'p-hŏr'n) Chile	56·00 S	67·00 W
161	Hornsby (hôrnz' bĭ) Austl. (Sydney In.)	33·43 S	151·06 E
118	Hornslandet (I.) Swe.	61·40 N	17·58 E
100	Horqueta (ŏr-kĕ'tä) Par.	23·20 S	57·00 W
72	Horse Cr. (hôrs) Colo.	38·49 N	103·48 W
70	Horse Cr. Wyo.	41·33 N	104·39 W
83	Horse Is. Can.	50·11 N	55·45 W
118	Horsens (hôrs'ĕns) Den.	55·50 N	9·49 E
65	Horseshoe B. (hôrs-shōō) Can. (Vancouver In.)	49·23 N	123·16 W
110	Horsforth (hôrs'fŭrth) Eng.	53·50 N	1·38 W
160	Horsham (hôr'shǎm) (hôrs'ǎm) Austl.	36·42 S	142·17 E
111	Horst (hôrst) Ger. (Hamburg In.)	53·49 N	9·37 E
118	Horten (hôr'tĕn) Nor.	59·26 N	10·27 E

ng-sing; ŋ-baŋk; N-nasalized n; nŏd; cŏmmit; ōld; ôbey ôrder; fōōd; fŏŏt; ou-out; s-soft; sh-dish; th-thin; pūre; ûnite; ûrn; stŭd; circŭs; ü-as "y" in study; '-indeterminate vowel.

är; finȧl; rāte; senåte; ärm; åsk; sofȧ; fâre; ch-choose; dh-as th in other; bē; ĕvent; bĕt; recĕnt; cratẽr; g-go; gh-guttural g; bĭt; ĭ-short neutral; rīde; ᴋ-guttural k as ch in German ich;

PRONOUNCING INDEX

Huntingdon–Inner Brass 217

Page	Name Pronunciation	Region	Lat. °′	Long. °′
78	Huntingdon	Tenn.	36·00 N	88·23 W
110	Huntingdon (Co.)	Eng.	52·26 N	0·19 W
80	Huntington	Ind.	40·55 N	85·30 W
84	Huntington	N. Y. (New York In.)	40·51 N	73·25 W
81	Huntington	Pa.	40·30 N	78·00 W
80	Huntington	W. Va.	38·25 N	82·25 W
74	Huntington Beach	Calif. (Los Angeles In.)	33·39 N	118·00 W
74	Huntington Park	Calif. (Los Angeles In.)	33·59 N	118·14 W
78	Huntsville (hŭnts'-vĭl)	Ala.	35·43 N	86·36 W
81	Huntsville	Can.	45·20 N	79·15 W
73	Huntsville	Mo.	39·24 N	92·32 W
77	Huntsville	Tex.	30·44 N	95·34 W
74	Huntsville	Utah (Salt Lake City In.)	41·16 N	111·46 W
91	Hunucmá (hōō-nōōk-mä')	Mex.	21·01 N	89·54 W
148	Huolu (hōōŭ lōō)	China	38·05 N	114·20 E
155	Huon G.	N. Gui. Ter.	7·15 S	147·45 E
147	Hupeh (Prov.)	China	31·20 N	111·58 E
80	Hurd, C. (hûrd)	Can.	45·15 N	81·45 W
71	Hurley (hûr'lĭ)	Wis.	46·26 N	90·11 W
100	Hurlingham (ōō'r-lēn-gäm)	Arg. (In.)	34·20 S	58·38 W
80	Huron (hū'rŏn)	Ohio	41·20 N	82·35 W
70	Huron	S. D.	44·22 N	98·15 W
63	Huron, L. (hū'rŏn)	U. S.-Can.	45·15 N	82·40 W
71	Huron Mts. (hū'rŏn)	Mich.	46·47 N	87·52 W
75	Huron R.	Mich. (Detroit In.)	42·12 N	83·26 W
64	Hurricane (hŭr'ĭ-kān)	Alaska	63·00 N	149·30 W
69	Hurricane	Utah	37·10 N	113·20 W
94	Hurricane Flats (Shoal) (hŭ-rĭ-kăn flăts)	Ba. Is.	23·35 N	78·30 W
112	Húsavik	Ice.	66·00 N	17·10 W
129	Huşi (kōōsh')	Sov. Un.	46·52 N	28·04 E
118	Huskvarna (hōōsk-vär'nȧ)	Swe.	57·48 N	14·16 E
120	Husum (hōō'zōōm)	Ger.	54·29 N	9·04 E
74	Hutchins (hŭch'ĭnz)	Tex. (Dallas, Fort Worth In.)	32·38 N	96·43 W
72	Hutchinson (hŭch'ĭn-sŭn)	Kans.	38·02 N	97·56 W
71	Hutchinson	Minn.	44·53 N	94·23 W
150	Hut'o Ho (R.) (hōō'tō'hō')	China	38·10 N	114·00 E
148	Huwu (hōō wōō)	China	31·17 N	119·48 E
117	Huy (û-ē') (hû'ē)	Bel.	50·33 N	5·14 E
112	Hvannadalshnukur (Mtn.)	Ice.	64·09 N	16·46 W
147	Hwang Ho (Yellow R.) (hwäng'hō')	China	35·06 N	113·39 E
146	Hwang Ho, Old beds of the	China	40 28 N	106·34 E
126	Hvar (I.) (ĸhvär)	Yugo.	43·08 N	16·28 E
152	Hwangju (hwäng'jōō')	Kor.	38·39 N	125·49 E
64	Hydaburg (hī-dă'bûrg)	Alaska	55·18 N	132·40 W
110	Hyde (hīd)	Eng.	53·27 N	2·05 W
143	Hyderābād (hī-dēr-ȧ-băd')	India	17·29 N	79·28 E
142	Hyderabad (hī-dēr-ȧ-băd')	W. Pak.	25·29 N	68·28 E
143	Hyderabad (State)	India	23·29 N	76·50 E
123	Hyères (ē-âr')	Fr.	43·09 N	6·08 E
123	Hyères, Iles d' (Is.) (ēl'dyâr')	Fr.	42·57 N	6·17 E
152	Hyesanjin (hyĕ'sän-jĭn')	Kor.	41·11 N	128·12 E
80	Hymera (hī-mē'rȧ)	Ind.	39·10 N	87·20 W
67	Hyndman Pk. (hīnd'măn)	Idaho	43·38 N	114·04 W
153	Hyōgo (Pref.) (hĭyō'gō)	Jap. (Ōsaka In.)	34·54 N	135·15 E
86	Hythe	Can.	55·18 N	119·34 W
153	Ia (R.) (ē'ä)	Jap. (Osaka In.)	34·54 N	135·34 E
121	Iaşi (yä'shē)	Rom.	47·10 N	27·40 E
155	Iba (ē'bä)	Phil. (Manila In.)	15·20 N	119·59 E
164	Ibadan (ē-bä'dän)	Nig.	7·26 N	3·48 E
98	Ibagué (ē-bȧ-gā')	Col. (In.)	4·27 N	75·13 W
127	Ibar (R.) (ē'bär)	Yugo.	43·22 N	20·35 E
153	Ibaragi (ē-bä'rä-gē)	Jap. (Ōsaka In.)	34·49 N	135·35 E
98	Ibarra (ē-bär'rä)	Ec.	0·19 N	78·08 W
163	Iberian Pen	Port.-Sp.	41·00 N	0·07 W
82	Iberville (ē-bȧr-vēl') (ī'bēr-vĭl)	Can.	45·14 N	73·01 W
164	Ibi (ē'bē)	Nig.	8·08 N	9·45 E
99	Ibiapaba, Serra da (Mts.) (sĕ'r-rä-dä-ē-byä-pȧ'bä)	Braz.	3·30 S	40·55 W
125	Ibiza (ē-bē'thä)	Sp.	38·55 N	1·24 E
125	Ibiza, Isla de (Iviza I.) (ē's-lä-dĕ-ē-bē'zä)	Sp.	39·07 N	1·05 E
167	Ibo (ē'bō)	Moz.	12·17 S	40·45 E
144	Ibrahim, Jabal (Mtn.)	Sau. Ar.	20·31 N	41·17 E
168	Ibrahim, Port	U. A. R. (Suez In.)	29·57 N	32·33 E
98	Ica (ē'kȧ)	Peru	14·09 S	75·42 W
98	Icá (R.) (ē-kȧ')	Braz.	2·56 S	69·12 W
98	Içana (ē-sä'nä)	Braz.	0·15 N	67·19 W
66	Ice Harbor Dam	Wash.	46·15 N	118·54 W
102	Iceland (īs'lănd)	Eur.	65·12 N	19·45 W
151	Ich'ang (ē'chäng')	China	30·38 N	111·22 E
142	Ichāpur	India (Calcutta In.)	22·47 N	88·21 E
153	Ichibusayama (Mt.) (ē'chē-bōō'sȧ-yä'mä)	Jap.	32·19 N	131·08 E
153	Ichikawa (ē'chē-kä'wä)	Jap. (Tōkyō In.)	35·44 N	139·54 E
153	Ichinomiya (ē'chē-nō-mē'yȧ)	Jap.	35·19 N	136·49 E
152	Ichinomiya	Jap.	35·23 N	140·33 E
153	Ichinomoto (ē-chē'nō-mō-tō)	Jap. (Ōsaka In.)	34·37 N	135·50 E
129	Ichnya (ĭch'nyä)	Sov. Un.	50·47 N	32·23 E
99	Icó (ē-kô')	Braz.	6·25 S	38·43 W
98	Icutú, Cerro (Mtn.) (sĕ'r-rô-ē-kōō-tōō')	Ven.	7·07 N	65·30 W
64	Icy C. (ī'sĭ)	Alaska	70·20 N	161·40 W
73	Idabel (ī'dȧ-bĕl)	Okla.	33·52 N	94·47 W
70	Idagrove (ī'dȧ-grōv)	Iowa	42·22 N	95·29 W
164	Idah (ē'dä)	Nig.	7·08 N	6·45 E
62	Idaho (State) (ī'dȧ-hō)	U. S.	44·00 N	115·10 W
67	Idaho Falls	Idaho	43·30 N	112·01 W
72	Idaho Springs	Colo.	39·43 N	105·32 W
124	Idanha-a-Nova (ē-dän'yȧ-ä-nō'vȧ)	Port.	39·58 N	7·13 W
146	Ideriin Gol (R.)	Mong.	48·58 N	98·38 E
168	Idfū (ĕd'fōō)	U. A. R. (Nile In.)	24·57 N	32·53 E
127	Idhra (I.)	Grc.	37·20 N	23·30 E
154	Idi (ē'dē)	Indon.	4·58 N	97·47 E
168	Idkū (ēd'kōō)	U. A. R. (Nile In.)	31·18 N	30·20 E
168	Idkū L.	U. A. R. (Nile In.)	31·13 N	30·22 E
110	Idle (R.) (īd''l)	Eng.	53·22 N	0·56 W
126	Idrija (ē'drē-ȧ)	Yugo.	46·01 N	14·01 E
167	Idutywa (ē-dōō-tī'wȧ)	S. Afr. (Natal In.)	32·06 S	28·18 E
117	Ieper	Bel.	50·50 N	2·53 E
126	Ierápetra	Grc. (Inset)	35·01 N	25·48 E
126	Iesi (yā'sē)	It.	43·37 N	13·20 E
164	Ife	Nig.	7·36 N	4·38 E
164	Iferouane (ēf'rōō-än')	Niger	19·23 N	8·24 E
163	Ifni (ēf'nē)	Afr.	29·45 N	11·00 W
134	Igarka (ē-gär'kȧ)	Sov. Un.	67·22 N	86·16 E
126	Iglesias (ē-lĕ'syôs)	It.	39·20 N	8·34 E
164	Igli (ē-glē')	Alg.	30·32 N	2·15 W
87	Igloolik	Can.	69·33 N	81·18 W
139	'Igma, Gebel el (Mts.)	U. A. R. (Palistine In.)	29·12 N	33·42 E
65	Ignacio (ĭg-nā'cĭ-ō)	Calif. (San Francisco In.)	38·05 N	122·32 W
100	Iguaçu (R.) (ē-gwä-sōō')	Braz. (In.)	22·42 S	43·19 W
90	Iguala (ē-gwä'lä)	Mex.	18·18 N	99·34 W
125	Igualada (ē-gwä-lä'dä)	Sp.	41·35 N	1·38 E
100	Iguassu (R.) (ē-gwä-sōō')	Braz.	25·45 S	52·30 W
100	Iguassu Falls (Falls)	Braz.	25·40 S	54·16 W
101	Iguatama (ē-gwä-tȧ'mä)	Braz (Rio de Janeiro In.)	20·13 S	45·40 W
99	Iguatu (ē-gwä-tōō')	Braz.	6·22 S	39·17 W
164	Iguidi, Erg (Dune)	Alg.	26·22 N	6·53 W
155	Iguig (ē-gēg')	Phil. (Manila In.)	17·46 N	121·44 E
150	Ihsien	China	41·30 N	121·15 E
148	I Ho (R.) (yē'hŭ)	China	34·38 N	118·07 E
150	Iian	China	46·10 N	129·40 E
153	Iida (ē'ē-dȧ)	Jap.	35·39 N	137·53 E
132	Iijoki (R.) (ē'yō'kĭ)	Fin.	65·28 N	27·00 E
153	Iizuka (ē'ē-zōō-kȧ)	Jap.	33·39 N	130·39 E
164	Ijebu Ode (ē-jĕ'bōō ōdȧ)	Nig.	6·46 N	3·59 E
117	IJsselmeer (L.) (ī'sĕl-mār)	Neth.	52·46 N	5·14 E
119	Ikaalinen (ē'kä-lĭ-nĕn)	Fin.	61·47 N	22·55 E
127	Ikaría (I.) (ē-kä'ryȧ)	Grc.	37·43 N	26·07 E
153	Ikeda-Kawanishi (ē'kȧ-dä kä-wä'nē-shē)	Jap. (Osaka In.)	34·49 N	135·26 E
127	Ikhtiman (ēk'tē-män)	Bul.	42·26 N	23·49 E
153	Iki (I.) (ē'kē)	Jap.	33·46 N	129·44 E
166	Ikoma (ē-kō'mä)	Tan.	2·08 S	34·47 E
136	Iksha (ĭk'shȧ)	Sov. Un. (Moscow In.)	56·10 N	37·30 E
155	Ilagen (ē-lä'gän)	Phil. (Manila In.)	17·09 N	121·52 E
151	Ilan (ē'län')	Taiwan	24·50 N	121·42 E
121	Iława (ē-lä'vȧ)	Pol.	53·35 N	19·36 E
85	Ile-Bizard Valois (yl-bē-zär vä-lōō-ä')	Can. (Montreal In.)	45·29 N	73·53 W
133	Ilek (ē'lyĕk)	Sov. Un.	51·30 N	53·10 E
133	Ilek (R.)	Sov. Un.	51·20 N	53·10 E
85	Ile-Perrot (yl-pĕ-rōt')	Can. (Montreal In.)	45·21 N	73·54 W
164	Ilesha	Nig.	7·45 N	4·50 E
110	Ilford (ĭl'fērd)	Eng. (London In.)	51·33 N	0·06 E
116	Ilfracombe (ĭl-frȧ-kōōm')	Eng.	51·13 N	4·08 W
101	Ilhabela (ē'lä-bĕ'lä)	Braz. (Rio de Janeiro In.)	23·47 S	45·21 W
101	Ilha Grande, Baia de (B.) (ēl'yȧ grän'dĕ)	Braz. (Rio de Janeiro In.)	23·17 S	44·25 W
124	Ilhavo (ēl'yȧ-vō)	Port.	40·36 N	8·41 W
99	Ilhéus (ē-lĕ'ōōs)	Braz.	14·52 S	39·00 W
64	Iliamna (ē-lē-ăm'nȧ)	Alaska	59·45 N	155·05 W
64	Iliamna (L.)	Alaska	59·25 N	155·30 W
64	Iliamna Vol.)	Alaska	60·18 N	153·25 W
134	Ilim (R.) (ē-lyēm')	Sov. Un.	57·28 N	103·00 E
134	Ilimsk (ē-lyēmsk')	Sov. Un.	56·47 N	103·43 E
155	Ilin (I.) (ē-lyēn')	Phil. (Manila In.)	12·16 N	120·57 E
129	Il'intsiy	Sov. Un.	49·07 N	29·13 E
127	Iliodhrómia (I.)	Grc.	39·18 N	23·35 E
81	Ilion (ĭl'ĭ-ŭn)	N. Y.	43·00 N	75·05 W
146	Ili R. (ē'lē)	Sov. Un.	43·46 N	77·41 E
110	Ilkeston (ĭl'kĕs-tŭn)	Eng.	52·58 N	1·19 W
98	Illampu, Nevado (Pk.) (nĕ-vȧ'dô-ēl-yäm-pōō')	Bol.	15·50 S	68·15 W
155	Illano B. (ēl-yä-nô)	Phil.	7·38 N	123·41 E
101	Illapel (ē-zhä-pĕ'l)	Chile (Santiago In.)	31·37 S	71·10 W
120	Iller R. (ĭl'er)	Ger.	47·52 N	10·06 E
98	Illimani, Nevado (Pk.) (nĕ-vȧ'dô-ēl-yē-mä'nē)	Bol.	16·50 S	67·38 W
63	Illinois (State) (ĭl-ĭ-noi') (ĭl-ĭ-noiz')	U. S.	40·25 N	90·40 W
73	Illinois (R.)	Ill.	40·52 N	89·31 W
128	Il'men', Ozero (L.) (ô'zĕ-rô el''men'') (ĭl'mĕn)	Sov. Un.	58·18 N	32·00 E
117	Ilmenau (ēl'mē-nou)	Ger.	50·37 N	13·02 E
117	Ilmenau (R.)	Ger.	53·20 N	10·20 E
164	Ilo (ē'lō)	Nig.	11·30 N	3·41 E
98	Ilo	Peru	17·46 S	71·13 W
92	Ilobasco (ē-lô-bäs'kô)	Sal.	13·57 N	88·46 W
154	Iloilo (ē-lô-ē'lō)	Phil.	10·49 N	122·33 E
92	Ilopango, L. (ē-lô-päŋ'gō)	Sal.	13·48 N	88·50 W
164	Ilorin (ē-lô-rēn')	Nig.	8·32 N	4·30 E
128	Ilūkste	Sov. Un.	55·59 N	26·20 E
65	Ilwaco (ĭl-wā'kô)	Wash. (Portland In.)	46·19 N	124·02 W
132	Ilych (R.) (ē'l'ĭch)	Sov. Un.	62·30 N	57·30 E
153	Imabari (ē'mä-bä'rē)	Jap.	34·05 N	132·58 E
153	Imai (ē-mī')	Jap. (Ōsaka In.)	34·30 N	135·47 E
152	Iman (R.) (ē-män')	Sov. Un.	45·40 N	134·31 E
135	Iman	Sov. Un.	46·07 N	133·21 E
132	Imandra (L.) (ē-män'drȧ)	Sov. Un.	67·40 N	32·30 E
168	Imbābah (ēm-bä'bȧ)	U. A. R. (Nile In.)	30·06 N	31·09 E
100	Imbarié (ēm-bä-ryĕ')	Braz. (In.)	22·38 S	43·13 W
136	Imeni Morozova (ĭm-yĕ'nyĭ mô rô'zô vȧ)	Sov. Un. (Leningrad In.)	59·58 N	31·02 E
128	Imeni Moskvy, Kanal (Moscow Can.) (kȧ-näl' ĭm-yă'nĭ mŏs-kvĭ)	Sov. Un.	56·33 N	37·15 E
152	Imienpo (yēmĭänpŭ)	China	44·59 N	127·56 E
80	Imlay City (ĭm'lā)	Mich.	43·00 N	83·15 W
120	Immenstadt (ĭm'ĕn-shtät)	Ger.	47·34 N	10·12 E
168	Immerpan (ĭmēr-pän)	S. Afr. (Johannesburg & Pretoria In.)	24·29 S	29·14 E
126	Imola (ē'mô-lä)	It.	44·19 N	11·43 E
126	Imotski (ē-môts'kē)	Yugo.	43·25 N	17·15 E
167	Impendle (ĭm-pĕnd'lȧ)	S. Afr. (Natal In.)	29·38 S	29·54 E
126	Imperia (ēm-pā'rē-ä)	It.	43·52 N	8·00 E
75	Imperial (ĭm-pē'rĭ-ăl)	Pa. (Pittsburgh In.)	40·27 N	80·15 W
68	Imperial Beach	Calif. (San Diego In.)	32·34 N	117·08 W
69	Imperial Res	Ariz.	32·57 N	114·19 W
68	Imperial Valley	Calif.	33·00 N	115·22 W
165	Impfondo (ĭmp-fōn'dô)	Con. B.	1·46 N	17·53 E
145	Imphal (ĭmp'hŭl)	India	24·42 N	94·00 E
127	Imroz (I.) (ĭm'rŏz)	Tur.	40·10 N	25·27 E
153	Ina (R.) (ē-nä')	Jap. (Ōsaka In.)	34·56 N	135·21 E
68	Inaja Ind. Res. (ē-nä'hä)	Calif.	32·56 N	116·37 W
112	Inari (L.)	Fin.	69·02 N	26·22 E
164	In Azaoua (Oasis) (ēn-ä-zou'ȧ)	Alg.	20·57 N	7·24 E
125	Inca (ēŋ'kä)	Sp.	39·43 N	2·53 E
133	Ince Burun (C.) (ĭn'jȧ)	Tur.	42·00 N	35·00 E
152	Inch'ŏn (ĭn'chŭn)	Kor.	37·26 N	126·46 E
126	Incudine, Mt. (Mtn.) (ēn-kōō-dē'nȧ) (ăɴ-kü-dēn')	Cor.	41·53 N	9·17 E
118	Indals-älven (R.)	Swe.	62·50 N	16·50 E
155	Indang (ēn'däng')	Phil. (Manila In.)	14·11 N	120·53 E
76	Indé (ēn'dȧ)	Mex.	25·53 N	105·15 W
73	Independence (ĭn-dē-pĕn'dĕns)	Kans.	37·14 N	95·42 W
74	Independence	Mo. (Kansas City In.)	39·06 N	94·26 W
75	Independence	Ohio (Cleveland In.)	41·23 N	81·39 W
66	Independence	Ore.	44·49 N	123·13 W
66	Independence Mts	Nev.	41·15 N	116·02 W
133	Inder (L.)	Sov. Un.	48·20 N	52·10 E
138	India (ĭn'dĭ-ȧ)	Asia	23·00 N	77·30 E
71	Indian (L.) (ĭn'dĭ-ăn)	Mich.	46·04 N	86·34 W
81	Indian (R.)	N. Y.	44·05 N	75·45 W
81	Indiana (ĭn-dĭ-än'ȧ)	Pa.	40·40 N	79·10 W
63	Indiana (State)	U. S.	39·50 N	86·45 W
75	Indianapolis (ĭn-dĭ-ăn-ăp'ô-lĭs)	Ind. (Indianapolis In.)	39·45 N	86·08 W
65	Indian Arm (R.) (ĭn'dĭ-ăn ärm)	Can. (Vancouver In.)	49·21 N	122·55 W
86	Indian Head (ĭn'dĭ-ăn hĕd)	Can.	50·36 N	103·42 W
7	Indian Ocean			
71	Indianola (ĭn-dĭ-ăn-ō'lȧ)	Iowa	41·22 N	93·33 W
78	Indianola	Miss.	33·29 N	90·35 W
135	Indigirka (R.) (ēn-dē-gēr'kȧ)	Sov. Un.	67·45 N	145·45 E
88	Indio (R.) (ē'n-dyô)	Pan. (Panama Canal In.)	9·13 N	78·28 W
154	Indochina (Reg.) (ĭn-dô-chī'nȧ)	Asia	17·22 N	105·18 E
154	Indonesia (ĭn'dô-nē-zhȧ)	Asia	4·38 S	118·45 E
142	Indore (ĭn-dōr')	India	22·48 N	76·51 E
154	Indragiri (R.) (ĭn-drȧ-jē'rē)	Indon.	0·27 S	102·05 E
142	Indrāvati (R.) (ĭn-drŭ-vä'tē)	India	19·15 N	80·54 E
122	Indre (R.) (ăɴ'dr')	Fr.	47·13 N	0·29 E
118	Indre Solund (I.) (ĭndrĕ-sô-lûnd)	Nor.	61·09 N	4·37 E
85	Indus (ĭn'dŭs)	Can. (Calgary In.)	50·55 N	113·45 W
142	Indus (R.)	W. Pak.	26·43 N	67·41 E
167	Indwe (ĭnd'wȧ)	S. Afr. (Natal In.)	31·30 S	27·21 E
133	Inebolu (ē-nȧ-bō'lōō)	Tur.	41·50 N	33·40 E
133	Inego (ē'nȧ-gŭ)	Tur.	40·05 N	29·20 E
155	Infanta (ēn-fän'tä)	Phil. (Manila In.)	14·44 N	121·39 E
155	Infanta	Phil. (Manila In.)	15·50 N	119·53 E
124	Infantes (ēn-fän'tȧs)	Sp.	38·44 N	3·00 W
91	Inferror, Laguna (L.) (lä-gōō'nä-ēn-fĕr-rôr)	Mex.	16·18 N	94·40 W
124	Infiesto (ēn-fyĕ's-tô)	Sp.	43·21 N	5·24 W
80	Ingersoll (ĭn'gēr-sŏl)	Can.	43·05 N	81·00 W
159	Ingham (ĭng'ăm)	Austl.	18·45 S	146·14 E
94	Ingles, Cayos (Is.) (kä'yōs-ē'n-glĕ's)	Cuba	21·55 N	82·35 W
74	Inglewood (ĭn'g'l-wōōd)	Calif. (Los Angeles In.)	33·57 N	118·22 W
85	Inglewood	Can. (Toronto In.)	43·48 N	79·56 W
135	Ingoda (R.) (ēn-gō'dȧ)	Sov. Un.	51·29 N	112·32 E
120	Ingolstadt (ĭŋ'gōl-shtät)	Ger.	48·46 N	11·27 E
129	Ingul (R.) (ēn-gōōl')	Sov. Un.	47·22 N	32.52 E
129	Ingulets (R.) (ēn-gōōl'yĕts')	Sov. Un.	47·12 N	33·12 E
133	Ingur (R.) (ēn-gōōr')	Sov. Un.	42·30 N	42·00 E
166	Inhambane (ēn'äm-bä'-nĕ)	Moz.	23·47 S	35·28 E
99	Inhambupe (ēn-yäm-bōō'pä)	Braz.	11·47 S	38·13 W
166	Inharrime (ēn-yär-rē'mä)	Moz.	24·17 S	35·07 E
100	Inhomirim (ē-nô-mē-rē'ɴ)	Braz. (In.)	22·34 S	43·11 W
167	Inhiuzan (Mtn.)	S. Afr. (Natal In.)	29·34 S	30·03 E
146	Ining (ē'nĭng')	China	43·58 N	80·49 E
98	Inirida (R.) (ē-nē-rē'dä)	Col.	2·25 N	70·38 W
160	Injune (ĭn'jōōn)	Austl.	25·52 S	148·30 E
125	Inkermann (ĭŋ-kēr-mȧn)	Alg.	35·55 N	0·57 E
119	Inkeroinem (ĭn'kĕr-oi-nĕn)	Fin.	60·42 N	26·50 E
75	Inkster (ĭngk'stēr)	Mich. (Detroit In.)	42·18 N	83·19 W
160	Innamincka (ĭnn-ȧ'mĭn-kȧ)	Austl.	27·50 S	140·48 E
89	Inner Brass (I.) (bräs)	Vir. Is. (U. S. A.) (St. Thomas In.)	18·23 N	64·58 W

ng-sing; ŋ-baŋk; ɴ-nasalized n; nŏd; cŏmmit; ōld; ôbey; ôrder; fōōd; fŏŏt; ou-out; s-soft; sh-dish; th-thin; pūre; ûnite; ûrn; stŭd; circŭs; ü as "y" in study; '-indeterminate vowel.

218 Inner Hebrides–Izamal PRONOUNCING INDEX

Page	Name Pronunciation Region	Lat. °′	Long. °′
116	Inner Hebrides (Is.)........Scot.	57·20 N	6·20 W
146	Inner Mongolian Aut. Reg. (mŏŋ-gō'lĭ-ăn). China	40·39 N	104·13 E
86	Innisfail.........Can.	52·01 N	113·57 W
114	Inn R. (ĭn)........Ger.-Aus.	48·19 N	13·16 E
120	Innsbruck (ĭns'brŏŏk).......Aus.	47·15 N	11·25 E
153	Ino (ē'nō)........Jap.	33·34 N	133·23 E
166	Inongo (ē-nôŋ'gō).......Con. L.	1·58 S	18·27 E
121	Inowroctaw (ē-nô-vrŏts'lăf)...Pol.	52·48 N	18·16 E
164	In Salah (ēn-sà-lä').......Alg.	27·13 N	2·22 E
69	Inscription House Ruin (ĭn'skrĭp-shŭn hous rōō'ĭn). Ariz.	36·45 N	110·47 W
90	Inter-American Hy. (ĭn'tēr ȧ-mĕr'ĭ-kăn). Mex.	22·30 N	99·08 W
71	International Falls (ĭn'tēr-năsh'ŭn-ăl fôlz). Minn.	48·34 N	93·26 W
86	Inuvik.........Can.	68·40 N	134·10 W
153	Inuyama (ē'nōō-yä'mä)......Jap.	35·24 N	137·01 E
159	Invercargill (ĭn-vēr-kär'gĭl) N. Z. (In.)	47·18 S	167·27 E
160	Inverel (ĭn-vēr-el').........Austl.	29·50 S	151·32 E
74	Invergrove (ĭn'vēr-grōv) Minn. (Minneapolis, St. Paul In.)	44·51 N	93·01 W
83	Inverness (ĭn-vēr-nĕs').......Can.	46·14 N	61·20 W
79	Inverness.........Fla.	28·48 N	82·22 W
116	Inverness.........Scot.	57·30 N	4·07 W
160	Investigator Str. (ĭn-vĕst'ĭ'gā-tôr) Austl.	35·33 S	137·00 E
166	Inyangani, Mt. (ēn-yän-gä'nē) S. Rh.	18·06 S	32·37 E
68	Inyo Mts. (ĭn'yō).........Calif.	36·55 N	118·04 W
136	Inzer R. (ĭn'zĕr) Sov. Un. (Urals In.)	54·24 N	57·17 E
164	In Zize (Oasis) (ēn-zē'zē).....Alg.	23·25 N	2·36 E
153	Iō (I.) (ē'wō).........Jap.	30·46 N	130·15 E
127	Ioánnina (Yannina) (yô-ä'nē-nà) (yä'nē-nà). Grc.	39·39 N	20·52 E
65	Ioco........Can. (Vancouver In.)	49·18 N	122·53 W
73	Iola (ī-ō'lȧ).........Kans.	37·55 N	95·23 W
80	Ionia (ī-ō'nĭ-ȧ).........Mich.	43·00 N	85·10 W
127	Ionian Is. (ī-ō'nĭ-ăn)........Grc.	39·10 N	20·05 E
115	Ionian Sea.........Eur.	38·59 N	18·48 E
127	Ios (I.) (ī'ŏs).........Grc.	36·48 N	25·25 E
63	Iowa (State) (ī'ō-wȧ).......U. S.	42·05 N	94·20 W
71	Iowa (R.).........Iowa	41·44 N	91·50 W
71	Iowa City.........Iowa	41·39 N	91·31 W
71	Iowa Falls.........Iowa	42·32 N	93·16 W
72	Iowa Park.........Tex.	33·57 N	98·39 W
99	Ipamerí (ē-pä-mâ-rē').......Braz.	17·44 S	48·03 W
121	Ipel R. (ē'pĕl)......Czech.-Hung.	48·08 N	19·00 E
98	Ipiales (ē-pē-ä'lâs).........Col.	0·48 N	77·45 W
151	Ipin (Süchow).........China	28·50 N	104·40 E
154	Ipoh.........Mala.	4·45 N	101·05 E
160	Ipswich (ĭps'wĭch).........Austl.	27·40 S	152·50 E
117	Ipswich.........Eng.	52·05 N	1·05 W
83	Ipswich.......Mass. (Boston In.)	42·41 N	70·50 W
70	Ipswich.........S. D.	45·26 N	99·01 W
99	Ipu (ē-pōō).........Braz.	4·11 S	40·45 W
128	Iput' (R.) (ē-pōōt')......Sov. Un.	52·53 N	31·57 E
98	Iquique (ē-kē'kĕ).........Chile	20·16 S	70·07 W
98	Iquitos (ē-kē'tōs).........Peru	3·39 S	73·18 W
75	Ira (ī'rä)....Ohio (Cleveland In.)	41·11 N	81·35 W
126	Iráklion (Candia).......Gr. (In.)	35·20 N	25·10 E
138	Iran (Persia) (ē-rän').......Asia	31·15 N	53·30 E
144	Iran, Plat. of.........Iran	32·28 N	58·00 E
154	Iran Mts.........Mala.	2·30 N	114·30 E
90	Irapuato (ē-rä-pwä'tō)......Mex.	20·41 N	101·24 W
138	Iraq (ē-räk').........Asia	32·00 N	42·30 E
93	Irazu Vol. (ē-rä-zōō').......C. R.	9·58 N	83·54 W
139	Irbid (ēr-bēd') Jordan (Palestine In.)	32·33 N	35·51 E
133	Irbil.........Iraq	36.10 N	44·00 E
132	Irbit (ēr-bēt')..........Sov. Un.	57·40 N	63·10 E
166	Irebu (ē-rā'bōō).........Con. L.	0·40 S	17·48 E
102	Ireland (īr-lănd).........Eur.	53·33 N	13·00 W
136	Iremel', Gora (Mt.) (gà-rä' ĭ-rĕ'mĕl). Sov. Un. (Urals In.)	54·32 N	58·52 E
167	Irene (ī-rē-nē).........S. Afr. (Johannesburg & Pretoria In.)	25·53 S	28·13 E
134	Irgiz (ĭr-gēz').........Sov. Un.	48·30 N	61·17 E
134	Irgiz (R.).........Sov. Un.	49·30 N	60·32 E
166	Iringa (ē-rĭŋ'gä).........Tan.	7·44 S	35·43 E
151	Iriomote Jima (I.) (ērē'-ō-mō-tä) Ryūkyū Is.	24·20 N	123·30 E
92	Iriona (ē-rē-ō'nä).........Hond.	15·53 N	85·12 W
116	Irish Sea (ī'rĭsh).........Eur.	53·55 N	5·25 W
134	Irkutsk (ĭr-kōōtsk')......Sov. Un.	52·16 N	104·00 E
110	Irlam (ûr'lăm).........Eng.	53·26 N	2·26 W
95	Irois, Cap des (C.).........Hai.	18·25 N	74·50 W
84	Irondale (ī'ērn-dăl) Ala. (Birmingham In.)	33·32 N	86·43 W
127	Iron Gate (Gorge)....Yugo.-Rom.	44·43 N	22·32 E
160	Iron Knob (ī-ăn nŏb).......Austl.	32·47 S	137·10 E
71	Iron Mountain (ī'ērn)......Mich.	45·49 N	88·04 W
71	Iron River.........Mich.	46·09 N	88·39 W
80	Ironton (ī'ērn-tŭn).........Ohio	38·30 N	82·45 W
71	Ironwood (ī'ērn-wŏŏd)......Mich.	46·28 N	90·10 W
80	Iroquois (R.) (ĭr'ō-kwoi)..Ill.-Ind.	40·55 N	87·20 W
87	Iroquois Falls.........Can.	48·41 N	80·39 W
153	Irō-Saki (C.) (ē'rō sä'kē)....Jap.	34·35 N	138·54 E
129	Irpen' (R.) (ĭr-pĕn')......Sov. Un.	50·13 N	29·55 E
145	Irrawaddy (R.).........Bur.	23·27 N	96·25 E
154	Irrawaddy, Mouths of the (ĭr-ȧ-wäd'ē). Bur.	15·40 N	94·32 E
146	Irrawaddy R.........Bur.	20·39 N	94·38 E
134	Irtysh (R.) (ĭr-tĭsh').....Sov. Un.	58·32 N	68·31 E
165	Irumu (ē-rōō'mōō).......Con. L.	1·30 N	29·52 E
124	Irun (ē-rōōn').........Sp.	43·20 N	1·47 W
74	Irvine (ûr'vĭn) Calif. (Los Angeles In.)	33·40 N	117·45 W
116	Irvine.........Scot.	55·39 N	4·40 W
80	Irvine.........Ky.	37·40 N	84·00 W
85	Irvine Cr...Can. (Edmonton In.)	53·23 N	113·27 W
74	Irving (ûr'vēng) Tex. (Dallas, Fort Worth In.)	32·49 N	96·57 W
84	Irvington (ûr'vēng-tŭn) N. J. (New York In.)	40·43 N	74·15 W
75	Irwin (ûr'-wĭn) Pa. (Pittsburgh In.)	40·19 N	79·42 W
136	Is (ēs).......Sov. Un. (Urals In.)	58·48 N	59·44 E
88	Isaacs, Mt. (ē-sä-ä'ks) Pan. (Panama Canal In.)	9·22 N	79·01 W
90	Isabela (I.) (ē-sä-bĕ'-lä).....Mex.	21·56 N	105·53 W
98	Isabela (I.) (ē-sä-bä'lä).......Ec.	0·47 S	91·35 W
95	Isabela, Cabo (C.) (kä'bô-ē-sä-bĕ'lä). Dom. Rep.	20·00 N	71·00 W
92	Isabella, Cord. (Mts.) (kôr-dēl-yĕ'rä-ē-sä-bĕlä). Nic.	13·20 N	85·37 W
80	Isabella Ind. Res. (ĭs-ȧ-bĕl'-lȧ) Mich.	43·35 N	84·55 W
129	Isaccea (ē-säk'chä).........Rom.	45·16 N	28·26 E
112	Isafjördhur (ēs'ä-fyûr-dōōr)...Ice.	66·09 N	22·39 W
165	Isangi (ē-säŋ'gē).........Con. L.	0·48 N	24·13 E
120	Isar R. (ē'zär).........Ger.	48·27 N	12·02 E
126	Isarco (R.) (ē-sär'kō).........It.	46·37 N	11·25 E
155	Isaroga, Vol. (ē-sä-rô-gä) Phil. (Manila In.)	13·40 N	123·23 E
125	Ischia (ēs'kyä)....It. (Naples In.)	40·29 N	13·58 E
168	Iscia Baidoa Som. (Horn of Afr. In.)	3·19 N	44·20 E
126	Iseo, Lago di (L.) (lä'-gō-dē-ē-zĕ'ō). It.	45·50 N	9·55 E
123	Isère (R.) (ē-zâr').........Fr.	45·24 N	6·04 E
123	Iserlohn (ē'zĕr-lōn) Ger. (Ruhr In.)	51·22 N	7·42 E
126	Isernia (ē-zĕr'nyä).........It.	41·35 N	14·14 E
153	Ise-Wan (B.) (ē'sĕ wän)......Jap.	34·49 N	136·44 E
164	Iseyin.........Nig.	8·13 N	3·21 E
151	Ishan.........China	24·32 N	108·42 E
152	Ishikari Wan (B.) (ē'shē-kä-rē wän). Jap.	43·30 N	141·05 E
134	Ishim (ĭsh-êm').........Sov. Un.	56·07 N	69·13 E
134	Ishim (R.).........Sov. Un.	53·17 N	67·45 E
136	Ishimbay (ē-shĕm-bī') Sov. Un. (Urals In.)	53·28 N	56·02 E
148	Ishing (yēsĭng).........China	31·26 N	119·57 E
152	Ishinomaki (ĭsh-nō-mä'kē)....Jap.	38·22 N	141·22 E
152	Ishinomaki Wan (B.) (ē-shē-nō-mä'kē wän). Jap.	38·10 N	141·40 E
136	Ishly (ĭsh'lĭ). Sov. Un. (Urals In.)	54·13 N	55·55 E
136	Ishlya (ĭsh'lyȧ) Sov. Un. (Urals In.)	53·54 N	57·48 E
127	Ishm.........Alb.	41·32 N	19·35 E
168	Ishmant......U. A. R. (Nile In.)	29·17 N	31·15 E
71	Ishpeming (ĭsh'pē-mĭng)....Mich.	46·28 N	87·42 W
148	Ishui (yē suĭ).........China	35·49 N	118·40 E
167	Isipingo (ĭs-ĭ-pĭŋg-gō) S. Afr. (Natal In.)	29·59 S	30·58 E
133	Iskenderun (ĭs-kĕn'dĕr-ōōn)..Tur.	36·45 N	36·15 E
115	İskenderun Körfezi (G.).....Tur.	36·22 N	35·25 E
133	Iskilip (ēs'kĭ-lēp').........Tur.	40·40 N	34·30 E
127	Iskūr (R.) (ĭs'k'r).........Bul.	43·05 N	23·37 E
124	Isla-Cristina (ĭs'lä-krē-stē'nä)..Sp.	37·13 N	7·20 W
145	Islamabad.........W. Pak.	33·55 N	73·05 E
92	Isla Mujeres (ē's-lä-mōō-kĕ'rĕs) Mex. (Yucatan In.)	21·25 N	86·53 W
86	Island (I.) (ī'lănd).........Can.	53·35 N	89·58 W
83	Islands, B. of (ī'lăndz).......Can.	49·11 N	58·45 W
116	Islay (I.) (ī'lā).........Scot.	55·45 N	6·35 W
122	Isle (R.) (ēl).........Fr.	45·02 N	0·29 E
110	Isle of Axholme (Reg.) (ăks'-hôm) Eng.	53·33 N	0·48 W
116	Isle of Man (măn).........Eur.	54·26 N	4·21 W
71	Isle Royale Nat'l Park (īl'roi-ăl') U. S.	47·57 N	88·37 W
69	Isleta (ēs-lā'tä) (ī-lē'tȧ)..N. Mex.	34·55 N	106·45 W
82	Isle Verte (ēl vĕrt').........Can.	48·01 N	69·20 W
85	Islington (ĭs'lĭng-tŏn) Can. (Toronto In.)	43·39 N	79·31 W
	Ismailia, see Al Ismā'īlīyah		
168	Ismā'īlīyah Can. U. A. R. (Suez In.)	30·25 N	31·45 E
111	Ismaning (ēz'mä-nēng) Ger. (Munich In.)	48·14 N	11·41 E
168	Isnā (ēs'nȧ)...U. A. R. (Nile In.)	25·17 N	32·33 E
119	Isojärvi (L.).........Fin.	61·47 N	22·00 E
133	Isparta (ē-spär'tȧ).........Tur.	37·50 N	30·40 E
138	Israel........Asia (Palestine In.)	31·00 N	35·00 E
65	Issaquah (ĭz'sȧ-kwăh) Wash. (Seattle In.)	47·32 N	122·02 W
123	Isselburg (ē'sĕl-bōōrg) Ger. (Ruhr In.)	51·50 N	6·28 E
122	Issoire (ē-swȧr').........Fr.	45·32 N	3·13 E
122	Issoudun (ē-sōō-dăN').........Fr.	46·56 N	2·00 E
123	Issum (ē'sōōm)...Ger. (Ruhr In.)	51·32 N	6·24 E
134	Issyk-Kul, Ozero (L.)....Sov. Un.	42·13 N	76·12 E
142	Istāda, Ab-i (L.).........Afg.	32·29 N	69·25 E
133	Istanbul (ē-stän-bōōl').......Tur.	41·02 N	29·00 E
127	Istiaía (ĭs-tyī'yä).........Grc.	38·58 N	23·11 E
98	Istmina (ēst-mē'nä)....Col. (In.)	5·10 N	76·40 W
79	Istokpoga (L.) (ĭs-tŏk-pō'gȧ) Fla. (In.)	27·20 N	81·33 W
126	Istra (pen.) (ē-strä).........Yugo.	45·18 N	13·48 E
127	Istranca Dağ (Mts.) (ĭ-strän'jȧ) Bul.-Turk.	41·50 N	27·25 E
122	Istres (ēs'tr')...Fr. (Marseille In.)	43·30 N	5·00 E
100	Itá (ē-tà').........Par.	25·39 S	57·14 W
99	Itabaiana (ē-tä-bä-yä-nä)...Braz.	10·42 S	37·17 W
101	Itabapoana (ē-tä'-bä-pôä'nä) Braz. (Rio de Janeiro In.)	21·19 S	40·58 W
101	Itabapoana (R.) Braz. (Rio de Janeiro In.)	21·11 S	41·18 W
101	Itabirito (ē-tä-bē-rē'tō) Braz. Rio de Janeiro (In.)	20·15 S	43·46 W
101	Itaboraí (ē-tä-bō-rāē') Braz. (Rio de Janeiro In.)	22·46 S	42·50 W
99	Itabuna (ē-tä-bōō'nä).......Braz.	14·47 S	39·17 W
101	Itacoara (ē-tä-kō'ä-rä) Braz. (Rio de Janeiro In.)	21·41 S	42·04 W
99	Itacoatiara (ē-tä-kwä-tyä'rä). Braz.	3·03 S	58·18 W
101	Itaguaí (ē-tä-gwä-ē') Braz. (Rio de Janeiro In.)	22·52 S	43·46 W
98	Itagüi (ē-tä'gwē).......Col. (In.)	6·11 N	75·36 W
100	Itagui (R.).........Braz. (In.)	22·53 S	43·43 W
100	Itaipava (ē-tī-pà'-vä)..Braz. (In.)	22·23 S	43·09 W
100	Itaipu (ē-tī'pōō).......Braz. (In.)	22·58 S	43·02 W
99	Itaituba (ē-tä'ī-tōō'bà)......Braz.	4·12 S	56·00 W
100	Itajái (ē-tä-zhī').........Braz.	26·52 S	48·39 W
101	Itajubá (ē-tä-zhōō-bà') Braz. (Rio de Janeiro In.)	22·26 S	45·27 W
168	Itala......Som. (Horn of Afr. In.)	2·45 N	46·15 E
102	Italy (ĭt'ȧ-lē).........Eur.	43·58 N	11·14 E
77	Italy.........Tex.	32·11 N	96·51 W
100	Itambi (ē-tä'm-bē)....Braz. (In.)	22·44 S	42·57 W
153	Itami (ē'tä'mē')..Jap. (Osaka In.)	34·47 N	135·25 E
101	Itapecerica (ē-tä-pĕ-sĕ-rē'kä) Braz. (Rio de Janeiro In.)	21·29 S	45·08 W
99	Itapecurú (R.) (ē-tä-pĕ-kōō-rōō') Braz.	4·05 S	43·49 W
99	Itapēcuru-Mirim (ē-tä-pĕ'kōō-rōō-mē-rēN')..Braz.	3·17 S	44·15 W
101	Itaperuna (ē-tä-pâ-rōō'nä) Braz. (Rio de Janeiro In.)	21·12 S	41·53 W
101	Itapetininga (ē-tä-pĕ-tē-nē'N-gä) Braz. (Rio de Janeiro In.)	23·37 S	48·03 W
99	Itapira (ē-tà-pē'rä).........Braz.	20·42 S	51·19 W
101	Itapira. Braz. (Rio de Janeiro In.)	21·27 S	46·47 W
142	Itarsi.........India	22·43 N	77·45 E
77	Itasca (ī-tăs'kȧ).........Tex.	32·09 N	97·08 W
71	Itasca (L.).........Minn.	47·13 N	95·14 W
101	Itatiaia, Pico da (Pk.) (pē'-kô-dà-ē-tä-tyà'ēä) Braz. (Rio de Janeiro In.)	22·18 S	44·41 W
101	Itatiba (ē-tä-tē'bä) Braz. (Rio de Janeiro In.)	23·01 S	46·48 W
101	Itaúna (ē-tä-ōō'nä) Braz. (Rio de Janeiro In.)	20·05 S	44·35 W
101	Itaverá (ē-tä-vĕ-rá') Braz. (Rio de Janeiro In.)	22·44 S	44·07 W
80	Ithaca (ĭth'ȧ-kȧ).........Mich.	43·20 N	84·35 W
81	Ithaca.........N. Y.	42·25 N	76·30 W
127	Itháki (I.) (ē'thä-kē).......Grc.	38·27 N	20·48 E
166	Itoko (ē-tō'kō).........Con. L.	1·13 S	22·07 E
168	Itsā (ēt'sȧ)....U. A. R. (Nile In.)	29·13 N	30·47 E
101	Itu (ē-tōō') Braz. (Rio de Janeiro In.)	23·16 S	47·16 W
148	Itu.........China	36·42 N	118·30 E
98	Ituango (ē-twäŋ'gō)....Col. (In.)	7·07 N	75·44 W
99	Ituiutaba (ē-tōō-ēōō-tä'bä)..Braz.	18·56 S	49·17 W
101	Itumirim (ē-tōō-mē-rē'N) Braz. (Rio de Janeiro In.)	21·20 S	44·51 W
91	Itundujia Santa Cruz (ē-tōōn-dōō-hē'ä sä'n-tä krōō'z). Mex.	16·50 N	97·43 W
152	It'ung.........China	43·15 N	125·10 E
92	Iturbide (ē'tōōr-bē'dhā) Mex. (Yucatan In.)	19·38 N	89·31 W
135	Iturup (I.) (ē-tōō-rōōp'). Sov. Un.	45·35 N	147·15 E
100	Ituzaingo (ē-tōō-zä-ē'n-gō) Arg. (In.)	34·24 S	58·40 W
111	Itzehoe (ē'tzĕ-hō) Ger. (Hamburg In.)	53·55 N	9·31 E
78	Iuka (ī-ū'kȧ).........Miss.	34·47 N	88·10 W
101	Iúna (ē-ōō'-nä) Braz. (Rio de Janeiro In.)	20·22 S	41·32 W
134	Iva (R.).........Sov. Un.	53·45 N	99·30 E
160	Ivanhoe (ĭv'ăn-hō).........Austl.	32·53 S	144·10 E
121	Ivano-Frankovsk (ē-vä'nō frän-kôvsk'). Sov. Un.	48·53 N	24·46 E
128	Ivanovo (ē-vä'nō-vō)....Sov. Un.	57·02 N	41·54 E
128	Ivanovo (Oblast).......Sov. Un.	56·55 N	40·30 E
129	Ivanpol' (ē-vän'pōl).....Sov. Un.	49·51 N	28·11 E
136	Ivanteyevka (ē-vàn-tyĕ'yĕf-kà) Sov. Un. (Moscow In.)	55·58 N	37·56 E
136	Ivdel' (ĭv'dyĕl) Sov. Un. (Urals In.)	60·42 N	60·27 E
75	Ives (ī'vĕs). Wis. (Milwaukee In.)	43·48 N	87·49 W
	Iviza I., see Ibiza, Isla de		
167	Ivohibé (ē-vō-hē-bā'). Malag. Rep.	22·28 S	46·59 E
163	Ivory Coast.........Afr.	7·43 N	6·30 W
126	Ivrea (ē-vrĕ'ä).........It.	45·25 N	7·54 E
87	Ivugivik.........Can.	62·17 N	77·52 W
152	Iwate Yama (Mt.) (ē-wä-tĕ-yä'mä). Jap.	39·50 N	140·56 E
153	Iwaya (ē'wä-yȧ)..Jap. (Osaka In.)	34·35 N	135·01 E
164	Iwo.........Nig.	7·52 N	4·04 E
90	Ixcateopán (ēs-kä-tä-ō-pän'). Mex.	18·29 N	99·49 W
111	Ixelles........Bel. (Brussels In.)	50·49 N	4·23 E
91	Ixhuatán (San Francisco) (ēs-hwä-tän'). Mex.	16·19 N	94·30 W
90	Ixhautlán (ēs-wät-län')......Mex.	20·41 N	98·01 W
90	Ixmiquilpan (ēs-mē-kēl'pän). Mex.	20·30 N	99·12 W
167	Ixopo........S. Afr. (Natal In.)	30·10 S	30·04 E
91	Ixtacalco (ēs-tä-käl'kō) Mex. (Mexico City In.)	19·23 N	99·07 W
91	Ixtacihuatl (Mtn.) (ē'ks-tä-sē-wä'tl). Mex. (Mexico City In.)	19·10 N	98·38 W
91	Ixtaltepec (Asunción) (ēs-täl-tĕ-pĕk'). Mex.	16·33 N	95·04 W
91	Ixtapalapa (ēs'tä-pä-lä'pä) Mex. (Mexico City In.)	19·21 N	99·06 W
91	Ixtapaluca (ēs'tä-pä-lōō'kä) Mex. (Mexico City In.)	19·18 N	98·53 W
91	Ixtepec (ēks-tĕ'pĕk').......Mex.	16·37 N	95·09 W
91	Ixtlahuaca (ēs-tlä-wä'kä) Mex. (Mexico City In.)	19·34 N	99·46 W
91	Ixtlán de Juárez (ēs-tlän' dā hwä'râz). Mex.	17·20 N	96·29 W
90	Ixtlán del Río (ēs-tlän'dĕl rē'ō) Mex.	21·05 N	104·22 W
151	Iyang (ē'yäng').........China	28·52 N	112·12 E
153	Iyo-Nada (Sea) (ē'yō nä-dä)..Jap.	33·33 N	132·07 E
92	Izabal (ē'zä-bäl').........Guat.	15·23 N	89·10 W
92	Izabal, L. (Golfo Dulce) (gôl'fō dōōl'sä). Guat.	15·30 N	89·04 W
92	Izalco (ē-zäl'kō).........Sal.	13·50 N	89·40 W
92	Izamal (ē-zä-mä'l). Mex. (Yucatan)	20·55 N	89·00 W

ăt; finăl; rāte: senāte: ärm: àsk: sofȧ: fâre: ch-choose: dh-as th in other; bē; ēvent; bĕt; recĕnt; cratēr; g-go; gh-guttural g; bĭt; ĭ-short neutral; rīde; K-guttural k as ch in German ich;

PRONOUNCING INDEX Izhevsk–John Day 219

Page	Name Pronunciation Region	Lat. °′	Long. °′
132	Izhevsk (ê-zhyĕfsk′)......Sov. Un.	56·50 N	53·15 E
132	Izhma (ĭzh′mȧ)..........Sov. Un.	65·00 N	54·05 E
132	Izhma (R.)..............Sov. Un.	64·00 N	53·00 E
136	Izhora R. (ēz′hô-rȧ) Sov. Un. (Leningrad In.)	59·36 N	30·20 E
129	Izmail (ēz-mȧ-ēl)........Sov. Un.	27·21 N	28·49 E
127	Izmir (Smyrna) (ĭz-mēr′) (smûr′nȧ).Tur.	38·25 N	27·05 E
127	Izmir Körfezi (G.)..........Tur.	38·43 N	26·37 E
133	Izmit (ĭz-mêt′)..............Tur.	40·45 N	29·45 E
153	Izu (I.) (ē′zōō)..............Jap.	34·32 N	139·25 E
153	Izuhara (ē′zōō-hä′rä)........Jap.	34·11 N	129·18 E
153	Izumo (ē′zōō-mō)...........Jap.	35·22 N	132·45 E
153	Izumu-Otsu (ē′zōō-mōō ō′tsōō) Jap. (Ōsaka In.)	34·30 N	135·24 E
111	Jaachimsthal (yä′kēm-stäl) Ger. (Berlin In.)	52·58 N	13·45 E
144	Jabal Rema (Mtn.).......Yemen	14·13 N	44·38 E
120	Jablonec (Nad Nisou) (yäb′lô-nyĕts).Czech.	50·43 N	15·12 E
121	Jablunkov P. (yäb′lōōn-kôf).Czech.	49·31 N	18·35 E
99	Jaboatão (zhä-bô-á-touN)...Braz.	8·14 S	35·08 W
144	Jabul Hadur Shuayb (Mtn.) Yemen	15·45 N	43·45 E
125	Jaca (hä′kä)................Sp.	42·35 N	0·30 W
90	Jacala (hä-kä′lä)...........Mex.	21·01 N	99·11 W
92	Jacaltenango (hä-käl-tĕ-näŋ′gō) Guat.	15·39 N	91·41 W
101	Jacareí (zhä-kȧ-rĕ-ē′) Braz. (Rio de Janeiro In.)	23·19 S	45·57 W
100	Jacarepagua (zhä-kä-rȧ′pä-gwä′) Braz. (In.)	22·55 S	43·22 W
99	Jacarézinho (zhä-kä-rĕ′zē-nyō) Braz.	23·13 S	49·58 W
120	Jachymov (yä′chĭ-môf)....Czech.	50·22 N	12·51 E
77	Jacinto City (hä-sēn′tō) (jȧ-sĭn′tō) Tex. (In.)	29·45 N	95·14 W
72	Jacksboro (jăks′bŭr-ô).......Tex.	33·13 N	98·11 W
78	Jackson (jăk′sŭn)...........Ala.	31·31 N	87·52 W
68	Jackson...................Calif.	38·22 N	120·47 W
78	Jackson....................Ga.	33·19 N	83·55 W
78	Jackson....................Ky.	37·32 N	83·17 W
77	Jackson....................La.	30·50 N	91·13 W
80	Jackson..................Mich.	42·15 N	84·25 W
71	Jackson..................Minn.	43·37 N	95·00 W
78	Jackson..................Miss.	32·17 N	90·10 W
73	Jackson....................Mo.	37·23 N	89·40 W
80	Jackson..................Ohio	39·00 N	82·40 W
78	Jackson..................Tenn.	35·37 N	88·49 W
161	Jackson, Port. Austl. (Sydney In.)	33·50 S	151·18 E
67	Jackson L...................Wyo.	43·57 N	110·28 W
167	Jacksontuin..............S. Afr. (Johannesburg & Pretoria In.)	25·44 S	27·45 E
78	Jacksonville (jăk′sŭn-vĭl).....Ala.	33·52 N	85·45 W
79	Jacksonville................Fla.	30·20 N	81·40 W
73	Jacksonville.................Ill.	39·43 N	90·12 W
77	Jacksonville................Tex.	31·58 N	95·18 W
79	Jacksonville Beach ....Fla.	31·18 N	81·25 W
95	Jacmel (zhȧk-mĕl′)..........Hai.	18·15 N	72·30 W
76	Jaco, L. (hä′kō).............Mex.	27·51 N	103·50 W
142	Jacobābad.............W. Pak.	28·22 N	28·27 E
99	Jacobina (zhä-kô-bē′nȧ).....Braz.	11·13 S	40·30 W
82	Jacques Cartier, Mt. (Tabletop) (zhȧk′kär-tyā′).Can.	48·59 N	65·59 W
85	Jacques-Cartier, R. Can. (Quebec In.)	47·04 N	71·28 W
83	Jacques Cartier Pass........Can.	50·04 N	63·43 W
82	Jacquet River (zhȧ-kĕ′) (jăk′ĕt) Can.	47·54 N	66·01 W
101	Jacuí (zhä-kōō-ē′) Braz. (Rio de Janeiro In.)	21·03 S	46·43 W
101	Jacutinga (zhä-kōō-tēn′gä) Braz. (Rio de Janeiro In.)	21·17 S	46·36 W
139	Jad′ah.....Jordan (Palestine In.)	31·23 N	35·45 E
120	Jade B. (yä′dĕ).............Ger.	53·28 N	8·17 E
166	Jadotville...............Con. L.	11·01 S	26·52 E
165	Jādū......................Libya	31·57 N	12·04 E
98	Jaén (ĸä-ĕ′n)..............Peru	5·38 S	78·49 W
124	Jaén........................Sp.	37·45 N	3·48 W
160	Jaffa, C. (jăf′ȧ)............Austl.	36·58 S	139·29 E
143	Jaffna (jăf′nȧ)............Ceylon	9·44 N	80·09 E
94	Jagüey Grande (hä′gwā grän′dā) Cuba	22·35 N	81·05 W
139	Jahore Str.. Mala. (Singapore In.)	1·22 N	103·37 E
95	Jaibo (R.) (hä-ē′bō)........Cuba	20·10 N	75·20 W
142	Jaipur....................India	26·45 N	77·00 E
142	Jaisaimer.................India	27·00 N	70·54 E
126	Jajce (yī′tsĕ)..............Yugo.	44·20 N	17·19 E
112	Jakobstad (yȧ′kôb-städh).....Fin.	63·33 N	22·31 E
91	Jalacingo (hä-lä-sĭŋ′gō)......Mex.	97·16 N	19·47 W
145	Jalalabād (jŭ-lä-lä-bäd′) Afg. (Khyber Pass In.)	34·25 N	70·27 E
92	Jalapa (hä-lä′pȧ)..........Guat.	14·38 N	89·58 W
91	Jalapa de Diaz (San Felipe) (dā dē-äz′) (sän fā-lē′pā).Mex.	18·06 N	96·33 W
91	Jalapa del Marqués (dĕl mär-kās′).Mex.	16·30 N	95·29 W
91	Jalapa Enriquez (ĕn-rē′käz)..Mex.	19·32 N	96·53 W
142	Jalgaon...................India	21·08 N	75·33 E
90	Jalisco (hä-lēs′kō)..........Mex.	21·27 N	104·54 W
88	Jalisco (State).............Mex.	20·07 N	104·45 W
127	Jalomita (R.)..............Rom.	44·37 N	26·42 E
124	Jalón (R.) (hä-lōn′)..........Sp.	41·22 N	1·46 W
90	Jalostotitlán (hä-lōs-tē-tlän′).Mex.	21·09 N	102·30 W
91	Jalpa (häl′pä)..............Mex.	18·12 N	93·06 W
90	Jalpa (häl′pä)..............Mex.	21·40 N	103·04 W
90	Jalpan (häl′pän)............Mex.	21·13 N	99·31 W
142	Jalpur....................India	20·49 N	86·37 E
91	Jaltepec (häl-tȧ-pĕk′).......Mex.	17·20 N	95·15 W
91	Jaltipan (häl-tȧ-pän′)........Mex.	17·59 N	94·42 W
90	Jaltocan (häl-tô-kän′)........Mex.	21·08 N	98·32 W
165	Jālū (Oasis)...............Libya	28·58 N	21·45 E
94	Jamaica (I.)...............N. A.	18·21 N	77·31 W
95	Jamaica Cay (I.)..........Ba. Is.	22·45 N	75·55 W
142	Jamalpur..............E. Pak.	24·56 N	89·58 E
90	Jamay (hä-mī′).............Mex.	20·16 N	103·43 W
127	Jambol (yȧm′bôl)...........Bul.	42·28 N	26·31 E
155	Jamdena (I.)..............Indon.	7·23 S	130·30 E
73	James (R.).................Mo.	36·51 N	93·22 W
79	James (R.)................N. C.	36·07 N	81·48 W
62	James (R.)................U. S.	46·25 N	98·55 W
81	James (R.)..................Va.	37·35 N	77·50 W
87	James B. (jāmz)............Can.	53·53 N	80·40 W
84	Jamesburg (jāmz′bûrg) N. J. (New York In.)	40·21 N	74·26 W
95	James Pt................Ba. Is.	25·20 N	76·30 W
158	James Ra..................Austl.	24·15 S	133·30 E
96	James Ross (I.)............Ant.	64·20 S	58·20 W
81	Jamestown (jāmz′toun)......N. Y.	42·05 N	79·15 W
70	Jamestown.................N. D.	46·54 N	98·42 W
84	Jamestown . R. I. (Providence In.)	41·30 N	71·21 W
167	Jamestown....S. Afr. (Natal In.)	31·07 S	26·49 E
70	Jamestown Res.............N. D.	47·16 N	98·40 W
91	Jamiltepec (hä-mēl-tȧ-pĕk)..Mex.	16·16 N	97·54 W
118	Jammerburgt (B.)..........Den.	57·20 N	9·28 E
142	Jammu...................India	32·50 N	32·51 E
142	Jammu and Kashmir (disputed reg.) (kȧsh-mēr′).India & Pak.	39·10 N	75·05 E
142	Jamnagar (jäm-nŭ′gŭr).....India	22·33 N	70·03 E
145	Jamrud (jäm′rōōd) W. Pak. (Khyber Pass In.)	34·00 N	71·22 E
142	Jamshedpur (jäm′shād-pōōr) India	22·52 N	86·11 E
98	Jamundí (hä-mōō′n-dē′).Col. (In.)	3·15 N	76·32 W
142	Janakpur...................Nep.	26·50 N	85·55 E
124	Jándula (R.) (hän′dōō-lä).....Sp.	38·28 N	3·52 W
71	Janesville (jānz′vĭl).........Wis.	42·41 N	89·03 W
139	Janin......Jordan (Palestine In.)	32·27 N	35·19 E
112	Jan Mayen (I.) (yän mī′ĕn)..Nor.	70·59 N	8·05 W
118	Jannelund (yän′ĕ-lōōnd).....Swe.	59·14 N	14·24 E
121	Jánoshalma (yä′nôsh-hôl-mô) Hung.	46·17 N	19·18 E
121	Janów Lubelski (yä′nōōf lŭ-bĕl′skĭ) Pol.	50·40 N	22·25 E
99	Januária (zhä-nwä′rē-ä).....Braz.	15·31 S	44·17 W
145	Janvo Pk...................India	25·32 N	94·33 E
148	Jaoyang (jä′ō-yäng′)........China	38·16 N	115·45 E
139	Japan (jȧ-păn′)..............Asia	36·30 N	133·30 E
152	Japan, Sea of (jȧ-păn′)......Asia	40·08 N	132·55 W
155	Japen (I.) (yä′pĕn)......W. Irian	1·30 S	136·15 E
100	Japeri (zhä-pĕ′rē).....Braz. (In.)	22·38 S	43·40 W
98	Japurá (R.) (zhä-pōō-rä′)...Braz.	1·30 S	67·54 W
95	Jarabacoa (ĸä-rä-bä-kô′ä) Dom. Rep.	19·05 N	70·40 W
90	Jaral del Progreso (hä-räl dĕl prô-grā′sō).Mex.	20·21 N	101·05 W
124	Jarama (R.) (hä-rä′mä).......Sp.	40·33 N	3·30 W
139	Jarash......Jordan (Palestine In.)	32·17 N	35·53 E
94	Jardines, Banco (Bk.) (bä′n-kō-här-dē′nȧs).Cuba	21·45 N	81·40 W
99	Jari (R.) (zhä-rē)..........Braz.	0·28 N	53·00 W
122	Jarnac (zhȧr-näk′)............Fr.	45·42 N	0·09 W
121	Jarocin (yä-rō′tsyēn)........Pol.	51·58 N	17·31 E
146	Jaro Pk. (hä′rō)............China	30·45 N	101·49 E
121	Jarosław (yȧ-rôs-wäf)........Pol.	50·01 N	22·41 E
139	Jasin......Mala. (Singapore In.)	2·19 N	102·26 E
119	Jašiūnai (dzä-shōō-nä′yĕ) Sov. Un.	54·27 N	25·25 E
144	Jāsk (jäsk).................Iran	25·46 N	57·48 E
121	Jasło (yäs′wō)..............Pol.	49·44 N	21·28 E
139	Jason B......Mala. (Singapore In.)	1·53 N	104·14 E
80	Jasonville (jā′sŭn-vĭl)........Ind.	39·10 N	87·15 W
78	Jasper (jăs′pēr).............Ala.	33·50 N	87·17 W
86	Jasper.....................Can.	52·54 N	118·18 W
78	Jasper.....................Fla.	30·30 N	82·56 W
80	Jasper.....................Ind.	38·20 N	86·55 W
70	Jasper....................Minn.	43·51 N	96·22 W
77	Jasper.....................Tex.	30·55 N	93·59 W
86	Jasper Natl. Park...........Can.	53·09 N	117·45 W
85	Jasper Place. Can. (Edmonton In.)	53·32 N	113·36 W
121	Jászapáti (yäs′ô-pä-tē)......Hung.	47·29 N	20·10 E
91	Jatate (R.) (hä-tä-tä′).......Mex.	16·30 N	91·29 W
94	Jatibonico (hä-tē-bô-nē′kô)..Cuba	22·00 N	79·15 W
125	Játiva (hä′tē-vä)..............Sp.	38·58 N	0·31 W
100	Jau′ (zhä-ōō′)..............Braz.	22·16 S	48·31 W
98	Jauja (ĸä-ōō′ĸ)..............Peru	11·43 S	75·32 W
90	Jaumave (hou-mä′vȧ).........Mex.	23·23 N	99·24 W
119	Jaunjelgava (youn′yĕl′gȧ-vȧ) Sov. Un.	56·37 N	25·06 E
128	Jaunlatgale (youn′lat′gȧ-lĕ) Sov. Un.	57·04 N	27·54 E
154	Java (I.) (jä′vȧ) (jă′vȧ)....Indon.	8·35 S	111·11 E
98	Javari (R.) (ĸä-vä-rē)...Col.-Peru	4·25 S	72·07 W
154	Java Sea (jä′vȧ) (jă′vȧ)....Indon.	5·10 S	110·30 E
125	Jávea (hȧ-vā′ä)...............Sp.	38·45 N	0·07 E
120	Jawor (yä′vôr)...............Pol.	51·04 N	16·12 E
121	Jaworzno (yä-vôzh′nô)........Pol.	50·11 N	19·18 E
136	Jayva R. (yäy′vȧ) Sov. Un. (Urals In.)	59·13 N	57·17 E
121	Jázberény (yäs′bĕ-rān′)....Hung.	47·30 N	19·56 E
139	Jazzin.......Leb. (Palestine In.)	33·34 N	35·37 E
77	Jeanerette (jĕn-ĕr-et′) (zhän-rĕt′) La.	29·54 N	91·41 W
114	Jebal Aures (Mts.)..........Alg.	35·16 N	5·53 E
164	Jebba (jĕb′ȧ)...............Nig.	9·07 N	4·46 E
165	Jebel, Bahr el (R.)..........Sud.	28·22 N	30·31 E
121	Jedrzejów (yăN-dzhā′yōōf)....Pol.	50·38 N	20·18 E
85	Jefferson (jĕf′ẽr-sŭn) Can. (Toronto In.)	43·55 N	79·26 W
78	Jefferson....................Ga.	34·05 N	83·35 W
71	Jefferson..................Iowa	42·10 N	94·22 W
77	Jefferson...................Tex.	32·47 N	94·21 W
71	Jefferson...................Wis.	42·59 N	88·45 W
66	Jefferson, Mt................Ore.	44·41 N	121·50 W
73	Jefferson City...............Mo.	38·34 N	92·10 W
67	Jefferson R................Mont.	45·37 N	112·22 W
75	Jeffersontown (jĕf′ẽr-sŭn-toun) Ky. (Louisville In.)	38·11 N	85·34 W
75	Jeffersonville (jĕf′ẽr-sŭn-vĭl) Ind. (Louisville In.)	38·17 N	85·44 W
	Jehol, see Ch′engte		
115	Jeib, Wadi el (R.).....Jordan-Isr.	30·30 N	35·20 E
119	Jēkabpils (yĕk′ȧb-pĭls)...Sov. Un.	56·29 N	25·50 E
120	Jelenia Góra (yĕ-lĕn′yȧ gōō′rä) Pol.	50·53 N	15·43 E
119	Jelgava (yĕl′gȧ-vȧ)......Sov. Un.	56·39 N	23·40 E
78	Jellico (jĕl′ĭ-kō)...........Tenn.	36·34 N	84·06 W
113	Jemmapes (zhē-mȧp′)........Alg.	36·43 N	7·21 E
120	Jena (yā′nä)...............Ger.	50·55 N	11·37 E
148	Jench′iu (rĕnchēō)..........China	38·44 N	116·05 E
79	Jenkins (jĕŋ′kĭnz)...........Ky.	37·09 N	82·38 W
84	Jenkintown (jĕŋ′kĭn-toun) Pa. (Philadelphia In.)	40·06 N	75·08 W
77	Jennings (jĕn′ĭngz)...........La.	30·14 N	92·40 W
80	Jennings..................Mich.	44·20 N	85·20 W
74	Jennings......Mo. (St. Louis In.)	38·43 N	90·16 W
99	Jequié (zhĕ-kyĕ′)...........Braz.	13·53 S	40·06 W
99	Jequitinhonha (R.) (zhĕ-kē-tĕŋ-ō′n-yä).Braz.	16·47 S	41·19 W
95	Jérémie (zhā-rȧ-mē′).........Hai.	18·40 N	74·10 W
99	Jeremoabo (zhĕ-rä-mō-á′bō).Braz.	10·03 S	38·13 W
91	Jerez, Punta (Pt.) (pōō′n-tä-ĸĕ-räz′).Mex.	23·04 N	97·44 W
124	Jerez de la Frontera (ĸĕ-rāth′ dā lä frôn-tā′rä).Sp.	36·42 N	6·09 W
124	Jerez de los Caballeros (ĸĕ-rath′ dā lōs kä-väl-yā′rôs).Sp.	38·20 N	6·45 W
159	Jericho (jĕr′ĭ-kō)..........Austl.	28·38 S	146·24 E
168	Jericho (jĕr-ĭkô) S. Afr. (Johannesburg & Pretoria In.)	25·16 S	27·47 E
	Jericho, see Arīhā		
69	Jerome (jē-rōm′)...........Ariz.	34·45 N	112·10 W
67	Jerome....................Idaho	42·44 N	114·31 W
122	Jersey (I.) (jûr′zĭ)..........Eur.	49·13 N	2·07 W
84	Jersey City. N. J. (New York In.)	40·43 N	74·05 W
81	Jersey Shore................Pa.	41·10 N	77·15 W
85	Jerseyville (jĕr′zē-vĭl) Can. (Toronto In.)	43·12 N	80·08 W
73	Jerseyville...................Ill.	39·07 N	90·18 W
139	Jerusalem (jē-rōō′sȧ-lĕm) Isr.-Jordan (Palestine In.)	31·46 N	35·14 E
154	Jesselton..................Mala.	5·55 N	116·05 E
84	Jesuit Bend (jĕz′ū-ĭt) La. (New Orleans In.)	29·45 N	90·02 W
79	Jesup (jĕs′ŭp)...............Ga.	31·36 N	81·53 W
91	Jesús Carranza (hē-sōō′s-kär-rä′n-zä).Mex.	17·26 N	95·01 W
70	Jewel Cave Natl. Mon......S. D.	43·44 N	103·52 W
65	Jewell (jū′ĕl)..Ore. (Portland In.)	45·56 N	123·30 W
142	Jhālawār..................India	24·29 N	79·09 E
142	Jhang Maghian.........W. Pak.	31·21 N	72·19 E
142	Jhansi (jän′sē).............India	25·29 N	78·32 E
142	Jharsuguda................India	22·51 N	86·13 E
142	Jhelum (R.) (jā′lŭm).....W. Pak.	31·40 N	71·51 E
146	Jibhalanta.................Mong.	47·49 N	97·00 E
69	Jicarilla Ind. Res. (ĸē-kä-rēl′yȧ) N. Mex.	36·45 N	107·00 W
93	Jicaron, Isla (I.) (ĸē-kä-rōn′).Pan.	7·14 N	81·41 W
121	Jiffa R....................Rom.	47·35 N	27·02 E
158	Jiggalong (jĭg′ȧ-lông).......Austl.	23·20 S	120·45 E
95	Jiguani (ĸē-gwä-nē′).........Cuba	20·20 N	76·30 W
94	Jigüey, Bahía (B.) (bä-ē′ȧ-ĸē′gwā).Cuba	22·15 N	78·10 W
148	Jihchao (rē′jou)............China	35·27 N	119·28 E
120	Jihlava (yē′hlȧ-vȧ).........Czech.	49·23 N	15·33 E
168	Jijiga.....Eth. (Horn of Afr. In.)	9·15 N	42·48 E
125	Jijona (ĸē-hō′nä)..............Sp.	38·31 N	0·29 W
142	Jikyop......................China	28·41 N	91·42 E
124	Jiloca (R.) (ĸē-lō′kȧ).........Sp.	41·13 N	1·30 W
92	Jilotepeque (ĸē-lô-tĕ-pĕ′kĕ) Guat.	14·39 N	89·36 W
165	Jima.......................Eth.	7·41 N	36·52 E
127	Jimbolia (zhĭm-bô′lyȧ)......Rom.	45·45 N	20·44 E
90	Jiménez (ĸē-mā′nåz)........Mex.	24·12 N	98·29 W
76	Jimenez....................Mex.	27·09 N	104·55 W
76	Jiménez....................Mex.	29·03 N	100·42 W
90	Jiménez del Téul (tĕ-ōō′l)...Mex.	21·28 N	103·51 W
81	Jim Thorpe (jĭm′ thôrp′)......Pa.	40·50 N	75·45 W
120	Jindřichov Hradec (yēn′d′r-zhĭ-kōōf hrä′dĕts).Czech.	49·09 N	15·02 E
165	Jinja (jĭn′jä)...............Ug.	0·29 N	33·11 E
92	Jinotega (kē-nô-tā′gä).......Nic.	13·07 N	86·00 W
92	Jinotepe (kē-nô-tā′pȧ).......Nic.	11·52 N	86·12 W
153	Jinzū-Gawa (Strm.) (jĕn′zōō gä′wä).Jap.	36·26 N	137·18 E
98	Jipijapa (ĸē-pē-hä′pä).......Ec.	1·36 S	80·52 W
92	Jiquilisco (ĸē-kē-lē′s-kô).......Sal.	13·18 N	88·32 W
90	Jiquilpan de Juarez (ĸē-kēl′pän dā hwä′räz).Mex.	20·00 N	102·43 W
91	Jiquipilco (hē-kē-pē′l-kô) Mex. (Mexico City In.)	19·32 N	99·37 W
168	Jirgā (jĕr′gȧ)..U. A. R. (Nile In.)	26·20 N	31·51 E
146	Jirgalanta.................Mong.	48·08 N	91·40 E
124	Jistredo, Sierra de (Mts.) (sē-ĕ′r-rä-dĕ-ĸēs-trĕ′dô).Sp.	42·50 N	6·15 W
91	Jitotol (ĸē-tô-tōl′)..........Mex.	17·03 N	92·54 W
99	João Pessoa (Paraíba) (zhô-ouN′ pĕ-sō′ȧ′) (pä-rä-ē′bȧ).Braz.	7·09 S	34·45 W
101	João Ribeiro (zhô-uN-rē-bā′rō) Braz. (Rio de Janeiro In.)	20·42 S	44·03 W
94	Jobabo (R.) (hō-bä′bä).......Cuba	20·50 N	77·15 W
85	Jock R. (jŏk) ..Can. (Ottawa In.)	45·08 N	75·51 W
90	Jocotepec (hō-kō-tā-pĕk′)....Mex.	20·17 N	103·26 W
124	Jodar (hō′där)................Sp.	37·54 N	3·20 W
142	Jodhpur (jōd′pōōr)..........India	26·23 N	83·00 E
119	Joensuu (yô-ĕn′sōō)..........Fin.	62·35 N	29·46 E
153	Jōga-Shima (I.) (jō′gä shē′mä) Jap. (Tōkyō In.)	35·07 N	139·37 E
128	Jōgeva (yû′gĕ-vȧ).......Sov. Un.	58·45 N	26·23 E
82	Jogins......................Can.	45·41 N	64·27 W
154	Jogjakarta (yŏg-yȧ-kär′tä).Indon.	7·50 S	110·20 E
167	Johannesburg (yô-hän′ĕs-bōōrgh) S. Afr. (Johannesburg & Pretoria In.)	26·08 S	27·54 E
66	John Day R. (jŏn dā).......Ore.	44·46 N	120·15 W
66	John Day R., Middle Fork...Ore.	44·53 N	119·04 W
66	John Day R., North Fork....Ore.	45·03 N	118·50 W

ng-sing; ŋ-baŋk; N-nasalized n; nŏd; cŏmmit; ōld; ôbey; ôrder; fōōd; fŏŏt; ou-out; s-soft; sh-dish; th-thin; pūre; ûnite; ûrn; stŭd; circŭs; ü-as "y" in study; ′-indeterminate vowel.

ăt; fĭnăl; rāte; senăte; ärm; ăsk; sofá; fâre; ch-choose; dh-as th in other; bē; ĕvent; bĕt; recĕnt; cratēr; g-go; gh-guttural g; bĭt; ɪ-short neutral; rīde; κ-guttural k as ch in German ich;

PRONOUNCING INDEX

Kameoka–Kawasaki 221

Page	Name Pronunciation Region	Lat. °′	Long. °′
153	Kameoka (kä'mā-ōkä) Jap. (Ōsaka In.)	35·01 N	135·35 E
142	Kàmet (Mt.) . . . . India	35·50 N	79·42 E
120	Kamień Pomorski . . . . Pol.	53·57 N	14·48 E
153	Kamikoma (kä'mē-kō'mä) Jap. (Ōsaka In.)	34·45 N	135·50 E
166	Kamina . . . . Con. L.	8·41 S	25·01 E
71	Kaministikwia (R.) (kȧ-mĭ-nĭ-stĭk'wĭ-ȧ) . Can.	48·40 N	89·41 W
86	Kamloops (kăm'lōōps) . . . . Can.	50·41 N	120·19 W
	Kammer, see Atter See		
142	Kampa Dzong . . . . China	28·23 N	89·42 E
165	Kampala (käm-pä'lä) . . . . Ug.	0·14 N	32·34 E
154	Kampar (Strm.) (käm'pär) Indon.	0·30 N	101·30 E
111	Kampenhout Bel. (Brussels In.)	50·56 N	4·33 E
123	Kamp-Lintfort (kämp-lĕnt'fōrt) Ger. (Ruhr In.)	51·30 N	6·34 E
154	Kampot (käm'pōt) . . . . Camb.	10·41 N	104·07 E
120	Kamp R. (kämp) . . . . Aus.	48·30 N	15·45 E
86	Kamsack (kăm'săk) . . . . Can.	51·32 N	102·00 W
103	Kamskoye (Res.) . . . . Sov. Un.	59·08 N	56·30 E
136	Kamskoye Vodokranilishche (L.) Sov. Un. (Urals In.)	59·03 N	56·48 E
93	Kamuk, Cerro (Mt.) (sĕ'r-rô-kä-mōō'k) . C. R.	9·18 N	83·02 W
152	Kamu Misaki (C.) (kä'mōō mē-sä'kē) . Jap.	43·25 N	139·35 E
129	Kamyshevatskaya (kȧ-mwĕsh'ĕ-vàt'skä-yȧ) . Sov. Un.	46·24 N	37·58 E
133	Kamyshin (kä-mwēsh'ĭn) Sov. Un.	50·08 N	45·20 E
132	Kamyshlov (kä-mēsh'lôf) Sov. Un.	56·50 N	62·32 E
151	Kan (R.) (kän) . . . . China	26·50 N	115·00 E
134	Kan (R.) . . . . Sov. Un.	56·30 N	94·17 E
69	Kanab (kăn'ăb) . . . . Utah	37·00 N	112·30 W
69	Kanab Plat . . . . Ariz.	36·31 N	112·55 W
136	Kanabeki (kȧ-nä'byĕ-kĭ) Sov. Un. (Urals In.)	57·48 N	57·16 E
64	Kanaga (I.) (kă-nă'gă) . . . . Alaska	52·02 N	177·38 W
153	Kanagawa (Pref.) (kä'nä-gä'wä) Jap. (Tōkyō In.)	35·29 N	139·32 E
153	Kanamachi (kä-nä-mä'chē) Jap. (Tōkyō In.)	35·46 N	139·52 E
136	Kananikol'skoye (kȧ-nȧ-nĭ-kôl'skô-yĕ) . Sov. Un. (Urals In.)	52·48 N	57·29 E
92	Kanasín (kä-nä-sē'n) Mex. (Yucatan In.)	20·54 N	89·31 W
64	Kanatak (kă-nă'tŏk) . . . . Alaska	57·35 N	155·48 W
63	Kanawha (R.) (kȧ-nô'wȧ) . . . U. S.	37·55 N	81·50 W
153	Kanaya (kä-nä'yä) Jap. (Tōkyō In.)	35·10 N	139·49 E
115	Kanayis, Rasel (C.) . . . . U. A. R.	31·14 N	28·08 E
153	Kanazawa (kä'nȧ-zä'wȧ) . . . . Jap.	36·34 N	136·38 E
142	Kanchenjunga, Mt. (kĭn-chĭn-jōōŋ'gȧ) . Nep.	32·40 N	88·18 E
145	Kandahār (kŭn-dŭ-här') . . . . Afg.	31·43 N	65·58 E
166	Kanda Kanda (kän'dȧ kän'dȧ) Con. L.	6·51 S	23·27 E
132	Kandalaksha (kȧn-dȧ-lȧk'shȧ) Sov. Un.	67·10 N	33·05 E
132	Kandalakshskiy Zaliv (B.) Sov. Un.	66·20 N	35·00 E
119	Kandava (kän'dȧ-vȧ) . . . Sov. Un.	57·03 N	22·45 E
164	Kandi (käN-dē') . . . . Dahomey	11·09 N	3·02 E
142	Kandiaro . . . . W. Pak.	27·09 N	68·12 E
142	Kandla (kŭnd'lŭ) . . . . India	23·00 N	70·20 E
143	Kandy (kän'dē) . . . . Ceylon	7·18 N	80·42 E
81	Kane (kān) . . . . Pa.	41·40 N	78·50 W
157	Kaneohe B. (kä-nā-ō'hä) Hawaii (In.)	21·32 N	157·40 W
129	Kanēv (kä-nyôf') . . . . Sov. Un.	49·46 N	31·27 E
129	Kanevskaya (kȧ-nyĕf'skȧ-yȧ) Sov. Un.	46·07 N	38·58 E
160	Kangaroo (I.) (kăŋ-gȧ-rōō') Austl.	36·05 S	137·05 E
144	Kangāvar (kŭŋ'gä-vär) . . . . Iran	34·37 N	46·45 E
154	Kangean (I.) (käŋ'gē-än) . . Indon.	6·50 S	116·22 E
152	Kanggye (käng'gyĕ) . . . . Kor.	40·55 N	126·40 E
152	Kanghwa (I.) (käng'hwä) . . . . Kor.	37·28 N	126·00 E
152	Kangnŭng(käng'nōōng) . . . . Kor.	37·42 N	128·50 E
166	Kango (käN-gō') . . . . Gabon	0·14 N	10·07 E
146	K'angting . . . . China	30·15 N	101·58 E
151	Kanhsien . . . . China	25·50 N	115·00 E
87	Kaniapiskau (L.) (kä-nĭ-ăp'ĭs-kô) Can.	54·04 N	71·20 W
87	Kaniapiskau (R.) . . . . Can.	56·52 N	68·53 W
132	Kanin, P-Ov. (Pen.) (kȧ-nēn') Sov. Un.	68·00 N	45·00 E
132	Kanin Nos, Mys (C.) . . . . Sov. Un.	68·40 N	44·00 E
127	Kanjiža (kä'nyē-zhä) . . . . Yugo.	46·05 N	20·02 E
75	Kankakee (kăŋ-kȧ-kē') Ill. (Chicago In.)	41·07 N	87·53 W
80	Kankakee (R.) . . . . Ill.	41·15 N	88·15 W
164	Kankan (käN-käN) (kän-kän') . Gui	10·20 N	9·16 W
150	Kannan . . . . China	47·50 N	123·30 E
79	Kannapolis (kăn-ăp'ō-lĭs) . . . N. C.	35·30 N	80·38 W
153	Kannoura (kä'nō-ōō'rä) . . . . Jap.	33·34 N	134·18 E
164	Kano (kä'nō) . . . . Nig.	12·03 N	8·32 E
166	Kanonberg (Mtn.) S. Afr. (Cape Town In.)	33·49 S	18·37 E
72	Kanopolis Res. (kăn-ŏp'ō-lĭs) Kans.	38·44 N	98·01 W
142	Kānpur (kän'pûr) . . . . India	26·33 N	80·19 E
62	Kansas (State) (kăn'zȧs) . . . . U. S.	38·30 N	99·40 W
73	Kansas (R.) . . . . Kans.	39·08 N	95·52 W
74	Kansas City Kans. (Kansas City In.)	39·06 N	94·39 W
74	Kansas City . Mo. (Kansas City In.)	39·05 N	94·35 W
134	Kansk . . . . Sov. Un.	56·14 N	95·43 E
152	Kansōng . . . . Kor.	38·09 N	128·29 E
146	Kansu (Prov.) (kän'sōō') . . . China	38·00 N	102·06 E
154	Kan Tang (kän'täng') . . . . Thai.	7·26 N	99·28 E
92	Kantunilkin (kän-tōō-nēl-kē'n) Mex. (Yucatan In.)	21·07 N	87·30 W
136	Kanzhakovskiy Kamen Gora (kȧn-zhă'kôvs-kēē kăm'ĭēn) Sov. Un. (Urals In.)	59·38 N	59·12 E
151	Kaoan . . . . China	28·30 N	115·02 E
148	Kaoch'eng (kä'ō-chĕng') . . . . China	34·56 N	114·57 E
149	Kaoch'iao . . . China (Shanghai In.)	31·21 N	121·35 E
151	Kaohsiung (kä'ō-syōōng') . Taiwan	22·35 N	120·25 E
148	Kaoi (gou'yē) . . . . China	37·37 N	114·39 E
164	Kaolack . . . . Senegal	14·02 N	16·16 W
148	Kaomi (gou'mē) . . . . China	36·23 N	119·46 E
148	Kaoshun (gou'shōōn) . . . . China	31·22 N	118·50 E
148	Kaot'ang (kä'ō-täng') . . . . China	36·52 N	116·12 E
151	Kaoteng Shan (Mtns.) . . . . China	26·30 N	110·00 E
165	Kaovar (Oasis) . . . . Niger	19·16 N	13·09 E
151	Kaoyao . . . . China	23·08 N	112·25 E
148	Kaoyu (gou'yü) . . . . China	32·46 N	119·26 E
151	Kaoyu Hu (L.) (kä'ō-yōō'hōō) China	32·42 N	118·40 E
134	Kapal (kȧ-päl') . . . . Sov. Un.	45·13 N	79·08 E
120	Kapfenberg (käp'fĕn-bĕrgh) . . Aus.	47·27 N	15·16 E
165	Kapoeta . . . . Sud.	4·45 N	33·35 E
121	Kaposvár (kô'pôsh-vär) . . . . Hung.	46·21 N	17·45 E
152	Kapsan (käp'sän') . . . . Kor.	40·59 N	128·22 E
154	Kapuas, Sungai (Strm.) (kä'pōō-äs) . Indon.	2·05 S	114·15 E
87	Kapuskasing . . . . Can.	49·28 N	82·22 W
133	Kapustin Yar (kä'pōōs-tēn yär') Sov. Un.	48·30 N	45·40 E
160	Kaputar, Mt. (kă-pû-tȧr) . . . Austl.	30·11 S	150·11 E
120	Kapuvár (kô'pōō-vär) . . . . Hung.	47·35 N	17·02 E
134	Kara (kärȧ) . . . . Sov. Un.	68·42 N	65·30 E
132	Kara (R.) . . . . Sov. Un.	68·30 N	65·20 E
136	Karabanovo (kä'rȧ-bȧ-nō-vô) Sov. Un. (Moscow In.)	56·19 N	38·43 E
136	Karabash (kó-rȧ-bäsh') Sov. Un. (Urals In.)	55·27 N	60·14 E
133	Kara-Bogaz-Gol, Zaliv (B.) (kȧrȧ' bŭ-gäs') . Sov. Un.	41·30 N	53·40 E
128	Karachev (kȧ-rȧ-chôf') . . . Sov. Un.	53·08 N	34·54 E
142	Karachi . . . . Pak.	24·59 N	68·56 E
103	Karacumy (Des.) . . . . Sov. Un.	39·08 N	59·53 E
133	Karadeniz Boğazi (Bosporous) (Str.) . Tur.	41·10 N	29·10 E
134	Karaganda (kȧ-rȧ-gän'dȧ) Sov. Un.	49·42 N	73·18 E
136	Karaidel (kä'rī-dĕl) Sov. Un. (Urals In.)	55·52 N	56·54 E
133	Kara-Khobda (R.) (kä-rä KÔb'dȧ) . Sov. Un.	50·40 N	55·00 E
145	Karakoram Pass . . . . India & Pak.	35·35 N	77·45 E
146	Karakoram Ra. (kä'rä kō'rōōm) India & Pak.	35·24 N	76·38 E
146	Karakorum (Ruins) . . . . Mong.	47·25 N	102·22 E
133	Karaköse (kä-rä-kŭ'sĕ) . . . . Tur.	39·50 N	43·10 E
130	Karakumy (kara-kum) (Des.) Sov. Un.	40·00 N	57·00 E
133	Karaman (kä-rä-män') . . . . Tur.	37·10 N	33·00 E
159	Karamea Bght. (kȧ-rȧ-mē'ȧ bĭt) N. Z. (In.)	41·10 S	170·42 E
144	Karand . . . . Iran	34·08 N	46·19 E
	Kara Sea, see Karskoye More		
153	Karatsu (kä'rȧ-tsōō) . . . . Jap.	33·28 N	129·59 E
134	Karaul (kä-rä-ōōl') . . . . Sov. Un.	70·13 N	83·46 E
120	Karawanken Mts. . . . . Aus.	46·32 N	14·07 E
144	Karbala (kŭr'bȧ-lä) . . . . Iraq	32·31 N	43·58 E
121	Karcag (kär'tsäg) . . . . Hung.	47·18 N	20·58 E
127	Kardhítsa . . . . Grc.	39·23 N	21·57 E
119	Kärdla (kĕrd'lȧ) . . . . Sov. Un.	58·59 N	22·44 E
165	Kareima (kä-rā'mȧ) . . . . Sud.	18·34 N	31·49 E
130	Karelian (A. S. S. R.) . . . Sov. Un.	62·30 N	32·35 E
166	Karema . . . . Tan.	6·47 S	30·29 E
134	Kargat (kär-gät') . . . . Sov. Un.	55·17 N	80·07 E
	Karghalik, see Yehch'eng		
132	Kargopol (kär-gō-pōl'') . . Sov. Un.	61·30 N	38·50 E
127	Kariaí . . . . Grc.	40·14 N	24·15 E
166	Kariba Res. . . . . N. Rh.	17·30 S	28·06 E
166	Karibib (kär'ȧ-bĭb) . . . . S. W. Afr.	21·55 S	15·50 E
143	Kārikāl (kä-rē-käl') . . . . India	10·58 N	79·49 E
164	Karimama (kä-rē-mä'mä) Dahomey	12·04 N	3·09 E
154	Karimata, Pulau-Pulau (Is.) (kä-rē-mä'tȧ) . Indon.	1·08 S	108·10 E
154	Karimata, Selat (Str.) . . . . Indon.	1·15 S	107·10 E
154	Karimundjawa (I.) (kä'rē-mōōn-yä'vä) . Indon.	5·36 S	110·15 E
168	Karin (kär'ĭn) Som. (Horn of Afr. In.)	10·43 N	45·50 E
155	Karkar (I.) (kär'kär) . N. Gui. Ter.	4·50 S	146·45 E
134	Karkaralinsk (kär-kär-ä-lēnsk') Sov. Un.	49·18 N	75·28 E
129	Karkinitskiy Zailv (B.) (kär-kē-net'skĭ-ē zä'lĭf) . Sov. Un.	45·50 N	32·45 E
120	Karl-Marx-Stadt (Chemnitz) . Ger.	50·48 N	12·53 E
126	Karlobag (kär-lō-bäg') . . . . Yugo.	44·30 N	15·03 E
126	Karlovac (kär'lō-vàts) . . . . Yugo.	45·29 N	15·16 E
129	Karlovka (kär'lôv-kȧ) . . . Sov. Un.	49·26 N	35·08 E
127	Karlovo (kär'lô-vō) . . . . Bul.	42·39 N	24·48 E
120	Karlovy Vary (kär'lô-vē vä'rē) Czech.	50·13 N	12·53 E
118	Karlshamn (kärls'häm) . . . . Swe.	56·11 N	14·50 E
118	Karlskrona (kärls'krō-nä) . . . . Swe.	56·10 N	15·33 E
120	Karlsruhe (kärls'rōō-ē) . . . . Ger.	49·00 N	8·23 E
118	Karlstad (kärl'städ) . . . . Swe.	59·23 N	13·28 E
64	Karluk (kär'lŭk) . . . . Alaska	57·30 N	154·22 W
118	Karmöy (I.) (kärm-ûe) . . . . Nor.	59·14 N	5·00 E
127	Karnobat (kär-nô'bät) . . . . Bul.	42·39 N	26·59 E
120	Kärnten (Carinthia) (State) (kĕrn'tĕn) . Aus.	46·55 N	13·42 E
166	Karonga (kȧ-rōŋ'gȧ) . . . . Nya.	9·52 S	33·57 E
115	Kárpathos (I.) . . . . Grc.	35·34 N	27·26 E
136	Karpinsk (kär'pĭnsk) Sov. Un. (Urals In.)	59·46 N	60·00 E
133	Kars (kärs) . . . . Tur.	40·35 N	43·00 E
134	Karsakpay (kär-säk-pī') . . Sov. Un.	47·47 N	67·07 E
128	Kārsava (kär'sȧ-vȧ) . . . . Sov. Un.	56·46 N	27·39 E
145	Karshi (kär'shē) . . . . Sov. Un.	38·30 N	66·08 E
134	Karskiye Vorota, Proliv (Str.) Sov. Un.	70·30 N	58·07 E
134	Karskoye More (Kara Sea) Sov. Un.	74·08 N	65·45 E
136	Kartaly (kȧr'tȧ lē) Sov. Un. (Urals In.)	53·05 N	60·40 E
143	Karunagapalli . . . . India	9·09 N	76·34 E
121	Karvina . . . . Czech.	49·50 N	18·30 E
166	Kasaï (R.) . . . . Con. L.	3·45 S	19·07 E
166	Kasama (kȧ-sä'mȧ) . . . . N. Rh.	10·15 S	31·13 E
166	Kasanga (kȧ-säŋ'gȧ) . . . . Tan.	8·27 S	31·13 E
153	Kasaoka (kä'sȧ-ō'kȧ) . . . . Jap.	34·33 N	133·29 E
152	Kasari Saki (C.) (kä'sä-rē sä-kē) Jap.	28·25 N	130·10 E
164	Kasba-Tadla (käs'bȧ-täd'lȧ) . Mor.	32·37 N	5·57 W
166	Kasempa (kȧ-sĕm'pȧ) . . . . N. Rh.	13·15 S	25·41 E
166	Kasenga (kȧ-seŋ'gȧ) . . . . Con. L.	10·27 S	28·42 E
144	Kash (R.) (kŭsh) . . . . Afg.	32·27 N	64·15 E
144	Kāshān (kä-shän') . . . . Iran	33·52 N	51·15 E
	Kashqar, see Sufu		
153	Kashihara (kä'shē-hä'rä) Jap. (Ōsaka In.)	34·35 N	135·38 E
128	Kashin (kä-shēn') . . . . Sov. Un.	57·20 N	37·38 E
128	Kashira (kä-shē'rȧ) . . . . Sov. Un.	54·49 N	38·11 E
153	Kashiwa (kä'shē-wä) Jap. (Tōkyō In.)	35·51 N	139·58 E
152	Kashiwazaki (kä'shē-wä-zä'kē) Jap.	37·06 N	138·17 E
	Kashmir, see Jammu and Kashmir		
142	Kashmor . . . . W. Pak.	28·33 N	69·34 E
136	Kashtak (käsh'tȧk) Sov. Un. (Urals In.)	55·18 N	61·25 E
128	Kasimov (kȧ-sē'môf) . . . . Sov. Un.	54·56 N	41·23 E
64	Kaskanak (kăs-kă'năk) . . . . Alaska	60·00 N	158·00 W
80	Kaskaskia (R.) (kăs-kăs'kĭ-ȧ) . . Ill.	38·45 N	89·15 W
	Kaskinem, see Kaskö		
119	Kaskö (Kaskinen) (käs'kû) (käs'kē-nĕn) . Fin.	62·24 N	21·18 E
136	Kasli (käs'lĭ) . Sov. Un. (Urals In.)	55·54 N	60·46 E
166	Kasongo (kä-sôŋ'gō) . . . . Con. L.	4·31 S	26·42 E
115	Kásos (I.) . . . . Grc.	35·20 N	26·55 E
165	Kassala (kä-sä'lä) . . . . Sud.	15·26 N	36·28 E
120	Kassel (käs'ĕl) . . . . Ger.	51·19 N	9·30 E
71	Kasson (kăs'ŭn) . . . . Minn.	44·01 N	92·45 W
133	Kastamonu (kä-stȧ-mō'nōō) . . Tur.	41·20 N	33·50 E
126	Kastélli . . . . Grc. (Inset)	35·13 N	24·11 E
115	Kastellórizon (C.) . . . . Tur.	36·01 N	30·00 E
127	Kastoría (kȧs-tō'rĭ-ȧ) . . . . Grc.	40·28 N	21·17 E
127	Kastron (käs'trôn) . . . . Grc.	39·52 N	25·01 E
142	Kasur . . . . W. Pak.	31·10 N	74·29 E
82	Katahdin, Mt. (kȧ-tä'dĭn) . . Maine	45·56 N	68·57 W
166	Katanga (Reg.) (kȧ-täŋ'gȧ) Con. L.	8·35 S	23·59 E
158	Katanning (kȧ-tăn'ĭng) . . . . Austl.	33·45 S	117·45 E
136	Katav-Ivanovsk (kä'tȧf ĭ-vä'nôfsk) . Sov. Un. (Urals In.)	54·46 N	58·13 E
136	Kateninskiy (kàtyĕ'nĭs-kĭ) Sov. Un. (Urals In.)	53·12 N	61·05 E
127	Kateríni . . . . Grc.	40·18 N	22·36 E
165	Katherina, G. (Pk.) . . . . U. A. R.	28·43 N	34·00 E
158	Katherine (kăth'ēr-ĭn) . . . . Austl.	14·15 S	132·20 E
142	Kathiawar Pen. (kä'tyȧ-wär') India	27·18 N	70·32 E
85	Kathryn (kăth'rĭn) Can. (Calgary In.)	51·13 N	113·42 W
74	Kathryn . . Calif. (Los Angeles In.)	33·42 N	117·45 W
142	Katiha . . . . India	25·39 N	87·39 E
64	Katmai Natl. Mon. (kăt'mī) Alaska	58·38 N	155·00 W
142	Kātmāndu (kät-män-dōō') . . . . Nep.	27·49 N	85·21 E
121	Katowice . . . . Pol.	50·15 N	19·00 E
118	Katrineholm (kȧ-trē'nĕ-hōlm) Swe.	59·01 N	16·10 E
136	Katsbakhskiy (kȧts-bȧk'skĭ) Sov. Un. (Urals In.)	52·57 N	59·37 E
164	Katsina (kät'sē-nȧ) . . . . Nig.	13·03 N	7·39 E
164	Katsina Ala (ä'lä) . . . . Nig.	7·15 N	9·12 E
153	Katsura (R.) (kä'tsōō-rä) Jap. (Ōsaka In.)	34·55 N	135·43 E
134	Katta-Kurgan (kȧ-tȧ-kōōr-gän') Sov. Un.	39·45 N	66·42 E
118	Kattegat (Str.) (kăt'ĕ-gät) . . . . Eur.	56·57 N	11·25 E
134	Katun' (R.) (kȧ-tōōn') . . . Sov. Un.	51·30 N	86·18 E
111	Katwijkaan Zee Neth. (Amsterdam In.)	52·12 N	4·23 E
157	Kauai (I.) . . . . Hawaii (In.)	22·09 N	159·15 W
157	Kauai Chan. (kä-ōō-ä'ē) Hawaii (In.)	21·35 N	158·52 W
120	Kaufbeuren (kouf'boi-rĕn) . . . Ger.	47·52 N	10·38 E
77	Kaufman (kôf'mȧn) . . . . Tex.	32·36 N	96·18 W
71	Kaukauna (kô-kô'nȧ) . . . . Wis.	44·17 N	88·15 W
157	Kaulakahi Chan. (kä'ōō-lȧ-kä'hē) Hawaii (In.)	22·00 N	159·55 W
157	Kaunakakai (kä'ōō-nȧ-kä'kī) Hawaii (In.)	21·06 N	156·59 E
119	Kaunas (Kovno) (kou'nȧs) (kôv'nô) . Sov. Un.	54·52 N	23·54 E
164	Kaure Namoda . . . . Nig.	12·41 N	7·32 E
127	Kavajë (kȧ-vä'yŭ) . . . . Alb.	41·11 N	19·36 E
127	Kaválla (kä-vä'lä) . . . . Grc.	40·55 N	24·24 E
127	Kavallas, Kólpos (G.) . . . . Grc.	40·45 N	24·20 E
155	Kavieng (kä-vē-ĕng') . N. Gui. Ter.	2·44 S	151·02 E
144	Kavir-E Lut (Des.) . . . . Iran	31·47 N	58·38 E
153	Kawagoe (kä-wä-gō'ā) Jap. (Tōkyō In.)	35·55 N	139·29 E
153	Kawaguchi (kä-wä-gōō-chē) Jap. (Tōkyō In.)	35·48 N	139·44 E
157	Kawaikini (Mtn.) (kä-wä'ē-kĭ-nĭ) . Hawaii (In.)	22·05 N	159·33 W
153	Kawasaki (kä-wä-sä'kē) Jap. (Tōkyō In.)	35·32 N	139·43 E

ng-sing; ŋ-baŋk; N-nasalized n; nŏd; cŏmmit; ōld; ôbey; ôrder; fōōd; fŏŏt; ou-out; s-soft; sh-dish; th-thin; pūre; ûnite; ûrn; stŭd; circŭs; ü-as "y" in study; '-indeterminate vowel.

ăt; fĭnăl; rāte; senâte; ârm; ȧsk; sofà; fâre; ch-choose; dh-as th in other; bē; ĕvent; bĕt; recĕnt; cratēr; g-go; gh-guttural g; bĭt; Ɩ-short neutral; rīde; ҡ-guttural k as ch in German ich;

PRONOUNCING INDEX Kilmarnock–Kolyma 223

Page	Name Pronunciation Region	Lat. °′	Long. °′
116	Kilmarnock (kĭl-mär'nŭk) . . . Scot.	55·38 N	4·25 W
116	Kilrush (kĭl'rŭsh) . . . Ire.	52·40 N	9·16 W
167	Kilwa Kivinje . . . Tan.	8·43 S	39·18 E
160	Kimba (kĭm'bȧ) . . . Austl.	33·08 S	136·25 E
70	Kimball (kĭm-bȧl) . . . Nebr.	41·14 N	103·41 W
70	Kimball . . . S. D.	43·44 N	98·58 W
86	Kimberley (kĭm'bĕr-lĭ) . . . Can.	49·48 N	115·55 W
166	Kimberley . . . S. Afr.	28·40 S	24·50 E
127	Kími . . . Grc.	38·38 N	24·05 E
127	Kímolos (I.) (kē'mô-lôs) . . . Grc.	36·52 N	24·20 E
128	Kimry (kĭm'rê) . . . Sov. Un.	56·53 N	37·24 E
154	Kinabalu, Mt. . . . Mala.	5·45 N	115·26 E
80	Kincardine (kĭn-kär'dĭn) . . . Can.	44·10 N	81·15 W
77	Kinder (kĭn'dēr) . . . La.	30·30 N	92·50 W
86	Kindersley (kĭn'dērz-lê) . . . Can.	51·30 N	109·10 W
164	Kindia (kĭn'dê-ȧ) . . . Gui.	10·02 N	12·49 W
166	Kindu-Port-Empain . . . Con. L.	2·59 S	25·59 E
132	Kinel'-Cherkassy . . . Sov. Un.	53·32 N	51·32 E
128	Kineshma (kê-nĕsh'mȧ) . . Sov. Un.	57·27 N	41·02 E
85	King (kĭng) . . . Can. (Toronto In.)	43·56 N	79·32 W
160	King (I.) . . . Austl.	39·35 S	143·40 E
160	Kingaroy (kĭŋ'gă-roi) . . . Austl.	26·37 S	151·50 E
68	King City (kĭng sĭ'tĭ) . . . Calif.	36·12 N	121·08 W
72	Kingfisher (kĭng'fĭsh-ẽr) . . . Okla.	35·51 N	97·55 W
158	King George Sd. (jôrj) . . . Austl.	35·17 S	118·30 E
128	Kingisepp (kĭŋ-gê-sep') . . Sov. Un.	59·22 N	28·38 E
158	King Leopold Ranges (lē'ô-pōld) Austl.	16·35 S	125·00 E
69	Kingman (kĭng'măn) . . . Ariz.	35·10 N	114·05 W
72	Kingman (kĭng'măn) . . . Kans.	37·38 N	98·07 W
68	Kings (R.) . . . Calif.	36·28 N	119·43 W
68	Kings Canyon Natl. Park (kăn'yŭn) Calif.	36·52 N	118·53 W
110	Kingsclere (kĭngs-clēr) Eng. (London In.)	51·18 N	1·15 W
160	Kingscote (kĭngz'kŭt) . . . Austl.	35·45 S	137·32 E
117	Kings Lynn (kĭngz lĭn') . . . Eng.	52·45 N	0·20 E
79	Kings Mt. . . . N. C.	35·13 N	81·30 W
110	Kings Norton (nôr'tŭn) . . . Eng.	52·25 N	1·54 W
158	King Sd. . . . Austl.	16·50 S	123·35 E
84	Kings Park (kĭngz pärk) N. Y. (New York In.)	40·53 N	73·16 W
67	Kings Pk. . . . Utah	40·46 N	110·20 W
79	Kingsport (kĭngz'pōrt) . . . Tenn.	36·33 N	82·36 W
160	Kingston (kĭngz'tŭn) . . . Austl.	37·52 S	139·52 E
81	Kingston . . . Can.	44·15 N	76·30 W
94	Kingston . . . Jam.	18·00 N	76·45 W
81	Kingston . . . N. Y.	42·00 N	74·00 W
81	Kingston . . . Pa.	41·15 N	75·50 W
65	Kingston . . . Wash. (Seattle In.)	47·04 N	122·29 W
93	Kingstown (kĭngz'toun) . . . St. Vincent (Le. & Wind. Is. In.)	13·10 N	61·14 W
79	Kingstree (kĭngz'trē) . . . S. C.	33·30 N	79·50 W
76	Kingsville (kĭngz'vĭl) . . . Tex.	27·32 N	97·52 W
86	King William I. (kĭng wĭl'yăm) Can.	69·25 N	97·00 W
167	King William's Town (kĭng-wĭl'-yŭmz-toun) . S. Afr. (Natal In.)	32·53 S	27·24 E
74	Kinloch (kĭn-lŏk) Mo. (St. Louis In.)	38·44 N	90·19 W
116	Kinnairds Hd. (kĭn-årds hĕd) Scot.	57·42 N	3·55 W
153	Kinomoto (kē'nō-mōtō) . . . Jap.	33·53 N	136·07 E
153	Kinosaki (kē'nō-sä'kê) . . . Jap.	35·38 N	134·47 E
116	Kinsale Hbr. (kĭn-sāl') . . . Ire.	51·35 N	8·17 W
72	Kinsley (kĭnz'lĭ) . . . Kans.	37·55 N	99·24 W
79	Kinston (kĭnz'tŭn) . . . N. C.	35·15 N	77·35 W
164	Kintampo (kēn-täm'pō) . . . Ghana	8·05 N	1·44 W
116	Kintyre Pen. . . . Scot.	55·50 N	5·40 W
	Kiorashi, see Ōmori		
72	Kiowa (kī'ô-wȧ) . . . Kans.	37·01 N	98·30 W
73	Kiowa . . . Okla.	34·42 N	95·53 W
127	Kiparissía . . . Grc.	37·17 N	21·43 E
127	Kiparissiakós Kólpos (G.) . . . Grc.	37·28 N	21·15 E
166	Kipembawe (kê-pĕm-bä'wȧ) . Tan.	7·43 S	33·22 E
74	Kirby (kŭr'bĭ) Tex. (San Antonio In.)	29·29 N	98·23 W
77	Kirbyville (kŭr'bĭ-vĭl) . . . Tex.	30·39 N	93·54 W
135	Kirenga (R.) (kê-rĕŋ'gȧ) . Sov. Un.	56·30 N	103·18 E
135	Kirensk (kē-rĕnsk') . . . Sov. Un.	57·47 N	108·22 E
145	Kirgizskiy Khrebet (Kirgiz) (Mts.) . Sov. Un.	37·58 N	72·23 E
130	Kirgiz S. S. R. (kĭr-gēz') . Sov. Un.	41·45 N	74·38 E
130	Kirgiz Steppe (Plain) . . . Sov. Un.	49·28 N	57·07 E
	Kirin, see Chilin		
	Kirin, see Chilung		
110	Kirkby-in-Ashfield (kûrk'bē-ĭn-ăsh'fēld) . . Eng.	53·06 N	1·16 W
116	Kirkcaldy (kẽr-kô'dĭ) . . . Scot.	56·06 N	3·15 W
85	Kirkfield Park (kûrk-fēld) Can. (Winnipeg In.)	49·53 N	97·16 W
110	Kirkham (kûrk'ăm) . . . Eng.	53·47 N	2·53 W
65	Kirkland (kûrk'lănd) Wash. (Seattle In.)	47·41 N	122·12 W
87	Kirkland Lake . . . Can.	48·14 N	80·06 W
127	Kirklareli (kêrk'lár-ĕ'lê) . . . Tur.	41·44 N	41·43 E
73	Kirksville (kûrks'vĭl) . . . Mo.	40·12 N	92·35 W
144	Kirkūk (kĭr-kōōk') . . . Iraq	35·28 N	44·22 E
116	Kirkwall (kûrk'wôl) . . . Scot.	58·58 N	2·59 W
74	Kirkwood (kûrk'wŏŏd) Mo. (St. Louis In.)	38·35 N	90·24 W
167	Kirkwood . . . S. Afr. (Natal In.)	33·26 S	25·24 E
120	Kirn (kêrn) . . . Ger.	49·47 N	7·23 E
128	Kirov . . . Sov. Un.	54·04 N	34·19 E
132	Kirov . . . Sov. Un.	58·35 N	49·35 E
133	Kirovabad (kē-rŭ-vŭ-băt') Sov. Un.	40·40 N	46·20 E
136	Kirovgrad (kē'rŭ-vŭ-grad) Sov. Un. (Urals In.)	57·26 N	60·03 E
129	Kirovograd (kē-rŭ-vŭ-grăt') Sov. Un.	48·33 N	32·17 E
129	Kirovograd (Oblast) . . . Sov. Un.	48·23 N	31·10 E
132	Kirovsk . . . Sov. Un.	67·40 N	33·58 E
136	Kirovsk (kê-rôfsk') Sov. Un. (Leningrad In.)	59·52 N	30·59 E
133	Kirsanov (kêr-sȧ'nôf) . . . Sov. Un.	52·40 N	42·40 E
133	Kirşehir (kêr-shĕ'hēr) . . . Tur.	39·10 N	34·00 E
142	Kirthar Ra. (kĭr-tŭr) . . . W. Pak.	30·40 N	67·20 E
110	Kirton (kûr'tŭn) . . . Eng.	53·29 N	0·35 W
112	Kiruna (kē-rōō'nä) . . . Swe.	67·49 N	20·08 E
72	Kirwin Res. (kûr'wĭn) . . . Kans.	39·34 N	99·04 W
153	Kiryū (kē'rĭ-ōō) . . . Jap.	36·26 N	139·18 E
128	Kirzhach (kêr-zhȧk') . . . Sov. Un.	56·08 N	38·53 E
167	Kisaki (kē-sȧ'kē) . . . Tan.	7·37 S	37·43 E
126	Kisámou, Kólpos (G) . . . Grc. (In.)	35·40 N	23·37 E
153	Kisarazu (kē'sȧ-rȧ'zōō) Jap. (Tōkyō In.)	35·23 N	139·55 E
134	Kiselëvsk (kē-sĭ-lyôfsk') . . Sov. Un.	54·05 N	86·19 E
166	Kisenyi (kē'sĕn'yē) . . . Rw.	1·43 S	29·15 E
129	Kishinëv (ke-shê-nyôf') . . Sov. Un.	47·02 N	28·52 E
153	Kishiwada (kē'shê-wä'dä) . . . Jap.	34·25 N	135·18 E
136	Kishkino (kēsh'kĭ-nô) Sov. Un. (Moscow In.)	55·15 N	38·04 E
64	Kiska (I.) (kĭs'kä) . . . Alaska	52·08 N	177·10 E
121	Kiskunfélegyháza (kĭsh'kŏŏn-fā'lĕd-y'hä'zô) . Hung.	46·42 N	19·52 E
121	Kiskunhalas (kĭsh'kŏŏn-hô'lôsh) Hung.	46·24 N	19·26 E
121	Kiskunmajsa (kĭsh'kŏŏn-mī'shô) Hung.	46·29 N	19·42 E
167	Kismayu . . . Som.	0·18 S	42·30 E
153	Kiso-Gawa (Strm.) (kē'sō-gä'wä) Jap.	35·29 N	137·12 E
153	Kiso-Sammyaku (Mts.) (kê'sō säm'myȧ-kōō) . Jap.	35·47 N	137·39 E
164	Kissidougou (kē'sê-dōō'gōō) . . Gui.	9·19 N	10·26 W
79	Kissimmee (kĭ-sĭm'ê) . . . Fla. (In.)	28·17 N	81·25 W
79	Kissimmee (L.) . . . Fla. (In.)	27·58 N	81·17 W
79	Kissimmee (R.) . . . Fla. (In.)	27·45 N	81·07 W
112	Kistrand (kē'stränd) . . . Nor.	70·29 N	25·01 E
121	Kisujszallás (kĭsh'ŏŏ'y'sä'läsh) Hung.	47·12 N	20·47 E
166	Kisumu (kē'sōō-mōō) . . . Ken.	0·05 S	34·49 E
139	Kiswah . . . Syr. (Palestine In.)	33·31 N	36·13 E
164	Kita (kē'tȧ) . . . Mali	13·05 N	9·33 W
152	Kitakami Gawa (R.) (kê'tȧ-kä'mē gä-wä) . Jap.	39·20 N	141·10 E
153	Kitakyūshū (kē'tȧ-kyōō'shōō') Jap.	34·15 N	130·23 E
80	Kitchener (kĭch'ĕ-nẽr) . . . Can.	43·25 N	80·35 W
166	Kitega (kê-tā'gȧ) . . . Burundi	3·39 S	30·05 E
165	Kitgum (kĭt'gŏŏm) . . . Ug.	3·29 N	33·04 E
115	Kíthira (I.) . . . Grc.	36·15 N	22·56 E
127	Kíthnos (I.) . . . Grc.	37·24 N	24·10 E
86	Kitimat . . . Can.	54·01 N	128·11 W
65	Kitsap (kĭt-săp) Wash. (Seattle In.)	47·45 N	122·32 W
153	Kitsuki (kêt'sŏŏ-kê) . . . Jap.	33·24 N	131·35 E
81	Kittaning (kĭ-tăn'ĭng) . . . Pa.	40·50 N	79·30 W
84	Kittatinny Mts. (kĭ-tŭ-tĭ'nê) N. J. (New York In.)	41·16 N	74·44 W
82	Kittery (kĭt'ẽr-ĭ) . . . Maine	43·07 N	70·45 W
111	Kittsee . . . Aus. (Vienna In.)	48·05 N	17·05 E
79	Kitty Hawk (kĭt'tê hôk) . . . N. C.	36·04 N	75·42 W
120	Kitzingen (kĭt'zĭng-ĕn) . . . Ger.	49·44 N	10·08 E
166	Kivu (L.) . . . Con. L.	2·00 S	28·30 E
133	Kiyev (kē'yĕf) . . . Sov. Un.	50·27 N	30·30 E
136	Kizel (kē'zĕl) . Sov. Un. (Urals In.)	59·05 N	57·42 E
133	Kizil Irmak (R.) (kĭz'ĭl ĭr-mäk') Tur.	40·15 N	34·00 E
136	Kizil'skoye (kĭz'ĭl-skô-yĕ) Sov. Un. (Urals In.)	52·43 N	58·53 E
133	Kizlyar (kĭz-lyär') . . . Sov. Un.	44·00 N	46·50 E
153	Kizu (kē'zōō) . . . Jap. (Ōsaka In.)	34·43 N	135·49 E
103	Kizyl-Arvat (kē'zĭl-ŭr-vät') Sov. Un.	38·55 N	56·33 E
111	Klaaswaal . Neth. (Amsterdam In.)	51·46 N	4·25 E
120	Kladno (kläd'nō) . . . Czech.	50·10 N	14·05 E
120	Klagenfurt (klä'gĕn-fŏŏrt) . . . Aus.	46·38 N	14·19 E
119	Klaipéda (Memel) (klī'pȧ-dȧ) (mā'mĕl) . Sov. Un.	55·43 N	21·10 E
66	Klamath Falls . . . Ore.	42·13 N	121·49 W
66	Klamath Ind. Res. (klăm'ȧth) . Ore.	42·48 N	121·40 E
66	Klamath Mts. . . . Calif.	42·00 N	123·25 W
66	Klamath R. . . . Calif.	41·27 N	123·35 W
139	Klang . . . Mala. (Singapore In.)	3·02 N	101·27 E
139	Klang (R.) . Mala. (Singapore In.)	3·00 N	101·38 E
118	Klar-älven (R.) . . . Swe.	60·40 N	13·00 E
65	Klaskanine (R.) (klăs'kȧ-nīn) Ore. (Portland In.)	46·02 N	123·43 W
120	Klatovy (klȧ'tô-vê) . . . Czech.	49·23 N	13·18 E
64	Klawak (klā'wăk) . . . Alaska	55·32 N	133·10 W
85	Kleinburg (klīn-bûrg) Can. (Toronto In.)	43·51 N	79·38 W
111	Kleinmachnow (klīn-mäĸ'nō) Ger. (Berlin In.)	52·22 N	13·12 E
167	Kleinmond . . . S. Afr. (Natal In.)	33·33 S	27·04 E
168	Klerksdorp (klẽrks'dôrp) . . . S. Afr. (Johannesburg & Pretoria In.)	26·52 S	26·40 E
168	Klerkskraal (klẽrks'kräl) . . . S. Afr. (Johannesburg & Pretoria In.)	26·15 S	27·10 E
128	Kletnya (klyĕt'nyȧ) . . . Sov. Un.	52·19 N	33·14 E
128	Kletsk (klĕtsk) . . . Sov. Un.	53·04 N	26·43 E
123	Kleve (klĕ'fĕ) . . . Ger. (Ruhr In.)	51·47 N	6·09 E
66	Klickitat R. . . . Wash.	46·01 N	121·07 W
128	Klimovichi (klē-mô-vē'chê) Sov. Un.	53·37 N	31·21 E
136	Klimovsk (klĭ'môfsk) Sov. Un. (Moscow In.)	55·21 N	37·32 E
128	Klin (klên) . . . Sov. Un.	56·18 N	36·43 E
118	Klintehamn (klēn'tē-häm) . . . Swe.	57·24 N	18·14 E
128	Klintsy (klĭn'tsĭ) . . . Sov. Un.	52·46 N	32·14 E
168	Klipgat . . . S. Afr. (Johannesburg & Pretoria In.)	25·26 S	27·57 E
168	Klip R. (klĭp) . . . S. Afr. (Johannesburg & Pretoria In.)	27·18 S	29·25 E
126	Ključ (klyōōch) . . . Yugo.	44·32 N	16·48 E
120	Klodzko (klôd'skô) . . . Pol.	50·26 N	16·38 E
64	Klondike Reg. (klŏn'dīk) Alaska-Can.	64·12 N	142·38 W
111	Klosterfelde (klōs'tĕr-fĕl-dĕ) Ger. (Berlin In.)	52·47 N	13·29 E
111	Klosterneuburg (klōs-tēr-noi'bŏŏrgh) . Aus. (Vienna In.)	48·19 N	16·20 E
139	Kluang . . . Mala. (Singapore In.)	2·01 N	103·19 E
121	Kluczbork (klōōch'bōrk) . . . Pol.	50·59 N	18·15 E
128	Klyaz'ma (R.) (klyäz'mȧ) . Sov. Un.	55·49 N	39·19 E
135	Klyuchevskaya (Vol.) (klyōō-chĕfskä'yä) . Sov. Un.	56·13 N	160·00 E
136	Klyuchi (klyōō'chĭ) Sov. Un. (Urals In.)	57·03 N	57·20 E
127	Knezha (knyā'zhȧ) . . . Bul.	43·27 N	24·03 E
70	Knife (R.) (nīf) . . . N. D.	47·06 N	102·33 W
80	Knightstown (nīts'toun) . . . Ind.	39·45 N	85·30 W
126	Knin (knēn) . . . Yugo.	44·02 N	16·14 E
120	Knittelfeld . . . Aus.	47·13 N	14·50 E
155	Knob Pk. (nŏb) . Phil. (Manila In.)	12·30 N	121·20 E
116	Knockmealdown Mts. (nŏk-mēl'doun) . Ire.	52·13 N	8·09 W
110	Knottingley (nŏt'ĭng-lĭ) . . . Eng.	53·42 N	1·14 W
80	Knox (nŏks) . . . Ind.	41·15 N	86·40 W
71	Knoxville (nŏks'vĭl) . . . Iowa	41·19 N	93·05 W
78	Knoxville . . . Tenn.	35·58 N	83·55 W
110	Knutsford (nŭts'fẽrd) . . . Eng.	53·18 N	2·22 W
121	Knyszyn (knĭ'shĭn) . . . Pol.	53·16 N	22·59 E
148	Ko (R.) (gōōŭ) . . . China	33·04 N	117·16 E
153	Kobayashi (kō'bȧ-yä'shê) . . . Jap.	31·58 N	130·59 E
153	Kōbe (kō'bĕ) . . . Jap. (Ōsaka In.)	34·30 N	135·10 E
129	Kobelyaki (kō-bĕl-yä'kê) . Sov. Un.	49·11 N	34·12 E
118	København (Copenhagen) (kû-b'n-houn') . Den.	55·43 N	12·27 E
120	Koblenz (kō'blĕntz) . . . Ger.	50·18 N	7·36 E
128	Kobozha (R.) (kô-bō'zhȧ) . Sov. Un.	58·55 N	35·18 E
121	Kobrin (kō'brên') . . . Sov. Un.	52·13 N	24·23 E
136	Kobrinskoye (kô-brĭn'skô-yĕ) Sov. Un. (Leningrad In.)	59·25 N	30·07 E
64	Kobuk (R.) (kō'bŭk) . . . Alaska	66·58 N	158·48 W
133	Kobuleti (kô-bŏŏ-lyā'tê) . Sov. Un.	41·50 N	41·40 E
127	Kocani (kô'chä-nĕ) . . . Yugo.	41·54 N	22·25 E
126	Kočevje (kô'chāv-ye) . . . Yugo.	45·38 N	14·51 E
74	Koch (kōk) . . . Mo. (St. Louis In.)	38·28 N	90·17 W
120	Kocher R. (kôĸ'ĕr) . . . Ger.	49·00 N	9·52 E
153	Kōchi (kō'chê) . . . Jap.	33·35 N	133·32 E
64	Kodiak (kō'dyăk) . . . Alaska	57·50 N	152·30 W
64	Kodiak (I.) . . . Alaska	57·24 N	153·32 W
165	Kodok (ko'dŏk) . . . Sud.	9·57 N	32·08 E
166	Koekenaap . . . S. Afr.	31·25 S	18·20 E
164	Koforidua (kō fô-rĭ-dōō'ȧ) . . Ghana	6·12 N	0·30 W
153	Kōfu (kō'fōō') . . . Jap.	35·41 N	138·34 E
153	Koga (kō'gȧ) . . . Jap.	36·13 N	139·40 E
153	Kogane (kō'gä-nȧ) Jap. (Tōkyō In.)	35·50 N	139·56 E
153	Koganei (kō'gä-nā) Jap. (Tōkyō In.)	35·42 N	139·31 E
118	Køge (kû'gĕ) . . . Den.	55·27 N	12·09 E
129	Kogil'nik (R.) (kȯ-gêl-nēk') Sov. Un.	46·08 N	29·10 E
142	Koh-i Baba Mt. . . . Afg.	39·39 N	67·09 E
145	Kohima (kô-ē'mȧ) . . . India	25·45 N	94·41 E
153	Koito (R.) (kȯ'ê-tō) Jap. (Tōkyō In.)	35·19 N	139·58 E
152	Kŏje (I.) (kû'jĕ) . . . Kor.	34·53 N	129·00 E
134	Kokand (kô-känt') . . . Sov. Un.	40·27 N	71·07 E
134	Kokchetav (kôk'chĕ-tȧf) . Sov. Un.	53·15 N	69·13 E
119	Kokemäen (R.) (kô'kē-mȧ'ĕn) . Fin.	61·23 N	22·03 E
128	Kokhma (kôĸ'mȧ) . . . Sov. Un.	56·57 N	41·08 E
143	Kokkanisseri . . . India	12·08 N	74·14 E
112	Kokkola (kô'kô-lȧ) . . . Fin.	63·47 N	22·58 E
80	Kokomo (kō'kô-mô) . . . Ind.	40·30 N	86·20 W
	Koko Nor, see Ch'ing Hai		
155	Kokopo (kô-kô'pō) . . . N. Gui. Ter.	4·25 S	152·27 E
87	Koksoak (R.) (kôk'sô-ăk) . . . Can.	57·42 N	69·50 W
167	Kokstad (kôk'shtät) S. Afr. (Natal In.)	30·33 S	29·27 E
148	Koku (gŏ'gōō) . . . China	39·00 N	117·30 E
153	Kokubu (kō'kōō-bōō) . . . Jap.	31·42 N	130·46 E
153	Kokubunji (kō'kōō-bŏŏn'jê) Jap. (Tōkyō In.)	35·43 N	139·29 E
153	Kokuou (kȯ'kōō-ȯ'ōō) Jap. (Ōsaka In.)	34·34 N	135·39 E
153	Kokura (kō'kŏŏ-rä) . . . Jap.	33·53 N	130·54 E
164	Kolahun (kô-lä'hŏŏn) . . . Lib.	8·24 N	10·11 W
	Kola Pen., see Kol'skiy P-Ov.		
143	Kolār (kȯl-är') . . . India	13·39 N	78·33 E
143	Kolār Gold Fields (kȯl-är') . . India	13·45 N	79·55 E
127	Kolarovgrad . . . Bul.	43·15 N	26·54 E
128	Kol'chugino (kôl-chŏŏ'gê-nô) Sov. Un.	56·19 N	39·29 E
118	Kolding (kŭl'dĭng) . . . Den.	55·29 N	9·24 E
166	Kole (kō'lȧ) . . . Con. L.	3·19 S	22·46 E
132	Kolguyev (I.) (kôl-gŏŏ'yĕf) Sov. Un.	69·00 N	49·00 E
120	Kolin (kō'lēn) . . . Czech.	50·01 N	15·11 E
119	Kolkasrags (Pt.) (kôl-käs'rȧgz) Sov. Un.	57·46 N	22·39 E
123	Köln (Cologne) . . . Ger. (Ruhr In.)	50·56 N	6·57 E
121	Kolno (kôw'nô) . . . Pol.	53·23 N	21·56 E
121	Koło (kô'wô) . . . Pol.	52·11 N	18·37 E
120	Kołobrzeg (kô-lôb'zhĕk) . . . Pol.	54·10 N	15·35 E
136	Kolomna (kȧl-ôm'nȧ) Sov. Un. (Moscow In.)	55·06 N	38·47 E
121	Kolomyya (kō'lô-mē'yȧ) . Sov. Un.	48·32 N	25 04 E
128	Kolp' (R.) (kôlp) . . . Sov. Un.	59·29 N	35·32 E
134	Kolpashevo (kŭl pȧ shô'vȧ) Sov. Un.	58·16 N	82·43 E
136	Kolpino (kôl'pê-nô) Sov. Un. (Leningrad In.)	59·45 N	30·37 E
128	Kolpny (kôlp'nyê) . . . Sov. Un.	52·14 N	36·54 E
132	Kol'skiy P-Ov. (Kola Pen.) Sov. Un.	67·15 N	37·40 E
132	Kolva (R.) . . . Sov. Un.	61·00 N	57·00 E
166	Kolwezi (kōl-wĕ'zē) . . . Con. L.	10·40 S	25·30 E
136	Kolyberovo (kô-lĭ-byâ'rô-vô) Sov. Un. (Moscow In.)	55·16 N	38·45 E
135	Kolyma (R.) . . . Sov. Un.	66·30 N	151·45 E

ng-sing; ŋ-baŋk; ĸ-nasalized n; nŏd; cŏmmit; ōld; ôbey; ôrder; fōōd; fŏŏt; ou-out; s-soft; sh-dish; th-thin; pūre; ûnite; ûrn; stŭd; circŭs; ü-as "y" in study; '-indeterminate vowel.

Page	Name Pronunciation Region	Lat. °′	Long. °′
	Kolymskiy (Mts.), see Gydan, Khrebet		
134	Kolyvan' (kôl-ê-vän')...Sov. Un.	55·28 N	82·59 E
130	Komadorskie Ostrova (Is.) Sov. Un.	55·40 N	167·13 E
164	Komadugu-Yobe R..........Nig.	12·14 N	10·00 E
121	Komárno (kô'mär-nô).....Czech.	47·46 N	18·08 E
121	Komarno..............Sov. Un.	49·38 N	23·43 E
121	Komaron (kô'mä-rôm).....Hung.	47·45 N	18·06 E
166	Komatipoort (kō-mä'tê-pōrt) S. Afr.	25·21 S	32·00 E
153	Komatsu (kō-mät'sōō).......Jap.	36·23 N	136·26 E
153	Komatsushima (kō-mät'sōō-shê'mä).Jap.	34·04 N	134 32 E
167	Komga (kōm'gà) S. Afr. (Natal In.)	32·36 S	27·54 E
130	Komi (A. S. S. R.) (kômê) Sov. Un.	61·31 N	53·15 E
166	Kommetijie S. Afr. (Cape Town In.)	34·09 S	18·19 E
146	Kommunizma, Pik (Pk.).Sov. Un.	39·46 N	71·23 E
127	Komotiní.................Grc.	41·07 N	25·22 E
154	Kompong Thom (kŏm'pŏng-tŏm) Camb.	12·41 N	104·39 E
129	Komrat (kôm-rät')......Sov. Un.	46·17 N	28·38 E
136	Komsomolets (kôm-sô-mô'lĕts) Sov. Un. (Urals In.)	53·45 N	63·04 E
133	Komsomolets Zaliv (B.)..Sov. Un.	45·40 N	52·00 E
135	Komsomol'sk-na-Amure (kŭm-sŭ-môlsk'nŭ-ŭ-mōōr'yĭ).Sov. Un.	50·46 N	137·14 E
129	Komsomol'skoye (kôm-sô-môl'skô-yĕ).Sov. Un.	48·42 N	28·44 E
132	Konda (R.) (kôn'dà)....Sov. Un.	60·50 N	64·00 E
136	Kondas R. (kôn'dȧs) Sov. Un. (Urals In.)	59·30 N	56·28 E
166	Kondoa (kôn-dō'ȧ)..........Tan.	4·52 S	36·00 E
164	Kong (kông).........Ivory Coast	9·05 N	4·41 W
164	Kong (Reg.).........Ivory Coast	9·19 N	4·03 W
166	Kongolo (kôŋ'gō'lō).......Con. L.	5·20 S	26·58 E
118	Kongsberg (kŭngs'bĕrg).....Nor.	59·40 N	9·36 E
118	Kongsvinger (kŭngs'vĭŋ-gĕr).Nor.	60·12 N	12·00 E
166	Koni (kō'nē)..............Con. L.	10·32 S	27·27 E
	Königsberg, see Kaliningrad		
111	Königsbrunn (kû'nĕgs-brōōn) Ger. (Munich In.)	48·16 N	10·53 E
111	Königs Wusterhausen (kû'nĕgs vōōs'tĕr-hou-zĕn) Ger. (Berlin In.)	52·18 N	13·38 E
121	Konin (kô'nyĕn)............Pol.	52·11 N	18·17 E
127	Kónitsa (kô'nyē'tsȧ).........Grc.	40·03 N	20·46 E
127	Konjic (kôn'yēts)..........Yugo.	43·38 N	17·59 E
152	Konju.....................Kor.	36·21 N	127·05 E
129	Konotop (kô-nô-tôp')....Sov. Un.	51·13 N	33·14 E
121	Końskie (koin''skyĕ).........Pol.	51·12 N	20·26 E
129	Konstantinovka (kôn-stȧn-tē'nôf-kȧ).Sov. Un.	48·33 N	37·42 E
120	Konstanz (kôn'-shtänts).......Ger.	47·39 N	9·10 E
164	Kontagora (kōn-tȧ-gō'rä)....Nig.	10·27 N	5 30 E
164	Kontcha (kōn'chä).........Cam.	8·03 N	12·21 E
133	Konya (kōn'yȧ)............Tur.	36·55 N	32·25 E
86	Kootenay Natl. Park (kōō'tê-nȧ) Can.	51·06 N	117·02 W
86	Kootenay (R.) (kōō'tê-nȧ)...Can.	50·28 N	115·50 W
153	Kōō-zan (Mtn.) (kōō'zän) Jap. (Ōsaka In.)	34·53 N	135·32 E
118	Kopervik (kô'pĕr-vĕk).......Nor.	59·18 N	5·20 E
144	Kopet, Mts................Iran	37·28 N	58·29 E
136	Kopeysk (kô-pāsk') Sov. Un. (Urals In.)	55·07 N	61·36 E
118	Köping (chû'pĭng)..........Swe.	59·32 N	15·58 E
118	Kopparberg (kŏp'pȧr-bĕrgh)..Swe.	59·53 N	15·00 E
168	Koppies..S. Afr. (Johannesburg & Pretoria In.)	27·15 S	27·35 E
126	Koprivnica (kô'prēv-nē'tsȧ).Yugo.	46·10 N	16·48 E
121	Kopychintsy (kô-pê-chēn'tsĕ) Sov. Un.	49·06 N	25·55 E
127	Korçë (kôr'chĕ)............Alb.	40·37 N	20·48 E
126	Korčula (I.) (kôr'chōō-lȧ)...Yugo.	42·50 N	17·05 E
165	Kordofan (Prov.) (kôr-dô-fän') Sud.	14·08 N	28·39 E
152	Korea B............China-Kor.	39·18 N	123·50 E
139	Korea (kô-rē'ȧ)..............Asia	38·45 N	130·00 E
152	Korean Arch..............Kor.	39·05 N	125·35 E
152	Korea Str...............Kor.-Jap.	33·30 N	128·30 E
121	Korets (kô-rĕts').........Sov. Un.	50·35 N	27·13 E
164	Korhogo (kôr-hō'gō)..Ivory Coast	9·22 N	5·21 W
127	Korinthiakós Kólpos (G.)....Grc.	38·15 N	22·33 E
127	Korinthos (Corinth) (kô-rēn'thôs) (kŏr'ĭnth).Grc.	37·56 N	22·54 E
152	Kōriyama (kō'rê-yä'mä).....Jap.	37·18 N	140·25 E
153	Kōriyama.........Jap. (Ōsaka In.)	34·39 N	135·48 E
136	Korkino (kôr'kē-nŭ) Sov. Un. (Urals In.)	54·53 N	61·25 E
120	Körmend (kûr'mĕnt).......Hung.	47·02 N	16·36 E
126	Kornat (I.) (kôr-nät').......Yugo.	43·46 N	15·10 E
111	Korneuburg (kôr'noi-bōōrgh) Aus. (Vienna In.)	48·22 N	16·21 E
129	Korocha (kô-rō'chȧ).....Sov. Un.	50·50 N	37·13 E
129	Korop (kō'rôp).........Sov. Un.	51·33 N	33·54 E
129	Korosten' (kô'rôs-tĕn)...Sov. Un.	50·51 N	28·39 E
129	Korostyshev (kô-rôs'tê-shôf) Sov. Un.	50·19 N	29·05 E
129	Korotoyak (kô'rô-tô-yȧk') Sov. Un.	51·00 N	39·06 E
135	Korsakov (kôr'sȧ-kôf')...Sov. Un.	46·42 N	143·16 E
119	Korsnas (kôrs'nĕs)..........Fin.	62·51 N	21·17 E
118	Korsør (kôrs'ûr')...........Den.	55·19 N	11·08 E
165	Körti (kôr'tê)...............Sud.	18·08 N	31·39 E
117	Kortrijk...................Bel.	50·49 N	3·10 E
135	Koryakskiy Khrebet (Mts.) Sov. Un.	62·00 N	168·45 E
129	Koryukovka (kôr-yōō-kôf'kȧ) Sov. Un.	51·44 N	32·24 E
142	Kosa.....................India	23·37 N	68·35 E
120	Kóscian (kŭsh'tsyȧn)........Pol.	52·05 N	16·38 E
121	Kóscierzyna (kŭsh-tsyĕ-zhē'nȧ) Pol.	54·08 N	17·59 E
78	Kosciusko (kŏs-ĭ-ŭs'kō).....Miss.	33·04 N	89·35 W
160	Kosciusko, Mt............Austl.	36·26 S	148·20 E
128	Kosel'sk (kô-zĕlsk')......Sov. Un.	54·01 N	35·49 E
165	Kosha (kō'shä).............Sud.	20·49 N	30·27 E
150	K'oshan (kō'shän')........China	48·00 N	126·30 E
153	Koshigaya (kō'shê-gä'yä) Jap. (Tōkyō In.)	35·53 N	139·48 E
153	Koshiki-Rettō (Is.) (kō-shē'kê rät'tō).Jap.	31·51 N	129·40 E
142	Kosi (R.) (kô'sē)..........India	26·00 N	86·20 E
121	Košice (kō'shê-tsĕ').......Czech.	48·43 N	21·17 E
167	Kosmos (kŏz'mŏs) S. Afr. (Johannesburg & Pretoria In.)	25·45 S	27·51 E
136	Kosobrodskiy (kä-sô'brôd-skĭ) Sov. Un. (Urals In.)	54·14 N	60·53 E
	Koso Lake, see Khöbsögol Dalai		
127	Kosovska Mitrovica (kō'sôv-skä' mē'trô-vê-tsä').Yugo.	42·51 N	20·50 E
126	Kostajnica (kôs'tä-ê-nē'tsȧ).Yugo.	45·14 N	16·32 E
168	Koster...S. Afr. (Johannesburg & Pretoria In.)	25·52 S	26·52 E
165	Kosti (kôs'tê)..............Sud.	13·09 N	32·39 E
136	Kostino (kôs'tĭ-nô) Sov. Un. (Moscow In.)	55·54 N	37·51 E
128	Kostroma (kôs-trô-mȧ')..Sov. Un.	57·46 N	40·55 E
128	Kostroma (Oblast)......Sov. Un.	57·50 N	41·10 E
120	Kostrzyn' (kôst'chĕn).......Pol.	52·35 N	14·38 E
136	Kos'va R. (kôs'vȧ) Sov. Un. (Urals In.)	58·44 N	57·08 E
120	Koszalin (kô-shä'lĭn).........Pol.	54·12 N	16·10 E
120	Köszeg (kû'sĕg)...........Hung.	47·21 N	16·32 E
142	Kota.....................India	25·17 N	75·49 E
154	Kotabaru.................Indon.	3·22 S	116·15 E
155	Kotabaru (Hollandia) (kō'tä-bä'rōō) (hôl-län'dĭ-ä) W. Irian	2·30 S	140·45 E
154	Kota Bharu (kō'tä bä'rōō)..Mala.	6·15 N	102·23 E
166	Kota Kota (kō-tȧ kō-tȧ)....Nya.	12·52 S	34·16 E
139	Kota Tinggi Mala. (Singapore In.)	1·43 N	103·54 E
127	Kotel (kō-tĕl')..............Bul.	42·54 N	26 28 E
132	Kotel'nich (kô-tyĕl'nēch).Sov. Un.	58·15 N	48·20 E
135	Kotel'nyy (I.) (kô-tyĕl'nê) Sov. Un.	74·51 N	134·09 E
143	Kothapur.................India	16·48 N	74·15 E
119	Kotka (kŏt'kȧ)..............Fin.	60·28 N	26·56 E
132	Kotlas (kôt'lȧs).........Sov. Un.	61·10 N	46·50 E
136	Kotlin, Ostrov (I.) (ôs-trôf' kôt'lĭn) Sov. Un. (Leningrad In.)	60·02 N	29·49 E
127	Kotor (kō'tôr)............Yugo.	42·26 N	18·48 E
128	Kotorosl' (R.) (kô-tô'rôsl) Sov. Un.	57·18 N	39·08 E
126	Kotor Varoš (kō'tôr vä'rôsh).Yugo.	44·37 N	17·23 E
129	Kotovsk (kô-tôfsk').....Sov. Un.	47·49 N	29·31 E
148	Kotse (hŏ'zhē)............China	35·13 N	115·28 E
165	Kotto R..........Cen. Afr. Rep.	5·17 N	22·04 E
135	Kotuy (R.) (kô-tōō')....Sov. Un.	71·00 N	103·15 E
64	Kotzebue (kôt'sē-bōō).....Alaska	66·48 N	162·42 W
64	Kotzebue Sd.............Alaska	67·00 N	164·28 W
165	Kouandé (kwän-dā') Cen. Afr. Rep.	6·08 N	14·32 E
164	Koudougou (kōō-dōō'gōō) Upper Volta	12·02 N	2·15 W
164	Koulikoro (kōō-lê-kō'rô).....Mali	13·00 N	7·29 W
166	Kouilou (R.)..............Con. B.	4·10 S	11·45 E
164	Koumbia (kōōm'bĭ-ä)........Gui.	11·35 N	13·01 W
164	Koundé (kōōn-dā').....Dahomey	10·19 N	1·42 E
134	Kounradskiy (kŭ-ōōn-rät'skē) Sov. Un.	47·25 N	75·10 E
164	Kouroussa (kōō-rōō'sä)......Gui.	10·43 N	9·59 W
165	Koussi, Emi (Mt.) (ā'mê kōō-sē') Chad	19·56 N	18·34 E
164	Koutiala (kōō-tê-ä'lä).......Mali	12·29 N	5·29 W
119	Kouvola (kō'ōō-vô-lä).......Fin.	60·51 N	26·40 E
132	Kovda (L.) (kôv'dȧ).....Sov. Un.	66·45 N	32·00 E
121	Kovel' (kō'vĕl).........Sov. Un.	51·13 N	24·45 E
	Kovno, see Kaunas		
128	Kovrov (kôv-rôf').......Sov. Un.	56·23 N	41·21 E
	Kowie, see Port Alfred		
151	Kowloon (kō'lōōn')...Hong Kong	22·28 N	114·20 E
148	Koyang (gōōŭ'yăng).......China	33·32 N	116·10 E
127	Koynare...................Bul.	43·23 N	24·07 E
64	Koyuk (kô-yōōk').........Alaska	65·00 N	161·18 W
64	Koyukuk (R.) (kô-yōō'kōōk) Alaska	66·25 N	153·50 W
127	Kozáni....................Grc.	40·16 N	21·51 E
129	Kozelets (kôzĕ-lyĕts)....Sov. Un.	50·53 N	31·07 E
121	Kozience (kô-zyĕ-nē'tsĕ).....Pol.	51·34 N	21·35 E
121	Koźle (kôzh'lĕ)..............Pol.	50·19 N	18·10 E
127	Kozloduy (kŭz'lô-dwĕ).......Bul.	43·45 N	23·42 E
153	Kōzu (I.) (kō'zōō)..........Jap.	34·16 N	139·03 E
154	Kra, Isth. of..............Thai.	9·30 S	99·45 E
167	Kraai (R.) (krä'ê) S. Afr. (Natal In.)	30·50 S	27·03 E
111	Krabbendijke Neth. (Amsterdam In.)	51·26 N	4·05 E
118	Kragerö (krä'gĕr-û).........Nor.	58·53 N	9·21 E
127	Kragujevac (krä'gōō'yĕ-väts) Yugo.	44·01 N	20·55 E
121	Kraków (krä'kōōf)..........Pol.	50·05 N	20·00 E
127	Kraljevo (kräl'ye-vô)......Yugo.	43·39 N	20·48 E
129	Kramatorsk (krȧ-mä'tôrsk) Sov. Un.	48·43 N	37·32 E
118	Kramfors (kräm'fôrs).......Swe.	62·54 N	17·49 E
126	Kranj (krän')..............Yugo.	46·16 N	14·23 E
167	Kranskop (kränz'kŏp) S. Afr. (Natal In.)	28·57 S	30·54 E
128	Krāslava (kräs'lä-vä)....Sov. Un.	55·53 N	27·12 E
120	Kraslice (kräs'lê-tsĕ).......Czech.	50·19 N	12·30 E
136	Krasnaya Gorka (kräs'nȧ-yȧ gôr'kȧ).Sov. Un. (Urals In.)	55·13 N	56·43 E
133	Krasnaya Sloboda.......Sov. Un.	43·20 N	44·30 E
121	Kraśnik (kräsh'nĭk).........Pol.	50·53 N	22·15 E
136	Krasnoarmeysk (kräs'nô-ȧr-maśk') Sov. Un. (Moscow In.)	56·06 N	38·09 E
129	Krasnoarmeyskoye.......Sov. Un.	48·19 N	37·04 E
129	Krasnodar (kräs'nô-dȧr).Sov. Un.	45·03 N	38·55 E
129	Krasnodarskiy (Oblast) Province (krȧs-nô-där'skĭ ôb'lȧst) Sov. Un.	47·28 N	38·13 E
136	Krasnogorskiy (kräs-nô-gôr'skĭ) Sov. Un. (Urals In.)	54·36 N	61·25 E
129	Krasnograd (kräs'nô-grät) Sov. Un.	49·23 N	35·26 E
136	Krasnogvardeyskiy (krȧ'sno-gvăr-dzyĕ ês-kēē) Sov. Un. (Urals In.)	57·17 N	62·05 E
132	Krasnokamsk (kräs-nô-kämsk') Sov. Un.	58·00 N	55·45 E
129	Krasnokutsk (krȧs-nô-kōōtsk') Sov. Un.	50·03 N	35·05 E
129	Krasnosel'ye (kräs'nô-sĕl'yĕ) Sov. Un.	48·44 N	32·24 E
132	Krasnoslobodsk (kräs'nô-slôbôtsk') Sov. Un.	54·20 N	43·50 E
136	Krasnotur'insk (krŭs-nŭ-tōō-rensk') Sov. Un. (Urals In.)	59·47 N	60·15 E
136	Krasnoufimsk (krŭs-nŭ-ōō-fēmsk') Sov. Un. (Urals In.)	56·38 N	57·46 E
136	Krasnoural'sk (kräs'nô-ōō-rälsk') Sov. Un. (Urals In.)	58·21 N	60·05 E
136	Krasnousol'skiy (kräs-nô-ōō-sôl'skĭ) Sov. Un. (Urals In.)	53·53 N	56·30 E
132	Krasnovishersk (kräs-nô-vêshersk').Sov. Un.	60·22 N	57·20 E
133	Krasnovodsk (kräs-nô-vôtsk') Sov. Un.	40·00 N	52.50 E
134	Krasnoyarsk (kräs-nô-yȧrsk') Sov. Un.	56·13 N	93·12 E
136	Krasnoye Selo (kräs'nŭ-yŭ sȧ'lō) Sov. Un. (Leningrad In.)	59·44 N	30·06 E
128	Krasny Kholm (kräs'nê kôlm) Sov. Un.	58·03 N	37·11 E
121	Krasnystaw (kräs-nê-stȧf')...Pol.	50·59 N	23·11 E
136	Krasnyy Bor (kräs'nê bôr) Sov. Un. (Leningrad In.)	59·41 N	30·40 E
136	Krasnyy Klyuch (kräs'nê klyûch') Sov. Un. (Urals In.)	55·24 N	56·43 E
133	Krasnyy Kut (krȧs-nê kōōt') Sov. Un.	50·50 N	47·00 E
154	Kratie (krȧ-tyā')..........Camb.	12·28 N	106·06 E
136	Kratovo (krȧ'tô-vô) Sov. Un. (Moscow In.)	55·35 N	38·10 E
127	Kratovo (krȧ'tô-vô)........Yugo.	42·04 N	22·12 E
123	Krefeld (krā'fĕlt).Ger. (Ruhr In.)	51·20 N	6·34 E
129	Kremenchug (krĕm'ĕn-chōōgh') Sov. Un.	49·04 N	33·26 E
129	Kremenchugskoye (Res.) (krĕm-ĕn-chōōgh'skô-ye) Sov. Un.	49·20 N	32·45 E
121	Kremenets (krĕ-mĕn-yĕts') Sov. Un.	50·06 N	25·43 E
111	Kremmen (krĕ'mĕn) Ger. (Berlin In.)	52·45 N	13·02 E
111	Krempe (krĕm'pĕ) Ger. (Hamburg In.)	53·50 N	9·29 E
120	Krems (krĕms).............Aus.	48·25 N	15·36 E
119	Krestsy................Sov. Un.	58·18 N	32·26 E
128	Kresttsy (krȧst'sê)......Sov. Un.	58·16 N	32·25 E
119	Kretinga (krĕ-tĭŋ'gȧ).....Sov. Un.	55·55 N	21·17 E
164	Kribi (krē'bê)..............Cam.	3·03 N	9·58 E
128	Krichëv (krē'chôf)......Sov. Un.	53·44 N	31·39 E
152	Krillon, Mys (Pt.) (mĭs krĭl' ôn) Sov. Un.	45·58 N	142·00 E
111	Krimpenald Ijssel Neth. (Amsterdam In.)	51·55 N	4·34 E
142	Krishnagar................India	23·29 N	88·33 E
118	Kristiansand (krĭs-tyȧn-sän'').Nor.	58·09 N	7·59 E
118	Kristianstad (krĭs-tyȧn-städ').Swe.	56·02 N	14·09 E
118	Kristiansund (krĭs-tyȧn-sōōn'') Nor.	63·07 N	7·49 E
118	Kristinehamn (krês-tē'nĕ-häm') Swe.	59·20 N	14·05 E
119	Kristinestad (krĭs-tē'nĕ-städh).Fin.	62·16 N	21·28 E
127	Kriva-Palanka (krē-vȧ-pȧ-läŋ'kȧ) Yugo.	42·12 N	22·21 E
129	Krivoy Rog (krê-voi' rôgh') Sov. Un.	47·54 N	33·22 E
129	Krivoye Ozero..........Sov. Un.	47·57 N	30·21 E
126	Križevci (krē'zhĕv-tsĭ).....Yugo.	46·02 N	16·30 E
126	Krk (I.) (k'rk)............Yugo.	45·06 N	14·33 E
121	Krnov (k'r'nôf)...........Czech.	50·05 N	17·41 E
118	Kröderen (krû'dĕ-rĕn).......Nor.	60·07 N	9·49 E
129	Krolevets (krô-lĕ'vyĕts)..Sov. Un.	51·33 N	33·21 E
121	Kroměříž (krô'myĕr-zhēzh).Czech.	49·18 N	17·23 E
128	Kromy (krô'mê).........Sov. Un.	52·44 N	35·41 E
135	Kronotskiy, Mys (C.) (krô'nôt'skĭ-ê).Sov. Un.	54·58 N	163·15 E
136	Kronshtadt (krōn'shtät) Sov. Un. (Leningrad In.)	59·59 N	29·47 E
168	Kroonstad (krōn'shtät)....S. Afr. (Johannesburg & Pretoria In.)	27·40 S	27·15 E
133	Kropotkin (krȧ-pôt'kĭn).Sov. Un.	45·25 N	40·30 E
121	Krosno (krôs'nô)............Pol.	49·41 N	21·46 E
121	Krotoszyn (krō-tō'shĭn).......Pol.	51·41 N	17·25 E
126	Krško (k'rsh'kô)...........Yugo.	45·58 N	15·30 E
166	Kruger Natl. Park (krōō'gĕr) (krü'gĕr).S. Afr.	23·22 S	30·18 E
167	Krugersdorp (krōō'gĕrz-dôrp) S. Afr. (Johannesburg & Pretoria In.)	26·06 S	27·46 E
127	Krujë (krōō'yȧ)..............Alb.	41·32 N	19·49 E
154	Krung Thep (Bangkok).....Thai.	13·50 N	100·29 E
127	Kruševac (krōō'shĕ-väts)...Yugo.	43·34 N	21·21 E
127	Krušovo (krōō'shô-vô)....Yugo.	41·20 N	21·15 E
119	Krustpils (krōōst'pêls)...Sov. Un.	56·31 N	25·51 E

ăt; finăl; rāte; senâte; ärm; ȧsk; sofȧ; fâre; ch-choose; dh-as th in other; bē; êvent; bĕt; recĕnt; cratẽr; g-go; gh-guttural g; bĭt; ĭ-short neutral; rīde; K-guttural k as ch in German ich;

PRONOUNCING INDEX
Krylbo–La Cresenta 225

Page Name Pronunciation Region Lat. °′ Long. °′
118 Krylbo (krŭl'bô) Swe. 60·07 N 16·14 E
129 Krymskaya (krĭm'skȧ-yȧ) Sov. Un. 44·58 N 38·01 E
129 Krymskaya (Oblast) Sov. Un. 45·08 N 34·05 E
129 Krymskiye Gory (Mts.) (krēm'skĭ-yĕ gô'rĭ) Sov. Un. 65·21 N 117·13 E
129 Krymskiy (Crimea) Poluostrov (Pen.) (krēm'skĭ pô-lōō-ôs'trôf) Sov. Un. 45·18 N 33·30 E
121 Krynki (krĭn'kė) Pol. 53·15 N 23·47 E
129 Kryukov (k'r'yōō-kôf') Sov. Un. 49·02 N 33·26 E
139 Ktima Cyprus (Palestine In.) 34·46 N 32·27 E
139 Kuala Klawang Mala. (Singapore In.) 2·57 N 102·04 E
139 Kuala Lumpur (kwä'lä lōōm-pōōr') Mala. (Singapore In.) 3·08 N 101·42 E
150 Kuan (kōō'än'). China (Peking In.) 39·25 N 116·18 E
148 Kuan (R.) (gōōäɴ) China 31·56 N 115·19 E
151 Kuangchang China 25·50 N 116·18 E
149 Kuangchou (Canton) (kăn'tŏn') China (Canton In.) 23·07 N 113·15 E
151 Kuangchou Wan (B.) China 20·40 N 111·00 E
Kuanghsi, see Kwangsi Chuang
148 Kuangjao (gōōäɴg'rou) China 37·04 N 118·24 E
148 Kuanglu Tao (I.) (gōōäng'lōō dou) China 39·13 N 122·21 E
148 Kuangp'ing (gōōäɴg'pĭng) China 36·30 N 114·57 E
148 Kuangshan (gōōäɴg'shan) China 32·02 N 114·53 E
146 Kuangsi Chuang (Aut. Reg.) (gōōäɴg'sē jwäng) China 23·52 N 108·30 E
151 Kuangte China 30·40 N 119·20 E
147 Kuangtung (Kwangtung) (Prov.) China 23·49 N 113·02 E
148 Kuanhsien (gōōäɴ'sĭäɴ) China 36·30 N 115·28 E
148 Kuanhu (gōōäɴ'hoo) China 34·26 N 117·59 E
148 Kuankü Shan (Mts.) (gōōäɴ'gōō shäɴ) China 35·20 N 117·27 E
148 Kuant'ao (gōōäɴ'tou) China 36·39 N 115·25 E
150 Kuantien China 40·40 N 24·50 E
148 Kuanyün (gōōän'yün) China 34·28 N 119·16 E
133 Kuba (kōō'bȧ) Sov. Un. 41·05 N 48·30 E
129 Kuban' (R.) (kōō-bȧn'') Sov. Un. 45·10 N 37·55 E
133 Kuban (R.) Sov. Un. 45·20 N 40·05 E
115 Kuban R. Sov. Un 45·14 N 38·20 E
132 Kubenskoye (L.) Sov. Un. 59·40 N 39·40 E
Kucha, see Kuch'e
146 Kuch'e (Kucha) (kōō'chĕ') (kō'chä') China 41·34 N 82·44 E
148 Kuchen (kōō'jĕn) China 33·20 N 117·18 E
148 Kuch'eng (kōō'chĕng') China 39·09 N 115·43 E
154 Kuching (kōō'chĭng) Mala. 1·30 N 110·26 E
153 Kuchinoerabo (I.) (kōō'chė nō ĕr'ȧ-bō) Jap. 30·31 N 129·53 E
153 Kudamatsu (kōō'dȧ-mä'tsōō) Jap. 34·00 N 131·51 E
154 Kudat (kōō-dät') Mala. 6·56 N 116·48 E
119 Kudirkos Naumiestis (kōōdĭr-kôs nä'ōō-mē'stĭs) Sov. Un. 54·51 N 23·00 E
134 Kudymkar (kōō-dĭm-kär') Sov. Un. 58·43 N 54·52 E
148 Kuei (R.) (kōōā) China 33·30 N 116·56 E
151 Kueichih China 30·35 N 117·28 E
149 Kueichou China (Canton In.) 22·46 N 113·15 E
146 Kueichou (Kweichow) (Prov.) China 27·03 N 106·31 E
151 Kueilin China 25·18 N 110·22 E
150 Kueisui China 41·05 N 111·50 E
151 Kueiyang China 26·45 N 107·00 E
146 K'uerhlo China 41·37 N 86·03 E
120 Kufstein (kōōf'shtīn) Aus. 47·34 N 12·11 E
111 Kuhstedt (kōō'shtĕt) Ger. (Hamburg In.) 53·23 N 8·58 E
Kuibyshev, see Kuybyshev
166 Kuilsrivier S. Afr. (Cape Town In.) 33·56 S 18·41 E
153 Kujū-san (Mt.) (kōō'jōō-sän') Jap. 33·07 N 131·14 E
165 Kukawa (kōō-kä'wä) Nig. 12·55 N 13·35 E
127 Kukës (kōō'kĕs) Alb. 42·03 N 20·25 E
127 Kula (kōō'lȧ) Bul. 43·52 N 23·13 E
133 Kula Tur. 38·32 N 28·30 E
142 Kula Kangri Mt. China 33·11 N 90·36 E
135 Kular, Khrebet (Mts.) (kōō-lär') Sov. Un. 69·00 N 131·45 E
119 Kuldīga (kōōl'dē-gȧ) Sov. Un. 56·59 N 21·59 E
132 Kulebaki (kōō-lĕ-bȧk'ĭ) Sov. Un. 55·22 N 42·30 E
120 Kulmbach (klōōlm'bäк) Ger. 50·07 N 11·28 E
126 Kulpa (R.) (kōōl'pȧ) Yugo. 45·32 N 14·50 E
134 Kulunda (kōō-lōōn'dȧ) Sov. Un. 52·38 N 74·00 E
134 Kulundinskoye (L.) Sov. Un. 52·45 N 77·18 E
152 Kum (R.) (kōōm) Kor. 36·50 N 127·30 E
133 Kuma (R.) (kōō'mä) Sov. Un. 44·50 N 45·10 E
153 Kumamoto (kōō'mä-mō'tō) Jap. 32·49 N 130·40 E
153 Kumano-Nada (Sea) (kōō-mä'nō nä-dä) Jap. 34·03 N 136·36 E
127 Kumanovo (kōō-mä'nō-vô) Yugo. 42·10 N 21·41 E
164 Kumasi (kōō-mä'sė) Ghana 6·45 N 1·39 W
164 Kumba (kōōm'bȧ) Cam. 4·41 N 9·26 E
143 Kumbakonam (kōōm'bŭ-kō'nŭm) India 10·59 N 79·25 E
127 Kumkale Tur. 39·59 N 26·10 E
143 Kumta India 14·19 N 75·28 E
136 Kunashak (kŭ-nä'shȧk) Sov. Un. (Urals In.) 55·43 N 61·35 E
152 Kunashir (I.) (kōō-nŭ-shēr') Sov. Un. 44·40 N 145·45 E
148 Kunch'eng Hu (L.) (kōōɴ'chĕng hoo) China 31·36 N 120·57 E
128 Kunda (kōō'dȧ) Sov. Un. 59·30 N 26·28 E
163 Kundelungu, Plateau des (Plat.) Bel. Congo' 9·00 S 25·30 E
136 Kundravy (kōōn'drȧ-vĭ) Sov. Un. (Urals In.) 54·50 N 60·14 E
139 Kundur (I.) Indon. (Singapore In.) 0·49 N 103·20 E
Kunene (R.), see Cunene
118 Kungälv (kŭng'ĕlf) Swe. 57·53 N 12·01 E
136 Kungur (kōōn-gōōr') Sov. Un. (Urals In.) 57·27 N 56·53 E
103 Kungrad (kōōn-grät') Sov. Un. 42·59 N 59·00 E
118 Kungsbacka (kŭngs'bä-kȧ) Swe. 57·31 N 12·04 E
142 Kungsherya China 31·33 N 84·38 E
146 K'un Lun Shan (Mts.) (kōōn'lōōn' shän') China 35·26 N 83·09 E
151 K'unming (Yünnanfu) (kōōn'mĭng') (yün'nän'fōō') China 25·10 N 102·50 E
152 Kunsan (kōōn'sän') Kor. 35·54 N 126·46 E
149 K'unshan (kōōn'shän') China (Shanghai In.) 31·23 N 120·57 E
136 Kuntsëvo (kōōn-tsyô'vô) Sov. Un. (Moscow In.) 55·43 N 37·27 E
136 Kun'ya Sov. Un. (Urals In.) 58·42 N 56·47 E
128 Kun'ya (R.) (kōōn'yȧ) Sov. Un. 56·45 N 30·53 E
112 Kuopio (kōō-ô'pē-ŏ) Fin. 62·48 N 28·30 E
155 Kupang Indon. 10·14 S 123·37 E
134 Kupino (kōō-pĭ'nô) Sov. Un. 54·00 N 77·47 E
119 Kupiškis (kōō-pĭsh'kĭs) Sov. Un. 55·50 N 24·55 E
129 Kupyansk (kōōp-yänsk') Sov. Un. 49·44 N 37·38 E
133 Kura (R.) (kōō'rä) Sov. Un. 41·10 N 45·40 E
146 Kurak Darya (R.) China 41·09 N 87·46 E
153 Kurashiki (kōō'rä-shē'kė) Jap. 34·37 N 133·44 E
153 Kurayoshi (kōō'rȧ-yō'shė) Jap. 35·25 N 133·49 E
133 Kurdistan (Reg.) (kûrd'ĭ-stăn) Tur.-Iran 37·40 N 43·30 E
127 Kŭrdzhali Bul. 41·39 N 25·21 E
153 Kure (kōō'rĕ) Jap. 34·17 N 132·35 E
119 Kuressaare (kōō'rĕ-sä'rĕ) Sov. Un. 58·15 N 22·26 E
134 Kurgan (kōōr-găn') Sov. Un. 55·28 N 65·14 E
134 Kurgan Tyube (kōōr-gän' tyōō'bĕ) Sov. Un. 38·00 N 68·49 E
144 Kuria Muria Is. (Br.) (kōō-rē-ȧ mōō'rē-ȧ) Aden 17·27 N 56·02 E
153 Kurihama (kōō-rē-hä'mä) Jap. (Tōkyō In.) 35·14 N 139·42 E
135 Kuril Is. (kōō'rĭl) Sov. Un. 46·20 N 149·30 E
119 Kurisches Haff (Bay) Sov. Un. 55·10 N 21·08 E
165 Kurmuk (kōōr'mōōk) Sud. 10·40 N 34·13 E
143 Kurnool (kōōr-nōōl') India 16·00 N 78·04 E
153 Kuro (I.) (kōō'rô) Jap. 30·49 N 129·56 E
161 Kurrajong Austl. (Sydney In.) 33·33 S 150·40 E
119 Kuršenai (kōōr'shȧ-nī) Sov. Un. 56·01 N 22·56 E
129 Kursk (kōōrsk) Sov. Un. 51·44 N 36·08 E
129 Kursk (Oblast) (kōōrsk) Sov. Un. 51·30 N 35·13 E
127 Kuršumlija (kōōr'shōōm'lĭ-yȧ) Yugo. 43·08 N 21·18 E
166 Kuruman (kōō-rōō-mȧn') S. Afr. 27·25 S 23·30 E
153 Kurume (kōō'rōō-mĕ) Jap. 33·20 N 130·26 E
153 Kururi (kōō'rōō-rē) Jap. (Tōkyō In.) 35·17 N 140·05 E
165 Kuruskū (kōō-rōōs-kōō') U. A. R. 22·33 N 32·24 E
136 Kusa (kōō'sȧ) Sov. Un. (Urals In.) 55·19 N 59·27 E
129 Kushchëvskaya Sov. Un. 46·34 N 39·40 E
134 Kushevat Sov. Un. 65·05 N 65·28 E
148 Kushih (gōō'sĕĭ) China 32·11 N 115·39 E
153 Kushikino (kōō'shĭ-kē'nō) Jap. 31·44 N 130·19 E
153 Kushimoto (kōō'shĭ-mō'tō) Jap. 33·29 N 135·47 E
152 Kushiro (kōō'shē-rō) Jap. 43·00 N 144·22 E
134 Kush-Murun (L.) (kōōsh-mōō-rōōn') Sov. Un. 52·30 N 64·15 E
133 Kushum (R.) (kōō-shōōm') Sov. Un. 50·30 N 50·40 E
136 Kushva (kōōsh'vȧ) Sov. Un. (Urals In.) 58·18 N 59·51 E
64 Kuskokwim (R.) Alaska 61·32 N 160·36 W
64 Kuskokwim B. (kŭs'kō-kwĭm) Alaska 59·25 N 163·14 W
64 Kuskokwim Mts. Alaska 62·08 N 158·00 W
64 Kuskovak (kŭs-kō'văk) Alaska 60·10 N 162·50 W
134 Kustanay (kōōs-tȧ-nī') Sov. Un. 53·10 N 63·39 E
133 Kutahya (kû-tä'hyȧ) Tur. 39·20 N 29·50 E
133 Kutaisi (kōō-tŭ-ē'sē) Sov. Un. 42·15 N 42·40 E
154 Kutaradja Indon. 5·30 N 95·20 E
142 Kutch, Gulf of India 22·45 N 68·33 E
142 Kutch, Rann of (Swp.) India 23·59 N 69·13 E
111 Kutenholz (kōō'tĕn-hōlts) Ger. (Hamburg In.) 53·29 N 9·20 E
136 Kutim (kōō'tĭm) Sov. Un. (Urals In.) 60·22 N 58·51 E
126 Kutina (kōō'tē-nȧ) Yugo. 45·29 N 16·48 E
121 Kutno (kōōt'nô) Pol. 52·14 N 19·22 E
132 Kutno (L.) Sov. Un. 65·15 N 31·30 E
134 Kutulik (kōō tōō'lyĭk) Sov. Un. 53·12 N 102·51 E
121 Kuty (kōō'tė) Sov. Un. 48·16 N 25·12 E
112 Kuusamo (kōō'sȧ-mô) Fin. 65·59 N 29·10 E
128 Kuvshinovo (kōōv-shē'nô-vô) Sov. Un. 57·01 N 34·09 E
Kuwait, see Al Kuwayt
138 Kuwait Asia 29·00 N 48·45 E
153 Kuwana (kōō'wȧ-nȧ) Jap. 35·02 N 136·40 E
132 Kuybyshev (Kuibyshev) (kōō'ē-bĭ-shĕf) Sov. Un. 53·10 N 50·05 E
134 Kuybyshev Sov. Un. 55·45 N 76·45 E
132 Kuybyshevskoye (Res.) Sov. Un. 53·40 N 49·00 E
148 Kuyeh (gōō'yĕ) China 39·46 N 118·23 E
133 Kuzey Anadolu Dağ'ari (Mts.) Tur. 41·20 N 34·30 E
133 Kuznetsk (kōōz-nyĕtsk') Sov. Un. 53·00 N 46·30 E
134 Kuznetsk Basin Sov. Un. 57·15 N 86·15 E
136 Kuznetsovka (kōōz-nyĕt'sôf-kȧ) Sov. Un. (Urals In.) 54·41 N 56·40 E
128 Kuznetsovo (kōōz-nyĕt-sô'vô) Sov. Un. 56·39 N 36·55 E
126 Kvarnerski Zaliv (B.) (kvär'nĕr-skė' zä'lĕv) Yugo. 44·41 N 14·05 E
64 Kvichak (vĭc'-hăk) Alaska 59·00 N 156·48 W
166 Kwango (R.) (kwäng'ō') Ang. 8·30 S 18·00 E
Kwangtung, see Kuangtung
Kweichow, see Kueichou
Kweitun, see Wusu
166 Kwenge (R.) (kwĕŋ'gĕ) Con. L. 6·45 S 18·34 E
121 Kwidzyń (kvē'dzĭn') Pol. 53·45 N 18·56 E
166 Kwilu (R.) (kwē'lōō) Con. L. 7·00 S 19·20 E
164 Kwitta (kwĭt'ȧ) Ghana 6·00 N 1·00 E
135 Kyakhta (kyäк'ta) Sov. Un. 51·00 N 107·30 E
142 Kyang Tsho (L.) China 30·37 N 88·33 E
142 Kyayisu (R.) India 38·05 N 74·36 E
146 Kyaukpyu (chouk'pyoo') Bur. 19·19 N 93·33 E
119 Kybartai (kē'bär-tī') Sov. Un. 54·40 N 22·46 E
151 Ky Lam Viet. 15·48 N 108·30 E
136 Kyn (kĭn') Sov. Un. (Urals In.) 57·52 N 58·42 E
159 Kynuna (kī-nōō'nȧ) Austl. 21·30 S 142·12 E
165 Kyoga L. Ug. 1·27 N 33·51 E
153 Kyōga-Saki (C.) (kyō'gä sa'kė) Jap. 35·46 N 135·14 E
152 Kyŏngju (kyŭng'yōō) Kor. 35·48 N 129·12 E
153 Kyōtō (kyō'tō') Jap. (Ōsaka In.) 35·00 N 135·46 E
153 Kyōto (Pref.) Jap. (Ōsaka In.) 34·56 N 135·42 E
134 Kyren (kĭ-rĕn') Sov. Un. 51·46 N 102·13 E
119 Kyrön (R.) (kü'rô) Fin. 63·03 N 22·20 E
136 Kyrya (kĕr'yȧ) Sov. Un. (Urals In.) 59·18 N 59·03 E
136 Kyshtym (kĭsh-tĭm') Sov. Un. (Urals In.) 55·43 N 60·33 E
136 Kytlym (kĭt'lĭm) Sov. Un. (Urals In.) 59·30 N 59·15 E
153 Kyūshū (I.) (kyōō'shōō') Jap. 32·27 N 131·03 E
127 Kyustendil (kyōōs-tĕn-dĭl') Bul. 42·16 N 22·39 E
134 Kyzyl (kĭ zĭl) Sov. Un. 51·37 N 93·38 E
103 Kyzylkum (Des.) (kĭ zĭl kōōm) Sov. Un. 42·47 N 64·45 E
146 Kyzylsu (R.) China 39·26 N 74·30 E
134 Kzyl-Orda (kzĕl-ôr'dȧ) Sov. Un. 44·58 N 65·45 E
120 Laa Aus. 48·42 N 16·23 E
124 La Almunia de Doña Godina (lä'äl-mōōn'yä dä dō nyä gō-dē'nä) Sp. 41·29 N 1·22 W
98 La Asunción (lä ä-sōōn-syōn') Ven. 11·02 N 63·57 W
100 La Banda (lä bän'dä) Arg. 27·48 S 64·12 W
90 La Barca (lä bär'kȧ) Mex. 20·17 N 102·33 W
164 Labé (lȧ-bā') Gui. 11·15 N 12·16 W
120 Labe (Elbe) R. (lȧ'bĕ) (ĕl'bĕ) Czech. 50·05 N 15·20 E
86 Laberge (R.) (lȧ-bĕrzh') Can. 61·08 N 136·42 W
94 Laberinto de las Doce Leguas (Is.) (lä-bȧ-rēn tô dā läs dō'sȧ lā'gwäs) Cuba 20·40 N 78·35 W
133 Labinsk Sov. Un. 44·30 N 40·40 E
139 Labis (läb'ĭs) Mala. (Singapore In.) 2·23 N 103·01 E
125 La Bisbal (lä bēs-bäl') Sp. 41·55 N 3·00 E
155 Labo (lä'bô) Phil. (Manila In.) 13·39 N 121·14 E
155 Labo Phil. (Manila In.) 14·11 N 122·49 E
155 Labo, Mt. Phil. (Manila In.) 14·00 N 122·47 E
85 L'Abord-a-Plouffe (lȧ-bôr'dȧ-plōōf) Can. (Montreal In.) 45·32 N 73·45 W
122 Labouheyre (lȧ-bōō-âr') Fr. 44·14 N 0·58 W
100 Laboulaye (lä-bô'ōō-lä-yĕ) Arg. 34·01 S 63·10 W
87 Labrador (Reg.) (lăb'rȧ-dôr) Can. 53·05 N 63·30 W
98 Lábrea (lä-brā'ä) Braz. 7·28 S 64·39 W
155 Labuan (lä-bwä'n) Phil. (Manila In.) 13·43 N 120·07 E
154 Labuan (I.) (lȧ-bōō-än') Mala. 5·28 N 115·11 E
155 Labuha Indon. 0·43 S 127·35 E
85 L'Acadie (lȧ-kȧ-dē') Can. (Montreal In.) 45·18 N 73·22 W
85 L'Acadie, Riviére (rê-vyâr') Can. (Montreal In.) 45·24 N 73·21 W
101 La Calera (lä-kä-lĕ-rä) Chile (Santiago In.) 32·47 S 71·11 W
98 La Calera Col. (In.) 4·43 N 73·58 W
113 La Calle (lȧ kȧl') Alg. 36·52 N 8·23 E
74 La Canada (lä kän-yä'dä) Calif. (Los Angeles In.) 34·13 N 118·12 W
91 Lacantum (R.) (lä-kän-tōō'm) Mex. 16·13 N 90·52 W
124 La Carolina (lä kä-rô-lē'nä) Sp. 38·16 N 3·48 W
91 La Catedral, Cerro (Mtn.) (sĕ'r-rô-lä-kä-tĕ-drä'l) Mex. (Mexico City In.) 19·32 N 99·31 W
82 Lac-au-Saumon Can. 48·24 N 67·23 W
85 Lac-Beauport (läk-bō-pōr') Can. (Quebec In.) 46·58 N 71·17 W
143 Laccadive Is. (lăk'ȧ-dīv) India 11·00 N 73·02 E
142 Laccadive Sea Asia 9·10 N 75·17 E
71 Lac Court Oreille Ind. Res. (lȧk kôrt-ô-rĕl) (lȧk kōōr tô-rā'y') Wis. 46·04 N 91·18 W
71 Lac du Flambeau Ind. Res. Wis. 46·12 N 89·50 W
92 La Ceiba (lȧ sēbä) Hond. 15·45 N 86·52 W
98 La Ceja (lä-sĕ-кä) Col. (In.) 6·02 N 75·25 W
87 Lac Frontiere Can. 46·41 N 70·04 W
132 Lacha (L.) (lȧ'chä) Sov. Un. 61·15 N 39·05 E
120 La Chaux de Fonds (lȧ shō-dē-fôɴ') Switz. 47·07 N 6·47 E
85 L'Achigan, R. (lȧ-shē-gäɴ) Can. (Montreal In.) 45·49 N 73·48 W
85 Lachine (lȧ-shēn') Can. (Montreal In.) 45·26 N 73·40 W
160 Lachlan (R.) (läk'lăn) Austl. 33·54 S 145·15 E
88 La Chorrera (láchōr-rā'rä) Pan. (Panama Canal In.) 8·54 N 79·47 W
85 Lachute (lȧ-shōōt') Can. (Montreal In.) 45·39 N 74·20 W
123 La Ciotat (lä syô-tȧ') Fr. 43·13 N 5·35 E
75 Lackawanna (lak-ȧ-wŏn'ȧ) N. Y. (Buffalo In.) 42·49 N 78·50 W
86 Lac la Biche Can. 54·46 N 112·04 W
82 Lac Megantic Can. 45·34 N 70·53 W
La Columna, see Bolivar
86 Lacombe Can. 52·29 N 113·41 W
91 La Concordia (lä-kōn-kô'r-dyä) Mex. 16·07 N 92·40 W
81 Laconia (lȧ-kō'nĭ-ȧ) N. H. 43·30 N 71·30 W
65 La Conner (lȧ kŏn'ĕr) Wash. (Seattle In.) 48·23 N 122·30 W
124 La Coruña (lä kô-rōōn'yä) Sp. 43·20 N 8·20 W
70 Lacreek (L.) (lă'krēk) S. D. 43·04 N 101·46 W
74 La Cresenta (lȧ krĕs'ĕnt-ȧ) Calif. (Los Angeles In.) 34·14 N 118·13 W

ng-sing; ŋ-baŋk; ɴ-nasalized n; nŏd; cŏmmit; ōld; ôbey; ôrder; fōōd; fŏŏt; ou-out; s-soft; sh-dish; th-thin; pūre; ůnite; ûrn; stŭd; circŭs; ü-as "y" in study; '-indeterminate vowel.

226 La Cross–Lansing PRONOUNCING INDEX

Page	Name Pronunciation Region	Lat. °′	Long. °′
72	La Cross (lȧ-krôs′) Kans.	38·30 N	99·20 W
71	La Crosse Wis.	43·48 N	91·14 W
92	La Cruz (lä-kro͞o′z) C. R.	11·05 N	85·37 W
98	La Cruz (lȧ kro͞oz′) Col.	1·37 N	77·00 W
70	Lacs, Riviere des (R.) (rē-vyĕr′ de läk) N. D.	48·30 N	101·45 W
85	Lac-St-Charles (läk-sĕn-shärl) Can. (Quebec In.)	46·55 N	71·23 W
93	La Cuesta (lä-kwĕ′s-tä) C. R.	8·32 N	82·51 W
124	La Culebra, Sierra de (Mts.) (sē-ĕ′r-rä-dĕ-lä-ko͞o-lĕ-brä) Sp.	41·52 N	6·21 W
73	La Cygne (lȧ-sēn′y′) (lȧ-sēn′) Kans.	38·20 N	94·45 W
80	Ladd (lăd) Ill.	41·25 N	89·25 W
124	La Demanda, Sierra de (Mts.) (sē-ĕ′r-rä-dĕ-lä-dĕ-mä′n-dä) Sp.	42·10 N	2·35 W
125	Ladíspoli (lä-dē′s-pô-lē) It. (Rome In.)	41·57 N	12·05 E
65	Ladner (lăd′nēr) Can. (Vancouver In.)	49·05 N	123·06 W
142	Lādnun (läd′no͞on) India	27·45 N	74·20 E
	Ladoga, Lake, see Ladozhskoye Ozero		
98	La Dorado (lä dō-rä′dä) Col. (In.)	5·28 N	74·42 W
119	Ladozhskoye Ozero (Lake Ladoga) (lä-dôsh′skô-yĕ ô′zĕ-rô) Sov. Un.	60·59 N	31·30 E
85	La Durantaye (lä dü-räN-tā′) Can. (Quebec In.)	46·51 N	70·51 W
167	Lady Frere (lā-dē frâ′r′) S. Afr. (Natal In.)	31·48 S	27·16 E
167	Lady Grey S. Afr. (Natal In.)	30·44 S	27·17 E
66	Ladysmith (lā′dĭ-smĭth) Can.	48·59 N	123·50 W
167	Ladysmith S. Afr. (Natal In.)	28·38 S	29·48 E
71	Ladysmith Wis.	45·27 N	91·07 W
155	Lae (lä′ā) N. Gui. Ter.	6·15 S	146·57 E
118	Laerdal (lâr′däl) Nor.	61·03 N	7·24 E
118	Laerdalsören (lâr′däls-û′rĕn) Nor.	61·08 N	7·26 E
118	Laesø (I.) (lâs′û) Den.	57·17 N	10·57 E
92	La Esperanza (lä ĕs-pä-rän′zä) Hond.	14·20 N	88·21 W
124	La Estrada (lä ĕs-trä′dä) Sp.	42·42 N	8·29 W
152	Lafa (lä′fä) China	43·49 N	127·19 E
122	La-Fare-les-Oliviers (lä-fär′lā-ô-lē-vyā) Fr. (Marseille In.)	43·33 N	5·12 E
78	Lafayette Ala.	32·52 N	85·25 W
65	Lafayette Calif. (San Francisco In.)	37·53 N	122·07 W
78	Lafayette (lă-fâ-yĕt′) Ga.	34·41 N	85·19 W
80	La Fayette Ind.	40·25 N	86·55 W
77	Lafayette La.	30·15 N	92·02 W
84	La Fayette R. I. (Providence In.)	41·34 N	71·29 W
123	La Ferté-Alais (lä-fĕr-tā′-ä-lā′) Fr. (Paris In.)	48·29 N	2·19 E
123	La Ferté-sous-Jouarre (lȧ fĕr-tā′so͞o-zho͞o-är′) Fr. (Paris In.)	48·56 N	3·07 E
84	Lafitte (lä-fēt′) La. (New Orleans In.)	29·45 N	90·08 W
122	La Flèche (lȧ flăsh′) Fr.	47·43 N	0·03 W
122	La Flotte (lȧ flôt′) Fr.	46·09 N	1·20 W
78	La Follette (lă-fŏl′ĕt) Tenn.	36·23 N	84·07 W
77	Lafourche, Bay. (bä-yo͞o′lȧ-fo͞orsh′) La.	29·25 N	90·15 W
99	La Gaiba (lä-gī′bä) Braz.	17·54 S	57·32 W
116	Lagan (lā′gȧn) N. Ire.	54·30 N	6·00 W
118	Lagan (R.) Swe.	56·34 N	13·25 E
112	Laganes (Pt.) Ice.	66·21 N	14·02 W
88	Lagarto, R. (lä-gä′r-tô) Pan. (Panama Canal In.)	9·08 N	80·05 W
92	Lagartos L. (lä-gä′r-tôs) Mex. (Yucatan In.)	21·32 N	88·15 W
118	Lågen (R.) (lô′ghĕn) Nor.	59·15 N	9·47 E
164	Laghouat (lä-gwät′) Alg.	33·45 N	2·49 E
123	Lagny (län-yē′) Fr. (Paris In.)	48·53 N	2·41 E
101	Lagoa da Prata (lä-gô′ä-dä-prä′tȧ) Braz. (Rio de Janeiro In.)	20·04 S	45·33 W
101	Lagoa Dourada (lȧ-gô′ä-do͞o-rä′dä) Braz. (Rio de Janeiro In.)	20·55 S	44·03 W
155	Lagonoy (lä-gô-noi′) Phil. (Manila In.)	13·44 N	123·31 E
155	Lagonoy G. Phil. (Manila In.)	13·34 N	123·46 E
164	Lagos (lä′gōs) Nig.	6·31 N	3·15 E
124	Lagos (lä′gōzh) Port.	37·08 N	8·43 W
90	Lagos de Moreno (lä′gōs dā mô-rā′nō) Mex.	21·21 N	101·55 W
122	La Grand′ Combe (lȧ gräN kaNb′) Fr.	44·12 N	4·03 E
66	La Grande (lȧ grănd′) Ore.	45·20 N	118·06 W
158	La Grange (lȧ grānj) Austl.	18·40 S	122·00 E
78	La Grange (lȧ-grānj′) Ga.	33·01 N	85·00 W
75	La Grange Ill. (Chicago In.)	41·49 N	87·53 W
80	Lagrange Ind.	41·40 N	85·25 W
80	La Grange Ky.	38·20 N	85·25 W
73	La Grange Mo.	40·04 N	91·30 W
75	Lagrange Ohio (Cleveland In.)	41·14 N	82·07 W
77	Lagrange Tex.	29·55 N	96·50 W
98	La Grita (lä grē′tä) Ven.	8.02 N	71·59 W
99	La Guaira (lä gwä′ē-rä) Ven. (In.)	10·36 N	66·54 W
124	La Guardia (lä gwär′dē-ä) Sp.	41·55 N	8·48 W
100	Laguna (lä-go͞o′nä) Braz.	28·19 S	48·42 W
94	Laguna, Cayos (Is.) (kä′yōs-lä-go͞o′nä) Cuba	22·15 N	82·45 W
155	Laguna de Bay (L.) (lä-go͞o′nä dä bä′ē) Phil. (Manila In.)	14·24 N	121·13 E
69	Laguna Ind. Res. N. Mex.	35·00 N	107·30 W
98	Lagunillas (lä-go͞o-nēl′yäs) Bol.	19·42 S	63·38 W
90	Lagunillas (lä-go͞o-nē′l-yäs) Mex.	21·34 N	99·41 W
95	La Habana (Havana) (lä-ä-bä′nä) Cuba (Havana In.)	23·08 N	82·23 W
74	La Habra (lȧ hăb′rȧ) Calif. (Los Angeles In.)	34·56 N	117·57 W
157	Lahaina (lä-hä′ē-nä) Hawaii (In.)	20·52 N	156·39 W
122	La Haye-Descartes (lȧ ȧ-dä-kärt′) Fr.	46·58 N	0·42 E
120	Lahn R. (län) Ger.	50·21 N	7·54 E
118	Laholm (lä′hôlm) Swe.	56·30 N	13·00 E
65	La Honda (lā hŏn′dă) Calif. (San Francisco In.)	37·20 N	122·16 W
142	Lahore (lä-hōr′) W. Pak.	31·39 N	74·22 E
120	Lahr (lär) Ger.	48·19 N	7·52 E
119	Lahti (lä′tē) Fin.	60·59 N	27·39 E
151	Lai, C. Viet.	17·08 N	107·30 E
148	Laian (läī′äN) China	32·27 N	118·25 E
148	Laichou Wan (B.) (läī′jō wäN) China	37·22 N	119·19 E
122	Laigle (lĕ′gl′) Fr.	48·45 N	0·37 E
151	Laipin (lī′pĭn′) China	23·42 N	109·20 E
148	Laiyang (läī′yäng) China	36·59 N	120·42 E
90	Laja, Rio de la (R.) (rē′ō-dĕ-lä-lä′kä) Mex.	20·17 N	100·57 W
94	Lajas (lä′häs) Cuba	22·25 N	80·20 W
100	Lajeado (lä-zhĕä′dô) Braz.	29·24 S	51·46 W
100	Lajes (lȧ′-zhĕs) Braz.	27·47 S	50·17 W
101	Lajinha (lä-zhē′nyä) Braz. (Rio de Janeiro In.)	20·08 S	41·36 W
68	La Jolla (lȧ hōl′yȧ) Calif. (San Diego In.)	32·51 N	117·16 W
68	La Jolla Ind. Res. Calif.	33·19 N	116·21 W
72	La Junta (lȧ ho͞on′tȧ) Colo.	37 59 N	103·35 W
168	Lak Dera (R.) (läk dā′rä) Som. (Horn of Afr. In.)	0·45 N	41·26 E
77	Lake Arthur (är′thŭr) La.	30·06 N	92·40 W
70	Lake Benton (bĕn′tŭn) Minn.	44·15 N	96·17 W
75	Lake Bluff (blŭf) Ill. (Chicago In.)	42·17 N	87·50 W
158	Lake Brown (broun) Austl.	31·03 S	118·30 E
77	Lake Charles (chärlz′) La.	30·15 N	93·14 W
79	Lake City Fla.	30·09 N	82·40 W
71	Lake City Iowa	42·14 N	94·43 W
71	Lake City Minn.	44·28 N	92·19 W
79	Lake City S. C.	33·57 N	79·45 W
71	Lake Crystal (krĭs′tȧl) Minn.	44·05 N	94·12 W
116	Lake Dist. (lāk) Eng.	54·25 N	3·20 W
74	Lake Elmo (ĕlmō) Minn. (Minneapolis, St. Paul In.)	45·00 N	92·53 W
75	Lake Forest (fŏr′ĕst) Ill. (Chicago In.)	42·16 N	87·50 W
69	Lake Fork (R.) Utah	40·30 N	110·25 W
71	Lake Geneva (jĕ-nē′vȧ) Wis.	42·36 N	88·28 W
87	Lake Harbour (här′bēr) Can.	62·43 N	69·40 W
74	Lake June (jo͞on) Tex. (Dallas, Fort Worth In.)	32·43 N	96·45 W
79	Lakeland (lāk′lănd) Fla. (In.)	28·02 N	81·58 W
78	Lakeland Ga.	31·02 N	83·02 W
74	Lakeland Minn. (Minneapolis, St. Paul In.)	44·57 N	92·47 W
71	Lake Linden (lĭn′dĕn) Mich.	47·11 N	88·26 W
71	Lake Mills (mĭlz′) Iowa	43·25 N	93·32 W
75	Lakemore (lāk-mōr) Ohio (Cleveland In.)	41·01 N	81·24 W
80	Lake Odessa Mich.	42·50 N	85·15 W
65	Lake Oswego (ŏs-wē′go) Ore. (Portland In.)	45·25 N	122·40 W
74	Lake Point Utah (Salt Lake City In.)	40·41 N	112·16 W
68	Lakeport (lāk′pōrt) Calif.	39·03 N	122·54 W
70	Lake Preston (prēs′tŭn) S. D.	44·21 N	97·23 W
77	Lake Providence (prŏv′ĭ-dĕns) La.	32·48 N	91·12 W
68	Lakeside (lāk′sīd) Calif. (San Diego In.)	32·52 N	116·55 W
166	Lakeside S. Afr. (Cape Town In.)	34·05 S	18·28 E
65	Lake Stevens Wash. (Seattle In.)	48·01 N	122·04 W
84	Lake Success (sŭk-sĕs′) N. Y. (New York In.)	40·46 N	73·43 W
74	Lakeview (lāk-vū′) Calif. (Los Angeles In.)	33·50 N	117·07 W
66	Lakeview Ore.	42·11 N	120·21 W
84	Lakeville (lāk′vĭl) N. Y. (New York In.)	41·12 N	74·16 W
67	Lake Walcott Res. Idaho	42·35 N	113·15 W
79	Lake Wales (wālz′) Fla. (In.)	27·54 N	81·35 W
72	Lakewood (lāk′wo͝od) Colo.	39·44 N	105·06 W
75	Lakewood Ohio (Cleveland In.)	41·29 N	81·48 W
81	Lakewood Pa.	40·05 N	74·10 W
65	Lakewood Wash. (Seattle In.)	47·10 N	122·31 W
65	Lakewood Wash. (Seattle In.)	48·09 N	122·13 W
74	Lakewood Village Calif. (Los Angeles In.)	33·50 N	118·09 W
79	Lake Worth (wûrth′) Fla. (In.)	26·37 N	80·04 W
74	Lake Worth Village Tex. (Dallas, Fort Worth In.)	32·49 N	97·26 W
75	Lake Zürich (tsü′rĭk) Ill. (Chicago In.)	42·11 N	88·05 W
119	Lakhdenpokh′ya (l′äk-dye′npōkyȧ) Sov. Un.	61·33 N	30·10 E
136	Lakhtinskiy (läk-tĭn′skĭ) Sov. Un. (Leningrad In.)	59·59 N	30·10 E
127	Lakonikós Kólpos (G.) Grc.	36·38 N	22·40 E
70	Lakota (lȧ-kō′tȧ) N. D.	48·04 N	98·21 W
92	La Libertad (lä lē-bĕr-tädh′) Guat.	15·31 N	91·44 W
92	La Libertad Guat. (Yucatan In.)	16·46 N	90·12 W
92	La Libertad Sal.	13·29 N	89·20 W
101	La Ligua (lä lē′gwä) Chile (Santiago In.)	32·21 S	71·13 W
124	Lalín (lä-lē′n) Sp.	42·40 N	8·05 W
124	La Línea (lä lē′nā-ä) Sp.	36·11 N	5·22 W
114	Lalla-Maghnia (lä′lä-mäg′nēä) Alg.	34·52 N	1·40 W
117	La Louviere (lȧ lo͞o-vyâr′) Bel.	50·30 N	4·10 E
90	La Luz (lä lo͞oz′) Mex.	21·04 N	101·19 W
122	La Machine (lȧ mȧ-shēn′) Fr.	46·53 N	3·26 E
82	La Malbaie (lȧ mäl-bâ′) Can.	47·39 N	70·11 W
124	La Mancha (Mts.) (lä män′chä) Sp.	38·55 N	4·20 W
72	Lamar (lȧ-mär′) Colo.	38·04 N	102·44 W
73	Lamar Mo.	37·28 N	94·15 W
126	La Marmora, Pta. (Mtn.) (lä-mä′r-mô-rä) It.	40·00 N	9·28 E
77	La Marque (lȧ-märk) Tex. (In.)	29·23 N	94·58 W
98	Lamas (lä′mȧs) Peru	6·24 S	76·41 W
122	Lamballe (läN-bäl′) Fr.	48·29 N	2·36 W
166	Lambaréné (läN-bȧ-rā-nā′) Gabon	0·48 S	10·07 E
101	Lambari (läm-bȧ′rē) Braz. (Rio de Janeiro In.)	21·58 S	45·22 W
98	Lambayeque (läm-bä-yā′kā) Peru	6·41 S	79·58 W
78	Lambert (lăm′bērt) Miss.	34·10 N	90·16 W
81	Lambertville (lăm′bērt-vĭl) N. J.	40·20 N	75·00 W
67	Lame Deer (lām dēr′) Mont.	45·36 N	106·40 W
124	Lamego (lä-mā′gō) Port.	41·07 N	7·47 W
68	La Mesa (lä mā′sä) Calif. (San Diego In.)	32·46 N	117·01 W
98	La Mesa Col. (In.)	4·38 N	74·27 W
72	Lamesa Tex.	32·44 N	101·54 W
127	Lamía (lȧ-mē′ȧ) Grc.	38·54 N	22·25 E
155	Lamon B. (lä-mōn′) Phil. (Manila In.)	14·35 N	121·52 E
101	La Mora (lä-mō′rä) Chile (Santiago In.)	32·28 S	70·56 W
70	La Moure (lȧ mo͞or′) N. D.	46·23 N	98·17 W
101	Lampa (R.) (lȧ′m-pä) Chile (Santiago In.)	33·15 S	70·55 W
76	Lampasas (lăm-păs′ȧs) Tex.	31·06 N	98·10 W
76	Lampasas R. Tex.	31·18 N	98·08 W
76	Lampazos (läm-pä′zōs) Mex.	27·03 N	100·30 W
113	Lampedusa (I.) (läm-pȧ-do͞o′sä) It.	35·29 N	12·58 E
111	Lamstedt (läm′shtĕt) Ger. (Hamburg In.)	53·38 N	9·06 E
167	Lamu (lä′mo͞o) Ken.	2·17 S	41·07 E
123	La Mure (lȧ mür′) Fr.	44·55 N	5·50 E
128	Lan′ (R.) (län′) Sov. Un.	52·38 N	27·05 E
157	Lanai (I.) (lä-nä′ē) Hawaii (In.)	20·48 N	157·06 W
142	Lanak La (P.) China	34·40 N	79·50 E
125	La Nao, Cabo de (C.) (kä′bô-dĕ-lä-nä′ō) Sp.	38·43 N	0·14 E
116	Lanark (lăn′ărk) Scot.	55·40 N	3·50 W
110	Lancashire (Co.) (lăŋ′kȧ-shĭr) Scot.	53·38 N	2·30 W
82	Lancaster (lăŋ′kăs-tēr) Can.	45·16 N	66·06 W
116	Lancaster Eng.	54·04 N	2·55 W
80	Lancaster Ky.	37·35 N	84·30 W
83	Lancaster Mass. (Boston In.)	42·28 N	71·40 W
81	Lancaster N. H.	44·25 N	71·30 W
75	Lancaster N. Y. (Buffalo In.)	42·54 N	78·42 W
80	Lancaster Ohio	39·40 N	82·35 W
81	Lancaster Pa.	40·05 N	76·20 W
79	Lancaster S. C.	34·42 N	80·45 W
74	Lancaster Tex. (Dallas, Fort Worth In.)	32·36 N	96·45 W
71	Lancaster Wis.	42·51 N	90·44 W
150	Lanchou (län′cho͞o) China	35·55 N	103·55 E
122	Lançon-Provence (läN-sôN′prô-vĕNs′) Fr. (Marseille In.)	43·35 N	5·08 E
166	Lândana (län-dä′nä) Ang.	5·15 S	12·07 E
120	Landau (län′dou) Ger.	49·13 N	8·07 E
67	Lander (lăn′dēr) Wyo.	42·49 N	108·24 W
122	Landerneau (läN-dĕr-nō′) Fr.	48·28 N	4·14 W
122	Landes (Moorland) (Plain) (läNd) Fr.	44·22 N	0·52 W
111	Landsberg (länds′bo͞orgh) Ger. (Munich In.)	48·03 N	10·53 E
116	Lands End Pt. Eng.	50·03 N	5·45 W
120	Landshut (länts′ho͞ot) Ger.	48·32 N	12·09 E
118	Landskrona (läns-kro͞o′nȧ) Swe.	55·51 N	12·47 E
78	Lanett (lȧ-nĕt′) Ala.	32·52 N	85·13 W
150	Lanfang China (Peking In.)	39·31 N	116·42 E
127	Langadhás Grc.	40·44 N	24·10 E
139	Langat (R.) Mala. (Singapore In.)	2·46 N	101·33 E
148	Langch′i (läng′che) China	31·10 N	119·09 E
151	Langchung China	31·40 N	106·05 E
85	Langdon (lăng′dŭn) Can. (Calgary In.)	50·58 N	113·40 W
74	Langdon Minn. (Minneapolis, St. Paul In.)	44·49 N	92·56 W
85	L′Ange-Gardien (läNzh gär-dyăN′) Can. (Quebec In.)	46·55 N	71·06 W
118	Lange Land Den.	54·52 N	10·46 E
65	Langeley Prairie (lăng′lĭ prâr′ĭ) Can. (Vancouver In.)	49·06 N	122·40 W
123	Langenthal Switz.	47·11 N	7·50 E
111	Langenzersdorf Aus. (Vienna In.)	48·30 N	16·22 E
118	Langesund (läng′ĕ-so͞on′) Nor.	58·59 N	9·38 E
118	Lang Fd. (läng′fyôr′) Nor.	62·40 N	7·45 E
84	Langhorne (lăng′hôrn) Pa. (Philadelphia In.)	40·10 N	74·55 W
112	Langjökoll (Gl.) (läng-yû′ko͞ol) Ice.	64·40 N	20·31 W
79	Langley (lăng′lĭ) S. C.	33·32 N	81·52 W
65	Langley Wash. (Seattle In.)	48·02 N	122·25 W
65	Langley Ind. Res. Can. (Vancouver In.)	49·12 N	122·31 W
120	Langnau (läng′nou) Switz.	46·56 N	7·46 E
122	Langogne (läN-gôn′y′) Fr.	44·43 N	3·50 E
122	Langon (läN-gôN′) Fr.	44·34 N	0·16 W
122	Langres (läN′gr′) Fr.	47·53 N	5·20 E
122	Langres, Plateaux de (Plat.) (plä-tō′dĕ-läN′grĕ) Fr.	47·39 N	5·00 E
154	Langsa (läng′sä) Indon.	4·33 N	97·52 E
154	Lang Son (läng′sŏn′) Viet.	21·52 N	106·42 E
85	Langstaff (lăng′stăf) Can. (Toronto In.)	43·51 N	79·25 W
73	L′Anguille (R.) (läN-gē′y′) Ark.	35·23 N	90·52 W
86	Lanigan (lăn′ĭ-gȧn) Can.	51·53 N	105·04 W
146	Lanisung Chiang (Mekong) China	24·45 N	100·31 E
81	Lansdale (lănz′dāl) Pa.	40·20 N	75·15 W
84	Lansdowne (lănz′doun) Md. (Baltimore In.)	39·14 N	76·39 W
84	Lansdowne Pa. (Philadelphia In.)	39·57 N	75·17 W
71	L′Anse (läns) Mich.	46·43 N	88·28 W
85	L′Anse-a-Giles (läNz-ȧ-zhēl) Can. (Quebec In.)	47·05 N	70·26 W
71	L′Anse and Vieux Desert Ind. Res. Mich.	46·41 N	88·12 W
81	Lansford (lănz′fērd) Pa.	40·50 N	75·50 W
85	Lansing (lăn′sĭng) Can. (Toronto In.)	43·46 N	79·24 W
75	Lansing Ill. (Chicago In.)	41·34 N	87·33 W
71	Lansing Iowa	43·22 N	91·16 W

ăt; finăl; rāte; senâte; ärm; ȧsk; sofȧ; fâre; ch-choose; dh-as th in other; bē; ēvent; bĕt; recĕnt; cratēr; g-go; gh-guttural g; bĭt; ĭ-short neutral; rīde; K-guttural k as ch in German ich;

PRONOUNCING INDEX Lansing–Legnano 227

Page	Name Pronunciation Region	Lat. °′	Long. °′
74	Lansing. . Kans. (Kansas City In.)	39·15 N	94·53 W
80	Lansing. . . . . Mich.	42·45 N	84·35 W
100	Lanús (lä-nōōs′). . . . . . . Arg. (In.)	34·27 S	58·24 W
126	Lanusei (lä-nōō-sĕ′y). . . . . It.	39·51 N	9·34 E
125	Lanúvio (lä-nōō′vyô) It. (Rome In.)	41·41 N	12·42 E
164	Lanzarote I. (län-zà-rō′tä). Can. Is.	29·04 N	13·03 W
154	Laoag (lä-wäg′). . . . . Phil.	18·13 N	120·38 E
147	Lao Ho (R.) (lä′ō hō′). . . . . . China	43·37 N	120·05 E
154	Lao Kay (lä′ōkä′ē). . . . . Viet.	22·30 N	102·32 E
122	Laon (läN). . . . . Fr.	49·36 N	3·35 E
98	La Oroya (lä-ô-rō′yä). . . . . . . Peru	11·44 S	76·12 W
138	Laos (lā′ōs) (là-ōs′). . . . . Asia	19·30 N	102·45 E
93	La Palma (lä-päl′mä). . . . . . . Pan.	8·25 N	78·07 W
124	La Palma. . . . . Sp.	37·24 N	6·36 W
164	La Palma I. . . . . Can. Is.	28·42 N	19·03 W
100	La Pampa (Prov.). . . . . Arg.	37·25 S	67·00 W
100	Lapa Rio Negro (lä-pä-rē′ō-nĕ′grô). Braz.	26·12 S	49·56 W
100	La Paz (lä päz′). . . . . Arg.	30·48 S	59·47 W
98	La Paz. Bol.	16·31 S	68·03 W
92	La Paz. . . . . Hond.	14·15 N	87·40 W
90	La Paz (lä-pà′z). . . . . Mex.	23·39 N	100·44 W
88	La Paz. . . . . Mex.	24·00 N	110·15 W
155	La Paz. . . . . Phil. (Manila In.)	17·41 N	120·41 E
80	Lapeer (lȧ-pēr′). . . . . Mich.	43·05 N	83·15 W
122	La-Penne-sur-Huveaune (la-pĕn′sür-ü-vōn′) Fr. (Marseille In.)	43·18 N	5·33 E
90	La Piedad Cabadas (lä pyā-dhädh′ kä-bä′dhäs). Mex.	20·20 N	102·04 W
112	Lapland (Reg.) (lăp′lănd). . . . Eur.	68·20 N	22·00 E
101	La Plata (lä plä′tä) Arg. (Buenos Aires In.)	34·54 S	57·57 W
73	La Plata (lȧ plā′tȧ). . . . . Mo.	40·03 N	92·28 W
69	La Plata Pk. . . . . Colo.	39·00 N	106·25 W
125	La Pobla de Lillet (lä-pô′blä-dĕ-lēl-yĕ′t). Sp.	42·14 N	1·58 E
155	Lapog (lä-pôg′) Phil. (Manila In.)	17·44 N	120·28 E
83	La Poile B. (lȧ pwäl′). . . . . . . Can.	47·28 N	58·35 W
80	La Porte (lȧ pōrt′). . . . . Ind.	41·35 N	86·45 W
75	Laporte. . . . . Ohio (Cleveland In.)	41·19 N	82·05 W
77	La Porte. . . . . Tex. (In.)	29·40 N	95·01 W
71	La Porte City. . . . . Iowa	42·20 N	92·10 W
119	Lappeenranta (lä′pēn-rän′tä). . Fin.	61·04 N	28·08 E
85	Laprairie (là-prâ-rē′) Can. (Montreal In.)	45·24 N	73·30 W
127	Lapseki (läp′sà-kē). . . . . Tur.	40·20 N	26·41 E
130	Laptev Sea (läp′tyĭf). . . . Sov. Un.	75·39 N	120·00 E
125	La Puebla (lä pwā′blä). . . . . . . Sp.	39·46 N	3·02 E
124	La Puebla de Montalbán (lä pwā′blä dā mōnt-äl-bän′) Sp.	39·54 N	4·21 W
121	Lapusul R. (lä′pōō-shōōl). . . Rom.	47·29 N	23·46 E
100	La Quiaca (lä kē-ä′kä). . . . . . . Arg.	22·15 S	65·44 W
126	L'Aquila (lä′kē-lä). . . . . It.	42·22 N	13·24 E
144	Lar (lär). . . . . Iran	27·31 N	54·12 E
161	Lara. . . . . . Austl. (Melbourne In.)	38·02 S	144·24 E
164	Larache (lä-räsh′). . . . . Mor.	35·15 N	6·09 W
62	Laramie (lăr′ȧ-mĭ). . . . . Wyo.	41·20 N	105·40 W
72	Laramie (R.). . . . . Colo.	40·56 N	105·55 W
125	L'Arba (l′är′bȧ). . . . . Alg.	36·35 N	3·10 E
84	Larchmont (lärch′mŏnt) N. Y. (New York In.)	40·56 N	73·46 W
65	Larch Mtn. (lärch) Ore. (Portland In.)	45·32 N	122·06 W
124	Laredo (lä-rā′dhō). . . . . Sp.	43·24 N	3·24 W
76	Laredo. . . . . Tex.	27·31 N	99·29 W
122	La Réole (lä rà-ōl′). . . . . Fr.	44·37 N	0·03 W
165	Largeau (lär-zhō′). . . . . Chad	17·45 N	19·26 E
94	Largo, Cayo (kä′yō-lär′gō). . Cuba	21·40 N	81·30 W
70	Larimore (lăr′ĭ-môr). . . . . . . N. D.	47·53 N	97·38 W
126	Larino (lä-rē′nō). . . . . It.	41·48 N	14·54 E
100	La Rioja (lä rē-ōhä). . . . . Arg.	29·18 S	67·42 W
100	La Rioja (Prov.) (lä-rē-ô′-kä). Arg.	28·45 S	68·00 W
127	Lárisa (lä′rē-sà). . . . . Grc.	39·38 N	22·25 E
142	Lārkāna. . . . . W. Pak.	27·40 N	68·12 E
139	Larnaca (lär′nà-kä) Cyprus (Palestine In.)	34·55 N	33·37 E
139	Larnaca (B.) Cyprus (Palestine In.)	34·55 N	33·51 E
72	Larned (lär′nĕd). . . . . Kans.	38·09 N	99·07 W
124	La Robla (lä rōb′lä). . . . . Sp.	42·48 N	5·36 W
122	La Rochelle (lȧ rô-shĕl′). . . . . . . Fr.	46·10 N	1·09 W
122	La Roche-sur-Yon (lȧ rôsh′sûr-yôN′). Fr.	46·39 N	1·27 W
124	La Roda (lä rō′dä). . . . . Sp.	39·13 N	2·08 W
95	La Romona (lä-rä-mô′nä) Dom. Rep.	18·25 N	69·00 W
158	Larrey Pt. (lăr′ē). . . . . Austl.	19·15 S	118·15 E
122	Laruns (lȧ-răNs′). . . . . Fr.	42·58 N	0·28 W
118	Larvik (lär′vēk). . . . . Nor.	59·06 N	10·03 E
99	La Sabana (lä-sä-bà′nä). Ven. (In.)	10·38 N	66·24 W
95	La Sabina (lä-sä-bē′nä) Cuba (Havana In.)	22·10 N	82·07 W
124	La Sagra (Mtn.) (lä sä′grä). . . Sp.	37·56 N	2·35 E
69	La Sal (lȧ säl′). . . . . Utah	38·10 N	109·20 W
75	La Salle (lȧ săl′) Can. (Detroit In.)	42·14 N	83·06 W
85	La Salle. . . . . Can. (Winnipeg In.)	49·41 N	97·16 W
80	La Salle. . . . . Ill.	41·20 N	89·05 W
72	Las Animas (lȧs ă′nĭ-mȧs). . . Colo.	38·03 N	103·16 W
168	Las Anod (läs ăn′ŏd) Som. (Horn of Afr. In.)	8·24 N	47·20 E
87	La Sarre. . . . . Can.	48·43 N	79·12 W
95	Lascahobas (läs-kä-ō′bäs). . . . Hai.	19·00 N	71·55 W
91	Las Cruces (läs-krōō′-sĕs). . . . Mex.	16·37 N	93·54 W
69	Las Cruces. . . . . N. Mex.	32·20 N	106·50 W
95	La Selle, Massif De (Mts.) (lä sĕl′). Hai.	18·25 N	72·05 W
100	La Serena (lä-sĕ-rĕ′nä). . . . . . Chile	29·55 S	71·24 W
123	La Seyne-sur-Mer (lä-sân′sür-mĕr′). Fr.	43·07 N	5·52 E
101	Las Flores (läs flo′rĕs) Arg. (Buenos Aires In.)	36·01 S	59·07 W
146	Lashio (lăsh′ē-ō). . . . . Bur.	22·58 N	98·03 E
74	La Sierra (lȧ sĭ-ĕr′ȧ) Calif. (Los Angeles In.)	33·54 N	117·29 W
92	Las Juntas (läs-kōō′n-täs). . . C. R.	10·15 N	85·00 W
168	Las Khoreh (läs kō′rå) Som. (Horn of Afr. In.)	11·13 N	48·19 E
124	Las Maismas (Reg.) (läs-mī′s-mäs). Sp.	37·05 N	6·25 W
124	La Solano (lä-sô-lä-nō). . . . . Sp.	38·56 N	3·13 W
164	Las Palmas (läs päl′mäs). Can. Is.	28·07 N	15·28 W
93	Las Palmas. . . . . Pan.	8·08 N	81·30 W
126	La Spezia (lä-spĕ′zyä). . . . . It.	44·07 N	9·48 E
101	Las Piedras (läs-pyĕ′dràs) Ur. (Buenos Aires In.)	34·42 S	56·08 W
92	Las Pilas (Vol.) (läs-pē′läs). . . Nic.	12·32 N	86·43 W
91	Las Rosas (läs rō thäs). . . . . . Mex.	16·24 N	92·23 W
125	Las Rozas de Madrid (läs rō′thas dā mä-dhrēdh′). Sp. (Madrid In.)	40·29 N	3·53 W
111	Lassee. . . . . Aus. (Vienna In.)	48·14 N	16·50 E
66	Lassen Pk. (lăs′ĕn). . . . . Calif.	40·30 N	121·32 W
66	Lassen Volcanic Natl. Park. . Calif.	40·43 N	121·35 W
85	L'Assomption (lás-sôm-syôN) Can. (Montreal In.)	45·50 N	73·25 W
93	Las Tablas (läs tä′bläs). . . . . . Pan.	7·48 N	80·16 W
86	Last Mountain (L.) (lȧst moun′tĭn). Can.	51·07 N	105·50 W
166	Lastoursville (läs-tōōr-vēl′) Gabon	1·00 S	12·49 E
88	Las Tres Marías (I.) (läs-trĕ′s mä-rē′äs). Mex.	21·30 N	106·40 W
88	Las Tres Virgenes, Vol. (vē′r-hĕ-nĕs). Mex.	26·00 N	111·45 W
91	Las Vacas (läs-và′käs). . . . . . Mex.	16·24 N	95·48 W
101	Las Vegas (läs-vĕ′gäs) Chile (Santiago In.)	30·50 S	70·59 W
68	Las Vegas (läs vā′gäs). . . . . . . Nev.	36·12 N	115·10 W
72	Las Vegas. . . . . N. Mex.	35·36 N	105·13 W
99	Las Vegas (läs-vĕ′gäs). . Ven. (In.)	10·26 N	64·08 W
90	Las Vigas. . . . . Mex.	19·38 N	97·03 W
94	Las Villas (State) (läs-vĕ′l-läs) Cuba	22·15 N	80·50 W
100	Las Vizcachas, Meseta de (Plat.) (mĕ-sĕ′tä-dĕ-läs-vêz-kä′-chäs) Arg.	49·35 S	71·00 W
98	Latacunga (lä-tä-kōōŋ′gä). . . . . Ec.	1·02 S	78·33 W
	Latakia, see El Ladhiqiya		
115	Latakia (Reg.) (lä-tä-kē′ä) U. A. R.	35·10 N	35·49 E
122	La Teste-de-Buch (lȧ-tĕst-dĕ-büsh). Fr.	44·38 N	1·11 W
73	Lathrop (lā′thrŭp). . . . . Mo.	39·32 N	94·21 W
	Latium (Reg.), see Lazio		
121	Latoritsa R. (là-tô′rĭ-tsà) Sov. Un.	48·27 N	22·30 E
85	La Tortue, R. (lä tōr-tü′) Can. (Montreal In.)	45·12 N	73·32 W
65	Latourell (lȧ-tou′rĕl) Ore. (Portland In.)	45·32 N	122·13 W
122	La Tremblade (lä-trĕN-bläd′). . Fr.	45·45 N	1·12 W
81	Latrobe (lȧ-trōb′). . . . . Pa.	40·25 N	79·15 W
82	La Tuque (lȧ tük′). . . . . Can.	47·27 N	72·49 W
143	Latūr (lä-tōōr′). . . . . India	18·20 N	76·35 E
130	Latvian (S. S. R.). . . . . Sov. Un.	57·28 N	24·29 E
160	Launceston (lôn′sĕs-tŭn). . . . Austl.	41·35 S	147·22 E
116	Launceston (lôrn′stŏn). . . . . . Eng.	50·38 N	4·26 W
100	La Unión (lä-ōō-nyô′n). . . . . . Chile	40·15 S	73·04 W
90	La Unión (lä ōōn-nyōn′). . . . . . Mex.	17·59 N	101·48 W
92	La Unión. . . . . Sal.	13·18 N	87·51 W
125	La Unión. . . . . Sp.	37·38 N	0·50 W
157	Laupahoehoe (lä′ōō-pä-hō′ĕ-hō-ĕ) Hawaii (In.)	19·58 N	155·13 W
159	Laura (lôrȧ). . . . . Austl.	15·40 S	144·45 E
128	Laura (lou′rà). . . . . Sov. Un.	57·36 N	27·29 E
81	Laurel (lô′rĕl). . . . . Del.	38·30 N	75·40 W
84	Laurel. . . . . . . Md. (Baltimore In.)	39·06 N	76·51 W
78	Laurel. . . . . Miss.	31·42 N	89·07 W
67	Laurel. . . . . Mont.	45·41 N	108·45 W
65	Laurel. . . . . Wash. (Vancouver In.)	48·52 N	122·29 W
65	Laurelwood (lô′rĕl-wōōd) Ore. (Portland In.)	45·25 N	123·05 W
79	Laurens (lô′rĕnz). . . . . S. C.	34·29 N	82·03 W
49	Laurentian Highlands (Reg.) (lô′rĕn-tĭ-ȧn). Can.	49·00 N	74·50 W
82	Laurentides Park (lô′rĕn-tīdz) Can.	47·53 N	71·26 W
126	Lauria (lou′rē-ä). . . . . It.	40·03 N	15·02 E
79	Laurinburg (lô′rĭn-bûrg). . . . N. C.	34·45 N	79·27 W
71	Laurium (lô′rĭ-ŭm). . . . . Mich.	47·13 N	88·28 W
154	Laurot Pulau-Pulau Is. . . . . Indon.	4·44 S	115·43 E
120	Lausanne (lō-zȧn′). . . . . Switz.	46·32 N	6·35 E
154	Laut (I.). . . . . Indon.	3·39 S	116·07 E
100	Lautaro (lou-tä′rô). . . . . Chile	38·40 S	72·24 W
85	Lauzon (lō-zōN′) Can. (Quebec In.)	46·50 N	71·10 W
66	Lava Beds Natl. Mon. (lä′vȧ bĕds). Calif.	41·38 N	121·44 W
77	Lavaca R. (lȧ-văk′ȧ). . . . . Tex.	29·05 N	96·50 W
67	Lava Hot Springs. . . . . Idaho	42·37 N	111·58 W
122	Laval (là-väl′). . . . . Fr.	48·05 N	0·47 W
122	Lavaur (là-vōr′). . . . . Fr.	43·41 N	1·48 E
122	Lavaveix-les-Mines (lá-vá-vĕ′lā-mēn′). Fr.	46·05 N	2·05 E
95	La Vega (lä-vĕ′-gä). . . . Dom. Rep.	19·15 N	70·35 W
159	Lavella (I.). . . . . Sol. Is.	7·50 S	155·45 E
126	Lavello (lä-vĕl′lô). . . . . It.	41·05 N	15·50 E
74	La Verne (lȧ vûrn′) Calif. (Los Angeles In.)	34·06 N	117·46 W
158	Laverton (lā′vēr-tŭn). . . . . . . Austl.	28·45 S	122·30 E
99	La Victoria (lä vēk-tō′rē-ä) Ven. (In.)	10·14 N	67·20 W
78	Lavonia (lȧ-vō′nĭ-ȧ). . . . . Ga.	34·26 N	83·05 W
77	Lavon Res. . . . . Tex.	33·06 N	96·20 W
101	Lavras (lä′vräzh) Braz. (Rio de Janeiro In.)	21·15 S	44·59 W
127	Lávrion (läv′rĭ-ŏn). . . . . Grc.	37·44 N	24·05 E
74	Lawndale (lôn′dāl) Calif. (Los Angeles In.)	33·54 N	118·22 W
75	Lawrence (lô′rĕns) Ind. (Indianapolis In.)	39·59 N	86·01 W
73	Lawrence. . . . . Kans.	38·57 N	95·13 W
83	Lawrence. . . . . Mass. (Boston In.)	42·42 N	71·09 W
75	Lawrence. . . . Pa. (Pittsburgh In.)	40·18 N	80·07 W
65	Lawrence. . Wash. (Vancouver In.)	48·52 N	122·18 W
75	Lawrenceburg (lô′rĕns-bûrg) Ind. (Cincinnati In.)	39·06 N	84·47 W
80	Lawrenceburg. . . . . Ky.	38·00 N	85·00 W
78	Lawrenceburg. . . . . Tenn.	35·13 N	87·20 W
78	Lawrenceville (lô-rĕns-vĭl). . . . . Ga.	33·56 N	83·57 W
80	Lawrenceville. . . . . Ill.	38·45 N	87·45 W
84	Lawrenceville N. J. (New York In.)	40·17 N	74·44 W
79	Lawrenceville. . . . . Va.	36·43 N	77·52 W
81	Lawsonia (lô-sō′nĭ-ȧ). . . . . Md.	38·00 N	75·50 W
72	Lawton (lô′tŭn). . . . . Okla.	34·36 N	98·25 W
139	Layang Layang (lä-yäng′ lä-yäng′). Mala. (Singapore In.)	1·49 N	103·28 E
74	Layton (lā′tŭn) Utah (Salt Lake City In.)	41·04 N	111·58 W
119	Laždijai (läzh′dē-yī′). . . . Sov. Un.	54·12 N	23·35 E
126	Lazio (Latium) (Reg.) (lä′zyô) (lā′t-zēōōm). It.	42·05 N	12·25 E
70	Lead (lēd). . . . . S. D.	44·22 N	103·47 W
72	Leadville (lĕd′vĭl). . . . . Colo.	39·14 N	106·18 W
87	Leaf (R.) (lēf). . . . . Can.	59·12 N	72·50 W
78	Leaf (R.). . . . . Miss.	31·43 N	89·20 W
77	League City (lēg). . . . . . . Tex. (In.)	29·31 N	95·05 W
80	Leamington (lĕm′ĭng-tŭn). . . . Can.	42·05 N	82·35 W
116	Leamington (lĕ′mĭng-tŭn). . . . Eng.	52·17 N	1·25 W
85	Leaside (lē′sīd) Can. (Toronto In.)	43·42 N	79·22 W
110	Leatherhead (lĕdh′ĕr-hĕd′) Eng. (London In.)	51·17 N	0·20 W
74	Leavenworth (lĕv′ĕn-wûrth) Kans. (Kansas City In.)	39·19 N	94·54 W
66	Leavenworth. . . . . Wash.	47·35 N	120·39 W
74	Leawood (lē′wōōd) Mo. (Kansas City In.)	38·58 N	94·37 W
121	Leba (lā′bä). . . . . Pol.	54·45 N	17·34 E
139	Lebam R. . . Mala. (Singapore In.)	1·35 N	104·09 E
74	Lebanon (lĕb′ȧ-nŭn) Ill. (St. Louis In.)	38·36 N	89·49 W
80	Lebanon. . . . . Ind.	40·00 N	86·30 W
80	Lebanon. . . . . Ky.	37·32 N	85·15 W
73	Lebanon. . . . . Mo.	37·40 N	92·43 W
81	Lebanon. . . . . N. H.	43·40 N	72·15 W
80	Lebanon. . . . . Ohio	39·25 N	84·10 W
66	Lebanon. . . . . Ore.	44·31 N	122·53 W
81	Lebanon. . . . . Pa.	40·20 N	76·20 W
78	Lebanon. . . . . Tenn.	36·10 N	86·16 W
138	Lebanon. . . . . Asia	34·00 N	35·00 E
115	Lebanon Mts. . . . . Leb.	33·30 N	35·32 E
129	Lebedin (lyĕ′bĕ-dĕn). . . . . Sov. Un.	48·56 N	31·35 E
129	Lebedin. . . . . Sov. Un.	50·34 N	34·27 E
128	Lebedyan′ (lyĕ′bĕ-dyän′) Sov. Un.	53·03 N	39·08 E
122	Le Blanc (lĕ-bläN′). . . . . Fr.	46·38 N	0·59 E
95	Le Borgne (lĕ bōrn′y′). . . . . Hai.	19·50 N	72·30 W
121	Lebork (lăN-bōōrk′). . . . . Pol.	54·33 N	17·46 E
122	Le Boucau (lĕ-bōō-kō′). . . . . Fr.	43·33 N	1·28 W
122	Le Bouscat (lĕ bōōs-kȧ). . . . . Fr.	44·53 N	0·38 W
124	Lebrija (lā-brē′hä). . . . . Sp.	36·55 N	6·06 W
100	Lebú (lĕ-bōō′). . . . . Chile	37·35 S	73·37 W
127	Lecce (lĕt′chā). . . . . It.	40·22 N	18·11 E
126	Lecco (lĕk′kō). . . . . It.	45·52 N	9·28 E
123	Le Châtelet-en-Brie (lĕ-shä-tĕ-lā′ ĕN-brē′). Fr. (Paris In.)	48·29 N	2·50 E
94	Leche, Laguna de (L.) (lä-gōō′nä-dĕ-lĕ′chĕ). Cuba	22·10 N	78·30 W
76	Leche, Laguna de la (L.). . . . Mex.	27·16 N	102·45 W
123	Lechenich (lĕ′kĕ-nēK) Ger. (Ruhr In.)	50·47 N	6·46 E
120	Lech R. (lĕk). . . . . Ger.	47·41 N	10·52 E
77	Lecompte. . . . . La.	31·06 N	92·25 W
122	Le Coteau (lĕ kō-tō′). . . . . Fr.	46·01 N	4·06 E
122	Le Creusot (lĕkrû-zō′). . . . . Fr.	46·48 N	4·23 E
122	Lectoure (lĕK-tōōr). . . . . Fr.	43·56 N	0·38 E
124	Ledesma (lā-dĕs′mä). . . . . Sp.	41·05 N	5·59 W
85	Leduc (lĕ-dōōk′) Can. (Edmonton In.)	53·16 N	113·34 W
71	Leech (L.) (lēch). . . . . Minn.	47·06 N	94·16 W
84	Leeds (lēdz) Ala. (Birmingham In.)	33·33 N	86·33 W
110	Leeds. . . . . Eng.	53·48 N	1·33 W
70	Leeds. . . . . N. D.	48·18 N	99·24 W
110	Leeds and Liverpool Can. (lĭv′ēr-pōōl). Eng.	53·36 N	2·38 W
111	Leegebruch (lĕh′gĕn-brōōK) Ger. (Berlin In.)	52·43 N	13·12 E
110	Leek (lēk). . . . . Eng.	53·06 N	2·01 W
120	Leer (lār). . . . . Ger.	53·14 N	7·27 E
116	Lee R. (lē). . . . . Ire.	51·52 N	8·30 W
79	Leesburg (lēz′bûrg). . . . . Fla.	28·49 N	81·53 W
81	Leesburg. . . . . Va.	39·10 N	77·30 W
69	Lees Ferry. . . . . Ariz.	36·55 N	111·45 W
74	Lees Summit Mo. (Kansas City In.)	38·55 N	94·23 W
95	Lee Stocking (I.). . . . . Ba. Is.	23·45 N	76·05 W
77	Leesville (lēz′vĭl). . . . . La.	31·09 N	93·17 W
80	Leetonia (lē-tō′nĭ-ȧ). . . . . Ohio	40·50 N	80·45 W
117	Leeuwarden (lā′wär-dĕn). . . Neth.	52·12 N	5·50 E
158	Leeuwin, C. (lōō′wĭn). . . . . . . Austl.	34·15 S	114·30 E
93	Leeward Is. (lē′wērd). . . . . . N. A.	12·25 N	62·15 W
93	Le Francois Mart. (Le. & Wind. Is. In.)	14·37 N	60·55 W
158	Lefroy (L.) (lē-froi′). . . . . . . Austl.	31·30 S	122·00 E
125	Leganés (lā-gä′nȧs) Sp. (Madrid In.)	40·20 N	3·46 W
155	Legaspi (lā-gäs′pē) Phil. (Manila In.)	13·09 N	123·44 E
160	Legge Pk. (lĕg). . . . . Austl.	41·33 S	148·10 E
	Leghorn, see Livorno		
126	Legnano (lā-nyä′nō). . . . . It.	45·35 N	8·53 E

ng-sing; ŋ-baŋk; N-nasalized n; nŏd; cŏmmit; ōld; ôbey; ôrder; fōōd; fŏŏt; ou-out; s-soft; sh-dish; th-thin; pūre; ûnite; ûrn; stŭd; circŭs; ü-as "y" in study; ′-indeterminate vowel.

228 Legnica–Limbe PRONOUNCING INDEX

Page	Name Pronunciation Region	Lat. °′	Long. °′
120	Legnica (lĕk-nĭt'sȧ) Pol.	51·13 N	16·10 E
142	Leh (lā) India	34·10 N	77·40 E
122	Le Havre (lẽ àv'r') Fr.	49·31 N	0·07 E
69	Lehi (lē'hī) Utah	40·25 N	111·55 W
69	Lehman Caves Natl. Mon. (lē'măn) Nev.	38·54 N	114·08 W
111	Lehnin (lĕh'nēn) Ger. (Berlin In.)	52·19 N	12·45 E
110	Leicester (lĕs'tẽr) Eng.	52·37 N	1·08 W
110	Leicester (Co.) Eng.	52·40 N	1·12 W
158	Leichhardt, (R.) (līk'härt) Austl.	18·30 S	139·45 E
111	Leiden (lī'dĕn) Neth. (Amsterdam In.)	52·09 N	4·29 E
160	Leigh Creek (lē krēk) Austl.	30·33 S	138·30 E
118	Leikanger (lī'kän-gẽr) Nor.	61·11 N	6·51 E
111	Leimuiden Neth. (Amsterdam In.)	52·13 N	4·40 E
120	Leine R. (lī'nĕ) Ger.	51·58 N	9·56 E
116	Leinster (lĕn-stẽr) Ire.	52·45 N	7·19 W
80	Leipsic (līp'sĭk) Ohio	41·05 N	84·00 W
120	Leipzig (līp'tsĭk) Ger.	51·20 N	12·24 E
124	Leiria (lā-rē'ä) Port.	39·45 N	8·50 W
78	Leitchfield (lēch'fēld) Ky.	37·28 N	86·20 W
111	Leitha (R.) Aus. (Vienna In.)	48·04 N	16·57 E
85	Leitrim Can. (Ottawa In.)	45·20 N	75·36 W
	Leixoes, see Matozinhos		
117	Lek (R.) (lĕk) Neth.	51·59 N	5·30 E
113	Lekef (lĕkĕf') Tun.	36·14 N	8·42 E
118	Leksand (lĕk'sänd) Swe.	60·45 N	14·56 E
65	Leland (lē'lănd) Wash. (Seattle In.)	47·54 N	122·53 W
120	Le Locle (lẽ lô'kl') Switz.	47·03 N	6·43 E
100	Le Maire, Estrecho de (Str.) (ĕs-trĕ'chô-dĕ-lĕ-mī'rĕ) Arg.	55·15 S	65·30 W
122	Le Mans (lẽ mäN') Fr.	48·01 N	0·12 E
93	Le Marin Mart. (Le. & Wind. Is. In.)	14·28 N	60·55 W
70	Le Mars (lê märz') Iowa	42·46 N	96·09 W
155	Lemery (lā-mā-rē') Phil. (Manila In.)	13·51 N	120·55 E
67	Lemhi Ra. (Mts.) (lĕm'hī) Idaho	44·35 N	113·33 W
67	Lemhi R. Idaho	44·40 N	113·27 W
70	Lemmon (lĕm'ŭn) S. D.	45·55 N	102·10 W
95	Le Môle (lẽ mōl') Hai.	19·50 N	73·20 W
68	Lemon Grove (lĕm'ŭn-grōv) Calif. (San Diego In.)	32·44 N	117·02 W
75	Lemont (lē'-mŏnt) Ill. (Chicago In.)	41·40 N	87·59 W
93	Le Moule (lẽ mōōl') Grande Terre (Le. & Wind. Is. In.)	16·19 N	61·22 W
92	Lempa R. (lĕm'pä) Sal.	13·20 N	88·46 W
118	Lemvig (lĕm'vēgh) Den.	56·33 N	8·16 E
118	Lena (lē'nä) Swe.	60·01 N	17·40 E
135	Lena (R.) Sov. Un.	68·39 N	124·15 E
100	Lençóes Paulista (lĕN-sôNs' pou-lēs'tȧ) Braz.	22·30 S	48·45 W
99	Lençóis (lĕn-sóis) Braz.	12·38 S	41·28 W
74	Lenexa (lē-nĕx'ȧ) Mo. (Kansas City In.)	38·58 N	94·44 W
103	Lenger (lyĭn'gyĕr) Sov. Un.	41·38 N	70·00 E
139	Lenik (R.) Mala. (Singapore In.)	1·59 N	102·51 E
134	Leninabad (lĕ-nyē-nȧ bät') Sov. Un.	40·15 N	69·49 E
133	Leninakan (lĕ-nyē-nȧ-kän') Sov. Un.	40·40 N	43·50 E
136	Leningrad (lyĕ-nēn-grät') Sov. Un. (Leningrad In.)	59·57 N	30 20 E
128	Leningrad (Oblast) Sov. Un.	59·15 N	30·30 E
129	Leningradskaya (lyĕ-nĭn-gräd'skȧ-yȧ) Sov. Un.	46·19 N	39·23 E
136	Lenino (lyĕ'nĭ-nô) Sov. Un. (Moscow In.)	55·37 N	47·41 E
134	Leninogorsk (lyĕ-nĭn ŭ gôrsk') Sov. Un.	50·29 N	83·25 E
133	Leninsk (lyĕ-nēnsk') Sov. Un.	48·40 N	45·10 E
134	Leninsk-Kuznetskiy (lyĕ-nênsk' kōōz-nyĕt'skĭ-ē) Sov. Un.	54·28 N	86·48 E
133	Lenkoran' (lĕn-kô-rän') Sov. Un.	38·52 N	48·58 E
70	Lennox (lĕn'ŭks) S. D.	43·22 N	96·53 W
79	Lenoir (lê-nōr') N. C.	35·54 N	81·35 W
78	Lenoir City Tenn.	35·47 N	84·16 W
71	Lenox Iowa	40·51 N	94·29 W
120	Leoben (lâ-ō'bĕn) Aus.	47·22 N	15·09 E
95	Léogane (lā-ô-gan') Hai.	18·30 N	72·35 W
70	Leola (lê-ō'lȧ) S. D.	45·43 N	99·55 W
83	Leominster (lĕm'ĭn-stẽr) Mass. (Boston In.)	42·32 N	71·45 W
71	Leon (lē'ŏn) Iowa	40·43 N	93·44 W
90	León (lā-ōn') Mex.	21·08 N	101·41 W
92	León (lĕ-ô'n) Nic.	12·28 N	86·53 W
124	León (lĕ-ô'n) Sp.	42·38 N	5·33 W
124	Leon (Reg.) (lĕ-ô'n) Sp.	41·18 N	5·50 W
126	Leonforte (lā-ôn-fôr'tä) It.	37·40 N	14·27 E
76	Leon R. (lē'ŏn) Tex.	31·54 N	98·20 W
101	Leopoldina (lā-ô-pôl-dē'nä) Braz. (Rio de Janeiro In.)	21·32 S	42·38 W
111	Leopoldsburg Bel. (Brussels In.)	51·07 N	5·18 E
111	Leopoldsdorf im Marchfelde (lā'ô-pôlts-dôrf') Aus. (Vienna In.)	48·14 N	16·42 E
166	Leopold II (L.) (lā'ô-pōld) Con. L.	2·16 S	19·00 E
166	Léopoldville (lā-ô-pōld-vēl') Con. L.	4·28 S	15·16 E
129	Leovo (lâ-ō'vô) Sov. Un.	46·30 N	28·16 E
124	Lepe (lā'pā) Sp.	37·15 N	7·12 W
128	Lepel' (lyĕ-pĕl') Sov. Un.	54·52 N	28·41 E
85	L'Épiphanie (lā-pē-fā-nē') Can. (Montreal In.)	45·51 N	73·29 W
123	Le Plessis-Belleville (lĕ-plĕ-sē' bĕl-vēl') Fr. (Paris In.)	49·05 N	2·46 E
120	Lepontine Alpi (Mts.) (lê-pŏn'tĭn) Switz.	46·28 N	8·38 E
82	Lepreau (lê-prō') Can.	45·10 N	66·28 W
134	Lepsinsh Sov. Un.	45·32 N	80·47 E
122	Le Puy-en-Velay (lẽ pwē') Fr.	45·02 N	3·54 E
126	Lercara (lĕr-kä'rä) It.	36·47 N	13·36 E
76	Lerdo (lĕr'dō) Mex.	25·31 N	103·30 W
165	Léré (lā-rā') Chad	9·42 N	14·14 E
167	Leribe Bas. (Natal In.)	28·53 S	28·02 E
125	Lérida (lā'rē-dhä) Sp.	41·38 N	0·37 E
91	Lerma (lĕr'mä) Mex.	19·49 N	90·34 W
91	Lerma Mex. (Mexico City In.)	19·17 N	99·30 W
124	Lerma (lĕ'r-mä) Sp.	42·03 N	3·45 W
90	Lerma (R.) Mex.	20·14 N	101·50 W
81	Le Roy (lê roi') N. Y.	43·00 N	78·00 W
116	Lerwick (lĕr'ĭk) (lûr'wĭk) Scot.	60·08 N	1·27 W
84	Lery, L. (lĕ'rē) La. (New Orleans In.)	29·48 N	89·45 W
123	Les Andelys (lā-zäN-dē-lē') Fr. (Paris In.)	49·15 N	1·25 E
95	Les Cayes Hai.	18·15 N	73·45 W
85	Les Cèdres (lā-sĕdr') Can. (Montreal In.)	45·18 N	74·03 W
127	Lesh (Alessio) (lĕshĕ) (ä-lā'sê-ō) Alb.	41·47 N	19·40 E
126	Lésina, Lago di (L.) (lä'gō dē lā'zē-nä) It.	41·48 N	15·12 E
127	Leskovac (lĕs'kô-vȧts) Yugo.	43·00 N	21·58 E
73	Leslie (lĕz'lĭ) Ark.	35·49 N	92·32 W
168	Leslie S. Afr. (Johannesburg & Pretoria In.)	26·23 S	28·57 E
132	Lesnoy (lĕs'noi) Sov. Un.	66·45 N	34·45 E
152	Lesogorsk (lyĕs'ô-gôrsk) Sov. Un.	49·28 N	141·59 E
152	Lesozavodsk (lyĕ-sô-zȧ-vôdsk') Sov. Un.	45·21 N	133·19 E
122	Lesparre (lẽ-spär) Fr.	45·18 N	0·57 W
122	Les-Pennes-Mirabeau (lā-pĕn' mĭ-rä-bō') Fr. (Marseille In.)	43·25 N	5·19 E
122	Les Sables-d'Olonne (lā sä'bl'dô-lŭn') Fr.	46·30 N	1·47 W
93	Les Saintes Is. (lā-săNt') Guad. (Le. & Wind. Is. In.)	15·50 N	61·40 W
	Lesser Khingan Mts. see Hsiaohsinganling Shanmo		
86	Lesser Slave L. (lĕs'ẽr slāv) Can.	55·10 N	116·18 W
122	L'Estaque (lĕs-tȧl) Fr. (Marseille In.)	43·22 N	5·20 E
123	Les Thilliers-en-Vexin (lā-tē-yā' ĕN-vĕ-săN') Fr. (Paris In.)	49·19 N	1·36 E
71	Le Sueur (lẽ sōōr') Minn.	44·27 N	93·53 W
127	Lésvos (I.) Grc.	39·15 N	25·40 E
120	Leszno (lĕsh'nô) Pol.	51·51 N	16·35 E
122	Le Teil (lẽ tā'y') Fr.	44·34 N	4·39 E
86	Lethbridge (lĕth'brĭj) Can.	49·40 N	112·39 W
166	Letiahau (R.) Bech.	21·16 S	22·17 E
129	Letichev (lyĕ-tē-chĕf') Sov. Un.	49·22 N	27·29 E
98	Leticia (lĕ-tē'syä) Col.	4·04 S	69·57 W
123	Letmathe (lĕt'mät-hĕ) Ger. (Ruhr In.)	51·22 N	7·37 E
122	Le Tréport (lẽ-trā-pôr') Fr.	50·03 N	1·21 E
154	Leuser, Gulung (Mtn.) Indon.	3·36 N	97·17 E
111	Leuven Bel. (Brussels In.)	50·53 N	4·42 E
127	Levádhia Grc.	38·25 N	22·51 E
123	Levallois-Perret (lē-vȧl-wä'pĕ-rĕ') Fr. (Paris In.)	48·53 N	2·17 E
112	Levanger (lĕ-väng'ẽr) Nor.	63·42 N	11·01 E
126	Levanna (Mtn.) (lå-vä'nä) Fr.-It.	45·25 N	7·14 E
158	Leveque, C. (lē-vĕk') Austl.	16·25 S	123·08 E
123	Leverkusen (lĕ'fĕr-kōō-zĕn) Ger. (Ruhr In.)	51·01 N	6·59 E
166	Leverville (lē-vā-vēl') Con. L.	5·13 S	18·43 E
121	Levice (lā'vēt-sĕ) Czech.	48·13 N	18·37 E
126	Levico (lā'vē-kō) It.	46·02 N	11·20 E
122	Le Vigan (lẽ vē-gäN') Fr.	43·59 N	3·36 E
85	Levis (lā-vē') (lē'vĭs) Can. (Quebec In.)	46·48 N	71·11 W
84	Levittown (lĕ'vĭt-toun) Pa. (Philadelphia In.)	40·08 N	74·50 W
127	Levkás (lyĕfkäs') Grc.	38·49 N	20·43 E
127	Levkás (I.) Grc.	38·42 N	20·22 E
121	Levoča (lā'vô-chä) Czech.	49·03 N	20·38 E
79	Levy (L.) (lē'vĭ) Fla.	29·31 N	82·23 W
81	Lewes (lōō'ĭs) Del.	38·45 N	75·10 W
116	Lewes Eng.	50·51 N	0·01 E
116	Lewis (I.) (lōō'ĭs) Scot.	58·05 N	6·07 W
65	Lewis (R.) East Fk. Wash. (Portland In.)	45·52 N	122·40 E
78	Lewisburg (lū'ĭs-bûrg) Tenn.	35·27 N	86·47 W
80	Lewisburg (lū'ĭs-bûrg) W. Va.	37·50 N	80·20 W
83	Lewis Hills Can.	48·49 N	58·28 W
83	Lewisporte (lū'ĭs-pōrt) Can.	49·15 N	55·06 W
67	Lewis Ra. (lū'ĭs) Mont.	48·05 N	113·06 W
66	Lewis R. Wash.	46·05 N	122·09 W
66	Lewiston (lū'ĭs-tŭn) Idaho	46·24 N	116·59 W
82	Lewiston Maine	44·05 N	70·14 W
75	Lewiston N. Y. (Buffalo In.)	43·11 N	79·02 W
67	Lewiston Utah	41·58 N	111·51 W
73	Lewistown (lū'ĭs-toun) Ill.	40·23 N	90·06 W
67	Lewistown Mont.	47·05 N	109·25 W
81	Lewistown Pa.	40·35 N	77·30 W
80	Lexington (lĕk'sĭng-tŭn) Ky.	38·05 N	84·30 W
83	Lexington Mass. (Boston In.)	42·27 N	71·14 W
78	Lexington Miss.	33·08 N	90·02 W
73	Lexington Mo.	39·11 N	93·52 W
72	Lexington Nebr.	40·46 N	99·44 W
79	Lexington N. C.	35·47 N	80·15 W
78	Lexington Tenn.	35·37 N	88·24 W
81	Lexington Va.	37·45 N	79·20 W
155	Leyte (I.) (lā'tā) Phil.	10·35 N	125·35 E
121	Lezajsk (lĕ'zhä-ĭsk) Pol.	50·14 N	22·25 E
128	Lezha (R.) (lĕ-zhä') Sov. Un.	58·59 N	40·27 E
122	Lézignan (lā-zē-nyäN') Fr.	43·13 N	2·48 E
129	L'gov (lgôf) Sov. Un.	51·42 N	35·15 E
142	Lhasa (läs'ä) China	29·41 N	91·12 E
148	Lhsien (yĕ'sĭăN) China	37·09 N	119·57 E
150	Lianghsiang (lyäng'syän') China (Peking In.)	39·43 N	116·08 E
136	Lianozovo (lĭ-á-nô'zô-vô) Sov. Un. (Moscow In.)	55·54 N	37·36 E
148	Liaoch'eng (lĭou'chĕng) China	36·27 N	115·56 E
150	Liao Ho (R.) (lyä'ō hō') China	41·40 N	122·40 E
147	Liaoning (Prov.) China	41·31 N	122·11 E
148	Liaotung Pantao (Pen.) (lĭou'dōōng bäN'dou) China	39·45 N	122·22 E
150	Liaotung Wan (B.) China	40·25 N	121·15 E
150	Liaoyang (lyä'ō-yäng') China	41·18 N	123·10 E
147	Liaoyüan (lyä'ō-yü-än') China	43·37 N	123·30 E
86	Liard (R.) (lê-är') Can.	59·43 N	126·42 W
98	Libano (lē'-bä-nō) Col. (In.)	4·55 N	75·05 W
124	Libar, Sierra de (Mts.) (sē-ĕ'r-rä-dĕ-lē-bär) Sp.	39·42 N	5·28 W
66	Libby (lĭb'ê) Mont.	48·27 N	115·35 W
165	Libenge (lê-bĕn'gä) Con. L.	3·39 N	18·40 E
72	Liberal (lĭb'ẽr-ăl) Kans.	37·01 N	100·56 W
120	Liberec (lē'bēr-ĕts) Czech.	15·47 N	15·06 E
163	Liberia (lī-bē'rĭ-ȧ) Afr.	6·30 N	9·55 W
92	Liberia C. R.	10·38 N	85·28 W
99	Libertad de Orituco (lē-bĕr-tä'd-dĕ-ō-rē-tōō'kô) Ven. (In.)	9·32 N	66·24 W
80	Liberty (lĭb'ẽr-tĭ) Ind.	39·35 N	84·55 W
74	Liberty Mo. (Kansas City In.)	39·15 N	94·25 W
79	Liberty S. C.	34·47 N	82·41 W
77	Liberty Tex.	30·03 N	94·46 W
74	Liberty Utah (Salt Lake City In.)	41·20 N	111·52 W
65	Liberty B. Wash. (Seattle In.)	47·43 N	122·41 W
75	Libertyville (lĭb'ẽr-tĭ-vĭl) Ill. (Chicago In.)	42·17 N	87·57 W
155	Libmanan (lĭb-mä'nän) Phil. (Manila In.)	13·42 N	123·04 E
167	Libode (lĭ-bō'dĕ) S. Afr. (Natal In.)	31·33 S	29·03 E
95	Libón, R. Hai.	19·30 N	71·45 W
122	Libourne (lē-bōōrn') Fr.	44·55 N	0·12 W
91	Libres (lē'bräs) Mex.	19·26 N	97·41 W
164	Libreville (lē-br'vēl') Gabon	0·29 N	9·26 E
84	Liburn (lĭb'ûrn) Ga. (Atlanta In.)	33·53 N	84·09 W
163	Libya (lĭb'ê-ä) Afr.	27·38 N	15·00 E
165	Libyan Des. (lĭb'ê-ăn) Libya	28·23 N	23·34 E
115	Libyan Plat. U. A. R.	30·58 N	26·20 E
100	Licancábur, Cerro (Mtn.) (sĕ'r-rô-lē-kän-kä'bōōr) Chile	22·45 S	67·45 W
101	Licanten (lē-kän-tĕ'n) Chile (Santiago In.)	34·58 S	72·00 W
110	Lichfield (lĭch'fēld) Eng.	52·41 N	1·49 W
146	Lichiang China	27·06 N	100·08 E
148	Liching (lē'jĭn) China	37·24 N	118·12 E
168	Lichtenburg (lĭk'tĕn-bĕrgh) S. Afr. (Johannesburg & Pretoria In.)	26·09 S	26·10 E
75	Lick Cr. (lĭk) Ind. (Indianapolis In.)	39·43 N	86·06 W
80	Licking (R.) (lĭk'ĭng) Ky.	38·30 N	84·10 W
126	Licosa, Pt. (lê-kō'sä) It.	40·17 N	14·40 E
121	Lida (lē'dȧ) Sov. Un.	53·53 N	25·19 E
70	Lidgerwood (lĭj'ẽr-wood) N. D.	46·04 N	97·10 W
118	Lidköping (lēt'chû-pĭng) Swe.	58·31 N	13·06 E
125	Lido di Roma (Ostia Lido) (lē'dô-dē-rō'mä) (ô's-tyä-lê-dô) It. (Rome In.)	41·19 N	12·17 E
121	Lidzbark (lĭts'bärk) Pol.	54·07 N	20·36 E
168	Liebenbergs R. S. Afr. (Johannesburg & Pretoria In.)	27·35 S	28·25 E
111	Liebenwalde (lē'bĕn-väl-dĕ) Ger. (Berlin In.)	52·52 N	13·24 E
151	Liechou Pan-Tao (Pen.) China	20·40 N	109·25 E
120	Liechtenstein (lĕk'tĕn-shtīn) Eur.	47·14 N	9·15 E
117	Liége (lê-äzh') Bel.	50·40 N	5·30 E
151	Lienchiang China	21·38 N	110·15 E
148	Lienshui (lĭăN'sōōā) China	33·46 N	119·15 E
147	Lienyün China	33·10 N	120·01 E
148	Lienyun (lĭăN'yüN) China	34·43 N	119·27 E
120	Lienz (lê-ĕnts') Aus.	46·49 N	12·45 E
119	Liepāja (le'pä-yä') Sov. Un.	56·31 N	20·59 E
111	Lier Bel. (Brussels In.)	5·08 N	4·34 E
111	Liesing (lē'sĭng) Aus. (Vienna In.)	48·09 N	16·17 E
120	Liestal (lēs'täl) Switz.	47·28 N	7·44 E
81	Lievre, Rivière du (R.) Can.	45·00 N	75·25 W
116	Liffey R. (lĭf'ĭ) Ire.	53·21 N	6·35 W
159	Lifou, (I.) N. Cal. Is.	21·15 S	167·32 E
155	Ligao (lê-gä'ô) Phil. (Manila In.)	13·14 N	123·33 E
160	Lightning Ridge Austl.	29·23 S	147·50 E
167	Ligonha (R.) (lê-gō'nyȧ) Moz.	16·14 S	39·00 E
80	Ligonier (lĭg-ô-nēr') Ind.	41·30 N	85·35 W
136	Ligovo (lē'gô-vô) Sov. Un. (Leningrad In.)	59·51 N	30·13 E
126	Liguria (Reg.) (lê-gōō-rē-ä) It.	44·24 N	8·27 E
126	Ligurian Sea (lĭ-gū'rĭ-ăn) Eur.	43·42 N	8·32 E
159	Lihou Rfs. (lê-hōō') Austl.	17·23 S	152·43 E
151	Lihsien (lē'hsyĕn') China	29·42 N	111·40 E
148	Lihsien China	38·30 N	115·38 E
148	Lihuang (lē'hōōăNg) China	31·32 N	115·46 E
157	Lihue (lê-hōō'ā) Hawaii (In.)	21·59 N	159·23 W
119	Lihula (lē'hŏŏ-lȧ) Sov. Un.	58·41 N	23·50 E
128	Likhoslavl' (lyê-kôslav''l) Sov. Un.	57·07 N	35·27 E
129	Likhovka (lyê-kôf'kȧ) Sov. Un.	48·52 N	33 57 E
122	Lille (lēl) Fr.	50·38 N	3·01 E
118	Lille Baelt (str.) Den.	55·09 N	9·53 E
118	Lillehammer (lēl'ĕ-häm'mĕr) Nor.	61·07 N	10·25 E
118	Lillesand (lēl'ĕ-sän') Nor.	58·16 N	8·19 E
118	Lillestrōm (lēl'ĕ-strûm) Nor.	59·56 N	11·04 E
65	Lilliwaup (lĭl'ĭ-wŏp) Wash. (Seattle In.)	47·28 N	123·07 W
86	Lillooet Can.	50·49 N	122·02 W
166	Lilongwe (lē-lô-än) Nya.	13·51 S	33·47 E
80	Lima (lī'mȧ) Ohio	40·40 N	84·05 W
98	Lima (lē'mä) Peru	12·06 S	76·55 W
124	Lima (R.) Port.	41·45 N	8·22 W
101	Lima Duarte (dwä'r-tĕ) Braz. (Rio de Janeiro In.)	21·52 S	43·47 W
67	Lima Res. Mont.	44·45 N	112·15 W
139	Limassol (lē-mä-sōl') Cyprus (Palestine In.)	34·39 N	33·02 E
100	Limay (lē-mä'ē) (R.) Arg.	39·50 S	69·15 W
119	Limbaži (lēm'bä-zĭ) Sov. Un.	57·32 N	24·44 E
95	Limbé Hai.	19·45 N	72·30 W

ăt; finăl; rāte; senâte; ärm; åsk; sofȧ; fâre; ch-choose; dh-as th in other; bē; ēvent; bĕt; recĕnt; cratẽr; g-go; gh-guttural g; bĭt; ĭ-short neutral; rīde; K-guttural k as ch in German ich;

PRONOUNCING INDEX Limboli–Lodgepole 229

Page	Name	Pronunciation	Region	Lat. °′	Long. °′
142	Limboli		India	22·39 N	71·49 E
120	Limburg	(lem-bŏŏrg′)	Ger.	50·22 N	8·03 E
118	Limedsforsen	(lē′mĕs-fōrs′ĕn)	Swe.	60·54 N	13·24 E
101	Limeira	(lē-mā′rä)	Braz. (Rio de Janeiro In.)	22·34 S	47·24 W
118	Limfjorden (Fd.)		Den.	56·14 N	7·55 E
118	Limfjorden (Fd.)		Den.	56·56 N	10·35 E
158	Limmen Bght.	(lĭm′ĕn)	Austl.	14·45 S	136·00 E
127	Limni	(lêm′nê)	Grc.	38·47 N	23·22 E
127	Limnos (I.)		Grc.	39·58 N	24·48 E
85	Limoges	(lê-môzh′)	Can. (Ottawa In.)	45·20 N	75·15 W
122	Limoges		Fr.	45·50 N	1·15 E
72	Limon	(lī′mŏn)	Colo.	39 15 N	103·41 W
93	Limón	(lê-mōn′)	C. R.	10·01 N	83·02 W
92	Limón	(lē-mô′n)	Hond.	15·53 N	85·34 W
95	Limon (R.)		Dom. Rep.	18·20 N	71·40 W
88	Limón B.		C. Z. (Panama Canal In.)	9·21 N	79·58 W
123	Limours	(lē-mōōr′)	Fr. (Paris In.)	48·39 N	2·05 E
122	Limousin, Plateaux du (Plat.)	(plä-tō′ dü lē-mōō-zäN′)	Fr.	45·44 N	1·09 E
122	Limoux	(lē-mōō′)	Fr.	43·03 N	2·14 E
166	Limpopo R.	(lĭm-pō′pō)	Afr.	23·15 S	27·46 E
101	Linares	(lê-nä′rās)	Chile (Santiago In.)	35·51 S	71·35 W
76	Linares		Mex.	24·53 N	99·34 W
124	Linares	(lē-nă′rĕs)	Sp.	38·07 N	3·38 W
101	Linares (Prov.)		Chile (Santiago In.)	35·53 S	71·30 W
126	Linaro, C.	(lê-nä′rä)	It.	42·02 N	11·53 E
148	Linchang	(lĭn′chäng′)	China	36·19 N	114·40 E
150	Linchiang	(lĭn′chäng′)	China	41·45 N	127·00 E
148	Linch′ing	(lĭn′chĭng)	China	36·49 N	115·42 E
151	Linch′uan		China	27·58 N	116·18 E
101	Lincoln	(lĭŋ′kŭn)	Arg. (Buenos Aires In.)	34·51 S	61·29 W
68	Lincoln		Calif.	38·51 N	121·19 W
110	Lincoln		Eng.	53·14 N	0·33 W
73	Lincoln		Ill.	40·09 N	89·21 W
72	Lincoln		Kans.	39·02 N	98·08 W
82	Lincoln		Maine	45·23 N	68·31 W
83	Lincoln		Mass. (Boston In.)	42·25 N	71·19 W
73	Lincoln		Nebr.	40·49 N	96·43 W
110	Lincoln (Co.)		Eng.	53·12 N	0·29 W
72	Lincoln, Mt.		Colo.	39·20 N	106·19 W
110	Lincoln Heights (Reg.)		Eng.	53·23 N	0·39 W
75	Lincoln Park		Mich. (Detroit In.)	42·14 N	83·11 W
84	Lincoln Park		N. J. (New York In.)	40·56 N	74·18 W
79	Lincolnton	–lĭŋ′kŭn-tŭn)	N. C.	35·27 N	81·15 W
116	Lincoln Wolds	(woldz′)	Eng.	53·25 N	0·23 W
78	Lindale	(lĭn′dāl)	Ga.	34·10 N	85·10 W
120	Lindau	(lĭn′dou)	Ger.	47·33 N	9·40 E
78	Linden	(lĭn′dĕn)	Ala.	32·16 N	87·47 W
74	Linden		Mo. (Kansas City In.)	39·13 N	94·35 W
84	Linden		N. J. (New York In.)	40·38 N	74·16 W
84	Lindenhurst	(lĭn′dĕn-hûrst)	N. Y. (New York In.)	40·41 N	73·23 W
84	Lindenwold	(lĭn′dĕn-wôld)	N. J. (Philadelphia In.)	39·50 N	75·00 W
118	Lindesberg	(lĭn′dĕs-bĕrgh)	Swe.	59·37 N	15·14 E
117	Lindesnes (C.)	(lĭn′ĕs-nĕs)	Nor.	58·00 N	7·05 E
150	Lindho		China	40·45 N	107·30 E
167	Lindi	(lĭn′dê)	Tan.	9·59 S	39·43 E
165	Lindi R		Con. L.	1·00 N	27·13 E
168	Lindley	(lĭnd′lê)	S. Afr. (Johannesburg & Pretoria In.)	27·52 S	27·55 E
111	Lindow	(lēn′dōv)	Ger. (Berlin In.)	52·58 N	12·59 E
81	Lindsay	(lĭn′zê)	Can.	44·20 N	78·45 W
72	Lindsay		Okla.	34·50 N	97·38 W
72	Lindsborg	(lĭnz′bôrg)	Kans.	38·34 N	97·42 W
110	Lindsey (Co.)	(lĭn′zĭ)	Eng.	53·25 N	0·32 W
148	Lineh′ü	(lĭn′chü)	China	36·31 N	118·33 E
78	Lineville	(līn′vĭl)	Ala.	33·18 N	85·45 W
150	Linfen		China	36·00 N	111·38 E
155	Lingayen	(lĭŋ′gä-yān′)	Phil. (Manila In.)	16·01 N	120·13 E
155	Lingayen G.		Phil. (Manila In.)	16·18 N	120·11 E
120	Lingen	(lĭŋ′gĕn)	Ger.	52·32 N	7·20 E
154	Lingga, Pulau-Pulau (Is.)	(lĭng-gä′)	Indon.	0·35 S	105·05 E
151	Lingling		China	26·10 N	111·40 E
148	Lingpi	(lĭng′pĭ′)	China	33·33 N	117·33 E
148	Lingtienchen	(ling′diäN′jĕn)	China	31·52 N	121·28 E
151	Lingting Yang (Can.)		China	22·00 N	114·00 E
164	Linguere	(lĭŋ-gĕr′)	Senegal	15·22 N	14·55 W
150	Lingwu		China	38·05 N	106·18 E
150	Lingyüan		China	41·12 N	119·20 E
151	Linhai		China	28·52 N	121·08 E
150	Linhsi		China	43·30 N	118·02 E
148	Linhuaikuan	(lĭnhōōäī′gōōäN)	China	32·55 N	117·38 E
148	Linhuanchi	(lĭn′hōōaN′jē)	China	33·42 N	116·33 E
148	Lini	(lĭn′yē)	China	35·04 N	118·21 E
151	Linkao		China	19·58 N	109·40 E
118	Linköping	(lĭn′chû-pĭng)	Swe.	58·25 N	15·35 E
148	Linmingkuan	(lĭN′mĭng′gōōän)	China	36·47 N	114·32 E
116	Linnhe (L.)	(lĭn′ê)	Scot.	56·35 N	4·30 W
99	Lins	(lê′Ns)	Braz.	21·42 S	49·41 W
84	Linthicum Heights	(lĭn′thĭ-kŭm)	Md. (Baltimore In.)	39·12 N	76·39 W
150	Lintien		China	42·08 N	124·59 E
80	Linton	(lĭn′tŭn)	Ind.	39·05 N	87·15 W
70	Linton		N. D.	46·16 N	100·15 W
151	Linwu	(lĭn′wōō′)	China	25·20 N	112·30 E
148	Linying	(lĭn′yĭng′)	China	33·48 N	113·56 E
148	Linyü	(lĭn′yü)	China	40·01 N	119·45 E
120	Linz	(lĭnts)	Aus.	48·18 N	14·18 E
155	Lipa	(lê-pä′)	Phil. (Manila In.)	13·55 N	121·10 E
126	Lipari	(lē′pä-rê)	It.	38·29 N	15·00 E
126	Lipari (I.)		It.	38·32 N	15·04 E
128	Lipetsk	(lyē′pĕtsk)	Sov. Un.	52·26 N	39·34 E
128	Lipetsk (Oblast)		Sov. Un.	52·18 N	38·30 E
151	Lip′ing	(lê′pĭng′)	China	26·18 N	109·00 E
121	Lipno	(lēp′nô)	Pol.	52·50 N	19·12 E
117	Lippe (R.)	(lĭp′ĕ)	Ger.	51·36 N	6·45 E
120	Lippstadt	(lĭp′shtät)	Ger.	51·39 N	8·20 E
84	Lipscomb	(lĭp′skŭm)	Ala. (Birmingham In.)	33·26 N	86·56 W
129	Liptsy	(lyēp′tsê)	Sov. Un.	50·11 N	36·25 E
151	Lip′u		China	24·38 N	110·35 E
126	Liri (R.)	(lē′rē)	It.	41·49 N	13·30 E
125	Liria	(lê′ryä)	Sp.	39·35 N	0·34 W
165	Lisala	(lê-sä′lä)	Con. L.	2·14 N	21·38 E
125	Lisboa (Lisbon)	(lêzh-bō′ä) (lĭz′bŭn)	Port. (Lisbon In.)	38·42 N	9·05 W
82	Lisbon		Maine	43·59 N	70·03 W
70	Lisbon		N. D.	46·21 N	97·43 W
80	Lisbon		Ohio	40·45 N	80·50 W
	Lisbon, see Lisboa				
116	Lisburn	(lĭs′bŭrn)	N. Ire.	54·35 N	6·05 W
64	Lisburne, C.		Alaska	68·20 N	165·40 W
150	Lishih		China	37·32 N	111·12 E
150	Lishu		China	43·12 N	124·18 E
150	Lishuchen		China	45·01 N	130·50 E
151	Lishui		China	28·28 N	120·00 E
148	Lishui	(lĭ′shwĭ′)	China	31·41 N	119·01 E
149	Lishui		China (Canton In.)	23·12 N	113·09 E
122	Lisieux	(lē-zyû′)	Fr.	49·10 N	0·13 E
136	Lisiy Nos	(lĭ′sĭy nôs)	Sov. Un. (Leningrad In.)	60·01 N	30·00 E
129	Liski	(lyēs′kê)	Sov. Un.	50·56 N	39·28 E
75	Lisle	(līl)	Ill. (Chicago In.)	41·48 N	88·04 W
123	L′Isle-Adam	(lēl-ädäN′)	Fr. (Paris In.)	49·05 N	2·13 E
160	Lismore	(lĭz′môr)	Austl.	28·48 S	153·18 E
47	Lister, Mt.	(lĭs′tēr)	Ant.	78·05 S	163·00 E
139	Litani (R.)		Leb. (Palestine In.)	33·28 N	35·42 E
73	Litchfield	(lĭch′fēld)	Ill.	39·10 N	89·38 W
71	Litchfield		Minn.	45·08 N	94·34 W
75	Litchfield		Ohio (Cleveland In.)	41·10 N	82·01 W
160	Lithgow	(lĭth′gō)	Austl.	33·23 S	149·31 E
126	Lithinon, Ark. (C.)		Grc. (In.)	34·59 N	24·35 E
84	Lithonia	(lĭ-thō′nĭ-ȧ)	Ga. (Atlanta In.)	33·43 N	84·07 W
130	Lithuanian S. S. R.	(lĭth-û-ā-′nĭ-ȧ)	Sov. Un.	55·42 N	23·30 E
129	Litin	(lê-tēn)	Sov. Un.	49·16 N	28·11 E
127	Litókhoron	(lē′tô-kō′rôn)	Grc.	40·05 N	22·29 E
120	Litomerice	(lē′tô-myĕr′zhĭ-tsĕ)	Czech.	50·33 N	14·10 E
120	Litomyšl	(lē′tô-mêsh′l)	Czech.	49·52 N	16·14 E
161	Little (R.)		Austl. (Melbourne In.)	37·54 S	144·27 E
78	Little (R.)		Tenn.-Mo.	36·28 N	89·39 W
77	Little R.		Tex.	30·48 N	96·50 W
94	Little Abaco (I.)	(ä′bä-kō)	Ba. Is.	26·55 N	77·45 W
47	Little America		Ant.	78·30 S	161·30 W
154	Little Andaman I.	(ăn-dȧ-măn′)	Andaman Is.	10·39 N	93·08 E
94	Little Bahama Bk.	(bȧ-hā′mȧ)	Ba. Is.	26·55 N	78·40 W
67	Little Belt Mts.	(bĕlt)	Mont.	47·00 N	110·50 W
67	Little Bighorn R.	(bĭg-hôrn)	Mont.	45·08 N	107·30 W
	Little Bitter, see el Buheirat el Murrat el Sughra				
66	Little Bitterroot R.	(bĭt′ēr-ōōt)	Mont.	47·45 N	114·45 W
72	Little Blue (R.)		Nebr.	40·15 N	98·01 W
74	Little Blue R.	(blōō)	Mo. (Kansas City In.)	38·52 N	94·25 W
110	Littleborough	(lĭt′′l-bŭr-ô)	Eng.	53·39 N	2·06 W
75	Little Calumet R.	(kăl-û-mĕt′)	Ill. (Chicago In.)	41·38 N	87·38 W
94	Little Cayman (I.)	(kā′mȧn)	Cayman Is.	19·40 N	80·05 W
69	Little Colorado (R.)	(kŏl-ô-rā′dō)	Ariz.	36·05 N	111·35 W
84	Little Compton	(kŏmp′tŏn)	R. I. (Providence In.)	41·31 N	71·07 W
93	Little Corn I.		Nic.	12·19 N	82·50 W
95	Little Exuma (I.)	(ĕk-sōō′mä)	Ba. Is.	23·25 N	75·40 W
71	Little Falls	(fôlz)	Minn.	45·58 N	94·23 W
81	Little Falls		N. Y.	43·05 N	74·55 W
72	Littlefield	(lĭt′′l-fēld)	Tex.	33·55 N	102·17 W
71	Little Fork (R.)	(fôrk)	Minn.	48·24 N	93·30 W
89	Little Hans Lollick (I.)	(hans lôl′lĭk)	Vir. Is. (U. S. A.) (St. Thomas In.)	18·25 N	64·54 W
66	Little Humboldt R.	(hŭm′bōlt)	Nev.	41·10 N	117·40 W
95	Little Inagua (I.)	(ê-nä′gwä)	Ba. Is.	21·30 N	73·00 W
94	Little Isaac (I.)	(ī′zȧk)	Ba. Is.	25·55 N	79·00 W
80	Little Kanawha (R.)	(kȧ-nô′wȧ)	W. Va.	39·05 N	81·30 W
166	Little Karroo (Mts.)	(kä-rōō)	S. Afr.	33·50 S	21·02 E
87	Little Mecatina (R.)	(mĕ cȧ tī nȧ)	Can.	52·40 N	62·21 W
75	Little Miami R.	(mī-ăm′ĭ)	Ohio (Cincinnati In.)	39·19 N	84·15 W
75	Little Miami R., E. Fk.		Ohio (Cincinnati In.)	39·01 N	84·03 W
73	Little Missouri (R.)	(mĭ-sōō′rĭ)	Ark.	34·15 N	93·54 W
70	Little Missouri (R.)		S. D.	45·46 N	103·48 W
83	Little or Gray (R.)	(lĭt′l) (grā)	Can.	47·50 N	57·05 W
79	Little Pee Dee (R.)	(pē-dē′)	S. C.	34·35 N	79·21 W
67	Little Powder R.	(pou′dēr)	Wyo.	44·51 N	105·20 W
73	Little Red (R.)	(rĕd)	Ark.	35·42 N	92·14 W
73	Little Red R.		Okla.	33·53 N	94·38 W
73	Little Rock	(rôk)	Ark.	34·42 N	92·16 W
123	Little St. Bernard P.	(sântbĕr-närd′) (săN bĕr-när′)	Fr.-It.	45·49 N	6·50 E
95	Little San Salvador (I.)	(săn săl′vȧ-dôr)	Ba. Is.	24·35 N	75·55 W
79	Little Satilla (R.)	(sȧ-tĭl′ȧ)	Ga.	31·43 N	82·47 W
70	Little Sioux (R.)	(sōō)	Iowa	42·22 N	95·47 W
67	Little Snake R.	(snāk)	Colo.	40·40 N	108·21 W
78	Little Tallapoosa (R.)	(tăl-ȧ-pŏŏ′să)	Ala.	32·25 N	85·28 W
78	Little Tennessee (R.)	(tĕn-ĕ-sē′)	Tenn.	35·36 N	84·05 W
72	Littleton	(lĭt′′l-tŭn)	Colo.	39·34 N	105·01 W
83	Littleton		Mass. (Boston In.)	42·32 N	71·29 W
81	Littleton		N. H.	44·15 N	71·45 W
80	Little Wabash (R.)	(wô′băsh)	Ill.	38·50 N	88·30 W
67	Little Wood R.	(wŏŏd)	Idaho	43·00 N	114·08 W
148	Liuan	(lyōō′än′)	China	31·45 N	116·29 E
151	Liuchou	(lōō′chōō)	China	24·25 N	109·30 E
148	Liuho	(lyōō′hō′)	China	32·22 N	118·50 E
150	Liuho		China	42·10 N	125·38 E
150	Liup′an Shan (Mts.)		China	36·20 N	105·30 E
151	Liuyang	(lyōō′yäng′)	China	28·10 N	113·35 E
148	Liuyüan	(lū′yüän)	China	36·09 N	114·37 E
128	Līvāni	(lē′vȧ-nê)	Sov. Un.	56·24 N	26·12 E
64	Livengood	(līv′ĕn-gŏŏd)	Alaska	65·30 N	148·35 W
78	Live Oak	(līv′ōk)	Fla.	30·15 N	83·00 W
65	Livermore	(lĭv′ēr-mōr)	Calif. (San Francisco In.)	37·41 N	121·46 W
80	Livermore		Ky.	37·30 N	87·05 W
161	Liverpool	(lĭv′ēr-pōōl)	Austl. (Sydney In.)	33·55 S	150·56 E
82	Liverpool		Can.	44·02 N	64·44 W
110	Liverpool		Eng.	53·25 N	2·52 W
77	Liverpool		Tex. (In.)	29·18 N	95·17 W
64	Liverpool B.		Alaska	70·25 N	129·35 W
159	Liverpool Ra.		Austl.	31·47 S	31·00 E
165	Livindo R.		Gabon	1·09 N	13·30 E
78	Livingston	(lĭv′ĭng-stŭn)	Ala.	32·35 N	88·09 W
92	Livingston		Guat.	15·50 N	88·45 W
74	Livingston		Ill. (St. Louis In.)	38·58 N	89·51 W
67	Livingston		Mont.	45·40 N	110·35 W
78	Livingston		Tenn.	36·23 N	85·20 W
166	Livingstone	(lĭv-ĭng-stôn)	N. Rh.	17·51 S	25·48 E
166	Livingstonia	(lĭv-ĭng-stō′nĭ-ȧ)	Nya.	10·35 S	34·07 E
126	Livno	(lēv′nô)	Yugo.	43·50 N	17·03 E
128	Livny	(lēv′nê)	Sov. Un.	52·28 N	37·36 E
75	Livonia	(lĭ-vō-nĭ-ȧ)	Mich. (Detroit In.)	42·25 N	83·23 W
126	Livorno (Leghorn)	(lê-vôr′nō) (lĕg′hôrn)	It.	43·32 N	11·18 E
100	Livramento	(lē-vrȧ-mĕ′n-tô)	Braz.	30·46 S	55·21 W
148	Liyang	(lē′yäng′)	China	31·30 N	119·29 E
116	Lizard Pt.	(lĭz′ȧrd)	Eng.	49·55 N	5·09 W
123	Lizy-sur-Ourcq	(lēk-sē′sür-ōōrk′)	Fr. (Paris In.)	49·01 N	3·02 E
111	Ljmuiden		Neth. (Amsterdam In.)	52·27 N	4·35 E
126	Ljubljana	(lyōō′blyä′na)	Yugo.	46·04 N	14·29 E
126	Ljubuški	(lyōō′bŏŏsh-kê)	Yugo.	43·11 N	17·29 E
118	Ljungan (R.)		Swe.	62·50 N	13·45 E
118	Ljungby	(lyŏŏng′bü)	Swe.	56·49 N	13·56 E
118	Ljusdal	(lyōōs′däl)	Swe.	61·50 N	16·11 E
118	Ljusnan (R.)		Swe.	61·55 N	15·33 E
116	Llandudno	(lăn-dūd′nō)	Wales	53·20 N	3·46 W
116	Llanelly	(lȧ-nĕl′ĭ)	Wales	51·44 N	4·09 W
124	Llanes	(lyä′nâs)	Sp.	43·25 N	4·41 W
76	Llano	(lä′nō) (lyä′nō)	Tex.	30·45 N	98·41 W
76	Llano R.		Tex.	30·38 N	99·04 W
98	Llanos	(lyȧ′nŏs) (Reg.)	Col.-Ven.	4·00 N	71·15 W
90	Llera	(lyā′rä)	Mex.	23·16 N	99·03 W
124	Llerena	(lyā-rā′nä)	Sp.	38·14 N	6·02 W
116	Lleyn Prom.	(lĭn)	Wales	52·55 N	3·10 W
125	Llobregat (R.)	(lyô-brĕ-gät′)	Sp.	41·55 N	1·55 E
85	Lloyd L.	(loid)	Can. (Calgary In.)	50·52 N	114·13 W
86	Lloydminster		Can.	53·18 N	109·50 W
125	Lluchmayor	(lyōōch-mä-yôr′)	Sp.	39·28 N	2·53 E
100	Llullaillaco (Vol.)	(lyōō-lyī-lyȧ′kō)	Arg.	24·50 S	68·30 W
166	Loange (R.)	(lô-äŋ′gā)	Con. L.	4·46 S	20·18 E
166	Lobatsi	(lō-bă′tsē)	Bech.	25·13 S	25·35 E
100	Lobería	(lô-bĕ-rē′ä)	Arg.	38·13 S	58·48 W
166	Lobito	(lô-bē′tō)	Ang.	12·15 S	13·35 E
136	Lobnya	(lôb′nyȧ)	Sov. Un. (Moscow In.)	56·01 N	37·29 E
101	Lobos	(lō′bôs)	Arg. (Buenos Aires In.)	35·10 S	59·08 W
94	Lobos, Cayo (I.)	(lō′bôs)	Ba. Is.	22·25 N	77·40 W
91	Lobos, Isla de (I.)	(ê′s-lă-dĕ-lô′bōs)	Mex.	21·24 N	97·11 W
98	Lobos de Tierra (I.)	(lô′bō-dĕ-tyĕ′r-ră)	Peru	6·29 S	80·55 W
136	Lobva	(lôb′vȧ)	Sov. Un. (Urals In.)	59·12 N	60·28 E
136	Lobva R.		Sov. Un. (Urals In.)	59·14 N	60·17 E
120	Locarno	(lô-kär′nō)	Switz.	46·10 N	8·43 E
122	Loches	(lôsh)	Fr.	47·08 N	0·56 E
151	Loching		China	28·02 N	120·40 E
79	Lochloosa (L.)	(lŏk-lō′sȧ)	Fla.	29·33 N	82·07 W
116	Lochy (L.)	(lŏk′ĭ)	Scot.	56·57 N	4·45 W
79	Lockhart	(lŏk′hȧrt)	S. C.	34·47 N	81·30 W
77	Lockhart		Tex.	29·54 N	97·40 W
81	Lock Haven	(lŏk′hā-vĕn)	Pa.	41·05 N	77·30 W
75	Lockland	(lŏk′lănd)	Ohio (Cincinnati In.)	39·14 N	84·27 W
85	Lockport	(lŏk′pōrt)	Can. (Winnipeg In.)	50·05 N	96·58 W
75	Lockport		Ill. (Chicago In.)	41·35 N	88·04 W
75	Lockport		N. Y. (Buffalo In.)	43·11 N	78·43 W
84	Lock Raven Res.	(lŏk ra′vĕn)	Md. (Baltimore In.)	39·28 N	76·38 W
154	Loc Ninh	(lōk′nĭng′)	Viet.	12·00 N	106·30 E
85	Locust Hill	(lō′kŭst hĭl)	Can. (Toronto In.)	43·54 N	79·11 W
139	Lod	(lôd)	Isr. (Palestine In.)	31·57 N	34·55 E
122	Lodève	(lô-dĕv′)	Fr.	43·43 N	3·18 E
119	Lodeynoye Pole	(lô-dĕy-nô′yĕ)	Sov. Un.	60·43 N	33·24 E
67	Lodge Cr.		Mont.	48·51 N	109·30 W
70	Lodgepole Cr.	(lŏj′pōl)	Wyo.	41·22 N	104·48 W

ng-sing; ŋ-baŋk; N-nasalized n; nŏd; cŏmmit; ōld; ôbey; ôrder; fōōd; fŏŏt; ou-out; s-soft; sh-dish; th-thin; pūre; ûnite; ûrn; stŭd; circŭs; ü-as "y" in study; ′-indeterminate vowel.

Page	Name Pronunciation Region	Lat. °′	Long. °′
142	Lodhran..........W. Pak.	29·40 N	71·39 E
68	Lodi (lō'dī)..........Calif.	38·07 N	121·17 W
126	Lodi (lô'dē)..........It.	45·18 N	9·30 E
75	Lodi (lō'dī)..Ohio (Cleveland In.)	41·02 N	82·01 W
124	Lodosa (lô-dô'-sä)..........Sp.	42·27 N	2·04 W
121	Łódź (wōōdzh)..........Pol.	51·46 N	19·13 E
125	Loeches (lô-ăch'ĕs) Sp. (Madrid In.)	40·22 N	3·25 W
112	Lofoten (Is.) (lô'fō-tĕn)......Nor.	68·26 N	13·42 E
80	Logan (lō'găn)..........Ohio	39·35 N	82·25 W
67	Logan..........Utah	41·46 N	111·51 W
80	Logan..........W. Va.	37·50 N	82·00 W
86	Logan, Mt..........Can.	60·54 N	140·33 W
80	Logansport (lō'gănz-pōrt)....Ind.	40·45 N	86·25 W
165	Logone R. (lō-gō'nä) (lô-gôn') Chad-Cam.	10·28 N	15·22 E
164	Logoualé (lô-gwä-lā').Ivory Coast	7·19 N	7·38 W
124	Logroño (lô-grō'nyō)..........Sp.	42·28 N	2·25 W
124	Logrosán (lô-grô-sän')..........Sp.	39·22 N	5·29 W
118	Løgstør (lûgh-stûr')..........Den.	56·56 N	9·15 E
148	Lohochai (lou'wŭ'jäï)......China	33·35 N	114·02 E
122	Loir (R.) (lwár)..........Fr.	47·40 N	0·07 E
122	Loire (R.)..........Fr.	47·19 N	1·11 W
98	Loja (lō'hä)..........Ec.	3·49 S	79·13 W
124	Loja (lô'-kä)..........Sp.	37·10 N	4·11 W
168	Lokala Drift (lô'kā-lȧ drĭft).S. Afr. (Johannesburg & Pretoria In.)	24·00 S	26·38 E
129	Lokhvitsa (lôĸ-vĕt'sȧ)...Sov. Un.	50·21 N	33·16 E
164	Lokoja (lô-kō'yä)..........Nig.	7·50 N	6·39 E
165	Lol R. (lōl)..........Sud.	9·06 N	28·09 E
118	Lolland (lôl'än')..........Den.	54·41 N	11·00 E
164	Lolo (lō'lō)..........Cam.	3·14 N	10·38 E
127	Lom (lōm)..........Bul.	43·48 N	23·15 E
74	Loma Linda (lō'mȧ lĭn'dȧ) Calif. (Los Angeles In.)	34·04 N	117·16 W
110	Lomas de Zamora (lō'mäs dā zä-mō'rä).Arg. (In.)	34·31 S	58·24 W
75	Lombard (lŏm-bärd) Ill. (Chicago In.)	41·53 N	88·01 W
126	Lombardia (Reg.) (lôm-bär-dē'ä).It.	45·20 N	9·30 E
155	Lomblen (I.) (lŏm-blĕn')...Indon.	8·08 S	123·45 E
154	Lombok (I.) (lŏm-bŏk')....Indon.	9·15 S	116·15 E
154	Lombok Selat (Str.).......Indon.	9·00 S	115·28 E
164	Lomé (lō-mā') (lō'mā)......Togo.	6·13 N	1·14 E
166	Lomela (lô-mā'lȧ)........Con. L.	2·19 S	23·33 E
166	Lomela (R.)..........Con. L.	0·21 S	21·11 E
76	Lometa (lō-mē'tȧ)..........Tex.	31·10 N	98·25 W
165	Lomié (lô-mê-ā')..........Cam.	3·14 N	13·34 E
74	Lomita (lō-mē'tȧ) Calif. (Los Angeles In.)	33·48 N	118·20 W
111	Lommel.......Bel. (Brussels In.)	51·14 N	5·21 E
116	Lomond, Loch (L.) (lŏk lō'mŭnd) Scot.	56·15 N	4·40 W
136	Lomonosov (lô-mô'nô-sof) Sov. Un. (Leningrad In.)	59·54 N	29·47 E
68	Lompoc (lŏm-pōk')..........Calif.	34·39 N	120·30 W
121	Lomza (lôm'zhȧ)..........Pol.	53·11 N	22·04 E
81	Lonaconing (lō-nȧ-kō'nĭng)...Md.	39·35 N	78·55 W
80	London (lŭn'dŭn)..........Can.	43·00 N	81·20 W
110	London.......Eng. (London In.)	51·30 N	0·07 W
78	London..........Ky.	37·07 N	84·06 W
80	London..........Ohio	39·50 N	83·30 W
82	Londonderry (lŭn'dŭn-dĕr-ĭ).Can.	45·29 N	63·40 W
116	Londonderry..........N. Ire.	54·60 N	6·80 W
158	Londonderry, C..........Austl.	13·30 S	127·00 E
99	Londrina (lôn-drē'nä).......Braz.	21·53 S	51·17 W
80	Lonely (I.) (lōn'lĭ)..........Can.	45·35 N	81·30 W
68	Lone Pine..........Calif.	36·36 N	118·03 W
93	Lone Star..........Nic.	13·58 N	84·25 W
95	Long (I.)..........Ba. Is.	23·25 N	75·10 W
82	Long (I.)..........Can.	44·21 N	66·25 W
155	Long (I.)..........N. Gui. Ter.	5·10 S	147·30 E
70	Long (L.)..........N. D.	46·47 N	100·14 W
65	Long (L.).....Wash. (Seattle In.)	47·29 N	122·36 W
166	Longa (R.) (lôŋ'gȧ)..........Ang.	10·20 S	15·10 E
79	Long B..........S. C.	33·30 N	78·54 W
74	Long Beach (lông bēch) Calif. (Los Angeles In.)	33·46 N	118·12 W
84	Long Beach.N. Y. (New York In.)	40·35 N	73·38 W
85	Long Branch (lông brȧnch) Can. (Toronto In.)	43·36 N	79·32 W
84	Long Branch.N. J. (New York In.)	40·18 N	73·59 W
70	Longdon (lông'-dŭn).......N. D.	48·45 N	98·23 W
110	Long Eaton (ē'tŭn)..........Eng.	52·54 N	1·16 W
116	Longford (lŏng'fērd)..........Ire.	53·43 N	7·40 W
74	Longhorn (lông-hôrn) Tex. (San Antonio In.)	29·33 N	98·23 W
81	Long I. (lông)..........N. Y.	40·50 N	72·50 W
81	Long Island Sd. (lông ī'lănd) Conn.-N. Y.	41·05 N	72·45 W
123	Longjumeau (lôɴ-zhü-mō') Fr. (Paris In.)	48·42 N	2·17 E
148	Longk'ou (lōōng'kō).......China	37·39 N	120·21 E
87	Longlac (lông'lăk)..........Can.	49·41 N	86·28 W
70	Longlake (lông-lāk).........S. D.	45·52 N	99·06 W
72	Longmont (lŏng'mŏnt)........Colo.	40·11 N	105·07 W
123	Longnes (lôɴ'yĕ)....Fr. (Paris In.)	48·56 N	1·37 W
110	Longnor (lông'nôr)..........Eng.	53·11 N	1·52 W
70	Long Pine (lông pīn).........Nebr.	42·31 N	99·42 W
81	Lont Pt..........Can.	42·35 N	80·05 W
83	Long Pt..........Can.	48·46 N	58·47 W
80	Long Point B..........Can.	42·40 N	80·10 W
71	Long Prairie (lông prâr'ĭ)...Minn.	45·58 N	94·49 W
83	Long Range Mts..........Can.	47·45 N	58·52 W
159	Longreach (lông'rēch).......Austl.	23·32 S	144·17 E
82	Long Reach (R.)..........Can.	45·26 N	66·05 W
161	Long Rf......Austl. (Sydney In.)	33·45 S	151·22 E
110	Longridge (lông'rĭj)..........Eng.	53·51 N	2·37 W
72	Longs Pk. (lôngz)..........Colo.	40·17 N	105·37 W
110	Longton (lông'tŭn)..........Eng.	52·59 N	2·08 W
85	Longueuil (lôɴ-gû'y')... Can. (Montreal In.)	45·32 N	73·30 W
65	Longview (lông-vū) Ore. (Portland In.)	46·06 N	123·02 W
77	Longview..........Tex.	32·29 N	94·44 W
77	Longville (lông'vĭl)..........La.	30·36 N	93·14 W
123	Longwy (lôɴ-wē')..........Fr.	49·32 N	6·14 E
154	Long Xuyen (loung' sōō'yĕn).Viet.	10·31 N	105·28 E
73	Lonoke (lō'nōk)..........Ark.	34·48 N	91·52 W
123	Lons-le-Saunier (lôɴ-lē-sō-nyā').Fr.	46·40 N	5·33 E
101	Lontué (lōn-tōōĕ') (R.) Chile (Santiago In.)	35.20 S	70·45 W
155	Looc (lô-ōk')...Phil. (Manila In.)	12·16 N	121·59 E
80	Loogootee..........Ind.	38·40 N	86·55 W
79	Lookout, C. (lŏŏk'out).....N. C.	34·34 N	76·38 W
66	Lookout Pt. Res..........Ore.	43·51 N	122·38 W
85	Looma (lōō'mă) Can. (Edmonton In.)	53·22 N	113·15 W
116	Loop Head (lōōp)..........Ire.	52·32 N	9·59 W
78	Loosahatchie (R.) (lōz-ȧ-hă'chē) Tenn.	35·20 N	89·45 W
111	Loosdrechtsche Plassen (L.) Neth. (Amsterdam In.)	52·11 N	5·09 E
135	Lopatka, Mys (C.) (lô-pät'kȧ) Sov. Un.	51·00 N	156·52 E
163	Lopez, Cap (C.)..........Gabon	0·41 S	9·00 E
155	Lopez B. (lō'päz) Phil. (Manila In.)	14·04 N	122·00 E
65	Lopez I.........Wash. (Seattle In.)	48·25 N	122·53 W
151	Lop'ing (lō'pĭng')..........China	29·02 N	117·12 E
165	Lopori R. (lō-pō'rē).......Con. L.	1·23 N	21·18 E
124	Lora (lō'rä)..........Sp.	37·40 N	5·31 W
142	Lora (R.)..........Afg.	31·43 N	67·08 E
75	Lorain (lô-rān') Ohio (Cleveland In.)	41·28 N	82·10 W
142	Loralai (lō-rŭ-lī')........W. Pak.	30·31 N	68·35 E
124	Lorca (lôr'kä)..........Sp.	37·39 N	1·40 W
159	Lord Howe (I.) (lôrd hou)..Austl.	31·44 S	157·56 E
69	Lordsburg (lôrdz'bûrg)...N. Mex.	32·20 N	108·45 W
101	Lorena (lô-rā'nȧ) Braz. (Rio de Janeiro In.)	22·45 S	45·07 W
99	Loreto (lô-rā'tō)..........Braz.	7·09 S	45·10 W
85	Loretteville (lô-rĕt-vēl') Can. (Quebec In.)	46·51 N	71·21 W
163	Loriami (R.)..........Con. L.	4·30 S	24·28 E
98	Lorica (lô-rē'kä)..........Col.	9·14 N	75·54 W
122	Lorient (lō-rē'äɴ')..........Fr.	47·45 N	3·22 W
116	Lorne, Firth of (fûrth ŏv lôrn') Scot.	56·10 N	6·09 W
85	Lorne Park (lôrn) Can. (Toronto In.)	43·31 N	79·36 W
120	Lörrach (lûr'äĸ)..........Ger.	47·36 N	7·38 E
74	Los Alamitos (lōs ăl-ȧ-mē'tōs) Calif. (Los Angeles In.)	33·48 N	118·04 W
69	Los Alamos (ăl-ȧ-mōs')...N. Mex.	35·53 N	106·20 W
65	Los Altos (ăl-tōs') Calif. (San Francisco In.)	37·23 N	122·06 W
101	Los Andes (ăn'dĕs) Chile (Santiago In.)	32·44 S	70·36 W
74	Los Angeles (ăŋ'gĕl-ĕs) (ăn'jĕl-ĕs) (äŋ'hȧ-lās) Calif. (Los Angeles In.)	34·00 N	118·15 W
100	Los Angeles (äŋ'hȧ-lās).....Chile	37·27 S	72·15 W
68	Los Angeles Aqueduct......Calif.	35·12 N	118·02 W
74	Los Angeles R. Calif. (Los Angeles In.)	33·50 N	118·13 W
101	Los Bronces (lōs brō'n-sĕs) Chile (Santiago In.)	33·09 S	70·18 W
66	Loscha R. (lōs'chă)........Idaho	46·20 N	115·11 W
100	Los Chonos, Archipielago de (är-chē-pyĕ'lä-gō dĕ lōs chō'nōs) Chile	44·35 S	76·15 W
100	Los Estados, Isla de (I.) (ē's-lä dĕ lōs ĕs-tä'dōs).Arg.	54·45 S	64·25 W
124	Los Filabres, Sierra de (Mts.) (sē-ĕ'r-rä dĕ lōs fē-lä'brĕs).Sp.	37·19 N	2·48 W
68	Los Gatos (gä'tōs)..........Calif.	37·13 N	121·59 W
151	Loshan (lō'shän')..........China	29·40 N	103·40 E
76	Los Herreras (ĕr-rä-räs)......Mex.	25·55 N	99·23 W
95	Los Ilanos (lōs ē-lä'nōs).Dom. Rep.	18·35 N	69·30 W
94	Los Indios, Cayos de (Is.) (kä'yōs dĕ lōs ē'n-dyō's).Cuba	21·50 N	83·10 W
126	Lošinj (lô'shēn')..........Yugo.	44·30 N	14·29 E
126	Lošinj (I.)..........Yugo.	44·35 N	14·34 E
168	Loskopdam (L.)..........S. Afr. (Johannesburg & Pretoria In.)	25·30 S	29·26 E
125	Los Monegros (Mts.) (mô-nĕ'grōs).Sp.	41·31 N	0·18 W
74	Los Nietos (nyā'tōs) Calif. (Los Angeles In.)	33·57 N	118·05 W
94	Los Patacios (pä-tȧ'sē-ōs)...Cuba	22·35 N	83·15 W
69	Los Pinos (R.) (pē'nōs) Colo.-N. Mex.	36·58 N	107·35 W
90	Los Reyes (rā'yĕs)..........Mex.	19·35 N	102·29 W
91	Los Reyes.Mex. (Mexico City In.)	19·21 N	98·58 W
93	Los Santos (săn'tōs).........Pan.	7·57 N	80·24 W
124	Los Santos (sän'tōs)..........Sp.	38·38 N	6·30 W
99	Los Teques (tĕ'kĕs)....Ven. (In.)	10·22 N	67·04 W
67	Lost R. (lôst)..........Idaho	43·56 N	113·38 W
66	Lost R..........Ore.	42·07 N	121·30 W
67	Lost River Mts. (rĭ'vēr)....Idaho	44·23 N	113·48 W
101	Los Vilos (vē'lōs) Chile (Santiago In.)	31·56 S	71·29 W
122	Lot (R.) (lôt)..........Fr.	44·32 N	1·08 E
100	Lota (lō'tä)..........Chile	37·11 S	73·14 W
149	Lotien (lō'tyĕn') China (Shanghai In.)	31·25 N	121·20 E
151	Loting (lō'tĭng')..........China	23·42 N	111·35 E
148	Lot'ing (lō'tĭng)..........China	39·26 N	118·53 E
120	Lötschen Tun. (lût'shĕn)...Switz.	46·26 N	7·54 E
78	Loudon (lou'dŭn)..........Tenn.	35·43 N	84·20 W
80	Loudonville (lou'dŭn-vĭl)....Ohio	40·40 N	82·15 W
122	Loudun (lōō-dŭɴ')..........Fr.	47·03 N	0·00
164	Louga (lōō'gä)..........Senegal	15·36 N	16·24 W
110	Loughborough (lŭf'bŭr-ō)...Eng.	56·46 N	1·12 W
80	Louisa (lōō'ēz-ȧ)..........Ky.	38·05 N	82·40 W
159	Louisade Arch. (lōō-ĭs-äd är-kĭ-pĕl-ĭ-gō).Austl.	10·44 S	153·58 E
79	Louisburg (lōō'ĭs-bûrg)......N. C.	36·05 N	79·19 W
83	Louisbourg (lōō'ĭs-bourg)....Can.	45·56 N	59·59 W
73	Louisiana (lōō-ē-zē-ăn'ȧ).....Mo.	39·24 N	91·03 W
63	Louisiana (State)..........U. S.	30·50 N	92·50 W
166	Louis Trichardt (lōō'ĭs trĭch'ärt) S. Afr.	22·52 S	29·53 E
72	Louisville (lōō'ĭs-vĭl) (lōō'ē-vĭl) Colo.	39·58 N	105·08 W
79	Louisville..........Ga.	33·00 N	82·25 W
75	Louisville.....Ky. (Louisville In.)	38·15 N	85·45 W
78	Louisville..........Miss.	33·10 N	89·02 W
166	Loukoléla..........Con B.	1·00 S	17·13 E
124	Loule (lō-lā')..........Port.	37·08 N	8·03 W
120	Louny (lō'nê)..........Czech.	50·20 N	13·47 E
70	Loup (R.) (lōōp)..........Nebr.	41·17 N	97·58 W
70	Loup City..........Nebr.	41·15 N	98·59 W
122	Lourdes (lōōrd)..........Fr.	43·06 N	0·03 W
166	Lourenço Marques, Baia de (B.) (bä-ē'ä dä lôw-rĕn'sô mär'kĕs).Moz.	26·14 S	33·30 E
125	Loures (lō'rĕzh).Port. (Lisbon In.)	38·49 N	9·10 W
124	Lousa (lō'zȧ)..........Port.	40·05 N	8·12 W
116	Louth (louth)..........Eng.	53·27 N	0·02 W
122	Louviers (lōō-vyā')..........Fr.	49·13 N	1·11 E
123	Louvres (lōōv'r')...Fr. (Paris In.)	49·02 N	2·28 E
128	Lovat' (lô-vät'y').......Sov. Un.	57·23 N	31·18 E
127	Lovech (lō'vĕts)..........Bul.	43·10 N	24·40 E
72	Loveland (lŭv'lănd)..........Colo.	40·24 N	105·04 W
75	Loveland...Ohio (Cincinnati In.)	39·16 N	84·15 W
67	Lovell (lŭv'ĕl)..........Wyo.	44·50 N	108·23 W
68	Lovelock (lŭv'lŏk)..........Nev.	40·10 N	118·37 W
84	Lovick (lŭ'vĭk) Ala. (Birmingham In.)	33·34 N	86·38 W
119	Loviisa (lô'vē-sȧ)..........Fin.	60·28 N	26·10 E
87	Low, C. (lō)..........Can.	62·58 N	86·50 W
166	Lowa (lō'wȧ)..........Con. L.	1·30 S	27·18 E
69	Lowell (lō'ĕl)..........Ariz.	31·25 N	109·55 W
75	Lowell........Ind. (Chicago In.)	41·17 N	87·26 W
83	Lowell.......Mass. (Boston In.)	42·38 N	71·18 W
80	Lowell..........Mich.	42·55 N	85·20 W
65	Lowell.......Wash. (Seattle In.)	47·57 N	122·12 W
111	Löwenberg (lû' vĕn-bĕrgh) Ger. (Berlin In.)	52·53 N	13·09 E
86	Lower Arrow (L.) (ăr'ō).....Can.	49·41 N	118·40 W
	Lower Austria (State), see Niederösterreich		
70	Lower Brule Ind. Res. (brü'lā) S. D.	44·15 N	100·21 W
159	Lower Hutt (hŭt).....N. Z. (In.)	41·08 S	175·00 E
66	Lower Klamath L. (klăm'ăth) Calif.	41·55 N	121·50 W
66	Lower L..........Calif.-Nev.	41·21 N	119·53 W
71	Lower Red (L.) (rĕd)......Minn.	47·58 N	94·31 W
68	Lower Otay Res. (ō'tā) Calif. (San Diego In.)	32·37 N	116·46 W
	Lower Saxony (State), see Niedersachsen		
117	Lowestoft (lō'stŏft)..........Eng.	52·31 N	1·45 E
121	Łowicz (lô'vĭch)..........Pol.	52·06 N	19·57 E
121	Low Tatra Mts..........Czech.	48·57 N	19·18 E
81	Lowville (lou'vĭl)..........N. Y.	43·45 N	75·30 W
91	Loxicha (Santa Caterina) (lô-zē'chä) (sän-tä kä-tä-rē'nä).Mex.	16·03 N	96·46 W
160	Loxton (lôks'tŭn)..........Austl.	34·25 S	140·38 E
75	Loyal Oak (loi'ăl ōk) Ohio (Cleveland In.)	41·03 N	81·38 W
150	Loyang..........China	34·45 N	112·32 E
159	Loyauté, Iles..........N. Cal.	21·17 S	168·16 E
144	Loz, Jabal Al (Mtn.).....Sau. Ar.	28·46 N	35·37 E
127	Ložnica (lôz'nê-tsȧ)........Yugo.	44·31 N	19·16 E
111	Lozorno.......Czech. (Vienna In.)	48·21 N	17·03 E
129	Lozova (lô-zô'vȧ).......Sov. Un.	48·54 N	36·17 E
129	Lozovatka (lô-zô-vät'kȧ).Sov. Un.	48·03 N	33·19 E
129	Lozovaya Pavlovka (lô-zo-vä'yä päv-lôf'kȧ).Sov. Un.	48·27 N	38·37 E
125	Lozoya, Canal de (kä-nä'l dĕ lô-thō'yä).Sp. (Madrid In.)	40·36 N	3·41 W
166	Lualaba (lōō-ȧ-lä'bȧ)......Con. L.	10·02 S	25·16 E
166	Luama (lōō-ä'mȧ).........Con. L.	4·47 S	27·32 E
150	Luan (R.)..........China	41·25 N	117·15 E
166	Luanda (lōō-än'dä)..........Ang.	8·50 S	13·15 E
154	Luang Prabang (lōō-ang'-prä-bäng').Laos	19·47 N	102·15 E
166	Luanguinga (R.) (lōō-än-gĭŋ'gȧ) Ang.	14·00 S	20·45 E
166	Luangwa (R.) (lōō-äŋ'gwȧ) N. Rh.	12·38 S	32·41 E
148	Luanhsien (lōōän'sĭän').....China	39·47 N	118·40 E
124	Luarca (lwär'kȧ)..........Sp.	43·33 N	6·30 W
113	Luarsens, Monts de (Mts.) (lwȧ-sôŋ).Alg.	35·44 N	0·50 E
121	Lubaczów (lōō-bä'chōōf).....Pol.	50·08 N	23·10 E
120	Lubán (lōō'bän')..........Pol.	51·08 N	15·17 E
119	Lubānas Ezers (L.) (lōō-bä'nȧs ā'zĕrs).Sov. Un.	56·48 N	26·30 E
155	Lubang (lōō-bäng') Phil. (Manila In.)	13·49 N	120·07 E
155	Lubang (Is.)...Phil. (Manila In.)	13·47 N	119·56 E
155	Lubao (lōō-bä'ō).Phil. (Manila In.)	14·55 N	120·36 E
121	Lubartow (lōō-bär'tōōf).....Pol.	51·27 N	22·37 E
121	Lubawa (lōō-bä'vä)..........Pol.	53·31 N	19·47 E
120	Lübben (lüb'ĕn)..........Ger.	51·56 N	13·53 E
72	Lubbock (lŭb'ŭk)..........Tex.	33·35 N	101·50 W
82	Lubec (lū'bĕk)..........Maine	44·49 N	67·01 W
120	Lübeck (lü'bĕk)..........Ger.	53·53 N	10·42 E
120	Lübecker Bucht (B.) (lü'bĕ-kĕr bōōĸt).Ger.	54·10 N	11·20 E
166	Lubilash (R.) (lōō-bē-lăsh') Con. L.	7·45 S	24·09 E
120	Lubin (lyōō'bĭn)..........Pol.	51·24 N	16·14 E
121	Lublin (lyōō'blĕn')..........Pol.	51·14 N	22·33 E
129	Lubny (lōōb'nê).........Sov. Un.	50·01 N	33·02 E
155	Lubuagan (lōō-bwä-gä'n) Phil. (Manila In.)	17·24 N	121·11 E
166	Lubudi (R.) (lōō-bōō'dê)..Con. L.	10·03 S	24·28 E
126	Lucca (lōōk'kä)..........It.	43·51 N	10·29 E
116	Luce B. (lūs)..........Scot.	54·45 N	4·45 W
94	Lucea..........Jam.	18·25 N	78·10 W

ăt; finăl; rāte; senāte; ärm; ȧsk; sofȧ; fâre; ch-choose; dh-as th in other; bē; ēvent; bĕt; recĕnt; cratēr; g-go; gh-guttural g; bĭt; ĭ-short neutral; rīde; ĸ-guttural k as ch in German ich;

PRONOUNCING INDEX Lucena–Macklin 231

Page	Name Pronunciation Region	Lat. °'	Long. °'
155	Lucena (lo͞o-sä'nä) Phil. (Manila In.)	13·55 N	121·36 E
124	Lucena (loō-thä'nä) Sp.	37·25 N	4·28 W
125	Lucena del Cid (lo͞o-thä'nä dä thēdh') Sp.	40·08 N	0·18 W
121	Lučenec (lo͞o'chå-nyĕts) Czech.	48·19 N	19·41 E
126	Lucera (lo͞o-chå'rä) It.	41·31 N	15·22 E
151	Luchi China	28·18 N	110·10 E
148	Luchia (lo͞o'jiä) China	32·12 N	115·53 E
148	Luchih (lo͞o'jĕ') China	31·17 N	120·54 E
67	Lucin (lů-sēn') Utah	41·23 N	113·59 W
155	Lucipara (I.) (lo͞o-sê-pä'rà) Indon.	5·45 S	128·15 E
111	Luckenwalde (lo͝ok-ĕn-väl'dĕ) Ger. (Berlin In.)	52·05 N	13·10 E
142	Lucknow (lŭk'nou) India	26·54 N	80·58 E
122	Luçon (lü-sôɴ') Fr.	46·27 N	1·12 W
95	Lucrecia, Cabo (C.) (kä'bô-lo͞o-krā'sē-à) Cuba	21·05 N	75·30 W
127	Luda Kamchiya (R.) Bul.	42·46 N	27·13 E
123	Lüdenscheid (lü'dĕn-shīt) Ger. (Ruhr In.)	51·13 N	7·38 E
166	Lüderitz (lü'dēr-ĭts) (lü'dĕ-rĭts) S. W. Afr.	26·35 S	15·15 E
166	Lüderitz B. S. W. Afr.	26·35 S	14·30 E
142	Ludhiana India	31·00 N	75·52 E
123	Lüdinghausen (lü'dēng-hou-zĕn) Ger. (Ruhr In.)	51·46 N	7·27 E
80	Ludington (lŭd'ĭng-tŭn) Mich.	44·00 N	86·25 W
110	Ludlow (lŭd'lō) Eng.	52·22 N	2·43 W
75	Ludlow Ky. (Cincinnati In.)	39·05 N	84·33 W
118	Ludvika (loodh-vē'kà) Swe.	60·10 N	15·09 E
120	Ludwigsburg (lo͞ot'vēks-bo͝orgh) Ger.	48·53 N	9·14 E
111	Ludwigsfelde (lo͞od'vēgs-fĕl-dĕ) Ger. (Berlin In.)	52·18 N	13·16 E
120	Ludwigshafen (lo͞ot'vēks-hä'fĕn) Ger.	49·29 N	8·26 E
120	Ludwigslust (lo͞ot'vēks-lo͞ost) Ger.	53·18 N	11·31 E
128	Ludza (lo͞od'zå) Sov. Un.	56·33 N	27·45 E
166	Luebo (lo͞o-ā'bô) Con. L.	5·15 S	21·22 E
166	Lufira (R.) (lo͞o-fē'rà) Con. L.	9·32 S	27·15 E
77	Lufkin (lŭf'kĭn) Tex.	31·21 N	94·43 W
128	Luga (lo͞o'gå) Sov. Un.	58·43 N	29·52 E
128	Luga (R.) Sov. Un.	59·00 N	29·25 E
120	Lugano (lo͞o-gä'nō) Switz.	46·01 N	8·52 E
129	Lugansk (lo͞o-gänsk') Sov. Un.	48·34 N	39·18 E
129	Lugansk (Oblast) (ôb'lást) Sov. Un.	49·08 N	38·37 E
167	Lugenda (R.) (lo͞o-zhĕn'dä) Moz.	12·16 S	37·29 E
168	Lugh Ferrandi Som. (Horn of Afr. In.)	3·38 N	42·35 E
116	Lugnaquilla, Mt. (lo͝ok-nȧ-kwĭ-lȧ) Ire.	52·56 N	6·30 W
126	Lugo (lo͞o'gô) It.	44·28 N	11·57 E
124	Lugo (lo͞o'gō) Sp.	43·01 N	7·32 W
115	Lugoi Rom.	45·42 N	22·00 E
127	Lugoj Rom.	45·51 N	21·56 E
	Luhe, see Winsen		
151	Luhsien China	28·58 N	105·25 E
165	Luī Chad	9·29 N	16·18 E
148	Lui (lo͞o'yī) China	33·52 N	115·32 E
166	Luilaka (R.) (lo͞o-ē-lä'kà) Con. L.	2·18 S	21·15 E
116	Luimneach (lĭm'nåk) Ire.	52·39 N	8·35 W
90	Luis Moya (lo͞oē's-mô-yä) Mex.	22·26 N	102·14 W
101	Luján (lo͞o-hän') Arg. (Buenos Aires In.)	34·36 S	59·07 W
101	Luján (R.) Arg. (Buenos Aires In.)	34·33 S	58·59 W
147	Lujchow Pen. China	20·40 N	110·30 E
166	Lukanga Swp. (lo͞o-käŋ'gà) N. Rh.	14·08 S	28·32 E
166	Lukenie (R.) (lo͞o-kä'nyå) Con. L.	2·48 S	18·45 E
127	Lukovit (lo͝o'kō-vēt') Bul.	43·13 N	24·07 E
121	Luków (wo͞o'ko͞of) Pol.	51·57 N	22·25 E
166	Lukuga (R.) (lo͞o-ko͞o'gä) Con. L.	5·47 S	27·48 E
132	Lule (R.) Swe.	66·20 N	20·25 E
112	Luleå (lo͞o'lĕ-ô) Swe.	65·39 N	21·52 E
127	Lüleburgaz (lü'lĕ-bo͝or-gäs') Tur.	41·25 N	27·23 E
148	Luling (lū'lĭng) China	39·54 N	118·53 E
77	Luling Tex.	29·41 N	97·38 W
65	Lulu (I.) (lū'lo͞o) Can. (Vancouver In.)	49·10 N	123·04 W
166	Lulua (R.) (lo͞o'lo͞o-à) Con. L.	6·30 S	22·15 E
166	Luluabourg (lo͞o'lo͞o-a-bo͞org') Con. L.	6·14 S	22·17 E
79	Lumber (R.) (lŭm'bēr) N. C.	35·12 N	79·35 W
78	Lumberton (lŭm'bēr-tŭn) Miss.	31·00 N	89·25 W
79	Lumberton N. C.	34·37 N	79·00 W
101	Luminárias (lo͞o-mē-nä'ryäs) Braz. (Rio de Janeiro In.)	21·32 S	44·53 W
65	Lummi (I.) Wash. (Vancouver In.)	48·42 N	122·43 W
65	Lummi B. (lŭm'ĭ) Wash. (Vancouver In.)	48·47 N	122·44 W
65	Lummi Island Wash. (Vancouver In.)	48·44 N	122·42 W
155	Luna (lo͞o'nä) Phil. (Manila In.)	16·51 N	120·22 E
118	Lund (lŭnd) Swe.	55·42 N	13·10 E
163	Lunda (Reg.) (lo͞on'dä) Ang.	8·53 S	20·00 E
166	Lundi (R.) (lo͞on'dē) S. Rh.	21·09 S	30·10 E
116	Lundy (I.) (lŭn'dē) Eng.	51·12 N	4·50 W
120	Lüneberger Heide (Reg.) (lü'nĕ-bo͝or-gĕr hī'dĕ) Ger.	53·08 N	10·00 E
120	Lüneburg (lü'nĕ-bo͝orgh) Ger.	53·16 N	10·25 E
122	Lunel (lü-nĕl') Fr.	43·41 N	4·07 E
123	Lünen (lü'nĕn) Ger. (Ruhr In.)	51·36 N	7·30 E
82	Lunenburg (lo͞o'nĕn-bûrg) Can.	44·24 N	64·16 W
83	Lunenburg Mass. (Boston In.)	42·36 N	71·44 W
123	Lunéville (lü-nà-vel') Fr.	48·37 N	6·29 E
166	Lunga (R.) (lo͞oŋ'gä) N. Rh.	12·58 S	26·18 E
152	Lungchen (lo͝ong'chĕn) China	48·38 N	122·12 E
135	Lungchen (lo͝ong'chĕn) China	48·47 N	126·43 E
151	Lungch'i China	24·35 N	117·45 E
151	Lungching China	22·20 N	107·02 E
150	Lungchingts'un (lo͝ong'chĭng'tso͞on') China	42·45 N	129·30 E
166	Lungé-Bungo (R.) (lŭn'gā bŭn'gō) Ang.	13·00 S	20·15 E
150	Lunghsi China	35·00 N	104·40 E
148	Lungku (lo͝ong'kō) China	34·52 N	116·48 E
149	Lungyentung China (Canton In.)	23·12 N	113·21 E
142	Lūni (R.) India	24·64 N	71·10 E
128	Luninets (R.) (lo͞o-nēn'yets) Sov. Un.	52·14 N	26·54 E
150	Lupei (lo͞o'pī) China	44·35 N	120·40 E
150	Lupin (Manchouli) (lo͞o'pĭn') (män-cho͞o'lē) China	49·25 N	117·15 E
100	Luque (lo͞o'kā) Par.	25·18 S	57·17 W
81	Luray (lū-rā') Va.	38·40 N	78·25 W
116	Lurgan (lûr'gǎn) N. Ire.	54·27 N	6·28 W
167	Lúrio (R.) (lo͞o'rē-ô) Moz.	13·17 S	40·29 E
167	Lúrio Moz.	13·58 S	37·52 E
166	Lusaka (lo͞o-sä'kà) N. Rh.	15·19 S	28·15 E
166	Lusambo (lo͞o-säm'bō) Con. L.	4·57 S	23·28 E
142	Lushai Hills Bur.	28·28 N	92·50 E
150	Lushan China	33·45 N	113·00 E
167	Lushoto (lo͞o-shō'tō) Tan.	4·47 S	38·17 E
148	Lüshun (Port Arthur) (lü'shŭn) China	38·49 N	121·15 E
167	Lusikisiki (lo͞o-sê-kê-sē'kê) S. Afr. (Natal In.)	31·22 S	29·37 E
70	Lusk (lŭsk) Wyo.	42·46 N	104·27 W
148	Lüta (lüdà) China	38·55 N	121·19 E
148	Lut'ai (lo͞o'tăī) China	39·20 N	117·50 E
77	Lutcher (lŭch'ẽr) La.	30·03 N	90·43 W
84	Lutherville (lo͞o'thŭr-vĭl) Md. (Baltimore In.)	39·26 N	76·38 W
116	Luton (lū'tŭn) Eng.	51·55 N	0·28 W
121	Lutsk (lo͞otsk) Sov. Un.	50·45 N	25·20 E
78	Luverne (lū-vûrn') Ala.	31·42 N	86·15 W
70	Luverne (lū-vûrn') Minn.	43·40 N	96·13 W
166	Luvua (R.) (lo͞o'vo͞o-à) Con. L.	6·49 S	27·17 E
166	Luvungi (lo͞o-vo͞oŋ'gē) Con. L.	2·54 S	29·00 E
78	Luxapalila Cr. (lŭk-sà-pôl'ĭ-lȧ) Ala.	33·36 N	88·08 W
123	Luxembourg (lŭk-sĕm-bûrg) (lük sän-bo͞or') (look-sĕm-bo͞orgh) Lux.	49·38 N	6·30 E
102	Luxembourg Eur.	49·30 N	6·22 E
84	Luxemburg Mo. (St. Louis In.)	38·32 N	90·17 W
123	Luxeuil (lük-sû'y') Fr.	47·49 N	6·19 E
84	Luxomni (lŭx'ôm-nī) Ga. (Atlanta In.)	33·54 N	84·07 W
	Luxor, see Al Uqşur		
150	Luya Shan (Mtn.) China	38·50 N	111·40 E
132	Luza (R.) (lo͞o'zä) Sov. Un.	60·30 N	47·10 E
120	Luzern (lo͞o-tsĕrn) Switz.	47·03 N	8·18 E
99	Luziânia (lo͞o-zyä'nēä) Braz.	16·17 S	47·44 W
154	Luzon (I.) (lo͞o-zŏn') Phil.	17·10 N	119·45 E
151	Luzon Str. (lo͞o-zŏn') Phil.	20·40 N	121·00 E
121	L'vov (l'vo͞of) Sov. Un.	49·51 N	24·01 E
135	Lyakhovskiye (Is.) (lya'ĸô'v-skyê) Sov. Un.	73·45 N	145·15 E
142	Lyallpur (lī'ǎl-pûr) W. Pak.	31·29 N	73·06 E
85	Lyalta Can. (Calgary In.)	51·07 N	113·36 W
136	Lyalya R. (lyà'lyà) Sov. Un. (Urals In.)	58·58 N	60·17 E
127	Lyaskovets Bul.	43·07 N	25·41 E
166	Lydenburg (lī'dĕn-bûrg) S. Afr.	25·06 S	30·21 E
68	Lyell, Mt. (lī'ĕl) Calif.	37·44 N	119·22 W
81	Lykens (lī'kĕnz) Pa.	40·35 N	76·45 W
121	Lyna R. (lĭn'à) Pol.	53·56 N	20·30 E
78	Lynch (lĭnch) Ky.	36·56 N	82·55 W
79	Lynchburg (lĭnch'bûrg) Va.	37·23 N	79·08 W
65	Lynch Cove (lĭnch) Wash. (Seattle In.)	47·26 N	122·54 W
85	Lynden (lĭn'dĕn) Can. (Toronto In.)	43·14 N	80·08 W
65	Lynden Wash. (Vancouver In.)	48·56 N	122·27 W
161	Lyndhurst Austl. (Melbourne In.)	38·03 S	145·14 E
75	Lyndon (lĭn'dǔn) Ky. (Louisville In.)	38·15 N	85·36 W
81	Lyndonville (lĭn'dǔn-vĭl) Vt.	44·35 N	72·00 W
83	Lynn (lĭn) Mass. (Boston In.)	42·28 N	70·57 W
84	Lynnhaven (lĭn'hā-vĕn) Va. (Norfolk In.)	36·50 N	76·04 W
86	Lynn Lake (lāk) Can.	56·48 N	101·10 W
74	Lynwood (lĭn'wo͝od) Calif. (Los Angeles In.)	33·56 N	118·13 W
122	Lyon (lē-ôɴ') Fr.	45·44 N	4·52 E
79	Lyons (lī'ŭnz) Ga.	32·08 N	82·19 W
72	Lyons Kans.	38·20 N	98·11 W
70	Lyons Nebr.	41·57 N	96·28 W
84	Lyons N. J. (New York In.)	40·41 N	74·33 W
81	Lyons N. Y.	43·05 N	77·00 W
118	Lyse Fd. (lü'sĕ fyôr') Nor.	58·59 N	6·35 E
118	Lysekil (lü'sĕ-kēl) Swe.	58·17 N	11·22 E
136	Lys'va (lĭs'vȧ) Sov. Un. (Urals In.)	58·07 N	57·47 E
110	Lytham (lĭth'ǎm) Eng.	53·44 N	2·58 W
167	Lyttelton (lĭt'l'ton) S. Afr. (Johannesburg & Pretoria In.)	25·51 S	28·13 E
86	Lytton (lĭt'ŭn) Can.	50·16 N	121·29 W
136	Lyuban' (lyo͞o' bàn) Sov. Un. (Leningrad In.)	59·21 N	31·15 E
129	Lyubar (lyo͞o'bär) Sov. Un.	49·56 N	27·44 E
136	Lyubertsy (lyo͞o'bĕr-tsê) Sov. Un. (Moscow In.)	55·40 N	37·55 E
128	Lyubim (lyo͞o-bēm') Sov. Un.	58·24 N	40·39 E
136	Lyublino (lyo͞ob'lĭ-nô) Sov. Un. (Moscow In.)	55·41 N	37·45 E
128	Lyudinovo (lū-dē'novô) Sov. Un.	53·52 N	34·28 E
146	Lyung Mong.	47·58 N	104·52 E
139	Ma'an (mä-än') Jordan (Palestine In.)	30·12 N	35·45 E
118	Maarianhamina (Mariehamn) (mä'rē-àn-hä'mē-na) (mà-rē'ĕ-häm''n) Fin.	60·07 N	19·57 E
111	Maartensdijk Neth. (Amsterdam In.)	52·09 N	5·10 E
123	Maas (R.) Neth. (Ruhr In.)	51·32 N	6·07 E
117	Maastricht (mäs'trĭkt) Bel.	50·51 N	5·35 E
165	Maaten Bishidra (Oasis) Libya	23·11 N	22·34 E
65	Mabana (mä-bä-nä) Wash. (Seattle In.)	48·06 N	122·25 W
77	Mabank (mā'bănk) Tex.	32·21 N	96·05 W
168	Mabeskraal S. Afr. (Johannesburg & Pretoria In.)	25·12 S	26·47 E
84	Mableton (mā'b'l-tŭn) Ga. (Atlanta In.)	33·49 N	84·34 W
114	Mabrouk (må-bro͞ok') Alg.	29·30 N	0·20 E
164	Mabrouk Mali	19·27 N	1·16 W
139	Mabruk (R.) Sau. Ar. (Palestine In.)	29·16 N	35·22 E
168	Mabula (mă'bo͞o-la) S. Afr. (Johannesburg & Pretoria In.)	24·49 S	27·59 E
82	McAdam (măk-ăd'ăm) Can.	45·37 N	67·21 W
101	Macaé (mä-kä-ā') Braz. (Rio de Janeiro In.)	22·22 S	41·47 W
84	McAfee (mǎk-ǎ'fē) N. J. (New York In.)	41·10 N	74·32 W
99	Macaira (R.) (mä-kī'rä) Ven. (In.)	9·37 N	66·16 W
155	Macalelon (mä-kä-lā-lōn') Phil. (Manila In.)	13·46 N	122·09 E
73	McAlester (mǎk ăl'ĕs-tēr) Okla.	34·55 N	95·45 W
76	McAllen (mǎk-ăl'ĕn) Tex.	26·12 N	98·14 W
99	Macapá (mä-kä-pä') Braz.	0·08 N	50·02 W
151	Macau (mà-kä'o͞o) Asia	22·10 N	113·35 E
99	Macau (mä-kä'o͞o) Braz.	5·12 S	36·34 W
95	Macaya, Pico de (Pk.) Hai.	18·25 N	74·00 W
86	McBride (mǎk-brīd) Can.	53·25 N	120·15 W
84	McCalla (mǎk-kăl'lā) Ala. (Birmingham In.)	33·20 N	87·00 W
76	McCamey (mǎ-kā'mĭ) Tex.	31·08 N	102·13 W
125	Maccarese (mäk-kä-rĕ'zĕ) It. (Rome In.)	41·53 N	12·13 E
74	McCarron (măk kăr'ŭn) Mich. (Sault Ste. Marie In.)	46·20 N	84·17 W
78	McCaysville (mǎ-kāz'vĭl) Ga.	34·57 N	84·21 W
110	Macclesfield (măk''lz-fēld) Eng.	53·15 N	2·07 W
110	Macclesfield Can. (măk''lz-fēld) Eng.	53·14 N	2·07 W
79	McColl (mȧ-kól') S. C.	34·40 N	79·34 W
78	McComb (mȧ-kōm') Miss.	31·14 N	90·27 W
70	McConaughy, L. (mǎk kŏ'nō ĭ') Nebr.	41·24 N	101·40 W
72	McCook (må-ko͝ok') Nebr.	40·13 N	100·37 W
79	McCormick (mȧ-kôr'mĭk) S. C.	33·56 N	82·20 W
116	Macdhui, Ben (Mtn.) (bĕn măk-do͞o'ê) Scot.	57·06 N	3·45 W
74	Macdona (măk-dō'nă) Tex. (San Antonio In.)	29·20 N	98·42 W
75	McDonald (mǎk-dŏn'ǎld) Pa. (Pittsburgh In.)	40·22 N	80·13 W
158	Macdonald (I.) (mǎk-dŏn'ǎld) Austl.	23·40 S	127·40 E
47	McDonald I Austl.	53·00 S	72·45 E
85	McDonald L. (mǎk-dŏn-ăld) Can. (Calgary In.)	51·12 N	113·53 W
158	Macdonnell Ra. (mǎk-dŏn'ĕl) Austl.	23·40 S	131·30 E
75	Macedonia (măs-ē-dō'nĭ-à) Ohio (Cleveland In.)	41·19 N	81·30 W
127	Macedonia (Reg.) (măs-ê-dō'nĭ-à) Eur.	41·05 N	22·15 E
99	Maceió (mä-sâ-yō') Braz.	9·33 S	35·35 W
126	Macerata (mä-chå-rä'tä) It.	43·18 N	13·28 E
160	Macfarlane, L. (măc'fär-lān) Austl.	32·10 S	137·00 E
73	McGehee (mȧ-gē') Ark.	33·39 N	91·22 W
68	McGill (mȧ-gĭl') Nev.	39·25 N	114·47 W
65	McGowan (mǎk-gou'ǎn) Wash. (Portland In.)	46·15 N	123·55 W
64	McGrath (măk grăth) Alaska	62·58 N	155·20 W
75	McGregor (mǎk-grĕg'ẽr) Can. (Detroit In.)	42·08 N	82·58 W
71	McGregor Iowa	42·58 N	91·12 W
77	McGregor Tex.	31·26 N	97·23 W
85	McGregor L. (măk-grĕg'ẽr) Can. (Ottawa In.)	45·38 N	75·44 W
167	Machache (Mtn.) Bas. (Natal In.)	29·22 S	27·53 E
101	Machado (mä-shä-dô) Braz. (Rio de Janeiro In.)	21·42 S	45·55 W
98	Machala (mä-chä'lä) Ec.	3·18 S	78·54 W
75	McHenry (măk-hĕn'rĭ) Ill. (Chicago In.)	42·21 N	88·16 W
74	Machens (măk'ĕns) Mo. (St. Louis In.)	38·54 N	90·20 W
82	Machias (mȧ-chī'ǎs) Maine	44·22 N	67·29 W
98	Machu Picchu (mä'cho͞o-pē'k-cho͞o) Peru	8·01 S	72·24 W
129	Măcin (mȧ-chēn') Rom.	45·15 N	28·09 E
70	McIntosh (măk'ĭn-tŏsh) S. D.	45·54 N	101·22 W
159	Mackay (mȧ-kī') Austl.	21·15 S	149·08 E
67	Mackay (mǎk-kā') Idaho	43·55 N	113·38 W
158	Mackay (I.) (mǎ-kī') Austl.	22·30 S	127·45 E
86	MacKay (L.) (măk-kā') Can.	64·00 N	113·13 W
65	McKay (R.) Ore.	45·43 N	123·00 W
85	MacKayville (măk-kā-vĭl) Can. (Montreal In.)	45·28 N	73·28 W
75	McKeesport (mȧ-kez'pōrt) Pa. (Pittsburgh In.)	40·21 N	79·51 W
75	McKees Rocks (mȧ-kēz' rŏks) Pa. (Pittsburgh In.)	40·29 N	80·05 W
78	McKenzie (mȧ-kĕn'zĭ) Tenn.	36·07 N	88·30 W
86	Mackenzie, Dist. of Can.	63·48 N	125·25 W
86	Mackenzie (R.) Can.	63·28 N	124·23 W
64	Mackenzie B. Alaska	69·20 N	137·10 W
86	Mackenzie Mts. (mȧ-kĕn'zĭ) Can.	63·41 N	129·27 W
66	McKenzie R. Ore.	44·07 N	122·20 W
80	Mackinac, Str. of (măk'ĭ-nô) (măk'ĭ-năk) Mich.	45·50 N	84·40 W
80	Mackinaw (R.) Ill.	40·35 N	89·25 W
80	Mackinaw City (măk'ĭ-nô) Mich.	45·45 N	84·45 W
64	McKinley, Mt. (mȧ-kĭn'lĭ) Alaska	63·00 N	151·02 W
73	McKinney (mȧ-kĭn'ĭ) Tex.	33·12 N	96·35 W
86	Macklin (măk'lĭn) Can.	52·22 N	109·51 W

ng-sing; ŋ-baŋk; ɴ-nasalized n; nŏd; cŏmmit; ōld; ôbey; ôrder; fo͞od; fo͝ot; ou-out; s-soft; sh-dish; th-thin; pūre; ûnite; ûrn; stŭd; circŭs; ü-as "y" in study; '-indeterminate vowel.

232 McLaughlin–Mallet Creek PRONOUNCING INDEX

Page Name Pronunciation Region Lat. °′ Long. °′

70 McLaughlin (mȧk-lŏf'lĭn) . . . S. D. 45·48 N 100·45 W
80 McLeansboro (mȧ-klānz'bŭr-ô) Ill. 38·10 N 88·35 W
167 Macleantown (măk-lān'toun) S. Afr. (Natal In.) 32·48 S 27·48 E
167 Maclear (mȧ-klēr') S. Afr. (Natal In.) 31·06 S 28·23 E
86 McLennan (măk-lĭn'ȧn) . . . . Can. 55·51 N 117·10 W
66 McLoughlin, Mt. (mȧk-lŏk'lĭn) Ore. 42·27 N 122·20 W
76 McMillan L. (mȧk-mĭl'ȧn) . . . Tex. 32·40 N 104·09 W
65 McMillin (mȧk-mĭl'ĭn) Wash. (Seattle In.) 47·08 N 122·14 W
66 McMinnville (mȧk-mĭn'vĭl) . . Ore. 45·13 N 123·13 W
78 McMinnville . . . . Tenn. 35·41 N 85·47 W
86 McMurray (mȧk-mŭr'ĭ) . . . . . Can. 56·45 N 111·15 W
65 McMurray . . . . Wash. (Seattle In.) 48·19 N 122·15 W
69 McNary (mȧk-nâr'ê) . . . . Ariz. 34·10 N 109·55 W
77 McNary . . . . La. 30·58 N 92·32 W
66 McNary Dam . . . . Ore.-Wash. 45·57 N 119·15 W
73 Macomb (mȧ-kōōm') . . . . Ill. 40·27 N 90·40 W
122 Mâcon (mä-kôɴ) . . . . Fr. 46·19 N 4·51 E
78 Macon (mā'kŏn) . . . . Ga. 32·49 N 83·39 W
78 Macon . . . . Miss. 32·07 N 88·31 W
73 Macon . . . . Mo. 39·42 N 92·29 W
73 McPherson (mȧk-fŭr's'n) . . . Kans. 38·21 N 97·41 W
160 Macquarie (R.) . . . . Austl. 31·43 S 148·04 E
47 Macquarie Is. (mȧ-kwŏr'ê) . Austl. 54·36 S 158·45 E
78 McRae (mȧk-rā') . . . . Ga. 32·02 N 82·55 W
78 McRoberts (mȧk-rŏb'ērts) . . . . Ky. 37·12 N 82·40 W
92 Macuelizo (mä-kwĕ-lē'zō) . . Hond. 15·22 N 88·32 W
139 Ma'dabā) . . Jordan (Palestine In.) 31·43 N 35·47 E
163 Madagascar (I.) (măd-ȧ-găs'kȧr) Malag. Rep. 23·30 S 46·00 E
83 Madame (I.) (mȧ-dȧm') . . . . . Can. 45·31 N 60·45 W
143 Madanapalle . . . . India 13·06 N 78·09 E
155 Madang (mä-däng') . N. Gui. Ter. 5·15 S 145·45 E
164 Madaoua (mȧ-dou'ȧ) . . . . Niger 14·04 N 6·03 E
74 Madart (mȧ'dărt) Minn. (Minneapolis, St. Paul In.) 44·48 N 93·02 W
81 Madawaska (R.) (măd-ȧ-wôs'kȧ) Can. 45·20 N 77·25 W
88 Madden, L. C. Z. (Panama Canal In.) 9·15 N 79·34 W
164 Madeira, Ilha da (I.) (mä-dā'rä) Mad. Is. 32·41 N 16·15 W
164 Madeira, Arquipelago da (Is.) (är-kē-pĕ'lä-gō-dä-mä-dĕý-rä) Port. 33·26 N 16·44 W
98 Madeira (R.) . . . . Braz. 6·48 S 62·43 W
82 Madeleine, C. (mȧd'lĕn') . . . . Can. 49·15 N 65·20 W
71 Madelia (mȧ-dē'lĭ-ȧ) . . . . Minn. 44·03 N 94·23 W
71 Madeline (I.) (măd'ĕ-lĭn) . . . . Wis. 46·47 N 91·30 W
68 Madera (mȧ-dā'rȧ) . . . . Calif. 36·57 N 120·04 W
92 Madera (Vol.) . . . . Nic. 11·27 N 85·30 W
142 Madhya Pradesh (State) ((mŭd'vŭ prŭ-dāsh') . India 27·04 N 77·48 E
73 Madill (mȧ-dĭl') . . . . Okla. 34·04 N 96·45 W
78 Madison (măd'ĭ-sŭn) . . . . Fla. 30·25 N 85·25 W
78 Madison . . . . Ga. 33·34 N 83·29 W
74 Madison . . . . . . Ill. (St. Louis In.) 38·40 N 90·09 W
80 Madison . . . . Ind. 38·45 N 85·25 W
73 Madison . . . . Kans. 38·08 N 96·07 W
82 Madison . . . . Maine 44·47 N 69·52 W
70 Madison . . . . Minn. 44·59 N 96·13 W
70 Madison . . . . Nebr. 41·49 N 97·27 W
84 Madison . . . . N. J. (New York In.) 40·46 N 74·25 W
79 Madison . . . . N. C. 36·22 N 79·59 W
70 Madison . . . . S. D. 44·01 N 97·08 W
71 Madison . . . . Wis. 43·05 N 89·23 W
67 Madison Res . . . . Mont. 45·25 N 111·28 W
67 Madison R . . . . Mont. 45·15 N 111·30 W
80 Madisonville (măd'ĭ-sŭn-vĭl) . . Ky. 37·20 N 87·30 W
77 Madisonville . . . . La. 30·22 N 90·10 W
77 Madisonville . . . . Tex. 30·57 N 95·55 W
154 Madjene . . . . Indon. 3·34 S 119·00 E
128 Madona (mä'dō'nȧ) . . . . . Sov. Un. 56·50 N 26·14 E
143 Madras (mȧ-drăs') (mŭ-drŭs') India 13·08 N 80·15 E
143 Madras (State) (mŭ-drŭs') (mȧ-drăs') . India 15·20 N 78·20 E
77 Madre, Laguna L. (lä-gōō'nä mä'drā) . Mex. 25·08 N 97·41 W
90 Madre, Sierra (Mts.) (sē-ĕ'r-rä-mä'drĕ) . Mex. 15·55 N 92·40 W
155 Madre, Sierra (Mts.) Phil. (Manila In.) 16·40 N 122·10 E
100 Madre de Dios, Arch. (mä'drā dā dê-ōs') . Chile 50·40 S 76·30 W
98 Madre de Dios, Rio (R.) (rē'ō-mä'drā dā dê-ōs') . Bol. 12·07 S 68·20 W
90 Madre del Sur, Sierra (Mts.) (sē-ĕ'r-rä-mä'drā dĕlsōōr') . Mex. 17·35 N 100·35 W
71 Madrid (măd'rĭd) . . . . Iowa 41·51 N 93·48 W
125 Madrid (mä-drē'd) Sp. (Madrid In.) 40·26 N 3·42 W
124 Madridejos (mä-dhrē-dhä'hōs).Sp. 39·29 N 3·32 W
66 Mad R. (măd) . . . . Calif. 40·38 N 123·37 W
143 Madura (mä-dōō'rä) . . . . India 9·57 N 78·04 E
154 Madura (I.) (mȧ-dōō'rä) . . . Indon. 6·45 S 113·30 E
100 Madureira, Serra do (Mtn.) (sĕ'r-rä-dô-mä-dōō-rā'rȧ) . Braz. (In.) 22·49 S 43·30 W
153 Maebashi (mä-ĕ-bä'shē) . . . . . . Jap. 36·26 N 139·04 E
125 Maella (mä-āl'yä) . . . . Sp. 41·10 N 0·07 E
94 Maestra, Sierra (Mts.) (sē-ĕ'r-rä-mä-ās'trä) . Cuba 20·05 N 77·05 W
159 Maewo (I.) . . . . New Hebr. 15·17 S 168·16 E
166 Mafeking (mäf'ĕ-kĭng) . . . . S. Afr. 25·46 S 24·45 E
167 Mafia (I.) (mä-fē'ä) . . . . Tan. 7·45 S 39·45 E
100 Mafra (mä'frä) . . . . Braz. 26·21 S 49·59 W
125 Mafra (mäf'rȧ) . Port. (Lisbon In.) 38·56 N 9·20 W
135 Magadan (mȧ-gȧ-dän') . . Sov. Un. 59·39 N 150·43 E
135 Magadan Oblast . . . . Sov. Un. 63·00 N 170·30 E
167 Magadi (L.) (mä-gä'dê) . . . . . Ken. 2·12 S 37·32 E
167 Magalies (R.) (mä-gä'lyĕs) S. Afr. (Johannesburg & Pretoria In.) 25·51 S 27·42 E
167 Magaliesberg (Mts.) S. Afr. (Johannesburg & Pretoria In.) 25·45 S 27·43 E
168 Magaliesburg . . . . S. Afr. (Johannesburg & Pretoria In.) 26·01 S 27·32 E
155 Magallanes (mä-gäl-yä'näs) Phil. (Manila In.) 12·48 N 123·52 E
100 Magallene, Estrecho de (Str.) (ĕs-trĕ'chô-dĕ-mä-gäl-yä'nĕs) Arg.-Chile 52·30 S 68·45 W
98 Magangué (mä-gän'gā) . . . . Col. 9·08 N 74·56 W
155 Magat (R.) (mä-gät') Phil. (Manila In.) 16·45 N 121·16 E
101 Magdalena (mäg-dä-lā'nä) Arg. (Buenos Aires In.) 35·05 S 57·32 W
98 Magdalena . . . . Bol. 13·17 S 63·57 W
62 Magdalena . . . . Mex. 30·34 N 110·50 W
69 Magdalena . . . . N. Mex. 34·10 N 107·45 W
100 Magdalena (I.) . . . . Chile 44·45 S 73·15 W
88 Magdalena, Bahia (B.) (bä-ē'ä-mäg-dä-lā'nȧ) . Mex. 24·30 N 114·00 W
98 Magdalena, Rio (R.) . . . . Col. 7·45 N 74·04 W
83 Magdalen Is. (măg'dȧ-lĕn) . . . Can. 47·27 N 61·25 W
120 Magdeburg (mäg'dĕ-bōōrgh) . Ger. 52·07 N 11·39 E
100 Magé (mä-zhā') . . . . Braz. (In.) 22·39 S 43·02 W
126 Magenta (mȧ-jĕn'tȧ) . . . . It. 45·26 N 8·53 E
112 Mageröy (I.) (mä'ghĕr-ûê) . . . Nor. 71·10 N 24·11 E
126 Maggiore, Lago di (L.) . . . . It. 46·03 N 8·25 E
168 Maghāghah . . . U. A. R. (Nile In.) 28·38 N 30·50 E
90 Magiscatzin (mä-kēs-kät-zēn') Mex. 22·48 N 98·42 W
127 Maglaj (mȧ'glä-ê) . . . . Yugo. 44·34 N 18·12 E
127 Maglić (mäg'lēch) . . . . Yugo. 43·36 N 20·36 E
127 Maglie (mäl'yā) . . . . It. 40·06 N 18·20 E
74 Magna (măg'nȧ) Utah (Salt Lake City In.) 40·43 N 112·06 W
136 Magnitogorsk (mäg-nyē'tô-gôrsk) . Sov. Un. (Urals In.) 53·26 N 59·05 E
73 Magnolia (măg-nō'lĭ-ȧ) . . . . . . Ark. 33·16 N 93·13 W
84 Magnolia . . . . Md. (Baltimore In.) 39·24 N 76·19 W
78 Magnolia . . . . Miss. 31·08 N 90·27 W
123 Magny-en-Vexin (mä-nyē' ĕɴ-vĕ-săɴ') . Fr. (Paris In.) 49·09 N 1·45 E
81 Magog (mȧ-gŏg') . . . . Can. 45·15 N 72·10 W
82 Magpie (L.) (măg'pī) . . . . Can. 50·56 N 64·30 W
71 Magpie (R.) . . . . Can. 48·13 N 84·50 W
86 Magrath . . . . Can. 49·22 N 112·52 W
166 Magude (mä-gōō'dȧ) . . . . Moz. 24·58 S 32·39 E
146 Magwe (mŭg-wā') . . . . Bur. 20·19 N 94·57 E
133 Mahabād . . . . Iran 36·55 N 45·50 E
165 Mahagi (mä-hä'gê) . . . . Con. L. 2·14 N 31·12 E
154 Mahakam, Sungai (Strm.) . . Indon. 0·30 S 116·15 E
167 Mahaly (mȧ-häl-ē') . . Malag. Rep. 24·09 S 46·20 E
154 Mahameru, Gunung (Mtn.) . . Java 8·00 S 112·50 E
142 Mahānadi (R.) (mŭ-hä-nŭd'ê) India 20·50 N 84·27 E
167 Mahanoro (mȧ-hȧ-nō'rō) Malag. Rep. 19·57 S 48·47 E
81 Mahanoy City (mä-hȧ-noi') . . . Pa. 40·50 N 76·10 W
142 Maharashtra (State) . . . . India 20·25 N 75·00 E
139 Mahasham (R.) U. A. R. (Palestine In.) 30·08 N 34·09 E
167 Mahavavy (R.) (mȧ-hȧ-vä'vê) Malag. Rep. 17·42 S 46·06 E
142 Mahaweli (R.) . . . . India 7·47 N 80·43 E
113 Mahdia (mä-dē'ä) (mȧ'dê-ȧ) . Tun. 35·30 N 11·09 E
143 Mahe (mä-ā') . . . . India 11·42 N 75·39 E
167 Mahenge (mä-hĕŋ'gä) . . . . Tan. 8·41 S 36·43 E
142 Mahi (R.) . . . . India 23·16 N 73·20 E
143 Māhīm Bay . . India (Bombay In.) 19·03 N 72·45 E
167 Mahlabatini (mä'lä-bä-tē'nê) S. Afr. (Natal In.) 28·15 S 31·29 E
111 Mahlow (mä'lōv) . Ger. (Berlin In.) 52·23 N 13·24 E
70 Mahnomen (mô-nō'mĕn) . . . Minn. 47·18 N 95·58 W
125 Mahón (mä-ōn') . . . . Sp. 39·52 N 4·15 E
82 Mahone Bay (mȧ-hōn') . . . . . . Can. 44·27 N 64·24 W
82 Mahone B. . . . . Can. 44·27 N 64·05 W
84 Mahopac, L. (mā-hō'păk) N. Y. (New York In.) 41·24 N 73·45 W
84 Mahwah (mȧ-wä') N. J. (New York In.) 41·05 N 74·09 W
110 Maidenhead (măd'ĕn-hĕd) Eng. (London In.) 51·30 N 0·44 W
Maidos, see Eceabat
110 Maidstone (mād'stŭn) Eng. (London In.) 51·17 N 0·32 E
165 Maiduguri (mä'ē-dä-gōō'rê) . . Nig. 11·53 N 13·12 E
98 Maigualide Sierra (Mts.) (sē-ĕ'r-rä-mī-gwä'lē-dĕ) . Ven. 6·30 N 65·50 W
142 Maijdi . . . . E. Pak. 22·59 N 91·08 E
Maikop, see Maykop
144 Maimana (mī-mä-nä') . . . . Afg. 35·53 N 64·38 E
160 Main Barrier Ra. (băr''ĕr) . Austl. 31·25 S 141·40 E
63 Maine (State) (mān) . . . . U. S. 45·25 N 69·50 W
116 Mainland (I.) (mān-lănd) Scot. (In.) 60·19 N 2·40 W
120 Main R. (mīn) . . . . Ger. 49·49 N 9·20 E
123 Maintenon (măɴ-tĕ-nôɴ') Fr. (Paris In.) 48·35 N 1·35 E
167 Maintirano (mä'ēn-tē-rä'nō) Malag. Rep. 18·05 S 44·08 E
120 Mainz (mīnts) . . . . Ger. 49·59 N 8·16 E
164 Maio I. (mä'yō) . . . . C. V. Is. (In.) 15·15 N 22·50 W
101 Maipo (mī'pô) (R.) Chile (Santiago In.) 33·45 S 71·08 W
100 Maipo (Vol.) . . . . Arg. 34·08 S 69·51 W
101 Maipú (mī'pōō') Arg. (Buenos Aires In.) 36·51 S 57·54 W
99 Maiquetía (mī-kĕ-tē'ä) . Ven. (In.) 10·37 N 66·56 W
95 Maisi, Punta (Pt.) (pōō'n-tä-mī-sē') . Cuba 20·10 N 74·00 W
123 Maison-Rouge (mā-zôɴ-rōōzh') Fr. (Paris In.) 48·34 N 3·09 E
168 Mait I. (māt) Som. (Horn. of Afr. In.) 11·24 N 46·38 E
160 Maitland (māt'lănd) . . . . Austl. 32·45 S 151·40 E
80 Maitland (R.) . . . . Can. 45·50 N 81·10 W
153 Maizuru (mä-ĭ'zōō-rōō) . . . . . . Jap. 35·26 N 135·15 E
Majorca I., see Mallorca, Isle de
167 Majunga (mȧ-jŭŋ'gä) Malag. Rep. 15·12 S 46·26 E
66 Makah Ind. Res. (mȧ kī') . . Wash. 48·17 N 124·52 W
165 Mak'alē . . . . Eth. 13·31 N 39·19 E
167 Makanya (mä-kän'yä) . . . . Tan. 4·15 S 37·49 E
166 Makarikari Salt Pan (L.) . . . Bech. 20·38 S 21·31 E
126 Makarska (mȧ'kär-skȧ) . . . . Yugo. 43·17 N 17·05 E
132 Makar'yev . . . . Sov. Un. 57·50 N 43·48 E
154 Makasar . . . . Indon. 5·08 S 119·28 E
154 Makasar, Selat (Str.) (mȧ-kăs'ĕr) Indon. 2·00 S 118·07 E
153 Make (I.) (mä'kȧ) . . . . Jap. 30·43 N 130·49 E
129 Makeyevka (mŭk-yā'ŭf-kȧ) Sov. Un. 48·03 N 38·00 E
133 Makhachkala (mȧᴋ'ȧch-kä'lä) Sov. Un. 43·00 N 47·40 E
167 Makhaleng (R.) . . Bas. (Natal In.) 29·53 S 27·33 E
127 Makhlata (mäᴋ'lä-tä) . . . . Bul. 43·27 N 24·16 E
144 Makkah (Mecca) (mĕk'ä) . Sau. Ar. 21·27 N 39·45 E
87 Makkovik . . . . Can. 55·01 N 59·10 W
121 Makó (mô'kō) . . . . Hung. 46·13 N 20·30 E
164 Makokou (mȧ-kô-kōō') . . . . Gabon 0·39 N 12·46 E
121 Maków Mazowiecki (mä'kōov mä-zō-vyĕts'kē) . Pol. 52·51 N 21·07 E
153 Makuhari (mä-kōō-hä'rē) Jap. (Tōkyō In.) 35·39 N 140·04 E
153 Makurazaki (mä'kōō-rä-zä'kê) Jap. 31·16 N 130·18 E
164 Makurdi . . . . Nig. 7·44 N 8·34 E
64 Makushin (mä-kōō'shĭn) . . . Alaska 53·57 N 166·28 W
134 Makushino (mȧ-kōō-shēn'ô) Sov. Un. 55·03 N 67·43 E
143 Malabar Coast (măl'ȧ-bär) . . India 16·30 N 75·33 E
139 Malacca (mȧ-lăk'ȧ) Mala. (Singapore In.) 2·11 N 102·15 E
139 Malacca (State) Mala. (Singapore In.) 2·19 N 102·09 E
154 Malacca, Str. of (mȧ-lăk'ȧ) . . Asia 4·15 N 99·44 E
67 Malad (mȧ-lăd') . . . . Idaho 42·11 N 112·15 W
125 Maladetta (Mts.) (mä-lä-dĕt'tä) Sp. 42·30 N 0·38 E
125 Malafede (R.) (mä-lä-fĕ'dĕ) It. (Rome In.) 41·43 N 12·28 E
98 Málaga (mȧ'lä-gȧ) . . . . Col. 6·41 N 72·46 W
124 Málaga . . . . Sp. 36·45 N 4·25 W
124 Málaga, Bahía de (B.) (bä-ē'ä-dĕ-mȧ'lä-gä) . Sp. 36·35 N 4·10 W
163 Malagasy Republic . . . . Afr. 18·05 S 43·12 E
124 Malagón (mä-lä-gōn') . . . . Sp. 39·12 N 3·52 W
159 Malaita (I.) (mȧ-lä'ē-tȧ) . . . Sol. Is. 8·38 S 161·15 E
165 Malakal (mȧ-lȧ-käl') . . . . Sud. 9·46 N 31·54 E
136 Malakhovka (mä-läk'ôf-kȧ) Sov. Un. (Moscow In.) 55·38 N 38·01 E
166 Malange (mä-läŋ'gȧ) . . . . Ang. 9·30 S 16·25 E
82 Malapedia (R.) . . . . Can. 48·11 N 67·08 W
93 Mala Punta (Pt.) (pōō'n-tä-mä'lä) Pan. 7·32 N 79·44 W
118 Mälaren (L.) . . . . Swe. 59·38 N 16·55 E
87 Malartic . . . . Can. 48·07 N 78·11 W
133 Malatya (mȧ-lä'tyȧ) . . . . Tur. 38·30 N 38·15 E
154 Malaya (Reg.) (mȧ-lā'yȧ) . . . Mala. 3·35 N 101·30 E
128 Malaya Vishera (vê-shā'rä) Sov. Un. 58·51 N 32·13 E
154 Malay Pen. (mȧ-lā') (mā'lā) . Asia 7·46 N 101·06 E
154 Malaysia (mȧ-lā'zhȧ) . . . . Asia 4·10 N 101·22 E
116 Mal B. (măl) . . . . Ire. 52·51 N 9·45 E
158 Malbon (măl'bŭn) . . . . Austl. 21·15 S 140·30 E
121 Malbork (măl'bŏrk) . . . . Pol. 54·02 N 19·04 E
125 Malcabran (R.) (mäl-kȧ-brän') Port. (Lisbon In.) 38·47 N 8·46 W
83 Malden (môl'dĕn) Mass. (Boston In.) 42·26 N 71·04 W
73 Malden . . . . Mo. 36·32 N 89·56 W
157 Malden (I.) . . . . Oceania 4·20 S 154·30 W
138 Maldive Is. (măl'dīv) . . . . Asia 4·30 N 71 30 E
110 Maldon (môrl'dŏn) Eng. (London In.) 51·44 N 0·39 E
100 Maldonado (mäl-dŏ-nä'dô) . . . . Ur. 34·54 S 54·57 W
90 Maldonado, Punta (Pt.) (pōō'n-tä) . Mex. 16·18 N 98·34 W
127 Maléa, Akr. (C.) . . . . Grc. 37·31 N 23·13 E
121 Male Karpaty (Mts.) . . . . . . Czech. 48·31 N 17·15 E
159 Malekula (I.) (mä-lā-kōō'lä) New Hebr. 16·44 S 167·45 E
124 Malhão da Estrêla (Mtn.) (mäl-you'ɴ-dä-ĕs-trĕ'lä) . Sp. 40·20 N 7·38 W
66 Malheur L. (mȧ-lōōr') . . . . Ore. 43·16 N 118·37 W
66 Malheur R. (mȧ-lōōr') . . . . Ore. 43·45 N 117·41 W
164 Mali . . . . Afr. 15·45 N 0·15 W
74 Malibu (mă'lĭ-bōō) Calif. (Los Angeles In.) 34·03 N 118·38 W
129 Malin (mȧ-lēn') . . . . Sov. Un. 50·44 N 29·15 E
90 Malinalco (mä-lē-näl'kō) . . . . Mex. 18·54 N 99·31 W
90 Malinaltepec (mä-lē-näl-tȧ-pĕk') Mex. 17·01 N 98·41 W
167 Malindi (mä-lēn'dê) . . . . Ken. 3·14 S 40·04 E
121 Malineč (mä'lē-nyets') . . . . . Czech. 48·31 N 19·40 E
116 Malin Hd . . . . N. Ire. 54·84 N 6·70 W
116 Malinmore Hd, (mă'lĭn-mōr) . . Ire. 54·45 N 8·30 W
136 Malino (mä'lĭ-nô) Sov. Un. (Moscow In.) 55·07 N 38·12 E
129 Malinovka (mȧ-lē-nôf'kȧ) . Sov. Un. 49·50 N 36·43 E
127 Malkara (măl'kȧ-rȧ) . . . . Tur. 40·51 N 26·52 E
127 Malko Tŭrnovo (mäl'kō-t'r'nô-vȧ) . Bul. 41·59 N 27·28 E
116 Mallaig (măl'ăg) . . . . Scot. 56·59 N 5·55 W
168 Mallawī (mȧ-lä'wê) U. A. R. (Nile In.) 27·43 N 30·49 E
75 Mallet Creek (măl'ĕt) Ohio (Cleveland In.) 41·10 N 81·55 W

ăt; finăl; rāte; senâte; ärm; ȧsk; sofȧ; fâre; ch-choose; dh-as th in other; bē; êvent; bĕt; recĕnt; cratĕr; g-go; gh-guttural g; bĭt; ĭ-short neutral; rīde; ᴋ-guttural k as ch in German ich;

PRONOUNCING INDEX Mallorca–Marennes 233

Page	Name Pronunciation Region	Lat. °′	Long. °′
125	Mallorca, Isla de (Majorca I.) (ĕ's-lä-dĕ-mäl-yô'r-kä) . Sp.	39·18 N	2·22 E
116	Mallow (măl'ō) Ire.	52·07 N	9·04 W
117	Malmédy (mȧl-mā-dē') Bel.	50·25 N	6·01 E
166	Malmesbury (mämz'bēr-ĭ) S. Afr.	33·30 S	18·35 E
118	Malmköping (mälm'chû'pĭng) Swe.	59·09 N	16·39 E
118	Malmö (mälm'û) Swe.	55·36 N	12·58 E
135	Malmyzh (mȧl-mêzh') Sov. Un.	49·58 N	137·07 E
132	Malmyzh Sov. Un.	56·30 N	50·48 E
128	Maloarkhangelsk (mä'lô-ȧr-кäŋ'gĕlsk) Sov. Un.	52·26 N	36·29 E
155	Malolos (mä-lō'lôs) Phil. (Manila In.)	14·58 N	120·53 E
136	Malomal'sk (mȧ-lô-mälsk') Sov. Un. (Urals In.)	58·47 N	59·55 E
81	Malone (mȧ-lōn') N. Y.	44·50 N	74·20 W
128	Maloyaroslavets (mä'lô-yä-rô-slä-vyĕts) Sov. Un.	55·01 N	36·25 E
132	Malozemel'skaya Tundra (Plains) Sov. Un.	67·30 N	50·00 E
110	Malpas (măl'pȧz) Eng.	53·01 N	2·46 W
98	Malpelo, Isla de (I.) (mäl-pä'lō) Col.	3·55 N	81·30 W
82	Malpeque B. (môl-pĕk') Can.	46·41 N	63·40 W
67	Malta (môl'tȧ) Mont.	48·20 N	107·50 W
113	Malta (I.) Eur.	35·52 N	14·26 E
166	Maltahöhe (mäl'tä-hō'ĕ) S. W. Afr.	24·45 S	16·45 E
85	Malton (môl'tŭn) Can. (Toronto In.)	43·42 N	79·39 W
91	Maltrata (mäl-trä'tä) Mex.	18·48 N	97·16 W
167	Maluti Mts. (mȧ-lōō-tĭ) Bas. (Natal In.)	29·00 S	28·29 E
143	Malvan India	16·08 N	73·32 E
73	Malvern (măl'vērn) Ark.	34·21 N	92·47 W
135	Malyy Anyuy (R.) Sov. Un.	67·52 N	164·30 E
135	Malyy Lyakhovskiye (I.) Sov. Un.	74·15 N	142·30 E
135	Malyy Tamir (I.) Sov. Un.	78·10 N	107·30 E
91	Mamantel (mä-män-tĕl') Mex.	18·36 N	91·06 W
84	Mamaroneck (măm'ȧ-rō-nĕk) N. Y (New York In.)	40·57 N	73·44 W
164	Mamau Gui.	10·26 N	12·07 W
155	Mamberamo (R.) (mäm-bȧ-rä'mō) W. Irian	2·30 S	138·00 E
166	Mambone (mäm-bō'nĕ) Moz.	21·04 S	35·13 E
155	Mamburao (mäm-bōō'rä-ō) Phil. (Manila In.)	13·14 N	120·35 E
124	Mamede, Serra de (Mts.) (sĕ'r-rä-dĕ-mä-mĕ'dĕ) Port.	39·29 N	7·11 W
164	Mamfe (mäm'fĕ) Cam.	9·06 E	5·52 N
153	Mamihara (mä'mê-hä-rä) Jap.	32·41 E	131·12 N
78	Mammoth Cave (măm'ŏth) Ky.	37·10 N	86·04 W
78	Mammoth Cave Natl. Park Ky.	37·20 N	86·21 W
67	Mammoth Hot Springs (măm'ŭth hôt sprĭngz) Wyo.	44·55 N	110·50 W
143	Mamnoli India (Bombay In.)	19·17 N	73·15 E
98	Mamoré (R.) (mä-mô-rā') Bol.	13·19 S	65·27 W
121	Mamry L. (mäm'rĭ) Pol.	54·10 N	21·28 E
139	Mamshit Isr. (Palestine In.)	31·02 N	35·04 E
125	Manacor (mä-nä-kôr') Sp.	39·35 N	3·15 E
155	Manado Indon.	1.29 N	124.50 E
95	Managua (mä-nä'gwä) Cuba (Havana In.)	22·14 N	82·17 W
92	Managua Nic.	12·10 N	86·16 W
92	Managua, Lago de (L.) (lä'gô-dĕ) Nic.	12·28 N	86·10 W
167	Manakara (mä-nä-kä'rŭ) Malag. Rep.	22·17 S	48·06 E
167	Mananara (R.) (mä-nä-nä'rŭ) Malag. Rep.	23·15 S	48·15 E
167	Mananjary (mä-nän-zhä'rê) Malag. Rep.	20·16 S	48·13 E
	Manáos, see Manaus		
142	Manasaroar (L.) China	30·40 N	81·58 E
81	Manassas (mȧ-năs'ȧs) Va.	38·45 N	77·30 W
99	Manaus (Manáos) (mä-nä'ōōzh) Braz.	3·01 S	60·00 W
80	Mancelona (măn-sê-lō'nȧ) Mich.	44·50 N	85·05 W
124	Mancha Real (män'chä rā-äl') Sp.	37·48 N	3·37 W
136	Manchazh (män'chȧsh) Sov. Un. (Urals In.)	56·30 N	58·10 E
81	Manchester (măn'chĕs-tēr) Conn.	41·45 N	72·30 W
110	Manchester Eng.	53·28 N	2·14 W
78	Manchester Ga.	32·50 N	84·37 W
71	Manchester Iowa	42·30 N	91·30 W
83	Manchester Mass. (Boston In.)	42·35 N	70·47 W
74	Manchester Mo. (St. Louis In.)	38·36 N	90·31 W
81	Manchester N. H.	43·00 N	71·30 W
80	Manchester Ohio	38·40 N	83·35 W
110	Manchester Ship Canal Eng.	53·20 N	2·40 W
	Manchouli, see Lupin		
147	Manchuria (Reg.) (măn-chōō'rē-ȧ) China	48·00 N	124·58 E
144	Mand, Rud-e (R.) Iran	28·30 N	51·43 E
118	Mandal (män'däl) Nor.	58·03 N	7·28 E
146	Mandalay (măn'dȧ-lā) Bur.	22·00 N	96·08 E
118	Mandalselv (R.) (män'dälsĕlv) Nor.	58·25 N	7·30 E
70	Mandan (măn'dăn) N. D.	46·49 N	100·54 W
165	Mandara Mts. (män-dä'rä) Cam.	10·55 N	14·10 E
139	Mandau Siak (R.) Indon. (Singapore In.)	1·03 N	101·25 E
93	Mandinga (män-dĭŋ'gä) Pan.	9·32 N	79·04 W
142	Mandla India	22·43 N	80·23 E
127	Mándra (män'drä) Grc.	38·06 N	23·32 E
167	Mandritsara (mȧn-drēt-sä'rȧ) Malag. Rep.	15·49 S	48·47 E
127	Manduria (män-dōō'rê-ä) It.	40·23 N	17·41 E
143	Mandve India (Bombay In.)	18·47 N	72·52 E
143	Māndvi (mŭnd'vē) India (Bombay In.)	19·29 N	72·53 E
142	Māndvi (mŭnd'vē) India	22·54 N	69·23 E
168	Manfalūṭ (män-fä-loot') U. A. R. (Nile In.)	27·18 N	30·59 E
126	Manfredonia (män-frä-dô'nyä) It.	41·39 N	15·55 E
126	Manfredónia, Golfo di (G.) (gôl-fô-dē) It.	41·34 N	16·05 E
99	Mangabeiras, Chap. das (Plains) (shä-pä'däs-däs-mäŋ-gä-bä'ê-räzh) Braz.	8·05 S	47·32 W
143	Mangalore (mŭŋ-gŭ-lōr') India	12·53 N	74·52 E
101	Mangaratiba (män-gä-rä-tē'bȧ) Braz. (Rio de Janeiro In.)	22·56 S	44·03 W
155	Mangatarem (män'gȧ-tä'rĕm) Phil. (Manila In.)	15·48 N	120·18 E
155	Mangguli (I.) (män-gōō-lē') Indon.	1·35 S	126·22 E
154	Mangkalihat, Tandjoeng (C.) (mäng'kä-lē-hät') Indon.	1·25 N	119·55 E
94	Mangles, Islas de (ē's-läs-dĕ-mäŋ'gläs) (măn'g'lz) Cuba	22·05 N	83·50 W
167	Mangoky (R.) (män-gō'kē) Malag. Rep.	22·02 S	44·11 E
124	Mangualde (män-gwäl'dĕ) Port.	40·38 N	7·44 W
100	Mangueira, L. da (L.) (män-gā'ê-rȧ) Braz.	33·15 S	52·45 W
72	Mangum (măŋ'gŭm) Okla.	34·52 N	99·31 W
133	Mangyshlak, P.-ov. (Pen.) Sov. Un.	44·30 N	50·40 E
75	Manhattan Ill. (Chicago In.)	41·25 N	87·29 W
73	Manhattan (măn-hăt'ăn) Kans.	39·11 N	96·34 W
74	Manhattan Beach Calif. (Los Angeles In.)	33·53 N	118·24 W
101	Manhuaçu (män-ōōȧ'sōō) Braz. (Rio de Janeiro In.)	20·17 S	42·01 W
101	Manhumirim (män-ōō-mê-rē'ɴ) Braz. (Rio de Janeiro In.)	20·22 S	41·57 W
167	Mania (R.) (män'yä) Malag. Rep.	19·52 S	46·02 E
99	Manicoré (mä-nē-kō-rā') Braz.	5·53 S	61·13 W
87	Manicouagan (R.) Can.	50·24 N	68·29 W
99	Manicuare (mä-nē-kwä'rĕ) Ven. (In.)	10·35 N	64·10 W
157	Manihiki Is. (mä'nē-hē'kê) Oceania	9·40 S	158·00 W
155	Manila (mȧ-nĭl'ȧ) Phil. (Manila In.)	14·37 N	121·00 E
155	Manila B. Phil. (Manila In.)	14·38 N	120·46 E
133	Manisa (mä'nê-sȧ) Tur.	38·40 N	27·30 E
80	Manistee (măn-ĭs-tē') Mich.	44·15 N	86·20 W
80	Manistee (R.) Mich.	44·25 N	85·45 W
71	Manistique (măn-ĭs-tēk') Mich.	45·58 N	86·16 W
71	Manistique (L.) Mich.	46·14 N	85·30 W
71	Manistique (R.) Mich.	46·05 N	86·09 W
86	Manitoba (Prov.) (măn-ĭ-tō'bȧ) Can.	55·12 N	97·29 W
86	Manitoba (L.) Can.	50·38 N	98·40 W
72	Manitou (măn'ĭ-tōō) Colo.	38·51 N	104·58 W
71	Manitou (I.) Mich.	47·21 N	87·33 W
71	Manitou (L.) Can.	49·21 N	93·01 W
80	Manitou Is. Mich.	45·05 N	86·00 W
80	Manitoulin I. (măn-ĭ-tōō'lĭn) Can.	45·45 N	81·30 W
71	Manitowoc (măn-ĭ-tô-wŏk') Wis.	44·05 N	87·42 W
98	Manizales (mä-nê-zä'lâs) Col. (In.)	5·05 N	75·31 W
166	Manjacaze (man'yä-kä'zĕ) Moz.	24·37 S	33·49 E
144	Manjil (mŭn-jēl') Iran	36·45 N	49·15 E
142	Mānjra (R.) India	18·18 N	77·00 E
72	Mankato (măn-kā'tō) Kans.	39·45 N	98·12 W
71	Mankato Minn.	44·10 N	93·59 W
125	Manlleu (män-lyā'ōō) Sp.	42·00 N	2·16 E
161	Manly (măn'lĭ) Austl. (Sydney In.)	33·48 S	151·16 E
143	Mannar (mȧ-när') Ceylon	9.48 N	80·03 E
142	Mannar, G. of India	8·47 N	78·33 E
111	Mannersdorf am Leithagebirge Aus. (Vienna In.)	47·58 N	16·36 E
120	Mannheim (män'hīm) Ger.	49·30 N	8·31 E
71	Manning (măn'ĭng) Iowa	41·53 N	95·04 W
79	Manning S. C.	33·41 N	80·12 W
80	Mannington (măn'ĭng-tŭn) W. Va.	39·30 N	80·55 W
126	Mannu (R.) (mä'n-nōō) It.	39·32 N	9·03 E
95	Man of War B. Ba. Is.	21·05 N	74·05 W
95	Man of War Chan. Ba. Is.	22·45 N	76·10 W
155	Manokwari (mä-nŏk-wä'rê) W. Irian	0·56 S	134·10 E
65	Manor (măn'ēr) Wash. (Portland In.)	45·45 N	122·36 W
143	Manori India (Bombay In.)	19·13 N	72·43 E
123	Manosque (mȧ-nôsh') Fr.	43·51 N	5·48 E
85	Manotick Can. (Ottawa In.)	45·13 N	75·41 W
125	Manresa (män-rā'sä) Sp.	41·44 N	1·52 E
87	Mansel (I.) (măn'sĕl) Can.	61·56 N	81·10 W
98	Manseriche, Pongo de (Water Gap) (pŏ'n-gô-dĕ-män-sĕ-rĕ'chĕ) Peru	4·15 S	77·45 W
110	Mansfield (mănz'fēld) Eng.	53·08 N	1·12 W
77	Mansfield La.	32·02 N	93·43 W
80	Mansfield Ohio	40·45 N	82·30 W
66	Mansfield Wash.	47·48 N	119·39 W
81	Mansfield, Mt. Vt.	44·30 N	72·45 W
110	Mansfield Woodhouse (wŏŏd-hous) Eng.	53·08 N	1·12 W
99	Manso (R.) Braz.	13·30 S	51·45 W
98	Manta (män'tä) Ec.	1·03 S	80·16 W
75	Manteno (măn-tē-nō) Ill. (Chicago In.)	41·15 N	87·50 W
123	Mantes-la-Jolie (mäɴt-ĕ-lä-zhō-lē') Fr. (Paris In.)	48·59 N	1·42 E
69	Manti (măn'tī) Utah	39·15 N	111·40 W
101	Mantiqueira, Serra da (Mts.) (sĕ'r-rä dä män-tê-kā'ê-rȧ) Braz. (Rio de Janeiro In.)	22·40 S	45·12 W
126	Mantova (Mantua) (män'tô-vä) (măn'tû-ȧ) It.	45·09 N	10·47 E
94	Mantua (män-tōō'ȧ) Cuba	22·20 N	84·15 W
74	Mantua (măn'tû-ȧ) Utah (Salt Lake City In.)	41·30 N	111·57 W
	Mantua, see Mantova		
82	Manuan (L.) (mä-nōō'ȧn) Can.	50·36 N	70·50 W
82	Manuan, Riviere (R.) Can.	49·50 N	70·55 W
155	Manui (Is.) (mä-nōō'ē) Indon.	3·35 S	123·38 E
155	Manus (I.) (mä'nōōs) N. Gui. Ter.	2·22 S	146·22 E
77	Manvel (măn'vĕl) Tex. (In.)	29·28 N	95·22 W
84	Manville (măn'vĭl) N. J. (New York In.)	40·33 N	74·36 W
84	Manville R. I. (Providence In.)	41·57 N	71·27 W
133	Manych (R.) (mä-nĭch') Sov. Un.	47·00 N	41·10 E
103	Manych Dep. Sov. Un.	46·32 N	42·44 E
133	Manych-Gudilo (Lake) Sov. Un.	46·40 N	42·50 E
168	Manzala L. U. A. R. (Nile In.)	31·14 N	32·04 E
98	Manzanares (män-sä-nä'rĕs) Col. (In.)	5·15 N	75·09 W
125	Manzanares (R.) (mänz-nä'rĕs) Sp. (Madrid In.)	40·36 N	3·48 W
125	Manzanares, Canal de (kä-nä'l-dĕ-män-thä-nä'rĕs) Sp. (Madrid In.)	40·20 N	3·38 W
94	Manzanillo (män'zä-nēl'yō) Cuba	20·20 N	77·05 W
90	Manzanillo Mex.	19·02 N	104·21 W
95	Manzanillo, Bahía de (B.) Hai.	19·55 N	71·50 W
90	Manzanillo, Bahía de (B.) (bä-ē'ä-dĕ-män-zä-nē'l-yō) Mex.	19·00 N	104·38 W
93	Manzanillo, Punta (Pt.) Pan.	9·40 N	79·33 W
152	Manzovka (mȧn-zhô'f-kȧ) Sov. Un.	44·16 N	132·13 E
165	Mao (mä'ô) Chad	14·07 N	15·15 E
151	Maoming China	21·55 N	110·40 E
91	Mapastepec (ma-päs-tā-pĕk') Mex.	15·24 N	92·52 W
155	Mapia (I.) (mä'pē-ä) W. Irian	0·57 N	134·22 E
76	Mapimi (mä-pê-mē') Mex.	25·50 N	103·50 W
85	Maple (mā'p'l) Can. (Toronto In.)	43·51 N	79·30 W
86	Maple Creek (krēk) Can.	49·52 N	109·32 W
85	Maple Grove (grōv) Can. (Montreal In.)	45·19 N	73·51 W
75	Maple Heights Ohio (Cleveland In.)	41·25 N	81·34 W
84	Maple Shade (shād) N. J. (Philadelphia In.)	39·57 N	75·01 W
65	Maple Valley (văl'ê) Wash. (Seattle In.)	47·24 N	122·02 W
74	Maplewood (wŏŏd) Mo. (St. Louis In.)	38·37 N	90·20 W
74	Maplewood Park (wŏŏd pärk) Ill. (St. Louis In.)	38·34 N	90·11 W
167	Mapumulo (mä-pä-mōō'lō) S. Afr. (Natal In.)	29·12 S	31·05 E
155	Maqueda Chan. (mä-kā'dä) Phil. (Manila In.)	13·40 N	123·52 E
166	Maquela do Zombo (mä-kā'lȧ dŏŏ zôm'bŏŏ) Ang.	6·08 S	15·15 E
71	Maquoketa (mȧ-kō-kê-tȧ) Iowa	42·04 N	90·42 W
71	Maquoketa (R.) Iowa	42·08 N	90·40 W
100	Mar, Serra do (Mts.) (sĕr'rȧ dŏŏ mär') Braz.	26·30 S	49·15 W
98	Maracaibo (mä-rä-kī'bō) Ven.	10·38 N	71·45 W
98	Maracaibo, Lago de (L.) (lä'gô-dĕ-mä-rä-kī'bō) Ven.	9·55 N	72·13 W
99	Maracay (mä-rä-käy') Ven. (In.)	10·15 N	67·35 W
165	Marādah Libya	29·10 N	19·07 E
164	Maradi (mȧ-rä-dē') Niger	13·30 N	7·11 E
133	Marāgheh Iran	37·20 N	46·10 E
167	Maraisburg S. Afr. (Johannesburg & Pretoria In.)	26·12 S	27·57 E
99	Marajó, Ilha de (I.) (mȧ-rȧ-zhō') Braz.	0·30 S	50·00 W
166	Marandelles (mä-rȧn-däl'ȧs) S. Rh.	18·08 S	31·36 E
99	Maranguape (mä-rȧŋ-gwä'pĕ) Braz.	3·48 S	38·38 W
	Maranhão, see São Luis		
99	Maranhão (State) (mä-rän-youɴ) Braz.	5·15 S	45·52 W
160	Maranoa (R.) (mä-rä-nō'ä) Austl.	27·01 S	148·03 E
125	Marano di Napoli (mä-rä'nô-dē-nä'pô-lē) It. (Naples In.)	40·39 N	14·12 E
98	Marañón, Rio (R.) (rē'ō-mä-rä-nyōn') Peru	4·26 S	75·08 W
99	Marapanim (mä-rä-pä-nē'ɴ) Braz.	0·45 S	47·42 W
133	Maras (mä-räsh') Tur.	37·40 N	36·50 E
79	Marathon (mär'ȧ-thŏn) Fla. (In.)	24·41 N	81·06 W
75	Marathon Ohio (Cincinnati In.)	39·09 N	83·59 W
154	Maratua (I.) Indon.	2·14 N	118·30 E
90	Maravatio (mä-rä-vä'tê-ō) Mex.	19·54 N	100·25 W
158	Marble Bar (märb''l bär) Austl.	21·15 S	119·15 E
69	Marble Can. (mär'b'l) Ariz.	36·21 N	111·48 W
168	Marble Hall (hâll) S. Afr. (Johannesburg & Pretoria In.)	24·59 S	29·19 E
83	Marblehead (mär'b'l-hĕd) Mass. (Boston In.)	42·30 N	70·51 W
120	Marburg (mär'bŏŏrgh) Ger.	50·49 N	8·46 E
92	Marcala (mär-kä-lä) Hond.	14·08 N	88·01 W
126	Marche (Reg.) (mär'kā) It.	43·35 N	12·33 E
111	Marchegg Aus. (Vienna In.)	48·18 N	16·55 E
124	Marchena (mär-chā'nä) Sp.	37·20 N	5·25 W
98	Marchena (I.) (ĕ's-lä-mär-chĕ'nä) Ec.	0·29 N	90·31 W
74	March Field (märch) Calif. (Los Angeles In.)	33·54 N	117·17 W
73	Marceline (mär-sê-lēn') Mo.	39·42 N	92·56 W
101	Marcos Paz (mär-kōs' päz) Arg. (Buenos Aires In.)	34·49 S	58·51 W
156	Marcus (I.) (mär'kŭs) Asia	24·00 N	155·00 E
84	Marcus Hook (mär'kŭs hŏŏk) Pa. (Philadelphia In.)	39·49 N	75·25 W
81	Marcy, Mt. (mär'sê) N. Y.	44·10 N	73·55 W
101	Mar de Espanha (mär-dĕ-ĕs-pä'nyä) Braz. (Rio de Janeiro In.)	21·53 S	43·00 W
100	Mar del Plata (mär dĕl plä'ta) Arg.	37·59 S	57·35 W
133	Mardin (mär-dēn') Tur.	37·25 N	40·40 E
159	Maré (I.) (mȧ-rā') N. Cal.	21·53 S	168·30 E
116	Maree (L.) (mȧ-rē') Scot.	57·40 N	5·44 W
71	Marengo (mȧ-rĕŋ'gō) Iowa	41·47 N	92·04 W
122	Marennes (mȧ-rĕn') Fr.	45·49 N	1·08 W

ng-sing; ŋ-baŋk; ɴ-nasalized n; nŏd; cŏmmit; ōld; ôbey; ôrder; fōōd; fŏŏt; ou-out; s-soft; sh-dish; th-thin; pūre; ûnite; ûrn; stŭd; circŭs; ü-as "y" in study; '-indeterminate vowel.

ăt; fīnȧl; rāte; senāte; ärm; ȧsk; sofȧ; fâre; ch-choose; dh-as th in other; bē; ĕvent; bĕt; recĕnt; cratêr; g-go; gh-guttural g; bĭt; ĭ-short neutral; rīde; κ-guttural k as ch in German ich;

PRONOUNCING INDEX Matatiele–Mendes 235

Page	Name Pronunciation Region	Lat. °′	Long. °′
167	Matatiele (mä-tä-tyā′lā) S. Afr. (Natal In.)	30·21 S	28·49 E
84	Matawana (mȧ-tȧ-wŏn′ȧ) N. J. (New York In.)	40·24 N	74·13 W
90	Matehuala (mä-tâ-wä′lä) . . . . Mex.	23·38 N	100·39 W
126	Matera (mä-tâ′rä) . . . . It.	40·42 N	16·37 E
113	Mateur (mȧ-tûr′) . . . . Tun.	37·09 N	9·43 E
143	Mātherān . . . . India (Bombay In.)	18·58 N	73·16 E
74	Mathews, L. (măth′ūz) Calif. (Los Agneles In.)	33·50 N	117·24 W
142	Mathura (mu-tōō′rŭ) . . . . India	27·39 N	77·39 E
101	Matias Barbosa (mä-tē′äs-bȧr-bô-sä) Braz. (Rio de Janeiro In.)	21·53 S	43·19 W
91	Matillas, Laguna (L.) (lä-gōō′nä-mä-tê′l-yäs) . Mex.	18·02 N	92·36 W
93	Matina (mä-tē′nä) . . . . C. R.	10·06 N	83·20 W
119	Matiši (mä′tê-sê) . . . . Sov. Un.	57·43 N	25·09 E
154	Matjan (I.) . . . . Indon.	6·52 S	121·45 E
90	Matlalcueyetl, Cerra (sĕ′r-rä-mä-tläl-kwĕ′yĕtl) . Mex.	19·13 N	98·02 W
110	Matlock (măt′lŏk) . . . . Eng.	53·08 N	1·33 W
110	Matlock Bath (măt′lŏk bäth) Eng.	53·06 N	1·34 W
134	Matochkin Shar (mä′tŏch-kĭn) Sov. Un.	73·57 N	56·16 E
99	Mato Grosso (mät′ŏŏ grōs′ŏŏ) Braz.	15·04 S	59·58 W
99	Mato Grosso (State) . . . . Braz.	14·38 S	55·36 W
99	Mato Grosso, Chapada de (Plain) (shä-pä′dä-dĕ) . Braz.	13·39 S	55·42 W
124	Matozinhos (Leixoes) (mȧ-tô-zēn′yōzh) (lĕ′y-shô′-ĕs) Port.	41·10 N	8·48 W
144	Matrah (mȧ-trä′) . . . . Mus. & Om.	23·36 N	58·27 E
165	Maţrūḩ . . . . U .A. R.	31·19 N	27·14 E
153	Matsudo (mät′sŏŏ-dô) Jap. (Tōkyō In.)	35·48 N	139·55 E
153	Matsue (mät′sŏŏ-ĕ) . . . . Jap.	35·29 N	133·04 E
153	Matsumoto (mät′sŏŏ-mō′tô) . . Jap.	36·15 N	137·59 E
153	Matsuyama (mät′sŏŏ-yä′mä) . Jap.	33·48 N	132·45 E
153	Matsuzaka (mät′sŏŏ-zä′kä) . . . Jap.	34·35 N	136·34 E
87	Mattagami (L.) (mâ-tä-gä′mê) Can.	50·10 N	78·49 W
79	Mattamuskeet (R.) (măt-tȧ-mŭs′kēt) . N. C.	35·34 N	76·03 W
81	Mattaponi (R.) (măt′ȧ-ponĭ′) . Va.	37·45 N	77·00 W
87	Mattawa (măt′ȧ-wȧ) . . . . Can.	46·15 N	78·49 W
82	Mattawin (R.) (măt′ȧ-wĭn) . . Can.	46·55 N	73·20 W
120	Matterhorn Mt. (mät′ēr-hôrn) Switz.	45·57 N	7·36 E
75	Matteson (mătt′ê-sŭn) Ill. (Chicago In.)	41·30 N	87·42 W
95	Matthew Town (măth′û toun) Ba. Is.	21·00 N	73·40 W
80	Mattoon (mă-tōōn′) . . . . Ill.	39·30 N	88·20 W
98	Maturín (mä-tōō-rēn′) . . . . Ven.	9·48 N	63·16 W
155	Mauban (mä′ōō-bän′) Phil. (Manila In.)	14·11 N	121·44 E
122	Maubeuge (mô-bûzh′) . . . . Fr.	50·18 N	3·57 E
75	Maud (môd) Ohio (Cincinnati In.)	39·21 N	84·23 W
111	Mauer (mou′ēr) . Aus. (Vienna In.)	48·09 N	16·16 E
99	Maués (mȧ-wĕ′s) . . . . Braz.	3·34 S	57·30 W
157	Maui (I.) (mä′ōō-ē) Hawaii (In.)	20·52 N	156·02 W
101	Maule (R.) (mȧ′ŏŏ-lĕ) Chile (Santiago In.)	35·45 S	70·50 W
80	Maumee (mô-mē′) . . . . Ohio	41·30 N	83·40 W
80	Maumee (R.) . . . . Ind.-Ohio	41·10 N	84·50 W
80	Maumee B. . . . . Ohio	41·50 N	83·20 W
166	Maun (mä-ŏŏn′) . . . . Bech.	19·52 S	23·40 E
157	Mauna Kea (Vol.) (mä′ŏŏ-näkā′ä) Hawaii (In.)	19·52 N	155·30 W
157	Mauna Loa (Vol.) (mä′ŏŏ-nälō′ä) Hawaii (In.)	19·28 N	155·38 W
154	Maung Nakhon Sawan . . . . . Thai.	16·00 N	99·52 E
77	Maurepas L. (mō-rē-pä′) . . . . . . La.	30·18 N	90·40 W
163	Mauritania (mô-rê-tā′nĭ-ȧ) . . . Afr.	19·38 N	13·30 W
47	Mauritius I. (mô-rĭsh′ĭ-ŭs) . . . . Afr.	20·18 S	57·36 E
65	Maury (mô′rĭ) Wash. (Seattle In.)	47·22 N	122·23 W
71	Mauston (môs′tŭn) . . . . Wis.	43·46 N	90·05 W
69	Maverick, (R.) (mā-vûr′ĭk) . . Ariz.	33·40 N	109·30 W
91	Maxcanú (mäs-kä-nōō′) . . . . . Mex.	20·35 N	89·59 W
85	Maxville (măks′vĭl) Can. (Ottawa In.)	45·17 N	74·52 W
74	Maxville . . . . . . Mo. (St. Louis In.)	38·26 N	90·24 W
135	Maya (R.) (mä′yä) . . . . . . Sov. Un.	58·00 N	135·45 E
95	Mayaguana (I.) . . . . Ba. Is.	22·25 N	73·00 W
95	Mayaguana Passage (Str.) . Ba. Is.	22·20 N	73·25 W
89	Mayagüez (mä-yä-gwāz′) P. R. (Puerto Rico In.)	18·12 N	67·10 W
95	Mayarí (mä-yä-rē′) . . . . Cuba	20·45 N	75·40 W
95	Mayari (R.) . . . . Cuba	20·25 N	75·35 W
92	Mayas, Montañas (Mts.) (mŏntăŋ′ăs mā′ăs) Br. Hond. (Yucatan In.)	16·43 N	89·00 W
120	Mayen (mī′ĕn) . . . . Ger.	50·19 N	7·14 E
122	Mayenne (mȧ-yĕn′) . . . . Fr.	48·19 N	0·35 W
122	Mayenne (R.) . . . . Fr.	48·14 N	0·45 W
78	Mayfield (mā′fēld) . . . . Ky.	36·44 N	88·19 W
79	Mayfield Cr. . . . . Ky.	36·54 N	88·47 W
75	Mayfield Heights Ohio (Cleveland In.)	41·31 N	81·26 W
66	Mayfield Res . . . . Wash.	46·31 N	122·34 W
133	Maykop (Maikop) (mī-kôp′) Sov. Un.	44·35 N	40·10 E
136	Maykor (mī-kôr′) Sov. Un. (Urals In.)	59·01 N	55·52 E
146	Maymyo (mī′myō′) . . . . Bur.	22·14 N	96·32 E
83	Maynard (mā′nȧrd) Mass. (Boston In.)	42·25 N	71·27 W
65	Maynard . . . . . Wash. (Seattle In.)	47·59 N	122·54 W
65	Mayne (mān) Can. (Vancouver In.)	48·51 N	123·18 W
65	Mayne (I.) . . Can. (Vancouver In.)	48·52 N	123·14 W
78	Mayo (mā-yō′) . . . . Fla.	30·02 N	83·08 W
64	Mayo (L.) . . . . Alaska	63·50 N	135·30 W
86	Mayo . . . . Can.	63·40 N	135·51 W
116	Mayo, Mts. of . . . . Ire.	54·01 N	9·01 W
79	Mayodan (mā-yō′dăn) . . . . . . N. C.	36·25 N	79·59 W
155	Mayon (Vol.) (mä-yōn′) Phil. (Manila In.)	13·21 N	123·43 E
167	Mayotte (I.) (mȧ-yôt′) Comores, Arch. des	13·07 S	45·32 E
94	May Pen . . . . Jam.	18·00 N	77·25 W
151	Mayraira Pt. . . . . Phil.	18·40 N	120·45 E
76	Mayran, Laguna de (L.) (lä-ŏŏ′nä-dĕ-mī-rän′) . . . . . . Mex.	25·40 N	102·35 W
80	Maysville (māz′vĭl) . . . . Ky.	38·35 N	83·45 W
166	Mayumba . . . . Gabon	3·15 S	10·10 E
81	Mayville (mā′vĭl) . . . . N. Y.	42·15 N	79·30 W
70	Mayville . . . . N. D.	47·30 N	97·20 W
71	Mayville . . . . Wis.	43·30 N	88·45 W
74	Maywood (mā′wŏŏd) Calif. (Los Angeles In.)	33·59 N	118·11 W
75	Maywood . . . . Ill. (Chicago In.)	41·53 N	87·51 W
166	Mazabuka (mä-zä-bōō′kä) . N. Rh.	16·00 S	27·43 E
99	Mazagão (mă-zȧ-gou′N) . . . . . Braz.	0·05 S	51·27 W
76	Mazapil (mä-zä-pēl′) . . . . Mex.	24·40 N	101·30 W
142	Mazar-i-Sharif (mȧ-zär′-ē-shȧ-rēf′) . Afg.	36·48 N	67·12 E
124	Mazarrón (mä-zär-rô′n) . . . . Sp.	36·37 N	1·29 W
99	Mazaruni (R.) (mä-zä-rōō′nê) Br. Gu.	5·58 N	59·37 W
92	Mazatenango (mä-zä-tâ-näŋ′gō) Guat.	14·30 N	91·30 W
91	Mazatla . . Mex. (Mexico City In.)	19·30 N	99·24 W
91	Mazatlán (San Juan) (mä-zä-tlän′) (sän hwän′) . Mex.	17·05 N	95·26 W
90	Mazatlán . . . . Mex.	23·14 N	106·27 W
119	Mažeikiai (mȧ-zhā′kê-ī) . . Sov. Un.	56·19 N	22·24 E
139	Mazhafah, Jabal (Mts.) Sau. Ar. (Palestine In.)	28·56 N	35·05 E
126	Mazzara del Vallo (mät-sä′rä dĕl väl′lō) . It.	37·40 N	12·37 E
126	Mazzarino (mät-sä-rē′nō) . . . . . . It.	37·16 N	14·15 E
166	Mbabane (m′bä-bä′nĕ) . . . . . Swaz.	26·18 S	31·14 E
165	Mbaiki (m′bȧ-ē′kê) . Cen. Afr. Rep.	3·54 N	17·57 E
166	Mbigou (m-bê-gōō′) . . . . . . Con. B.	2·07 S	12·07 E
165	M′Bomu R. (m′bō′mōō) . . Con. L.	4·38 N	23·48 E
164	M′Bout (m′bōō′) . . . . . Mauritania	16·03 N	12·31 W
72	Meade (mēd) . . . . Kans.	37·17 N	100·21 W
69	Meade, L. . . . . Nev.-Ariz.	36·20 N	114·14 W
67	Meade Pk. . . . . Idaho	42·19 N	111·16 W
65	Meadowdale (mĕd′ō-dāl) Wash. (Seattle In.)	47·51 N	122·20 W
86	Meadow Lake (mĕd′ō lāk) . . . Can.	54·10 N	108·30 W
85	Meadows (mĕd′ōz) Can. (Winnipeg In.)	50·02 N	97·35 W
81	Meadville (mēd′vĭl) . . . . Pa.	41·40 N	80·10 W
80	Meaford (mē′fērd) . . . . Can.	44·35 N	80·40 W
87	Mealy Mts. (mē′lē) . . . . Can.	53·32 N	57·58 W
160	Meandarra (mē-ȧn-dä′rȧ) . . . Austl.	27·47 S	149·40 E
123	Meaux (mō) . . . . Fr. (Paris In.)	48·58 N	2·53 E
91	Mecapalapa (mā-kä-pä-lä′pä) Mex.	20·32 N	97·52 W
83	Mecatina (I.) (mā-kȧ-tē′nȧ) . Can.	50·50 N	58·33 W
83	Mecatina (R.) (mā-kȧ-tē′nȧ) . Can.	50·50 N	59·45 W
	Mecca, see Makkah		
82	Mechanic Falls (mê-kăn′ĭk) . Maine	44·05 N	70·23 W
81	Mechanicsburg (mê-kăn′ĭks-bŭrg) . Pa.	40·15 N	77·00 W
81	Mechanicsville (mê-kăn′ĭks-vĭl) N. Y.	42·55 N	73·45 W
111	Mechelen . . . . . . Bel. (Brussels In.)	51·01 N	4·28 E
114	Mecheria . . . . Mor.	33·30 N	0·13 W
120	Mecklenburg (Reg.) (mĕk′lĕn-bŏŏrgh) . Ger.	53·34 N	12·18 E
154	Medan (mâ-dän′) . . . . Indon.	3·35 N	98·35 E
100	Medanosa, Punta (Pt.) (pōō′n-tä-mĕ-dä-nô′sä) . Arg.	47·50 S	65·53 W
110	Medden (R.) (mĕd′ĕn) . . . . . . Eng.	53·14 N	1·05 W
125	Médéa (mā-dā′ä) . . . . Alg.	36·18 N	2·40 E
98	Medellín (mâ-dhĕl-yēn′) . Col. (In.)	6·15 N	75·34 W
91	Medellín (mĕ-dĕl-yĕ′n) . . . . . . Mex.	19·03 N	96·08 W
114	Medenine (mā-dē-nēn′) . . . . . . Tun.	33·22 N	10·33 E
83	Medfield (mĕd′fēld) Mass. (Boston In.)	42·11 N	71·19 W
83	Medford (mĕd′fērd) Mass. (Boston In.)	42·25 N	71·07 W
84	Medford . . N. J. (Philadelphia In.)	39·54 N	74·50 W
72	Medford . . . . Okla.	36·47 N	97·44 W
66	Medford . . . . Ore.	42·19 N	122·52 W
71	Medford . . . . Wis.	45·09 N	90·22 W
84	Media (mē′dĭ-ȧ) Pa. (Philadelphia In.)	39·55 N	75·24 W
121	Medias (mĕd-yäsh′) . . . . Rom.	46·09 N	24·21 E
66	Medical Lake (mĕd′ĭ-kăl) . . Wash.	47·34 N	117·40 W
72	Medicine Bow Ra. (mĕd′ĭ-sĭn bō) . Colo.-Wyo.	40·55 N	106·02 W
67	Medicine Bow R. . . . . Wyo.	41·58 N	106·30 W
86	Medicine Hat (mĕd′ĭ-sĭn hăt) . Can.	50·09 N	110·50 W
67	Medicine L. (mĕd′ĭ-sĭn) . . . . Mont.	48·24 N	104·15 W
72	Medicine Lodge . . . . Kans.	37·17 N	98·37 W
72	Medicine Lodge (R.) . . . . Kans.	37·20 N	98·57 W
81	Medina (mê-dī′nȧ) . . . . N. Y.	43·15 N	78·20 W
75	Medina . . . . . Ohio (Cleveland In.)	41·08 N	81·52 W
124	Medina del Campo (mâ-dē′nä dĕl käm′pō) . Sp.	41·18 N	4·54 W
124	Medina de Rioseco (mâ-dē′nä dā rê-ô-sā′kô) . Sp.	41·53 N	5·05 W
76	Medina L. . . . . Tex.	29·36 N	98·47 W
76	Medina R. . . . . Tex.	29·45 N	99·13 W
124	Medina Sidonia (sê-dō′nyä) . . . Sp.	36·28 N	5·58 W
101	Medio (mĕ′dyô) (R.) Arg. (Buenos Aires In.)	33·40 S	60·30 W
114	Mediterranean Sea (mĕd-ĭ-tēr-ā′nê-ăn) . Afr.-Asia-Eur.	36·22 N	13·25 E
113	Medjerda, Oued (R.) (wĕd mĕ-jĕr′dȧ) . Tun.	36·43 N	9·54 E
134	Mednogorsk . . . . Sov. Un.	51·27 N	57·22 E
133	Medveditsa (R.) (mĕd-vyĕ′dê tsȧ) . Sov. Un.	50·10 N	43·40 E
132	Medvezhegorsk (mĕd-vyĕzh′yĕ-gôrsk′) . Sov. Un.	63·00 N	34·20 E
135	Medvezh′y (Is.) . . . . Sov. Un.	71·00 N	161·25 E
83	Medway (mĕd′wā) Mass. (Boston In.)	42·08 N	71·23 W
128	Medyn′ (mĕ-dēn′) . . . . Sov. Un.	54·58 N	35·53 E
129	Medzhibozh (mĕd-zhê-bōzh′) Sov. Un.	49·23 N	27·29 E
158	Meekatharra (mē-kȧ-thăr′ȧ) . Austl.	26·30 S	118·38 E
69	Meeker (mēk′ēr) . . . . Colo.	40·00 N	107·55 W
120	Meerane (mā-rä′nē) . . . . Ger.	50·51 N	12·27 E
142	Meerut (mē′rŏŏt) . . . . India	28·59 N	77·43 E
165	Mēgā . . . . Eth.	6·14 N	35·34 E
127	Megalópolis (mĕg-ȧ lŏ′pô-lĭs) . Grc.	37·22 N	22·08 E
129	Meganom, M. (C.) (mĭs mĕ-gȧ-nôm′) . Sov. Un.	44·48 N	35·17 E
127	Mégara (mĕg′ȧ-rȧ) . . . . Grc.	37·59 N	23·21 E
79	Megget (mĕg′ĕt) . . . . S. C.	32·44 N	80·15 W
65	Megler (mĕg′lēr) Wash. (Portland In.)	46·15 N	123·52 W
128	Meglino (L.) (mâ-glē′nô) . Sov. Un.	58·32 N	35·27 E
79	Meherrin (R.) (mê-hĕr′ĭn) . . . . Va.	36·40 N	77·49 W
142	Mehsāna . . . . India	23·42 N	72·23 E
122	Mehun-sur-Yèvre (mē-ŭN-sür-yĕvr′) . Fr.	47·11 N	2·14 E
148	Meichu (mā′jĕōō) . . . . China	31·17 N	119·12 E
151	Meihsien . . . . China	24·20 N	116·10 E
151	Meiling Pass (mā′lĭng′) . . . . . China	25·22 N	115·00 E
123	Meinerzhagen (mī′nĕrts-hä-gĕn) Ger. (Ruhr In.)	51·06 N	7·39 E
120	Meiningen (mī′nĭng-ĕn) . . . . . . Ger.	50·35 N	10·25 E
120	Meiringen . . . . Switz.	46·45 N	8·11 E
100	Mejillones (mâ-KĒ-lyō′nâs) . . Chile	23·07 S	70·31 W
164	Meknés (mĕk′nĕs) (mĕk-nĕs′) . Mor.	33·56 N	5·44 W
	Mekong, see Lanisung Chiang		
154	Mekong, Mouths of the (mē′kông′) . . . Viet.	10·09 N	107·15 E
154	Mekong R. . . . . Thai.-Laos	17·53 N	103·57 E
161	Melbourne (mĕl′bŭrn) Austl. (Melbourne In.)	37·52 S	145·08 E
79	Melbourne . . . . Fla. (In.)	28·02 N	28·37 W
110	Melbourne . . . . Eng.	52·49 N	1·26 W
75	Melbourne . . . Ky. (Cincinnati In.)	39·02 N	84·22 W
71	Melcher (mĕl′chēr) . . . . Iowa	41·13 N	93·11 W
132	Melekess (mĕl-yĕk ĕs) . . . . Sov. Un.	54·20 N	49·30 E
128	Melenki (mĕ-lyĕŋ′kê) . . . . Sov. Un.	55·25 N	41·34 E
86	Melfort (mĕl′fôrt) . . . . Can.	52·55 N	104·31 W
165	Melik, Wadi el (R.) . . . . Sud.	16·48 N	29·30 E
164	Melilla (Sp.) (mā-lēl′yä) . . . . . . Afr.	35·24 N	3·03 W
101	Melipilla (mâ-lê-pē′lyä) Chile (Santiago In.)	33·40 S	71·12 W
129	Melitopol′ (mā-lê-tô′pôl-y′) Sov. Un.	46·49 N	35·19 E
168	Melkrivier . . . . S. Afr. (Johannesburg & Pretoria In.)	24·01 S	28·23 E
71	Mellen (mĕl′ĕn) . . . . Wis.	46·20 N	90·40 W
118	Mellerud (mâl′ĕ-rōōdh) . . . . . . Swe.	58·43 N	12·25 E
167	Melmoth . . . . . . S. Afr. (Natal In.)	28·38 S	31·26 E
100	Melo (mā′lō) . . . . Ur.	32·18 S	54·07 W
85	Melocheville (mĕ-lôsh-vēl′) Can. (Montreal In.)	45·24 N	73·56 W
136	Melozha R. (myĕ′lô-zhȧ) Sov. Un. (Moscow In.)	56·06 N	38·34 E
164	Melrhir Chott (L.) (mĕl′rēr) . . Alg.	33·52 N	5·22 E
83	Melrose (mĕl′rōz) Mass. (Boston In.)	42·29 N	71·06 W
71	Melrose . . . . Minn.	45·39 N	94·49 W
75	Melrose Park . . . . Ill. (Chicago In.)	41·54 N	87·52 W
166	Melsetter (mĕl-sĕt′ēr) . . . . . . S. Rh.	19·44 S	32·51 E
110	Meltham (mĕl′thăm) . . . . Eng.	53·35 N	1·51 W
161	Melton (mĕl′tŭn) Austl. (Melbourne In.)	37·41 S	144·35 E
110	Melton Mowbray (mō′brâ) . . Eng.	52·45 N	0·52 W
123	Melun (mē-lŭN′) . . . Fr. (Paris In.)	48·32 N	2·40 E
165	Melut (mâ-lōōt′) . . . . Sud.	10·30 N	32·17 E
86	Melville (mĕl′vĭl) . . . . Can.	51·00 N	102·52 W
77	Melville . . . . La.	30·39 N	91·45 W
159	Melville, C. . . . . Austl.	14·15 S	145·50 E
158	Melville (I.) . . . . Austl.	11·30 S	131·12 E
87	Melville (R.) . . . . Can.	53·46 N	59·31 W
86	Melville Hills . . . . Can.	69·18 N	124·57 W
87	Melville Pen . . . . Can.	67·44 N	84·09 W
75	Melvindale (mĕl′vĭn-dāl) Mich. (Detroit In.)	42·17 N	83·11 W
121	Mélykút (mā′l′kōōt) . . . . Hung.	46·14 N	19·21 E
168	Memal (mĕ′mĕl) S. Afr. (Johannesburg & Pretoria In.)	27·42 S	29·35 E
167	Memba (mĕm′bȧ) . . . . Moz.	14·12 S	40·35 E
	Memel, see Klaipéda		
120	Memmingen (mĕm′ĭng-ĕn) . . . Ger.	47·59 N	10·10 E
99	Memo (R.) (mĕ′mō) . . . . Ven. (In.)	9·32 N	66·30 W
73	Memphis (mĕm′fĭs) . . . . Mo.	40·27 N	92·11 W
78	Memphis (mĕm′fĭs) . . . . Tenn.	35·07 N	90·03 W
72	Memphis . . . . Tex.	34·42 N	100·33 W
168	Memphis (Ruins) U. A. R. (Nile In.)	29·50 N	31·12 E
81	Memphremagog (L.) (mĕm′frê-mā′gŏg) . Can.	45·05 N	72·10 W
73	Mena (mē′nȧ) . . . . Ark.	34·35 N	94·09 W
129	Mena (mā-nȧ′) . . . . Sov. Un.	51·31 N	32·14 E
161	Menangle . . . . . Austl. (Sydney In.)	34·08 S	150·48 E
76	Menard (mê-närd′) . . . . Tex.	30·56 N	99·48 W
71	Menasha (mê-năsh′ȧ) . . . . Wis.	44·12 N	88·29 W
122	Mende (mäNd) . . . . Fr.	44·31 N	3·30 E
123	Menden (mĕn′dĕn) Ger. (Ruhr In.)	51·26 N	7·47 E
133	Menderes (R.) (mĕn′dĕr-ĕs) . . Tur.	37·50 N	28·20 E
100	Mendes (mĕ′n-dĕs) . . . . Braz. (In.)	22·32 S	43·44 W

ng-sing; ŋ-baŋk; N-nasalized n; nŏd; cŏmmit; ōld; ôbey; ôrder; fōōd; fŏŏt; ou-out; s-soft; sh-dish; th-thin; pūre; ûnite; ûrn; stŭd; circŭs; ü-as "y" in study; ′-indeterminate vowel.

236 Mendocino–Mikuni PRONOUNCING INDEX

Page	Name	Pronunciation	Region	Lat. °′	Long. °′
66	Mendocino, C.	(mĕn'dô-sē'nō)	Calif.	40·25 N	124·22 W
71	Mendota	(mĕn-dō'tȧ)	Ill.	41·34 N	89·06 W
71	Mendota (L.)		Wis.	43·09 N	89·41 W
100	Mendoza	(mĕn-dō'sä)	Arg.	32·48 S	68·45 W
100	Mendoza (Prov.)		Arg.	35·10 S	69·00 W
151	Mengtzu		China	23·22 N	103·20 E
160	Menindee	(mẽ-nĭn-dē)	Austl.	32·23 S	142·30 E
65	Menlo Park	(mĕn'lō pärk)	Calif. (San Francisco In.)	37·27 N	122·11 W
70	Menno	(mĕn'ô)	S. D.	43·14 N	97·34 W
71	Menominee	(mê-nŏm'ĭ-nē)	Mich.	45·08 N	87·40 W
71	Menominee (R.)		Mich.-Wis.	45·37 N	87·54 W
75	Menomonee Falls	(fôls)	Wis. (Milwaukee In.)	43·11 N	88·06 W
71	Menominee Ra.		Mich.	46·07 N	88·53 W
75	Menomonee R.		Wis. (Milwaukee In.)	43·09 N	88·06 W
71	Menomonie		Wis.	44·53 N	91·55 W
125	Menorca, Isla de (Minorca) (I.)	(ē's-lä-dĕ-mĕ-nô'r-kä)	Sp.	40·05 N	3·58 E
125	Mentana	(mĕn-tá'nä)	It. (Rome In.)	42·02 N	12·40 E
154	Mentawai, Pulau-Pulau (Is.)	(mĕn-tä-vī')	Indon.	1·08 S	98·10 E
123	Menton	(mäN-tôN')	Fr.	43·46 N	7·37 E
74	Mentone	(mĕn'tōne)	Calif. (Los Angeles In.)	34·05 N	117·08 W
167	Mentz (R.)	(mĕnts)	S. Afr. (Natal In.)	33·13 S	25·15 E
132	Menzelinsk	(mĕn'zyĕ-lênsk')	Sov. Un.	55·40 N	53·15 E
158	Menzies	(mĕn'zēz)	Austl.	29·45 S	122·15 E
76	Meogui	(mâ-ō'gē)	Mex.	28·17 N	105·28 W
117	Meppel	(mĕp'ĕl)	Neth.	52·41 N	6·08 E
120	Meppen	(mĕp'ĕn)	Ger.	52·40 N	7·18 E
126	Merabéllou, Kólpos (G.)		Grc. (In.)	35·16 N	25·55 E
73	Meramec (R.)	(mĕr'ȧ-mĕk)	Mo.	38·06 N	91·06 W
126	Merano	(mā-rä'nō)	It.	46·39 N	11·10 E
83	Merasheen (I.)	(mē'rá-shēn)	Can.	47·23 N	54·15 W
155	Merauke	(mâ-rou'kä)	W. Irian	8·32 S	140·17 E
84	Meraux	(mē-rō')	La. (New Orleans In.)	29·56 N	89·56 W
168	Merca	(mĕr'kä)	Som. (Horn of Afr. In.)	1·45 N	44·47 E
125	Mercato San Severino	(mĕr-kä'tō sän sĕ-vĕ-rē'nō)	It. (Naples In.)	40·34 N	14·38 E
68	Merced	(mẽr-sĕd')	Calif.	37·17 N	120·30 W
68	Merced (R.)		Calif.	37·25 N	120·31 W
101	Mercedario, Cerro (Mtn.)	(mĕr-sâ-dhä'rê-ō)	Chile (Santiago In.)	31·58 S	70·07 W
100	Mercedes	(mĕr-sā'dhās)	Arg.	29·04 S	58·01 W
101	Mercedes		Arg. (Buenos Aires In.)	34·41 S	59·26 W
76	Mercedes		Tex.	26·09 N	97·55 W
101	Mercedes		Ur. (Buenos Aires In.)	33·17 S	58·04 W
101	Mercedita	(mĕr-sĕ-dē'tä)	Chile (Santiago In.)	33·51 S	71·10 W
65	Mercer Island	(mûr'sẽr)	Wash. (Seattle In.)	47·35 N	122·15 W
101	Mercês	(mĕr-sĕ's)	Braz. (Rio de Janeiro In.)	21·13 S	43·20 N
139	Merchong (R.)		Mala. (Singapore In.)	3·08 N	103·13 E
111	Merchtem		Bel. (Brussels In.)	50·57 N	4·13 E
125	Mercier-Lacombe	(mĕr-syā' lâ-kôNb)	Alg.	35·18 N	0·11 W
87	Mercy, C.		Can.	64·48 N	63·22 W
81	Meredith	(mĕr'ê-dĭth)	N. H.	43·35 N	71·35 W
129	Merefa	(mâ-rĕf'ȧ)	Sov. Un.	49·49 N	36·04 E
92	Merendón, Serrania de (Mts.)	(sĕr-rä-nē'ä-dā mâ-rĕn-dōn')	Hond.	15·01 N	89·05 W
110	Mereworth	(mĕ-rĕ'wûrth)	Eng. (London In.)	51·15 N	0·23 E
	Mergen, see Nench'eng				
154	Mergui	(mẽr-gē')	Bur.	12·29 N	98·39 E
154	Mergui Archip.		Asia	12·04 N	97·02 E
91	Mérida	(mā'rē-dhä)	Mex. (Yucatan In.)	20·57 N	89·38 W
98	Mérida		Ven.	8·30 N	71·15 W
98	Mérida, Sierra Nevada de (Mts.)	(sē-ĕ'r-rä-nĕ-vä'dä-dĕ-mĕ'rê-dhä)	Ven.	8·30 N	70·45 W
81	Meriden	(mĕr'ĭ-dĕn)	Conn.	41·30 N	72·50 W
78	Meridian	(mê-rĭd-ĭ-ăn)	Miss.	32·21 N	88·41 W
77	Meridian		Tex.	31·56 N	97·37 W
119	Merikarvia	(mā'rē-kár'vê-ä)	Fin.	61·51 N	21·30 E
111	Mering	(mĕ'rĕng)	Ger. (Munich In.)	48·16 N	11·00 E
78	Meriwether Lewis Natl. Mon.	(mĕr'ĭ-wĕth-ẽr lōō'ĭs)	Tenn.	35·25 N	87·25 W
76	Merkel	(mûr'kĕl)	Tex.	32·26 N	100·02 W
119	Merkine	(mĕr'kĭ-nê)	Sov. Un.	54·09 N	24·10 E
111	Merksem		Bel. (Brussels In.)	51·15 N	4·27 E
121	Merkys R.	(măr'kĭs)	Sov. Un.	54·23 N	25·00 E
100	Merlo	(mĕr-lô)	Arg. (In.)	34·25 S	58·44 W
165	Merowe		Sud.	18·07 N	31·57 E
74	Merriam	(mĕr-rĭ-yăm)	Minn. (Minneapolis, St. Paul In.)	44·44 N	93·36 W
74	Merriam		Mo. (Kansas City In.)	39·01 N	94·42 W
84	Merrick	(mĕr'ĭk)	N. Y. (New York In.)	40·40 N	73·33 W
71	Merrill	(mĕr'ĭl)	Wis.	45·11 N	89·42 W
83	Merrimac	(mĕr'ĭ-măk)	Mass. (Boston In.)	42·50 N	71·00 W
83	Merrimack		N. H. (Boston In.)	42·51 N	71·25 W
81	Merrimack (R.)	(mĕr'ĭ-măk)	Mass.-N. H.	43·10 N	71·30 W
83	Merrimack R.		Mass. (Boston In.)	42·49 N	70·44 W
86	Merritt	(mĕr'ĭt)	Can.	50·10 N	120·48 W
85	Merritton	(mĕr'ĭt-tŭn)	Can. (Toronto In.)	43·14 N	79·13 W
77	Merryville	(mĕr'ĭ-vĭl)	La.	30·46 N	93·34 W
120	Merseburg	(mĕr'zĕ-bōōrgh)	Ger.	51·21 N	11·59 E
110	Mersey (R.)	(mûr'zê)	Eng.	52·52 N	2·04 W
116	Mersey (R.)		Eng.	53·15 N	2·51 W
133	Mersin	(mĕr-sēn')	Tur.	37·00 N	34·40 E
139	Mersing		Mala. (Singapore In.)	2·25 N	103·51 E
142	Merta Road	(mār'tŭ rōd)	India	26·50 N	73·54 E
116	Merthyr Tydfil	(mûr'thẽr tĭd'vĭl)	Wales	51·46 N	3·30 W
124	Mértola Almodóvar	(mĕr-tô-lȧ-äl-mô-dô'vär)	Port.	37·39 N	8·04 W
123	Méru	(mā-rü')	Fr. (Paris In.)	49·14 N	2·08 E
165	Meru	(mā'rōō)	Ken.	00·01 N	37·45 E
99	Merume Mts.	(mĕr-ü'mẽ)	Br. Gu.	5·45 N	60·15 W
111	Merwerde, Kanal (Can.)		Neth. (Amsterdam In.)	52·15 N	5·01 E
65	Merwin (L.)	(mẽr'wĭn)	Wash. (Portland In.)	45·58 N	122·27 W
133	Merzifon	(mẽr'ze-fōn)	Tur.	40·50 N	35·30 E
123	Merzig	(mĕr'tsēg)	Ger.	49·27 N	6·54 E
69	Mesa	(mā'sȧ)	Ariz.	33·25 N	111·50 W
71	Mesabi Ra.	(mā-sŏb'bē)	Minn.	47·17 N	93·04 W
127	Mesagne	(mā-sän'yâ)	It.	40·34 N	17·51 E
69	Mesa Verde Natl. Park.	(vẽr'dē)	Colo.	37·22 N	108·27 W
69	Mescalero Ind. Res.	(mĕs-kä-lā'rō)	N. Mex.	33·10 N	105·45 W
128	Meshchovsk	(myĕsh'chĕfsk)	Sov. Un.	54·17 N	35·19 E
165	Meshra er Req		Sud.	8·28 N	29·15 E
69	Mesilla	(mâ-sē'yä)	N. Mex.	32·15 N	106·45 W
127	Mesolóngion	(mĕ-sô-lôŋ'gê-ôn)	Grc.	38·23 N	21·28 E
126	Messina	(mĕ-sē'nȧ)	It.	38·11 N	15·34 E
166	Messina		S. Afr.	22·17 S	30·13 E
126	Messina, Stretto di (Str.)	(strĕ't-tô dē)	It.	38·10 N	15·34 E
127	Messíni		Grc.	37·05 N	22·00 E
127	Messiniakós Kólpos (G.)		Grc.	36·59 N	22·00 E
127	Mesta (R.)	(mĕ-stá')	Bul.	41·42 N	23·40 E
126	Mestre	(mĕs'trā)	It.	45·29 N	12·15 E
98	Meta (Dept.)	(mĕ'tȧ)	Col. (In.)	3·28 N	74·07 W
98	Meta (R.)		Col.	4·33 N	72·09 W
83	Metabetchouan (R.)	(mĕ-tȧ-bĕt-chōō-än')	Can.	47·45 N	72·00 W
77	Metairie	(mĕ-trâr'ĭ)	La.	30·00 N	90·11 W
100	Metán	(mĕ-tá'n)	Arg.	25·32 S	64·51 W
92	Metapán	(mâ-tä-pän')	Sal.	14·21 N	89·26 W
85	Metcalfe	(mĕt-käf)	Can. (Ottawa In.)	45·14 N	75·27 W
65	Metchosin		Can. (Seattle In.)	48·22 N	123·33 W
90	Metepec	(mā-tĕ-pĕk')	Mex.	18·56 N	98·31 W
91	Metepec		Mex. (Mexico City In.)	19·15 N	99·36 W
66	Methow R.	(mĕt'hou) (mĕt hou')	Wash.	48·26 N	120·15 W
83	Methuen	(mê-thū'ĕn)	Mass. (Boston In.)	42·44 N	71·11 W
82	Metis Beach	(mâ-tē') (mā-tĭs')	Can.	48·40 N	68·04 W
127	Metkovic'	(mĕt'kô-vĭch)	Yugo.	43·02 N	17·40 E
64	Metlakatla	(mĕt-lȧ-kăt'lȧ)	Alaska	55·10 N	131·30 W
73	Metropolis	(mê-trŏp'ô-lĭs)	Ill.	37·09 N	88·46 W
79	Metter	(mĕt'ẽr)	Ga.	32·21 N	82·05 W
123	Mettmann	(mĕt'män)	Ger. (Ruhr In.)	51·15 N	6·58 E
84	Metuchen	(mĕ-tŭ'chĕn)	N. J. (New York In.)	40·32 N	74·21 W
123	Metz	(mĕtz)	Fr.	49·08 N	6·10 E
90	Metztitlán	(mĕtz-tēt-län')	Mex.	20·36 N	98·45 W
122	Meuse (R.)	(mûz) (müz)	Eur.	50·32 N	5·22 E
110	Mexborough	(mĕks'bŭr-ô)	Eng.	53·30 N	1·17 W
77	Mexia	(mâ-hē'ä)	Tex.	31·32 N	96·29 W
91	Mexicalcingo	(mĕ-kĕ-käl-sēn'gō)	Mex. (Mexico City In.)	19·13 N	99·34 W
68	Mexicali	(mäk-sê-kä'lê)	Mex.	32·28 N	115·29 W
69	Mexican Hat	(mĕk'sĭ-kăn hăt)	Utah	37·10 N	109·55 W
82	Mexico	(mĕk'sĭ-kō)	Maine	44·34 N	70·33 W
73	Mexico		Mo.	39·09 N	91·51 W
88	Mexico (State)	(mäk'sê-kō)	Mex.	19·50 N	99·50 W
49	Mexico		N. A.	23·45 N	104·00 W
88	Mexico, G. of		N. A.	25·15 N	93·45 W
91	Mexico City	(mĕk'sĭ-kō)	Mex. (Mexico City In.)	19·28 N	99·09 W
90	Mexticacán	(mĕs'tê-kä-kän')	Mex.	21·12 N	102·43 W
144	Meydān-e Naftūn		Iran	31·45 N	49·17 E
81	Meyersdale	(mī'ẽrz-dāl)	Pa.	39·55 N	79·00 W
168	Meyerton	(mī'ẽr-tŭn)	S. Afr. (Johannesburg & Pretoria In.)	26·35 S	28·01 E
132	Mezen'		Sov. Un.	65·50 N	44·05 E
132	Mezen' (R.)		Sov. Un.	65·20 N	44·45 E
122	Mézenc, Mt.	(mōN-mä-zĕN')	Fr.	44·55 N	4·12 E
128	Mezha (R.)	(myā'zhä)	Sov. Un.	55·53 N	31·44 E
122	Mézières	(mā-zyâr')	Fr.	49·45 N	4·40 E
123	Mézières-sur-Seine	(mā-zyâr'sür-sān')	Fr. (Paris In.)	48·58 N	1·49 E
121	Mezőkövesd	(mĕ'zû-kû'vêsht)	Hung.	47·49 N	20·36 E
121	Mezötur	(mĕ'zû-tōōr)	Hung.	47·00 N	20·36 E
90	Mezquital	(mâz-kê-täl')	Mex.	23·30 N	104·20 W
90	Mezquital (R.)		Mex.	23·07 N	104·52 W
90	Mezquitic	(mâz-kê-tĕk')	Mex.	22·25 N	103·43 W
90	Mezquitic (R.)		Mex.	22·25 N	103·45 W
136	Mga	(m'gá)	Sov. Un. (Leningrad In.)	59·45 N	31·04 E
128	Mglin	(m'glēn')	Sov. Un.	53·03 N	32·52 E
90	Miacatlán	(mē'ä-kä-tlän')	Mex.	18·42 N	99·17 W
91	Miahuatlán	(mē'ä-wä-tlän')	Mex.	16·20 N	96·38 W
124	Miajadas	(mê-ä-hä'däs)	Sp.	39·10 N	5·53 W
69	Miami	(mī-ăm'ĭ)	Ariz.	33·20 N	110·55 W
79	Miami		Fla. (In.)	25·45 N	80·11 W
73	Miami		Okla.	36·51 N	94·51 W
72	Miami		Tex.	35·41 N	100·39 W
80	Miami (R.)		Ohio	39·20 N	84·45 W
79	Miami Beach		Fla. (In.)	25·47 N	80·07 W
94	Miami Drainage Can.		Fla.	26·25 N	80·50 W
80	Miamisburg	(mī-ăm'ĭz-bûrg)	Ohio	39·40 N	84·20 W
75	Miamitown	(mī-ăm'ĭ-toun)	Ohio (Cincinnati In.)	39·13 N	84·43 W
144	Mīāneh		Iran	37·15 N	47·13 E
155	Miangas (I.)	(myä'n-gäs)	Phil.	5·30 N	127·00 E
148	Miaochen	(mĭou'zhen)	China	31·44 N	121·28 E
151	Miaoli	(mê-ou'lĭ)	Taiwan	24·30 N	120·48 E
148	Miao Liehtao (Is.)	(miou' lĭĕdou)	China	38·06 N	120·35 E
136	Miass	(mī-äs')	Sov. Un. (Urals In.)	55·00 N	60·03 E
120	Miastko	(myäst'kô)	Pol.	54·01 N	17·00 E
121	Michalovce	(mē'Kä-lôf'tsĕ)	Czech.	48·44 N	21·56 E
83	Michel (L.)	(mê-shĕl') (mĭch'ĕl)	Can.	50·21 N	56·45 W
64	Michelson, Mt.	(mĭch'ĕl-sŭn)	Alaska	69·11 N	144·12 W
111	Michendorf	(mē'Kĕn-dōrf)	Ger. (Berlin In.)	52·19 N	13·02 E
95	Miches	(mē'-chĕs)	Dom. Rep.	19·00 N	69·05 W
63	Michigan (State)	(mĭsh'ĭ-găn)	U.S.	45·55 N	87·00 W
63	Michigan, L.		U. S.	43·20 N	87·10 W
80	Michigan City		Ind.	41·40 N	86·55 W
87	Michikamau (L.)		Can.	54·11 N	63·21 W
71	Michipicoten (I.)	(mĭ-shĭ-pĭ-kō'tĕn)	Can.	47·49 N	85·50 W
71	Michipicoten (R.)		Can.	47·56 N	84·42 W
71	Michipicoten Harbour		Can.	47·58 N	84·58 W
128	Michurinsk	(mĭ-chōō-rĭnsk')	Sov. Un.	52·53 N	40·32 E
93	Mico, Punta (Pt.)	(pōō'n-tä-mē'kô)	Nic.	11·38 N	83·24 W
66	Midas	(mī'dȧs)	Nev.	41·15 N	116·50 W
166	Middelburg	(mĭd'ĕl-bûrg)	S. Afr.	31·30 S	25·00 E
168	Middelburg		S. Afr. (Johannesburg & Pretoria In.)	25·47 S	29·30 E
168	Middelwit	(mĭd'l'wĭt)	S. Afr. (Johannesburg & Pretoria In.)	24·50 S	27·00 E
154	Middle Andaman I.	(ăn-dȧ-măn')	Andaman Is.	12·44 N	93·21 E
77	Middle Bay	(mĭd''l bā)	Tex. (In.)	29·38 N	95·06 W
94	Middle Bight (B.)	(bīt)	Ba. Is.	24·20 N	77·35 W
81	Middlebury	(mĭd''l-bĕr-ĭ)	Vt.	44·00 N	73·10 W
76	Middle Concho	(kŏn'chō)	Tex.	31·21 N	100·50 W
118	Middlefart	(mēd''l-fårt)	Den.	55·30 N	9·45 E
70	Middle Loup (R.)	(lōōp)	Nebr.	41·49 N	100·20 W
80	Middleport	(mĭd''l-pōrt)	Ohio	39·00 N	82·05 W
84	Middle River		Md. (Baltimore In.)	39·20 N	76·27 W
78	Middlesboro	(mĭd''lz-bŭr-ô)	Ky.	36·36 N	83·42 W
116	Middlesbrough	(mĭd''lz-brŭ)	Eng.	54·35 N	1·18 W
84	Middlesex	(mĭd''l-sĕks)	N. J. (New York In.)	40·34 N	74·30 W
110	Middleton	(mĭd''l-tŭn)	Eng.	53·04 N	2·12 W
64	Middleton (I.)		Alaska	59·35 N	146·35 W
82	Middletown	(mĭd''l-toun)	Can.	44·56 N	65·03 W
81	Middletown		Conn.	41·35 N	72·40 W
81	Middletown		Del.	39·30 N	75·40 W
83	Middletown		Mass. (Boston In.)	42·35 N	71·01 W
84	Middletown		N. Y. (New York In.)	41·26 N	74·25 W
80	Middletown		Ohio	39·30 N	84·25 W
110	Middlewich	(mĭd''l-wĭch)	Eng.	53·11 N	2·27 W
125	Midi, Canal du	(kä-näl-dü-mê-dē')	Fr.	43·22 N	1·35 E
167	Mid Illovo	(mĭd ĭl'ô-vō)	S. Afr. (Natal In.)	29·59 S	30·32 E
81	Midland	(mĭd'lănd)	Can.	44·45 N	79·50 W
80	Midland		Mich.	43·40 N	84·20 W
76	Midland		Tex.	32·00 N	102·04 W
85	Midnapore	(mĭd'-nȧ-pōr)	Can. (Calgary In.)	50·56 N	114·04 W
74	Midvale	(mĭd'vāl)	Utah (Salt Lake City In.)	40·37 N	111·54 W
78	Midway	(mĭd'wā)	Ala.	32·03 N	85·30 W
156	Midway Is.		Pac. O.	28·00 N	179·00 W
67	Midwest	(mĭd-wĕst')	Wyo.	43·25 N	106·15 W
133	Midye	(mēd'yĕ)	Tur.	41·35 N	28·10 E
120	Miedzyrzecz	(myĕ-dzû'zhĕch)	Pol.	52·26 N	15·35 E
121	Mielec	(myĕ'lĕts)	Pol.	50·17 N	21·27 E
76	Mier	(myâr)	Mex.	26·26 N	99·08 W
124	Mieres	(myā'räs)	Sp.	43·14 N	5·45 W
90	Mier y Noriega	(myâr'ê nô-rê-ä'gä)	Mex.	22·28 N	100·08 W
120	Miessen	(mē'sĕn)	Ger.	51·11 N	13·28 E
139	Migdal Ashkelon	(mĭg'dăl ăsh'kĕ-lōn)	Isr. (Palestine In.)	31·40 N	34·36 E
129	Migorod		Sov. Un.	49·56 N	33·36 E
90	Miguel Auza	(mē-gĕ'l-ä-ōō'zä)	Mex.	24·17 N	103·27 W
100	Miguel Pereira	(pĕ-rā'-rä)	Braz. (In.)	22·27 S	43·28 W
95	Mija, Monte (Mtn.)	(mô'n-tĕ-mē'kä)	Dom. Rep.	19·10 N	71·15 W
125	Mijares (R.)	(mē-hä'räs)	Sp.	40·05 N	0·42 W
153	Mikage	(mē'kä-gå)	Jap. (Ōsaka In.)	34·42 N	135·15 E
153	Mikawa-Wan (B.)	(mē'kä-wä wän)	Jap.	34·43 N	137·09 E
128	Mikhaylov	(mē-Käy'lôf)	Sov. Un.	54·14 N	39·03 E
129	Mikhaylovka		Sov. Un.	47·16 N	35·12 E
133	Mikhaylovka		Sov. Un.	50·05 N	43·10 E
136	Mikhaylovka	(mē-kä'ê-lôf-kä)	Sov. Un. (Urals In.)	55·35 N	57·57 E
136	Mikhaylovka		Sov. Un. (Leningrad In.)	59·20 N	30·21 E
136	Mikhněvo	(mĭk-nyô'vô)	Sov. Un. (Moscow In.)	55·08 N	37·57 E
153	Miki	(mē'kê)	Jap. (Ōsaka In.)	34·47 N	134·59 E
167	Mikindani	(mê-kên-dä'nê)	Tan.	10·17 S	40·06 E
119	Mikkeli	(mĭk'ĕ-lĭ)	Fin.	61·42 N	27·14 E
127	Míkonos (I.)		Grc.	37·26 N	25·30 E
120	Mikulov	(mĭ'kōō-lôf)	Czech.	48·47 N	16·39 E
153	Mikuni	(mē'kōō-nê)	Jap.	36·09 N	136·14 E

ăt; finăl; rāte; senâte; ärm; ȧsk; sofȧ; fâre; ch-choose; dh-as th in other; bē; ēvent; bĕt; recĕnt; cratẽr; g-go; gh-guttural g; bĭt; ĭ-short neutral; rīde; K-guttural k as ch in German ich;

PRONOUNCING INDEX Mikuni-Sammyaku–Moapa River 237

Page	Name Pronunciation Region	Lat. °'	Long. °'
153	Mikuni-Sammyaku (Mts.) (săm'myä-kōō). Jap.	36·51 N	138·38 E
153	Mikura (I.) (mē'kōō-rä) Jap.	33·53 N	139·26 E
164	Mila (mē'lä) Alg.	36·30 N	6.16 E
71	Milaca (mē-lăk'ȧ) Minn.	45·45 N	93·41 W
80	Milan (mĭ'lăn) Mich.	42·05 N	83·40 W
73	Milan Mo.	40·13 N	93·07 W
78	Milan Tenn.	35·54 N	88·47 W
	Milan, see Milano		
126	Milano (Milan) (mē-lä'nō) It.	45·29 N	9·12 E
133	Milas (mē'läs) Tur.	37·10 N	27·25 E
126	Milazzo (mē-lät'sō) It.	38·13 N	15·17 E
70	Milbank (mĭl'băŋk) S. D.	45·13 N	96·38 W
160	Mildura (mĭl-dū'rȧ) Austl.	34·10 S	142·18 E
67	Miles City (mīlz) Mont.	46·24 N	105·50 W
81	Milford (mĭl'fērd) Conn.	41·15 N	73·05 W
81	Milford Del.	38·55 N	75·25 W
83	Milford Mass. (Boston In.)	42·09 N	71·31 W
75	Milford Mich. (Detroit In.)	42·35 N	83·36 W
81	Milford N. H.	42·50 N	71·40 W
75	Milford Ohio (Cincinnati In.)	39·11 N	84·18 W
69	Milford Utah	38·20 N	113·05 W
116	Milford Haven (hāv'n) Wales	51·40 N	5·10 W
113	Miliana (mēl-yä'nä) Alg.	36·19 N	1·56 E
158	Miling (mĭl'ĭng) Austl.	30·30 S	116·25 E
65	Milipitas (mĭl-ĭ-pĭ'tăs) Calif. (San Francisco In.)	37·26 N	121·54 W
67	Milk R. (mĭlk) Mont.	48·25 N	108·45 W
68	Mill Cr. Calif.	40·07 N	121·55 W
85	Mill Cr. (mĭl). Can. (Edmonton In.)	53·13 N	113·25 W
122	Millau (mē-yō') Fr.	44·06 N	3·04 E
65	Millbrae (mĭl'brā) Calif. (San Francisco In.)	37·36 N	122·23 W
83	Millbury (mĭl'bĕr-ĭ) Mass. (Boston In.)	42·12 N	71·46 W
78	Milledgeville (mĭl'ĕj-vĭl) Ga.	33·05 N	83·15 W
85	Mille Iles, R. des (rē-vyâr' dā mĭl'ĭl') Can. (Montreal In.)	45·41 N	73·40 W
71	Mille Lac Ind. Res. (mĭl lăk') Minn.	46·14 N	94·13 W
71	Mille Lacs (L.) Minn.	46·25 N	93·22 W
71	Mille Lacs, Lac des (L.) (läk dē mēl läks). Can.	48·52 N	90·53 W
79	Millen (mĭl'ĕn) Ga.	32·47 N	81·55 W
70	Miller (mĭl'ēr) S. D.	44·31 N	99·00 W
129	Millerovo (mĭl'ĕ-rō-vō) Sov. Un.	48·58 N	40·27 E
80	Millersburg (mĭl'ērz-bûrg) Ky.	38·15 N	84·10 W
80	Millersburg Ohio	40·35 N	81·55 W
81	Millersburg Pa.	40·35 N	76·55 W
82	Millerton (mĭl'ēr-tŭn) Can.	46·56 N	65·40 W
83	Millertown (mĭl'ēr-toun) Can.	48·48 N	56·33 W
160	Millicent (mĭl-ĭ'sĕnt) Austl.	37·30 S	140·20 E
82	Millinocket (mĭl-ĭ-nŏk'ĕt) Maine	45·40 N	68·44 W
83	Millis (mĭl'ĭs) Mass. (Boston In.)	42·10 N	71·22 W
74	Millstadt (mĭl'stăt) Ill. (St. Louis In.)	38·27 N	90·06 W
84	Millstone R. (mĭl'stōn) N. J. (New York In.)	40·27 N	74·38 W
158	Millstream (mĭl'strēm) Austl.	21·45 S	117·10 E
82	Milltown (mĭl'toun) Can.	45·13 N	67·19 W
75	Millvale (mĭl'vāl) Pa. (Pittsburgh In.)	40·29 N	79·58 W
65	Mill Valley (mĭl) Calif. (San Francisco In.)	37·54 N	122·32 W
81	Millville (mĭl'vĭl) N. J.	39·25 N	75·00 W
123	Milly-la-Forêt (mē-yē'-la-fō-rĕ') Fr. (Paris In.)	48·24 N	2·28 E
166	Milnerton (mĭl'nēr-tŭn) S. Afr. (Cape Town In.)	33·52 S	18·30 E
70	Milnor (mĭl'nēr) N. D.	46·17 N	97·29 W
82	Milo (mī'lō) Maine	44·16 N	69·01 W
	Milo (I.), see Mílos		
127	Mílos (Milo) (I.) (mē'lŏs) Grc.	36·45 N	24·35 E
91	Milpa Alta (mē'l-pä-ȧ'l-tä) Mex. (Mexico City In.)	19·11 N	99·01 W
78	Milton (mĭl'tŭn) Fla.	30·37 N	87·02 W
74	Milton Ill. (St. Louis In.)	38·54 N	90·08 W
83	Milton Mass. (Boston In.)	42·16 N	71·03 W
81	Milton Pa.	41·00 N	76·50 W
74	Milton Utah (Salt Lake City In.)	41·04 N	111·44 W
65	Milton Wash. (Seattle In.)	47·15 N	122·20 W
71	Milton Wis.	42·45 N	89·00 W
66	Milton-Freewater Ore.	45·57 N	118·25 W
85	Milton West. Can. (Toronto In.)	43·31 N	79·53 W
75	Milwaukee. Wis. (Milwaukee In.)	43·03 N	87·55 W
89	Milwaukee Depth Atl. O.	19·45 N	68·00 W
75	Milwaukee R. Wis. (Milwaukee In.)	43·10 N	87·56 W
65	Milwaukie (mĭl-wô'kē) Ore. (Portland In.)	45·27 N	122·38 W
91	Mimiapan (mē-myä-pȧn') Mex. (Mexico City In.)	19·26 N	99·28 W
85	Mimico (mĭ'mĭ-kō) Can. (Toronto In.)	43·37 N	79·30 W
101	Mimoso do Sul (mē-mō'sō-dō-sōō'l) Braz. (Rio de Janeiro In.)	21·03 S	41·21 W
125	Mina (R.) (mē'nȧ) Alg.	35·24 N	0·51 E
153	Minakuchi (mē'nȧ-kōō'chē) Jap.	34·59 N	136·06 E
94	Minas (mē'näs) Cuba	21·30 N	77·35 W
139	Minas Indon. (Singapore In.)	0·52 N	101·29 E
100	Minas (mē'näs) Ur.	34·18 S	55·12 W
92	Minas, Sierra de las (Mts.) (syĕr'rä dā läs mē'näs). Guat.	15·08 N	90·25 W
82	Minas Basin (mī'nȧs) Can.	45·19 N	64·10 W
82	Minas Chan. Can.	45·13 N	64·55 W
92	Minas de Oro (mē'-näs-dĕ-ŏ-rō) Hond.	14·52 N	87·19 W
124	Minas de Ríontinto (mē'näs dā rē-ô-tēn'tō). Sp.	37·43 N	6·35 W
99	Minas Gerais (State) (mē'näzh-zhĕ-rä'ēs). Braz.	17·45 S	43·50 W
99	Minas Novas (mē'näzh nō'väzh) Braz.	17·20 S	42·19 W
70	Minatare (L.) (mĭn'ȧ-târ) Nebr.	41·56 N	103·07 W
91	Minatitlán (mē-nä-tē-tlän') Mex.	17·59 N	94·33 W
90	Minatitlán Mex.	19·21 N	104·02 W
153	Minato (mē'nȧ-tō) Jap. (Tōkyō In.)	35·13 N	139·52 E
116	Minch, The (Chan.) Scot.	58·04 N	6·04 W
116	Minch, The Little (Chan.) (mĭnch). Scot.	56·85 N	6·42 W
151	Min Chiang (R.) China	26·30 N	118·30 E
151	Min Chiang (R.) China	29·30 N	104·00 E
155	Mindanao (I.) (mĭn-dä-nou') Phil.	7·30 N	125·10 E
155	Mindanao Sea Phil.	8·55 N	124·00 E
120	Minden (mĭn'dĕn) Ger.	52·17 N	8·58 E
77	Minden La.	32·36 N	93·19 W
72	Minden Nebr.	40·30 N	98·54 W
155	Mindoro (I.) (mĭn-dō'rō) Phil. (Manila In.)	13·04 N	121·06 E
155	Mindoro Str. Phil. (Manila In.)	12·28 N	120·33 E
136	Mindyak (mēn'dyȧk) Sov. Un. (Urals In.)	54·01 N	58·48 E
84	Mineola (mĭn-ē-ō'lȧ) N. Y. (New York In.)	40·43 N	73·38 W
77	Mineola Tex.	32·39 N	95·31 W
90	Mineral del Chico (mē-nȧ-räl'dĕl chē'kō). Mex.	20·13 N	98·46 W
90	Mineral del Monte (mē-nȧ-räl dĕl mōn'tȧ). Mex.	20·18 N	98·39 W
133	Mineral'nyye Vody Sov. Un.	44·10 N	43·15 E
71	Mineral Point (mĭn'ēr-ȧl) Wis.	42·50 N	90·10 W
76	Minerál Wells (mĭn'ēr-ȧl wĕlz) Tex.	32·48 N	98·06 W
80	Minerva (mĭ-nûr'vȧ) Ohio	40·45 N	81·10 W
126	Minervino (mē-nĕr-vē'nō) It.	41·07 N	16·05 E
153	Mineyama (mē-nĕ-yä'mä) Jap.	35·38 N	135·05 E
82	Mingan (mĭŋ'gȧn) Can.	50·19 N	64·02 W
133	Mingechaur (R.) Sov. Un.	41·00 N	47·20 E
158	Mingenew (mĭn'gĕ-nū) Austl.	29·15 S	115·45 E
148	Mingkuang (mĭng'gōōäng) China	32·41 N	118·00 E
80	Mingo Junction (mĭŋ'gō) Ohio	40·15 N	80·40 W
124	Minho (Reg.) (mēn yōō) Port.	41·32 N	8·13 W
94	Minho (R.) Jam.	17·55 N	77·20 W
124	Minho, Rio (R.) (rē'ō-mē'n-yō) Port.	41·48 N	9·05 W
85	Ministik L. (mĭ-nĭs'tĭk) Can. (Edmonton In.)	53·23 N	113·05 W
164	Minna (mĭn'ä) Nig.	9·40 N	6·34 E
73	Minneapoli (mĭn-ē-ăp'ō-lĭ) Kans.	39·07 N	97·41 W
74	Minneapolis (mĭn-ē-ăp'ō-lĭs) Minn. (Minneapolis, St. Paul In.)	44·58 N	93·15 W
86	Minnedosa (mĭn-ē-dō'sȧ) Can.	50·16 N	99·50 W
70	Minneota (mĭn-ē-ō'tȧ) Minn.	44·34 N	95·59 W
63	Minnesota (State) (mĭn-ē-sō'tȧ) U. S.	46·10 N	90·20 W
70	Minnesota (R.) Minn.	45·04 N	96·03 W
71	Minnetonka (L.) (mĭn-ē-tŏŋ'kȧ) Minn.	44·52 N	93·34 W
69	Minnie Maud Cr. (mĭn'ĭmôd') Utah	39·50 N	110·30 W
153	Mino (R.) (mē'nō) Jap. (Ōsaka In.)	34·56 N	135·06 E
124	Miño (R.) (mē'nyō) Sp.	42·28 N	7·48 W
80	Minonk (mī'nŏnk) Ill.	40·55 N	89·00 W
75	Minooka (mĭ-nōō'kȧ) Ill. (Chicago In.)	41·27 N	88·15 W
	Minorca (I.), see Menorca, Isla de		
70	Minot (mī'nŏt) N. D.	48·13 N	101·16 W
128	Minsk (mēnsk) Sov. Un.	53·54 N	27·35 E
128	Minsk (Oblast) Sov. Un.	53·50 N	27·43 E
121	Mińsk Mazowiecki (mēn'sk mä-zō-vyĕt'skĭ) Pol.	52·10 N	21·35 E
110	Minsterley (mĭnstēr-lē) Eng.	52·38 N	2·55 W
82	Minto (mĭn'tō) Can.	46·05 N	66·05 W
87	Minto (L.) Can.	57·18 N	75·50 W
126	Minturno (mēn-tōōr'nō) It.	41·17 N	13·44 E
168	Minūf (mē-nōōf') U. A. R. (Nile In.)	30·26 N	30·55 E
134	Minusinsk (mē-nōō-sēnsk') Sov. Un.	53·47 N	86·43 E
146	Minya Konka (Mt.) (mēn'yȧ kôŋ'kȧ). China	29·16 N	101·46 E
136	Min'yar (mēn'yȧr) Sov. Un. (Urals In.)	55·06 N	57·33 E
85	Miquelon L. (mĭ'kē-lôn) Can. (Edmonton In.)	53·16 N	112·55 W
90	Miquihuana (mē-kē-wä'nä) Mex.	23·36 N	99·45 W
121	Mir (mēr) Sov. Un.	53·27 N	26·25 E
124	Mira (R.) (mē'rä) Port.	37·29 N	8·15 W
101	Miracema (mē-rä-sĕ'mä) Braz. (Rio de Janeiro In.)	21·24 S	42·10 W
99	Mirador (mē-rȧ-dōr') Braz.	6·19 S	44·12 W
98	Miraflores (mē-rä-flō'räs) Col.	5·10 N	73·13 W
98	Miraflores Peru	16·19 S	71·20 W
88	Miraflores Locks C. Z. (Panama Canal In.)	9·00 N	79·35 W
95	Miragoâne (mē-rȧ-gwän') Hai.	18·25 N	73·05 W
101	Miraí (mē-rä-ē') Braz. (Rio de Janeiro In.)	21·13 S	42·36 W
143	Miraj (mē-rŭj') India	16·55 N	74·40 E
74	Mira Loma (mĭ'rȧ lō'mȧ) Calif. (Los Angeles In.)	34·01 N	117·32 W
68	Miramar (mĭr'ȧ-mär) Calif. (San Diego In.)	32·53 N	117·08 W
122	Miramas Fr. (Marseille In.)	43·35 N	5·00 E
82	Miramichi (R.) Can.	46·36 N	66·08 W
82	Miramichi B. (mĭr'ȧ-mē'shē). Can.	47·14 N	64·45 W
98	Miranda (mē-rä'n-dä) Col. (In.)	3·14 N	76·11 W
99	Miranda Ven. (In.)	10·09 N	68·24 W
99	Miranda (State) Ven. (In.)	10·17 N	66·41 W
124	Miranda de Ebro (mē-rä'n-dä-dĕ-ĕ'l-brō). Sp.	42·42 N	2·59 W
124	Miranda de Ebro (mē-rän'dä dōō-dwĕ'rō). Port.	41·30 N	6·17 W
124	Mirandela (mē-rän-dā'lȧ) Port.	41·28 N	7·10 W
76	Mirando City (mĭr-ăn'dō) Tex.	27·25 N	99·03 W
95	Mira Por Vos Islets (Is.) (mē'rä pôr vōs'). Ba. Is.	22·05 N	74·30 W
95	Mira Por Vos Pass (Str.) Ba. Is.	22·10 N	74·35 W
144	Mirbāt Mus. & Om.	16·58 N	54·42 E
95	Mirebalais (mēr-bȧ-lĕ') Hai.	18·50 N	72·05 W
123	Mirecourt (mēr-kōōr') Fr.	48·20 N	6·08 E
122	Mirepoix (mēr-pwä') Fr.	43·06 N	1·52 E
110	Mirfield (mûr'fēld) Eng.	53·41 N	1·42 W
154	Miri (mē'rē) Mala.	4·13 N	113·56 E
100	Mirim, L. (mē-rēɴ') Braz.-Ur.	33·00 S	53·15 W
129	Miropol'ye (mē-rō-pôl'yĕ) Sov. Un.	51·02 N	35·13 E
142	Mīrpur Khās (mēr'pōōr ĸäs) W. Pak.	25·36 N	69·10 E
142	Mirzapur (mēr'zä-pōōr) India	25·12 N	82·38 E
164	Misa Togo	7·00 N	00·34 E
153	Misaki (mē'sȧ-kē) Jap. (Tōkyō In.)	35·08 N	139·37 E
91	Misantla (mē-sän'tlä) Mex.	19·55 N	96·49 W
82	Miscou (I.) (mĭs'kō) Can.	47·58 N	64·35 W
82	Miscou Pt. Can.	48·04 N	64·25 W
125	Miseno, C. (mē-zĕ'nō) It. (Naples In.)	40·33 N	14·12 E
93	Misery, Mt. (mĭz'rē-ĭ) St. Christopher (Le. & Wind. Is. In.)	17·28 N	62·47 W
152	Mishan (mĭ'shäɴ) China	45·32 N	132·19 E
80	Mishawaka (mĭsh-ȧ-wôk'ȧ) Ind.	41·45 N	86·15 W
153	Mishima (mē'shē-mä) Jap.	35·09 N	138·56 E
100	Misiones (Prov.) (mē-syō'näs) Arg.	27·00 S	54·30 W
93	Miskito, Cayos (Is.) Nic.	14·34 N	82·30 W
121	Miskolc (mĭsh'kōlts) Hung.	48·07 N	20·50 E
155	Misol (I.) (mē-sōl') W. Irian	2·00 S	130·05 E
71	Misquah Hills (mĭs-kwä' hĭlz) Minn.	47·50 N	90·30 W
168	Miṣr al Jadīdah (Ruins) U. A. R. (Nile In.)	30·06 N	31·35 E
165	Misratāh Libya	32·23 N	14·58 E
87	Missinaibi (R.) (mĭs'ĭn-ä'ē-bē) Can.	50·27 N	83·01 W
74	Mission (mĭsh'ŭn) Mo. (Kansas City In.)	39·02 N	94·39 W
76	Mission Tex.	26·14 N	98·19 W
65	Mission City (sĭ'tĭ) Can. (Vancouver In.)	49·08 N	122·19 W
80	Mississinewa (R.) (mĭs-ĭ-sĭn'ē-wä) Ind.	40·30 N	85·45 W
63	Mississippi (State) (mĭs-ĭ-sĭp'ē) U. S.	32·30 N	89·45 W
81	Mississippi (L.) Can.	45·05 N	76·15 W
63	Mississippi (R.) U. S.	31·50 N	91·30 W
84	Mississippi Delta, The La. (New Orleans In.)	28·59 N	89·14 W
78	Mississippi Sd. Miss.	34·16 N	89·10 W
67	Missoula (mĭ-zōō'lȧ) Mont.	46·52 N	114·00 W
63	Missouri (State) (mĭ-sōō'rē) U. S.	38·00 N	93·40 W
63	Missouri (R.) U. S.	40·40 N	96·00 W
77	Missouri City Tex. (In.)	29·37 N	95·32 W
62	Missouri Coteau, (Plat.) U. S.	47·30 N	101·00 W
70	Missouri Valley Iowa	41·35 N	95·53 W
65	Mist (mĭst) Ore. (Portland In.)	46·00 N	123·15 W
82	Mistassibi (R.) (mĭs-tȧ-sĭ'bē). Can.	49·45 N	71·58 W
82	Mistassini (mĭs-tȧ-sĭ'nē) Can.	48·56 N	71·55 W
87	Mistassini (L.) (mĭs-tȧ-sĭ'nē). Can.	50·48 N	75·00 W
120	Mistelbach (mĭs'tĕl-bäk) Aus.	48·34 N	16·33 E
92	Misteriosa, L. (mēs-tĕ-ryō'sä) Mex. (Yucatan In.)	18·05 N	90·15 W
126	Mistretta (mē-strĕt'tä) It.	37·54 N	14·22 E
90	Mita, Punta de (Pt.) (pōō'n-tä-dĕ-mē'tä). Mex.	20·44 N	105·34 W
153	Mitaka (mē'tä-kä) Jap. (Tōkyō In.)	35·42 N	139·34 E
74	Mitchell (mĭch'ĕl) Ill. (St. Louis In.)	38·46 N	90·05 W
80	Mitchell Ind.	38·45 N	86·25 W
70	Mitchell Nebr.	41·56 N	103·49 W
70	Mitchell S. D.	43·42 N	98·01 W
159	Mitchell (R.) Austl.	15·30 S	142·15 E
79	Mitchell, Mt. N. C.	35·47 N	82·15 W
168	Mit Ghamr U. A. R. (Nile In.)	30·43 N	31·20 E
127	Mitilíni Grc.	39·09 N	26·35 E
153	Mito (mē'tō') Jap.	36·20 N	140·23 E
153	Mitsu (mēt'sōō) Jap.	34·21 N	132·49 E
120	Mittelland (can.) (mĭt'ĕl-länd) Ger.	52·18 N	10·42 E
111	Mittenwalde (mē'tĕn-väl-dĕ) Ger. (Berlin In.)	52·16 N	13·33 E
120	Mittweida (mĭt-vī'dä) Ger.	50·59 N	12·58 E
136	Mityayevo (mĭt-yä'yĕ-vō) Sov. Un. (Urals In.)	60·17 N	61·02 E
129	Mius (R.) (mē-ōōs') Sov. Un.	47·30 N	38·48 E
153	Miwa (mē'wä) Jap. (Ōsaka In.)	34·32 N	135·51 E
92	Mixico (mēs'kō) Guat.	14·37 N	90·37 W
90	Mixquiahuala (mēs-kē-wä'lä). Mex.	20·12 N	99·13 W
90	Mixteco (R.) (mēs-tä'kō) Mex.	17·45 N	98·10 W
153	Miyake (mē'yä-kȧ) Jap. (Ōsaka In.)	34·35 N	135·34 E
153	Miyake (I.) (mē'yä-kȧ) Jap.	34·06 N	139·21 E
153	Miyakonojō (mē'yȧ-kō'nô-jō). Jap.	31·42 N	131·03 E
153	Miyazaki (mē'yä-zä'kē) Jap.	31·55 N	131·27 E
153	Miyoshi (mē-yō'shē') Jap.	34·48 N	132·49 E
114	Mizdah (mēz'dä) Libya	31·29 N	13·09 E
127	Mizil (mē'zēl) Rom.	45·01 N	26·30 E
	Mizonokuchi, see Takatsu		
118	Mjölby (myûl'bü) Swe.	58·20 N	15·09 E
118	Mjörn (L.) Swe.	57·55 N	12·22 E
118	Mjösa (myûsä) Nor.	60·41 N	11·25 E
118	Mjösvatn (myûs-vät'n) Nor.	59·55 N	7·50 E
166	Mkalamo (m'kä-lä'mō) Tan.	4·07 S	34·38 E
120	Mladá Boleslav (mlä'dä bô'lĕ-släf) Czech.	50·26 N	14·52 E
121	Mława (mwä'vȧ) Pol.	53·07 N	20·25 E
127	Mljet (I.) (mlyĕt) Yugo.	42·40 N	17·45 E
155	Moa (I.) Indon.	8·30 S	128·30 E
69	Moab (mō'ăb) Utah	38·35 N	109·35 W
68	Moapa River Ind. Res. (mō-ăp'ȧ) Nev.	36·44 N	115·01 W

ng-sing; ŋ-baŋk; ɴ-nasalized n; nŏd; cŏmmit; ōld; ôbey; ôrder; fōōd; fŏŏt; ou-out; s-soft; sh-dish; th-thin; pūre; ûnite; ûrn; stŭd; circŭs; ü-as "y" in study; '-indeterminate vowel.

238 Mobaye–Montmorency PRONOUNCING INDEX

Page	Name Pronunciation Region	Lat. °′	Long. °′
165	Mobaye (mô-bä'y') Cen. Afr. Rep.	4·30 N	21·10 E
73	Moberly (mō'bēr-lĭ) Mo.	39·24 N	92·25 W
78	Mobile (mô-bēl') Ala.	30·42 N	88·03 W
78	Mobile (R.) Ala.	31·15 N	88·00 W
78	Mobile B. Ala.	30·26 N	87·56 W
70	Mobridge (mō'brĭj) S. D.	45·32 N	100·26 W
95	Moca (mô'kä) Dom. Rep.	19·25 N	70·35 W
167	Moçambique (mō-säN-bē'kĕ) Moz.	15·07 S	40·48 E
166	Moçâmedes Ang.	15·10 S	12·15 E
166	Moçâmedes (Reg.) (mô-zà-mĕ-dĕs) Ang.	16·00 S	12·15 E
144	Mocha (mō'kà) Yemen	13·11 N	43·20 E
90	Mochitlán (mō-chê-tlän') Mex.	17·10 N	99·19 W
166	Mochudi (mō-chōō'dê) Bech.	24·13 S	26·07 E
167	Mocímboa da Praia (mō-sē'êm-bô-à dä prä'ëà) Moz.	11·25 S	40·18 E
101	Mococa (mô-kô'kà) Braz. (Rio de Janeiro In.)	21·29 S	46·58 W
90	Moctezuma (môk'tâ-zōō'mä) Mex.	22·44 N	101·06 W
167	Modderfontein S. Afr. (Johannesburg & Pretoria In.)	26·06 S	28·10 E
168	Modderpoort S. Afr. (Johannesburg & Pretoria In.)	29·08 S	27·27 E
126	Modena (mô'dĕ-nä) It.	44·38 N	10·54 E
68	Modesto (mô-dĕs'tō) Calif.	37·39 N	121·00 W
113	Modica (mô'dē-kä) It.	36·50 N	14·43 E
111	Mödling (mûd'lĭng) Aus. (Vienna In.)	48·06 N	16·17 E
99	Moengo Fr. Gu.	5·43 N	54·19 W
166	Moero, L. Con. L.	8·45 S	27·45 E
123	Moers (mûrs) Ger. (Ruhr In.)	51·27 N	6·38 E
72	Moffat Tun. (môf'ăt) Colo.	39·52 N	106·20 W
168	Mogadiscio (mô-gä-dē'shō) Som. (Horn of Afr. In.)	2·08 N	45·22 E
75	Mogadore (mŏg-à-dōr') Ohio (Cleveland In.)	41·04 N	81·23 W
146	Mogaung (mô-gä'ŏŏng) Bur.	25·30 N	96.52 E
101	Mogi das Cruzes (mô-gê-däs-krōō'sĕs) Braz. (Rio de Janeiro In.)	23·33 S	46·10 W
101	Mogi-Guaçu (R.) (mô-gê-gwà'sōō) Braz. (Rio de Janeiro In.)	22·06 S	47·12 W
128	Mogilëv (mô-gê-lyôf') Sov. Un.	53·53 N	30·22 E
128	Mogilëv (Oblast) (mô-gê-lyôf') Sov. Un.	53·28 N	30·15 E
129	Mogilëv-Podol'skiy (mô-gê-lyôf) (pô-dôl'skĭ) Sov. Un.	48·27 N	27·51 E
121	Mogilno (mô-gēl'nô) Pol.	52·38 N	17·58 E
101	Mogi-Mirim (mô-gê-mē-rē'N) Braz. (Rio de Janeiro In.)	22·26 S	46·57 W
146	Mogok (mô-gōk') Bur.	23·14 N	96·38 E
69	Mogollon (mō-gō-yōn') N. Mex.	33·25 N	108·45 W
69	Mogollon, Plat. (mō-gô-yōn') Ariz.	34·26 N	111·17 W
168	Mogol R. (mô-gŏl) S. Afr. (Johannesburg & Pretoria In.)	24·12 S	27·55 E
124	Moguer (mô-gĕr') Sp.	37·15 N	6.50 W
121	Mohács (mô'häch) Hung.	45·59 N	18·38 E
167	Mohales Hoek Bas. (Natal In.)	30·09 S	27·28 E
70	Mohall (mō'hôl) N. D.	48·46 N	101·29 W
68	Mohave (L.) (mô-hä'vä) Nev.	35·23 N	114·40 W
81	Mohawk (R.) (mō'hôk) N. Y.	43·15 N	75·20 W
167	Mohéli (I.) (mô-â-lē') (mô-hā'lê) Comores, Arch. des	12·23 S	43·38 E
147	Moho (mō'hō') China	53·33 N	122·30 E
119	Mõisaküla (mẽē'sà-kü'lä) Sov. Un.	58·07 N	25·12 E
87	Moisie (R.) (mwà-zē') Can.	51·24 N	66·11 W
122	Moissac (mwä-säk') Fr.	44·07 N	1·05 E
125	Moita (mô-ē'tà) Port. (Lisbon In.)	38·39 N	9·00 W
68	Mojave Calif.	35·06 N	118·09 W
68	Mojave (R.) (mô-hä'vä) Calif.	34·46 N	117·24 W
68	Mojave Desert Calif.	35·05 N	117·30 W
153	Moji (mō'jê) Jap.	33·56 N	130·59 E
68	Mokelumne (R.) (mō-kê-lŭm'nē) Calif.	38·12 N	121·09 W
167	Mokhotlong Bas. (Natal In.)	29·18 S	29·06 E
152	Mokpo (môk'pō') Kor.	34·50 N	126·30 E
132	Moksha (R.) (môk-shä') Sov. Un.	54·50 N	43·20 E
111	Mol Bel. (Brussels In.)	51·21 N	5·09 E
126	Molat (I.) (mō'lät) Yugo.	44·15 N	14·40 E
121	Moldavia (Reg.) Rom.	47·20 N	27·12 E
118	Molde (môl'dĕ) Nor.	62·44 N	7·15 E
118	Molde Fd. (môl'dĕ fyôrd) Nor.	62·40 N	7·05 E
121	Moldova R. Rom.	47·17 N	26·27 E
166	Molepolole (mō-lā-pô-lō'lā) Bech.	24·15 S	25·33 E
126	Molfetta (môl-fĕt'tä) It.	41·11 N	16·38 E
101	Molina (mŏ-lē'nä) Chile (Santiago In.)	35·07 S	71·17 W
124	Molina de Aragón (mô-lē'nä dĕ ä-rä-gô'n) Sp.	41·40 N	1·54 W
124	Molína de Segura (mô-lē'nä dĕ sĕ-gōō'rä) Sp.	38·03 N	1·07 W
71	Moline (mô-lēn') Ill.	41·31 N	90·34 W
166	Moliro Con. L.	8·08 S	30·30 E
126	Moliterno (mōl-ê-tĕr'nō) It.	40·13 N	15·54 E
98	Mollendo (mô-lyĕn'dō) Peru	17·02 S	71·59 W
64	Moller, Port (pōrt mōl'ĕr) Alaska	56·18 N	161·30 W
118	Mölndal (mûln'däl) Swe.	57·39 N	12·01 E
129	Molochnaya (R.) (mô-lôch'nà-yà) (rĕ-kä') Sov. Un.	47·05 N	35·22 E
129	Molochnoye, Ozero (L.) (ô'zĕ-rô mô-lôch'nô-yĕ) Sov. Un.	46·35 N	35·32 E
128	Molodechno (mô-lô-dĕch'nô) Sov. Un.	54·18 N	26·57 E
128	Molodechno (Oblast) Sov. Un.	54·27 N	27·38 E
136	Molody Tud (mō-lō-dô'ê tōō'd) Sov. Un. (Moscow In.)	55·17 N	37·31 E
128	Mologa (R.) (mô-lô'gà) Sov. Un.	58·05 N	35·43 E
157	Molokai (I.) (mō-lô-kä'ê) Hawaii (In.)	21·15 N	157·05 E
136	Molokcha R. (mô'lôk-chä) Sov. Un. (Moscow In.)	56·15 N	38·29 E
166	Molopo (R.) (mō-lō-pō) S. Afr.	27·45 S	20·45 E
167	Molteno (môl-tā'nô) S. Afr. (Natal In.)	31·24 S	26·23 E
155	Molucca Pass. (mô-lŭk'à) Indon.	1·55 N	126·30 E
155	Moluccas (Is.) (mô-lŭk'àz) Indon.	2·40 S	127·15 E
155	Molucca Sea Indon.	0·15 N	125·41 E
167	Mombasa (mōm-bä'sä) Ken.	4·01 S	39·43 E
152	Mombetsu (mōm'bĕt-sōō') Jap.	44·21 N	142·48 E
75	Momence (mô-mĕns') Ill. (Chicago In.)	41·09 N	87·40 W
92	Momostenango (mô-môs-tā-näŋ'gô) Guat.	15·02 N	91·25 W
92	Momotombo Nig.	12·25 N	86·43 W
155	Mompog Pass (mōm-pōg') Phil. (Manila In.)	13·35 N	122·09 E
98	Mompos (mōm-pōs') Col.	8·05 N	74·30 W
118	Møn (I.) (mûn) Den.	54·54 N	12·30 E
75	Monaca (mŏ-nă'kō) Pa. (Pittsburgh In.)	40·41 N	80·17 W
123	Monaco (mŏn'ȧ-kō) Eur.	43·43 N	7·47 E
116	Monaghan (mŏn'à-găn) Ire.	54·16 N	7·20 W
89	Mona Pass. (mō'nä) N. A.	18·00 N	68·10 W
113	Monastir (mŏn-às-tēr') Tun.	35·49 N	10·56 E
	Monastir, see Bitola		
129	Monastyrishche (mô-nás-tē-rēsh'châ) Sov. Un.	48·57 N	29·53 E
128	Monastyrshchina (mô-nás-tērsh'chĭ-nà) Sov. Un.	54·19 N	31·49 E
99	Monção (moŋ-souN') Braz.	3·39 S	45·23 W
124	Moncayo (Mtn.) (môn-kä'yō) Sp.	41·44 N	1·48 W
132	Monchegorsk (mōn'chĕ-gôrsk) Sov. Un.	69·00 N	33·35 E
123	Mönchengladbach (mûn'ĸĕn gläd'bäĸ) Ger. (Ruhr In.)	51·12 N	6·28 E
124	Moncique, Serra de (Mts.) (sĕr'rä dä môn-chē'kĕ) Port.	37·22 N	8.37 W
76	Monclova (mōn-klō'vä) Mex.	26·53 N	101·25 W
82	Moncton (mŭŋk'tŭn) Can.	46·06 N	64·49 W
124	Mondego, Cabo (C.) (kà'bō môn-dā'gōō) Port.	40·12 N	8·55 W
124	Mondêgo (R.) (mōn-dĕ'gō) Port.	40·10 N	8·36 W
166	Mondombe (môn-dôm'bà) Con. L.	0·45 S	23·06 E
124	Mondoñedo (môn-dô-nyā'dō) Sp.	43·35 N	7·18 W
126	Mondoví (mōn-dô'vē') It.	44·23 N	7·53 E
71	Mondovi (mŏn-dō'vĭ) Wis.	44·35 N	91·42 W
75	Monee (mŏ-nĭ) Ill. (Chicago In.)	41·25 N	87·45 W
75	Monessen (mŏ-nĕs'sĕn) Pa. (Pittsburgh In.)	40·09 N	79·53 W
73	Monett (mô-nĕt') Mo.	36·55 N	93·55 W
124	Monforte de Lemos (môn-fôr'tā dĕ lĕ'môs) Sp.	42·30 N	7·30 W
165	Mongala R. (mŏn-gȧl'ȧ) Con. L.	3·20 N	21·30 E
165	Mongalla Sud.	5·11 N	31·46 E
142	Monghyr (mŏn-gēr') India	25·23 N	86·34 E
138	Mongolia (mŏŋ-gō'lĭ-ȧ) Asia	46·00 N	100·00 E
165	Mongoumba (mŏŋ-gōōm'bà) Con. B.	3·41 N	18·21 E
166	Mongu (mŏŋ-gōō') N. Rh.	15·14 S	23·07 E
92	Monkey River (mŭŋ'kĭ) Br. Hond. (Yucatan In.)	16·22 N	88·33 W
85	Monkland Sta. (mŭngk-lănd) Can. (Ottawa In.)	45·12 N	74·52 W
166	Monkoto (mōn-kō'tô) Con. L.	1·45 S	20·51 E
73	Monmouth (mŏn'mŭth) (mŏn'mouth) Ill.	40·54 N	90·38 W
84	Monmouth Junction (mŏn'mouth jŭngk'shŭn) N. J. (New York In.)	40·23 N	74·33 W
68	Mono (L.) (mō'nō) Calif.	38·04 N	119·00 W
80	Monon (mō'nŏn) Ind.	40·55 N	86·55 W
81	Monongah (mô-nŏŋ'gȧ) W. Va.	39·25 N	80·10 W
75	Monongahela (mô-nŏn-gà-hē'là) Pa. (Pittsburgh In.)	40·11 N	79·55 W
81	Monongahela (R.) W. Va.	39·30 N	80·10 W
127	Monopoli (mô-nô'pô-lê) It.	40·55 N	17·17 E
125	Monovar (mō-nō'vär) Sp.	38·26 N	0·50 W
126	Monreale (mōn-rà-ä'lä) It.	38·04 N	13·15 E
78	Monroe (mŭn-rō') Ga.	33·47 N	83·43 W
77	Monroe La.	32·30 N	92·06 W
80	Monroe Mich.	41·55 N	83·25 W
84	Monroe N. Y. (New York In.)	41·19 N	74·11 W
79	Monroe N. C.	34·58 N	80·34 W
69	Monroe Utah	38·35 N	112·10 W
65	Monroe Wash. (Seattle In.)	47·52 N	121·58 W
71	Monroe Wis.	42·35 N	89·40 W
79	Monroe (L.) Fla.	28·50 N	81·15 W
73	Monroe City Mo.	39·38 N	91·41 W
78	Monroeville (mŭn-rō'vĭl) Ala.	31·33 N	87·19 W
74	Monrovia (mŏn-rō'vĭ-ȧ) Calif. (Los Angeles In.)	34·09 N	118·00 W
164	Monrovia Lib.	6·21 N	10·59 W
117	Mons (môN') Bel.	50·29 N	3·55 E
82	Monson (mŏn'sŭn) Maine	45·17 N	69·28 W
118	Mönsterås (mŭn'stēr-ôs) Swe.	57·04 N	16·24 E
146	Montagh Ata (Mt.) China	38·26 N	75·23 E
87	Montagne Tremblante Park Can.	46·30 N	75·51 W
83	Montague (mŏn'tȧ-gū) Can.	46·11 N	62·35 W
80	Montague Mich.	43·30 N	86·25 W
64	Montague (I.) Alaska	60·10 N	147·00 W
155	Montalban (mōnt-äl-bän) Phil. (Manila In.)	14·47 N	121·11 E
99	Montalbán Ven. (In.)	10·14 N	68·19 W
126	Montalcone (mōn-tāl-kō'nĕ) It.	45·49 N	13·30 E
124	Montalegre (mōn-tä-lā'grĕ) Port.	41·49 N	7·48 W
62	Montana (State) (mŏn-tăn'ȧ) U. S.	47·10 N	111·50 W
124	Montánchez (môn-tän'chàth) Sp.	39·18 N	6·09 W
122	Montargis (môN-tàr-zhē') Fr.	47·59 N	2·42 E
123	Montataire (môN-tà-târ) Fr. (Paris In.)	49·15 N	2·26 E
122	Montauban (môN-tô-bäN') Fr.	44·01 N	1·22 E
81	Montauk Pt. (mŏn-tôk') N. Y.	41·05 N	71·55 W
125	Montbanch (mônt-bän'ch) Sp.	41·20 N	1·08 E
122	Montbard (môN-bàr') Fr.	47·40 N	4·19 E
123	Montbéliard (môN-bā-lyàr') Fr.	47·32 N	6·45 E
77	Mont Belvieu (mŏnt bĕl'vū) Tex. (In.)	29·51 N	94·53 W
123	Mont Blanc Tunnel (môN bläN) Fr.-It.	45·53 N	6·53 E
122	Montbrison (môN-brē-zôN') Fr.	45·38 N	4·06 E
122	Montcalm, Pic de (Pk.) (pēk dē môN-kàm') Fr.	42·43 N	1·13 E
122	Montceau-les-Mines (môN-sō'lā-mēn') Fr.	46·39 N	4·22 E
84	Montclair (mŏnt-klâr') N. J. (New York In.)	40·49 N	74·13 W
122	Mont-de-Marsan (môN-dē-màr-säN') Fr.	43·54 N	0·32 W
122	Montdidier (môN-dē-dyā') Fr.	49·42 N	2·33 E
101	Monte (mŏ'n-tĕ) Arg. (Buenos Aires In.)	35·25 S	58·49 W
98	Monteagudo (mōn'tâ-ä-gōō'dhō) Bol.	19·49 S	63·48 W
74	Montebello (mŏn-tê-bĕl'ō) Calif. (Los Angeles In.)	34·01 N	118·06 W
85	Montebello Can. (Ottawa In.)	45·40 N	74·56 W
158	Monte Bello (Is.) Austl.	20·30 S	114·10 E
100	Monte Caseros (mŏ'n-tĕ-kä-sĕ'rôs) Arg.	30·16 S	57·39 W
92	Mont Ecillos, Cord. de (Mts.) (kôr-dēl-yĕ'rä dĕ mô'nt ĕ-sē'l-yōs) Hond.	14·19 N	87·52 W
95	Monte Cristi (mô'n-tĕ-krē's-tē) Dom. Rep.	19·50 N	71·40 W
126	Montecristo, I. di (mōn'tâ-krēs'tō) It.	42·20 N	10·19 E
90	Monte Escobedo (mōn'tâ ĕs-kô-bā'dhō) Mex.	22·18 N	103·34 W
125	Monteforte Irpino (môn-tĕ-fô'r-tĕ ē'r-pē'nō) It. (Naples In.)	40·39 N	14·42 E
124	Montefrío (mōn-tà-frē'ō) Sp.	37·20 N	4·02 W
94	Montego Bay (mŏn-tē'gō) Jam.	18·30 N	77·55 W
100	Monte Grande (mô'n-tĕ grän'dĕ) Arg. (In.)	34·34 S	58·28 W
125	Montelavar (mōn-tĕ-là-vär') Port. (Lisbon In.)	38·51 N	9·20 W
122	Montélimar (môN-tā-lē-mär') Fr.	44·33 N	4·47 E
124	Montellano (mōn-tâ-lyä'nō) Sp.	37·00 N	5·34 W
71	Montello (mŏn-tĕl'ō) Wis.	43·47 N	89·20 W
76	Montemorelos (mōn'tâ-mō-rā'lōs) Mex.	25·14 N	99·50 W
124	Montemor-o-Novo (mōN-tĕ-môr'ōō-nô'vōō) Port.	38·39 N	8·11 W
	Montenegro (Reg.), see Črna Gora		
126	Montepulciano (mōn'tâ-pōōl-chä'nō) It.	43·05 N	11·48 E
122	Montereau-faut-Yonne (môN-t'rō'fō-yôn') Fr.	48·24 N	2·57 E
68	Monterey (mŏn-tĕ-rā') Calif.	36·36 N	121·53 W
78	Monterey Tenn.	36·06 N	85·15 W
68	Monterey B. Calif.	36·48 N	122·01 W
74	Monterey Park Calif. (Los Angeles In.)	34·04 N	118·08 W
98	Montería (mōn-tà-rā'ä) Col.	8·47 N	75·57 W
100	Monteros (mōn-tĕ'rôs) Arg.	27·14 S	65·29 W
125	Monterotondo (môn-tĕ-rō-tô'n-dō) It. (Rome In.)	42·03 N	12·39 E
76	Monterrey (mōn-tĕr-rā') Mex.	25·43 N	100·19 W
126	Monte Sant' Angelo (mô'n-tĕ sän ä'n-gzhĕ-lô) It.	41·43 N	15·59 E
66	Montesano (mŏn-tê-sä'nō) Wash.	46·59 N	123·35 W
99	Montes Claros (môn-tĕs-klä'rôs) Braz.	16·44 S	43·41 W
78	Montevallo (mōn-tê-văl'ō) Ala.	33·05 N	86·49 W
126	Montevarchi (mōn-tâ-vär'kē) It.	43·30 N	11·45 E
101	Montevideo (mōn'tâ-vê-dhā'ō) Ur. (Buenos Aires In.)	34·50 S	56·10 W
69	Monte Vista (mŏn'tê vĭs'tȧ) Colo.	37·35 N	106·10 W
78	Montezuma (mŏn-tê-zōō'mȧ) Ga.	32·17 N	84·00 W
69	Montezuma Castle Natl. Mon. Ariz.	34·38 N	111·50 W
111	Montfoort Neth. (Amsterdam In.)	52·02 N	4·56 E
123	Montfort l'Amaury (mŏN-fôr'lä-mō-rē') Fr. (Paris In.)	48·47 N	1·49 E
122	Montfort-sur-Meu (mŏN-fôr-sür-mû') Fr.	48·09 N	1·58 W
78	Montgomery (mŏnt-gŭm'ēr-ĭ) Ala.	32·23 N	86·17 W
142	Montgomery W. Pak.	30·43 N	73·04 E
80	Montgomery W. Va.	38·10 N	81·25 W
73	Montgomery City Mo.	38·58 N	91·29 W
73	Monticello (mŏn-tĭ-sĕl'ō) Ark.	33·38 N	91·47 W
78	Monticello Fla.	30·32 N	83·53 W
78	Monticello Ga.	33·00 N	83·11 W
80	Monticello Ill.	40·05 N	88·35 W
80	Monticello Ind.	40·40 N	86·50 W
71	Monticello Iowa	42·14 N	91·13 W
78	Monticello Ky.	36·47 N	84·50 W
82	Monticello Maine	46·19 N	67·53 W
71	Monticello Minn.	45·18 N	93·48 W
81	Monticello N. Y.	41·35 N	74·40 W
69	Monticello Utah	37·55 N	109·25 W
123	Montigny-lès-Metz (môN-tēn-yē'lā-mĕts') Fr.	49·06 N	6·07 E
125	Montijo (môn-tē'zhō) Port. (Lisbon In.)	38·42 N	8·58 W
124	Montijo (môn-tē'hō) Sp.	38·55 N	6·35 W
93	Montijo, Bahia (B.) (bä-ē'ä môn-tē'hō) Pan.	7·36 N	81·11 W
82	Mont Joli (môN zhō-lē') Can.	48·37 N	68·09 W
122	Montluçon (môN-lü-sôN') Fr.	46·20 N	2·35 E
85	Montmagny (môN-màn-yē') Can. (Quebec In.)	46·59 N	70·33 W
85	Montmorency (mŏnt-mô-rĕn'sĭ) Can. (Quebec In.)	46·53 N	71·09 W
123	Montmorency (môN'mô-räN-sē') Fr. (Paris In.)	48·59 N	2·19 E
85	Montmorency, Rivière (R.) (rê-vyâr' mŏnt-mô-rĕn'sĭ) Can (Quebec In.)	47·04 N	71·12 W

ăt; finăl; rāte; senâte; ārm; åsk; sofȧ; fâre; ch-choose; dh-as th in other; bē; ēvent; bĕt; recĕnt; cratēr; g-go; gh-guttural g; bĭt; ĭ-short neutral; rīde; ĸ-guttural k as ch in German ich;

PRONOUNCING INDEX Montmorillon–Mount Rainier 239

Page	Name	Pronunciation	Region	Lat. °'	Long. °'
122	Montmorillon	(môn'mô-rê-yôn')	Fr.	46·26 N	0·50 E
126	Montone (R.)	(môn-tô'nĕ)	It.	44·03 N	11·45 E
124	Montoro	(môn-tō'rô)	Sp.	38·01 N	4·22 W
80	Montpelier	(mŏnt-pēl'yẽr)	Ind.	40·35 N	85·20 W
67	Montpelier		Idaho	42·19 N	111·19 W
80	Montpelier		Ohio	41·35 N	84·35 W
81	Montpelier		Vt.	44·20 N	72·35 W
122	Montpellier	(môn-pĕ-lyā')	Fr.	43·38 N	3·53 E
85	Montreal	(mŏn-trê-ôl')	Can. (Montreal In.)	45·30 N	73·35 W
85	Montreal North		Can. (Montreal In.)	45·36 N	73·38 W
85	Montreal South		Can. (Montreal In.)	45·31 N	73·30 W
120	Montreux	(môn-trû')	Switz.	46·26 N	6·52 E
74	Montrose	(mŏnt-rōz)	Calif. (Los Angeles In.)	34·13 N	118·13 W
69	Montrose	(mŏn-trōz')	Colo.	38·30 N	107·55 W
116	Montrose		Scot.	56·45 N	2·25 W
75	Montrose		Ohio (Cleveland In.)	41·08 N	81·38 W
81	Montrose	(mŏnt-rōz')	Pa.	41·50 N	75·50 W
82	Monts, Pointe des (Pt.)	(pwăNt' dā môN')	Can.	49·19 N	67·22 W
123	Mont St. Martin	(môN săN mär-tăN')	Fr.	49·34 N	6·13 E
93	Montserrat I.	(mŏnt-sĕ-răt')	N. A. (Le. & Wind. Is. In.)	16·48 N	62·00 W
84	Montvale	(mŏnt-vāl')	N. J. (New York In.)	41·02 N	74·01 W
154	Monywa	(mŏn'yōō-wa)	Bur.	22·02 N	95·16 E
126	Monza	(mōn'tsä)	It.	45·34 N	9·17 E
125	Monzón	(mōn-thōn')	Sp.	41·54 N	1·09 E
77	Moody	(mōō'dĭ)	Tex.	31·18 N	97·20 W
168	Mooi (R.)	(mōō'ĭ)	S. Afr. (Johannesburg & Pretoria In.)	26·34 S	27·03 E
167	Mooi (R.)		S. Afr. (Natal In.)	29·00 S	30·15 E
167	Mooirivier		S. Afr. (Natal In.)	29·14 S	29·59 E
161	Moolap		Austl. (Melbourne In.)	38·11 S	144·26 E
160	Moonta	(mōōn'tȧ)	Austl.	34·05 S	137·42 E
158	Moora	(mŏŏr'ȧ)	Austl.	30·35 S	116·12 E
67	Moorcroft	(mōr'krôft)	Wyo.	44·17 N	104·59 W
158	Moore (L.)	(mōr)	Austl.	29·50 S	128·12 E
111	Moorenweis	(mō'rĕn-vīz)	Ger. (Munich In.)	48·10 N	11·05 E
81	Moore Res.		Vt.-N. H.	44·20 N	72·10 W
84	Moorestown	(morz'toun)	N. J. (Philadelphia In.)	39·58 N	74·56 W
75	Mooresville	(mōrz'vĭl)	Ind. (Indianapolis In.)	39·37 N	86·22 W
79	Mooresville	(mōrz'vĭl)	N. C.	35·34 N	80·48 W
70	Moorhead	(mōr'hĕd)	Minn.	46·52 N	96·44 W
78	Moorhead		Miss.	33·25 N	90·30 W
	Moorland, see Landes				
86	Moose (L.)	(mōōs)	Can.	54·14 N	99·28 W
87	Moose (R.)		Can.	51·01 N	80·42 W
85	Moose Creek		Can. (Ottawa In.)	45·16 N	74·58 W
82	Moosehead	(mōōs'hĕd)	Maine	45·37 N	69·15 W
86	Moose Jaw	(mōōs jô)	Can.	50·26 N	105·40 W
82	Mooselookmeguntic (L.)	(mōō-sĕ-lŏŏk-mê-gŭn'tĭk)	Maine	44·54 N	70·20 W
86	Moose Mtn.		Can.	50·10 N	102·54 W
81	Moosilauke (Mtn.)	(mōō-sĭ-lȧ'kē)	N. H.	44·00 N	71·50 W
111	Moosinning	(mō'zē-nēng)	Ger. (Munich In.)	48·17 N	11·51 E
87	Moosonee	(mōō'sô-nê)	Can.	51·20 N	80·44 W
164	Mopti	(mŏp'tê)	Mali	14·27 N	3·56 W
98	Moquegua	(mô-kā'gwä)	Peru	17·15 S	70·54 W
121	Mór	(mōr)	Hung.	47·51 N	18·14 E
71	Mora	(mō'rȧ)	Minn.	45·52 N	93·18 W
72	Mora		N. Mex.	35·58 N	105·17 W
124	Mora	(mô-rä)	Sp.	39·42 N	3·45 W
125	Mora		Sp.	41·06 N	0·25 E
142	Morādābād	(mô-rä-dȧ-bäd')	India	28·57 N	78·48 E
92	Morales	(mô-rä'lĕs)	Guat.	15·29 N	88·46 W
167	Moramanga	(mō-rä-mäŋ'gä)	Malag. Rep.	18·48 S	48·09 E
95	Morant Pt.	(mô-rănt')	Jam.	17·55 N	76·10 W
118	Morastrand	(mō'rä-strănd)	Swe.	61·00 N	14·29 E
125	Morata de Tajuña	(mô-rä'tä dā tä-hōō'nyä)	Sp. (Madrid In.)	40·14 N	3·27 W
121	Morava (Moravia) (Prov.)	(mô'rä-vä) (mô-rā'vĭ-ȧ)	Czech.	49·21 N	16·57 E
120	Morava R.		Czech.	49·53 N	16·53 E
	Moravia, see Morava				
99	Morawhanna	(mô-rȧ-hwä'nȧ)	Br. Gu.	8·12 N	59·33 W
116	Moray Firth	(mŭr'ȧ)	Scot.	57·41 N	3·55 W
118	Mörbylånga	(mûr'bü-lôŋ'gȧ)	Swe.	56·32 N	16·23 E
86	Morden	(mōr'dĕn)	Can.	49·08 N	98·19 W
161	Mordialloc	(môr-dĭ-ăl'ŏk)	Austl. (Melbourne In.)	38·00 S	145·05 E
116	More, Ben (Mtn.)	(bĕn môr)	Scot.	58·09 N	5·01 W
70	Moreau (R.)	(mô-rō')	S. D.	45·13 N	102·22 W
116	Morecambe B.	(mōr'kăm)	Eng.	53·55 N	3·25 W
160	Moree	(mō'rē)	Austl.	29·20 S	149·50 E
80	Morehead		Ky.	38·10 N	83·25 W
79	Morehead City	(mōr'hĕd)	N. C.	34·43 N	76·43 W
73	Morehouse	(mōr'hous)	Mo.	36·49 N	89·41 W
90	Morelia	(mô-rā'lyä)	Mex.	19·43 N	101·12 W
125	Morella	(mô-rāl'yä)	Sp.	40·38 N	0·07 W
90	Morelos	(mô-rā'lōs)	Mex.	22·46 N	102·36 W
76	Morelos		Mex.	28·24 N	100·51 W
91	Morelos		Mex. (Mexico City In.)	19·41 N	99·29 W
76	Morelos, R.		Mex.	25·27 N	99·35 W
65	Morena, Sierra (Mt.)	(syĕr'rä mô-rā'nä)	Calif. (San Francisco In.)	37·24 N	122·19 W
124	Morena, Sierra (Mts.)	(syĕr'rä mô-rā'nä)	Sp.	38·15 N	5·45 W
69	Morenci	(mô-rĕn'sĭ)	Ariz.	33·05 N	109·25 W
80	Morenci		Mich.	41·50 N	84·05 W
100	Moreno	(mô-rĕ'nō)	Arg. (In.)	34·25 S	58·47 W
74	Moreno		Calif. (Los Angeles In.)	33·55 N	117·09 W
94	Mores (I.)	(mōrz)	Ba. Is.	26·20 N	77·35 W
65	Moresby (I.)	(mōrz'bĭ)	Can. (Vancouver In.)	48·43 N	123·15 W
86	Moresby I.		Can	52·54 N	131·00 W
160	Moreton (I.)	(môr'tŭn)	Austl.	26·53 S	152·42 E
160	Moreton B.	(môr'tŭn)	Austl.	27·12 S	153·10 E
85	Morewood	(mōr'wŏŏd)	Can. (Ottawa In.)	45·11 N	75·17 W
67	Morgan	(môr'găn)	Utah	41·04 N	111·42 W
77	Morgan City		La.	29·41 N	91·11 W
80	Morganfield	(môr'găn-fēld)	Ky.	37·40 N	87·55 W
167	Morgansbaai		S. Afr. (Natal In.)	32·42 S	28·19 E
79	Morganton	(môr'găn-tŭn)	N. C.	35·44 N	81·42 W
81	Morgantown	(môr'găn-toun)	W. Va.	39·40 N	79·55 W
168	Morganzon	(môr'gănt-sŏn)	S. Afr. (Johannesburg & Pretoria In.)	26·44 S	29·39 E
145	Morga Ra.		Afg. (Khyber Pass In.)	34·02 N	70·38 E
161	Moriac		Austl. (Melbourne In.)	38·15 S	144·12 E
153	Moriguchi	(mō'rê-gōō'chê)	Jap. (Ōsaka In.)	34·44 N	135·34 E
85	Morinville	(mō'-rĭn-vĭl)	Can. (Edmonton In.)	53·47 N	113·40 W
152	Morioka	(mō'rê-ō'kȧ)	Jap.	39·40 N	141·21 E
135	Morkoka (R.)	(môr-kô'kȧ)	Sov. Un.	65·35 N	111·00 E
122	Morlaix	(mŏr-lĕ')	Fr.	48·36 N	3·48 W
85	Morley	(mŏr'lē)	Can. (Calgary In.)	51·10 N	114·51 W
123	Mormant		Fr. (Paris In.)	48·35 N	2·54 E
93	Morne Diablotin, Mt.	(môrn dē-ȧ-blô-tăN')	Dominica (Le. & Wind. Is. In.)	15·31 N	61·24 W
93	Morne Gimie, Mt.	(môrn' zhê-mē')	St. Lucia (Le. & Wind. Is. In.)	13·53 N	61·03 W
161	Mornington		Austl. (Melbourne In.)	38·13 S	145·02 E
74	Moro	(mō'rō)	Ill. (St. Louis In.)	38·56 N	90·01 W
155	Morobe		N. Gui. Ter.	8·03 S	147·45 E
165	Morocco	(mô-rŏk'ō)	Afr.	32·00 N	7·00 W
167	Morogoro	(mō-rō-gō'rō)	Tan.	6·49 S	37·46 E
90	Moroleón	(mō-rō-lā-ōn')	Mex.	20·07 N	101·15 W
167	Morombé	(mōō-rōōm'bā)	Malag. Rep.	21·39 S	43·34 E
100	Morón	(mō-rŏ'n)	Arg. (In.)	34·24 S	58·37 W
94	Morón	(mô-rōn')	Cuba	22·05 N	78·35 W
99	Morón	(mô-rŏ'n)	Ven. (In.)	10·29 N	68·11 W
167	Morondava	(mô-rōn-dȧ'vȧ)	Malag. Rep.	20·17 S	44·18 E
124	Morón de la Frontera	(mô-rōn'dā lāf rôn-tā'rä)	Sp.	37·08 N	5·20 W
68	Morongo Ind. Res.	(mō-rôŋ'gō)	Calif.	33·54 N	116·47 W
69	Moroni	(mô-rō'nĭ)	Utah	39·30 N	111·40 W
155	Morotai (I.)	(mō-rô-tä'ē)	Indon.	2·12 N	128·30 E
133	Morozovsk		Sov. Un.	48·20 N	41·50 E
70	Morrill	(mŏr'ĭl)	Nebr.	41·59 N	103·54 W
73	Morrilton	(mŏr'ĭl-tŭn)	Ark.	35·09 N	92·42 W
99	Morrinhos	(mô-rēn'yōzh)	Braz.	17·45 S	48·56 W
86	Morris	(mŏr'ĭs)	Can.	49·19 N	97·32 W
80	Morris		Ill.	41·20 N	88·25 W
70	Morris		Minn.	45·35 N	95·53 W
71	Morrison	(mŏr'ĭ-sŭn)	Ill.	41·48 N	89·58 W
84	Morris Plains	(mŏr'ĭs pláns)	N. J. (New York In.)	40·49 N	74·29 W
74	Morris Res.		Calif. (Los Angeles In.)	34·11 N	117·49 W
84	Morristown	(mŏr'rĭs-toun)	N. J. (New York In.)	40·48 N	74·29 W
78	Morristown		Tenn.	36·10 N	83·18 W
84	Morrisville	(mŏr'ĭs vĭl)	Pa. (Philadelphia In.)	40·12 N	74·46 W
82	Morrisville		Vt.	44·33 N	72·39 W
99	Morro do Chapéu	(môr-ōō dōō-shä-pĕ'ōō)	Braz.	11·34 S	41·03 W
75	Morrow	(mŏr'ō)	Ohio (Cincinnati In.)	39·21 N	84·07 W
133	Morshansk	(môr-shȧnsk')	Sov. Un.	53·25 N	41·35 E
118	Mors (I.)		Den.	56·46 N	8·38 E
126	Mortara	(môr-tä'rä)	It.	45·13 N	8·47 E
100	Morteros	(môr-tĕ'rôs)	Arg.	30·47 S	62·00 W
101	Mortes, Rio das (R.)	(rē'-o-däs-mô'r-tĕs)	Braz. (Rio de Janeiro In.)	21·04 S	44·29 W
71	Morton Ind. Res.	(mŏr'tŭn)	Minn.	44·35 N	94·48 W
111	Mortsel	(môr-sĕl')	Bel. (Brussels In.)	51·10 N	4·28 E
122	Morvan, Mts. du	(môr-văN')	Fr.	46·45 N	4·00 E
132	Morzhovets (I.)	(môr'zhô-vyĕts')	Sov. Un.	66·40 N	42·30 E
128	Mosal'sk	(mō-zȧlsk')	Sov. Un.	54·27 N	34·57 E
66	Moscow	(mŏs'kō)	Idaho	46·44 N	116·57 W
	Moscow, see Moskva				
	Moscow Canal, see Imeni Moskvy, Kanal				
120	Mosel R.	(mō'sĕl) (mô-zĕl)	Ger.	49·49 N	7·00 E
66	Moses Lake		Wash.	47·08 N	119·15 W
66	Moses L.	(mō'zĕz)	Wash.	47·09 N	119·30 W
168	Moses R.		S. Afr. (Johannesburg & Pretoria In.)	25·17 S	29·04 E
119	Moshchnyy (Is.)	(môsh'chnĭ)	Sov. Un.	59·56 N	28·07 E
167	Moshi	(mō'shê)	Tan.	3·17 S	37·18 E
136	Moskva (Moscow)	(mŏs-kvä')	Sov. Un. (Moscow In.)	55·45 N	37·37 E
128	Moskva (Oblast)		Sov. Un.	55·38 N	36·48 E
128	Moskva (R.)		Sov. Un.	55·50 N	37·05 E
121	Mosonmagyaróvár		Hung.	47·51 N	17·16 E
93	Mosquitos, Costa de	(kôs-tä-dĕ-mōs-kē'tō)	Nic.	12·05 N	83·49 W
93	Mosquitos, Gulfo de los (G.)	(gōō'l-fô-dĕ-lōs-mōs-kē'tōs)	Pan.	9·17 N	80·59 W
118	Moss	(mōs)	Nor.	59·29 N	10·39 E
65	Moss Beach	(môs bēch)	Calif. (San Francisco In.)	37·32 N	122·31 W
166	Mossel Bay	(mô'sŭl bā)	S. Afr.	34·06 S	22·23 E
110	Mossley	(môs'lĭ)	Eng.	53·31 N	2·02 W
99	Mossoró	(mō-sô-rōō')	Braz.	5·13 S	37·14 W
78	Moss Point	(môs)	Miss.	30·25 N	88·32 W
120	Most	(môst)	Czech.	50·32 N	13·37 E
164	Mostaganem	(mŏs'tä-gä-nĕm')	Alg.	36·04 N	0·11 E
127	Mostar	(môs'tär)	Yugo.	43·20 N	17·51 E
125	Móstoles	(mōs-tō'läs)	Sp. (Madrid In.)	40·19 N	3·52 W
92	Motagua R.	(mô-tä'gwä)	Guat.	15·29 N	88·39 W
118	Motala	(mô-tô'lä)	Swe.	58·34 N	15·00 E
116	Motherwell	(mŭdh'ẽr-wĕl)	Scot.	55·45 N	4·05 W
124	Motril	(mô-trēl')	Sp.	36·44 N	3·32 W
92	Motul	(mō-tōō'l)	Mex. (Yucatan In.)	21·07 N	89·14 W
166	Mouanda		Gabon	1·37 S	13·09 E
95	Mouchoir Bk.	(mōō-shwȧr')	Ba. Is.	21·35 N	70·40 W
95	Mouchoir Passage (Str.)		Ba. Is.	21·05 N	71·05 W
123	Moudon		Switz.	46·40 N	6·47 E
166	Mouille Pt.		S. Afr. (Cape Town In.)	33·54 S	18·19 E
122	Moulins	(mōō-lăN')	Fr.	46·34 N	3·19 E
85	Moulin Vallie're	(mōō-lĕN' vȧ-lē-ĕr')	Can. (Quebec In.)	46·58 N	71·12 W
154	Moulmein	(mōl-mān')	Bur.	16·30 N	97·39 E
114	Moulouya Oued (R.)	(mōō-lōō'yȧ)	Mor.	34·07 N	3·27 W
78	Moultrie	(mōl'trĭ)	Ga.	31·10 N	83·48 W
79	Moultrie (Dam)		S. C.	33·12 N	80·00 W
73	Mound City	(mound)	Ill.	37·06 N	89·13 W
73	Mound City		Mo.	40·08 N	95·13 W
80	Mound City Group Natl. Mon.		Ohio	39·25 N	83·00 W
80	Moundsville	(moundz'vĭl)	W. Va.	39·50 N	80·50 W
123	Mounier, Mt.	(mōō-nyā')	Fr.	44·10 N	6·59 E
84	Mountain Brook	(moun'tĭn brŏŏk)	Ala. (Birmingham In.)	33·30 N	86·45 W
74	Mountain Creek L.		Tex. (Dallas, Fort Worth In.)	32·43 N	97·03 W
65	Mountaindale	(dāl)	Ore. (Portland In.)	45·37 N	123·02 W
73	Mountain Grove	(grōv)	Mo.	37·07 N	92·16 W
66	Mountain Home	(hōm)	Idaho	43·08 N	115·43 W
86	Mountain Park	(pärk)	Can.	52·57 N	117·22 W
65	Mountain View	(moun'tĭn vū)	Calif. (San Francisco In.)	37·25 N	122·07 W
73	Mountain View		Mo.	36·59 N	91·46 W
84	Mountain View		N. J. (New York In.)	40·55 N	74·17 W
79	Mount Airy	(âr'ĭ)	N. C.	36·28 N	80·37 W
	Mount Athos (Reg.), see Áyion Óros				
167	Mount Ayliff	(ā'lĭf)	S. Afr. (Natal In.)	30·48 S	29·24 E
71	Mount Ayr	(âr)	Iowa	40·43 N	94·06 W
80	Mount Carmel	(kär'mĕl)	Ill.	38·25 N	87·45 W
81	Mount Carmel		Pa.	40·50 N	76·25 W
71	Mount Carroll		Ill.	42·05 N	89·55 W
75	Mount Clemens	(klĕm'ĕnz)	Mich. (Detroit In.)	42·36 N	82·52 W
166	Mount Darwin		S. Rh.	15·44 S	31·40 E
82	Mount Desert (I.)	(dê-zûrt')	Can.	44·15 N	68·08 W
79	Mount Dora	(dō'rȧ)	Fla. (In.)	28·45 N	81·38 W
161	Mount Duneed		Austl. (Melbourne In.)	38·15 S	144·20 E
161	Mount Eliza		Austl. (Melbourne In.)	38·11 S	145·05 E
70	Mountevideo	(mōn'tȧ-vê-dhā'ō)	Minn.	44·56 N	95·42 W
167	Mount Fletcher	(flĕ'chẽr)	S. Afr. (Natal In.)	30·42 S	28·32 E
80	Mount Forest	(fŏr'ĕst)	Can.	44·00 N	80·45 W
167	Mount Frere	(frâr')	S. Afr. (Natal In.)	30·54 S	29·02 E
160	Mount Gambier	(găm'bēr)	Austl.	37·30 S	140·53 E
80	Mount Gilead	(gĭl'ĕăd)	Ohio	40·30 N	82·50 W
75	Mount Healthy	(hĕlth'ē)	Ohio (Cincinnati In.)	39·14 N	84·32 W
84	Mount Holly	(hŏl'ĭ)	N. J. (Philadelphia In.)	39·59 N	74·47 W
85	Mount Hope		Can. (Toronto In.)	43·09 N	79·55 W
84	Mount Hope	(hōp)	N. J. (New York In.)	40·55 N	74·32 W
80	Mount Hope		W. Va.	37·55 N	81·10 W
158	Mount Isa	(ī'zȧ)	Austl.	21·00 S	139·45 E
84	Mount Kisco	(kĭs'kō)	N. Y. (New York In.)	41·12 N	73·44 W
65	Mountlake Terrace	(mount lāk tĕr'ĭs)	Wash. (Seattle In.)	47·48 N	122·19 W
75	Mount Lebanon	(lĕb'ȧ-nŭn)	Pa. (Pittsburgh In.)	40·22 N	80·03 W
64	Mount McKinley Natl. Park	(mȧ-kĭn'lĭ)	Alaska	63·48 N	153·02 W
158	Mount Magnet	(măg-nĕt)	Austl.	28·00 S	118·00 E
161	Mount Martha		Austl. (Melbourne In.)	38·17 S	145·01 E
159	Mount Morgan	(môr-găn)	Austl.	23·42 S	150·45 E
161	Mount Moriac		Austl. (Melbourne In.)	38·13 S	144·12 E
80	Mount Morris	(mŏr'ĭs)	Mich.	43·10 N	83·45 W
81	Mount Morris		N. Y.	42·45 N	77·50 W
79	Mount Olive	(ŏl'ĭv)	N. C.	35·11 N	78·05 W
69	Mount Peale		Utah	38·26 N	109·16 W
71	Mount Pleasant	(plĕz'ănt)	Iowa	40·59 N	91·34 W
80	Mount Pleasant		Mich.	43·35 N	84·45 W
79	Mount Pleasant		S. C.	32·46 N	79·51 W
78	Mount Pleasant		Tenn.	35·31 N	87·12 W
73	Mount Pleasant		Tex.	33·10 N	94·56 W
69	Mount Pleasant		Utah	39·35 N	111·20 W
75	Mount Prospect	(prŏs'pĕkt)	Ill. (Chicago In.)	42·03 N	87·56 W
66	Mount Rainier Natl. Park	(rȧ-nēr')	Wash.	46·47 N	121·17 W

ng-sing; ŋ-baŋk: N-nasalized n; nŏd; cŏmmit; ōld; ōbey; ôrder; fōōd; fŏŏt; ou-out; s-soft; sh-dish; th-thin; pūre; ûnite; ûrn; stŭd; circŭs; ü-as "y" in study; '-indeterminate vowel.

240 Mount Revelstoke–Nagua PRONOUNCING INDEX

Page	Name Pronunciation Region	Lat. °′	Long. °′
86	Mount Revelstoke Natl. Park (rĕv'ĕl-stōk). Can.	51·22 N	120·15 W
81	Mount Savage (săv'âj) Md.	39·45 N	78·55 W
66	Mount Shasta (shăs'tȧ) Calif.	41·18 N	122·17 W
73	Mount Sterling (stûr'lĭng) Ill.	39·59 N	90·44 W
80	Mount Sterling Ky.	38·05 N	84·00 W
83	Mount Stewart (stū'ărt) Can.	46·21 N	62·54 W
81	Mount Union (ūn'yŭn) Pa.	40·25 N	77·50 W
80	Mount Vernon (vûr'nŭn) Ill.	38·20 N	88·50 W
80	Mount Vernon Ind.	37·55 N	87·50 W
73	Mount Vernon Mo.	37·09 N	93·48 W
84	Mount Vernon N. Y. (New York In.)	40·55 N	73·51 W
80	Mount Vernon Ohio	40·25 N	82·30 W
65	Mount Vernon. Wash. (Seattle In.)	48·25 N	122·20 W
155	Mount Wilhelm New Guinea	5·45 S	144·30 E
148	Moup'ing (mō'pĭng) China	37·23 N	121·36 E
99	Moura (mō'rȧ) Braz.	1·33 S	61·38 W
124	Moura Port.	38·08 N	7·28 W
116	Mourne, Mts. (môrn) N. Ire.	54·10 N	6·09 W
123	Moûtiers (mōō-tyâr') Fr.	45·31 N	6·34 E
160	Mowbullan, Mt. (mō'bōō-lăn) Austl.	26·50 S	151·34 E
90	Moyahua (mô-yä'wä) Mex.	21·16 N	103·10 W
165	Moyale (mô-yä'lä) Ken.	3·28 N	39·04 E
164	Moyamba (mô-yäm'bä) S. L.	8·11 N	12·27 W
114	Moyen Atlas (Mts.) Mor.	32·49 N	5·28 W
123	Moyeuvre Grande Fr.	49·15 N	6·26 E
66	Moyie R. (moi'yē) Idaho	48·50 N	116·10 W
98	Moyobamba (mō-yō-bäm'bä) Peru	6·12 S	76·56 W
92	Moyuta (mô-ē-ōō'tä) Guat.	14·01 N	90·05 W
135	Moyyero (R.) Sov. Un.	67·15 N	104·10 E
163	Mozambique (Portuguese East Africa) (mō-zăm-bēk') Afr.	20·15 S	33·53 E
84	Mozambique, Pt. La. (New Orleans In.)	29·38 N	89·26 W
167	Mozambique Chan. (mō-zăm-bek') Ind. O.	52·18 S	4·28 E
133	Mozdok (môz-dôk') Sov. Un.	43·45 N	44·35 E
128	Mozhaysh (mô-zhäysh') Sov. Un.	55·31 N	36·02 E
136	Mozhayskiy (mô-zhäy'skĭ) Sov. Un. (Leningrad In.)	59·42 N	30·08 E
129	Mozyr' (mô-zür') Sov. Un.	52·03 N	29·14 E
166	Mporokoso ('m-pō-rô-kō'sō) N. Rh.	9·28 S	30·06 E
167	Mpwapwa ('m-pwä'pwä) Tan.	6·20 S	36·39 E
167	Mqanduli ('m-kän'dōō-lē) S. Afr. (Natal In.)	31·50 S	28·42 E
121	Mragowo (mrăŋ'gô-vô) Pol.	53·52 N	21·18 E
164	M'sila (m'sē'lȧ) Alg.	35·47 N	4·34 E
128	Msta (R.) (m'stȧ') Sov. Un.	58·33 N	32·08 E
128	Mstislavl' (m'stē-slävl') Sov. Un.	54·01 S	31·42 E
166	Mtengula ('m-tĕŋ-gōō'lȧ) Moz.	12·42 S	34·48 E
166	Mtetwe Pan (Basin) ('m-tĕt'wĕ) Bech.	20·00 S	24·18 E
128	Mtsensk (m'tsĕnsk) Sov. Un.	53·17 N	36·33 E
154	Muang Khon Kaen Thai.	16·37 N	102·41 E
154	Muang Lamphum Thai.	18·40 N	98·59 E
154	Muang Phitsanulok Thai.	16·51 N	100·15 E
154	Muang Sakon Thai.	17·00 N	104·06 E
139	Muar (R.) Mala. (Singapore In.)	2·18 N	102·43 E
123	Much (mōōk) Ger. (Ruhr In.)	50·54 N	7·24 E
110	Much Wenlock (mŭch wĕn'lŏk) Eng.	52·35 N	2·33 W
78	Muckalee Cr. (mŭk'ȧ lē) Ga.	31·55 N	84·10 W
65	Muckleshoot Ind. Res. (mŭck''l-shōōt) Wash. (Seattle In.)	47·21 N	122·04 W
99	Mucugê (mōō-kōō-zhĕ') Braz.	13·02 S	41·19 W
71	Mud (L.) (mŭd) Mich.	46·12 N	84·32 W
68	Mud (L.) Nev.	40·28 N	119·11 W
68	Muddy (R.) (mŭd'ĭ) Nev.	36·56 N	114·42 W
73	Muddy Boggy Cr. (mud'ĭ bôg'ĭ) Okla.	34·42 N	96·11 W
69	Muddy Cr. (mŭd'ĭ) Utah	38·45 N	111·10 W
160	Mudgee (mŭ-jē) Austl.	32·47 S	149·10 E
124	Mugía (mōō-kē'ä) Sp.	43·05 N	9·14 W
133	Muğla (mōōg'lä) Tur.	37·10 N	28·20 E
120	Mühldorf (mül-dôrf) Ger.	48·15 N	12·33 E
120	Mühlhausen (mül'hou-zĕn) Ger.	51·13 N	10·25 E
119	Muhu (I.) (mōō'hōō) Sov. Un.	58·41 N	22·55 E
151	Mui Ron, C. Viet.	18·05 N	106·45 E
68	Muir Woods Natl. Mon. (mūr) Calif.	37·54 N	123·22 W
166	Muizenberg (mwĭz-ĕn-bûrg') S. Afr. (Cape Town In.)	34·07 S	18·28 E
121	Mukachëvo (mōō-kȧ-chyô'vô) Sov. Un.	48·25 N	22·43 E
	Mukden, see Shenyang		
135	Mukhtuya (mōōk-tōō'yȧ) Sov. Un.	61·00 N	113·00 E
65	Mukilteo (mū-kĭl-tā'ō) Wash. (Seattle In.)	47·57 N	122·18 W
153	Muko (R.) (mōō'kô) Jap. (Ōsaka In.)	34·52 N	135·17 E
75	Mukwonago (mū-kwō-nȧ'gō) Wis. (Milwaukee In.)	42·52 N	88·19 W
124	Mula (mōō'lä) Sp.	38·05 N	1·12 W
120	Mulde R. (mōōl'dē) Ger.	50·30 N	12·30 E
150	Muleng China	44·32 N	130·18 E
150	Muleng (R.) China	44·40 N	130·30 E
90	Muleros (mōō-lā'rōs) Mex.	23·44 N	104·00 W
84	Mulga (mŭl'gȧ) Ala. (Birmingham In.)	33·33 N	86·59 W
83	Mulgrave (mŭl'grāv) Can.	45·37 N	61·22 W
159	Mulgrave (I.) Austl.	10·08 S	142·14 E
124	Mulhacén (Mtn.) Sp.	37·04 N	3·18 W
123	Mülheim (mül'hīm) Ger. (Ruhr In.)	51·25 N	6·53 E
123	Mulhouse (mü-lōōz') Fr.	47·46 N	7·20 E
116	Mull (I.) (mŭl) Scot.	56·40 N	6·19 W
66	Mullan (mŭl'ăn) Idaho	47·26 N	115·50 W
154	Müller Mts. (mül'ĕr) Indon.	0·22 N	113·05 E
116	Mullet Pen. Ire.	54·15 N	10·12 W
116	Mullinger (mŭl-ĭn-gär) Ire.	53·31 N	7·26 W
79	Mullins (mŭl'ĭnz) S. C.	34·11 N	79·13 W
92	Mullins River Br. Hond. (Yucatan In.)	17·08 N	88·18 W
142	Multan (mōōl-tän') W. Pak.	30·17 N	71·13 E
65	Multnomah Chan. (mŭl nō mȧ) Ore. (Portland In.)	45·41 N	122·53 W
154	Mulu, Gunung (Mtn.) Mala.	3·56 N	115·11 E
73	Mulvane (mŭl-vān') Kans.	37·30 N	97·13 W
166	Mumbwa (mōōm'bwä) N. Rh.	14·58 S	27·06 E
92	Muna (mōō'nä) Mex. (Yucatan In.)	20·28 N	89·42 W
111	München (Munich) (mün'kĕn) Ger. (Munich In.)	48·08 N	11·35 E
80	Muncie (mŭn'sĭ) Ind.	40·10 N	85·30 W
75	Mundelein (mŭn-dē-lĭn') Ill. (Chicago In.)	42·16 N	88·00 W
98	Mundonueva, Pico de (Pk.) (pē'kô-dĕ-mōō'n-dô-nwĕ'vä) Col. (In.)	4·18 N	74·12 W
91	Muneco, Cerro (Mtn.) (sĕ'r-rô-mōō-nĕ'kō) Mex. (Mexico City In.)	19·13 N	99·20 W
159	Mungana (mŭn-găn'ȧ) Austl.	17·15 S	144·18 E
74	Munger (mŭn'gẽr) Minn. (Duluth In.)	46·48 N	92·20 W
160	Mungindi (mŭn-gĭn'dē) Austl.	32·00 S	148·45 E
75	Munhall (mŭn'hôl) Pa. (Pittsburgh In.)	40·24 N	79·53 W
166	Munhanga (mōōn-häŋ'gȧ) Ang.	12·15 S	18·55 E
	Munich, see München		
71	Munising (mū'nĭ-sĭng) Mich.	46·24 N	86·41 W
134	Munku Sardyk (Mtn.) (mōōn'kōō sär-dĭk') Sov. Un.-Mong.	51·45 N	100·30 E
155	Muños (mōōn-nyōth') Phil. (Manila In.)	15·44 N	120·53 E
123	Münster (mün'stẽr) Ger. (Ruhr In.)	51·57 N	7·38 E
75	Munster (mŭn'stẽr) Ind. (Chicago In.)	41·34 N	87·31 W
116	Munster (mŭn-stẽr) Ire.	52·30 N	9·24 W
154	Muntok (mōōn-tŏk') Indon.	2·05 S	105·11 E
101	Munzi Freire (mōō-nē'z-frā'rĕ) Braz. (Rio de Janeiro In.)	20·29 S	41·25 W
154	Muong Sing (mōō'ông-sĭng') Laos	21·06 N	101·17 E
112	Muonio (R.) Fin.-Swe.	68·15 N	23·00 E
101	Muqui (mōō-kōōē) Braz. (Rio de Janeiro In.)	20·56 S	41·20 W
133	Muradiye (mōō-rä'dē-yĕ) Tur.	39·00 N	43·40 E
122	Murat (mü-rä') Fr.	45·05 N	2·56 E
133	Murat (R.) (mōō-rät') Tur.	38·50 N	40·40 E
158	Murchison (R.) (mûr'chĭ-sŭn) Austl.	26·45 S	116·15 E
165	Murchison Falls (mûr'chĭ-sŭn) Ug.	2·19 N	31·50 E
124	Murcia (mōōr'thyä) Sp.	38·00 N	1·10 W
124	Murcia (Reg.) Sp.	38·35 N	1·51 W
70	Murdo (mûr'dô) S. D.	43·53 N	100·42 W
82	Murdochville (mŭr-dŏk'vĭl) Can.	48·56 N	65·37 W
121	Muresul R. (mōō'rĕsh-ōōl) Rom.	46·02 N	21·50 E
122	Muret (mü-rĕ') Fr.	43·28 N	1·17 E
78	Murfreesboro (mûr'frēz-bŭr-ô) Tenn.	35·50 N	86·19 W
103	Murgab (R.) (mōōr-gäb') Sov. Un.	37·07 N	62·32 E
101	Muriaé (mōō-ryä-ĕ') Braz. (Rio de Janeiro In.)	21·10 S	42·21 W
101	Muriaé (R.) Braz. (Rio de Janeiro In.)	21·20 S	41·40 W
136	Murino (mōō'rĭ-nô) Sov. Un. (Leningrad In.)	60·03 N	30·28 E
120	Müritz See (L.) (mür'ĭts) Ger.	53·20 N	12·33 E
146	Murku Sardyk (Pk.) Sov. Un.-Mong.	51·56 N	100·21 E
132	Murmansk (mōōr-mänsk') Sov. Un.	69·00 N	33·20 E
132	Murom (mōō'rôm) Sov. Un.	55·30 N	42·00 E
152	Muroran (mōō'rô-rän) Jap.	42·21 N	141·05 E
124	Muros (mōō'rōs) Sp.	42·48 N	9·00 W
153	Muroto-Zaki (Pt.) (mōō'rô-tô zä'kē) Jap.	33·14 N	134·12 E
74	Murphy (mŭr'fĭ) Mo. (St. Louis In.)	38·29 N	90·29 W
78	Murphy N. C.	35·05 N	84·00 W
73	Murphysboro (mŭr'fĭz-bŭr-ô) Ill.	37·46 N	89·21 W
78	Murray (mŭr'ĭ) Ky.	36·39 N	88·17 W
74	Murray Utah (Salt Lake City In.)	40·40 N	111·53 W
79	Murray (R.) (mŭr'ĭ) S. C.	34·07 N	81·18 W
160	Murray Bridge Austl.	35·10 S	139·35 E
159	Murray Reg. (mŭ'rē) Austl.	33·20 S	142·30 E
160	Murray R. Austl.	34·12 S	141·20 E
120	Mur R. (mōōr) Aus.	47·10 N	14·08 E
160	Murrumbidgee (R.) (mŭr-ŭm-bĭd'jē) Austl.	34·30 S	145·20 E
142	Murshidabad (mōōr'shē-dä-bäd') India	24·08 N	87·11 E
126	Murska Sobota (mōōr'skä sô'bô-tä) Yugo.	46·40 N	16·14 E
142	Murwāra India	23·54 N	80·23 E
160	Murwillumbah (mŭr-wĭl'lŭm-bŭ) Austl.	28·15 S	153·30 E
120	Mürz R. (mürts) Aus.	47·30 N	15·21 E
165	Murzūq Libya	26·00 N	14·09 E
120	Murzzuschlag (mürts'tsōō-shlägh) Aus.	47·37 N	15·41 E
133	Mus (mōōsh) Tur.	38·55 N	41·30 E
127	Musala (Mtn.) Bul.	42·05 N	23·24 E
152	Musan (mōō'sän) Kor.	41·11 N	129·10 E
153	Musashino (mōō-sä'shē-nō) Jap. (Tōkyō In.)	35·43 N	139·35 E
144	Muscat (mŭs-kăt') Mus. & Om.	23·23 N	58·30 E
144	Muscat & Oman Asia	18·50 N	56·45 E
71	Muscatine (mŭs-kȧ-tēn') Iowa	41·26 N	91·00 W
78	Muscle Shoals (mŭs''l shōlz) Ala.	34·44 N	87·38 W
158	Musgrave Ra. (mŭs'grāv) Austl.	26·15 S	131·15 E
166	Mushie (mŭsh'ē) Con. L.	3·04 S	16·50 E
154	Musi, Air (Strm.) (mōō'sē) Indon.	2·40 S	103·42 E
98	Musinga, Alto (Ht.) (ȧ'l-tô-mōō-sĕ'n-gä) Col. (In.)	6·40 N	76·13 W
75	Muskego L. (mŭs-kē'gō) Wis. (Milwaukee In.)	42·53 N	88·10 W
80	Muskegon (mŭs-kē'gŭn) Mich.	43·15 N	86·20 W
80	Muskegon (R.) Mich.	43·20 N	85·55 W
80	Muskegon Heights Mich.	43·10 N	86·20 W
80	Muskingum (R.) (mŭs-kĭŋ'gŭm) Ohio	39·45 N	81·55 W
73	Muskogee (mŭs-kō'gē) Okla.	35·44 N	95·21 W
81	Muskoka (L.) (mŭs-kō'kȧ) Can.	45·00 N	79·30 W
155	Mussau (I.) (mōō-sä'ōō) N. Gui. Ter.	1·30 S	149·32 E
116	Musselburgh (mŭs''l-bŭr-ô) Scot.	55·55 N	3·08 W
67	Musselshell R. (mŭs''l-shĕl) Mont.	46·25 N	108·20 W
133	Mustafakemalpasa Tur.	40·05 N	28·30 E
77	Mustang Bay Tex. (In.)	29·22 N	95·12 W
72	Mustang Cr. (mŭs'tăng) Tex.	36·22 N	102·46 W
77	Mustang I. Tex.	27·43 N	97·00 W
93	Mustique I. (müs-tēk') N. A. (Le. & Wind. Is. In.)	12·53 N	61·03 W
128	Mustvee (mōōst'vĕ-ĕ) Sov. Un.	58·50 N	26·54 E
147	Musu Dan (C.) (mōō'sōō dän) Kor.	40·51 N	130·00 E
152	Musu Dan (Pt.) (mōō'sōō dän) Sov. Un.	40·48 N	129·50 E
160	Muswellbrook (mŭs'wŭl-brōōk) Austl.	32·15 S	150·50 E
150	Mutan (R.) China	45·30 N	129·40 E
150	Mutanchiang China	44·28 N	129·38 E
166	Mutombo Mukulu (mōō-tôm'bō mōō-kōō'lōō) Con. L.	8·12 S	23·56 E
152	Mutsu Wan (B.) (mōōt'sōō wän) Jap.	41·20 N	140·55 E
83	Mutton B. (mŭt''n) Can.	50·47 N	58·58 W
101	Mutum (mōō-tōō'm) Braz. (Rio de Janeiro In.)	19·48 S	41·24 W
134	Muyun-Kum, Peski (Des.) (mōō-yōōn' kōōm') Sov. Un.	44·30 N	70·00 E
142	Muzaffargarh W. Pak.	30·09 N	71·15 E
76	Muzquiz (mōōz'kēz) Mex.	27·53 N	101·31 W
166	Mwanza (mwän'zä) Tan.	2·31 S	32·52 E
167	Mwatate (mwä-tä'tä) Ken.	3·28 S	38·19 E
166	Mwaya (mwä'yä) Tan.	9·19 S	33·51 E
114	Mya R. (myä') Alg.	29·26 N	3·15 E
146	Myingyan (myĭng-yŭn') Bur.	21·37 N	95·26 E
154	Myinmoletkat (Pk.) Bur.	13·58 N	98·34 E
146	Myitkyina (myĭ'chē-nȧ) Bur.	25·33 N	97·25 E
121	Myjava (mûē'yȧ-vä) Czech.	48·45 N	17·33 E
142	Mymensingh (mī-mŭn-sĭng') E. Pak.	24·48 N	90·28 E
152	Myohyang San (Mtn.) (myō'hyang) Kor.	40·00 N	126·12 E
112	Mýrdalsjökull (Gl.) (mür'dȧls-yû'kōōl) Ice.	63·34 N	18·04 W
79	Myrtle Beach (mûr't'l) S. C.	33·42 N	78·53 W
84	Myrtle Grove (grōv) La. (New Orleans In.)	29·38 N	89·57 W
66	Myrtle Point Ore.	43·04 N	124·08 W
128	Myshkino (mêsh'kē-nô) Sov. Un.	57·48 N	38·21 E
143	Mysore (mī-sōr') India	12·31 N	76·42 E
143	Mysore (State) India	20·15 N	75·32 E
119	Mysovka (mē' sôf-kȧ) Sov. Un.	55·11 N	21·17 E
71	Mystic (mĭs'tĭk) Iowa	40·47 N	92·54 W
136	Mytishchi (mê-tēsh'chi) Sov. Un. (Moscow In.)	55·55 N	37·46 E
166	Mzimba ('m-zĭm'bä) Nya.	11·41 S	33·39 E
120	Naab R. (näp) Ger.	49·38 N	12·15 E
111	Naaldwijk. Neth. (Amsterdam In.)	52·00 N	4·11 E
164	Naama (nä'ä-mä) Lib.	7·18 N	9·31 W
119	Naantali (nän'tȧ-lē) Fin.	60·29 N	22·03 E
158	Nabberu (L.) (năb'ẽr-ōō) Austl.	26·05 S	120·35 E
164	Nabeul (nā-bûl') Tun.	36·34 N	10·45 E
168	Naboomspruit S. Afr. (Johannesburg & Pretoria In.)	24·32 S	28·43 E
139	Nābulus Jordan (Palestine In.)	32·13 N	35·16 E
167	Nacala (nä-kä'lȧ) Moz.	14·33 S	40·52 E
92	Nacaome (nä-kä-ō'mâ) Hond.	13·32 N	87·28 W
114	Naceur, Bou Mt. Mor.	33·50 N	3·55 W
151	Na Cham (nä chäm') Viet.	22·02 N	106·30 E
66	Naches R. (năch'ĕz) Wash.	46·51 N	121·03 W
120	Nachod (näk'ôt) Czech.	50·25 N	16·08 E
87	Nachvak Can.	59·08 N	63·57 W
68	Nacimiento (R.) (nȧ-sĭ-myĕn'tō) Calif.	35·50 N	121·00 W
77	Nacogdoches (năk'ô-dō'chĕz) Tex.	31·36 N	94·40 W
76	Nadadores (nä-dä-dō'räs) Mex.	27·04 N	101·36 W
142	Nadaid India	22·45 N	72·51 E
89	Nadir Vir. Is. (U. S. A.) (St. Thomas In.)	18·19 N	64·53 W
127	Nădlac Rom.	46·09 N	20·52 E
	Nad Nisou, see Jablonec		
	Nad Vahom, see Nové Mesto		
121	Nadvornaya (näd-vōōr'nȧ-yȧ) Sov. Un.	48·37 N	24·35 E
134	Nadym (R.) (nȧ'dĭm) Sov. Un.	64·30 N	72·48 E
118	Naestved (nĕst'vĭdh) Den.	55·14 N	11·46 E
168	Nafishah U. A. R.	30·34 N	32·15 E
155	Naga (nä'gä) Phil. (Manila In.)	13·37 N	123·12 E
153	Naga (I.) Jap.	32·09 N	130·16 E
153	Nagahama (nä'gä-hä'mä) Jap.	33·32 N	132·29 E
153	Nagahama Jap.	35·23 N	136·16 E
146	Nagaland (State) India	25·47 N	94·15 E
153	Nagano (nä'gä-nô) Jap.	36·42 N	138·12 E
153	Nagaoka (nä'gȧ-ō'kȧ) Jap.	37·22 N	138·49 E
143	Nagapatam India	10·48 N	79·51 E
92	Nagarote (nä-gä-rô'tĕ) Nic.	12·17 N	86·35 W
153	Nagasaki (nä'gȧ-sä'kē) Jap.	32·48 N	129·53 E
153	Nagasu (nä'gäs-ōō) Jap.	33·31 N	131·22 E
142	Nāgaur India	27·19 N	73·41 E
136	Nagaybakskiy (nȧ-gáy-bák'skĭ) Sov. Un. (Urals In.)	53·33 N	59·33 E
155	Nagcarlan (näg-kär-län') Phil. (Manila In.)	14·07 N	121·24 E
143	Nagercoil India	8·15 N	77·29 E
133	Nagornokarabakh (Reg.) (nu-gôr'nŭ-kŭ-rŭ-bäk') Sov. Un.	40·10 N	46·50 E
153	Nagoya (nä'gō'yȧ) Jap.	35·09 N	136·53 E
142	Nagpur (näg'pōōr) India	21·12 N	79·09 E
95	Nagua (nȧ'gwä) Dom. Rep.	19·20 N	69·40 W

ăt; finăl; rāte; senâte; ärm; àsk; sofȧ; fâre; ch-choose; dh-as th in other; bē; ēvent; bĕt; recĕnt; cratẽr; g-go; gh-guttural g; bĭt; ĭ-short neutral; rīde; K-guttural k as ch in German ich;

Page	Name Pronunciation Region	Lat. °′	Long. °′
155	Naguilian (nä-gwê-lē'än) Phil. (Manila In.)	16·33 N	120·23 E
120	Nagykanizsa (nôd'y'kô'nê-shô) Hung.	46·27 N	17·00 E
121	Nagykörös (nôd'y'kŭ'rŭsh) Hung.	47·02 N	19·46 E
152	Naha (nä'hä) ... Ryūkyū Is.	26·02 N	127·43 E
83	Nahant (nȧ-hănt) Mass. (Boston In.)	42·26 N	70·55 W
139	Nahariya ... Isr. (Palestine In.)	33·01 N	35·06 E
133	Nahr al Khābur (R.) ... U. A. R.	35·50 N	41·00 E
125	Nahr-Ouassel (R.) (när-wä-sěl') Alg.	35·30 N	1·55 E
100	Nahuel Huapi (L.) (nä'wål wä'pê) Arg.	41·00 S	71·30 W
92	Nahuizalco (nä-wê-zäl'kō) ... Sal.	13·50 N	89·43 W
155	Naic (nä'ēk) ... Phil. (Manila In.)	14·20 N	120·46 E
76	Naica (nä-ē'kä) ... Mex.	27·53 N	105·30 W
99	Naiguatá (nī-gwä-tȧ') .. Ven. (In.)	10·37 N	66·44 W
99	Naiguata, Pico (Mtn.) (pē'kô) Ven. (In.)	10·32 N	66·44 W
142	Naihāti ... India (Calcutta In.)	22·54 N	88·25 E
87	Nain (nīn) ... Can.	56·29 N	61·52 W
84	Nairn (nărn) La. (New Orleans In.)	29·27 N	89·37 W
116	Nairn (nârn) ... Scot.	57·35 N	3·54 W
167	Nairobi (nī-rō'bê) ... Ken.	1·18 S	36·47 E
167	Naivasha (nī-vä'shȧ) ... Ken.	0·47 S	36·29 E
144	Najd (Des.) ... Sau. Ar.	25·18 N	42·38 E
168	Naj 'Ḥammādi (näg'hä-mä'dê) U. A. R. (Nile In.)	26·02 N	32·12 E
152	Najin (nä'jĭn) ... Kor.	42·04 N	136·06 E
144	Najran (Des.) (nŭj-rän') . Sau. Ar.	17·29 N	45·30 E
152	Naju (nä'jōō') ... Kor.	35·02 N	126·42 E
94	Najusa (R.) (nä-hōō'sä) ... Cuba	21·55 N	77·55 W
150	Nakadorishima (I.) (nä'kä'dô'rê-shê'mä) . Jap.	33·00 N	128·20 E
165	Nak'amet ... Eth.	9·09 N	36·29 E
153	Nakatsu (nä'käts-ōō) ... Jap.	33·34 N	131·10 E
133	Nakhichevan' (nȧ-ᴋē-chě-vȧn') Sov. Un.	49·10 N	45·30 E
135	Nakhodka (nŭ-ᴋôt'kŭ) ... Sov. Un.	43·03 N	133·08 E
154	Nakhon Ratchasima ... Thai.	14·56 N	102·14 E
154	Nakhon Si Thammarat ... Thai.	8·27 N	99·58 E
87	Nakina ... Can.	50·10 N	86·40 W
118	Nakskov (näk'skou) ... Den.	54·51 N	11·06 E
121	Nakto nad Notecia (näk'wō näd nō-tě'chōɴ).Pol.	53·10 N	17·35 E
152	Naktong (R.) (näk'tŭng) ... Kor.	36·10 N	128·30 E
133	Nal'chik (nȧl-chēk') ... Sov. Un.	43·30 N	43·35 E
124	Nalón (R.) (nä-lōn') ... Sp.	43·15 N	5·38 W
164	Nālūt (nä-lōōt') ... Libya	31·51 N	10·49 E
144	Namak, Daryacheh-ye (L.) .. Iran	34·58 N	51·33 E
71	Namakan (L.) (nă'mȧ-kȧn) . Minn.	48·20 N	92·43 W
166	Namakwaland (Reg.) (nă-mä'kwă'lănd) . S. W. Afr.	25·30 S	16·30 E
144	Namakzār E Shahdād (L.) (nŭ-mŭk-zär') . Iran	31·20 N	57·59 E
134	Namangan (nȧ-mȧn-gän') Sov. Un.	41·08 N	71·59 E
85	Namao ... Can. (Edmonton In.)	53·43 N	113·30 W
155	Namatanai (nä'mä-tȧ-nä'ê) N. Gui. Ter.	3·43 S	152·26 E
69	Nambe Pueblo Ind. Res. (näm'bå pwěb'lô) . N. Mex.	35·52 N	105·39 W
160	Nambour (năm'bŏŏr) ... Austl.	26·48 S	153·00 E
154	Nam Dinh (näm dēnᴋ') ... Viet.	20·30 N	106·10 E
74	Nameoki (nă'mē-ō-kē) Ill. (St. Louis In.)	38·44 N	90·07 W
152	Namhae (I.) (näm'hī') ... Kor.	34·23 N	128·05 E
166	Namib Des. (nä-mēb') .. S. W. Afr.	24·00 S	15·00 E
160	Namoi (R.) (năm'oi) ... Austl.	30·10 S	148·43 E
114	Namous, Oued en (R.) (nȧ-mōōs') Alg.	31·48 N	00·19 W
66	Nampa (năm'pȧ) ... Idaho	43·35 N	116·35 W
112	Namsos (näm'sôs) ... Nor.	64·28 N	11·14 E
142	Nam Tsho (L.) ... China	30·30 N	91·10 E
117	Namur (nȧ-mür') ... Bel.	50·29 N	4·55 E
166	Namutoni (nȧ-mōō-tō'nê) S. W. Afr.	18·45 S	17·00 E
154	Nan, Mae Nam (R.) ... Thai.	18·11 N	100·29 E
91	Nanacamilpa (nä-nä-kä-mê'l-pä) Mex. (Mexico City In.)	19·30 N	98·33 W
66	Nanaimo (nȧ-nī'mō) ... Can.	49·09 N	123·57 W
152	Nanam (nä'nän') ... Kor.	41·38 N	129·37 E
153	Nanao (nä'nä-ō) ... Jap.	37·03 N	136·59 E
151	Nanao Tao (I.) (nä'nä-ō dou) China	23·30 N	117·30 E
151	Nanch'ang (nän'chäng') ... China	28·38 N	115·48 E
151	Nancheng ... China	26·50 N	116·40 E
150	Nancheng ... China	33·02 N	107·00 E
148	Nanch'enghuang Tai (I.) (naɴ'chěng'hōōäɴg'dou) . China	38·22 N	120·54 E
148	Nanching (Nanking) (nän'jĭng) (nän'kĭng) . China	32·04 N	118·46 E
151	Nanch'ung ... China	30·45 N	106·05 E
123	Nancy (näɴ-sē') ... Fr.	48·42 N	6·11 E
84	Nancy Cr. (năn'cē) Ga. (Atlanta In.)	33·51 N	84·25 W
142	Nanda Devi (Mt.) (nän'dä dā'vē) India	30·30 N	80·25 E
142	Nander ... India	19·13 N	77·21 E
142	Nandurbār ... India	21·29 N	74·13 E
143	Nandyal ... India	15·54 N	78·09 E
142	Nanga Parbat (Pk.) ... India	40·05 N	74·35 E
123	Nangis (näɴ-zhē') .. Fr. (Paris In.)	48·33 N	3·01 E
149	Nanhai (Fatshan) China (Canton In.)	23·02 N	113·07 E
149	Nanhsiang .. China (Shanghai In.)	31·17 N	121·17 E
151	Nanhsiung ... China	25·10 N	114.20 E
149	Nanhui ... China (Shanghai In.)	31·03 N	121·45 E
148	Naniana ... China	35·14 N	116·24 E
151	Nani Dinh ... Viet.	20·25 N	106·08 E
148	Nani Hu (L.) (näɴ'yi' hōō) . China	31·12 N	119·05 E
	Nanking, see Nanching		
148	Nankung (nän'kŏŏng') ... China	37·22 N	115·22 E
151	Nan Ling (Mtns.) ... China	25·15 N	111·40 E
148	Nanlo (nän'lō') ... China	36·03 N	115·13 E
158	Nannine (nă-nēn') ... Austl.	26·50 S	118·30 E
151	Nanning (nän'nĭng') ... China	22·56 N	108·10 E
151	Nanp'an (R.) ... China	24·50 N	105·30 E
151	Nanpling ... China	26·40 N	118·05 E
84	Nansemond (năn'sê-mŭnd) Va. (Norfolk In.)	36·46 N	76·32 W
84	Nansemond R. . Va. (Norfolk In.)	36·50 N	76·34 W
146	Nan Shan (Mts.)(nän'shän').China	38·43 N	98·00 E
153	Nantai Zan (Mtn.) (nän-täê zän) Jap.	36·47 N	139·28 E
122	Nantes (näɴt') ... Fr.	47·13 N	1·37 W
123	Nanteuil-le-Haudouin (näɴ-tû-lĕ-ō-dwȧɴ') . Fr. Paris In.)	49·08 N	2·49 E
81	Nanticoke (năn'tī-kōk) ... Pa.	41·10 N	76·00 W
81	Nantucket (I.) (năn-tŭk'ĕt) . Mass.	41·15 N	70·05 W
148	Nantung (nän'tŏŏng') ... China	32·02 N	120·51 E
110	Nantwich (nănt'wĭch) ... Eng.	53·04 N	2·31 W
150	Nanyang ... China	33·00 N	112·42 E
150	Nanyüan ... China (Peking In.)	39·48 N	116·24 E
148	Nanyün (näɴ'yün') ... China	38·11 N	116·37 E
151	Nao Chou (I.) ... China	20·58 N	110·58 E
91	Naolinco (nä-ō-lēŋ'kō) ... Mex.	19·39 N	96·50 W
84	Naomi (nă-ō'mĭ) La. (New Orleans In.)	29·42 N	89·59 W
127	Náousa (nä'ōō-sȧ) ... Grc.	40·38 N	22·05 E
68	Napa (năp'ȧ) ... Calif.	38·20 N	122·17 W
81	Napanee (năp'ȧ-nē) ... Can.	44·15 N	77·00 W
75	Naperville (nā'pēr-vĭl) Ill. (Chicago In.)	41·46 N	88·09 W
159	Napier (nā'pĭ-ēr) ... N. Z. (In.)	39·30 S	177·00 E
85	Napierville (nā'pĭ-ēr-vĭl) Can. (Montreal In.)	45·11 N	73·24 W
79	Naples (nă'p'lz) ... Fla. (In.)	26·07 N	81·46 W
	Naples, see Napoli		
98	Napo (R.) (nä'pō) ... Peru	1·49 S	74·20 W
80	Napoleon (nȧ-pō'lē-ŭn) ... Ohio	41·20 N	84·10 W
77	Napoleonville (nȧ-pō'lê-ŭn-vĭl).La.	29·56 N	91·03 W
125	Napoli (Naples) (nä'pô-lē) It. (Naples In.)	40·37 N	14·12 E
125	Napoli, Golfo di (G.) (gôl-fô-dē) . It. (Napoli In.)	40·29 N	14·08 E
80	Nappanee (năp'ȧ-nē) ... Ind.	41·30 N	86·00 W
153	Nara (nä'rä) ... Jap. (Osaka In.)	34·41 N	135·50 E
164	Nara ... Mali	15·09 N	7·27 W
153	Nara (Pref.) ... Jap. (Osaka In.)	34·36 N	135·49 E
128	Nara (R.) ... Sov. Un.	55·05 N	37·16 E
160	Naracoorte (nȧ-rȧ-kōōn'tê) . Austl.	36·50 S	140·50 E
143	Naraspur ... India	16·32 N	81·43 E
84	Narberth (när'bûrth) Pa. (Philadelphia In.)	40·01 N	75·17 W
122	Narbonne (nȧr-bôn') ... Fr.	43·12 N	3·00 E
127	Nardò (när-dô') ... It.	40·11 N	18·02 E
98	Nare (nä'rě) ... Col. (In.)	6·12 N	74·37 W
121	Narew R. (nä'rĕf) ... Pol.	52·43 N	21·19 E
142	Narmada (R.) ... India	22·17 N	74·45 E
128	Naroch' (L.) (nä'rôch) ... Sov. Un.	54·51 N	27·00 E
132	Narodnaya, Gora (Mtn.) (nȧ-rôd'nȧ-yȧ) . Sov. Un.	65·10 N	60·10 E
128	Naro Fominsk (nä'rô-fô-mēnsk') Sov. Un.	55·23 N	36·43 E
119	Närpeså (R.) ... Fin.	62·35 N	21·24 E
161	Narrabeen (năr-ȧ-bĭn) Austl. (Sydney In.)	33·44 S	151·18 E
160	Narrabri (nä-rä'brê) ... Austl.	30·17 S	149·46 E
84	Narragansett (năr-ă-găn'sĕt) R. I. (Providence In.)	41·26 N	71·27 W
81	Narragansett B ... R. I.	41·20 N	71·15 W
160	Narrandera (nȧ-rȧn-dē'rȧ) .. Austl.	34·40 S	146·40 E
158	Narrogin (năr'ô-gĭn) ... Austl.	33·00 S	117·15 E
128	Narva (nȧr'vȧ) ... Sov. Un.	59·24 N	28·12 E
155	Narvacan (när-vä-kän') Phil. (Manila In.)	17·27 N	120·29 E
128	Narva Jõesuu (nȧr'vȧ ŏŏ-ô-ă'sōō-ŏŏ) . Sov. Un.	59·26 N	28·02 E
112	Narvik (när'vêk) ... Nor.	68·21 N	17·18 E
119	Narvskiy Zaliv (B.) (nȧr'vskĭ zä'lĭf) . Sov. Un.	59·35 N	27·25 E
132	Nar'yan-Mar (när'yȧn mär') Sov. Un.	67·42 N	53·30 E
160	Naryilco (năr-ĭl'kô) ... Austl.	28·40 S	141·50 E
134	Narym (nä-rēm') ... Sov. Un.	58·47 N	82·05 E
145	Naryn (R.) (nŭ-rĭn') ... Sov. Un.	41·46 N	73·00 E
110	Naseby (nāz'bĭ) ... Eng.	52·23 N	0·59 W
74	Nashua (năsh'ŭ-ȧ) Mo. (Kansas City In.)	39·18 N	94·34 W
83	Nashua ... N. H. (Boston In.)	42·47 N	71·23 W
73	Nashville (năsh'vĭl) ... Ark.	33·56 N	93·50 W
78	Nashville ... Ga.	31·12 N	83·15 W
73	Nashville ... Ill.	38·21 N	89·42 W
80	Nashville ... Mich.	42·35 N	85·05 W
78	Nashville ... Tenn.	36·10 N	86·48 W
71	Nashwauk (năsh'wôk) ... Minn.	47·21 N	93·12 W
127	Našice (nä'shê-tsě) ... Yugo.	45·29 N	18·06 E
121	Nasielsk (nä'syělsk) ... Pol.	52·35 N	20·50 E
142	Nāsik (nä'sĭk) ... India	20·02 N	73·49 E
165	Nasir (nä-zēr') ... Sud.	8·30 N	33·06 E
142	Nasirabād ... India	26·13 N	74·48 E
87	Naskaupi (R.) (năs'kô-pĭ) ... Can.	53·59 N	61·10 W
94	Nassau (năs'ô) ... Ba. Is.	25·05 N	77·20 W
155	Nassau-Gebergte (Mts.) .. W. Irian	3·48 S	136·45 E
111	Nassenheide (nä'sěn-hī-dě) Ger. (Berlin In.)	52·49 N	13·13 E
118	Nässjö (něs'shû) ... Swe.	57·39 N	14·39 E
155	Nasugbu (nȧ-sŏŏg-bōō') Phil. (Manila In.)	14·05 N	120·37 E
76	Nasworthy L. (năz'wûr-thê) .. Tex.	31·17 N	100·30 W
151	Nata ... China	19·30 N	109·38 E
93	Natá (nä-tȧ') ... Pan.	8·20 N	8·30 W
98	Natagaima (nä-tä-gī'mä) . Col. (In.)	3·38 N	75·07 W
99	Natal (nä-täl') ... Braz.	6·00 S	35·13 W
166	Natal (Prov.) (nȧ-täl') ... S. Afr.	28·50 S	30·07 E
83	Natashguan (nä-tăsh'kwän) .. Can.	50·09 N	61·46 W
87	Natashguan (R.) ... Can.	51·34 N	61·46 W
78	Natchez (năch'ĕz) ... Miss.	31·35 N	91·20 W
77	Natchitoches (năk'ĭ-tŏsh) (nȧch-ĭ-tōsh') . La.	31·46 N	93·06 W
139	Nathanya ... Isr. (Palestine In.)	32·19 N	34·52 E
83	Natick (nā'tĭk) . Mass. (Boston In.)	42·17 N	71·21 W
135	National Area (Reg.) ... Sov. Un.	66·30 N	170·30 E
67	National Bison Ra. (Mts.) (năsh'ŭn-ăl bī's'n) . Mont.	47·18 N	113·58 W
68	National City Calif. (San Diego In.)	32·38 N	117·01 W
85	Nation R. (nā'shŭn) Can. (Ottawa In.)	45·21 N	75·07 W
99	Natividade (nä-tê-vê-dä'dĕ) . Braz.	11·43 S	47·34 W
75	Natrona (nā'trŏ nā) Pa. (Pittsburgh In.)	40·38 N	79·43 W
166	Natron L. (nā'trŏn) ... Tan.	2·29 S	35·17 E
168	Natrum, Wadi el (Val.) U. A. R. (Nile In.)	30·33 N	30·12 E
154	Natuna, Pulau-Pulau (Is.) . Indon.	3·22 N	108·00 E
69	Natural Bridges Natl. Mon. (năt'û-răl brĭj'ĕs) . Utah	37·20 N	110·20 W
158	Naturaliste, C. (năt-û-rȧ-lĭst') Austl.	33·30 S	115·10 E
91	Naucalpan (nä'ōō-käl-pȧ'n) Mex. (Mexico City In.)	19·28 N	99·14 W
91	Nauchampatepetl (Mtn.) (näōō-chäm-pä-tě'pětl) . Mex.	19·32 N	97·09 W
82	Naudville ... Can.	48·36 N	71·40 W
111	Nauen (nou'ĕn) .. Ger. (Berlin In.)	52·36 N	12·53 E
81	Naugatuck (nô'gȧ-tŭk) ... Conn.	41·25 N	73·05 W
155	Naujan (nä-ŏŏ-hän') Phil. (Manila In.)	13·19 N	121·17 E
120	Naumburg (noum'bŏŏrgh) ... Ger.	51·10 N	11·50 E
156	Nauru I ... Oceania	0·30 S	167·00 E
91	Nautla (nä-ōōt'lä) ... Mex.	20·14 N	96·44 W
76	Nava (nä'vä) ... Mex.	28·25 N	100·44 W
124	Nava, L. de la ... Sp.	42·05 N	4·42 W
124	Nava del Rey (nä-vä děl rā'ê) . Sp.	41·22 N	5·04 W
124	Navahermosa (nä-vä-ĕr-mō'sä).Sp.	39·39 N	4·28 W
94	Navajas (nä-vä-häs') ... Cuba	22·40 N	81·20 W
69	Navajo Ind. Res. (năv'ȧ-hō) Ariz.-N. Mex.	36·31 N	109·24 W
69	Navajo Natl. Mon. ... Ariz.	36·43 N	110·39 W
69	Navajo Res ... N. Mex.	36·57 N	107·26 W
125	Navalcarnero (nä-väl'kär-nā'rō) Sp. (Madrid In.)	40·17 N	4·05 W
124	Navalmoral de la Mata (nä-väl'mōräl' dā lä mä'tä) . Sp.	39·53 N	5·32 W
85	Navan (nă'vȧn) . Can. (Ottawa In.)	45·25 N	75·26 W
100	Navarino (nȧ-vä-rê'nô) (I.) .. Chile	55·30 S	68·15 W
124	Navarra (Reg.) (nä-vär'rä) ... Sp.	42·40 N	1·35 W
101	Navarro (nä-vȧ'r-rō) Arg. (Buenos Aires In.)	35·00 S	59·16 W
77	Navasota (năv-ȧ-sō'tȧ) ... Tex.	30·24 N	96·05 W
77	Navasota R ... Tex.	31·03 N	96·11 W
95	Navassa (I.) (nȧ-vȧs'ȧ) ... N. A.	18·25 N	75·15 W
124	Navia (R.) (nä-vē'ä) ... Sp.	43·10 N	6·45 W
101	Navidad (nä-vê-dä'd) Chile (Santiago In.)	34·57 S	71·51 W
95	Navidad Bk. (nä-vê-dädh') . Ba. Is.	20·05 N	69·00 W
101	Navidade do Carangola (nȧ-vē-dä'dě-dô-kȧ-rän-gô'la) Braz. (Rio de Janeiro In.)	21·04 S	41·58 W
88	Navojoa (nä-vô-kô'ä) ... Mex.	27·00 N	109·40 W
127	Návplion ... Grc.	37·33 N	22·46 E
142	Nawābshāh (nȧ-wäb'shä) . W. Pak.	26·20 N	68·30 E
145	Nawagai (nŭ-wŭ-gī') W. Pak. (Khyber Pass In.)	34·40 N	71·18 E
127	Náxos (I.) (nȧk'sôs) ... Grc.	37·15 N	25·20 E
88	Nayarit (State) (nä-yä-rēt') . Mex.	22·00 N	105·15 W
90	Nayarit, Sierra de (Mts.) (sē-ĕ'r-rä-dě) . Mex.	23·20 N	105·07 W
99	Nazaré (nä-zä-rě') ... Braz.	13·04 S	38·49 W
124	Nazaré (nä-zä-rā') ... Port.	39·38 N	9·04 W
99	Nazaré da Mata (dä-mä-tä) . Braz.	7·46 S	35·13 W
139	Nazareth (năz'ȧ-rěth) Isr. (Palestine In.)	32·43 N	35·19 E
76	Nazas (nä'zäs) ... Mex.	25·14 N	104·08 W
76	Nazas, R ... Mex.	25·08 N	104·20 W
133	Nazilli (nȧ-zĭ-lē') ... Tur.	37·40 N	28·10 E
136	Naziya R. (nȧ-zē'yȧ) Sov. Un. (Leningrad In.)	59·48 N	31·18 E
165	Ndélé (n'dā-lā') ... Cen. Afr. Rep.	8·21 N	20·43 E
166	Ndjolé (n'dzhô-lā') ... Gabon	0·15 S	10·45 E
166	Ndola (n'dō'lä) ... N. Rh.	12·52 S	28·44 E
116	Neagh Lough (B.) (lŏk nā) . N. Ire.	54·40 N	6·47 W
161	Neapean (R.) . Austl. (Sydney In.)	33·40 S	150·39 E
127	Neápolis (nå-ŏp' ô-lĭs) ... Grc.	36·35 N	23·08 E
126	Neápolis ... Grc. (In.)	35·17 N	25·37 E
64	Near Is. (nēr) ... Alaska	52·20 N	172·40 E
116	Neath (nēth) ... Wales	51·41 N	3·50 W
160	Nebine Cr. (nĕ-bēne') ... Austl.	27·50 S	147·00 E
133	Nebit-Dag (nyĕ-bēt'däg') . Sov. Un.	39·30 N	54·20 E
62	Nebraska (State) (nê-brăs'kȧ) U. S.	41·45 N	101·30 W
73	Nebraska City ... Nebr.	40·40 N	95·50 W
77	Neches R. (nĕch'ĕz) ... Tex.	31·03 N	94·40 W
120	Neckar R. (nĕk'är) ... Ger.	49·16 N	9·06 E
100	Necochea (nā-kô-chā'ä) ... Arg.	38·30 S	58·45 W
129	Nedrigaylov (nĕ-drĭ-gī'lôf). Sov. Un.	50·49 N	33·52 E
83	Needham (nēd'ăm) Mass. (Boston In.)	42·17 N	71·14 W
68	Needles (nē'd'lz) ... Calif.	34·51 N	114·39 W
71	Neenah (nē'nȧ) ... Wis.	44·10 N	88·30 W
86	Neepawa ... Can.	50·17 N	99·31 W
72	Nee Res. (nĕĕ) ... Colo.	38·26 N	102·56 W
117	Neetze (R.) (nĕ'tzĕ) ... Ger.	53·04 N	11·00 E
153	Negareyama (nå'gä-rå-yä'mä) Jap. (Tōkyō In.)	35·52 N	139·54 E
71	Negaunee (nê-gô'nê) ... Mich.	46·30 N	87·37 W
139	Negev (Des.) (nĕ'gĕv) Isr. (Palestine In.)	30·34 N	34·43 E
127	Negoi (Mtn.) (nā-goi') ... Rom.	45·33 N	24·38 E
143	Negombo ... Ceylon	7·39 N	79·49 E
127	Negotin (nĕ'gô-tên) ... Yugo.	44·13 N	22·33 E
154	Negrais, C. (nĕ'grīs) ... Bur.	16·08 N	93·34 E

ng-sing; ŋ-baŋk; ɴ-nasalized n; nŏd; cŏmmit; ōld; ôbey; ôrder; fōōd; fŏŏt; ou-out; s-soft; sh-dish; th-thin; pūre; ûnite; ûrn; stŭd; circŭs; ü-as "y" in study; '-indeterminate vowel.

ăt; finál; rāte; senâte; ärm; àsk; sofá; fâre; ch-choose; dh-as th in other; bē; ĕvent; bĕt; recĕnt; cratēr; g-go; gh-guttural g; bĭt; ɪ-short neutral; rīde; κ-guttural k as ch in German ich;

ng-sing; ŋ-baŋk; N-nasalized n; nŏd; cŏmmit; ōld; ŏbey; ôrder; fōōd; fŏŏt; ou-out; s-soft; sh-dish; th-thin; pūre; ūnite; ûrn; stŭd; circ̬us; ū-as "y" in study; '-indeterminate vowel.

ăt; finăl; rāte; senăte; ärm; ȧsk; sofȧ; fâre; ch-choose; dh-as th in other; bē; ĕvent; bĕt; recĕnt; cratēr; g-go; gh-guttural g; bĭt; ĭ-short neutral; rīde; ĸ-guttural k as ch in German ich;

PRONOUNCING INDEX Nowy Dwor Mazowiecki–Oglio 245

Page	Name Pronunciation Region	Lat. °′	Long. °′
121	Nowy Dwór Mazowiecki (nō′vĭ dvōōr mä-zō-vyĕts′ke) Pol.	52·26 N	20·46 E
121	Nowy Sacz (nô′vê sônch′) Pol.	49·36 N	20·42 E
121	Nowy Targ (tärk′) Pol.	49·29 N	20·02 E
66	Noxon Res. Mont.	47·50 N	115·40 W
78	Noxubee (R.) (nŏks′ū-bē) Miss.	33·20 N	88·55 W
124	Noya (nō′yä) Sp.	42·46 N	8·50 W
153	Nozaki (nō′zä-kê) Jap. (Ōsaka In.)	34·43 N	135·39 E
167	Nqamakwe (′n-gä-mä′kwå) S. Afr. (Natal In.)	32·13 S	27·57 E
167	Nqutu (′n-kōō′tōō) S. Afr. (Natal In.)	28·17 S	30·41 E
165	Nubian Des. (nōō′bĭ-ăn) Sud.	21·13 N	33·09 E
98	Nudo Coropuna (Mt.) (nōō′dô kō-rō-pōō′nä) Peru	15·53 S	72·04 W
98	Nudo de Pasco (Mt.) (dĕ päs′kô) Peru	10·34 S	76·12 W
76	Nueces R. (nû-ā′sås) Tex.	28·20 N	98·08 W
86	Nueltin (L.) (nwĕl′tin) Can.	60·14 N	101·00 W
92	Nueva Armenia (nwā′vä är-mā′nê-ä) Hond.	15·47 N	86·32 W
99	Nueva Esparta (State) (nwĕ′vä ĕs-pä′r-tä) Ven. In.	10·50 N	64·35 W
94	Nueva Gerona (kĕ-rō′nä) Cuba	21·55 N	82·45 W
101	Nueva Palmira (päl-mē′rä) Ur. (Buenos Aires In.)	33·53 S	58·23 W
62	Nueva Rosita (nōōĕ′vä rô-sē′tä) Mex.	27·55 N	101·10 W
92	Nueva San Salvador (Santa Tecla) (sän′ säl-vä-dōr) (sän′tä tĕ′klä) Sal.	13·41 N	89·16 W
101	Nueve de Julio (nwā′vå dā hōō′lyô) Arg. (Buenos Aires In.)	35·26 S	60·51 W
94	Nuevitas (nwā-vē′täs) Cuba	21·35 N	77·15 W
94	Nuevitas, Bahía de (bä-ē′ä dĕ nwā-vē′täs) Cuba	21·30 N	77·05 W
74	Nuevo (nwā′vō) Calif. (Los Angeles In.)	33·48 N	117·09 W
76	Nuevo Laredo (lä-rā′dhō) Mex.	27·29 N	99·30 W
88	Nuevo Leon (State) (lå-ōn′) Mex.	26·00 N	100·00 W
88	Nuevo San Juan (nwĕ′vô sän kōō-ä′n) C. Z. (Panama Canal In.)	9·14 N	79·43 W
136	Nugumanovo (nû-gû-mä′nô-vô) Sov. Un. (Urals In.)	55·28 N	61·50 E
133	Nukha (nōō′kä) Sov. Un.	41·10 N	47·10 E
64	Nulato (nōō-lä′tō) Alaska	64·40 N	158·18 W
158	Nullagine (nŭ-lă′jēn) Austl.	22·00 S	120·07 E
158	Nullarbor Plain, (Reg.) (nŭ-lär′bôr) Austl.	31·45 S	126·30 E
111	Numansdorp Neth. (Amsterdam In.)	51·43 N	4·25 E
153	Numazu (nōō′mä-zōō) Jap.	35·06 N	138·55 E
101	No. 1, Canal Arg. (Buenos Aires In.)	36·43 S	58·14 W
101	No. 9, Canal Arg. (Buenos Aires In.)	36·22 S	58·19 W
101	No. 12, Canal Arg. (Buenos Aires In.)	36·47 S	57·20 W
167	Numolani Bas. (Natal In.)	29·06 S	28·59 E
110	Nuneaton (nŭn′ē-tŭn) Eng.	52·31 N	1·28 W
150	Nungan China	44·25 N	125·10 E
64	Nunivak (I.) (nōō′nĭ-văk) Alaska	60·25 N	167·42 W
92	Nunkiní (nōōn-kē-nē′) Mex. (Yucatan In.)	20·19 N	90·14 W
64	Nunyama (nûn-yä′mȧ) Sov. Un.	65·49 N	170·32 W
126	Nuoro (nwô′rō) It.	40·29 N	9·20 E
134	Nura (R.) (nōō′rä) Sov. Un.	49·48 N	73·54 E
134	Nurata (nōōr′ät′ȧ) Sov. Un.	40·33 N	65·28 E
120	Nürnberg (nürn′bĕrgh) Ger.	49·28 N	11·07 E
95	Nurse Cay (I.) Ba. Is.	22·30 N	75·50 W
133	Nusabyin (nōō′sĭ-bên) Tur.	37·05 N	41·10 E
64	Nushagak (R.) (nū-shă-găk′) Alaska	59·28 N	157·40 W
148	Nushan Hu (L.) (nū′shän hōō) China	32·50 N	117·59 E
145	Nushki (nŭsh′kê) W. Pak.	29·30 N	66·02 E
111	Nuthe R. (nōō′tê) Ger. (Berlin In.)	52·15 N	13·11 E
84	Nutley (nŭt′lê) N. J. (New York In.)	40·49 N	74·09 W
81	Nutter Fort (nŭt′ĕr fôrt) W. Va.	39·15 N	80·15 W
74	Nutwood (nŭt′wŏŏd) Ill. (St. Louis In.)	39·05 N	90·34 W
139	Nuwaybi ′al Muzayyinah U. A. R. (Palestine In.)	28·59 N	34·40 E
84	Nyack (nī′ăk) N. Y. (New York In.)	41·05 N	73·55 W
165	Nyala Sud.	12·00 N	24·52 E
166	Nyangwe (nyăng′wā) Con. L.	4·09 S	26·16 E
166	Nyasa, L. (nyä′sä) Tan.-Moz.	11·32 S	35·15 E
166	Nyasaland (nyä′sä-lănd) Afr.	11·15 S	33·45 E
136	Nyazepetrovsk (nyȧ′zĕ-pĕ-trôvsk′) Sov. Un. (Urals In.)	56·04 N	59·38 E
118	Nyborg (nü′bôr″) Den.	55·20 N	10·45 E
118	Nybro (nü′brō) Swe.	56·44 N	15·56 E
146	Nyenchhen Thanglha (Mts.) China	29·55 N	88·08 E
118	Nyhem (nü′hĕm) Swe.	56·39 N	12·50 E
121	Nyiregyháza (nyē′rĕd-y′hä′zä) Hung.	47·58 N	21·45 E
118	Nykøbing (nü′kû-bĭng) Den.	56·46 N	8·47 E
118	Nykøbing Falster Den.	54·45 N	11·54 E
118	Nykøbing Sjaelland Den.	55·55 N	11·37 E
118	Nyköping (nü′chû-pĭng) Swe.	58·46 N	16·58 E
168	Nyl R. (nĭl) S. Afr. (Johannesburg & Pretoria In.)	24·30 S	28·55 E
168	Nylstroom (nĭl′strōm) S. Afr. (Johannesburg & Pretoria In.)	24·42 S	28·25 E
160	Nymagee (nī-mȧ-gē′) Austl.	32·17 S	146·18 E
120	Nymburk (nĕm′bŏŏrk) Czech.	50·12 N	15·03 E
116	Nymphe Bk. (nĭmpf) Ire.	51·36 N	7·35 W
118	Nynashamn (nü-nĕs-häm′n) Swe.	58·53 N	17·55 E
160	Nyngan (nĭŋ′găn) Austl.	31·31 S	147·25 E
164	Nyong R. (nyông) Cam.	3·41 N	12·21 E
120	Nýrány (nĕr-zhä′nê) Czech.	49·43 N	13·13 E
121	Nysa (nē′sȧ) Pol.	50·29 N	17·20 E
	Nystad, see Uusikaupunki		
132	Nytva Sov. Un.	58·00 N	55·10 E
135	Nyuya (R.) (nyōō′yȧ) Sov. Un.	60·30 N	111·45 E
70	Oahe Dam (ō-ȧ-hē) S. D.	44·28 N	100·34 W
70	Oahe Res. S. Dak.	45·20 N	100·00 W
157	Oahu (I.) (ō-ä′hōō) (ō-ä′hú) Hawaii (In.)	21·38 N	157·48 W
85	Oak Bluff (ōk blŭf) Can. (Winnipeg In.)	49·47 N	97·21 W
67	Oak Creek (ōk krēk′) Colo.	40·20 N	106·50 W
68	Oakdale (ōk′dāl) Calif.	37·45 N	120·52 W
80	Oakdale Ky.	38·15 N	85·50 W
77	Oakdale La.	30·49 N	92·40 W
75	Oakdale Pa. (Pittsburgh In.)	40·24 N	80·11 W
110	Oakengates (ōk′ĕn-gāts) Eng.	52·41 N	2·27 W
70	Oakes (ōks) N. D.	46·10 N	98·50 W
82	Oakfield (ōk′fēld) Maine	46·08 N	68·10 W
84	Oakford (ōk′fōrd) Pa. (Philadelphia In.)	40·08 N	74·58 W
65	Oak Grove (grōv) Ore. (Portland In.)	45·25 N	122·38 W
110	Oakham (ōk′ăm) Eng.	52·40 N	0·38 W
80	Oakharbor (ōk′här′bēr) Ohio	41·30 N	83·05 W
65	Oak Harbor Wash. (Seattle In.)	48·18 N	122·39 W
74	Oak Knoll (nōl) Tex. (Dallas, Fort Worth In.)	32·47 N	97·17 W
65	Oakland (ōk′lănd) Calif. (San Francisco In.)	37·48 N	122·16 W
70	Oakland Nebr.	41·50 N	96·28 W
80	Oakland City Ind.	38·20 N	87·20 W
75	Oaklawn (ōk′lôn) Ill. (Chicago In.)	41·43 N	87·45 W
161	Oakleigh (ōk′lȧ) Austl. (Melbourne In.)	37·54 S	145·05 E
67	Oakley (ōk′lĭ) Idaho	42·15 N	113·53 W
72	Oakley Kans.	39·08 N	100·49 W
78	Oakman (ōk′măn) Ala.	33·42 N	87·20 W
75	Oakmont (ōk′mōnt) Pa. (Pittsburgh In.)	40·31 N	79·50 W
84	Oak Mtn. Ala. (Birmingham In.)	33·22 N	86·42 W
75	Oak Park (pärk) Ill. (Chicago In.)	41·53 N	87·48 W
65	Oak Point Wash. (Portland In.)	46·11 N	123·11 W
78	Oak Ridge (rĭj) Tenn.	36·01 N	84·15 W
74	Oak Ridge Park Mich. (Sault Ste. Marie In.)	46·18 N	84·12 W
85	Oakville (ōk′vĭl) Can. (Toronto In.)	43·27 N	79·40 W
85	Oakville Can. (Winnipeg In.)	49·56 N	98·00 W
84	Oakville La. (New Orleans In.)	29·47 N	90·02 W
74	Oakville Mo. (St. Louis In.)	38·27 N	90·18 W
85	Oakville Cr. Can. (Toronto In.)	43·34 N	79·54 W
77	Oakwood (ōk′wŏŏd) Tex.	31·36 N	95·48 W
75	Oakwood Wis. (Milwaukee In.)	42·51 N	88.30 W
69	Oatman (ōt′măn) Ariz.	34·00 N	114·25 W
88	Oaxaca (State) (wä-hä′kä) Mex.	16·45 N	97·00 W
91	Oaxaca, Sierra de (Mts.) (sē-ĕ′r-rä dĕ) Mex.	16·15 N	97·25 W
91	Oaxaca de Juárez (kōōä′rĕz) Mex.	17·03 N	96·42 W
134	Ob′ (R.) Sov. Un.	62·15 N	67·00 E
87	Oba (ō′bȧ) Can.	48·58 N	84·09 W
153	Obama (ō′bä-mä) Jap.	35·29 N	135·44 E
116	Oban (ō′băn) Scot.	56·25 N	5·35 W
75	O'Bannon (ō-băn′nŏn) Ky. (Louisville In.)	38·17 N	85·30 W
82	Obatogamau (L.) (ō-bä-tō′găm-ô) Can.	49·38 N	74·10 W
168	Obbia (ôb′byä) Som. (Horn of Afr. In.)	5·24 N	48·28 E
123	Oberhausen (ō′bĕr-hou′zĕn) Ger. (Ruhr In.)	51·27 N	6·51 E
72	Oberlin (o′bĕr-lĭn) Kans.	39·49 N	100·30 W
80	Oberlin Ohio	41.15 N	82·15 W
120	Oberösterreich (Prov.) Aus.	48·05 N	13·15 E
111	Oberroth (ō′bĕr-rōt) Ger. (Munich In.)	48·19 N	11·20 E
111	Ober-Schleissheim (ō′bĕr-shlīs-hēm) Ger. (Munich In.)	48·15 N	11·34 E
155	Obi (I.) (ō′bê) Indon.	1·25 S	128·15 E
99	Óbidos (ō′bê-dŏŏzh) Braz.	1·57 S	55·32 W
152	Obihiro (ō′bē-hē′rō) Jap.	42·55 N	142·50 E
78	Obion (R.) Tenn.	36·10 N	89·25 W
78	Obion (R.), North Fk. (ô-bī′ŏn) Tenn.	35·49 N	89·06 W
129	Obitochnaya, Kosa (C.) (kô-sä′ ô-bē-tôch′nä-yȧ) Sov. Un.	46·32 N	36·07 E
153	Obitsu (R.) (ō′bĕt′sōō) Jap. (Tōkyō In.)	35·19 N	140·03 E
168	Obock (ō-bŏk′) Fr. Som. (Horn of Afr. In.)	11·55 N	43·15 E
128	Obol′ (R.) (ō-bŏl′) Sov. Un.	55·24 N	29·24 E
129	Oboyan′ (ō-bō-yän′) Sov. Un.	51·14 N	36·16 E
134	Obskaya Guba (R.) Sov. Un.	67·13 N	73·45 E
129	Obukhov (ō′bōō-kôf) Sov. Un.	50·07 N	30·36 E
79	Ocala (ō-kä′lȧ) Fla.	29·11 N	82·09 W
90	Ocampo (ō-käm′pō) Mex.	22·49 N	99·23 W
98	Ocaña (ō-kän′yä) Col.	8·15 N	73·37 W
124	Ocaña (ō-kä′n-yä) Sp.	39·58 N	3·31 W
164	Occidental, Grand Erg (Dunes) Alg.	29·30 N	00·45 W
98	Occidental, Cordillera (Mts.) (kôr-dēl-yĕ′rä ôk-sê-dĕn-täl′) Col. (In.)	5·05 N	76·04 W
98	Occidental, Cordillera (Mts.) Peru	10·12 S	76·58 W
88	Occidental, Sierra Madre, (Mts.) (sē-ĕ′r-rä-mä′drĕ-ôk-sē-dĕn-tä′l) Mex.	29·30 N	107·30 W
84	Oceana (ō′shĕ′ăn-ȧ) Va. (Norfolk In.)	36·51 N	76·01 W
68	Ocean Beach (ō′shăn bēch) Calif. (San Diego In.)	32·44 N	117·14 W
95	Ocean Bight (B.) Ba. Is.	21·15 N	73·15 W
81	Ocean City Md.	38·20 N	75·10 W
81	Ocean City N. J.	39·15 N	74·35 W
86	Ocean Falls (Fôls) Can.	52·27 N	127·50 W
161	Ocean Grove Austl. (Melbourne In.)	38·16 S	144·32 E
81	Ocean Grove (grōv) N. J.	40·10 N	74·00 W
74	Ocean Park (pärk) Calif. (Los Angeles In.)	34·00 N	118·28 W
84	Oceanport (ō′-shăn-pōrt) N. J. (New York In.)	40·18 N	74·02 W
68	Oceanside (ō′shăn-sīd) Calif.	33·11 N	117·22 W
78	Ocean Springs (sprĭngs) Miss.	30·25 N	88·49 W
127	Ocenele Mari Rom.	45·05 N	24·17 E
129	Ochakov (ō-chä′kôf) Sov. Un.	46·38 N	31·33 E
146	Ochina Ho (R.) China	41·15 N	100·46 E
150	Ochir China	45·38 N	115·35 E
78	Ochlockonee R. (ŏk-lô-kō′nē) Fla.-Ga.	30·10 N	84·38 W
78	Ocilla (ô-sĭl′ȧ) Ga.	31·36 N	83·15 W
118	Ockelbo (ôk′ĕl-bô) Swe.	60·54 N	16·35 E
79	Ocmulgee, (R.) Ga.	32·35 N	83·30 W
78	Ocmulgee Natl. Mon. (ôk-mŭl′gē) Ga.	32·45 N	83·28 W
127	Ocna-Sibiului (ôk′nȧ-sê-byōō-lōō-ê) Rom.	45·52 N	24·04 E
95	Ocoa, Bahai de (B.) (bä-ä′ē-ô-kō′ä) Dom. Rep.	18·20 N	70·40 W
91	Ococingo (ô-kô-sê′n-gô) Mex.	17·03 N	92·18 W
92	Ocom, L. (ô-kō′m) Mex. (Yucatan In.)	19·26 N	88·18 W
78	Oconee, (R.) (ô-kō′nē) Ga.	32·45 N	83·00 W
71	Oconomowoc (ô-kŏn′ô-mô-wŏk′) Wis.	43·06 N	88·24 W
71	Oconto (ô-kŏn′tō) Wis.	44·54 N	87·55 W
71	Oconto (R.) Wis.	45·08 N	88·24 W
71	Oconto Falls Wis.	44·53 N	88·11 W
92	Ocós (ô-kōs′) Guat.	14·31 N	92·12 W
92	Ocotal (ō-kô-täl′) Nic.	13·36 N	86·31 W
92	Ocotepeque (ô-kô-tä-pä′kå) Hond.	14·25 N	89·13 W
90	Ocotlán (ō-kô-tlän′) Mex.	20·19 N	102·44 W
91	Ocotlán de Morelos (dā mô-rā′lōs) Mex.	16·46 N	96·41 W
91	Ocozocoautla (ô-kō′zô-kwä-ōō′tlä) Mex.	16·44 N	93·22 W
99	Ocumare del Tuy (ō-kōō-mä′rä del twē′) Ven. (In.)	10·07 N	66·47 W
155	Ocussi Port. Tim.	9·00 S	128·53 E
153	Odawara (ō′dȧ-wä′rä) Jap.	35·15 N	139·10 E
118	Odda (ôdh-ȧ) Nor.	60·04 N	6·30 E
168	Oddur Som. (Horn of Afr. In.)	3·55 N	43·45 E
70	Odebolt (ō′dê-bōlt) Iowa	42·20 N	95·14 W
124	Odemira (ō-dâ-mē′rȧ) Port.	37·35 N	8·40 W
133	Ödemis (û′dĕ-mēsh) Tur.	38·12 N	28·00 E
168	Odendaalsrus (ō′dĕn-däls-rûs′) S. Afr. (Johannesburg & Pretoria In.)	27·52 S	26·41 E
118	Odense (ō′dhĕn-sĕ) Den.	55·24 N	10·20 E
84	Odenton (ō′dĕn-tŭn) Md. (Baltimore In.)	39·05 N	76·43 W
120	Odenwald (For.) (ō′dĕn-väld) Ger.	49·39 N	8·55 E
120	Oder R. (ō′dĕr) Ger.	52·40 N	14·19 E
129	Odessa (ô-dĕs′sä) Sov. Un.	46·28 N	30·44 E
76	Odessa (ô-dĕs′ȧ) Tex.	31·52 N	102·21 W
66	Odessa Wash.	47·20 N	118·42 W
129	Odessa (Oblast) Sov. Un.	46·05 N	29·48 E
124	Odiel (R.) (ō-dê-ĕl′) Sp.	37·47 N	6·42 W
164	Odienné (ō-dê-ĕn-nā′) Ivory Coast	9·47 N	7·32 W
110	Odiham (ŏd′ē-ăm) Eng. (London In.)	51·14 N	0·56 W
138	Odintsovo (ô-dēn′tsô-vô) Sov. Un. (Moscow In.)	55·40 N	37·16 E
155	Odioñgan (ō-dê-ōŋ′gän) Phil. (Manila In.)	12·24 N	121·59 E
125	Odivelas (ō-dê-vā′lyäs) Port. (Lisbon In.)	38·47 N	9·11 W
121	Odobesti (ô-dô-bĕsh′t′) Rom.	45·46 N	27·08 E
72	O'Donnell (ō-dŏn′ĕl) Tex.	32·59 N	101·51 W
121	Odorhei (ō-dôr-hā′) Rom.	46·18 N	25·17 E
121	Odra R. (ô′drä) Pol.	50·28 N	17·55 E
99	Oeiras (wä-ê-räzh′) Braz.	7·05 S	42·01 W
125	Oeirás (ô-ĕ′y-rä′s) Port. (Lisbon In.)	38·42 N	9·18 W
71	Oelwein (ōl′wīn) Iowa	42·40 N	91·56 W
74	O'Fallon (ō-făl′ŭn) Ill. (St. Louis In.)	38·36 N	89·55 W
67	O'Fallon Cr. Mont.	46·25 N	104·47 W
126	Ofanto (R.) (ô-fän′tō) It.	41·08 N	15·33 E
120	Offenbach (ôf′ĕn-bäk) Ger.	50·06 N	8·50 E
120	Offenburg (ôf′ĕn-bŏŏrgh) Ger.	48·28 N	7·57 E
153	Ofuna (ō′fōō-nä) Jap. (Tōkyō In.)	35·21 N	139·32 E
168	Ogaden Plat. Eth. (Horn of Afr. In.)	6·45 N	44·53 E
153	Ōgaki Jap.	35·21 N	136·36 E
70	Ogallala (ō-gä-lä′lä) Nebr.	41·80 N	101·44 W
164	Ogbomosho (ŏg-bô-mō′shō) Nig.	8·06 N	4·04 E
71	Ogden (ŏg′dĕn) Iowa	42·10 N	94·20 W
74	Ogden Utah (Salt Lake City In.)	41·14 N	111·58 W
74	Ogden Pk. Utah (Salt Lake City In.)	41·11 N	111·51 W
74	Ogden R. Utah (Salt Lake City In.)	41·16 N	111·54 W
84	Ogdensburg (ŏg′dĕnz-bûrg) N. J. (New York In.)	41·05 N	74·36 W
81	Ogdensburg N. Y.	44·40 N	75·30 W
79	Ogeechee, (R.) (ô-gē′chê) Ga.	32·35 N	81·50 W
168	Ogies S. Afr. (Johannesburg & Pretoria In.)	26·03 S	29·04 E
86	Ogilvie Ra. (ō′g′l-vĭ) Can.	64·43 N	138·36 W
80	Oglesby (ō′g′lz-bĭ) Ill.	41·20 N	89·00 W
126	Oglio (R.) (ôl′yō) It.	45·15 N	10·19 E

ng-sing; ŋ-baŋk; n-nasalized n; nŏd; cŏmmit; ōld; ôbey; ôrder; fōōd; fŏŏt; ou-out; s-soft; sh-dish; th-thin; pūre; ûnite; ûrn; stŭd; circŭs; ü-as "y" in study; ′-indeterminate vowel.

246 Ogo–Oregon Caves PRONOUNCING INDEX

Page	Name Pronunciation Region	Lat. °′	Long. °′
153	Ōgo (ō'gô) Jap. (Ōsaka In.)	34·49 N	135·06 E
154	Ogoamas, Bulu (Mtn.) Indon.	0·45 N	120·15 E
166	Ogooué (R.) Gabon	0·20 S	11·07 E
136	Ogudněvo (ôg-ōō-nyô'vô) Sov. Un. (Moscow In.)	56·04 N	38·17 E
126	Ogulin (ō-gōō-lēn') Yugo.	45·17 N	15·11 E
157	Ohia (ō-hī'ä) Hawaii (In.)	19·35 N	155·01 W
101	O'Higgins (Prov.) (ō-kē'gēns) Chile (Santiago In.)	34·17 S	70·52 W
63	Ohio, (State) (ô'hī'ō) U. S.	40·30 N	83·15 W
80	Ohio R. U. S.	37·25 N	88·05 W
79	Ohoopee (R.) (ô-hōō'pē) Ga.	32·32 N	82·38 W
120	Ohre (Eger) R. (ōr'zhě) (ā'gěr) Czech.	50·08 N	12·45 E
127	Ohrid (ō'ĸrēd) Yugo.	41·08 N	20·46 E
127	Ohrid (L.) Alb.-Yugo.	40·58 N	20·35 E
153	Ōi (oi') Jap. (Tōkyō In.)	35·51 N	139·31 E
118	Oieren (L.) (ûïě'rěn) Nor.	59·50 N	11·25 E
153	Oi-Gawa (Strm.) (ō'ē-gä'wà) Jap.	35·09 N	138·05 E
81	Oil City (oil sĭ'tĭ) Pa.	41·25 N	79·40 W
111	Oirschot Neth. (Amsterdam In.)	51·30 N	5·20 E
122	Oise (R.) (wäz) Fr.	49·30 N	2·56 E
111	Oisterwijk Neth. (Amsterdam In.)	51·34 N	5·13 E
153	Oita (ō'ē-tä) Jap.	33·14 N	131·38 E
153	Oji (ō'jê) Jap. (Ōsaka In.)	34·36 N	135·43 E
76	Ojinaga (ō-Kê-nä'gä) Mex.	29·34 N	104·26 W
91	Ojitlán (San Lucas) (ōkê-tlän') (sän-lōō'kās) Mex.	18·04 N	96·23 W
90	Ojo Caliente (ōĸō kāl-yěn'tā) Mex.	21·50 N	100·43 W
90	Ojocaliente (ō-ĸō-kä-lyě'n-tě) Mex.	22·39 N	102·15 W
94	Ojo del Toro, Pico (Pk.) (pē'kô-ô-ĸō-děl-tô'rô) Cuba	19·55 N	77·25 W
85	Oka (ō-kä) Can. (Montreal In.)	45·28 N	74·05 W
133	Oka (R.) (ô-kä') Sov. Un.	52·10 N	35·20 E
134	Oka (R.) (ō-kä') Sov. Un.	53·28 N	101·09 E
132	Oka (R.) (ô-kà') Sov. Un.	55·10 N	42·10 E
166	Okahandja S. W. Afr.	21·50 S	16·45 E
86	Okanagan (ō'kȧ-näg'ȧn) Can.	49·56 N	120·23 W
66	Okanogan Wash.	48·20 N	119·34 W
66	Okanogan R. Wash.	48·36 N	119·33 W
164	Okano R. (ô'kä'nō) Gabon	0·15 N	11·08 E
78	Okatibbee (R.) (ō'kä-tĭb'ē) Miss.	32·37 N	88·54 W
78	Okatoma Cr. (ô-kȧ-tō'mă) Miss.	31·43 N	89·34 W
153	Okaya (ō'kȧ-yȧ) Jap.	36·04 N	138·01 E
153	Okayama (ō'kȧ-yä'mȧ) Jap.	34·39 N	133·54 E
153	Okazaki (ō'kȧ-zä'kê) Jap.	34·58 N	137·09 E
79	Okeechobee (ō-kê-chō'bē) Fla. (In.)	27·15 N	26·48 W
79	Okeechobee, L. Fla. (In.)	27·00 N	80·49 W
72	Okeene (ô-kēn') Okla.	36·06 N	98·19 W
79	Okefenokee Swp. (ō'kê-fê-nō'kê) Ga.	30·54 N	82·20 W
73	Okemah (ô-kē'mä) Okla.	35·26 N	96·18 W
117	Oker (R.) (ō'kěr) Ger.	52·23 N	10·00 E
135	Okha (ŭ-ĸä') Sov. Un.	53·44 N	143·12 E
136	Okhotino (ô-ĸô'tĭ-nô) Sov. Un. (Moscow In.)	56·14 N	38·24 E
135	Okhotsk (ô-ĸôtsk') Sov. Un.	59·28 N	143·32 E
139	Okhotsk, Sea of (ô-kôtsk') Asia	56·45 N	146·00 E
153	Oki-Guntō (Arch.) (ō'kê gōōn'tō) Jap.	36·17 N	133·05 E
152	Okinawa (I.) (ō'kê-nä'wȧ) Ryūkyū Is.	26·30 N	128·30 E
152	Okinawa Guntō (Is.) (gōōn'tō') Ryūkyū Is.	26·50 N	127·25 E
153	Okino (I.) (ō'kê-nô) Jap.	36·22 N	133·27 E
152	Ōkino Erabu (I.) (ō-kē'nô-ȧ-rä'bōō) Jap.	27·18 N	129·00 E
62	Oklahoma (State) (ô-klȧ-hō'mȧ) U. S.	36·00 N	98·20 W
73	Oklahoma City Okla.	35·27 N	97·32 W
79	Oklawaha (R.) (ŏk-lȧ-wô'hô) Fla.	29·13 N	82·00 W
73	Okmulgee (ôk-mŭl'gē) Okla.	35·37 N	95·58 W
75	Okolona (ō-kô-lō'nȧ) Ky. (Louisville In.)	38·08 N	85·41 W
78	Okolona Miss.	33·59 N	88·43 W
166	Okovanggo (R.) Ang.-S. W. Afr.	17·50 S	19·30 E
166	Okovanggo Swp. Bech.	19·30 S	23·02 E
152	Okushiri (I.) (ō'koo-shē'rê) Jap.	42·12 N	139·30 E
65	Olalla (ō-lä'lȧ) Wash. (Seattle In.)	47·26 N	122·33 W
92	Olanchito (ō'län-chē'tô) Hond.	15·28 N	86·35 W
118	Öland (I.) (û-lând') Swe.	57·03 N	17·15 E
74	Olathe (ô-lā'thê) Mo. (Kansas City In.)	38·53 N	94·49 W
100	Olavarría (ŏ-lä-vär-rē'ä) Arg.	36·49 S	60·15 W
121	Oława (ô-lä'vȧ) Pol.	50·57 N	17·18 E
101	Olazcoago (ô-läz-kôä'gô) Arg. (Buenos Aires In.)	35·14 S	60·37 W
126	Olbia (ô'l-byä) It.	40·55 N	9·28 E
111	Olching (ōl'ĸēng) Ger. (Munich In.)	48·13 N	11·21 E
94	Old Bahama Chan. (bȧ-hā'mȧ) N. A.	22·45 N	78·30 W
95	Old Bight Ba. Is.	24·15 N	75·20 W
84	Old Bridge (brĭj) N. J. (New York In.)	40·24 N	74·22 W
110	Oldbury (ōld'bēr-ĭ) Eng.	52·30 N	2·01 W
86	Old Crow (crō) Can.	67·51 N	139·58 W
120	Oldenburg (ôl'děn-bŏŏrgh) Ger.	53·09 N	8·13 E
81	Old Forge (fôrj) Pa.	41·20 N	75·50 W
110	Oldham (ōld'ȧm) Eng.	53·32 N	2·07 W
64	Old Harbor (här'bēr) Alaska	57·18 N	153·20 W
116	Old Head of Kinsale (ōld hěd ŏv kĭn-sāl) Ire.	51·35 N	8·35 W
77	Old R. Tex. (In.)	29·54 N	94·52 W
86	Olds (ōldz) Can.	51·50 N	114·00 W
82	Old Town (toun) Maine	44·55 N	68·42 W
81	Olean (ō-lê-ăn') N. Y.	42·05 N	78·25 W
82	O'Leary (ō-lēr'ē) Can.	46·43 N	64·10 W
121	Olecko (ō-lět'skô) Pol.	54·02 N	22·29 E
135	Olekma (R.) (ô-lyěk-mȧ') Sov. Un.	55·41 N	120·33 E
135	Olëkminsk (ô-lyěk-mênsk') Sov. Un.	60·39 N	120·40 E
135	Oleněk (R.) (ô-lyě-nyôk') Sov. Un.	70·18 N	121·15 E
122	Oléron Île, d' (I.) (ēl' dō lā-rôɴ') Fr.	45·52 N	1·58 W
121	Olesnica (ô-lěsh-nĭ'tsȧ) Pol.	51·13 N	17·24 E
123	Olfen (ōl'fěn) Ger. (Ruhr In.)	51·43 N	7·22 E
135	Ol'ga (ôl'gȧ) Sov. Un.	43·48 N	135·44 E
84	Olga (ōl'gȧ) La. (New Orleans In.)	29·22 N	89·25 W
152	Ol'gi, Zaliv (B.) (zä'lĭf ôl'gĭ) Sov. Un.	43·43 N	135·25 E
129	Ol'gopol (ôl-gô-pôl'y') Sov. Un.	48·11 N	29·28 E
124	Olhão (ôl-youɴ') Port.	37·02 N	7·54 W
167	Olievenhoutpoort S. Afr. (Johannesburg & Pretoria In.)	25·58 S	27·55 E
166	Olifants (R.) (ŏl'ĭ-fȧnts) S. Afr.	23·58 S	31·00 E
167	Olifantsfontein S. Afr. (Johannesburg & Pretoria In.)	25·58 S	28·19 E
127	Ólimbos Grc.	40·03 N	22·22 E
90	Olinalá (ô-lê-nä-lä') Mex.	17·47 N	98·51 W
99	Olinda (ō-lê'n-dä) Braz.	8·00 S	34·58 W
74	Olinda (ō-lĭn'dȧ) Calif. (Los Angeles In.)	33·55 N	117·51 W
125	Oliva (ô-lê'vä) Sp.	38·54 N	0·07 W
124	Oliva de Jerez (ô-lē'vä dā hā'rěth) Sp.	38·33 N	6·55 W
125	Olivais (ô-lê-vá'ys) Port. (Lisbon In.)	38·46 N	9·06 W
74	Olive (ŏl'ĭv) Calif. (Los Angeles In.)	33·50 N	117·51 W
80	Olive Hill Ky.	38·15 N	83·10 W
101	Oliveira (ô-lē-vä'rä) Braz. (Rio de Janeiro In.)	20·42 S	44·49 W
124	Olivenza (ō-lē-věn'thä) Sp.	38·42 N	7·06 W
86	Oliver (ŏ'lĭ-vēr) Can.	49·09 N	119·36 W
85	Oliver Can. (Edmonton In.)	53·38 N	113·21 W
74	Oliver (ŏ'lĭvēr) Wis. (Duluth In.)	46·39 N	92·12 W
85	Oliver L. Can. (Edmonton In.)	53·19 N	113·00 W
71	Olivia (ō-lĭv'ē-ȧ) Minn.	44·46 N	95·00 W
100	Olivos (ōlē'vōs) Arg. (In.)	34·15 S	58·29 W
121	Olkusz (ôl'kŏŏsh) Pol.	50·16 N	19·41 E
98	Ollagüe (ô-lyä'gā) Chile	21·17 S	68·17 W
110	Ollerton (ŏl'ēr-tŭn) Eng.	53·12 N	1·02 W
74	Olmos Park (ōl'mŭs pärk') Tex. (San Antonio In.)	29·27 N	98·32 W
80	Olney (ŏl'nĭ) Ill.	38·45 N	88·05 W
65	Olney (ŏl'nē) Ore. (Portland In.)	46·06 N	123·45 W
72	Olney Tex.	33·24 N	98·43 W
83	Olomane (R.) (ō'lō mä'nē) Can.	50·50 N	60·30 W
121	Olomouc (ô'lô-mōts) Czech.	49·37 N	17·15 E
119	Olonets (ô-lô'něts) Sov. Un.	60·58 N	32·54 E
122	Oloron, Gave d' (Strm.) (gäv-dŏ-lō-rŏɴ') Fr.	43·21 N	0·44 W
122	Oloron-Ste. Marie (ō-lō-rôɴt'săɴt mȧ-rē') Fr.	43·11 N	1·37 W
125	Olot (ô-lōt') Sp.	42·09 N	2·30 E
123	Olpe (ōl'pě) Ger. (Ruhr In.)	51·02 N	7·51 E
129	Ol'shanka (ôl'shäŋ-kȧ) Sov. Un.	48·14 N	30·52 E
129	Ol'shany (ôl'shȧn-ê) Sov. Un.	50·02 N	35·54 E
120	Olsnitz (ōlz'nētz) Ger.	50·25 N	12·11 E
121	Olsztyn (ôl'shtên) Pol.	53·47 N	20·28 E
120	Olten (ôl'těn) Switz.	47·20 N	7·53 E
127	Oltenita (ôl-tā'nĭ-tsȧ) Rom.	44·05 N	26·39 E
115	Olt R. Rom.	44·09 N	24·40 E
124	Olvera (ôl-vě'rä) Sp.	36·55 N	7·16 W
66	Olympia (ô-lĭm'pĭ-ȧ) Wash.	47·02 N	122·52 W
66	Olympic Mts. Wash.	47·54 N	123·58 W
66	Olympic Natl. Park (ô-lĭm'pĭk) Wash.	47·54 N	123·00 W
66	Olympus Mt. (ô-lĭm'pŭs) Wash.	47·43 N	123·30 W
139	Olympus Mts. Cyprus (Palestine In.)	34·50 N	32·44 E
81	Olyphant (ŏl'ĭ-fănt) Pa.	41·30 N	75·40 W
135	Olyutorskiy, Mys (C.) (ŭl-yōō'tŏr-skē) Sov. Un.	59·49 N	167·16 E
153	Omae-Zaki (Pt.) (ō'mä-ȧ zä'kê) Jap.	34·37 N	138·15 E
165	Om Ager Eth.	14·06 N	36·46 E
116	Omagh (ō'mä) N. Ire.	54·35 N	7·25 W
70	Omaha (ō'mȧ-hä) Nebr.	41·18 N	95·57 W
70	Omaha Ind. Res. Nebr.	42·09 N	96·08 W
144	Oman, G. of Asia	24·24 N	58·58 E
166	Omaruru (ō-mä-rōō'rōō) S. W. Afr.	21·25 S	16·50 E
126	Ombrone (R.) (ôm-brō'nā) It.	42·48 N	11·18 E
165	Omdurman (ŏm-dōōr-män') Sud.	15·45 N	32·30 E
91	Omealca (ōmȧ-äl'kō) Mex.	18·44 N	96·45 W
90	Ometepec (ō-mā-tā-pěk') Mex.	16·41 N	98·27 W
153	Ōmiya (ō'mê-yȧ) Jap. (Tōkyō In.)	35·54 N	139·38 E
92	Omoa (ō-mō'rä) Hond.	15·43 N	88·03 W
135	Omolon (R.) (ō'mō) Sov. Un.	67·43 N	159·15 E
153	Ōmori (Kioroshi) (ō'mô-rê) (kê'ō-rō'shē) Jap. (Tōkyō In.)	35·50 N	140·09 E
165	Omo R. (ō'mō) Eth.	5·54 N	36·09 E
92	Omotepe, Isla de (I.) (ē's-lä-dě-ō-mō-tā'pā) Nic.	11·32 N	85·30 W
71	Omro (ŏm'rō) Wis.	44·01 N	89·46 W
134	Omsk (ômsk) Sov. Un.	55·12 N	73·19 E
153	Ōmura (ō'mōō-rä) Jap.	32·56 N	129·57 E
153	Ōmuta (ō'mōō-tȧ) Jap.	33·02 N	130·28 E
132	Omutninsk (ō'mōō-tēnsk) Sov. Un.	58·38 N	52·10 E
70	Onawa (ŏn-ȧ-wȧ) Iowa	42·02 N	96·05 W
80	Onaway Mich.	45·25 N	84·10 W
125	Onda (ōn'dä) Sp.	39·58 N	0·13 W
121	Ondava R. (ōn'dȧ-vȧ) Czech.	48·51 N	21·40 E
150	Öndör Haan Mong.	47·20 N	110·40 E
132	Onega (ô-nyě'gȧ) Sov. Un.	63·50 N	38·08 E
132	Onega (R.) Sov. Un.	63·20 N	39·20 E
	Onega, L., see Onezhskoye Ozero		
81	Oneida (ô-nī'dȧ) N. Y.	43·05 N	75·40 W
81	Oneida (L.) N. Y.	43·10 N	76·00 W
70	O'Neill (ō-nēl') Nebr.	42·28 N	98·38 W
135	Onekotan (ŭ-nyě-kŭ-tän') Sov. Un.	49·45 N	153·45 E
81	Oneonta (ō-nê-ŏn'tȧ) N. Y.	42·25 N	75·05 W
132	Onezhskaja Guba (B.) Sov. Un.	64·30 N	36·00 E
132	Onezhskiy, P-Ov. (Pen.) Sov. Un.	64·30 N	37·40 E
132	Onezhskoye Ozero (L. Onega) (ô-năsh'skô-yě ô'zě-rô) Sov. Un.	62·02 N	34·35 E
146	Ongin (ŏn'gĭn') Mong.	46·00 N	102·46 E
143	Ongole India	15·36 N	80·03 E
167	Onilahy (R.) Malag. Rep.	23·41 S	45·00 E
164	Onitsha (ô-nĭt'shȧ) Nig.	6·13 N	5·47 E
153	Onomichi (ō'nô-mē'chê) Jap.	34·27 N	133·12 E
135	Onon (R.) (ô'nôn) Sov. Un.	50·33 N	114·18 E
135	Onon Gol (R.) (ô'nôn) Sov. Un.	48·30 N	110·38 E
99	Onoto (ô-nŏ'tô) Ven. (In.)	9·38 N	65·03 W
158	Onslow (ŏnz'lō) Austl.	21·53 S	115·00 E
79	Onslow B. (ônz'lō) N. C.	34·22 N	77·35 W
153	Ontake San (Mtn.) (ôn'tä-kȧ sän) Jap.	35·55 N	137·29 E
74	Ontario (ŏn-tā'rĭ-ō) Calif. (Los Angeles In.)	34·04 N	117·39 W
66	Ontario Ore.	44·02 N	116·57 W
87	Ontario (Prov.) Can.	50·47 N	88·50 W
63	Ontario, L. U. S.-Can.	43·35 N	79·05 W
125	Onteniente (ōn-tā-nyěn'tā) Sp.	38·48 N	0·35 W
71	Ontonagon (ŏn-tô-năg'ŏn) Mich.	46·50 N	89·20 W
153	Ōnuki (ō'nōō-kê) Jap. (Tōkyō In.)	35·17 N	139·51 E
158	Oodnadatta (ōōd'nȧ-dȧ'tȧ) Austl.	27·38 S	135·40 E
158	Ooldea Station (ōōl-dā'ȧ) Austl.	30·35 S	132·08 E
73	Oologah Res. Okla.	36·43 N	95·32 W
111	Ooltgensplaat Neth. (Amsterdam In.)	51·41 N	4·19 E
78	Oostanaula (R.) (ōō-stȧ-nô'lȧ) Ga.	34·25 N	85·10 W
117	Oostende (ōst-ěn'dě) Bel.	51·14 N	2·55 E
111	Oosterhout Neth. (Amsterdam In.)	51·38 N	4·52 E
117	Ooster Schelde (R.) Neth.	51·40 N	3·40 E
92	Opalaca, Sierra de (Mts.) (sē-ě'r-rä-dě-ô-pä-lȧ'kä) Hond.	14·30 N	88·29 W
121	Opatow (ô-pä'tŏŏf) Pol.	50·47 N	21·25 E
121	Opava (ō'pä-vä) Czech.	49·56 N	17·52 E
118	Opdal (ôp'däl) Nor.	62·37 N	9·41 E
78	Opelika (ŏp-ê-lī'kȧ) Ala.	32·39 N	85·23 W
77	Opelousas (ŏp-ē-lōō'sȧs) La.	30·33 N	92·04 W
81	Opeongo (L.) (ŏp-ê-ôŋ'gō) Can.	45·40 N	78·20 W
67	Opheim (ō-fīm') Mont.	48·51 N	106·19 W
64	Ophir (ō'fēr) Alaska	63·10 N	156·28 W
139	Ophir, Mt. Mala. (Singapore In.)	2·22 N	102·37 E
92	Opico (ô-pē'kō) Sal.	13·50 N	89·23 W
87	Opinaca (R.) (ŏp-ĭ-nä'kȧ) Can.	52·28 N	77·40 W
123	Opladen (ōp'lä-děn) Ger. (Ruhr In.)	51·04 N	7·00 E
128	Opochka (ō-pôch'kȧ) Sov. Un.	56·43 N	28·39 E
121	Opoczno (ô-pôch'nô) Pol.	51·22 N	20·18 E
121	Opole (ô-pôl'ä) Pol.	50·42 N	17·55 E
121	Opole Lubelskie (ō-pō'lă lōō-běl'skyě) Pol.	51·09 N	21·58 E
	Oporto, see Pôrto		
66	Oportunity (ŏp-ŏr tū'nĭ tĭ) Wash.	47·37 N	117·20 W
129	Oposhnya (ô-pôsh'nyȧ) Sov. Un.	49·57 N	34·34 E
78	Opp (ŏp) Ala.	31·18 N	86·15 W
74	Oquirrh Mts. (ō'kwēr) Utah (Salt Lake City In.)	40·38 N	112·11 W
121	Oradea (ô-räd'yä) Rom.	47·02 N	21·55 E
164	Oran (ō-rän') (ô-räɴ') Alg.	35·46 N	0·45 W
100	Orán (ô-rä'n) Arg.	23·13 S	64·17 W
73	Oran (ôr'ȧn) Mo.	37·05 N	89·39 W
160	Orange (ŏr'ěnj) Austl.	33·15 S	149·08 E
74	Orange Calif. (Los Angeles In.)	33·48 N	117·51 W
81	Orange Conn.	41·15 N	73·00 W
122	Orange (ô-räɴzh') Fr.	44·08 N	4·48 E
84	Orange N. J. (New York In.)	40·46 N	74·14 W
77	Orange Tex.	30·07 N	93·44 W
99	Orange, Cabo (C.) (kä-bô-rä'n-zhě) Braz.	4·25 N	51·30 W
79	Orange (L.) Fla.	29·30 N	82·12 W
166	Orange (R.) S. W. Afr.-S. Afr.	29·15 S	17·30 E
79	Orangeburg (ŏr'ěnj-bûrg) S. C.	33·30 N	80·50 W
94	Orange Cay (I.) (ŏr-ěnj kē) Ba. Is.	24·55 N	79·05 W
70	Orange City Iowa	43·01 N	96·06 W
166	Orange Free State (Prov.) S. Afr.	28·15 S	26·00 E
85	Orangeville (ŏr'ěnj-vĭl) Can. (Toronto In.)	43·55 N	80·06 W
168	Orangeville S. Afr. (Johannesburg & Pretoria In.)	27·05 S	28·13 E
92	Orange Walk (wôl'k) Br. Hond. (Yucatan In.)	18·09 N	88·32 W
155	Orani (ō-rä'nê) Phil. (Manila In.)	14·47 N	120·32 E
111	Oranienburg (ō-rä'nê-ěn-bŏŏrgh) Ger. (Berlin In.)	52·45 N	13·14 E
155	Oranje-Gebergte (Mts.) W. Irian	4·22 S	139·25 E
166	Oranjemund S. W. Afr.	28·33 S	16.20 E
127	Orastie (ô-rûsh'tyě) Rom.	45·50 N	23·14 E
	Orașul-Stalin, see Brașov		
126	Orbetello (ôr-bȧ-těl'lō) It.	42·27 N	11·15 E
124	Orbigo (R.) (ôr-bē'gō) Sp.	42·30 N	5·55 W
160	Orbost (ôr'bŭst) Austl.	37·43 S	148·20 E
65	Orcas (I.) (ôr'kȧs) Wash. (Vancouver In.)	48·43 N	122·52 W
74	Orchard Farm (ôr'chērd färm) Mo. (St. Louis In.)	38·53 N	90·27 W
75	Orchard Park N. Y. Buffalo In.)	42·46 N	78·46 W
65	Orchards (ôr'chēdz) Wash. (Portland In.)	45·40 N	122·33 W
98	Orchilla (ôr-kēl-ȧ) Ven.	11·47 N	66·34 W
70	Ord (ôrd) Nebr.	41·35 N	98·57 W
158	Ord (R.) Austl.	17·30 S	128·40 E
136	Orda (ôr'dȧ) Sov. Un. (Urals In.)	56·50 N	57·12 E
124	Órdenes (ōr'dě-näs) Sp.	43·46 N	8·24 W
150	Ordos Des. China	39·12 N	108·10 E
69	Ord Pk. Ariz.	33·55 N	109·40 W
133	Ordu (ôr'dōō) Tur.	41·00 N	37·50 E
124	Orduña (ôr-dōō'nyä) Sp.	42·59 N	3·01 W
72	Ordway (ôrd'wā) Colo.	38·11 N	103·46 W
133	Ordzhonikidze (Ora ghō nĭ kĭd ze) Sov. Un.	43·05 N	44·35 E
118	Örebro (û'rē-brō) Swe.	59·16 N	15·11 E
136	Oredezh R. (ô'rě-dězh) Sov. Un. (Leningrad In.)	59·23 N	30·21 E
71	Oregon Ill.	42·01 N	89·21 W
62	Oregon (State) U. S.	43·40 N	121·50 W
66	Oregon Caves Natl. Mon. (cāvz) Ore.	42·05 N	123·13 W

ăt; finȧl; rāte; senāte; ärm; ȧsk; sofȧ; fâre; ch-choose; dh-as th in other; bē; ēvent; bět; recěnt; cratēr; g-go; gh-guttural g; bĭt; ĭ-short neutral; rīde: ĸ-guttural k as ch in German ich;

PRONOUNCING INDEX Oregon City–Oxford 247

Page	Name Pronunciation Region	Lat. °′	Long. °′
65	Oregon City...Ore. (Portland In.)	45·21 N	122·36 W
118	Oregrund (û′rĕ-grŏŏnd)......Swe.	60·20 N	18·26 E
129	Orekhov (ôr-yĕ′кôf).....Sov. Un.	47·34 N	35·51 E
128	Orekhovo-Zuyevo (ôr-yĕ′кô-vô zōō′yĕ-vô).Sov Un.	55·46 N	39·00 E
128	Orël (ôr-yôl′)..........Sov. Un.	52·54 N	36·03 E
128	Orël (Oblast)..........Sov. Un.	52·35 N	36·08 E
129	Orel′ (R.).............Sov. Un.	49·08 N	34·55 E
69	Orem (ō′rĕm).............Utah	40·15 N	111·50 W
	Ore Mts., see Erzgebirge		
133	Orenburg (ô′rĕn-bōōrg)..Sov. Un.	51·50 N	55·05 E
124	Orense (ō-rĕn′sā)............Sp.	42·20 N	7·52 W
118	Øresund (Sd) (ûr′ŭ-sōōn)....Den.	55·30 N	12·25 E
94	Organos, Sierra de los (Mts.) (sē-ĕ′r-rä-dĕ-lôs-ŏ′r-gä-nôs).Cuba	22·20 N	84·10 W
69	Organ Pipe Cactus Natl. Mon. (ôr′găn pīp kăk′tŭs).Ariz.	32·14 N	113·05 W
101	Orgãos, Serra das (Mtn.) (sĕ′r-rä-däs-ôr-gouɴ′s) Braz. (Rio de Janeiro In.)	22·30 S	43·01 W
129	Orgeyev (ôr-gyĕ′yĕf).....Sov. Un.	47·27 N	28·49 E
146	Orhon Gol (R.)..........Mong.	48·33 N	103·07 E
98	Oriental, Cordillera (Mts.) (kôr-dēl-yĕ′rä ō-rē-ĕn-täl′).Bol.	14·00 S	68·33 W
98	Oriental, Cordillera (Mts.) (kôr-dēl-yĕ′rä).Col. (In.)	3·30 N	74·27 W
95	Oriental, Cordillera (Mts.) (kôr-dēl-yĕ′rä-ô-ryĕ′n-täl) Dom. Rep.	18·55 N	69·40 W
88	Oriental, Sierra Madre, (Mts.) (sē-ĕ′r-rä-mä′drē-ô-ryĕ′n-täl′) Mex.	25·30 N	100·45 W
95	Oriente (State) (ō-rē-ĕn′tâ)..Cuba	20·25 N	76·15 W
125	Orihuela (ō′rē-wā′lä).........Sp.	38·04 N	0·55 W
119	Orihvesi (L.) (ô′rĭ-vĕ-sĭ)......Fin.	62·15 N	29·55 E
81	Orillia (ô-rĭl′ĭ-ȧ)...........Can.	44·35 N	79·25 W
98	Orinoco, Rio (R.) (rē′ō-ō-rĭ-nō′kô).Ven.	8·32 N	63·13 W
155	Orion (ō-rē-ōn′).Phil. (Manila In.)	14·37 N	120·34 E
142	Orissa (State) (ŏ-rĭs′ȧ)......India	25·09 N	83·50 E
126	Oristano (ō-rēs-tä′nō).........It.	39·53 N	8·38 E
126	Oristano, Golfo di (G.) (gôl-fô-dē-ô-rēs-tä′nō).It.	39·53 N	8·12 E
99	Orituco (R.) (ô-rē-tōō′kō) Ven. (In.)	9·37 N	66·25 W
99	Oriuco (ô-rêōō′kō) (R.).Ven. (In.)	9·36 N	66·25 W
91	Orizaba (ô-rē-zä′bä)........Mex.	18·52 N	97·05 W
118	Orkdal (ôr′k-däl)...........Nor.	63·19 N	9·54 E
112	Örkedalen (ûr′kĕ-dä-lĕn).....Nor.	63·13 N	9·53 E
118	Örken (L.) (ûr′kĕn).........Swe.	57·11 N	14·45 E
118	Orkla (R.) (ôr′klä)..........Nor.	62·55 N	9·50 E
168	Orkney (ôrk′nĭ)...........S. Afr. (Johannesburg & Pretoria In.)	26·58 S	26·39 E
116	Orkney (Is.)..............Scot.	59·01 N	2·08 W
79	Orlando (ôr-lăn′dō).....Fla. (In.)	28·32 N	81·22 W
167	Orlando (ôr-lăn-dô)........S. Afr. (Johannesburg & Pretoria In.)	26·15 S	27·56 E
75	Orland Park (ôr-lăn′) Ill. (Chicago In.)	41·38 N	87·52 W
85	Orleans (ôr-lâ-äɴ′) Can. (Ottawa In.)	45·28 N	75·31 W
122	Orléans (ôr-lā-äɴ′)..........Fr.	47·55 N	1·56 E
80	Orleans (ôr-lēnz′)...........Ind.	38·40 N	86·25 W
164	Orléansville (ôr-lâ-äɴ-vēl′).Alg.	36·14 N	1·32 E
79	Ormond (ôr′mŏnd)..........Fla.	29·15 N	81·05 W
110	Ormskirk (ôrms′kērk).......Eng.	53·34 N	2·53 W
85	Ormstown (ôrms′toun) Can. (Montreal In.)	45·07 N	74·00 W
122	Orne (R.) (ôrn′)............Fr.	49·05 N	0·32 W
121	Orneta (ôr-nyĕ′tä)..........Pol.	54·07 N	20·10 E
118	Ornö (I.)..................Swe.	59·02 N	18·35 E
112	Örnsköldsvik (ûrn′skôlts-vēk).Swe.	63·10 N	18·32 E
90	Oro, Rio del (R.) (rē′ō dĕl ō′rō) Mex.	18·04 N	100·59 W
76	Oro, Rio del (R.)...........Mex.	26·04 N	105·40 W
126	Orobie, Alpi (Mts.) (äl′pē-ô-rŏ′byĕ).It.	46·05 N	9·47 E
98	Orocué (ô-rô-kwā′)..........Col.	4·48 N	71·26 W
116	Oronsay, Pass. of (ō′rŏn-sā)..Scot.	55·55 N	6·25 W
126	Orosei, Golfo di (G.) (gôl-fô-dē-ō-rô-sā′ē).It.	40·12 N	9·45 E
121	Orosháza (ô-rôsh-hä′sô)....Hung.	46·33 N	20·31 E
92	Orosi Vol. (ō-rō′sē)........C. R.	11·00 N	85·30 W
68	Oroville (ōr′ô-vĭl)..........Calif.	39·29 N	121·34 W
66	Oroville.................Wash.	48·55 N	119·25 W
80	Orrville (ôr′vĭl)............Ohio	40·45 N	81·50 W
118	Orsa (ōr′sä)...............Swe.	61·08 N	14·35 E
118	Örsdals Vand (L.) (ûrs-däls vän) Nor.	58·39 N	6·06 E
128	Orsha (ôr′shȧ)..........Sov. Un.	54·29 N	30·28 E
133	Orsk (ôrsk)..............Sov. Un.	51·15 N	58·50 E
127	Orşova (ôr′shô-vä).........Rom.	44·43 N	22·26 E
98	Ortega (ôr-tĕ′gä).......Col. (In.)	3·56 N	75·12 W
124	Ortegal, Cabo (C.) (kä′bô-ôr-tå-gäl′).Sp.	43·46 N	8·15 W
111	Orth..........Aus. (Vienna In.)	48·09 N	16·42 E
125	Orthez (ôr-tĕz′)..............Fr.	43·29 N	0·43 W
124	Ortigueira (ôr-tē-gā′ē-rä)......Sp.	43·40 N	7·50 W
65	Orting (ôrt′ĭng) Wash. (Seattle In.)	47·06 N	122·12 W
126	Ortona (ôr-tō′nä).............It.	42·22 N	14·22 E
70	Ortonville (ôr-tŭn-vĭl)......Minn.	45·18 N	96·26 W
98	Oruro (ô-rōō′rō).............Bol.	17·57 S	66·59 W
126	Orvieto (ôr-vyâ′tō)...........It.	42·43 N	12·08 E
127	Oryakhovo..................Bul.	43·43 N	23·59 E
118	Os (ôs).....................Nor.	60·24 N	5·22 E
132	Osa (ô′sȧ)..............Sov. Un.	57·18 N	55·25 E
93	Osa, Pen. de (ō′sä).........C. R.	8·30 N	83·25 W
71	Osage (ō′sāj)...............Iowa	43·16 N	92·49 W
73	Osage (R.)..................Mo.	38·10 N	93·12 W
73	Osage City (ō′sāj sĭ′tĭ).....Kans.	38·28 N	95·53 W
153	Ōsaka (ō′sä-kä)..Jap. (Ōsaka In.)	34·40 N	135·27 E
153	Ōsaka (Pref.)....Jap. (Ōsaka In.)	34·45 N	135·36 E
153	Ōsaka-Wan (B.) (wän).......Jap.	34·34 N	135·16 E
71	Osakis (ô-sā′kĭs)...........Minn.	45·51 N	95·09 W
71	Osakis (L.)................Minn.	45·55 N	94·55 W
153	Ōsawa (ō′sä-wä).Jap. (Tōkyō In.)	35·54 N	129·48 E
73	Osawatomie (ŏs-ȧ-wät′ô-mē).Kans.	38·29 N	94·57 W
72	Osborne (ŏz′bŭrn)..........Kans.	39·25 N	98·42 W
71	Osceola (ŏs-ē-ō′lȧ)..........Iowa	41·04 N	93·45 W
73	Osceola.....................Mo.	38·02 N	93·41 W
70	Osceola....................Nebr.	41·11 N	97·34 W
73	Osceola....................Tenn.	35·42 N	89·58 W
80	Oscoda (ŏs-kō′dȧ)...........Mich.	44·25 N	83·20 W
128	Osëtr (R.) (ô′sĕt′r)......Sov. Un.	54·27 N	38·15 E
80	Osgood (ŏz′gŏŏd)............Ind.	39·10 N	85·20 W
85	Osgoode Sta....Can. (Ottawa In.)	45·09 N	75·37 W
134	Osh (ôsh)...............Sov. Un.	40·28 N	72·47 E
81	Oshawa (ŏsh′ȧ-wȧ)..........Can.	43·50 N	78·50 W
153	Ōshima (I.) (ō′shē′mä).......Jap.	34·47 N	139·35 E
70	Oshkosh (ŏsh′kŏsh)........Nebr.	41·24 N	102·22 W
71	Oshkosh....................Wis.	44·01 N	88·35 W
119	Oshmyany (ôsh-myä′nĭ)..Sov. Un.	54·27 N	25·55 E
164	Oshogbo...................Nig.	7·53 N	4·23 E
127	Osijek (ôs′ĭ-yĕk)..........Yugo.	45·33 N	18·48 E
134	Osinniki (ŭ-sē′nyĭ-kē)....Sov. Un.	53·29 N	85·19 E
129	Osipenko (ŭ-sē′pyĭn-kō)..Sov. Un.	46·45 N	36·47 E
71	Oskaloosa (ŏs-kȧ-lōō′sȧ).......Iowa	41·16 N	92·40 W
118	Oskarshamn (ôs′kärs-häm′n).Swe.	57·16 N	16·24 E
118	Oskarsström (ôs′kärs-strûm).Swe.	56·48 N	12·55 E
129	Oskol (R.) (ôs-kôl′)......Sov. Un.	49·25 N	37·41 E
118	Oslo (ôs′lō)................Nor.	59·56 N	10·41 E
118	Oslo Fd (fyôrd).............Nor.	59·03 N	10·35 E
124	Osma (ôs′mä)...............Sp.	41·35 N	3·02 W
133	Osmaniye....................Tur.	37·10 N	36 30 E
120	Osnabrück (ôs-nä-brük′).....Ger.	52·16 N	8·05 E
100	Osorno (ô-sō′r-nō)..........Chile	40·42 S	73·13 W
159	Osprey Reef (I.) (ŏs′prâ)...Austl.	14·00 S	146·45 E
160	Ossa, Mt. (ŏsȧ).............Austl.	41·45 S	146·05 E
74	Osseo (ŏs′sē-ō)............Minn. (Minneapolis, St. Paul In.)	45·07 N	93·24 W
84	Ossining (ŏs′ĭ-nĭng) N. Y. (New York In.)	41·09 N	73·51 W
82	Ossipee (ŏs′ĭ-pē)...........N. H.	43·42 N	71·08 W
118	Ossjöen (L.) (ôs-syûĕn).......Nor.	61·20 N	12·00 E
128	Ostashkov (ôs-täsh′kôf)..Sov. Un.	57·07 N	33·04 E
117	Oste (R.) (ōz′tĕ)............Ger.	53·20 N	9·19 E
129	Oster (ōs′tĕr)...........Sov. Un.	50·55 N	30·52 E
118	Oster-daläven (R.)..........Swe.	61·40 N	13·00 E
118	Oster Fd. (ûs′tĕr fyôr′)......Nor.	60·40 N	5·25 E
118	Ostersund (ûs′tĕr-sōōnd)......Swe.	63·09 N	14·49 E
118	Östhammar (ûst′häm′är).....Swe.	60·16 N	18·21 E
125	Ostia Antica (ô′s-tyä-än-tē′kä) It. (Rome In.)	41·46 N	12·24 E
	Ostia Lido, see Lido di Roma		
121	Ostrava...................Czech.	49·51 N	18·18 E
121	Ostróda (ôs′trōōt-ȧ)..........Pol.	53·41 N	19·58 E
129	Ostróg (ôs-trôk′)........Sov. Un.	50·21 N	26·40 E
129	Ostrogozhsk (ôs-trô-gôzhk′) Sov. Un.	50·53 N	39·03 E
121	Ostrołeka (ôs-trô-woɴ′kȧ)....Pol.	53·04 N	21·35 E
129	Ostropol′ (ôs-trô-pôl′)...Sov. Un.	49·48 N	27·32 E
128	Ostrov (ôs-trôf′)........Sov. Un.	57·21 N	28·22 E
121	Ostrowiec Świetokrzyski (ôs-trô′vyĕts shvyĕɴ-tô-kzhĭ′ske) Pol.	50·55 N	21·24 E
121	Ostrów Lubelski (ôs′trŏŏf lōō′bĕl-skĭ).Pol.	51·32 N	22·49 E
121	Ostrów Mazowiecka (mä-zô-vyĕt′skȧ).Pol.	52·47 N	21·54 E
121	Ostrow Wielkopolski (ôs′trōōv vyĕl-kô-pôl′skē).Pol.	51·38 N	17·49 E
121	Ostrzeszów (ôs-tzhä′shōōf)....Pol.	51·26 N	17·56 E
127	Ostuni (ôs-tōō′nē)............It.	40·44 N	17·35 E
127	Osum (R.) (ō′sōōm)........Alb.	40·37 N	20·00 E
153	Ōsumi-Guntō (Arch.) (ō′sōō-mē gōōn′tō).Jap.	30·34 N	130·30 E
153	Ōsumi (Van Diemen) Kaikyō (Str.) (văn dē′mĕn) (käē′kyō) Jap.	31·02 N	130·10 E
124	Osuna (ô-sōō′nä)............Sp.	37·18 N	5·05 W
128	Osveya (ôs′vĕ-yȧ).......Sov. Un.	56·00 N	28·08 E
110	Oswaldtwistle (ŏz-wȧld-twĭs″l) Eng.	53·44 N	2·23 W
81	Oswegatchie (R.) (ŏs-wê-găch′ĭ) N. Y.	44·15 N	75·20 W
73	Oswego (ŏs-wē′gō)........Kans.	37·10 N	95·08 W
81	Oswego....................N. Y.	43·25 N	76·30 W
121	Oswiecim (ôsh-vyăɴ′tsyĭm)...Pol.	50·02 N	19·17 E
152	Otaru (ō′tȧ-rōō)............Jap.	43·07 N	141·00 E
98	Otavalo (ōtä-vä′lō)...........Ec.	0·14 N	78·16 W
166	Otavi (ô-tä′vē)........S. W. Afr.	19·35 S	17·20 E
68	Otay (ō′tä)..Calif. (San Diego In.)	32·36 N	117·04 W
128	Otepää (ô′tĕ-pâ).......Sov. Un.	58·03 N	26·31 E
127	Othonoí (I.).................Grc.	40·51 N	19·26 E
127	Óthris, Óros (Mts.)..........Grc.	39·00 N	22·15 E
87	Otish Mts. (ô-tĭsh′).........Can.	52·24 N	70·01 W
166	Otjiwarongo (ŏt-jē-wä-rôŋ′gō) Ang.	20·20 S	16·25 E
126	Otočac (ō′tô-chȧts)........Yugo.	44·53 N	15·15 E
136	Otradnoye (ô-trȧ′d-nôyĕ) Sov. Un. (Leningrad In.)	59·46 N	30·50 E
127	Otranto (ō′trän-tô) (ô-trăn′tō)..It.	40·07 N	18·30 E
127	Otranto, C. di..............It.	40·06 N	18·32 E
127	Otranto, Strait of.........It.-Alb.	40·30 N	18·45 E
136	Otra R. (ôt′rȧ) Sov. Un. (Moscow In.)	55·22 N	38·20 E
80	Otsego (ŏt-sē′gō)..........Mich.	42·25 N	85·45 W
153	Otsu (ō′tsōō)....Jap. (Ōsaka In.)	35·00 N	135·54 E
118	Ottavand (L.) (ôt′tä-vän).....Nor.	61·53 N	8·40 E
85	Ottawa (ŏt′ȧ-wȧ) Can. (Ottawa In.)	45·25 N	75·43 W
80	Ottawa.......................Ill.	41·20 N	88·50 W
73	Ottawa.....................Kans.	38·37 N	95·16 W
80	Ottawa.....................Ohio	41·00 N	84·00 W
87	Ottawa (R.)................Can.	46·05 N	77·20 W
87	Ottawa Is...................Can.	59·50 N	81·00 W
168	Ottensville (ŏt′ĕns-vĭl)......S. Afr. (Johannesburg & Pretoria In.)	24·46 S	29·34 E
118	Otteråen (ôt′ĕr-ôĕn).........Nor.	59·13 N	7·20 E
69	Otter Cr. (ŏt′ēr)............Utah	38·20 N	111·55 W
81	Otter Cr.....................Vt.	44·05 N	73·15 W
65	Otter Pt.......Can. (Seattle In.)	48·21 N	123·50 W
70	Otter Tail (L.)............Minn.	46·21 N	95·52 W
74	Otterville (ŏt′ĕr-vĭl) Ill. (St. Louis In.)	39·03 N	90·24 W
166	Ottery (ŏt′ĕr-ĭ) S. Afr. (Cape Town In.)	34·02 S	18·31 E
71	Ottumwa (ô-tŭm′wȧ).........Iowa	41·00 N	92·26 W
91	Otumba (ô-tŭm′bä) Mex. (Mexico City In.)	19·41 N	98·46 W
160	Otway, C. (ŏt′wā)..........Austl.	38·55 S	153·40 E
100	Otway, Seno (B.) (sĕ′nō-ô′t-wä′y) Chile	53·00 S	73·00 W
121	Otwock (ôt′vôtsk)...........Pol.	52·05 N	21·18 E
63	Ouachita, (R.).............U. S.	33·25 N	92·30 W
73	Ouachita Mts. (wŏsh′ĭ-tô)...Okla.	34·29 N	95·01 W
165	Ouaddai (Reg.) (wä-dī′)....Chad	13·04 N	20·00 E
164	Ouagadougou (wä′gȧ-dōō′gōō) Upper Volta	12·20 N	1·43 W
164	Ouahigouya (wä-ê-gōō′yȧ) Upper Volta	13·34 N	2·22 W
164	Oualata (wä-lä′tä)....Mauritania	17·11 N	6·50 W
164	Ouallène (wäl-lân′)..........Alg.	24·43 N	1·15 E
95	Ouanaminthe...............Hai.	19·35 N	71·45 W
165	Ouanda-Djalé (wän′dȧ jä-lā′) Cen. Afr. Rep.	8·56 N	22·46 E
164	Ouarane (Dunes).....Mauritania	20·44 N	10·27 W
164	Ouargla (wär′glä)...........Alg.	32·00 N	5·18 E
111	Oude Rijn (R.) Neth. (Amsterdam In.)	52·09 N	4·33 E
111	Oudewater.Neth. (Amsterdam In.)	52·01 N	4·52 E
111	Oud Gastel Neth. (Amsterdam In.)	51·35 N	4·27 E
114	Oudrhes, L. (Mt.)..........Mor.	32·33 N	4·49 W
166	Oudtshoorn (outs′hōrn)....S. Afr.	33·33 S	23·36 E
164	Oued-Zem (wĕd-zĕm′).......Mor.	33·05 N	5·49 W
122	Ouessant, I. d′ (ēl-dwĕ-säɴ′)...Fr.	48·28 N	5·00 W
165	Ouesso.................Con. B.	1·38 N	16·04 E
95	Ouest, Pt...................Hai.	19·00 N	73·25 W
164	Ouezzane (wĕ-zan′).........Mor.	34·48 N	5·40 W
116	Oughter (L.) (lŏк oк′tĕr).....Ire.	54·02 N	7·40 W
164	Ouidah (wē-dä′)........Dahomey	6·25 N	2·05 E
114	Ouled Nail, Montes des (Mts.).Alg.	34·43 N	2·44 E
123	Oulins (ōō-läɴ′)....Fr. (Paris In.)	48·52 N	1·27 E
122	Oullins (ōō-läɴ′)..............Fr.	45·44 N	4·46 E
112	Oulu (ō′lōō)..................Fin.	64·58 N	25·43 E
112	Oulu-jarvi (L.)..............Fin.	64·20 N	25·48 E
165	Oum Chalouba (ōōm shä-lōō′bä) Chad	15·48 N	20·30 E
112	Ounas (R.) (ō′nȧs)..........Fin.	67·46 N	24·40 E
110	Oundle (ōn′d′l)..............Eng.	52·28 N	0·28 W
165	Ounianga Kébir (ōō-nē-äŋ′gȧ kē-bēr′).Chad	19·04 N	20·22 E
69	Ouray (ōō-rā′)..............Colo.	38·00 N	107·40 W
99	Ourinhos (ôōō-rē′nyôs)......Braz.	23·04 S	49·45 W
124	Ourique (ō-rē′kĕ)...........Port.	37·39 N	8·10 W
101	Ouro Fino (ōū-rô-fē′nō) Braz. (Rio de Janeiro In.)	22·18 S	46·21 W
101	Ouro Prêto (ō′rōō prā′tōō) Braz. (Rio de Janeiro In.)	20·24 S	43·30 W
116	Ouse (R.)..................Eng.	53·45 N	1·09 W
87	Outardes, R. aux (ōō-tärdz′).Can.	50·33 N	69·10 W
164	Outat el Hadj.............Mor.	33·25 N	3·44 W
83	Outer (I.) (out′ĕr)..........Can.	51·06 N	58·23 W
71	Outer (I.) (out′ĕr)..........Wis.	47·03 N	90·20 W
89	Outer Brass (I.) (brȧs)....Vir. Is. (U. S. A.) (St. Thomas In.)	18·24 N	64·58 W
116	Outer Hebrides (Is.)........Scot.	57·20 N	7·50 W
166	Outjo (ōt′yō)..........S. W. Afr.	20·05 S	17·10 E
85	Outremont (ōō-trē-môɴ′) Can. (Montreal In.)	45·31 N	73·36 W
160	Ouyen (ōō-ĕn)..............Austl.	35·05 S	142·10 E
100	Ovalle (ô-väl′yä)............Chile	30·43 S	71·16 W
166	Ovamboland (Reg.)....S. W. Afr.	18·10 S	15·00 E
95	Ovando, Bahía de (B.) (bä-ē′ä-dĕ-ô-vä′n-dō).Cuba	20·10 N	74·05 W
124	Ovar (ô-vär′)...............Port.	40·52 N	8·38 W
111	Overijsche.....Bel. (Brussels In.)	50·46 N	4·32 E
74	Overland (ō′vēr-lȧnd) Mo. (St. Louis In.)	38·42 N	90·22 W
74	Overland Park Mo. (Kansas City In.)	38·59 N	94·40 W
84	Overlea (ō′vēr-lā) (ō′vēr-lē) Md. (Baltimore In.)	39·21 N	76·31 W
112	Overtornea.................Swe.	66·19 N	23·31 E
129	Ovidiopol′ (ô-vē-dē-ô′pôl′) Sov. Un.	46·15 N	30·28 E
95	Oviedo (ō-vyĕ′dō).....Dom. Rep.	17·50 N	71·25 W
124	Oviedo (ō-vē-ā′dhō)..........Sp.	43·22 N	5·50 W
129	Ovruch (ôv′rōōch)......Sov. Un.	51·19 N	28·51 E
153	Owada (ō′wä-dȧ).Jap. (Tōkyō In.)	35·43 N	140·06 E
153	Owada..........Jap. (Tōkyō In.)	35·49 N	139·33 E
81	Owasco (L.) (ō-wăs′kō).....N. Y.	42·50 N	76·30 W
153	Owashi (ō′wä-shē)...........Jap.	34·03 N	136·12 E
81	Owego (ō-wē′gō)............N. Y.	42·05 N	76·15 W
71	Owen (ō′ĕn).................Wis.	44·56 N	90·35 W
68	Owens (L.) (ō′ĕnz)..........Calif.	36·27 N	117·45 W
68	Owens (R.).................Calif.	37·13 N	118·20 W
80	Owensboro (ō′ĕnz-bŭr-ô)......Ky.	37·45 N	87·05 W
80	Owen Sound (ō′ĕn)..........Can.	44·30 N	80·55 W
155	Owen Stanley Ra. (stăn′lē)..Pap.	9·00 S	147·30 E
80	Owensville (ō′ĕnz-vĭl)........Ind.	38·15 N	87·40 W
73	Owensville...................Mo.	38·20 N	91·29 W
75	Owensville..Ohio (Cincinnati In.)	39·08 N	84·07 W
80	Owenton (ō′ĕn-tŭn)...........Ky.	38·35 N	84·55 W
164	Owerri (ô-wĕr′ē).............Nig.	5·26 N	7·04 E
67	Owl Cr. (oul)...............Wyo.	43·45 N	108·46 W
80	Owosso (ô-wŏs′ō)...........Mich.	43·00 N	84·15 W
66	Owyhee Mts. (ô-wī′hē).....Idaho	43·15 N	116·48 W
66	Owyhee Res..................Ore.	43·27 N	117·30 W
66	Owyhee R...................Ore.	43·04 N	117·45 W
66	Owyhee R., South Fork....Idaho	42·07 N	116·43 W
91	Oxchuc (ôs-chōōk′)..........Mex.	16·47 N	92·24 W
78	Oxford (ŏks′fērd)............Ala.	33·38 N	8·46 W

ng-sing; ŋ-baŋk; ɴ-nasalized n; nŏd; cŏmmit; ōld; ôbey; ôrder; fōōd; fŏŏt; ou-out; s-soft; sh-dish; th-thin; pūre; ûnite; ûrn; stŭd; circŭs; ü-as "y" in study; ′-indeterminate vowel.

Page	Name Pronunciation Region	Lat. °′	Long. °′
82	Oxford (ŏks'fẽrd) Can.	45·44 N	63·51 W
110	Oxford Eng. (London In.)	51·43 N	1·16 W
83	Oxford Mass. (Boston In.)	42·07 N	71·52 W
80	Oxford Mich.	42·50 N	83·15 W
78	Oxford Miss.	34·22 N	89·30 W
79	Oxford N. C.	36·17 N	78·35 W
80	Oxford Ohio	39·30 N	84·45 W
92	Oxkutzcab (ōx-kōō'tz-kȧb) Mex. (Yucatan In.)	20·18 N	89·22 W
84	Oxmoor (ŏks'mōōr) Ala. (Birmingham In.)	33·25 N	86·52 W
116	Ox Mts. (ŏks) Ire.	54·05 N	9·05 W
68	Oxnard (ŏks'närd) Calif.	34·08 N	119·12 W
91	Oxtotepec (ôx-tô-tĕ'pĕk) Mex. (Mexico City In.)	19·10 N	99·04 W
168	Oxyrhyncus (Ruins) U. A. R. (Nile In.)	28·37 N	30·48 E
99	Oyapock (ō-yȧ-pŏk').Braz.-Fr. Gu.	2·45 N	52·15 W
164	Oyem (ô-yĕm) (ô-yăɴ') Gabon	1·42 N	11·38 E
135	Oymyakon (oi-myŭ-kôn').Sov. Un.	63·14 N	142·58 E
164	Oyo (ō'yō) Nig.	7·52 N	3·51 E
123	Oyonnax (ô-yô-nȧks') Fr.	46·16 N	5·40 E
84	Oyster Bay. N. Y. (New York In.)	40·52 N	73·32 W
77	Oyster Bay Tex. (In.)	29·41 N	94·33 W
77	Oyster Cr. (ois'tẽr) Tex. (In.)	29·13 N	95·29 W
95	Ozama (R.) (ō-zä'mä). Dom. Rep.	18·45 N	69·55 W
155	Ozamiz (ô-zä'mēz) Phil.	8·06 N	123·43 E
78	Ozark (ō'zärk) Ala.	31·28 N	85·28 W
73	Ozark Ark.	35·29 N	93·49 W
73	Ozarks, L. of the (ō'zärkz) Mo.	38·06 N	93·26 W
73	Ozark Plat. Mo.	36·37 N	93·56 W
128	Ozëry (ô-zyô'rê) Sov. Un.	54·53 N	38·31 E
126	Ozieri Sard.	40·38 N	8·53 E
121	Ozorków (ô-zôr'kōōf) Pol.	51·58 N	19·20 E
91	Ozuluama (ō'zōō-lōō-ȧ'mä). Mex.	21·34 N	97·52 W
91	Ozumba (ô-zōō'm-bä) Mex. (Mexico City In.)	19·02 N	98·48 W
146	Paan China	30·08 N	99·00 E
166	Paarl (pärl) S. Afr.	33·45 S	18·55 E
157	Paauilo (pä-ä-ōō'ê-lō).Hawaii (In.)	20·03 N	155·25 W
121	Pabianice (pä-byȧ-nē'tsĕ) Pol.	51·40 N	19·29 E
98	Pacaás Novos, Massiço de (Mts.) (mä-sē'sô-dĕ-pä-kȧ's-nô'vōs) Braz.	11·03 S	64·02 W
98	Pacaraima, Serra (Mts.) (sĕr'rȧ pä-kä-rä-ē'mȧ) Braz. -Ven.	3·45 N	62·30 W
98	Pacasmayo (pä-käs-mä'yō) Peru	7·24 S	79·30 W
146	Pach'u (pä'chōō') China	39·50 N	78·23 E
90	Pachuca (pä-chōō'kä) Mex.	20·07 N	98·43 W
65	Pacific (pȧ-sĭf'ĭk) Wash. (Seattle In.)	47·16 N	122·15 W
65	Pacifica (pȧ-sĭf'ĭ-kä) Calif. (San Francisco In.)	37·38 N	122·29 W
68	Pacific Beach Calif. (San Diego In.)	32·47 N	117·22 W
68	Pacific Grove Calif.	36·37 N	121·54 W
157	Pacific O.		
79	Pacolet (R.) (pă'cō-lĕt) S. C.	34·55 N	81·49 W
123	Pacy-sur-Eure (pä-sē-sür-ûr') Fr. (Paris In.)	49·01 N	1·24 E
154	Padang (pä-däng') Indon.	1·01 S	100·28 E
139	Padang, Palau (I.) Indon. (Singapore In.)	1·12 N	102·21 E
80	Paden City (pā'dĕn) W. Va.	39·30 N	80·55 W
120	Paderborn (pä-dĕr-bôrn') Ger.	51·43 N	8·46 E
110	Padiham (păd'ĭ-hăm) Eng.	53·48 N	2·19 W
90	Padilla (pä-dēl'yä) Mex.	24·00 N	98·45 W
65	Padilla B. (pä-dĭl'lȧ) Wash. (Seattle In.)	48·31 N	122·34 W
126	Padova (Padua) (pä'dô-vä) (păd'ū-ȧ). It.	45·24 N	11·53 E
77	Padre I. (pä'drā) Tex.	27·09 N	97·15 W
	Padua, see Padova		
78	Paducah (pȧ-dū'kȧ) Ky.	37·05 N	88·36 W
152	Paektu San (Mt.) (pâk'tōō-sän') China-Kor.	42·00 N	128·03 E
126	Pag (I.) (päg) Yugo.	44·30 N	14·48 E
154	Pagai Selatan (I.) Indon.	2·48 S	100·22 E
154	Pagai Utara (I.) Indon.	2·45 S	100·02 E
127	Pagasitikós Kólpos (G.) Grc.	39·15 N	23·00 E
69	Pagosa Springs (pȧ-gō'sȧ). Colo.	37·15 N	107·05 W
157	Pahala (pä-hä'lä) Hawaii (In.)	19·11 N	155·28 W
139	Pahang (State) Mala. (Singapore In.)	3·02 N	102·57 E
154	Pahang R. Mala.	3·39 N	102·41 E
79	Pahokee (pȧ-hō'kē) Fla. (In.)	26·45 N	80·40 W
148	Paichü (bäī'gü) China	33·04 N	120·17 E
150	Paich'uan China	47·22 N	126·00 E
119	Paide (pī'dĕ) Sov. Un.	58·54 N	25·30 E
150	Paiho China	32·30 N	110·15 E
148	Pai Hu (L.) (bäī' hōō) China	31·22 N	117·38 E
119	Päijänna (L.) (pĕ'ē-yĕn-nĕ) Fin.	61·38 N	25·05 E
148	Paikouchen (bäī'gō'jen) China	39·08 N	116·02 E
150	Pailingmiao China	41·42 N	110·55 E
157	Pailolo Chan. (pä-ê-lō'lō) Hawaii (In.)	21·05 N	156·41 W
101	Paine (pī'nĕ). Chile (Santiago In.)	33·49 S	70·44 W
80	Painesville (pānz'vĭl) Ohio	41·40 N	81·15 W
69	Painted Des. (pānt'ĕd) Ariz.	36·15 N	111·35 W
80	Paintsville (pānts'vĭl) Ky.	37·50 N	82·50 W
148	Paip'u (bäī'pōō) China	32·15 N	120·47 E
151	Paise China	24·00 N	106·38 E
116	Paisley (pāz'lĭ) Scot.	55·50 N	4·30 W
98	Paita (pä-ē'tä) Peru	5·11 S	81·12 W
150	Pai T'ou Shan (Mts.) Korea	40·30 N	127·20 E
69	Paiute Ind. Res. Utah	38·17 N	113·50 W
150	Paiyü Shan (Mtns.) China	37·02 N	108·30 E
91	Pajápan (pä-hä'pän) Mex.	18·16 N	94·41 W
154	Pakanburu Indon.	0·43 N	101·15 E
154	Pakhoi (päk'hoi') China	21·58 N	108·51 E
136	Pakhra R. (päᴋ'rá) Sov. Un. (Moscow In.)	55·29 N	37·51 E
138	Pakistan Asia	28·00 N	67·30 E
142	Pakistan, East Asia	24·15 N	89·50 E
142	Pakistan, West Asia	32·20 N	71·30 E
154	Pakokku (pȧ-kŏk'kōō) Bur.	21·29 N	95·00 E
126	Pakrac (pä'kräts) Yugo.	45·25 N	17·13 E
121	Paks (pôksh) Hung.	46·38 N	18·53 E
77	Palacios (pȧ-lä'syōs) Tex.	28·42 N	96·12 W
125	Palafrogell (pä-lä-frô-gĕl) Sp.	41·55 N	3·09 E
126	Palagruža (Is.) (pä'lä-grōō'zhä) Yugo.	42·20 N	16·23 E
123	Palaiseau (pȧ-lĕ-zō'). Fr. (Paris In.)	48·44 N	2·16 E
135	Palana Sov. Un.	59·07 N	159·58 E
155	Palanan B. (pä-lä'nän) Phil. (Manila In.)	17·14 N	122·35 E
155	Palanan Pt. Phil. (Manila In.)	17·12 N	122·40 E
127	Palanka (pä'län-kä) Yugo.	45·14 N	19·24 E
142	Pālanpur (pä'lŭn-pōōr) India	24·08 N	73·29 E
166	Palapye (pȧ-läp'yĕ) Bech.	22·34 S	27·28 E
75	Palatine (păl'ȧ-tīn) Ill. (Chicago In.)	42·07 N	88·03 W
79	Palatka (pȧ-lăt'kȧ) Fla.	29·39 N	81·40 W
155	Palau (Pelew) Is. (pä-lä'ōō) Pac. Is. Trust. Ter.	7·15 N	134·30 E
155	Palauig (pä-lou'ēg) Phil. (Manila In.)	15·27 N	119·54 E
155	Palauig Pt. Phil. (Manila In.)	15·28 N	119·41 E
154	Palawan (I.) (pä-lä'wăn) Phil.	9·50 N	117·38 E
119	Paldiski (päl'dĭ-skĭ) Sov. Un.	59·22 N	24·04 E
154	Palembang (pä-lĕm-bäng'). Indon.	2·57 S	104·40 E
92	Palencia (pä-lĕn'sê-ȧ) Guat.	14·40 N	90·22 W
124	Palencia (pä-lĕ'n-syä) Sp.	42·02 N	4·32 W
91	Palenque (pä-lĕŋ'kä) Mex.	17·34 N	91·58 W
95	Palenque, Punta (Pt.) (pōō'n-tä) Dom. Rep.	18·10 N	70·10 W
85	Palermo (pä-lĕr'mô) Can. (Toronto In.)	43·26 N	79·47 W
98	Palermo Col. (In.)	2·53 N	75·26 W
126	Palermo It.	38·08 N	13·24 E
77	Palestine Tex.	31·46 N	95·38 W
139	Palestine (Reg.) (păl'ĕs-tīn) Asia (Palestine In.)	31·33 N	35·00 E
146	Paletwa (pŭ-lĕt'wä) Bur.	21·19 N	92·52 E
143	Palghāt India	10·49 N	76·40 E
142	Pali India	25·53 N	73·18 E
92	Palín (pä-lēn') Guat.	14·42 N	90·42 W
66	Palisade (păl-ĭ-sād') Nev.	40·39 N	116·11 W
91	Palizada (pä-lê-zä'dä) Mex.	18·17 N	92·04 W
142	Palk Str. (pôk) India	10·00 N	79·23 E
101	Palma (päl'mä) Braz. (Rio de Janeiro In.)	21·23 S	42·18 W
125	Palma, Ba. de (B.) (bä-ē'ä-dĕ). Sp.	39·24 N	2·37 E
124	Palma del Río (dĕl rē'ō) Sp.	37·43 N	5·19 W
125	Palma de Mallorca (dĕ-mäl-yô'r-kä). Sp.	39·35 N	2·38 E
99	Palmares (päl-mà'rĕs) Braz.	8·46 S	35·28 W
100	Palmas (päl'mäs) Braz.	26·20 S	51·56 W
164	Palmas, C. Lib.	4·30 N	9·20 W
95	Palma Soriano (sô-rê-ä'nō). Cuba	20·15 N	76·00 W
79	Palm Beach (päm bēch'). Fla. (In.)	26·43 N	80·03 W
99	Palmeira dos Índios (päl-mā'rä-dôs-ē'n-dyōs). Braz.	9·26 S	36·33 W
125	Palmela (päl-mä'lä) Port. (Lisbon In.)	38·34 N	8·54 W
64	Palmer (päm'ẽr) Alaska	61·38 N	149·15 W
65	Palmer Wash. (Seattle In.)	47·19 N	121·53 W
47	Palmer Pen. Ant.	70·00 S	65·00 W
159	Palmerston North (päm'ẽr-stŭn) N. Z. (In.)	40·21 S	175·43 E
159	Palmerville (päm'ẽr-vĭl) Austl.	16·08 S	144·15 E
79	Palmetto (pāl-mĕt'ō) Fla. (In.)	27·32 N	82·34 W
95	Palmetto Pt. Ba. Is.	21·15 N	73·25 W
126	Palmi (päl'mē) It.	38·21 N	15·54 E
98	Palmira (päl-mē'rä) Col. (In.)	3·33 N	76·17 W
94	Palmira Cuba	22·15 N	80·25 W
73	Palmyra (păl-mī'rȧ) Mo.	39·45 N	91·32 W
84	Palmyra. N. J. (Philadelphia In.)	40·01 N	75·00 W
157	Palmyra (I.) Oceania	6·00 N	162·20 W
142	Palmyras Pt. India	25·42 N	87·45 E
103	Palmyre Syr.	30·35 N	37·58 E
65	Palo Alto (pä'lō äl'tō) Calif. (San Francisco In.)	37·27 N	122·09 W
72	Paloduro Cr. (pä-lô-dōō'rō). Tex.	36·16 N	101·12 W
139	Paloh Mala. (Singapore In.)	2·11 N	103·12 E
76	Paloma, L. (pä-lō'mä) Mex.	26·53 N	104·02 W
101	Palomo, Cerro el (Mtn.) (sĕ'r-rô-ĕl-pä-lô'mô) Chile (Santiago In.)	34·36 S	70·20 W
125	Palos, Cabo de (C.) (kä'bô-dĕ-pä'lôs). Sp.	39·38 N	0·43 W
74	Palos Verdes Estates (pȧ'lŭs vûr'dĭs) Calif. (Los Angeles In.)	33·48 N	118·24 W
66	Palouse (pȧ-lōōz') Wash.	46·54 N	117·04 W
66	Palouse Hills Wash.	46·48 N	117·47 W
66	Palouse R. Wash.	47·02 N	117·35 W
133	Palu (pä-loo') Tur.	38·55 N	40·10 E
98	Palúa (pä-lōō'ȧ) Ven.	8·30 N	62·30 W
155	Paluan (pä-lōō'än) Phila. (Manila In.)	13·25 N	120·29 E
135	Pamamushir (I.) Sov. Un.	50·42 N	153·45 E
122	Pamiers (pȧ-myā') Fr.	43·07 N	1·34 E
145	Pamirs (Plat.) Sov. Un.	38·14 N	72·27 E
79	Pamlico R. (păm'lĭ-kō) N. C.	35·25 N	76·59 W
79	Pamlico Sd. N. C.	35·10 N	76·10 W
72	Pampa (păm'pȧ) Tex.	35·32 N	100·56 W
100	Pampa de Castillo (Plat.) (pä'm-pä-dĕ-käs-tē'l-yō). Arg.	45·30 S	67·30 W
155	Pampanga (R.) (päm-päŋ'gä) Phil. (Manila In.)	15·20 N	120·48 E
100	Pampas (Reg.) (päm'päs) Arg.	37·00 S	64·30 W
124	Pampilhosa do Botão (päm-pê-lyō'sȧ-dô-bō-to'uɴ) Port.	40·21 N	8·23 W
98	Pamplona (päm-plō'nä) Col.	7·19 N	72·41 W
124	Pamplona (päm-plō'nä) Sp.	42·49 N	1·39 W
81	Pamunkey (R.) (pȧ-mŭŋ'kĭ). Va.	37·40 N	77·20 W
80	Pana (pā'nȧ) Ill.	39·25 N	89·05 W
92	Panabá (pä-nä-bä') Mex. (Yucatan In.)	21·18 N	88·15 W
127	Panagyurishte (pȧ-nȧ-gyōō'rêsh-tĕ). Bul.	42·30 N	24·11 E
88	Panamá (păn-ȧ-mä') N. A. (Panama Canal In.)	8·35 N	81·08 W
89	Panama, G. of Pan.	7·45 N	79·20 W
89	Panama, Isth. of Pan.	9·00 N	81·00 W
93	Panama, B. of Pan.	8·50 N	79·08 W
78	Panama City (păn-ȧ mä' sĭ'tĭ). Fla.	30·08 N	85·39 W
68	Panamint Ra. (păn-ȧ-mĭnt') Calif.	36·40 N	117·30 W
126	Panaria (Is.) (pä-nä'rê-ä) It.	38·37 N	15·05 E
126	Panaro (R.) (pä-nä'rô) It.	44·47 N	11·06 E
154	Panay (I.) (pä-nī') Phil.	11·15 N	121·38 E
127	Pančevo (pän'chĕ-vô) Yugo.	44·52 N	20·42 E
139	Panchor. Mala. (Singapore In.)	2·10 N	102·43 E
166	Panda (pän'dä') Con. L.	10·59 S	27·24 E
94	Pan de Guajaibon (Mtn.) (pän dä gwä-jȧ-bōn'). Cuba	22·50 N	83·20 W
154	Pandjang, Selat (Str.) Indon.	1·00 N	102·00 E
119	Panevėžys (pä'nyĕ-väzh'ēs) Sov. Un.	55·44 N	24·21 E
134	Panfilov (pŭn-fē'lôf) Sov. Un.	44·12 N	79·58 E
165	Panga (päŋ'gä) Con. L.	1·58 N	26·45 E
167	Pangani (pän-gä'nē) Tan.	5·28 S	38·58 E
149	P'angchiang. China (Canton In.)	22·57 N	113·15 E
148	Pangfou (bäng'fōō) China	32·54 N	117·22 E
154	Pangkalpinang (päng-käl'pê-näng') Indon.	2·11 S	106·04 E
142	Pangkong Tsho (L.) China	33·40 N	79·30 E
87	Pangnirtung Can.	66·08 N	65·26 W
69	Panguitch (păŋ'gwĭch) Utah	37·50 N	112·30 W
101	Panimávida (pä-nē-mà'vē-dä) Chile (Santiago In.)	36·44 S	71·26 W
	Panjim, see Nova Goa		
150	Panshih China	42·50 N	126·48 E
151	Pan Si Pan (Mtn.) Viet.	22·25 N	103 50 E
155	Pantar (I.) (pän'tär) Indon.	8·40 S	123·45 E
74	Pantego (păn'tĭ-gō) Tex. (Dallas, Fort Worth In.)	32·45 N	97·06 W
113	Pantelleria (I.) (pän-tĕl-lȧ-rē'ä) It.	36·43 N	11·59 E
91	Pantepec (pän-tä-pĕk') Mex.	17·11 N	93·04 W
90	Panuco (pä'nōō-kô) Mex.	22·04 N	98·11 W
90	Pánuco (pä'nōō-kô) Mex.	29·47 N	105·55 W
90	Panuco (R.) Mex.	21·59 N	98·20 W
76	Pánuco de Coronado (pä'nōō-kô dä kō-rô-nä'dhō) Mex.	24·33 N	104·20 W
143	Panvel India (Bombay In.)	18·59 N	73·06 E
92	Panzós (pän-zós') Guat.	15·26 N	89·40 W
99	Pao (pà'ō) (R.) Ven. (In.)	9·52 N	67·57 W
150	Paochang China	41·52 N	115·25 E
150	Paocheng China	33·15 N	106·58 E
150	Paochi China	34·10 N	106·58 E
73	Paola (pā-ō'lȧ) Kans.	38·34 N	94·51 W
80	Paoli (pȧ-ō'lĭ) Ind.	38·35 N	86·30 W
84	Paoli Pa. (Philadelphia In.)	40·03 N	75·29 W
69	Paonia (pā-ō'nyȧ) Colo.	38·50 N	107·40 W
146	Paoshan (pä'ô-shän') China	25·14 N	99·03 E
149	Paoshan China (Shanghai In.)	31·25 N	121·29 E
148	Paoti (pä'ô-tē') China	39·44 N	117·19 E
150	Paot'ou China	40·28 N	110·10 E
148	Paoying (pä'ô-yĭng) China	33·14 N	119·20 E
121	Pápa (pä'pô) Hung.	47·18 N	17·27 E
92	Papagayo, Golfo del (G.) (gôl-fô-dĕl-pä-pä-gä'yō). C. R.	10·44 N	85·56 W
90	Papagayo, Laguna (L.) (lä-ōō-nä) Mex.	16·44 N	99·44 W
90	Papagayo (R.) (pä-pä-gä'yō) Mex.	16·52 N	99·41 W
69	Papago Ind. Res. (pä'pä-gō). Ariz.	32·33 N	112·12 W
88	Papantla de Olarte (pä-pän'tlä dä-ô-lä'r-tĕ). Mex.	20·30 N	97·15 W
91	Papatoapan (R.) (pä-pä-tô-ä-pä'n). Mex.	18·00 N	96·22 W
120	Papenburg (päp'ĕn-bōōrgh). Ger.	53·05 N	7·23 E
101	Papinas (pä-pē'näs) Arg. (Buenos Aires In.)	35·30 S	57·19 W
85	Papineauville (pä-pē-nō'vĕl) Can. (Ottawa In.)	45·38 N	75·01 W
155	Papua (păp'ōōȧ) Oceania	7·30 S	142·30 E
155	Papua, Gulf of (păp-ōō-ȧ). Pap.	8·20 S	144·45 E
101	Papudo (pä-pōō'dô) Chile (Santiago In.)	32·30 S	71·25 W
100	Paquequer Pequeno (pä-kĕ-kĕ'r-pĕ-kĕ'nô). Braz. (In.)	22·19 S	43·02 W
	Pará, see Belém		
99	Pará (State) (pä-rä') Braz.	4·45 S	53·30 W
101	Pará (pä-rä') (R.) Braz. (Rio de Janeiro In.)	20·21 S	44·38 W
99	Pará, Rio do (R.) (rē'ō-dô-pä-rä') Braz.	1·09 S	48·48 W
128	Para (R.) Sov. Un.	53·45 N	40·58 E
155	Paracale (pä-rä-kä'lā) Phil. (Manila In.)	14·17 N	122·47 E
100	Paracambi (pä-rä-kä'm-bē) Braz. (In.)	22·36 S	43·43 W
99	Paracatu (pä-rä-kä-tōō') Braz.	17·17 S	46·43 W
160	Parachilna (pä-rä-chĭl'nä). Austl.	31·09 S	138·20 E
127	Paraćin (pä'rä-chēn) Yugo.	43·51 N	21·26 E
101	Para de Minas (pä-rä-dĕ-mē'näs) Braz. (Rio de Janeiro In.)	19·52 S	44·37 W
66	Paradise Valley (păr'ȧ-dīs). Nev.	41·28 N	117·32 W
98	Parados, Cerro de los (Mtn.) (sĕ'r-rô-dĕ-lôs-pä-rä'dôs) Col. (In.)	5·44 N	75·13 W
73	Paragould (păr'ȧ-gōōld) Ark.	36·03 N	90·29 W
99	Paraguaçu (R.) (pä-rä-gwä-zōō') Braz.	12·25 S	39·46 W
98	Paraguaná, Pen. de (Pen.) (pĕ-nē'ng-sōō-lä-dĕ-pä-rä-gwä-nä'). Ven.	12·00 N	69·55 W
96	Paraguay (păr'ȧ-gwā) S. A.	24·00 S	57·00 W
99	Paraguay, Rio (R.) (rē'ō-pä-rä-gwä'y). S. A.	21·12 S	57·31 W
	Paraíba, see João Pessoa		
99	Paraíba (State) (pä-rä-ē'bä). Braz.	7·11 S	37·05 W

ăt; finăl; rāte; senâte; ärm; ȧsk; sofȧ; fâre; ch-choose; dh-as th in other; bē; êvent; bĕt; recĕnt; cratẽr; g-go; gh-guttural g; bĭt; ĭ-short neutral; rīde; ᴋ-guttural k as ch in German ich;

ng-sing; ŋ-baŋk; N-nasalized n; nŏd; cŏmmit; ōld; ŏbey; ôrder; fōōd; fŏŏt; ou-out; s-soft; sh-dish; th-thin; pūre; ūnite; ûrn; stŭd; circŭs; ū-as "y" in study; '-indeterminate vowel.

ăt; fïnăl; rāte; senâte; ärm; àsk; sofà; fâre; ch-choose; dh-as th in other; bē; ĕvent; bĕt; recĕnt; cratĕr; g-go; gh-guttural g; bĭt; ĭ-short neutral; rīde; κ-guttural k as ch in German ich;

PRONOUNCING INDEX Petseri–Plain City 251

Page	Name Pronunciation Region	Lat. °′	Long. °′
128	Petseri (pĕt'sĕ-rē) Sov. Un.	57·48 N	27·33 E
75	Pewaukee (pĭ-wô'kē) Wis. (Milwaukee In.)	43·05 N	88·15 W
75	Pewaukee L. Wis. (Milwaukee In.)	43·03 N	88·18 W
75	Pewee Valley (pe wē) Ky. (Louisville In.)	38·19 N	85·29 W
132	Peza (R.) (pyâ'zâ) Sov. Un.	65·35 N	46·50 E
122	Pézenas (pā-zē-nä') Fr.	43·26 N	3·24 E
120	Pforzheim (pfôrts'hīm) Ger.	48·52 N	8·43 E
142	Phalodi India	27·13 N	72·22 E
154	Phan Rang (p'hän'räng') Viet.	11·30 N	108·43 E
	Pharsalus, see Fársala		
78	Phenix City (fē'nĭks) Ala.	32·29 N	85·00 W
154	Phet Buri Thai.	13·07 N	99·53 E
78	Philadelphia (fĭl-à-dĕl'phĭ-à) Miss.	32·45 N	89·07 W
84	Philadelphia Pa. (Philadelphia In.)	40·00 N	75·13 W
70	Philip (fĭl'ĭp) S. D.	44·03 N	101·35 W
164	Philippeville (fē-lēp'vēl') Alg.	36·58 N	6·51 E
155	Philippines (fĭl'ĭ-pēnz) Asia	14·25 N	125·00 E
156	Philippine Sea (fĭl'ĭ-pēn) Asia	16·00 N	133·00 E
155	Philippine Trench Phil.	10·30 N	127·15 E
	Philippopolis, see Plovdiv		
81	Philipsburg (fĭl'lĭps-bẽrg) Pa.	40·55 N	78·10 W
67	Philipsburg Wyo.	46·19 N	113·19 W
160	Phillip (I.) (fĭl'ĭp) Austl.	38·32 S	145·10 E
139	Phillip Chan. Indon. (Singapore In.)	1·04 N	103·40 E
81	Phillipi (fĭ-lĭp'ĭ) W. Va.	39·10 N	80·00 W
71	Phillips (fĭl'ĭps) Wis.	45·41 N	90·24 W
72	Phillipsburg (fĭl'lĭps-bẽrg) Kans.	39·44 N	99·19 W
81	Phillipsburg Pa.	40·45 N	75·10 W
154	Phnom Penh (nŏm'pĕn') Camb.	11·39 N	104·53 E
84	Phoebus (fē'bŭs) Va. (Norfolk In.)	37·02 N	76·19 W
69	Phoenix (fē'nĭks) Ariz.	33·30 N	112·00 W
84	Phoenix La. (New Orleans In.)	29·39 N	89·56 W
156	Phoenix Is Oceania	4·00 S	174·00 W
84	Phoenixville (fē'nĭks-vĭl) Pa. (Philadelphia In.)	40·08 N	75·31 W
154	Phu Bia (Pk.) Laos	19·36 N	103·00 E
154	Phuket Thai.	7·57 N	98·19 E
148	P'i (R.) (pē') China	32·06 N	116·31 E
126	Piacenza (pyä-chĕnt'sä) It.	45·02 N	9·42 E
126	Pianosa (I.) (pyä-nō'sä) It.	42·13 N	15·45 E
121	Piatra-Neamt (pyä'trà-nä-ämts') Rom.	46·54 N	26·24 E
99	Piauí (State) (pyou'ē) Braz.	7·40 S	42·25 W
99	Piauí, Serra do (Mts.) (sĕr'rà dōō pyou'ē) Braz.	10·45 S	44·36 W
126	Piave (R.) (pyä'vā) It.	45·45 N	12·15 E
126	Piazza Armerina (pyät'sä är-mā-rē'nä) It.	37·23 N	14·26 E
165	Pibor R. (pē'bôr) Sud.	7·21 N	32·54 E
71	Pic (R.) (pēk) Can.	48·48 N	86·28 W
89	Picara Pt. (pē-kä'rä) Vir. Is. (U. S. A.) (St. Thomas In.)	18·23 N	64·57 W
78	Picayune (pĭk'á yōōn) Miss.	30·32 N	89·41 W
126	Piccole Alpi Dolomitche (Mts.) (pē'k-kô-le-äl'pē-dô-lô'mē-tē'chĕ) It.	46·05 N	12·17 E
125	Pic du Midi d'Ossau (Mtn.) (pēk dü mē-dē' dôs-sō') Fr.	42·51 N	0·25 W
73	Picher (pĭch'ẽr) Okla.	36·58 N	94·49 W
151	Pichieh China	27·20 N	105·18 E
101	Pichilemu (pē-chē-lĕ'mōō) Chile (Santiago In.)	34·22 S	72·01 W
91	Pichucalco (pē-chōō-käl'kō) Mex.	17·34 N	93.06 W
91	Pichucalco (R.) Mex.	17·40 N	93·02 W
71	Pickerel (L.) (pĭk'ẽr-ĕl) Can.	48·35 N	91·10 W
78	Pickwick (R.) (pĭk'wĭck) Tenn.	35·04 N	88·05 W
74	Pico (pē'kō) Calif. (Los Angeles In.)	34·01 N	118·05 W
125	Pico de Aneto (Mtn.) (pē'kō-dĕ-ä-nĕ'tô) Sp.	42·35 N	0·38 E
164	Pico I. (pē'kōō) Azores (In.)	38·16 N	28·49 W
99	Picos (pē'kōzh) Braz.	7·13 S	41·23 W
161	Picton (pĭk'tŭn) Austl. (Sydney In.)	34·11 S	150·37 E
83	Pictou (pĭk-tōō') Can.	45·43 N	62·44 W
143	Pidurutalagala Mt. (pē'dōō-rōō-tà'lá-gä'là) Ceylon	12·27 N	80·45 E
71	Pie (I.) (pī) Can.	48·10 N	89·07 W
101	Piedade (pyä-dä'dĕ) Braz. (Rio de Janeiro In.)	23·42 S	47·25 W
78	Piedmont (pēd'mŏnt) Ala.	33·54 N	85·36 W
65	Piedmont Calif. (San Francisco In.)	37·50 N	122·14 W
73	Piedmont Mo.	37·09 N	90·42 W
79	Piedmont S. C.	34·40 N	82·27 W
81	Piedmont W. Va.	39·30 N	79·05 W
124	Piedrabuena (pyā-drä-bwā'nä) Sp.	39·01 N	4·10 W
101	Piedras, Punta (Pt.) (pōō'n-tä-pyĕ'dräs) Arg. (Buenos Aires In.)	35·25 S	57·10 W
76	Piedras Negras (pyā'dräs nā'gräs) Mex.	28·41 N	100·33 W
119	Pieksämäki (pyĕk'sĕ-mĕ-kĕ) Fin.	62·18 N	27·14 E
124	Piélagos (pyā'lä-gōs) Sp.	43·23 N	3·55 W
126	Piemonte (Reg.) (pyĕ-mô'n-tĕ) It.	44·30 N	7·42 E
168	Pienaars R. S. Afr. (Johannesburg & Pretoria In.)	25·13 S	28·05 E
168	Pienaarsrivier S. Afr. (Johannesburg & Pretoria In.)	25·12 S	28·18 E
70	Pierce (pērs) Nebr.	42·11 N	97·33 W
81	Pierce W. Va.	39·15 N	79·30 W
84	Piermont (pēr'mŏnt) N. Y. (New York In.)	41·03 N	73·55 W
70	Pierre (pēr) S. D.	44·22 N	100·20 W
121	Piešťany (pyĕsh'tyä-nŭ'ĭ) Czech.	48·36 N	17·48 E
167	Pietermaritzburg (pē-tẽr-mä-rĭts-bûrg) S. Afr. (Natal In.)	29·36 S	30·23 E
168	Pietersburg (pē'tẽrz-bûrg) S. Afr. (Johannesburg & Pretoria In.)	23·56 S	29·30 E
81	Pieton Can.	44·00 N	77·15 W
166	Piet Retief (pēt rĕ-tēf') S. Afr.	27·00 S	30·58 E
121	Pietrosul Pk. Rom.	47·35 N	24·49 E
126	Pieve di Cadore (pyā'vå dē kä-dō'rā) It.	46·26 N	12·22 E
71	Pigeon (R.) (pĭj'ŭn) Can.-Minn.	48·05 N	90·13 W
85	Pigeon Lake Can. (Winnipeg In.)	49·57 N	97·36 W
73	Piggott (pĭg'ŭt) Ark.	36·22 N	90·10 W
91	Pijijiapan (pēkē-kē-ä'pän) Mex.	15·40 N	93·12 W
111	Pijnacker Neth. (Amsterdam In.)	52·01 N	4·25 E
72	Pikes Pk. (pīks) Colo.	38·49 N	105·03 W
79	Pikeville (pīk'vĭl) Ky.	37·28 N	82·31 W
120	Piła (pē'là) Pol.	53·09 N	16·44 E
168	Pilansberg (pē'ăns'bûrg) S. Afr. (Johannesburg & Pretoria In.)	25·08 S	26·55 E
101	Pilar (pē'lär) Arg. (Buenos Aires In.)	34·27 S	58·55 W
100	Pilar Par.	27·00 S	58·15 W
155	Pilar (pē'lär) Phil. (Manila In.)	12·55 N	123·41 E
155	Pilar Phil. (Manila In.)	17·24 N	120·36 E
99	Pilar de Goiás (dĕ-gô'yà's) Braz.	14·47 S	49·33 W
65	Pilchuck (R.) Wash. (Seattle In.)	48·03 N	121·58 W
65	Pilchuck Cr. (pĭl'chŭk) Wash. (Seattle In.)	48·19 N	122·11 W
65	Pilchuck Mtn. Wash. (Seattle In.)	48·03 N	121·48 W
100	Pilcomayo (R.) (pēl-cō-mī'ō) Par.	24·45 S	69·15 W
155	Pili (pē'lē) Phil. (Manila In.)	13·34 N	123·17 E
121	Pilica R. (pē-lēt'sä) Pol.	51·00 N	19·48 E
65	Pillar Pt. (pĭl'ár) Can. (Seattle In.)	48·14 N	124·06 W
65	Pillar Rock Wash. (Portland In.)	46·16 N	123·35 W
90	Pilón (R.) (pē-lōn') Mex.	24·13 N	99·03 W
73	Pilot Point (pī'lŭt) Tex.	33·24 N	97·00 W
84	Pilottown (pī'lŭt-toun) La. (New Orleans In.)	29·11 N	89·15 W
	Pilsen, see Plzeň		
119	Piltene (pĭl'tĕ-nĕ) Sov. Un.	57·17 N	21·40 E
90	Pimal, Cerra (Mtn.) (sĕ'r-rä-pē-mäl') Mex.	22·58 N	104·19 W
158	Pimba (pĭm'bá) Austl.	31·15 S	146·50 E
167	Pimville (pĭm'vĭl) S. Afr. (Johannesburg & Pretoria In.)	26·17 S	27·54 E
88	Pinacate, Cerro (Mtn.) (sĕ'r-rō-pē-nä-kä'tĕ) Mex.	31·45 N	113·30 W
155	Pinamalayan (pē-nä-mä-lä'yän) Phil. (Manila In.)	13·04 N	121·31 E
133	Pinarbasi (pē'när-bä'shĭ) Tur.	38·50 N	36·10 E
94	Pinar del Rio (pē-när' dĕl rē'ō) Cuba	22·25 N	83·35 W
94	Pinar del Rio (State) Cuba	22·45 N	83·25 W
155	Pinatubo (Mtn.) (pē-nä-tōō'bō) Phil. (Manila In.)	15·09 N	120·19 E
73	Pinckneyville (pĭnk'nĭ-vĭl) Ill.	38·06 N	89·22 W
121	Pińczow (pēn''chōōf) Pol.	50·32 N	20·33 E
101	Pindamonhangaba (pē'n-dä-mōnyà'n-gä-bä) Braz. (Rio de Janeiro In.)	22·56 S	45·26 W
127	Píndhos Oros (Mts.) Grc.	39·48 N	21·19 E
83	Pine, C (pīn) Can.	46·36 N	53·35 W
71	Pine (R.) Wis.	45·50 N	88·37 W
73	Pine Bluff (pīn blŭf) Ark.	34·13 N	92·01 W
71	Pine City (pīn) Minn.	45·50 N	93·01 W
158	Pine Creek Austl.	13·45 S	132·00 E
68	Pine Cr. Nev.	40·15 N	116·17 W
66	Pine Forest Ra. Nev.	41·35 N	118·45 W
132	Pinega (pê-nyĕ'gà) Sov. Un.	64·40 N	43·30 E
132	Pinega (R.) Sov. Un.	64·10 N	42·30 E
84	Pine Hill (pīn hĭl) N. J. (Philadelphia In.)	39·47 N	74·59 W
65	Pinehurst (pīn'hûrst) Wash. (Seattle In.)	47·56 N	122·13 W
79	Pine Is. Fla. (In.)	24·48 N	81·32 W
79	Pine Island Sd. Fla. (In.)	26·32 N	82·30 W
84	Pine Lake Estates (lăk ĕs-tāts') Ga. (Atlanta In.)	33·47 N	84·13 W
166	Pinelands (pīn'lănds) S. Afr. (Cape Town In.)	33·57 S	18·30 E
74	Pine Lawn (lôn) Mo. (St. Louis In.)	38·42 N	90·17 W
84	Pine Mountain (moun'tĭn) Ga. (Atlanta In.)	33·39 N	84·09 W
70	Pine Ridge Ind. Res. (rĭj) S. D.	43·33 N	102·13 W
126	Pinerola (pē-nâ-rô'lō) It.	44·47 N	7·18 E
77	Pines, Lake o' the Tex.	32·50 N	94·40 W
167	Pinetown (pīn'toun) S. Afr. (Natal In.)	29·47 S	30·52 E
74	Pine View Res. (vū) Utah (Salt Lake City In.)	41·17 N	111·54 W
78	Pineville (pīn'vĭl) Ky.	36·48 N	83·43 W
77	Pineville La.	31·20 N	92·25 W
154	Ping, Mae Nam (R.) Thai.	17·54 N	98·29 E
149	Pingchoupao China (Canton In.)	23·01 N	113·11 E
150	Pingchüan China	40·58 N	118·40 E
139	Pinggir Indon. (Singapore In.)	1·05 N	101·12 E
151	P'ingho (pĭng'hō') China	24·30 N	117·02 E
151	Pinghsiang China	27·40 N	113·50 E
150	Pingliang (pĭng'lyăng') China	35·12 N	106·50 E
151	P'inglo (pĭng'lō') China	24·30 N	110·22 E
151	P'ingt'an China	25·30 N	119·45 E
150	Pingting (pĭng'tĭng') China	37·50 N	113·30 E
148	P'ingtu (pĭng'tōō') China	36·46 N	119·57 E
151	P'ingtung Taiwan	22·40 N	120·35 E
150	P'ingwu China	32·20 N	104·40 E
148	P'ingyuan (pĭng'yü-än') China	37·11 N	116·26 E
101	Pinhal (pē-nyá'l) Braz. (Rio de Janeiro In.)	22·11 S	46·43 W
125	Pinhal Novo (nô vōō) Port. (Lisbon In.)	38·38 N	8·54 W
124	Pinhel (pēn-yĕl') Port.	40·45 N	7·03 W
148	Pinhsien (pĭn'sĭän) China	38·29 N	117·58 E
150	Pinhsien China	45·40 N	127·20 E
154	Pini (I.) (pē'nē) Indon.	0·07 N	98·38 E
127	Piniós (R.) Grc.	40·33 N	21·40 E
68	Pinnacles Natl. Mon. (pĭn'á-k'lz) Calif.	36·30 N	121·00 W
111	Pinneberg (pĭn'ĕ-bĕrg) Ger. (Hamburg In.)	53·40 N	9·48 E
65	Pinole (pĭ-nō'lē) Calif. (San Francisco In.)	38·01 N	122·17 W
94	Pinos, Isla de (I.) (ē's-lä-dĕ-pē'nôs) Cuba	21·40 N	82·45 W
124	Pinos-Puente (pwān'tå) Sp.	37·15 N	3·43 W
90	Pinotepa Nacional (pē-nô-tā'pä nä-syô-näl') Mex.	16·21 N	98·04 W
159	Pins, Ile des N. Cal.	22·44 S	167·44 E
121	Pinsk (pēn'sk) Sov. Un.	52·07 N	26·05 E
98	Pinta (I.) Ec.	0·41 N	90·47 W
85	Pintendre (pĕn-tändr') Can. (Quebec In.)	46·45 N	71·07 W
125	Pinto (pēn'tō) Sp. (Madrid In.)	40·14 N	3·42 W
69	Pioche (pī-ō'chē) Nev.	37·56 N	114·28 W
126	Piombino (pyôm-bē'nō) It.	42·56 N	10·33 E
65	Pioneer (pī'ô-nēr') Wash. (Portland In.)	45·49 N	122·40 W
67	Pioneer Mts. Mont.	45·23 N	112·51 W
121	Piotrków Trybunalski (pyōtr'kōōv trĭ-bōō-nal'skē) Pol.	51·23 N	19·44 E
78	Piper (pī'pẽr) Ala.	33·04 N	87·00 W
74	Piper Kans. (Kansas City In.)	39·09 N	94·51 W
127	Pipéri (I.) (pē'per-ē) Grc.	39·19 N	24·20 E
69	Pipe Spring Natl. Mon. (pīp sprĭng) Ariz.	36·50 N	112·45 W
70	Pipestone (pīp'stōn) Minn.	44·00 N	96·19 W
71	Pipestone (R.) Can.	48·34 N	92·22 W
70	Pipestone Natl. Mon. Minn.	44·03 N	96·24 W
82	Pipmaukin, L. (pĭp-mä-kän') Can.	49·36 N	69·55 W
80	Piqua (pĭk'wȧ) Ohio	40·10 N	84·15 W
101	Piracaia (pē-rä-kä'yä) Braz. (Rio de Janeiro In.)	23·04 S	46·20 W
101	Piracicaba (pē-rä-sē-kä'bä) Braz. (Rio de Janeiro In.)	22·43 S	47·39 W
101	Piraí (pē-rä-ē') Braz. (Rio de Janeiro In.)	22·38 S	43·54 W
101	Piraíba (R.) (pä-rä-ē'bà) Braz. (Rio de Janeiro In.)	21·38 S	41·29 W
134	Piramida, Gol'tsy (Mtn.) Sov. Un.	54·00 N	96·00 E
126	Piran (pē-rä'n) Yugo.	45·31 N	13·34 E
101	Piranga (pē-rä'n-gä) Braz. (Rio de Janeiro In.)	20·41 S	43·17 W
101	Pirapetinga (pē-rä-pĕ-tē'n-gä) Braz. (Rio de Janeiro In.)	21·40 S	42·20 W
99	Pirapóra (pē-rä-pō'rȧ) Braz.	17·39 S	44·54 W
101	Pirassununga (pē-rä-sōō-nōō'n-gä) Braz. (Rio de Janeiro In.)	22·00 S	47·24 W
99	Pirenópolis (pē-rĕ-nô'pō-lēs) Braz.	15·56 S	48·49 W
127	Pírgos Grc.	37·51 N	21·28 E
99	Piritu, Laguna de (L.) (lä-gōō'nä-dĕ-pē-rē'tōō) Ven. (In.)	10·00 N	64·57 W
120	Pirmasens (pĭr-mä-zĕns') Ger.	49·12 N	7·34 E
120	Pirna (pĭr'nä) Ger.	50·57 N	13·56 E
155	Piroe (pē-rōō') Indon.	3·15 S	128·25 E
127	Pirot (pē'rōt) Yugo.	43·09 N	22·35 E
69	Pirtleville (pûr't'l-vĭl) Ariz.	31·25 N	109·35 W
129	Piryatin (pēr-yä-tēn') Sov. Un.	50·13 N	32·31 E
126	Pisa (pē'sä) It.	43·52 N	10·24 E
98	Pisagua (pē-sä'gwä) Chile	18·43 S	70·12 W
98	Pisco (pēs'kō) Peru	13·43 S	76·07 W
98	Pisco, Bahia de (B.) (bä-ē'ä-dĕ) Peru	13·43 S	77·48 W
81	Piseco (L.) (pĭ-sā'kō) N. Y.	43·25 N	74·35 W
120	Pisek (pē'sĕk) Czech.	49·18 N	14·08 E
100	Pissis, Monte (Vol.) (mô'n-tĕ-pē-sēs') Arg.	27·50 S	68·35 W
139	Pissouri Cyprus (Palestine In.)	34·39 N	32·42 E
126	Pisticci (pēs-tē'chē) It.	40·24 N	16·34 E
126	Pistoia (pēs-tô'yä) It.	43·57 N	11·54 E
83	Pistolet B. (pĭs-tō-lā') Can.	51·40 N	55·43 W
124	Pisuerga (R.) (pē-swĕr'gä) Sp.	41·48 N	4·28 W
98	Pitalito (pē-tä-lē'tō) Col.	1·45 N	75·09 W
75	Pitcairn (pĭt'kârn) Pa. (Pittsburgh In.)	40·29 N	79·47 W
157	Pitcairn (I.) Oceania	24·30 S	133·00 W
112	Pite (R.) (pē'tĕ) Swe.	66·08 N	18·51 E
112	Piteå (pē'tĕ-ô') Swe.	65·21 N	21·10 E
127	Pitesti (pē-tĕsht') Rom.	44·51 N	24·51 E
158	Pithara (pĭt'ărȧ) Austl.	30·27 S	116·45 E
122	Pithiviers (pē-tē-vyā') Fr.	48·12 N	2·14 E
84	Pitman (pĭt'mȧn) N. J. (Philadelphia In.)	39·44 N	75·08 W
93	Pitons du Carbet, Mt. Mart. (Le. & Wind. Is. In.)	14·40 N	61·05 W
66	Pit R. (pĭt) Calif.	40·58 N	121·42 W
167	Pitseng Bas. (Natal In.)	29·03 S	28·13 E
65	Pitt (R.) Can. (Vancouver In.)	49·19 N	122·39 W
64	Pitt Pt. (pĭt) Alaska	70·48 N	152·00 W
65	Pittsburg (pĭts'bûrg) Calif. (San Francisco In.)	38·01 N	121·52 W
73	Pittsburg Kans.	37·25 N	94·43 W
65	Pittsburg Ore. (Portland In.)	45·54 N	123·09 W
73	Pittsburg Tex.	32·00 N	94·57 W
75	Pittsburgh Pa. (Pittsburgh In.)	40·26 N	80·01 W
73	Pittsfield (pĭts'fēld) Ill.	39·37 N	90·47 W
82	Pittsfield Maine	44·45 N	69·44 W
81	Pittsfield Mass.	42·25 N	73·15 W
81	Pittston (pĭts'tŭn) Pa.	41·20 N	75·50 W
148	P'itzuwo (Hsinchin) (pē'zhĕ'wŏ) (sĭn'jĭn) China	39·25 N	122·19 E
101	Piūi (pē-ōō'ē) Braz. (Rio de Janeiro In.)	20·27 S	45·57 W
98	Piura (pē-ōō'rä) Peru	5·13 S	80·46 W
136	Piya (pē'yä) Sov. Un. (Urals In.)	58·34 N	61·12 E
74	Placentia (plä-sĕn'shĭ-ȧ) Calif. (Los Angeles In.)	33·52 N	117·50 W
83	Placentia Can.	47·16 N	53·59 W
83	Placentia B. Can.	47·14 N	54·30 W
68	Placerville (plăs'ẽr-vĭl) Calif.	38·43 N	120·47 W
94	Placetas (plä-thā'täs) Cuba	22·10 N	79·40 W
81	Placid (L.) (plăs'ĭd) N. Y.	44·20 N	74·00 W
74	Plain City (plān) Utah (Salt Lake City In.)	41·18 N	112·06 W

ng-sing; ŋ-baŋk; N-nasalized n; nŏd; cŏmmit; ōld; ôbey; ôrder; fōōd; fo͝ot; ou-out; s-soft; sh-dish; th-thin; pūre; ûnite; ûrn; stŭd; circŭs; ü-as "y" in study; '-indeterminate vowel.

252 Plainfield–Port Bolivar PRONOUNCING INDEX

Page	Name Pronunciation Region	Lat. °′	Long. °′
75	Plainfield (plān′fēld) Ill. (Chicago In.)	41·37 N	88·12 W
75	Plainfield..Ind. (Indianapolis In.)	39·42 N	86·23 W
84	Plainfield...N. J. (New York In.)	40·38 N	74·25 W
73	Plainview (plān′vū)........Ark.	34·59 N	93·15 W
71	Plainview..........Minn.	44·09 N	93·12 W
70	Plainview..........Nebr.	42·20 N	97·47 W
72	Plainview..........Tex.	34·11 N	101·42 W
80	Plainwell (plān′wĕl)........Mich.	42·25 N	85·40 W
85	Plaisance (plĕ-zäNs′) Can. (Ottawa In.)	45·37 N	75·07 W
95	Plana or Flat Cays (Is.) (plä′nä) Ba. Is.	22·35 N	73·35 W
122	Plan-de-Cuques (plä-dĕ-kük′) Fr. (Marseille In.)	43·22 N	5·29 E
111	Planegg (plä′nĕg) Ger. (Munich In.)	48·06 N	11·27 E
73	Plano (plā′nō)..........Tex.	33·01 N	96·42 W
85	Plantagenet (plăN-tàzh-nĕ′) Can. (Ottawa In.)	45·33 N	75·00 W
79	Plant City (plȧnt sĭ′tĭ)..Fla. (In.)	28·00 N	82·07 W
77	Plaquemine (plăk′mēn′)......La.	30·17 N	91·14 W
124	Plasencia (plä-sĕn′thê-ä)......Sp.	40·02 N	6·07 W
136	Plast (plást)..Sov. Un. (Urals In.)	54·22 N	60·48 E
82	Plaster Rock (plȧs′tẽr rŏk)..Can.	46·54 N	67·22 W
152	Plastun (plȧs-tōōn′).....Sov. Un.	44·41 N	136·08 E
100	Plata, R. de la (R.) (dālä plä′tä) Arg.-Ur.	34·35 S	58·15 W
126	Platani (R.) (plä-tä′nē).......It.	37·26 N	13·28 E
95	Plateforme, Pte..........Hai.	19·35 N	73·50 W
64	Platinum (plăt′ĭ-nŭm).....Alaska	59·00 N	161·27 W
98	Plato (plä′tō)..........Col.	9·49 N	74·48 W
90	Platón Sánchéz (plä-tōn′ sän′chĕz).Mex.	21·14 N	98·20 W
73	Platt Natl. Park (plăt)......Okla.	34·31 N	96·44 W
70	Platte (plăt)..........S. D.	43·22 N	98·51 W
73	Platte (R.)..........Mo.	40·09 N	94·40 W
62	Platte (R.)..........U. S.	40·50 N	100·40 W
71	Platteville (plăt′vĭl)........Wis.	42·44 N	90·31 W
73	Plattsburg (plăts′bûrg)........Mo.	39·33 N	94·26 W
81	Plattsburgh..........N. Y.	44·40 N	73·30 W
70	Plattsmouth (plăts′mŭth)...Nebr.	41·00 N	95·53 W
120	Plauen (plou′ĕn)..........Ger.	50·30 N	12·08 E
95	Playa de Guanabo (plä-yä-dĕ-gwä-nä′bô) Cuba (Havana In.)	23·10 N	82·07 W
95	Playa de Santa Fe (sä′n-tä-fĕ′) Cuba (Havana In.)	23·05 N	82·31 W
69	Playas (L.) (plä′yȧs).....N. Mex.	31·50 N	108·30 W
91	Playa Vicente (vē-sĕn′tā)....Mex.	17·49 N	95·49 W
91	Playa Vicente (R.)........Mex.	17·36 N	96·13 W
81	Pleasant (L.) (plĕz′ănt).....N. Y.	43·25 N	74·25 W
65	Pleasant Hill Calif. (San Francisco In.)	37·57 N	122·04 W
73	Pleasant Hill..........Mo.	38·46 N	94·18 W
65	Pleasanton (plĕz′ăn-tŭn) Calif. (San Francisco In.)	37·40 N	121·53 W
73	Pleasanton..........Kans.	38·10 N	94·41 W
76	Pleasanton..........Tex.	28·58 N	98·30 W
75	Pleasant Plain (plĕz′ănt) Ohio (Cincinnati In.)	39·17 N	84·06 W
75	Pleasant Ridge.Mich. (Detroit In.)	42·28 N	83·09 W
75	Pleasure Ridge Park (plĕzh′ẽr rĭj) Ky. (Louisville In.)	38·09 N	85·49 W
74	Pleasant View (plĕz′ănt vū) Utah (Salt Lake City In.)	41·20 N	112·02 W
84	Pleasantville (plĕz′ănt-vĭl) N. Y. (New York In.)	41·08 N	73·47 W
159	Plenty, B. of (plĕn′tê) . N. Z. (In.)	37·23 S	177·10 E
67	Plentywood (plĕn′tê-wŏŏd) . Mont.	48·47 N	104·38 W
128	Ples (plyĕs)..........Sov. Un.	57·26 N	41·29 E
128	Pleshcheyevo (L.) (plĕsh-chă′yĕ-vô) . Sov. Un.	56·50 N	38·22 E
82	Plessisville (plĕ-sē′vēl′).......Can.	46·12 N	71·47 W
121	Pleszew (plĕ′zhĕf)..........Pol.	51·54 N	17·48 E
123	Plettenberg (plĕ′tĕn-bĕrgh) Ger. (Ruhr In.)	51·13 N	7·53 E
127	Pleven (plĕ′vĕn)..........Bul.	43·24 N	24·26 E
127	Pljevlja (plĕv′lyä)........Yugo.	43·20 N	19·21 E
121	Płock (pwôtsk)..........Pol.	52·32 N	19·44 E
122	Ploërmel (plô-ĕr-mĕl′)........Fr.	47·56 N	2·25 W
127	Ploești (plô-yĕsht′′)........Rom.	44·56 N	26·01 E
127	Plomárion (plô-mä′rĭ-ŏn).....Grc.	38·51 N	26·24 E
122	Plomb du Cantal (Mt.) (plôN′dükăN-tàl′) . Fr.	45·30 N	2·49 E
127	Plovdiv (Philippopolis) (plôv′dĭf) (fĭl-ĭp-ŏp′ô-lĭs) .Bul.	42·09 N	24·43 E
91	Pluma Hidalgo (plōō′mä ē-däl′gō) Mex.	15·54 N	96·23 W
119	Plunge (plōōn′gä).......Sov. Un.	55·56 N	21·45 E
116	Plymouth (plĭm′ŭth)........Eng.	50·25 N	4·14 W
80	Plymouth..........Ind.	41·20 N	86·20 W
81	Plymouth..........Mass.	42·00 N	70·45 W
75	Plymouth.....Mich. (Detroit In.)	42·23 N	83·27 W
81	Plymouth..........N. H.	43·50 N	71·40 W
79	Plymouth..........N. C.	35·50 N	76·44 W
81	Plymouth..........Pa.	41·15 N	75·55 W
93	Plymouth Montserrat (Le. & Wind. Is. In.)	16·43 N	62·12 W
71	Plymouth..........Wis.	43·45 N	87·59 W
128	Plyussa (R.) (plyōō′sȧ)..Sov. Un.	58·33 N	28·30 E
120	Plzeň (Pilsen)..........Czech.	49·46 N	13·25 E
126	Po, Bocche del (Mouth) (bô′chĕ-dĕl-pô′) . It.	44·57 N	12·38 E
126	Po, Fiume (R.) (fyōō′mĕ-pô)...It.	45·00 N	11·23 E
150	Poar..........China	35·10 N	113·08 E
164	Pobé (pô-bā′)........Dahomey	6·56 N	2·32 E
73	Pocahontas (pō-kȧ-hŏn′tȧs)..Ark.	36·15 N	91·01 W
71	Pocahontas..........Iowa	42·43 N	94·41 W
67	Pocatello (pō-kȧ-tĕl′ō).......Idaho	42·54 N	112·30 W
128	Pochĕp (pô-chĕp′).......Sov. Un.	52·56 N	32·27 E
128	Pochinok (pô-chē′nôk)...Sov. Un.	54·14 N	32·27 E
132	Pochinski..........Sov. Un.	54·40 N	44·50 E
90	Pochotitán (pô-chô-tē-tä′n)..Mex.	21·37 N	104·33 W
91	Pochutla (San Pedro) (pō-chōō′tlä) (sän pā′drō) .Mex.	15·46 N	96·28 W
81	Pocomoke City (pō-kō-mōk′).Md.	38·05 N	75·35 W
81	Pocono Mts. (pō-cō′nō).......Pa.	41·10 N	75·05 W
101	Poços de Caldas (pō-sôs-dĕ-käl′dȧs) Braz. (Rio de Janeiro In.)	21·48 S	46·34 W
164	Poder (pô-dôr′)........Senegal	16·35 N	15·04 W
134	Podkamennaya (Stony) Tunguska (R.).Sov. Un.	61·43 N	93·45 E
136	Podol′sk (pô-dôl′′sk) Sov. Un. (Moscow In.)	55·26 N	37·33 E
129	Podvolochisk..........Sov. Un.	49·32 N	26·16 E
126	Poggibonsi (pôd-jē-bôn′sē).....It.	43·27 N	11·12 E
128	Pogodino (pô-gô′dē-nô)..Sov. Un.	54·17 N	31·00 E
152	Pohai Str. (pō′hī′)........China	38·05 N	121·40 E
152	P′ohangdong..........Kor.	35·57 N	129·23 E
148	Pohsien..........China	33·52 N	115·47 E
148	Pohsing (pō′hsĭng′)........China	37·09 N	118·08 E
85	Pointe-a′-Gatineau (pōō-ăNt′ä-gä-tē-nō′) Can. (Ottawa In.)	45·28 N	75·42 W
84	Pointe a la Hache (point′ à là ȧsh′) La. (New Orleans In.)	29·35 N	89·47 W
93	Pointe-à-Pitre (pwăNt′ à pē-tr′) Guad. (Le. & Wind. Is. In.)	16·15 N	61·32 W
85	Pointe-aux-Pins (pōō-ăNt′ ō-pĕN) Can. (Edmonton In.)	53·38 N	113·15 W
85	Pointe-aux-Trembles (pōō-ăNt′ ō-trāNbl) Can. (Montreal In.)	45·39 N	73·30 W
85	Pointe Claire (pōō-ăNt′ klĕr) Can. (Montreal In.)	45 26 N	73 50 W
85	Pointe Fortune (fôr′tūn) Can. (Montreal In.)	45·34 N	74·23 W
166	Pointe Noire..........Con. B.	4·48 S	11·50 E
64	Point Hope (hōp)........Alaska	68·18 N	166·38 W
80	Point Pleasant (plĕz′ănt)..W. Va.	38·50 N	82·10 W
65	Point Roberts (rŏb′ẽrts) Wash. (Vancouver In.)	48·59 N	123·04 W
123	Poissy (pwȧ-sē′)....Fr. (Paris In.)	48·55 N	2·02 E
122	Poitiers (pwȧ-tyā′)..........Fr.	46·35 N	0·18 E
142	Pokaran (pō′kŭr-ŭn).......India	27·00 N	72·05 E
150	Pok′ot′u (pō′kô-tōō′)......China	48·45 N	121·42 E
128	Pokrov (pô′krôf).......Sov. Un.	55·56 N	39·09 E
129	Pokrovskoye (pô-krôf′skô-yĕ) Sov. Un.	47·27 N	38·54 E
128	Pola (R.) (pō′lä)........Sov. Un.	54·44 N	31·53 E
124	Pola de Allade (dĕ-äl-yä′dĕ)...Sp.	43·18 N	6·35 W
124	Pola de Laviana (dĕ-lä-vyä′nä).Sp.	43·15 N	5·29 W
102	Poland (pō′lănd)..........Eur.	52·37 N	17·01 E
155	Polangui (pô-läŋ′gē) Phil. (Manila In.)	13·18 N	123·29 E
136	Polazna (pô′làz-nȧ) Sov. Un. (Urals In.)	58·18 N	56·25 E
119	Polessk (pô′lĕsk).......Sov. Un.	54·50 N	21·14 E
133	Poles′ye (Pripyat′ Marshes) Sov. Un.	52·10 N	27·30 E
136	Polevskoy (pô-lĕ′vs-kô′ê) Sov. Un. (Urals In.)	56·28 N	60·14 E
121	Polgár (pôl′gär)..........Hung.	47·54 N	21·10 E
150	P′oli (pō′lī)..........China	45·40 N	130·38 E
126	Policastro, Golfo di (G.).......It.	41·00 N	13·23 E
123	Poligny (pō-lē-nyē′)..........Fr.	46·48 N	5·42 E
127	Políkhnitos..........Grc.	39·05 N	26·11 E
155	Polillo (pô-lēl′yō) Phil. (Manila In.)	14·42 N	121·56 E
155	Polillo Is.......Phil. (Manila In.)	15·05 N	122·15 E
155	Polillo Str.......Phil. (Manila In.)	15·02 N	121·40 E
128	Polist′ (R.) (pô′lĭst).....Sov. Un.	57·42 N	31·02 E
126	Polistena (pō-lēs-tä′nä)........It.	40·25 N	16·05 E
127	Políyiros..........Grc.	40·23 N	23·27 E
134	Polkan, Gol′tsy (Mtn.)..Sov. Un.	60·18 N	92·08 E
125	Pollensa (pôl-yĕn′sä)..........Sp.	39·50 N	3·00 E
92	Polochic R. (pō-lô-chēk′)...Guat.	15·19 N	89·45 W
129	Polonnoye (pô′lô-nô-yĕ)..Sov. Un.	50·07 N	27·31 E
128	Polotsk (pô′lôtsk)........Sov. Un.	55·30 N	28·48 E
101	Polpaico (pôl-pá′y-kô) Chile (Santiago In.)	33·10 S	70·53 W
67	Polson (pōl′sŭn)..........Mont.	47·40 N	114·10 W
129	Poltava (pôl-tä′vä)......Sov. Un.	49·35 N	34·33 E
129	Poltava (Oblast)........Sov. Un.	49·53 N	32·58 E
128	Põltsamaa (pōlt′sȧ-mä)..Sov. Un.	58·39 N	26·00 E
128	Põltsamaa (R.)........Sov. Un.	58·35 N	25·55 E
136	Polunochnoye (pô-lōō-nô′ch-nô′yĕ) Sov. Un. (Urals In.)	60·52 N	60·27 E
134	Poluy (R.) (pôl′wē).....Sov. Un.	65·45 N	68·15 E
136	Polyakovka (pŭl-yä′kôv-kȧ) Sov. Un. (Urals In.)	54·38 N	59·42 E
132	Polyarnyy (pŭl-yär′nē)..Sov. Un.	69·10 N	33·30 E
101	Pomba (pô′m-bȧ) (R.) Braz. (Rio de Janeiro In.)	21·28 S	42·28 W
120	Pomerania (Reg.) (pŏm-ê-rā′nĭ-ȧ) Pol.	53·50 N	15·20 E
118	Pomeranian B. (pō′mĕ-rā-ny-ăn) Ger.	54·10 N	14·20 E
80	Pomeroy..........Ohio	39·00 N	82·00 W
167	Pomeroy (pŏm′ẽr-roi) S. Afr. (Natal In.)	28·36 S	30·26 E
66	Pomeroy (pŏm′ẽr-oi).......Wash.	46·28 N	117·35 W
125	Pomezia (pô-mĕ′t-zyä) It. (Rome In.)	41·41 N	12·31 E
125	Pomigliano d′Arco (pô-mē-lyá′nô-d-ä′r-kô) It. (Naples In.)	40·39 N	14·23 E
70	Pomme de Terre (pôm dē tĕr′) Minn.	45·22 N	95·52 W
74	Pomona (pô-mō′nȧ) Calif. (Los Angeles In.)	34·04 N	117·45 W
127	Pomorie..........Bul.	42·24 N	27·41 E
142	Pomo Tsho (L.)........China	23·38 N	89·58 E
79	Pompano (pŏm′pȧ-nō)..Fla. (In.)	26·12 N	80·07 W
84	Pompton Lakes (pŏmp′tŏn) N. J. (New York In.)	41·01 N	74·16 W
92	Pomuch (pô-mōō′ch) Mex. (Yucatan In.)	20·12 N	90·10 W
70	Ponca (pŏn′kȧ)..........Nebr.	42·34 N	96·43 W
73	Ponca City..........Okla.	36·42 N	97·07 W
85	Ponce (pōn′sä) P. R. (Puerto Rico In.)	18·01 N	66·43 W
143	Pondicherry (pôn-dĭ-shĕr′ē′) (pŏn-dĭ-shĕr′ē).India	11·58 N	79·48 E
124	Ponferrada (pŏn-fĕr-rä′dhä)...Sp.	42·33 N	6·38 W
86	Ponoca (pō-nō′cȧ)..........Can.	52·43 N	113·32 W
132	Ponoy..........Sov. Un.	66·58 N	41·00 E
132	Ponoy (R.)........Sov. Un.	65·50 N	38·40 E
164	Ponta Delgada (pôn′tȧ dĕl-gä′dȧ) Azores (In.)	37·40 N	25·45 W
100	Ponta Grossa (grō′sȧ).......Braz.	25·09 S	50·05 W
123	Pont-à-Mousson (pôN′tȧ-mōōsôN′) Fr.	48·55 N	6·02 E
99	Ponta Porã..........Braz.	22·30 S	55·31 W
123	Pontarlier (pôN′tȧr-lyā′)......Fr.	46·53 N	6·22 E
122	Pont-Audemer (pôN′tōd′mâr′).Fr.	49·23 N	0·28 E
123	Pontcarré (pôN-kȧ-rā′) Fr. (Paris In.)	48·48 N	2·42 E
77	Pontchartrain L. (pôN-shȧr-trăn′) La.	30·10 N	90·10 W
126	Pontedera (pōn-tā-dā′rä)......It.	43·37 N	10·37 E
124	Ponte de Sor (pōŋ′tĕ dā sōr′) Port.	39·14 N	8·03 W
110	Pontefract (pŏn′tē-frăkt)....Eng.	53·41 N	1·18 W
101	Ponte Nova (pô′n-tĕ-nô′vȧ) Braz. (Rio de Janeiro In.)	20·26 S	42·52 W
124	Pontevedra (pōn-tĕ-vĕ-drä)...Sp.	42·28 N	8·38 W
166	Ponthierville (pôN-tyā-vēl′) Con. L.	0·28 S	25·19 E
80	Pontiac (pŏn′tĭ-ăk)..........Ill.	40·55 N	88·35 W
75	Pontiac.......Mich. (Detroit In.)	42·37 N	83·17 W
154	Pontianak (pôn-tē-ä′nȧk)..Indon.	0·04 S	109·20 E
139	Pontian Kechil Mala (Singapore In.)	1·29 N	103·24 E
122	Pontivy (pôN-tē-vē′)........Fr.	48·05 N	2·57 W
122	Pont-l′Abbe (pôN-lȧ-bā′)......Fr.	47·53 N	4·12 W
123	Pontoise (pôN-twȧz′) Fr. (Paris In.)	49·03 N	2·05 E
136	Pontonnyy (pôn′tôn-nyĭ) Sov. Un. (Leningrad In.)	59·47 N	30·39 E
78	Pontotoc (pŏn-tô-tŏk′)......Miss.	34·11 N	88·59 W
126	Pontremoli (pôn-trĕm′ô-lē).....It.	44·21 N	9·50 E
126	Ponza, Isole di (I.) (ē′sō-lĕ-dē-pōn′tsä)..........It.	40·55 N	12·58 E
116	Poole (pōōl)..........Eng.	50·43 N	2·00 W
142	Poona (pōō′nŭ)..........India	18·38 N	73·53 E
98	Poopó, Lago de (L.) (lä′gô-dĕ-pō-ô-pô′).Bol.	18·16 S	67·57 W
98	Popayán (pō-pä-yän′)........Col.	2·21 N	76·43 W
67	Poplar (pŏp′lẽr)..........Mont.	48·08 N	105·10 W
73	Poplar Bluff (blŭf)..........Mo.	36·43 N	90·22 W
80	Poplar Plains (plāns).........Ky.	38·20 N	83·40 W
85	Poplar Point.Can. (Winnipeg In.)	50·04 N	97·58 W
67	Poplar R..........Mont.	48·34 N	105·20 W
67	Poplar R., West Fork......Mont.	48·59 N	106·06 W
78	Poplarville (pŏp′lẽr-vĭl).....Miss.	30·50 N	89·33 W
91	Popocatépetl (Mtn.) (pô-pô-kä-tā′pĕt′l) Mex. (Mexico City In.)	19·01 N	98·38 W
166	Popokabaca (pō′pô-kȧ-bä′kȧ) Con. L.	5·38 S	16·47 E
129	Popovka (pô′pôf-kȧ).....Sov. Un.	50·03 N	33·41 E
129	Popovka..........Sov. Un.	51·13 N	33·08 E
127	Popovo (pô′pô-vō)..........Bul.	43·23 N	26·17 E
142	Porbandar (pōr-bŭn′dŭr)....India	21·44 N	69·40 E
98	Porce (pôr-sĕ) (R.).....Col. (In.)	7·11 N	74·55 W
124	Porcuna (pôr-kōō′nä)........Sp.	37·54 N	4·10 W
64	Porcupine (R.)..........Alaska	67·00 N	143·25 W
86	Porcupine (R.)..........Can.	67·38 N	140·07 W
67	Porcupine Cr. (pôr′kû-pīn).Mont.	46·38 N	107·04 W
67	Porcupine Cr..........Mont.	48·27 N	106·24 W
126	Pordenone (pōr-dā-nō′nä)......It.	45·58 N	12·38 E
126	Poreč (pô′rĕch)..........Yugo.	45·13 N	13·37 E
119	Pori (Björneborg) (pô′rē) (byûr′nē-bôrgh)....Fin.	61·29 N	21·45 E
101	Poriúncula (po-rēōō′n-kōō-lä) Braz. (Rio de Janeiro In.)	20·58 S	42·02 W
112	Porjus (pôr′yōōs)..........Swe.	66·54 N	19·40 E
128	Porkhov (pôr′Kôf).......Sov. Un.	57·46 N	29·33 E
98	Porlamar (pôr-lä-mär′)......Ven.	11·00 N	63·55 W
122	Pornic (pôr-nēk′)..........Fr.	47·08 N	2·07 W
135	Poronaysk (pô′rō-nīsk)..Sov. Un.	49·21 N	143·23 E
120	Porrentruy (pô-răN-trüē′)..Switz.	47·25 N	7·02 E
118	Porsgrunn (pôrs′grōōn′).....Nor.	59·09 N	9·36 E
98	Portachuelo (pôrt-ä-chwä′lô).Bol.	17·20 S	63·12 W
81	Portage (pôr′tāj)..........Pa.	40·25 N	78·35 W
71	Portage..........Wis.	43·33 N	89·29 W
74	Portage Des Sioux (dē sōō) Mo. (St. Louis In.)	38·56 N	90·21 W
85	Portage-la-Prairie (lä-prā′rĭ) Can. (Winnipeg In.)	49·58 N	98·18 W
86	Port Alberni (pôr äl-bĕr-nē′).Can.	49·20 N	124·51 W
124	Portalegre (pôr-tä-lā′grĕ)....Port.	39·18 N	7·26 W
72	Portales (pôr-tä′lĕs)......N. Mex.	34·10 N	103·11 W
82	Port-Alfred (ăl′frĕd)........Can.	48·19 N	70·55 W
167	Port Alfred (Kowie) (kou′ĭ) S. Afr. (Natal In.)	33·36 S	26·55 E
86	Port Alice..........Can.	50·29 N	127·29 W
81	Port Allegany (ăl-ē-gā′nĭ).....Pa.	41·50 N	78·10 W
166	Port Ambim..........Ang.	11·01 S	13·45 E
66	Port Angeles (ăn′jē-lĕs)....Wash.	48·07 N	123·26 W
95	Port Antonio..........Jam.	18·10 N	76·25 W
161	Portarlington Austl. (Melbourne In.)	38·07 S	144·39 E
87	Port Arthur (är′thẽr).......Can.	48·28 N	89·12 W
77	Port Arthur..........Tex.	29·52 N	93·59 W
	Port Arthur, see Lüshun		
160	Port Augusta (ô-gŭs′tȧ)....Austl.	32·28 S	137·50 E
83	Port au Port B. (pôr′tō pôr′) Can.	48·41 N	58·45 W
95	Port-au-Prince (prăNs′)......Hai.	18·35 N	72·20 W
80	Port Austin (ŏs′tĭn)..........Mich.	44·00 N	83·00 W
166	Port Beaufort (bō′fẽrt).....S. Afr.	34·14 S	20·59 E
154	Port Blair (blâr)......Andaman Is.	12·07 N	92·45 E
77	Port Bolivar (bŏl′ĭ-vȧr).Tex. (In.)	29·22 N	94·46 W

ăt; finăl; rāte; senâte; ärm; åsk; sofȧ; fâre; ch-choose; dh-as th in other; bē; ēvent; bĕt; recĕnt; cratẽr; g-go; gh-guttural g; bĭt; ĭ-short neutral; rīde; K-guttural k as ch in German ich;

PRONOUNCING INDEX Port Chester–Prince Edward Is. 253

Page	Name Pronunciation Region	Lat. °′	Long. °′
84	Port Chester (chĕs'tẽr) N. Y. (New York In.)	40·59 N	73·40 W
65	Port Chicago (shĭ-kô'gō) Calif. (San Francisco In.)	38·03 N	122·01 W
80	Port Clinton (klĭn'tŭn) Ohio	41·30 N	83·00 W
75	Port Colborne (kōl'bŏrn) Can. (Buffalo In.)	43·53 N	79·13 W
65	Port Coquitlam (kô-kwĭt'lăm) Can. (Vancouver In.)	49·16 N	122·47 W
85	Port Credit (krĕd'ĭt) Can. (Toronto In.)	43·33 N	79·35 W
85	Port Dalhousie (dăl-hōō'zĭ) Can. (Toronto In.)	43·12 N	79·17 W
122	Port-de-Bouc (pôr-dē-bōōk') Fr. (Marseille In.)	43·24 N	5·00 E
95	Port de Paix (pĕ') Hai.	19·55 N	72·50 W
139	Port Dickson (dĭk'sŭn) Mala. (Singapore In.)	2·33 N	101·49 E
65	Port Discovery (B.) (dĭs-kŭv'ẽr-ĭ) Wash. (Seattle In.)	48·05 N	122·55 W
167	Port Edward (ĕd'wẽrd) S. Afr. (Natal In.)	31·04 S	30·14 E
82	Port Elgin (ĕl'jĭn) Can.	46·03 N	64·06 W
167	Port Elizabeth (ê-lĭz'ȧ-bĕth) S. Afr. (Natal In.)	33·57 S	25·37 E
78	Porterdale (pōr'tẽr-dāl) Ga.	33·34 N	83·53 W
68	Porterville (pōr'tẽr-vĭl) Calif.	36·03 N	119·05 W
164	Port Étienne (pôr tȧ-tyĕn') Mauritania	21·02 N	17·09 W
100	Portezuelo de Tupungato (Vol.) (pôr-tĕ-zwĕ-lō-dĕ-tōō-pōō'n-gä-tô) Arg-Chile	33·30 S	69·52 W
166	Port Francqui (fräN-kē') Con. L.	4·15 S	20·43 E
65	Port Gamble (găm'bŭl) Wash. (Seattle In.)	47·52 N	122·36 W
65	Port Gamble Ind. Res. Wash. (Seattle In.)	47·54 N	122·33 W
166	Port Gentil (zhäN-tē') Gabon	1·30 S	8·45 E
78	Port Gibson (gĭb'sŭn) Miss.	31·56 N	90·57 W
164	Port Harcourt (här'kŭrt) Nig.	4·47 N	7·00 E
158	Port Headland (hĕd'lănd) Austl.	20·30 S	118·30 E
166	Port Herald (hĕr'ăld) Nya.	16·52 S	35·16 E
83	Port Hood (hŏŏd) Can.	46·03 N	61·30 W
81	Port Hope (hōp) Can.	43·55 N	78·10 W
80	Port Huron (hū rŏn) Mich.	43·00 N	82·30 W
125	Portici (pôr'tē-chē) It. (Naples In.)	40·34 N	14·20 W
101	Portillo (pôr-tē'l-yô) Chile (Santiago In.)	32·51 N	70·09 W
124	Portimão (pôr-tē-mo'uN) Port.	37·09 N	8·34 W
84	Port Jarvis (jûr'vĭs) N. Y. (New York In.)	41·22 N	74·41 W
160	Portland (pōrt'lănd) Austl.	38·20 S	142·40 E
80	Portland Ind.	40·25 N	85·00 W
82	Portland Maine	43·40 N	70·16 W
80	Portland Mich.	42·50 N	85·00 W
65	Portland Ore. (Portland In.)	45·31 N	123·41 W
94	Portland Bight (B.) Jam.	17·45 N	77·05 W
94	Portland Pt. Jam.	17·40 N	77·20 W
77	Port Lavaca (lȧ-vä'kȧ) Tex.	28·36 N	96·38 W
160	Port Lincoln (lĭŋ'kŭn) Austl.	34·39 S	135·50 E
65	Port Ludlow (lŭd'lō) Wash. (Seattle In.)	47·26 N	122·41 W
	Port Lyautey, see Kenitra		
160	Port Macquarie (mȧ-kwŏ'rĭ) Austl.	31·25 S	152·45 E
65	Port Madison Ind. Res. (măd'ĭ-sŭn) Wash. (Seattle In.)	47·46 N	122·38 W
94	Port Maria (mȧ-rī'ȧ) Jam.	18·20 N	76·55 W
82	Port Menier (mē-nyā') Can.	49·51 N	64·19 W
65	Port Moody (mōōd'ĭ) Can. (Vancouver In.)	49·17 N	122·51 W
155	Port Moresby (mōrz'bē) Pap.	9·34 S	147·20 E
77	Port Neches (nĕch'ĕz) Tex.	29·59 N	93·57 W
49	Port Nelson (nĕl'sŭn) Can.	56·59 N	92·57 W
82	Portneuf-Sur-Mer (pôr-nûf'sür mĕr) Can.	48·40 N	69·10 W
166	Port Nolloth (nŏl'ŏth) S. Afr.	29·10 S	17·00 E
124	Pôrto (Oporto) (pōr'tōō) Port.	41·10 N	8·38 W
98	Pôrto Acre (ä'krĕ) Braz.	9·38 S	67·34 W
100	Pôrto Alegre (ä-lā'grĕ) Braz.	29·58 S	51·11 W
166	Porto Alexandre (ä-lĕ-zhän'drĕ) Ang.	16·00 S	11·50 E
167	Pôrto Amélia (ȧ-mĕ'lyȧ) Moz.	12·59 S	40·32 E
93	Portobelo (pôr'tô-bā'lō) Pan.	9·32 N	79·40 W
99	Pôrto de Pedras (pā'drȧzh) Braz.	9·09 S	35·20 W
101	Pôrto Feliz (fĕ-lē's) Braz. (Rio de Janeiro In.)	23·12 S	47·30 W
126	Portoferraio (pōr'tô-fĕr-rä'yō) It.	42·47 N	10·20 E
99	Port-of-Spain (spān) Trin.	10·44 N	61·24 W
126	Portogruaro (pōr'tô-grōō-ä'rō) It.	45·48 N	12·49 E
99	Pôrto Guaira (gwä-ē-rä) Braz.	24·03 S	44·02 W
68	Portola (pôr'tō-lȧ) Calif.	39·47 N	120·29 W
99	Pôrto Mendes (mĕ'n-dĕs) Braz.	24·41 S	54·13 W
99	Pôrto Murtinho (mōōr-tēn'yōō) Braz.	21·43 S	57·43 W
99	Pôrto Nacional (nȧ-syô-näl') Braz.	10·43 S	48·14 W
164	Porto Novo (pōr'tô-nō'vō) Dahomey	6·31 N	2·32 E
65	Port Orchard (ôr'chẽrd) Wash. (Seattle In.)	47·32 N	122·38 W
65	Port Orchard (B.) Wash. (Seattle In.)	47·40 N	122·39 W
164	Porto Santo, Ilha de (I.) (säN'tōō) Mad. Is.	32·41 N	16·15 W
99	Pôrto Seguro (sā-gōō'rōō) Braz.	16·26 S	38·59 W
126	Porto Torres (tôr'rĕs) It.	40·49 N	8·25 E
126	Porto-Vecchio (vĕk'ê-ô) Fr.	41·36 N	9·17 E
98	Pôrto Velho (väl'yōō) Braz.	8·45 S	63·43 W
98	Portoviejo (pôr-tô-vyā'hō) Ec.	1·11 S	80·28 W
160	Port Phillip B. (fĭl'ĭp) Austl.	37·57 S	144·50 E
160	Port Pirie (pĭ'rê) Austl.	33·10 S	138·00 E
86	Port Radium (rā'dē-ŭm) Can.	66·06 N	118·03 W
94	Port Royal (B.) (roi'ăl) Jam.	17·50 N	76·45 W
	Port Said, see Būr Sa'īd		
167	Port St. Johns (sânt jŏnz) S. Afr. (Natal In.)	31·37 S	29·32 E
167	Port Shepstone (shĕps'tŭn) S. Afr. (Natal In.)	30·45 S	30·23 E
116	Portsmouth (pôrts'mŭth) Eng.	50·45 N	1·03 W
81	Portsmouth N. H.	43·05 N	70·50 W
80	Portsmouth Ohio	38·45 N	83·00 W
84	Portsmouth Va. (Norfolk In.)	36·50 N	76·19 W
93	Portsmouth Dominica (Le. & Wind. Is. In.)	15·33 N	61·28 W
100	Port Stanley Falk. Is.	51·46 S	57·59 W
165	Port Sudan (sōō-dän') Sud.	19·30 N	37·10 E
84	Port Sulphur (sŭl'fẽr) La. (New Orleans In.)	29·28 N	89·41 W
65	Port Susan (B.) (sū-zăn') Wash. (Seattle In.)	48·11 N	122·25 W
139	Port Swettenham (swĕt'ĕn-hăm) Mala. (Singapore In.)	3·00 N	101·25 E
79	Port Tampa (tăm'pȧ) Fla. (In.)	27·50 N	82·30 W
65	Port Townsend (tounz'ĕnd) Wash. (Seattle In.)	48·07 N	122·46 W
65	Port Townsend (B.) Wash. (Seattle In.)	48·05 N	122·47 W
102	Portugal (pōr'tū-găl) Eur.	38·15 N	8·08 W
124	Portugalete (pōr-tōō-gä-lā'tā) Sp.	43·18 N	3·05 W
	Portuguese East Africa, see Mozambique		
163	Portuguese Guinea (gĭn'ê) Afr.	12·00 N	20·00 W
	Portuguese India, see Damão, Diu & Gôa		
155	Portuguese Timor (tê-mōr') Asia	4·22 S	126·15 E
	Portuguese West Africa, see Angola		
122	Port Vendres (pôr väN'dr') Fr.	42·32 N	3·07 E
160	Port Wakefield (wāk'fēld) Austl.	34·12 S	138·10 E
84	Port Washington (wôsh'ĭng-tŭn) N. Y. (New York In.)	40·49 N	73·42 W
71	Port Washington Wis.	43·24 N	87·52 W
100	Posadas (pō-sä'dhäs) Arg.	27·32 S	55·56 W
124	Posadas (pô-sä-däs) Sp.	37·48 N	5·09 W
148	Poshan (pō'shän') China	36·32 N	117·51 E
128	Poshekhon'ye Volodarsk (pô-shyĕ'kôn-yĕ vôl'ô-därsk) Sov. Un.	58·31 N	39·07 E
154	Poso, Danau (L.) (pō'sō) Indon.	2·00 S	119·40 E
136	Pospelkova (pôs-pyĕl'kô-vȧ) Sov. Un. (Urals In.)	59·25 N	60·50 E
65	Possession Sd. (pŏ-zĕsh'ŭn) Wash. (Seattle In.)	47·59 N	122·17 W
76	Possum Kingdom Res. (pŏs'ŭm kĭng'dŭm) Tex.	32·58 N	98·12 W
72	Post (pōst) Tex.	33·12 N	101·21 W
126	Postojna (pôs-tōyná) Yugo.	45·45 N	14·13 E
152	Pos'yet (pos-yĕt') Sov. Un.	42·27 N	130·47 E
84	Potash (pŏ'tăsh) La. (New Orleans In.)	29·29 N	89·43 W
73	Potawatomi Ind. Res. (pŏt-ȧ-wă'tō mē) Kans.	39·30 N	96·11 W
168	Potchefstroom (pŏch'ĕf-strōm) S. Afr. (Johannesburg & Pretoria In.)	26·42 S	27·06 E
73	Poteau (pô-tō') Okla.	35·03 N	94·37 W
76	Poteet (pô-tēt) Tex.	29·05 N	98·35 W
126	Potenza (pô-tĕnt'sä) It.	40·39 N	15·49 E
126	Potenza (R.) It.	43·09 N	13·00 E
168	Potgiertersrus (pôt-kē'tĕrs-rûs) S. Afr. (Johannesburg & Pretoria In.)	24·09 S	29·04 E
66	Potholes Res. Wash.	47.00 N.	119·20 W
133	Poti (pô'tê) Sov. Un.	42·10 N	41·40 E
164	Potiskum Nig.	11·45 N	11·05 E
81	Potomac (R.) (pô-tō'măk) Va.	38·15 N	76·55 W
98	Potosí (pō-tō-sē') Bol.	19·42 S	65·42 W
73	Potosi (pŏ-tō'sĭ) Mo.	37·56 N	90·46 W
76	Potosi, R. (pō-tō-sē') Mex.	25·04 N	99·36 W
148	Pot'ou (bŭ'tō) China	38·05 N	116·35 E
92	Potrerillos (pō-trȧ-rēl'yôs) Hond.	15·13 N	87·58 W
111	Potsdam (pŏts'dăm) Ger. (Berlin In.)	52·24 N	13·04 E
81	Potsdam (pŏts'dăm) N. Y.	44·40 N	75·00 W
111	Potsdam (Dist.) (pŏts'dăm) Ger. (Berlin In.)	52·31 N	12·45 E
111	Pottenstein Aus. (Vienna In.)	47·58 N	16·06 E
110	Potters Bar (pŏt'ẽrz bär) Eng. (London In.)	51·41 N	0·12 W
81	Pottstown (pŏts'toun) Pa.	40·15 N	75·40 W
81	Pottsville (pŏts'vĭl) Pa.	40·40 N	76·15 W
143	Pottuvil Ceylon	6·33 N	81·48 E
81	Poughkeepsie (pô-kĭp'sĭ) N. Y.	41·45 N	73·55 W
154	Poulo Condore, Iles de (I.) Viet.	8·30 N	106·28 E
65	Poulsbo (pōlz'bōō) Wash. (Seattle In.)	47·44 N	122·38 W
110	Poulton-le-Fylde (pōl'tŭn-lē-fīld') Eng.	53·52 N	2·59 W
101	Pouso Alegre (pō'zōō ä-lā'grĕ) Braz. (Rio de Janeiro In.)	22·13 S	45·56 W
124	Póvoa de Varzim (pō-vō'ȧ dā vär'zēN) Port.	41·23 N	8·44 W
87	Povungnituk Can.	59·12 N	77·51 W
67	Powder River Wyo.	43·06 N	106·55 W
67	Powder R. (pou'dẽr) Mont.-Wyo.	45·18 N	105·37 W
66	Powder R. Ore.	44·55 N	117·35 W
67	Powder R., South Fk. Wyo.	43·13 N	106·54 W
67	Powell (pou'ĕl) Wyo.	44·44 N	108·44 W
69	Powell, L. Utah	37·26 N	110·25 W
95	Powell Pt. Ba. Is.	24·50 N	76·20 W
78	Powell Res. Ky.-Tenn.	36·30 N	83·35 W
86	Powell River Can.	49·54 N	124·25 W
151	Poyang (pō'yäng) China	29·00 N	116·42 E
151	P'oyang Hu (L.) China	29·20 N	116·28 E
71	Poygan (R.) (poi'găn) Wis.	44·10 N	89·05 W
127	Požarevac (pō'zhä'rĕ-váts) Yugo.	44·38 N	21·12 E
120	Poznań (pôz'nän'') Pol.	52·24 N	16·55 E
124	Pozoblanco (pō-thō-bläŋ'kō) Sp.	38·23 N	4·50 W
91	Pozo Rica (pô-zô-rē'kä) Mex.	20·32 N	97·25 W
90	Pozos (pô'zōs) Mex.	22·05 N	100·50 W
125	Pozuelo de Alarcón (pô-thwā'lō dā ä-lär-kōn') Sp. (Madrid In.)	40·27 N	3·49 W
125	Pozzuoli (pôt-swô'lē) It. (Naples In.)	40·34 N	14·08 E
128	Pra (R.) (prȧ) Sov. Un.	55·00 N	40·13 E
154	Prachin Buri (prä'chĕn) Thai.	13·59 N	101·15 E
98	Pradera (prä-dĕ'rä) Col. (In.)	3·24 N	76·13 W
122	Prades (prȧd) Fr.	42·37 N	2·23 E
98	Prado (prä'dô) Col. (In.)	3·44 N	74·55 W
74	Prado Dam (prä'dō) Calif. (Los Angeles In.)	33·53 N	117·39 W
101	Prados (prä'dôs) Braz. (Rio de Janeiro In.)	21·05 S	44·04 W
	Prague, see Praha		
120	Praha (Prague) (prä'hȧ) (präg) Czech.	50·05 N	14·30 E
164	Praia (prä'yȧ) C. V. Is. (In.)	15·00 N	23·30 W
100	Praia Funda, Ponta da (Pt.) (pôn'tä-dȧ-prä'yȧ-fōō'n-dä) Braz. (In.)	23·04 S	43·34 W
66	Prairie City (prā'rĭ) Ore.	44·25 N	118·42 W
71	Prairie du Chien (prā'rĭ dōō shēn') Wis.	43·02 N	91·10 W
85	Prairie Grove (prā'rĭ grōv) Can. (Winnipeg In.)	49·48 N	96·57 W
71	Prairie Island Ind. Res. Minn.	44·42 N	92·32 W
85	Prairies, R. des (rē-vyâr' dā prâ-rē') Can. (Montreal In.)	45·40 N	73·35 W
74	Prairietown (prā'rĭ-toun) Ill. (St. Louis In.)	38·58 N	89·55 W
151	Pratas (Is.) China	20·40 N	116·30 E
126	Prato (prä'tō) It.	43·53 N	11·03 E
122	Prats-de-Mollo (prá-dĕ-mô-lō') Fr.	42·26 N	2·36 E
72	Pratt (prăt) Kans.	37·37 N	98·43 W
78	Prattville (prăt'vĭl) Ala.	32·28 N	86·27 W
119	Pravdinsk Sov. Un.	54·26 N	20·11 E
136	Pravdinskiy (pràv-dēn'skĭ) Sov. Un. (Moscow In.)	56·03 N	37·52 E
124	Pravia (prä'vē-ä) Sp.	43·30 N	6·08 W
119	Pregolya (R.) (prĕ-gô'lă) Sov. Un.	54·37 N	20·50 E
76	Premont (prē-mŏnt') Tex.	27·20 N	98·07 W
120	Prenzlau (prĕnts'lou) Ger.	53·19 N	13·52 E
121	Přerov (przhĕ'rôf) Czech.	49·28 N	17·28 E
91	Presa Aleman (L.) (prä'sä-lĕ-mä'n) Mex.	18·20 N	96·35 W
110	Prescot (prĕs'kŭt) Eng.	53·25 N	2·48 W
69	Prescott (prĕs'kŏt) Ariz.	34·30 N	112·30 W
73	Prescott Ark.	33·47 N	93·23 W
81	Prescott (prĕs'kŭt) Can.	44·45 N	75·35 W
74	Prescott (prĕs'kŏt) Wis. (Minneapolis, St. Paul In.)	44·45 N	92·48 W
70	Presho (prĕsh'ô) S. D.	43·56 N	100·04 W
100	Presidencia Rogue Sáenz Peña (prĕ-sē-dĕ'n-sēä-rô'kĕ-sà'ĕnz-pĕ'n-yä) Arg.	26·52 S	60·15 W
99	Presidente Epitácio (prā-sē-dĕn'tĕ å-pê-tä'syōō) Braz.	21·56 S	52·01 W
76	Presidio (prĕ-sĭ'dĭ-ô) Tex.	29·33 N	104·23 W
90	Presidio, Rio del (R.) (rê'ō-dĕl-prĕ-sē'dyô) Mex.	23·54 N	105·44 W
121	Prešov (prĕ'shôf) Czech.	49·00 N	21·18 E
127	Prespa (L.) (prĕs'pä) Alb.-Yugo.	40·49 N	20·50 E
99	Prespuntal (R.) (prĕs-pōōn-täl') Ven. (In.)	9·55 N	64·32 W
82	Presque Isle (prĕsk'ēl') Maine	46·41 N	68·03 W
111	Pressbaum Aus. (Vienna In.)	48·12 N	16·06 E
110	Preston (prĕs'tŭn) Eng.	53·46 N	2·42 W
67	Preston (pres'tŭn) Idaho	42·05 N	111·54 W
71	Preston (prĕs'tŭn) Minn.	43·42 N	92·06 W
65	Preston Wash. (Seattle In.)	47·31 N	121·56 W
80	Prestonburg (prĕs'tŭn-bûrg) Ky.	37·35 N	82·50 W
110	Prestwich (prĕst'wĭch) Eng.	53·32 N	2·17 W
167	Pretoria (prē-tō'rĭ-ȧ) S. Afr. (Johannesburg & Pretoria In.)	25·43 S	28·16 E
167	Pretoria North (prĕ-tô'rĭ-ȧ nōōrd) S. Afr. (Johannesburg & Pretoria In.)	25·41 S	28·11 E
127	Préveza (prĕ'vȧ-zä) Grc.	38·58 N	20·44 E
64	Pribilof (Is.) (prĭ'bĭ-lof) Alaska	57·00 N	169·20 W
127	Priboj (prē'boi) Yugo.	43·33 N	19·33 E
69	Price (prīs) Utah	39·35 N	110·50 W
69	Price (R.) Utah	39·21 N	110·35 W
85	Priddis (prĭd'dĭs) Can. (Calgary In.)	50·53 N	114·20 W
85	Priddis Cr. Can. (Calgary In.)	50·56 N	114·32 W
124	Priego (prê-ā'gō) Sp.	37·27 N	4·13 W
119	Prienai (prê-ĕn'ī) Sov. Un.	54·38 N	23·56 E
166	Prieska (prê-ĕs'kȧ) S. Afr.	29·40 S	22·50 E
66	Priest L. (prēst) Idaho	48·30 N	116·43 W
66	Priest Rapids Dam Wash.	46·39 N	119·55 W
66	Priest Rapids Res. Wash.	46·42 N	119·58 W
136	Priiskovaya (prĭ-ĕs'kô-va-yȧ) Sov. Un. (Urals In.)	60·50 N	58·55 E
126	Prijedor (prē'yĕ-dôr) Yugo.	44·58 N	16·43 E
127	Prijepolje (prē'yĕ-pô'lyĕ) Yugo.	43·22 N	19·41 E
127	Prilep (prē'lĕp) Yugo.	41·20 N	21·35 E
129	Priluki (prê-lōō'kê) Sov. Un.	50·36 N	32·21 E
119	Primorsk (prē-môrsk') Sov. Un.	60·24 N	28·35 E
129	Primorsko-Akhtarskaya (prē-môr'skô äk-tär'skĭ-ê) Sov. Un.	46·03 N	38·09 E
74	Primrose (prĭm'rōz) Tex. (Dallas, Fort Worth In.)	32·36 N	97·28 W
167	Primrose S. Afr. (Johannesburg & Pretoria In.)	26·11 S	28·11 E
86	Prince Albert (prĭns ăl'bẽrt) Can.	53·17 N	105·33 W
86	Prince Albert Natl. Park Can.	54·10 N	105·25 W
86	Prince Albert Sd. Can.	70·23 N	116·57 W
87	Prince Charles I. (chärlz) Can.	67·41 N	74·10 W
82	Prince Edward Natl. Park (ĕd'wẽrd) Can.	46·33 N	63·35 W
83	Prince Edward I. (Prov.) Can.	46·45 N	63·10 W
47	Prince Edward Is. S. Afr.	46·36 S	37·57 E

ng-sing; ŋ-baŋk; N-nasalized n; nŏd; cŏmmit; ōld; ôbey; ôrder; fōōd; fŏŏt; ou-out; s-soft; sh-dish; th-thin; pūre; ûnite; ûrn; stŭd; circŭs; ü-as "y" in study; '-indeterminate vowel.

254 Prince Edward Pen.–Qezel Owzan PRONOUNCING INDEX

Page Name Pronunciation Region Lat. °′ Long. °′

81 Prince Edward Pen. . . . . Can. 44·00 N 77·15 W
86 Prince George (jôrj) . . . . Can. 53·51 N 122·57 W
64 Prince of Wales (I.) . . . . Alaska 55·48 N 133·46 W
159 Prince of Wales (I.) . . . . Austl. 10·47 S 142·15 E
64 Prince of Wales, C. (wālz) . Alaska 65·48 N 169·08 W
86 Prince Rupert (roo'pērt) . . . . . Can. 54·20 N 130·11 W
110 Princes Risborough
(prĭns'ĕz rĭz'brŭ)
Eng. (London In.) 51·41 N 0·51 W
84 Princess Anne (prĭn'sĕs ăn)
Va. (Norfolk In.) 36·44 N 76·03 W
159 Princess Charlotte B. (shär'lŏt)
Austl. 13·45 S 144·15 E
47 Princess Martha Coast (mär'thå)
Ant. 72·00 S 5·00 W
86 Princeton (prĭns'tŭn) . . . . Can. 49·21 N 120·20 W
80 Princeton . . . . Ill. 41·20 N 89·25 W
80 Princeton . . . . Ind. 38·20 N 87·35 W
78 Princeton . . . . Ky. 37·07 N 87·52 W
71 Princeton . . . . Mich. 46·16 N 87·33 W
71 Princeton . . . . Minn. 45·34 N 93·36 W
73 Princeton . . . . Mo. 40·23 N 93·34 W
84 Princeton . . . N. J. (New York In.) 40·21 N 74·40 W
79 Princeton . . . . W. Va. 37·21 N 81·05 W
71 Princeton . . . . Wis. 43·50 N 89·09 W
64 Prince William Sd. (wĭl'yăm)
Alaska 60·40 N 147·10 W
164 Príncipe, Ilha do (I.)
(ēl'yå dô prēn'sē-pĕ) . Afr. 1·42 N 5·38 E
66 Prineville (prīn'vĭl) . . . . Ore. 44.17 N 120.48 W
66 Prineville Res. . . . . Ore. 44·07 N 120·45 W
93 Prinzapolca (prēn-zä-pōl'kä) . . Nic. 13·18 N 83·35 W
93 Prinzapolca R. . . . . Nic. 13·23 N 84·23 W
74 Prior Lake (prī'ēr)
Minn. (Minneapolis,
St. Paul In.) 44·43 N 93·26 W
119 Priozërsk (prĭ-ô'zĕrsk) . . . Sov. Un. 61·03 N 30·08 E
133 Pripyat (Pripet) (R.) (prē'pyåt)
Sov. Un. 51·50 N 29·45 E
Pripyat' Marshes, see Poles'ye
127 Priština (prēsh'tĭ-nä) . . . . Yugo. 42·39 N 21·12 E
78 Pritchard (prĭt'chârd) . . . . Ala. 30·44 N 87·04 W
120 Pritzwalk (prēts'välk) . . . . Ger. 53·09 N 12·12 E
122 Privas (prē-väs') . . . . Fr. 44·44 N 4·37 E
129 Privol'noye (prē'vôl-nô-yĕ)
Sov. Un. 47·30 N 32·21 E
127 Prizren (prē'zrĕn) . . . . Yugo. 42·11 N 20·45 E
125 Procida (prô'chē-dä)
It. (Naples In.) 40.31 N 14.02 E
125 Procida, I. di . . . . . It. (Naples In.) 40·32 N 13·57 E
74 Proctor (prŏk'tēr)
Minn. (Duluth In.) 46·45 N 92·14 W
81 Proctor . . . . Vt. 43·40 N 73·00 W
65 Proebstel (prōb'stĕl)
Wash. (Portland In.) 45·40 N 122·29 W
124 Proenca-a-Nova
(prô-ān'så-å-nō'vå) . . . . Port. 39·44 N 7·55 W
92 Progreso (prô-grĕ'sô) . . . . Hond. 15·28 N 87·49 W
91 Progreso (prô-grā'sō) . . . . Mex. 21·14 N 89·39 W
76 Progreso . . . . Mex. 27·29 N 101·05 W
134 Prokop'yevsk . . . . Sov. Un. 53·52 N 86·38 E
127 Prokuplje (prô'kŏop'l-yĕ) . . . Yugo. 43·16 N 21·40 E
154 Prome (prōm) . . . . Bur. 18·46 N 95·15 E
128 Pronya (R.) (prô'nyä) . . . Sov. Un. 54·08 N 30·58 E
128 Pronya (R.) . . . . Sov. Un. 54·08 N 39·30 E
99 Propriá (prō-prē-ä') . . . . Braz. 10·17 S 36·47 W
75 Prospect (prŏs'pĕkt)
Ky. (Louisville In.) 38·21 N 85·36 W
84 Prospect Park (prŏs'pĕkt pärk)
Pa. (Philadelphia In.) 39·53 N 75·18 W
66 Prosser (prŏs'ēr) . . . . Wash. 46·10 N 119·46 W
121 Prostějov (prôs'tyĕ-yôf) . . . . Czech. 49·28 N 17·08 E
65 Protection (I.) (prô-tĕk'shŭn)
Wash. (Seattle In.) 48·07 N 122·56 W
128 Protoka (R.) (prôt'ô-kå)
Sov. Un. 55·00 N 36·42 E
127 Provadiya (prō-väd'ē-yå) . . . . Bul. 43·13 N 27·28 E
80 Providence (prŏv'ĭ-dĕns) . . . . . Ky. 37·25 N 87·45 W
84 Providence . . R. I. (Providence In.) 41·50 N 71·23 W
67 Providence . . . . Utah 41·42 N 111·50 W
93 Providencia, Isla de (I.) . . . . . . Col. 13·21 N 80·55 W
95 Providenciales (I.)
(prō-vē-dĕn-sē-ä'lås)
(prŏ-vĭ-dĕn'shålz) . Caicos 21·50 N 72·15 W
64 Provideniya (prô-vĭ-dă'nĭ-yå)
Sov. Un. 64·30 N 172·54 W
69 Provo (prō'vō) . . . . Utah 40·15 N 111·40 W
126 Prozor (prô'zôr) . . . . Yugo. 43·48 N 17·59 E
84 Prudence I. (proo'dĕns)
R. I. (Providence In.) 41·38 N 71·20 W
121 Prudnik (prŏod'nĭk) . . . . Pol. 50·19 N 17·34 E
119 Prunkkala (prōōŋk'å-lå) . . . . . . Fin. 60·38 N 22·32 E
120 Prussia (Reg.) (prŭsh'å) . . . . . Ger. 50·43 N 8·35 E
121 Pruszków (prŏosh'kŏof) . . . . . . Pol. 52·09 N 20·50 E
129 Prut (R.) (prōōt) . . . . Sov. Un. 48·05 N 27·07 E
73 Pryor (prī'ēr) . . . . Okla. 36·16 N 95·19 W
133 Prypeć (R.) . . . . Sov. Un. 51·50 N 25·35 E
121 Przedbórz (pzhĕd'bōōzh) . . . . . Pol. 51·05 N 19·53 E
121 Przedbórz . . . . Pol. 53·01 N 20·54 E
121 Przemyśl (pzhĕ'mĭsh'l) . . . . Pol. 49·47 N 22·45 E
134 Przheval'sk (p'r-zhĭ-välsk')
Sov. Un. 42·25 N 78·18 E
127 Psará (I.) (psä'rå) . . . . Grc. 38·39 N 25·26 E
129 Psël (R.) (psĕl) . . . . Sov. Un. 49·45 N 33·42 E
127 Psevdhókavos (Pen.) . . . . Grc. 39·58 N 24·05 E
128 Pskov (pskôf) . . . . Sov. Un. 57·48 N 28·19 E
128 Pskov (Oblast) . . . . Sov. Un. 57·33 N 29·05 E
128 Pskovskoye Ozero (L.)
(p'skôv'skô'yĕ ôzĕ-rô) . Sov. Un. 58·05 N 28·15 E
128 Ptich' (R.) (p'tēch) . . . . . . Sov. Un. 53·17 N 28·16 E
126 Ptuj (ptōō'ē) . . . . Yugo. 46·24 N 15·54 E
139 Puak (pōō'ä)
Indon. (Singapore In.) 1·39 N 101·31 E
151 Pucheng (pōō'chĕng') . . . . . . China 28·02 N 118·25 E
121 Puck (pŏotsk) . . . . Pol. 54·43 N 18·23 E
146 Pudog . . . . China 33·29 N 79·26 E
132 Pudozh (pōō'dôzh) . . . . . . Sov. Un. 61·50 N 36·50 E
90 Puebla (pwā'blä) . . . . Mex. 19·02 N 98·11 W
124 Puebla de Don Fadrique
(pwĕ'blä dā dōn fä-drē'kā) . . Sp. 37·55 N 2·55 W
72 Pueblo (pwā'blō) . . . . Colo. 38·15 N 104·36 W
90 Pueblo Nuevo (nwā'vō) . . . . . Mex. 23·23 N 105·21 W
91 Pueblo Viejo (vyā'hō) . . . . Mex. 17·23 N 93·46 W
74 Puente (pwĕn'tē)
Calif. (Los Angeles In.) 34·01 N 117·57 W
101 Puente Alto (pwĕ'n-tĕ ål'tô)
Chile (Santiago In.) 33·36 S 70·34 W
124 Puenteareas (pwĕn-tā-ä-rā'äs) . Sp. 42·09 N 8·23 W
124 Puente Ceso (pwĕn'tå thā'sō) . . Sp. 43·15 N 8·53 W
124 Puentedeume
(pwĕn-tå-dhå-ōō'må) . Sp. 43·28 N 8·09 W
124 Puente-Genil (pwĕn'tå-hå-nēl')
Sp. 37·25 N 4·18 W
69 Puerco (R.) (pwĕr'kō) . . . N. Mex. 35·15 N 107·05 W
100 Puerto Aisén (pwĕ'r-tō å'y-sĕ'n)
Chile 45·28 S 72·44 W
91 Puerto Ángel (pwĕ'r-tō äŋ'hål)
Mex. 15·42 N 96·32 W
93 Puerto Armuelles
(pwe'r-tô år-mōō-ā'lyās) . . Pan. 8·18 N 82·52 W
92 Puerto Barrios (pwĕ'r-tô bär'rē-ôs)
Guat. 15·43 N 88·36 W
98 Puerto Bermúdez
(pwĕ'r-tō bĕr-mōō'dāz) . Peru 10·17 S 74·57 W
98 Puerto Berrío (pwĕ'r-tō bĕr-rē'ō)
Col. (In.) 6·29 N 74·27 W
99 Puerto Cabello
(pwĕ'r-tō kä-bĕl'yō) . Ven. (In.) 10·28 N 68·01 W
93 Puerto Cabezas
(pwĕ'r-tô kå-bā'zås) . Nic. 14·01 N 83·26 W
100 Puerto Casado (pwĕ'r-tō kå-sä'dō)
Par. 22·16 S 57·57 W
92 Puerto Castilla
(pwĕ'r-tô käs-tēl'yō) Hond. 16·01 N 86·01 W
98 Puerto Chicama
(pwĕ'r-tō chē-kä'må) . Peru 7·46 S 79·18 W
98 Puerto Columbia
(pwĕr'tô kô-lôm'bē-å) . Col. 11·08 N 75·09 W
93 Puerto Cortés (pwĕ'r-tô kôr-tās')
C. R. 9·00 N 83·37 W
92 Puerto Cortés (pwĕ'r-tô kôr-tās')
Hond. 15·48 N 87·57 W
98 Puerto Cumarebo
(pwĕ'r-tō kōō-mä-rĕ'bô) . Ven. 11·25 N 69·17 W
125 Puerto de Beceite (Mts.)
(pwĕ'r-tō dĕ bĕ-sĕ'y-tĕ) . Sp. 40·43 N 0·05 W
72 Puerto de Luna
(pwĕr'tō då lōō'nå) . N. Mex. 34·49 N 104·36 W
98 Puerto de Nutrias
(pwĕ'r-tō dĕ nōō-trē-ås') . Ven. 8·02 N 69·19 W
100 Puerto Deseado
(pwĕ'r-tō dā-sā-ä'dhō) . Arg. 47·38 S 66·00 W
98 Puerto Eten (pwĕ'r-tō ĕ-tĕ'n) . Peru 6·59 S 79·51 W
93 Puerto Jimenez
(pwĕ'r-tô ĸē-mĕ'nĕz) . C. R. 8·35 N 83·23 W
99 Puerto La Cruz
(pwĕ'r-tō lä krōō'z) . Ven. (In.) 10·14 N 64·38 W
124 Puertollano (pwĕr-tôl-yä'nō) . . Sp. 38·41 N 4·05 W
100 Puerto Madryn
(pwĕ'r-tō må-drĕn') . Arg. 42·45 S 65·01 W
98 Puerto Maldonado
(pwĕ'r-tō mål-dō-nå'dô) . Peru 12·43 S 69·01 W
Puerto Mexico, see Coatzacoalcos
90 Puerto Miniso (pwĕ'r-tō mē-nē'sô)
Mex. 16·06 N 98·02 W
100 Puerto Montt (pwĕ'r-tō mô'nt)
Chile 41·29 S 73·00 W
100 Puerto Natales (pwĕ'r-tō nä-tå'lĕs)
Chile 51·48 S 72·01 W
98 Puerto Niño (pwĕ'r-tō nē'n-yô)
Col. (In.) 5·57 N 74·36 W
98 Puerto Ordaz (pwĕ'r-tō ōōr-då's)
Ven. 8·30 N 62·45 W
94 Puerto Padre (pwĕ'r-tō på'drā)
Cuba 21·10 N 76·40 W
88 Puerto Peñasco
(pwĕ'r-tô pĕn-yå's-kô) . Mex. 31·39 N 113·15 W
100 Puerto Pinasco
(pwĕ'r-tō pē-nå's-kō) . Par. 22·31 S 57·50 W
99 Puerto Píritu (pwĕ'r-tō pē'rē-tōō)
Ven. (In.) 10·05 N 65·04 W
95 Puerto Plata (pwĕ'r-tô plä'tä)
Dom. Rep. 19·50 N 70·40 W
154 Puerto Princesa
(pwĕr-tô prēn-sā'så) . Phil. 9·45 N 118·41 E
89 Puerto Rico (pwĕr'tô rē'kō)
N. A. (In.) 18·16 N 66·50 W
89 Puerto Rico Trough . . . . N. A. 19·45 N 66·30 W
98 Puerto Salgar
(pwĕ'r-tō säl-gär') . Col (In.) 5·30 N 74·39 W
100 Puerto Santa Cruz
(pwĕ'r-tō sän'tä krōōz') . Arg. 50·04 S 68·32 W
99 Puerto Suárez
(pwĕ'r-tō swä'råz) . Bol. 18·55 S 57·39 W
98 Puerto Tejada
(pwĕ'r-tō tĕ-ĸä'dä) . Col. (In.) 3·13 N 76·23 W
90 Puerto Vallarta
(pwĕ'r-tō väl-yär'tä) . Mex. 20·36 N 105·13 W
100 Puerto Varas (pwĕ'r-tō vä'rås)
Chile 41·16 S 73·03 W
98 Puerto Wilches
(pwĕ'r-tō vēl'c-hĕs) . Col. 7·19 N 73·54 W
133 Pugachëv (pōō'gå-chyôf) . Sov. Un. 52·00 N 48·40 E
65 Puget (pū'jĕt)
Wash. (Portland In.) 46·10 N 123·23 W
66 Puget Sd. . . . . Wash. 47·49 N 122·26 W
126 Puglia (Apulia) (Reg.)
(pōō'lyä) (ä-pōō'lyä) . It. 41·13 N 16·10 E
148 Puhsien (pōō'sĭān) . . . . China 35·43 N 115·22 E
139 Pukin (R.) . . Mala. (Singapore In.) 2·53 N 102·54 E
126 Pula (pōō'lä) . . . . Yugo. 44·52 N 13·55 E
98 Pulacayo (pōō-lä-kä'yō) . . . . . . Bol. 20·12 S 66·33 W
148 P'ulantien (pōō'lăn'chĕn') . . China 39·23 N 121·57 E
78 Pulaski (pŭ-lăs'kĭ) . . . . Tenn. 35·11 N 87·03 W
79 Pulaski . . . . Va. 37·00 N 81·45 W
121 Puławy (pŏŏ-wä'vĕ) . . . . Pol. 51·24 N 21·59 E
142 Pulizat (R.) . . . . India 13·58 N 79·52 E
66 Pullman (pōōl'măn) . . . . Wash. 46·44 N 117·10 W
155 Pulog (Mtn.) (pōō'lôg)
Phil. (Manila In.) 16·38 N 120·53 E
112 Pultusk (pōōl'tŏosk) . . . . Pol. 52·40 N 21·09 E
67 Pumpkin Cr. (pŭmp'kĭn) . . . Mont. 45·47 N 105·35 W
142 Punakhapoo-nŭk'ŭ) . . . . Bhu. 27·45 N 89·59 E
98 Punata (pōō-nä'tä) . . . . Bol. 17·43 S 65·43 W
142 Punjab (State) (pŭn'jäb') . . . India 35·50 N 75·20 E
98 Puno (pōō'nô) . . . . Peru 15·58 S 7·02 W
100 Punta Arenas (pōō'n-tä-rĕ'näs)
Chile 53·09 S 70·48 W
99 Punta de Piedras
(pōō'n-tä dĕ pyĕ'drås)
Ven. (In.) 10·54 N 64·06 W
92 Punta Gorda (pōōn'tä gôr'dä)
Br. Hond. 16·07 N 88·50 W
79 Punta Gorda (pŭn'tå gôr'då)
Fla. (In.) 26·55 N 82·02 W
93 Punta Gorda, Rio (R.)
(pōō'n-tä gô'r-dä) . Nic. 11·34 N 84·13 W
101 Punta Indio, Can.
(pōō'n-tä ē'n-dyô)
Arg. (Buenos Aires In.) 34·56 S 57·20 W
93 Puntarenas (pōōnt-ä-rā'näs) . C. R. 9·59 N 84·49 W
98 Punto Fijo (pōō'n-tō fē'ĸô) . . Ven. 11·48 N 70·14 W
164 Punto Grande (grä'n-dĕ)
C. V. Is. (In.) 16·53 N 25·00 W
81 Punxsutawney (pŭnk-sŭ-tô'nē)
Pa. 40·55 N 79·00 W
98 Puquio (pōō'kyô) . . . . Peru 14·43 S 74·02 W
134 Pur (R.) . . . . Sov. Un. 65·30 N 77·30 E
73 Purcell (pûr-sĕl') . . . . Okla. 35·01 N 97·22 W
65 Purdy (pûr'dē)
Wash. (Seattle In.) 47·23 N 122·37 W
90 Purépero (pōō-rā'pā-rō) . . . . . Mex. 19·56 N 102·02 W
72 Purgatoire (R.) (pûr-gå-twär')
Colo. 37·25 N 103·53 W
142 Puri (pōō'rē) . . . . India 19·52 N 85·51 E
95 Purial, Sierra de (Mts.)
(sē-ĕ'r-rå-dĕ-pōō-rē-äl') . Cuba 20·15 N 74·40 W
98 Purificacion (pōō-rē-fē-kä-syōn')
Col. (In.) 3·52 N 74·54 W
90 Purificación (pōō-rē-fē-kä-syō'n)
Mex. 19·44 N 104·38 W
90 Purificación (R.) . . . . Mex. 19·30 N 104·54 W
111 Purkersdorf . . . . Aus. (Vienna In.) 48·13 N 16·11 E
154 Pursat (pōōr-sät') . . . . Camb. 12·33 N 103·51 E
90 Puruandiro (pōō-rōō-än'dē-rō)
Mex. 20·04 N 101·33 W
98 Purús (R.) (pōō-rōō's) . . . . . . Braz. 6·45 S 64·34 W
152 Pusan . . . . Kor. 35·08 N 129·05 E
136 Pushkin (pōōsh'kĭn)
Sov. Un. (Leningrad In.) 59·43 N 30·25 E
136 Pushkino (pōōsh'kē-nô)
Sov. Un. (Moscow In.) 56·01 N 37·51 E
128 Pustoshka (pûs-tôsh'kå) . Sov. Un. 56·20 N 29·33 E
91 Pustunich (pōōs-tōō'nēch) . . . Mex. 19·10 N 90·29 W
101 Putaendo (pōō-tä-ĕn-dô)
Chile (Santiago In.) 32·37 S 70·42 W
123 Puteaux (pü-tō') . . Fr. (Paris In.) . 48·52 N 2·12 E
167 Putfontein (pōōt'fŏn-tān) . . S. Afr.
(Johannesburg & Pretoria In.) 26·08 S 28·24 E
151 P'ut'ien . . . . China 25·40 N 119·02 E
129 Putivl' (pōō-tēv'l') . . . . . . Sov. Un. 51·22 N 33·24 E
91 Putla de Guerrero
(pōō'tlä-dĕ-gĕr-rĕ'rō) . Mex. 17·03 N 97·55 W
81 Putnam (pŭt'năm) . . . . Conn. 41·55 N 71·55 W
134 Putorana, Gory (Mts.) . . . Sov. Un. 68·45 N 93·15 E
143 Puttālām . . . . Ceylon 8·02 N 79·44 E
98 Putumayo (R.) (pōō-tōō-mä'yō)
Col.-Peru 1·02 S 73·50 W
149 Putung (pōō'tōōng')
China (Shanghai In.) 31·14 N 121·29 E
154 Putung, Tandjung (C.) . . . . Indon. 3·35 S 111·50 E
119 Puulavesi (L.) . . . . Fin. 61·49 N 27·10 E
65 Puyallup (pū-ăl'ŭp)
Wash. (Seattle In.) 47·12 N 122·18 W
148 P'uyang (pōō'yäng) . . . . China 35·42 N 114·58 E
166 Pweto (pwä'tō) . . . . Con. L. 8·29 S 28·58 E
134 Pyasina (R.) (pyä-sē'nå) . Sov. Un. 72·45 N 87·37 E
133 Pyatigorsk (pyå-tē-gôrsk')
Sov. Un. 44·00 N 43·00 E
119 Pyhäjärvi (L.) . . . . Fin. 60·57 N 21·50 E
146 Pyinmana (pyēn-mä'nŭ) . . . . . Bur. 19·47 N 96·15 E
80 Pymatuning Res. (pī-må-tŭn'ĭng)
Pa. 41·40 N 80·30 W
152 Pyŏnggang (pyŭng'gäng') . . . . Kor. 38·21 N 127·18 E
152 P'yŏngyang . . . . Kor. 39·03 N 125·48 E
68 Pyramid (L.) (pĭ'rå-mĭd) . . . . . Nev. 40·02 N 119·50 W
68 Pyramid Lake Ind. Res. . . . . . Nev. 40·17 N 119·52 W
168 Pyramids . . . . . U. A. R. (Nile In.) 29·53 N 31·10 E
125 Pyrenees (Mts.) (pĭr-e-nēz')
Fr.-Sp. 43·00 N 0·05 E
120 Pyrzyce (pĕzhĭ'tsĕ) . . . . Pol. 53·09 N 14·53 E
168 Qana el Suweis (Suez Can.)
U. A. R. (Suez In.) 30·53 N 32·21 E
115 Qārah (Oasis) . . . . U. A. R. 29·28 N 26·29 E
133 Qareh Sū (R.) . . . . Iran 38·50 N 47·10 E
168 Qārūn, Birket (L.)
U. A. R. (Nile In.) 29·34 N 30·34 E
144 Qaryat al Ulya . . . . Sau. Ar. 27·43 N 47·43 E
165 Qasr Banī Walid . . . . Libya 31·45 N 14·04 E
138 Qatar (kä'tår) . . . . Asia 25·00 N 52·45 E
115 Qattarah, Munkhafad al (Dep.)
U. A. R. 30·07 N 27·30 E
144 Qāyen . . . . Iran 33·45 N 59·08 E
168 Qena, Wadi (val.)
U. A. R. (Nile In.) 26·38 N 32·53 E
144 Qeshm . . . . Qeshm (Isl.) 26·51 N 56·10 E
144 Qeshm (I.) . . . . Iran 26·52 N 56·15 E
144 Qezel Owzan . . . . Iran 37·00 N 48·23 E

ăt; finăl; rāte; senāte; ärm; åsk; sofå; fâre; ch-choose; dh-as th in other; bē; ēvent; bĕt; recĕnt; cratēr; g-go; gh-guttural g; bĭt; ĭ-short neutral; rīde; ĸ-guttural k as ch in German ich;

PRONOUNCING INDEX Qezel Owzan–Raul Soares 255

Page	Name Pronunciation Region	Lat. °′	Long. °′
133	Qezel Owzan (R.)..........Iran	37·00 N	47·35 E
139	Qiblîya, el (cliff) U. A. R. (Palestine In.)	28·47 N	32·22 E
168	Qift (kêft).....U. A. R. (Nile In.)	25·58 N	32·52 E
168	Qinā (kā'nà)...U. A. R. (Nile In.)	26·10 N	32·48 E
139	Qiraiya (R.) U. A. R. (Palestine In.)	30·14 N	34·21 E
144	Qom.....................Iran	34·28 N	50·53 E
	Qomul, see Hami		
81	Quabbin Res. (kwā'bĭn)....Mass	42·20 N	72·10 W
73	Quachita, L. (kwä shĭ'tô)....Ark.	34·47 N	93·37 W
81	Quakertown (kwā'kẽr-toun)...Pa.	40·30 N	75·20 W
72	Quanah (kwä'nà)..........Tex.	34·19 N	99·43 W
151	Quang Ngai (kwäng n'gä'è)..Viet.	15·05 N	108·58 E
151	Quang Ngai (Mtn.)..........Viet.	15·10 N	108·20 E
154	Quang Tri (kwäng'trē')......Viet.	16·39 N	107·05 E
86	Qu'Appelle (R.) (kà-pĕl')....Can.	50·55 N	104·12 W
126	Quartu Sant' Elena (kwär-tōō' sänt a'lâ-nä) .It.	39·16 N	9·12 E
85	Quebec (kwê-bĕk') (kå-bĕk') Can. (Quebec In.)	46·49 N	71·14 W
87	Quebec (Prov.)............Can.	51·07 N	70·25 W
120	Quedlinburg (kvĕd'lên-bōōrgh) Ger.	51·49 N	11·10 E
86	Queen Charlotte Is. (kwēn shär'lŏt) .Can.	53·40 N	132·50 W
86	Queen Charlotte Str. (strāt) .Can.	51·19 N	128·42 W
49	Queen Elizabeth Is. (ê-lĭz'á-bĕth) Can.	78·20 N	110·00 W
86	Queen Maud G. (mäd)......Can.	68·27 N	102·55 W
47	Queen Maud Land..........Ant.	75·00 S	10·00 E
47	Queen Maud Ra............Ant.	85·00 S	179·00 W
158	Queens Chan. (kwēnz).....Austl.	14·25 S	129·10 E
161	Queenscliff .Austl. (Melbourne In.)	38·16 S	144·39 E
159	Queensland (State) (kwēnz'lánd) Austl.	22·45 S	141·01 E
160	Queenstown (kwēnz'toun)..Austl.	42·00 S	145·40 E
167	Queenstown....S. Afr. (Natal In.)	31·54 S	26·53 E
124	Queija, Sierra de (Mts.) (sē-ĕ'r-rä-dĕ-kĕ'y-kä) .Sp.	42·08 N	7·23 W
100	Queimados (kā-mà'dôs) Braz. (In.)	22·42 S	43·34 W
166	Quelimane (kā lê-mä'nĕ)....Moz.	17·48 S	37·05 E
	Quelpart, see Cheju		
94	Quemado de Güines (kā-mä'dhā-dĕ-gwē'nĕs)...Cuba	22·45 N	80·20 W
151	Quemoy (Chinmen)......Taiwan	24·30 N	118·20 E
93	Quepos (kā'pôs)..........C. R.	9·26 N	84·10 W
93	Quepos, Punta (pt.) (pōō'n-tä) .C. R.	9·23 N	84·20 W
166	Que Que (kwĕ'kwĕ).......S. Rh.	18·49 S	29·45 E
90	Querétaro (kå-rā'tä-rō)......Mex.	20·37 N	100·25 W
124	Quesada (kå-sä'dhä).........Sp.	37·51 N	3·04 W
86	Quesnel (kā-nĕl')..........Can.	53·00 N	122·28 W
86	Quesnel (L.)..............Can.	52·28 N	121·40 W
98	Quetame (kĕ-tä'mĕ)....Col. (In.)	4·20 N	73·50 W
87	Quetico Park (kwĕ'tĭ-kô)...Can.	48·29 N	91·50 W
142	Quetta (kwĕt'ä).........W. Pak.	30·19 N	67·01 E
92	Quezaltenango (kå-zäl'tâ-näŋ'gō) Guat.	14·50 N	91·30 W
92	Quezaltepeque (kå-zäl'tâ-pā'kå) Guat.	14·39 N	89·26 W
92	Quezaltepeque (kĕ-zäl'tĕ'pĕ-kĕ) Sal.	13·50 N	89·17 W
155	Quezon City (kā-zōn) Phil. (Manila In.)	14·40 N	121·02 E
98	Quibdo (kēb'dō).......Col. (In.)	5·42 N	76·41 W
122	Quiberon (kê-bē-rôN')........Fr.	47·29 N	3·08 W
92	Quiché (kē-shā')..........Guat.	15·05 N	91·08 W
111	Quicksborn (kvēks'bōrn) Ger. (Hamburg In.)	53·44 N	9·54 E
65	Quilcene (kwĭl-sēn') Wash. (Seattle In.)	47·50 N	122·53 W
101	Quilimari (kē-lē-mä'rē) Chile (Santiago In.)	32·06 S	71·28 W
86	Quill (L.) (kwĭl)...........Can.	52·10 N	103·34 W
122	Quillan (kê-yäN')............Fr.	43·53 N	2·13 E
101	Quillota (kēl-yō'tä) Chile (Santiago In.)	32·52 S	71·14 W
100	Quilmes (kēl'màs)......Arg. (In.)	34·28 S	58·16 W
143	Quilon (kwê-lōn')..........India	8·58 N	76·16 E
160	Quilpie (kwĭl'pê)..........Austl.	26·34 S	149·20 E
101	Quilpué (kēl-pōō ĕ') Chile (Santiago In.)	33·03 S	71·22 W
98	Quimbaya (kēm-bä'yä) .Col. (In.)	4·38 N	75·46 W
122	Quimper (kăN-pĕr')..........Fr.	47·59 N	4·04 W
155	Quinabucasan Pt. (kē-nä-bōō-kä'sän) Phil. (Manila In.)	14·09 N	123·33 E
66	Quinalt R..............Wash.	47·23 N	124·10 W
66	Quinault Ind. Res.........Wash.	47·27 N	124·34 W
78	Quincy (kwĭn'sê)............Fla.	30·35 N	84·35 W
73	Quincy.....................Ill.	39·55 N	91·23 W
83	Quincy.......Mass. (Boston In.)	42·15 N	71·00 W
80	Quincy.....................Mich.	42·00 N	84·50 W
65	Quincy.......Ore. (Portland In.)	46·08 N	123·10 W
154	Qui Nhon (kwĭnyôn)........Viet.	13·51 N	109·03 E
66	Quinn R. (kwĭn)...........Nev.	41·42 N	117·45 W
124	Quintana de la Serena (kēn-tä'nä dä lä sâ-rā'nä) .Sp.	38·45 N	5·39 W
124	Quintanar (kēn-tä-när').......Sp.	39·36 N	3·02 W
88	Quintana Roo (Ter.) (rō'ō)..Mex.	19·30 N	88·35 W
101	Quintero (kēn-tĕ'rô) Chile (Santiago In.)	32·48 S	71·30 W
90	Quiroga (kē-rō'gä)..........Mex.	19·39 N	101·30 W
124	Quiroga (kē-rô'gä)..........Sp.	42·28 N	7·18 W
78	Quitman (kwĭt'măn).........Ga.	30·46 N	83·35 W
78	Quitman...................Miss.	33·02 N	88·43 W
98	Quito (kē'tō)..............Ec.	0·17 S	78·32 W
99	Quixadá (kê-shä-dä').......Braz.	4·58 S	38·58 W
168	Qulūṣanā (kōō-lōōs'nä) U. A. R. (Nile In.)	28·22 N	30·44 E
167	Qumbu (kōōm'bōō) S. Afr. (Natal In.)	29·12 S	28·53 E
139	Qumran....Jordan (Palestine In.)	31·45 N	35·28 E
84	Quonset Point (kwän'sĕt) R. I. (Providence In.)	41·36 N	71·25 W
160	Quorn (kwôrn)..............Austl.	32·20 S	138·00 E
168	Qūs (kōōs)....U. A. R. (Nile In.)	25·53 N	32·48 E
167	Quthing.........Bas. (Natal In.)	30·35 S	27·42 E
159	Quvea (I.)...............N. Cal.	20·43 S	166·48 E
144	Quzvīn....................Iran	36·10 N	49·59 E
120	Raab R. (räp)..............Aus.	46·55 N	15·55 E
112	Raahe (rä'ĕ)...............Fin.	64·39 N	24·22 E
126	Rab (I.) (räb)............Yugo.	44·45 N	14·40 E
154	Raba.....................Indon.	8·32 S	118·49 E
121	Raba R...................Hung.	47·28 N	17·12 E
164	Rabat (rä-bät')............Mor.	33·59 N	6·47 W
155	Rabaul (rä'boul).....N. Gui. Ter.	4·15 S	152·19 E
127	Rača (rä'chà)..............Yugo.	44·13 N	21·01 E
71	Raccoon (R.) (ră-kōōn').....Iowa	42·07 N	94·45 W
95	Raccoon Cay (I.).........Ba. Is.	22·25 N	75·50 W
83	Race, C. (rās)..............Can.	46·37 N	52·55 W
139	Rachado, C. Mala. (Singapore In.)	2·26 N	101·29 E
121	Racibórz (rä-chē'bōōzh)......Pol.	50·06 N	18·14 E
75	Racine (rá-sēn') Wis. (Milwaukee In.)	42·43 N	87·49 W
74	Raco (rá cō) Mich. (Sault Ste. Marie In.)	46·22 N	84·43 W
121	Rădăuti (rû-dû-ōōts'')......Rom.	47·53 N	25·55 E
110	Radcliffe (răd'klĭf)..........Eng.	53·34 N	2·20 W
123	Radevormwald (rä'dĕ-fōrm-väld) Ger. (Ruhr In.)	51·12 N	7·22 E
79	Radford (răd'fērd)...........Va.	37·06 N	81·33 W
142	Rādhanpur................India	23·57 N	71·38 E
74	Radio Center (rā'dĭ-ō cĕn'tēr) Minn. (Minneapolis, St. Paul In.)	44·50 N	93·06 W
168	Radium (rā'dĭ-ŭm)........S. Afr. (Johannesburg & Pretoria In.)	25·06 S	28·18 E
116	Radnor Forest (răd'nôr).....Wales	52·11 N	3·25 W
121	Radom (rä'dôm)..............Pol.	51·24 N	21·11 E
127	Radomir (rä'dô-mêr)........Bul.	42·33 N	22·58 E
121	Radomsko (rä-dôm'skô)......Pol.	51·04 N	19·27 E
129	Radomyshl (rä-dô-mēsh''l) Sov. Un.	50·30 N	29·13 E
127	Radoviš (rä'dô-vêsh).......Yugo.	41·39 N	22·28 E
118	Radöy (I.) (räd-ûê).........Nor.	60·43 N	4·40 E
129	Radul' (rá'dōōl)........Sov. Un.	51·52 N	30·46 E
119	Radviliškis (räd'vê-lēsh'kēs) Sov. Un.	55·49 N	23·31 E
144	Radwah, Jabal (Mtn.)...Sau. Ar.	24·44 N	38·14 E
121	Radzyń Podlaski (räd'zēn-y' pŭd-lä'skĭ) .Pol.	51·49 N	22·40 E
79	Raeford (rā'fērd)..........N. C.	34·57 N	79·15 W
123	Raesfeld (răz'fĕld) Ger. (Ruhr In.)	51·46 N	6·50 E
158	Raeside (rā'sīd)...........Austl.	29·20 S	122·30 E
86	Rae Str. (rā)...............Can.	68·40 N	95·03 W
100	Rafaela (rä-fä-å'lä)..........Arg.	31·15 S	61·21 W
115	Rafah (rä'fä)............U. A. R.	31·14 N	34·12 E
165	Rafai (rä-fī')......Cen. Afr. Rep.	4·59 N	23·58 E
144	Rafhā....................Sau. Ar.	29·43 N	43·13 E
67	Raft R. (răft)..............Idaho	42·20 N	113·17 W
142	Raga.....................China	29·31 N	85·52 E
155	Ragay (rä-gī') .Phil. (Manila In.)	13·49 N	122·45 E
155	Ragay G.......Phil. (Manila In.)	13·44 N	122·38 E
133	Ragga...................U. A. R.	36·00 N	39·00 E
118	Ragunda (rä-gōōn'dä)........Swe.	63·07 N	16·24 E
113	Ragusa (rä-gōō'sä)...........It.	36·58 N	14·41 E
	Ragusa, see Dubrovnik		
84	Rahway (rô'wā) N. J. (New York In.)	40·37 N	74·16 W
143	Raichur (rä'ê-chōōr').......India	16·23 N	77·18 E
142	Raigarh (rī'gŭr)...........India	21·57 N	83·32 E
69	Rainbow Bridge Natl. Mon. (rān'bō) .Utah	37·05 N	111·00 W
88	Rainbow City..............C. Z. (Panama Canal In.)	9.20·N	79·23 W
65	Rainier.......Ore. (Portland In.)	46·05 N	122·56 W
66	Rainier, Mt. (rā-nēr')......Wash.	46·52 N	121·46 W
71	Rainy (L.) (rān'ê)....Can.-Minn.	48·50 N	93·06 W
71	Rainy (R.)...........Can.-Minn.	48·36 N	94·14 W
87	Rainy River...............Can.	48·42 N	94·29 W
142	Raipur (rä'jŭ-bōō-rē')......India	21·25 N	81·37 E
80	Raisin (R.) (rā'zĭn)........Mich.	42·00 N	83·35 W
84	Raitan (rā-tăn) N. J. (New York In.)	40·34 N	74·40 W
154	Raja, Bukit (Mtn.).......Indon.	0·45 S	112·11 E
143	Rajahmundry (räj-ŭ-mŭn'drê) India	17·03 N	81·51 E
154	Rajang, Balang (strm.).....Mala.	2·10 N	113·30 E
142	Rājasthān (State) (rä'jŭs-tän) India	31·20 N	72·00 E
142	Rājkot (räj'kôt)...........India	22·20 N	70·48 E
142	Rakers Tal (L.)............China	30·42 N	80·40 E
121	Rakhov (rä'kôf).........Sov. Un.	48·02 N	24·13 E
136	Rakh'ya (räk'yä) Sov. Un. (Leningrad In.)	60·06 N	30·50 E
129	Rakitnoye (rá-kēt'nô-yĕ) .Sov. Un.	50·51 N	35·53 E
120	Rakovnik (rä'kôv-nyĕk)....Czech.	50·07 N	13·45 E
128	Rakvere (räk'vĕ-rĕ).....Sov. Un.	59·22 N	26·14 E
79	Raleigh (rô'lă)............N. C.	35·45 N	78·39 W
79	Raleigh, B.................N. C.	34·50 N	76·15 W
93	Rama (rä'mä)...............Nic.	12·11 N	84·14 W
101	Ramallo (rä-mä'l-yō) Arg. (Buenos Aires In.)	33·28 S	60·02 W
123	Rambouillet (räN-bōō-yĕ') Fr. (Paris In.)	48·39 N	1·49 E
167	Rame Hd......S. Afr. (Natal In.)	31·48 S	29·22 E
136	Ramenskoye (rá'mĕn-skô-yĕ) Sov. Un. (Moscow In.)	55·34 N	38·15 E
144	Ramlat As Sab Atayn (Reg.) Sau. Ar.	16·02 N	45·30 E
139	Ramm, Jabal (Mts.) Jordan (Palestine In.)	29·37 N	35·32 E
143	Rāmnād...................India	9·13 N	78·52 E
90	Ramos (rä'mōs).............Mex.	22·46 N	101·52 W
76	Ramos Arizpe (ä-rēz'pä).....Mex.	25·33 N	100·57 W
64	Rampart (răm'pärt)........Alaska	65·28 N	150·18 W
84	Rampo Mts. (răm'pō) N. J.-N. Y. (New York In.)	41·06 N	74·12 W
142	Rāmpur (räm'pōōr)........India	28·53 N	79·03 E
142	Rāmpur-Boālia (bô-ä'lê-ä) E. Pak.	24·26 N	88·39 E
154	Ramree (I.) (räm'rē')........Bur.	19·01 N	93·23 E
85	Ramsayville (răm'zê vĭl) Can. (Ottawa In.)	45·23 N	75·34 W
110	Ramsbottom (rămz'bŏt-ŭm) Eng.	53·39 N	2·20 W
116	Ramsey (răm'zê).....Isle of Man	54·20 N	4·25 W
84	Ramsey....N. J. (New York In.)	41·03 N	74·09 W
117	Ramsgate (rămz''gāt).......Eng.	51·19 N	1·20 E
118	Ramsjö (räm'shû)...........Swe.	62·11 N	15·44 E
155	Ramu (R.) (rä'mōō)..N. Gui. Ter.	5·35 S	145·16 E
154	Ranau, L. (rä-nä'ōō)......Indon.	4·52 S	103·52 E
101	Rancagua (rän-kä'gwä) Chile (Santiago In.)	34·10 S	70·43 W
122	Rance (räNs)................Fr.	48·17 N	2·30 W
142	Rānchi (rän'chē)...........India	23·24 N	85·18 E
95	Rancho Boyeros (rä'n-chô-bô-yĕ'rôs) Cuba (Havana In.)	23·00 N	82·23 W
84	Randallstown (răn'dălz-toun) Md. (Baltimore In.)	39·22 N	76·48 W
118	Randers (rän'ĕrs)...........Den.	56·28 N	10·03 E
167	Randfontein (rănt'fŏn-tän) .S. Afr. (Johannesburg & Pretoria In.)	26·10 S	27·42 E
79	Randleman (răn'd'l-măn)...N. C.	35·49 N	79·50 W
83	Randolph (răn'dôlf) Mass. (Boston In.)	42 10 N	71·03 W
70	Randolph..................Nebr.	42·22 N	97·22 W
81	Randolph...................Vt.	43·55 N	72·40 W
83	Random I. (răn'dŭm).......Can.	48·12 N	53·25 W
118	Rands Fd. (räns' fyôr)......Nor.	60·35 N	10·10 E
82	Rangeley (rānj'lê).........Maine	44·56 N	70·38 W
81	Rangeley (L.)..............Maine	44·55 N	70·40 W
76	Ranger (rān'jēr)............Tex.	32·26 N	98·41 W
142	Rangia....................India	26·32 N	91·39 E
154	Rangoon (răŋ-gōōn')........Bur.	16·46 N	96·09 E
142	Rangpur (rŭng'pōōr).....E. Pak.	25·48 N	89·19 E
139	Rangsang, Palau (I.) (räng'säng') Indon. (Singapore In.)	1·03 N	102·54 E
111	Rangsdorf (rängs'dōrf) Ger. (Berlin In.)	52·17 N	13·25 E
142	Raniganj (rä-nē-gŭnj')......India	23·40 N	87·08 E
86	Rankin Inlet (răŋ'kĕn)......Can.	62·45 N	94·27 W
128	Ranova (R.) (rä'nô-vá)..Sov. Un.	53·55 N	40·03 E
75	Ransomville (răn'sum-vĭl) N. Y. (Buffalo In.)	43·15 N	78·54 W
139	Rantau.....Mala. (Singapore In.)	2·35 N	101·58 E
154	Rantemario, Bulu (Mtn.)..Indon.	3·22 S	119·50 E
80	Rantoul (răn-tōōl')...........Ill.	40·25 N	88·05 W
126	Rapallo (rä-päl'lō)............It.	44·21 N	9·14 E
157	Rapa Nui (Easter) (I.) (rä'pä nōō'ê) (ēs'tēr) .Chile	26·50 S	109·00 W
101	Rapel (rä-päl') (R.) Chile (Santiago In.)	34·05 S	71·30 W
71	Rapid (R.) (răp'ĭd).........Minn.	48·21 N	94·50 W
70	Rapid City................S. D.	44·06 N	103·14 W
119	Rapla (räp'lá)...........Sov. Un.	59·02 N	24·46 E
81	Rappahannock (R.) (răp'á-hăn'ŭk) .Va.	38·20 N	75·25 W
81	Raquette (L.) (răk'ĕt)......N. Y.	43·50 N	74·35 W
81	Raquette (R.)..............N. Y.	44·20 N	74·50 W
121	Rara Mazowiecka (rä'rä mä-zō-vyĕts'kä) .Pol.	51·46 N	20·17 E
84	Raritan R. (răr'ĭ-tăn) N. J. (New York In.)	40·32 N	74·27 W
157	Rarotonga (rä'rô-tŏŋ'gá) .Cook Is.	20·40 S	163·00 W
144	Ras Al Hadd (C.).....Mus. & Om.	22·29 N	59·46 E
139	Ra's an Naqb Jordan (Palestine In.)	30·00 N	35·29 E
163	Ras Dashan (Mtn.) (räs dä-shän') Eth.	12·49 N	38·14 E
119	Raseiniai (rä-syā'nyĭ)...Sov. Un.	55·23 N	23·04 E
144	Ra's Fartak (C.)...........Aden	15·43 N	52·17 E
139	Rashayya.....Leb. (Palestine In.)	33·30 N	35·50 E
168	Rashīd (Rosetta) (rá-shēd') (rô-zĕt'á) U. A. R. (Nile In.)	31·22 N	30·25 E
168	Rashīd, Masabb (R. Mth.) U. A. R. (Nile In.)	31·30 N	29·58 E
136	Rashkina (rásh'kĭ-ná) Sov. Un. (Urals In.)	59·57 N	61·30 E
129	Rashkov (räsh'kôf)......Sov. Un.	47·55 N	28·51 E
144	Rasht......................Iran	37·13 N	49·45 E
127	Raška (räsh'kå)............Yugo.	43·16 N	20·40 E
142	Ras Kuh Mt...............W. Pak.	34·03 N	65·10 E
144	Ras Madrakah (C.)..Mus. & Om.	18·53 N	57·48 E
133	Rasskazovo (rás-kä'sô-vô) Sov. Un.	52·40 N	41·40 E
144	Ra's Tannūrah..........Sau. Ar.	26·45 N	49·59 E
120	Rastatt (rä-shtät')..........Ger.	48·51 N	8·12 E
136	Rastes (rás'tĕs) Sov. Un. (Urals In.)	59·24 N	58·49 E
136	Rastunovo (rás-tōō'nô-vô) Sov. Un. (Moscow In.)	55·15 N	37·50 E
124	Ras Uarc (C.)..............Mor.	35·28 N	2·58 W
142	Ratangarh (rŭ-tŭn'gŭr).....India	28·10 N	74·30 E
154	Rat Buri...................Thai.	13·30 N	99·46 E
77	Ratcliff (răt'klĭf)...........Tex.	31·22 N	95·09 W
120	Rathenow (rä'tĕ-nō)........Ger.	52·36 N	12·20 E
116	Rathlin (I.) (răth-lĭn).......Ire.	54·80 N	6·10 W
123	Ratingen (rä'tĕn-gĕn) Ger. (Ruhr In.)	51·18 N	6·51 E
64	Rat Is. (răt)..............Alaska	51·35 N	176·48 E
142	Ratlam....................India	23·19 N	75·05 E
143	Ratnāgir...................India	17·04 N	73·24 E
72	Raton (rá-tōn')...........N. Mex.	36·52 N	104·26 W
66	Rattlesnake Cr. (răt''l snāk) .Ore.	42·38 N	117·39 W
118	Rättvik (rĕt'vēk)............Swe.	60·54 N	15·07 E
120	Ratzeburger See (L.) (rä'tzĕ-bōōr-gĕr-zā) .Ger.	53·48 N	11·02 E
101	Rauch (rá'ōōch) Arg. (Buenos Aires In.)	36·47 S	59·05 W
118	Raufoss (rou'fôs)...........Nor.	60·44 N	10·30 E
101	Raúl Soares (rä-ōō'l-sôä'rĕs) Braz. (Rio de Janeiro In.)	20·05 S	42·28 W

ng-sing; ŋ-baŋk; N-nasalized n; nŏd; cŏmmit; ōld; ôbey; ôrder; fōōd; fŏŏt; ou-out; s-soft; sh-dish; th-thin; pūre; ûnite; ûrn; stŭd; circŭs; ü-as "y" in study; '-indeterminate vowel.

Page	Name Pronunciation Region	Lat. °′	Long. °′
119	Rauma (rä'ōō-mȧ) . . . . . Fin.	61·07 N	21·31 E
119	Rauna (räū'-nȧ) . . . . . Sov. Un.	57·21 N	25·31 E
154	Raung, Gunung (Mtn.) . . . . Indon.	8·15 S	113·56 E
119	Rautalampi (ra'ōō-tē-lăm'pō) . Fin.	62·39 N	26·25 E
121	Rava-Russkaya (rä'vȧ rōōs'kä-yȧ) Sov. Un.	50·14 N	23·40 E
126	Ravenna (rä-vĕn'nä) . . . . . It.	44·27 N	12·13 E
70	Ravenna (rȧ-vĕn'ȧ) . . . . . Nebr.	41·20 N	98·50 W
80	Ravenna . . . . . Ohio	41·10 N	81·20 W
120	Ravensburg (rä'vĕns-bōōrgh) . Ger.	47·48 N	9·35 E
65	Ravensdale (rā'vĕnz-dāl) Wash. (Seattle In.)	47·22 N	121·58 W
158	Ravensthorpe (rā'vĕns-thôrp) Austl.	33·30 S	120·20 E
80	Ravenswood (rā'vĕnz-wŏŏd) W. Va.	38·55 N	81·50 W
142	Rawalpindi (rä-wŭl-pēn'dē) W. Pak.	33·42 N	73·04 E
144	Rawanduz . . . . . Iraq	36·37 N	44·30 E
120	Rawicz (rä'vēch) . . . . . Pol.	51·36 N	16·51 E
158	Rawlina (rôr-lēnȧ) . . . . . Austl.	31·13 S	125·45 E
67	Rawlins (rô'lĭnz) . . . . . Wyo.	41·46 N	107·15 W
100	Rawson (rô'sŭn) . . . . . Arg.	43·16 S	65·09 W
101	Rawson . . . Arg. (Buenos Aires In.)	34·36 S	60·03 W
110	Rawtenstall (rô'tĕn-stôl) . . . . Eng.	53·42 N	2·17 W
83	Ray, C. (rā) . . . . . Can.	47·38 N	59·25 W
135	Raychikinsk (rī'chĭ-kēnsk) Sov. Un.	49·52 N	129·17 E
110	Rayleigh (rā'lē) Eng. (London In.)	51·35 N	0·36 E
86	Raymond (rā'mŭnd) . . . . . Can.	49·32 N	112·38 W
66	Raymond . . . . . Wash.	46·41 N	123·42 W
77	Raymondville (rā'mŭnd-vĭl) . . Tex.	26·30 N	97·46 W
64	Ray Mts. . . . . . Alaska	65·40 N	151·45 W
77	Rayne (rān) . . . . . La.	30·12 N	92·15 W
90	Rayón (rä-yōn') . . . . . Mex.	21·49 N	99·39 W
167	Rayton (rā'tŭn) . . . . . S. Afr. (Johannesburg & Pretoria In.)	25·45 S	28·33 E
74	Raytown (rā'toun) Mo. (Kansas City In.)	39·01 N	94·48 W
77	Rayville (rā-vĭl) . . . . . La.	32·28 N	91·46 W
122	Raz, Pte. du (Pt.) (pwănt dü rä) . Fr.	48·02 N	4·43 W
129	Razdel'naya (räz-dĕl'nä-yȧ) Sov. Un.	46·47 N	30·08 E
152	Razdol'noye (räz-dôl'nô-yĕ) Sov. Un.	43·38 N	131·58 E
127	Razgrad . . . . . Bulg.	43·32 N	26·32 E
127	Razlog (räz'lôk) . . . . . Bul.	41·54 N	23·32 E
122	Ré, Île de (I.) (ēl dē rā') . . . . Fr.	46·10 N	1·53 W
110	Rea (R.) (rē) . . . . . Eng.	52·25 N	2·31 W
85	Reaburn (rā'bûrn) Can. (Winnipeg In.)	50·06 N	97·53 W
110	Reading (rĕd'ĭng) Eng. (London In.)	51·25 N	0·58 W
83	Reading . . . . Mass. (Boston In.)	42·32 N	71·07 W
80	Reading . . . . . Mich.	41·45 N	84·45 W
75	Reading . . . . Ohio (Cincinnati In.)	39·14 N	84·26 W
81	Reading . . . . . Pa.	40·20 N	75·55 W
100	Realango (rĕ-ä-lăn-gô) . Braz. (In.)	22·25 S	43·25 W
165	Rebiana (Oasis) . . . . . Libya	24·10 N	22·03 E
152	Rebun (I.) (rē'bōōn) . . . . . Jap.	45·25 N	140·54 E
126	Recanati (rā-kä-nä'tē) . . . . . It.	43·25 N	13·35 E
158	Recherche, Arch. of the (rē-shârsh') . Austl.	34·17 S	122·30 E
128	Rechitsa (ryĕ'chēt-sȧ) . . . Sov. Un.	52·22 N	30·24 E
99	Recife (Pernambuco) (rā-sē'fĕ) (pĕr-năm-bōō'kō) . Braz.	8.09 S	34·59 W
167	Recife, C. (rȧ-sē'fĕ) S. Afr. (Natal In.)	34·03 S	25·43 E
100	Reconquista (rā-kōn-kēs'tä) . . Arg.	29·01 S	59·41 W
73	Rector (rĕk'tēr) . . . . . Ark.	36·16 N	90·21 W
78	Red (R.) . . . . . Tenn.	36·30 N	87·10 W
72	Red (R.), North Fk. . . . . Tex.	35·20 N	100·08 W
63	Red. (R.) . . . . . U. S.	31·40 N	92·55 W
62	Red (R.) (rĕd) . . . . . U. S.-Can.	48·10 N	97·00 W
84	Redan (rē-dăn') (rĕd'ăn) Ga. (Atlanta In.)	33·44 N	84·09 W
84	Red Bank (băngk) N. J. (New York In.)	40·21 N	74·06 W
68	Red Bluff (blŭf) . . . . . Calif.	40·10 N	122·14 W
76	Red Bluff Res. . . . . . Tex.	32·03 N	103·52 W
71	Redby (rĕd'bē) . . . . . Minn.	47·52 N	94·55 W
71	Red Cedar (R.) (sē'dēr) . . . . Wis.	45·03 N	91·48 W
86	Redcliff (rĕd'clĭf) . . . . . Can.	50·10 N	111·09 W
71	Red Cliff Ind. Res. . . . . . Wis.	46·48 N	91·22 W
160	Redcliffe (rĕd'clĭf) . . . . . Austl.	27·20 S	153·12 E
72	Red Cloud (kloud) . . . . . Nebr.	40·06 N	98·32 W
86	Red Deer (dēr) . . . . . Can.	52·12 N	113·52 W
86	Red Deer (R.) . . . . . Can.	50·55 N	111·32 W
75	Reddick (rĕd'dĭk) Ill. (Chicago In.)	41·06 N	88·16 W
84	Redding (rĕd'ĭng) Ala. (Birmingham In.)	33·27 N	86·54 W
66	Redding . . . . . Calif.	40·36 N	122·25 W
101	Redenção da Serra (rĕ-dĕn-souN-dä-sĕ'r-rä) Braz. (Rio de Janeiro In.)	23·17 S	45·31 W
70	Redfield (rĕd'fēld) . . . . . S. D.	44·53 N	98·30 W
77	Red Fish Bar . . . . . Tex. (In.)	29·29 N	94·53 W
83	Red Indian L. (ĭn'dĭ-ăn) . . . . Can.	48·42 N	56·40 W
123	Redklinghausen (rĕk'lĭng-hou-zĕn) Ger. (Ruhr In.)	51·36 N	7·13 E
87	Red Lake (lāk) . . . . . Can.	51·01 N	93·55 W
70	Red Lake (R.) . . . . . Minn.	48·02 N	96·04 W
71	Red Lake Falls (lāk fôls) . . . Minn.	47·52 N	96·17 W
70	Red Lake Ind. Res. . . . . . Minn.	48·09 N	95·55 W
74	Redlands (rĕd'lăndz) Calif. (Los Angeles In.)	34·04 N	117·11 W
81	Red Lion (lī'ŭn) . . . . . Pa.	39·55 N	76·30 W
67	Red Lodge . . . . . Mont.	45·13 N	107·16 W
65	Redmond (rĕd'mŭnd) Wash. (Seattle In.)	47·40 N	122·07 W
120	Rednitz R. (rĕd'nētz) . . . . . Ger.	49·49 N	10·57 E
70	Red Oak (ōk) . . . . . Iowa	41·00 N	95·12 W
122	Redon (rē-dôN') . . . . . Fr.	47·42 N	2·03 W
100	Redonda, Isla (ē's-lä-rĕ-dô'n-dä) Braz. (In.)	23·05 S	43·11 W
93	Redonda I. N. A. (Le. & Wind. Is. In.)	16·55 N	62·28 W
124	Redondela (rā-dhôn-dā'lä) . . . . Sp.	42·16 N	8·34 W
124	Redondo (rȧ-dôn'dōō) . . . . . Port.	38·40 N	7·32 W
65	Redondo (rē-dŏn'dō) Wash. (Seattle In.)	47·21 N	122·19 W
74	Redondo Beach Calif. (Los Angeles In.)	33·50 N	118·23 W
72	Red R., Prairie Dog Town Fk. (prā'rĭ) . Tex.	34·54 N	101·31 W
72	Red R., Salt Fk. . . . . . Tex.	35·04 N	100·31 W
146	Red R. . . . . . Viet.	22·25 N	103·50 E
67	Red Rock Cr. . . . . . Mont.	44·54 N	112·44 W
165	Red Sea . . . . . Afr.-Asia	23·15 N	37·00 E
67	Redwater Cr. (rĕd-wô'tēr) . . Mont.	47·37 N	105·25 W
72	Red Willow Cr. . . . . . Nebr.	40·34 N	100·48 W
71	Red Wing . . . . . Minn.	44·34 N	92·35 W
65	Redwood City (rĕd' wŏŏd) Calif. (San Francisco In.)	37·29 N	122·13 W
71	Redwood Falls . . . . . Minn.	44·32 N	95·06 W
116	Ree, Lough (B.) (lŏk'rē') . . . . Ire.	53·30 N	7·45 W
80	Reed City (rēd) . . . . . Mich.	43·50 N	85·35 W
68	Reedley (rēd'lē) . . . . . Calif.	36·37 N	119·27 W
71	Reedsburg (rēdz'bûrg) . . . . Wis.	43·32 N	90·01 W
66	Reedsport (rēdz'pôrt) . . . . Ore.	43·42 N	124·08 W
78	Reelfoot (R.) (rēl'fŏŏt) . . . . Tenn.	36·18 N	89·20 W
123	Rees (rĕz) . . . . Ger. (Ruhr In.)	51·46 N	6·25 E
74	Reese (rēs) Utah (Salt Lake City In.)	41·15 N	112·09 W
160	Reeves, Mt. (rēv's) . . . . . Austl.	33·50 S	149·56 E
77	Reform (rē-fôrm') . . . . . Ala.	33·23 N	88·00 W
77	Refugio (rå-fōō'hyō) (rĕ-fū'jō) . Tex.	28·18 N	97·15 W
120	Rega (R.) (rĕ-gä) . . . . . Pol.	53·48 N	15·30 E
120	Regen R. (rā'ghĕn) . . . . . Ger.	49·09 N	12·21 E
120	Regensburg (rā'ghĕns-bōōrgh) . Ger.	49·02 N	12·06 E
126	Reggio (rĕ'jō) . . . . . It.	44·43 N	10·34 E
84	Reggio (rĕg'jĭ-ō) La. (New Orleans In.)	29·50 N	89·46 W
126	Reggio di Calabria (rĕ'jō dē kä-lä'brē-ä) . It.	38·07 N	15·42 E
121	Reghin (rā-gēn') . . . . . Rom.	46·47 N	24·44 E
86	Regina (rē-jī'nȧ) . . . . . Can.	50·31 N	104·30 W
144	Registan (Reg.) . . . . . Afg.	30·53 N	64·42 E
95	Regla (rāg'lä) Cuba (Havana In.)	23·08 N	82·20 W
124	Reguengos de Monsaraz (rā-gĕn'gōzh dā mōn-sä-räzh') Port.	38·26 N	7·30 W
84	Rehoboth (rē-hō'bŏth) Mass. (Providence In.)	41·50 N	71·13 W
166	Rehoboth . . . . . S. W. Afr.	23·10 S	17·15 E
139	Rehovoth . . . . Isr. (Palestine In.)	31·53 N	34·49 E
120	Reichenbach (rī'kĕn-bäk) . . . . Ger.	50·36 N	12·18 E
79	Reidsville (rēdz'vĭl) . . . . . N. C.	36·20 N	79·37 W
110	Reigate (rī'gāt) . Eng. (London In.)	51·12 N	0·12 W
122	Reims (răns) . . . . . Fr.	49·16 N	4·00 E
100	Reina Adelaida, Arch. (är-chē'-pyĕ'lä-gō-rā'nä-ä-dĕ-lī'dä) Chile	52·00 S	74·15 W
71	Reinbeck (rīn'bĕk) . . . . . Iowa	42·22 N	92·34 W
86	Reindeer (L.) (rān'dēr) . . . . Can.	57·36 N	101·23 W
124	Reinosa (rā-ē-nō'sä) . . . . . Sp.	43·01 N	4·08 W
84	Reistertown (rēs'tēr-toun) Md. (Baltimore In.)	39·28 N	76·50 W
168	Reitz . . . . . S. Afr. (Johannesburg & Pretoria In.)	27·48 S	28·25 E
84	Relay (rē'lā) . . Md. (Baltimore In.)	39·14 N	76·44 W
125	Relizane (rē-lē-zän') . . . . . Alg.	35·43 N	0·34 E
139	Rembau . . . . Mala. (Singapore In.)	2·36 N	102·06 E
98	Remedios (rē-mā'dyōs) . . Col. (In.)	7·03 N	74·42 W
94	Remedios (rā-mā'dhē-ōs) . . . . Cuba	22·30 N	79·35 W
93	Remedios (rĕ-mĕ'dyōs) . . . . . Pan.	8·14 N	81·46 W
123	Remiremont (rē-mēr-môN') . . . . Fr.	48·01 N	6·35 E
139	Rempang I. Indon. (Singapore In.)	0·51 N	104·04 E
123	Remscheid (rĕm'shīt) Ger. (Ruhr In.)	51·10 N	7·11 E
159	Rendova (I.) (rĕn'dô-vȧ) . . Sol. Is.	8·38 S	156·26 E
120	Rendsburg (rĕnts'bōōrgh) . . . . Ger.	54·19 N	9·39 E
81	Renfrew (rĕn'frōō) . . . . . Can.	45·30 N	76·30 W
139	Rengam (rĕn'gäm') Mala. (Singapore In.)	1·53 N	103·24 E
101	Rengo (rĕn'gō) Chile (Santiago In.)	34·22 S	70·50 W
129	Reni (ran') . . . . . Sov. Un.	45·26 N	28·18 E
160	Renmark (rĕn'märk) . . . . . Austl.	34·10 S	140·50 E
159	Rennel (I.) (rĕn-nĕl') . . . . . Sol. Is.	11·50 S	160·38 E
122	Rennes (rĕn) . . . . . Fr.	48·07 N	1·02 W
81	Rensselaer (rĕn'sē-lâr) . . . . . N. Y.	42·40 N	73·45 W
68	Reno (rē'nō) . . . . . Nev.	39·32 N	119·49 W
126	Reno (R.) (rā'nô) . . . . . It.	44·10 N	10·55 E
81	Renovo (rē-nō'vō) . . . . . Pa.	41·20 N	77·50 W
80	Rensselaer (rĕn'sē-lâr) . . . . . Ind.	41·00 N	87·10 W
74	Rentchler (rĕnt'chlēr) Ill. (St. Louis In.)	38·30 N	89·52 W
65	Renton (rĕn'tŭn) Wash. (Seattle In.)	47·29 N	122·13 W
71	Renville (rĕn'vĭl) . . . . . Minn.	44·44 N	95·13 W
84	Republic (rē-pŭb'lĭk) Ala. (Birmingham In.)	33·37 N	86·54 W
66	Republic . . . . . Wash.	48·38 N	118·44 W
72	Republican (R.), South Fk. (rē-pŭb'lĭ-kăn) . Colo.	39·35 N	102·28 W
73	Republican (R.) . . . . . Kans.	39·22 N	97·14 W
159	Repulse B. (rē-pŭls') . . . . . Austl.	20·56 S	149·22 E
124	Requena (rā-kā'nä) . . . . . Sp.	39·29 N	1·03 W
101	Resende (rĕ-sĕ'n-dĕ) Braz. (Rio de Janeiro In.)	22·30 S	44·26 W
101	Resende Costa (kôs-tä) Braz. (Rio de Janeiro In.)	20·55 S	44·12 W
129	Reshetilovka (ryĕ' shĕ-tē-lôf-kȧ) Sov. Un.	49·34 N	34·04 E
100	Resistencia (rä-sēs-tĕn'syä) . . . Arg.	27·24 S	58·54 W
127	Reşita (rå'shē-tȧ) . . . . . Rom.	45·18 N	21·56 E
87	Resolution (I.) (rĕz-ô-lū'shŭn) Can.	61·30 N	63·58 W
159	Resolution (I.) (rĕz-ŏl-ûshŭn) N. Z. (In.)	45·43 S	166·00 E
82	Restigouche (R.) (rĕs-tē-gōōsh') Can.	47·35 N	67·35 W
98	Restrepo (rĕs-trĕ'pô) . . . . Col. (In.)	3·49 N	76·31 W
98	Restrepo . . . . . Col. (In.)	4·16 N	73·32 W
92	Retalhuleu (rā-täl-ōō-lān') . . Guat.	14·31 N	91·41 W
122	Rethel (r-tĕl') . . . . . Fr.	49·34 N	4·20 E
126	Réthimnon . . . . . Grc. (In.)	35·21 N	24·30 E
111	Retie . . . . . Bel. (Brussels In.)	51·16 N	5·08 E
65	Retsil (rĕt'sĭl) . Wash. (Seattle In.)	47·33 N	122·37 W
47	Reunion I. (rā-ü-nyôn') . . . . . Afr.	21·06 S	55·36 E
125	Reus (rā'ōōs) . . . . . Sp.	41·08 N	1·05 E
120	Reutlingen (roit'lĭng-ĕn) . . . . . Ger.	48·29 N	9·14 E
136	Reutov (rĕ-ōōt'ôf) Sov. Un. (Moscow In.)	55·45 N	37·52 E
	Reval, see Tallinn		
136	Revda (ryåv'dȧ) Sov. Un. (Urals In.)	56·48 N	59·57 E
86	Revelstoke (rĕv'ĕl-stōk) . . . . . Can.	51·02 N	118·19 W
93	Reventazon, R. (rā-vĕn-tä-zōn') C. R.	10·10 N	83·30 W
83	Revere (rē-vēr') Mass. (Boston In.)	42·24 N	71·01 W
88	Revillagigedo, Islas De (I.) (ē's-läs-dĕ-rĕ-vēl-yä-hĕ'gĕ-dô) Mex.	18·45 N	111·00 W
122	Revin (rē-văN') . . . . . Fr.	49·56 N	4·34 E
142	Rewa (rā'wä) . . . . . India	24·41 N	81·11 E
142	Rewāri . . . . . India	28·19 N	76·39 E
67	Rexburg (rĕks'bûrg) . . . . . Idaho	43·50 N	111·48 W
76	Rey, L. (rā) . . . . . Mex.	27·00 N	103·33 W
93	Rey, Isla del (I.) (ē's-lä-dĕl-rā'ē) . Pan.	8·20 N	78·40 W
98	Reyes (rā'yĕs) . . . . . Bol.	14·19 S	67·16 W
68	Reyes, Pt. . . . . . Calif.	38·00 N	123·00 W
102	Reykjanes (C.) (rā'kyȧ-nĕs) . . . Ice.	63·37 N	24·33 W
112	Reykjavik (rā'kyȧ-vēk) . . . . . Ice.	64·09 N	21·39 W
76	Reynosa (rā-ē-nō'sä) . . . . . Mex.	26·05 N	98·21 W
144	Rezā'īyeh (Urmia) (rĕ-zī'ȧ) (ōōr'mē-ȧ) . Iran	37·30 N	45·15 E
128	Rēzekne (rå'zĕk-nĕ) . . . . Sov. Un.	56·31 N	27·19 E
136	Rezh (rĕzh') . . Sov. Un. (Urals In.)	57·22 N	61·23 E
129	Rezina (ryĕzh'ĕ-nĭ) . . . . . Sov. Un.	47·44 N	28·56 E
126	Rhaetien Alps (Mts.) . . . . . It.	46·22 N	10·33 E
117	Rheden (rā'dĕn) . . . . . Neth.	52·02 N	6·02 E
123	Rheinberg (rīn'bĕrgh) Ger. (Ruhr In.)	51·33 N	6·37 E
120	Rheine (rī'nĕ) . . . . . Ger.	52·16 N	7·26 E
120	Rheinland-Pfalz (Rhineland-Palatinate) (State) . Ger.	50·05 N	6·40 E
120	Rhein R. (rīn) . . . . . Ger.	50·34 N	7·21 E
123	Rheydt (rĕ'yt) . . . . Ger. (Ruhr In.)	51·10 N	6·28 E
71	Rhinelander (rīn'lăn-dēr) . . . . Wis.	45·39 N	89·25 W
111	Rhin Kanal (Can.) (rēn kä-näl') Ger. (Berlin In.)	52·47 N	12·40 E
111	Rhin R. (rēn) . . . . Ger. (Berlin In.)	52·52 N	12·49 E
63	Rhode Island (State) (rōd ī'lănd) U. S.	41·35 N	71·40 W
167	Rhodes (rōdz) . . S. Afr. (Natal In.)	30·48 S	27·56 E
127	Rhodope Mts. (rô'dô-pĕ) . . . . . Bul.	42·00 N	24·08 E
116	Rhondda (rŏn'dhȧ) . . . . . Wales	51·40 N	3·40 W
122	Rhône (R.) (rōn) . . . . . Fr.	45·14 N	4·53 E
111	Rhoon . . . . Neth. (Amsterdam In.)	51·52 N	4·24 E
116	Rhum (I.) (rŭm) . . . . . Scot.	56·63 N	6·20 W
99	Riachão (rē-ä-chouN') . . . . . Braz.	6·55 S	46·33 W
74	Rialto (rē-äl'tō) Calif. (Los Angeles In.)	34·06 N	117·23 W
124	Riaza (R.) (rē-ä'thä) . . . . . Sp.	41·25 N	3·25 W
124	Ribadavia (rē-bä-dhä'vē-ä) . . . . Sp.	42·18 N	8·06 W
124	Ribadeo (rē-bä-dhä'ō) . . . . . Sp.	37·32 N	7·05 W
124	Ribadesella (rē'bä-dä-säl'yä) . . Sp.	43·30 N	5·02 W
116	Ribble, R. (rĭb''l) . . . . . Eng.	53·10 N	3·15 W
118	Ribe (rē'bĕ) . . . . . Den.	55·20 N	8·45 E
101	Ribeirão Prêto (rē-bā-rouN-prĕ'tô) Braz. (Rio de Janeiro In.)	21·11 S	47·47 W
72	Ribera (rē-bĕ'rä) . . . . . N. Mex.	35·23 N	105·27 W
98	Riberalta (rē-bȧ-räl'tä) . . . . . Bol.	11·06 S	66·02 W
71	Rib Lake (rĭb lāk) . . . . . Wis.	45·20 N	90·11 W
68	Rice (rīs) . . . . . Calif.	34·05 N	114·50 W
81	Rice (L.) . . . . . Can.	44·05 N	78·10 W
74	Rice L. . . . . . Minn. (Minneapolis, St. Paul In.)	45·10 N	93·09 W
71	Rice Lake . . . . . Wis.	45·30 N	91·44 W
64	Richards I. (rĭch'ērds) . . . . . Can.	69·45 N	135·30 W
74	Richards Landing (lănd'ĭng) Can. (Sault Ste. Marie In.)	46·18 N	84·02 W
74	Richardson (rĭch'ērd-sŭn) Tex. (Dallas, Fort Worth In.)	32·56 N	96·44 W
65	Richardson . . . . Wash. (Seattle In.)	48·27 N	122·54 W
86	Richardson Mts. . . . . . Can.	66·58 N	136·19 W
81	Richardson Park (pärk) . . . . . Del.	39·45 N	75·35 W
81	Richelieu (R.) (rēsh'lyû') . . . . Can.	45·05 N	73·25 W
74	Richfield (rĭch'fēld) Minn. (Minneapolis, St. Paul In.)	44·53 N	93·17 W
75	Richfield . . . . Ohio (Cleveland In.)	41·14 N	81·38 W
69	Richfield . . . . . Utah	38·45 N	112·05 W
81	Richford (rĭch'fērd) . . . . . Vt.	45·00 N	72·35 W
73	Rich Hill (rĭch hĭl) . . . . . Mo.	38·05 N	94·21 W
82	Richibucto (rĭ-chĭ-bŭk'tō) . . . . Can.	46·42 N	64·55 W
78	Richland (rĭch'lănd) . . . . . Ga.	32·05 N	84·40 W
66	Richland . . . . . Wash.	46·17 N	119·19 W
71	Richland Center (sĕn'tēr) . . . Wis.	43·20 N	90·25 W
159	Richmond (rĭch'mŭnd) . . . . . Austl.	20·47 S	143·14 E
161	Richmond . . . . Austl. (Sydney In.)	33·36 S	150·45 E
65	Richmond Calif. (San Francisco In.)	37·56 N	122·21 W
82	Richmond . . . . . Can.	45·40 N	72·07 W
85	Richmond . . . . . Can. (Ottawa In.)	45·12 N	75·49 W
75	Richmond . . . . . Ill. (Chicago In.)	42·29 N	88·18 W
80	Richmond . . . . . Ind.	39·50 N	85·00 W
80	Richmond . . . . . Ky.	37·45 N	84·20 W
73	Richmond . . . . . Mo.	39·16 N	93·58 W

ăt; finăl; rāte; senāte; ärm; ȧsk; sofȧ; fâre; ch-choose; dh-as th in other; bē; ēvent; bĕt; recĕnt; cratēr; g-go; gh-guttural g; bĭt; ĭ-short neutral; rīde; K-guttural k as ch in German ich;

PRONOUNCING INDEX Richmond–Rogoaguado 257

Page	Name Pronunciation Region	Lat. °′	Long. °′
77	Richmond....Tex.	29·35 N	95·45 W
167	Richmond.....S. Afr. (Natal In.)	29·52 S	30·17 E
167	Richmond.....S. Afr. (Natal In.)	33·44 S	26·36 E
67	Richmond....Utah	41·55 N	111·50 W
81	Richmond....Va.	37·35 N	77·30 W
65	Richmond Beach Wash. (Seattle In.)	47·47 N	122·23 W
74	Richmond Heights Mo. (St. Louis In.)	38·38 N	90·20 W
85	Richmond Hill (hĭl) Can. (Toronto In.)	43·53 N	79·26 W
93	Richmond Pk. St. Vincent (Le. & Wind. Is. In.)	13·19 N	61·12 W
78	Richton (rĭch′tŭn)....Miss.	31·20 N	89·54 W
80	Richwood (rĭch′wo͝od).....W. Va.	38·10 N	80·30 W
111	Ridderkerk Neth. (Amsterdam In.)	51·52 N	4·35 E
81	Rideau L. (rē-dō′)....Can.	44·40 N	76·20 W
85	Rideau R......Can. (Ottawa In.)	45·17 N	75·41 W
84	Ridgefield (rĭj′fēld) Conn. (New York In.)	41·16 N	73·30 W
65	Ridgefield...Wash. (Portland In.)	45·49 N	122·40 W
81	Ridgeley (rĭj′lē)....W. Va.	39·40 N	78·45 W
75	Ridgeway (rĭj′wā) Can. (Buffalo In.)	42·53 N	79·02 W
81	Ridgeway....Pa.	41·25 N	78·40 W
84	Ridgewood (rĭdj′wo͝od) N. J. (New York In.)	40·59 N	74·08 W
86	Riding Mountain Natl. Park (rīd′ĭng). Can.	50·59 N	99·19 W
94	Riding Rocks (Is.)....Ba. Is.	25·20 N	79·10 W
167	Riebeek-Oos...S. Afr. (Natal In.)	33·14 S	26·09 E
120	Ried (rēd)....Aus.	48·13 N	13·30 E
120	Riesa (rē′zȧ)....Ger.	51·17 N	13·17 E
167	Riet (R.) (rēt)....S. Afr. (Johannesburg & Pretoria In.)	25·54 S	27·54 E
126	Rieti (rē-ā′tē)....It.	42·25 N	12·51 E
167	Rievleidam (L.)....S. Afr. (Johannesburg & Pretoria In.)	25·52 S	28·18 E
69	Rifle (rī′f′l)....Colo.	39·35 N	107·50 W
119	Rīga (rē′gȧ)....Sov. Un.	56·55 N	24·05 E
119	Riga, G. of....Sov. Un.	57·56 N	23·05 E
144	Rīgān....Iran	28·45 N	58·55 E
85	Rigaud (rē-gō′) Can. (Montreal In.)	45·29 N	74·18 W
67	Rigby (rĭg′bē)....Idaho	43·40 N	111·55 W
87	Rigolet (rĭg-ō-lā′)....Can.	54·10 N	58·40 W
126	Rijeka (Fiume) (rĭ-yĕ′kä)...Yugo.	45·22 N	14·24 E
111	Rijkevorsel....Bel. (Brussels In.)	51·21 N	4·46 E
111	Rijswijk..Neth. (Amsterdam In.)	52·03 N	4·19 E
121	Rika R. (rē′kȧ)....Sov. Un.	48·21 N	23·37 E
122	Rille (R.) (rēl)....Fr.	49·12 N	0·43 E
144	Rimach, Wādī ar (R.)....Sau. Ar.	26·17 N	41·13 E
121	Rimavska Sobota (rĕ′mäf-skä sô′bô-tȧ). Czech.	48·25 N	20·01 E
118	Rimbo (rēm′bo͞o)....Swe.	59·45 N	18·22 E
126	Rimini (rē′mē-nē)....It.	44·03 N	12·33 E
127	Rîmnicul Sărat....Rom.	45·24 N	27·06 E
127	Rîmnicu Valcea....Rom.	45·07 N	24·22 E
82	Rimouski (rē-mo͞os′kē)....Can.	48·27 N	68·32 W
90	Rincón de Romos (rēn-kōn dā rō-mōs′). Mex.	22·13 N	102·21 W
154	Rindjani, Gunung (Mtn.)..Indon.	8·39 S	116·22 E
118	Ringkøbing (rĭng′kûb-ĭng)...Den.	56·06 N	8·14 E
118	Ringkøbing Fd....Den.	55·55 N	8·04 E
118	Ringsaker (rĭngs′äk-ĕr)....Nor.	60·55 N	10·40 E
118	Ringsted (rĭng′stĕdh)....Den.	55·27 N	11·49 E
112	Ringvassöy (I.) (rĭng′väs-ûê). Nor.	69·58 N	16·43 E
161	Ringwood. Austl. (Melbourne In.)	37·49 S	145·14 E
88	Rio Abajo (rē′ō-ȧ-bä′kō) Pan. (Panama Canal In.)	9·01 N	78·30 W
90	Rio Balsas (rē′ō-bäl-säs)....Mex.	17·59 N	99·45 W
98	Riobamba (rē′ō-bäm′bä)....Ec.	1·45 S	78·37 W
101	Rio Bonito (rē′o͞o bō-nē′to͞o) Braz. (Rio de Janeiro In.)	22·44 S	42·38 W
98	Rio Branco (rē′o͞o brăŋ′ko͞o). Braz.	9·57 S	67·50 W
99	Rio Branco (Ter.)....Braz.	2·35 N	61·25 W
101	Rio Casca (rē′ō-kȧ′s-kä) Braz. (Rio de Janeiro In.)	20·15 S	42·39 W
99	Rio Chico (rē′ō chē′kō). Ven. (In.)	10·20 N	65·58 W
101	Rio Claro (rē′o͞o klä′ro͞o) Braz. (Rio de Janeiro In.)	21·25 S	47·33 W
100	Río Cuarto (rē′ō kwär′tō)...Arg.	33·05 S	64·15 W
101	Rio das Flores (rē′ō-däs-flō-rĕs) Braz. (Rio de Janeiro In.)	22·10 S	43·35 W
100	Rio de Janeiro (rē′o͞o dā zhä-nâ′ē-ro͞o) Braz. (In.)	22·50 S	43·20 W
99	Rio de Janeiro (State)....Braz.	22·27 S	42·43 W
93	Río de Jesús (rē′ō-dĕ-kĕ-so͞o′s) Pan.	7·54 N	80·59 W
164	Rio del Rey (rē′ō dĕl rā′ē)...Nig.	4·41 N	8·38 E
164	Rio de Oro (Ter.) (rē′ō dā ō′rō) Sp. Sah.	23·11 N	14·15 W
100	Río Dercero (rē′ō dĕr-sĕ′rō)..Arg.	32·12 S	63·59 W
91	Río Frío (rē′ō-frē′ō) Mex. (Mexico City In.)	19·21 N	98·40 W
100	Río Gallegos (rē′ō gä-lā′gōs)..Arg.	51·43 S	69·15 W
100	Rio Grande (rē′o͞o grän′dĕ)..Braz.	31·04 S	52·14 W
90	Rio Grande (rē′ō grän′dä)...Mex.	23·51 N	102·59 W
76	Riogrande (rē′ō grän′dä)....Tex.	26·23 N	98·48 W
69	Rio Grande (R.) (rē′ō grän′dē) Colo.	37·44 N	106·51 W
99	Rio Grande do Norte (State) (rē′o͞o grän′dĕ do͞o nôr′tĕ). Braz.	5·26 S	37·20 W
100	Rio Grande do Sul (State) (rē′o͞o grän′dĕ-dô-so͞o′l). Braz.	29·00 S	54·00 W
98	Ríohacha (rē′ō-ä′chä)....Col.	11·30 N	72·54 W
93	Río Hato (rē′ō-ä′tō)....Pan.	8·19 N	80·11 W
122	Riom (rē-ôN′)....Fr.	45·54 N	3·08 E
163	Rio Muni (Col.) (rē′ō mo͞o′nē). Afr.	1·47 N	8·33 E
98	Ríonegro (rē′ō-nĕ′grō)...Col. (In.)	6·09 N	75·22 W
100	Río Negro (Prov.) (rē′ō nā′grō) Arg.	40·15 S	68·15 W
101	Río Negro (Dept.) (rē′ō-nĕ′grō) Ur. (Buenos Aires In.)	32·48 S	57·45 W
100	Rio Negro, Embalse del (Res.) (ĕm-bä′l-sĕ-dĕl-rĕ′ō-nĕ′grō). Ur.	32·45 S	55·50 W
126	Rionero (rē-ō-nā′rō)....It.	40·55 N	15·42 E
101	Rio Novo (rē′ō-nô′vō) Braz. (Rio de Janeiro In.)	21·30 S	43·08 W
99	Rio Pardo de Minas (rē′ō pär′dō-dĕ-mē′näs). Braz.	15·43 S	42·24 W
101	Rio Pombo (rē′ō pôm′bä) Braz. (Rio de Janeiro In.)	21·17 S	43·09 W
101	Rio Sorocaba, Represado (Res.) (rĕ-prĕ-sä-dô-rē′ō-sô-rō-kä′bä) Braz. (Rio de Janeiro In.)	23·37 S	47·19 W
98	Ríosucio (rē′ō-so͞o′syō)..Col. (In.)	5·25 N	75·41 W
125	Riou, Oued (R.) (o͞o-ĕd rĭ-o͞o) Alg.	35·45 N	1·18 E
139	Riouw Arch. Indon. (Singapore In.)	0·49 N	103·45 E
154	Riouw, Pulau-Pulau (Is.)..Indon.	0·30 N	104·55 E
139	Riouw, Selat (Str.) Indon. (Singapore In.)	0·49 N	104·24 E
99	Rio Verde (vĕr′dĕ)....Braz.	17·47 S	50·49 W
90	Ríoverde (rē′ō-vĕr′dä)....Mex.	21·54 N	99·59 W
110	Ripley (rĭp′lē)....Eng.	53·03 N	1·24 W
78	Ripley....Miss.	34·44 N	88·55 W
78	Ripley....Tenn.	35·44 N	89·34 W
125	Ripoll (rē-pōl′′)....Sp.	42·10 N	2·10 E
71	Ripon (rĭp′ŏn)....Wis.	43·49 N	88·50 W
158	Ripon (I.)....Austl.	20·05 S	118·10 E
165	Ripon Falls....Ug.	0·38 N	33·02 E
159	Risdon (rĭz′dŭn)....Austl.	42·37 S	147·32 E
152	Rishiri (I.) (rē-shē′rē)....Jap.	45·10 N	141·08 E
139	Rishon le Zion. Isr. (Palestine In.)	31·57 N	34·48 E
80	Rising Sun (rĭz′ĭng sŭn)....Ind.	38·55 N	84·55 W
118	Risør (rēs′ûr)....Nor.	58·44 N	9·10 E
98	Ritacuva, Alto (Mtn.) (ä′l-tô-rē-tä-ko͞o′vä). Col.	6·22 N	72·13 W
75	Rittman (rĭt′măn) Ohio (Cleveland In.)	40·58 N	81·47 W
66	Ritzville (rĭts′vĭl)....Wash.	47·08 N	118·23 W
118	Riuvenfjeld (Mts.) (rĭû-vĕn-fyĕl′) Nor.	59·20 N	6·55 E
95	Riva (rē′vä)....Dom. Rep.	19·10 N	69·55 W
126	Riva (rē′vä)....It.	45·54 N	10·49 E
92	Rivas (rē′väs)....Nic.	11·25 N	85·51 W
122	Rive-de-Gier (rēv-dē-zhē-ā′)...Fr.	45·32 N	4·37 E
100	Rivera (rē-vā′rä)....Ur.	30·52 S	55·32 W
164	River Cess (rĭv′ēr sĕs)....Lib.	5·46 N	9·52 W
75	Riverdale (rĭv′ēr dāl) Ill. (Chicago In.)	41·38 N	87·36 W
74	Riverdale Utah (Salt Lake City In.)	41·11 N	112·00 W
78	River Falls....Ala.	31·20 N	86·25 W
71	River Falls....Wis.	44·48 N	92·38 W
81	Riverhead (rĭv′ēr hĕd)....N. Y.	40·55 N	72·40 W
160	Riverina (Reg.) (rĭv-ēr-ē′nȧ). Austl.	34·55 S	144·30 E
65	River Jordan (jôr′dăn) Can. (Seattle In.)	48·26 N	124·02 W
74	River Oaks (ōkz) Tex. (Dallas, Fort Worth In.)	32·47 N	97·24 W
75	River Rouge (ro͞ozh) Mich. (Detroit In.)	42·16 N	83·09 W
74	Riverside (rĭv′ēr-sīd) Calif. (Los Angeles In.)	33·59 N	117·21 W
75	Riverside......Can. (Detroit In.)	42·20 N	82·57 W
84	Riverside. N. J. (Philadelphia In.)	40·02 N	74·58 W
161	Riverstone....Austl. (Sydney In.)	33·41 S	150·52 E
86	Riverton (rĭv′ēr-tŭn)....Can.	51·02 N	97·12 W
81	Riverton....Va.	39·00 N	78·15 W
67	Riverton....Wyo.	43·02 N	108·24 W
122	Rivesaltes (rēv′zält′)....Fr.	42·48 N	2·48 E
79	Riviera Beach (rĭv-ĭ-ĕr′ȧ bēch) Fla. (In.)	26·46 N	80·04 W
82	Riviere (rē-vyâr′)....Can.	46·43 N	72·00 W
82	Riviere (R.)....Can.	49·05 N	72·04 W
85	Rivie′re Beaudette (bō-dĕt′) Can. (Montreal In.)	45·14 N	74·20 W
82	Riviere du Loup (rē-vyâr′ dü lo͞o′) Can.	47·50 N	69·34 W
85	Rivie′re-Qui-Barre (rēv-yĕr′ kē-bär) Can. (Edmonton In.)	53·47 N	113·51 W
133	Rize (rē′zĕ)....Tur.	41·00 N	40·30 E
127	Rizzuto, C. (rēt-so͞o′tō)....It.	38·53 N	17·05 E
118	Rjukan (ryo͞o′kän)....Nor.	59·53 N	8·30 E
122	Roanne (rō-än′)....Fr.	46·02 N	4·04 E
78	Roanoke (rō′ȧ-nōk)....Ala.	33·08 N	85·21 W
79	Roanoke....Va.	37·16 N	79·55 W
79	Roanoke (R.)....N. C.-Va.	36·17 N	77·22 W
79	Roanoke Rapids....N. C.	36·25 N	77·40 W
79	Roanoke Rapids, L....N. C.	36·28 N	77·37 W
69	Roan Plat. (rōn)....Colo.	39·25 N	108·50 W
92	Roatan (rō-ä-tän′)....Hond.	16·18 N	86·33 W
92	Roatan I....Hond.	16·19 N	86·46 W
166	Robben Island S. Afr. (Cape Town In.)	33·48 S	18·22 E
75	Robbins (rŏb′ĭnz). Ill. (Chicago In.)	41·39 N	87·42 W
74	Robbinsdale (rŏb′ĭnz-dāl) Minn. (Minneapolis, St. Paul In.)	45·03 N	93·22 W
65	Robe (rōb)....Wash. (Seattle In.)	48·06 N	121·50 W
159	Roberts, Mt. (rŏb′ērts)....Austl.	32·05 S	152·30 E
65	Roberts, Pt. (rŏb′ērts) Wash. (Vancouver In.)	48·58 N	123·05 W
83	Robertson (rŏb′ērt-sŭn)....Can.	51·05 N	59·07 W
164	Robertsport (rŏb′ērts-pōrt)...Lib.	6·45 N	11·31 W
82	Roberval (rŏb′ēr-văl) (rō-bĕr-väl′) Can.	48·32 N	72·15 W
80	Robinson (rŏb′ĭn-sŭn)....Ill.	39·00 N	87·45 W
83	Robinson's....Can.	48·16 N	58·50 W
160	Robinvale (rŏb-ĭn′văl)....Austl.	34·45 S	142·45 E
86	Robson, Mt. (rŏb′sŭn)....Can.	53·13 N	119·02 W
77	Robstown (rŏbz′toun)....Tex.	27·46 N	97·41 W
125	Roca, Cabo da (C.) (kȧ′bō-dä-rō′kȧ) Port. (Lisbon In.)	38·47 N	9·30 W
99	Rocas, Atol das (Atoll) (ȧ-tôl-däs-rō′kȧs). Braz.	3·50 S	33·46 W
168	Rocca Littotorio Som. (Horn of Afr. In.)	7·00 N	47·30 E
96	Rocedos São Pedro E São Paulo (I.) (rô-zĕ′dôs-souN-pĕ′drô-ĕ-souN-pä͞o-lô). Braz.	1·50 N	30·00 W
100	Rocha (rō′chäs)....Ur.	34·26 S	54·14 W
110	Rochdale (rŏch′dāl)....Eng.	53·37 N	2·09 W
95	Roche à Bateau (rôsh ȧ bȧ-tō′) Hai.	18·10 N	74·00 W
122	Rochefort (rôsh-fŏr′)....Fr.	45·55 N	0·57 W
71	Rochelle (rô-shĕl′)....Ill.	41·53 N	89·06 W
80	Rochester (rŏch′ĕs-tēr)....Ind.	41·05 N	86·20 W
75	Rochester.....Mich. (Detroit In.)	42·41 N	83·09 W
71	Rochester....Minn.	44·01 N	92·30 W
81	Rochester....N. H.	43·20 N	71·00 W
81	Rochester....N. Y.	43·15 N	77·35 W
75	Rochester....Pa. (Pittsburgh In.)	40·42 N	80·16 W
71	Rock (R.)....Ill.	41·40 N	89·52 W
70	Rock (R.)....Iowa	43·17 N	96·13 W
65	Rock (R.).....Ore. (Portland In.)	45·34 N	122·52 W
65	Rock (R.).....Ore. (Portland In.)	45·52 N	123·14 W
84	Rockaway (rŏck′ȧ-wā) N. J. (New York In.)	40·54 N	74·30 W
161	Rockbank. Austl. (Melbourne In.)	37·44 S	144·40 E
85	Rockcliffe Park (rok′klĭf pärk) Can. (Ottawa In.)	45·27 N	75·40 W
75	Rock Cr. (rŏk)...Ill. (Chicago In.)	41·16 N	87·54 W
67	Rock Cr....Mont.	46·25 N	113·40 W
66	Rock Cr....Ore.	45·30 N	120·06 W
66	Rock Cr....Wash.	47·09 N	117·50 W
77	Rockdale (rŏck′dāl)....Tex.	30·39 N	97·00 W
71	Rock Falls (rŏck fôlz)....Ill.	41·45 N	89·42 W
71	Rockford (rŏck′fērd)....Ill.	42·16 N	89·07 W
159	Rockhampton (rŏk-hămp′tŭn) Austl.	23·26 S	150·29 E
79	Rockhill (rŏk′hĭl)....S. C.	34·55 N	81·01 W
79	Rockingham (rŏk′ĭng-hăm)..N. C.	34·54 N	79·45 W
110	Rockingham For. (rok′ĭng-hăm) Eng.	52·29 N	0·43 W
71	Rock Island....Ill.	41·31 N	90·37 W
66	Rock Island Dam (ī lănd)..Wash.	47·17 N	120·33 W
85	Rockland (rŏk′lănd) Can. (Ottawa In.)	45·33 N	75·17 W
82	Rockland....Maine	44·06 N	69·09 W
83	Rockland.....Mass. (Boston In.)	42·07 N	70·55 W
160	Rockland Res....Austl.	36·55 S	142·20 E
78	Rockmart (rŏk′märt)....Ga.	33·58 N	85·00 W
74	Rockmont (rŏk′mŏnt) Wis. (Duluth In.)	46·34 N	91·54 W
80	Rockport (rŏk′pōrt)....Ind.	38·20 N	87·00 W
83	Rockport.....Mass. (Boston In.)	42·39 N	70·37 W
73	Rockport....Mo.	40·25 N	95·30 W
77	Rockport....Tex.	28·03 N	97·03 W
70	Rock Rapids (răp′ĭdz)....Iowa	43·26 N	96·10 W
95	Rock Sd....Ba. Is.	24·50 N	76·05 W
76	Rocksprings (rŏk sprĭngs)....Tex.	30·02 N	100·12 W
67	Rock Springs....Wyo.	41·35 N	109·13 W
99	Rockstone (rŏk′stōn)....Br. Gu.	5·55 N	57·27 W
85	Rockton (rŏk′tŭn) Can. (Toronto In.)	43·18 N	80·08 W
70	Rock Valley (văl′ĭ)....Iowa	43·13 N	96·17 W
80	Rockville (rŏk′vĭl)....Ind.	39·45 N	87·15 W
84	Rockville Centre (sĕn′tēr) N. Y. (New York In.)	40·39 N	73·39 W
73	Rockwall (rŏk′wôl)....Tex.	32·55 N	96·23 W
71	Rockwell City (rŏk′wĕl)....Iowa	42·22 N	94·37 W
85	Rockwood (rŏk-wo͝od) Can. (Toronto In.)	43·37 N	80·08 W
82	Rockwood....Maine	45·39 N	69·45 W
78	Rockwood....Tenn.	35·51 N	84·41 W
67	Rocky Boys Ind. Res....Mont.	48·08 N	109·34 W
72	Rocky Ford....Colo.	38·02 N	103·43 W
84	Rocky Hill (hĭl) N. J. (New York In.)	40·24 N	74·38 W
79	Rocky Mount....N. C.	35·55 N	77·47 W
72	Rocky Mountain Natl. Park. Colo.	40·29 N	106·06 W
49	Rocky Mts. (rŏk′ē)....N. A.	50·00 N	114·00 W
75	Rocky River. Ohio (Cleveland In.)	41·29 N	81·51 W
75	Rocky R., E. Br. Ohio (Cleveland In.)	41·13 N	81·43 W
75	Rocky R., W. Br. Ohio (Cleveland In.)	41·17 N	81·54 W
95	Rodas (rō′dhäs)....Cuba	22·20 N	80·35 W
110	Roden (R.) (rō′dĕn)....Eng.	52·49 N	2·38 W
65	Rodeo (rō′dēō) Calif. (San Francisco In.)	38·02 N	122·16 W
76	Rodeo (rō-dā′ō)....Mex.	25·12 N	104·34 W
122	Rodez (rō-dĕz′)....Fr.	44·22 N	2·34 E
115	Rōdhos....Grc.	36·24 N	28·15 E
115	Ródhos (I.)....Grc.	36·00 N	28·29 E
121	Rodnei, Muntii (Mts.) (rôd′nĕ-ê) Rom.	47·41 N	24·05 E
128	Rodniki (rôd′nĕ-kē)....Sov. Un.	57·08 N	41·48 E
127	Rodonit, Kep I (C.)....Alb.	41·38 N	19·01 E
	Rodosto, see Tekirdağ		
84	Roebling (rōb′lĭng) N. J. (Philadelphia In.)	40·07 N	74·48 W
158	Roebourne (rō′bŭrn)....Austl.	20·50 S	117·15 E
158	Roebuck, B. (rō′bŭck)....Austl.	18·15 S	121·10 E
168	Roedtan....S. Afr. (Johannesburg & Pretoria In.)	24·37 S	29·08 E
117	Roermond (ro͞or′mônt)....Neth.	41·11 N	5·59 E
117	Roeselare....Bel.	50·55 N	3·05 E
65	Roesiger (L.) (rōz′ĭ-gēr) Wash. (Seattle In.)	47·59 N	121·56 W
87	Roes Welcome Sd. (rōz)....Can.	64·10 N	87·23 W
128	Rogachëv (rôg′ȧ-chyôf)..Sov. Un.	53·07 N	30·04 E
127	Rogatica (rô-gȧ′tē-tsȧ)....Yugo.	43·46 N	19·00 E
121	Rogatin (rô-gȧ′tĭn)....Sov. Un.	49·22 N	24·37 E
73	Rogers (rŏj-ērz)....Ark.	36·19 N	94·07 W
80	Rogers City....Mich.	45·30 N	83·50 W
78	Rogersville (rŏj′ērz-vĭl)....Tenn.	36·21 N	83·00 W
122	Rognac (rŏn-yăk′) Fr. (Marseille In.)	43·29 N	5·15 E
98	Rogoaguado (L.) (rō′gō-ȧ-gwȧ′dō) Bol.	12·42 S	66·46 W

ng-sing; ŋ-baŋk; N-nasalized n; nŏd; cŏmmit; ōld; ôbey; ôrder; fo͞od; fo͝ot; ou-out; s-soft; sh-dish; th-thin; pūre; ûnite; ûrn; stŭd; circŭs; ü-as "y" in study; ′-indeterminate vowel.

258 Rogovskaya–Rybatskoye PRONOUNCING INDEX

Page	Name Pronunciation Region	Lat. °′	Long. °′
129	Rogovskaya (rô-gôf'skȧ-yȧ) Sov. Un.	45·43 N	38·42 E
120	Rogózno (rô'gôzh-nô)........Pol.	52·44 N	16·53 E
66	Rogue R. (rōg).............Ore.	42·32 N	124·13 W
118	Röikenviken (rûē'kĕn-vêk-ĕn) Nor.	60·27 N	10·26 E
101	Rojas (rō'häs) Arg. (Buenos Aires In.)	34·11 S	60·42 W
91	Rojo, Cabo (C.) (rō'hō).....Mex.	21·35 N	97·16 W
89	Rojo, Cabo (C.) (rō'hō) P. R. (Puerto Rico In.)	17·55 N	67·14 W
153	Rokkō-Zan (Mtn.) (rôk'kō zăn) Jap. (Osaka In.)	34·46 N	135·16 E
120	Rokycany (rô'kĭ'tsȧ-nĭ)....Czech.	49·44 N	13·37 E
98	Roldanillo (rôl-dă-nē'l-yō) Col. (In.)	4·24 N	76·09 W
73	Rolla (rŏl'ȧ)................Mo.	37·56 N	91·45 W
70	Rolla......................N. D.	48·52 N	99·32 W
118	Rollag (rōō'lȧgh)...........Nor.	59·55 N	8·48 E
95	Rolleville................Ba. Is.	23·40 N	76·00 W
160	Roma (rō'mȧ)............Austl.	26·30 S	148·48 E
167	Roma..........Bas. (Natal In.)	29·28 S	27·43 E
125	Roma (Rome) (rō'mä) (rōm) It. (Rome In.)	41·52 N	12·37 E
126	Romagna (Reg.) (rô-mȧ'n-yă). It.	44·18 N	10·48 E
83	Romaine (rô-mĕn')..........Can.	50·12 N	60·38 W
87	Romaine (R.).............Can.	51·22 N	63·23 W
121	Roman (rō'män)...........Rom.	46·56 N	26·57 E
102	Romania (rō-mā'nê-ȧ).......Eur.	46·18 N	22·53 E
79	Romano, C. (rō-mā'nō). Fla. (In.)	25·48 N	82·00 W
94	Romano, Cayo (I.) (kä'yō-rô-mȧ'nô). Cuba	22·15 N	78·00 W
136	Romanovo (rô-mă'nô-vô) Sov. Un. (Urals In.)	59·09 N	61·24 E
122	Romans-sur-Isère (rô-mäɴ'-sür-ē-sĕr'). Fr.	45·04 N	4·49 E
64	Romanzof, C. (rō'măn zôf). Alaska	62·00 N	167·18 W
155	Romblon (rōm-blōn') Phil. (Manila In.)	12·34 N	122·16 E
155	Romblon (I.). Phil. (Manila In.)	12·33 N	122·17 E
78	Rome (rōm)................Ga.	34·14 N	85·10 W
81	Rome.....................N. Y.	43·15 N	75·25 W
	Rome, see Roma		
80	Romeo (rō'mê-ō)..........Mich.	42·50 N	83·00 W
110	Romford (rŭm'fērd) Eng. (London In.)	51·35 N	0·11 E
122	Romilly-sur-Seine (rô-mê-yē'sür-sān'). Fr.	48·32 N	3·41 E
90	Romita (rō-mē'tă)..........Mex.	20·53 N	101·32 W
129	Romny (rôm'nĭ)........Sov. Un.	50·46 N	33·31 E
118	Rømø (I.) (rûm'û)..........Den.	55·08 N	8·17 E
74	Romoland (rŏ'mō'lănd) Calif. (Los Angeles In.)	33·44 N	117·11 W
122	Romorantin (rô-mô-räɴ-tăɴ')..Fr.	47·24 N	1·46 E
139	Rompin....Mala. (Singapore In.)	2·42 N	102·30 E
139	Rompin (R.) Mala. (Singapore In.)	2·54 N	103·10 E
75	Romulus (rom'ū lŭs) Mich. (Detroit In.)	42·14 N	83·24 W
116	Ronaldsay, North (I.)......Scot.	59·21 N	2·23 W
116	Ronaldsay, South (I.) (rŏn'ăld-s'ā). Scot.	59·48 N	2·55 W
67	Ronan (rō'năn)...........Mont.	47·28 N	114·03 W
99	Roncador, Serra do (Mts.) (sĕr'rȧ dōō rôn-kă-dôr'). Braz.	12·44 S	52·19 W
124	Roncesvalles (rôn-sĕs-vă'l-yĕs). Sp.	43·00 N	1·17 W
80	Ronceverte (rŏn'sê-vûrt)..W. Va.	37·45 N	80·30 W
124	Ronda (rōn'dä).............Sp.	37·45 N	5·10 W
98	Rondônia (Ter.)...........Braz.	10·15 S	63·07 W
86	Ronge, Lac la (L.)..........Can.	55·16 N	104·16 W
118	Rønne (rûn'ĕ)..............Den.	55·08 N	14·46 E
118	Ronneby (rōn'ĕ-bü).........Swe.	56·13 N	15·17 E
72	Ront Ra. (Mts.) (rŏnt).....Colo.	40·59 N	105·29 W
167	Roodepoort (rō'dĕ-pōrt)....S. Afr. (Johannesburg & Pretoria In.)	26·10 S	27·52 E
73	Roodhouse (rōōd'hous).......Ill.	39·29 N	90·21 W
168	Rooiberg.................S. Afr. (Johannesburg & Pretoria In.)	24·46 S	27·42 E
111	Roosendaal (rō'zĕn-dāl) Neth. (Amsterdam In.)	51·32 N	4·27 E
69	Roosevelt (rōz''vĕlt)........Utah	40·20 N	110·00 W
69	Roosevelt (R.).............Ariz.	33·45 N	111·00 W
99	Roosevelt (R.) (rô'sĕ-vĕlt)..Braz.	9·22 S	60·28 W
47	Roosevelt I...............Ant.	79·30 S	168·00 W
75	Root R. (rōōt) Wis. (Milwaukee In.)	42·49 N	87·54 W
158	Roper (R.) (rōp'ēr)........Austl.	14·50 S	134·00 E
136	Ropsha (rôp'shȧ) Sov. Un. (Leningrad In.)	59·44 N	29·53 E
122	Roquefort...................Fr.	43·59 N	3·00 E
98	Roques, Islas los (Is.).......Ven.	21·25 N	67·40 W
101	Roque Pérez (rô'kĕ-pĕ'rĕz) Arg. (Buenos Aires In.)	35·23 S	59·22 W
125	Roquetas (rô-kā'täs).........Sp.	40·50 N	0·32 E
99	Roraima, Mtn. (rô-rä-ē'mă) Ven.-Br. Gu.	5·12 N	60·52 W
118	Röros (rûr'ôs)..............Nor.	62·36 N	11·25 E
120	Rorschach (rōr'shäk).......Switz.	47·27 N	9·28 E
129	Ros' (R.) (rôs).........Sov. Un.	49·40 N	30·22 E
120	Rosa, Monte (Mt.) (mōn'tā rō'ză). It.	45·56 N	7·51 E
76	Rosales (rō-zä'lās)..........Mex.	28·15 N	100·43 W
155	Rosales (rô-sä'lĕs) Phil. (Manila In.)	15·54 N	120·38 E
90	Rosamorada (rō'zä-mō-rä'dhä) Mex.	22·06 N	105·16 W
91	Rosaria, Laguna (L.) (lä-gōō'nä-rô-sȧ'ryä). Mex.	17·50 N	93·51 W
101	Rosario (rô-zä'rê-ō) Arg. (Buenos Aires In.)	32·58 S	60·42 W
99	Rosario (rô-zä'rê-ōō)........Braz.	2·49 S	44·15 W
90	Rosario....................Mex.	22·58 N	105·54 W
155	Rosario........Phil. (Manila In.)	13·49 N	121·13 E
101	Rosario....Ur. (Buenos Aires In.)	34·19 S	57·24 W
94	Rosario, Cayo (I.) (kä'yō-rô-sä'ryō). Cuba	21·40 N	81·55 W
100	Rosário do Sul (rô-zä'rê-ōō-dô-sōō'l). Braz.	30·17 S	54·52 W
99	Rosário Oeste (ō'ĕst'ĕ)......Braz.	14·47 S	56·20 W
65	Rosario Str...Wash. (Seattle In.)	48·27 N	122·45 W
125	Rosas, Golfo de (G.) (gôl-fô-dĕ-rō'zäs). Sp.	42·10 N	3·20 E
123	Rosbach (rōz'bäĸ). Ger. (Ruhr In.)	50·47 N	7·38 E
76	Roscoe (rôs'kō).............Tex.	32·26 N	100·38 W
70	Roseau (rô-zō')............Minn.	48·52 N	95·47 W
93	Roseau Dominica (Le. & Wind. Is. In.)	15·17 N	61·23 W
70	Roseau (R.)..............Minn.	48·52 N	96·11 W
66	Roseberg (rōz'bûrg).........Ore.	43·13 N	123·20 W
67	Rosebud Cr...............Mont.	45·48 N	106·34 W
70	Rosebud Ind. Res. (rōz'bud). S. D.	43·13 N	100·42 W
78	Rosedale (rōz'dāl).........Miss.	33·49 N	90·56 W
65	Rosedale......Wash. (Seattle In.)	47·20 N	122·39 W
75	Roselle (rō-zĕl')..Ill. (Chicago In.)	41·59 N	88·05 W
85	Rosemere (rōz'mēr) Can. (Montreal In.)	45·38 N	73·48 W
74	Rosemount (rōz'mount) Minn. (Minneapolis, St. Paul In.)	44·44 N	93·08 W
168	Rosendal (rô-sĕn'täl)......S. Afr. (Johannesburg & Pretoria In.)	28·32 S	27·56 E
120	Rosenheim (rō'zĕn-hīm)......Ger.	47·52 N	12·06 E
86	Rosetown (rōz'toun)........Can.	51·37 N	108·10 W
	Rosetta, see Rashīd		
167	Rosettenville............S. Afr. (Johannesburg & Pretoria In.)	26·15 S	28·04 E
68	Roseville (rōz'vĭl).........Calif.	38·44 N	121·19 W
75	Roseville.....Mich. (Detroit In.)	42·30 N	82·55 W
74	Roseville.................Minn. (Minneapolis, St. Paul In.)	45·01 N	93·10 W
80	Rosiclare (rōz'ĭ-klâr)..........Ill.	37·30 N	88·15 W
99	Rosignol (rŏs-ĭg-nŏl)......Br. Gu.	6·16 N	57·37 W
127	Rosiorii de Vede (rô-shôr'ê dĕ vĕ-dĕ). Rom.	44·06 N	25·00 E
118	Roskilde (rôs'kêl-dĕ)........Den.	55·39 N	12·04 E
128	Roslavl' (rôs'läv'l)......Sov. Un.	53·56 N	32·52 E
66	Roslyn (rŏz'lĭn)...........Wash.	47·14 N	121·00 W
129	Rosovka..............Sov. Un.	47·14 N	36·35 E
123	Rösrath (rûz'rät). Ger. (Ruhr In.)	50·53 N	7·11 E
75	Ross (rôs)...Ohio (Cincinnati In.)	39·19 N	84·39 W
126	Rossano (rô-sä'nō)............It.	39·34 N	16·38 E
85	Ross Cr.....Can. (Edmonton In.)	53·50 N	113·08 W
66	Ross Dam...............Wash.	48·40 N	121·07 W
81	Rosseau (L.) (rôs-sō')........Can.	45·15 N	79·30 W
159	Rossel (I.) (rô-sĕl')........Austl.	11·31 S	154·00 E
85	Rosser (rôs'sēr) Can. (Winnipeg In.)	49·59 N	97·27 W
82	Rossignol (rô-sê-nyôl').......Can.	44·15 N	65·25 W
86	Rossland (rôs'lȧnd).........Can.	49·00 N	118·08 W
129	Rossosh' (rôs'sŭsh)......Sov. Un.	50·12 N	39·32 E
167	Rossouw......S. Afr. (Natal In.)	31·12 S	27·18 E
47	Ross Sea..................Ant.	76·00 S	178·00 W
47	Ross Shelf Ice..............Ant.	81·30 S	175·00 W
78	Rossville (rôs'vĭl)............Ga.	34·57 N	85·22 W
120	Rostock (rôs'tŭk)...........Ger.	54·04 N	12·06 E
128	Rostov................Sov. Un.	57·13 N	39·23 E
129	Rostov (Oblast)........Sov. Un.	47·38 N	39·15 E
133	Rostov-na-Donu (rôstôv-nȧ-dô-nōō). Sov. Un.	47·16 N	39·47 E
112	Rösvatn (L.) (rûs-vät'n).....Nor.	65·36 N	13·08 E
78	Roswell (rôz'wĕl).............Ga.	34·02 N	84·21 W
72	Roswell...............N. Mex.	33·23 N	104·32 W
72	Rotan (rô-tăn')..............Tex.	32·51 N	100·27 W
120	Rothenburg................Ger.	49·20 N	10·10 E
110	Rotherham (rŏdh'ēr-ăm)....Eng.	53·26 N	1·21 W
82	Rothesay..................Can.	45·25 N	65·59 W
116	Rothesay (rôth'sȧ).........Scot.	55·50 N	3·14 W
110	Rothwell (rôth'wĕl)........Eng.	53·44 N	1·30 W
154	Roti (I.) (rō'tê)..........Indon.	10·30 S	122·52 E
160	Roto (rō'tô)..............Austl.	33·07 S	145·30 E
111	Rotterdam (rôt'ĕr-dām') Neth. (Amsterdam In.)	51·55 N	4·27 E
120	Rottweil (rōt'vīl)..........Ger.	48·10 N	8·36 E
122	Roubaix (rōō-bĕ')............Fr.	50·42 N	3·10 E
122	Rouen (rōō-äɴ')..............Fr.	49·25 N	1·05 E
75	Rouge, R.....Mich. (Detroit In.)	42·30 N	83·15 W
85	Rouge R. (rōōzh) Can. (Toronto In.)	43·53 N	79·21 W
75	Round Lake....Ill. (Chicago In.)	42·21 N	88·05 W
83	Round Pd. (round)..........Can.	48·12 N	53·50 W
65	Round Top (Mtn.) (tŏp) Ore. (Portland In.)	45·41 N	123·22 W
67	Roundup (round'ŭp).......Mont.	46·25 N	108·35 W
116	Rousay (I.) (rōō'zȧ)........Scot.	59·10 N	3·04 W
87	Rouyn (rōōn)..............Can.	48·22 N	79·03 W
112	Rovaniemi (rô'vȧ-nyĕ'mĭ)....Fin.	66·29 N	25·45 E
126	Rovato (rô-vä'tō).............It.	45·33 N	10·00 E
129	Roven'ki (rô-vĕn'ki')....Sov. Un.	48·06 N	39·44 E
129	Roven'ki..............Sov. Un.	49·54 N	38·54 E
126	Rovereto (rō-vȧ-rā'tô).........It.	45·53 N	11·05 E
126	Rovigo (rô-vē'gô).............It.	45·05 N	11·48 E
126	Rovinj (rô'vên')............Yugo.	45·05 N	13·40 E
98	Rovira (rô-vē'rä).......Col. (In.)	4·14 N	75·13 W
121	Rovno (rôv'nô).........Sov. Un.	50·37 N	26·17 E
129	Rovno (Oblast).........Sov. Un.	50·55 N	27·00 E
129	Rovnoye (rôv'nô-yĕ).....Sov. Un.	48·11 N	31·46 E
83	Rowley (rou'lē) Mass. (Boston In.)	42·43 N	70·53 W
74	Roxana (rŏks'ăn-nȧ) Ill. (St. Louis In.)	38·51 N	90·05 W
154	Roxas (rô-xäs)..............Phil.	11·30 N	122·47 E
79	Roxboro (rŏks' bŭr-ô)......N. C.	36·22 N	78·58 W
72	Roy (roi)...............N. Mex.	35·54 N	104·09 W
74	Roy....Utah (Salt Lake City In.)	41·10 N	112·02 W
94	Royal (I.)..............Ba. Is.	25·30 N	76·50 W
116	Royal Can. (roi-ăl)...........Ire.	53·28 N	6·45 W
167	Royal Natal Natl. Pk. (roi'ăl) S. Afr. (Natal In.)	28·35 S	28·54 E
65	Royal Oak (roi'ăl ōk) Can. (Seattle In.)	48·30 N	123·24 W
75	Royal Oak....Mich. (Detroit In.)	42·29 N	83·09 W
80	Royalton (roi'ăl-tŭn).......Mich.	42·00 N	86·25 W
122	Royan (rwä-yäɴ')............Fr.	45·40 N	1·02 W
122	Roye (rwä)..................Fr.	49·43 N	2·40 E
84	Royersford (rô' yērz-fērd) Pa. (Philadelphia In.)	40·11 N	75·32 W
78	Royston (roiz'tŭn)...........Ga.	34·15 N	83·06 W
110	Royton (roi'tŭn)...........Eng.	53·34 N	2·07 W
123	Rozay-en-Brie (rô-zā-ĕɴ-brē') Fr. (Paris In.)	48·41 N	2·57 E
136	Rozhaya R. (rô'zhȧ-yȧ) Sov. Un. (Moscow In.)	55·20 N	37·37 E
121	Rožňava (rôzh'nyȧ-vȧ)....Czech.	48·39 N	20·32 E
133	Rtishchevo ('r-tĭsh'chĕ-vô) Sov. Un.	52·15 N	43·40 E
167	Ruaha (R.) (rwä'hȧ)........Tan.	7·51 S	37·00 E
159	Ruapehu (Mtn.) (rōō-ȧ-pā'hōō) N. Z. (In.)	39·15 S	175·37 E
139	Ruâq (R.). U. A. R. (Palestine In.)	29·48 N	33·59 E
134	Rubtsovak.............Sov. Un.	51·31 N	81·17 E
64	Ruby (rōō'bê)...........Alaska	64·38 N	155·22 W
68	Ruby (L.)..................Nev.	40·11 N	115·20 W
68	Ruby Mts.................Nev.	40·11 N	115·36 W
67	Ruby R..................Mont.	45·06 N	112·10 W
95	Rucilla, Loma (Hill) (lô'mä-rōō-sê'l-yä). Dom. Rep.	19·05 N	70·55 W
144	Rūd-E-Kar (R.).............Iran	33·15 N	47·31 E
118	Rudkøbing (rōōdh'kûb-ĭng)..Den.	54·56 N	10·44 E
111	Rüdnitz (rüd'nētz) Ger. (Berlin In.)	52·44 N	13·38 E
142	Rudok (rōō'dôk)..........China	33·42 N	79·56 E
165	Rudolf, L. (rōō'dŏlf)...Ken.-Eth.	3·43 N	35·49 E
117	Rudolstadt (rōō'dôl-shtät)...Ger.	50·46 N	13·30 E
165	Rufa'a (rōō-fä'ä)...........Sud.	14·52 N	33·30 E
122	Ruffec (rü-fĕk')..............Fr.	46·03 N	0·11 E
167	Rufiji (R.) (rōō-fē'jê)........Tan.	8·29 S	37·39 E
164	Rufisque (rü-fēsk').......Senegal	14·41 N	17·13 W
66	Rufus Woods.............Wash.	48·02 N	119·33 W
110	Rugby (rŭg'bê)............Eng.	52·22 N	1·15 W
70	Rugby...................N. D.	48·22 N	100·00 W
110	Rugeley (rōōj'lē)...........Eng.	52·46 N	1·56 W
120	Rügen (Pen.) (rü'ghĕn)......Ger.	54·28 N	13·47 E
119	Ruhnu-Saar (I.) (rōōnōō-sȧ'ȧr) Sov. Un.	57·46 N	23·15 E
120	Ruhr R. (rōōr).............Ger.	51·18 N	8·17 E
90	Ruiz (rōōē'z)..............Mex.	21·55 N	105·09 W
98	Ruiz, Nevado del (Pk.) (nĕ-vȧ'dô-dĕl-rōōē'z). Col. (In.)	4·52 N	75·20 W
119	Rūjiena (rōō'yĭ-ă-nȧ)....Sov. Un.	57·54 N	25·19 E
166	Rukwa (L.) (rōōk-wä')......Tan.	8·15 S	33·14 E
71	Rum (R.) (rŭm)...........Minn.	45·52 N	93·45 W
127	Ruma (rōō'mȧ)............Yugo.	45·00 N	19·53 E
165	Rumbek (rŭm'bĕk)..........Sud.	6·52 N	29·43 E
95	Rum Cay (I.)............Ba. Is.	23·40 N	74·50 W
82	Rumford (rŭm'fērd).......Maine	44·32 N	70·35 W
139	Rummānah U. A. R. (Palestine In.)	31·01 N	32·39 E
110	Runcorn (rŭŋ'kôrn).........Eng.	53·20 N	2·44 W
139	Rupat, Palau (I.) (rōō'pät) Indon. (Singapore In.)	1·55 N	101·35 E
139	Rupat, Selat (Str.) Indon. (Singapore In.)	1·55 N	101·17 E
67	Rupert (rōō'pērt)..........Idaho	42·36 N	113·41 W
87	Rupert (R.)................Can.	76·27 N	77·47 W
127	Ruse (Russe) (rōō'sĕ) (rōō'sĕ) Bul.	43·50 N	25·59 E
71	Rush City................Minn.	45·40 N	92·59 W
65	Rushton (rŭsh'tŭn) Wash. (Seattle In.)	47·18 N	122·30 W
73	Rushville (rŭsh'vĭl)...........Ill.	40·08 N	90·34 W
80	Rushville..................Ind.	39·35 N	85·30 W
70	Rushville.................Nebr.	42·43 N	102·27 W
77	Rusk (rŭsk)................Tex.	31·49 N	95·09 W
65	Ruskin (rŭs'kĭn) Can. (Vancouver In.)	49·10 N	122·25 W
111	Russ (R.)......Aus. (Vienna In.)	48·12 N	16·55 E
99	Russas (rōō's-säs)..........Braz.	4·48 S	37·50 W
	Russe, see Ruse		
65	Russell..Calif. (San Francisco In.)	37·39 N	122·08 W
86	Russell (rŭs'ĕl).............Can.	50·47 N	101·20 W
85	Russell........Can. (Ottawa In.)	45·15 N	75·22 W
72	Russell..................Kans.	38·51 N	98·51 W
80	Russell....................Ky.	38·30 N	82·45 W
159	Russell...............N. Z. (In.)	35·38 S	174·13 E
159	Russell Is................Sol. Is.	9·16 S	158·30 E
78	Russellville (rŭs'ĕl-vĭl).......Ala.	34·29 N	87·44 W
73	Russellville................Ark.	35·16 N	93·08 W
78	Russelville.................Ky.	36·48 N	86·51 W
130	Russian S. F. S. R.......Sov. Un.	61·00 N	60·00 E
68	Russian (R.) (rŭsh'ăn)......Calif.	38·59 N	123·10 W
168	Rustenburg (rŭs'tĕn-bûrg). S. Afr. (Johannesburg & Pretoria In.)	25·40 S	26·15 E
77	Ruston (rŭs'tŭn).............La.	32·32 N	92·39 W
129	Rutchenkovo (rōō-chĕn'kô-vô) Sov. Un.	47·54 N	37·36 E
124	Rute (rōō'tā)................Sp.	37·20 N	4·34 W
68	Ruth (rōōth)..............Nev.	39·17 N	115·00 W
121	Ruthenia (Reg.)........Sov. Un.	48·25 N	23·00 E
79	Rutherfordton (rŭdh'ēr-fērd-tŭn) N. C.	35·23 N	81·58 W
81	Rutland (rŭt'lănd)...........Vt.	43·35 N	72·55 W
110	Rutland (Co.).............Eng.	52·40 N	0·37 W
166	Rutshuru (rōōt-shōō'rōō)..Con. L.	1·13 S	29·15 E
126	Ruvo (rōō'vô)................It.	41·07 N	16·32 E
163	Ruwenzori Ra. (rōō-wĕn-zō'rê) Afr.	0·53 N	30·00 E
128	Ruza (rōō'zȧ)..........Sov. Un.	55·42 N	36·12 E
121	Ruzhany (rōō-zhän'ĭ)....Sov. Un.	52·49 N	24·54 E
166	Rwanda....................Afr.	2·10 S	29·37 E
136	Ryabovo (ryä'bô-vô) Sov. Un. (Leningrad In.)	59·24 N	31·08 E
128	Ryazan' (ryä-zän'')......Sov. Un.	54·37 N	39·43 E
128	Ryazan' (Oblast)........Sov. Un.	54·10 N	39·37 E
128	Ryazhsk (ryäzh'sk').....Sov. Un.	53·43 N	40·04 E
132	Rybachiy, P-Ov. (Pen.)..Sov. Un.	69·50 N	33·20 E
136	Rybatskoye (rĭ-bät'skô-yĕ) Sov. Un. (Leningrad In.)	59·50 N	30·31 E

ăt; finăl; rāte; senâte; ärm; ȧsk; sofȧ; fâre; ch-choose; dh-as th in other; bē; êvent; bĕt; recĕnt; cratēr; g-go; gh-guttural g; bĭt; ĭ-short neutral; rīde; ĸ-guttural k as ch in German ich;

PRONOUNCING INDEX
Rybinsk–St. Girons 259

Page	Name Pronunciation Region	Lat. °′	Long. °′
128	Rybinsk (ry-bĭ'nsk) ... Sov. Un.	58·02 N	38·52 E
	Rybinsk, L., see Rybinskoye Vodokhranilishche		
128	Rybinskoye Vodokhranilishche (Rybinsk) (L.) . Sov. Un.	58·23 N	38·15 E
121	Rybnik (rĭb'nêk) ... Pol.	50·06 N	18·37 E
129	Rybnitsa (rĭb'nēt-sȧ) ... Sov. Un.	47·45 N	29·02 E
116	Ryde (rīd) ... Eng.	50·43 N	1·16 W
84	Rye (rī) ... N. Y. (New York In.)	40·58 N	73·42 W
129	Ryl'sk (rēl''sk) ... Sov. Un.	51·33 N	34·42 E
152	Ryōtsu (ryōt'sōō) ... Jap.	38·02 N	138·23 E
121	Rypin (rĭ'pēn) ... Pol.	53·04 N	19·25 E
156	Ryūkyū Rettō (Is.) (ryōō'kyōō) Asia	26·00 N	119·00 E
121	Rzeszów (zhâ'shōōf) ... Pol.	50·02 N	22·00 E
128	Rzhev ('r-zhĕf) ... Sov. Un.	56·16 N	34·17 E
129	Rzhishchëv ('r-zhĭsh'chĕf) Sov. Un.	49·58 N	31·05 E
120	Saale R. (sä'lĕ) ... Ger.	51·14 N	11·52 E
120	Saalfeld (säl'fĕlt) ... Ger.	50·38 N	11·20 E
120	Saar (State) (zär) ... Ger.	49·25 N	6·50 E
120	Saarbrücken (zähr'brü-kĕn) .. Ger.	49·15 N	7·01 E
119	Saaremaa (Ezel) (I.) (sä'rĕ-mä) Sov. Un.	58·28 N	21·30 E
100	Saavedra (sä-ä-vä'drä) ... Arg.	37·45 S	62·23 W
127	Šabac (shä'bȧts) ... Yugo.	44·45 N	19·49 E
125	Sabadell (sä-bä-dhäl') ... Sp.	41·32 N	2·07 E
154	Sabah (Reg.) ... Asia	5·10 N	116·25 E
93	Saba I. (sä'bä) N. A. (Le. & Wind. Is. In.)	17·39 N	63·20 W
154	Sabalana (I.) ... Indon.	6·56 S	118·10 E
94	Sabana, Arch. de (är-chē-pyĕ'lä-gô dĕ sä-bä'nä) Cuba	23·05 N	80·00 W
93	Sabana, R. (sä-bä'nä) ... Pan.	8·40 N	78·02 W
95	Sabana de la Mar (sä-bä'nä dā lä mär') Dom. Rep.	19·05 N	69·30 W
99	Sabana de Uchire (sä-bà'nä dĕ ōō-chē'rĕ) Ven. (In.)	10·02 N	65·32 W
92	Sabanagrande (sä-bä'nä-grä'n-dĕ) Hond.	13·47 N	87·16 W
98	Sabanalarga (sä-bà'nä-lär'gä) . Col.	10·38 N	75·02 W
98	Sabanas Páramo (Mtn.) (sä-bá'näs pá'rä-mô) ... Col. (In.)	6·28 N	76·08 W
91	Sabancuy (sä-bäŋ-kwē') ... Mex.	18·58 N	91·09 W
154	Sabang (sä'bäng) ... Indon.	5·52 N	95·26 E
126	Sabaudia (sȧ-bou'dê-ä) ... It.	41·19 N	13·00 E
165	Sabderat (säb-dȧ-rät') ... Eth.	15·30 N	36·45 E
73	Sabetha (sȧ-bĕth'ȧ) ... Kans.	39·54 N	95·49 W
166	Sabi (R.) (sä'bê) ... S. Rh.	20·18 S	32·07 E
119	Sabile (sä'bē-lĕ) ... Sov. Un.	57·03 N	22·34 E
76	Sabinal (sȧ-bī'nȧl) ... Tex.	29·19 N	99·27 W
94	Sabinal, Cayo (I.) (kä'yō sä-bē-näl') .. Cuba	21·40 N	77·20 W
88	Sabinas ... Mex.	28·05 N	102·30 W
76	Sabinas, R. (sä-bē'näs) ... Mex.	26·37 N	99·52 W
76	Sabinas, Rio (R.) (rē'ō sä-bē'näs) Mex.	27·25 N	100·33 W
76	Sabinas Hidalgo (ê-däl'gô) . Mex.	26·30 N	100·10 W
77	Sabine (sȧ-bēn') ... Tex.	29·44 N	93·54 W
47	Sabine, Mt. ... Ant.	72·05 S	169·10 E
63	Sabine (R.) ... U. S.	31·35 N	94·00 W
77	Sabine L. ... La.-Tex.	29·53 N	93·41 W
155	Sablayan (säb-lä-yän') Phil. (Manila In.)	12·49 N	120·47 E
82	Sable, C. (sā'b'l) ... Can.	43·25 N	65·24 W
79	Sable, C. ... Fla. (In.)	25·12 N	81·10 W
122	Sablé-sur-Sarthe (säb-lā-sür-särt') Fr.	47·50 N	0·17 W
132	Sablya, Gora (Mtn.) ... Sov. Un.	64·50 N	59·00 E
124	Sàbor (R.) (sä-bōr') ... Port.	41·18 N	6·54 W
73	Sac (R.) (sôk) ... Mo.	38·11 N	93·45 W
81	Sacandaga Res. (să-kăn-dȧ'gȧ) N. Y.	43·10 N	74·15 W
125	Sacavém (sä-kä-vĕN') Port. (Lisbon In.)	38·47 N	9·06 W
125	Sacavem (R.) .. Port. (Lisbon In.)	38·52 N	9·06 W
71	Sac City (sŏk) ... Iowa	42·25 N	95·00 W
120	Sachsen (Reg.) (zäk'sĕn) ... Ger.	50·45 N	12·17 E
81	Sacketts Harbor (săk'ĕts) ... N. Y.	43·55 N	76·05 W
82	Sackville (săk'vĭl) ... Can.	45·54 N	64·26 W
82	Saco (sô'kô) ... Maine	43·30 N	70·28 W
100	Saco (R.) (sä'kô) ... Braz. (In.)	22·20 S	43·26 W
82	Saco (R.) ... Maine	43·53 N	70·46 W
100	Sacra Famalia do Tinguá (sä-krä fä-mä'lyä dô tĕn-gwá') Braz. (In.)	22·29 S	43·36 W
68	Sacramento (săk-rȧ-mĕn'tō) . Calif.	38·35 N	121·30 W
76	Sacramento ... Mex.	25·45 N	103·22 W
76	Sacramento ... Mex.	27·05 N	101·45 W
68	Sacramento (R.) ... Calif.	40·20 N	122·07 W
166	Sa'da Bandeira (sä'dȧ bän-dā'rȧ) Ang.	14·50 S	13·30 E
65	Saddle Mtn. (săd''l) Ore. (Portland In.)	45·58 N	123·40 W
145	Sadiya (sŭ-dē'yä) ... India	27·53 N	95·35 E
152	Sado (I.) (sä'dō) ... Jap.	38·05 N	138·26 E
124	Sado (R.) (sä'dōō) ... Port.	38·15 N	8·20 W
118	Saeby (sĕ'bü) ... Den.	57·21 N	10·29 E
153	Saeki (sä'ȧ-kĕ) ... Jap.	32·56 N	131·51 E
139	Safad ... Isr. (Palestine In.)	32·58 N	35·30 E
69	Safford (săf'fērd) ... Ariz.	32·50 N	109·45 W
164	Safi (Asfi) (sä'fê) (ȧs'fê) ... Mor.	32·24 N	9·09 W
133	Safid Rud (R.) ... Iran	36·50 N	49·40 E
153	Saga (sä'gä) ... Jap.	33·15 N	130·18 E
153	Sagami-Nada (Sea) (sä'gä'mē nä-dä) . Jap.	35·06 N	139·24 E
75	Sagamore Hills (săg'ȧ-môr hĭlz) Ohio (Cleveland In.)	41·19 N	81·34 W
71	Saganaga (L.) (să-gȧ-nă'gȧ) Can.-Minn.	48·13 N	91·17 W
80	Saginaw (săg'ĭ-nô) ... Mich.	43·25 N	84·00 W
74	Saginaw ... Minn. (Duluth In.)	46·51 N	92·26 W
74	Saginaw Tex. (Dallas, Fort Worth In.)	32·52 N	97·22 W
80	Saginaw B. ... Mich.	43·50 N	83·40 W
133	Sagiz (R.) (sä'gēz) ... Sov. Un.	48·30 N	56·10 E
69	Saguache (sȧ-wăch') (sȧ-gwä'chê) Colo.	38·05 N	106·10 W
69	Saguache Cr. ... Colo.	38·05 N	106·40 W
95	Sagua de Tánamo (sä-gwä dĕ tä'nä-mō) ... Cuba	20·40 N	75·15 W
94	Sagua la Grande (sä-gwä lä grä'n-dĕ) ... Cuba	22·45 N	80·05 W
69	Saguaro Natl. Mon. (säg-wä'rō) Ariz.	32·12 N	110·40 W
87	Saguenay (R.) (săg-ē-nā') ... Can.	48·05 N	70·26 W
164	Saguia el Hamra (Ter.) (säg-yä ĕl häm'rȧ) . Sp. Sah.	27·01 N	10·58 W
125	Sagunto (sä-gōōn'tō) ... Sp.	39·40 N	0·17 W
163	Sahara Des. (sȧ-hä'rȧ) ... Afr.	23·44 N	1·40 W
114	Saharan Atlas (Mts.) ... Mor.-Alg.	32·51 N	1·02 W
142	Sahāranpur (sŭ-hä'rŭn-pōōr') India	29·58 N	77·41 E
74	Sahara Village (sȧ-hä'rȧ) Utah (Salt Lake City In.)	41·06 N	111·58 W
139	Saheira (R.) U. A. R. (Palestine In.)	29·55 N	33·18 E
90	Sahuayo (sä-wä'yō) ... Mex.	20·03 N	102·43 W
164	Saïda (sä'ê-dä) ... Alg.	34·51 N	00·07 E
144	Sa'īdabād (sä'ê-dȧ-bät) ... Iran	29·30 N	55·43 E
154	Saigon (sȧ-ê-gôN') (sī-gŏn') .. Viet.	10·46 N	106·34 E
153	Saijō (sä'ê-jō) ... Jap.	33·55 N	133·13 E
119	Saimaa (sä'ĭ-mȧ) ... Fin.	61·24 N	28·45 E
90	Sain Alto (sä-ēn' äl'tō) ... Mex.	23·35 N	103·13 W
85	St. Adolphe (sânt a'dŏlf) (săN' tȧ-dôlf') Can. (Winnipeg In.)	49·40 N	97·07 W
122	St. Affrique (săN' tȧ-frēk') ... Fr.	43·58 N	2·52 E
161	St. Albans (sânt ôl'bănz) Austl. (Melbourne In.)	37·44 S	144·47 E
110	St. Albans ... Eng. (London In.)	51·44 N	0·20 W
81	St. Albans ... Vt.	44·50 N	73·05 W
80	St. Albans ... W. Va.	38·20 N	81·50 W
116	St. Albans Hd. ... Eng.	50·34 N	2·00 W
85	St. Albert (sânt ăl'bērt) Can. (Edmonton In.)	53·38 N	113·38 W
122	St. Amand Montrond (săN't ȧ-măN' môN-rôN') . Fr.	46·44 N	2·28 E
167	St. André, Cap (C.) .. Malag. Rep.	16·15 S	44·31 E
78	St. Andrew, B. ... Fla.	30·20 N	85·45 W
83	St. Andrew Chan. ... Can.	46·06 N	60·28 W
82	St. Andrews (ăn'drōōz) ... Can.	43·42 N	65·05 W
116	St. Andrews ... Scot.	56·20 N	2·40 W
85	St. Andrews East Can. (Montreal In.)	45·33 N	74·19 W
85	Ste. Angele-de-Laval (săNt' ăN-zhĕl'-dē-lȧväl') Can. (Montreal In.)	45·33 N	73·42 W
85	St. Anicet (sĕNt ȧ-nē-sĕ') Can. (Montreal In.)	45·07 N	74·23 W
74	St. Ann (sânt ăn') Mo. (St. Louis In.)	38·44 N	90·23 W
82	Ste. Anne (săNt' ȧn') (sânt ăn') Can.	46·55 N	71·46 W
85	Ste. Anne ... Can. (Montreal In.)	45·24 N	73·57 W
75	St. Anne ... Ill. (Chicago In.)	41·01 N	87·44 W
93	Ste. Anne Grande Terre (Le. & Wind. Is. In.)	16·15 N	61·23 W
85	Ste. Anne, R. ... Can. (Quebec In.)	47·07 N	70·50 W
85	Ste. Anne-de-Beaupré (dē bō-prā') Can. (Quebec In.)	47·01 N	70·56 W
82	St. Anne de la Pocatière (dĕ lȧ pô-kȧ-tyâr') . Can.	47·24 N	70·01 W
85	Ste. Anne-des-Plaines Can. (Montreal In.)	45·46 N	73·49 W
83	St. Anns B. (ănz) ... Can.	46·28 N	60·10 W
94	St. Ann's Bay ... Jam.	18·25 N	77·15 W
85	St. Anselme (săN' tăN-sĕlm') Can. (Quebec In.)	46·37 N	70·58 W
83	St. Anthony (săN ăn'thō-nê) . Can.	51·24 N	55·35 W
67	St. Anthony (sânt ăn'thô-nê) Idaho	43·59 N	111·42 W
155	St. Antonio, Mt. Phil. (Manila In.)	13·23 N	122·00 E
85	St. Apollinaire (săN' tȧ-pôl-ê-nâr') Can. (Quebec In.)	46·36 N	71·30 W
123	St. Arnoult-en-Yvelines (săN-tär-nōō'ĕN-nēv-lēn') Fr. (Paris In.)	48·33 N	1·55 E
85	St. Augustin (sânt ô'gŭs-tĕn) Can. (Montreal In.)	45·38 N	73·59 W
85	St. Augustin ... Can. (Quebec In.)	46·45 N	71·27 W
79	St. Augustine (sânt ô'gŭs-tēn) Fla.	29·53 N	81·21 W
85	Ste. Barbe (sânt bärb') Can. (Montreal In.)	45·14 N	74·12 W
125	Ste. Barbe du Tlelat (săNt bärb' dü tlē-lȧ') . Alg.	35·33 N	0·28 W
82	St. Barthélémy (săN' bȧr-tȧ-lĕ-me) Can.	46·09 N	73·10 W
93	St. Barthelemy I. N. A. (Le. & Wind. Is. In.)	17·55 N	62·32 W
116	St. Bees Hd. (sânt bēz' hĕd) Eng.	54·30 N	3·40 W
85	St. Benoit (sĕN bĕ-nōō-ä') Can. (Montreal In.)	45·34 N	74·05 W
84	St. Bernard (bēr-närd') La. (New Orleans In.)	29·52 N	89·52 W
75	St. Bernard . Ohio (Cincinnati In.)	39·10 N	84·30 W
85	St. Boniface (bŏn'ĭ fȧs) Can. (Winnipeg In.)	49·53 N	97·06 W
116	St. Brides B. (sânt brīdz') Wales	51·17 N	4·45 W
122	St. Brieuc (săN' brēs') ... Fr.	48·32 N	2·47 W
85	St. Bruno (brü'nō) Can. (Montreal In.)	45·31 N	73·20 W
85	St. Canut (săN' kȧ-nü') Can. (Montreal In.)	45·43 N	74·04 W
82	St. Casimir (kȧ-zê-mēr') ... Can.	46·45 N	72·34 W
85	St. Catharines (kăth'ȧ-rĭnz) Can. (Toronto In.)	43·10 N	79·14 W
93	St. Catherine, Mt. Grenada (Le. & Wind. Is. In.)	12·10 N	62·42 W
122	St. Chamas (săN-shä-mä') Fr. (Marseille In.)	43·32 N	5·03 E
122	St. Chamond (săN' shȧ-môN') .. Fr.	45·30 N	4·17 E
85	St. Charles (săN' shärlz') Can. (Quebec In.)	46·47 N	70·57 W
75	St. Charles (sânt chärlz') Ill. (Chicago In.)	41·55 N	88·19 W
80	St. Charles ... Mich.	43·20 N	84·10 W
71	St. Charles ... Minn.	43·56 N	92·05 W
74	St. Charles ... Mo. (St. Louis In.)	38·47 N	90·29 W
93	St. Christopher I. (St. Kitts) (sânt kĭts') St. Kitts-Nevis-Anguilla (Le. & Wind. Is. In.)	17·24 N	62·25 W
80	St. Clair (sânt klâr) ... Mich.	42·55 N	82·30 W
80	St. Clair (L.) ... Mich.-Can.	42·25 N	82·30 W
80	St. Clair (R.) ... Mich.-Can.	42·45 N	82·25 W
85	Ste. Claire ... Can. (Quebec In.)	46·36 N	70·52 W
75	St. Clair Shores Mich. (Detroit In.)	42·30 N	82·54 W
123	St. Claude (săN' klōd') ... Fr.	46·24 N	5·53 E
85	St. Clet (săNt' klā') Can. (Montreal In.)	45·22 N	74·21 W
79	St. Cloud (sânt kloud') .. Fla. (In.)	28·13 N	81·17 W
71	St. Cloud ... Minn.	45·33 N	94·08 W
85	St. Constant (kŏn'stănt) Can. (Montreal In.)	45·22 N	73·35 W
167	St. Croix (I.) (săN krwä) S. Afr. (Natal In.)	33·48 S	25·45 E
89	Saint Croix (I.) (sânt kroi') Vir. Is. (U. S. A.) (Puerto Rico In.)	17·40 N	64·43 W
82	St. Croix (R.) (kroi') ... Can.	45·17 N	67·32 W
71	St. Croix Ind. Res. ... Wis.	45·40 N	92·21 W
71	St. Croix R. (sânt kroi') Minn.-Wis.	45·00 N	92·44 W
85	St. Damien (sânt dā'mê-ĕn) Can. (Quebec In.)	46·37 N	70·39 W
85	St. David (dā'vĭd) Can. (Quebec In.)	46·47 N	71·11 W
116	St. David's Hd. ... Wales	51·54 N	5·25 W
123	St.-Denis (săN'dē-nē') Fr. (Paris In.)	48·26 N	2·22 E
123	St. Dié (dē-ā') ... Fr.	48·18 N	6·55 E
122	St. Dizier (dē-zyā') ... Fr.	48·49 N	4·55 E
85	St. Dominique (sĕN dō-mē-nēk') Can. (Montreal In.)	45·19 N	74·09 W
85	St. Edouard (sĕN-tē-dōō-är') Can. (Montreal In.)	45·14 N	73·31 W
64	St. Elias, Mt. (sânt ê-lī'ăs) ... Can.	60·25 N	141·00 W
85	St. Elzear (sĕN-tĕl-zē-är') Can. (Montreal In.)	45·36 N	73·44 W
85	St. Etienne (săN' tā-tyĕn') Can. (Montreal In.)	45·15 N	73·55 W
85	St. Etienne ... Can. (Quebec In.)	46·39 N	71·19 W
122	St.-Étienne ... Fr.	45·26 N	4·22 E
85	Ste. Euphémie (sĕNt û-fē-mē') Can. (Quebec In.)	46·47 N	70·27 W
85	St. Eustache (săN' tû-stȧsh') Can. (Montreal In.)	45·34 N	73·54 W
85	St. Eustache . Can. (Winnipeg In.)	49·58 N	97·47 W
85	St. Eustache sur le Lac (sĕN tû-stȧsh' sür lē läk) Can. (Montreal In.)	45·33 N	73·54 W
93	St. Eustatius I. (sânt u-stā'shŭs) N. A. (Le. & Wind. Is. In.)	17·32 N	62·45 W
85	Ste. Famille (săNt' fȧ-mē'y') Can. (Quebec In.)	46·58 N	70·58 W
82	St. Felicien (săN fā-lē-syăN') . Can.	48·39 N	72·30 W
82	Ste. Felicite ... Can.	48·54 N	67·22 W
85	St. Féréol (fa-rā-ôl') Can. (Quebec In.)	47·07 N	70·52 W
126	St. Florent, Golfe de (G.) ... Cor.	42·55 N	9·08 E
122	St. Florent-sur-Cher (săN' flô-răN'sür-shâr') . Fr.	46·58 N	2·15 E
122	St. Flour (săN flōōr') ... Fr.	45·02 N	3·09 E
85	Ste. Foy (săNt fwä) Can. (Quebec In.)	46·45 N	71·20 W
73	St. Francis (R.) (sânt frăn'sĭs) Ark.	35·56 N	90·27 W
82	St. Francis (R.) (frăn'sĭs) ... Can.	45·55 N	72·25 W
81	St. Francis L. (săN frăn'sĭs) ... Can.	45·00 N	74·20 W
85	St. François (săN'frăN-swä') Can. (Quebec In.)	47·01 N	70·49 W
122	St. Gaudens (gō-dăNs') ... Fr.	43·07 N	0·43 E
73	Ste. Genevieve (sânt jĕn'ĕ-vēv) Mo.	37·58 N	90·02 W
160	St. George (sânt jôrj') ... Austl.	28·02 S	148·40 E
82	St. George (săN jôrj') ... Can.	45·08 N	66·49 W
85	St. George (săN'zhôrzh') Can. (Toronto In.)	43·14 N	80·15 W
79	St. George (sânt jôrj') ... S. C.	33·11 N	80·35 W
69	St. George ... Utah	37·05 N	113·40 W
64	St. George (I.) ... Alaska	56·30 N	169·40 W
83	St. George, C. ... Can.	48·28 N	59·24 W
78	St. George, C. ... Fla.	29·30 N	85·20 W
82	St. Georges (jôrj'ĕs) ... Can.	46·09 N	70·42 W
83	St. George's ... Can.	48·29 N	58·26 W
99	St. Georges ... Fr. Gu.	3·48 N	51·47 W
93	St. Georges Grenada (Le. & Wind. Is. In.)	12·02 N	61·57 W
83	St. Georges B. ... Can.	48·28 N	59·00 W
116	St. George's Chan. (jôr-jĕz) Eng.-Ire.	51·45 N	6·30 W
123	St. Germain-en-Laye (săN' zhĕr-măN-ăN-lā') Fr. (Paris In.)	48·53 N	2·05 E
85	St. Gervais (zhĕr-vĕ') Can. (Quebec In.)	46·43 N	70·53 W
122	St. Girons (zhē-rôN') ... Fr.	42·58 N	1·08 E

ng-sing; ŋ-baŋk; N-nasalized n; nŏd; cŏmmit; ōld; ôbey; ôrder; fōōd; fŏŏt; ou-out; s-soft; sh-dish; th-thin; pūre; ûnite; ûrn; stŭd; circŭs; ü-as "y" in study; '-indeterminate vowel.

ăt; fĭnȧl; rāte; senâte; ärm; ȧsk; sofȧ; fâre; ch-choose; dh-as th in other; bē; ĕvent; bĕt; recĕnt; cratēr; g-go; gh-guttural g; bĭt; ï-short neutral; rīde; ĸ-guttural k as ch in German ich;

PRONOUNCING INDEX

Salamat–Sand Springs 261

Page	Name	Pronunciation	Region	Lat. °′	Long. °′
165	Salamat, Bahr (R.)	(bär sä-lä-mät′)	Chad.	10·06 N	19·16 E
155	Salamaua	(sä-lä-mä′wä)	N. Gui. Ter.	6·50 S	146·55 E
98	Salamina	(sä-lä-mē′-nä)	Col. (In.)	5·25 N	75·29 W
127	Salamis	(săl′à-mĭs)	Grc.	37·58 N	23·30 E
98	Salaverry	(sä-lä-vā′rē)	Peru	8·16 S	78·54 W
155	Salawati (I.)	(sä-lä-wä′tē)	W. Irian	1·22 S	130·15 E
157	Sala-y-Gómez (I.)		Chile	26·50 S	105·50 W
95	Salcedo	(säl-sā′dō)	Dom. Rep.	19·25 N	70·30 W
98	Saldaña (R.)	(säl-dà′n-yä)	Col. (In.)	3·42 N	75·16 W
166	Saldanha		S. Afr.	32·55 S	18·05 E
119	Saldus	(sál′dŏŏs)	Sov. Un.	56·39 N	22·30 E
160	Sale	(sāl)	Austl.	38·10 S	147·07 E
110	Sale		Eng.	53·24 N	2·20 W
164	Salé	(sà-lā′)	Mor.	34·09 N	6·42 W
85	Sale, Riviére (R.)	(sál′rê-vyâr′)	Can. (Winnipeg In.)	49·44 N	97·11 W
132	Salekhard	(sŭ-lyĭ-kärt)	Sov. Un.	66·35 N	66·50 E
80	Salem	(sā′lĕm)	Ill.	38·40 N	89·00 W
143	Salem		India	11·39 N	78·11 E
80	Salem		Ind.	38·35 N	86·00 W
83	Salem		Mass. (Boston In.)	42·31 N	70·54 W
73	Salem		Mo.	37·36 N	91·33 W
83	Salem		N. H. (Boston In.)	42·46 N	71·16 W
81	Salem		N. J.	39·35 N	75·30 W
80	Salem		Ohio	40·55 N	80·50 W
66	Salem		Ore.	44·55 N	123·03 W
70	Salem		S. D.	43·43 N	97·23 W
167	Salem		S. Afr. (Natal In.)	33·29 S	26·30 E
79	Salem		Va.	37·16 N	80·05 W
80	Salem		W. Va.	39·15 N	80·35 W
126	Salemi	(sä-lä′mē)	It.	37·48 N	38·50 E
125	Salerno	(sä-lĕr′nō)	It. (Naples In.)	40·27 N	14·46 E
126	Salerno, Golfo di (G.)	(gôl-fô-dē)	It.	40·30 N	14·40 E
110	Salford	(săl′fērd)	Eng.	53·26 N	2·19 W
129	Salgir (R.)	(sál′gēr)	Sov. Un.	45·25 N	34·22 E
121	Salgōtarjan	(shôl′gô-tôr-yån)	Hung.	48·06 N	19·50 E
72	Salida	(sá-lī′dá)	Colo.	38·31 N	106·01 W
122	Salies	(sá-lēs′)	Fr.	43·27 N	0·58 W
73	Salina	(sá-lī′ná)	Kans.	38·50 N	97·37 W
69	Salina		Utah	39·00 N	111·55 W
126	Salina (I.)	(sä-lē′nä)	It.	38·35 N	14·48 E
95	Salina Pt.		Ba. Is.	22·10 N	74·20 W
91	Salina Cruz	(sä-lē′nä krōōz′)	Mex.	16·10 N	95·12 W
68	Salinas	(sá-lē′nás)	Calif.	36·41 N	121·40 W
90	Salinas		Mex.	22·38 N	101·42 W
89	Salinas		P. R. (Puerto Rico In.)	17·58 N	66·16 W
68	Salinas (R.)		Calif.	36·33 N	121·29 W
91	Salinas (R.)	(sä-lē′näs)	Mex.	16·15 N	90·31 W
92	Salinas, Bahia de (B.)	(bä-ē′ä-dĕ-sá-lē′nás)	Nic.-C. R.	11·05 N	85·55 W
125	Salinas, Cape	(sä-lēnàs)	Sp.	39·14 N	1·02 E
76	Salinas Victoria	(sä-lē′näs vêk-tō′rē-ä)	Mex.	25·59 N	100·19 W
73	Saline (R.)	(sá-lēn′)	Ark.	34·06 N	92·30 W
72	Saline (R.)		Kans.	39·05 N	99·43 W
123	Salins-les-Bains	(sá-lăN′-lā-băN′)	Fr.	46·55 N	5·54 E
166	Salisbury		S. Rh.	17·49 S	30·52 E
116	Salisbury	(sôlz′bē-rē)	Eng.	50·35 N	1·51 W
82	Salisbury		Can.	46·03 N	65·05 W
81	Salisbury		Md.	38·20 N	75·40 W
73	Salisbury		Mo.	39·24 N	92·47 W
79	Salisbury		N. C.	35·40 N	80·29 W
87	Salisbury (I.)		Can.	63·36 N	76·20 W
116	Salisbury Plain		Eng.	51·15 N	1·52 W
164	Sal I.	(sääl)	C. V. Is. (In.)	16·45 N	22·39 W
79	Salkehatchie (R.)	(sô-kê-hăch′ê)	S. C.	33·09 N	81·10 W
73	Sallisaw	(săl′ĭ-sô)	Okla.	35·27 N	94·48 W
67	Salmon	(săm′ŭn)	Idaho	45·11 N	113·54 W
66	Salmon Falls R.		Idaho	42·22 N	114·53 W
158	Salmon Gums	(gŭmz)	Austl.	33·00 S	122·00 E
82	Salmon (R.)		Can.	46·19 N	65·36 W
81	Salmon (R.)		N. Y.	44·35 N	74·15 W
65	Salmon (R.)		Wash. (Portland In.)	45·44 N	122·36 W
66	Salmon R.		Idaho	45·30 N	115·45 W
66	Salmon R., Middle Fork		Idaho	44·54 N	114·50 W
66	Salmon R., South Fork		Idaho	44·51 N	115·47 W
66	Salmon River Mts.		Idaho	44·15 N	115·44 W
123	Salon-de-Provence	(sà-lôN-dē-prô-văNs′)	Fr.	43·48 N	5·09 E
121	Salonta	(sá-lôn′tá)	Rom.	46·46 N	21·38 E
133	Sal'sk	(sälsk)	Sov. Un.	46·30 N	41·20 E
69	Salt, (R.)	(sôlt)	Ariz.	33·28 N	111·35 W
73	Salt (R.)		Mo.	39·54 N	92·11 W
100	Salta	(säl′tä)	Arg.	24·50 S	65·16 W
100	Salta (Prov.)		Arg.	25·15 S	65·00 W
74	Saltair	(sôlt′âr)	Utah (Salt Lake City In.)	40·46 N	112·09 W
95	Salt Cay (I.)		Turks & Caicos Is.	21·20 N	71·15 W
75	Salt Cr.	(sôlt)	Ill. (Chicago In.)	42·01 N	88·01 W
76	Saltillo	(säl-tēl′yō)	Mex.	25·24 N	100·59 W
74	Salt Lake City	(sôlt lāk sĭ′tĭ)	Utah (Salt Lake City In.)	40·45 N	111·52 W
101	Salto	(säl′tō)	Arg. (Buenos Aires In.)	34·17 S	60·15 W
100	Salto		Ur.	31·18 S	57·45 W
101	Salto, Serra do (Mtn.)	(sĕ′r-rä-dô)	Braz. (Rio de Janeiro In.)	20·26 S	43·28 W
90	Salto (R.)		Mex.	22·16 N	99·18 W
99	Salto Grande	(grän′dä)	Braz.	22·57 S	49·58 W
68	Salton Sea	(sôlt′ŭn)	Calif.	33·28 N	115·43 W
164	Saltpond		Ghana	5·16 N	1·07 W
69	Salt River Ind. Res.	(sôlt rĭv′ẽr)	Ariz.	33·40 N	112·01 W
95	Saltrou	(sál-trōō′)	Hai.	18·15 N	72·00 W
118	Saltsjöbaden	(sält′shû-bäd′ĕn)	Swe.	59·15 N	18·20 E
79	Saltville	(sôlt′vĭl)	Va.	36·50 N	81·45 W
136	Saltykovka	(sål-tē′kôf-kå)	Sov. Un. (Moscow In.)	55·45 N	37·56 E
88	Salud, Mt.	(sä-lōō′th)	Pan. (Panama Canal In.)	9·14 N	79·42 W
79	Saluda	(sá-lōō′dá)	S. C.	34·02 N	81·46 W
79	Saluda (R.)		S. C.	34·07 N	81·48 W
126	Saluzzo	(sä-lōōt′sō)	It.	44·39 N	7·31 E
99	Salvador (Bahia)	(säl-vä-dōr′) (bä-ē′ä)	Braz.	12·59 S	38·27 W
77	Salvador L.		La.	29·45 N	90·20 W
94	Salvador Pt.		Ba. Is.	24·30 N	77·45 W
90	Salvatierra	(säl-vä-tyĕr′rä)	Mex.	20·13 N	100·52 W
146	Salween R.	(săl-wēn′)	Bur.	26·46 N	98·19 E
133	Sal'yany		Sov. Un.	39·40 N	49·10 E
120	Salzburg	(sälts′bōōrgh)	Aus.	47·48 N	13·04 E
120	Salzburg (State)		Aus.	47·30 N	13·18 E
120	Salzwedel	(sälts-vā′dĕl)	Ger.	52·51 N	11·10 E
168	Samālūt	(sä-mä-lōōt′)	U. A. R. (Nile In.)	28·17 N	30·43 E
95	Samaná	(sä-mä-nä′)	Dom. Rep.	19·15 N	69·25 W
95	Samana, Cabo (C.)	(kà′bô)	Dom. Rep.	19·20 N	69·00 W
95	Samana or Atwood Cay (I.)		Ba. Is.	23·05 N	73·45 W
155	Samar (I.)	(sä′mär)	Phil.	11·30 N	126·07 E
133	Samara (R.)		Sov. Un.	52·50 N	50·35 E
129	Samara (R.)	(sà-mä′rà)	Sov. Un.	48·47 N	35·30 E
155	Samarai	(sä-mä-rä′ē)	Pap.	10·45 S	150·49 E
134	Samarkand	(sà-màr-känt′)	Sov. Un.	39·42 N	67·00 E
142	Sambalpur	(sŭm′bŭl-pōōr)	India	21·30 N	84·05 E
142	Sāmbhar (R.)		India	27·00 N	74·58 E
121	Sambor	(säm′bôr)	Sov. Un.	49·31 N	23·12 E
101	Samborombón, Bahia (B.)	(bä-ē′ä-säm-bô-rôm-bô′n)	Arg. (Buenos Aires In.)	35·57 S	57·05 W
101	Samborombón (R.)		Arg. (Buenos Aires In.)	35·20 S	57·52 W
117	Sambre (R.)	(säN′br′)	Bel.	50·20 N	4·15 E
65	Sammamish, L.	(sà-măm′ĭsh)	Wash. (Seattle In.)	47·35 N	122·02 W
65	Sammamish (R.)		Wash. (Seattle In.)	47·43 N	122·08 W
127	Samokov	(sä′mô-kôf)	Bul.	42·20 N	23·33 E
125	Samora Correia	(sä-mô′rä-kôr-rĕ′yä)	Port. (Lisbon In.)	38·55 N	8·52 W
134	Samorovo	(sà-mà-rô′vô)	Sov. Un.	60·47 N	69·13 E
127	Sámos (I.)	(să′mŏs)	Grc.	37·53 N	26·35 E
127	Samothráki (I.)		Grc.	40·23 N	25·10 E
155	Sampaloc Pt.	(säm-pä′lŏk)	Phil. (Manila In.)	14·43 N	119·56 E
118	Samsø (I.)	(säm′sû)	Den.	55·49 N	10·47 E
78	Samson	(săm′sŭn)	Ala.	31·06 N	86·02 W
152	Samsu	(säm′sōō′)	Kor.	41·12 N	128·00 E
133	Samsun	(sàm′sōōn′)	Tur.	41·20 N	36·05 E
133	Samtredia	(sàm′trĕ-dê)	Sov. Un.	42·18 N	42·25 E
65	Samuel (I.)	(săm′ū-ĕl)	Can. (Vancouver In.)	48·50 N	123·10 W
133	Samur (R.)	(sà-mōōr′)	Sov. Un.	41·40 N	47·20 E
164	San	(sän)	Mali	13·37 N	4·45 W
144	San'a	(sän′ä)	Yemen	15·45 N	44·00 E
164	Sanaga R.	(sä-nä′gä)	Cam.	4·33 N	11·50 E
96	San Ambrosio, Isla de (I.)	(ē′s-lä-dĕ-sän äm-brō′zē-ō)	Chile	26·40 S	80·00 W
155	Sanana (I.)		Indon.	2·15 S	126·38 E
144	Sanandaj		Iran	36·44 N	46·43 E
68	San Andreas	(săn ăn′drē-ăs)	Calif.	38·10 N	120·42 W
65	San Andreas (L.)		Calif. (San Francisco In.)	37·36 N	122·26 W
98	San Andrés	(sän-än-drĕ′s)	Col. (In.)	6·57 N	75·41 W
91	San Andrés	(sän än-drās′)	Mex. (Mexico City In.)	19·15 N	99·10 W
91	San Andres, Laguna de (L.)		Mex.	22·40 N	97·50 W
62	San Andres, Mts.	(săn ăn′drē-ăs)	U. S.	33·00 N	106·40 W
	San Andrés, see Petén, Laguna de				
101	San Andrés de Giles	(sän-än-drĕ′s-dĕ-gē′lĕs)	Arg. (Buenos Aires In.)	34·26 S	59·28 W
93	San Andres I.		Col.	12·32 N	81·34 W
69	San Andres Mts.		N. Mex.	23·45 N	106·40 W
91	San Andrés Tuxtla	(sän-än-drā′s-tōōs′tlä)	Mex.	18·27 N	95·12 W
76	San Angelo	(săn ăn′jĕ-lō)	Tex.	31·28 N	100·22 W
126	San Antioco, I. di	(ē′sō-lä-dē-sän-än-tyō′kō)	It.	39·00 N	8·25 E
101	San Antonio	(sän-àn-tô′nyō)	Chile (Santiago In.)	33·34 S	71·36 W
98	San Antonio		Col. (In.)	2·57 N	75·06 W
98	San Antonio		Col. (In.)	3·55 N	75·38 W
155	San Antonio		Phil. (Manila In.)	14·57 N	120·05 E
74	San Antonio	(săn ăn-tō′nē-ō)	Tex. (San Antonio In.)	29·25 N	98·30 W
68	San Antonio (R.)		Calif.	36·00 N	121·13 W
94	San Antonio, Cabo (C.)	(kà′bô-sän-än-tô′nyō)	Cuba	21·55 N	84·55 W
125	San Antonio Abad	(sän än-tō′nyô ä-bädh′)	Sp.	38·59 N	1·17 E
77	San Antonio B.		Tex.	28·20 N	97·08 W
101	San Antonio de Areco	(dā ä-rä′kō)	Arg. (Buenos Aires In.)	34·16 S	59·30 W
95	San Antonio de las Vegas	(sän än-tô′nyō-dĕ-läs-vĕ′gäs)	Cuba (Havana In.)	22·07 N	82·16 W
95	San Antonio de los Baños	(dā lōs bän′yōs)	Cuba (Havana In.)	22·08 N	82·30 W
100	San Antonio de los Cobres	(dā lōs kō′brās)	Arg.	24·15 S	66·29 W
101	San Antônio de Pádua	(dĕ-pà′dwä)	Braz. (Rio de Janeiro In.)	21·32 S	42·09 W
99	San Antonio de Tamanaco	(sän-àn-tô-nyō-dĕ-tä-mä-nà′kô)	Ven. (In.)	9·42 N	66·03 W
100	San Antonio Oeste	(sän-än-tō′nyō ô-ĕs′tå)	Arg.	40·49 S	64·56 W
74	San Antonio Pk.	(săn ăn-tō′nĭ-ô)	Calif. (Los Angeles In.)	34·17 N	117·39 W
76	San Antonio R.		Tex.	29·00 N	97·58 W
92	Sanarate	(sä-nä-rä′tĕ)	Guat.	14·47 N	90·12 W
77	San Augustine	(săn ô′gŭs-tēn)	Tex.	31·33 N	94·08 W
76	San Bartolo		Mex.	24·43 N	103·12 W
91	San Bartolo	(săn bär-tō′lô)	Mex. (Mexico City In.)	19·36 N	99·43 W
126	San Bartolomeo	(bär-tô-lô-mā′ô)	It.	41·25 N	15·04 E
126	San Benedetto del Tronto	(bā′nå-dĕt′tō dĕl trōn′tô)	It.	42·58 N	13·54 E
77	San Benito	(săn bĕ-nē′tō)	Tex.	26·07 N	97·37 W
68	San Benito (R.)		Calif.	36·40 N	121·20 W
74	San Bernardino	(bûr-när-dē′nô)	Calif. (Los Angeles In.)	34·07 N	117·19 W
68	San Bernardino Mts.		Calif.	34·05 N	116·23 W
101	San Bernardo	(sän bĕr-när′dô)	Chile (Santiago In.)	33·35 S	70·42 W
90	San Blas	(sän bläs′)	Mex.	21·33 N	105·19 W
78	San Blas, C.		Fla.	29·38 N	85·38 W
93	San Blas, Cord. de (Mts.)	(kôr-dēl-yĕ′rä-dĕ)	Pan.	9·17 N	78·20 W
93	San Blas, Golfo de (G.)		Pan.	9·33 N	78·42 W
93	San Blas, Punta (Pt.)		Pan.	9·35 N	78·55 W
65	San Bruno	(săn brū-nô)	Calif. (San Francisco In.)	37·38 N	122·25 W
76	San Buenaventura	(bwā′nä-vĕn-tōō′rä)	Mex.	27·07 N	101·30 W
65	San Carlos	(săn kär′lōs)	Calif. (San Francisco In.)	37·30 N	122·15 W
100	San Carlos	(sän-kà′r-lŏs)	Chile	36·23 S	71·58 W
98	San Carlos		Col. (In.)	6·11 N	74·58 W
91	San Carlos	(sän kär′lōs)	Mex.	17·49 N	92·33 W
76	San Carlos		Mex.	24·36 N	98·52 W
93	San Carlos	(sän-kà′r-lôs)	Nic.	11·08 N	84·48 W
155	San Carlos		Phil. (Manila In.)	15·56 N	120·20 E
98	San Carlos		Ven.	9·36 N	68·35 W
100	San Carlos de Bariloche	(sän-kà′r lŏs-dĕ-bä-rē-lô′chĕ)	Arg.	41·15 S	71·26 W
69	San Carlos Ind. Res.	(săn kär′lōs)	Ariz.	33·27 N	110·15 W
69	San Carlos Res.		Ariz.	33·05 N	110·29 W
93	San Carlos R.		C. R.	10·36 N	84·18 W
99	San Casimiro	(kä-sē-mē′rô)	Ven. (In.)	10·01 N	67·02 W
126	San Cataldo	(kä-täl′dō)	It.	37·30 N	13·59 E
95	Sanchez	(sän′chĕz)	Dom. Rep.	19·15 N	69·40 W
90	Sanchez, Río de los (R.)	(rē′ō-dĕ-lôs)	Mex.	20·31 N	102·29 W
90	Sánchez Román (Tlaltenango)	(rô-mà′n) (tlä′l-tĕ-nän-gô)	Mex.	21·48 N	103·20 W
124	San Clemente	(sän klâ-mĕn′tå)	Sp.	39·25 N	2·24 W
68	San Clemente (I.)		Calif.	33·02 N	118·36 W
95	San Cristobal	(krēs-tô′bäl)	Dom. Rep.	18·25 N	70·05 W
92	San Cristóbal		Guat.	15·22 N	90·26 W
98	San Cristóbal		Ven.	7·43 N	72·15 W
98	San Cristobal (I.)		Ec.	1·05 S	89·15 W
159	San Cristobal (I.)		Sol. Is.	10·47 S	162·17 E
126	San Croce, C.	(krô′chä)	It.	37·15 N	15·18 E
94	Sancti Spíritus	(säŋk′tê spē′rê-tōōs)	Cuba	21·55 N	79·25 W
122	Sancy, Puy de (Pk.)	(pwē-dĕ-säN-sē′)	Fr.	45·30 N	2·53 E
65	Sand (I.)	(sănd)	Ore. (Portland In.)	46·16 N	124·01 W
71	Sand (I.)		Wis.	46·03 N	91·09 W
168	Sand (R.)		S. Afr. (Johannesburg & Pretoria In.)	28·09 S	26·46 E
153	Sanda	(sän′dä)	Jap. (Ōsaka In.)	34·53 N	135·14 E
154	Sandakan	(sån-dä′kån)	Mala.	5·51 N	118·03 E
116	Sanday (I.)	(sănd′ā)	Scot.	59·17 N	2·25 W
110	Sandbach	(sănd′băch)	Scot.	53·08 N	2·22 W
118	Sandefjord	(sän′dĕ-fyôr′)	Nor.	59·09 N	10·14 E
65	San de Fuca	(de-fōō-cä)	Wash. (Seattle In.)	48·14 N	122·44 W
76	Sanderson	(săn′dēr-sŭn)	Tex.	30·09 N	102·24 W
78	Sandersville	(săn′dērz-vĭl)	Ga.	32·57 N	82·50 W
167	Sandflats	(sănd-flăts)	S. Afr. (Natal In.)	33·26 S	25·57 E
118	Sandhammar, C.	(sänt′häm-mår)	Swe.	55·24 N	14·37 E
70	Sand Hills (Reg.)	(sănd)	Nebr.	41·57 N	101·29 W
84	Sand Hook	(sănd hŏŏk)	N. J. (New York In.)	40·29 N	74·05 W
110	Sandhurst	(sănd′hûrst)	Eng. (London In.)	51·20 N	0·48 W
68	San Diego	(săn dē-ā′gô)	Calif. (San Diego In.)	32·43 N	117·10 W
76	San Diego		Tex.	27·47 N	98·13 W
68	San Diego (R.)		Calif.	32·53 N	116·57 W
90	San Diego de la Unión	(sän dē-å′gô dā lä ōō-nyōn′)	Mex.	21·27 N	100·52 W
77	Sandies Cr.	(sănd′ēz)	Tex.	29·13 N	97·34 W
74	San Dimas	(săn dē′màs)	Calif. (Los Angeles In.)	34·07 N	117·49 W
90	San Dimas	(dē-mäs′)	Mex.	24·08 N	105·57 W
118	Sandnes	(sänd′nĕs)	Nor.	58·52 N	5·44 E
166	Sandoa	(sän-dō′ä)	Con. L.	9·39 S	23·00 E
121	Sandomierz	(sän-dô′myĕzh)	Pol.	50·39 N	21·45 E
126	San Donà di Piave	(sän dô-nà′ dē pyä′vĕ)	It.	45·38 N	12·34 E
146	Sandoway	(sän-dô-wī′)	Bur.	18·24 N	94·28 E
66	Sandpoint	(sănd point)	Idaho	48·17 N	116·34 W
101	Sandringham	(săn′drĭng-ăm)	Austl. (Melbourne In.)	37·57 S	145·01 E
126	Sandrio	(sä′n-dryô)	It.	46·11 N	9·53 E
73	Sand Springs	(sănd sprĭnz)	Okla.	36·08 N	96·06 W

ng-sing; ŋ-baŋk; N-nasalized n; nŏd; cŏmmit; ōld; ôbey; ôrder; fōōd; fŏŏt; ou-out; s-soft; sh-dish; th-thin; pūre; ûnite; ûrn; stŭd; circŭs; ü-as "y" in study; ′-indeterminate vowel.

262 Sandstone–San Miguel de Allende PRONOUNCING INDEX

Page	Name Pronunciation Region	Lat. °′	Long. °′
158	Sandstone (sănd′stōn) . . . . . . Austl.	28·00 s	119·25 E
71	Sandstone . . . . Minn.	46·08 N	92·53 W
84	Sandusky (săn-dŭs′kē) Ala. (Birmingham In.)	33·32 N	86·50 W
80	Sandusky . . . . Mich.	43·25 N	82·50 W
80	Sandusky . . . . Ohio	41·25 N	82·45 W
80	Sandusky (R.) . . . . Ohio	41·10 N	83·20 W
80	Sandwich (sănd′wĭch) . . . . Ill.	42·35 N	88·35 W
65	Sandy (sănd′ē) . Ore. (Portland In.)	45·24 N	122·16 W
74	Sandy . . Utah (Salt Lake City In.)	40·36 N	111·53 W
83	Sandy (I.) . . . . Can.	51·13 N	58·10 W
65	Sandy (R.) . . . . Ore. (Portland In.)	45·28 N	122·17 W
160	Sandy C . . . . Austl.	24·25 s	153·10 E
67	Sandy Cr . . . . Mont.	48·20 N	110·08 W
67	Sandy Cr . . . . Wyo.	42·08 N	109·35 W
84	Sandy Hook (hŏŏk) Conn. (New York In.)	41·25 N	73·17 W
85	Sandy L . . . . Can. (Edmonton In.)	53·46 N	113·58 W
77	Sandy Point . . . . Tex. (In.)	29·22 N	95·27 W
65	Sandy Pt . . Wash. (Vancouver In.)	48·48 N	122·42 W
84	Sandy Springs (sprinz) Ga. (Atlanta In.)	33·55 N	84·23 W
101	San Enrique (sän-ĕn-rē′kĕ) Arg. (Buenos Aires In.)	35·47 s	60·22 W
100	San Estanislao (ĕs-tä-nēs-lȧ′ô) Par.	24·38 s	56·20 W
92	San Esteban (ĕs-tĕ′bän) . . . . Hond.	15·13 N	85·53 W
155	San Fabian (fä-byä′n) Phil. (Manila In.)	16·14 N	120·28 E
101	San Felipe (fȧ-lē′pȧ) Chile (Santiago In.)	32·45 s	70·43 W
90	San Felipe (fĕ-lē′pĕ) . . . . Mex.	21·29 N	101·13 W
90	San Felipe . . . . Mex.	22·21 N	105·26 W
98	San Felipe (fĕ-lē′pĕ) . . . . Ven.	10·13 N	68·45 W
	San Felipe, see Jalapa de Diaz		
68	San Felipe, Cr. (sän fē-lēp′ȧ) Calif.	33·10 N	116·03 W
94	San Felipe, Cayos de (Is.) (kä′yōs-dĕ-sän-fĕ-lē′pĕ) . Cuba	22·00 N	83·30 W
125	San Felíu de Guixols (sän fȧ-lē′ōō dȧ gē-hôls) . Sp.	41·45 N	3·01 E
96	San Felix, Isla de (I.) (ē′s-lä-dĕ-sän fȧ-lēks′) . Chile	26·20 s	80·10 W
124	San Fernanda (fĕr-nä′n-dä) . . . . Sp.	36·28 N	6·13 W
100	San Fernando (fĕr-nȧ′n-dô) Arg. (In.)	34·11 s	58·34 W
74	San Fernando (fĕr-nän′dô) Calif. (Los Angeles In.)	34·17 N	118·27 W
101	San Fernando . Chile (Santiago In.)	36·36 s	70·58 W
76	San Fernando (fĕr-nän′dô) . . Mex.	24·52 N	98·10 W
155	San Fernando (sän fĕr-nä′n-dō) Phil. (Manila In.)	16·38 N	120·19 E
98	San Fernando de Apure (sän-fĕr-nä′n-dō-dĕ-ä-pōō′rȧ) Ven.	7·46 N	67·29 W
98	San Fernando de Atabapo (dĕ-ä-tä-bä′pô) . Ven.	3·58 N	67·41 W
125	San Fernando de Henares (dĕ-ā-nä′rȧs) . Sp. (Madrid In.)	40·23 N	3·31 W
76	San Fernando R. (sän fĕr-nän′dô) . Mex.	25·07 N	98·25 W
118	Sånfjället (Mtn.) . . . . Swe.	62·19 N	13·30 E
85	Sanford (săn′fērd) Can. (Winnipeg In.)	49·41 N	97·27 W
79	Sanford (săn′fôrd) . . . . . . Fla. (In.)	28·46 N	80·18 W
82	Sanford (săn′fērd) . . . . Maine	43·26 N	70·47 W
79	Sanford . . . . N. C.	35·26 N	79·10 W
100	San Francisco (săn frăn-sĭs′kô) Arg.	31·23 s	62·09 W
65	San Francisco Calif. (San Francisco In.)	37·45 N	122·26 W
92	San Francisco . . . . Sal.	13·48 N	88·11 W
	San Francisco, see Ixhuatán		
69	San Francisco (R.) . . . . . . N. Mex.	33·35 N	108·55 W
65	San Francisco B. (săn frăn-sĭs′kô) Calif. (San Francisco In.)	37·45 N	122·21 W
88	San Francisco del Oro (dĕl ō′rō) Mex.	27·00 N	106·37 W
90	San Francisco del Rincón (dĕl rēn-kōn′) . Mex.	21·01 N	101·51 W
99	San Francisco de Macaira (dĕ-mä-kī′rä) . Ven. (In.)	9·58 N	66·17 W
95	San Francisco de Macoris (dā-mä-kō′rēs) . Dom. Rep.	19·20 N	70·15 W
95	San Francisco de Paula (dā pou′lȧ) . Cuba (Havana In.)	23·04 N	82·18 W
62	San Francisco Mts . . . . U. S.	35·30 N	112·35 W
74	San Gabriel (săn gä-brē-ĕl′) (gā′brē-ĕl) Calif. (Los Angeles In.)	34·06 N	118·06 W
90	San Gabriel Chilac (sän-gä-brē-ĕl-chē-läk′) . Mex.	18·19 N	97·22 W
74	San Gabriel Mts. Calif. (Los Angeles In.)	34·17 N	118·03 W
74	San Gabriel Res. Calif. (Los Angeles In.)	34·14 N	117·48 W
74	San Gabriel R. Calif. (Los Angeles In.)	33·47 N	118·06 W
73	Sangamon (R.) (săn′gȧ-mŭn) . . Ill.	40·08 N	90·08 W
165	Sanga R. (sän-gä) . . . . Afr.	3·41 N	16·12 E
68	Sanger (săng′ēr) . . . . Calif.	36·42 N	119·33 W
120	Sangerhausen (säng′ĕr-hou-zĕn) Ger.	51·28 N	11·17 E
155	Sangihe (I.) (säŋ′gē-ē) . . . . . Indon.	3·30 N	125·30 E
98	San Gil (sän-Kē′l) . . . . Col.	6·32 N	73·13 W
126	San Giovanni in Fiore (sän jô-vän′nē ēn fyō′rȧ) . It.	39·15 N	16·40 E
125	San Giuseppe Vesuviano (sän-zhēōō-sĕ′p-pĕ-vĕ-sōō-vyȧ′nô) It. (Naples In.)	40·36 N	14·31 E
152	Sangju (säng′jōō′) . . . . Kor.	36·20 N	128·07 E
124	Sangonera (R.) (säŋ-gô-nā′rä) . Sp.	37·43 N	1·58 W
74	San Gorgonio Mt. (săn gôr-gō′nī-ō) Calif. (Los Angeles In.)	34·06 N	116·50 W
62	Sangre De Cristo, Mts. (săng′ēr-de-krēs-tō) . U. S.	37·45 N	105·50 W
65	San Gregoria (sän grĕ-gôr′ā) Calif. (San Francisco In.)	37·20 N	122·23 W
126	Sangro (R.) (säŋ′grô) . . . . It.	41·38 N	13·56 E
124	Sangüesa (sän-gwĕ′sä) . . . . Sp.	42·36 N	1·15 W
148	Sanho (sän′hŏ) . . . . China	39·59 N	117·06 E
79	Sanibel I. (săn′ĭ-bĕl) . . . . Fla. (In.)	26·26 N	82·15 W
	San Ildefonso, see Villa Alta		
155	San Ildefonso, C. (sän-ēl-dĕ-fôn-sô) Phil. (Manila In.)	16·03 N	122·10 E
124	San Ildefonso o la Granja (ō lä grän′khä) . Sp.	40·54 N	4·02 W
100	San Isidro (ē-sē′drô) . . . . Arg. (In.)	34·13 s	58·31 W
93	San Isidro . . . . C. R.	9·24 N	83·43 W
74	San Jacinto (săn jȧ-sĭn′tô) Calif. (Los Angeles In.)	33·47 N	116·57 W
155	San Jacinto (sän hä-sēn′tô) Phil. (Manila In.)	12·33 N	123·43 E
77	San Jacinto (R.), West Fork . Tex.	30·35 N	95·37 W
74	San Jacinto R. (săn jȧ-sĭn′tô) Calif. (Los Angeles In.)	33·44 N	117·14 W
77	San Jacinto R . . . . Tex.	30·25 N	95·05 W
101	San Javier (sän-hȧ-vē-ĕr) Chile (Santiago In.)	35·35 s	71·43 W
91	San Jerónimo Mex. (Mexico City In.)	19·31 N	98·46 W
90	San Jerónimo de Juárez (hȧ-rō′nē-mô dȧ hwä′rȧz) . Mex.	17·08 N	100·30 W
99	San Joaquin (hô-ä-kē′n) Ven. (In.)	10·16 N	67·47 W
68	San Joaquin (R.) (săn hwä-kēn′) Calif.	37·10 N	120·51 W
68	San Joaquin Valley . . . . Calif.	36·45 N	120·30 W
100	San Jorge, Golfo (G.) (gôl-fô-săn-Kô′r-Kĕ) . Arg.	46·15 s	66·45 W
99	San José (săn hô-sā′) . . . . Bol.	17·54 s	60·42 W
65	San Jose (săn hô-zā′) Calif. (San Francisco In.)	37·20 N	121·54 W
93	San Jose (sän hô-sā′) . . . . C. R.	9·57 N	84·05 W
92	San José . . . . Guat.	13·56 N	90·49 W
155	San Jose . . . . . . Phil. (Manila In.)	12·22 N	121·04 E
155	San Jose (sān-Kô-sĕ′) Phil. (Manila In.)	13·52 N	121·07 E
155	San José . . . . Phil. (Manila In.)	14·49 N	120·47 E
155	San Jose . . . . Phil. (Manila In.)	15·49 N	120·57 E
101	San José (hô-sĕ′) Ur. (Buenos Aires In.)	34·20 s	56·43 W
101	San José (Dept.) Ur. (Buenos Aires In.)	34·17 s	56·23 W
88	San Jose (I.) (Kô-sĕ′) . . . . Mex.	25·00 N	110·35 W
69	San Jose (R.) (săn hô-zā′) N. Mex.	35·15 N	108·10 W
93	San Jose, Isla de (I.) (ē′s-lä-dĕ-sän hô-sā′) . Pan.	8·17 N	79·20 W
101	San José (R.) (sän-hô-sĕ′) Ur. (Buenos Aires In.)	34·05 s	56·47 W
100	San José de Feliciano (dȧ lä ĕs-kē′nȧ) . Arg.	30·26 s	58·44 W
99	San José de Gauribe (sän-hô-sĕ′dĕ-gȧōō-rē′bĕ) Ven. (In.)	9·51 N	65·49 W
95	San Jose de las Lajas (sän-Kô-sĕ′dĕ-läs-lȧ′käs) Cuba (Havana In.)	22·13 N	82·10 W
90	San José Iturbide (ē-tōōr-bē′dĕ) Mex.	21·00 N	100·24 W
100	San Juan (hwän′) . . . . Arg.	31·36 s	68·29 W
98	San Juan (hŏŏȧ′n) . . . . . . Col. (In.)	3·23 N	73·48 W
95	San Juan (sän hwän′) . . Dom. Rep.	18·50 N	71·15 W
155	San Juan (sän-Kōōȧ′n) Phil. (Manila In.)	14·30 N	121·14 E
155	San Juan . . . . . . Phil. (Manila In.)	16·41 N	120·20 E
89	San Juan (sän hwän′) P. R. (Puerto Rico In.)	18·30 N	66·10 W
	San Juan, see Guichicovi		
	San Juan, see Mazatlán		
100	San Juan (Prov.) . . . . Arg.	31·00 s	69·30 W
89	San Juan, Cabezas de (C.) P. R. (Puerto Rico In.)	18·29 N	65·30 W
94	San Juan, Pico (Pk.) (pē′kô-sän-kŏŏȧ′n) . Cuba	21·55 N	80·00 W
91	San Juan (R.) (sän-hōō-än′) . Mex.	18·10 N	95·23 W
76	San Juan, Rio (R.) (rē′ō-sän hwän) . Mex.	25·35 N	99·15 W
69	San Juan (R.) . . . . Utah	37·10 N	110·30 W
100	San Juan Bautista (sän hwän′ bou-tēs′tä) . Par.	26·48 s	57·09 W
90	San Juan Capistrano (sän-hōō-än′ kä-pēs-trä′nô) Mex.	22·41 N	104·07 W
68	San Juan Cr. (săn hwän′) . . . Calif.	35·24 N	120·12 W
76	San Juan de Guadalupe (sän hwan dȧ gwä-dhä-lōō′pȧ) Mex.	24·37 N	102·43 W
93	San Juan del Norte (Greytown) (dĕl nôr-tȧ) (grā′toun) . Nic.	10·55 N	83·44 W
93	San Juan del Norte Bahia de (B.) (bä-ē′ä-dĕ-sän hwän dĕl nôr′tȧ) Nic.	11·12 N	83·40 W
90	San Juan de los Lagos (sän-hōō-än′dȧ los lä′gôs) . Mex.	21·15 N	102·18 W
90	San Juan de los Lagos (R.) (dȧ lōs lä′gôs) . Mex.	21·13 N	102·12 W
99	San Juan de los Morros (dĕ-lôs-mô′r-rôs) . Ven. (In.)	9·54 N	67·22 W
90	San Juan del Rio (dĕl rē′ô) . . Mex.	20·21 N	99·59 W
76	San Juan del Rio (săn hwän del rē′ô) . Mex.	24·47 N	104·29 W
92	San Juan del Sur (dĕl sōōr) . . . Nic.	11·15 N	85·53 W
76	San Juan de Sabinas (dĕ-sä-bē′näs) . Mex.	27·56 N	101·23 W
91	San Juan Evangelista (sän-hōō-ä′n-ȧ-väŋ-kȧ-lēs′ta′) Mex.	17·57 N	95·08 W
74	San Juan Hot Springs (săn hwän′) . Calif. (Los Angeles In.)	33·37 N	117·28 W
65	San Juan I . . . . Wash. (Seattle In.)	48·28 N	123·08 W
65	San Juan Is. (săn hwän) Can. (Vancouver In.)	48·49 N	123·14 W
91	San Juan Ixtenco (ēx-tĕ′n-kô) Mex.	19·14 N	97·52 W
94	San Juan Martinez (sän kōō ȧ′n-mär-tē′nĕz) . Cuba	22·15 N	83·50 W
69	San Juan Mts. (san hwán′) . . Colo.	37·50 N	107·30 W
93	San Juan R . . . . Nic.	10·58 N	84·18 W
100	San Julián (sän hōō-lyȧ′n) . . . Arg.	49·17 s	68·02 W
100	San Justo (hōōs′tô) . . . . . Arg. (In.)	34·25 s	58·33 W
164	Sankarani R. (sän′kä-rä′nē) Mali-Gui.	11·15 N	8·01 W
120	Sankt Gallen . . . . Switz.	47·25 N	9·22 E
166	Sankuru (R.) (sän-kōō′rōō) Con. L.	4·12 s	22·08 E
88	San Lazaro, C. (sän-lȧ′zä-rō) Mex.	24·58 N	113·30 W
65	San Leandro (săn lē-ăn′drô) Calif. (San Francisco In.)	37·43 N	122·10 W
101	San Lorenzo (săn lô-rĕn′zô) Arg. (Buenos Aires In.)	32·46 s	60·44 W
65	San Lorenzo (săn lô-rĕn′zô) Calif. (San Francisco In.)	37·41 N	122·08 W
92	San Lorenzo (sän lô-rĕn′zô) . Hond.	13·24 N	87·24 W
125	San Lorenzo de El Escorial (sän lô-rĕn′tho dĕl ĕs-kō-rē-äl′) Sp. (Madrid In.)	40·36 N	4·09 W
124	Sanlúcar (sän-lōō′kär) . . . . Sp.	36·46 N	6·21 W
98	San Lucas (lōō′kȧs) . . . . Bol.	20·12 s	65·06 W
	San Lucas, see Ojitlán		
88	San Lucas, C . . . . Mex.	22·45 N	109·45 W
100	San Luis (lōō-ēs′) . . . . Arg.	33·16 s	66·15 W
98	San Luis (lŏŏē′s) . . . . Col. (In.)	6·03 N	74·57 W
95	San Luis . . . . Cuba	20·15 N	75·50 W
92	San Luis . . . . Guat.	14·38 N	89·42 W
100	San Luis (Prov.) . . . . Arg.	32·45 s	66·00 W
88	San Luis (State) . . . . Mex.	22·45 N	101·45 W
90	San Luis de la Paz (dȧ lä päz′) Mex.	21·17 N	100·32 W
76	San Luis del Cordero (dĕl kôr-dā′rô) . Mex.	25·25 N	104·20 W
68	San Luis Obispo (ô-bĭs′pō) . . Calif.	35·18 N	120·40 W
68	San Luis Obispo, B . . . . Calif.	35·07 N	121·05 W
90	San Luis Potosi (pō-tô-sē′) . . Mex.	22·08 N	100·58 W
68	San Luis Rey (R.) (rā′ē) . . . . Calif.	133·22 N	117·06 W
69	San Manuel (sän măn′ū-ĕl) . . Ariz.	32·30 N	110·45 W
69	San Marcial (săn mär-shäl′) N. Mex.	33·40 N	107·00 W
126	San Marco (sän mär′kô) . . . . It.	41·53 N	15·50 E
92	San Marcos (mär′kôs) . . . . . . Guat.	14·57 N	91·49 W
90	San Marcos . . . . Mex.	16·46 N	99·23 W
76	San Marcos (săn mär′kôs) . . . Tex.	29·53 N	97·56 W
92	San Marcos de Colón (sän-mȧ′r-kōs-dĕ-kô-lô′n) . Hond.	13·17 N	86·50 W
76	San Marcos R . . . . Tex.	30·08 N	98·15 W
92	San Maria (Vol.) (sän-mä-rē′ä) Guat.	14·45 N	91·33 W
127	San Maria di Léuca, C. (dē-lĕ′ōō-kä) . It.	39·47 N	18·20 E
155	San Mariano (săn mä-rē-ä′nô) Phil. (Manila In.)	17·00 N	121·58 E
74	San Marino (săn mēr-ē′nô) Calif. (Los Angeles In.)	34·07 N	118·06 W
126	San Marino (sän mä-rē′nô) . . . Eur.	43·52 N	12·38 E
126	San Marino . . . . San Marino	44·55 N	12·26 E
98	San Martín (sän mär-tē′n) Col. (In.)	3·42 N	73·44 W
91	San Martín (mär-tē′n) . . . . . . Mex.	18·36 N	95·11 W
100	San Martín (L.) . . . . Arg.-Chile	48·15 s	72·30 W
90	San Martin Chalchicuautla (sän mär-tē′n chäl-chē-kwä-ōō′ tlä) . Mex.	21·22 N	98·39 W
125	San Martin de la Vega (sän mär ten′ dȧ lä vā′gä) Sp. (Madrid In.)	40·12 N	3·34 W
90	San Martín Hidalgo (sän mär-tē′n-ē-däl′gô) . Mex.	20·27 N	103·55 W
65	San Mateo (săn mä-tā′ô) Calif. (San Francisco In.)	37·34 N	122·20 W
91	San Mateo (Etlatongo) (sän-mä-tĕ′ô) (ĕ-tlä-tô′n-gō) Mex.	16·59 N	97·04 W
125	San Mateo (sän mä-tā′ō) . . . . . . Sp.	40·26 N	0·09 E
99	San Mateo (sän mȧ-tĕ′ô) Ven. (In.)	9·45 N	64·34 W
100	San Matías, Golfo (G.) (sän mä-tē′äs) . Arg	41·30 s	63·45 W
151	Sanmen Wan (B.) . . . . China	29·00 N	122·15 E
100	San Miguel (sän mē-gĕ′l) Arg. (In.)	34·17 s	58·43 W
91	San Miguel (sän mē-gȧl′) . . . . Mex.	18·18 N	97·09 W
93	San Miguel . . . . Pan.	8·26 N	78·55 W
155	San Miguel (sän mē-gĕ′l) Phil. (Manila In.)	15·09 N	120·56 E
92	San Miguel (sän mē-gȧl′) . . . . . Sal.	13·28 N	88·11 W
99	San Miguel (sän mē-gĕ′l) Ven. (In.)	9·56 N	64·58 W
	San Miguel, see Sola de Vega		
	San Miguel, see Talea de Castro		
93	San Miguel, Bahia (B.) (bä-ē′ä-sän mē-gȧl′) . Pan.	8·17 N	78·26 W
68	San Miguel (I.) . . . . Calif.	34·03 N	120·23 W
98	San Miguel (R.) (sän-mē-gĕl′) Bol.	13·34 s	63·58 W
69	San Miguel (R.) (săn mē-gĕl′) Colo.	38·15 N	108·40 W
91	San Miguel (R.) (sän mē-gȧl′) Mex.	15·27 N	92·00 W
92	San Miguel (Vol.) . . . . Sal.	13·27 N	88·17 W
155	San Miguel B . . Phil. (Manila In.)	13·55 N	123·12 E
90	San Miguel de Allende (dȧ ä-lyĕn′dȧ) . Mex.	20·54 N	100·44 W

ăt; finăl; rāte; senȧte; ärm; ȧsk; sofȧ; fâre; ch-choose; dh-as th in other; bē; ēvent; bĕt; recĕnt; cratēr; g-go; gh-guttural g; bĭt; ĭ-short neutral; rīde; K-guttural k as ch in German ich;

PRONOUNCING INDEX San Miguel el Alto–Santiago del Estero 263

Page	Name Pronunciation Region	Lat. °′	Long. °′
90	San Miguel el Alto (ĕl äl′tō) . Mex.	21·03 N	102·26 W
168	Sanmur, Wadi (Val.) U. A. R. (Nile In.)	28·48 N	31·12 E
155	San Narcisco . . . Phil. (Manila In.)	15·01 N	120·05 E
155	San Narciso (sän när-sē′sō) Phil. (Manila In.)	13·34 N	123·33 E
101	San Nicolás (sän nē-kō-lä′s) Arg. (Buenos Aires In.)	33·20 S	60·14 W
155	San Nicolas (nē-kō-läs′) Phil. (Manila In.)	16·05 N	120·45 E
68	San Nicolas (I.) (săn nĭ′kō-là) Calif.	33·14 N	119·10 W
90	San Nicolás (R.) . . . . Mex.	19·40 N	105·08 W
121	Sanok (sä′nôk) . . . . Pol.	49·31 N	22·13 E
65	San Pablo (săn păb′lō) Calif. (San Francisco In.)	37·58 N	122·21 W
155	San Pablo (sän-pä-blō) Phil. (Manila In.)	14·05 N	121·20 E
155	San Pablo . . . . . . Phil. (Manila In.)	17·29 N	121·49 E
99	San Pablo (sän-pä′blō) . Ven. (In.)	9·46 N	65·04 W
65	San Pablo B. (săn păb′lō) Calif (San Francisco In.)	38·04 N	122·25 W
65	San Pablo Res. Calif. (San Francisco In.)	37·55 N	122·12 W
93	San Pablo R. (sän päb′lō) . . . . Pan.	8·12 N	81·12 W
155	San Pascual (päs-kwäl′) Phil. (Manila In.)	13·08 N	122·59 E
100	San Pedro (sän pā′drō) . . . . . . Arg.	24·15 S	64·51 W
101	San Pedro . Arg. (Buenos Aires In.)	33·41 S	59·42 W
74	San Pedro (săn pē′drō) Calif. (Los Angeles In.)	33·44 N	118·17 W
101	San Pedro (săn pē′drō) Chile (Santiago In.)	33·54 S	71·27 W
91	San Pedro (sän pā′drō) . . . . . . Mex.	18·38 N	92·25 W
100	San Pedro (sän-pĕ′drō) . . . . . . Par.	24·13 S	57·00 W
92	San Pedro (sän pā′drō) . . . . Sal.	13·49 N	88·58 W
	San Pedro, see Amusgos		
	San Pedro, see Pochutla		
69	San Pedro (R.) . . . . Ariz.	32·48 N	110·37 W
94	San Pedro (R.) (sän-pĕ′drō) . Cuba	21·05 N	78·15 W
91	San Pedro, Rio de (R.) (rē′ō-dē-sän-pĕ′drō) . Mex.	18·23 N	92·13 W
90	San Pedro, Río de (R.) . . . . . . Mex.	21·51 N	102·24 W
90	San Pedro (R.) (sän pā′drō) . Mex.	22·08 N	104·59 W
74	San Pedro B. (săn pē′drō) Calif. (Los Angeles In.)	33·42 N	118·12 W
76	San Pedro de las Colonias (dĕ-läs-kō-lō′nyäs) . Mex.	25·47 N	102·58 W
95	San Pedro de Macorís (sän-pĕ′drō-dā mä-kō-rēs′) Dom. Rep.	18·30 N	69·30 W
90	San Pedro Lagunillas (sän pā′drō lä-gōō-nēl′yäs) . Mex.	21·12 N	104·47 W
92	San Pedro R. (sän pā′drō) Guat. (Yucatan In.)	17·11 N	90·23 W
76	San Pedro R. . . . . Mex.	27·56 N	105·50 W
92	San Pedro Sula (sän pā′drō sōō′lä) Hond.	15·29 N	88·01 W
	San Pedro y San Pablo, see Teposcolula		
126	San Pietro, I. di (ē′sō-lä-dē-sän pyā′trō) . It.	39·09 N	8·15 E
65	San Quentin (săn kwĕn-tēn′) Calif. (San Francisco In.)	37·57 N	122·29 W
155	San Quintin (sän kēn-tēn′) Phil. (Manila In.)	15·59 N	120·47 E
100	San Rafael (sän rä-fä-äl′) . . . . Arg.	34 30 S	68·13 W
65	San Rafael (săn rà-fĕl) Calif. (San Francisco In.)	37·58 N	122·31 W
98	San Rafael (sän-rä-fä-ĕ′l) Col. (In.)	6·18 N	75·02 W
69	San Rafael (R.) (săn rà-fĕl′) Utah	39·05 N	110·50 W
95	San Rafael, Cabo (C.) (kä′bō) Dom. Rep.	19·00 N	68·50 W
65	San Ramon (săn rà-mōn′) Calif. (San Francisco In.)	37·47 N	122·59 W
93	San Ramōn . . . . C. R.	10·07 N	84·30 W
126	San Remo (sän rā′mō) . . . . It.	43·48 N	7·46 E
121	San R. . . . . Pol.	50·33 N	22·12 E
89	San Roman, C. (sän-rō-mä′n) Ven.	12·00 N	69·45 W
98	San Roque (sän-rō′kĕ) . . Col. (In.)	6·29 N	75·00 W
124	San Roque . . . . Sp.	36·13 N	5·23 W
76	San Saba (săn sä′bȧ) . . . . Tex.	31·12 N	98·43 W
76	San Saba R. . . . . Tex.	30·58 N	99·12 W
92	San Salvador (sän säl-vä-dōr′) . Sal.	13·45 N	89·11 W
98	San Salvador (I.) . . . . Ec.	0·14 S	90·50 W
95	San Salvador (Watling) (I.) (săn săl′vȧ-dôr) . Ba. Is.	24·05 N	74·30 W
101	San Salvador (R.) (sän-säl-vä-dō′r) Ur. (Buenos Aires In.)	33·42 S	58·04 W
164	Sansanné-Mango (sän-sä-nā′ mäɴ′gō) . Togo	10·31 N	0·23 E
164	San Sebastian (sän sȧ-bäs-tyän′) Can. Is.	28·09 N	17·11 W
124	San Sebastian . . . . Sp.	43·19 N	1·59 W
99	San Sebastián (sän-sĕ-bäs-tyá′n) Ven. (In.)	9·58 N	67·11 W
125	San Sebastián de los Reyes (sän sä-bäs-tyän′dā lōs rā′yĕs) Sp. (Madrid In.)	40·33 N	3·38 W
126	San Severo (sän sĕ-vâ′rō) . . . . . . It.	41·43 N	15·24 E
150	San She (Mtn.) . . . . China	33·00 N	103·50 E
147	San Shui . . . . China	23·14 N	112·51 E
69	San Simon Cr. (săn sī-mōn′) Ariz.	32·45 N	109·30 W
74	Santa Ana (săn′tȧ ăn′ȧ) Calif. (Los Angeles In.)	33·45 N	117·52 W
90	Santa Ana (sän′tä ä′nä) . . . . . Mex.	19·18 N	98·10 W
92	Santa Ana . . . . Sal.	14·02 N	89·35 W
74	Santa Ana Mts. Calif. (Los Angeles In.)	33·44 N	117·36 W
74	Santa Ana R. Calif. (Los Angeles In.)	33·41 N	117·57 W
76	Santa Anna . . . . Tex.	31·44 N	99·18 W
100	Santa Anna, Cochilha de (Mts.) (kō-chē′lä dĕ sän-tä-nä) . Braz.	30·30 S	56·30 W
125	Sant' Antimo . . . . . It. (Naples In.)	40·40 N	14·11 E
101	Santa Bárbara (sän-tä-bà′r-bä-rä) Braz. (Rio de Janeiro In.)	19·57 S	43·25 W
68	Santa Barbara (săn′tȧ bär′bȧ-rȧ) Calif.	34·26 N	119·43 W
92	Santa Barbara (sän′tä bär′bä-rä) Hond.	14·52 N	88·20 W
76	Santa Barbara . . . . Mex.	26·48 N	105·50 W
68	Santa Barbara (I.) . . . . Calif.	33·30 N	113·01 W
68	Santa Barbara (Is.) . . . . Calif.	33·45 N	119·46 W
68	Santa Barbara Chan. . . . . Calif.	34·15 N	120·00 W
101	Santa Branca (sän-tä-brä′ɴ-kä) Braz. (Rio de Janeiro In.)	23·25 S	45·52 W
68	Santa Catalina (I.) . . . . Calif.	33·29 N	118·37 W
93	Santa Catalina, Cerro de (Mt.) (sĕ′r-rō-dĕ-sän-tä-kä-tä-lē′nä) Pan.	8·39 N	81·36 W
68	Santa Catalina, G. of (săn′tȧ kă-tȧ-lē′nȧ) . Calif.	33·00 N	117·58 W
76	Santa Catarina (sän′tä kä-tä-rē′nä) Mex.	25·41 N	100·27 W
	Sta. Catarina, see Loxicha		
	Sta. Catarina, see Yosonotú		
100	Santa Catarina (State) (sän-tä-kä-tä-rē′nä) . Braz.	27·15 S	50·30 W
90	Santa Catarina (R.) . . . . Mex.	16·31 N	98·39 W
65	Santa Clara (săn′tȧ klâr′ȧ) Calif. (San Francisco In.)	37·21 N	121·56 W
94	Santa Clara (sän′tä klä′rä) . . Cuba	22·25 N	80·00 W
76	Santa Clara . . . . Mex.	24·29 N	103·22 W
100	Santa Clara . . . . Ur.	32·46 S	54·51 W
68	Santa Clara (R.) (săn′tȧ klă′rȧ) Calif.	34·22 N	118·53 W
92	Santa Clara, (Vol.) . . . . Nic.	12·44 N	87·00 W
94	Santa Clara, Bahía de (B.) (bä-ē′ä-dĕ-sän-tä-klä-rä) . . Cuba	23·05 N	80·50 W
88	Santa Clara, Sierra, (Mts.) (sē-ĕ′r-rä-sän′tä klä′rä) . Mex.	27·30 N	113·50 W
98	Santa Cruz (sän′tä krōōz′) . . . Bol.	17·45 S	63·03 W
100	Santa Cruz (sän-tä-krōō′s) . . Braz.	29·43 S	52·15 W
100	Santa Cruz . . . . Braz. (In.)	22·55 S	43·41 W
68	Santa Cruz (săn′tȧ krōōz′) . . Calif.	36·59 N	122·02 W
101	Santa Cruz . . . Chile (Santiago In.)	34·38 S	71·21 W
92	Santa Cruz . . . . C. R.	10·16 N	85·37 W
76	Santa Cruz . . . . Mex.	25·50 N	105·25 W
155	Santa Cruz . . . . . Phil. (Manila In.)	13·28 N	122·02 E
155	Santa Cruz . . . . . Phil. (Manila In.)	14·17 N	121·25 E
155	Santa Cruz . . . . . Phil. (Manila In.)	15·46 N	119·53 E
155	Santa Cruz . . . . . Phil. (Manila In.)	17·06 N	120·27 E
100	Santa Cruz (Prov.) . . . . Arg.	48·00 S	70·00 W
68	Santa Cruz (I.) (săn′tȧ krōōz′) Calif.	34·05 N	119·55 W
98	Santa Cruz (I.) (sän-tä-krōō′z) . Ec.	0·38 S	90·20 W
69	Santa Cruz (R.) (săn′tȧ krōōz′) Ariz.	32·30 N	111·30 W
100	Santa Cruz (R.) (sän′tä krōōz′) Arg.	50·05 S	66·30 W
92	Santa Cruz Barillas (sän-tä-krōō′z-bä-rē′l-yäs) Guat.	15·47 N	91·22 W
	Santa Cruz Chico, see Pedro Antonio Santos		
94	Santa Cruz del Sur (sän-tä-krōō′s-dĕl-sōō′r) . Cuba	20·45 N	78·00 W
164	Santa Cruz de Tenerife (sän′tä krōōz dā tā-nā-rē′fā) Can. Is.	28·07 N	15·27 W
159	Santa Cruz Is. . . . . Sol. Is.	10·58 S	166·47 E
65	Santa Cruz Mts. (săn′tȧ krōōz′) Calif. (San Francisco In.)	37·30 N	122·19 W
95	Santa Domingo, Cay (I.) . . Ba. Is.	21·50 N	75·45 W
126	Sant'Eufemia, Golfo di (G.) (gôl-fō-dē-sän-tĕ′ōō-fĕ′myä) . . It.	38·53 N	15·53 E
124	Santa Eugenia de Ribeira (sän-tä-ĕōō-hĕ′nyä-dĕ-rē-bĕ′y-rä) Sp.	42·34 N	8·55 W
125	Santa Eulalia del Rio (sän′ta ä-ōō-lä′lē-ä dĕl rē′ō) . Sp.	38·58 N	1·29 E
100	Santa Fe (sän′tä fā′) . . . . Arg.	31·33 S	60·45 W
94	Santa Fe (sän-tä-fĕ′) . . . . Cuba	21·45 N	82·40 W
69	Santa Fe (săn′tȧ fā′) . . . . . N. Mex.	35·10 N	106·00 W
124	Santafé (sän′tä-fā′) . . . . Sp.	37·12 N	3·43 W
100	Santa Fe (Prov.) (sän′tä fā′) . Arg.	32·00 S	61·15 W
99	Santa Filomena (sän-tä-fē-lō-mĕ′nä) . Braz.	9·09 S	44·45 W
88	Santa Genoveva, (Mtn.) (sän-tä-hĕ-nō-vĕ′vä) . Mex.	23·30 N	110·00 W
151	Sant'ai . . . . China	31·02 N	105·02 E
99	Santa Inés (sän′tä ē-nĕ′s) Ven. (In.)	9·54 N	64·21 W
100	Santa Inés (I.) (sän′tä ē-näs′) Chile	53·45 S	74·15 W
164	Santa Isabel (ē-sä-bĕl′) Fernando Poo	3·43 N	8·42 E
159	Santa Isabel, (I.) . . . . Sol. Is.	7·57 S	159·28 E
94	Santa Lucia (sän′tä lōō-sē′ä) . Cuba	21·50 N	77·30 W
101	Santa Lucia (sän-tä-lōō-sē′ä) Ur. (Buenos Aires In.)	34·27 S	56·23 W
99	Santa Lucia . . . . Ven. (In.)	10·18 N	66·40 W
101	Santa Lucia (R.) (sän-tä-lōō-sē′ä) Ur. (Buenos Aires In.)	34·19 S	56·13 W
94	Santa Lucia B. (sän′tȧ lōō-sē′ȧ) Cuba	22·55 N	84·20 W
88	Santa Magarita (I.) (sän′tȧ mär-gȧ-rē′tȧ) . Mex.	24·15 N	112·00 W
100	Santa Maria (sän′tȧ mä-rē′ȧ) Braz.	29·40 S	28·45 W
68	Santa Maria (săn-tȧ mȧ-rē′ȧ) Calif.	34·57 N	120·28 W
126	Santa Maria (sän-tä mä-rē′ä) . . It.	41·05 N	14·15 E
155	Santa Maria (sän-tä-mä-rē′ä) Phil. (Manila In.)	14·48 N	120·57 E
	Santa Maria, see Huazolotitlán		
90	Santa Maria (R.) (sän′tä mä-rē′ä) . Mex.	21·33 N	100·17 W
95	Santa Maria, C. . . . . Ba. Is.	23·45 N	75·30 W
124	Santa Maria, Cabo de (C.) (kä′bō-dĕ-sän-tä-mä-rē′ä) . Port.	36·58 N	7·54 W
94	Santa Maria, Cayo (I.) (kä′yō-săn′tȧ mȧ-rē′ȧ) . Cuba	22·40 N	79·00 W
90	Santa María del Oro (sän′tä-mä-rē′ä-dĕl-ô-rō) . Mex.	21·21 N	104·35 W
90	Santa Maria de los Angeles (dĕ-lôs-ä′n-hĕ-lĕs) . Mex.	22·10 N	103·34 W
90	Santa María del Rio (sän′tä mä-rē′ä dĕl rē′ō) . Mex.	21·46 N	100·43 W
90	Santa Maria de Ocotán (sän′tä-mä-rē′ä-dĕ-ō-kō-tá′n) Mex.	22·56 N	104·30 W
164	Santa Maria I. (sän-tä-mä-rē′ä) Azores (In.)	37·09 N	26·02 W
101	Santa Maria Madalena (sän-tä-mà-rē′ä-mä-dä-lĕ-nä) Braz. (Rio de Janeiro In.)	22·00 S	42·00 W
98	Santa Marta (sän′tä mär′tä) . Col.	11·15 N	74·13 W
74	Santa Monica (săn′tȧ mŏn′ĭ-kȧ) Calif. (Los Angeles In.)	34·01 N	118·29 W
74	Santa Monica Mts. Calif. (Los Angeles In.)	34·08 N	118·38 W
100	Santana (R.) (sän-tä′nä) Braz. (In.)	22·33 S	43·37 W
98	Santander (sän-tän-dĕr′) Col. (In.)	3·00 N	76·25 W
124	Santander (sän-tän-dâr′) . . . . . . Sp.	43·27 N	3·50 W
125	Sant'Angelo Romano (sän-tä′n-gzhĕ-lō-rō-mä′nō) It. (Rome In.)	42·02 N	12·45 E
125	Sant' Antimo . . . . . It. (Naples In.)	40·40 N	14·11 E
125	Santañy (sän-tän′yē) . . . . Sp.	39·21 N	3·08 E
68	Santa Paula (săn′tȧ pô′lȧ) . . Calif.	34·24 N	119·05 W
99	Santarém (sän-tä-rĕɴ′) . . . . . . Braz.	2·28 S	54·37 W
124	Santarém . . . . Port.	39·18 N	8·48 W
94	Santaren Chan. (săn-tȧ-rĕn′) Ba. Is.	24·15 N	79·30 W
69	Santa Rita (săn′tȧ rē′tȧ) . N. Mex.	32·45 N	108·05 W
101	Santa Rita do Passo Quatro (sän-tä-rē′tä-dō-pä′sō-kwà′trō) Braz. (Rio de Janeiro In.)	21·43 S	47·27 W
101	Santa Rita do Sapucai (sä-pōō-kà′ē) Braz. (Rio de Janeiro In.)	22·15 S	45·41 W
100	Santa Rosa (sän-tä-rō-sä) . . . . Arg.	36·45 S	64·10 W
68	Santa Rosa (săn′tȧ rō′zȧ) . . . Calif.	38·27 N	122·42 W
98	Santa Rosa (sän-tä-rō-sä) Col. (In.)	6·38 N	75·26 W
98	Santa Rosa . . . . Ec.	3·29 S	78·55 W
92	Santa Rosa (sän′tä rō′sȧ) . . . Guat.	14·21 N	90·16 W
92	Santa Rosa . . . . Hond.	14·45 N	88·51 W
72	Santa Rosa (săn′tȧ rō′sȧ) N. Mex.	34·55 N	104·41 W
155	Santa Rosa (sän′tä rō′sä) Phil. (Manila In.)	14·18 N	121·07 E
99	Santa Rosa (sän-tä-rō-sä) Ven. (In.)	9·37 N	64·10 W
98	Santa Rosa de Cabal (sän-tä-rô-sä-dĕ-kä-bä′l) Col. (In.)	4·53 N	75·38 W
101	Santa Rosa de Viterbo (sän-tä-rô-sä-dĕ-vē-tĕr′-bō) Braz. (Rio de Janeiro In.)	21·30 S	47·21 W
68	Santa Rosa Ind. Res. (săn′tȧ rō′zȧ) . Calif.	33·28 N	116·50 W
88	Santa Rosalía (sän′tä rô-zä′lē-ä) Mex.	27·13 N	112·15 W
	Santa Rosalia, see Ciudad Camargo		
66	Santa Rosa Mts. (săn′tȧ rō′zȧ) Nev.	41·33 N	117·50 W
74	Santa Susana (săn′tȧ sōō-ză′nȧ) Calif. (Los Angeles In.)	34·16 N	118·42 W
	Santa Tecla, see Nueva San Salvador		
101	Santa Teresa (sän-tä-tĕ-rĕ′sä) Arg. (Buenos Aires In.)	33·27 S	60·47 W
99	Santa Teresa . . . . Ven. (In.)	10·14 N	66·40 W
100	Santa Vitória do Palmar (sän-tä-vē-tô′ryä-dō-päl-mär) Braz.	33·30 S	53·16 W
68	Santa Ynez (R.) (săn′tȧ ē-nĕz′) Calif.	34·40 N	120·20 W
68	Santa Ysabel Ind. Res. (săn′tȧ ĭ-zȧ-bĕl′) . Calif.	33·05 N	116·46 W
68	Santee (săn-tē′) Calif. (San Diego In.)	32·50 N	116·58 W
79	Santee (R.) . . . . S. C.	33·27 N	80·02 W
100	Santiago (sän-tyà′gō) . . . . Braz.	29·05 S	54·46 W
101	Santiago (sän-tē-ä′gō) Chile (Santiago In.)	33·26 S	70·40 W
93	Santiago . . . . Pan.	8·07 N	80·58 W
155	Santiago (sän-tyä′gō) Phil. (Manila In.)	16·42 N	121·33 E
124	Santiago . . . . Sp.	42·52 N	8·32 W
	Santiago, see Tejupan		
	Santiago, see Zacatepec		
101	Santiago (Prov.) (sän-tyà′gō) Chile (Santiago In.)	33·28 S	70·55 W
90	Santiago, Rio Grande de (R.) (rē′ō-grä′n-dĕ-dĕ-sän-tyà′gō) Mex.	21·15 N	104·05 W
155	Santiago (I.) . . . Phil. (Manila In.)	16·29 N	120·03 E
95	Santiago de los Cabelleros (sän-tyà′gō-dā lōs kä-bä-yä′rōs) Dom. Rep.	19·30 N	70·45 W
95	Santiago de Cuba (sän-tyà′gō-dā kōō′bä) . . . . Cuba	20·00 N	75·50 W
95	Santiago de las Vegas (sän-tyà′gō-dĕ-läs-vĕ′gäs) Cuba (Havana In.)	22·13 N	82·23 W
100	Santiago del Estero (sän-tē-ä′gō-dĕl ĕs-tā′rō) . Arg.	27·50 S	64·14 W

Page	Name Pronunciation Region	Lat. °'	Long. °'
100	Santiago del Estero (Prov.) (sän-tē-ä'gō-děl ěs-tā'rò).Arg.	27·15 s	63·30 w
76	Santiago Mts. (sän-tē-ä'gō)..Tex.	30·00 N	103·30 w
74	Santiago Res. Calif. (Los Angeles In.)	33·47 N	117·42 w
95	Santiago Rodriguez (sän-tyä'gō-rō-drē'gěz) Dom. Rep.	19·30 N	71·25 w
91	Santiago Tuxtla (sän-tyá'gō-tōō'x-tlä).Mex.	18·28 N	95·18 w
76	Santiaguillo, Laguna de (L.) (lä-ōō'nä-dě-sän-tē-ä-gēl'yō) Mex.	24·51 N	104·43 w
66	Santiam R. (sǎn'tyǎm)......Ore.	44·42 N	122·26 w
124	Santisteban del Puerto (sän'tě stä-bän'děl pwěr'tò).Sp.	38·15 N	3·12 w
148	Santo (sän'tŏ)............China	32·49 N	119·39 E
99	Santo Amaro (sä-mä'rŏō) Braz.	12·32 s	38·33 w
101	Santo Amaro de Campos (sän-tô-ä-mä'rŏ-dě-kám'pôs) Braz. (Rio de Janeiro In.)	22·01 s	41·05 w
101	Santo André (sän-tô-än-drě') Braz. (Rio de Janeiro In.)	23·40 s	46·31 w
100	Santo Angelo (sän-tô-ä'n-zhě-lò) Braz.	28·16 s	53·59 w
164	Santo Antào I. (sän-tô-än-tä-ò) C. V. Is. (In.)	17·20 N	26·05 w
166	Santo Antonio (sän'tŏō än-tō'ně-ŏō).Ang.	6·10 s	12·25 E
101	Santo Antônio do Monte (sän-tô-än-tō'nyô-dô-môn'tě) Braz. (Rio de Janeiro In.)	20·06 s	45·18 w
94	Santo Domingo (sän'tô-dōmǐn'gò) Cuba	22·35 N	80·20 w
92	Santo Domingo (sän-tô-dô-mě'n-gō).Nic.	12·15 N	84·56 w
155	Santo Domingo.Phil. (Manila In.)	17·39 N	120·24 E
95	Santo Domingo (sän'tô dô-mǐn'gô) Dom. Rep.	18·30 N	69·55 w
	Santo Domingo, see Zanatepec		
124	Santo Domingo de la Calzada (dä lä käl-thä'dä).Sp.	42·27 N	2·55 w
124	Santoña (sän-tō'nyä).......Sp.	43·25 N	3·27 w
101	Santos (sän'tozh) Braz. (Rio de Janeiro In.)	23·58 s	46·20 w
101	Santos Dumont (sän'tôs-dōō-mô'nt) Braz. (Rio de Janeiro In.)	21·28 s	43·33 w
155	Santo Thomas (sän-tô-tō-mä's) Phil. (Manila In.)	14·07 N	121·09 E
155	Santo Tomas (Mtn.) Phil. (Manila In.)	16·23 N	120·32 E
100	Santo Tomé (sän-tô-tô-mě')..Arg.	28·32 s	56·04 w
153	Sanuki (sä'nōō-kè) Jap. (Tōkyō In.)	35·16 N	139·53 E
101	San Urbano (sän-ōōr-bä'nò) Arg. (Buenos Aires In.)	33·39 s	61·28 w
100	San Valentin, M. (Mtn.) (sän-vä-lěn-tē'n) Chile	46·41 s	73·30 w
122	Sanvic (sàn-vēk')...........Fr.	49·34 N	0·08 E
101	San Vicente (sän-vē-sěn'tě) Arg. (Buenos Aires In.)	35·00 s	58·26 w
101	San Vicente..Chile (Santiago In.)	34·25 s	71·06 w
92	San Vicente (sän vê-sěn'tä)...Sal.	13·41 N	88·43 w
124	San Vicente de Alcántara (sän vê-thěn'tä dä äl-kán'tä-rä) Sp.	39·24 N	7·08 w
126	San Vito (sän vē'tô)........It.	45·53 N	12·52 E
151	Sanya...................China	18·10 N	109·32 E
166	Sanyati (R.) (sän-yä'tě)..S. Rh.	17·08 s	29·11 E
149	Sanyüanli.....China (Canton In.)	23·11 N	113·16 E
68	San Ysidro (sän ysǐ-drō') Calif. (San Diego In.)	32·33 N	117·02 w
101	São Bernardo do Campo (soun-běr-när'dô-dô-kä'm-pô) Braz. (Rio de Janeiro In.)	23·44 s	46·33 w
100	São Borja (soun-bôr-zhä)...Braz.	28·44 s	55·59 w
101	São Carlos (soun kär'lŏzh) Braz. (Rio de Janeiro In.)	22·02 s	47·54 w
99	São Cristovão (soun-krěs-tō-voun) Braz.	11·04 s	37·11 w
101	São Fidélis (soun-fē-dě'lēs) Braz. (Rio de Janeiro In.)	21·41 s	41·45 w
99	São Francisco (soun frän-sēsh'kòō) Braz.	15·59 s	44·42 w
99	São Francisco, Rio (R.) (rě'ō-sän-frän-sě's-kō).Braz.	8·56 s	40·20 w
100	São Francisco do Sul (soun frän-sēsh'kŏō-dô-sōō'l) Braz.	26·15 s	48·42 w
100	São Gabriel (soun'gä-brě-ěl') Braz.	30·28 s	54·11 w
101	São Geraldo (soun-zhě-rä'l-dô) Braz. (Rio de Janeiro In.)	21·01 s	42·49 w
100	São Gonçalo (soun'gŏn-gä'lŏō) Braz. (In.)	22·55 s	43·04 w
101	São Gonçalo do Sapucaí (soun-gŏn-sä'lŏ-dô-sä-pōō-kī') Braz. (Rio de Janeiro In.)	21·55 s	45·34 w
101	São João da Barra (soun-zhŏun-dä-bä'rä) Braz. (Rio de Janeiro In.)	21·40 s	41·03 w
101	São João da Boa Vista (soun-zhŏun-dä-bôä-vě's-tä) Braz. (Rio de Janeiro In.)	21·58 s	46·45 w
101	São João del Rei (soun zhŏun'děl-rä) Braz. (Rio de Janeiro In.)	21·08 s	44·14 w
100	São João de Meriti (soun-zhŏun-dě-mě-rē-tě) Braz. (In.)	22·47 s	43·22 w
99	São João do Araguaia (soun zhŏ-ŏun'dô-ä-rä-gwä'yä) Braz.	5·29 s	48·44 w
125	São João dos Lampas (soun' zhô-oun' dŏzh län-päzh') Port. (Lisboa In.)	38·52 N	9·24 w
101	São João Nepomuceno (soun-zhŏun-ně-pô-mōō-sě-nō) Braz. (Rio de Janeiro In.)	21·33 s	43·00 w
164	São Jorge I. (soun zhôr' zhě) Azores (In.)	38·28 N	27·34 w
101	São José do Rio Pardo (soun-zhô-sě'dô-rě'ō-pà'r-dō) Braz. (Rio de Janeiro In.)	21·36 s	46·50 w
99	São José do Rio Prêto (soun zhô-zě'dô-rě'ō-prě-tō) Braz.	20·57 s	49·12 w
101	São José dos Campos (soun zhô-zä'dŏzh kän pŏzh') Braz.	23·12 s	45·53 w
100	São Leopoldo (soun-lě-ô-pôl'dô) Braz.	29·46 s	51·09 w
99	São Luis (Maranhão) (soun-lōōē's-mä-rän-youn').Braz.	2·31 s	43·14 w
101	São Luis do Paraitinga (soun-lōōē's-dô-pä-rä-ē-tě'n-gä) Braz.	23·15 s	44·18 w
99	São Mateus (soun mä-tä'ōōzh) Braz.	18·44 s	39·45 w
101	São Miguel Arcanjo (soun-mē-gě'l-är-kän-zhō) Braz.	23·54 s	47·59 w
164	São Miguel I.......Azores (In.)	37·59 N	26·38 w
95	Saona (I.) (sä-ō'nä)..Dom. Rep.	18·10 N	68·55 w
122	Saône (R.) (sōn)...........Fr.	46·27 N	4·58 E
164	São Nicolau (soun' ně-kô-loun') C. V. Is. (In.)	16·19 N	25·19 w
101	São Paulo (soun' pou'lŏō) Braz. (Rio de Janeiro In.)	23·34 s	46·38 w
99	São Paulo (State) (soun pou'lŏō) Braz.	21·45 s	50·47 w
98	São Paulo de Olivença (soun'pou'lŏōdä ô-lē-věn'sá) Braz.	3·32 s	68·46 w
101	São Pedro (soun-pě'drò) Braz. (Rio de Janeiro In.)	22·34 s	47·54 w
101	São Pedro de Aldeia (soun-pě'drô-dě-äl-dě'yä) Braz. (Rio de Janeiro In.)	22·50 s	42·04 w
99	São Raimundo Nonato (soun' rī-mŏō'n-do nô-nä'tŏō) Braz.	9·09 s	42·32 w
101	São Roque (soun' rō'kě) Braz. (Rio de Janeiro In.)	23·32 s	47·08 w
99	São Roque, Cabo de (C) (kä'bo-dě-soun' rō'kě).Braz.	5·06 s	35·11 w
166	São Salvador (soun säl-vä-dôr) Ang.	6·30 s	14·10 E
101	São Sebastião (soun sä-bäs-tê-oun') Braz. (Rio de Janeiro In.)	23·48 s	45·25 w
101	São Sebastião, Ilha de (I.) (ēl'yá dä soun' sä-bäs-tê-oun') Braz. (Rio de Janeiro In.)	23·52 s	45·22 w
101	São Sebastião do Paraíso (soun-sě-bäs-tê-oun-dô-pä-rä-ē'sô). Braz. (Rio de Janeiro In.)	20·54 s	46·58 w
101	São Simão (soun-sē-moun) Braz. (Rio de Janeiro In.)	21·30 s	47·33 w
164	São Tiago I. (soun tê-ä'gŏō) C. V. Is. (In.)	15·09 N	24·45 w
164	São Tomé (soun tô-mä')....Afr.	0·16 N	6·44 E
101	São Tomé, Cabo de (C.) (kä'bō-dě-soun-tô-mě') Braz. (Rio de Janeiro In.)	22·00 s	40·00 w
164	São Tomé, Ilhade (I.) (ě'lä-dě).Afr.	0·41 N	6·01 E
114	Saoura, Oued (soun).....Alg.	29·39 N	1·42 w
124	São Vinente, Cabo de (C.) (kä'bō-dě-sän-vê-sě'n-tě).Port.	37·03 N	9·31 w
101	São Vicente (soun ve-se'n-tě) Braz. (Rio de Janeiro In.)	23·57 s	46·25 w
164	Sao Vincente I. (soun vê-sěn'tä) C. V. Is. (In.)	16·51 N	24·35 w
164	Sapele (sä-pā'lā)........Nig.	5·57 N	5·22 E
128	Sapozhok (sä-pô-zhôk')..Sov. Un.	53·58 N	40·44 E
152	Sapporo (säp-pô'rō)......Jap.	43·02 N	141·29 E
136	Sapronovo (säp-rô'nô-vô) Sov. Un. (Moscow In.)	55·13 N	38·25 E
101	Sapucaí (R.) (sä-pōō-kä-ē') Braz. (Rio de Janeiro In.)	21·07 s	45·53 w
101	Sapucaia (sä-pōō-kä'yä) Braz. (Rio de Janeiro In.)	22·01 s	42·54 w
101	Sapucaí Mirim (R.) (sä-pōō-kä-ē'mē-rěn) Braz. (Rio de Janeiro In.)	21·06 s	47·03 w
73	Sapulpa (sá-pŭl'pá).........Okla.	36·01 N	96·05 w
101	Saquarema (sä-kwä-rě-mä) Braz. (Rio de Janeiro In.)	22·56 s	42·32 w
65	Sara (sä'rä)..Wash. (Portland In.)	45·45 N	122·42 w
127	Sara, Bahr (R.) (bär) Chad-Cen. Afr. Rep.	8·19 N	17·44 E
127	Sarajevo (sä-rä-yěv'ô) (sä-rä'ya-vô).Yugo.	43·15 N	18·26 E
136	Sarana (sä-rä'nä) Sov. Un. (Urals In.)	56·31 N	57·44 E
81	Saranac Lake.........N. Y.	44·20 N	74·05 w
81	Saranac L. (săr'ä-năk)......N. Y.	44·15 N	74·20 w
100	Sarandí (sä-rän'dě).....Arg. (In.)	34·26 s	58·21 w
101	Sarandí Grande (sä-rän'dē-grän'dě) Ur. (Buenos Aires In.)	33·42 N	56·21 w
142	Sarangpur................India	23·39 N	76·32 E
132	Saransk (sá-ränsk')....Sov. Un.	54·10 N	45·10 E
136	Sarany (sä-rä'nǐ) Sov. Un. (Urals In.)	58·33 N	58·48 E
132	Sarapul (sä-rä'pŏōl')....Sov. Un.	56·28 N	53·50 E
79	Sarasota (săr-á-sōtá)....Fla. (In.)	27·27 N	82·30 w
77	Saratoga (săr-ä-tō'gä).....Tex.	30·17 N	94·31 w
65	Saratoga......Wash. (Seattle In.)	48·04 N	122·29 w
65	Saratoga Pass. Wash. (Seattle In.)	48·09 N	122·33 w
81	Saratoga Springs (sprǐngz')..N. Y.	43·05 N	74·50 w
133	Saratov (sä rä'tôf).......Sov. Un.	51·30 N	45·00 E
151	Saravane...............Laos	15·48 N	106·40 E
154	Sarawak (Reg.) (sä-rä'wäk).Asia	2·30 N	112·45 E
121	Sárbogárd (shär'bō-gärd)..Hung.	46·53 N	18·38 E
85	Sarcee Ind. Res. (sär'sě) Can. (Calgary In.)	50·58 N	114·23 w
164	Sardalas................Libya	25·59 N	10·33 E
126	Sardinia (I.) (sär-dǐn'ǐá)....It.	40·08 N	9·05 E
78	Sardis (sär'dǐs)..........Miss.	34·26 N	89·55 w
70	Sargent (sär'jěnt).......Nebr.	41·40 N	99·38 w
133	Sarikamis...............Tur.	40·30 N	42·40 E
125	Sariñena (sä-rěn-yě'nä)......Sp.	41·46 N	0·11 w
150	Sariwŏn (sä're-wŭn').....Korea	38·40 N	125·45 E
122	Sark (I.) (särk)......Chan. Is.	49·28 N	2·22 w
127	Şarkoy (shär'kû-ê).......Tur.	40·39 N	27·07 E
122	Sarlat (sär-lä')...........Fr.	44·52 N	1·13 E
100	Sarmiento, Monte (Mt.) (mô'n-tě-sär-myěn'tō).Chile	54·28 s	70·40 w
80	Sarnia (sär'ně-á).........Can.	43·00 N	82·25 w
125	Sarno (sä'r-nō)...It. (Naples In.)	40·35 N	14·38 E
121	Sarny (sär'ně).........Sov. Un.	51·17 N	26·39 E
127	Saronikós Kólpos (G.)......Grc.	37·51 N	23·30 E
127	Saros Körfezi (G.) (sä'rôs)...Tur.	40·30 N	26·20 E
121	Sárospatak (shä'rôsh-pô'tôk) Hung.	48·19 N	21·35 E
127	Šar Planina (Mts.) (shär plä'ně-na).Yugo.	42·07 N	21·54 E
118	Sarpsborg (särps'bôrg).....Nor.	59·17 N	11·07 E
123	Sarrebourg (sär-bōōr').....Fr.	48·44 N	7·02 E
123	Sarreguemines (sär-gě-mēn').Fr.	49·06 N	7·05 E
124	Sarria (sär'ě-ä)...........Sp.	42·14 N	7·17 w
92	Sarstun R. (särs-tōō'n)...Guat.	15·50 N	89·26 w
126	Sartène (sär-těn')........Fr.	41·36 N	8·59 E
122	Sarthe (R.) (särt)..........Fr.	47·44 N	0·32 w
	Sartor, see Store Sotra		
120	Sárvár (shär'vär).......Hung.	47·14 N	16·55 E
133	Sarych, Mys (C.) (mǐs sä-rēch') Sov. Un.	44·25 N	33·00 E
134	Sary Ishikotrau, Peski (des.) (sä'rě ē' shěk-ō'trou).Sov. Un.	46·12 N	75·30 E
134	Sarysu (R.) (sä'rě-sōō)....Sov. Un.	47·47 N	69·14 E
142	Sasaram (sŭs-ŭ-räm')......India	25·00 N	84·00 E
153	Sasayama (sä-sä-yä'mä)....Jap.	35·05 N	135·14 E
153	Sasebo (sä'sä-bō)........Jap.	33·12 N	129·43 E
	Saseno, see Sazan		
120	Sašice (sä'shǐ-tse).......Czech.	49·14 N	13·31 E
86	Saskatchewan (Prov.)......Can.	54·46 N	107·40 w
86	Saskatchewan (R.) (săs-kăch'ě-wän).Can.	53·30 N	103·41 w
86	Saskatoon (săs-ká-tōōn')..Can.	52·11 N	106·42 w
119	Saslauka (säs-lä'û-kà)...Sov. Un.	57·22 N	22·34 E
168	Sasolburg S. Afr. (Johannesburg & Pretoria In.)	26·52 s	27·47 E
132	Sasovo (säs'ô-vô).......Sov. Un.	54·20 N	42·00 E
74	Saspamco (säs-päm'cō) Tex. (San Antonio In.)	29·13 N	98·18 w
164	Sassandra R. (säs-sän'drä) Ivory Coast	6·23 N	6·52 w
126	Sassari (säs'sä-rě)..........It.	40·44 N	8·33 E
120	Sassnitz (säs'něts).........Ger.	54·31 N	13·37 E
164	Satadougou (sä-tä-dōō-gōō')..Mali	12·31 N	11·26 w
118	Säter (sě'tēr)............Swe.	60·21 N	15·50 E
79	Satilla (R.) (sä-tǐl'á)........Ga.	31·15 N	82·13 w
136	Satka (sät'ká) Sov. Un. (Urals In.)	55·03 N	59·02 E
121	Sátoraljaujhely (shä'tô-rô-lyô-ōō'yěl').Hung.	48·24 N	21·40 E
121	Satu-Mare (sä-tōō-mä'rě)..Rom.	47·50 N	22·53 E
65	Saturna (sä-tûr'nä) Can. (Vancouver In.)	48·48 N	123·12 w
65	Saturna (I.).Can. (Vancouver In.)	48·47 N	123·03 w
118	Saude (sou'dě)............Nor.	59·40 N	6·21 E
112	Saudhárkrokur............Ice.	65·41 N	19·38 w
138	Saudi Arabia (sä-ōō'dǐ ä-rä'bǐ-á) Asia	22·40 N	46·00 E
111	Sauerlach (zou'ěr-läk) Ger. (Munich In.)	47·58 N	11·39 E
80	Saugatuck (sô'gá-tŭk)....Mich.	42·40 N	86·10 w
80	Saugeen Pen. (sô'gěn).....Can.	44·55 N	81·20 w
80	Saugeer (R.) (sô'gěr)......Can.	44·20 N	81·20 w
81	Saugerties (sô'gěr-tēz)....N. Y.	42·05 N	73·55 w
142	Saugor (sä-gûr') (sä-gōr')..India	23·55 N	78·45 E
83	Saugus (sô'gŭs).Mass. (Boston In.)	42·28 N	71·01 w
71	Sauk (R.) (sôk)..........Minn.	45·30 N	94·45 w
71	Sauk Centre............Minn.	45·43 N	94·58 w
71	Sauk City.............Wis.	43·16 N	89·45 w
71	Sauk Rapids (răp'ǐd)....Minn.	45·35 N	94·08 w
	Saulai, see Shyaulyay		
82	Sault-au-Mouton.......Can.	48·34 N	69·20 w
74	Sault Ste. Marie (sōō sänt má-rē') Mich. (Sault Ste. Marie In.)	46·29 N	84·21 w
95	Saumatre, Etang (L.)......Hai.	18·40 N	72·10 w
159	Saunders, C. (sôrn'děrs).N. Z. (In.)	45·55 s	170·50 E
85	Saunders L. (sän'děrs) Can. (Edmonton In.)	53·18 N	113·25 w
65	Sausalito (sô-sá-lē'tô) Calif. (San Francisco In.)	37·51 N	122·29 w
122	Sausset-les-Pins Fr. (Marseille In.)	43·20 N	5·08 E
65	Sauvie I. (sô'vē) Ore. (Portland In.)	45·43 N	123·49 w
127	Sava (R.) (sä'vä)........Yugo.	44·50 N	19·07 E
84	Savage (sä'věj) Md. (Baltimore In.)	39·07 N	76·49 w
74	Savage Minn. (Minneapolis, St. Paul In.)	44·47 N	93·20 w
133	Savalan (Mtn.)..........Iran	38·20 N	48·00 E
164	Savalou (sä'vä-lōō)....Dahomey	7·58 N	2·00 E
71	Savanna (sá-vän'á)........Ill.	42·05 N	90·09 w
79	Savannah (sá-văn'á)........Ga.	32·04 N	81·07 w
73	Savannah................Mo.	39·58 N	94·49 w
73	Savannah................Tenn.	35·13 N	88·14 w
79	Savannah (R.).......Ga.-S. C.	33·11 N	81·51 w

ăt; fĭnăl; rāte; senâte; ärm; àsk; sofá; fâre; ch-choose; dh-as th in other; bē; ěvent; bět; recĕnt; cratĕr; g-go; gh-guttural g; bĭt; ɪ-short neutral; rīde; ĸ-guttural k as ch in German ich;

PRONOUNCING INDEX Savanna la Mar–Sepik 265

Page	Name Pronunciation Region	Lat. °′	Long. °′
94	Savanna la Mar (sȧ-văn′ȧ lȧ mär′) Jam.	18·10 N	78·10 W
120	Sávava R. Czech.	49·36 N	15·24 E
164	Savé (sȧ-vā′) Dahomey	8·09 N	2·30 E
122	Save (R.) Fr.	43·32 N	0·50 E
166	Save, Rio (R.) (rē′ō-sä′vě) Moz.	21·28 S	34·14 E
123	Saverne (sȧ-věrn′) Fr.	48·40 N	7·22 E
126	Savigliano (sä-vēl-yä′nō) It.	44·38 N	7·42 E
126	Savona (sä-vō′nä) It.	44·19 N	8·28 E
119	Savonlinna (sȧ′vôn-lēn′nȧ) Fin.	61·53 N	28·49 E
129	Savran′ (säv-rän′) Sov. Un.	48·07 N	30·09 E
154	Savu Sea (sä′vōō) Indon.	9·15 S	122·15 E
154	Sawahlunto Indon.	0·37 S	100·50 E
154	Sawankhalok Thai.	17·16 N	99·48 E
165	Sawda, Jabal as (Mts.) Libya	28·14 N	13·46 E
114	Sawfjjin, Wadi (R.) Libya	31·18 N	13·16 E
168	Sawhāj U. A. R. (Nile In.)	26·34 N	31·40 E
165	Sawknah Libya	29·04 N	15·53 E
154	Sawu (I.) Indon.	10·15 S	122·00 E
65	Sawyer (L.) (sô′yẽr) Wash. (Seattle In.)	47·20 N	122·02 W
164	Say (sä′ē) Niger	13·09 N	2·16 E
134	Sayan Khrebet (Mts.) (sŭ-yän′) Sov. Un.	51·30 N	90·00 E
139	Sayda (Sidon) (sä′ê-dȧ) (sī′dŏn) Leb. (Palestine In.)	33·34 N	35·23 E
74	Sayers (sā′ẽrs) Tex. (San Antonio In.)	29·22 N	98·18 W
144	Sayhūt Aden	15·23 N	51·28 E
72	Sayre (sā′ẽr) Okla.	35·19 N	99·40 W
81	Sayre Pa.	41·55 N	76·30 W
84	Sayreton (sā′ẽr-tŭn) Ala. (Birmingham In.)	33·34 N	86·51 W
84	Sayreville (sâr′vĭl) N. J. (New York In.)	40·28 N	74·21 W
146	Sayr Usa Mong.	44·51 N	107·00 E
91	Sayula (sä-yōō′lä) Mex.	17·51 N	94·56 W
90	Sayula Mex.	19·50 N	101·33 W
90	Sayula, Luguna de (L.) (lȧ-gŏŏ′nä-dě) Mex.	20·00 N	103·33 W
144	Say′ūn Aden	16·00 N	48·59 E
81	Sayville (sā′vĭl) N. Y.	40·45 N	73·10 W
127	Sazan (Saseno) (I.) Alb.	40·30 N	19·17 E
136	Sazhino (sáz-hē′nô) Sov. Un. (Urals In.)	56·20 N	58·15 E
118	Scäffle Swe.	59·10 N	12·55 E
138	Scandinavian Pen. Eur.	62·00 N	14·00 E
74	Scanlon (skăn′lŏn) Minn. (Duluth In.)	46·27 N	92·26 W
65	Scappoose (skă-pōōs′) Ore. (Portland In.)	45·46 N	122·53 W
65	Scappoose (R.) Ore. (Portland In.)	45·47 N	122·57 W
85	Scarborough (skär′bẽr-ô) Can. (Toronto In.)	43·45 N	79·12 W
116	Scarborough (skär′bŭr-ô) Eng.	54·16 N	0·19 W
85	Scarborough Junction Can. (Toronto In.)	43·43 N	79·15 W
84	Scarsdale (skärz′dāl) N. Y. (New York In.)	41·01 N	73·47 W
165	Sceui Ghimira Eth.	7·13 N	35·49 E
111	Schaerbeek (skär′bāk) Bel. (Brussels In.)	50·53 N	4·23 E
120	Schaffhausen (shäf′hou-zĕn) Switz.	47·43 N	8·38 E
87	Schefferville Can.	54·52 N	67·01 W
117	Schelde, R. Bel.	51·04 N	3·55 E
81	Schenectady (skĕ-nĕk′tȧ-dê) N. Y.	42·50 N	73·55 W
111	Scheveningen Neth. (Amsterdam In.)	52·06 N	4·15 E
111	Schiedam Neth. (Amsterdam In.)	51·55 N	4·23 E
123	Schiltigheim (shēl′tegh-hīm) Fr.	48·48 N	7·47 E
126	Schio (skē′ô) It.	45·43 N	11·23 E
120	Schleswig (shlĕs′vēgh) Ger.	54·32 N	9·32 E
120	Schleswig-Holstein (State) (shlĕs′vēgh-hōl′shtīn) Ger.	54·40 N	9·10 E
120	Schmalkalden (shmäl′käl-dĕn) Ger.	50·41 N	10·25 E
75	Schneider (schnīd′ẽr) Ind. (Chicago In.)	41·12 N	87·26 W
71	Schofield (skō′fēld) Wis.	44·52 N	89·37 W
120	Schönebeck (shû′nĕ-bergh) Ger.	52·01 N	11·44 E
111	Schoonhoven Neth. (Amsterdam In.)	51·56 N	4·51 E
155	Schouten (I.) (skou′tĕn) W. Irian	0·45 S	136·40 E
120	Schramberg (shräm′bĕrgh) Ger.	48·14 N	8·24 E
81	Schroon (L.) (skrōōn) N. Y.	43·50 N	73·50 W
111	Schultzendorf (shōōl′tzĕn-dōrf) Ger. (Berlin In.)	52·21 N	13·35 E
70	Schuyler (skī′ler) Nebr.	41·28 N	97·05 W
81	Schuylkill (skōōl′kĭl) Pa.	40·35 N	76·10 W
120	Schwabach (shvä′bäk) Ger.	49·19 N	11·02 E
120	Schwäbische Alb (Mts.) (shvă′bē-shĕ älb) Ger.	48·11 N	9·09 E
120	Schwäbisch Gmünd (shvă′bēsh gmünd) Ger.	48·47 N	9·49 E
120	Schwäbisch Hall (häl) Ger.	49·08 N	9·44 E
120	Schwandorf (shvän′dôrf) Ger.	49·19 N	12·08 E
154	Schwaner Mts. (skvän′ẽr) Indon.	1·38 S	111·08 E
120	Schwarzwald (For.) (shvärts′ väld) Ger.	47·54 N	7·57 E
120	Schwaz Aus.	47·20 N	11·45 E
111	Schwechat (shvĕk′ät) Aus. (Vienna In.)	48·09 N	16·29 E
120	Schwedt (shvĕt) Ger.	53·04 N	14·17 E
120	Schweinfurt (shvīn′fŏŏrt) Ger.	50·03 N	10·14 E
123	Schwelm (shvĕlm) Ger. (Ruhr In.)	51·17 N	7·18 E
120	Schwenningen (shvĕn′ĭng-ĕn) Ger.	48·04 N	8 33 E
120	Schwerin (shvĕ-rēn′) Ger.	53·36 N	11·25 E
120	Schweriner See (L.) (shvĕ′rē-nĕr zā) Ger.	53·40 N	11·06 E
123	Schwerte (shvĕr′tĕ) Ger. (Ruhr In.)	51·26 N	7·34 E
111	Schwielow L. (shvē′lōv) Ger. (Berlin In.)	52·20 N	12·52 E
120	Schwyz (shvēts) Switz.	47·01 N	8·38 E

Page	Name Pronunciation Region	Lat. °′	Long. °′
126	Sciacca (shê-äk′kä) It.	37·30 N	13·09 E
116	Scilly (Is.) (sĭl′ê) Eng.	49·56 N	6·50 W
80	Scioto (R.) (sī-ō′tō) Ohio	39·10 N	82·55 W
83	Scituate (sĭt′ū-āt) Mass. (Boston In.)	42·12 N	70·45 W
67	Scobey (skō′bê) Mont.	48·48 N	105·29 W
65	Scoggin (skŏ′gĭn) Ore. (Portland In.)	45·28 N	123·14 W
85	Scotch R. (skŏch) Can. (Ottawa In.)	45·21 N	74·56 W
66	Scotia (skō′shȧ) Calif.	40·29 N	124·06 W
116	Scotland (skŏt′lȧnd) U. K.	57·05 N	5·10 W
70	Scotland S. D.	43·08 N	97·43 W
79	Scotland Neck (nĕk) N. C.	36·06 N	77·25 W
81	Scotstown (skŏts′toun) Can.	45·35 N	71·15 W
86	Scott, C. (skŏt) Can.	50·48 N	129·34 W
66	Scott, Mt. Ore.	42·55 N	122·00 W
65	Scott, Mt. Ore. (Portland In.)	45·27 N	122·33 W
74	Scott Air Force Base Ill. (St. Louis In.)	38·33 N	89·52 W
167	Scottburgh (skŏt′bŭr-ô) S. Afr. (Natal In.)	30·18 S	30·42 E
72	Scott City Kans.	38·28 N	100·54 W
84	Scottdale (skŏt′ dāl Ga. (Atlanta In.)	33·47 N	84·16 W
47	Scott Is. Ant.	67·24 S	179·55 W
47	Scott Ra. Ant.	68·00 S	55·00 E
70	Scottsbluff (skŏts′blŭf) Nebr.	41·52 N	103·40 W
70	Scotts Bluff Natl. Mon. Nebr.	41·45 N	103·47 W
78	Scottsboro (skŏts′bŭro) Ala.	34·40 N	86·03 W
80	Scottsburg (skŏts′ bûrg) Ind.	38·40 N	85·50 W
160	Scottsdale (skŏts′dāl) Austl.	41·12 S	147·37 E
78	Scottsville (skŏts′vĭl) Ky.	36·45 N	86·10 W
80	Scottville Mich.	44·00 N	86·20 W
81	Scranton (skrăn′tŭn) Pa.	41·45 N	75·45 W
81	Scugog (L.) (skū′gôg) Can.	44·05 N	78·55 W
110	Scunthorpe (skŭn′thôrp) Eng.	53·36 N	0·38 W
	Scutari, see Shkodër		
127	Scutari (R.) (skōō′tä-rê) Alb.	42·14 N	19·33 E
79	Sea, Is. (sē) Ga.-S. C.	31·21 N	81·05 W
65	Seabeck (sē′bĕck) Wash. (Seattle In.)	47·38 N	122·50 W
65	Seabold (sē′bōld) Wash. (Seattle In.)	47·42 N	122·33 W
84	Sea Bright (sē brīt) N. J. (New York In.)	40·22 N	73·58 W
77	Seabrook (sē′brŏŏk) Tex. (In.)	29·34 N	95·01 W
81	Seaford (sē′fẽrd) Del.	38·35 N	75·40 W
72	Seagraves (sē′grāvs) Tex.	32·51 N	102·38 W
86	Seal (R.) Can.	59·08 N	96·37 W
74	Seal Beach Calif. (Los Angeles In.)	33·44 N	118·06 W
95	Seal Cays (Is.) Turks & Caicos Is.	21·10 N	71·45 W
95	Seal Cays (Is.) Ba. Is.	22·40 N	75·55 W
166	Seal I. (sēl) S. Afr. (Cape Town In.)	34·07 S	18·36 E
77	Sealy (sē′lê) Tex.	29·46 N	96·10 W
166	Sea Point (sē point) S. Afr. (Cape Town In.)	33·55 S	18·23 E
73	Searcy (sûr′sê) Ark.	35·13 N	91·43 W
68	Searles (L.) (sûrl′s) Calif.	35·44 N	117·22 W
82	Searsport (sērz′pōrt) Maine	44·28 N	68·55 W
66	Seaside (sē′sīd) Ore.	45·59 N	123·55 W
65	Seattle (sê-ăt′′l) Wash. (Seattle In.)	47·36 N	122·20 W
92	Sebaco (sĕ-bä′kô) Nic.	12·50 N	86·03 W
82	Sebago (sē-bā′gō) Maine	43·52 N	70·20 W
88	Sebastion Vizcaino, Bahia (B.) (bä-ē′ä-sĕ-bäs-tyô′n-vēs-kä-ē′nô) Mex.	28·45 N	115·15 W
68	Sebastopol (sē-bȧs′tô-pôl) Calif.	38·27 N	122·50 W
154	Sebatik (I.) Indon.	3·52 N	118·14 E
127	Sebes Rom.	45·58 N	23·34 E
80	Sebewaing (se′bê-wăng) Mich.	43·45 N	83·25 W
128	Sebezh (syĕ′bĕzh) Sov. Un.	56·16 N	28·29 E
133	Sebinkarahisar Tur.	40·15 N	38·10 E
124	Sebkha bou Areg (Marsh) Mor.	35·09 N	3·02 W
125	Sebkhan d'Oran (L.) Alg.	35·28 N	0·28 W
120	Sebnitz (zĕb′nĕts) Ger.	51·01 N	14·16 E
125	Seborbe (sĕ-bôr-dĕ) Sp.	39·50 N	0·30 W
114	Sebou, Oued R. Mor.	34·23 N	5·18 W
80	Sebree (sē-brē′) Ky.	37·35 N	87·30 W
79	Sebring (sē′brĭng) Fla. (In.)	27·30 N	81·26 W
80	Sebring Ohio	40·55 N	81·05 W
126	Secchia (R.) (sĕ′kyä) It.	44·25 N	10·25 E
91	Seco (R.) (sĕ′kô) Mex.	18·11 N	93·18 W
165	Second Cataract Sud.	21·52 N	31·18 E
73	Sedalia (sê-dä′lê-ȧ) Mo.	38·42 N	93·12 W
122	Sedan (sē-dän′) Fr.	49·49 N	4·55 E
73	Sedan (sê-dăn′) Kans.	37·07 N	96·08 W
110	Sedgley (sĕdj′lĭ) Eng.	52·32 N	2·07 W
139	Sedom Isr. (Palestine In.)	31·04 N	35·24 E
65	Sedro Woolley (sē′drô-wŏŏl′ê) Wash. (Seattle In.)	48·30 N	122·14 W
119	Šeduva (shĕ′dōō-vȧ) Sov. Un.	55·46 N	23·45 E
166	Seekoevlei (L.) (zä′kōōf-lī) S. Afr. (Cape Town In.)	34·04 S	18·33 E
111	Seestall (zā′shtäl) Ger. (Munich In.)	47·58 N	10·52 E
114	Sefrou (sē-frōō′) Mor.	33·49 N	4·46 W
132	Seg (L.) (syĕgh) Sov. Un.	64·00 N	33·30 E
139	Segamat (sä′gȧ-mȧt) Mala. (Singapore In.)	2·30 N	102·49 E
164	Ségou (sā-gōō′) Mali	13·24 N	6·20 W
98	Segovia (sĕ-gō′vēä) Col. (In.)	7·08 N	74·42 W
124	Segovia (sā-gō′vê-ä) Sp.	40·58 N	4·05 W
	Segovia, see Coco		
125	Segre (R.) (sā′grä) Sp.	41·54 N	1·10 E
64	Seguam (I.) (sē′gwäm) Alaska	52·16 N	172·10 W
64	Seguam P. Alaska	52·20 N	173·00 W
164	Séguela (sā-gä-lä′) Ivory Coast	8·03 N	7·05 W
76	Seguin (sĕ-gēn′) Tex.	29·35 N	97·58 W
64	Segula (I.) (sē-gū′lȧ) Alaska	52·08 N	178·35 E
125	Segura (R.) (sä-gōō′rä) Sp.	38·07 N	0·33 W
124	Segura, Sierra de (Mts.) (sē-ĕ′r-rä-dĕ) Sp.	38·05 N	2·45 W

Page	Name Pronunciation Region	Lat. °′	Long. °′
124	Segura (R.) Sp.	38·24 N	2·12 W
142	Sehwān W. Pak.	26·33 N	67·51 E
95	Seibo (sĕ′y-bō) Dom. Rep.	18·45 N	69·05 W
119	Seinäjoki (sā′ê-nĕ-yô′kê) Fin.	62·47 N	22·50 E
122	Seine, Baie de la (B.) (bī dĕ lä sån) Fr.	49·37 N	0·53 W
71	Seine (R.) (sån) Can.	49·04 N	91·00 W
122	Seine, Rivière (R.) (rēv-yâr′) Fr.	49·21 N	1·17 E
85	Seine R. (sån) Can. (Winnipeg In.)	49·48 N	97·04 W
100	Seio do Venus (Mtn.) (sĕ-yô-dô-vĕ′nōōs) Braz. (In.)	22·28 S	43·12 W
125	Seixal (sā-ê-shäl′) Port. (Lisbon In.)	38·38 N	9·06 W
164	Sekondi-Takoradi (sĕ-kôn′dê tä-kô-rä′dê) Ghana	4·55 N	1·53 W
139	Selangor (State) (sȧ-län′gōr) Mala. (Singapore In.)	2·53 N	101·29 E
127	Selanoutsi (sâl′ȧ-nôv-tsĭ) Bul.	43·42 N	24·05 E
155	Selaru (I.) Indon.	8·30 S	130·30 E
154	Selatan, Tandjung (C.) (sȧ-lä′tän) Indon.	4·09 S	114·40 E
64	Selawik (sē-lȧ-wĭk) Alaska	66·30 N	160·09 W
118	Selbu (L.) (sĕl′bōō) Nor.	63·18 N	11·55 E
110	Selby (sĕl′bê) Eng.	53·47 N	1·03 W
64	Seldovia (sĕl-dō′vê-ȧ) Alaska	59·26 N	151·42 W
135	Selemdzha (R.) (sâ-lĕmt-zhä′) Sov. Un.	52·28 N	131·50 E
135	Selenga (R.) (sĕ lĕŋ gä′) Sov. Un.	51·00 N	106·40 E
146	Selenge Gol (R.) Mong.	49·04 N	102·23 E
135	Selennyakh (R.) (sĕl-yĭn-yäk) Sov. Un.	67·42 N	141·45 E
123	Sélestat (sē-lē-stä′) Fr.	48·16 N	7·27 E
164	Selibaby (sȧ-lê-bȧ-bē′) Mauritania	15·21 N	12·11 W
128	Seliger (L.) (sĕl′lē-gĕr) Sov. Un.	57·14 N	33·18 E
142	Seling Tsho (L.) China	31·55 N	89·00 E
142	Selipuk Gömpa China	31·37 N	82·42 E
128	Selizharovo (sâ′lê-zhä′rô-vô) Sov. Un.	56·51 N	33·28 E
86	Selkirk (sĕl′kûrk) Can.	50·13 N	97·07 W
86	Selkirk Mts. Can.	50·14 N	116·42 W
65	Selleck (sĕl′ĕck) Wash. (Seattle In.)	47·22 N	121·52 W
75	Sellersburg (sĕl′ẽrs-bûrg) Ind. (Louisville In.)	38·25 N	85·45 W
135	Sellya Khskaya, Guba (B.) (sĕl-yäk′skȧ-yȧ) Sov. Un.	72·30 N	136·00 E
78	Selma (sĕl′mȧ) Ala.	32·25 N	87·00 W
68	Selma Calif.	36·34 N	119·37 W
79	Selma N. C.	35·33 N	78·16 W
74	Selma Tex. (San Antonio In.)	29·33 N	98·19 W
111	Selsingen (zĕl′zĕn-gĕn) Ger. (Hamburg In.)	53·22 N	9·13 E
166	Selukwe (sê-lŭk′wê) S. Rh.	19·34 S	30·03 E
66	Selway R. (sĕl′wȧ) Idaho	46·07 N	115·12 W
86	Selwyn (L.) (sĕl′wĭn) Can.	59·41 N	104·30 W
127	Seman (R.) Alb.	40·48 N	19·53 E
154	Semarang (sĕ-mä′räng) Indon.	7·03 S	110·27 E
154	Semarinda Indon.	0·30 S	117·10 E
	Semendria, see Smederevo		
129	Semënovka (sĕ-myôn′ôf-kȧ) Sov. Un.	52·10 N	32·34 E
65	Semiahmoo Ind. Res. Can. (Vancouver In.)	49·01 N	122·43 W
65	Semiahmoo Spit (sĕm′ĭ-ȧ-mōō) Wash. (Vancouver In.)	48·59 N	122·52 W
64	Semichi Is. (sē mē′chī) Alaska	52·40 N	174·50 E
67	Seminoe Res. (sĕm′ĭ nô) Wyo.	42·08 N	107·10 W
73	Seminole (sĕm′ĭ-nōl) Okla.	35·13 N	96·41 W
79	Seminole Ind. Res. Fla. (In.)	26·19 N	81·11 W
79	Seminole Ind. Res. Fla. (In.)	27·05 N	81·25 W
78	Seminole, L. Fla.-Ga.	30·57 N	84·46 W
134	Semipalatinsk (sĕ′mê-pȧ-lȧ-tyĕnsk′) Sov. Un.	50·28 N	80·29 E
64	Semisopochnoi (I.) (sĕ-mē-sȧ-pôsh′ noi) Alaska	51·45 N	179·25 E
134	Semiyarskoye (sĕ′mê-yär′skô-yĕ) Sov. Un.	51·03 N	78·28 E
165	Semliki R. (sĕm′lê-kē) Con. L.-Ug.	0·45 N	29·36 E
	Semlin, see Zemun		
120	Semmering P. (sĕm′ẽr-ĭng) Aus.	47·39 N	15·50 E
133	Semnān Iran	35·30 N	53·30 E
99	Senador Pompeu (sĕ-nä-dōr-pôm-pĕ′ōō) Braz.	5·34 S	39·18 W
78	Senatobia (sĕ-nȧ-tō′bê-ȧ) Miss.	34·36 N	89·56 W
152	Sendai (sĕn-dī′) Jap.	38·18 N	141·02 E
73	Seneca (sĕn′ĕ-kȧ) Kans.	39·49 N	96·03 W
78	Seneca S. C.	34·40 N	82·58 W
81	Seneca (L.) N. Y.	42·30 N	76·55 W
81	Seneca Falls N. Y.	42·55 N	76·55 W
163	Senegal (sĕn-ĕ-gôl′) Afr.	14·53 N	14·58 W
164	Senegal R. Senegal-Mauritania	16·45 N	14·37 W
168	Senekal (sĕn′ĕ-kȧl) S. Afr. (Johannesburg & Pretoria In.)	28·20 S	27·37 E
120	Senftenberg (zĕnf′tĕn-bĕrgh) Ger.	51·32 N	14·00 E
99	Senhor do Bomfim (sĕn-yôr dô bôn-fē′n) Braz.	5·21 S	40·09 W
126	Senigallia (sâ-nê-gäl′lyä) It.	43·42 N	13·16 E
126	Senj (sĕn′) Yugo.	44·58 N	14·55 E
112	Senja (I.) (sĕnyä) Nor.	69·28 N	16·10 E
123	Senlis (sän-lēs′) Fr. (Paris In.)	49·13 N	2·35 E
165	Sennar (sĕn-när′) Sud.	13·34 N	33·32 E
165	Sennar Dam Sud.	13·38 N	33·38 E
87	Senneterre Can.	48·20 N	77·22 W
128	Senno (syĕ′nô) Sov. Un.	54·48 N	29·43 E
122	Sens (säns) Fr.	48·05 N	3·18 E
92	Sensuntepeque (sĕn-sōōn-tȧ-pä′kȧ) Sal.	13·53 N	88·34 W
127	Senta (sĕn′tä) Yugo.	45·54 N	20·05 E
153	Senzaki (sĕn′zä-kē) Jap.	34·22 N	131·09 E
	Seoul, see Sŏul		
139	Sepang Mala. (Singapore In.)	2·43 N	101·45 E
100	Sepetiba, Baia de (B.) (baē′ä dĕ sä-pȧ-tē′bȧ) Braz. (In.)	23·01 S	43·42 W
155	Sepik (R.) (sĕp-ēk′) N. Gui. Ter.	4·07 S	142·40 E

ng-sing; ŋ-baŋk; n-nasalized n; nŏd; cŏmmit; ōld; ôbey; ôrder; fōōd; fŏŏt; ou-out; s-soft; sh-dish; th-thin; pūre; ûnite; ûrn; stŭd; circŭs; ü-as "y" in study; ′-indeterminate vowel.

266 Septemes-les-Vallons–Shibeli PRONOUNCING INDEX

Page	Name Pronunciation Region	Lat. °'	Long. °'
122	Septèmes-les-Vallons (sĕ-tàm'la-vä-ôɴ') Fr. (Marseille In.)	43·25 N	5·23 E
95	Septentrional, Cordillera (Mts.) (kôr-dēl-yĕ'rä sĕp-tĕn-tryô-nä'l) Dom. Rep.	19·50 N	71·15 W
123	Septeuil (sĕ-tû') Fr. (Paris In.)	48·53 N	1·40 E
82	Sept-Iles Can.	50·11 N	66·21 W
78	Sequatchie (R.) (sê-kwăch'ê) Tenn	35·33 N	85·14 W
65	Sequim (sē'kwĭm) Wash. (Seattle In.)	48·05 N	123·07 W
65	Sequim B. Wash. (Seattle In.)	48·04 N	122·58 W
68	Sequoia Natl. Park (sê-kwoi'à) Calif.	36·34 N	118·37 W
117	Seraing (sē-răɴ') Bel.	50·38 N	5·28 E
155	Seram (I.) Indon.	2·45 S	129·30 E
142	Sèrampore India (Calcutta In.)	22·44 N	88·21 E
154	Serang (sâ-räng') Indon.	6·13 S	106·10 E
139	Seranggung. Indon. (Singapore In.)	0·49 N	104·11 E
	Serbia (Reg.), see Srbija		
133	Serdobsk (sĕr-dôpsk') Sov. Un.	52·30 N	44·20 E
129	Seredina-Buda (sĕ-rā-dē'nà-bōō'dà) Sov. Un.	52·11 N	34·03 E
139	Seremban (sĕr-ĕm-bän') Mala. (Singapore In.)	2·44 N	101·57 E
166	Serenje (sē-rĕn'yê) N. Rh.	13·12 S	30·49 E
168	Serenli (sâ-rĕn'lē) Som. (Horn of Afr. In.)	2·28 N	42·15 E
	Seres, see Sérrai		
121	Seret Czech.	48·17 N	17·43 E
121	Seret Rom.	47·58 N	26·01 E
121	Seret R. (sĕr'ĕt) Sov. Un.	49·45 N	25·30 E
134	Sergeya Kirova (I.) (sĕr-gyĕ'yà kē'rô-và) Sov. Un.	77·30 N	86·10 E
99	Sergipe (State) (sĕr-zhē'pĕ) Braz.	10·27 S	37·04 W
132	Sergiyevsk Sov. Un.	53·58 N	51·00 E
127	Sérifos Grc.	37·10 N	24·32 E
127	Sérifos (I.) Grc.	37·42 N	24·17 E
101	Serodino (sĕ-rô-dê'nō) Arg. (Buenos Aires In.)	32·36 S	60·56 W
100	Seropédica (sĕ-rô-pĕ'dē-kä) Braz. (In.)	22·44 S	43·43 W
136	Serov (syĕ-rôf') Sov. Un. (Urals In.)	59·36 N	60·30 E
166	Serowe (sĕ-rō'wĕ) Bech.	22·18 S	26·39 E
124	Serpa (sĕr-pä) Port.	37·56 N	7·38 W
128	Serpukhov (syĕr'pōō-ĸôf) Sov. Un.	54·53 N	37·27 E
127	Sérrai (Seres) (sĕr'rĕ) (sĕr'ĕs) Grc.	41·06 N	23·36 E
76	Serranias Del Burro (sĕr-rä-nē'äs dĕl bōō'r-rô) Mex.	29·39 N	102·07 W
99	Serrinha (sĕr-rēn'yà) Braz.	11·43 S	38·49 W
124	Serta (sĕr'tà) Port.	39·48 N	8·01 W
99	Sertânia (sĕr-tà'nyä) Braz.	8·28 S	37·13 W
101	Sertãozinho (sĕr-touɴ-zē'n-yô) Braz. (Rio de Janeiro In.)	21·10 S	47·58 W
139	Serting (R.). Mala. (Singapore In.)	3·01 N	102·32 E
100	Seruí (sĕ-rōō-ē') Braz. (In.)	22·40 S	43·08 W
126	Sesia (R.) (sâz'yä) It.	45·33 N	8·25 E
125	Sesimbra (sĕ-sē'm-brä) Port. (Lisbon In.)	38·27 N	9·06 W
167	Sesmyl (R.) S. Afr. (Johannesburg & Pretoria In.)	25·51 S	28·06 E
126	Sestri Levante (sĕs'trē lâ-vän'tå) It.	44·15 N	9·24 E
136	Sestroretsk (sĕs-trô'rĕtsk) Sov. Un. (Leningrad In.)	60·06 N	29·58 E
136	Sestroretskiy Razliv, Ozero (L.) (ô'zĕ-rô sĕs-trô' rĕts-kĭ räz'lĭf) Sov. Un. (Leningrad In.)	60·05 N	30·07 E
153	Seta (sĕ'tä) Jap. (Ōsaka In.)	34·58 N	135·56 E
122	Sète (Cette) (sĕt) Fr.	43·24 N	3·42 E
99	Sete Lagoas (sĕ-tĕ lä-gô'äs) Braz.	19·23 S	43·58 W
164	Setif (sâ-tēf') Alg.	36·18 N	5·21 E
153	Seto (sĕ'tō) Jap.	35·11 N	137·07 E
153	Seto-Naikai (Sea) (sĕ'tô nī'kī) Jap.	33·50 N	132·25 E
164	Settat (sĕt-ät') (sē-tà') Mor.	33·02 N	7·30 W
166	Setté-Cama (sĕ-tĕ-kä-mä') Gabon	2·29 S	9·40 E
94	Settlement Pt. (sĕt'l-mĕnt) Ba. Is.	26·40 N	79·00 W
168	Settlers (sĕt'lẽrs) S. Afr. (Johannesburg & Pretoria In.)	24·57 S	28·33 E
125	Setúbal (sâ-tōō'bäl) Port. (Lisbon In.)	30·32 N	8·54 W
124	Setúbal, B. de (bä-ē'ä) Port.	38·27 N	9·08 W
87	Seul, Lac (L.) (läk sûl) Can.	50·28 N	91·26 W
118	Sevalen (L.) (sĕ'vä-lĕn) Nor.	62·19 N	10·15 E
133	Sevan (L.) (syĭ-vän') Sov. Un.	40·10 N	45·20 E
129	Sevastopol' (Akhiar) (syĕ-väs-tô'pôl'') (äĸ'yär) Sov. Un.	44·34 N	33·34 E
	Seven Is., see Shichitō		
110	Sevenoaks (sĕ-vĕn-ôks') Eng. (London In.)	51·16 N	0·12 E
136	Severka R. (sâ'vĕr-kà) Sov. Un. (Moscow In.)	55·11 N	38·41 E
87	Severn (R.) (sĕv'ẽrn) Can.	55·21 N	88·42 W
116	Severn (R.) Eng.	51·42 N	2·25 W
84	Severna Park (sĕv'ẽrn-â) Md. (Baltimore In.)	39·04 N	76·33 W
132	Severnaya Dvina (Northern Dvina) (R.) Sov. Un.	63·00 N	42·40 E
130	Severnaya Zemlya (Northern Land) (Is.) (sĕ-vyĭr-nī'u zĭ-m'lyä') Sov. Un.	79·33 N	101·15 E
136	Severoural'sk (sĕ-vyĭ-rŭ-ōō-rälsk') Sov. Un. (Urals In.)	60·08 N	59·53 E
69	Sevier (L.) (sê-vēr') Utah	38·55 N	113·10 W
69	Sevier R. Utah	39·25 N	112·20 W
69	Sevier R., East Fork Utah	37·45 N	112·10 W
98	Sevilla (sĕ-vē'l-yä) Col. (In.)	4·16 N	75·56 W
124	Sevilla (sâ-vēl'yä) Sp.	37·29 N	5·58 W
75	Seville (sĕ'vĭl) Ohio (Cleveland In.)	41·01 N	81·54 W
127	Sevlievo (sĕv'lyĕ-vô) Bul.	41·02 N	25·05 E
122	Sèvre Nantaise (R.) (sâ'vrĕ näɴ-tàz') Fr.	47·00 N	1·02 W
122	Sèvre Niortaise (R.) (sâ'vr' nyôr-tâz') Fr.	46·23 N	1·05 W
128	Sevsk (syĕfsk) Sov. Un.	52·08 N	34·28 E
64	Seward (sū'ärd) Alaska	60·18 N	149·28 W
73	Seward Nebr.	40·55 N	97·06 W
64	Seward Pen. Alaska	65·40 N	164·00 W
100	Sewell (sĕ'ōō-ĕl) Chile	34·01 S	70·18 W
75	Sewickley (sê-wĭk'lê) Pa. (Pittsburg In.)	40·33 N	80·11 W
91	Seybaplaya (sā-ê-bä-plä'yä) Mex.	19·38 N	90·40 W
47	Seychelles (Is.) (sā-shĕl') Afr.	5·20 S	55·10 E
112	Seydhisfjördhur (sā'dēs-fyûr-dōōr) Ice.	65·21 N	14·08 W
92	Seyé (sĕ-yĕ') Mex. (Yucatan In.)	20·51 N	89·22 W
115	Seyhan (R.) Tur.	37·28 N	35·40 E
129	Seym (R.) (sĕym) Sov. Un.	51·23 N	33·22 E
80	Seymour (sē'mōr) Ind.	38·55 N	85·55 W
71	Seymour Iowa	40·41 N	93·03 W
72	Seymour Tex.	33·35 N	99·16 W
167	Seymour (sē'môr) S. Afr. (Natal In.)	32·33 S	26·48 E
167	Sezela S. Afr. (Natal In.)	30·33 S	30·37 W
126	Sezze (sĕt'så) It.	41·32 N	13·03 E
127	Sfântul-Gheorghe Rom.	45·53 N	25·49 E
164	Sfax (sfäks) Tun.	34·51 N	10·45 E
111	's Gravenhage (The Hague) ('s Krä'vĕn-hä'ĸĕ) (hāg) Neth. (Amsterdam In.)	52·05 N	4·16 E
147	Sha (R.) (shä) China	33·33 N	114·30 E
148	Sha (R.) China	34·47 N	118·27 E
148	Sha (R.) China	39·26 N	122·08 E
166	Shabani S. Rh.	20·15 S	30·28 E
136	Shablykino (sháb-lē'kĭ-nô) Sov. Un. (Moscow In.)	56·22 N	38·37 E
149	Shaching China (Canton In.)	22·44 N	113·48 E
47	Shackleton Shelf Ice (shăk''l-tŭn) Ant.	65·00 S	100·00 E
84	Shades Cr. (shādz) Ala. (Birmingham In.)	33·20 N	86·55 W
84	Shades Mtn. Ala. (Birmingham In.)	33·22 N	86·51 W
144	Shagrā (shăg'rä) Sau. Ar.	25·13 N	45·15 E
144	Shahdād Iran	30·45 N	57·45 E
142	Shah Fuladi (Mt.) Afg.	39·33 N	67·38 E
165	Shahhāt Libya	32·49 N	21·46 E
142	Shāhjahānpur (shä-jŭ-hän'pōōr) India	27·58 N	79·58 E
150	Shaho (shä-hō') China (Peking In.)	40·08 N	116·16 E
144	Shahrezā (shä-rä'zä) Iran	31·47 N	51·47 E
133	Shahsavār Iran	36·40 N	51·00 E
75	Shaker Hts. (shā'kẽr) Ohio (Cleveland In.)	41·28 N	81·34 W
129	Shakhty (shäĸ'tê) Sov. Un.	47·41 N	40·11 E
74	Shakopee (shăk'ô-pe) Minn. (Minneapolis, St. Paul In.)	44·48 N	93·31 W
165	Shala L. (shä'lä) Eth.	7·34 N	39·00 E
144	Sham, Jabal ash (Mtn.) Mus. & Om.	23·01 N	57·45 E
165	Shambe (shäm'bå) Sud.	7·08 N	30·46 E
144	Shammar, Jabal (Mts.) (jĕb'ĕl shŭm'år) Sau. Ar.	27·13 N	40·16 E
81	Shamokin (shà-mō'kĭn) Pa.	40·45 N	76·30 W
72	Shamrock (shăm'rŏk) Tex.	35·14 N	100·12 W
166	Shamva (shäm'vá) S. Rh.	17·18 S	31·35 E
75	Shandon (shăn-dŭn) Ohio (Cincinnati In.)	39·20 N	84·13 W
148	Shangch'eng (shäng'chĕng) China	31·47 N	115·22 E
148	Shangchialin (shäng'jĭä'lĭn) China	38·20 N	116·05 E
148	Shangch'iu (shäng'chĭō) China	34·24 N	115·39 E
149	Shanghai (shäng'hī') China (Shanghai In.)	31·14 N	121·27 E
149	Shanghaihsien China (Shanghai In.)	31·02 N	121·24 E
148	Shanghai Shih (Prov.) China	31·30 N	121·45 E
148	Shangho (shäng'hō) China	37·18 N	117·10 E
151	Shangjao China	28·25 N	117·58 E
148	Shangts'ai (shäng'tsī') China	33·16 N	114·16 E
150	Shangtu China	41·38 N	113·22 E
147	Shanhsi (Shansi) (Prov.) China	37·31 N	111·30 E
148	Shanhsien (shän'hsyĕn') China	34·47 N	116·04 E
84	Shannon (shăn'ŭn) Ala. (Birmingham In.)	33·23 N	86·52 W
116	Shannon R. (shăn'ŏn) Ire.	52·30 N	9·58 W
146	Shanshan (shän'shän') China	42·51 N	89·53 E
	Shansi, see Shanhsi		
135	Shantar (I.) (shän'tär) Sov. Un.	55·13 N	138·42 E
151	Shant'ou (Swatow) (swä'tō') China	23·20 N	116·40 E
147	Shantung (Prov.) China	36·08 N	117·09 E
151	Shantung Pantao (Pen.) China	37·00 N	120·10 E
151	Shantung Pt. (shän'tōōng') China	37·28 N	122·40 E
151	Shaohsing China	30·00 N	120·40 E
148	Shaopo (shou'pō') China	32·33 N	119·30 E
148	Shaopo Hu (L.) (shou'pō' hōō) China	32·07 N	119·13 E
136	Shapki (shäp'kĭ) Sov. Un. (Leningrad In.)	59·36 N	31·11 E
158	Shark B. (shärk) Austl.	25·30 S	113·00 E
83	Sharon (shăr'ŏn) Mass. (Boston In.)	42·07 N	71·11 W
80	Sharon Pa.	41·15 N	80·30 W
72	Sharon Springs Kan.	38·51 N	101·45 W
75	Sharonville (shăr'ŏn vĭl) Ohio (Cincinnati In.)	39·16 N	84·24 W
75	Sharpsburg (shärps'bûrg) Pa. (Pittsburgh In.)	40·30 N	79·54 W
144	Sharr, Jabal (Mtn.) Sau. Ar.	28·00 N	36·07 E
151	Shashih China	30·20 N	112·18 E
66	Shasta, Mt. Calif.	41·35 N	122·12 W
66	Shasta L. (shăs'tà) Calif.	40·51 N	122·32 W
132	Shatsk (shätsk) Sov. Un.	54·00 N	41·40 E
72	Shattuck (shăt'ŭk) Okla.	36·16 N	99·53 W
86	Shaunavon Can.	49·37 N	108·29 W
78	Shaw (shô) Miss.	33·36 N	90·44 W
71	Shawano (shá-wô'nô) Wis.	44·41 N	88·13 W
87	Shawinigan Falls Can.	46·32 N	72·46 W
74	Shawnee (shô-nē') Mo. (Kansas City In.)	39·01 N	94·43 W
73	Shawnee Okla.	35·20 N	96·54 W
80	Shawneetown (shô'nē-toun) Ill.	37·40 N	88·05 W
151	Shayang China	31·00 N	112·38 E
121	Shchara (R.) (sh-chä'rå) Sov. Un.	53·17 N	25·12 E
136	Shchëlkovo (shchĕl'kô-vô) Sov. Un. (Moscow In.)	55·55 N	38·00 E
129	Shchëtovo (shchĕ'tô-vô) Sov. Un.	48·11 N	39·13 E
129	Shchigry (shchē'grê) Sov. Un.	51·52 N	36·54 E
129	Shchors (shchôrs) Sov. Un.	51·38 N	31·58 E
136	Shchuch'ye Ozero (shchōōch'yĕ ô'zĕ-rō) Sov. Un. (Urals In.)	56·31 N	56·35 E
142	Sheakhala India (Calcutta In.)	22·47 N	88·10 E
168	Shebeli R. (shä'bå-lē) Eth. (Horn of Afr. In.)	6·07 N	43·10 E
71	Sheboygan (shê-boi'găn) Wis.	43·45 N	87·44 W
71	Sheboygan Falls Wis.	43·43 N	87·51 W
164	Shebshi Mts. Nig.-Cam.	8·22 N	12·14 E
82	Shediac (shĕ'dê-ăk) Can.	46·16 N	64·33 W
116	Sheelin (L.) (shē'lĭn) Ire.	53·46 N	7·34 W
110	Sheerness (shēr'nĕs) Eng. (London In.)	51·26 N	0·46 E
78	Sheffield (shĕf'fēld) Ala.	35·42 N	87·42 W
85	Sheffield Can. (Toronto In.)	43·20 N	80·13 W
110	Sheffield Eng.	53·23 N	1·28 W
75	Sheffield Ohio (Cleveland In.)	41·26 N	82·05 W
75	Sheffield Lake Ohio (Cleveland In.)	41·30 N	82·03 W
148	Shehsien (shĕ'hsyĕn') China	36·34 N	113·42 E
116	Shehy, Mts Ire.	51·46 N	9·35 W
132	Sheksna (R.) (shĕks'nå) Sov. Un.	59·50 N	38·40 E
135	Shelagskiy, Mys (C.) (shĭ-läg'skē) Sov. Un.	70·08 N	170·52 E
73	Shelbina (shĕl-bī'nå) Ark.	39·41 N	92·03 W
82	Shelbourne (shĕl'bŭrn) Can.	43·46 N	65·20 W
80	Shelburn (shĕl'bŭrn) Ind.	39·10 N	87·30 W
81	Shelburne Can.	44·05 N	80·05 W
75	Shelby (shĕl'bê) Ind. (Chicago In.)	41·12 N	87·21 W
80	Shelby Mich.	43·35 N	86·20 W
78	Shelby Miss.	33·56 N	90·44 W
67	Shelby Mont.	48·26 N	111·50 W
79	Shelby N. C.	35·16 N	81·35 W
80	Shelby Ohio	40·50 N	82·40 W
80	Shelbyville (shĕl'bê-vĭl) Ill.	39·20 N	88·45 W
80	Shelbyville Ind.	39·30 N	85·45 W
80	Shelbyville Ky.	38·10 N	85·15 W
78	Shelbyville Tenn.	35·30 N	86·28 W
70	Sheldon (shĕl'dŭn) Iowa	43·10 N	95·50 W
77	Sheldon Tex. (In.)	29·52 N	95·07 W
135	Shelekhova, Zaliv (B.) Sov. Un.	60·00 N	156·00 E
64	Shelikof Str. (shĕ'lê-kôf) Alaska	57·56 N	154·20 W
84	Shell Beach (bĕch) La. (New Orleans In.)	29·52 N	89·41 W
67	Shelley (shĕl'lê) Idaho	43·24 N	112·06 W
84	Shell I. (shĕl) La. (New Orleans In.)	29·17 N	89·42 W
71	Shellrock (R.) (shĕl'rŏk) Iowa	43·25 N	93·19 W
128	Shelon' (R.) (shå'lôn) Sov. Un.	57·50 N	29·40 E
81	Shelton (shĕl'tŭn) Conn.	41·15 N	73·05 W
72	Shelton Nebr.	40·46 N	98·41 W
66	Shelton Wash.	47·14 N	123·05 W
136	Shemakha (shĕ-mà-kä') Sov. Un. (Urals In.)	56·16 N	59·19 E
133	Shemakha Sov. Un.	40·35 N	48·40 E
73	Shenandoah (shĕn-ăn-dō'à) Iowa	40·46 N	95·23 W
81	Shenandoah Pa.	40·50 N	76·15 W
81	Shenandoah Va.	38·30 N	78·30 W
81	Shenandoah Natl. Park Va.	38·35 N	78·25 W
81	Shenandoah (R.) Va.	38·55 N	78·05 W
148	Shenchiu (shenchĭō) China	33·11 N	115·06 E
165	Shendi (shĕn'dê) Sud.	16·44 N	33·29 E
148	Shengfang (shengfäng) China	39·05 N	116·40 E
146	Shenhsi (Shensi) (Prov.) (shĕn'sē') China	35·04 N	108·45 E
148	Shenhsien (shen'sĭän') China	38·02 N	115·33 E
132	Shenkursk (shĕn-kōōrsk') Sov. Un.	62·10 N	43·08 E
150	Shenmu China	38·55 N	110·35 E
	Shensi, see Shenhsi		
148	Shentse (shen'zhō) China	38·12 N	115·12 E
150	Shenyang (Mukden) (shĕn'yäng') (mōōk'dĕn) China	41·45 N	123·22 E
142	Sheopur India	25·37 N	78·10 E
85	Shepard (shĕ'pȧrd) Can. (Calgary In.)	50·57 N	113·54 W
129	Shepetovka (shĕ-pĕ-tôf'kȧ) Sov. Un.	50·10 N	27·01 E
160	Shepparton (shĕp'ăr-tŭn) Austl.	36·15 S	145·25 E
83	Sherborn (shûr'bŭrn) Mass. (Boston In.)	42·15 N	71·22 W
81	Sherbrooke (shûr'brōōk) Can.	45·25 N	72·00 W
110	Sherburn (shûr'bŭrn) Eng.	53·47 N	1·15 W
121	Shereshevo (shĕ-rĕ-shĕ-vô) Sov. Un.	52·31 N	24·08 E
73	Sheridan (shĕr'ĭ-dăn) Ark.	34·19 N	92·21 W
66	Sheridan Ore.	45·06 N	123·22 W
67	Sheridan Wyo.	44·48 N	106·56 W
73	Sherman (shĕr'măn) Tex.	33·39 N	96·37 W
136	Sherna R. (shĕr'nȧ) Sov. Un. (Moscow In.)	56·08 N	38·45 E
86	Sherridon Can.	55·08 N	101·00 W
111	's Hertogenbosch (sĕr-tō'ghĕn-bôs) Neth. (Amsterdam In.)	51·41 N	5·19 E
65	Sherwood (shûr'wŏŏd) Ore. (Portland In.)	45·21 N	122·50 W
110	Sherwood For. Eng.	53·11 N	1·07 W
116	Shetland (Is.) (shĕt'lănd) Scot.	60·35 N	2·10 W
139	Sheva R. Isr. (Palestine In.)	31·15 N	34·38 E
70	Sheyenne (R.) (shī-ĕn') N. D.	46·42 N	97·52 W
80	Shiawassee (R.) (shī-â-wôs'ê) Mich.	43·15 N	84·05 W
144	Shibām (shē'bäm) Aden	16·02 N	48·40 E
168	Shibeli R. Som. (Horn of Afr. In.)	1·38 N	43·50 E

ăt; finăl; rāte; senâte; ärm; àsk; sofà; fâre; ch-choose; dh-as th in other; bē; êvent; bĕt; recĕnt; cratẽr; g-go; gh-guttural g; bĭt; ĭ-short neutral; rīde; ĸ-guttural k as ch in German ich;

PRONOUNCING INDEX

Shibin al Kawn–Singapore Str. 267

Page	Name Pronunciation Region	Lat. °′	Long. °′
168	Shibīn al Kawn (shē-bēn′ĕl kōm′) U. A. R. (Nile In.)	30·31 N	31·01 E
168	Shibīn al Qanāţir (kȧ-nä′tēr) U. A. R. (Nile In.)	30·18 N	31·21 E
153	Shichitō (Seven Is.) (shē′chē-tō) Jap.	34·18 N	139·28 E
67	Shields R. (shēldz) . . . . Mont.	45·54 N	110·40 W
110	Shifnal (shĭf′nȧl) . . . . Eng.	52·40 N	2·22 W
148	Shih (R.) (shē hǒ) . . . . China	32·09 N	114·11 E
148	Shihchiangchen (shē′kĭäng′zhen) China	32·16 N	120·59 E
149	Shihch′iao . . . . China (Canton In.)	22·56 N	113·22 E
148	Shihchiu Hu (L.) (shē′jĭō′hōō) China	31·29 N	119·07 E
	Shihkiachwang, see Shihmen		
151	Shihlung . . . . China	23·05 N	113·58 E
148	Shihmen (Shihkiachwang) (shē mĕn) (shē′jĭá′zhōōäng) China	38·04 N	114·31 E
148	Shihohienfou . . . . China	31·27 N	117·51 E
144	Shihr . . . . Aden	14·45 N	49·32 E
149	Shiht′ou . . . . . . China (Canton In.)	23·01 N	113·23 E
148	Shihts′un (shē′chōōen) . . . . . China	33·47 N	117·18 E
148	Shihtzu Shan (Mts.) (shē′jē shän) China	37·17 N	121·38 E
149	Shihwan . . . . . . China (Canton In.)	23·01 N	113·04 E
151	Shihwanta Shan (Mtns.) . . . China	22·10 N	107·30 E
150	Shihwei Pk . . . . China	47·11 N	119·59 E
142	Shikarpur . . . . W. Pak.	27·51 N	68·52 E
153	Shiki (shē′kē) . . . . Jap. (Tōkyō In.)	35·50 N	139·35 E
153	Shikoku (I.) (shē′kō′kōō) . . . . . Jap.	33·43 N	133·33 E
135	Shilka (R.) (shĭl′kȧ) . . . . . Sov. Un.	53·00 N	118·45 E
142	Shilla (Mt.) . . . . India	37·18 N	78·17 E
142	Shillong (shĕl-lông′) . . . . India	25·39 N	91·58 E
74	Shiloh (shī′lō) . . Ill. (St. Louis In.)	38·34 N	89·54 W
153	Shimabara (shē′mä-bä′rä) . . . . Jap.	32·46 N	130·22 E
153	Shimada (shē′mä-dä) . . . . Jap.	34·49 N	138·13 E
153	Shimizu (shē′mē-zōō) . . . . Jap.	35·00 N	138·29 E
153	Shimminato (shĕm′mē′nä-tō) . Jap.	36·47 N	137·05 E
153	Shimoda (shē′mō-dä) . . . . Jap.	34·41 N	138·58 E
143	Shimoga . . . . India	13·59 N	75·38 E
153	Shimonoseki (shē′mō-nō-sĕ′kē) (shē-mō-nô′sĕ-kĭ) . Jap.	33·58 N	130·55 E
153	Shimo-Saga (shē′mō sä′gä) Jap. (Ōsaka In.)	35·01 N	135·41 E
116	Shin, Loch (L.) (lŏk shĭn) . . . Scot.	58·08 N	4·20 W
153	Shinagawa-Wan (B.) (shē′nä-gä′wä wän) Jap. (Tōkyō In.)	35·37 N	139·49 E
153	Shinano-Gawa (Strm.) (shē-nä′nō gä′wä) . Jap.	36·43 N	138·22 E
65	Shine (shīn) . . . Wash. (Seattle In.)	47·52 N	122·40 W
153	Shingū (shĭn′gōō) . . . . Jap.	33·43 N	135·59 E
153	Shinji (L.) (shĭn′jē) . . . . Jap.	35·23 N	133·05 E
165	Shinko R. (shĭn′kō) . Cen. Afr. Rep.	6·37 N	24·31 E
166	Shinyanga (shĭn-yäŋ′gä) . . . . . Tan.	3·35 S	33·07 E
152	Shiono Misaki (C.) (shē-ô′nō mē′sä-kē) . Jap.	33·20 N	136·10 E
94	Ship Channel Cay (I.) (shĭp chă-nĕl kē) . Ba. Is.	24·50 N	76·50 W
110	Shipley (shĭp′lē) . . . . Eng.	53·50 N	1·47 W
82	Shippegan . . . . Can.	47·44 N	64·45 W
82	Shippegan (I.) . . . . Can.	47·50 N	64·38 W
81	Shippenburg (shĭp′ĕn bûrg) . . . Pa.	40·00 N	77·30 W
82	Shipshaw (R.) (shĭp′shô) . . . . . Can.	48·50 N	71·03 W
139	Shiqma (R.) . . . Isr. (Palestine In.)	31·31 N	34·40 E
153	Shirane-san (Mtn.) (shē′rä′nȧ-sän′) . Jap.	35·44 N	138·14 E
152	Shira Saki (C.) (shē′rä sä′kē) . Jap.	41·25 N	142·10 E
166	Shirati (shē-rä′tē) . . . . Tan.	1·15 S	34·02 E
144	Shiraz (shē-räz′) . . . . Iran	29·32 N	52·27 E
166	Shire (R.) (shē′rȧ) . . . . Nya.	15·10 S	34·58 E
129	Shirokoye (shē′rô-kô-yĕ) . Sov. Un.	47·40 N	33·18 E
142	Shirpuri . . . . India	25·31 N	77·46 E
64	Shishaldin Vol. (shī-shăl′dĭn) Alaska	54·48 N	164·00 W
75	Shively (shīv′lē) Ky. (Louisville In.)	38·11 N	85·47 W
139	Shivta . . . . Isr. (Palestine In.)	30·53 N	34·38 E
69	Shivwits (Shebit) Ind. Res. (shĭv′wĭts) (shē′bĭt) . Utah	37·10 N	113·50 W
69	Shivwits Plat . . . . Ariz.	36·13 N	113·42 W
83	Shirley (shûr′lē) Mass. (Boston In.)	42·33 N	71·39 W
153	Shizuki (shĭ′zōō-kē) . . . . Jap.	34·29 N	134·51 E
153	Shizuoka (shē′zōō′ōkȧ) . . . . . . Jap.	34·58 N	138·24 E
128	Shklov (shklôf) . . . . Sov. Un.	54·11 N	30·23 E
127	Shkodër (Scutari) (shkô′dûr) (skōō′tȧrē) . Alb.	42·04 N	19·30 E
152	Shkotovo (shkô′tô-vô) . . . Sov. Un.	43·15 N	132·21 E
73	Shoal Cr. (shōl) . . . . Ill.	38·37 N	89·25 W
80	Shoals (shōlz) . . . . Ind.	38·40 N	86·45 W
142	Shoapur . . . . India	25·53 N	76·45 E
153	Shodo (I.) (shō′dō) . . . . Jap.	34·27 N	134·27 E
143	Sholāpur (shō′lä-pōōr) . . . . . . India	17·42 N	75·51 E
139	Shoniron . . . Jordan (Palestine In.)	32·18 N	35·14 E
75	Shorewood (shōr′wōōd) Wis. (Milwaukee In.)	43·05 N	77·54 W
67	Shoshone (shō-shōn′ē) . . . . . . Idaho	42·56 N	114·24 W
67	Shoshone L . . . . Wyo.	44·17 N	110·50 W
67	Shoshone R . . . . Wyo.	44·20 N	109·28 W
129	Shostka (shôst′kȧ) . . . . . . Sov. Un.	51·51 N	33·31 E
148	Sh′ouchang (shō′zhäng) . . . . China	35·59 N	115·52 E
148	Shouhsien . . . . China	32·36 N	116·45 E
148	Shoukuang (shō′gōōäng) . . . . China	36·53 N	118·45 E
129	Shpola (shpô′lȧ) . . . . Sov. Un.	49·01 N	31·36 E
77	Shreveport (shrēv′pōrt) . . . . La.	32·30 N	93·46 W
110	Shrewsbury (shrōōz′bĕr-ĭ) . . . . Eng.	52·43 N	2·44 W
83	Shrewsbury . . . Mass. (Boston In.)	42·18 N	71·43 W
110	Shropshire (Co.) (shrŏp′shĭr) . Eng.	52·36 N	2·45 W
94	Shroud Cay (I.) (shroud) . . Ba. Is.	24·20 N	76·40 W
150	Shuangch′eng . . . . China	45·18 N	126·18 E
148	Shuangho (shōōäng hō) . . . . . China	31·33 N	116·48 E
148	Shuanglunho (shōōäng′lōōĕn′hō) China	31·50 N	115·07 E
150	Shuangyang . . . . China	43·28 N	125·45 E
71	Shullsburg (shŭlz′bûrg) . . . . . . Wis.	42·35 N	90·16 W
148	Shulyehehen (shōōlĭēhŭhĕn) . China	36·08 N	114·07 E
64	Shumagin (Is.) (shōō′mȧ-gēn) Alaska	55·22 N	159·20 W
151	Shunan (shōō′nän′) . . . . China	29·38 N	119·00 E
64	Shungnak (shŭng′nȧk) . . . . . Alaska	66·55 N	157·20 W
150	Shuni (shōōn′yĭ′) China (Peking In.)	40·09 N	116·38 E
146	Shunning (shŭ′nĭng′) . . . . China	24·34 N	99·49 E
149	Shunte . . . . China (Canton In.)	22·50 N	113·15 E
136	Shunut, ′Gora (Mt.) (gá-rä shōō′nōōt) Sov. Un. (Urals In.)	56·33 N	59·45 E
144	Shuqrah . . . . Aden	13·32 N	46·02 E
144	Shūrāb (R.) (shōō räb) . . . . . . Iran	31·02 N	55·43 E
152	Shuri (shōō′rē) . . . . Ryūkyū Is.	26·10 N	127·48 E
133	Shur R. (shōōr) . . . . Iran	35·40 N	50·10 E
144	Shūstar (shōōsh′tŭr) . . . . Iran	31·50 N	48·46 E
128	Shuya (shōō′yȧ) . . . . Sov. Un.	56·52 N	41·23 E
148	Shuyang (shōō yäng) . . . . China	34·09 N	118·47 E
145	Shweba . . . . Bur.	22·23 N	96·13 E
	Shyaulyay, see Šiauliai		
152	Siakin (L.) (sĭä′jĭn) . . . . China	42·25 N	132·45 E
139	Siak Ketjil (R.) Indon. (Singapore In.)	1·01 N	101·45 E
139	Siak Sri Indrapura (sē-äks′rĭ ĕn′drá-pōō′rä) Indon. (Singapore In.)	0·48 N	102·05 E
142	Sialkot (sē-äl′kōt) . . . . W. Pak.	32·39 N	74·30 E
	Siam, see Thailand		
154	Siam, G. of (sī-ăm′) . . . . Thai.	11·37 N	100·46 E
150	Sian (Hsian) (syän′) . . . . China	34·20 N	109·00 E
148	Siaowu Shan (Mts.) (sĭou′wōō shän) . China	39·48 N	114·52 E
127	Siátista (syä′tĭs-ta) . . . . Grc.	40·15 N	21·32 E
155	Siau (I.) . . . . Indon.	2·40 N	126·00 E
119	Šiauliai (Shyaulyay) (shē-ou′lē-ī) Sov. Un.	55·57 N	23·19 E
136	Sibay (sē′báy) . Sov. Un. (Urals In.)	52·41 N	58·40 E
126	Šibenik (shē-bä′nĕk) . . . . Yugo.	43·44 N	15·55 E
138	Siberia (Reg.) . . . . Asia	57·00 N	97·00 E
154	Siberut (I.) (sē′bȧ-rōōt) . . . . Indon.	1·22 S	99·45 E
142	Sibi . . . . W. Pak.	29·41 N	67·52 E
166	Sibiti (sē-bē-tē′) . . . . Con. B.	3·35 S	13·10 E
127	Sibiu (sē-bĭ-ōō′) . . . . Rom.	45·47 N	24·09 E
70	Sibley (sĭb′lē) . . . . Iowa	43·24 N	95·33 W
154	Sibolga (sē-bō′gä) . . . . Indon.	1·45 N	98·45 E
145	Sibsagar (sēb-sŭ′gŭr) . . . . India	26·47 N	94·45 E
154	Sibuti . . . . Phil.	4·40 N	119·30 E
155	Sibuyan (I.) (sē-bōō-yän′) Phil. (Manila In.)	12·19 N	122·25 E
154	Sibuyan Sea . . . . Phil.	12·43 N	122·38 E
154	Sicapoo (Mtn.) (sē-kä-pōō′) . . Phil.	18·05 N	121·03 E
113	Sicily (I.) (sĭs′ĭ-lē) . . . . It.	37·38 N	13·30 E
92	Sico R. (sē′kō) . . . . Hond.	15·32 N	85·42 W
98	Sicuani (sē-kwä′nē) . . . . Peru	14·12 S	71·12 W
165	Sidamo (Prov.) (sē-dä′mō) . . . Eth.	5·08 N	37·45 E
126	Siderno Marina (sē-dĕr′nō mä-rē′nä) . It.	38·18 N	16·19 E
126	Sídheros, Akr. (C.) . . . Grc. (Inset)	35·19 N	26·20 E
127	Sidhiró Kastron . . . . Grc.	41·13 N	23·27 E
125	Sidi-Aïsa . . . . Alg.	35·53 N	3·44 E
165	Sidi Barrānī . . . . U. A. R.	31·41 N	26·09 E
164	Sidi-bel Abbès (sē′dē-bĕl à-bĕs′) Alg.	35·15 N	0·43 W
164	Sidi Ifni (ēf′nē) . . . . Ifni	29·22 N	10·15 W
47	Sidley, Mt. (sĭd′lē) . . . . Ant.	77·25 S	129·00 W
67	Sidney (sĭd′nē) . . . . Mont.	47·43 N	104·07 W
70	Sidney . . . . Nebr.	41·10 N	103·00 W
80	Sidney . . . . Ohio	40·20 N	84·10 W
78	Sidney Lanier, L. (lăn′yēr) . . . . Ga.	34·27 N	83·56 W
	Sidon, see Sayda		
121	Siedlce (syĕd′′l-tsĕ) . . . . Pol.	52·09 N	22·20 E
123	Siegburg (zĕg′bōōrgh) Ger. (Ruhr In.)	50·48 N	7·13 E
123	Siegen (zē′ghĕn) . . Ger. (Ruhr In.)	50·52 N	8·01 E
111	Sieghartskirchen Aus. (Vienna In.)	48·16 N	16·00 E
120	Sieg R. (zēg) . . . . Ger.	50·51 N	7·53 E
121	Siemiatycze (syĕm′yȧ′tē-chĕ) . Pol.	52·26 N	22·52 E
121	Siemionówka (sĕĕ-mēō′-nôf-kȧ) Pol.	52·53 N	43·50 E
154	Siem Reap (syĕm′rä′äp) . . . Camb.	13·32 N	103·54 E
126	Siena (sē-ĕn′ä) . . . . It.	43·19 N	11·21 E
121	Sieradz (syĕ′rädz) . . . . Pol.	51·35 N	18·45 E
124	Siero (syä′rō) . . . . Sp.	43·24 N	5·39 W
121	Sierpc (syĕrpts) . . . . Pol.	52·51 N	19·42 E
76	Sierra Blanca (sē-ĕ′rȧ blaŋ-kȧ) Tex.	31·10 N	105·20 W
69	Sierra Blanca Pk. (blăn′kȧ) N. Mex.	33·25 N	105·50 W
163	Sierra Leone (sē-ĕr′rä lā-ō′nä) . Afr.	8·48 N	12·30 E
74	Sierra Madre (mä′drē) Calif. (Los Angeles In.)	34·10 N	118·03 W
76	Sierra Mojada (sē-ĕ′r-rä-mō-ĸä′dä) . Mex.	27·22 N	103·42 W
127	Sífnos (I.) . . . . Grc.	36·58 N	24·30 E
118	Sigdal (sēgh′däl) . . . . Nor.	60·01 N	9·35 E
122	Sigean (sē-zhŏɴ′) . . . . Fr.	43·02 N	2·56 E
71	Sigeurney (sē-gûr-nĭ) . . . . Iowa	41·16 N	92·10 W
121	Sighet (sē-gât′) . . . . Rom.	47·57 N	23·55 E
121	Sighisoara (sē-gē-shwä′rȧ) . . . Rom.	46·11 N	24·48 E
112	Siglufjördhur . . . . Ice.	66·06 N	18·45 W
133	Signakhi . . . . Sov. Un.	41·45 N	45·50 E
74	Signal Hill (sĭg′nȧl hĭl) Calif. (Los Angeles In.)	33·48 N	118·11 W
98	Sigsig (sēg-sēg′) . . . . Ec.	3·05 S	78·44 W
118	Sigtuna (sēgh-tōō′nȧ) . . . . Swe.	59·40 N	17·39 E
94	Siguanea, Ensenada de la (B.) (ĕn-sĕ-nä-dä-dĕ-lä-sē-gwä-nā′ä) Cuba	21·45 N	83·15 W
92	Siguatepeque (sē-gwȧ′tĕ-pĕ-kĕ) Hond.	14·33 N	87·51 W
124	Sigüenza (sē-gwĕ′n-zä) . . . . Sp.	41·03 N	2·38 W
164	Siguiri (sē-gē-rē′) . . . . Gui.	11·30 N	9·04 W
133	Siirt (sĭ-ērt′) . . . . Tur.	38·00 N	42·00 E
164	Sikasso (sē-käs′sō) . . . . Mali	11·15 N	5·43 W
73	Sikeston (sīks′tŭn) . . . . Mo.	36·50 N	89·35 W
135	Sikhote Alin′, Khrebet (Mts.) (se-ĸō′ta a-lēn′) . Sov. Un.	45·00 N	135·45 E
127	Sikinos (I.) (sĭ′kĭ-nōs) . . . . Grc.	36·45 N	24·55 E
142	Sikkim . . . . Asia	27·42 N	88·25 E
121	Siklós (sĭ′klōsh) . . . . Hung.	45·51 N	18·18 E
124	Sil (R.) (sē′l) . . . . Sp.	42·20 N	7·13 W
155	Silang (sē-läng′) . Phil. (Manila In.)	14·14 N	120·58 E
90	Silao (sē-lä′ō) . . . . Mex.	20·56 N	101·25 W
142	Silchar (sĭl-chär′) . . . . India	24·52 N	92·50 E
168	Silent Valley (sī′lĕnt vă′lē) . S. Afr. (Johannesburg & Pretoria In.)	24·32 S	26·40 E
79	Siler City (sī′lēr) . . . . N. C.	35·45 N	79·29 W
121	Silesia (Reg.) (sĭ-lē′shȧ) . . . . . . Pol.	50·58 N	16·53 E
133	Silifke . . . . Tur.	36·20 N	34·00 E
115	Silistra (sē-lēs′trȧ) . . . . Bul.	44·01 N	27·13 E
118	Siljan (R.) (sēl′yän) . . . . Swe.	60·48 N	14·28 E
118	Silkeborg (sĭl′kĕ-bôr′) . . . . Den.	56·10 N	9·33 E
85	Sillery (sēl′-re′) . Can. (Quebec In.)	46·46 N	71·15 W
73	Siloam Springs (sī-lōm) . . . . Ark.	36·10 N	94·32 W
90	Silocayoápan (sē-lô-kä-yô-ȧ′pän) Mex.	17·29 N	98·09 W
77	Silsbee (sĭlz′ bē) . . . . Tex.	30·19 N	94·09 W
119	Šilutė (shĭ-lōō′tȧ) . . . . Sov. Un.	55·23 N	21·26 E
101	Silva Jardim (sē′l-vä-zhär-dēɴ) Braz. (Rio de Janeiro In.)	22·40 S	42·24 W
65	Silvana (sĭl-vän′ȧ) Wash. (Seattle In.)	48·12 N	122·16 W
99	Silvânia (sēl-vá′nyä) . . . . Braz.	16·43 S	48·33 W
166	Silva Porto (sĭl′vȧ pôr′tōō) . . . Ang.	12·20 S	17·05 E
73	Silver (L.) . . . . Mo.	39·38 N	93·12 W
74	Silverado (sĭl-vēr-ä′dō) Calif. (Los Angeles In.)	33·45 N	117·40 W
95	Silver Bk . . . . Ba. Is.	20·40 N	69·40 W
95	Silver Bank Passage (Str.) . Ba. Is.	20·40 N	70·20 W
71	Silver Bay . . . . Minn.	47·24 N	91·07 W
69	Silver City (sĭl′vēr sĭ′tĭ) . . N. Mex.	32·45 N	108·20 W
93	Silver City . . . . Pan.	9·20 N	79·54 W
81	Silver Creek (crēk) . . . . N. Y.	42·35 N	79·10 W
69	Silver Cr . . . . Ariz.	34·30 N	110·05 W
75	Silver Cr . . . . . . Ind. (Louisville In.)	38·20 N	85·45 W
75	Silver Cr., Muddy Fk. Ind. (Louisville In.)	38·26 N	85·52 W
65	Silverdale (sĭl′vēr-dāl) Wash. (Seattle In.)	49·39 N	122·42 W
75	Silver Lake (lāk) Wis. (Milwaukee In.)	42·33 N	88·10 W
75	Silver L . . . . Wis. (Milwaukee In.)	42·35 N	88·08 W
81	Silver Spring (sprĭng) . . . . Md.	39·00 N	77·00 W
65	Silver Star Mtn. Wash. (Portland In.)	45·45 N	122·15 W
69	Silverton (sĭl′vēr-tŭn) . . . . Colo.	37·50 N	107·40 W
75	Silverton . . . . Ohio (Cincinnati In.)	39·12 N	84·24 W
66	Silverton . . . . Ore.	45·02 N	122·46 W
167	Silverton . . . . S. Afr. (Johannesburg & Pretoria In.)	25·45 S	28·13 E
124	Silves (sēl′vĕzh) . . . . Port.	37·15 N	8·24 W
66	Silvies R. (sĭl′vēz) . . . . Ore.	43·44 N	119·15 W
168	Silwá (Baḩrī) . . U. A. R. (Nile In.)	24·43 N	32·58 E
136	Sim (sĭm) . . . . Sov. Un. (Urals In.)	55·00 N	57·42 E
80	Simcoe (sĭm′kō) . . . . Can.	42·50 N	80·20 W
81	Simcoe (L.) . . . . Can.	44·30 N	79·20 W
154	Simeuloee (I.) . . . . Indon.	2·27 N	95·30 E
129	Simferopol′ (Akmechet) (sēm-fĕ-rô′pôl′) (ák-mĕch′ĕt) Sov. Un.	44·58 N	34·04 E
115	Simi (I.) . . . . Grc.	36·27 N	27·41 E
65	Similk Beach (sē′mĭlk) Wash. (Seattle In.)	48·27 N	122·35 W
142	Simla (sĭm′lȧ) . . . . India	31·09 N	77·15 E
121	Simleul-Silvaniei (shēm-lā′ōōl-sēl-vä′nyĕ-ē) . Rom.	47·14 N	22·46 E
94	Simms Pt . . . . Ba. Is.	25·00 N	77·40 W
91	Simojovel (sē-mō-hô-vĕl′) . . . Mex.	17·12 N	92·43 W
119	Simola (sē′mô-lȧ) . . . . Fin.	60·55 N	28·06 E
101	Simonésia (sē-mô-nĕ′syä) Braz. (Rio de Janeiro In.)	20·04 S	41·53 W
166	Simonstown (sī′mŭnztoun) S. Afr. (Cape Town In.)	34·11 S	18·25 E
120	Simplon P. (sĭm′plŏn) (săɴ-plôɴ′) Switz.	46·13 N	7·53 E
120	Simplon Tun . . . . It.-Switz.	46·16 N	8·20 E
71	Simpson (I.) . . . . Can.	48·43 N	87·44 W
158	Simpson Des. (sĭmp-sŭn) . . . Austl.	24·40 S	136·40 E
86	Simpson Pen . . . . Can.	68·58 N	89·20 W
118	Simrishamn (sĕm′rēs-häm′n) . Swe.	55·35 N	14·19 E
136	Sim R . . . . Sov Un. (Urals In.)	55·00 N	57·42 E
77	Sims Bay, (sĭmz bī-yōō′) . Tex. (In.)	29·37 N	95·23 W
135	Simushir (I.) (se-mōō′shēr) Sov. Un.	47·15 N	150·47 E
127	Sinaia (sĭ-nä′yȧ) . . . . Rom.	45·20 N	25·30 E
165	Sinai Pen. (sī′nī) . . . . U. A. R.	29·24 N	33·29 E
155	Sinait (sē-nä′ēt) . Phil. (Manila In.)	15·54 N	120·28 E
88	Sinaloa (State) (sē-nä-lô-ä) . . Mex.	25·15 N	107·45 W
152	Sinanju (sĭ′nän-jōō′) . . . . Kor.	39·39 N	125·41 E
133	Sinap . . . . Tur.	42·00 N	35·05 E
98	Sincé (sēn′sā) . . . . Col.	9·15 N	75·14 W
98	Sincelejo (sēn-sä-lā′hō) . . . . . . Col.	9·12 N	75·30 W
65	Sinclair Inlet (sĭn-klâr′) Wash. (Seattle In.)	47·31 N	122·41 W
119	Sindi (sēn′dē) . . . . Sov. Un.	58·20 N	24·40 E
129	Sinel′nikovo (sē′nyĕl-nē′kô′vô) Sov. Un.	49·19 N	35·33 E
124	Sines (sē′nȧzh) . . . . Port.	37·57 N	8·50 W
165	Singa (sĭŋ′gȧ) . . . . Sud.	13·09 N	33·52 E
139	Singapore (sĭn′gȧ-pōr′) Singapore I. (Singapore In.)	1·18 N	103·52 E
139	Singapore I . . . Asia (Singapore In.)	1·22 N	103·45 E
139	Singapore Str. Indon. (Singapore In.)	1·14 N	104·20 E

ng-sing; ŋ-baŋk; ɴ-nasalized n; nŏd; cŏmmit; ōld; ôbey; ôrder; fōōd; fŏŏt; ou-out; s-soft; sh-dish; th-thin; pūre; ûnite; ûrn; stŭd; circŭs; ü-as "y" in study; ′-indeterminate vowel.

268 Singaradjac–Solomon R. PRONOUNCING INDEX

Page	Name Pronunciation Region	Lat. °′	Long. °′
154	Singaradjac (sĭŋ′gȧ-rä′jȧ) Indon.	8·15 S	115·03 E
127	Singitikós Kólpos (G.) Grc.	40·15 N	24·00 E
146	Singu (sĭn′gŭ) Bur.	22·37 N	96·04 E
167	Singunyane (R.) Bas. (Natal In.)	29·35 S	28·08 E
129	Siniye Lipyagi (sēn′ē-ĕ lēp′yȧ-gē) Sov. Un.	51·24 N	38·29 E
126	Sinj (sēn′) Yugo.	43·42 N	16·39 E
146	Sinkiang Uighur (Aut. Reg.) China	40·15 N	82·15 E
136	Sin′kovo (sĭn-kô′vô) Sov. Un. (Moscow In.)	56·23 N	37·19 E
99	Sinnamary Fr. Gu.	5·15 N	57·52 W
126	Sinni (R.) (sēn′nē) It.	40·05 N	16·15 E
168	Sinnūris U. A. R. (Nile In.)	29·25 N	30·52 E
100	Sino, Pedra do (Mtn.) (pĕ′drä-dô-sē′nô) Braz. (In.)	22·27 S	43·02 W
166	Sinoia (sĭ-noi′ȧ) S. Rh.	17·17 S	30·09 E
111	Sint Niklaas Bel. (Brussels In.)	51·10 N	4·07 E
77	Sinton (sĭn′tŭn) Tex.	28·03 N	97·30 W
125	Sintra (sēn′trȧ) Port. (Lisbon In.)	38·48 N	9·23 W
111	Sint Truiden Bel. (Brussels In.)	50·49 N	5·14 E
152	Sinŭiju (sĭ′nōōĭ-jōō) Kor.	40·04 N	124·33 E
136	Sinyavino (sĭn-yä′vĭ-nô) Sov. Un. (Leningrad In.)	59·50 N	31·07 E
128	Sinyaya (R.) (sēn′yȧ-yȧ) Sov. Un.	56·40 N	28·20 E
129	Sinyukha (R.) (sē′nyōō-ĸȧ) Sov. Un.	48·34 N	30·49 E
120	Sion (sē′ôɴ′) Switz.	46·15 N	7·17 E
70	Sioux City (sōō) Iowa	42·30 N	96·25 W
70	Sioux Falls (fôlz) S. D.	43·33 N	96·43 W
87	Sioux Lookout Can.	50·11 N	91·42 W
98	Sipí (sē-pē′) Col. (In.)	4·39 N	76·38 W
86	Sipiwesk Can.	55·36 N	97·24 W
78	Sipsey (R.) (sĭp′sē) Ala.	33·26 N	87·42 W
154	Sipura (I.) Indon.	2·15 S	99·33 E
90	Siqueros (sē-kā′rōs) Mex.	23·19 N	106·14 W
93	Siquia, R. (sē-kē′ä) Nic.	12·23 N	84·36 W
113	Siracusa (sē-rä-koo′sä) It.	37·02 N	15·19 E
142	Sirājganj (sĭ-räj′gŭnj) E. Pak.	24·23 N	89·43 E
92	Sirama (sē-rä-mä) Sal.	13·23 N	87·55 W
158	Sir Edward Pellew Group (Is.) (pĕl′ū) Austl.	15·15 S	137·15 E
121	Siretul R Rom.	46·10 N	27·18 E
144	Sirham, Wadi (R.) Sau. Ar.	31·02 N	37·16 E
127	Síros (Ermoúpolis) Grc.	37·30 N	24·56 E
127	Síros (I.) Grc.	37·23 N	24·55 E
142	Sirsa India	29·39 N	75·02 E
119	Širvintos (shēr′vĭn-tôs) Sov. Un.	55·02 N	24·59 E
91	Sisal (sē-säl′) Mex.	21·09 N	90·03 W
126	Siska (sē′sȧk) Yugo.	45·29 N	16·20 E
68	Sisquoc (R.) (sĭs′kwŏk) Calif.	34·47 N	120·13 W
70	Sisseton (sĭs′tŭn) S. D.	45·39 N	97·04 W
144	Sistān, Daryacheh-ye (L.) Iran-Afg.	31·45 N	61·15 E
123	Sisteron (sēst′rôɴ′) Fr.	44·10 N	5·55 E
80	Sisterville (sĭs′tēr-vĭl) W. Va.	39·30 N	81·00 W
126	Sitía (sē′tĭ-ȧ) Grc. (In.)	26·10 N	35·09 E
64	Sitka (sĭt′kȧ) Alaska	57·08 N	135·18 W
64	Sitka Natl. Mon Alaska	57·20 N	136·10 W
110	Sittingbourne (sĭt-ĭng-bôrn) Eng. (London In.)	51·20 N	0·44 E
133	Sivas (sē′väs) Tur.	39·50 N	36·50 E
129	Sivash (L.) (sē′vȧsh) Sov. Un.	45·55 N	34·42 E
133	Siverek (sē′vĕ-rĕk) Tur.	37·50 N	39·20 E
119	Siverskaya (sē′vĕr-skȧ-yȧ) Sov. Un.	59·17 N	30·03 E
165	Sīwah (Oasis) (sē′wä) U. A. R.	29·33 N	25·11 E
93	Sixaola R. (sē-ĸä-ō′lä) (sĕk-sä-ō′lä) C. R.	9·31 N	83·07 W
165	Sixth Cataract Sud.	16·26 N	32·44 E
118	Sjaelland (I.) (shĕl′län′) Den.	55·34 N	11·35 E
127	Sjenica (syĕ′nē-tsä) Yugo.	43·15 N	20·02 E
129	Skadovsk (skä′dôfsk) Sov. Un.	46·08 N	32·54 E
118	Skagen (skä′ghĕn) Den.	57·43 N	10·32 E
118	Skagen (Pt.) Den.	57·43 N	10·31 E
118	Skagerrak (Str.) (skä-ghĕ-räk′) Eur.	57·43 N	8·28 E
65	Skagit B. (skăg′ĭt) Wash. (Seattle In.)	48·20 N	122·32 W
66	Skagit R Wash.	48·29 N	121·52 W
64	Skagway (skăg-wā) Alaska	59·30 N	135·28 W
118	Skälderviken (B.) Swe.	56·20 N	12·25 E
135	Skalistyy, Golets (Mtn.) Sov. Un.	57·28 N	119·48 E
65	Skamania (skȧ-mā′nĭ-ȧ) Wash. (Portland In.)	45·37 N	122·03 W
65	Skamokawa (skȧ-mā′nĭ-ȧ) Wash. (Portland In.)	46·16 N	123·27 W
118	Skanderborg (skän′ĕr-bôr′) Den.	56·04 N	9·55 E
81	Skaneateles (skăn-ĕ-ăt′lĕs) N. Y.	42·55 N	76·25 W
81	Skaneateles (L.) N. Y.	42·50 N	76·20 W
118	Skänninge (shĕn′ĭng-ĕ) Swe.	58·24 N	15·02 E
118	Skanör (skän′ûr) Swe.	55·24 N	12·49 E
127	Skantzoúra (Is.) (skän′tsōō-rä) Grc.	39·03 N	24·05 E
118	Skara (skä′rȧ) Swe.	58·25 N	13·24 E
86	Skeena (R.) Can.	54·31 N	129·21 W
167	Skeerpoort S. Afr. (Johannesburg & Pretoria In.)	25·49 S	27·45 E
167	Skeerpoort (R.) S. Afr. (Johannesburg & Pretoria In.)	25·58 S	27·41 E
99	Skeldon (skĕl′dŭn) Br. Gu.	5·49 N	57·15 W
112	Skellefte (R.) (shĕl′ĕ-ftĕ) Swe.	65·18 N	19·08 E
112	Skellefteå (shĕl′ĕf-tĕ-å′) Swe.	64·47 N	20·48 E
118	Skern (R.) (skĕrn) Den.	55·56 N	8·52 E
116	Skerries (Is.) (skĕr′ēz) Wales	53·30 N	4·59 W
136	Skhodnya R. (skôd′nyȧ) Sov. Un. (Moscow In.)	55·55 N	37·16 E
127	Skíathos (I.) (skē′ȧ-thôs) Grc.	39·15 N	23·25 E
116	Skibbereen (skĭb′ēr-ēn) Ire.	51·32 N	9·25 W
77	Skidmore (skĭd′mōr) Tex.	28·16 N	97·40 W
118	Skien (skē′ĕn) Nor.	59·13 N	9·35 E
121	Skierniewice (skyĕr-nyĕ-vēt′sĕ) Pol.	51·58 N	20·13 E
168	Skilpadfontein S. Afr. (Johannesburg & Pretoria In.)	25·02 S	28·50 E
127	Skíros Grc.	38·53 N	24·32 E
127	Skiros (I.) Grc.	38·50 N	24·43 E
118	Skive (skē′vĕ) Den.	56·34 N	8·56 E
112	Skjalfandá (R.) (skyäl′fänd-ô) Ice.	65·24 N	16·40 W
112	Skjerstad (skyĕr-städ) Nor.	67·12 N	15·37 E
126	Škofja Loka (shkôf′yȧ lō′kȧ) Yugo.	46·10 N	14·20 E
75	Skokie (skō′kē) Ill. (Chicago In.)	42·02 N	87·45 W
65	Skokomish Ind. Res. (skŏ-kō′mĭsh) Wash. (Seattle In.)	47·22 N	123·07 W
121	Skole (skô′lĕ) Sov. Un.	49·03 N	23·32 E
127	Skópelos (I.) (skô′pȧ-lôs) Grc.	39·04 N	23·31 E
128	Skopin (skô′pēn) Sov. Un.	53·49 N	39·35 E
127	Skopje (skôp′yĕ) Yugo.	42·02 N	21·26 E
118	Skövde (shûv′dĕ) Swe.	58·25 N	13·48 E
135	Skovorodino (skô′vô-rô′dĭ-nô) Sov. Un.	53·53 N	123·56 E
82	Skowhegan (skou-hē′gŭn) Maine	44·45 N	69·27 W
126	Skradin (skrä′dēn) Yugo.	43·49 N	17·58 E
118	Skreia (skrā′ȧ) Nor.	60·40 N	10·55 E
118	Skudeneshavn (skōō′dĕ-nes-houn′) Nor.	59·10 N	5·19 E
118	Skulerud (skōō′lĕ-rōōdh) Nor.	59·40 N	11·30 E
69	Skull Valley Ind. Res. (skŭl) Utah	40·25 N	112·50 W
78	Skuna, (R.) (skû′nȧ) Miss.	33·57 N	89·36 W
71	Skunk (R.) (skŭnk) Iowa	41·12 N	92·14 W
119	Skuodas (skwô′dȧs) Sov. Un.	56·16 N	21·32 E
118	Skurup (skû′rŏŏp) Swe.	55·29 N	13·27 E
129	Skvira (skvē′rä) Sov. Un.	49·43 N	29·41 E
100	Skvring, Seno (B.) (sĕ′nô-s-krē′ng) Chile	52·35 S	72·30 W
120	Skwierzyna (skvē-ĕr′zhĭ-nȧ) Pol.	52·35 N	15·30 E
116	Skye (I.) (skī) Scot.	57·25 N	6·17 W
65	Skykomish (R.) (skī′kō-mĭsh) Wash. (Seattle In.)	47·50 N	121·55 W
118	Slagese Den.	55·25 N	11·19 E
154	Slamet, Gunung (Mtn.) (slä′mĕt) Indon.	7·15 S	109·15 E
127	Slanic (slŭ′nĕk) Rom.	45·13 N	25·56 E
71	Slate (I.) (slāt) Can.	48·38 N	87·14 W
73	Slater (slāt′ēr) Mo.	39·13 N	93·03 W
127	Slatina (slä′tē-nä) Rom.	44·26 N	24·21 E
72	Slaton (slā′tŭn) Tex.	33·26 N	101·38 W
86	Slave (R.) (slāv) Can.	59·40 N	111·21 W
134	Slavgorod (slȧf′gô-rôt) Sov. Un.	52·58 N	78·43 E
127	Slavonija (Reg.) (slä-vô′nē-yä) Yugo.	45·29 N	17·31 E
126	Slavonska Požega (slä-vôn′skä pô′zhĕ-gä) Yugo.	45·18 N	17·42 E
127	Slavonski Brod (slä-vôn′skē brôd) Yugo.	45·10 N	18·01 E
129	Slavuta (slȧ-vōō′tȧ) Sov. Un.	50·18 N	27·01 E
129	Slavyansk (slȧv′yänsk′) Sov. Un.	48·52 N	37·34 E
129	Slavyanskaya (slȧv-yan′skȧ-yȧ) Sov. Un.	45·14 N	38·09 E
70	Slayton (slā′tŭn) Minn.	44·00 N	95·44 W
110	Sleaford (slē′fērd) Eng.	53·00 N	0·25 W
71	Sleepy Eye (slēp′ĭ ī) Minn.	44·17 N	94·44 W
77	Slidell (slĭ-dĕl′) La.	30·17 N	89·47 W
111	Sliedrecht Neth (Amsterdam In.)	51·49 N	4·46 E
116	Sligo (slĭ′gō) Ire.	54·17 N	8·19 W
118	Slite (slē′tĕ) Swe.	57·41 N	18·47 E
127	Sliven (slē′vĕn) Bul.	42·41 N	26·20 E
84	Sloatsburg (slōts′bûrg) N. Y. (New York In.)	41·09 N	74·11 W
119	Slobodka (slô′bôd-kȧ) Sov. Un.	54·34 N	26·12 E
132	Slobodskoy (slô′bôt-skoi) Sov. Un.	58·48 N	50·02 E
119	Sloka (slô′kȧ) Sov. Un.	56·57 N	23·37 E
121	Slonim (swô′nêm) Sov. Un.	53·05 N	25·19 E
110	Slough (slou) Eng. (London In.)	51·29 N	0·36 W
	Slovakia, see Slovensko		
126	Slovenija (Reg.) (slô-vĕ′nê-yä) Yugo.	45·58 N	14·43 E
121	Slovensko (Slovakia) (Prov.) (slô-vĕn′skô) (slô-vȧk′ĭ-ȧ) Czech.	48·40 N	19·00 E
121	Sluch′ (R.) Sov. Un.	50·56 N	26·48 E
126	Sluderno (slōō-dĕr′nô) It.	46·38 N	10·37 E
126	Slunj (slōōn′) Yugo.	45·08 N	15·46 E
121	Slupsk (swŏŏpsk) Pol.	54·28 N	17·02 E
128	Slutsk (slōōtsk) Sov. Un.	53·02 N	27·34 E
116	Slyne Head (slīn) Ire.	53·25 N	10·05 W
73	Smackover (smăk′ō-vēr) Ark.	33·22 N	92·42 W
127	Smederevo (Semendria) (smĕ′dĕ-rĕ-vô) (sĕ-mĕn′drĭ-ȧ) Yugo.	44·39 N	20·54 E
127	Smederevska Palanka (smĕ-dĕ-rĕv′skä pä-län′kä) Yugo.	44·21 N	21·00 E
118	Smedjebacken (smĭ′tyĕ-bä-kĕn) Swe.	60·09 N	15·19 E
129	Smela (smyä′lȧ) Sov. Un.	49·14 N	31·52 E
129	Smeloye (smyä′lô-ĕ) Sov. Un.	50·55 N	33·36 E
81	Smethport (smĕth′pōrt) Pa.	41·50 N	78·25 W
128	Smiltene (smēl′tĕ-nĕ) Sov. Un.	57·26 N	25·57 E
86	Smith (smĭth) Can.	55·10 N	113·53 W
65	Smith (I.) Wash. (Seattle In.)	48·20 N	122·53 W
72	Smith Center (sĕn′tēr) Kans.	39·45 N	98·46 W
86	Smithers (smĭth′ērs) Can.	54·13 N	127·22 W
79	Smithfield (smĭth′fēld) N. C.	35·30 N	78·21 W
74	Smithfield Tex. (Dallas, Fort Worth In.)	32·52 N	97·12 W
67	Smithfield Utah	41·50 N	111·49 W
80	Smithland (smĭth′lănd) Ky.	37·10 N	88·25 W
77	Smith Point Tex. (In.)	29·32 N	94·45 W
67	Smith R Mont.	47·00 N	111·20 W
81	Smiths Falls (smĭths) Can.	44·55 N	76·05 W
83	Smith Sd Can.	48·15 N	53·50 W
160	Smithton (smĭth′tŭn) Austl.	40·55 S	145·12 E
74	Smithton Ill. (St. Louis In.)	38·24 N	89·59 W
77	Smithville (smĭth′vĭl) Tex.	30·00 N	97·08 W
167	Smits (R.) S. Afr. (Natal In.)	31·45 S	26·33 E
166	Smitswinkel Flats S. Afr. (Cape Town In.)	34·16 S	18·25 E
68	Smoke Creek Des. (smōk crēk) Nev.	40·28 N	119·40 W
73	Smoky Hill (R.) (smōk′ĭ hĭl) Kans.	38·40 N	97·32 W
118	Smöla (I.) (smûlä) Nor.	63·16 N	7·40 E
128	Smolensk (smô-lyĕnsk′) Sov. Un.	54·46 N	32·03 E
128	Smolensk (Oblast) Sov. Un.	55·00 N	32·18 E
127	Smyadovo Bul.	43·04 N	27·00 E
81	Smyrna (smûr′nȧ) Del.	39·20 N	75·35 W
84	Smyrna Ga. (Atlanta In.)	33·53 N	84·31 W
	Smyrna, see Izmir		
64	Snag (snăg) Can.	62·18 N	140·30 W
71	Snake (R.) (snāk) Minn.	45·58 N	93·20 W
69	Snake Ra Nev.	39·20 N	114·15 W
67	Snake R., Henrys Fork Idaho	43·52 N	111·55 W
66	Snake R Wash.	46·33 N	118·18 W
66	Snake River Pln. (rĭv′ēr) Idaho	43·08 N	114·46 W
94	Snap Pt Ba. Is.	23·45 N	77·30 W
69	Sneffels Pk. (snĕf′ĕlz) Colo.	38·00 N	107·50 W
85	Snelgrove (snĕl′grōv) Can. (Toronto In.)	43·44 N	79·50 W
121	Sniardwy L. (snyärt′vĭ) Pol.	53·46 N	21·59 E
118	Snöhetta (Mtn.) (snû-hĕttä) Nor.	62·18 N	9·12 E
65	Snohomish (snō-hō′mĭsh) Wash. (Seattle In.)	47·55 N	122·05 W
65	Snohomish (R.) Wash. (Seattle In.)	47·53 N	122·04 W
65	Snoqualmie (snō qwäl′mē) Wash. (Seattle In.)	47·32 N	121·50 W
66	Snoqualmie R Wash.	47·32 N	121·53 W
129	Snov (R.) (snôf) Sov. Un.	51·38 N	31·38 E
116	Snowdon, Mt. (snō′dŭn) Wales	53·05 N	4·04 W
81	Snow Hill (hĭl) Md.	38·15 N	75·20 W
159	Snowy Mts. (snō′ē) Austl.	36·17 S	148·30 E
72	Snyder (snī′dēr) Okla.	34·40 N	98·57 W
76	Snyder Tex.	32·48 N	100·53 W
110	Soar (R.) (sōr) Eng.	52·44 N	1·09 W
165	Sobat R. (sō′bȧt) Sud.	9·04 N	32·02 E
128	Sobinka (sô-bĭŋ′kȧ) Sov. Un.	55·59 N	40·02 E
153	Sobo Zan (Mt.) (sô′bô zän) Jap.	32·47 N	131·27 E
99	Sobral (sô-brä′l) Braz.	3·39 S	40·16 W
121	Sochaczew (sô-ĸä′chĕf) Pol.	52·14 N	20·18 E
146	Soché (Yarkand) (sō′chĕ) (yär-känt′) China	38·15 N	77·15 E
133	Sochi (sôch′ĭ) Sov. Un.	43·35 N	39·50 E
157	Society Is. (sô-sī′ĕ-tē) Fr. Polynesia	15·00 S	157·30 W
84	Socola (sŏ-kō′lȧ) La. (New Orleans In.)	29·32 N	89·46 W
91	Socoltenango (sô-kôl-tĕ-näŋ′gō) Mex.	16·17 N	92·20 W
101	Socorro (sŏ-kô′r-rō) Braz. (Rio de Janeiro In.)	22·35 S	46·32 W
98	Socorro (sô-kôr′rō) Col.	6·23 N	73·19 W
69	Socorro N. Mex.	34·05 N	106·55 W
168	Socotra I. (sô-kō′trȧ) Som. (Horn of Afr. In.)	13·00 N	52·30 E
124	Socuellamos (sō-kōō-āl′yä-môs) Sp.	39·18 N	2·48 W
68	Soda (L.) (sō′dȧ) Calif.	35·12 N	116·25 W
65	Soda Pk Wash. (Portland In.)	45·53 N	122·04 W
67	Soda Springs (sprĭngz) Idaho	42·39 N	111·37 W
118	Söderhamn (sû-dĕr-häm′′n) Swe.	61·20 N	17·00 E
118	Söderköping Swe.	58·30 N	16·14 E
118	Södertälje (sû-dĕr-tĕl′yĕ) Swe.	59·12 N	17·35 E
150	Sodi Soruksum (Mtn.) China	37·20 N	102·00 E
165	Sodo Eth.	7·03 N	37·46 E
118	Södra Dellen (L.) Swe.	61·45 N	16·30 E
120	Soest (zōst) Ger.	51·35 N	8·05 E
	Sofia, see Sofiya		
127	Sofiya (Sofia) (sô′fē-yȧ) (sô′fê-ȧ) Bul.	42·43 N	23·20 E
129	Sofiyevka (sô-fē′yĕf-kȧ) Sov. Un.	48·03 N	33·53 E
153	Sōga (sô′gä) Jap. (Tōkyō In.)	35·35 N	140·08 E
98	Sogamoso (sô-gä-mô′sō) Col.	5·42 N	72·51 W
118	Sogndal (sôghn′dȧl) Nor.	58·20 N	6·17 E
118	Sogndal Nor.	61·14 N	7·04 E
118	Sogne Fd. (sôgn′ĕ fyôrd) Nor.	61·09 N	5·30 E
128	Sogozha (R.) (sô′gô-zhȧ) Sov. Un.	58·35 N	39·08 E
122	Soissons (swä-sôɴ′) Fr.	49·23 N	3·17 E
153	Sōka (sō′kä) Jap. (Tōkyō In.)	35·50 N	139·49 E
121	Sokal (sô′käl′) Sov. Un.	50·28 N	24·20 E
133	Soke (sû′kĕ) Tur.	37·40 N	27·10 E
164	Sokodé (sô-kô-dā′) Togo	8·56 N	1·08 E
121	Sokolka (sô-kōōl′kȧ) Pol.	53·23 N	23·30 E
164	Sokolo (sô-kô-lō′) Mali	14·51 N	6·09 W
164	Sokoto (sō′kô-tō) Nig.	13·03 N	5·14 E
164	Sokoto (Reg.) Nig.	12·29 N	6·34 E
121	Sokotów Podlaski (sô-kô-wōōf′ pŭd-lä′skĭ) Pol.	52·24 N	22·15 E
91	Sola de Vega (San Miguel) (sō′lä dā vā′gä) (sän mē-gāl′) Mex.	16·31 N	96·58 W
155	Solana (sō-lä′nä) Phil. (Manila In.)	17·40 N	121·41 E
161	Solander, C. Austl. (Sydney In.)	34·03 S	151·16 E
155	Solano (sō-lä′nō) Phil. (Manila In.)	16·31 N	121·11 E
98	Soledad (sō-lĕ-dä′d) Col.	10·47 N	75·00 W
90	Soledad Díez Gutierrez (sô-lä-dhädh′dē′äz gōō-tyä′rĕz) Mex.	22·19 N	100·54 W
66	Soleduck R. (sōl′dŭk) Wash.	47·59 N	124·28 W
92	Solentiname, Islas de (Is.) (ĕ′s-läs-dĕ-sô-lĕn-tē-nä′mȧ) Nic.	11·15 N	85·16 W
110	Solihull (sō′lĭ-hŭl) Eng.	52·25 N	1·46 W
136	Solikamsk (sô-lē-kȧmsk′) Sov. Un. (Urals In.)	59·38 N	56·48 E
98	Solimões, Rio (R.) (rē′ō-sô-lē-mô′ĕs) Braz.	2·45 S	67·44 W
123	Solingen (zô′lĭng-ĕn) Ger. (Ruhr In.)	51·10 N	7·05 E
118	Sollefteå (sôl-lĕf′tĕ-ô) Swe.	63·06 N	17·17 E
125	Sóller (sō′lyĕr) Sp.	39·45 N	2·40 E
133	Sol′-Iletsk Sov. Un.	51·10 N	55·05 E
122	Sologne (Reg.) (sō-lōn′yĕ) Fr.	47·36 N	1·53 E
92	Solola (sô-lō′lä) Guat.	14·45 N	91·12 W
159	Solomon Is. Prot. (sŏ′ô-mŭn) Oceania	8·50 S	157·52 E
156	Solomon Is. Oceania	7·00 S	148·00 E
72	Solomon R Kans.	39·24 N	98·19 W
72	Solomon R. North Fk Kans.	39·34 N	99·52 W
72	Solomon R., South Fk Kans.	39·19 N	99·52 W

ăt; finăl; rāte; senâte; ärm; ȧsk; sofȧ; fâre; ch-choose; dh-as th in other; bē; ēvent; bĕt; recĕnt; cratẽr; g-go; gh-guttural g; bĭt; ĭ-short neutral; rīde; ĸ-guttural k as ch in German ich;

Page	Name Pronunciation Region	Lat. °′	Long. °′
75	Solon (sō'lŭn) Ohio (Cleveland In.)	41·23 N	81·26 W
120	Solothurn (zō'lō-thōōrn) Switz.	47·13 N	7·30 E
132	Solov'etskiy (I.) Sov. Un.	65·10 N	35·40 E
126	Šolta (I.) (shôl'tä) Yugo.	43·20 N	16·15 E
144	Soltānābād Iran	28·06 N	55·24 E
120	Soltau (sôl'tou) Ger.	53·00 N	9·50 E
128	Sol'tsy (sôl'tsė) Sov. Un.	58·04 N	30·13 E
150	Solun (sô-lōōn') China	47·32 N	121·18 E
81	Solvay (sŏl'vā) N. Y.	43·05 N	76·10 W
118	Sölvesborg (sûl'vĕs-bôrg) Swe.	56·04 N	14·35 E
132	Sol'vychegodsk (sôl'vê-chĕ-gôtsk') Sov. Un.	61·18 N	46·58 E
116	Solway Firth (sŏl'wāfûrth') Eng.-Scot.	54·42 N	3·55 W
163	Somali Republic (sō-mä'lē) Afr.	3·28 N	44·47 E
127	Sombor (sôm'bôr) Yugo.	45·45 N	19·10 E
90	Sombrerete (sōm-brā-rā'tā) Mex.	23·38 N	103·37 W
99	Sombrero, Cayo (C.) (kä-yō-sôm-brĕ'rō) Ven. (In.)	10·52 N	68·12 W
78	Somerset (sŭm'ēr-sĕt) Ky.	37·05 N	84·35 W
84	Somerset Mass. (Providence In.)	41·46 N	71·05 W
81	Somerset Pa.	40·00 N	79·05 W
74	Somerset Tex. (San Antonio In.)	29·13 N	98·39 W
167	Somerset East S. Afr. (Natal In.)	32·44 S	25·36 E
82	Somersworth (sŭm'ērz-wûrth) N. H.	43·16 N	70·53 W
68	Somerton (sŭm'ēr-tŭn) Ariz.	32·36 N	114·43 W
83	Somerville (sŭm'ēr-vĭl) Mass. (Boston In.)	42·23 N	71·06 W
84	Somerville N.J. (New York In.)	40·34 N	74·37 W
78	Somerville Tenn.	35·14 N	89·21 W
77	Somerville Tex.	30·21 N	96·31 W
121	Somesul R. (sô-mā'shōōl) Rom.	47·43 N	23·09 E
125	Somma Vesuviana (sôm'mä vä-zōō-vē-ä'nä) It. (Naples In.)	40·38 N	14·27 E
122	Somme (R.) (sŏm) Fr.	50·02 N	2·04 E
111	Sommerfeld (zō'mĕr-fĕld) Ger. (Berlin In.)	52·48 N	13·02 E
161	Sommerville Austl. (Melbourne In.)	38·14 S	145·10 E
92	Somoto (sô-mō'tō) Nic.	13·28 N	86·37 W
100	Somuncurá, Meseta de (Plat.) (mĕ-sĕ'tä-dĕ-sô-mōō'n-kōō-rä') Arg.	41·15 S	68·00 W
142	Son (R.) (sōn) India	24·40 N	82·35 E
93	Soná (sō'nä) Pan.	8·00 N	81·19 W
152	Sŏnchŏn (sŭn'shŭn) Kor.	39·49 N	124·56 E
118	Sønderborg (sûn"ĕr-bôrgh) Den.	54·55 N	9·47 E
120	Sondershausen (zôn'dērz-hou'zĕn) Ger.	51·17 N	10·45 E
151	Song Ca (R.) Viet.	19·15 N	105·00 E
166	Songea (sôn-gā'ä) Tan.	10·39 S	35·44 E
152	Sŏngjin (sŭng'jĭn') Kor.	40·38 N	129·10 E
154	Songkhla (sông'klä') Thai.	7·09 N	100·34 E
120	Sonneberg (sôn'ē-bĕrgh) Ger.	50·20 N	11·14 E
68	Sonora (sō-nō'rȧ) Calif.	37·58 N	120·22 W
76	Sonora Tex.	30·33 N	100·38 W
88	Sonora (State) Mex.	29·45 N	111·15 W
88	Sonora (R.) Mex.	28·45 N	111·35 W
68	Sonora Pk. Calif.	38·22 N	119·39 W
124	Sonseca (sôn-sā'kä) Sp.	39·41 N	3·56 W
98	Sonsón (sôn-sôn') Col. (In.)	5·42 N	75·28 W
92	Sonsonate (sōn-sō-nä'tå) Sal.	13·46 N	89·43 W
155	Sonsorol Is. (sŏn-sō-rōl') Pac. Is. Trust Ter.	5·03 N	132·33 E
148	Soochow (Wuhsien) (sōō'jō) (wōō'sĭän) China	31·19 N	120·37 E
65	Sooke Basin (sŏŏk) Can. (Seattle In.)	48·21 N	123·47 W
74	Soo Locks (sōō lŏks) U. S.-Can.	46·30 N	84·30 W
98	Sopetrán (sō-pĕ-trä'n) Col. (In.)	6·30 N	75·44 W
118	Sopot (sô'pôt) Pol.	54·26 N	18·25 E
120	Sopron (shŏp'rōn) Hung.	47·41 N	16·36 E
126	Sora (sō'rä) It.	41·43 N	13·37 E
118	Sör Aurdal (sûr äûr-däl) Nor.	60·54 N	9·24 E
124	Sorbas (sôr'bäs) Sp.	37·05 N	2·07 W
91	Sordo (R.) (sô'r-dō) Mex.	16·39 N	97·33 W
82	Sorel (sô-rĕl') Can.	46·01 N	73·07 W
160	Sorell, C. Austl.	42·10 S	144·50 E
126	Soresina (sō-rå-zē'nä) It.	45·17 N	9·51 E
124	Soria (sō'rē-ä) Sp.	41·46 N	2·28 W
101	Soriano (sŏ-rēä'nō) (Dept.) Ur. (Buenos Aires In.)	33·25 S	58·00 W
101	Sorocaba (sō-rō-kä'bȧ) Braz. (Rio de Janeiro In.)	23·29 S	47·27 W
129	Soroki (sō-rō'kē) Sov. Un.	48·09 N	28·17 E
155	Sorong (sō-rông') W. Irian	1·15 S	131·30 E
128	Sorot' (R.) (sō-rō'tzh) Sov. Un.	57·08 N	29·23 E
165	Soroti (sō-rō'tē) Ug.	1·51 N	33·33 E
112	Söröy (I.) (sûr-ûê) Nor.	70·37 N	20·58 E
124	Sorraia (R.) (sôr-rī'ä) Port.	38·55 N	8·42 W
125	Sorrento (sôr-rĕn'tō) It. (Naples In.)	40·23 N	14·23 E
155	Sorsogon (sôr-sôgōn') Phil.	12·51 N	124·02 E
119	Sortavala (sôr'tä-vä-lä) Sov. Un.	61·43 N	30·40 E
150	Sŏsan (sŭ'sän) Korea	36·40 N	126·25 E
129	Sosna (R.) (sôs'nä) Sov. Un.	50·33 N	38·15 E
129	Sosnitsa (sôs-nē'tsä) Sov. Un.	51·30 N	32·29 E
134	Sosnogorsk Sov. Un.	63·13 N	54·09 E
121	Sosnowiec (sôs-nô'vyĕts) Pol.	50·17 N	19·10 E
152	Sosunova, Mys (Pt.) (mĭs sô'sōō-nôf'ȧ) Sov. Un.	46·28 N	138·06 E
136	Sos'va (R.) (sôs'vȧ) Sov. Un. (Urals In.)	59·55 N	60·40 E
132	Sos'va (R.) (sôs'vȧ) Sov. Un.	63·10 N	63·30 E
90	Sota la Marina (sô-tä-lä-mä-rē'nä) Mex.	22·45 N	98·11 W
91	Soteapan (sō-tå-ä'pän) Mex.	18·14 N	94·51 W
90	Soto la Marina, Rio (R.) (rē'ō-sō'tō lä mä-rē'nä) Mex.	23·55 N	98·30 W
92	Sotuta (sō-tōō'tä) Mex. (Yucatan In.)	20·35 N	89·00 W
99	Soublette (sō-ōō-blĕ'tĕ) Ven. (In.)	9·55 N	66·06 W
126	Soúdhas, Kólpos (G.) Grc. (Inset)	35·33 N	24·22 E
115	Soueïda Syr.	32·41 N	36·41 E
127	Souflion Grc.	41·12 N	26·17 E
93	Soufrière (sōō-frē-âr') St. Lucia (Le. & Wind. Is. In.)	13·50 N	61·03 W
93	Soufrière (Vol.) Basse Terre (Le. & Wind. Is. In.)	16·02 N	61·41 W
93	Soufrière Vol. Montserrat (Le. & Wind. Is. In.)	16·43 N	62·10 W
113	Souk-Ahras (sōōk-ä-räs') Alg.	36·18 N	8·19 E
152	Sŏul (Seoul) Kor.	37·35 N	127·03 E
167	Sources, Mt. aux (môɴ'tō sōōrs') Bas. (Natal In.)	28·47 S	29·04 E
124	Soure (sōr-ĕ) Port.	40·04 N	8·37 W
83	Souris (sōō-rē') Can.	46·20 N	62·17 W
86	Souris Can.	49·32 N	100·23 W
86	Souris (R.) Can.	48·46 N	101·32 W
77	Sourlake (sour'lāk) Tex.	30·09 N	94·24 W
164	Sousse (sōōs) Tun.	36·00 N	10·39 E
122	Soustons (sōōs-tôɴ') Fr.	43·46 N	1·22 W
79	South (R.) N. C.	34·49 N	78·33 W
167	South Africa Afr. (Natal In.)	31·50 S	28·05 E
84	South Amboy (south'ăm'boi) N. J. (New York In.)	40·28 N	74·17 W
6	South America		
116	Southampton (south-ămp'tŭn) Eng.	50·54 N	1·30 W
87	Southampton I. Can.	64·38 N	84·00 W
154	South Andaman I. (ăn-dȧ-măn') India	11·57 N	93·24 E
158	South Australia (State) (ôs-trā'lĭ-ȧ) Austl.	29·45 S	132·00 E
95	South B. Ba. Is.	20·55 N	73·35 W
80	South Bend (bĕnd) Ind.	41·40 N	86·20 W
66	South Bend (bĕnd) Wash.	46·39 N	123·48 W
94	South Bight (B.) Ba. Is.	24·20 N	77·35 W
94	South Bimini (I.) (bē'mē-nē) Ba. Is.	25·40 N	79·20 W
83	Southboro (south'bŭr-ô) Mass. (Boston In.)	42·18 N	71·33 W
79	South Boston (bôs'tŭn) Va.	36·41 N	78·55 W
81	Southbridge (south'brĭj) Mass.	42·05 N	72·00 W
95	South Caicos (I.) (kī'kōs) Caicos	21·30 N	71·35 W
155	South C. Pap.	10·40 S	149·00 E
63	South Carolina (State) (kăr-ô-lī'nȧ) U. S.	34·15 N	81·10 W
110	South Cave (cāv) Eng.	53·45 N	0·35 W
80	South Charleston (south chärlz'tŭn) W. Va.	38·20 N	81·40 W
154	South China Sea (chī'nȧ) Asia	15·23 N	114·12 E
161	South Cr. Austl. (Sydney In.)	33·43 S	167·00 E
62	South Dakota (State) (dȧ-kō'tȧ) U. S.	44·20 N	101·55 W
116	South Downs (dounz) Eng.	50·55 N	1·13 W
159	Southeast, C. Austl.	43·47 S	146·03 E
110	Southend-on-Sea (south-ĕnd') Eng. (London In.)	51·33 N	0·41 E
159	Southern Alps (Mts.) (sŭ-thûrn ălps) N. Z. (In.)	44·08 S	169·18 E
158	Southern Cross Austl.	31·13 S	119·30 E
86	Southern Indian (L.) (sŭth'ērn ĭn'dĭ-ăn) Can.	57·20 N	99·29 W
79	Southern Pines (sŭth'ērn pīnz) N. C.	35·10 N	79·23 W
166	Southern Rhodesia (rō-dē'zhĭ-ȧ) Afr.	17·50 S	29·30 E
116	Southern Uplands (ŭp'lȧndz) Scot.	55·15 N	4·28 W
69	Southern Ute Ind. Res. (ūt) Colo.	37·05 N	108·23 W
75	South Euclid (ū'klĭd) Ohio (Cleveland In.)	41·30 N	81·34 W
80	South Fox (I.) (fŏks) Mich.	45·25 N	85·55 W
74	South Gate (gāt) Calif. (Los Angeles In.)	33·57 N	118·13 W
96	South Georgia (I.) (jôr'jȧ) Falk. Is.	54·00 S	37·00 W
80	South Haven (hāv"n) Mich.	42·25 N	86·15 W
81	Southington (sŭdh'ĭng-tŭn) Conn.	41·35 N	72·55 W
159	South I. N. Z. (In.)	43·15 S	167·00 E
70	South Loup (R.) (lōōp) Nebr.	41·21 N	100·08 W
83	South Merrimack (mĕr'ĭ-măk) N. H. (Boston In.)	42·47 N	71·36 W
75	South Milwaukee (mĭl-wô'kē) Wis. (Milwaukee In.)	42·55 N	87·52 W
94	South Negril Pt. (nå-grēl') Jam.	18·15 N	78·25 W
84	South Norfolk (nôr'fŏk) Va. (Norfolk In.)	36·48 N	76·16 W
74	South Ogden (ŏg'dĕn) Utah (Salt Lake City In.)	41·12 N	111·58 W
82	South Paris (păr'ĭs) Maine	44·13 N	70·32 W
75	South Park (pärk) Ky. (Louisville In.)	38·06 N	85·43 W
74	South Pasadena (păs-å-dē'nȧ) Calif. (Los Angeles In.)	34·06 N	118·08 W
72	South Pease (R.) (pēz) Tex.	33·54 N	100·45 W
65	South Pender (I.) (pĕn'dēr) Can. (Vancouver In.)	48·45 N	123·09 W
78	South Pittsburg (pĭts'bûrg) Tenn.	35·00 N	85·42 W
62	South Platte (R.) (plăt) U. S.	40·40 N	102·40 W
80	South Pt. Mich.	44·50 N	83·20 W
93	South Pt. W. I. F. (Le. & Wind. Is. In.)	13·00 N	59·43 W
47	South Polar Plat. Ant.	87·00 S	2·00 W
160	Southport (south'pōrt) Austl.	27·57 S	153·27 E
79	Southport N. C.	35·55 N	78·02 W
110	Southport (south'pôrt) Eng.	53·38 N	3·00 W
75	Southport Ind. (Indianapolis In.)	39·40 N	86·07 W
82	South Portland (pōrt-lănd) Maine	43·37 N	70·15 W
65	South Prairie (prā'rĭ) Wash. (Seattle In.)	47·08 N	122·06 W
74	South Range (rānj) Wis. (Duluth In.)	46·37 N	91·59 W
84	South River (rĭv'ēr) N. J. (New York In.)	40·27 N	74·23 W
84	South R. Ga. (Atlanta In.)	33·40 N	84·15 W
74	South St. Paul Minn. (Minneapolis, St. Paul In.)	44·54 N	93·02 W
74	South Salt Lake (sôlt lāk) Utah (Salt Lake City In.)	40·44 N	111·53 W
96	South Sandwich Is. (sănd'wĭch) Falk. Is.	58·00 S	27·00 W
96	South Sandwich Trench S. A.-Ant.	55·00 S	27·00 W
65	South San Francisco (săn frăn-sĭs'kō) Calif. (San Francisco In.)	37·39 N	122·24 W
86	South Saskatchewan (R.) (săs-kăch'ê-wän) Can.	50·29 N	110·25 W
116	South Shields (shēldz) Eng.	55·00 N	1·22 W
116	South Shropshire Hills (shrŏp'shĭr) Eng.	52·30 N	3·02 W
70	South Sioux City (sōō sĭt'ē) Nebr.	42·28 N	96·26 W
159	South Taranaki Bght. (tä-rä-nä'kē) N. Z. (In.)	39·27 S	171·44 E
74	Southton (south'tŭn) Tex. (San Antonio In.)	29·18 N	98·26 W
116	South Uist (I.) (ū'ĭst) Scot.	56·83 N	6·64 W
66	South Umpqua R. (ŭmp'kwå) Ore.	43·00 N	122·54 W
110	Southwell (south'wĕl) Eng.	53·04 N	0·56 W
163	South-West Africa (ăf'rĭ-kä) Afr.	19·30 S	16·13 E
159	Southwest C. N. Z. (In.)	47·17 S	167.12 E
65	South Westminster (wĕst'mĭn-stēr) Can. (Vancouver In.)	49·12 N	122·53 W
95	Southwest Pt. Ba. Is.	23·55 N	74·30 W
94	Southwest Pt. Ba. Is.	25·50 N	77·10 W
94	Southwest Pt. Ba. Is.	26·35 N	78·35 W
119	Sovetsk (Tilsit) (sô-vyĕtsk') Sov. Un.	55·04 N	21·54 E
135	Sovetskaya Gavan' (sŭ-vyĕt'skī-u gä'vŭn') Sov. Un.	48·59 N	140·14 E
138	Soviet Union (sō-vĭ-ĕt') Eur.-Asia	60·30 N	64·00 E
110	Sow (R.) (sou) Eng.	52·45 N	2·12 W
152	Sōya Kaikyō (Str.) (sō'ya kī'kyō) Jap.-Sov. Un.	45·45 N	141·38 E
152	Sōya Misaki (C.) (sō'yȧ mē'sä-kē) Jap.	45·35 N	141·25 E
128	Sozh (R.) (sôzh) Sov. Un.	52·17 N	31·00 E
127	Sozopol (sôz'ō-pôl') Bul.	42·18 N	27·50 E
117	Spa (spä) Bel.	50·30 N	5·50 E
74	Spadra (spăd'rȧ) Calif. (Los Angeles In.)	34·03 N	117·48 W
102	Spain (spān) Eur.	40·15 N	4·30 W
70	Spalding (spôl'dĭng) Nebr.	41·43 N	98·23 W
65	Spanaway (spăn'ȧ-wā) Wash. (Seattle In.)	47·06 N	122·26 W
81	Spangler (spăng'lēr) Pa.	40·40 N	78·50 W
69	Spanish Fork (spăn'ĭsh fôrk) Utah	40·10 N	111·40 W
163	Spanish Sahara (sȧ hä'rȧ) Afr.	23·05 N	15·33 W
94	Spanish Town Jam.	18·00 N	76·55 W
68	Sparks (spärks) Nev.	39·34 N	119·45 W
84	Sparrows Point (spăr'ōz) Md. (Baltimore In.)	39·13 N	76·29 W
78	Sparta (spär'tȧ) Ga.	33·16 N	82·59 W
73	Sparta Ill.	38·07 N	89·42 W
80	Sparta Mich.	43·10 N	85·45 W
78	Sparta Tenn.	35·54 N	85·26 W
71	Sparta Wis.	43·56 N	90·50 W
	Sparta, see Spárti		
84	Sparta Mts. N. J. (New York In.)	41·00 N	74·38 W
79	Spartanburg (spär'tăn-bûrg) S. C.	34·57 N	82·13 W
124	Spartel (C.) (spär-tĕl') Mor.	35·48 N	5·50 W
127	Spárti (Sparta) Grc.	37·07 N	22·28 E
126	Spartivento, C. (spär-tē-vĕn'tō) It.	37·55 N	16·09 E
126	Spartivento, C. It.	38·54 N	8·52 E
128	Spas-Demensk (spȧs dyĕ-mĕnsk') Sov. Un.	54·24 N	34·02 E
128	Spas-Klepiki (spȧs klĕp'ē-kē) Sov. Un.	55·09 N	40·11 E
135	Spassk-Dal'niy (spŭsk'däl'nyē) Sov. Un.	44·30 N	133·00 E
128	Spassk-Ryazanskiy (ryä-zän'skĭ) Sov. Un.	54·24 N	40·21 E
126	Spátha, Akr. (C.) Grc. (Inset)	35·42 N	23·45 E
84	Spaulding (spôl'dĭng) Ala. (Birmingham In.)	33·27 N	86·50 W
83	Spear, C. (spēr) Can.	47·28 N	52·30 W
70	Spearfish (spēr'fĭsh) S. D.	44·28 N	103·52 W
75	Speed (spēd) Ind. (Louisville In.)	38·25 N	85·45 W
75	Speedway (spēd'wā) Ind. (Indianapolis In.)	39·47 N	86·14 W
111	Speicher L. (shpī'kēr) Ger. (Munich In.)	48·12 N	11·47 E
80	Spencer (spĕn'sēr) Ind.	39·15 N	86·45 W
71	Spencer Iowa	43·09 N	95·08 W
79	Spencer N. C.	35·43 N	80·25 W
80	Spencer W. Va.	38·55 N	81·20 W
160	Spencer G. (spĕn'sēr) Austl.	34·20 S	136·55 E
111	Sperenberg (shpĕ'rĕn-bĕrgh) Ger. (Berlin In.)	52·09 N	13·22 E
127	Sperkhiós (R.) Grc.	38·54 N	22·02 E
116	Sperrin Mts. (spĕr'ĭn) N. Ire.	54·55 N	6·45 W
120	Spessart (Mts.) (shpĕ'särt) Ger.	50·07 N	9·32 E
116	Spey (L.) (spā) Scot.	57·25 N	3·29 W
120	Speyer (shpī'ēr) Ger.	49·18 N	8·26 E
168	Sphinx (Pyramid) (sfĭnks) U. A. R. (Nile In.)	29·57 N	31·08 E
111	Spijkenisse Neth. (Amsterdam In.)	51·51 N	4·18 E
126	Spinazzola (spē-nät'zō-lä) It.	40·58 N	16·05 E
66	Spirit Lake (spĭr'ĭt) Idaho	47·58 N	116·51 W
71	Spirit Lake (lăk) Iowa	43·25 N	95·08 W
86	Spirit River Can.	55·50 N	118·50 W
121	Spišská Nová Ves (spēsh'skä nō'vä vĕs) Czech.	48·56 N	20·35 E
120	Spittal (shpē-täl') Aus.	46·48 N	13·28 E
	Spitzbergen (Is.), see Svalbard		
126	Split (splĭt) Yugo.	43·30 N	16·28 E
66	Spokane (spōkăn') Wash.	47·39 N	117·25 W
66	Spokane R. Wash.	47·47 N	118·00 W
126	Spoleto (spō-lā'tō) It.	42·44 N	12·44 E
73	Spoon (R.) (spōōn) Ill.	40·36 N	90·22 W
71	Spooner (spōōn'ēr) Wis.	45·50 N	91·53 W

ng-sing; ŋ-baŋk; ɴ-nasalized n; nŏd; cŏmmit; ōld; ôbey; ôrder; fōōd; fŏŏt; ou-out; s-soft; sh-dish; th-thin; pūre; ûnite; ûrn; stŭd; circŭs; ü-as "y" in study; '-indeterminate vowel.

Page	Name Pronunciation Region	Lat. °′	Long. °′
127	Sporádhes (Is.) Grc.	38·55 N	24·05 E
84	Spotswood (spŏtz'wood) N. J. (New York In.)	40·23 N	74·22 W
66	Sprague R. (sprāg) Ore.	42·30 N	121·42 W
154	Spratly (I.) (sprăt'lē) China	8·38 N	11·54 E
79	Spray (sprā) N. C.	36·30 N	79·44 W
120	Spree R. (shprā) Ger.	51·53 N	14·08 E
120	Spremberg (shprĕm'bĕrgh) Ger.	51·35 N	14·23 E
73	Spring (R.) Ark.	36·25 N	91·35 W
166	Springbok (spring'bŏk) S. Afr.	29·35 S	17·55 E
68	Spring, Cr. (spring) Nev.	40·18 N	117·45 W
77	Spring Cr. Tex.	30·03 N	95·43 W
76	Spring Cr. Tex.	31·08 N	100·50 W
73	Springdale (spring'dāl) Ark.	36·10 N	94·07 W
83	Springdale Can.	49·30 N	56·05 W
84	Springdale Conn. (New York In.)	41·05 N	73·31 W
75	Springdale Pa. (Pittsburgh In.)	40·33 N	79·46 W
72	Springer (spring'ēr) N. Mex.	36·21 N	104·37 W
72	Springfield (spring'fēld) Colo.	37·24 N	102·40 W
71	Springfield Minn.	44·14 N	94·59 W
66	Springfield Ore.	44·01 N	123·02 W
73	Springfield Ill.	39·46 N	89·37 W
80	Springfield Ky.	37·35 N	85·10 W
81	Springfield Mass.	42·05 N	72·35 W
73	Springfield Mo.	37·13 N	93·17 W
80	Springfield Ohio	39·55 N	83·50 W
78	Springfield Tenn.	36·30 N	86·53 W
81	Springfield Vt.	43·20 N	72·35 W
166	Springfontein (spring'fŏn-tīn) S. Afr.	30·16 S	25·45 E
82	Springhill (spring-hĭl') Can.	45·39 N	64·04 W
68	Spring Mts. Nev.	36·18 N	115·49 W
167	Springs (springs) S. Afr. (Johannesburg & Pretoria In.)	26·16 S	28·27 E
85	Springstein (spring'stīn) Can. (Winnipeg In.)	49·49 N	97·29 W
84	Springton Res. (spring-tŭn) Pa. (Philadelphia In.)	39·57 N	75·26 W
161	Springvale Austl. (Melbourne In.)	37·57 S	145·09 E
68	Spring Valley Calif. (San Diego In.)	32·46 N	117·01 W
80	Springvalley (spring-văl'ĭ) Ill.	41·20 N	89·15 W
71	Spring Valley Minn.	43·41 N	92·26 W
84	Spring Valley N. Y. (New York In.)	41·07 N	74·03 W
69	Springville (spring-vĭl) Utah	40·10 N	111·40 W
161	Springwood Austl. (Sydney In.)	33·42 S	150·34 E
85	Spruce Grove (sprōōs grōv) Can. (Edmonton In.)	53·33 N	113·55 W
72	Spur (spûr) Tex.	33·29 N	100·51 W
81	Squam (L.) (skwôm) N. H.	43·45 N	71·30 W
126	Squillace, Gulfo di (G.) (gōō'l-fō-dē skwēl-lä'chä) It.	38·44 N	16·47 E
127	Srbija (Serbia) (Reg.) (sr bē-yä) (sĕr'bē-ä) Yugo.	44·05 N	20·35 E
127	Srbobran (s'r'bō-brän') Yugo.	45·32 N	19·50 E
135	Sredne-Kolymsk (s'rĕd'nyĕ kô-lēmsk') Sov. Un.	67·49 N	154·55 E
136	Sredne Rogartka (s'red'nä-ya) (rô gär'tkä) Sov. Un. (Leningrad In.)	59·49 N	30·20 E
136	Sredniy Ik (R.) (srĕd'nĭ ĭk) Sov. Un. (Urals In.)	55·46 N	58·50 E
136	Sredniy Ural (Mts.) (ōō'rál) Sov. Un. (Urals In.)	57·47 N	59·00 E
121	Šrem (shrĕm) Pol.	52·06 N	17·01 E
127	Sremska Karlovci (srĕm'skē kär'lov-tsē) Yugo.	45·10 N	19·57 E
127	Sremska Mitrovica (srĕm'skä mē'trô-vê-tsä') Yugo.	44·59 N	19·39 E
135	Sretensk (s'rĕ'tĕnsk) Sov. Un.	52·13 N	117·39 E
142	Srinagar (srē-nŭg'ŭr) India	34·11 N	74·49 E
121	Sroda (shrô'dä) Pol	52·14 N	17·17 E
146	Ssuch'uan (Szechwan) (Prov.) China	31·30 N	102·52 E
151	Ssuen China	24·50 N	108·18 E
148	Ssuhsien (sü'sĭän) China	33·29 N	116·57 E
146	Ssumao China	22·56 N	101·07 E
151	Ssŭnan China	27·50 N	108·30 E
150	Ssup'ing China	43·05 N	124·24 E
148	Ssushui (sē'sōōĭ) China	35·40 N	117·17 E
149	Ssut'uan China (Shanghai In.)	30·57 N	121·43 E
111	Stabroek Bel. (Brussels In.)	51·20 N	4·21 E
111	Stade (shtä'dĕ) Ger. (Hamburg In.)	53·36 N	9·28 E
112	Stadhur Ice.	65·08 N	20·56 W
118	Städjan (Mtn.) (stĕd'yän) Swe.	61·53 N	12·50 E
110	Stafford (stăf'fērd) Eng.	52·48 N	2·06 W
72	Stafford Kans.	37·58 N	78·37 W
110	Stafford (Co.) Eng.	52·45 N	2·00 W
111	Stahnsdorf (shtäns'dôrf) Ger. (Berlin In.)	52·22 N	13·10 E
	Stalin, see Varna		
	Stalinabad, see Dushanbe		
	Stalingrad, see Volgograd		
	Stalino, see Donetsk		
129	Stalino (Oblast) (stä'lĭ-nô) (ôb'låst) Sov. Un.	47·54 N	37·13 E
134	Stalino, Pik (Mtn.) Sov. Un.	39·00 N	72·15 E
128	Stalinogorsk (stä'lyin-ŭ-gôrsk') Sov. Un.	54·06 N	38·08 E
	Stalinsk, see Novokuznetsk		
110	Stalybridge (stā'lē-brij) Eng.	53·29 N	2·03 W
71	Stambaugh (stăm'bô) Mich.	46·03 N	88·38 W
84	Stamford (stăm'fērd) Conn. (New York In.)	41·03 N	73·32 W
110	Stamford Eng.	52·39 N	0·28 W
72	Stamford Tex.	32·57 N	99·48 W
111	Stammersdorf (shtäm'ĕrs-dôrf) Aus. (Vienna In.)	48·19 N	16·25 E
73	Stamps (stămps) Ark.	33·22 N	93·31 W
73	Stanberry (stan'bĕr-ē) Mo.	40·12 N	94·34 W
168	Standerton (stăn'dēr-tŭn) S. Afr. (Johannesburg & Pretoria In.)	26·57 S	29·17 E

Page	Name Pronunciation Region	Lat. °′	Long. °′
70	Standing Rock Ind. Res. (stănd'ĭng rŏk) N. D.	47·07 N	101·05 W
110	Standish (stăn'dĭsh) Eng.	53·36 N	2·39 W
78	Stanford (stăn'fērd) Ky.	37·29 N	84·40 W
167	Stanger (stăŋ-ger) S. Afr. (Natal In.)	29·22 S	31·18 E
118	Stangvik Fd. (stang'vêk fyôrd) Nor.	62·54 N	8·55 E
94	Staniard Creek Ba. Is.	24·50 N	77·55 W
68	Stanislaus (R.) (stăn'ĭs-lô) Calif.	38·10 N	120·16 W
82	Stanley (stăn'lē) Can.	46·19 N	66·45 W
70	Stanley N. D.	48·20 N	102·25 W
71	Stanley Wis.	44·56 N	90·56 W
165	Stanley Falls Con. L.	0·12 N	25·34 E
166	Stanley Pool (L.) Con. L.	4·15 S	16·00 E
142	Stanley Res. (stăn'lē) India	12·07 N	77·27 E
165	Stanleyville (stan'lē-vĭl) Con.L.	0·32 N	25·14 E
92	Stann Creek (stăn krēk) Br. Hond. (Yucatan In.)	17·01 N	88·14 W
135	Stanovoy Khrebet (Mts.) (stŭn-ȧ-voi') Sov. Un.	56·12 N	127·12 E
74	Stanton (stăn'tŭn) Calif. (Los Angeles In.)	33·48 N	118·00 W
70	Stanton Nebr.	41·57 N	97·15 W
76	Stanton Tex.	32·08 N	101·46 W
65	Stanwood (stăn'wood) Wash. (Seattle In.)	48·14 N	122·23 W
71	Staples (stā'p'lz) Minn.	46·21 N	94·48 W
127	Stara Planina (Balkan Mts.) Bul.	42·50 N	24·45 E
136	Staraya Kupavna (stä'rȧ-yȧ kû-päf'nȧ) Sov. Un. (Moscow In.)	55·48 N	38·10 E
128	Staraya Russa (stä'rȧ-yȧ rōōsȧ) Sov. Un.	57·58 N	31·21 E
127	Stara Zagora (zä'gô-rȧ) Bul.	42·26 N	25·37 E
85	Starbuck (stär'bŭk) Can. (Winnipeg In.)	49·46 N	97·38 W
120	Stargard Szczecinski (shtär'gärt shchĕ-chyn'skē) Pol.	53·19 N	15·03 E
128	Staritsa (stä'rê-tsȧ) Sov. Un.	56·29 N	34·58 E
79	Starke (stärk) Fla.	29·55 N	82·07 W
72	Starkville (stärk'vĭl) Colo.	37·06 N	104·34 W
78	Starkville Miss.	33·27 N	88·47 W
111	Starnberg (shtärn-bĕrgh) Ger. (Munich In.)	47·59 N	11·20 E
129	Starobel'sk (stä-rô-byĕlsk') Sov. Un.	49·19 N	38·57 E
128	Starodub (stä-rô-drōōp') Sov. Un.	52·25 N	32·49 E
121	Starogard Gdenski (stä'rō-gärd gdĕn'skē) Pol.	53·58 N	18·33 E
129	Staro-Konstantinov (stä'rô kôn-stán-tē'nôf) Sov. Un.	49·45 N	27·12 E
129	Staro-Minskaya (stä'rô mĭn'skȧ-yȧ) Sov. Un.	46·19 N	38·51 E
129	Staro-Shcherbinovskaya Sov. Un.	46·38 N	38·38 E
136	Staro-Subkhangulovo (stăro-sōōb-kan-gōō'lōvō) Sov. Un. (Urals In.)	53·08 N	57·24 E
136	Staroutkinsk (stä-rô-ōōt'kĭnsk) Sov. Un. (Urals In.)	57·14 N	59·21 E
129	Staroverovka Sov. Un.	49·31 N	35·48 E
116	Start Pt. (stärt) Eng.	50·14 N	3·34 W
121	Stary Sącz (stä-rê sōnch') Pol.	49·32 N	20·36 E
129	Staryy Oskol (stä'rê ôs-kôl') Sov. Un.	51·18 N	37·51 E
120	Stassfurt (shtäs'fōōrt) Ger.	51·52 N	11·35 E
121	Staszów (stä'shōōf) Pol.	50·32 N	21·13 E
81	State College (stāt kŏl'ĕj) Pa.	40·50 N	77·55 W
74	State Line (līn) Minn. (Duluth In.)	46·36 N	92·18 W
84	Staten I. (stăt'ĕn) N. Y. (New York In.)	40·35 N	74·10 W
79	Statesboro (stāts'bŭr-ô) Ga.	32·26 N	81·47 W
79	Statesville (stāts'vĭl) N. C.	35·45 N	80·54 W
74	Staunton (stôn'tŭn) Ill. (St. Louis In.)	39·01 N	89·47 W
81	Staunton Va.	38·10 N	79·05 W
118	Stavanger (stä'väng'ĕr) Nor.	58·59 N	5·44 E
65	Stave (R.) (stāv) Can. (Vancouver In.)	49·12 N	122·24 W
110	Staveley (stāv'lē) Eng.	53·17 N	1·21 W
111	Stavenisse Neth.(Amsterdam In.)	51·35 N	3·59 E
132	Stavropol' (stäv'rô-pôl') Sov. Un.	53·30 N	49·10 E
133	Stavropol' Sov. Un.	45·05 N	41·50 E
120	Stawno (swav'nō) Pol.	54·21 N	16·38 E
72	Steamboat Springs (stēm'bōt') Colo.	40·30 N	106·48 W
129	Steblëv (styĕp'lyôf) Sov. Un.	49·23 N	31·03 E
71	Steel (R.) (stēl) Can.	49·08 N	86·55 W
81	Steelton (stĕl'tŭn) Pa.	40·15 N	76·45 W
111	Steenbergen Neth. (Amsterdam In.)	51·35 N	4·18 E
66	Steens Mts. (stēnz) Ore.	42·15 N	118·52 W
158	Steep Pt. (stēp) Austl.	26·15 S	112·05 E
165	Stefanie L. (stĕf-ȧ-nē') Eth.	4·46 N	37·31 E
75	Steger (stē'gēr) Ill. (Chicago In.)	41·28 N	87·38 W
120	Steiermark (Styria) (state) (shtī'ĕr-märk) Aus.	47·22 N	14·40 E
86	Steinbach Can.	49·28 N	96·52 W
112	Steinkjer (stĕĭn-kyĕr) Nor.	64·00 N	11·19 E
65	Stella (stĕl'ȧ) Wash. (Portland In.)	46·11 N	123·12 W
83	Stellarton (stĕl'ár-tŭn) Can.	45·34 N	62·41 W
120	Stendal (shtĕn'däl) Ger.	52·37 N	11·51 E
133	Stepanakert (styĕ'pän-ȧ-kĕrt) Sov. Un.	39·50 N	46·40 E
160	Stephens, Port (stē'fĕns) Austl.	32·43 S	152·55 E
83	Stephenville (stē'vĕn-vĭl) Can.	48·31 N	58·38 W
84	Stepney Depot (stĕp-nē) Conn. (New York In.)	41·17 N	73·15 W
134	Stepnyak (styĭp-nyäk') Sov. Un.	52·37 N	70·43 E
123	Sterkrade (shtĕr'krädē) Ger. (Ruhr In.)	51·31 N	6·51 E
167	Sterkstroom S. Afr. (Natal In.)	31·33 S	26·36 E

Page	Name Pronunciation Region	Lat. °′	Long. °′
72	Sterling (stûr'lĭng) Colo.	40·38 N	103·14 W
71	Sterling Ill.	41·48 N	89·42 W
72	Sterling Kans.	38·11 N	98·11 W
83	Sterling Mass. (Boston In.)	42·26 N	71·41 W
76	Sterling Tex.	31·53 N	100·58 W
136	Sterlitamak (styĕr'lē-ta-mȧk') Sov. Un. (Urals In.)	53·38 N	55·56 E
121	Sternberk (shtĕrn'bĕrk) Czech.	49·44 N	17·18 E
	Stettin, see Szczec'in		
120	Stettiner Haff (L.) (shtĕ'tē-nēr häf) Ger.	53·47 N	14·02 E
86	Stettler Can.	52·19 N	112·50 W
80	Steubenville (stū'bĕn-vĭl) Ohio	40·20 N	80·40 W
65	Stevens (L.) (stē'vĕnz) Wash. (Seattle In.)	47·59 N	122·06 W
71	Stevens Point Wis.	44·30 N	89·35 W
67	Stevensville (stē'vĕnz-vĭl) Mont.	46·31 N	114·03 W
65	Steveston (stēvz'tŭn) Can. (Vancouver In.)	49·08 N	123·11 W
86	Stewart (R.) (stū'ērt) Can.	63·27 N	138·48 W
159	Stewart I. N. Z. (In.)	46·50 S	168·06 E
82	Stewiacke (stū'wê-ăk) Can.	45·08 N	63·22 W
168	Steynsrus (stīns'rōōs) S. Afr. (Johannesburg & Pretoria In.)	27·58 S	27·33 E
120	Steyr (shtīr) Aus.	48·03 N	14·24 E
86	Stikine (R.) (stĭ-kēn') Can.	58·17 N	103·10 W
86	Stikine Mts. Can.	59·24 N	129·12 W
65	Stillaguamish (R.) Wash. (Seattle In.)	48·11 N	122·18 W
65	Stillaguamish (R.), South Fk. (stĭl-ȧ-gwä'mĭsh) Wash. (Seattle In.)	48·05 N	121·59 W
74	Stillwater (stĭl'wô-tēr) Minn. (Minneapolis, St. Paul In.)	45·04 N	92·48 W
67	Stillwater Mont.	45·23 N	109·45 W
73	Stillwater Okla.	36·06 N	97·03 W
68	Stillwater Ra. Nev.	39·43 N	118·11 W
66	Stillwater R. Mont.	48·47 N	114·40 W
127	Štip (shtĭp) Yugo.	41·43 N	22·07 E
116	Stirling (stûr'lĭng) Scot.	56·05 N	3·59 W
85	Stittsville (stĭts'vĭl) Can. (Ottawa In.)	45·15 N	75·54 W
118	Stjördalshalsen (styûr-däls-hälsĕn) Nor.	63·26 N	11·00 E
71	Stockbridge Munsee Ind. Res. (stŏk'brĭdj mŭn-sē) Wis.	44·49 N	89·00 W
111	Stockerau (shtŏ'kĕ-rou) Aus. (Vienna In.)	48·24 N	16·13 E
82	Stockholm (stŏk'hōlm) Maine	47·05 N	68·08 W
118	Stockholm (stôk'hôlm') Swe.	59·23 N	18·00 E
110	Stockport (stŏk'pôrt) Eng.	53·24 N	2·09 W
68	Stockton (stŏk'tŭn) Calif.	37·56 N	121·16 W
116	Stockton Eng.	54·35 N	1·25 W
72	Stockton Kans.	39·26 N	99·16 W
71	Stockton (I.) Wis.	46·56 N	90·25 W
76	Stockton Plat Tex.	30·34 N	102·35 W
118	Stöde (stû'dĕ) Swe.	62·26 N	16·35 E
110	Stoke-on-Trent (stōk-ŏn-trĕnt) Eng.	53·01 N	2·12 W
121	Stokhod (R.) (stō-kōd) Sov. Un.	51·24 N	25·20 E
127	Stolac (stô'lȧts) Yugo.	43·03 N	17·59 E
135	Stolbovoy (Is.) (stôl-bô-voi') Sov. Un.	73·43 N	133·05 E
121	Stolin (stô'lĕn) Sov. Un.	51·54 N	26·52 E
123	Stommeln (shtō'mĕln) Ger. (Ruhr In.)	51·01 N	6·46 E
118	Stömstad Swe.	58·58 N	11·09 E
110	Stone Eng.	52·54 N	2·09 W
85	Stoneham (stōn'ăm) Can. (Quebec In.)	46·59 N	71·22 W
83	Stoneham Mass. (Boston In.)	42·30 N	71·05 W
116	Stonehaven (stōn'hā-v'n) Scot.	56·57 N	2·09 W
84	Stone Mountain (stōn) Ga. (Atlanta In.)	33·49 N	84·10 W
85	Stonewall (stōn'wôl) Can. (Winnipeg In.)	50·08 N	97·19 W
78	Stonewall Miss.	32·08 N	88·44 W
85	Stoney Creek (stō'nē) Can. (Toronto In.)	43·13 N	79·45 W
85	Stoney Ind. Res. Can (Calgary In.)	51·10 N	114·45 W
81	Stonington (stōn'ĭng-tŭn) Conn.	41·20 N	71·55 W
68	Stony Cr. (stō'nē) Calif.	39·28 N	122·35 W
85	Stony Mountain Can. (Winnipeg In.)	50·05 N	97·13 W
85	Stony Plain (stō'nē plān) Can. (Edmonton In.)	53·23 N	114·00 W
84	Stony Point N. Y. (New York In.)	41·13 N	73·58 W
118	Storå (R.) Den.	56·22 N	8·35 E
132	Stora Lule (R.) (stōō'rä lōō'lē) Swe.	67·00 N	19·30 E
118	Stord (I.) (stôrd) Nor.	59·54 N	5·15 E
118	Store Baelt (Str.) Den.	55·25 N	10·50 E
112	Stören (stûrĕn) Nor.	62·58 N	10·21 E
118	Store Sotra (Sartor) (stô-rĕ-sô'-trä) (sär'tôr) Nor.	60·24 N	4·35 E
118	Stor Fd. (stôr fyôrd) Nor.	62·17 N	6·19 E
167	Stormberg (Mts.) (stôrm'bûrg) S. Afr. (Natal In.)	31·28 S	26·35 E
71	Storm Lake Iowa	42·39 N	95·12 W
89	Stormy Pt. (stôrm'ē) Vir. Is. (U. S. A.) (St. Thomas In.)	18·22 N	65·01 W
116	Stornoway (stôr'nō-wā) Scot.	58·13 N	6·21 W
121	Storozhinets (stô-rô'zhên-yĕts) Sov. Un.	48·10 N	25·44 E
118	Storsjö (stôr'shû) Swe.	62·49 N	13·08 E
118	Storsjöen (L.) (stôr-syûĕn) Nor.	61·32 N	11·30 E
118	Storsjön (L.) Swe.	63·06 N	14·00 E
118	Storvik (stôr'vêk) Swe.	60·37 N	16·31 E
83	Stoughton (stō'tŭn) Mass. (Boston In.)	42·07 N	71·06 W
71	Stoughton Wis.	42·54 N	89·15 W
117	Stour (R.) (stour) Eng.	52·09 N	0·29 E
110	Stourbridge (stour'brĭj) Eng.	52·27 N	2·08 W
83	Stow (stō) Mass. (Boston In.)	42·56 N	71·31 W
75	Stow Ohio (Cleveland In.)	41·09 N	81·26 W

ăt; finăl; rāte; senāte; ärm; ȧsk; sofȧ; fâre; ch-choose; dh-as th in other; bē; êvent; bĕt; recĕnt; cratēr; g-go; gh-guttural g; bĭt; ĭ-short neutral· rīde; K-guttural k as ch in German ich;

PRONOUNCING INDEX Straatsdrif–Susung 271

Page	Name Pronunciation Region	Lat. °′	Long. °′
168	Straatsdrif, S. Afr. (Johannesburg & Pretoria In.)	25·19 S	26·22 E
116	Strabane (strä-băn'), N. Ire.	54·52 N	6·60 W
159	Stradbroke Is. (străd'brōk), Austl.	27·45 S	154·18 E
123	Straelen (shträ'lĕn), Ger. (Ruhr In.)	51·26 N	6·16 E
159	Strahan (strā'ăn), Austl.	42·08 S	145·28 E
120	Strakonice (strä'kô-nyĕ-tsĕ), Czech.	49·18 N	13·52 E
127	Straldzha (strāl'dzhȧ), Bul.	42·37 N	26·44 E
120	Stralsund (shräl'sōōnt), Ger.	54·18 N	13·04 E
118	Strand (strănd), Nor.	59·05 N	5·59 E
116	Strangford, Lough (B.) (lŏĸ străng'fērd), Ire.	54·30 N	5·34 W
118	Strängnas (strĕng'nĕs), Swe.	59·23 N	16·59 E
116	Stranraer (străn-rär'), Scot.	54·55 N	5·05 W
123	Strasbourg (stràs-bōōr'), Fr.	48·36 N	7·49 E
80	Stratford (străt'fērd), Can.	43·20 N	81·05 W
81	Stratford, Conn.	41·10 N	73·05 W
116	Stratford, Eng.	52·13 N	1·41 W
71	Stratford, Wis.	44·16 N	90·02 W
120	Straubing (strou'bĭng), Ger.	48·52 N	12·36 E
120	Strausberg (strous'bĕrgh), Ger.	52·35 N	13·50 E
69	Strawberry (R.), Utah	40·05 N	110·55 W
66	Strawberry Mts. (strô'bĕr'ĭ), Ore.	44·19 N	119·20 W
76	Strawn (strôn), Tex.	32·38 N	98·28 W
80	Streator (strē'tēr), Ill.	41·05 N	88·50 W
70	Streeter, N. D.	46·40 N	99·22 W
85	Streetsville (strētz'vĭl), Can. (Toronto In.)	43·34 N	79·43 W
127	Strehaia (strĕ-ĸä'yȧ), Rom.	44·37 N	23·13 E
136	Strel'na (strĕl'nȧ), Sov. Un. (Leningrad In.)	59·52 N	30·01 E
110	Stretford (strĕt'fērd), Eng.	53·25 N	2·19 W
155	Strickland (R.) (strĭk'lănd), Pap.	6·15 S	142·00 E
111	Strijen, Neth. (Amsterdam In.)	51·44 N	4·32 E
127	Strimonikós Kólpos (G.), Grc.	40·40 N	23·55 E
126	Strómboli (Vol.) (strôm'bô-lē), It.	38·46 N	15·16 E
136	Stromyn (strô'mĭn), Sov. Un. (Moscow In.)	56·02 N	38·29 E
78	Strong (R.) (strông), Miss.	32·03 N	89·42 W
75	Strongsville (strôngz'vĭl), Ohio (Cleveland In.)	41·19 N	81·50 W
116	Stronsay (I.) (strŏn'sā), Scot.	59·09 N	2·35 W
81	Stroudsburg (stroudz'bûrg), Pa.	41·00 N	75·15 W
118	Struer, Den.	56·29 N	8·34 E
128	Strugi Krasnyye (strōō'gĭ krä's-ny'yĕ), Sov. Un.	58·14 N	29·10 E
127	Struma (R.) (strōō'mȧ), Bul.	41·55 N	23·05 E
127	Strumica (strōō'mĭ-tsȧ), Yugo.	41·26 N	22·38 E
80	Struthers (strŭdh'ērz), Ohio	41·00 N	80·35 W
111	Struvenhütten (shtrōō'vĕn-hü-tĕn), Ger. (Hamburg In.)	53·52 N	10·04 E
168	Strydpoortberg (Mts.), S. Afr. (Johannesburg & Pretoria In.)	24·08 S	29·18 E
121	Stryy (strē'), Sov. Un.	49·16 N	23·51 E
121	Strzelce Opolskie (stzhĕl'tsĕ o-pŏl'skyĕ), Pol.	50·31 N	18·20 E
121	Strzelin (stzhĕ-lĭn), Pol.	50·48 N	17·06 E
121	Strzelno (stzhăl'nô), Pol.	52·37 N	18·10 E
79	Stuart (stū'ērt), Fla. (In.)	27·10 N	80·14 W
71	Stuart, Iowa	41·31 N	94·20 W
64	Stuart (I.), Alaska	63·25 N	162·45 W
65	Stuart (I.), Wash. (Vancouver In.)	48·42 N	123·10 W
158	Stuart Ra, Austl.	29·00 S	134·30 E
154	Stung Treng (stŏŏng'trĕng'), Camb.	13·36 N	106·00 E
111	Stupava, Czech. (Vienna In.)	48·17 N	17·02 E
121	Stupsk (swōōpsk), Pol.	54·28 N	17·02 E
71	Sturgeon (R.), Mich.	46·43 N	88·43 W
71	Sturgeon Bay, Wis.	44·50 N	87·22 W
87	Sturgeon Falls, Can.	46·19 N	79·49 W
85	Sturgeon R. (stûr'jŭn), Can. (Edmonton In.)	53·41 N	113·46 W
80	Sturgis, Ky.	37·35 N	88·00 W
80	Sturgis (stûr'jĭs), Mich.	41·45 N	85·25 W
70	Sturgis, S. D.	44·25 N	103·31 W
158	Sturt Cr, Austl.	19·40 S	127·40 E
75	Sturtevant (stŭr'tē-vănt), Wis. (Milwaukee In.)	42·42 N	87·54 W
167	Stutterheim (stŭrt'ēr-hīm), S. Afr. (Natal In.)	32·34 S	27·27 E
73	Stuttgart (stŭt'gärt), Ark.	34·30 N	91·33 W
120	Stuttgart (shtōōt'gärt), Ger.	48·48 N	9·15 E
112	Stykkisholmur, Ice.	65·00 N	21·48 W
121	Styr' R. (stēr), Sov. Un.	51·44 N	26·07 E
	Styria, see Steiermark		
165	Suakin (swä'kĕn), Sud.	19·02 N	37·19 E
151	Suao (sōō'ou), Taiwan	24·35 N	121·45 E
142	Subarnarakha (R.), India	22·38 N	86·26 E
119	Subata (sōō'bȧ-tȧ), Sov. Un.	56·02 N	25·54 E
155	Subic (sōō'bĭk), Phil. (Manila In.)	14·52 N	120·15 E
155	Subic B, Phil. (Manila In.)	14·41 N	120·11 E
127	Subotica (sōō'bô'tē-tsȧ), Yugo.	46·06 N	19·41 E
84	Succasunna (sŭk'kȧ-sŭn'nȧ), N. J. (New York In.)	40·52 N	74·37 W
121	Suceava (sōō-chȧ-ä'vȧ), Rom.	47·39 N	26·17 E
121	Suceava R, Rom.	47·45 N	26·10 E
121	Sucha (sōō'ĸȧ), Pol.	49·44 N	19·40 E
135	Suchan (sōō-chän'), Sov. Un.	43·15 N	133·19 E
91	Suchiapa (sōō-chē-ä'pä), Mex.	16·38 N	93·08 W
91	Suchiapa (R.), Mex.	16·27 N	93·26 W
148	Such'ien (sü'chĭăn), China	33·57 N	118·17 E
92	Suchitoto (sōō-chē-tō'tō), Sal.	13·58 N	89·03 W
	Süchow, see Hsüchou		
	Süchow, see Ipin		
65	Sucia Is. (sōō'sē-ȧ), Wash. (Vancouver In.)	48·46 N	122·54 W
98	Sucio (R.) (sōō'syō), Col. (In.)	6·55 N	76·15 W
116	Suck (sŭk), Ire.	53·34 N	8·16 W
98	Sucre (sōō'krä), Bol.	19·06 S	65·16 W
99	Sucre (State) (sōō'krĕ), Ven. (In.)	10·18 N	64·12 W
99	Suçuapara (sōō-sōōȧ-pà'rä), Braz.	16·57 S	48·47 W
95	Sud, Canal du (Chan.), Hai.	18·40 N	73·15 W
85	Sud, Rivière du (rē-vyâr'dü süd'), Can. (Quebec In.)	46·56 N	70·35 W
136	Suda (sōō'dá), Sov. Un. (Urals In.)	56·58 N	56·45 E
128	Suda (R.) (sōō'dȧ), Sov. Un.	59·24 N	36·40 E
144	Sudair (sŭ-dä'ēr), Sau. Ar.	25·48 N	46·28 E
163	Sudan, Afr.	14·00 N	28·00 E
163	Sudan (Reg.) (sōō-dän'), Afr.	16·48 N	3·11 E
87	Sudbury (sŭd'bēr-ê), Can.	46·28 N	81·00 W
83	Sudbury, Mass. (Boston In.)	42·23 N	71·25 W
120	Sudetes (Mts.), Czech.	50·41 N	15·37 E
128	Sudogda (sōō'dôk-dȧ), Sov. Un.	55·57 N	40·29 E
128	Sudost' (R.) (sōō-dôst'), Sov. Un.	52·43 N	33·13 E
139	Sudr (R.), U. A. R. (Palestine In.)	29·46 N	32·57 E
129	Sudzha (sōōd'zhȧ), Sov. Un.	51·14 N	35·11 E
125	Sueca (swā'kä), Sp.	39·12 N	0·18 W
	Suez, see As Suways		
	Suez Canal, see Qana el Suweis		
168	Suez, G. of (sōō-ĕz'), U. A. R. (Suez In.)	29·53 N	32·33 E
84	Suffern (sŭf'fērn), N. Y. (New York In.)	41·07 N	74·09 W
84	Suffolk (sŭf'ŭk), Va. (Norfolk In.)	36·43 N	76·35 W
146	Sufu (Kashgar), China	39·29 N	76·00 E
134	Sufu, Sov. Un.	39·47 N	76·17 E
80	Sugar (Cr.), Ind.	39·55 N	87·10 W
72	Sugar City, Colo.	38·12 N	103·42 W
74	Sugar Creek, Mo. (Kansas City In.)	39·07 N	94·27 W
73	Sugar Cr. (shŏŏg'ēr), Ill.	40·14 N	89·28 W
74	Sugar I., Mich. (Sault Ste. Marie In.)	46·31 N	84·12 W
77	Sugarland Jct. (shŏŏg'ēr-lȧnd), Tex. (In.)	29·29 N	95·31 W
160	Sugarloaf Pt. (sŏŏgēr'lōf), Austl.	32·19 S	153·04 E
142	Suget Pass (sōō'gĕt), China	36·35 N	77·40 E
120	Suhl (zōōl), Ger.	50·37 N	10·41 E
148	Suhsien (sōō'sĭān), China	33·37 N	117·51 E
151	Suichuan (Mtn.), China	26·25 N	114·10 E
148	Suichung (sōōĭ'jŏŏng), China	40·22 N	120·20 E
135	Suifenho (swā'fŭn'hŭ'), Sov. Un.	44·47 N	131·13 E
150	Suihua (Peilintzu), China	41·38 N	126·42 E
146	Suilai (sōō'ē-lī'), China	44·30 N	86·00 E
148	Suining (sōō'ē-nĭng'), China	33·54 N	117·57 E
101	Suipacha (swē-pä'chä), Arg. (Buenos Aires In.)	34·45 S	59·43 W
148	Suip'ing (sōō'ē-pĭng), China	33·09 N	113·58 E
116	Suir R. (sūr), Ire.	52·20 N	7·32 W
65	Suisun B. (sōō-ē-sōōn'), Calif. (San Francisco In.)	38·07 N	122·02 W
153	Suita (sōō'ē-tä), Jap. (Osaka In.)	34·45 N	135·32 E
150	Suite, China	37·32 N	110·12 E
146	Suiyuan (Prov.) (sōō'ē-yän'), China	41·31 N	107·04 E
154	Sukabumi, Indon.	6·52 S	106·56 E
154	Sukadana, Indon.	1·15 S	110·30 E
153	Sukagawa (sōō'kä-gä'wä), Jap.	37·08 N	140·07 E
128	Sukhinichi (sōō'ĸē'nē-chē), Sov. Un.	54·07 N	35·18 E
132	Sukhona (R.) (sōō-ĸô'nȧ), Sov. Un.	59·30 N	42·20 E
136	Sukhoy Log (sōō'kôy lôg), Sov. Un. (Urals In.)	56·55 N	62·03 E
133	Sukhumi (sōō-kōōm'), Sov. Un.	43·00 N	41·00 E
142	Sukkur (sŭk'ŭr), W. Pak.	27·49 N	68·50 E
136	Suksun (sōōk'sōōn), Sov. Un. (Urals In.)	57·08 N	57·22 E
153	Sukumo (sōō'kōō-mô), Jap.	32·58 N	132·45 E
153	Sukurai (sōō'kōō-rī), Jap. (Ōsaka In.)	34·31 N	135·51 E
155	Sula (I.), Indon.	2·20 S	125·20 E
129	Sula (R.) (sōō-lä'), Sov. Un.	50·36 N	33·13 E
92	Sulaco R. (sōō-lä'kō), Hond.	14·55 N	87·31 W
142	Sulaiman Ra. (sōō-lä-ê-män'), W. Pak.	34·22 N	69·10 E
133	Sulak (R.) (sōō-làk'), Sov. Un.	43·30 N	47·00 E
154	Sulawesi (Prov.), Indon.	1·30 S	120·22 E
118	Suldals Vand (L.) (sül-dâls vän), Nor.	59·35 N	6·59 E
136	Suleya (sōō-lĕ'yá), Sov. Un. (Urals In.)	55·12 N	58·52 E
111	Sulfeld (zōōl'fĕld), Ger. (Hamburg In.)	53·48 N	10·13 E
129	Sulina (sōō-lē'nȧ), Rom.	45·08 N	29·38 E
112	Sulitjema (Mtn.) (sōō-lê-tyĕl'mȧ), Nor.-Swe.	67·03 N	16·09 E
98	Sullana (sōō-lyä'nä), Peru	4·57 N	80·47 W
78	Sulligent (sŭl'ĭ-jĕnt), Ala.	33·52 N	88·06 W
80	Sullivan (sŭl'ĭ-vȧn), Ill.	41·35 N	88·35 W
80	Sullivan, Ind.	39·05 N	87·20 W
73	Sullivan, Mo.	38·13 N	91·09 W
126	Sulmona (sōōl-mō'nä), It.	42·02 N	13·58 E
146	Sulo, China	41·29 N	80·15 E
146	Sulo Ho (R.), China	40·53 N	94·55 E
73	Sulphur (sŭl'fŭr), Okla.	34·31 N	96·58 W
73	Sulphur (R.), Tex.	33·26 N	95·06 W
73	Sulphur Springs (sprĭngz), Tex.	33·09 N	95·36 W
65	Sultan (sŭl'tăn), Wash. (Seattle In.)	47·52 N	121·49 W
65	Sultan (R.), Wash. (Seattle In.)	47·55 N	121·49 W
90	Sultepec (sōōl-tȧ-pĕk'), Mex.	18·50 N	99·51 W
154	Sulu Arch. (sōō'lōō), Phil.	5·52 N	122·00 E
115	Suluntah, Libya	32·39 N	21·49 E
115	Sulūq, Libya	31·41 N	20·23 E
154	Sulu Sea, Phil.	8·25 N	119·00 E
153	Suma (sōō'mä), Jap. (Osaka In.)	34·39 N	135·08 E
65	Sumas (sū'mȧs), Wash. (Vancouver In.)	49·00 N	122·16 W
154	Sumatera (Sumatra) (I.) (sōō-mä-tĕr'ȧ), Indon.	2·06 N	99·40 E
139	Sumatera Tenga (Prov.), Indon. (Singapore In.)	0·56 N	101 25 E
154	Sumba (I.) (sŭm'bȧ), Indon.	9·52 S	119·00 E
154	Sumbawa (I.) (sōōm-bä'wä), Indon.	9·00 S	118·18 E
154	Sumbawa-Besar, Indon.	8·32 S	117·20 E
121	Sümeg (shü'mĕg), Hung.	46·59 N	17·19 E
153	Sumida (R.) (sōō'mê-dä), Jap.	36·01 N	139·24 E
101	Sumidouro (sōō-mê-dō'rōō), Braz. (Rio de Janeiro In.)	22·04 S	42·41 W
153	Sumiyoshi (sōō'mê-yō'shê), Jap. (Ōsaka In.)	34·43 N	135·16 E
66	Summer L. (sŭm'ēr), Ore.	42·50 N	120·35 W
82	Summerside (sŭm'ēr-sīd), Can.	46·25 N	63·47 W
79	Summerton (sŭm'ēr-tŭn), S. C.	33·37 N	80·22 W
79	Summerville (sŭm'ēr-vĭl), S. C.	33·00 N	80·10 W
75	Summit (sŭm'mĭt), Ill. (Chicago In.)	41·47 N	87·48 W
84	Summit, N. J. (New York In.)	40·43 N	74·21 W
66	Summit Lake Ind. Res, Nev.	41·35 N	119·30 W
69	Summit Pk, Colo.	37·20 N	106·40 W
65	Sumner (sŭm'nēr), Wash. (Seattle In.)	47·12 N	122·14 W
120	Šumperk (shŏŏm'pĕrk), Czech.	49·57 N	17·02 E
78	Sumrall (sŭm'rôl), Miss.	31·25 N	89·34 W
79	Sumter (sŭm'tēr), S. C.	33·55 N	80·21 W
129	Sumy (sōō'mĭ), Sov. Un.	50·54 N	34·47 E
129	Sumy (Oblast), Sov. Un.	51·02 N	34·05 E
81	Sunbury (sŭn'bēr-ê), Pa.	40·50 N	76·45 W
154	Sunda Is, Indon.	9·00 S	108·40 E
118	Sundals Fd. (sŏŏn'däls), Nor.	62·50 N	7·55 E
67	Sundance (sŭn'dăns), Wyo.	44·24 N	104·27 W
142	Sundarbans (Swp.) (sŏŏn'dēr-bŭns), E. Pak.-India	21·50 N	89·00 E
154	Sunda Selat (Str.), Indon.	5·45 S	106·15 E
154	Sunda Trench (sŏŏn'dä), Indon.	9·45 S	107·30 E
167	Sundays (R.) (sŭn'dās), S. Afr. (Natal In.)	33·17 S	25·14 E
158	Sunday Str. (sŭn'dā), Austl.	15·50 S	122·45 E
118	Sundbyberg (sōōn'bü-bĕrgh), Swe.	59·24 N	17·56 E
116	Sunderland (sŭn'dēr-lȧnd), Eng.	54·55 N	1·25 W
118	Sundsvall (sōōnds'väl), Swe.	62·24 N	19·19 E
78	Sunflower, (R.) (sŭn-flou'ēr), Miss.	32·57 N	90·40 W
150	Sungari Res. (sōōn'gä-rē), China	42·55 N	127·50 E
	Sungari, see Sung Hua (R.)		
149	Sungchiang, China (Shanghai In.)	31·01 N	121·14 E
147	Sung Hua (R.) (Sungari) (sōōn'gä-rē), China	46·09 N	127·53 E
150	Sungtzu (Mtn.), China	39·40 N	114·50 E
133	Sungurlu (sōōn'gŏŏr-lōō'), Tur.	40·08 N	34·20 E
142	Sun Kosi (R.), Nepal	27·13 N	85·52 E
74	Sunland (sŭn-lănd), Calif. (Los Angeles In.)	34·16 N	118·18 W
118	Sunne (sōōn'ĕ), Swe.	59·51 N	13·07 E
110	Sunninghill (sŭnĭng'hĭl), Eng. (London In.)	51·23 N	0·40 W
65	Sunnydale (sŭn-nê-dāl), Calif. (San Francisco In.)	37·23 N	122·02 W
74	Sunnymead (sŭn'ĭ-mēd), Calif. (Los Angeles In.)	33·56 N	117·15 W
69	Sunnyside (sŭn'ĭ-sīd), Utah	39·35 N	110·20 W
66	Sunnyside, Wash.	46·19 N	120·00 W
65	Sunol (sōō'nŭl), Calif. (San Francisco In.)	37·36 N	122·53 W
67	Sun R. (sŭn), Mont.	47·34 N	111·53 W
74	Sunset (sŭn-sĕt), Utah (Salt Lake City In.)	41·08 N	112·02 W
69	Sunset Crater Natl. Mon. (krā'tēr), Ariz.	35·20 N	111·30 W
161	Sunshine, Austl. (Melbourne In.)	37·47 S	144·50 E
135	Suntar (sōōn-tär'), Sov. Un.	62·14 N	117·49 E
119	Suoyarvi (sōō'ô-yĕr'vê), Sov. Un.	62·12 N	32·29 E
69	Superior (su-pē'rĭ-ēr), Ariz.	33·15 N	111·10 W
72	Superior, Nebr.	40·04 N	98·05 W
74	Superior, Wis. (Duluth In.)	46·44 N	92·06 W
67	Superior, Wyo.	41·45 N	108·57 W
91	Superior, Laguna (L.) (lä-gōō'nȧ sōō-pä-rê-ōr'), Mex.	16·20 N	94·55 W
63	Superior, L., U. S.-Can.	47·38 N	89·20 W
74	Superior Village, Wis. (Duluth In.)	46·38 N	92·07 W
152	Sup'ung Res. (sōō'pōōng), Kor.-China	40·35 N	126·00 E
65	Suquamish (sōō-gwä'mĭsh), Wash. (Seattle In.)	47·44 N	122·34 W
139	Sūr (Tyre) (sōōr) (tīr), Leb. (Palestine In.)	33·16 N	35·13 E
144	Şūr, Muscat and Oman	22·23 N	59·28 E
154	Surabaja, Indon.	7·23 S	112·45 E
168	Surad Ad (Mt.) (sōō'răd-ăd), Som. (Horn of Afr. In.)	10·40 N	47·23 E
154	Surakarta, Indon.	7·35 S	110·45 E
121	Šurany (shōō'rȧ-nû'), Czech.	48·05 N	18·11 E
160	Surat (sū-răt), Austl.	27·18 S	149·00 E
142	Surat (sōō'rŭt), India	21·08 N	73·22 E
154	Surat Thani, Thai.	8·59 N	99·14 E
128	Surazh (sōō-räzh'), Sov. Un.	53·02 N	32·27 E
128	Surazh, Sov. Un.	55·24 N	30·46 E
122	Surgères (sür-zhâr'), Fr.	46·06 N	0·51 W
134	Surgut (sōōr-gōōt'), Sov. Un.	61·18 N	73·38 E
154	Surin, Thai.	14·59 N	103·57 E
99	Surinam (Neth. Guiana) (sōō-rê-näm') (gē-ăn'ȧ), S. A.	3·45 N	56·30 W
99	Suriname (R.), Sur.	4·15 N	55·38 W
119	Sur-Sari (I.) (sōōr-sä'rĭ), Sov. Un.	60·04 N	26·55 E
153	Suruga-Wan (B.) (sōō'rōō-gä wän), Jap.	34·52 N	138·36 E
165	Surt, Libya	31·14 N	16·37 E
115	Surt, Khalij (G.), Afr.	31·30 N	18·28 E
126	Susa (sōō'sä), It.	45·01 N	7·09 E
153	Susa, Jap.	34·40 N	131·39 E
126	Sušac (sōō'shäts), Yugo.	44·31 N	14·15 E
126	Sušak (sōō'shäk), Yugo.	45·20 N	14·24 E
126	Sušak (I.), Yugo.	42·45 N	16·30 E
153	Susaki (sōō'sä-kê), Jap.	33·23 N	133·16 E
64	Susitna (sōō-sĭt'nȧ), Alaska	61·28 N	150·28 W
64	Susitna (R.), Alaska	62·00 N	150·28 W
81	Susquehanna (sŭs'kwê-hăn'ȧ), Pa.	41·55 N	75·35 W
81	Susquehanna (R.), Pa.	39·50 N	76·20 W
75	Sussex, Wis. (Milwaukee In.)	43·08 N	88·12 W
82	Sussex (sŭs'ĕks), Can.	45·42 N	65·32 W
84	Sussex, N. J. (New York In.)	41·12 N	74·36 W
151	Susung (sōō'sōōng'), China	30·18 N	116·08 E

ng-sing; ŋ-baŋk: ɴ-nasalized n; nŏd; cŏmmit; ōld; ôbey; ôrder; fōōd; fŏŏt; ou-out; s-soft; sh-dish; th-thin; pūre; ûnite; ûrn; stŭd; circŭs; ü-as "y" in study; '-indeterminate vowel.

272 Sutherland–Tal'ai PRONOUNCING INDEX

Page Name Pronunciation Region Lat. °′ Long. °′

161 Sutherland (sŭdh′ ẽr-lănd) Austl. (Sydney In.) 34·02 s 151·04 e
166 Sutherland (sŭ′thẽr-lănd) . . S. Afr. 32·25 s 20·40 e
142 Sutlej (R.) (sŭt′lĕj) . . . . Pak.-India 29·53 n 72·25 e
110 Sutton (sut′′n) . Eng. (London In.) 51·21 n 0·12 w
83 Sutton . . . . Mass. (Boston In.) 42·09 n 71·46 w
110 Sutton Coldfield (kōld′fēld) . . Eng. 52·34 n 1·49 w
110 Sutton-in-Ashfield (ĭn-ăsh′fēld) Eng. 53·07 n 1·15 w
153 Suwa (sōō′wä) . . . . Jap. 36·03 n 138·08 e
121 Suwatki (sōō-vou′kē) . . . . Pol. 54·05 n 22·58 e
78 Suwannee (R.) (sōō-wô′nē) Fla.-Ga. 29·42 n 83·00 w
128 Suzdal′ (sōōz′dȧl) . . . . Sov. Un. 56·26 n 40·29 e
152 Suzu Misaki (C.) (sōō′zōō mē′sä-kē) . Jap. 37·30 n 137·35 e
130 Svalbard (Spitzbergen) (Is.) (sväl′bärt) (spĭts′bûr-gĕn) . Eur. 77·00 n 20·00 e
118 Svaneke (svä′nĕ-kĕ) . . . . Den. 55·08 n 15 07 e
129 Svatovo (svä′tō-vō) . . . . . Sov. Un. 49·23 n 38·10 e
118 Svedala (svĕ′dä-lä) . . . . Swe. 55·29 n 13·11 e
118 Sveg . . . . Swe. 62·03 n 14·22 e
118 Svelvik (svĕl′vêk) . . . . Nor. 59·37 n 10·18 e
118 Svendborg (svĕn-bôrgh) . . . . . Den. 55·05 n 10·35 e
65 Svensen (svĕn′sĕn) Ore. (Portland In.) 46·10 n 123·39 w
136 Sverdlovsk (svĕrd-lôfsk′) Sov. Un. (Urals In.) 56·48 n 60·37 e
152 Svetlaya (svyĕt′lȧ-yȧ) . . . Sov. Un. 46·09 n 137·53 e
127 Svilajnac (svē′lȧ-ē-nȧts) . . . . Yugo. 44·12 n 21·14 e
127 Svilengrad (svĕl′ĕn-grȧt) . . . . . Bul. 41·44 n 26·11 e
132 Svir′ (R.) . . . . Sov. Un. 60·55 n 33·40 e
119 Svir Kanal (can.) (kȧ-näl′) Sov. Un. 60·10 n 32·40 e
127 Svishtov (svēsh′tôf) . . . . Bul. 43·36 n 25·21 e
128 Svisloch′ (svēs′lôk) . . . . . . Sov. Un. 53·38 n 28·10 e
120 Svitavy . . . . Czech. 49·46 n 16·28 e
121 Svitsa (R.) (svĭ-tsä) . . . . . Sov. Un. 49·09 n 24·10 e
135 Svobodnyy (svō-bôd′nĭ) . . Sov. Un. 51·28 n 128·28 e
112 Svolvaer (svôl′vĕr) . . . . Nor. 68·15 n 14·29 e
135 Svyatoy Nos, Mys (C.) (svyŭ′toi nôs) . Sov. Un. 72·18 n 139·28 e
119 Svyentsyany (shvyĕn′tsyȧ-nĭ) Sov. Un. 55·09 n 26·09 e
110 Swadlincote (swŏd′lĭn-kōt) . . . Eng. 52·46 n 1·33 w
159 Swain Rfs. (swān) . . . . Austl. 22·12 s 152·08 e
79 Swainsboro (swānz′bŭr-ō) . . . . . Ga. 32·37 n 82·21 w
166 Swakopmund (svä′kôp-mōōnt) (swä′kôp-mōōnd) . S. W. Afr. 22·40 s 14·30 e
116 Swale (R.) (swāl) . . . . Eng. 54·12 n 1·30 w
110 Swallowfield (swŏl′ō-fēld) Eng. (London In.) 51·21 n 0·58 w
83 Swampscott (swômp′skŏt) Mass. (Boston In.) 42·28 n 70·55 w
161 Swan, I. (swŏn) Austl. (Melbourne In.) 38·15 s 144·41 e
158 Swan (R.) . . . . Austl. 31·30 s 126·30 e
160 Swan Hill . . . . Austl. 35·20 s 143·30 e
86 Swan Hills (hĭlz) . . . . Can. 54·50 n 118·10 w
158 Swanland (Reg.) (swŏn′lănd) Austl. 31·45 s 119·15 e
86 Swan River (swŏn rĭv′ẽr) . . . . Can. 52·01 n 101·29 w
67 Swan R . . . . Mont. 47·40 n 113·45 w
85 Swansea (swän′sē) Can. (Toronto In.) 43·38 n 79·28 w
116 Swansea . . . . Wales 51·37 n 3·59 w
74 Swansea (swŏn′sē) Ill. (St. Louis In.) 38·32 n 89·59 w
84 Swansea . . . Mass. (Providence In.) 41·45 n 71·09 w
116 Swansea B . . . . Wales 51·25 n 4·12 w
72 Swanson Res. (swŏn′sŭn) . . . Nebr. 40·13 n 101·30 w
166 Swartkop (Mtn.) S. Afr. (Cape Town In.) 34·13 s 18·27 e
168 Swartruggens S. Afr. (Johannesburg & Pretoria In.) 25·59 s 26·40 e
167 Swartspruit S. Afr. (Johannesburg & Pretoria In.) 25·44 s 28·01 e
Swatow, see Shant′ou
166 Swaziland (Swä′zē-lănd) . . . . . Afr. 26·45 s 31·30 e
102 Sweden (swē′dĕn) . . . . Eur. 60·10 n 14·10 e
84 Swedesboro (swēdz′bē-rō) N. J. (Philadelphia In.) 39·45 n 75·22 w
78 Sweetwater (swēt′wô-tẽr) . . . Tenn. 35·36 n 84·29 w
76 Sweetwater . . . . Tex. 32·28 n 100·25 w
70 Sweetwater (L.) . . . . N. D. 48·15 n 98·35 w
168 Sweetwater (can.) U. A. R. (Suez In.) 30·14 n 32·25 e
68 Sweetwater Res. Calif. (San Diego In.) 32·42 n 116·54 w
67 Sweetwater R . . . . Wyo. 42·19 n 108·35 w
120 Świdnica (shvĭd-nē′tsȧ) . . . . . . Pol. 50·50 n 16·30 e
120 Swidwin (shvĭd′vĭn) . . . . Pol. 53·46 n 15·48 e
120 Swiebodziec (shvyĕn-bô′ jĕts) . Pol. 52·16 n 15·36 e
120 Swiebodzin (shvyăn-bôd′jĕn) . . Pol. 50·51 n 16·17 e
121 Swiecie (shvyăn′tsyĕ) . . . . Pol. 53·23 n 18·26 e
121 Swietokrzyskie Góry (Mts.) (shvyĕn-tō-kzhĭ′skyĕ gōō′rĭ) Pol. 50·57 n 21·02 e
110 Swift (R.) . . . . Eng. 52·26 n 1·08 w
82 Swift (R.) (swĭft) . . . . Maine 44·42 n 70·40 w
86 Swift Current (swĭft kûr′ĕnt) . Can. 50·20 n 107·59 w
66 Swift Res . . . . Wash. 46·03 n 122·10 w
116 Swilly, Lough (B.) (lŏk swĭ-lē) Ire. 54·84 n 8·04 w
116 Swindon (swĭn′dŭn) . . . . Eng. 51·35 n 1·55 w
65 Swinomish Ind. Res. (swĭ-nō′mĭsh) Wash. (Seattle In.) 48·25 n 122·27 w
120 Swinoujscie (slvĭ-nĭ-ô-wēsh′chyĕ) . Pol. 53·56 n 14·14 e
110 Swinton (swĭn′tŭn) . . . . Eng. 53·30 n 1·19 w
75 Swissvale (swĭs′vāl) Pa. (Pittsburgh In.) 40·25 n 79·53 w
102 Switzerland (swĭt′zẽr-lănd) . . . Eur. 46·30 n 7·43 e

128 Syas′ (R.) (syäs) . . . . Sov. Un. 59·28 n 33·24 e
71 Sycamore (sĭk′ȧ-mōr) . . . . Ill. 42·00 n 88·42 w
128 Sychëvka (sē-chôf′kȧ) . . . Sov. Un. 55·52 n 34·18 e
161 Sydney (sĭd′nē) . Austl. (Sydney In.) 33·55 s 151·17 e
83 Sydney . . . . Can. 46·08 n 60·11 w
Syene, see Aswān
83 Sydney Mines . . . . Can. 46·15 n 60·15 w
132 Syktyvkar (sük-tüf′kär) . . Sov. Un. 61·35 n 50·40 e
78 Sylacauga (sĭl-ȧ-kô′gȧ) . . . . Ala. 33·10 n 86·15 w
118 Sylfjällen (Mtn.) (sül′fyĕl-ĕn) . Swe. 63·00 n 12·10 e
118 Sylling (sül′lĭng) . . . . Nor. 59·52 n 10·12 e
120 Sylt I. (sĭlt) . . . . Ger. 54·55 n 8·30 e
79 Sylvania (sĭl-vā′nĭ-ȧ) . . . . Ga. 32·44 n 81·40 w
78 Sylvester (sĭl-vĕs′tẽr) . . . . Ga. 31·32 n 83·50 w
81 Syracuse . . . . N. Y. 43·05 n 76·10 w
72 Syracuse (sĭr′ȧ-kūs) . . . . Kans. 37·59 n 101·44 w
74 Syracuse Utah (Salt Lake City In.) 41·06 n 112·04 w
115 Syra I . . . . Grc. 37·19 n 25·10 e
103 Syr-Dar′ya (R.) . . . . Sov. Un. 44·15 n 65·45 e
165 Syria (sĭr′ĭ-ȧ) . . . . Asia 35·00 n 37·15 e
144 Syrian Des. (sĭr′ĭ-ȧn) . . . . Asia 32·03 n 39·30 e
136 Sysert′ (sĕ′sĕrt) Sov. Un. (Urals In.) 56·30 n 60·48 e
132 Syso′la (R.) . . . . Sov. Un. 60·50 n 50·40 e
133 Syzran′ (sĕz-rän′) . . . . Sov. Un. 53·10 n 48·10 e
121 Szabadszallas (sô′bôd-sä′lăsh) Hung. 46·52 n 19·15 e
120 Szamotuty (shȧ-mô-tōō′wē) . . . Pol. 52·36 n 16·34 e
121 Szarvas (sôr′vôsh) . . . . Hung. 46·51 n 20·36 e
121 Szczebrzeszyn (shchĕ-bzhä′shĕn) Pol. 50·41 n 22·58 e
120 Szczecin (Stettin) (shchĕ′tsĭn) (shtĕ-tēn′) . Pol. 53·25 n 14·35 e
120 Szczecinek (shchĕ′tsĭ-nĕk) . . . . Pol. 53·42 n 16·42 e
121 Szczuczyn (shchōō′chĕn) . . . . . Pol. 53·32 n 22·17 e
121 Szczytno (shchĭt′nô) . . . . Pol. 53·33 n 21 00 e
Szechwan, see Ssuchuan
121 Szeged (sĕ′gĕd) . . . . Hung. 46·15 n 20·12 e
121 Székesfehérvar (sā′kĕsh-fĕ′hăr-vär) . Hung. 47·12 n 18·26 e
121 Szekszard (sĕk′särd) . . . . Hung. 46·19 n 18·42 e
146 Szengen . . . . China 23·39 n 107·45 e
121 Szentendre (sĕnt′ĕn-drĕ) . . . . Hung. 47·40 n 19·07 e
121 Szentes (sĕn′tĕsh) . . . . Hung. 46·38 n 20·18 e
121 Szigetvar (sĕ′gĕt-vär) . . . . . . Hung. 46·05 n 17·50 e
121 Szolnok (sôl′nôk) . . . . Hung. 47·11 n 20·12 e
121 Szombathely (sôm′bôt-hĕl′) . Hung. 47·13 n 16·35 e
120 Szprotawa . . . . Pol. 51·34 n 15·29 e
121 Sztálinváros . . . . Hung. 46·57 n 18·55 e
121 Szydlowiec (shid-wô′vyets) . . . Pol. 51·13 n 20·53 e
155 Taal (L.) (tä-äl′) Phil. (Manila In.) 13·58 n 121·06 e
155 Tabaco (tä-bä′kō) Phil. (Manila In.) 13·27 n 123·40 e
167 Tabankulu (tä-bän-kōō′la) S. Afr. (Natal In.) 30·56 s 29·19 e
93 Tabasara, Serrania de (Ra.) (sĕr-rä-nē′ä dā tä-bä-sä′rä) . Pan. 8·29 n 81·22 w
90 Tabasco (tä-bäs′kō) . . . . Mex. 21·47 n 103·04 w
86 Taber . . . . Can. 49·47 n 112·20 w
155 Tablas (I.) (tä′bläs) Phil. (Manila In.) 12·26 n 112·15 e
155 Tablas Str . . . . . Phil. (Manila In.) 12·17 n 121·41 e
166 Table B. (tā′b′l) S. Afr. (Cape Town In.) 33·41 s 18·27 e
166 Table Mt . S. Afr. (Cape Town In.) 33·58 s 18·26 e
73 Table Rock Lake . . . . Mo. 36·37 n 93·29 w
Tabletop, see Jacques Cartier, Mt.
88 Taboga (I.) (tä-bō′gä) Pan. (Panama Canal In.) 8·48 n 79·35 w
88 Taboguilla (I.) (tä-bô-gē′l-yä) Pan. (Panama Canal In.) 8·48 n 79·31 w
99 Taboleiro (Plat.) (tä-bô-lā′rō) Braz. 9·34 s 39·22 w
120 Tábor (tä′bôr) . . . . Czech. 49·25 n 14·40 e
166 Tabora (tä-bō′rä) . . . . Tan. 5·07 s 32·47 e
164 Tabou (tȧ-bōō′) . . . . . . Ivory Coast 4·30 n 7·25 w
144 Tabriz (tȧ-brēz′) . . . . Iran 38·00 n 46·13 e
90 Tacámbaro (R.) (tä-käm′bä-rō) Mex. 18·55 n 101·25 w
90 Tacambaro de Codallos (dā kō-däl′yōs) . Mex. 19·12 n 101·28 w
92 Tacaná (Vol.) (tä-kä-nä′) Mex.-Guat. 15·09 n 92·07 w
99 Tacarigua, Laguna de la (L.) (lä-gōō′nä-dĕ-lä-tä-kä-rē′gwä) Ven. (In.) 10·18 n 65·43 w
93 Tacarouna, Cerro (Mt.) (sĕ′r-rô-tä-kä-rô-ōō′nä) . Pan. 8·07 n 77·18 w
149 Tach′ang . . . . China (Shanghai In.) 31·18 n 121·25 e
148 Tach′angshan Tao (I.) (dȧ′chäng′shän dou) . China 39·21 n 122·31 e
146 T′ach′eng (Chuguchak) (tä′chĕng′) . China 46·50 n 83·24 e
148 Tach′iao (dȧ′chĭou) . . . . China 32·23 n 119·41 e
148 Tach′in Tao (I.) (dä′chĭn dou) China 38·18 n 120·50 e
155 Tacloban (tä-klō′bän) . . . . Phil. 11·06 n 124·58 e
98 Tacna (täk′nä) . . . . Peru 18·34 s 70·16 w
65 Tacoma (tȧ-kō′mȧ) Wash. (Seattle In.) 47·14 n 122·27 w
81 Taconic Ra. (tȧ-kŏn′ĭk) . . . . N. Y. 41·55 n 73·40 w
91 Tacotalpa (tä-kô-täl′pä) . . . . . Mex. 17·37 n 92·51 w
91 Tacotalpa (R.) . . . . Mex. 17·24 n 92·38 w
100 Tacuarembó (tä-kwä-rĕm′bō) . . Ur. 31·44 s 55·56 w
164 Tademaït, Plat. du (tä-dē-mä′ēt) Alg. 28·00 n 2·15 e
168 Tadjoura (tȧd-zhōō′rȧ) Fr. Som. (Horn of Afr. In.) 11·48 n 42·54 e
110 Tadley (tăd′lē) . Eng. (London In.) 51·19 n 1·08 w
98 Tadó (tä-dō′) . . . . Col. (In.) 5·15 n 76·30 w
153 Tadotsu (tä′dô-tsōō) . . . . Jap. 34·14 n 133·43 e
82 Tadoussac (tȧ-dōō-sȧk′) . . . . . Can. 48·09 n 69·44 w
130 Tadzhik (S. S. R.) (tát′zhĕk) Sov. Un. 39·22 n 69·30 e

152 Taebaek Sanmaek (Mts.) (tī-bĭk′ sän-mĭk′) . Kor. 37·20 n 128·50 e
152 Taedong R. (tī-dŏng) . . . . Kor. 38·38 n 124·32 e
152 Taegu (tī′gōō′) . . . . Kor. 35·49 n 128·41 e
124 Tafalla (tä-fäl′yä) . . . . Sp. 42·30 n 1·42 w
149 Tafan . . . . China (Canton In.) 23·27 n 113·06 e
114 Tafilelt (Oasis) (tä-fē′lĕlt) . . . Mor. 31·49 n 4·44 w
125 Tafna (R.) (täf′nä) . . . . Alg. 35·28 n 1·00 w
68 Taft (tȧft) . . . . Calif. 35·09 n 119·27 w
129 Taganrog (tȧ-gȧn-rôk′) . . Sov. Un. 47·13 n 38·44 e
129 Taganrogskiy Zaliv (B.) (tȧ-gȧn-rôk′skĭ zä′lĭf) . Sov. Un. 46·55 n 38·17 e
126 Tagliamento (R.) (täl-yä-mĕn′tō) It. 46·11 n 12·53 e
159 Tagula (I.) (tä′gōō-lȧ) . . . . . . Austl. 11·45 s 153·46 e
Tagus, see Tajo, Río
154 Tahan, Gunong (Pk.) . . . . . . Mala. 4·33 n 101·52 e
164 Tahat, Mt. (tä-hät′) . . . . Alg. 23·22 n 5·21 e
148 Taheishan Tao (I.) (dȧ′hā′shän dou) . China 37·57 n 120·37 e
157 Tahiti (I.) (tä-hē′tē) (tä′ē-tē′) Fr. Polynesia 17·30 s 149·30 w
119 Tahkuna Nina (tȧh-kōō′nȧ nē′nȧ) Sov. Un. 59·08 n 22·03 e
73 Tahlequah (tă-lē-kwä′) . . . . . Okla. 35·54 n 94·58 w
68 Tahoe (L.) (tä′hō) . . . . Calif.-Nev. 39·09 n 120·18 w
164 Tahoua (tä′ōō-ä) . . . . Niger 14·52 n 5·16 e
151 Tahsien . . . . China 31·12 n 107·30 e
148 Tahsien Shan (Mts.) (dä′sĭän shän) . China 36·28 n 117·42 e
150 Tahsing . . . . China (Peking In.) 39·44 n 116·19 e
150 Tahsingaling Shanmo (Greater Khingan Mts.) . China 46·30 n 120·00 e
168 Ṭahṭā (tä′tä) . . U. A. R. (Nile In.) 26·48 n 31·29 e
65 Tahuya (tȧ-hū-yā′) Wash. (Seattle In.) 47·23 n 123·03 w
65 Tahuya (R.) . . Wash. (Seattle In.) 47·28 n 122·55 w
148 T′aian (tĭ′än′) . . . . China 36·13 n 117·08 e
148 Taich′iao (dăĭ′chĭou) . . . . China 31·43 n 120·40 e
151 T′aichung (tī′chōōng) . . . . . Taiwan 24·10 n 120·42 e
148 T′aierhchuang (tăĭ′ē′jōōäng) . China 34·34 n 117·44 e
148 Taifou (dăĭ′fōō) . . . . China 31·22 n 119·29 e
Taigones, see Taygonos
150 T′aihang Shan (Mts.) (tī′häng′ shän′) . China 35·45 n 112·00 e
148 T′aiho (tăĭ′hŭ) . . . . China 33·10 n 115·38 e
148 Taihsien (tăĭ′sĭän) . . . . China 32·31 n 119·54 e
148 T′aihsing (tăĭ′sĭng) . . . . China 32·12 n 119·58 e
148 T′ai Hu (L.) (tăĭ′hōō) . . . . . . China 31·13 n 120·00 e
150 Taiku . . . . China 37·25 n 112·35 e
146 Tailagein Khara (Reg.) (tī′lȧ-gän′ kä′rä) . Mong. 43·39 n 105·54 e
150 T′ailai . . . . China 46·20 n 123·10 e
160 Tailem Bend (tā-lĕm) . . . . . . Austl. 35·15 s 139·30 e
Taimyr, see Taymyr
151 T′ainan (tī′nan′) . . . . Taiwan 23·08 n 120·18 e
115 Tainaron, Akra (C.) . . . . Grc. 36·20 n 21·20 e
151 Taining (tī′nĭng′) . . . . China 26·58 n 117·15 e
150 T′aipai Shan (Mtn.) . . . . China 33·42 n 107·25 e
151 T′aipei (tī′pä′) . . . . Taiwan 25·02 n 121·38 e
154 Taiping . . . . Mala. 4·56 n 100·39 e
152 Taira (tī′rä) . . . . Jap. 37·03 n 140·57 e
153 Taisha (tī′shä) . . . . Jap. 35·23 n 132·40 e
151 T′aishan . . . . China 22·15 n 112·50 e
148 T′ai Shan (Mtn.) (tăĭ′ shän) China 36·16 n 117·05 e
Taishet, see Tayshet
100 Taitao, Peninsula de (pĕ-nē′ng-sōō-lä-dĕ-tä-ē-tä′ō) Chile 46·20 s 77·15 w
149 T′aits′ang (tī′tsäng′) China (Shanghai In.) 31·26 n 121·06 e
151 T′aitung (tī′tōōng′) . . . . Taiwan 22·45 n 121·02 e
150 Taiwan (Formosa) (I.) (tī-wän) (fŏr-mō′sȧ) . . . . Asia 23·30 n 122·20 e
150 T′aiyüan (tī′yü-än′) . . . . China 37·32 n 112·38 e
151 Taiyün (Mtn.) (tī′yü-än′) . . China 25·40 n 118·08 e
101 Tajano de Morais (tĕ-zhä′nô-dĕ-mô-rä′ēs) Braz. (Rio de Janeiro In.) 22·05 s 42·04 w
124 Tajo, Río (Tagus) (R.) (rē′ō-tä′hō) (tā′gŭs) . Sp. 39·43 n 5·52 w
92 Tajumulco (Vol.) (tä-hōō-mōōl′kō) Guat. 15·03 n 91·53 w
124 Tajuña (R.) (tä-kōō′n-yä) . . . . Sp. 40·23 n 2·36 w
114 Tājūrā . . . . Libya 32·56 n 13·24 w
154 Tak . . . . Thai. 16·57 n 99·12 e
153 Taka (I.) (tä′kä) . . . . Jap. 30·47 n 130·23 e
153 Takada (tä′kȧ-dä) . . . . Jap. 37·08 n 138·30 e
153 Takahashi (tä′kä′hä-shĭ′) . . . . . Jap. 34·47 n 133·35 e
153 Takamatsu (tä′kä′mä-tsōō′) . . Jap. 34·20 n 134·02 e
153 Takamori (tä′kä′mô-rē′) . . . . . Jap. 32·50 n 131·08 e
149 Takang . . . . China (Canton In.) 22·48 n 113·24 e
153 Takaoka (tä′kä′ô-kä′) . . . . Jap. 36·45 n 136·59 e
153 Takarazuka (tä′kä-rä-zōō′kä) Jap. (Ōsaka In.) 34·48 n 135·22 e
153 Takasaki (tä′kät′sōō-kē′) . . . . . Jap. 36·20 n 139·00 e
153 Takatsu (Mizonokuchi) (tä-kät′sōō) (mē′zō-nō-kōō′chē) Jap. (Tōkyō In.) 35·36 n 139·37 e
153 Takatsuki (tä′kät′sōō-kē′) Jap. (Ōsaka In.) 34·51 n 135·38 e
167 Takaungu (tä′kä′ōōŋ-gōō′) . . . Ken. 3·41 s 39·48 e
153 Takayama (tä′kä′yä′mä) . . . . . Jap. 36·11 n 137·16 e
153 Takefu (tä′kĕ-fōō) . . . . Jap. 35·57 n 136·09 e
165 Takkaze R. (täk′ä-zä) . . . . Eth. 13·38 n 38·00 e
86 Takla (L.) (tă′klä) . . . . Can. 55·33 n 125·22 w
146 Takla Makan (Des.) (mȧ-kän′) China 39·22 n 82·34 e
148 Taku . . . . China 39·00 n 117·42 e
148 Taku (R.) (dä′gōō) . . . . China 37·07 n 120·14 e
90 Tala (tä′lä) . . . . Mex. 20·39 n 103·42 w
101 Talagante (tä-lä-gä′n-tĕ) Chile (Santiago In.) 33·39 s 70·54 w
150 Tal′ai . . . . China 45·25 n 124·22 e

ng-sing; ŋ-banŋ; ɴ-nasalized n; nŏd; cŏmmit; ōld; ŏbey; ôrder; fōōd; fŏŏt; ou-out; s-soft; sh-dish; th-thin; pūre; ûnite; ûrn; stŭd; circŭs; ū-as "y" in study; '-indeterminate vowel.

Page	Name Pronunciation	Region	Lat. ° '	Long. ° '
151	Tattien Ting (Mtn.)	China	22·25 N	111·20 E
151	Tatu Ho (R.)	China	29·20 N	103·30 E
101	Tatuí (tä-tōō-ē′)			
		Braz. (Rio de Janeiro In.)	23·21 S	47·49 W
150	Tat'ung (tä′tōŏng′)	China	40·00 N	113·30 E
101	Taubaté (tou-bà-tā′)			
		Braz. (Rio de Janeiro In.)	23·03 S	45·32 W
120	Tauern Tun	Aus.	47·12 N	13·17 E
165	Taufikia (tou-fēk′yà)	Sud.	9·30 N	31·47 E
166	Taungs (tä′ōŏngs)	S. Afr.	27·25 S	29·45 E
84	Taunton (tàn′tŭn)			
	Mass. (Providence In.)	41·54 N	71·03 W
84	Taunton R...R. I. (Providence In.)	41·50 N	71·02 W
117	Taunus (Mts.) (tou′nŏŏz)	Ger.	50·15 N	8·33 E
159	Taupo, L. (tä′ōō-pō)	N. Z.	38·38 S	175·27 E
119	Taurage (tou′rà-gä)	Sov. Un.	55·15 N	22·18 E
	Taurus Mts., see Toros Dağlari			
124	Tauste (tä-ōōs′tä)	Sp.	41·55 N	1·15 W
134	Tavda (tàv-dà′)	Sov. Un.	58·00 N	64·44 E
132	Tavda (R.)	Sov. Un.	59·20 N	63·28 E
123	Taverny (tà-vēr-nē′)			
		Fr. (Paris In.)	49·02 N	2·13 E
91	Taviche (tä-vē′chě)	Mex.	16·43 N	96·35 W
124	Tavira (tä-vē′rá)	Port.	37·09 N	7·42 W
154	Tavoy	Bur.	14·04 N	98·19 E
133	Tavşanli (tàv′shän-lĭ)	Tur.	39·30 N	29·30 E
77	Tawakoni (L.)	Tex.	32·51 N	95·59 W
153	Tawaramoto (tä′wä-rä-mô-tô)			
		Jap. (Ōsaka In.)	34·33 N	135·48 E
80	Tawas City	Mich.	44·15 N	83·30 W
80	Tawas Pt. (tô′wàs)	Mich.	44·15 N	83·25 W
148	Tawen (R.)	China	35·58 N	116·53 E
154	Tawitawi Group (Is.)			
		Phil.	4·52 N	120·35 E
90	Taxco de Alarcón			
	(täs′kō dě ä-lär-kô′n)	Mex.	18·34 N	99·37 W
116	Tay, Firth of (fûrth ŏv tā)	Scot.	56·26 N	2·45 W
116	Tay (L.)	Scot.	56·25 N	5·07 W
116	Tay (R.)	Scot.	56·35 N	3·37 W
155	Tayabas B. (tä-yä′bäs)			
		Phil. (Manila In.)	13·44 N	121·40 E
134	Tayga (tī′gä)	Sov. Un.	56·12 N	85·47 E
135	Taygonos, Mys (Taigonos) (C.)			
		Sov. Un.	60·37 N	160·17 E
77	Taylor (tā′lēr)	Tex.	30·35 N	97·25 W
69	Taylor, Mt.	N. Mex.	35·17 N	107·40 W
80	Taylorville (tā′lēr-vĭl)	Ill.	39·30 N	89·20 W
144	Taymā	Sau. Ar.	27·45 N	38·55 E
135	Taymyr (Taimyr) (L.) (tī-mĭr′)			
		Sov. Un.	74·13 N	100·45 E
134	Taymyr, P-Ov (Taimyr) (Pen.)			
		Sov. Un.	75·15 N	95·00 E
134	Tayshet (Taishet) (tī-shět′)			
		Sov. Un.	56·09 N	97·49 E
154	Taytay (tī-tī)	Phil.	10·37 N	119·10 E
151	Tayü	China	25·20 N	114·20 E
155	Tayung (tä-yōōng′)			
		Phil. (Manila In.)	16·01 N	120·45 E
134	Taz (B.) (tàz)	Sov. Un.	67·15 N	80·45 E
164	Taza (tä′zä)	Mor.	34·08 N	4·00 W
134	Tazovskoye	Sov. Un.	66·58 N	78·28 E
133	Tbilisi (′tbĭl-yē′sē)	Sov. Un.	41·40 N	44·45 E
166	Tchibanga (chê-bán′gä)	Gabon	2·48 S	10·50 E
121	Tczew (t′chēf′)	Pol.	54·06 N	18·48 E
92	Teabo (tě-ä′bô)			
		Mex. (Yucatan In.)	20·25 N	89·14 W
77	Teague (tēg)	Tex.	31·39 N	96·16 W
91	Teapa (tě-ä′pä)	Mex.	17·35 N	92·56 W
164	Tébessa (tā′bēs′ä)	Alg.	35·27 N	8·13 E
139	Tebingtinggi, Palau (I.)			
	(teb′ĭng-tĭng′gä)			
	Indon. (Singapore In.)	0·54 N	102·39 E
90	Tecalitlán (tā-kä-lē-tlän′)	Mex.	19·28 N	103·17 W
90	Tecoanapa (tā-kwä-nä-pä′)	Mex.	16·33 N	98·46 W
92	Tecoh (tě-kô) Mex. (Yucatan In.)	20·46 N	89·27 W
90	Tecolotlán (tā-kô-lō′tlän′)	Mex.	20·13 N	103·57 W
91	Tecolutla (R.)	Mex.	20·33 N	97·00 W
91	Tecolutla (R.)	Mex.	20·16 N	97·14 W
90	Tecomán (tā-kô-män′)	Mex.	18·53 N	103·53 W
91	Tecómitl (tě-kô′mětl)			
		Mex. (Mexico City In.)	19·13 N	98·59 W
90	Tecozautla (tā′kô-zä-ōō′tlä).Mex.	20·33 N	99·38 W
90	Tecpan de Galeana			
	(těk-pän′ dā gä-lā-ä′nä). Mex.	17·13 N	100·41 W
91	Tecpatán (těk-pä-tá′n)	Mex.	17·08 N	93·18 W
90	Tecuala (tě-kwä-lä′)	Mex.	22·24 N	105·29 W
121	Tecuci (ta-kōōch′)	Rom.	45·51 N	27·30 E
75	Tecumseh (tě-kŭm′sě)			
		Can. (Detroit In.)	42·19 N	82·53 W
80	Tecumseh	Mich.	42·00 N	84·00 W
76	Tecumseh	Nebr.	40·21 N	96·09 W
73	Tecumseh	Okla.	35·18 N	96·55 W
116	Tees (R.) (tēz)	Eng.	54·40 N	2·10 W
98	Tefé (těf-ä′)	Braz.	3·27 S	64·43 W
153	Teganuna (L.) (tä′gä-nōō′nä)			
		Jap. (Tōkyō In.)	35·50 N	140·02 E
92	Tegucigalpa (tâ-gōō-sē-gäl′pä)			
		Hond.	14·08 N	87·15 W
68	Tehachapi Mts. (tě-hǎ-shä′pǐ)			
		Calif.	34·50 N	118·55 W
144	Tehrān (tě-hrän′)	Iran	35·45 N	51·30 E
148	Tehsien (dü′sîän)	China	37·28 N	116·17 E
151	Tehua	China	25·30 N	118·15 E
91	Tehuacan (tā-wä-kän′)	Mex.	18·27 N	97·23 W
91	Tehuantepec (Sto. Domingo)			
	(tā-wän-tâ-pěk′)			
	(sän-tô dô-mě′n-gô).Mex.	16·20 N	95·14 W
88	Tehuantepec, Golfo de (G.)			
	(gôl-fô dě).Mex.	15·45 N	95·00 W
91	Tehuantepec, Istmo de (Isth.)			
	(ê′st-mô dě).Mex.	17·55 N	94·35 W
91	Tehuantepec (R.)	Mex.	16·30 N	95·23 W
90	Tehuehuetla Arroyo (R.)			
	(tě-wě-wě′tlä à-rô-yô).Mex.	17·54 N	100·26 W
90	Tehuitzingo (tě-wě-tzĭn′gô).Mex.	18·21 N	98·16 W

Page	Name Pronunciation	Region	Lat. ° '	Long. ° '
124	Tejeda, Sierra de. (Mts.)			
	(sē-ě′r-rä dě tě-kě′dä).Sp.	36·55 N	5·57 W
124	Tejo, Rio (R.) (rê-ōtä′hōō)..Port.	39·23 N	8·01 W
91	Tejúpan (Santiago)			
	(tě-kōō-pä′n) (sän-tyä′gô).Mex.	17·39 N	97·34 W
90	Tejupilco, Punta (Pt.) (pōō′n-tä			
		Mex.	18·19 N	103·30 W
90	Tejupilco de Hidalgo			
	(tâ-hōō-pēl′kô dä ê-dhäl′gô)			
		Mex.	18·52 N	100·07 W
70	Tekamah (tě-kä′má)	Nebr.	41·46 N	96·13 W
92	Tekax de Alvaro Obregon			
	(tě-kä′x dě á′l-vä-rô-brě-gô′n)			
		Mex. (Yucatan In.)	20·12 N	89·11 W
127	Tekirdağ (Rodosto) (tě-kēr′dägh′)			
		Tur.	41·00 N	27·28 E
92	Tekit (tě-kě′t).Mex. (Yucatan In.)	20·35 N	89·18 W
66	Tekoa (tě-kō′á)	Wash.	47·15 N	117·03 W
92	Tela (tě′lä)	Hond.	15·45 N	87·25 W
92	Tela, Bahia de (B.) (bä-ē′ä dě)			
		Hond.	15·53 N	87·29 W
139	Telapa Burok, Gunong (Mt.)			
	Mala. (Singapore In.)	2·51 N	102·04 E
133	Telavi	Sov. Un.	42·00 N	45·20 E
139	Tel Aviv-Jaffa (těl-ä-vēv′ja′fá)			
	Isr. (Palestine In.)	32·03 N	34·46 E
86	Telegraph Creek (těl′ê-grăf)..Can.	57·59 N	131·22 W
129	Teleneshty (tyě-lě-nĕsht′i).Sov.Un.	47·31 N	28·22 E
68	Telescope Pk. (těl′ê skōp) ... Calif.	36·12 N	117·05 W
99	Teles Pirez (R.) (tě-lěs pē′rěz)			
		Braz.	8·28 S	57·07 W
139	Telesung...Indon. (Singapore In.)	1·07 N	102·53 E
92	Telica (Vol.) (tä-lē′kä)	Nic.	12·38 N	86·52 W
146	Telii Nuur (L.)	China	45·49 N	86·08 E
80	Tell City (těl)	Ind.	38·00 N	86·45 W
64	Teller (těl′ēr)	Alaska	65·17 N	166·28 W
98	Tello (tě′l-yō)	Col. (In.)	3·05 N	75·08 W
69	Telluride (těl′ú-rīd)	Colo.	37·55 N	107·50 W
139	Telok Datok			
	Mala. (Singapore In.)	2·51 N	101·33 E
90	Teloloapan (tā′lô-lô-ä′pän) ... Mex.	18·19 N	99 54 W
132	Tel'pos-Iz, Gora (Mtn.)			
	(tyěl′pôs-ēz′).Sov. Un.	63·50 N	59·20 E
139	Tel Sharuhea... Isr. (Palestine In.)	31·16 N	34·29 E
119	Telšiai (těl′-shä′ē)	Sov. Un.	55·59 N	22·17 E
111	Teltow (těl′tō) ... Ger. (Berlin In.)	52·24 N	13·12 E
154	Telukbetung	Indon.	5·30 S	105·04 E
139	Telukletjak			
	Indon. (Singapore In.)	1·53 N	101·45 E
164	Tema (tē′má)	Ghana	5·45 N	0.00
90	Temascalcingo			
	(tā′mäs-käl-sǐŋ′gō).Mex.	19·55 N	100·00 W
90	Temascaltepec			
	(tā′mäs-käl-tâ pěk).Mex.	19·00 N	100·03 W
92	Temax (tě′mäx)			
		Mex. (Yucatan In.)	21·10 N	88·51 W
133	Temir (tyě′mēr)	Sov. Un.	49·10 N	57·15 E
134	Temir-Tau	Sov. Un.	50·08 N	73·13 E
82	Temiscouata (L.)			
	(tě′mĭs-kōō-ä′tä).Can.	47·46 N	69·10 W
91	Temoaya			
	Mex. (Mexico City In.)	19·28 N	99·36 W
100	Temperley (tě′m-pěr-lä).Arg. (In.)	34·32 S	58·24 W
126	Tempio Pausania			
	(těm′pē-ō pou-sä′nē-ä).Sard.	40·55 N	9·05 E
77	Temple (těm′p′l)	Tex.	31·06 N	97·20 W
74	Temple City			
	Calif. (Los Angeles In.)	34·07 N	118·02 W
85	Templeton (těm′p′l-tŭn)			
	Can. (Ottawa In.)	45·29 N	75·37 W
120	Templin (těm-plēn′)	Ger.	53·08 N	13·30 E
90	Tempoal (R.) (tyěm-pô-ä′l)...Mex.	21·38 N	98·23 W
129	Temryuk (tyěm-ryōōk′).Sov. Un.	45·17 N	37·21 E
100	Temuco (tâ-mōō′kō)	Chile	38·46 S	72·38 W
136	Temyasovo (těm-yä′sô-vô)			
	Sov. Un. (Urals In.)	53·00 N	58·06 E
92	Tenabó (tě-nä-bô′)			
	Mex. (Yucatan In.)	20·05 N	90·11 W
90	Tenamaxtlán (tä′nä-mäs-tlän′)			
		Mex.	20·13 N	104·06 W
90	Tenancingo (tâ-nän-sēŋ′gō) ..Mex.	18·54 N	99·36 W
91	Tenango (tä-näŋ′gō)			
	Mex. (Mexico City In.)	19·09 N	98·51 W
154	Tenasserim (těn-äs′ēr-ĭm)...Bur.	12·09 N	99·01 E
129	Tenderovskaya Kosa (C.)			
	(těn-dě-rôf′skä-yä kô-sä′)			
	Sov. Un.	46·12 N	31·17 E
	Tenedos, see Bozcaada			
164	Tenéré (Reg.)	Niger	18·45 N	11·16 E
164	Tenerife I. (tā-nä-rē′fä)			
	(těn-ēr-ĭf′) Can. Is.	28·41 N	17·02 W
113	Ténés (tā-něs′)	Alg.	36·28 N	1·22 E
148	T'enghsien (těng′hsē-ěn′)..China	35·07 N	117·08 E
134	Tengiz (L.) (tyǐn-gēs′)...Sov. Un.	50·45 N	68·39 E
146	Tengri Khan (těŋ′grě kän′).China	42·10 N	80·20 E
153	Tenjin (těn′jĕn).Jap. (Ōsaka In.)	34·54 N	135·04 E
166	Tenke (těŋ′kä)	Con. L.	10·36 S	26·12 E
73	Tenkiller Ferry Res. (těn-kĭl′ēr)			
		Okla.	35·42 N	94·47 W
164	Tenkodogo (těŋ-kô-dō′gô)			
		Upper Volta	11·42 N	0·30 W
65	Tenmile (R.) (těn mǐl)			
	Wash. (Vancouver In.)	48·52 N	122·32 W
158	Tennant Creek (těn′ănt) ... Austl.	19·45 S	134·00 E
63	Tennessee (State) (těn-ê-sē′) U. S.	35·50 N	88·00 W
63	Tennessee (L.)	U. S.	35·35 N	88·20 W
78	Tennessee (R.)	U. S.	35·10 N	88·20 W
78	Tennille (těn′ĭl)	Ga.	32·55 N	86·50 W
101	Teno (tě′nô) (R.)			
	Chile (Santiago In.)	34·55 S	71·00 W
160	Tenora (těn-ôrá)	Austl.	34·23 S	147·33 E
91	Tenosique (tä-nô-sē′kä)....Mex.	17·27 N	91·25 W
153	Tenryū-Gawa (Strm.)			
	(těn′ryōō′gä′wä).Jap.	35·16 N	137·54 E
77	Tensas R. (těn′sô)	La.	31·54 N	91·30 W

Page	Name Pronunciation	Region	Lat. ° '	Long. ° '
78	Tensaw (R.) (těn′sô)	Ala.	30·45 N	87·52 W
160	Tenterfield (těn′tēr-fēld)....Austl.	29·00 S	52·06 E
79	Ten Thousand, Is.			
	(těn thou′zǎnd). Fla (In.)	25·45 N	81·35 W
90	Teocaltiche (tā′ô-käl-tē′chä)..Mex.	21·27 N	102·38 W
91	Teocelo (tā-ô-sā′lō)	Mex.	19·22 N	96·57 W
90	Teocuitatlán de Corona			
	(tā′ô-kwē′tä-tlän′ dä kô-rō′nä)			
		Mex.	20·06 N	103·22 W
99	Teófilo Otoni (tě-ô′fē-lō-tô′ně)			
		Braz.	17·49 S	41·18 W
90	Teoloyucan (tā′ô-lô-yōō′kän).Mex.	19·43 N	99·12 W
91	Teopisca (tā-ô-pēs′kä)	Mex.	16·30 N	92·33 W
91	Teotihuacán (tě-ô-tē-wä-kä′n)			
	Mex. (Mexico City In.)	19·40 N	98·52 W
91	Teotitlán del Camino			
	(tā-ô-tē-tlän′ děl kä-mē′nô).Mex.	18·07 N	97·04 W
90	Tepalcatepec (tā′päl-kä-tä′pěk)			
		Mex.	19·11 N	102·51 W
90	Tepalcatepec (R.)	Mex.	18·54 N	102·25 W
90	Tepalcingo (tā-päl-sēŋ′gô)....Mex.	18·34 N	98·49 W
91	Tepatitlan de Morelos			
	(tā-pä-tê-tlän′ dä mô-rä′los)			
		Mex.	20·15 N	102·47 W
91	Tepeaca (tā-pâ-ä′kä)	Mex.	18·57 N	97·54 W
91	Tepecoacuilco de Trujano			
	(tā′pä-kô′ä-kwēl′kô dä			
	trōō-hä′nô).Mex.	19·15 N	99·29 W
90	Tepeji del Rio (tā-pâ-κe′ děl rē′ō)			
		Mex.	19·55 N	99·22 W
91	Tepelmeme (tā′pěl-mā′mä)....Mex.	17·51 N	97·23 W
91	Tepetlaoxtoc (tā′pä-tlä′ôs-tōk′)			
	Mex. (Mexico City In.)	19·34 N	98·49 W
90	Tepezala (tā-pä-zä-lä′)	Mex.	22·12 N	102·12 W
90	Tepic (tā-pēk′)	Mex.	21·32 N	104·53 W
148	Tep'ing (dü′pǐng)	China	37·28 N	116·57 E
136	Tĕplaya Gora			
	(tyôp′lä-yä gô-rä)			
	Sov. Un. (Urals In.)	58·32 N	59·08 E
120	Teplice Sanov (těp′li-tsě shä′nôf)			
		Czech.	50·39 N	13·50 E
91	Teposcolula (San Pedro y San			
	Pablo) (tā-pôs-kô-lōō′lä)			
	(sän pā′drō ē sän pä′blō).Mex.	17·33 N	97·29 W
98	Tequendama, Salto de (Falls)			
	(sä′l-tô dě tě-kěn-dä′mä)			
	Col. (In.)	4·34 N	74·18 W
90	Tequila (tâ-kē′lä)	Mex.	20·53 N	103·48 W
91	Tequisistlán (R.) (tě-kē-sěs-tlä′n)			
		Mex.	16·20 N	95·40 W
90	Tequisquiapan			
	(tâ-kēs-kê-ä′pän).Mex.	20·33 N	99·57 W
125	Ter (R.) (těr)	Sp.	42·04 N	2·52 E
124	Tera (R.) (tä′rä)	Sp.	42·05 N	6·24 W
126	Teramo (tā′rä-mô)	It.	42·40 N	13·41 E
123	Terborg			
	Neth. (Ruhr In.)	51·55 N	6·23 E
133	Tercan (těr′jän)	Tur.	39·40 N	40·12 E
164	Terceira I. (těr-sä′rä)			
	Azores (In.)	38·49 N	26·36 W
121	Terebovlya (tě-rä′bôv-lyä)			
	Sov. Un.	49·18 N	25·43 E
133	Terek (R.)	Sov. Un.	43·30 N	45·10 E
136	Terenkul' (tě-rěn′kōōl)			
	Sov. Un. (Urals In.)	55·38 N	62·18 E
99	Teresina (těr-ä-sē′ná)	Braz.	5·04 S	42·42 W
100	Teresópolis (těr-ā-sô′pō-lězh)			
	Braz. (In.)	22·25 S	42·59 W
132	Teribërka (tyěr-ê-byôr′kä)			
	Sov. Un.	69·00 N	35·15 E
133	Terme (těr′mě)	Tur.	41·05 N	42·00 E
142	Termez (tyěr′měz)	Sov. Un.	37·19 N	67·20 E
126	Termini (těr′mě-ně)	It.	37·58 N	13·39 E
91	Términos, Laguna de (L.)			
	(lä-gōō′nä dě ě′r-mē-nòs).Mex.	18·37 N	91·32 W
126	Termoli (těr′mô-lě)	It.	42·00 N	15·01 E
110	Tern (R.) (tûrn)	Eng.	52·49 N	2·31 W
155	Ternate (těr-nä′tä)	Indon.	0·52 N	127·25 E
126	Terni (těr′nē)	It.	42·38 N	12·41 E
121	Ternopol' (těr-nō-pōl′)..Sov. Un.	49·32 N	25·36 E
152	Terpeniya, Zaliv (B.)			
	(zä′lĭf těr-pä′nĭ-yä).Sov. Un.	49·10 N	143·05 E
135	Terpeniya, Mys (C.)....Sov. Un.	48·44 N	144·42 E
86	Terrace (těr′ĭs)	Can.	54·36 N	128·38 W
126	Terracina (těr-rä-chē′nä)	It.	41·18 N	13·14 E
83	Terra Nova Natl. Park....Can.	48·37 N	54·15 W
85	Terrebonne			
	Can. (Montreal In.)	45·42 N	73·38 W
77	Terrebonne B.	La.	28·55 N	90·30 W
80	Terre Haute (těr-ê hōt′)	Ind.	39·25 N	87·25 W
77	Terrell (těr′ěl)	Tex.	32·44 N	96·15 W
65	Terrell...Wash. (Vancouver In.)	48·53 N	122·44 W
74	Terrell Hills			
	Tex. (San Antonio In.)	29·28 N	98·27 W
117	Terschelling (I.) (těr-sκěl′ĭng)			
		Neth.	53·25 N	5·12 E
124	Teruel (tā-rōō-ěl′)	Sp.	40·20 N	1·05 W
127	Tešanj (tě′shän′)	Yugo.	44·36 N	17·59 E
111	Teschendorf (tě′shěn-dôrf)			
	Ger. (Berlin In.)	52·51 N	13·10 E
91	Tesecheacan (tě-sě-chě-ä-kä′n)			
		Mex.	18·10 N	95·41 W
64	Teshekpuk (L.) (tē-shěk′pŭk)			
		Alaska	70·18 N	152·36 W
152	Teshio Dake (Mt.)			
	(těsh′ê-ō-dä′kä).Jap.	44·00 N	142·50 E
152	Teshio Gawa			
	(těsh′ê-ô gä′wä).Jap.	44·35 N	114·55 E
86	Teslin (L.) (těs-lĭn)	Can.	60·12 N	132·08 W
86	Teslin (R.)	Can.	61·18 N	134·14 W
146	Tesiin Gol (L.)	Mong.	50·30 N	94·30 E
164	Tessaoua (těs-sä′ōō-ä)	Niger	13·53 N	7·53 E
111	Tessenderlo....Bel. (Brussels In.)	51·04 N	5·08 E
116	Test (R.) (těst)	Eng.	51·10 N	2·20 W
126	Testa del Gargano (Pt.)			
	(tās′tä děl gär-gä′nô).It.	41·48 N	16·13 E

Page	Name Pronunciation Region	Lat. °'	Long. °'
166	Tete (tā'tĕ)....Moz.	15·13 s	33·40 e
129	Teterev (R.) (tyĕ'tyĕ-rĕf) Sov. Un.	50·35 n	29·18 e
120	Teterow (tā'tĕ-rō)....Ger.	53·46 n	12·33 e
127	Teteven (tĕt'ĕ-ven')....Bul.	42·57 n	24·15 e
67	Teton R. (tē'tŏn)....Mont.	47·54 n	111·37 w
127	Tetovo (tā'tô-vô)....Yugo.	42·01 n	21·00 e
110	Tettenhall (tĕt'ĕn-hôl)....Eng.	52·36 n	2·10 w
164	Tetuán (tâ-twän')....Mor.	35·42 n	5·34 w
152	Tetyukhe-Pristan (tĕt-yōō'кĕ pri-stän').Sov. Un.	44·21 n	135·44 e
132	Tetyushi (tyĕt-yōō'shĭ)..Sov. Un.	54·58 n	48·40 e
111	Teupitz (toi'pētz).Ger. (Berlin In.)	52·08 n	13·37 e
126	Tevere (Tiber) (R.) (tā'vâ-rā) (tī'bĕr).It.	42·30 n	12·14 e
83	Tewksbury (tūks'bĕr-ĭ) Mass. (Boston In.)	42·37 n	71·14 w
73	Texarkana (tĕk-sär-kăn'a)...Ark.	33·26 n	94·02 w
73	Texarkana....Tex.	33·26 n	94·04 w
73	Texarkana Dam....Tex.	33·18 n	94·09 w
84	Texas (tĕk'sas) Md. (Baltimore In.)	39·28 n	76·40 w
62	Texas (State)....U. S.	31·00 n	101·00 w
77	Texas City....Tex. (In.)	29·23 n	94·54 w
90	Texcaltitlán (tās-käl'tē-tlän') Mex.	18·54 n	99·51 w
117	Texel (I.) (tĕk'sĕl)....Neth.	53·10 n	4·45 e
91	Texcoco (tās-kō'kō) Mex. (Mexico City In.)	19·31 n	98·53 w
90	Texcoco, Lago de (L.) (lä'gô-dĕ) Mex.	19·28 n	98·59 w
91	Texistepec (tĕk-sēs-tā-pĕk')..Mex.	17·51 n	94·46 w
91	Texmelucan (tās-mā-lōō'kän) Mex. (Mexico City In.)	19·17 n	98·26 w
73	Texoma, L. (tĕk'ō-mă)....Okla.	34·03 n	96·28 w
167	Teyateyaneng....Bas. (Natal In.)	29·11 s	27·43 e
128	Teykovo (tĕy-kô-vô)....Sov. Un.	56·52 n	40·34 e
91	Teziutlán (tā-zē-ōō-tlän')....Mex.	19·48 n	97·21 w
90	Tezontepec (tā-zōn-tā-pĕk')..Mex.	19·52 n	98·48 w
90	Tezontepec de Aldama (dā äl-dä'mä).Mex.	20·19 n	99·19 w
142	Tezpur....India	26·42 n	92·52 e
86	Tha-anne (R.)....Can.	60·50 n	96·56 w
167	Thaba Putsua (Mtn.) Bas. (Natal In.)	29·44 s	27·58 e
168	Thabazimbi....S. Afr. (Johannesburg & Pretoria In.)	24·36 s	27·22 e
138	Thailand (Siam)....Asia	16·30 n	101·00 e
154	Thale Luang (L.)....Thai.	7·51 n	99·39 e
110	Thame (tām)..Eng. (London In.)	51·43 n	0·59 w
80	Thames (R.) (tĕmz)....Can.	42·40 n	81·45 w
117	Thames, R....Eng.	51·26 n	0·54 e
115	Thamit R....Libya	30·39 n	16·23 e
143	Thāna (thā'nŭ) India (Bombay In.)	19·13 n	72·58 e
143	Thāna Cr....India (Bombay In.)	19·03 n	72·58 e
146	Thang Ha Ri (Mts.)....China	33·15 n	89·07 e
151	Thanh-Hoa (tän'hō'ä)....Viet.	19·46 n	105·42 e
123	Thann (tän)....Fr.	47·49 n	7·05 e
123	Thaon-les-Vosges (tä-ŏn-lā-vōzh') Fr.	48·16 n	6·24 e
160	Thargomindah (thär'gō-mĭn'da) Austl.	27·58 s	143·57 e
127	Thásos (I.) (thă'sôs)....Grc.	40·41 n	24·53 e
89	Thatch Cay (I.) (thăch) Vir. Is. (U. S. A.) (St. Thomas In.)	18·22 n	64·53 w
120	Thaya R. (tä'yä)....Aus.-Czech.	48·48 n	15·40 e
73	Thayer (thâ'ĕr)....Mo.	36·30 n	91·34 w
	Thebes, see Thivai		
168	Thebes (Ruins) (thēbz) U. A. R. (Nile In.)	25·47 n	32·39 e
65	The Brothers (Mtn.) (brŭth'ĕrs) Wash. (Seattle In.)	47·39 n	123·08 w
66	The Dalles (dălz)....Ore.	45·36 n	121·10 w
155	The Father, (Mtn.)..N. Gui. Ter.	5·10 s	151·55 e
	The Hague, see 's Gravenhage		
142	Thelum....W. Pak.	32·59 n	73·43 e
161	The Oaks....Austl. (Sydney In.)	34·04 s	150·36 e
160	Theodore (thē'ō'dôr)....Austl.	24·51 s	150·09 e
69	Theodore Roosevelt Dam (thē-ô-dôr rōō-sa-vĕlt).Ariz.	33·46 n	111·25 w
70	Theodore Roosevelt Natl. Mem. Park....N. D.	47·20 n	103·42 w
86	The Pas (pä)....Can.	53·48 n	101·17 w
67	Thermopolis (thĕr-mŏp'ō-lĭs) Wyo.	43·38 n	108·11 w
160	The Round Mtn....Austl.	30·17 s	152·19 e
127	Thessalía (Reg.)....Grc.	39·50 n	22·09 e
87	Thessalon....Can.	46·11 n	83·37 w
127	Thessaloníki (thĕs-sä-lô-nē'kē) Grc.	40·38 n	22·59 e
82	Thetford Mines (thĕt'fĕrd mīns) Can.	46·05 n	71·20 w
167	The Twins (Mtn.) (twĭnz) S. Afr. (Natal In.)	30·09 s	28·29 e
168	Theunissen....S. Afr. (Johannesburg & Pretoria In.)	28·25 s	26·44 e
77	Thibodaux (tē-bō-dō')....La.	29·48 n	90·48 w
86	Thickwood Hills (thĭk'wŏŏd).Can.	53·28 n	108·30 w
70	Thief (L.) (thēf)....Minn.	48·32 n	95·46 w
70	Thief (R.)....Minn.	48·18 n	96·07 w
70	Thief River Falls (thēf rĭv'ĕr fôlz).Minn.	48·07 n	96·11 w
84	Thiells (thĕlz) N. Y. (New York In.)	41·12 n	74·01 w
122	Thiers (tyâr)....Fr.	45·51 n	3·32 e
164	Thiès (tē-ĕs')....Senegal	14·43 n	16·56 w
146	Thimbu....Bhu.	27·31 n	89·45 e
112	Thingvallavatn (L.)....Ice.	64·12 n	20·22 w
123	Thionville (tyôn-vēl')....Fr.	49·23 n	6·31 e
165	Third Cataract....Sud.	19·53 n	30·11 e
118	Thisted (tēs'tĕdh)....Den.	56·57 n	8·38 e
112	Thistil Fd. (tēs'tĕl)....Ice.	66·29 n	14·59 w
160	Thistle (I.) (thĭs''l)....Austl.	34·55 s	136·11 e
127	Thivai (Thebes)....Grc.	38·20 n	23·18 e

Page	Name Pronunciation Region	Lat. °'	Long. °'
112	Thjórsá (R.) (tyûr'sä)....Ice.	64·23 n	19·18 w
111	Tholen....Neth. (Amsterdam In.)	51·32 n	4·11 e
72	Thomas (tŏm'ăs)....Okla.	35·44 n	98·43 w
81	Thomas....W. Va.	39·15 n	79·30 w
78	Thomaston (tŏm'ăs-tŭn)....Ga.	32·51 n	84·17 w
78	Thomasville (tŏm'ăs-vĭl)....Ala.	31·55 n	87·43 w
79	Thomasville....N. C.	35·52 n	80·05 w
86	Thompson (tŏmp'sŭn)....Can.	55·48 n	97·59 w
73	Thompson (R.)....Mo.	40·32 n	93·49 w
66	Thompson Falls....Mont.	47·35 n	115·20 w
75	Thompsonville (tomp'sŭn-vĭl) Wis. (Milwaukee In.)	42·47 n	87·57 w
79	Thomson (tŏm'sŭn)....Ga.	33·28 n	82·29 w
159	Thomson (R.) (tŏm-sŏn)...Austl.	29·30 s	143·07 e
123	Thonon-les-Bains (tō-nôn'lā-băn') Fr.	46·22 n	6·27 e
112	Thórisvatn (L.)....Ice.	64·02 n	119·09 w
110	Thorne (thôrn)....Eng.	53·37 n	0·58 w
85	Thornhill (thôrn-hĭl) Can. (Toronto In.)	43·49 n	79·25 w
80	Thorntown (thôrn'tŭn)....Ind.	40·05 n	86·35 w
85	Thorold (thō'rōld) Can. (Toronto In.)	43·13 n	79·12 w
122	Thouars (tōō-är')....Fr.	47·00 n	0·17 w
81	Thousand Is. (thou'zănd) N. Y.-Can.	44·15 n	76·10 w
127	Thrace (Reg.) (thrās)...Grc.-Tur.	41·20 n	26·07 e
110	Thrapston (thrăp'stŭn)....Eng.	52·23 n	0·32 w
67	Three Forks (thrē fôrks)...Mont.	45·56 n	111·35 w
80	Three Oaks (thrē ōks)....Mich.	41·50 n	86·40 w
164	Three Points, C....Ghana	4·27 n	2·29 w
80	Three Rivers....Mich.	42·00 n	83·40 w
120	Thun (tōōn)....Switz.	46·46 n	7·34 e
71	Thunder B. (thŭn'dĕr)....Can.	48·29 n	88·52 w
120	Thuner See (L.)....Switz.	46·40 n	7·30 e
76	Thurber (thûr'bĕr)....Tex.	32·30 n	98·23 w
120	Thüringen (Thuringia) (former state or region) (tü'rĭng-ĕn).Ger.	51·07 n	10·45 e
116	Thurles (thûrlz)....Ire.	52·44 n	7·45 w
110	Thurrock (thŭ'rŏk) Eng. (London In.)	51·28 n	0·19 e
159	Thursday (I.) (thûrz-dā)...Austl.	10·17 s	142·23 e
85	Thurso (thŭr'sô) Can. (Ottawa In.)	45·36 n	75·15 w
116	Thurso....Scot.	58·35 n	3·40 w
47	Thurston Pen. (thûrs'tŭn)...Ant.	71·20 s	98·00 w
166	Thysville (tēs-vēl')....Con. L.	5·08 s	14·58 e
155	Tiaong (tē-ä-ông') Phil. (Manila In.)	13·56 n	121·20 e
164	Tiaret (tyä-rĕ')....Alg.	35·28 n	1·15 e
100	Tibagi (tē-bä-zhē)....Braz.	24·40 s	50·35 w
165	Tibasti, Sarir (Des.)....Chad	24·00 n	16·30 e
	Tiber (R.), see Tévere		
139	Tiberias (tī-bē'rĭ-ăs) Isr. (Palestine In.)	32·48 n	35·32 e
165	Tibesti Massif (Mts.)....Chad	20·43 n	17·16 e
146	Tibet Aut. Reg. (tĭ-bĕt')...China	31·15 n	84·48 e
146	Tibet, Plat. of....China	32·22 n	83·30 e
139	Tibnīn....Leb. (Palestine In.)	33·12 n	35·23 e
65	Tiburon (tē-bōō-rōn') Calif. (San Francisco In.)	37·53 n	122·27 w
95	Tiburon....Hai.	18·35 n	74·25 w
88	Tiburón (I.)....Mex.	28·45 n	113·10 w
93	Tiburon, Cabo (C.) (kä'bô)..Pan.	8·42 n	77·19 w
65	Tiburon I. Calif. (San Francisco In.)	37·52 n	122·26 w
155	Ticaco Pass (tē-kä-kō) Phil. (Manila In.)	12·38 n	123·50 e
155	Ticao (I.) (tē-kä'ō) Phil. (Manila In.)	12·40 n	123·30 e
110	Tickhill (tĭk'ĭl)....Eng.	53·26 n	1·06 w
81	Ticonderaga (tī-kŏn-dĕr-ō'gä) N. Y.	43·50 n	73·30 w
92	Ticul (tē-kōō'l) Mex. (Yucatan In.)	20·22 n	89·32 w
118	Tidaholm (tē'dä-hôlm)....Swe.	58·11 n	13·53 e
110	Tideswell (tīdz'wĕl)....Eng.	53·17 n	1·47 w
164	Tidikelt (Reg.) (tē-dē-kĕlt')...Alg.	25·53 n	2·11 e
164	Tidjikdja (tē-jĭk'jä)....Mauritania	18·37 n	11·30 w
150	T'iehling (tyâ'lĭng)....China	42·18 n	123·50 e
125	Tielmes (tyâl-mäs') Sp. (Madrid In.)	40·15 n	3·20 w
151	Tien Ch'ih (L.) (tyĕn)....China	24·58 n	103·18 e
148	T'ienching (Tientsin) (tyĕn'tsĕn') China	39·08 n	117·14 e
111	Tienen....Bel. (Brussels In.)	50·49 n	4·58 e
148	Tienerhwan (dĭăn'ĕ'hōōän).China	31·39 n	114·08 e
148	Tienfou (dĭăn'fōō)....China	31·53 n	117·28 e
148	T'ienma Shan (Mts.) (tĭăn'mă shän).China	36·02 n	117·57 e
151	Tienmen (tyĕn'mĕn')....China	30·40 n	113·10 e
151	Tienpai....China	21·30 n	111·20 e
151	T'ienpao....China	23·18 n	106·40 e
	Tien-Shan (Mts.), see Tyan' Shan'		
148	Tienshan Hu (L.) (dĭăn'shän'hōō) China	31·08 n	120·30 e
150	T'ienshui....China	34·25 n	105·40 e
150	T'ientsaokang....China	45·58 n	126·00 e
	Tientsin, see T'ienching		
151	T'ientung....China	23·32 n	107·10 e
118	Tierp (tyĕrp)....Swe.	60·21 n	17·28 e
167	Tierpoort....S. Afr. (Johannesburg & Pretoria In.)	25·53 s	28·26 e
91	Tierra Blanca (tyĕ'r-rä-blä'n-kä) Mex.	18·28 n	96·19 w
100	Tierra del Fuego (Reg.) (tyĕr'rä dĕl fwā'gō).Chile-Arg.	53·50 s	68·45 w
124	Tiétar (R.) (tē-ā'tär)....Sp.	39·56 n	5·44 w
101	Tietê (tyā-tā') Braz. (Rio de Janeiro In.)	23·08 s	47·42 w
99	Tieté (R.)....Braz.	20·46 s	50·46 w
80	Tiffin (tĭf'ĭn)....Ohio	41·10 n	83·15 w
78	Tifton (tĭf'tŭn)....Ga.	31·25 n	83·34 w
65	Tigard (tī'gärd) Ore. (Portland In.)	45·25 n	122·46 w
82	Tignish (tĭg'nĭsh)....Can.	46·56 n	64·03 w

Page	Name Pronunciation Region	Lat. °'	Long.
136	Tigoda R. (tē'gô-dä) Sov. Un. (Leningrad In.)	59·29 n	31·15 e
100	Tigre (tē'grĕ)....Arg. (In.)	34·09 s	58·35 w
98	Tigre (R.)....Peru	2·20 s	75·41 w
166	Tigres, Peninsula dos (Pen.) (pĕ-nē'ŋ-sōō-lä-dôs-tē'grĕs).Ang.	16·30 s	11·45 e
144	Tigris, R....Asia	34·30 n	44·00 e
139	Tīh, Gebel el (Mts.) U. A. R. (Palestine In.)	29·24 n	33·42 e
146	Tihua (Urumchi) (ōō-rōōm'chē) China	43·49 n	87·43 e
91	Tihuatlán (tē-wä-tlän')....Mex.	20·43 n	97·34 w
68	Tijuana (tē-hwä'nä) Mex. (San Diego In.)	32·32 n	117·02 w
100	Tijuca, Pico da (Mtn.) (pĕ'kō-dä-tē-zhōō'kä).Braz. (In.)	22·56 s	43·17 w
92	Tikal (Ruins) (tē-käl') Guat. (Yucatan In.)	17·16 n	89·49 w
133	Tikhoretsk (tē kôr-yĕtsk') Sov. Un.	45·55 n	40·05 e
128	Tikhvin (tēк-vēn')....Sov. Un.	59·36 n	33·38 e
144	Tikrīt....Iraq	34·36 n	43·31 e
135	Tiksi (tēk-sē')....Sov. Un.	71·42 n	128·32 e
111	Tilburg (tĭl'bûrg) Neth. (Amsterdam In.)	51·33 n	5·05 e
164	Tilemsi, Vallée du (Valley)...Mali	18·09 n	0·02 w
135	Tilichiki (tyĭ-le-chĭ-kē)...Sov. Un.	60·49 n	166·14 e
129	Tiligul (R.) (tē'lĭ-gûl)...Sov. Un.	47·25 n	30·27 e
164	Tillabéri (tē-yä-bā-rē')....Niger	14·14 n	1·30 e
66	Tillamook (tĭl'a-mŏŏk)....Ore.	45·27 n	123·50 w
66	Tillamook B....Ore.	45·32 n	124·26 w
118	Tillberga (tēl-bĕr'ghá)....Swe.	59·40 n	16·34 e
80	Tillsonburg (tĭl'sŭn-bûrg)....Can.	42·50 n	80·50 w
	Tilsit, see Sovetsk		
129	Tim (têm)....Sov. Un.	51·39 n	37·07 e
159	Timaru (tĭm'á-rōō)....N. Z. (In.)	44·26 s	171·17 e
129	Timashevskaya (tēmă-shĕfś-kă'yă).Sov. Un.	45·47 n	38·57 e
77	Timbalier B. (tĭm'bá-lēr)....La.	28·55 n	90·14 w
65	Timber (tĭm'bĕr) Ore. (Portland In.)	45·43 n	123·17 w
164	Timbo (tĭm'bō)....Gui.	10·41 n	11·51 w
	Timbuktu, see Tombouctou		
118	Time (tē'mĕ)....Nor.	58·45 n	5·39 e
164	Timimoun (tē-mē-mōōn')....Alg.	29·14 n	0·22 e
164	Timiris, Cap (C.)....Mauritania	19·37 n	17·38 w
127	Timiş (R.)....Rom.	45·28 n	21·06 e
87	Timiskaming (L.)....Can.	47·27 n	81·00 w
87	Timiskaming Station (tē-mĭs'ká-mĭng).Can.	46·41 n	79·01 w
87	Timmins (tĭm'ĭnz)....Can.	48·25 n	81·22 w
164	Timmissao (tē-mē-sä'ō)....Alg.	22·03 n	2·56 e
79	Timmonsville (tĭm'ŭnz-vĭl)..S. C.	34·09 n	79·55 w
155	Timor (I.) (tê-mōr')....Indon.	10·08 s	125·00 e
156	Timor Sea....Asia	12·40 s	125·00 e
127	Timoşoara....Rom.	45·44 n	21·21 e
69	Timpanogos Cave Natl. Mon. (tĭ-măn'ō-gŏz).Utah	40·25 n	111·45 w
77	Timpson (tĭmp'sŭn)....Tex.	31·55 n	94·24 w
135	Timpton (R.) (tĕmp'tôn).Sov. Un.	57·15 n	126·35 e
168	Timsāh (L.) (tĭm'sä) U. A. R. (Suez In.)	30·34 n	32·22 e
95	Tina, Monte (Mtn.) (mô'n-tĕ-tē'nä).Dom. Rep.	18·50 n	70·40 w
167	Tina (R.) (tē'nă) S. Afr. (Natal In.)	30·50 s	28·44 e
99	Tinaguillo (tē-nä-gē'l-yō) Ven. (In.)	9·55 n	68·18 w
164	Tindouf (tēn-dōōf')....Alg.	27·43 n	7·44 w
139	Tinggi, Palau (I.) Mala. (Singapore In.)	2·16 n	104·16 e
148	T'ingho (dĭng'hŭ)....China	37·45 n	118·29 e
148	Tinghsien (dĭng'sĭän)....China	38·30 n	115·00 e
148	Tinghsing (dĭng'sĭng)....China	39·18 n	115·50 e
149	Tinglin....China (Shanghai In.)	30·53 n	121·18 e
98	Tingo María (tē'ngō-mä-rē'ä).Peru	9·15 s	76·04 w
118	Tingsryd (tĭngs'rüd)....Swe.	56·32 n	14·58 e
148	Tingtzu Wan (B.) (dĭng'tze wän) China	36·33 n	121·06 e
90	Tinguindio Paracho (tēn-kē'n-dyō-pärä-chō).Mex.	19·38 n	102·02 w
101	Tinguiririca (R.) (tē'n-gē-rē-rē'kä) Chile (Santiago In.)	36·48 s	70·45 w
148	Tingyüan (tĭng'yü-än')....China	32·32 n	117·40 e
75	Tinley Park (tĭn'lē) Ill. (Chicago In.)	41·34 n	87·47 w
118	Tinnosset (tĕn'nôs'sĕt)....Nor.	49·44 n	9·00 e
118	Tinnsjö (tĭnnsyû)....Nor.	59·55 n	8·49 e
100	Tinogasta (tē-nō-gäs'tä)....Arg.	28·07 s	67·30 w
127	Tinos (I.)....Grc.	37·45 n	25·12 e
145	Tinsukia (tĭn-sōō'kĭ-á)....India	27·18 n	95·29 e
69	Tintic (tĭn'tĭk)....Utah	39·55 n	112·15 w
165	Tin Toumma Steppe (Plat.) (tĭn tōōm'ä).Niger	16·16 n	13·06 e
139	Tioman (I.).Mala. (Singapore In.)	2·25 n	104·30 e
92	Tipitapa (tē-pē-tä'pä)....Nic.	12·14 n	86·05 w
92	Tipitapa R....Nic.	12·13 n	85·57 w
78	Tippah Cr., (R.) (tĭp'pá)....Miss.	34·43 n	88·15 w
80	Tippecanoe (R.) (tĭp-ē-ká-nōō') Ind.	40·55 n	86·45 w
166	Tipperary (tĭ-pē-râ'rē)....Ire.	52·28 n	8·13 w
73	Tippo Bay. (tĭp'ō bīōō')....Miss.	33·35 n	90·06 w
110	Tipton (tĭp'tŭn)....Eng.	52·32 n	2·04 w
80	Tipton....Ind.	40·15 n	86·00 w
71	Tipton....Iowa	41·46 n	91·10 w
127	Tiranë (tē-rä'nä)....Alb.	41·18 n	19·50 e
126	Tirano (tē-rä'nō)....It.	46·12 n	10·09 e
129	Tiraspol' (tē-räs'pôl')....Sov. Un.	46·52 n	29·38 e
168	Tir'at el'Abbâsîya R. U. A. R. (Suez In.)	32·45 n	32·15 e
133	Tire (tē'rĕ)....Tur.	38·05 n	27·48 e
116	Tiree (I.) (tī-rē')....Scot.	56·34 n	6·30 w
127	Tîrgovişte....Rom.	44·54 n	25·29 e
121	Tîrgu-Mureş....Rom.	46·33 n	24·35 e
121	Tîrgu Neamt....Rom.	47·14 n	26·23 e
121	Tîrgu-Ocna....Rom.	46·18 n	26·38 e

ng-sing; ŋ-baŋk; n-nasalized n; nŏd; cŏmmit; ōld; ôbey; ôrder; fōōd; fŏŏt; ou-out; s-soft; sh-dish; th-thin; pūre; ûnite; ûrn; stŭd; circŭs; ü-a "y" in study; '-indeterminate vowel.

ăt; fĭnăl; rāte; senâte; ärm; ȧsk; sofá; fâre; ch-choose; dh-as th in other; bē; ēvent; bĕt; recĕnt; crātēr; g-go; gh-guttural g; bĭt; ł-short neutral; rīde; к-guttural k as ch in German ich;

PRONOUNCING INDEX Totonicapan–Tudela 277

Page	Name Pronunciation Region	Lat. °′	Long. °′
92	Totonicapán (tô-tō-nē-kä'pän) Guat.	14·55 N	91·20 W
101	Totoras (tô-tô'räs) Arg. (Buenos Aires In.)	32·33 S	61·13 W
153	Totsuka (tōt'sōō-kä) Jap.	35·24 N	139·32 E
110	Tottenham (tŏt'ĕn-ăm) Eng. (London In.)	51·35 N	0·06 W
153	Tottori (tô'tô-rē) Jap.	35·30 N	134·15 E
164	Touat (Oases) (tōō'ät) Alg.	27·22 N	00·38 W
164	Toubkal Pk. Mor.	31·15 N	7·46 W
164	Touggourt (tōō-gōōrt') (tōō-gōōr') Alg.	33·09 N	6·07 E
114	Touil R. (tōō-ēl') Alg.	34·42 N	2·16 E
123	Toul (tōōl) Fr.	48·39 N	5·51 E
82	Toulnustouc, Riviere (R.) Can.	50·30 N	67·55 W
123	Toulon (tōō-lôn') Fr.	43·09 N	5·54 E
122	Toulouse (tōō-lōōz') Fr.	43·37 N	1·27 E
154	Toungoo (tŏ-ōōŋ-gōō') Bur.	19·00 N	96·29 E
151	Tourane (tōō-rän') Viet.	16·08 N	108·22 E
122	Tourcoing (tōōr-kwăn') Fr.	50·44 N	3·06 E
123	Tournan-en-Brie (tōōr-nän-ĕn-brē') Fr. (Paris In.)	48·45 N	2·47 E
122	Tours (tōōr) Fr.	47·23 N	0·39 E
165	Toussidé, Pic (Pk.) (tōō-sē-dā') Chad	21·10 N	16·30 E
118	Tovdalselv (R.) (tôv-däls-ĕlv) Nor.	58·23 N	8·16 E
81	Towanda (tô-wän'dȧ) Pa.	41·45 N	76·30 W
70	Towner (tou'nẽr) N. D.	48·21 N	100·24 W
83	Townsend (toun'zĕnd) Mass. (Boston In.)	42·41 N	71·42 W
67	Townsend Mont.	46·19 N	111·35 W
65	Townsend, Mt. Wash. (Seattle In.)	47·52 N	123·03 W
159	Townsville (tounz'vĭl) Austl.	19·18 S	146·50 E
84	Towson (tou'sŭn) Md. (Baltimore In.)	39·24 N	76·36 W
154	Towuti, Danau (L.) (tô-wōō'tē) Indon.	3·00 S	121·45 E
76	Toyah (tô'yȧ) Tex.	31·19 N	103·46 W
153	Toyama (tō'yä-mä) Jap.	36·42 N	137·14 E
153	Toyama-Wan (B.) Jap.	36·58 N	137·16 E
153	Toyohashi (tō'yô-hä'shē) Jap.	34·44 N	137·21 E
153	Toyonaka (tō'yô-nä'kä) Jap. (Ōsaka In.)	34·47 N	135·28 E
114	Tozeur (tô-zûr') Tun.	33·59 N	8·11 E
124	Trabancos (R.) (trä-bäŋ'kōs) Sp.	41·15 N	5·13 W
133	Trabzon (träb'zôn) Tur.	41·00 N	39·45 E
68	Tracy (trā'sē) Calif.	37·45 N	121·27 W
70	Tracy Minn.	44·13 N	95·37 W
78	Tracy City Tenn.	35·15 N	85·44 W
124	Trafalgar, Cabo de (C.) (kä'bô-dĕ-trä-fäl-gä'r) Sp.	36·10 N	6·02 W
167	Trafonomby (Mtn.) Malag. Rep.	24·32 S	46·35 E
86	Trail (trāl) Can.	49·04 N	117·56 W
111	Traisen (R.) Aus. (Vienna In.)	48·15 N	15·55 E
111	Traiskirchen Aus. (Vienna In.)	48·01 N	16·18 E
119	Trakai (trȧ-kày) Sov. Un.	54·38 N	24·59 E
121	Trakiszki (trȧ-kē'-sh-kē) Pol.	54·16 N	23·07 E
116	Tralee (trȧ-lē') Ire.	52·16 N	9·20 W
118	Trälleborg (trĕl'ĕ-bôrg) Swe.	55·24 N	13·07 E
118	Tranas (trän'ōs) Swe.	58·03 N	14·56 E
142	Tranbonsha (Mt.) China	35·27 N	86·25 E
124	Trancoso (träŋ-kō'sōō) Port.	40·46 N	7·23 W
155	Trangan (I.) (träŋ'gän) Indon.	6·52 S	133·30 E
126	Trani (trä'nē) It.	41·15 N	16·25 E
103	Transcaucasia (Reg.) Sov. Un.	41·17 N	44·30 E
85	Transcona (trăns-kō'nȧ) Can. (Winnipeg In.)	49·54 N	97·00 W
146	Trans-Himalays Mts. (trăns'hĭ-mä'lȧ-yȧ) China	31·15 N	81·56 E
166	Transvaal (Prov.) (trăns-väl') S. Afr.	24·21 S	28·18 E
121	Transylvania (Reg.) (trăn-sĭl-vā'nĭ-ȧ) Rom.	46·30 N	22·35 E
	Transylvanian Alps (Mts.), see Carpatii Meridionali		
126	Trapani (trä'pä-nē) It.	38·02 N	14·34 E
123	Trappes (trȧp) Fr. (Paris In.)	48·47 N	2·01 E
160	Traralgon (tră'răl-gŏn) Austl.	38·15 S	146·33 E
126	Trasimeno, Lago (L.) (lä'gō trä-sē-mä'nō) It.	43·00 N	12·12 E
124	Tras os Montes (Mts.) (träzh'ōzh môn'täzh) Port.	41·33 N	7·13 W
124	Trasparga (träs-pär-gä) Sp.	43·13 N	7·50 W
120	Traun R. (troun) Aus.	48·10 N	14·15 E
120	Traunstein (troun'stīn) Ger.	47·52 N	12·38 E
70	Traverse, L. (trăv'ẽrs) Minn.-S. D.	45·46 N	96·53 W
80	Traverse City Mich.	44·45 N	85·40 W
126	Travnik (träv'nēk) Yugo.	44·13 N	17·43 E
65	Treasure I. (trĕzh'ẽr) Calif. (San Francisco In.)	37·49 N	122·22 W
111	Trebbin (trĕ'bēn) Ger. (Berlin In.)	52·13 N	13·13 E
120	Třebič (t'rzhĕ'bēch) Czech.	49·13 N	15·53 E
127	Trebinje (trā'bēn-yĕ) Yugo.	42·43 N	18·21 E
121	Trebisow (trĕ'bē-shôf) Czech.	48·36 N	21·32 E
120	Třebŏn (t'rzhĕ'bôn') Czech.	49·00 N	14·48 E
159	Tregrosse Is. (trē-grōs') Austl.	18·08 S	150·53 E
100	Treinta y Tres (trā-ĕn'tä ē träs') Ur.	33·14 S	54·17 W
122	Trélazé (trā-lȧ-zā') Fr.	47·27 N	0·32 W
100	Trelew (trē'lū) Arg.	43·15 S	65·25 W
116	Tremadoc B. (trē-mă'dŏk) Wales	52·43 N	4·27 W
126	Tremiti, Isole di (Is.) (ē'sō-lĕ dē trä-mē'tē) It.	42·07 N	16·33 E
121	Trenčín (trĕn'chēn) Czech.	48·52 N	18·02 E
154	Trengganu (State) (trĕng-gä'nōō) Mala.	4·53 N	102·26 E
100	Trenque Lauquén (trĕn'kĕ-lä'ōō-kĕ'n) Arg.	35·50 S	62·44 W
81	Trent (R.) (trĕnt) Can.	44·15 N	77·55 W
116	Trent (R.) Eng.	53·05 N	1·00 W
110	Trent and Mersey Can. (trĕnt) (mûr'zē) Eng.	53·11 N	2·24 W
126	Trento (trĕn'tô) It.	46·04 N	11·07 E
126	Trento (Reg.) It.	46·16 N	10·47 E
81	Trenton (trĕn'tŭn) Can.	44·05 N	77·35 W
83	Trenton Can.	45·39 N	62·40 W
75	Trenton Mich. (Detroit In.)	42·08 N	83·12 W
73	Trenton Mo.	40·05 N	93·36 W
84	Trenton N. J. (New York In.)	40·13 N	74·46 W
78	Trenton Tenn.	35·57 N	88·55 W
83	Trepassey (trē-păs'ē) Can.	46·47 N	53·20 W
83	Trepassey B. Can.	46·35 N	53·25 W
100	Tres Arroyos (träs'är-rō'yōs) Arg.	38·18 S	60·16 W
101	Três Coraçoes (trĕ's kō-rä-zô'ĕs) Braz. (Rio de Janeiro In.)	21·41 S	45·14 W
91	Tres Cumbres (trĕ's kōō'm-brĕs) Mex. (Mexico City In.)	19·03 N	99·14 W
99	Três Lagoas (trĕ's lä-gō'äs) Braz.	20·48 S	51·42 W
99	Três Marias, Reprêsa (Res.) (rĕ-prā'sä trĕs' mä-rē'äs) Braz.	18·15 S	45·30 W
98	Tres Morros, Alto de (Mtn.) (ä'l-tō dĕ trĕ's mô'r-rôs) Col. (In.)	7·08 N	76·10 W
101	Três Pontas (trĕ's pô'n-täs) Braz. (Rio de Janeiro In.)	21·22 S	45·30 W
101	Três Rios (trĕ's rē'ōs) Braz. (Rio de Janeiro In.)	22·07 S	43·13 W
111	Treuenbrietzen (troi'ĕn-brē-tzĕn) Ger. (Berlin In.)	52·06 N	12·52 E
126	Treviglio (trā-vē'lyô) It.	45·30 N	9·34 E
126	Treviso (trĕ-vē'sō) It.	45·39 N	12·15 E
146	Triangle, The (Reg.) Asia	26·00 N	98·00 E
168	Trichardt (trĭ-kärt') S. Afr. (Johannesburg & Pretoria In.)	26·32 S	29·16 E
126	Trieste (Trst) (trē-ĕs'tā) It.	45·39 N	13·48 E
126	Trieste, G. of It.	45·38 N	13·40 E
124	Trigueros (trē-gā'rōs) Sp.	37·23 N	6·50 W
142	Trigu Tsho (L.) China	28·47 N	91·37 E
127	Tríkkala Grc.	39·33 N	21·49 E
75	Trim Cr. (trĭm) Ill. (Chicago In.)	41·19 N	87·39 W
143	Trincomalee (trĭŋ-kô-mȧ-lē') Ceylon	8·39 N	81·12 E
110	Tring (trĭng) Eng. (London In.)	51·46 N	0·40 W
98	Trinidad (trē-nē-dhädh') Bol.	14·48 S	64·43 W
72	Trinidad (trĭn'ĭ-dăd) Colo.	37·11 N	104·31 W
94	Trinidad (trē-nē-dhädh') Cuba	21·50 N	80·00 W
101	Trinidad Ur. (Buenos Aires In.)	33·29 S	56·55 W
94	Trinidad, Sierra de (Mts.) (sē-ĕ'r-rä dĕ trē-nē-dä'd) Cuba	21·50 N	79·55 W
99	Trinidad (I.) (trĭn'ĭ-dăd) Trin.	10·00 N	61·00 W
89	Trinidad and Tobago (trĭn'ĭ-dăd) (tô-bā'gō) N. A.	11·00 N	61·00 W
96	Trinidade, Ilha de (I.) (ē'lä dĕ trē-nē-dä-dĕ) Braz.	21·00 S	32·00 W
88	Trinidad R. Pan. (Panama Canal In.)	8·55 N	80·01 W
91	Trinitaria (trē-nē-tä'ryä) Mex.	16·09 N	92·04 W
93	Trinité Mart. (Le. & Wind. Is. In.)	14·47 N	61·00 W
83	Trinity (trĭn'ĭ-tē) Can.	48·22 N	53·24 W
77	Trinity Tex.	30·52 N	95·27 W
64	Trinity (Is.) Alaska	56·25 N	153·15 W
74	Trinity (R.), West Fk. Tex.	33·22 N	98·26 W
73	Trinity (R.), East Fk. Tex.	33·24 N	96·42 W
83	Trinity B. Can.	47·55 N	53·30 W
66	Trinity Res. Calif.	40·51 N	122·41 W
66	Trinity R. Calif.	40·50 N	123·20 W
77	Trinity R. Tex.	30·50 N	95·09 W
126	Trino (trē'nô) It.	45·11 N	8·16 E
78	Trion (trī'ŏn) Ga.	34·32 N	85·18 W
	Tripoli, see T'arābulus		
	Tripoli, see Tarābulus		
127	Tripolis (trĭ'pô-lĭs) Grc.	37·32 N	22·32 E
	Tripolitania, see Tarābulus		
70	Tripp (trĭp) S. D.	43·13 N	97·58 W
142	Tripura (Mts.) W. Pak.	28·38 N	91·37 E
47	Tristan da Cunha Is. (três-tän'dȧ kōōn'yȧ) Atl. O.	35·30 S	12·15 W
99	Triste, Golfo (G.) (gôl-fô trĕ's-tĕ) Ven. (In.)	10·40 N	68·05 W
84	Triticus Res. (trī tĭ-cŭs) N. Y. (New York In.)	41·20 N	73·36 W
84	Triumph (trī'ŭmf) La. (New Orleans In.)	29·21 N	89·29 W
143	Trivandrum (trē-vŭn'drŭm) India	8·34 N	76·58 E
121	Trnava (t'r'nȧ-vȧ) Czech.	48·22 N	17·34 E
155	Trobriand Is. (trō-brē-ănd') Pap.	8·25 S	151·45 E
126	Trogir (trō'gēr) Yugo.	43·32 N	16·17 E
82	Trois Pistoles (trwä' pēs-tôl') Can.	48·07 N	69·10 W
82	Trois-Riviéres (rē-vyâr') Can.	46·21 N	72·35 W
136	Troitsk (trô'ētsk) Sov. Un. (Urals In.)	54·06 N	61·34 E
134	Troitsko-Pechorsk (trô'ĭtsk-ô-pyĕ-chôrsk') Sov. Un.	62·18 N	56·07 E
129	Troitskoye Sov. Un.	47·39 N	30·16 E
118	Trollhättan (trôl'hĕt-ĕn) Swe.	58·17 N	12·17 E
118	Trollheim (Mts.) (trôll-hĕĭm) Nor.	62·48 N	9·05 E
112	Tromsö (trôm'sû) Nor.	69·38 N	19·12 E
68	Trona (trō'nȧ) Calif.	35·49 N	117·20 W
100	Tronador, Cerro (Mtn.) (sĕ'r-rô trō-nä-dôr) Arg.	41·17 S	71·56 W
90	Troncoso (trôn-kô'sō) Mex.	22·43 N	102·22 W
118	Trondheim (Nidaros) (trôn'hăm) (nē'dhä-rôs) Nor.	63·25 N	11·35 E
139	Troodos, Mt. Cyprus (Palestine In.)	34·56 N	32·52 E
118	Trosa (trō'sä) Swe.	58·54 N	17·25 E
87	Trout (L.) Can.	51·16 N	92·46 W
66	Trout Cr. Ore.	42·18 N	118·31 W
65	Troutdale (trout'dāl) Ore. (Portland In.)	45·32 N	122·23 W
122	Trouville-sur-Mer (trōō-vēl'sür-mâr') Fr.	49·23 N	0·05 E
78	Troy (troi) Ala.	31·47 N	85·46 W
74	Troy Ill. (St. Louis In.)	38·44 N	89·53 W
73	Troy Kans.	39·46 N	95·07 W
73	Troy Mo.	38·56 N	90·57 W
66	Troy Mont.	48·28 N	115·56 W
81	Troy N. Y.	42·45 N	73·45 W
79	Troy N. C.	35·21 N	79·58 W
80	Troy Ohio	40·00 N	84·10 W
127	Troy (Ruins) Tur.	39·59 N	26·14 E
122	Troyes (trwȧ) Fr.	48·18 N	4·03 E
	Trst, see Trieste		
127	Trstenik (t'r'stĕ-nēk) Yugo.	43·36 N	20·00 E
128	Trubchëvsk (trōōp'chĕfsk) Sov. Un.	52·36 N	32·46 E
138	Trucial Coast (trōō'shăl) Asia	23·30 N	53·00 E
68	Truckee (trŭk'ē) Calif.	39·20 N	120·12 W
68	Truckee (R.) Calif.-Nev.	39·25 N	120·07 W
161	Truganina Austl. (Melbourne In.)	37·49 S	144·44 E
98	Trujillo (trōō-kē'l-yō) Col. (In.)	4·10 N	76·20 W
92	Trujillo (trōō-kēl'yō) Hond.	15·55 N	85·58 W
98	Trujillo Peru	8·08 S	79·00 W
124	Trujillo (trōō-kē'l-yô) Sp.	39·27 N	5·50 W
98	Trujillo Ven.	9·15 N	70·28 W
90	Trujillo (R.) Mex.	23·12 N	103·10 W
95	Trujin, L. (trōō-kēn') Dom. Rep.	17·45 N	71·25 W
73	Trumann (trōō'măn) Ark.	35·41 N	90·31 W
127	Trŭn (trŭn) Bul.	42·49 N	22·39 E
82	Truro (trōō'rō) Can.	45·22 N	63·20 W
116	Truro Eng.	50·17 N	5·05 W
84	Trussville (trŭs'vĭl) Ala. (Birmingham In.)	33·37 N	86·37 W
69	Truth or Consequences (trōōth ŏr kŏn'sē-kwĕn-sĭs) N. Mex.	33·10 N	107·20 W
120	Trutnov (trōōt'nôf) Czech.	50·36 N	15·36 E
120	Trzcianka (tchyän'kȧ) Pol.	53·02 N	16·27 E
120	Trzebiatowo (tchĕ-byä'tōō-vô) Pol.	54·03 N	15·16 E
146	Tsaidam Swp. (tsī'dăm) China	37·19 N	94·08 E
150	Ts'aiyü China (Peking In.)	39·39 N	116·36 E
79	Tsala Apopka (R.) (tsä'lȧ ȧ-pŏp'kȧ) Fla.	28·57 N	82·11 W
148	Ts'anghsien (chäng'sĭän) China	38·21 N	116·53 E
149	Ts'angmen China (Canton In.)	22·42 N	113·09 E
	Tsangwu, see Wuchou		
148	Tsaochuang (jou'jōōäng) China	34·51 N	117·34 E
148	Ts'aohsien (tsou'sĭän) China	34·48 N	115·33 E
146	Tsasata Bogda Uula (Mt.) Mong.	46·44 N	92·34 E
65	Tsawwassen Ind. Res. Can. (Vancouver In.)	49·03 N	123·11 W
134	Tselinograd (tsĕ'lē-nô-grä'd) Sov. Un.	51·10 N	71·43 E
149	Tsengch'en China (Canton In.)	23·18 N	113·49 E
136	Tsentral'nyy-Kospashskiy (tsĕn-träl'nyĭ-kôs-pàsh'skĭ) Sov. Un. (Urals In.)	59·03 N	57·48 E
142	Tsethang China	29·20 N	91·49 E
166	Tshela (tshā'lȧ) Con. L.	4·50 S	13·05 E
166	Tshikapa (tshē-kä'pȧ) Con. L.	6·29 S	20·53 E
166	Tshilongo (tshē-lôŋ'gō) Con. L.	10·28 S	26·09 E
166	Tshuapa (R.) Con. L.	0·25 S	22·07 E
167	Tsiafajovona (Mtn.) Malag. Rep.	19·17 S	47·27 E
167	Tsiandra (tsē-än-drō') Malag. Rep.	18·46 S	44·58 E
133	Tsimlyanskiy (Res.) (tsym-lyȧ'ns-kēē) Sov. Un.	47·50 N	43·40 E
139	Tsin (R.) Isr. (Palestine In.)	30·52 N	35·05 E
148	Tsinan (Chinan) (je'năn) China	36·40 N	117·01 E
	Tsinghai (Prov.), see Chinghai		
	Tsingtao, see Ch'ingtao		
167	Tsiribihina (R.) (tsē'rē-bē-hē-nä') Malag. Rep.	19·45 S	43·30 E
167	Tsitsa (R.) (tsē'tsȧ) S. Afr. (Natal In.)	31·28 S	28·53 E
	Tsitsihar, see Ch'ich'ihaerh		
167	Tsolo (tsŏ'lō) S. Afr. (Natal In.)	31·19 S	28·47 E
167	Tsomo S. Afr. (Natal In.)	32·03 S	27·49 E
167	Tsomo (R.) S. Afr. (Natal In.)	31·53 S	27·48 E
153	Tsu (tsōō) Jap.	34·42 N	136·31 E
153	Tsuchiura (tsōō'chē-ōō-rä) Jap.	36·04 N	140·09 E
153	Tsuda (tsōō'dä) Jap. (Ōsaka In.)	34·48 N	135·43 E
152	Tsugaru Kaikyō (str.) (tsōō'gä-rōō kī'kyō) Jap.	41·25 N	140·20 E
166	Tsumeb (tsōō'mĕb) S. W. Afr.	19·10 S	17·45 E
153	Tsunashima (tsōō'nä-shē'mä) Jap. (Tōkyō In.)	35·32 N	139·37 E
151	Ts'unghua China	23·30 N	113·40 E
148	Tsunhua (zhōōn'hooä) China	40·12 N	117·55 E
153	Tsuruga (tsōō'rōō-gä) Jap.	35·39 N	136·04 E
153	Tsurugi San (Mtn.) (tsōō'rōō-gē sän) Jap.	33·52 N	134·07 E
152	Tsuruoka (tsōō'rōō-ō'kä) Jap.	38·43 N	139·51 E
153	Tsurusaki (tsōō'rōō-sä'kē) Jap.	33·15 N	131·42 E
153	Tsu Shima (I.) (tsōō shē'mä) Jap.	34·28 N	129·30 E
153	Tsushima Kaikyō (Str.) (tsōō'shē-mä kī'kyō) Asia	33·52 N	129·30 E
153	Tsuwano (tsōō'wä-nô') Jap.	34·28 N	131·47 E
153	Tsuyama (tsōō'yä-mä') Jap.	35·05 N	134·00 E
124	Tua (R.) (tōō'ä) Port.	41·23 N	7·18 W
65	Tualatin (R.) (tōō'ȧ-lȧ-tĭn) Ore. (Portland In.)	45·25 N	122·54 W
157	Tuamotu (Low), Arch. (tōō-ä-mō'tōō) Fr. Polynesia	19·00 S	141·20 W
155	Tuao (tōō-ä'ō) Phil. (Manila In.)	17·44 N	121·26 E
133	Tuapse (tōō'äp-sĕ) Sov. Un.	44·00 N	39·10 E
164	Tuareg (Reg.) Alg.	21·26 N	2·51 E
144	Tuayq, Jabal (Mts.) Sau. Ar.	20·45 N	46·30 E
100	Tubarão (tōō-bä-roun') Braz.	28·23 S	48·56 W
120	Tübingen (tü'bĭng-ĕn) Ger.	48·33 N	9·05 E
136	Tubinskiy (tû bĭn'skĭ) Sov. Un. (Urals In.)	52·53 N	58·15 E
165	Tubruq (Tobruk) Libya	32·03 N	24·04 E
99	Tucacas (tōō-kä'käs) Ven. (In.)	10·48 N	68·20 W
84	Tucker (tŭk'ẽr) Ga (Atlanta In.)	33·51 N	84·13 W
69	Tucson (tōō-sŏn') Ariz.	32·15 N	111·00 W
100	Tucumán (tōō-kōō-män') Arg.	26·52 S	65·08 W
100	Tucumán (Prov.) Arg.	26·30 S	65·30 W
72	Tucumcari (tōō'kŭm-kâr-ē) N. Mex.	35·11 N	103·43 W
98	Tucupita (tōō-kōō-pē'tä) Ven.	9·00 N	62·09 W
99	Tucuruí (tōō-kōō-tōō-ē') Braz.	3·34 S	49·44 W
124	Tudela (tōō-dhä'lä) Sp.	42·03 N	1·37 W

ng-sing; ŋ-baŋk; N-nasalized n; nŏd; cŏmmit; ōld; ōbey; ôrder; fōōd; fŏŏt; ou-out; s-soft; sh-dish; th-thin; pūre; ûnite; ûrn; stŭd; circŭs; ü-as "y" in study; '-indeterminate vowel.

278 Tugaloo–Ueckermunde PRONOUNCING INDEX

Page	Name Pronunciation Region	Lat. °′	Long. °′
78	Tugaloo (R.) (tŭg'ȧ-lo͞o) . Ga.-S. C.	34·35 N	83·05 W
167	Tugela (R.) (to͞o-gel'ȧ) S. Afr. (Natal In.)	28·50 S	30·52 E
167	Tugela Ferry . . S. Afr. (Natal In.)	29·16 S	30·24 E
80	Tug Fork (R.) (tŭg) . . . . . . W. Va.	37·50 N	82·30 W
155	Tuguegarao (to͞o-gā-gȧ-rä'ō) Phil. (Manila In.)	17·37 N	121·44 E
148	T'uhsieh (R.) (to͞o'hăĭ) . . . . . China	37·05 N	116·56 E
168	Tuinplaas . . . . S. Afr. (Johannesburg & Pretoria In.)	24·54 S	28·46 E
74	Tujunga (to͞o-jŭŋ'gȧ) Calif. (Los Angeles In.)	34·15 N	118·16 W
136	Tukan (to͞o'kȧn) Sov. Un. (Urals In.)	53·52 N	57·25 E
155	Tukengbesi, Palau-Palau (Is.) Indon.	6·00 S	124·15 E
165	Tukrah . . . . Libya	32·34 N	20·47 E
86	Tuktoyaktuk (to͞ok-tō-yăk'to͞ok) Can.	69·32 N	132·37 W
132	Tukum (to͝o'ko͝om) . . . . . . Sov. Un.	57·00 N	22·50 E
119	Tukums (to͝o'ko͝oms) . . . . Sov. Un.	56·57 N	23·09 E
166	Tukuyu (to͞o-ko͞o'yȧ) . . . . Tan.	9·13 S	33·43 E
65	Tukwila (tŭk'wĭ-lȧ) Wash. (Seattle In.)	47·28 N	122·16 W
90	Tula (to͞o'lä) . . . . Mex.	20·04 N	99·22 W
128	Tula (to͞o'lȧ) . . . . Sov. Un.	54·12 N	37·37 E
128	Tula (Oblast) . . . . Sov. Un.	53·45 N	37·19 E
90	Tula (R.) (to͞o'lä) . . . . Mex.	20·40 N	99·27 W
159	Tulagi (I.) (to͞o-lä'gē) . . . . . Sol. Is.	9·15 S	160·17 E
65	Tulalip (tū-lă'lĭp) Wash. (Seattle In.)	48·04 N	122·18 W
65	Tulalip Ind. Res. Wash. (Seattle In.)	48·06 N	122·16 W
90	Tulancingo (to͞o-län-sĭŋ'gō) . . Mex.	20·04 N	98·24 W
68	Tulare (to͞o-lä'rā) (tûl-âr') . . Calif.	36·12 N	119·22 W
68	Tulare Basin . . . . Calif.	35·57 N	120·18 W
69	Tularosa (to͞o-lȧ-rō'zȧ) . . . N. Mex.	33·05 N	106·05 W
98	Tulcán (to͞ol-kän') . . . . Ec.	0·44 N	77·52 W
129	Tulcea (to͝ol'chȧ) . . . . Rom.	45·10 N	28·47 E
129	Tul'chin (to͝ol'chĕn) . . . . Sov. Un.	48·42 N	28·53 E
90	Tulcingo (to͞ol-sĭŋ'gō) . . . . Mex.	18·03 N	98·27 W
68	Tule (R.) (to͞o'lā) . . . . Calif.	36·08 N	118·50 W
167	Tuléar (to͞o-lā-är') . . . Malag. Rep.	20·16 S	43·44 E
68	Tule River Ind. Res. (to͞o'lā) Calif.	36·05 N	118·35 W
166	Tuli (to͞o'lē) . . . . S. Rh.	20·58 S	29·12 E
72	Tulia (to͞o'lĭ-ȧ) . . . . Tex.	34·32 N	101·46 W
91	Tulijá (R.) (to͞o-lē-ĸä') . . . . . . Mex.	17·28 N	92·11 W
64	Tulik Vol. (to͝o'lĭk) . . . . Alaska	53·28 N	168·10 W
139	Tūl Karm (to͞ol kärm) Jordan (Palestine In.)	32·19 N	35·02 E
78	Tullahoma (tŭl-ȧ-hō'mȧ) . . . Tenn.	35·21 N	86·12 W
116	Tullamore (tŭl-ȧ-mōr') . . . . Ire.	53·15 N	7·29 W
122	Tulle (tül) . . . . Fr.	45·15 N	1·45 E
111	Tulln (to͝oln) . . . Aus. (Vienna In.)	48·21 N	16·04 E
111	Tullner Feld (Reg.) Aus. (Vienna In.)	48·20 N	15·59 E
165	Tulmaythah . . . . Libya	32·44 N	21·08 E
91	Tulpetlac (to͞ol-pā-tlȧk') Mex. (Mexico City In.)	19·33 N	99·04 W
73	Tulsa (tŭl'sȧ) . . . . Okla.	36·08 N	95·58 W
98	Tuluá (to͞o-lo͞o-ä') . . . . . . Col. (In.)	4·06 N	76·12 W
146	T'ulufan (Turfan) (to͞o'lo͞o-fän') (to͞or-făn') . China	43·06 N	88·41 E
92	Tulum (to͞o-lo͝o'm) Mex. (Yucatan In.)	20·17 N	87·26 W
134	Tulun (to͝o-lo͞on') . . . . Sov. Un.	54·29 N	100·43 E
69	Tumacacori Natl. Mon. (to͞o-mä-kä'kô-rē) . Ariz.	31·36 N	110·20 W
98	Tumaco (to͞o-mä'kô) . . . . Col.	1·41 N	78·44 W
92	Tuma R. (to͞o'mä) . . . . Nic.	13·07 N	85·32 W
166	Tumba (L.) (to͝om'bä) . . . . Con. L.	1·03 S	18·28 E
98	Tumbes (to͞o'm-bĕs) . . . . Peru	3·39 S	80·27 W
90	Tumbiscatío (to͞om-bē-skȧ-tē'ō) Mex.	18·32 N	102·23 W
65	Tumbo (I.) . . Can. (Vancouver In.)	48·49 N	123·04 W
150	T'umen (to͞o'mĕn) . . . . China	43·00 N	129·50 E
152	Tumen (R.) . . . . China	42·08 N	128·40 E
99	Tumeremo (to͞o-mā-rā'mō) . . . Ven.	7·15 N	61·28 W
99	Tumuc-Humac Mts. (to͞o-mo͝ok'o͞o-mäk') . S. A.	2·15 N	54·50 W
94	Tunas de Zaza (to͞o'näs dā zä'zä) Cuba	21·40 N	79·35 W
116	Tunbridge Wells (tŭn'brĭj welz') Eng.	51·05 N	0·09 E
134	Tundra (Reg.) . . . . Sov. Un.	70·45 N	84·00 E
147	Tung (R.) . . . . China	24·13 N	115·08 E
148	Tunga (do͞ong'ä) . . . . China	36·11 N	116·16 E
142	Tungabhadra Res. . . . . India	15·26 N	75·57 E
151	T'ungan (to͞on'gän') . . . . China	24·48 N	118·02 E
148	T'ungch'engi (to͞ong'chĕng'yē) China	36·21 N	116·14 E
147	T'ungchiang . . . . China	47·38 N	132·54 E
148	Tungeh'angshou (to͞ong'chăng'shō) China	38·21 N	114·41 E
148	Tunghai (do͞ong'hăĭ) . . . . China	34·35 N	119·05 E
150	T'ungho . . . . China	45·58 N	128·40 E
151	Tunghsiang . . . . China	28·18 N	116·38 E
150	Tunghsien . . . . . China (Peking In.)	39·55 N	116·40 E
148	Tung Hu (L.) (to͞ong' ho͞o') . China	32·22 N	116·32 E
151	Tungjen (to͝ong'jĕn') . . . . China	27·45 N	109·12 E
149	Tungkuan . . . . China (Canton In.)	23·03 N	113·14 E
150	T'ung-Kuan . . . . China	34·48 N	110·25 E
148	Tungkuang (do͞ong'go͞oäng) . China	37·54 N	116·33 E
151	T'ungku Chiao (Pt.) . . . . China	19·40 N	111·15 E
150	Tungliao (Payintala) . . . . China	43·30 N	122·15 E
148	Tungming (to͝ong'mĭng') . . . . China	35·16 N	115·06 E
148	Tungpa (to͞ong'bä) . . . . China	31·40 N	119·02 E
148	Tungpa . . . . China	35·56 N	116·19 E
150	T'ungpei (to͞ong'pā) . . . . China	48·00 N	126·48 E
148	Tungping (to͞ong'pĭng) . . . . . China	35·50 N	116·24 E
148	Tungp'ing Hu (L.) (ho͞o) . . . China	36·06 N	116·24 E
148	Tungt'antien (do͞ong'tän'dĭăn) China	35·26 N	116·54 E
151	Tungt'ing Hŭ (L.) (to͞ong'tĕng' ho͞o) . China	29·10 N	112·30 E
148	Tungwen (R.) (do͞ong'wĕn) . China	36·24 N	119·00 E
150	Tunhua . . . . China	48·18 N	128·10 E
143	Tuni . . . . India	17·29 N	82·38 E
78	Tunica (tū'nĭ-kȧ) . . . . Miss.	34·41 N	90·23 W
164	Tunis (tū'nĭs) . . . . Tun.	36·59 N	10·06 E
113	Tunis, Golfe de (G.) . . . . Tun.	37·06 N	10·43 E
163	Tunisia (tû-nĭzh'ē-ȧ) . . . . Afr.	35·00 N	10·11 E
98	Tunja (to͞o'n-hȧ) . . . . Col.	5·32 N	73·19 W
81	Tunkhannock (tŭnk-hăn'ŭk) . . Pa.	41·35 N	75·55 W
65	Tunnel (R.) (tŭn'ĕl) Wash. (Seattle In.)	47·48 N	123·04 W
68	Tuolumne (R.) (twô-lŭm'nē) . Calif.	37·35 N	120·37 W
135	Tuostakh (R.) . . . . Sov. Un.	67·09 N	137·30 E
99	Tupã (to͞o-pȧ) . . . . Braz.	21·47 S	50·33 W
78	Tupelo (tū'pē-lō) . . . . Miss.	34·14 N	88·43 W
99	Tupinambaranas, Ilha (I.) (ē'lă-to͞o-pē-năɴ-bă-ră'năs) . Braz.	3·04 S	58·09 W
98	Tupiza (to͞o-pē'zä) . . . . Bol.	21·26 S	65·43 W
81	Tupper Lake (tŭp'ēr) . . . . . . N. Y.	44·15 N	74·25 W
98	Tuquerres (to͞o-kĕ'r-rĕs) . . . . . . Col.	1·12 N	77·44 W
134	Tura (to͝or'ȧ) . . . . Sov. Un.	64·08 N	99·58 E
103	Tura (R.) . . . . Sov. Un.	57·15 N	64·23 E
144	Turayf . . . . Sau. Ar.	31·32 N	38·30 E
90	Turbio (R.) (to͞or-byô) . . . . . . Mex.	20·28 N	101·40 W
98	Turbo (to͞o'bō) . . . . Col.	8·02 N	76·43 W
121	Turciansky Sväty Martin (to͞or'chyȧn-skû'svă'tû' mär'tyēn) . Czech.	49·02 N	18·48 E
121	Turda (to͝or'dȧ) . . . . Rom.	46·35 N	23·47 E
	Turfan, see T'ulufan		
146	Turfan Depression . . . . China	42·16 N	90·00 E
167	Turffontein . . . . S. Afr. (Johannesburg & Pretoria In.)	26·15 S	28·03 E
134	Turgay (to͞or'gī) . . . . Sov. Un.	49·42 N	63·39 E
103	Turgayka (R.) (to͞or-gī'kă) Sov. Un.	49·44 N	66·15 E
127	Tŭrgovishte . . . . Bul.	43·14 N	26·36 E
133	Turgutlu . . . . Tur.	38·30 N	27·20 E
119	Türi (tü'rĭ) . . . . Sov. Un.	58·49 N	25·29 E
124	Turia (R.) (to͞o'ryä) . . . . Sp.	40·12 N	1·18 W
90	Turicato (to͞o-rē-kä'tō) . . . . . . Mex.	19·03 N	101·24 W
94	Turiguano (I.) (to͞o-rē-gwä'nō) Cuba	22·20 N	78·35 W
	Turin, see Torino		
121	Turka (to͝or'kȧ) . . . . Sov. Un.	49·10 N	23·02 E
134	Turkestan (tûr-kĕ-stăn') (to͝or-kĕ-stan') . Sov. Un.	42·40 N	65·00 E
130	Turkestan (Reg.) . . . . Sov. Un.	43·27 N	62·14 E
138	Turkey . . . . Eur.-Asia	38·45 N	32·00 E
71	Turkey (R.) (tûrk'ē) . . . . Iowa	43·20 N	92·16 W
130	Turkmen (S. S. R.) (to͞ork-mĕn') Sov. Un.	40·46 N	56·01 E
95	Turks I. Pass . . Turks & Caicos Is.	21·15 N	71·25 W
95	Turks Is. (tûrks) Turks & Caicos Is.	21·25 N	71·10 W
119	Turku (Åbo) (to͝or'ko͝o) (ô'bô) . Fin.	60·28 N	22·12 E
68	Turlock (tûr'lŏk) . . . . Calif.	37·30 N	120·51 W
92	Turneffe I. (tûr-nĕf'fē) Br. Hond. (Yucatan In.)	17·25 N	87·43 W
74	Turner (tûr'nēr) Mo. (Kansas City In.)	39·05 N	94·42 W
94	Turner Sd . . . . Ba. Is.	24·20 N	78·05 W
111	Turnhout (tŭrn-hout') Bel. (Brussels In.)	51·19 N	4·58 E
120	Turnov (to͝or'nôf) . . . . Czech.	50·36 N	15·12 E
127	Tŭrnovo . . . . Bul.	43·06 N	25·38 E
127	Turnu Măgurele (to͝or'no͝o mŭ-go͞o-rĕ'ly') . Rom.	43·54 N	24·49 E
127	Turnu-Severin (sĕ-vĕ-rēn') . . Rom.	44·37 N	22·38 E
94	Turquino, Pico de (Pk.) (pē'kō dā to͞or-kē'nō) . Cuba	20·00 N	76·50 W
93	Turrialba (to͞or-ryä'l-bä) . . . . C. R.	9·54 N	83·41 W
127	Turski Trstenik . . . . Bul.	43·26 N	24·50 E
103	Turtkul' (to͝ort-ko͞ol') . . . . Sov. Un.	41·28 N	61·02 E
77	Turtle B. (tûr't'l) . . . . . . Tex. (In.)	29·48 N	94·38 W
70	Turtle Cr . . . . S. D.	44·40 N	98·53 W
70	Turtle Mountain Ind. Res . . N. D.	48·45 N	99·57 W
70	Turtle Mts . . . . N. D.	48·57 N	100·11 W
134	Turukhansk (to͞o-ro͞o-ĸänsk') Sov. Un.	66·03 N	88·39 E
121	Turya R. (to͞or'yȧ) . . . . . . Sov. Un.	51·18 N	24·55 E
78	Tuscaloosa (tŭs-kȧ-lo͞o'sȧ) . . . . Ala.	33·10 N	87·35 W
66	Tuscarora (tŭs-kȧ-rō'rȧ) . . . . . Nev.	41·18 N	116·15 W
75	Tuscarora Ind. Res. N. Y. (Buffalo In.)	43·10 N	78·51 W
80	Tuscola (tŭs-kō'lȧ) . . . . Ill.	39·50 N	88·20 W
78	Tuscumbia (tŭs-kŭm'bĭ-ȧ) . . . . Ala.	35·41 N	87·42 W
151	Tushan (do͞o'shän) . . . . China	25·50 N	107·42 E
148	Tushan . . . . China	31·38 N	116·16 E
136	Tushino (to͞o'shĭ-nô) Sov. Un. (Moscow In.)	55·51 N	37·22 E
78	Tuskegee (tŭs-kē'gē) . . . . Ala.	32·25 N	85·40 W
148	T'ussuk'ou (to͞o'sĕ'kō) . . . . . . China	36·19 N	117·37 E
74	Tustin (tŭs'tĭn) Calif. (Los Angeles In.)	33·44 N	117·49 W
128	Tutayev (to͞o-tȧ-yĕf') . . . . Sov. Un.	57·53 N	39·34 E
110	Tutbury (tŭt'bēr-ē) . . . . Eng.	52·52 N	1·51 W
143	Tuticorin (to͞o-tē-kô-rĭn') . . . . India	8·51 N	78·09 E
91	Tutitlan (to͞o-tē-tlä'n) Mex. (Mexico City In.)	19·38 N	99·10 W
99	Tutóia (to͞o-tō'yȧ) . . . . Braz.	2·42 S	42·21 W
127	Tutrakan . . . . Bul.	44·02 N	26·36 E
73	Tuttle Creek Res. . . . . Kans.	39·30 N	96·38 W
120	Tuttlingen (to͝ot'lĭng-ĕn) . . . . . Ger.	47·58 N	8·50 E
78	Tutwiler (tŭt'wĭ-lēr) . . . . Miss.	34·01 N	90·25 W
134	Tuva Aut. Oblast . . . . Sov. Un.	51·15 N	90·45 E
85	Tuxedo (tŭk-sē'dō) Can. (Winnipeg In.)	49·51 N	97·13 W
84	Tuxedo Park (tŭk-sē'dō pärk) N. Y. (New York In.)	41·11 N	74·11 W
110	Tuxford (tŭks'fērd) . . . . Eng.	53·14 N	0·54 W
90	Tuxpan (to͞os'pän) . . . . Mex.	19·34 N	103·22 W
91	Túxpan . . . . Mex.	20·57 N	97·26 W
91	Túxpan (R.) (to͞os'pän) . . . . . Mex.	20·55 N	97·52 W
91	Túxpan, Arrecife (Rf.) (är-rĕ-sē'fĕ-to͞o'x-pä'n) . Mex.	21·01 N	97·12 W
91	Tuxtepec (to͝os-tā-pĕk') . . . . . Mex.	18·06 N	96·09 W
91	Tuxtla Gutiérrez (to͝os'tlä go͞o-tyâr'rĕs) . Mex.	16·44 N	93·08 W
112	Tuy . . . . Sp.	42·07 N	8·49 W
99	Tuy (to͞o'ē) (R.) . . . . Ven. (In.)	10·15 N	66·03 W
93	Tuyra R. (to͞o-ē'rȧ) . . . . Pan.	7·55 N	77·37 W
151	Tuyün (to͞o'yün') . . . . China	26·18 N	107·40 E
133	Tuz Gölü (L.) . . . . Tur.	39·00 N	33·30 E
127	Tuzla (to͝oz'lä) . . . . Yugo.	44·33 N	18·46 E
118	Tvedestrand (tvĭ'dhĕ-stränd) . Nor.	58·39 N	8·54 E
118	Tveitsund (tvāt'so͝ond) . . . . . . Nor.	59·03 N	8·29 E
	Tver, see Kalinin		
128	Tvertsa (L.) (tvĕr'tsȧ) . . . Sov. Un.	56·58 N	35·22 E
116	Tweed (R.) (twēd) . . . . Scot.	55·32 N	2·35 W
168	Tweeling (twē'lĭng) . . . . S. Afr. (Johannesburg & Pretoria In.)	27·34 S	28·31 E
75	Twelvemile Cr. (twĕlv'mīl) N. Y. (Buffalo In.)	43·13 N	78·58 W
85	Twenty Mile Cr. (twĕn'tĭ mīl) Can. (Toronto In.)	43·09 N	79·49 W
110	Twickenham (twĭk''n-ăm) Eng. (London In.)	51·26 N	0·20 W
83	Twillingate (twĭl'ĭn-gāt) . . . . . Can.	49·41 N	54·49 W
67	Twin Bridges (twĭn brĭ-jĕz) . Mont.	45·34 N	112·17 W
67	Twin Falls (fôls) . . . . Idaho	42·33 N	114·29 W
75	Twinsburg (twĭnz'bŭrg) Ohio (Cleveland In.)	41·19 N	81·26 W
72	Two Butte Cr. (to͞o būt) . . . . Colo.	37·39 N	102·45 W
71	Two Harbors . . . . Minn.	47·00 N	91·42 W
73	Two Prairie Bay. (prā'rĭ bī o͞o') Ark.	34·48 N	92·07 W
71	Two Rivers (rĭv'ērz) . . . . Wis.	44·09 N	87·36 W
161	Tyabb . . . . Austl. (Melbourne In.)	38·16 S	145·11 E
121	Tyachev (tyä'chĕf) . . . . . . Sov. Un.	48·01 N	23·42 E
146	Tyan' Shan' (Tien-Shan) (Mts.) Sov. Un.-China	42·00 N	78·46 E
129	Tyasmin (R.) (tyȧs-mĭn') Sov. Un.	49·14 N	32·23 E
167	Tylden (tĭl-dĕn) . S. Afr. (Natal In.)	32·08 S	27·06 E
110	Tyldesley (tĭldz'lē) . . . . Eng.	53·32 N	2·28 W
70	Tyler (tī'lēr) . . . . Minn.	44·18 N	96·08 W
77	Tyler . . . . Tex.	32·21 N	95·19 W
78	Tylertown (tī'lēr-toun) . . . . . . Miss.	31·08 N	90·06 W
70	Tyndall (tĭn'dȧl) . . . . S. D.	42·58 N	97·52 W
135	Tyndinskiy . . . . Sov. Un.	55·22 N	124·45 E
116	Tyne (R.) (tīn) . . . . Eng.	54·59 N	1·56 W
116	Tynemouth (tīn'mŭth) . . . . . . Eng.	55·04 N	1·39 W
118	Tynest (tün'sĕt) . . . . Nor.	62·17 N	10·45 E
83	Tyngsboro (tĭnj-bûr'ō) Mass. (Boston In.)	42·40 N	71·27 W
	Tyre, see Sūr		
118	Tyri Fd. (tü'rē) . . . . Nor.	60·03 N	10·25 E
69	Tyrone (tī'rōn) . . . . N. Mex.	32·40 N	108·20 W
81	Tyrone . . . . Pa.	40·40 N	78·15 W
160	Tyrrell, L. (tir'ĕll) . . . . Austl.	35·12 S	143·00 E
113	Tyrrhenian Sea (tĭr-rē'nĭ-ăn) . . . It.	40·10 N	12·15 E
119	Tyrvää (tür'vâ) . . . . Fin.	61·19 N	22·51 E
133	Tyub-Karagan, Mys (C.) Sov. Un.	44·30 N	50·10 E
134	Tyukalinsk (tyo͝o-kȧ-lĭnsk') Sov. Un.	56·03 N	71·43 E
135	Tyukyan (R.) (tyo͝ok'yȧn) Sov. Un.	65·42 N	116·09 E
133	Tyuleniy (I.) . . . . Sov. Un.	44·30 N	48·00 E
134	Tyumen' (tyo͞o-mĕn') . . . . Sov. Un.	57·02 N	65·28 E
134	Tyura-Tam . . . . Sov. Un.	46·00 N	63·15 E
92	Tzucacab (tzo͞o-kä-kä'b) Mex. (Yucatan In.)	20·06 N	89·03 W
148	Tz'uhsien (tsĕ'sĭän) . . . . China	36·22 N	114·23 E
151	Tzu Shui (R.) (tso͞o) . . . . China	26·50 N	111·00 E
148	Tzuya (R.) (zhĕ'yä) . . . . China	38·38 N	116·31 E
148	Tzuyang (tsĕ'yäng) . . . . China	35·35 N	116·50 E
114	Uarc, Ras (C.) . . . . Mor.	35·31 N	2·45 W
98	Uaupés (wä-o͞o'pās) . . . . Braz.	0·02 S	67·03 W
101	Ubá (o͝o-bȧ') Braz. (Rio de Janeiro In.)	21·08 S	42·55 W
163	Ubangi R. (o͞o-băŋ'gē) . . . . Afr.	0·45 N	17·28 E
101	Ubatuba (o͞o-bā-to͞o'bȧ) Braz. (Rio de Janeiro In.)	23·25 S	45·06 W
153	Ube (o͞o'bā) . . . . Jap.	33·57 N	131·18 E
124	Ubeda (o͞o'bā-dä) . . . . Sp.	38·01 N	3·23 W
99	Uberaba (o͞o-bā-rä'bȧ) . . . . . . Braz.	19·47 S	47·47 W
99	Uberlândia (o͞o-bĕr-lȧ'n-dyä) . Braz.	18·54 S	48·11 W
166	Ubombo (o͞o-bôm'bô) . . . . . . S. Afr.	27·33 S	32·13 E
154	Ubon Ratchathani (o͞o'bŭn rä'chätá-nē) . Thai	15·15 N	104·52 E
129	Ubort' (R.) (o͞o-bôrt') . . . . Sov. Un.	51·18 N	27·43 E
124	Ubrique (o͞o-brē'kā) . . . . Sp.	36·43 N	5·36 W
146	Ubsa Nuur (L.) . . . . Mong.	50·29 N	93·32 E
98	Ucayali (R.) (o͞o'kä-yä'lē) . . . . Peru	8·58 S	74·13 W
111	Uccle (ü'kl') . . . Bel. (Brussels In.)	50·48 N	4·17 E
136	Uchaly (û-chä'lĭ) Sov. Un. (Urals In.)	54·22 N	59·28 E
134	Uch-Aral (o͝och'ȧ-ral') . . . Sov. Un.	46·14 N	80·58 E
153	Uchiko (o͞o'chē-kō) . . . . Jap.	33·30 N	132·39 E
153	Uchinoura (o͞o'chē-nô-o͞o'rȧ) . . Jap.	31·16 N	131·03 E
136	Uchinskoye Vodokhranilishche L. (o͞och-ēn'skô-yĕ vô-dô-ĸrȧ-nĭ'lĭ-shchĕ) Sov. Un. (Moscow In.)	56·08 N	37·44 E
152	Uchiura-Wan (B.) (o͞o'chē-o͞o'rä wän) . Jap.	42·20 N	140·44 E
142	Uch-Korgon . . . . Sov. Un.	37·22 N	68·41 E
	Uch Turfan, see Wushih		
135	Uchur (R.) (o͝o-cho͝or') . . . Sov. Un.	58·27 N	131·34 E
135	Uda (R.) (o͝o'dȧ) . . . . Sov. Un.	52·28 N	110·51 E
135	Uda (R.) . . . . Sov. Un.	53·54 N	131·29 E
142	Udaipur (o͝o-dŭ'ē-po͞or) . . . . . India	24·41 N	73·41 E
129	Uday (R.) (o͝o-dī') . . . . . . Sov. Un.	50·45 N	32·13 E
118	Uddevalla (o͞od'dĕ-väl-ȧ) . . . . Swe.	58·21 N	11·55 E
126	Udine (o͞o'dē-nā) . . . . It.	46·05 N	13·14 E
134	Udmurt (A. S. S. R.) . . . . Sov. Un.	52·30 N	52·17 E
154	Udon Thani . . . . Thai.	17·31 N	102·51 E
135	Udskaya Guba (B.) . . . . . Sov. Un.	55·00 N	136·30 E
165	Ueb Gestro R. (wĕb gĕs'tro) . . Eth.	6·25 N	41·21 E
120	Ueckermünde (ü'kĕr-mün-dĕ) . Ger.	53·43 N	14·01 E

ăt; finăl; rāte; senāte; ärm; ȧsk; sofȧ; fâre; ch-choose; dh-as th in other; bē; ēvent; bĕt; recĕnt; cratēr; g-go; gh-guttural g; bĭt; ĭ-short neutral; rīde: ĸ-guttural k as ch in German ich;

Page	Name Pronunciation Region	Lat. °′	Long. °′
75	Utica (ū'tĭ-kȧ) Ind. (Louisville In.)	38·20 N	85·39 W
81	Utica....N. Y.	43·05 N	75·10 W
124	Utiel (ōō-tyȧl')....Sp.	39·34 N	1·13 W
75	Utika (ū'tĭ-kȧ) Mich. (Detroit In.)	42·37 N	83·02 W
92	Utila I. (ōō-tē'lä)....Hond.	16·07 N	87·05 W
153	Uto (ōō'tō')....Jap.	32·43 N	130·39 E
111	Utrecht (ū'trĕkt) (ü'trĕkt) Neth. (Amsterdam In.)	52·05 N	5·06 E
124	Utrera (ōō-trā'rä)....Sp.	37·12 N	5·48 W
118	Utsira (I.) (ütsĭrä)....Nor.	59·21 N	4·50 E
153	Utsunomiya (ōōt'sōō-nō'mē-yȧ') Jap.	36·35 N	139·52 E
154	Uttaradit....Thai.	17·47 N	100·10 E
142	Uttar Pradesh (State) (ōōt-tär-prä-dēsh). India	34·19 N	78·40 E
110	Uttoxeter (ŭt-tôk'sē-tēr)....Eng.	52·54 N	1·52 W
89	Utuado (ōō-tōō-ä'dhō) P. R. (Puerto Rico In.)	18·16 N	66·40 W
119	Uusikaupunki (Nystad) (ōō'sĭ-kou'pōōŋ-kĭ) (nü'städh) Fin.	60·48 N	21·24 E
76	Uvalde (ū-văl'dē)....Tex.	29·14 N	99·47 W
136	Uvel'skiy (ōō-vyĕl'skĭ) Sov. Un. (Urals In.)	54·27 N	60·22 E
166	Uvira (ōō-vē'rä)....Con. L.	3·28 S	29·03 E
128	Uvod' (R.) (ōō-vôd')....Sov. Un.	56·52 N	41·03 E
167	Uvongo....S. Afr. (Natal In.)	30·49 S	30·23 E
153	Uwajima (ōō-wä'jē-mä)....Jap.	33·12 N	132·35 E
83	Uxbridge (ŭks'brĭj) Mass. (Boston In.)	42·05 N	71·38 W
92	Uxmal (Ruins) (ōō'x-mä'l) Mex. (Yucatan In.)	20·22 N	89·44 W
136	Uy R. (ōōy)..Sov. Un. (Urals In.)	54·05 N	62·11 E
136	Uyskoye (ûy'skô-yĕ) Sov. Un. (Urals In.)	54·22 N	60·01 E
98	Uyuni (ōō-yōō'nē)....Bol.	20·28 S	66·45 W
98	Uyuni, Salar de (Salt Flat) (sä-lär-dĕ). Bol.	20·58 S	67·09 W
130	Uzbek S. S. R. (ōōz-bĕk').Sov. Un.	42·42 N	60·00 E
133	Uzen, Bol'shoy (R.)....Sov. Un.	49·50 N	49·35 E
129	Uzh (R.) (ōōzh)....Sov. Un.	51·07 N	29·05 E
121	Uzhgorod (ōōzh'gô-rôt)..Sov. Un.	48·38 N	22·18 E
127	Uzunköpru (ōō'zōōn'kû-prü)..Tur.	41·17 N	26·42 E
166	Vaal (R.) (väl)....S. Afr.	28·15 S	24·30 E
168	Vaaldam (L.)....S. Afr. (Johannesburg & Pretoria In.)	26·58 S	28·37 E
168	Vaalplaas....S. Afr. (Johannesburg & Pretoria In.)	25·39 S	28·56 E
168	Vaalwater....S. Afr. (Johannesburg & Pretoria In.)	24·17 S	28·08 E
119	Vaasa (vä'sȧ)....Fin.	63·06 N	21·39 E
121	Vác (väts)....Hung.	47·46 N	19·10 E
95	Vache, Ile À (I.) (väsh)....Hai.	18·05 N	73·40 W
112	Vadsö (vädh'sû)....Nor.	70·08 N	29·52 E
118	Vadstena (väd'stĭ'nȧ)....Swe.	58·27 N	14·53 E
120	Vaduz (vä'dōōts)....Liech.	47·10 N	9·32 E
132	Vaga (R.) (va'gȧ)....Sov. Un.	61·55 N	42·30 E
118	Vågsöy (I.)....Nor.	61·58 N	4·44 E
121	Vah R. (väk)....Czech.	48·07 N	17·52 E
142	Vaigai (R.)....India	10·20 N	78·13 E
134	Vakh (R.) (väk)....Sov. Un.	61·30 N	81·33 E
127	Valachia (Reg.)....Rom.	44·45 N	24·17 E
85	Valcartier-Village (väl-kärt-yā' vē-läzh') Can. (Quebec In.)	46·56 N	71·28 W
128	Valdai Hills (vál-dī' gô'rĭ) Sov. Un.	57·50 N	32·35 E
128	Valday (Valdai) (vál-dī').Sov. Un.	57·58 N	33·13 E
125	Valdemorillo (väl-dȧ-mô-rēl'yō) Sp. (Madrid In.)	40·30 N	4·04 W
124	Valdepeñas (väl-dȧ-pān'yäs)...Sp.	38·46 N	3·22 W
124	Valderaduey (R.) (väl-dĕ-rä-dwĕ'y).Sp.	41·39 N	5·35 W
100	Valdés, Pen. (väl-dĕ's)....Arg.	42·15 S	63·15 W
64	Valdez (văl'dĕz)....Alaska	61·10 N	146·18 W
125	Valdilecha (väl-dē-lā'chä) Sp. (Madrid In.)	40·17 N	3·19 W
100	Valdivia (väl-dē'vä)....Chile	39·47 S	73·13 W
98	Valdivia (väl-dē'vēä)....Col. (In.)	7·10 N	75·26 W
87	Val d' Or....Can.	48·03 N	77·50 W
78	Valdosta (văl-dŏs'tȧ)....Ga.	30·50 N	83·18 W
124	Valdovino (väl-dô-vē'nō)....Sp.	43·36 N	8·05 W
66	Vale (vāl)....Ore.	43·59 N	117·14 W
99	Valença (vä-lĕn'sȧ)....Braz.	13·43 S	38·58 W
122	Valence-sur-Rhône (vä-lĕns-sür-rōn').Fr.	44·56 N	4·54 E
124	Valencia (vä-lĕ'n-syä)....Port.	42·03 N	8·36 W
125	Valencia (vä-lĕn'thē-ä)....Sp.	39·26 N	0·23 W
124	Valencia....Sp.	39·34 N	7·13 W
99	Valencia (vä-lĕn'syä)...Ven. (In.)	10·11 N	68·00 W
125	Valencia (Reg.) (vä-lĕn'thē-ä).Sp.	39·08 N	0·43 W
116	Valencia (I.) (vȧ-lĕn'shȧ)....Ire.	51·55 N	10·26 W
99	Valencia, Lago de (L.)..Ven. (In.)	10·11 N	67·45 W
122	Valenciennes (vȧ-län-syĕn')....Fr.	50·24 N	3·36 E
70	Valentine (vȧ län-tē-nyĕ')...Nebr.	42·52 N	100·34 W
98	Valera (vä-lĕ'rä)....Ven.	9·12 N	70·45 W
136	Valerianovsk (vä-lĕ-rĭ-ä'nôvsk) Sov. Un. (Urals In.)	58·47 N	59·34 E
128	Valga (väl'gȧ)....Sov. Un.	57·47 N	26·03 E
167	Valhalla (văl-hăl-ȧ)....S. Afr. (Johannesburg & Pretoria In.)	25·49 S	28·09 E
67	Valier (vă-lēr')....Mont.	48·17 N	112·14 W
127	Valjevo (väl'yȧ-vō)....Yugo.	44·17 N	19·57 E
129	Valki (väl'kē)....Sov. Un.	49·49 N	35·40 E
92	Valladolid (väl-yä-dhō-lēdh') Mex. (Yucatan In.)	20·39 N	88·13 W
124	Valladolid (väl-yä-dhō-lēdh')..Sp.	41·41 N	4·41 W
125	Vall de Uxo' (väl-dĕ-ōōx-ô')...Sp.	39·50 N	0·15 W
98	Valle (Dept.) (vä'l-yĕ)..Col. (In.)	4·03 N	76·13 W
68	Valle, Arroyo del (ä-rō'yō dĕl väl'yȧ).Calif.	37·36 N	121·43 W
125	Vallecas (väl-yä'käs) Sp. (Madrid In.)	40·23 N	3·37 W
76	Valle de Allende (väl'yä dä äl-yĕn'dȧ).Mex.	26·55 N	105·25 W
90	Valle de Bravo (brä'vô)....Mex.	19·12 N	100·07 W
99	Valle de Guanape (vä'l-yĕ-dĕ-gwä-nä'pĕ) Ven. (In.)	9·54 N	65·41 W
98	Valle de la Pascua (lä-pä's-kōōä) Ven.	9·12 N	65·08 W
90	Valle de Santiago (sän-tē-ä'gô) Mex.	20·23 N	101·11 W
98	Valledupar (dōō-pär')....Col.	10·13 N	73·39 W
98	Valle Grande (grän'dä)....Bol.	18·27 S	64·03 W
65	Vallejo (vä-yā'hō) (vȧ-lā'hō) Calif. (San Francisco In.)	38·06 N	122·15 W
90	Vallejo, Sierra de (Mts.) (sē-ĕ'r-rä-dĕ-väl-yĕ'kô).Mex.	21·00 N	105·10 W
100	Vallenar (väl-yȧ-när')....Chile	28·39 S	70·52 W
125	Vallerano (R.) (vä-lĕ-rä'nō) It. (Rome In.)	41·46 N	12·29 E
114	Valletta (väl-lĕt'ä)....Malta	35·50 N	14·29 E
74	Valle Vista (văl'yä vĭs'tȧ) Calif. (Los Angeles In.)	33·45 N	116·53 W
70	Valley City....N. D.	46·55 N	97·59 W
75	Valley City (văl'ĭ) Ohio (Cleveland In.)	41·14 N	81·56 W
73	Valley Falls....Kans.	39·21 N	95·26 W
84	Valley Falls (fôls) R. I. (Providence In.)	41·55 N	71·23 W
85	Valleyfield (văl'ē-fēld) Can. (Montreal In.)	45·16 N	74·09 W
74	Valley Park (văl'ē pärk) Mo. (St. Louis In.)	38·33 N	90·30 W
84	Valley Stream (văl'ĭ strēm) N. Y. (New York In.)	40·39 N	73·42 W
126	Valli di Comácchio (L.) (vä'lē-dē-kô-mä'chyô).It.	44·38 S	12·15 E
95	Vallière (väl-yâr')....Hai.	19·30 N	71·55 W
101	Vallimanca (R.) (väl-yē-mä'n-kä) Arg. (Buenos Aires In.)	36·21 S	60·55 W
125	Valls (väls)....Sp.	41·15 N	1·15 E
86	Val Marie....Can.	49·10 N	107·59 W
119	Valmiera (väl'myĕ-rȧ)...Sov. Un.	57·34 N	25·54 E
122	Valognes (vá-lôn'y')....Fr.	49·32 N	1·30 W
	Valona, see Vlorë		
101	Valparaíso (väl'pä-rä-ē'sô) Chile (Santiago In.)	33·02 S	71·32 W
80	Valparaiso (văl-pȧ-rā'zô)....Ind.	41·25 N	87·05 W
90	Valparaiso....Mex.	22·49 N	103·33 W
101	Valpariso (Prov.) Chile (Santiago In.)	32·58 S	71·23 W
122	Valréas (vȧl-rà-ä')....Fr.	45·25 N	4·56 E
	Valsbaai, see False B.		
155	Valsch, Kap (C.) (välsh).W. Irian	8·30 S	137·15 E
168	Valsch R....S. Afr. (Johannesburg & Pretoria In.)	27·32 S	26·51 E
136	Valuyevo (vȧ-lōō'yĕ-vô) Sov. Un. (Moscow In.)	55·34 N	37·21 E
129	Valuyki (vȧ-lōō-ē'kē)....Sov. Un.	50·14 N	38·04 E
74	Val Verde (văl vûr'dē) Calif. (Los Angeles In.)	33·51 N	117·15 W
95	Valverde (väl-vĕ'r-dĕ).Dom. Rep.	19·35 N	71·10 W
124	Valverde del Camino (väl-vĕr-dĕ-dĕl-kä-mē'nō).Sp.	37·34 N	6·44 W
142	Vambanād (R.)....India	10·00 N	76·03 E
133	Van (vȧn)....Tur.	38·04 N	43·10 E
73	Van Buren (văn bū'rĕn)....Ark.	35·26 N	94·20 W
82	Van Buren....Maine	47·09 N	67·58 W
80	Vanceburg (văns'bûrg)....Ky.	38·35 N	83·20 W
65	Vancouver (văn-kōō'vēr) Can. (Vancouver In.)	49·16 N	123·06 W
65	Vancouver..Wash. (Portland In.)	45·37 N	122·40 W
86	Vancouver I....Can.	49·47 N	128·23 W
80	Vandalia (văn-dā'lĭ-ȧ)....Ill.	39·00 N	89·00 W
73	Vandalia....Mo.	39·19 N	91·30 W
168	Vanderbijlpark....S. Afr. (Johannesburg & Pretoria In.)	26·43 S	27·50 E
86	Vanderhoof....Can.	53·59 N	124·10 W
	Van Diemen, see Ōsumi Kaikyō		
158	Van Diemen, C. (văndē'mĕn).Austl.	11·05 S	130·15 E
158	Van Diemen G....Austl.	11·50 S	131·30 E
75	Van Dyke (văn dīk) Mich. (Detroit In.)	42·27 N	83·01 W
90	Vanegas (vä-nĕ'gäs)....Mex.	23·54 N	100·54 W
118	Vänern (L.)....Swe.	58·52 N	13·17 E
118	Vänersborg (vĕ'nĕrs-bôr')....Swe.	58·24 N	12·15 E
167	Vanga (väŋ'gä)....Ken.	4·38 S	39·10 E
143	Vangani....India (Bombay In.)	19·07 N	73·15 E
133	Van Gölü (L.)....Tur.	38·45 N	43·00 E
80	Van Lear (văn lēr')....Ky.	37·45 N	82·50 W
122	Vannes (vȧn)....Fr.	47·42 N	2·46 W
74	Van Nuys (văn nīz') Calif. (Los Angeles In.)	34·11 N	118·27 W
119	Vantaan (R.)....Fin.	60·25 N	24·43 E
80	Van Wert (văn wûrt')....Ohio	40·50 N	84·35 W
118	Vara (vä'rä)....Swe.	58·17 N	12·55 E
128	Varaklāni....Sov. Un.	56·38 N	26·46 E
126	Varallo (vä-räl'lō)....It.	45·44 N	8·14 E
142	Vārānasi (Banaras)....India	25·25 N	83·00 E
112	Varanger Fd. (vä-räng'gĕr)..Nor.	70·05 N	30·53 E
126	Varano, Lago di (L.) (lä'gō-dē-vä-rä'nō).It.	41·52 N	15·55 E
126	Varaždin (vä'räzh'dĕn)....Yugo.	46·17 N	16·20 E
126	Varazze (vä-rät'sä)....It.	44·23 N	8·34 E
118	Varberg (vär'bĕrg)....Swe.	57·06 N	12·16 E
127	Vardar (R.) (vär'där)....Yugo.	41·40 N	21·50 E
118	Varde (vär'dĕ)....Den.	55·39 N	8·28 E
112	Vardö (värd'û)....Nor.	70·23 N	30·43 E
154	Varella, C....Viet.	12·58 N	109·50 E
119	Varėna (vä-rā'nȧ)....Sov. Un.	54·16 N	24·35 E
85	Varennes (vȧ-rĕn') Can. (Montreal In.)	45·41 N	73·27 W
127	Varěs (vä'rĕsh)....Yugo.	44·10 N	18·20 E
126	Varese (vä-rā'sā)....It.	45·45 N	8·49 E
101	Varginha (vär-zhē'n-yä) Braz. (Rio de Janeiro In.)	21·33 S	45·25 W
119	Varkaus (vär'kous)....Fin.	62·19 N	27·51 E
136	Varlamovo (vár-lá'mô-vô) Sov. Un. (Urals In.)	54·37 N	60·41 E
127	Varna (Stalin) (vär'nȧ) (stä'lĭn) Bul.	43·14 N	27·58 E
136	Varna....Sov. Un. (Urals In.)	53·22 N	60·59 E
118	Värnamo (vĕr'nȧ-mô)....Swe.	57·11 N	13·45 E
120	Varnsdorf (värns'dôrf)....Czech.	50·54 N	14·36 E
79	Varnville (värn'vĭl)....S. C.	32·49 N	81·05 W
85	Vars (värz)....Can. (Ottawa In.)	45·21 N	75·21 W
129	Varvaropolye (vär'vär'ô-pô-lyĕ) Sov. Un.	48·38 N	38·37 E
124	Vascongadas (Reg.) (väs-kôn-gä'däs).Sp.	42·35 N	2·46 W
132	Vashka (R.)....Sov. Un.	63·20 N	47·50 E
65	Vashon (văsh'ŭn) Wash. (Seattle In.)	47·27 N	122·28 W
65	Vashon Heights (hītz) Wash. (Seattle In.)	47·30 N	122·28 W
65	Vashon I....Wash. (Seattle In.)	47·27 N	122·27 W
129	Vasil'kov (vá-sēl'-kôf')...Sov. Un.	50·10 N	30·22 E
121	Vaslui (vás-lōō'ē)....Rom.	46·39 N	27·49 E
80	Vassar (văs'ĕr)....Mich.	43·25 N	83·35 W
100	Vassouras (väs-sō'räzh).Braz. (In.)	22·25 S	43·40 W
118	Västanfors (vĕst'án-fôrs)....Swe.	59·59 N	15·49 E
118	Västerås (vĕs'tĕr-ôs)....Swe.	59·39 N	16·30 E
118	Väster-dalälven (R.)....Swe.	61·06 N	13·10 E
118	Västervik (vĕs'tĕr-vēk)....Swe.	57·45 N	16·35 E
126	Vasto (väs'tô)....It.	42·06 N	12·42 E
134	Vasyugan (R.) (vás-yōō-gán') Sov. Un.	58·52 N	77·30 E
125	Vatican City (Cittádel Vaticano) (văt'ĭ-kăn sĭt'ē) (chē-tà'del vä-tē-kä'nô).Eur. (Rome In.)	41·54 N	12·22 E
126	Vaticano, C. (vä-tē-kä'nô)....It.	38·38 N	15·52 E
112	Vatnajökull (Gl.) (vät'nȧ-yû-kōōl) Ice.	64·34 N	16·41 W
167	Vatomandry (vä-tōō-män'drē) Malag. Rep.	18·53 S	48·13 E
121	Vatra Dornei (vät'rȧ dôr'nā') Rom.	47·22 N	25·20 E
118	Vättern (L.)....Swe.	58·15 N	14·24 E
85	Vaudreuil (vô-drû'y') Can. (Montreal In.)	45·24 N	74·02 W
65	Vaugh (vôn)..Wash. (Seattle In.)	47·21 N	122·47 W
72	Vaughn....N. Mex.	34·37 N	105·13 W
98	Vaupés (R.) (vá'ōō-pĕ's)....Col.	1·18 N	71·14 W
118	Vaxholm (väks'hōlm)....Swe.	59·26 N	18·19 E
118	Växjo (vĕks'shû)....Swe.	56·53 N	14·46 E
132	Vaygach (I.) (vī-gäch')..Sov. Un.	70·00 N	59·00 E
99	Veadeiros, Chapadas dos (Mts.) (shä-pä'däs-dôs-vĕ-ä-dā'rōs) Braz.	15·20 S	48·43 W
118	Veblungsnares (vib'lōōngs-nĕs) Nor.	62·33 N	7·46 E
127	Vedea (R.) (vȧ'dyȧ)....Rom.	44·25 N	24·45 E
101	Vedia (vĕ'dyä) Arg. (Buenos Aires In.)	34·29 S	61·30 W
80	Veedersburg (vē'dērz-bûrg)...Ind.	40·05 N	87·15 W
91	Vega de Alatorre (vä'gä dä ä-lä-tōr'rȧ).Mex.	20·02 N	96·39 W
95	Vega Real (Mts.) (vĕ'gä-rĕ-ä'l) Dom. Rep.	19·30 N	71·05 W
112	Vegen (I.) (vĕ'ghĕn)....Nor.	65·38 N	10·51 E
86	Vegreville....Can.	53·26 N	112·27 W
143	Vehār L....India (Bombay In.)	19·11 N	72·50 E
101	Veinticinco de Mayo (vā-ēn'tē-sēn'kō dä mä'yō) Arg. (Buenos Aires In.)	35·26 S	60·09 W
124	Vejer (vā-kĕr')....Sp.	36·15 N	5·58 W
118	Vejle (vī'lĕ)....Den.	55·41 N	9·29 E
123	Velbert (fĕl'bĕrt)..Ger. (Ruhr In.)	51·20 N	7·03 E
126	Velebit (Mts.) (vā'lĕ-bēt)...Yugo.	44·25 N	15·23 E
123	Velen (fĕ'lĕn)....Ger. (Ruhr In.)	51·54 N	7.00 E
124	Vélez-Málaga (vā'lāth-mä'lä-gä) Sp.	36·48 N	4·05 W
124	Vélez Rubio (rōō'bē-ô)....Sp.	37·38 N	2·05 W
126	Velika Kapela (Mts.) (vĕ'lē-kä kä-pĕ'lä).Yugo.	45·03 N	15·20 E
127	Velika Morava (R.) (mô'rä-vä) Yugo.	44·20 N	21·10 E
128	Velikaya (R.) (vȧ-lē'kȧ-yȧ) Sov. Un.	57·25 N	28·07 E
121	Velikiy Bychkov (vĕ-lē'kē bōōch-kôf').Sov. Un.	47·59 N	24·01 E
128	Velikiye Luki (vyē-lē'-kyē lōō'ke) Sov. Un.	56·19 N	30·32 E
132	Velikiy Ustyug (vȧ-lē'kĭ ōōs-tyōōg').Sov. Un.	60·45 N	46·38 E
128	Velikoye (vȧ-lē'kô-yĕ)...Sov. Un.	57·21 N	39·45 E
128	Velikoye (L.)....Sov. Un.	57·00 N	36·53 E
128	Velizh (vȧ'lēzh)....Sov. Un.	55·37 N	31·11 E
120	Velke Meziříčí (vĕl'kä mězh'r-zhyĭ-chĭ).Czech.	49·21 N	16·01 E
159	Vella (I.) (vāl'yä)....Sol. Is.	8·00 S	156·42 E
125	Velletri (vĕl-lā'trē).It. (Rome In.)	41·42 N	12·48 E
143	Vellore (vĕl-lōr')....India	12·57 N	79·09 E
136	Vels (vĕls)...Sov. Un. (Urals In.)	60·35 N	58·47 E
132	Vel'sk (vĕlsk)....Sov. Un.	61·00 N	42·18 E
111	Velten (fel'tĕn)..Ger. (Berlin In.)	52·41 N	13·11 E
136	Velya R. (vĕl'yȧ) Sov. Un. (Moscow In.)	56·23 N	37·54 E
98	Venadillo (vĕ-nä-dē'l-yō) Col. (In.)	4·43 N	74·55 W
90	Venado (vā-nä'dō)....Mex.	22·54 N	101·07 W
100	Venado Tuerto (vĕ-nä'dō-tōōĕ'r-tō).Arg.	33·28 S	61·47 W
122	Vendée, Collines de (hills) (kō-lēn' dĕ vĕn-dā').Fr.	46·44 N	0·17 W
122	Vendôme (vän-dōm')....Fr.	47·46 N	1·05 E
126	Veneto (Reg.) (vĕ-nĕ'tô)....It.	45·58 N	11·24 E
128	Venëv (vĕn-ĕf')....Sov. Un.	54·19 N	38·14 E
126	Venezia (Venice) (vä-nät'sē-ä).It.	45·25 N	12·18 E
126	Venezia, Golfo di (G.) (gôl-fô-dē-vĕ-nät'sē-ä).It.	45·23 N	13·00 E

ăr; finăl; rāte; senāte; ärm; ȧsk; sofȧ; fâre; ch-choose; dh-as th in other; bē; ēvent; bĕt; recĕnt; cratēr; g-go; gh-guttural g; bĭt; ĭ-short neutral; rīde; k-guttural k as ch in German ich;

PRONOUNCING INDEX Venezuela–Villafranca del Bierzo 281

Page	Name Pronunciation Region	Lat. °′	Long. °′
96	Venezuela (vĕn-ê-zwē'lȧ)....S. A.	8·00 N	65·00 W
98	Venezuela, Golfo de (G.) (gôl-fô-dĕ).Ven.	11·34 N	71·02 W
64	Veniaminof, Mt..........Alaska	56·12 N	159·20 W
74	Venice (vĕn'ĭs) Calif. (Los Angeles In.)	33·59 N	118·28 W
74	Venice.........Ill. (St. Louis In.)	38·40 N	90·10 W
84	Venice.....La. (New Orleans In.)	29·17 N	89·22 W
	Venice, see Venezia		
123	Venlo..........Neth. (Ruhr In.)	51·22 N	6·11 E
119	Venta (R.) (vĕn'tȧ).....Sov. Un.	57·05 N	21·45 E
100	Ventana, Sierra de la (Mts.) (sē-ĕ'r-rȧ-dĕ-lä-vĕn-tȧ'nȧ).Arg.	38·00 S	63·00 W
168	Ventersburg (vĕn-tērs'bûrg) S. Afr. (Johannesburg & Pretoria In.)	28·06 S	27·10 E
168	Ventersdorp (vĕn-tērs'dôrp) S. Afr. (Johannesburg & Pretoria In.)	26·20 S	26·48 E
126	Ventimiglia (vĕn-tê-mēl'yä)....It.	43·46 N	7·37 E
81	Ventnor (vĕnt'nẽr)..........N. J.	39·20 N	74·25 W
119	Ventspils (vĕnt'spêls)....Sov. Un.	57·24 N	21·41 E
98	Ventuari (R.) (vĕn-tōōä'rē)..Ven.	4·47 N	65·56 W
68	Ventura (vĕn-tōō'rȧ).......Calif.	34·18 N	119·18 W
136	Venukovsky (vĕ-nōō'kôv-skĭ) Sov. Un. (Moscow In.)	55·10 N	37·26 E
90	Venustiano Carranza (vĕ-nōōs-tyä'nō-kär-rä'n-zä) Mex.	19·44 N	103·48 W
91	Venustiano Carranzo (kär-rä'n-zō) Mex.	16·21 N	92·36 W
100	Vera (vĕ-rä)................Arg.	29·22 S	60·09 W
124	Vera (vä'rä)................Sp.	37·18 N	1·53 W
88	Vera Cruz (State) (vā-rä-krōōz') Mex.	20·30 N	97·15 W
91	Veracruz Llave (l-yä'vĕ)....Mex.	19·13 N	96·07 W
142	Verāval (vĕr'ŭ-väl)..........India	20·59 N	70·49 E
126	Vercelli (vĕr-chĕl'lê)..........It.	45·18 N	8·27 E
85	Verchères (vĕr-shâr') Can. (Montreal In.)	45·46 N	73·21 W
69	Verde (R.) (vûrd)..........Ariz.	34·04 N	111·40 W
95	Verde, Cap (C.)..........Ba. Is.	22·50 N	75·00 W
95	Verde, Cay (I.)...........Ba. Is.	22·00 N	75·05 W
91	Verde (R.)................Mex.	16·05 N	97·44 W
90	Verde (R.)................Mex.	20·50 N	103·00 W
90	Verde (R.)................Mex.	21·48 N	99·50 W
155	Verde (I.) (vĕr'dȧ) Phil. (Manila In.)	13·34 N	121·11 E
155	Verde Island Pass. (vĕr'dē) Phil. (Manila In.)	13·36 N	120·39 E
74	Verdemont (vûr'dê-mŏnt) Calif. (Los Angeles In.)	34·12 N	117·22 W
120	Verden (fĕr'dĕn)............Ger.	52·55 N	9·15 E
73	Verdigris (R.) (vûr'dê-grēs).Okla.	36·50 N	95·29 W
85	Verdun (vĕr'dŭN') Can. (Montreal In.)	45·27 N	73·34 W
122	Verdun-sur-Meuse (vâr-dûN'sür-mûz').Fr.	49·09 N	5·21 E
168	Vereeniging (vĕ-rä'nĭ-gĭng).S. Afr. (Johannesburg & Pretoria In.)	26·40 S	27·56 E
168	Verena (vĕr-ĕn ȧ).........S. Afr. (Johannesburg & Pretoria In.)	25·30 S	29·02 E
128	Vereya (vĕ-rȧ'yȧ).......Sov. Un.	55·21 N	36·08 E
124	Vergara (vĕr-gä'rä)..........Sp.	43·08 N	2·23 W
124	Verin (vå-rēn').............Sp.	41·56 N	7·26 W
136	Verkhne Chusovskiye Gorodki (vyĕrk'nyĕ chōō-sôv'skĭ-ye gȧ-rôd'kĭ).Sov. Un. (Urals In.)	58·13 N	75·06 E
135	Verkhne-Kamchatsk (vyĕrk'nyĕ kȧm-chatsk') Sov. Un.	54·42 N	158·41 E
136	Verkhne Neyvinskiy (nā-vĭn'skĭ) Sov. Un. (Urals In.)	57·17 N	60·10 E
136	Verkhne Ural'sk (ŏŏ-ralsk') Sov. Un. (Urals In.)	53·53 N	59·15 E
129	Verkhneye (vyĕrĸ'nĕ-yĕ) Sov. Un.	48·53 N	38·29 E
136	Verkhniy Avzyan (vyĕrk'nyĕ åv-zyȧn') Sov. Un. (Urals In.)	53·32 N	57·30 E
136	Verkhniye Kigi (vyĕrk'nĭ-yĕ kĭ'gĭ) Sov. Un. (Urals In.)	55·23 N	58·37 E
136	Verkhniy Ufaley (ōō-fá'lā) Sov. Un. (Urals In.)	56·04 N	60·15 E
121	Verkhniy Yasenov (vyĕ'rĸ-nēē yä'syĕ-ŋĕf).Sov. Un.	48·17 N	24·21 E
136	Verkhnyaya Pyshma (vyĕrk'nyä-yä pōōsh'mȧ) Sov. Un. (Urals In.)	56·57 N	60·37 E
136	Verkhnyaya Salda (säl'dȧ) Sov. Un. (Urals In.)	58·03 N	60·33 E
134	Verkhnyaya Tunguska (Angara) (R.) (tōōn-gōōs'kȧ).Sov. Un.	58·13 N	97·00 E
136	Verkhnyaya Tura (tōō'rȧ) Sov. Un. Urals. In.)	58·22 N	59·51 E
136	Verkhnyaya Yayva (yäy'vȧ) Sov. Un. (Urals In.)	59·28 N	59·38 E
136	Verkhotur'ye (vyĕr-kô-tōōr'yĕ) Sov. Un. (Urals In.)	58·52 N	60·47 E
135	Verkhoyansk (vyĕr-kô-yänsk') Sov. Un.	67·43 N	133·33 E
135	Verkhoyanskiy Khrebet (Mts.) (vyĕr-ĸô-yänsk').Sov. Un.	67·45 N	128·00 E
86	Vermilion (vẽr-mĭl'yŭn).....Can.	53·19 N	110·53 W
82	Vermilion (R.)..............Can.	47·30 N	73·15 W
80	Vermilion (R.)...............Ill.	41·05 N	89·00 W
71	Vermilion (L.)............Minn.	47·49 N	92·35 W
71	Vermilion Ra...............Minn.	47·55 N	91·59 W
71	Vermilion (R.).............Minn.	48·09 N	92·31 W
70	Vermillion................S. D.	42·46 N	96·56 W
70	Vermillion (R.)............S. D.	43·54 N	97·14 W
77	Vermillion B................La.	29·47 N	92·00 W
63	Vermont (State) (vẽr-mŏnt') U. S.	43·50 N	72·50 W
67	Vernal (vûr'nȧl)............Utah	40·29 N	109·40 W
166	Verneuk Pan (L.) (vĕr-nŭk') S. Afr.	30·10 S	21·46 E
74	Vernon (vûr'nŭn) Calif. (Los Angeles In.)	34·01 N	118·12 W
86	Vernon (vĕr-nôN')..........Can.	50·18 N	119·15 W
85	Vernon........Can. (Ottawa In.)	45·10 N	75·27 W
80	Vernon (vûr'nŭn)............Ind.	39·00 N	85·40 W
84	Vernon.....N. J. (New York In.)	41·12 N	74·29 W
72	Vernon.....................Tex.	34·09 N	99·16 W
79	Vero Beach (vē'rô).....Fla. (In.)	27·36 N	80·25 W
127	Véroia......................Grc.	40·30 N	22·13 E
126	Verona (vā-rō'nä)............It.	45·28 N	11·02 E
65	Vernonia (vûr-nō'nyȧ) Ore. (Portland In.)	45·52 N	123·12 W
123	Versailles (vĕr-sī'y') Fr. (Paris In.)	48·48 N	2·07 E
80	Versailles (vẽr-sālz').........Ky.	38·05 N	84·45 W
73	Versailles...................Mo.	38·27 N	92·52 W
82	Verte, B. (vûrt)............Can.	46·03 N	63·57 W
164	Vert, Cap (C.)..........Senegal	14·52 N	17·49 W
167	Verulam (vĕ-rōō-lăm) S. Afr. (Natal In.)	29·39 S	31·08 E
117	Verviers (vĕr-vyā')..........Bel.	50·35 N	5·57 E
129	Vesëloye (vĕ-syô'lô-yĕ)..Sov. Un.	46·59 N	34·56 E
119	Vesijärvi (L.)..............Fin.	61·09 N	25·10 E
123	Vesoul (vē-sōōl')............Fr.	47·38 N	6·11 E
112	Vester Aalen (Is.) (vĕs'tĕr ô'lĕn) Nor.	68·54 N	14·03 E
112	Vestfjord...................Nor.	67·33 N	12·59 E
112	Vestmannaeyjar (vĕst'mȧn-ȧ-ā'yȧr).Ice.	63·12 N	20·17 W
125	Vesuvio (vesuvius) (Mtn.) (vĕ-sōō'vyä).It. (Naples In.)	40·35 N	14·26 E
128	Ves'yegonsk (vĕ-syĕ-gônsk') Sov. Un.	58·42 N	37·09 E
121	Veszprem (vĕs'prām)......Hung.	47·05 N	17·53 E
121	Vesztö (vĕs'tû)............Hung.	46·55 N	21·18 E
128	Vetka (vyĕt'kȧ).........Sov. Un.	52·36 N	31·05 E
118	Vetlanda (vĕt-län'dȧ).......Swe.	57·26 N	15·05 E
132	Vetluga (vyĕt-lōō'gȧ)....Sov. Un.	57·50 N	45·42 E
132	Vetluga (R.)............Sov. Un.	56·50 N	45·50 E
127	Vetovo (vä'tô-vô)...........Bul.	43·42 N	26·18 E
127	Vetren (vĕt'rĕn')...........Bul.	42·16 N	24·04 E
168	Vet R. (vĕt)..............S. Afr. (Johannesburg & Pretoria In.)	28·25 S	26·37 E
80	Vevay (vē'vā)..............Ind.	38·45 N	85·05 W
123	Veynes (vān'')..............Fr.	44·31 N	5·47 E
122	Vézère (R.) (vā-zer').........Fr.	45·01 N	1·00 E
98	Viacha (vēȧ'chȧ)............Bol.	16·43 S	68·16 W
126	Viadana (vê-ȧ-dä'nä)..........It.	44·55 N	10·30 E
73	Vian (vī'ǎn)...............Okla.	35·30 N	95·00 W
99	Viana (vē-ä'nä)............Braz.	3·09 S	44·44 W
124	Viana del Bollo (vê-ä'nä dĕl bôl'yô) Sp.	42·10 N	7·07 W
124	Viana do Alentejo (vê-ä'nȧ dōō ä-lĕN-tä'hōō).Port.	38·20 N	8·02 W
124	Viana do Castélo (dōō käs-tă'lōō) Port.	41·41 N	8·45 W
124	Viar (R.) (vê-ä'rä)...........Sp.	38·15 N	6·08 W
126	Viareggio (vē-ä-rĕd'jô)........It.	43·52 N	10·14 E
118	Viborg (vē'bôr)..............Den.	56·27 N	9·22 E
126	Vibo Valentia (vē'bô-vä-lĕ'n-tyä) It.	38·47 N	16·06 E
125	Vicálvero (vē-kȧ'l-vĕ-rō) Sp. (Madrid In.)	40·25 N	3·37 W
100	Vicente López (vē-sĕ'n-tĕ-lō'pĕz) Arg. (In.)	34·15 S	58·29 W
126	Vicenza (vê-chĕnt'sȧ).........It.	45·33 N	11·33 E
125	Vich (vēch).................Sp.	41·55 N	2·14 E
128	Vichuga (vē-chōō'gȧ)....Sov. Un.	57·13 N	41·58 E
122	Vichy (vê-shē')..............Fr.	46·06 N	3·28 E
80	Vicksburg (vĭks'bûrg)......Mich.	42·10 N	85·30 W
78	Vicksburg..................Miss.	32·20 N	90·50 W
101	Viçosa (vē-sô'sä) Braz. (Rio de Janeiro In.)	23·46 S	42·51 W
101	Victoria (vēk-tô'rêä) Arg. (Buenos Aires In.)	32·36 S	60·09 W
65	Victoria (vĭk-tō'rĭ-ȧ) Can. (Seattle In.)	48·26 N	123·23 W
100	Victoria (vēk-tô-rêä)........Chile	38·15 S	72·16 W
149	Victoria (vĭk-tō'rĭ-ȧ)..Hong Kong	22·10 N	114·18 E
98	Victoria (vēk-tô'rêä)....Col. (In.)	5·19 N	74·54 W
164	Victoria (vĭk-tō'rĭ-ȧ)........Nig.	4·06 N	9·13 E
155	Victoria (vēk-tô-ryä) Phil. (Manila In.)	15·34 N	120·41 E
77	Victoria (vĭk-tō'rĭ-ȧ)........Tex.	28·48 N	97·00 W
79	Victoria.....................Va.	36·57 N	78·13 W
159	Victoria (State)............Austl.	36·46 S	143·15 E
158	Victoria (R.)..............Austl.	17·25 S	130·50 E
146	Victoria, Mt...............Bur.	21·26 N	93·59 E
155	Victoria, Mt...............Pap.	9·35 S	147·45 E
166	Victoria (L.)..............Tan.	2·00 S	32·16 E
90	Victoria de Durango (vēk-tō'ryä-dĕ-dōō-rä'n-gô) Mex.	24·02 N	104·42 W
94	Victoria de las Tunas (vêk-tō'rê-ä dä läs tōō'näs) Cuba	20·55 N	77·05 W
166	Victoria Falls.............S. Rh.	18·15 S	25·35 E
86	Victoria I.................Can.	70·13 N	107·45 W
47	Victoria Land...............Ant.	75·00 S	160·00 E
92	Victoria Pk. (vêk-tōrĭ'ȧ) Br. Hond. (Yucatan In.)	16·47 N	88·40 W
158	Victoria River Downs (vĭc-tôr'ĭȧ) Austl.	16·30 S	131·10 E
86	Victoria Str. (vĭk-tō'rĭ-ȧ)....Can.	69·10 N	100·58 E
82	Victoriaville (vĭk-tō'rĭ-ȧ-vĭl).Can.	46·04 N	71·59 W
166	Victoria West (wĕst).......S. Afr.	31·25 S	23·10 E
79	Vidalia (vĭ-dā'lĭ-ȧ)..........Ga.	32·10 N	82·26 W
77	Vidalia.....................La.	31·33 N	91·28 W
127	Vidin (vĭ'dĕn)...............Bul.	44·00 N	22·53 E
128	Vidzy (vĕ'dzĭ)...........Sov. Un.	55·23 N	26·46 E
100	Viedma (vyäd'mä)...........Arg.	40·55 S	63·03 W
100	Viedma (L.)................Arg.	49·40 S	72·35 W
92	Viejo R. (vyä'hô)............Nic.	12·45 N	86·19 W
78	Vienna (vê-ĕn'ȧ)............Ga.	32·03 N	83·50 W
73	Vienna.......................Ill.	37·24 N	88·50 W
	Vienna, see Wien		
122	Vienne (vyĕn')...............Fr.	45·31 N	4·54 E
122	Vienne (R.).................Fr.	47·06 N	0·20 E
154	Vientiane (vyān'tyān')......Laos	18·07 N	102·33 E
89	Vieques (vyā'kås) P. R. (Puerto Rico In.)	18·09 N	65·27 W
89	Vieques (I.) (vyā'kås) P. R. (Puerto Rico In.)	18·05 N	65·28 W
168	Vierfontien (vẽr'fŏn-tān)...S. Afr. (Johannesburg & Pretoria In.)	27·06 S	26·45 E
123	Viersen (fēr'zĕn).Ger. (Ruhr In.)	51·15 N	6·24 E
120	Vierwaldstätter See (L.)....Switz.	46·54 N	8·36 E
122	Vierzon (vyâr-zôN')..........Fr.	47·14 N	2·04 E
76	Viesca (vê-ās'kä)...........Mex.	25·21 N	102·47 W
76	Viesca, Laguna de (L.) (lä-ōō'nä-dĕ).Mex.	25·30 N	102·40 W
126	Vieste (vyĕs'tå)..............It.	41·52 N	16·10 E
139	Vietnam (vyĕt'näm')........Asia	18·00 N	106·20 E
155	Vigan (vēgän)..Phil. (Manila In.)	17·36 N	120·22 E
126	Vigevano (vê-jȧ-vä'nô)........It.	45·18 N	8·52 E
123	Vigny (vēn-y'ē')...Fr. (Paris In.)	49·05 N	1·54 E
124	Vigo (vē'gō).................Sp.	42·18 N	8·42 W
119	Vihti (vē'tĭ)................Fin.	60·27 N	24·18 E
	Viipuri, see Vyborg		
127	Vijosë (R.).................Alb.	40·15 N	20·30 E
112	Vik.........................Ice.	63·22 N	18·58 W
118	Vik (vĭk)...................Nor.	61·06 N	6·35 E
159	Vila.................New Hebr.	18·00 S	168·30 E
166	Vila de João Belo (vē'lä-dĕ-zho'uN-bĕ'lô).Moz.	25·00 S	33·45 E
166	Vila de Manica (vē'lä dä mä-nē'kȧ).Moz.	18·48 S	32·49 E
124	Vila de Rei (vē'lȧ dä rā'ĭ)...Port.	39·42 N	8·03 W
124	Vila do Conde (vē'lä dōō kôn'dĕ) Port.	41·21 N	8·44 W
124	Vila Franca de Xira (fräŋ'kȧ dä shē'rȧ).Port.	38·58 N	8·59 W
166	Vila Henrique De Carvalho (vē'lä-ĕn-rē'kĕ-dĕ-kär-vä'lô) Ang.	9·25 S	20·30 E
122	Vilaine (R.) (vē-lân')........Fr.	47·34 N	0·20 W
166	Vila Luso (vē'lä-lōō'sô)......Ang.	11·45 S	19·55 E
166	Vila Marechal Carmona (mä-rĕ-zhäl-kär-mô-nä).Ang.	7·30 S	15·05 E
166	Vilanculos (vê-län-kōō'lôs)..Moz.	22·03 S	35·13 E
128	Vilāni (vē'lȧ-nĭ).........Sov. Un.	56·31 N	27·00 E
124	Vila Nova de Fozcoa (nō'vȧ dä fôz-kō'ȧ).Port.	41·08 N	7·11 W
124	Vila Nova de Gaia (vē'lä nō'vȧ dä gä'yä).Port.	41·08 N	8·40 W
124	Vila Nova de Milfontes (nō'vȧ dä mêl-fôn'tāzh).Port.	37·44 N	8·48 W
124	Vila Real (rā-äl')...........Port.	41·18 N	7·48 W
124	Vila Real de Santo Antonio (vê'lä-rĕ-ä'l-dĕ-sän-tô-än-tô'nyô) Port.	37·14 N	7·25 W
166	Vila Rocadas (rô-kä'däs)....Ang.	16·50 S	15·05 E
124	Vila Vicosa (vē-sō'zä).......Port.	38·47 N	7·24 W
128	Vileyka (vê-lā'ē-kȧ).....Sov. Un.	54·19 N	26·58 E
112	Vilhelmina..................Swe.	64·37 N	16·30 E
119	Viljandi (vēl'yän-dê)....Sov. Un.	58·24 N	25·34 E
168	Viljoenskroon............S. Afr. (Johannesburg & Pretoria In.)	27·13 S	26·58 E
119	Vilkaviškis (vêl-kȧ-vēsh'kēs) Sov. Un.	54·40 N	23·08 E
119	Vilkija (vêl-kē'ēä).......Sov. Un.	55·04 N	23·30 E
134	Vil'kitskogo (I.) (vyl-kēts-kōgō) Sov. Un.	73·25 N	76·00 E
133	Vilkovo (vĭl-kô-vô)......Sov. Un.	45·24 N	29·36 E
76	Villa Acuña (vêl'yä-kōō'n-yä) Mex.	29·20 N	100·56 W
76	Villa Ahumada (ä-ōō-mä'dä).Mex.	30·43 N	106·30 W
91	Villa Alta (San Ildefonso) (äl'tä) (sän ēl-dā-fōn'sō).Mex.	17·20 N	96·08 W
100	Villa Angela (vē'l-yä ȧ'n-ĸĕ-lä) Arg.	27·31 S	60·42 W
124	Villaba (vēl-yä'bä)...........Sp.	43·18 N	7·43 W
100	Villa Ballester (vē'l-yä-bäl-yĕs-tĕr) Arg. (In.)	34·18 S	58·33 W
98	Villa Bella (bĕ'l-yä)........Bol.	10·25 S	65·22 W
164	Villa Bens (bĕns)...........Mor.	27·54 N	12·41 W
124	Villablino (vêl-yä-blē'nō).....Sp.	42·58 N	6·18 W
124	Villacañas (vêl-yä-kän'yäs)....Sp.	39·39 N	3·20 W
124	Villacarrillo (vêl-yä-kä-rēl'yō) Sp.	38·09 N	3·07 W
120	Villach (fē'läĸ)..............Aus.	46·38 N	13·50 E
126	Villacidro (vē-lä-chē'drô)......It.	39·28 N	8·41 E
164	Villa Cisneros (vēl'yä thēs-nä'rōs) Sp. Sah.	23·45 N	16·04 W
101	Villa Constitución (kōn-stê-tōō-syōn') Arg. (Buenos Aires In.)	33·15 S	60·19 W
76	Villa Coronado (kō-rō-nä'dhō) Mex.	26·45 N	105·10 W
91	Villa Cuauhtémoc (vêl'yä-kōō-äŏŏ-tĕ'môk).Mex.	22·11 N	97·50 W
76	Villa de Allende (vēl'yä dä äl-yĕn'dä).Mex.	25·18 N	100·01 W
90	Villa de Alvarez (vēl'yä-dĕ-ä'l-vä-rĕz).Mex.	19·17 N	103·44 W
99	Villa de Cura (dĕ-kōō'rä) Ven. (In.)	10·03 N	67·29 W
90	Villa de Guadalupe (dĕ-gwä-dhä-lōō'pā).Mex.	23·22 N	100·44 W
90	Villa de Reyes (dä rä'yĕs)...Mex.	21·45 N	100·55 W
100	Villa Dolores (vēl'yä dō-lō'räs) Arg.	31·50 S	65·05 W
90	Villa Escalante (vēl'yä-ĕs-kä-lán'tĕ) Mex.	19·24 N	101·36 W
125	Villafamés (vēl'yä-fä-mās')....Sp.	40·07 N	0·05 W
91	Villa Flores (vēl'yä-flō'räs)...Mex.	16·13 N	93·17 W
126	Villafranca (vēl-lä-fräŋ'kä)....It.	45·22 N	10·53 E
124	Villafranca del Bierzo (vēl-yä-fräŋ'kä dĕl byĕr'thō).Sp.	42·37 N	6·49 W

ng-sing; ŋ-baŋk; N-nasalized n; nŏd; cŏmmit; ōld; ôbey; ôrder; fōōd; fŏŏt; ou-out; s-soft; sh-dish; th-thin; pūre; ûnite; ûrn; stŭd; circŭs; ü-as "y" in study; '-indeterminate vowel.

282 Villafranca de los Barros–Wabash PRONOUNCING INDEX

Page	Name Pronunciation Region	Lat. °′	Long. °′
124	Villafranca de los Barros (vēl-yä-fräŋ′kä dā lōs bär′rōs) Sp.	38·34 N	6·22 W
125	Villafranca del Panadés (vēl-yä frän′kä děl pä-nä-dās′) Sp.	41·20 N	1·40 E
90	Villa García (gär-sē′ä) . . . . . . Mex.	22·07 N	101·55 W
124	Villagarcia (vēl′yä-gär-thē′ä) . . Sp.	42·38 N	8·43 W
168	Villaggio Duca degli Abruzzi Som. (Horn of Afr. In.)	2·40 N	45·20 E
76	Villagran (vēl-yä-grän′) . . . . . Mex.	24·28 N	99·30 W
80	Villa Grove (vĭl′ȧ grōv′) . . . . Ill.	39·55 N	88·15 W
100	Villaguay (vē′l-yä-gwī) . . . . Arg.	31·47 N	58·53 W
100	Villa Hayes (vēl′yä äyȧs) (hāz) Par.	25·07 S	57·31 W
91	Villahermosa (vēl′yä-ĕr-mō′sä) Mex.	17·59 N	92·56 W
90	Villa Hidalgo (vēl′yäē-däl′gō) Mex.	21·39 N	102·41 W
125	Villajoyosa (vēl′yä-hô-yō′sä) . . Sp.	38·30 N	0·14 W
76	Villaldama (vēl-yäl-dä′mä) . . Mex.	26·30 N	100·26 W
76	Villa Lopez (vēl′yä lō′pěz) . . . Mex.	27·00 N	105·02 W
124	Villalpando (vēl-yäl-pän′dō) . . . Sp.	41·54 N	5·24 W
100	Villa María (vē′l-yä-mä-rē′ä) . Arg.	32·17 S	63·08 W
124	Villamatín (vēl-yä-mä-tē′n) . . . Sp.	36·50 N	5·38 W
100	Villa Mercedes (měr-sā′dȧs) . . Arg.	33·38 S	65·16 W
98	Villa Montes (vē′l-yä-mô′n-těs) Bol.	21·13 S	63·26 W
90	Villa Morelos (mô-rě′lōs) . . . . Mex.	20·01 N	101·24 W
98	Villanueva (vē′l-yä-nōōĕ′vä) . . Col.	10·44 N	73·08 W
92	Villanueva (vēl′yä-nwä′vä) . Hond.	15·19 N	88·02 W
90	Villanueva (vēl′yä-nōōĕ′vä) . . Mex.	22·25 N	102·53 W
124	Villanueva de Córdoba (vêl-yä-nwě′vä-dä kôr′dô-bä) Sp.	38·18 N	4·38 W
124	Villanueva de la Serena (lä sä-rā′nä) . Sp.	38·59 N	5·56 W
125	Villanueva y Geltrú (ēκěl-trōō′) Sp.	41·13 N	1·44 E
91	Villa Obregón (vē′l-yä-ô-brě-gô′n) Mex. (Mexico City In.)	19·21 N	99·11 W
76	Villa Ocampo (ô-käm′pō) . . . . Mex.	26·26 N	105·30 W
90	Villa Pedro Montoya (vēl′yä-pě′drō-môn-tô′yȧ) . Mex.	21·38 N	99·51 W
123	Villard-Bonnot (vēl-yär′bôn-nô′) Fr.	45·15 N	5·53 E
125	Villarreal (vêl-yär-rě-äl) . . . . . . Sp.	39·55 N	0·07 W
100	Villarrica (vēl-yä-rē′kä) . . . . . . Par.	25·55 S	56·23 W
124	Villarrobledo (vēl-yär-rô-blā′dhō) Sp.	39·15 N	2·37 W
124	Villa Sanjurjo (vêl-yä-sän-kōō′r-kō) . Sp.	35·15 N	3·55 W
90	Villa Union (vēl′yä-ōō-nyōn′) Mex.	23·10 N	106·14 W
98	Villavicencio (vē′l-yä-vē-sě′n-syō) Col. (In.)	4·09 N	73·38 W
125	Villaviciosa de Odón (vēl′yä-vē-thē-ō′sä dä ō-dōn′) Sp. (Madrid In.)	40·22 N	3·54 W
98	Villavieja (vē′l-yä-vē-ě′κä) Col. (In.)	3·13 N	75·13 W
100	Villazón (vē′l-yä-zô′n) . . . . Bol.	22·02 S	65·42 W
122	Villefranche-de-Lauragais (vēl-fränsh′dě-lô-rä-gā′) . . . . . Fr.	43·25 N	1·41 E
122	Villefranche-de-Rouergue (dě-rōō-ĕrg′) . Fr.	44·21 N	2·02 E
122	Villefranche sur-Saône (sür-sä-ōn′) . Fr.	45·59 N	4·43 E
123	Villejuif (vēl′zhüst′) Fr. (Paris In.)	48·48 N	2·22 E
87	Ville Marie . . . . Can.	47·18 N	79·22 W
125	Villena (vē-lyā′nä) . . . . Sp.	38·37 N	0·52 W
85	Villeneuve (vēl′nûv′) Can. (Edmonton In.)	53·40 N	113·49 W
123	Villeneuve-St. Georges (sǎN-zhôrzh′) . Fr. (Paris In.)	48·43 N	2·27 E
122	Villeneuve-sur-Lot (sür-lō′) . . . . Fr.	44·25 N	0·41 E
77	Ville Platte (vēl plăt′) . . . . La.	30·41 N	92·17 W
122	Villers Cotterêts (vē-är′kô-trā′) Fr. (Paris In.)	49·15 N	3·05 E
123	Villerupt (vēl′rüp′) . . . . Fr.	49·28 N	6·16 E
98	Villeta (vē′l-yě′tȧ) . . . . . . Col. (In.)	5·02 N	74·29 W
122	Villeurbanne (vēl-ûr-bän′) . . . . . Fr.	45·43 N	4·55 E
168	Villiers (vĭl′ĭ-ērs) . . . . S. Afr. (Johannesburg & Pretoria In.)	27·03 S	28·38 E
120	Villingen (fĭl′ĭng-ěn) . . . . Ger.	48·04 N	8·28 E
71	Villisca (vĭ-lĭs′kȧ) . . . . Iowa	40·56 N	94·56 W
143	Villupuram . . . . India	11·59 N	79·33 E
119	Vilnius (Wilno) (vĭl′nê-ōōs) Sov. Un.	54·40 N	25·26 E
119	Vilppula (vĭl′pŭ-lȧ) . . . . Fin.	62·01 N	24·24 E
111	Vilvoorde . . . . . . Bel. (Brussels In.)	50·56 N	4·25 E
135	Vilyuy (R.) (vēl′yȧ) . . . . . Sov. Un.	65·22 N	108·45 E
135	Vilyuysk (vē-lyōō′ĭsk′) . . . Sov. Un.	63·41 N	121·47 E
135	Vilyuyskiye Gory (Mts.) (vē-lyōōs-kē-yě) . Sov. Un.	67·45 N	109·45 E
118	Vimmerby (vĭm′ěr-bü) . . . . . . Swe.	57·41 N	15·51 E
120	Vimperk (vĭm-pěrk′) . . . . Czech.	49·04 N	13·41 E
101	Viña del Mar (vē′nyä děl mär′) Chile (Santiago In.)	33·00 S	71·33 W
82	Vinalhaven (vī-nȧl-hā′věn) . Maine	44·03 N	68·49 W
125	Vinaroz (vē-nä′rōth) . . . . Sp.	40·29 N	0·27 E
123	Vincennes (văN-sěn′) Fr. (Paris In.)	48·51 N	2·27 E
80	Vincennes (vĭn-zěnz′) . . . . Ind.	38·40 N	87·30 W
78	Vincent (vĭn′sěnt) . . . . Ala.	33·21 N	86·25 W
112	Vindelälven (R.) . . . . Swe.	65·02 N	18·30 E
112	Vindeln (vĭn′děln) . . . . Swe.	64·10 N	19·52 E
142	Vindhya Ra. (vĭnd′yä) . . . . . . India	22·30 N	75·50 E
81	Vineland (vīn′lănd) . . . . N. J.	39·30 N	75·00 W
151	Vinh (vên′y′) . . . . Viet.	18·38 N	105·42 E
124	Vinhais (vēn-yä′ēzh) . . . . Port.	41·51 N	7·00 W
84	Vinings (vī′nĭngz) Ga. (Atlanta In.)	33·52 N	84·28 W
73	Vinita (vĭ-nē′tȧ) . . . . Okla.	36·38 N	95·09 W
127	Vinkovci (vēn′kôv-tsě) . . . . . Yugo.	45·17 N	18·47 E

Page	Name Pronunciation Region	Lat. °′	Long. °′
129	Vinnitsa (vê′nêt-sȧ) . . . . . Sov. Un.	49·13 N	28·31 E
129	Vinnitsa (Oblast) . . . . Sov. Un.	48·45 N	28·01 E
136	Vinogradovo (vĭ-nô-grä′do-vô) Sov. Un. (Moscow In.)	55·25 N	38·33 E
47	Vinson Massif (Mtn.) . . . . Ant.	77·40 S	87·00 W
71	Vinton (vĭn′tŭn) . . . . Iowa	42·08 N	92·01 W
77	Vinton . . . . La.	30·12 N	93·35 W
143	Vinukonda . . . . India	16·05 N	79·48 E
84	Violet (vī′ô-lět) La. (New Orleans In.)	29·54 N	89·54 W
151	Virac (vê-räk′) . . . . Phil.	13·38 N	124·20 E
119	Virbalis (vêr′bá-lês) . . . . . Sov. Un.	54·38 N	22·55 E
86	Virden (vûr′děn) . . . . Can.	49·48 N	101·00 W
73	Virden . . . . Ill.	39·28 N	89·46 W
69	Virgin (R.) . . . . . . Ariz.-Nev.-Utah	36·51 N	113·50 W
71	Virginia (vēr-jĭn′yȧ) . . . . Minn.	47·32 N	92 36 W
168	Virginia . . . . S. Afr. (Johannesburg & Pretoria In.)	28·07 S	26·54 E
63	Virginia (State) . . . . U. S.	37·00 N	80·45 W
84	Virginia Beach . . Va. (Norfolk In.)	36·50 N	75·58 W
68	Virginia City . . . . Nev.	39·18 N	119·40 W
89	Virgin Is. (vûr′jĭn) . . . . N. A.	18·15 N	64·00 W
119	Virmo (vĭr′mô) . . . . Fin.	60·41 N	21·58 E
71	Viroqua (vĭ-rō′kwȧ) . . . . Wis.	43·33 N	90·54 W
126	Virovitica (vê-rô-vē′tê-tsä) . Yugo.	45·50 N	17·24 E
127	Virpazar (vēr′pä-zär′) . . . . . . Yugo.	42·16 N	19·06 E
119	Virrat (vĭr′ät) . . . . Fin.	62·15 N	23·45 E
118	Virserum (vĭr′sě-rōōm) . . . . . . Swe.	57·22 N	15·35 E
126	Vis (vês) . . . . Yugo.	43·03 N	16·11 E
126	Vis (I.) . . . . Yugo.	43·00 N	16·10 E
126	Visa, Mt. (Mtn.) (vē′sä) . . . . It.	45·42 N	7·08 E
143	Visākhapatnan (vĭ-zä′kȧ-pŭt′nän) India	17·48 N	83·21 E
68	Visalia (vĭ-sā′lĭ-ȧ) . . . . Calif.	36·20 N	119·18 W
118	Visby (vĭs′bü) . . . . Swe.	57·39 N	18·19 E
49	Viscount Mellville Sound (vī′kount′) . Can.	74·80 N	110·00 W
127	Višegrad (vē′shě-gräd) . . . . . . Yugo.	43·45 N	19·19 E
136	Vishera R. (vĭ′shě-rȧ) Sov. Un. (Urals In.)	60·40 N	58·46 E
136	Visim (vē′sĭm) . Sov. Un. (Urals In.)	57·38 N	59·32 E
118	Viskan (R.) . . . . Swe.	57·20 N	12·25 E
128	Višķi (vēs′kĭ) . . . . Sov. Un.	56·02 N	26·47 E
127	Visoko (vē′sô-kô) . . . . Yugo.	43·59 N	18·10 E
127	Vistonís (L.) (vēs′tô-nĭs) . . . . . Grc.	40·58 N	25·12 E
	Vistula, see Wisla		
127	Vitanovac (vē′tä′nô-vȧts) . . . Yugo.	43·44 N	20·50 E
128	Vitebsk (vē′tyěpsk) . . . . . Sov. Un.	55·12 N	30·16 E
128	Vitebsk (Oblast) . . . . Sov. Un.	55·05 N	29·18 E
126	Viterbo (vē-těr′bō) . . . . It.	42·24 N	12·08 E
135	Vitim (vē′têm) . . . . Sov. Un.	59·22 N	112·43 E
135	Vitim (R.) (vē′têm) . . . . . Sov. Un.	56·12 N	115·30 E
136	Vitino (vē′tĭ-nô) Sov. Un. (Leningrad In.)	59·40 N	29·51 E
99	Vitória (vê-tō′rē-ä) . . . . Braz.	20·09 S	40·17 W
124	Vitoria (vē-tô-ryä) . . . . Sp.	42·43 N	2·43 W
99	Vitória da Conquista (-dä-kōn-kwē′s-tä) . Braz.	14·51 S	40·44 W
122	Vitré (vē-trā′) . . . . Fr.	48·09 N	1·15 W
122	Vitrolles (vē-trōl′) Fr. (Marseille In.)	43·27 N	5·15 E
122	Vitry-le-François (vē-trē′lě-fräN-swȧ′) . Fr.	48·44 N	4·34 E
113	Vittoria (vē-tô′rê-ô) . . . . It.	37·01 N	14·31 E
126	Vittorio (vē-tô′rê-ô) . . . . It.	45·59 N	12·17 E
155	Vitu Is. (vē′tōō) . . . . N. Gui. Ter.	4·45 S	149·50 E
124	Vivero (vê-vä′rō) . . . . Sp.	43·39 N	7·37 W
77	Vivian (vĭv′ĭ-ȧn) . . . . La.	32·51 N	93·59 W
127	Vize (vē′zě) . . . . Tur.	41·34 N	27·46 E
143	Vizianagram (vē-zē-ȧ-nŭ′grŭm′) India	18·10 N	83·29 E
111	Vlaardingen (vlär′dĭng-ěn) Neth. (Amsterdam In.)	51·54 N	4·20 E
128	Vladimir (vlä-dyē′mēr) . . Sov. Un.	56·08 N	40·24 E
128	Vladimir (Oblast) (vlä-dyē′mēr) Sov. Un.	56·08 N	39·53 E
152	Vladimiro-Aleksandrovskoye (vlȧ-dyē′mē-rô ȧ-lěk-sän′drôf-skô-yě) . Sov. Un.	42·50 N	133·00 E
121	Vladimir-Volynskiy (vlȧ-dyē′mēr vô-lēn′skĭ) Sov. Un.	50·50 N	24·20 E
135	Vladivostok (vlȧ-dê-vôs-tôk′) Sov. Un.	43·06 N	131·47 E
127	Vlasenica (vlä′sě-nēt′sä) . . . . Yugo.	44·11 N	18·58 E
127	Vlasotinci (vlä′sô-tēn-tsě) . . . Yugo.	42·58 N	22·08 E
117	Vlieland (I.) (vlē′länt) . . . . . . Neth.	53·19 N	4·55 E
117	Vlissingen (vlĭs′sĭng-ěn) . . . . . . Neth.	51·30 N	3·34 E
127	Vlorë (Valona) (vlō′rŭ) . . . . Alb.	40·28 N	19·31 E
120	Vltana R. . . . . Czech.	49·24 N	14·18 E
132	Vodl (L.) (vôd″l) . . . . Sov. Un.	62·20 N	37·20 E
167	Vogel (R.) (vô′gěl) S. Afr. (Natal In.)	32·52 S	25·12 E
155	Vogelkop Pen. (fō′gěl-kôp) W. Irian	1·25 S	133·15 E
126	Voghera (vô-gā′rä) . . . . It.	44·58 N	9·02 E
167	Vohémar (vô-ā-mär′) . Malag. Rep.	13·35 S	50·05 E
65	Voight (R.) . . . Wash. (Seattle In.)	47·03 N	122·08 W
123	Voiron (vwä-rôN′) . . . . Fr.	45·23 N	5·48 E
127	Voïvïïs (L.) . . . . Grc.	39·34 N	22·50 E
129	Volchansk (vôl-chänsk′) . Sov. Un.	50·18 N	36·56 E
129	Volch′ya (R.) (vôl-chyä′) . Sov. Un.	49·42 N	34·39 E
133	Volga (R.) (vôl′gä) . . . . . . Sov. Un.	47·30 N	46·20 E
133	Volga, Mouths of the . . . . Sov. Un.	46·00 N	49·10 E
113	Volgograd (Stalingrad) (vŏl′gō-grä′t) (stä′lēn-grat) Sov. Un.	48·40 N	42·20 E
133	Volgogradskoye (Res.) (vôl-gō-grad′skô-yě) . Sov. Un.	51·10 N	45·10 E
128	Volkhov (vôl′kôf) . . . . Sov. Un.	59·54 N	32·21 E
128	Volkhov (R.) . . . . Sov. Un.	58·45 N	31·40 E
121	Volkovysk (vôl-kô-vēsk′) . Sov. Un.	53·11 N	24·29 E
85	Volmer (vŏl′měr) Can. (Edmonton In.)	53·43 N	113·40 W
136	Volodarskiy (vô-lô-där′skĭ) Sov. Un. (Leningrad In.)	59·49 N	30·06 E

Page	Name Pronunciation Region	Lat. °′	Long. °′
128	Vologda (vô′lôg-dȧ) . . . . . Sov. Un.	59·12 N	39·52 E
128	Vologda (Oblast) . . . . Sov. Un.	59·00 N	37·26 E
129	Volokonovka (vô-lô-kô′nôf-kȧ) Sov. Un.	50·28 N	37·52 E
128	Volokolamsk (vô-lô-kôlȧmsk) Sov. Un.	56·02 N	35·58 E
127	Vólos (vô′lôs) . . . . Grc.	39·23 N	22·56 E
128	Volozhin (vô′lô-shên) . . . . Sov. Un.	54·04 N	26·38 E
133	Vol′sk (vôl′sk) . . . . Sov. Un.	52·10 N	47·00 E
164	Volta R. (vôl′tȧ) . . . . Ghana	8·15 N	0·57 W
101	Volta Redonda (vōl′tä-rä-dôn′dä) Braz. (Rio de Janeiro In.)	22·32 S	44·05 W
126	Volterra (vôl-těr′rä) . . . . It.	43·22 N	10·51 E
126	Voltri (vōl′trē) . . . . It.	44·25 N	8·45 E
126	Volturno (R.) (vôl-tōōr′nô) . . . . It.	41·12 N	14·20 E
128	Volzhskoye (L.) (vôl′sh-skô-yě) Sov. Un.	56·43 N	36·18 E
74	Von Ormy (vŏn ôr′mê) Tex. (San Antonio In.)	29·18 N	98·36 W
128	Vōōpsu (vōōp′-sōō) . . . . . . Sov. Un.	58·06 N	27·30 E
111	Voorberg . . Neth. (Amsterdam In.)	52·04 N	4·21 E
167	Voortrekkerhoogte . . . . S. Afr. (Johannesburg & Pretoria In.)	25·48 S	28·10 E
168	Voortrekkerspos (vôr′trě-kērs-pŏs) . S. Afr. (Johannesburg & Pretoria In.)	24·12 S	27·00 E
128	Vop′ (R.) (vôp) . . . . Sov. Un.	55·20 N	32·40 E
112	Vopnafjördhur . . . . Ice.	65·43 N	14·58 W
120	Vorarlberg (Prov.) . . . . Aus.	47·20 N	9·55 E
118	Vordingborg (vôr′dĭng-bôr) . . Den.	55·10 N	11·55 E
127	Voríai (Is.) . . . . Grc.	39·12 N	24·03 E
127	Vorios Evvïkós Kólpos (G.) . . Grc.	38·48 N	23·02 E
132	Vorkuta (vôr-kōō′tȧ) . . . . Sov. Un.	67·28 N	63·40 E
119	Vormsi (I.) (vôrm′sĭ) . . . . Sov. Un.	59·06 N	23·05 E
133	Vorona (R.) (vô-rô′nȧ) . . . Sov. Un.	51·50 N	42·00 E
132	Voron′ya (R.) (vô-rô′nyȧ) Sov. Un.	68·20 N	35·20 E
129	Voronezh (vô-rô′nyězh) . . Sov. Un.	51·39 N	39·11 E
129	Voronezh (Oblast) . . . . Sov. Un.	51·10 N	39·13 E
128	Voronezh (R.) . . . . Sov. Un.	52·17 N	39·32 E
121	Voronovo (vô′rô-nô-vô) . . Sov. Un.	54·07 N	25·16 E
136	Vorontsovka (vô-rônt′sôv-kȧ) Sov. Un. (Urals In.)	59·40 N	60·14 E
128	Võrts-Järv (L.) (vôrts yärv) Sov. Un.	58·15 N	26·12 E
128	Võru (vô′rû) . . . . Sov. Un.	57·50 N	26·58 E
136	Vorya R. (vôr′yȧ) Sov. Un. (Moscow In.)	55·55 N	38·15 E
123	Vosges (Mts.) (vōzh) . . . . Fr.	48·09 N	6·57 E
136	Voskresensk (vôs-krě-sěnsk′) Sov. Un. (Moscow In.)	55·20 N	38·42 E
118	Voss (vôs) . . . . Nor.	60·40 N	6·24 E
132	Votkinsk (vôt-kēnsk′) . . . Sov. Un.	57·00 N	54·00 E
124	Vouga (R.) (vō′gȧ) . . . . Port.	40·43 N	7·51 W
122	Vouziers (vōō-zyā′) . . . . Fr.	49·25 N	4·40 E
118	Voxna älv (R.) . . . . Swe.	61·30 N	15·24 E
132	Vozhe (L.) (vôzh′yě) . . . . Sov. Un.	60·40 N	39·00 E
129	Voznesensk (vôz-nyě-sěnsk′) Sov. Un.	47·34 N	31·22 E
130	Vrangelya (Wrangel) (I.) . Sov. Un.	71·25 N	173·38 E
127	Vranje (vrän′yě) . . . . Yugo.	42·33 N	21·55 E
127	Vratsa (vrät′tsȧ) . . . . Bul.	43·12 N	23·31 E
127	Vrbas (v′r′bȧs) . . . . Yugo.	45·34 N	19·43 E
126	Vrbas (R.) . . . . Yugo.	44·25 N	17·17 E
120	Vrchlabi (v′r′chlȧ-bě) . . . . . . Czech.	50·32 N	15·51 E
168	Vrede (vrĭ′dě) (vrēd) . . . . . . S. Afr. (Johannesburg & Pretoria In.)	27·25 S	29·11 E
168	Vredefort (vrĭ′dě-fôrt) (vrēd′fôrt) S. Afr. (Johannesburg & Pretoria In.)	27·00 S	27·21 E
111	Vreeswijk . Neth. (Amsterdam In.)	52·00 N	5·06 E
127	Vršac (v′r′shȧts) . . . . Yugo.	45·08 N	21·18 E
121	Vrutky (vrōōt′kě) . . . . Czech.	49·09 N	18·55 E
166	Vryburg (vrī′bûrg) . . . . S. Afr.	26·55 S	29·45 E
166	Vryheid (vrī′hīt) . . . . S. Afr.	27·43 S	30·58 E
121	Vsetín (fsět′yēn) . . . . Czech.	49·21 N	18·01 E
136	Vsevolozhskiy (vsyě′vôlô′zh-skēē) Sov. Un. (Leningrad In.)	60·01 N	30·41 E
94	Vuelta Abajo (Mts.) (vwěl′tä ä-bä′hō) . Cuba	22·20 N	83·45 W
111	Vught . . . . Neth. (Amsterdam In.)	51·38 N	5·18 E
127	Vukovar (vōō′kô-vär) . . . . . . Yugo.	45·20 N	19·00 E
80	Vulcan (vŭl′kăn) . . . . Mich.	45·45 N	87·50 W
126	Vulcano (I.) (vōōl-kä′nô) . . . . . . It.	38·23 N	15·00 E
127	Vŭlchedrŭm . . . . Bul.	43·43 N	23·29 E
119	Vyartsilya (vyär-tsē′lyä) . Sov. Un.	62·10 N	30·40 E
132	Vyatka (R.) (vyät′kȧ) . . . Sov. Un.	58·25 N	51·25 E
152	Vyazemskiy (vyȧ-zěm′skĭ) Sov. Un.	47·29 N	134·39 E
128	Vyaz′ma (vyȧz′mȧ) . . . . . Sov. Un.	55·12 N	34·17 E
132	Vyazniki (vyȧz′nê-kê) . . . Sov. Un.	56·10 N	42·10 E
119	Vyborg (Viipuri) (vwē′bôrk) Sov. Un.	60·43 N	28·46 E
132	Vychegda (R.) (vē′chěg-dȧ) Sov. Un.	61·40 N	48·00 E
132	Vyg (L.) . . . . Sov. Un.	63·40 N	35·00 E
132	Vym (R.) (vwēm) . . . . Sov. Un.	63·15 N	51·20 E
136	Vyritsa (vē′rĭ-tsȧ) Sov. Un. (Leningrad In.)	59·24 N	30·20 E
128	Vyshnevolotskoye (L.) (vŭy′sh-ŋě′vôlôt′s-kô′yě) Sov. Un.	57·30 N	34·27 E
128	Vyshniy Volochëk (vêsh′nyĭ vôl-ô-chěk′) . Sov. Un.	57·34 N	34·35 E
120	Výškov (vêsh′kôf) . . . . Czech.	49·17 N	16·58 E
120	Vysoké Myto (vŭ′sô-kä mû′tô) Czech.	49·58 N	16·07 E
128	Vysokovsk (vĭ-sô′kôfsk) . . Sov. Un.	56·16 N	36·32 E
132	Vytegra (vŭ′těg-rȧ) . . . . . . Sov. Un.	61·00 N	36·20 E
132	Vyur . . . . Sov. Un.	57·55 N	27·00 E
117	Waal (L.) (väl) . . . . Neth.	51·46 N	5·00 E
111	Waalwijk . Neth. (Amsterdam In.)	51·41 N	5·05 E
87	Wabana (wä bä-nä) Can. (Newfoundland In.)	47·32 N	52·29 W
80	Wabash (wô′băsh) . . . . Ind.	40·45 N	85·50 W
80	Wabash (R.) . . . . Ill.-Ind.	38·00 N	88·00 W

ăt; finȧl; rāte; senâte; ärm; àsk; sofȧ; fâre; ch-choose; dh-as th in other; bē: êvent; bět; recěnt; cratēr; g-go; gh-guttural g; bĭt; ĭ-short neutral; rīde; κ-guttural k as ch in German ich;

PRONOUNCING INDEX Wabasha–Waukegan 283

Page	Name Pronunciation Region	Lat. °'	Long. °'
71	Wabasha (wä'bȧ-shô) Minn.	44·24 N	92·04 W
121	Wabrzeźno (vôn-bzězh'nô) Pol.	53·17 N	18·59 E
79	Waccamaw (R.) (wăk'ȧ-mô) S. C.	33·47 N	78·55 W
78	Waccasassa B. (wă-kȧ-să'sȧ) Fla.	29·02 N	83·10 W
111	Wachow (vä'kōv) Ger. (Berlin In.)	52·32 N	12·46 E
77	Waco (wā'kō) Tex.	31·35 N	97·06 W
153	Wadayama (wä'dä'yä-mä) Jap.	35·19 N	134·49 E
117	Waddenzee (Sea) Neth.	53·00 N	4·50 E
86	Waddington, Mt. (wŏd'dĭng-tŭn) Can.	51·30 N	125·23 W
165	Wadelai (wä-dĕ-lä'ē) Ug.	2·45 N	31·34 E
71	Wadena (wŏ-dē'nȧ) Minn.	46·26 N	95·09 W
79	Wadesboro (wādz'bŭr-ō) N. C.	34·57 N	80·05 W
165	Wādi Halfa (wä'dē häl'fä) Sud.	21·58 N	31·23 E
139	Wadī Musa Jordan (Palestine In.)	30·19 N	35·29 E
79	Wadley (wŏd'lē) Ga.	32·54 N	82·25 W
165	Wad Medani (wäd mē-dä'nē) Sud.	14·27 N	33·31 E
121	Wadowice (vȧ-dô'vēt-sĕ) Pol.	49·53 N	19·31 E
87	Wager B. (wā'jẽr) Can.	65·48 N	88·19 W
160	Wagga Wagga (wôg'ȧ wôg'ȧ) Austl.	35·10 S	147·30 E
73	Wagoner (wăg'ŭn-ẽr) Okla.	35·58 N	95·22 W
72	Wagon Mound (wăg'ŭn mound) N. Mex.	35·59 N	104·45 W
121	Wagrowiec (vôn-grô'vyĕts) Pol.	52·47 N	17·14 E
70	Wahoo (wä-hōō') Nebr.	41·14 N	96·39 W
70	Wahpeton (wô'pē-tŭn) N. D.	46·17 N	96·38 W
157	Waialua (wä'ē-ä-lōō'ä) Hawaii (In.)	21·33 N	158·08 W
157	Waianae (wä'ē-ä-nä'ā) Hawaii (In.)	21·25 N	158·11 W
120	Waidhofen (vīd'hôf-ĕn) Aus.	47·58 N	14·46 E
155	Waigeo (I.) (wä-ē-gä'ō) W. Irian	0·07 N	131·00 E
149	Waikang (wäī'käng) China (Shanghai In.)	31·23 N	121·11 E
159	Waikato (R.) (wä'ē-kä'to) N. Z. (In.)	38·00 S	175·47 E
160	Waikerie (wā'kẽr-ē) Austl.	34·15 S	140·00 E
157	Wailuku (wä'ē-lōō'kōō) Hawaii (In.)	20·55 N	156·30 W
157	Waimanalo (wä-ē-mä'nä-lô) Hawaii (In.)	21·19 N	157·53 W
157	Waimea (wä-ē-mā'ä) Hawaii (In.)	20·01 N	155·40 W
157	Waimea Hawaii (In.)	21·56 N	159·38 W
142	Wainganga (R.) (wä-ēn-gŭn'gä) India	20·24 N	79·41 E
154	Waingapu Indon.	9·32 S	120·00 E
64	Wainwright (wān-rīt) Alaska	74·40 N	159·00 W
86	Wainwright Can.	52·53 N	110·40 W
157	Waipahu (wä'ē-pä'hōō) Hawaii (In.)	21·20 N	158·02 W
74	Waiska R. (wȧ-ĭz-kȧ) Mich. (Sault Ste. Marie In.)	46·20 N	84·38 W
66	Waitsburg (wāts'bûrg) Wash.	46·17 N	118·08 W
153	Wajima (wä'jē-mä) Jap.	37·23 N	136·56 E
153	Wakamatsu (wä-kä'mät-sōō) Jap.	33·54 N	130·44 E
153	Wakamatsu Jap.	37·27 N	139·51 E
153	Wakasa-Wan (B.) (wä'kä-sä wän) Jap.	35·43 N	135·39 E
159	Wakatipu (R.) (wä-kä-tē'pōō) N. Z. (In.)	44·24 S	169·00 E
153	Wakayama (wä-kä'yä-mä) Jap.	34·14 N	135 11 E
156	Wake (I.) (wāk) Oceania	15·30 N	165·00 E
72	Wakeeney (wô-kē'nē) Kans.	39·01 N	99·53 W
85	Wakefield (wāk-fēld) Can. (Ottawa In.)	45·39 N	75·55 W
110	Wakefield Eng.	53·41 N	1·25 W
83	Wakefield Mass. (Boston In.)	42·31 N	71·05 W
71	Wakefield Mich.	46·28 N	89·55 W
70	Wakefield Nebr.	42·15 N	96·52 W
84	Wakefield R. I. (Providence In.)	41·26 N	71·30 W
79	Wake Forest (wāk fŏr'ĕst) N. C.	35·58 N	78·31 W
153	Waki (wä'kē) Jap.	34·05 N	134·10 E
152	Wakkanai (wä'kä-nä'ē) Jap.	45·19 N	141·43 E
166	Wakkerstroom (vȧk'ẽr-strōm) (wăk'ẽr-strōōm) S. Afr.	27·19 S	30·04 E
120	Walbrzych (väl'bzhûk) Pol.	50·46 N	16·16 E
82	Waldoboro (wôl'dô-bŭr-ô) Maine	44·06 N	69·22 W
66	Waldo L. (wôl'dō) Ore.	43·46 N	122·10 W
74	Waldron (wôl'drŭn) Mo. (Kansas City In.)	39·14 N	94·47 W
65	Waldron (I.) Wash. (Vancouver In.)	48·42 N	123·02 W
64	Wales (wālz) Alaska	65·35 N	168·14 W
116	Wales U. K.	52·12 N	3·40 W
120	Wałez (välch) Pol.	53·16 N	16·30 E
160	Walgett (wôl'gĕt) Austl.	30·00 S	148·10 E
47	Walgreen Coast (wôl'grĕn) Ant.	73·00 S	110·00 W
78	Walhalla (wŏl-hăl'ȧ) S. C.	34·45 N	83·04 W
71	Walker (wôk'ẽr) Minn.	47·06 N	94·37 W
68	Walker (R.) Nev.	39·07 N	119·10 W
65	Walker, Mt. Wash. (Seattle In.)	47·47 N	122·54 W
68	Walker L. Nev.	38·46 N	118·30 W
68	Walker River Ind. Res. Nev.	39·06 N	118·20 W
67	Walkerville (wôk'ẽr-vĭl) Mont.	46·20 N	112·32 W
66	Wallace (wŏl'ās) Idaho	47·27 N	115·55 W
161	Wallacia Austl. (Sydney In.)	33·52 S	150·40 E
66	Wallapa B. (wŏl ȧ pä) Wash.	46·39 N	124·30 W
160	Wallaroo (wŏl-ȧ-rōō) Austl.	33·52 S	137·45 E
110	Wallasey (wŏl'ȧ-sē) Eng.	53·25 N	3·03 W
66	Walla Walla (wŏl'ȧ wŏl'ȧ) Wash.	46·03 N	118·20 W
75	Walled Lake (wôl'd lāk) Mich. (Detroit In.)	42·32 N	83·29 W
165	Wallel, Tulu (Mt.) Eth.	9·00 N	34·52 E
110	Wallingford (wŏl'ĭng-fẽrd) Eng. (London In.)	51·34 N	1·08 W
81	Wallingford Vt.	43·30 N	72·55 W
156	Wallis Is. Oceania	13·00 S	183·50 E
77	Wallisville (wŏl'ĭs-vĭl) Tex. (In.)	29·50 N	94·44 W
66	Wallowa (wôl'ô-wȧ) Ore.	45·34 N	117·32 W
66	Wallowa Mts. Ore.	45·10 N	117·22 W
66	Wallowa R. Ore.	45·28 N	117·28 W
116	Walney (C.) (wôl'nē) Eng.	54·04 N	3·13 W
74	Walnut (wôl'nŭt) Calif. (Los Angeles In.)	34·00 N	117·51 W
73	Walnut (R.) Kans.	37·28 N	97·06 W
69	Walnut Canyon Natl. Mon. Ariz.	35·10 N	111·30 W
65	Walnut Creek Calif. (San Francisco In.)	37·54 N	122·04 W
74	Walnut Cr. Tex. (Dallas, Fort Worth In.)	32·37 N	97·03 W
73	Walnut Ridge (rĭj) Ark.	36·04 N	90·56 W
83	Walpole (wôl'pōl) Mass. (Boston In.)	42·09 N	71·15 W
81	Walpole N. H.	43·05 N	72·25 W
110	Walsall (wôl-sôl) Eng.	52·35 N	1·58 W
72	Walsenburg (wôl'sĕn-bûrg) Colo.	37·38 N	104·46 W
72	Walters (wôl'tẽrz) Okla.	34·21 N	98·19 W
83	Waltham (wôl'thăm) Mass. (Boston In.)	42·22 N	71·14 W
110	Walthamstow (wôl'tăm-stō) Eng. (London In.)	51·34 N	0·01 W
81	Walton (wôl'tŭn) N. Y.	42·10 N	75·05 W
110	Walton-le-Dale (lē-dāl') Eng.	53·44 N	2·40 W
166	Walvis Bay (wôl'vĭs) S. Afr.	22·50 S	14·30 E
71	Walworth (wôl'wŭrth) Wis.	42·33 N	88·39 W
165	Wamba (wăm'bä) Con. L.	2·15 N	28·05 E
166	Wamba (R.) Con. L.	6·45 S	17·51 E
73	Wamego (wŏ-mē'gō) Kans.	39·13 N	96·17 W
167	Wami (R.) (wä'mē) Tan.	6·31 S	37·17 E
84	Wanaque (wŏn'ȧ-kū) N. J. (New York In.)	41·03 N	74·16 W
84	Wanaque Res. N. J. (New York In.)	41·06 N	74·20 W
148	Wanchih (wän'chĭ') China	31·11 N	118·31 E
111	Wandsbek (vänds'bĕk) Ger. (Hamburg In.)	53·34 N	10·07 E
110	Wandsworth (wŏndz'wûrth) Eng.	51·26 N	0·12 W
159	Wanganui (wŏn'gȧ-nōō'ē) N. Z. (In.)	39·53 S	175·01 E
160	Wangaratta (wŏn'gȧ-răt'ȧ) Austl.	36·23 S	146·18 E
152	Wangching (wäng'chĕng) China	43·14 N	129·33 E
148	Wangch'ingt'o (wäng'chĭng'tōōŭ) China	39·14 N	116·56 E
120	Wangeroog I. (vän'gĕ-rōg) Ger.	53·49 N	7·57 E
151	Wanhsien (wän'hsyĕn') China	30·48 N	108·22 E
148	Wanhsien (wän'sĭän) China	38·51 N	115·10 E
166	Wankie (wăn'kē) S. Rh.	18·27 S	26·30 E
110	Wantage (wŏn'tăj) Eng. (London In.)	51·33 N	1·26 W
151	Wantsai China	28·05 N	114·25 E
160	Waodoan (wôd'ôn) Austl.	26·12 S	149·52 E
80	Wapakoneta (wä'pȧ-kô-nĕt'ȧ) Ohio	40·35 N	84·10 W
71	Wapello (wŏ-pĕl'ō) Iowa	41·10 N	91·11 W
73	Wappapello Res. (wä'pȧ-pĕl-lō) Mo.	37·07 N	90·10 W
81	Wappingers Falls (wŏp'ĭn-jẽrz) N. Y.	41·35 N	73·55 W
71	Wapsipinicon (R.) (wŏp'sĭ-pĭn'ĭ-kŏn) Iowa	42·16 N	91·35 W
153	Warabi (wä'rä-bē) Jap. (Tōkyō In.)	35·50 N	139·41 E
143	Warangal (wŭ'răn-gȧl) India	18·03 N	17·39 E
158	Warburton, The (R.) (wŏr'bûr-tŭn) Austl.	27·30 S	138·45 E
139	Wardan (R.) U. A. R. (Egypt) (Palestine In.)	29·29 N	32·52 E
168	Warden (wôr'dĕn) S. Afr. (Johannesburg & Pretoria In.)	27·52 S	28·59 E
142	Wardha (wŭr'dä) India	20·46 N	78·42 E
75	Wardsworth (wôrdz'wûrth) Ohio (Cleveland In.)	41·01 N	81·44 W
80	War Eagle (wôr ē'g'l) W. Va.	37·30 N	81·50 W
120	Waren (vä'rĕn) Ger.	53·32 N	12·43 E
123	Warendorf (vä'rĕn-dōrf) Ger. (Ruhr In.)	51·57 N	7·59 E
166	Warmbad (värm'bäd) (wôrm'băd) S. W. Afr.	28·25 S	18·45 E
168	Warmbad S. Afr. (Johannesburg & Pretoria In.)	24·52 S	28·18 E
65	Warm Beach (wôrm) Wash. (Seattle In.)	48·10 N	122·22 W
66	Warm Springs Ind. Res. (wôrm sprĭngz) Ore.	44·55 N	121·30 W
66	Warm Springs Res. Ore.	43·42 N	118·40 W
118	Warnemünde (vär'nĕ-mün-dĕ) Ger.	54·11 N	12·04 E
66	Warner Ra. (Mts.) (wôrn'ẽr) Calif.-Ore.	41·30 N	120·17 W
120	Warnow R. (vär'nō) Ger.	53·51 N	11·55 E
160	Warracknabeal Austl.	36·20 S	142·28 E
161	Warragamba (R.) Austl. (Sydney In.)	33·55 S	150·32 E
159	Warrego (R.) (wôr'ē-gô) Austl.	27·13 S	145·58 E
73	Warren (wŏr'ĕn) Ark.	33·37 N	92·03 W
80	Warren Ind.	40·40 N	85·25 W
75	Warren Mich. (Detroit In.)	42·33 N	83·03 W
70	Warren Minn.	48·11 N	96·44 W
80	Warren Ohio	41·15 N	80·50 W
65	Warren Ore. (Portland In.)	45·49 N	122·51 W
81	Warren Pa.	41·50 N	79·10 W
84	Warren R. I. (Providence In.)	41·44 N	71·14 W
75	Warrendale (wŏr'ĕn-dāl) Pa. (Pittsburgh In.)	40·39 N	80·04 W
73	Warrensburg (wŏr'ĕnz-bûrg) Mo.	38·45 N	93·42 W
85	Warrenton (wŏr'ĕn-tŭn) Can. (Winnipeg In.)	50·08 N	97·32 W
79	Warrenton Ga.	33·26 N	82·37 W
65	Warrenton Ore. (Portland In.)	46·10 N	123·56 W
81	Warrenton Va.	38·45 N	77·50 W
164	Warri (wär'ē) Nig.	5·33 N	5·43 E
110	Warrington Eng.	53·22 N	2·30 W
78	Warrington (wŏr'ĭng-tŭn) Fla.	30·21 N	87·15 W
160	Warrnambool (wôr'năm-bōōl) Austl.	36·20 S	142·28 E
71	Warroad (wôr'rōd) Minn.	48·55 N	95·20 W
159	Warrumbungle Ra. (wôr'ŭm-bŭn-g'l) Austl.	31·18 S	150·00 E
73	Warsaw (wôr'sô) Ill.	40·21 N	91·26 W
80	Warsaw Ind.	41·15 N	85·50 W
81	Warsaw N. Y.	42·45 N	78·10 W
79	Warsaw N. C.	35·00 N	78·07 W
	Warsaw, see Warszawa		
110	Warsop (wôr'sŭp) Eng.	53·13 N	1·05 W
121	Warszawa (Warsaw) (vȧr-shä'vȧ) Pol.	52·15 N	21·05 E
120	Warta R. (vär'tȧ) Pol.	52·35 N	15·07 E
167	Wartburg S. Afr. (Natal In.)	29·26 S	30·39 E
160	Warwick (wŏr'ĭk) Austl.	28·05 S	152·10 E
82	Warwick Can.	45·58 N	71·57 W
116	Warwick Eng.	52·19 N	1·46 W
84	Warwick N. Y. (New York In.)	41·15 N	74·22 W
84	Warwick R. I. (Providence In.)	41·42 N	71·27 W
110	Warwick (Co.) Eng.	52·22 N	1·34 W
74	Wasatch Mts. (wô'săch) Utah (Salt Lake City In.)	40·45 N	111·46 W
69	Wasatch Plat. Utah	38·55 N	111·40 W
62	Wasatch Ra. U. S.	39·10 N	111·30 W
167	Wasbank S. Afr. (Natal In.)	28·27 S	30·09 E
167	Waschbank Pk. (Mtn.) (väsh'bȧnk) S. Afr. (Natal In.)	31·17 S	27·26 E
66	Wasco (wăs'kō) Ore.	45·36 N	120·42 W
71	Waseca (wô-sē'kȧ) Minn.	44·04 N	93·31 W
117	Wash, The (Est.) (wŏsh) Eng.	53·00 N	0·20 E
82	Washburn (wŏsh'bŭrn) Maine	46·46 N	68·10 W
71	Washburn Wis.	46·41 N	90·55 W
67	Washburn, Mt. Wyo.	44·55 N	110·10 W
81	Washington (wŏsh'ĭng-tŭn) D. C.	38·50 N	77·00 W
78	Washington Ga.	33·43 N	82·46 W
80	Washington Ind.	38·40 N	87·10 W
71	Washington Iowa	41·17 N	91·42 W
73	Washington Kans.	39·48 N	97·04 W
73	Washington Mo.	38·33 N	91·00 W
79	Washington N. C.	35·32 N	77·01 W
75	Washington Pa. (Pittsburgh In.)	40·10 N	80·14 W
62	Washington (State) U. S.	47·30 N	121·10 W
81	Washington, Mt. N. H.	44·15 N	71·15 W
65	Washington, L. Wash. (Seattle In.)	47·34 N	122·12 W
71	Washington (I.) Wis.	45·18 N	86·42 W
80	Washington Court House Ohio	39·30 N	83·25 W
74	Washington Park Ill. (St. Louis In.)	38·38 N	90·06 W
72	Washita (R.) (wŏsh'ĭ-tô) Okla.	35·33 N	99·16 W
65	Washougal (wŏ-shōō'gȧl) Wash. (Portland In.)	45·35 N	122·21 W
65	Washougal (R.) Wash. (Portland In.)	45·38 N	122·17 W
121	Wasilkow (vȧ-sēl'kōōf) Pol.	53·12 N	23·13 E
123	Wassenberg (vä'sĕn-bĕrgh) Ger. (Ruhr In.)	51·06 N	6·07 E
68	Wassuk Ra. (wȧs'sŭk) Nev.	38·58 N	119·00 W
74	Watauga (wȧ tō gä') Tex. (Dallas, Fort Worth In.)	32·51 N	97·16 W
89	Water (I.) (wô'tẽr) Vir. Is. (U. S. A.) (St. Thomas In.)	18·20 N	64·57 W
168	Waterberg (Mts.) (wôrtẽr'bûrg) S. Afr. (Johannesburg & Pretoria In.)	24·25 S	27·53 E
79	Waterboro (wô'tẽr-bŭr-ō) S. C.	32·50 N	80·40 W
81	Waterbury (wô'tẽr-bĕr-ē) Conn.	41·30 N	73·00 W
82	Waterbury Vt.	44·20 N	72·44 W
95	Water Cay (I.) Ba. Is.	22·55 N	75·50 W
85	Waterdown (wô'tẽr-doun) Can. (Toronto In.)	43·20 N	79·54 W
79	Wateree (R.) (wô'tẽr-ē) S. C.	34·40 N	80·48 W
116	Waterford (wô'tẽr-fẽrd) Ire.	52·20 N	7·03 W
75	Waterford Wis. (Milwaukee In.)	42·46 N	88·13 W
167	Waterkloof S. Afr. (Johannesburg & Pretoria In.)	25·48 S	28·15 E
111	Waterloo Bel. (Brussels In.)	50·44 N	4·24 E
80	Waterloo (wô-tẽr-lōō') Can.	43·30 N	80·40 W
81	Waterloo Can.	45·25 N	72·30 W
73	Waterloo Ill.	38·19 N	90·08 W
71	Waterloo Iowa	42·30 N	92·22 W
81	Waterloo N. Y.	42·55 N	76·50 W
67	Waterton-Glacier Intl. Peace Park (wô'ter-tŭn-glā'shûr) Mont.-Can.	48·55 N	114·10 W
83	Watertown (wô'tẽr-toun) Mass. (Boston In.)	42·22 N	71·11 W
81	Watertown N. Y.	44·00 N	75·55 W
70	Watertown S. D.	44·53 N	97·07 W
71	Watertown Wis.	43·13 N	88·40 W
78	Water Valley (văl'ē) Miss.	34·08 N	89·38 W
82	Waterville (wô'tẽr-vĭl) Maine	44·34 N	69·37 W
71	Waterville Minn.	44·10 N	93·35 W
66	Waterville Wash.	47·38 N	120·04 W
81	Watervliet (wô'tẽr-vlēt') N. Y.	42·45 N	73·45 W
110	Watford (wŏt'fŏrd) Eng. (London In.)	51·38 N	0·24 W
	Watling I., see San Salvador I.		
110	Watlington (wŏt'lĭng-tŭn) Eng. (London In.)	51·37 N	1·01 W
72	Watonga (wŏ-tŏn'gȧ) Okla.	35·50 N	98·26 W
86	Watrous Can.	51·40 N	105·32 W
165	Watsa (wät'sä) Con. L.	3·02 N	29·30 E
80	Watseka (wŏt-sē'kȧ) Ill.	40·45 N	87·45 W
75	Watson (wŏt'sŭn) Ind. (Louisville In.)	38·21 N	85·42 W
86	Watson Lake Can.	60·18 N	128·50 W
68	Watsonville (wŏt'sŭn-vĭl) Calif.	36·55 N	121·46 W
123	Wattenscheid (vä'tĕn-shīd) Ger. (Ruhr In.)	51·30 N	7·07 E
74	Watts (wŏts) Calif. (Los Angeles In.)	33·56 N	118·15 W
78	Watts Bar (R.) (bär) Tenn.	35·45 N	84·49 W
165	Wau (wä'ōō) Sud.	7·41 N	28·00 E
165	Wāu al Kebir Libya	25·23 N	16·52 E
70	Waubay (wô'bā) S. D.	45·19 N	97·18 W
79	Wauchula (wô-chōō'lȧ) Fla. (In.)	27·32 N	81·48 W
75	Wauconda (wô-kŏn'dȧ) Ill. (Chicago In.)	42·15 N	88·08 W
75	Waukegan (wŏ-kē'găn) Ill. (Chicago In.)	42·22 N	87·51 W

ng-sing; ŋ-baŋk; N-nasalized n; nŏd; cŏmmit; ōld; ôbey; ôrder; fōōd; fōōt; ou-out; s-soft; sh-dish; th-thin; pūre; ûnite; ûrn; stŭd; circŭs; ü-as "y" in study; '-indeterminate vowel.

PRONOUNCING INDEX Weymouth–Winsford 285

Page	Name Pronunciation Region	Lat. °′	Long. °′
75	Weymouth .. Ohio (Cleveland In.)	41·11 N	81·48 W
94	Whale Cay (I.) ... Ba. Is.	24·50 N	77·45 W
94	Whale Cay Chans ... Ba. Is.	26·45 N	77·10 W
116	Wharfe (R.) (hwôr'fė) ... Eng.	54·01 N	1·53 W
84	Wharton (hwôr'tŭn) N. J. (New York In.)	40·54 N	74·35 W
77	Wharton ... Tex.	29·19 N	96·06 W
71	What Cheer (hwŏt chēr) ... Iowa	41·23 N	92·24 W
65	Whatcom, L. (hwät'kŭm) Wash. (Portland In.)	48·44 N	123·34 W
75	Wheatland (hwēt'lănd) Wis. (Milwaukee In.)	42·36 N	88·12 W
67	Wheatland ... Wyo.	42·04 N	104·52 W
75	Wheaton (hwē'tŭn) Ill. (Chicago In.)	41·52 N	88·06 W
81	Wheaton ... Md.	39·05 N	77·05 W
70	Wheaton ... Minn.	45·48 N	96·29 W
69	Wheeler Pk. (hwē'lẽr) ... Nev.	38·58 N	114·15 W
75	Wheeling (hwēl'ĭng) Ill. (Chicago In.)	42·08 N	87·54 W
80	Wheeling ... W. Va.	40·05 N	80·45 W
101	Wheelwright (ōōē'l-rē'gt) Arg. (Buenos Aires In.)	33·46 S	61·14 W
65	Whidbey I. (hwĭd'bė) Wash. (Seattle In.)	48·13 N	122·50 W
84	Whippany (hwĭp'ȧ-nē) N. J. (New York In.)	40·49 N	74·25 W
78	Whistler (hwĭs'lẽr) ... Ala.	30·46 N	88·07 W
81	Whitby (hwĭt'bė) ... Can.	43·50 N	79·00 W
110	Whitchurch (hwĭt'chûrch) ... Eng.	52·58 N	79·00 W
73	White (R.) ... Ark.	34·32 N	91·11 W
68	White Mt. ... Calif.	37·38 N	118·13 W
81	White (L.) ... Can.	45·15 N	76·35 W
71	White (L.) ... Can.	48·47 N	85·50 W
71	White (R.) ... Can.	48·34 N	85·46 W
69	White (R.) ... Colo.	40·10 N	108·55 W
80	White (R.) ... Ind.	39·15 N	86·45 W
70	White (R.) ... S. D.	43·41 N	99·48 W
70	White (R.), South Fork ... S. D.	43·13 N	101·04 W
72	White (R.) ... Tex.	36·25 N	102·20 W
81	White (R.) ... Vt.	43·45 N	72·35 W
83	White B. ... Can.	50·07 N	56·24 W
83	White Bear B. ... Can.	47·28 N	57·55 W
74	White Bear Lake ... Minn. (Minneapolis, St. Paul In.)	45·05 N	93·01 W
74	White Bear L. ... Minn. (Minneapolis, St. Paul In.)	45·04 N	92·58 W
77	White Castle ... La.	30·10 N	91·09 W
80	White Cloud ... Mich.	43·35 N	85·45 W
86	White Court ... Can.	54·09 N	115·34 W
70	White Earth (R.) ... N. D.	48·30 N	102·44 W
70	White Earth Ind. Res. ... Minn.	47·18 N	95·42 W
71	Whiteface (R.) (whīt'fās) ... Minn.	47·12 N	92·13 W
81	Whitefield (hwĭt'fēld) ... N. H.	44·20 N	71·35 W
67	Whitefish (hwĭt'fĭsh) ... Mont.	48·24 N	114·25 W
71	Whitefish (B.) ... Mich.	46·36 N	84·50 W
71	Whitefish (R.) ... Mich.	46·12 N	86·56 W
75	Whitefish Bay Wis. (Milwaukee In.)	43·07 N	77·54 W
73	White Hall ... Ill.	39·26 N	90·23 W
80	Whitehall (hwĭt'hôl) ... Mich.	43·20 N	86·20 W
81	Whitehall ... N. Y.	43·30 N	73·25 W
116	Whitehaven (hwĭt'hā-vĕn) ... Eng.	54·35 N	3·30 W
65	Whitehorn, Pt. (hwĭt'hôrn) Wash. (Vancouver In.)	48·54 N	122·48 W
86	Whitehorse (whīt'hôrs) ... Can.	60·39 N	135·01 W
84	White House . N. J. (New York In.)	40·37 N	74·46 W
77	White L. ... La.	29·40 N	92·35 W
82	White Mts. ... Maine	44·22 N	71·15 W
81	White Mts. ... N. H.	42·20 N	71·05 W
70	Whitemouth (L.) (hwĭt'mŭth) Can.	49·18 N	95·50 W
	White Nile, see El Abyad, Bahr		
71	White Otter (L.) ... Can.	49·15 N	91·48 W
86	White P. ... Alaska-Can.	59·35 N	135·03 W
84	White Plains N. Y. (New York In.)	41·02 N	73·47 W
80	White R., East Fork ... Ind.	38·45 N	86·20 W
66	White R. ... Wash.	47·07 N	121·48 W
69	White River Plat. ... Colo.	39·45 N	107·50 W
65	White Rock . Can. (Vancouver In.)	49·01 N	122·49 W
74	Whiterock Res. (hwĭt'rŏk) Tex. (Dallas, Fort Worth In.)	32·51 N	96·40 W
168	Whites (wīts) ... S. Afr. (Johannesburg & Pretoria In.)	28·02 S	27·00 E
69	White Sands Natl. Mon. . N. Mex.	32·50 N	106·20 W
132	White Sea ... Sov. Un.	66·00 N	40·00 E
74	White Settlement Tex. (Dallas, Fort Worth In.)	32·45 N	97·28 W
67	White Sulphur Springs ... Mont.	46·32 N	110·49 W
167	White Umfolosi (R.) (ŭm-fō-lō'zė) S. Afr. (Natal In.)	28·12 S	30·55 E
79	Whiteville (hwĭt'vĭl) ... N. C.	34·18 N	78·45 W
71	Whitewater (whit-wŏt'ẽr) ... Wis.	42·49 N	88·40 W
70	Whitewater (L.) ... Can.	49·14 N	100·39 W
79	Whitewater B. ... Fla. (In.)	25·16 N	80·21 W
67	Whitewater Cr. ... Mont.	48·50 N	107·50 W
75	Whitewater R. Ind. (Cincinnati In.)	39·19 N	84·55 W
78	Whitewell (hwĭt'wĕl) ... Tenn.	35·11 N	85·31 W
73	Whitewright (hwĭt'rĭt) ... Tex.	33·33 N	96·25 W
116	Whitham (R.) (wĭth'ăm) ... Eng.	53·08 N	0·15 W
75	Whiting (hwĭt'ĭng) Ind. (Chicago In.)	41·41 N	87·30 W
83	Whitinsville (hwĭt'ĕns-vĭl) Mass. (Boston In.)	42·06 N	71·40 W
83	Whitman (hwĭt'măn) Mass. (Boston In.)	42·05 N	70·57 W
66	Whitman Natl. Mon. ... Ore.	45·58 N	118·10 W
79	Whitmire (hwĭt'mīr) ... S. C.	34·30 N	81·40 W
68	Whitney, Mt. ... Calif.	36·34 N	118·18 W
77	Whitney L. (hwĭt'nė) ... Tex.	32·02 N	97·36 W
110	Whitstable (wĭt'stăb'l) Eng. (London In.)	51·22 N	1·03 E
159	Whitsunday (I.) (hwĭt's'n-dā) Austl.	20·16 S	149·00 E
74	Whittier (hwĭt'ĭ-ẽr) Calif. (Los Angeles In.)	33·58 N	118·02 W
167	Whittlesea (wĭt'l'sē) S. Afr. (Natal In.)	32·11 S	26·51 E
110	Whitworth (hwĭt'wûrth) ... Eng.	53·40 N	2·10 W
160	Whyalla (hwī-ăl'ȧ) ... Austl.	33·00 S	137·32 E
80	Wiarton (wī'ȧr-tŭn) ... Can.	44·45 N	80·45 W
73	Wichita (wĭch'ĭ-tô) ... Kans.	37·42 N	97·21 W
72	Wichita (R.) ... Tex.	33·50 N	99·38 W
72	Wichita Falls (fôls) ... Tex.	33·54 N	98·29 W
72	Wichita Mts. ... Okla.	34·48 N	98·43 W
116	Wick (wĭk) ... Scot.	58·25 N	3·05 W
84	Wickatunk (wĭk'ȧ-tŭnk) N. J. (New York In.)	40·21 N	74·15 W
84	Wickford (wĭk'fẽrd) R. I. (Providence In.)	41·34 N	71·26 W
75	Wickliffe (wĭk'klĭf) Ohio (Cleveland In.)	41·37 N	81·29 W
	Wicklow, see Cill Mantainn		
116	Wicklow Mts. (wĭk'lō) ... Ire.	52·49 N	6·20 W
65	Wickup Mtn. (wĭk'ŭp) Ore. (Portland In.)	46·06 N	123·35 W
81	Wiconisco (wĭ-kŏn'ĭs-kō) ... Pa.	40·35 N	76·45 W
80	Widen (wī'dĕn) ... W. Va.	38·25 N	80·55 W
110	Widnes (wĭd'nĕs) ... Eng.	53·21 N	2·44 W
120	Wieden (vē'dĕn) ... Ger.	49·41 N	12·09 E
121	Wieliczka (vyĕ-lēch'kȧ) ... Pol.	49·58 N	20·06 E
121	Wieluń (vyĕ'lōōn') ... Pol.	51·13 N	18·33 E
111	Wien (Vienna) (vēn) (vė-ĕn'ȧ) Aus. (Vienna In.)	48·13 N	16·22 E
111	Wien (State) ... Aus. (Vienna In.)	48·11 N	16·23 E
120	Wiener Neustadt (vē'nẽr noi'shtät) .. Aus.	47·48 N	16·15 E
111	Wiener Wald (For.) Aus. (Vienna In.)	48·09 N	16·05 E
121	Wieprz, R. (vyĕpzh) ... Pol.	51·25 N	22·45 E
77	Wiergate (wẽr'gāt) ... Tex.	31·00 N	93·42 W
120	Wiesbaden (vēs'bä-dĕn) ... Ger.	50·05 N	8·15 E
110	Wigan (wĭg'ăn) ... Eng.	53·33 N	2·37 W
78	Wiggins (wĭg'ĭnz) ... Miss.	30·51 N	89·05 W
116	Wight, Isle of (I.) (wīt) ... Eng.	50·44 N	1·17 W
73	Wilber (wĭl'bẽr) ... Nebr.	40·29 N	96·57 W
73	Wilburton (wĭl'bẽr-tŭn) ... Okla.	34·54 N	95·18 W
160	Wilcannia (wĭl-căn-ĭȧ) ... Austl.	31·30 S	143·30 E
111	Wildau (vēl'dou) . Ger. (Berlin In.)	52·20 N	13·39 E
111	Wildberg (vēl'bĕrgh) Ger. (Berlin In.)	52·52 N	12·39 E
74	Wildomar (wĭl'dô-mär) Calif. (Los Angeles In.)	33·35 N	117·17 W
70	Wild Rice (R.) ... Minn.	47·10 N	96·40 W
70	Wild Rice (R.) ... N. D.	46·10 N	97·12 W
74	Wild Rice L. . Minn. (Duluth In.)	46·54 N	92·10 W
120	Wild Spitze Pk. ... Aus.	46·49 N	10·50 E
81	Wildwood (wīld'wŏŏd) ... N. J.	39·00 N	74·50 W
72	Wiley (wī'lė) ... Colo.	38·08 N	102·41 W
168	Wilge R. (wĭl'jė) ... S. Afr. (Johannesburg & Pretoria In.)	25·38 S	29·09 E
168	Wilge R. ... S. Afr. (Johannesburg & Pretoria In.)	27·27 S	28·46 E
155	Wilhelm, Mt. ... N. Gui. Ter.	5·58 S	144·58 E
99	Wilhelmina Gebergte (Mts.) .. Sur.	4·30 N	57·00 W
155	Wilhelmina-Top (Pk.) (vêl-hĕl-mē'nȧ) . W. Irian	3·55 S	138·26 E
120	Wilhelmshaven (vêl-hĕlms-hä'fĕn) Ger.	53·30 N	8·10 E
111	Wilhemina, Kanal (can.) Neth. (Amsterdam In.)	51·37 N	4·55 E
81	Wilkes-Barre (wĭlks'băr-ė) ... Pa.	41·15 N	75·50 W
47	Wilkes Land ... Ant.	71·00 S	126·00 E
65	Wilkeson (wĭl-kē'sŭn) Wash. (Seattle In.)	47·06 N	122·03 W
86	Wilkie (wĭlk'ē) ... Can.	52·29 N	108·50 W
75	Wilkinsburg (wĭl'kĭnz-bûrg) Pa. (Pittsburgh In.)	40·26 N	79·53 W
66	Willamette R. ... Ore.	44·15 N	123·13 W
80	Willard (wĭl'ȧrd) ... Ohio	41·00 N	82·50 W
74	Willard . Utah (Salt Lake City In.)	41·24 N	112·02 W
69	Willcox (wĭl'kŏks) ... Ariz.	32·15 N	109·50 W
98	Willemstad ... Curaçao	12·12 N	68·58 W
110	Willenhall (wĭl'ĕn-hôl) ... Eng.	52·35 N	2·03 W
110	Willesden (wĭlz'dĕn) Eng. (London In.)	51·31 N	0·17 W
158	William Creek (wĭl'yăm) ... Austl.	28·45 S	136·20 E
69	Williams (wĭl'yămz) ... Ariz.	35·15 N	112·15 W
94	Williams (I.) ... Ba. Is.	25·30 N	78·30 W
78	Williamsburg (wĭl'yămz-bûrg) . Ky.	36·42 N	84·09 W
75	Williamsburg Ohio (Cincinnati In.)	39·04 N	84·02 W
79	Williamsburg ... Va.	37·15 N	76·41 W
80	Williamson (wĭl'yăm-sŭn) .. W. Va.	37·40 N	82·15 W
81	Williamsport (wĭl'yămz-pōrt) . Md.	39·35 N	77·45 W
81	Williamsport ... Pa.	41·15 N	77·05 W
79	Williamston (wĭl'yămz-tŭn) . N. C.	35·50 N	77·04 W
79	Williamston ... S. C.	34·36 N	82·30 W
80	Williamstown (wĭl'yămz-toun) W. Va.	39·20 N	81·30 W
75	Williamsville (wĭl'yăm-vĭl) N. Y. (Buffalo In.)	42·58 N	78·46 W
81	Willimantic (wĭl-ĭ-măn'tĭk) . Conn.	41·40 N	72·10 W
77	Willis (wĭl'ĭs) ... Tex.	30·24 N	95·29 W
159	Willis Is. ... Austl.	16·15 S	150·30 E
70	Williston (wĭl'ĭs-tŭn) ... N. D.	48·08 N	103·38 W
75	Willoughby (wĭl'ô-bė) Ohio (Cleveland In.)	41·39 N	81·25 W
67	Willow Cr. (wĭl'ō) ... Mont.	48·45 N	111·34 W
66	Willow Cr. ... Ore.	44·21 N	117·34 W
85	Willowdale (wĭl'ō-dāl) Can. (Toronto In.)	43·47 N	79·25 W
84	Willow Grove Pa. (Philadelphia In.)	40·07 N	75·07 W
74	Willowick (wĭl'ô-wĭk) Calif. (Los Angeles In.)	33·45 N	117·55 W
75	Willowick .. Ohio (Cleveland In.)	41·39 N	81·28 W
166	Willowmore (wĭl'ô-mōr) ... S. Afr.	33·15 S	23·37 E
75	Willow Run (wĭl'ô rŭn) Mich. (Detroit In.)	42·16 N	83·34 W
68	Willows (wĭl'ōz) ... Calif.	39·32 N	122·11 W
73	Willow Springs (sprĭngz) ... Mo.	36·59 N	91·56 W
167	Willowvale (wĭ-lô'vāl) S. Afr. (Natal In.)	32·17 S	28·32 E
77	Wills Point (wĭlz point) ... Tex.	32·42 N	96·02 W
71	Wilmar (wĭl'mär) ... Minn.	45·07 N	95·05 W
74	Wilmer (wĭl'mẽr) Tex. (Dallas, Fort Worth In.)	32·35 N	96·40 W
75	Wilmette (wĭl-mĕt') Ill. (Chicago In.)	42·04 N	87·42 W
74	Wilmington (wĭl'mĭng-tŭn) Calif. (Los Angeles In.)	33·46 N	118·16 W
84	Wilmington . Del. (Philadelphia In.)	39·45 N	75·33 W
75	Wilmington ... Ill. (Chicago In.)	41·19 N	88·09 W
83	Wilmington ... Mass. (Boston In.)	42·34 N	71·10 W
79	Wilmington ... N. C.	34·12 N	77·56 W
80	Wilmington ... Ohio	39·20 N	83·50 W
80	Wilmore (wĭl'mōr) ... Ky.	37·50 N	84·35 W
110	Wilmslow (wĭlmz' lō) ... Eng.	53·19 N	2·14 W
	Wilno, see Vilnius		
73	Wilson (wĭl'sŭn) ... Ark.	35·35 N	90·02 W
79	Wilson ... N. C.	35·42 N	77·55 W
73	Wilson ... Okla.	34·09 N	97·27 W
78	Wilson, L. ... Ala.	34·45 N	86·58 W
78	Wilson (R.) ... Ala.	34·53 N	87·28 W
161	Wilson, Pt. . Austl. (Melbourne In)	38·05 S	144·31 E
74	Wilson, Mt. Calif. (Los Angeles In.)	34·15 N	118·06 W
71	Wilson (I.) ... Can.	48·48 N	87·23 W
67	Wilson Pk. ... Utah	40·46 N	110·27 W
160	Wilson's Prom. (wĭl'sŭnz) ... Austl.	39·05 S	146·50 E
74	Wilsonville (wĭl'sŭn-vĭl) Ill. (St. Louis In.)	39·04 N	89·52 W
111	Wilstedt (vēl'shtĕt) Ger. (Hamburg In.)	53·45 N	10·04 E
111	Wilster (vēl'stẽr) Ger. (Hamburg In.)	53·55 N	9·23 E
84	Wilton (wĭl'tŭn) Conn. (New York In.)	41·11 N	73·25 W
70	Wilton ... N. D.	47·90 N	100·47 W
158	Wiluna (wĭ-lōō'nȧ) ... Austl.	26·35 S	120·25 E
80	Winamac (wĭn'ȧ măk) ... Ind.	41·05 N	86·40 W
169	Winburg (wĭm-bûrg) ... S. Afr. (Johannesburg & Pretoria In.)	28·31 S	27·02 E
74	Winchester (wĭn'chĕs-tẽr) Calif. (Los Angeles In.)	33·41 N	117·06 W
116	Winchester ... Eng.	3·03 N	1·20 W
66	Winchester ... Idaho	46·14 N	116·39 W
80	Winchester ... Ind.	40·10 N	84·50 W
80	Winchester ... Ky.	38·00 N	84·15 W
83	Winchester ... Mass. (Boston In.)	42·28 N	71·09 W
81	Winchester ... N. H.	42·45 N	72·25 W
78	Winchester ... Tenn.	35·11 N	86·06 W
81	Winchester ... Va.	39·40 N	78·10 W
81	Windber (wĭnd'bẽr) ... Pa.	40·15 N	78·45 W
70	Wind Cave Natl. Park ... S. D.	43·36 N	103·53 W
78	Winder (wĭn'dẽr) ... Ga.	33·58 N	83·43 W
116	Windermere (wĭn'dẽr-mēr) ... Eng.	54·25 N	2·59 W
81	Windham (wĭnd'ăm) ... Conn.	41·45 N	72·05 W
83	Windham ... N. H. (Boston In.)	42·49 N	71·21 W
166	Windhoek (vĭnt'hŏŏk) .. S. W. Afr.	22·05 S	17·10 E
75	Wind L. ... Wis. (Milwaukee In.)	42·49 N	88·06 W
76	Wind Mtn. ... N. Mex.	32·02 N	105·30 W
71	Windom (wĭn'dŭm) ... Minn.	43·50 N	95·04 W
160	Windora (wĭn-dō'rȧ) ... Austl.	25·15 S	142·50 E
67	Wind R. ... Wyo.	43·17 N	109·02 W
67	Wind River Ind Res. ... Wyo.	43·07 N	109·08 W
67	Wind River Ra. ... Wyo.	43·19 N	109·47 W
161	Windsor (wĭn'zẽr) Austl. (Sydney In.)	33·37 S	150·49 E
75	Windsor ... Can. (Detroit In.)	42·19 N	83·00 W
82	Windsor ... Can.	44·59 N	64·07 W
83	Windsor ... Can.	49·00 N	55·39 W
72	Windsor ... Colo.	40·27 N	104·51 W
110	Windsor ... Eng. (London In.)	51·27 N	0·37 W
73	Windsor ... Mo.	38·32 N	93·31 W
82	Windsor ... Vt.	43·30 N	72·25 W
79	Windsor ... N. C.	35·58 N	76·57 W
89	Windward Is. (wĭnd'wẽrd) .. N. A.	12·45 N	61·40 W
95	Windward Pass ... N. A.	19·30 N	74·20 W
73	Winfield (wĭn'fēld) ... Kans.	37·14 N	97·00 W
87	Wingham (wĭn'găm) ... Can.	43·48 N	81·23 W
67	Winifred (wĭn ĭ frĕd) ... Mont.	47·35 N	109·20 W
76	Wink (wĭnk) ... Tex.	31·48 N	103·06 W
164	Winneba (wĭn'ė-bȧ) ... Ghana	5·29 N	0·43 W
71	Winnebago (wĭn'ė-bā'gō) ... Minn.	43·45 N	94·08 W
71	Winnebago, L. ... Wis.	44·09 N	88·10 W
70	Winnebago Ind. Res. ... Nebr.	42·15 N	96·06 W
66	Winnemucca (wĭn-ė-mŭk'ȧ) .. Nev.	40·59 N	117·43 W
68	Winnemucca (L.) ... Nev.	40·06 N	119·07 W
70	Winner (wĭn'ẽr) ... S. D.	43·22 N	99·50 W
75	Winnetka (wĭ-nĕt'kȧ) Ill. (Chicago In.)	42·07 N	87·44 W
67	Winnett (wĭn'ĕt) ... Mont.	47·01 N	108·20 W
77	Winnfield (wĭn'fēld) ... La.	31·56 N	92·39 W
71	Winnibigoshish (L.) (wĭn'ĭ-bĭ-gō'shĭsh) . Minn.	47·30 N	93·45 W
85	Winnipeg (wĭn'ĭ-pĕg) Can. (Winnipeg In.)	49·55 N	97·09 W
86	Winnipeg, L. ... Can.	53·29 N	98·41 W
86	Winnipeg (R.) ... Can.	50·30 N	95·34 W
86	Winnipegosis (wĭn'ĭ-pė-gō'sĭs) Can.	51·40 N	100·01 W
86	Winnipegosis (L.) ... Can.	52·19 N	101·40 W
81	Winnipesaukee (L.) (wĭn'ė-pė-sô'kė) . N. H.	43·40 N	71·20 W
77	Winnsboro (wĭnz'bŭr-ô) ... La.	32·09 N	91·42 W
79	Winnsboro ... S. C.	34·29 N	81·05 W
73	Winnsboro ... Tex.	32·56 N	95·15 W
85	Winona (wĭ-nō'nȧ) Can. (Toronto In.)	43·13 N	79·39 W
71	Winona ... Minn.	44·03 N	91·40 W
78	Winona ... Miss.	33·29 N	89·43 W
81	Winooski (wĭ-nōōs'kė) ... Vt.	44·30 N	73·10 W
111	Winsen (Luhe) (vēn'zĕn) (lōō'hĕ) Ger. (Hamburg In.)	53·22 N	10·13 E
110	Winsford (wĭnz'fẽrd) ... Eng.	53·11 N	2·30 W

ng-sing; ŋ-baŋk; N-nasalized n; nŏd; cŏmmit; ōld; ōbey; ôrder; fōōd; fŏŏt; ou-out; s-soft; sh-dish; th-thin; pūre; ûnite; ûrn; stŭd; circŭs; ü-as "y" in study; '-indeterminate vowel.

ăt; fînăl; rāte; senâte; ärm; àsk; sofà; fâre; ch-choose; dh-as th in other: bē; êvent; bĕt; recĕnt; cratēr; g-go; gh-guttural g; bĭt; ĭ-short neutral; rīde; κ-guttural k as ch in German ich;

PRONOUNCING INDEX Yamashina–Zacualpan 287

Page	Name Pronunciation Region	Lat. °′	Long. °′
153	Yamashina (yä'mä-shē'nä) Jap. (Ōsaka In.)	34·59 N	135·50 E
153	Yamashita (yä'mä-shē'tä) Jap. (Ōsaka In.)	34·53 N	135·25 E
153	Yamato-takada (yä'mä-tō tä'kä-dä) Jap. (Ōsaka In.)	34·31 N	135·45 E
98	Yambi, Mesa de (mě'sä-dě-yà'm-bē) Col.	1·55 N	71·45 W
146	Yamdrog Tsho (L.) China	29·11 N	91·26 E
146	Yamethin (yŭ-mē'thěn) Bur.	20·14 N	96·27 E
65	Yamhill (yăm'hĭl) Ore. (Portland In.)	45·20 N	123·11 W
136	Yamkino (yäm'kĭ-nô) Sov. Un. (Moscow In.)	55·56 N	38·25 E
160	Yamma Yamma, L. (yăm'à yăm'à) Austl.	26·15 S	141·30 E
67	Yampa R. (yăm'pa) Colo.	40·29 N	108·12 W
135	Yamsk (yämsk) Sov. Un.	59·41 N	154·09 E
142	Yamuna (R.) India	26·50 N	79·45 E
135	Yana (R.) (yä'nà) Sov. Un.	69·42 N	135·45 E
160	Yanac (yăn'ak) Austl.	36·10 S	141·30 E
153	Yanagawa (yä-nä'gä-wä) Jap.	33·11 N	130·24 E
143	Yanam (yŭnŭm') India	16·48 N	82·15 E
144	Yanbu al Bahr Sau. Ar.	23·57 N	38·02 E
148	Yangch'eng Hu (L.) (yäng'chěng'hōō) China	31·30 N	120·31 E
151	Yangchiang China	21·52 N	111·58 E
148	Yangchiaokou (yang'jēou'gō) China	37·16 N	118·53 E
148	Yangchiat'an (yäng'jēä'tän) China	31·43 N	115·53 E
148	Yangch'uanchan China	37·52 N	113·36 E
151	Yangch'un (yäng'chōōn') China	22·08 N	111·48 E
148	Yangerhchuang (yäng'ē'jōōäng) China	38·18 N	117·31 E
148	Yangho (yäng'hŭ) China	33·48 N	118·23 E
148	Yanghsin (yäng'sĭn) China	37·39 N	117·34 E
150	Yangkochuang China (Peking In.)	40·10 N	116·48 E
148	Yangku (yäng'kōō') China	36·06 N	115·46 E
148	Yangsanmu (yäng'sän'mōō) China	38·28 N	117·18 E
147	Yangtze (R.) (yäng'tsě) China	30·30 N	117·25 E
152	Yangyang (yäng'yäng') Kor.	38·02 N	128·38 E
70	Yankton (yănk'tŭn) S. D.	42·51 N	97·24 W
	Yannina, see Ioánnina		
136	Yanychi (yà'nĭ-chĭ) Sov. Un. (Urals In.)	57·42 N	56·24 E
165	Yao (yä'ō) Chad	13·00 N	17·38 E
153	Yao Jap. (Ōsaka In.)	34·37 N	135·36 E
164	Yaounde (yà-ōōn-dā') Cam.	3·58 N	11·45 E
156	Yap (yăp) (I.) Pac. Is. Trust Ter.	11·00 N	138·00 E
95	Yaque del Norte (R.) (yä'kà děl nôr'tā) Dom. Rep.	19·40 N	71·25 W
95	Yaque del Sur (R.) (yä-kě-děl-sōō'r) Dom. Rep.	18·35 N	71·05 W
88	Yaqui (R.) (yä'kē) Mex.	28·15 N	109·40 W
99	Yaracuy (State) (yä-rä-kōō'ē) Ven. (In.)	10·10 N	68·31 W
160	Yaraka (yà-răk'à) Austl.	24·50 S	144·08 E
132	Yaransk (yä-ränsk') Sov. Un.	57·18 N	48·05 E
165	Yarda (Well) (yär'dà) Chad	18·29 N	19·13 E
	Yarkand, see Soch'e		
142	Yarkand (R.) (yär-känt') India	36·11 N	76·10 E
82	Yarmouth (yär'mŭth) Can.	43·49 N	66·08 W
136	Yaroslavka (yà-rô-släv'kà) Sov. Un. (Urals In.)	55·52 N	57·59 E
128	Yaroslavl' (yà-rô-släv''l) Sov. Un.	57·57 N	39·54 E
128	Yaroslavl' (Oblast) Sov. Un.	58·05 N	38·05 E
132	Yarra-to (L.) (yà'rô-tô') Sov. Un.	68·30 N	71·30 E
128	Yartsevo (yär'tsyê-vô) Sov. Un.	55·04 N	32·38 E
134	Yartsevo Sov. Un.	60·13 N	89·52 E
98	Yarumal (yä-rōō-mäl') Col. (In.)	6·57 N	75·24 W
121	Yasel'da R. (yä-syŭl'dà) Sov. Un.	52·13 N	25·53 E
95	Yateras (yä-tā'räs) Cuba	20·00 N	75·00 W
73	Yates Center (yāts) Kans.	37·53 N	95·44 W
86	Yathkyed (L.) (yàth-kĭ-ĕd') Can.	62·38 N	97·12 W
153	Yatsuga-dake (Mtn.) (yät'sōō-gä dä'kä) Jap.	36·01 N	138·21 E
153	Yatsushiro (yät'sōō'shê-rô) Jap.	32·30 N	130·35 E
90	Yautepec (yä-ōō-tà-pěk') Mex.	18·53 N	99·04 W
121	Yavoroy (yä'vō-rō'yē) Sov. Un.	49·56 N	23·24 E
153	Yawata (yä'wä-tä) Jap. (Osaka In.)	34·52 N	135·43 E
153	Yawatahama (yä'wä'tä'hä-mä) Jap.	33·24 N	132·25 E
144	Yazd Iran	31·59 N	54·03 E
78	Yazoo (R.) (yă'zōō) Miss.	32·32 N	90·40 W
78	Yazoo City Miss.	32·50 N	90·18 W
154	Ye (yā) Bur.	15·13 N	97·52 E
84	Yeadon (yē'dŭn) Pa. (Philadelphia In.)	39·56 N	75·16 W
124	Yecla (yā'klä) Sp.	38·35 N	1·09 W
128	Yefremov (yĕ-frĕ'mŏf) Sov. Un.	53·08 N	38·04 E
128	Yegor'yevsk (yĕ-gôr'yĕfsk) Sov. Un.	55·23 N	38·59 E
148	Yehch'eng (Karghalik) (yĕ'chĕng') China	37·30 N	79·26 E
148	Yehhsien (yĕ'sĭän) China	33·37 N	113·23 E
132	Yelabuga (yĕ-lä'bŏŏ-gà) Sov. Un.	55·50 N	52·18 E
133	Yelan Sov. Un.	50·50 N	44·00 E
128	Yelets (yĕ-lyĕts') Sov. Un.	52·35 N	38·28 E
136	Yelizavetpol'skiy (yĕ'lĭ-za-vĕt-pôl-skĭ) Sov. Un. (Urals In.)	52·51 N	60·38 E
135	Yelizavety, Mys (C.) (yĕ-lyē-sà-vyĕ'tà) Sov. Un.	54·28 N	142·59 E
116	Yell (I.) (yĕl) Scot.	60·35 N	1·27 W
78	Yellow (R.) (yĕl'ō) Fla.	30·33 N	86·53 W
86	Yellowknife (yĕl'ō-nīf) Can.	62·29 N	114·38 W
	Yellow R., see Hwang Ho		
150	Yellow Sea China	35·20 N	122·15 E
67	Yellowstone L. Wyo.	44·27 N	110·03 W
67	Yellowstone Natl. Park (yĕl'ô-stōn) Wyo.	44·45 N	110·35 W
67	Yellowstone R. Mont.	46·28 N	105·39 W
67	Yellowstone R., Clark Fk. Wyo.	44·55 N	109·05 W
128	Yel'nya (yĕl'nyà) Sov. Un.	54·34 N	33·12 E
164	Yelwa (yĕl'wä) Nig.	8·57 N	9·44 E
136	Yemanzhelinsk (yĕ-män-zhä'lĭnsk) Sov. Un. (Urals In.)	54·47 N	61·24 E
138	Yemen (yĕm'ĕn) Asia	15·45 N	44·30 E
132	Yemetsk Sov. Un.	63·28 N	41·28 E
129	Yenakiyevo (yĕ-nä'kĭ-yĕ-vô) Sov. Un.	48·14 N	38·12 E
150	Yenan (yĕn'än') China	36·35 N	109·32 E
145	Yenangyaung (yä'nän-d oung) Bur.	20·27 N	94·59 E
148	Yench'eng (yĕn'chĕng) China	33·23 N	120·11 E
148	Yencheng (yĕn'chĕng) China	33·38 N	113·59 E
146	Yench'i (yĕn'chĭ') China	42·14 N	86·28 E
150	Yenchi China	42·55 N	129·35 E
148	Yenchiaha (yen'jēä'hŭ) China	31·47 N	114·50 E
148	Yenchianchi (yĕn'jēä'jē) China	31·52 N	115·57 E
148	Yenching (yĕn'jĭn) China	35·09 N	114·13 E
148	Yenchuang (yĕn'jōōäng) China	36·08 N	117·47 E
164	Yendi (yĕn'dē) Ghana	9·21 N	0·02 E
133	Yenice (R.) Tur.	41·10 N	33·00 E
134	Yenisey (R.) (yĕ-nê-sĕ'ê) Sov. Un.	67·48 N	87·15 E
134	Yeniseysk (yĕ-nĭ-sā'ĭsk) Sov. Un.	58·27 N	90·28 E
148	Yenling (yĕn'lĭng') China	34·07 N	114·12 E
148	Yenshan (yĕn'shän') China	38·05 N	117·15 E
150	Yenshou China	45·25 N	128·43 E
148	Yent'ai (Chefoo) China	37·32 N	121·22 E
158	Yeo (I.) (yō) Austl.	28·15 S	124·00 E
133	Yerevan (yĕ-rĕ-vän') Sov. Un.	40·10 N	44·30 E
116	Yerington (yē'rĭng-tŭn) Nev.	38·59 N	119·10 W
132	Yermak (I.) Sov. Un.	66·30 N	71·30 E
124	Yeste (yĕs'tâ) Sp.	38·23 N	2·19 W
122	Yeu, Île d' (I.) (ēl dyû) Fr.	46·43 N	2·45 W
129	Yevpatoriya (yĕf-pà'tô-rĭ-yà) Sov. Un.	45·13 N	33·22 E
129	Yeya (R.) (yä'yà) Sov. Un.	46·25 N	39·17 E
135	Yevrey Aut. Oblast Sov Un.	48·45 N	132·00 E
129	Yeysk (yĕysk) Sov. Un.	46·41 N	38·13 E
	Yg, see Yug		
127	Yiannitsá Grc.	40·47 N	22·26 E
150	Yinch'uan (Nīnghsia) China	38·22 N	106·22 E
146	Yingchisha China	39·01 N	75·29 E
150	Yingk'ou (yĭng'kō') China	40·35 N	122·10 E
149	Yinhang China (Shanghai In.)	31·20 N	121·30 E
150	Yin Shan (Mtn.) (yĭng'shän') China	40·50 N	110·30 E
	Yinhsien, see Ningpo		
127	Yioúra (I.) Grc.	37·52 N	24·42 E
127	Yíthion Grc.	36·50 N	22·37 E
153	Ynasa (yōō'ä-sä) Jap.	34·02 N	135·10 E
77	Yoakum (yō'kŭm) Tex.	29·18 N	97·09 W
78	Yockanookany, (R.) (yŏk'á-nōō-kă-nī) Miss.	32·47 N	89·38 W
153	Yodo-Gawa (Str.) (yō'dō'gä-wä) Jap. (Ōsaka In.)	34·46 N	135·35 E
151	Yog Pt. (yōg) Phil.	14·00 N	124·30 E
86	Yoho Natl. Park (yō'hō) Can.	51·32 N	117·06 W
92	Yojoa, Lago de (L.) (lä'gô dě yô-hō'ä) Hond.	14·49 N	87·53 W
153	Yokkaichi (yō'kä'ē-chê) Jap.	34·58 N	136·35 E
153	Yokohama (yō'kō-hä'mä) Jap. (Tōkyō In.)	35·37 N	139·40 E
153	Yokosuka (yô-kō'sōō-kä) Jap. (Tōkyō In.)	35·17 N	139·40 E
153	Yokota (yō-kō'tä) Jap. (Tōkyō In.)	35·23 N	140·02 E
164	Yola (yō'lä) Nig.	9·13 N	12·27 E
93	Yolaina, Cord. de (Mts.) (kôr-dēl-yě'rä dě yō-lä-ē'nä) Nic.	11·34 N	84·34 W
98	Yolombó (yô-lôm-bŏ') Col. (In.)	6·37 N	74·59 W
153	Yonago (yō'nä-gō) Jap.	35·27 N	133·19 E
152	Yonezawa (yō'nĕ'zä-wä) Jap.	37·50 N	140·07 E
152	Yŏngdŏk (yŭng'dŭk') Kor.	36·28 N	129·25 E
152	Yŏnghŭng (yŭng'hōōng') Kor.	39·31 N	127·11 E
152	Yŏnghŭng Man (B.) Kor.	39·10 N	128·00 E
84	Yonkers (yŏŋ'kĕrz) N. Y. (New York In.)	40·57 N	73·54 W
122	Yonne (R.) (yôn) Fr.	48·18 N	3·15 E
153	Yono (yō'nō) Jap. (Tōkyō In.)	35·53 N	139·36 E
74	Yorba Linda (yôr'bà lĭn'dà) Calif. (Los Angeles In.)	33·55 N	117·51 W
78	York (yôrk) Ala.	32·33 N	88·16 W
158	York Austl.	32·00 S	117·00 E
116	York Eng.	53·58 N	1·10 W
73	York Nebr.	40·52 N	97·36 W
81	York Pa.	40·00 N	76·40 W
79	York S. C.	34·59 N	81·14 W
159	York, C. Austl.	10·45 S	142·35 E
49	York, Kap (C.) Grnld.	75·30 N	73·00 W
160	Yorketown Austl.	35·00 S	137·28 E
87	York Factory (făk'tō-rĭ) Can.	56·59 N	92·27 W
160	York Pen. Austl.	34·24 S	137·20 E
116	Yorkshire Wolds (Hills) (yôrk'shĭr) Eng.	54·00 N	0·35 W
86	Yorkton (yôrk'tŭn) Can.	51·11 N	102·40 W
77	Yorktown (yôrk'toun) Tex.	28·57 N	97·30 W
79	Yorktown Va.	37·12 N	76·31 W
92	Yoro (yō'rô) Hond.	15·09 N	87·05 W
68	Yosemite Natl. Park (yô-sĕm'ĭ-tê) Calif.	38·03 N	119·36 W
153	Yoshida (yō'shē-dà) Jap.	34·39 N	132·41 E
153	Yoshikawa (yō-shē'kä'wä') Jap. (Tōkyō In.)	35·53 N	139·51 E
153	Yoshino (R.) (yō'shē-nō) Jap.	34·04 N	133·57 E
153	Yoshiwara (yō-shē'wä'rä') Jap.	35·11 N	138·44 E
132	Yoshkar-Ola (yôsh-kär'ô-lä') Sov. Un.	56·35 N	48·05 E
91	Yosonotú (Santa Catarina) (yô-sō-nô-tōō') (sän'tä kä-tä-rē'nä) Mex.	16·51 N	97·37 W
152	Yŏsu (yŭ'sōō') Kor.	34·42 N	127·42 E
116	Youghal B. (yōō'ôl) (yôl) Ire.	51·52 N	7·46 W
116	Youhal Ire.	51·58 N	7·57 W
165	Youkadouma (yōō-kà-dōō'mä) Cam.	3·29 N	15·04 E
160	Young (yŭng) Austl.	34·15 S	148·18 E
101	Young (yô-ōō'ng) Ur. (Buenos Aires In.)	32·42 S	57·38 W
65	Youngs (L.) (yŭngz) Wash. (Seattle In.)	47·25 N	122·08 W
75	Youngstown (yŭngz'toun) N. Y. (Buffalo In.)	43·15 N	79·02 W
80	Youngstown Ohio	41·05 N	80·40 W
133	Yozgat (yôz'gàd) Tur.	39·50 N	34·50 E
75	Ypsilanti (ĭp-sĭ-lăn'tĭ) Mich. (Detroit In.)	42·15 N	83·37 W
66	Yreka (wī-rē'kà) Calif.	41·43 N	122·36 W
84	Yscloskey (ĭs-klŏs'kĕ) La. (New Orleans In.)	29·51 N	89·42 W
76	Ysleta (ēz-lĕ'tà) Tex.	31·42 N	106·18 W
122	Yssingeaux (ē-săN-zhō') Fr.	45·09 N	4·08 E
118	Ystad (ü'städ) Swe.	55·29 N	13·28 E
118	Ytre Solund (I.) (ü'trĕ sōō'lĕn) Nor.	61·01 N	4·25 E
151	Yüan (R.) (yōō'än') China	28·50 N	110·50 E
151	Yüanan (yōō'ä-nän') China	31·08 N	111·28 E
151	Yüanling China	28·30 N	110·18 E
148	Yüanshih China	37·45 N	114·32 E
68	Yuba City (yōō'bà) Calif.	39·08 N	121·38 W
164	Yubi C. (yōō'bē) Mor.	28·01 N	13·21 W
74	Yucaipa (yŭ-kà-ē'pà) Calif. (Los Angeles In.)	34·02 N	117·02 W
88	Yucatan (State) (yōō-kä-tän') Mex.	20·45 N	89·00 W
88	Yucatán Chan. Mex.	22·30 N	87·00 W
151	Yu Chiang (R.) (yōō) China	23·55 N	106·50 E
148	Yüch'eng (yü'chĕng') China	34·31 N	115·54 E
148	Yüch'eng China	36·55 N	116·39 E
135	Yudoma (R.) (yōō-dō'mà) Sov. Un.	59·13 N	137·00 E
148	Yüehchuang (yüĕ'jōōäng) China	36·13 N	118·17 E
151	Yüehyang China	29·25 N	113·05 E
132	Yug (R.) (yōōg) Sov. Un.	59·50 N	45·55 E
102	Yugoslavia (yōō-gô-slä-vĭ-à) Eur.	44·48 N	17·29 E
148	Yühsien (yüsĭän) China	34·09 N	113·25 E
150	Yühsien (yōō'hsyĕn') China	39·40 N	114·38 E
128	Yukhnov (yōōk'-nof) Sov. Un.	54·44 N	35·15 E
86	Yukon (Ter.) (yōō'kŏn) Can.	63·16 N	135·30 W
64	Yukon R. Alaska	62·10 N	163·10 W
64	Yukutat B. (yōō-kū tăt') Alaska	59·34 N	140·50 W
136	Yuldybayevo (yōōld'-bä'yĕ-vô) Sov. Un. (Urals In.)	52·20 N	57·52 E
151	Yülin China	22·38 N	110·10 E
150	Yülin (yōō'lĭn') China	38·18 N	109·45 E
69	Yuma (yōō'mä) Ariz.	32·40 N	114·40 W
72	Yuma Colo.	40·08 N	102·50 W
95	Yuma, Bahia de (B.) (bä-ē'ä-dĕ-yōō'mä) Dom. Rep.	18·20 N	68·05 W
95	Yuma (R.) Dom. Rep.	19·05 N	70·05 W
146	Yümen (yü'mĕn') China	40·14 N	96·56 E
150	Yünch'eng (yün'chĕng) China	35·00 N	110·40 E
151	Yüngan (yōōn'gän') China	26·00 N	117·22 E
	Yungchia, see Wenchow		
150	Yungch'ing (yōōng'chĭng') China (Peking In.)	39·18 N	116·27 E
	Yungchow, see Lingling		
148	Yungnien (yōōng'nĭän) China	36·41 N	114·46 E
151	Yungshun (yōōng'shōōn') China	29·05 N	109·58 E
150	Yungting Ho (R.) (yōōng'tĭng' hō') China	40·25 N	115·00 E
148	Yün Ho (R.) (Grand Canal) (yün'hŭ) China	34·23 N	117·57 E
151	Yünhsiao China	24·00 N	117·20 E
150	Yünhsien China	32·50 N	110·55 E
147	Yün Ling Shan (Mts.) (yün lĭng shän) China	26·35 N	117·15 E
146	Yünnan (Prov.) (yün'nän') China	24·23 N	101·03 E
	Yünnanfu, see K'unming		
146	Yünnan Plat. China	26·03 N	101·26 E
153	Yura (yōō'rä) Jap.	34·18 N	134·54 E
90	Yurécuaro (yōō-rā'kwä-rô) Mex.	20·21 N	102·16 W
98	Yurimaguas (yōō-rê-mä'gwäs) Peru	5·59 S	76·12 W
90	Yuriria (yōō'rê-rē'ä) Mex.	20·11 N	101·08 W
132	Yur'yevets Sov. Un.	57·15 N	43·08 E
136	Yuryuzan' (yōōr-yōō-zän') Sov. Un. (Urals In.)	54·47 N	58·45 E
92	Yuscarán (yōōs-kä-rän') Hond.	13·57 N	86·48 W
151	Yüshan (yōō'shän') China	28·42 N	118·20 E
150	Yüshu China	44·58 N	126·32 E
142	Yutien (Keriya) (yōō'tĕn') China	36·55 N	81·39 E
148	Yut'ien (yü'tyĕn') China	39·54 N	117·45 E
100	Yuty (yōō-tē') Par.	26·45 S	56·13 W
150	Yützu China	37·32 N	112·40 E
148	Yuwangcheng (yü'wäng'chĕng) China	31·32 N	114·26 E
132	Yuzha (yōō'zhà) Sov. Un.	56·38 N	42·20 E
136	Yuzhnny Ural (Mts.) (yōō'zhnĭ ŏŏ-räl') Sov. Un. (Urals In.)	52·51 N	57·48 E
135	Yuzhno-Sakhalinsk (yōōzh'nô-sä-kä-lĭnsk') Sov. Un.	47·11 N	143·04 E
136	Yuzhnoural'skiy (yōōzh-nô-ŏŏ-räl'skĭ) Sov. Un. (Urals In.)	54·26 N	61·17 E
120	Yverdon (ê-vĕr-dôn) Switz.	46·46 N	6·35 E
122	Yvetot (ēv-tō') Fr.	49·39 N	0·45 E
114	Za R. Mor.	34·19 N	2·23 W
91	Zaachila (sä-ä-chē'lä) Mex.	16·56 N	96·45 W
111	Zaandam (zän'dàm) Neth. (Amsterdam In.)	52·25 N	4·49 E
139	Zabdānī Syr. (Palestine In.)	33·45 N	36·06 E
120	Zabkowice (zaNb'kō-vē'tsĕ) Pol.	50·35 N	16·48 E
121	Zabrze (zäb'zhĕ) Pol.	50·18 N	18·48 E
92	Zacapa (sä-kä'pä) Guat.	14·56 N	89·30 W
91	Zacapoaxtla (sä-kä-pô-äs'tlä) Mex.	19·51 N	97·34 W
90	Zacatecas (sä-kä-tā'käs) Mex.	22·44 N	102·32 W
88	Zacatecas (State) Mex.	24·00 N	102·45 W
92	Zacatecoluca (sä-kä-tĕ-kô-lōō'kä) Sal.	13·31 N	88·50 W
90	Zacateko (zä-kä-tĕ'kō) Mex.	19·12 N	98·12 W
91	Zacatepec (Santiago) (sä-kä-tä-pĕk') (sän-tê-ä'gô) Mex.	17·10 N	95·53 W
91	Zacatlán (sä-kä-tlän') Mex.	19·55 N	97·57 W
90	Zacoalco de Torres (sä-kō-äl'kō dā tōr'rĕs) Mex.	20·12 N	103·33 W
90	Zacualpan (sä-kōō-äl-pän') Mex.	18·43 N	99·46 W

ng-sing; ŋ-baŋk; N-nasalized n; nŏd; cŏmmit; ōld; ôbey; ôrder; fōōd; fŏŏt; ou-out; s-soft; sh-dish; th-thin; pūre; ûnite; ûrn; stŭd; circŭs; ü-as "y" in study; '-indeterminate vowel.

Page	Name	Pronunciation	Region	Lat. °′	Long. °′
90	Zacualtipan	(så-kōō-äl-tē-pän') Mex.		20·38 N	98·39 W
126	Zadar	(zä'där)	Yugo.	44·08 N	15·16 E
128	Zadonsk	(zä-dônsk')	Sov. Un.	52·22 N	38·55 E
139	Za'farānah	U. A. R. (Egypt) (Palestine In.)		29·07 N	32·38 E
120	Zagan	(zhä'gän')	Pol.	51·34 N	15·32 E
125	Zagarolo	(tzä-gä-rô'lô) It. (Rome In.)		41·51 N	12·53 E
119	Žagare	(zhå'gårĕ)	Sov. Un.	56·21 N	23·14 E
139	Zaghartā	Leb. (Palestine In.)		34·24 N	35·53 E
164	Zaghouan	(zá-gwän')	Tun.	36·30 N	10·04 E
127	Zagorá	(zä'gô-rä)	Grc.	39·29 N	23·04 E
136	Zagorsk	(zä-gôrsk') Sov. Un. (Moscow In.)		56·18 N	38·08 E
126	Zagreb	(zä'grĕb)	Yugo.	45·50 N	15·58 E
144	Zagro Mts.		Iran	33·30 N	46·30 E
144	Zahedān	(zä'hä-dän)	Iran	29·37 N	60·31 E
139	Zahlah	(zä-lä'). Leb. (Palestine In.)		33·50 N	35·54 E
111	Zahorska-Ves. Czech. (Vienna In.)			48·24 N	16·51 E
125	Zahrez Chergui	(L.)	Alg.	35·10 N	2·17 E
127	Zaječar	(zä'yĕ-chär')	Yugo.	43·54 N	22·16 E
127	Zákinthos		Grc.	37·48 N	20·55 E
127	Zákinthos	(Zante) (I.)	Grc.	37·45 N	20·32 E
121	Zakopane	(zä-kô-pä'nĕ)	Pol.	49·18 N	19·57 E
120	Zalaegerszeg	(zŏ'lô-ĕ'gĕr-sĕg) Hung.		46·50 N	16·50 E
121	Zalău	(zä-lŭ'ōō)	Rom.	47·11 N	23·06 E
111	Zaltbommel	Neth. (Amsterdam In.)		51·48 N	5·15 E
166	Zambezi	(R.) (zäm-bä'zĕ)	Afr.	16·33 S	29·22 E
154	Zamboanga	(säm-bô-aṇ'gä)	Phil.	6·58 N	122·02 E
121	Zambrów	(zäm'brōōf)	Pol.	52·59 N	22·17 E
90	Zamora	(sä-mō rä)	Mex.	19·59 N	102·16 W
124	Zamora	(thä-mō'rä)	Sp.	41·32 N	5·43 W
121	Zamość	(zä'môshch)	Pol.	50·42 N	23·17 E
91	Zanatepec	(Sto. Domingo) (sä-nä-tä-pek') (sän-tô dō-miṇ'gô). Mex.		16·30 N	94·22 W
111	Zandvoort	Neth. (Amsterdam In.)		52·22 N	4·30 E
80	Zanesville	(zānz'vĭl)	Ohio	39·55 N	82·00 W
144	Zanjān		Iran	36·26 N	48·24 E
167	Zanzibar	(zän'zǐ-bär)	Zan.	6·13 S	39·12 E
167	Zanzibar	(I.)	Afr.	6·00 S	39·30 E
165	Zanzūr	(zän-zōōr')	Libya	32·40 N	12·49 E
128	Zapadnaya Dvina	(R.) (zä'pád-nä-yä dvē'nä). Sov. Un.		55·30 N	28·27 E
100	Zapala	(zä-pä'lä)	Arg.	38·53 S	70·02 W
119	Zapa-naya Dvina	(R.) (zä'pád-nä-yä dvē nä). Sov. Un.		56·40 N	24·40 E
76	Zapata	(sä-pä'tä)	Tex.	26·52 N	99·18 W
94	Zapata, Ciénaga de	(Swp.) (syē'nä-gä-dē-zä-pä'tä). Cuba		22·30 N	81·20 W
94	Zapata, Península de	(pĕ-nē'n-sōō-lä-dĕ-zä-pä'tä)	Cuba	22·20 N	81·30 W
92	Zapatera, Isla	(I.) (ē's-lä-sä-pä-tä'rō)	Nic.	11·45 N	85·45 W
90	Zapopan	(sä-pō'pän)	Mex.	20·42 N	102·23 W
119	Zaporoshskoye	(zä-pô-rôsh'skô-yĕ). Sov. Un.		60·36 N	30·31 E
129	Zaporozh'ye	(zä-pô-rôzh'yĕ) Sov. Un.		47·53 N	35·25 E
129	Zaporozhye	(Oblast) (zä-pô-rôzh'yĕ ôb'låst).Sov. Un.		47·20 N	35·05 E
90	Zapotiltic	(sä-pô-tēl-tēk')	Mex.	19·37 N	103·25 W
90	Zapotitlán	(sä-pô-tē-tlän')	Mex.	17·13 N	98·58 W
91	Zapotitlán, Punta	(Pt.)	Mex.	18·34 N	94·48 W
90	Zapotlanejo	(sä-pô-tlä-nä'hô)	Mex.	20·38 N	103·05 W
90	Zaragoza		Mex.	23·59 N	99·45 W
90	Zaragoza		Mex.	22·02 N	100·45 W
125	Zaragoza	(thä-rä-gō'thä)	Sp.	41·39 N	0·53 W
121	Zărandului, Muntii	(Mts.)	Rom.	46·07 N	22·21 E
119	Zarasay	(zä-rä-sī')	Sov. Un.	55·45 N	26·18 E
101	Zárate	(zä-rä'tä) Arg. (Buenos Aires In.)		34·05 S	59·05 W
128	Zaraysk	(zä-rä'ĕsk)	Sov. Un.	54·46 N	38·53 E
142	Zardālu		W. Pak.	30·20 N	67·40 E
164	Zaria	(zä'rē-ä)	Nig.	11·08 N	7·45 E
133	Zarineh, Rūd-é	(R.)	Iran	36·40 N	46·35 E
139	Zarga	(R.)	Jordan (Palestine In.)	32·13 N	35·43 E
120	Zary	(zhä'rĕ)	Pol.	51·38 N	15·08 E
98	Zarzal	(zä-zä'l)	Col. (In.)	4·23 N	76·04 W
135	Zashiversk	(zä'shǐ-vĕrsk') Sov. Un.		67·08 N	144·02 E
121	Zastavna	(zás-täf'nä)	Sov. Un.	48·32 N	25·50 E
167	Zastron	(zás'trŭn) S. Afr. (Natal In.)		30·19 S	27·07 E

Page	Name	Pronunciation	Region	Lat. °′	Long. °′
120	Žatec	(zhä'tĕts)	Czech.	50·19 N	13·32 E
135	Zavitinsk		Sov. Un.	50·12 N	129·44 E
121	Zawiercie	(zä-vyĕr'tsyĕ)	Pol.	50·28 N	19·25 E
144	Zāyantleh Rud	(R.)	Iran	32·16 N	50·48 E
134	Zaysan	(zī'sän)	Sov. Un.	47·43 N	84·44 E
134	Zaysan	(L.)	Sov. Un.	48·16 N	84·05 E
94	Zaza	(R.) (zä'zä)	Cuba	21·40 N	79·25 W
121	Zbarazh	(zbä-räzh')	Sov. Un.	49·39 N	25·48 E
121	Zbruch R	(zbrōōch)	Sov. Un.	48·56 N	26·18 E
121	Zdolbunov	(zdôl-bōō'nôôf) Sov. Un.		50·31 N	26·17 E
121	Zdunska Wola	(zdōōn''skä vō'lä) Pol.		51·36 N	18·27 E
168	Zebediela	S. Afr. (Johannesburg & Pretoria In.)		24·19 S	29·21 E
117	Zeebrugge	(zä'brōōg'gĕ)	Bel.	51·20 N	3·00 W
80	Zeeland	(zē'länd)	Mich.	42·50 N	86·00 W
111	Zehdenick	(tsä'dĕ-nĕk) Ger. (Berlin In.)		52·59 N	13·20 E
111	Zehlendorf	(tsä'lĕn-dôrf) Ger. (Berlin In.)		52·47 N	13·23 E
168	Zeila	(zä'lä) Som. (Horn of Afr. In.)		11·19 N	43·20 E
111	Zeist	Neth. (Amsterdam In.)		52·05 N	5·14 E
121	Zelechów	(zhĕ-lĕ'ĸōōf)	Pol.	51·48 N	21·55 E
119	Zelenogorsk	(zĕ-lä'nô-gôrsk) Sov. Un.		60·13 N	29·39 E
120	Zella-Mehlis	(tsäl'ä-mä'lĕs)	Ger.	50·40 N	10·38 E
165	Zémio	(zä-myō') Cen. Afr. Rep.		5·03 N	25·11 E
130	Zemlya Frantsa Iosifa	(Franz Josef Land) (Is.) . Sov. Un.		81·32 N	40·00 E
91	Zempoala	(Pt.) (pōō'n-tä-sĕm-pô-ä'lä) .Mex.		19·30 N	96·18 W
91	Zempoatlépetl	(Mtn.) (sĕm-pô-ä-tlä'pĕt'l) . Mex.		17·13 N	95·59 W
127	Zemun	(Semlin) (zĕ'mōōn) (sĕm'lǐn)	Yugo.	44·50 N	20·25 E
127	Zenica	(zĕ'nĕt-sä)	Yugo.	44·10 N	17·54 E
153	Zeni-Su	(Is.) (zĕ'nē sōō)	Jap.	33·55 N	138·55 E
129	Zen'kov	(zĕn-kof')	Sov. Un.	50·13 N	34·23 E
127	Žepče	(zhĕp'chĕ)	Yugo.	44·26 N	18·01 E
111	Zepernick	(tsĕ'pĕr-nĕk) Ger. (Berlin In.)		52·39 N	13·32 E
103	Zeravshan	(R.) (zä-räf-shän') Sov. Un.		40·00 N	65·42 E
120	Zerbst	(tsĕrbst)	Ger.	51·58 N	12·03 E
111	Zerpenschleuse	(tsĕr'pĕn-shloi-zĕ) Ger. (Berlin In.)		52·51 N	13·30 E
111	Zeuthen	(tsoi'tĕn) . Ger. (Berlin In.)		52·21 N	13·38 E
123	Zevenaar	Neth. (Ruhr In.)		51·56 N	6·06 E
111	Zevenbergen	Neth. (Amsterdam In.)		51·38 N	4·36 E
135	Zeya	(zå'yä)	Sov. Un.	53·43 N	127·29 E
135	Zeya	(R.)	Sov. Un.	52·31 N	128·30 E
133	Zeytun	(zā-tōōn')	Tur.	38·00 N	36·40 E
124	Zezere	(R.) (zĕ'zä-rĕ)	Port.	39·54 N	8·12 W
121	Zgierz	(zgyĕzh)	Pol.	51·51 N	19·26 E
129	Zgurovka	(zgōō'rôf-kä)	Sov. Un.	50·31 N	31·43 E
129	Zhdanov	(zhdä'nôf)	Sov. Un.	47·07 N	37·32 E
134	Zhelaniya, Mys	(C.) (zhĕ'lä-nǐ-yä) Sov. Un.		75·43 N	69·10 E
135	Zhigalovo	(zhĕ-gä'lô-vô) . Sov. Un.		54·52 N	105·05 E
135	Zhigansk	(zhĕ-gänsk') . . . Sov. Un.		66·45 N	123·20 E
142	Zhikatse		China	29·22 N	88·57 E
129	Zhitomir	(zhĕ'tô'mĕr)	Sov. Un.	50·15 N	28·40 E
129	Zhitomir	(Oblast)	Sov. Un.	50·40 N	28·07 E
128	Zhizdra	(zhĕz'drä)	Sov. Un.	53·47 N	34·41 E
128	Zhizhitskoye	(R.) (zhĕ-zhĕt'skô-yĕ) . Sov. Un.		56·08 N	31·34 E
129	Zhmerinka	(zhmyĕ'rĕṇ-kä) Sov. Un.		49·02 N	28·09 E
136	Zhukovskiy	(zhŏŏ-kôf'skǐ) Sov. Un. (Moscow In.)		55·33 N	38·09 E
158	Ziel, Mt.	(zēl)	Austl.	23·15 S	132·45 E
120	Zietona Gora	(zhyĕ'lô'nä gōō'rä) Pol.		51·56 N	15·30 E
136	Zigazinskiy	(zǐ-gazinskēĕ) Sov. Un. (Urals In.)		53·50 N	57·18 E
164	Ziguichor		Senegal	12·28 N	16·27 W
136	Zilair	(zē'lä-lr) .Sov. Un. (Urals In.)		52·12 N	57·23 E
133	Zile	(zē-lē')	Tur.	40·20 N	35·50 E
121	Žilina	(zhĕ'lǐ-nä)	Czech.	49·14 N	18·45 E
165	Zillah		Libya	28·26 N	17·52 E
134	Zima	(zē'mä)	Sov. Un.	53·58 N	102·08 E
90	Zimapan	(sē-mä'pän)	Mex.	20·43 N	99·23 W

Page	Name	Pronunciation	Region	Lat. °′	Long. °′
91	Zimatlán de Alvarez	(sē-mä-tlän' dä äl'vä-räz) .Mex.		16·52 N	96·47 W
127	Zimnicea	(zĕm-nē'chä)	Rom.	43·39 N	25·22 E
91	Zinacatepec	(zē-nä-kä-tĕ'pĕk) Mex.		18·19 N	97·15 W
	Zinántectl, see Toluca, Nevado de				
90	Zinapécuaro	(sē-nä-pä'kwä-rô) Mex.		19·50 N	100·49 W
164	Zinder	(zĭn'dĕr)	Niger	13·49 N	8·54 E
75	Zion	(zī'ŭn) . . . . Ill. (Chicago In.)		42·27 N	87·50 W
69	Zion Natl. Park		Utah	37·20 N	113·00 W
75	Zionsville	(zĭunz-vǐl) Ind. (Indianapolis In.)		39·57 N	86·15 W
98	Zipaquirá	(sē-pä-kē-rä') .Col. (In.)		5·01 N	74·01 W
90	Zirandaro	(sē-rän-dä'rō)	Mex.	18·28 N	101·02 W
90	Zitacuaro	(sē-tä-kwä'rō)	Mex.	19·25 N	100·22 W
90	Zitlala	(sē-tlä'lä)	Mex.	17·38 N	99·09 W
120	Zittau	(tsē'tou)	Ger.	50·55 N	14·48 E
127	Zlatograd		Bul.	41·24 N	25·05 E
136	Zlatoust	(zlä-tô-ōōst') Sov. Un. (Urals In.)		55·13 N	59·39 E
165	Zlitan		Libya	32·27 N	14·33 E
121	Złoczew	(zwô'chĕf)	Pol.	51·23 N	18·34 E
128	Zlynka	(zlĕṇ'kä)	Sov. Un.	52·28 N	31·39 E
129	Znamenka	(znä'mĕn-kä) . Sov. Un.		48·43 N	32·35 E
119	Znamensk	(znä'mĕnsk) . . Sov. Un.		54·39 N	21·49 E
120	Znojomo	(znoi'mô)	Czech.	48·52 N	16·03 E
111	Zoetermeer	Neth. (Amsterdam In.)		52·03 N	4·29 E
111	Zoeterwoude	Neth. (Amsterdam In.)		52·03 N	4·29 E
111	Zohor	Czech. (Vienna In.)		48·20 N	17·00 E
121	Zolochĕv	(zô'lô-chĕf) . . . Sov. Un.		49·48 N	24·55 E
129	Zolotonosha	(zô'lô-tô-nô'shä) Sov. Un.		49·41 N	32·03 E
152	Zolotoy, Mys	(Pt.) (mǐs zô-lô-tôy') . Sov. Un.		47·24 N	139·10 E
166	Zomba	(zôm'bä)	Nya.	15·19 S	35·17 E
165	Zongo	(zôṇ'gô)	Con. L.	4·19 N	18·36 E
133	Zonguldak	(zôn'gōōl'däk) . . . Tur.		41·25 N	31·50 E
111	Zonhoven	Bel. (Brussels In.)		50·59 N	5·24 E
91	Zoquitlán	(sō-kēt-län')	Mex.	18·09 N	97·02 W
124	Zorita	(thô-rē'tä)	Sp.	39·18 N	5·41 W
111	Zossen	(tsō'sĕn) . Ger. (Berlin In.)		52·13 N	13·27 E
128	Zubtsov	(zōōp-tsôf') . . . Sov. Un.		56·13 N	34·34 E
125	Zuera	(thwä'rä)	Sp.	41·40 N	0·48 W
120	Zuger See	(L.) (tsōōg)	Switz.	47·10 N	8·40 E
120	Zugspitze Pk.		Aus.-Ger.	47·25 N	11·00 E
124	Zújar	(R.) (thōō'här)	Sp.	38·55 N	5·05 W
94	Zulueta	(zōō-lōō-ĕ'tä)	Cuba	22·20 N	79·35 W
166	Zululand	(Reg.) (zōō'lōō-länd) S. Afr.		27·45 S	31·29 E
166	Zumbo	(zōōm'bŏô)	Moz.	15·32 S	30·30 E
71	Zumbro	(R.) (zŭm'brô)	Minn.	44·18 N	92·14 W
71	Zumbrota	(zŭm-brō'tä)	Minn.	44·16 N	92·39 W
90	Zumpango	(sŏŏm-päṇ-gō) . Mex.		19·48 N	99·06 W
111	Zundert	Neth. (Amsterdam In.)		51·28 N	4·39 E
164	Zungeru	(zōōṇ-gä'rōō)	Nig.	9·45 N	6·13 E
69	Zuni	(R.)	Ariz.-N. Mex.	34·40 N	109·30 W
69	Zuni Ind. Res.	(zōō'nē) . N. Mex.		35·10 N	108·40 W
69	Zuni Mts.		N. Mex.	35·10 N	108·10 W
120	Zürich	(tsü'rĭk)	Switz.	47·22 N	8·32 E
120	Zürich See	(L.)	Switz.	47·18 N	8·47 E
153	Zushi	(zōō'shē) . Jap. (Tōkyō In.)		35·17 N	139·35 E
167	Zuurberg	(Mts.) (zōō'bûrg) S. Afr. (Natal In.)		33·15 S	25·32 E
165	Zuwārah		Libya	32·58 N	12·07 E
139	Zuwayzā	Jordan (Palestine In.)		31·42 N	35·58 E
128	Zvenigorod	(zvä-nē'gô-rôt) Sov. Un.		55·46 N	36·54 E
129	Zvenigorodka	(zvä-nē'gô-rôt'kä) Sov. Un.		49·07 N	30·59 E
121	Zvolen	(zvô'lĕn)	Czech.	48·35 N	19·10 E
127	Zvornik	(zvôr'nēk)	Yugo.	44·24 N	19·08 E
165	Zwai L.	(zwä'ē)	Eth.	8·08 N	39·11 E
167	Zwartberg	(Mtn.) (zvärt-bĕrk) S. Afr. (Natal In.)		30·08 S	29·34 E
120	Zwickau	(tsvĭk'ou)	Ger.	50·43 N	12·30 E
120	Zwiebrücken	(tsvī-brük'ĕn)	Ger.	49·16 N	7·20 E
117	Zwolle	(zvôl'ĕ)	Neth.	52·33 N	6·05 E
121	Zyrardow	(zhĕ-rär'dōōf)	Pol.	52·04 N	20·28 E
135	Zyryanka	(zĕ-ryän'kä) . Sov. Un.		65·45 N	151·15 E
134	Zyryanovsk	(zĕ-ryä'nôfsk) Sov. Un.		49·43 N	83·52 E
121	Zywiec	(zhǐ'vyĕts)	Pol.	49·42 N	19·14 E

ăt: fĭnăl; rāte; senâte; ârm; àsk; sofá; fâre; ch-choose; dh-as th in other; bē; ĕvent; bĕt; recĕnt; cratēr; g-go; gh-guttural g; bĭt; ɫ-short neutral; rīde; ĸ-guttural k as ch in German ich;